computing		informatique
pejorative	*pej, péj*	péjoratif
philosophy	*Phil*	philosophie
photography	*Photo*	photographie
plural	*pl*	pluriel
politics	*Pol*	politique
possessive	*poss*	possessif
past participle	*pp*	participe passé
prefix	*pref, préf*	préfixe
preposition	*prep, prép*	préposition
present participle	*pres p*	participe présent
pronoun	*pron*	pronom
psychology	*Psych*	psychologie
past	*pt*	prétérit
something	*qch*	quelque chose
somebody	*qn*	quelqu'un
railway	*Rail*	chemin de fer
relative pronoun	*rel pron, pron rel*	pronom relatif
religion	*Relig*	religion
somebody	*sb*	quelqu'un
school	*School, Scol*	scolaire
sport	*Sport*	sport
something	*sth*	quelque chose
technology	*Tech*	technologie
theatre	*Theat, Théât*	théâtre
television	*TV*	télévision
university	*Univ*	université
American English	*US*	anglais américain
auxiliary verb	*v aux*	verbe auxiliaire
intransitive verb	*vi*	verbe intransitif
reflexive verb	*vpr*	verbe pronominal
transitive verb	*vt*	verbe transitif
transitive and intransitive verb	*vt/i*	verbe transitif et intransitif
approximate translation	≈	équivalent approximatif
trademark	®	marque déposée
colloquial	🗈	familier
slang	⊠	argot

Oxford
French
Mini Dictionary

FIFTH EDITION

French–English
English–French

Français–Anglais
Anglais–Français

Contents/Table des matières

Introduction/Introduction   vi–vii

Pronunciation/Prononciation

    French/français   viii

    English/anglais   ix

French–English/français–anglais   **1–308**

Phrasefinder/Mini guide de conversation

English–French/anglais–français   **309–598**

French Verbs   599

Verbes irréguliers anglais   609

Numbers/Les nombres   611

Proprietary terms

This dictionary includes some words which are, or are asserted to be, proprietary terms or trademarks. The presence or absence of such assertions should not be regarded as affecting the legal status of any proprietary name or trademark. In cases where the editorial staff has evidence that a word is used as a proprietary name or trademark, this is indicated by the symbol ®. No judgement concerning the legal status of such words is made or implied thereby.

Les marques déposées

Les mots qui, à notre connaissance, sont considérés comme des marques ou des noms déposés sont signalés dans cet ouvrage par ®. La présence ou l'absence de cette mention ne peut pas être considérée comme ayant valeur juridique.

Contributors/Collaborateurs

**Fifth Edition/
Cinquième édition**

Joanna Rubery

Isabelle Stables-Lemoine

Proofreader/Correcteur

Amanda Leigh

**Fourth Edition/
Quatrième édition**

Nicholas Rollin

Jean Benoit Ormal-Grenon

**Data capture/
Saisie des données**

Susan Wilkin

Proofreaders/Correcteurs

Isabelle Stables-Lemoine

Meic Haines

Mary O'Neill

**Third Edition/
Troisième édition**

Isabelle Stables-Lemoine

Marianne Chalmers

Rosalind Combley

Catherine Roux

Laura Wedgeworth

**Phrasefinder/
Mini guide de conversation**

Hélène Haenen

Neil and Roswitha Morris

**First and Second Edition/
Première et deuxième
éditions**

Michael Janes

Dora Latiri-Carpenter

Edwin Carpenter

Introduction

This new edition of the *Oxford French Mini Dictionary* has been designed to be a practical reference tool for the student, adult learner, traveller and business professional. It provides user-friendly treatment of core vocabulary across a broad spectrum of written and spoken language.

Enhanced coverage

The wordlist has been revised to reflect recent additions to both languages. The *Phrasefinder* has been expanded and enables the user to communicate in commonly encountered situations such as travel, shopping, eating out, and organizing leisure activities.

The more complex grammatical words, or *function words*, are given special treatment in highlighted entries to make them easily accessible. All verbs in the French-English section are cross-referenced to the verb tables at the end of the book. Here information is given on regular, irregular and reflexive verbs as well as the translation of French verb tenses.

Easy reference

The dictionary layout has been designed to be clear, streamlined and easy to use. Bullet points separate each new part of speech within an entry. Nuances of meaning or usage are pinpointed by semantic indicators or by typical collocates with which the headword frequently occurs. Extra help is given with symbols to mark the register of language. A boxed exclamation mark ⚠ indicates colloquial language and a cross ✖ indicates slang.

The pronunciation of French is given in the International Phonetic Alphabet. Irregular parts of French verbs appear as headwords with a cross-reference to the main entry of the verb.

Introduction

Cette nouvelle édition de l'*Oxford French Mini Dictionary* a été conçue comme un outil de référence pratique destiné aux étudiants, aux touristes et aux professionnels. Il offre un traitement convivial du vocabulaire de base représentatif de la langue écrite et parlée.

Une édition augmentée

La nomenclature a été révisée de façon à refléter les récents apports de vocabulaire dans les deux langues. La partie centrale intitulée *Mini guide de conversation* aidera l'utilisateur à communiquer dans les situations les plus courantes telles que le voyage, le shopping, les sorties au restaurant ou les loisirs.

Les mots grammaticaux, qui forment les structures de base des deux langues, font l'objet d'une présentation distincte qui les rend rapidement accessibles, les choix de traduction et des exemples étant clairement signalés. De courtes notes d'usage indiquent les pièges éventuels. Une liste de verbes irréguliers anglais se trouve à la fin de l'ouvrage.

Une consultation facilitée

La présentation du dictionnaire a été conçue de façon à être claire, simplifiée et à faciliter la consultation de l'ouvrage. Des puces séparent chaque nouvelle partie du discours à l'intérieur d'une entrée, ce qui facilite leur repérage. Les nuances de sens ou d'usage sont marquées au moyen d'indicateurs sémantiques ou par des collocateurs types avec lesquels le mot s'emploie fréquemment, guidant ainsi rapidement l'utilisateur à la traduction appropriée. Un point d'exclamation 🅸 indique un niveau de langue familier et une croix 🗙 indique un niveau argotique.

Les symboles utilisés pour la prononciation sont ceux de l'Alphabet Phonétique International. Les pluriels irréguliers ainsi que les conjugaisons ou les formes du comparatif et du superlatif irrégulières anglaises sont indiqués entre parenthèses.

Pronunciation of French

a	*as in*	patte	/pat/	ɑ	*as in*	pâte	/pɑt/
ã		clan	/klã/	e		dé	/de/
ɛ		belle	/bɛl/	ɛ̃		lin	/lɛ̃/
ə		demain	/dəmɛ̃/	i		gris	/gʀi/
o		gros	/gʀo/	ɔ		corps	/kɔʀ/
ɔ̃		long	/lɔ̃/	œ		leur	/lœʀ/
œ̃		brun	/bʀœ̃/	ø		deux	/dø/
u		fou	/fu/	y		pur	/pyʀ/

Semi-Vowels

j	*as in*	fille	/fij/
ɥ		huit	/ɥit/
w		oui	/wi/

Consonants

Aspiration of 'h'
Where it is impossible to make a liaison this is indicated by /'/ immediately after the slash e.g. haine /'ɛn/.

b	*as in*	bal	/bal/	ŋ	*as in*	camping	/kɑ̃piŋ/
d		dent	/dã/	p		porte	/pɔʀt/
f		foire	/fwaʀ/	R		rire	/ʀiʀ/
g		gomme	/gɔm/	s		sang	/sã/
k		clé	/kle/	ʃ		chien	/ʃjɛ̃/
l		lien	/ljɛ̃/	t		train	/tʀɛ̃/
m		mer	/mɛʀ/	v		voile	/vwal/
n		nage	/naʒ/	z		zèbre	/zɛbʀ/
ɲ		oignon	/ɔɲɔ̃/	ʒ		jeune	/ʒœn/

La prononciation de l'anglais

Voyelles et diphtongues

iː	see	ɔː	saw	eɪ	page	ɔɪ	join
ɪ	sit	ʊ	put	əʊ	home	ɪə	near
e	ten	uː	too	aɪ	five	eə	hair
æ	hat	ʌ	cup	aɪə	fire	ʊə	poor
ɑː	arm	ɜː	fur	aʊ	now		
ɒ	got	ə	ago	aʊə	flour		

Consonnes

p	pen	tʃ	chin	s	so	n	no
b	bad	dʒ	June	z	zoo	ŋ	sing
t	tea	f	fall	ʃ	she	l	leg
d	dip	v	voice	ʒ	measure	r	red
k	cat	θ	thin	h	how	j	yes
g	got	ð	then	m	man	w	wet

L'accent d'intensité

L'accent d'intensité est indiqué au moyen du signe /'/, placé devant la syllabe qu'il affecte.

Aa

a /a/ ➡AVOIR **5**.

à /a/
● *préposition*

à+le = au
à+les = aux

····➤ (avec verbe de mouvement) to.

····➤ (pour indiquer où l'on se trouve) ~ **la maison** at home; ~ **Nice** in Nice.

····➤ (âge, date, heure) ~ **l'âge de...** at the age of...; **au XIXe siècle** in the 19th century; ~ **deux heures** at two o'clock.

····➤ (description) with; **aux yeux verts** with green eyes.

····➤ (appartenance) ~ **qui est ce stylo?** whose pen is this?; **c'est** ~ **vous?** is this yours?

····➤ (avec nombre) ~ **90 km/h** at 90 km per hour; ~ **10 minutes d'ici** 10 minutes from here; **des tomates** ~ **2 euros le kilo** tomatoes at 2 euros a kilo; **un timbre** ~ **2 euros** a 2-euro stamp; **nous avons fait le travail** ~ **deux** two of us did the work; **mener 5** ~ **4** to lead 5 (to) 4.

····➤ (avec être) **c'est** ~ **moi** it's my turn; **je suis** ~ **vous tout de suite** I'll be with you in a minute; **c'est** ~ **toi de décider** it's up to you to decide.

····➤ (hypothèse) ~ **ce qu'il paraît** apparently; ~ **t'entendre** to hear you talk.

····➤ (exclamatif) ~ **ta santé!** cheers!; ~ **demain/bientôt!** see you tomorrow/soon!

····➤ (moyen) ~ **la main** by hand; ~ **vélo** by bike; ~ **pied** on foot; **chauffage au gaz** gas heating.

abaissement /abɛsmɑ̃/ *nm* (de taux, de prix) cut; (de seuil) lowering.

abaisser /abese/ **1** *vt* lower; (*levier*) pull *ou* push down; (fig) humiliate. □ **s'**~ *vpr* go down, drop; (fig) demean oneself; **s'**~ **à** to stoop to.

abandon /abɑ̃dɔ̃/ *nm* abandonment; (de personne) desertion; (de course) withdrawal; (naturel) abandon; **à l'**~ in a state of neglect.

abandonner /abɑ̃dɔne/ **1** *vt* abandon; (*épouse, cause*) desert; (renoncer à) give up, abandon; (céder) give (à to); (*course*) withdraw from; (Ordinat) abort. □ **s'**~ **à** *vpr* give oneself up to.

abasourdir /abazurdir/ **2** *vt* stun.

abat-jour /abaʒur/ *nm inv* lampshade.

abats /aba/ *nmpl* offal.

abattement /abatmɑ̃/ *nm* dejection; (faiblesse) exhaustion; (Comm) reduction; (fig) ~ **fiscal** tax allowance.

abattre /abatr/ **11** *vt* knock down; (*arbre*) cut down; (*animal*) slaughter; (*avion*) shoot down; (*affaiblir*) weaken; (*démoraliser*) demoralize; **ne pas se laisser** ~ not let things get one down. □ **s'**~ *vpr* come down, fall (down).

abbaye /abei/ *nf* abbey.

abbé /abe/ *nm* priest; (supérieur d'une abbaye) abbot.

abcès /apsɛ/ *nm* abscess.

abdiquer /abdike/ **1** *vt/i* abdicate.

abdomen /abdɔmɛn/ *nm* abdomen.

abdominal (*pl* -aux) /abdɔminal/ *adj* abdominal. **abdominaux** *nmpl* (Sport) stomach exercises.

abeille /abɛj/ *nf* bee.

aberrant, ∼e /abɛrã, -t/ *adj* absurd.

abêtir /abetir/ **2** *vt* turn into a moron.

abîme /abim/ *nm* abyss.

abîmer /abime/ **1** *vt* damage, spoil. □ **s'∼** *vpr* get damaged ou spoilt.

ablation /ablasjɔ̃/ *nf* removal.

aboiement /abwamã/ *nm* bark, barking; **∼s** barking.

abolir /abɔlir/ **2** *vt* abolish.

abondance /abɔ̃dãs/ *nf* abundance; (prospérité) affluence. **abondant, ∼e** *adj* abundant, plentiful.

abonder /abɔ̃de/ **1** *vi* abound (en in); **∼** dans le sens de qn agree wholeheartedly with sb.

abonné, ∼e /abɔne/ *nm, f* (lecteur) subscriber; (voyageur, spectateur) season-ticket holder.

abonnement /abɔnmã/ *nm* (à un journal) subscription; (de bus, Théât) season-ticket; (au gaz) standing charge.

abonner (s') /(s)abɔne/ **1** *vpr* subscribe (à to).

abord /abɔr/ *nm* access; **∼s** surroundings; **d'∼** first.

abordable /abɔrdabl/ *adj* (*prix*) affordable; (*personne*) approachable; (*texte*) accessible.

aborder /abɔrde/ **1** *vt* approach;

(lieu) reach; (*problème*) tackle. ● *vi* reach land.

aborigène /abɔriʒɛn/ *nm* aborigine.

aboutir /abutir/ **2** *vi* succeed, achieve a result; **∼** à end (up) in, lead to; **n'∼** à rien come to nothing.

aboutissement /abutismã/ *nm* outcome; (de carrière, d'évolution) culmination.

aboyer /abwaje/ **31** *vi* bark.

abrégé /abreʒe/ *nm* summary.

abréger /abreʒe/ **14** **40** *vt* (*texte*) shorten, abridge; (*mot*) abbreviate, shorten; (*visite*) cut short.

abreuver /abrœve/ **1** *vt* water; (fig) overwhelm (de with). □ **s'∼** *vpr* drink.

abréviation /abrevjasjɔ̃/ *nf* abbreviation.

abri /abri/ *nm* shelter; à l'∼ under cover; (en lieu sûr) safe; à l'∼ de sheltered from; se mettre à l'∼ take shelter.

abricot /abriko/ *nm* apricot.

abriter /abrite/ **1** *vt* shelter; (recevoir) house. □ **s'∼** *vpr* (take) shelter.

abrupt, ∼e /abrypt/ *adj* steep, sheer; (fig) abrupt.

abruti, ∼e /abryti/ *nm, f* **1** idiot.

absence /apsãs/ *nf* absence; il a des **∼s** sometimes his mind goes blank.

absent, ∼e /apsã, -t/ *adj* (*personne*) absent, away; (*chose*) missing; il est toujours **∼** he's still away; d'un air **∼** absently. ● *nm, f* absentee.

absenter (s') /(s)apsãte/ **1** *vpr* go ou be away; (sortir) go out, leave.

absolu, ∼e /apsɔly/ *adj* absolute.

absorbant, ∼e /apsɔrbã, -t/ *adj*

(*travail*) absorbing; (*matière*) absorbent.

absorber /apsɔʀbe/ **1** *vt* absorb; **être absorbé par qch** be engrossed in sth.

abstenir (s') /(s)apstəniʀ/ **58** *vpr* abstain; **s'~** de refrain from.

abstrait, **~e** /apstʀɛ, -t/ *adj & nm* abstract.

absurde /apsyʀd/ *adj* absurd.

abus /aby/ *nm* abuse, misuse; (*injustice*) abuse; **~ de confiance** breach of trust.

abuser /abyze/ **1** *vt* deceive. ● *vi* go too far; **~ de** abuse, misuse; (*profiter de*) take advantage of; (*alcool*) overindulge in. □ **s'~** *vpr* be mistaken.

abusif, **-ive** /abyzif, -v/ *adj* excessive; (*impropre*) wrong; (*injuste*) unfair.

académie /akademi/ *nf* academy; (*circonscription*) local education authority.

Académie française A scholarly body composed of 40 life members selected on the basis of their contribution to scholarship or literature. It monitors developments in the French language and rules on French usage, as encoded in the *Dictionnaire de l'Académie française* (which is not always taken seriously by the public at large).

acajou /akaʒu/ *nm* mahogany.

accablant, **~e** /akablɑ̃, -t/ *adj* (*chaleur*) oppressive; (*fait, témoignage*) damning.

accabler /akable/ **1** *vt* overwhelm; **~ d'impôts** burden with taxes; **~ d'injures** heap insults upon.

accéder /aksede/ **14** *vi* **~ à** (*lieu*) reach; (*pouvoir, trône*) accede to; (*requête*) grant; (*Ordinat*) access; **~ à la propriété** become a homeowner.

accélérateur /akseleʀatœʀ/ *nm* accelerator.

accélérer /akseleʀe/ **14** *vt/i* accelerate. □ **s'~** *vpr* speed up.

accent /aksɑ̃/ *nm* accent; (*sur une syllabe*) stress, accent; **mettre l'~ sur** stress; **~ aigu/grave/circonflexe** acute/grave/circumflex accent.

accentuer /aksɑ̃tɥe/ **1** *vt* (*lettre, syllabe*) accent; (*fig*) emphasize, accentuate. □ **s'~** *vpr* become more pronounced, increase.

accepter /aksɛpte/ **1** *vt* accept; **~ de faire** agree to do.

accès /aksɛ/ *nm* access; (*porte*) entrance; (*de fièvre*) bout; (*de colère*) fit; (*d'enthousiasme*) burst; (*Ordinat*) access; **les ~ de** (*voies*) the approaches to; **facile d'~** easy to get to.

accessoire /akseswaʀ/ *adj* secondary, incidental. ● *nm* accessory; (*Théât*) prop.

accident /aksidɑ̃/ *nm* accident; **~ de train/d'avion** train/plane crash; **par ~** by accident. **accidenté**, **~e** *adj* (*personne*) injured (in an accident); (*voiture*) damaged; (*terrain*) uneven, hilly. **accidentel**, **~le** *adj* accidental.

acclamer /aklame/ **1** *vt* cheer, acclaim.

accommoder /akɔmɔde/ **1** *vt* adapt (à to); (*cuisiner*) prepare; (*assaisonner*) flavour. □ **s'~ de** *vpr* make the best of.

accompagnateur, **-trice** /akɔ̃paɲatœʀ, -tʀis/ *nm, f* (*Mus*) accompanist; (*guide*) guide; **~ d'enfants** accompanying adult.

accompagner /akɔ̃paɲe/ **1** vt accompany. □ s'~ de vpr be accompanied by.

accomplir /akɔ̃pliʀ/ **2** vt carry out, fulfil. □ s'~ vpr take place, happen; (vœu) be fulfilled.

accord /akɔʀ/ nm agreement; (harmonie) harmony; (Mus) chord; être d'~ agree (pour to); se mettre d'~ come to an agreement, agree; d'~! all right ⚑, OK!

accorder /akɔʀde/ **1** vt grant; (couleurs) match; (Mus) tune; (attribuer) (valeur, importance) assign. □ s'~ vpr (se mettre d'accord) agree; (s'octroyer) allow oneself; s'~ avec (s'entendre avec) get on with.

accotement /akɔtmɑ̃/ nm verge; ~ non stabilisé soft verge.

accouchement /akuʃmɑ̃/ nm childbirth; (travail) labour.

accoucher /akuʃe/ **1** vi give birth (de to); (être en travail) be in labour. ● vt deliver. **accoucheur** nm médecin ~ obstetrician.

accoudoir /akudwaʀ/ nm arm-rest.

accoupler /akuple/ **1** vt (Tech) couple. □ s'~ vpr mate.

accourir /akuʀiʀ/ **20** vi run up.

accoutumance /akutymɑ̃s/ nf familiarization; (Méd) addiction.

accoutumer /akutyme/ **1** vt accustom. □ s'~ vpr get accustomed.

accro /akʀo/ nmf ⚑ (drogué) addict; (amateur) fan.

accroc /akʀo/ nm tear, rip; (fig) hitch.

accrochage /akʀɔʃaʒ/ nm hanging; hooking; (Auto) collision; (dispute) clash; (Mil) encounter.

accrocher /akʀɔʃe/ **1** vt (suspendre) hang up; (attacher) hook, hitch; (déchirer) catch; (heurter) hit;

(attirer) attract. □ s'~ vpr cling, hang on (à to); (se disputer) clash.

accroissement /akʀwasmɑ̃/ nm increase (de in).

accroître /akʀwatʀ/ **24** vt increase. □ s'~ vpr increase.

accroupir (s') /(s)akʀupiʀ/ **2** vpr squat.

accru, ~e /akʀy/ adj increased, greater.

accueil /akœj/ nm reception, welcome.

accueillant, ~e /akœjɑ̃, -t/ adj friendly, welcoming.

accueillir /akœjiʀ/ **25** vt receive, welcome; (film, livre) receive; (prendre en charge) (réfugiés, patients) take care of, cater for.

accumuler /akymyle/ **1** vt (énergie) store up; (capital) accumulate. □ s'~ vpr (neige, ordures) pile up; (dettes) accrue.

accusation /akyzasjɔ̃/ nf accusation; (Jur) charge; l'~ (magistrat) the prosecution.

accusé, ~e /akyze/ adj marked. ● nm, f defendant, accused.

accuser /akyze/ **1** vt accuse (de of); (blâmer) blame (de for); (Jur) charge (de with); (fig) emphasize; ~ réception de acknowledge receipt of.

acharné, ~e /aʃaʀne/ adj relentless, ferocious. **acharnement** nm (énergie) furious energy; (ténacité) determination.

acharner (s') /(s)aʃaʀne/ **1** vpr persevere; s'~ sur set upon; (poursuivre) hound; s'~ à faire (s'évertuer) try desperately; (s'obstiner) keep on doing.

achat /aʃa/ nm purchase; ~s shopping; faire l'~ de buy; faire des ~s do some shopping.

acheminer /aʃ(ə)mine/ **1** vt dis-

patch, convey; (*courrier*) handle.
□ s'~ vers *vpr* head for.

acheter /aʃ(ə)te/ **6** *vt* buy; ~ qch
à qn (pour lui) buy sth for sb; (chez
lui) buy sth from sb. **acheteur,
-euse** *nm, f* buyer; (*client de magasin*) shopper.

achèvement /aʃɛvmɑ̃/ *nm* completion.

achever /aʃ(ə)ve/ **6** *vt* finish (off).
□ s'~ *vpr* end.

acide /asid/ *adj* acid, sharp.
● *nm* acid.

acier /asje/ *nm* steel.

acné /akne/ *nf* acne.

acompte /akɔ̃t/ *nm* deposit, part-
payment.

à-côté (*pl* ~s) /akote/ *nm* side
issue; ~s (*argent*) extras.

acoustique /akustik/ *nf* acoustics
(+ *sg*). ● *adj* acoustic.

acquéreur /akerœr/ *nm* pur-
chaser, buyer.

acquérir /akerir/ **7** *vt* acquire,
gain; (*biens*) purchase, acquire.

acquis, ~e /aki, -z/ *adj* acquired;
(*fait*) established; tenir qch pour
~ take sth for granted. ● *nm* experience. **acquisition** *nf* acquisition;
purchase.

acquitter /akite/ **1** *vt* acquit;
(*dette*) settle. □ s'~ de *vpr* (*promesse*) fulfil; (*devoir*) discharge.

âcre /akr/ *adj* acrid.

acrobatie /akrɔbasi/ *nf* acrobatics
(+ *pl*); ~ aérienne aerobatics (+ *pl*).

acte /akt/ *nm* act, action, deed;
(*Théât*) act; (*Jur*) deed; ~ de
naissance/mariage birth/marriage
certificate; ~s (*compte rendu*) proceedings; prendre ~ de note.

acteur /aktœr/ *nm* actor.

actif, -ive /aktif, -v/ *adj* active; (*population*) working. ● *nm* (Comm) as-
sets; avoir à son ~ have to one's

credit *ou* name.

action /aksjɔ̃/ *nf* action; (Comm)
share; (Jur) action; (*effet*) effect;
(*initiative*) initiative. **actionnaire**
nmf shareholder.

activer /aktive/ **1** *vt* speed up;
(*feu*) boost. □ s'~ *vpr* hurry up;
(s'affairer) be very busy.

activité /aktivite/ *nf* activity; en
~ (*volcan*) active; (*fonctionnaire*)
working; (*usine*) in operation.

actrice /aktris/ *nf* actress.

actualité /aktyalite/ *nf* topicality;
l'~ current affairs; les ~s news;
d'~ topical.

actuel, ~le /aktyɛl/ *adj* current,
present; (d'actualité) topical. **ac-
tuellement** *adv* currently, at the
present time.

acupuncture /akypɔ̃ktyr/ *nf* acupuncture.

adaptateur /adaptatœr/ *nm*
(Électr) adapter.

adapter /adapte/ **1** *vt* adapt;
(fixer) fit. □ s'~ *vpr* adapt (oneself);
(Tech) fit.

additif /aditif/ *nm* (note) rider;
(substance) additive.

addition /adisjɔ̃/ *nf* addition; (au
café) bill; (US) check. **additionner**
1 *vt* add; (totaliser) add (up).

adepte /adɛpt/ *nmf* follower; (d'activité) enthusiast.

adéquat, ~e /adekwa, -t/ *adj* suitable; (suffisant) adequate.

adhérent, ~e /aderɑ̃, -t/ *nm, f*
member.

adhérer /adere/ **14** *vi* adhere, stick
(à to); ~ à (*club*) be a member of;
(s'inscrire à) join.

adhésif, -ive /adezif, -v/ *adj* adhesive; ruban ~ sticky tape.

adhésion /adezjɔ̃/ *nf* membership;
(soutien) support.

adieu (*pl* ~x) /adjø/ *interj & nm*

a

goodbye, farewell.

adjectif /adʒɛktif/ nm adjective.

adjoint, ~e /adʒwɛ̃, -t/ nm, f assistant; ~ au maire deputy mayor.
● adj assistant.

adjuger /adʒyʒe/ **40** vt award; (aux enchères) auction. □ s'~ vpr take (for oneself).

ADM abrév fpl (armes de destruction massive) WMD.

admettre /admɛtʀ/ **42** vt let in, admit; (tolérer) allow; (reconnaître) admit, acknowledge; (candidat) pass.

administrateur, -trice /administʀatœʀ, -tʀis/ nm, f administrator, director; (Jur) trustee; ~ de site Internet Webmaster.

administratif, -ive /administʀatif, -v/ adj administrative; (document) official. **administration** nf administration; (gestion) management; l'A~ Civil Service.

administrer /administʀe/ **1** vt run, manage; (justice, biens, antidote) administer.

admirateur, -trice /admiʀatœʀ, -tʀis/ nm, f admirer.

admiration /admiʀasjɔ̃/ nf admiration.

admirer /admiʀe/ **1** vt admire.

admission /admisjɔ̃/ nf admission.

ADN abrév m (acide désoxyribonucléique) DNA.

adolescence /adɔlesɑ̃s/ nf adolescence. **adolescent, ~e** nm, f adolescent, teenager.

adopter /adɔpte/ **1** vt adopt. **adoptif, -ive** adj (enfant) adopted; (parents) adoptive.

adorer /adɔʀe/ **1** vt love; (plus fort) adore; (Relig) worship, adore.

adosser /adose/ **1** vt lean (à, contre against). □ s'~ vpr lean

back (à, contre against).

adoucir /adusiʀ/ **2** vt soften; (boisson) sweeten; (chagrin) ease. □ s'~ vpr soften; (chagrin) ease; (temps) become milder. **adoucissant** nm (fabric) softener.

adresse /adʀɛs/ nf address; (habileté) skill; ~ électronique email address.

adresser /adʀese/ **1** vt send; (écrire l'adresse sur) address; (remarque) address; ~ la parole à speak to. □ s'~ à vpr address; (aller voir) (personne) go and ask one; (bureau) enquire at; (viser, intéresser) be directed at.

adroit, ~e /adʀwa, -t/ adj skilful, clever.

ADSL abrév m (asymmetrical digital subscriber line) ADSL.

adulte /adylt/ nmf adult. ● adj adult; (plante, animal) fully grown.

adultère /adyltɛʀ/ adj adulterous.
● nm adultery.

adverbe /advɛʀb/ nm adverb.

adversaire /advɛʀsɛʀ/ nmf opponent, adversary.

aérer /aeʀe/ **1** vt air; (texte) space out. □ s'~ vpr get some air.

aérien, -ienne /aeʀjɛ̃, -jɛn/ adj air; (photo) aerial; (câble) overhead.

aérobic /aeʀɔbik/ nm aerobics (+ sg).

aérogare /aeʀɔgaʀ/ nf air terminal.

aéroglisseur /aeʀɔglisœʀ/ nm hovercraft.

aérogramme /aeʀɔgʀam/ nm airmail letter; (US) aerogram.

aéronautique /aeʀɔnotik/ adj aeronautical. ● nf aeronautics (+ sg).

aéroport /aeʀɔpɔʀ/ nm airport.

aérospatial, ~e (mpl -iaux) /aeʀɔspasjal, -jo/ adj aerospace.

affaiblir /afeblir/ ② vt weaken. □ s'~ vpr get weaker.

affaire /afɛr/ nf affair, matter; (Jur) case; (histoire, aventure) affair; (occasion) bargain; (entreprise) business; (transaction) deal; (question, problème) matter; ~s (Comm) business; (Pol) affairs; (problèmes personnels) business; (effets personnels) things; c'est mon ~ that's my business; avoir ~ à deal with; ça fera l'~ that will do the job; ça fera leur ~ that's just what they need; tirer qn d'~ help sb out of a tight spot; se tirer d'~ get out of trouble.

affairé, ~e /afere/ adj busy.

affaisser (s') /(s)afese/ ① vpr (terrain, route) sink, subside; (poutre) sag; (personne) collapse.

affamé, ~e /afame/ adj starving.

affectation /afɛktasjɔ̃/ nf (nomination) (à une fonction) appointment; (dans un lieu) posting; (de matériel, d'argent) allocation; (comportement) affectation.

affecter /afɛkte/ ① vt (feindre) affect; (toucher, affliger) affect; (destiner) assign; (nommer) appoint, post.

affectif, -ive /afɛktif, -v/ adj emotional.

affection /afɛksjɔ̃/ nf affection; (maladie) complaint.

affectueux, -euse /afɛktɥø, -z/ adj affectionate.

affichage /afiʃaʒ/ nm billposting; (électronique) display.

affiche /afiʃ/ nf (public) notice; (publicité) poster; (Théât) bill; être à l'~ (film) be showing; (pièce) be on.

afficher /afiʃe/ ① vt (annonce) put up; (événement) announce; (sentiment) display; (Ordinat) display.

affirmatif, -ive /afirmatif, -v/ adj affirmative. **affirmation** nf assertion.

affirmer /afirme/ ① vt assert; (soutenir) maintain.

affligé, ~e /afliʒe/ adj distressed; ~ de afflicted with.

affluer /aflye/ ① vi flood in; (sang) rush.

affolant, ~e /afɔlɑ̃, -t/ adj alarming.

affoler /afɔle/ ① vt throw into a panic. □ s'~ vpr panic.

affranchir /afrɑ̃ʃir/ ② vt stamp; (à la machine) frank; (esclave) emancipate; (fig) free. **affranchissement** nm (tarif) postage.

affreux, -euse /afrø, -z/ adj (laid) hideous; (mauvais) awful.

affrontement /afrɔ̃tmɑ̃/ nm confrontation.

affronter /afrɔ̃te/ ① vt confront. □ s'~ vpr confront each other.

affûter /afyte/ ① vt sharpen.

afin /afɛ̃/ prép & conj ~ de faire in order to do; ~ que so that.

africain, ~e /afrikɛ̃, -ɛn/ adj African. A~, ~e nm, f African.

Afrique /afrik/ nf Africa; ~ du Sud South Africa.

agacer /agase/ ⑩ vt irritate, annoy.

âge /aʒ/ nm age; (vieillesse) (old) age; quel ~ avez-vous? how old are you?; ~ adulte adulthood; ~ mûr maturity; d'un certain ~ middle-aged.

âgé, ~e /aʒe/ adj elderly; ~ de cinq ans five years old.

agence /aʒɑ̃s/ nf agency, bureau, office; (succursale) branch; ~ d'interim employment agency; ~ de voyages travel agency; ~ publicitaire advertising agency.

agenda /aʒɛ̃da/ nm diary; ~ électronique electronic organizer.

agent /aʒɑ̃/ *nm* agent; (fonctionnaire) official; ~ **(de police)** policeman; ~ **de change** stockbroker; ~ **commercial** sales representative.

agglomération /aglɔmeʁasjɔ̃/ *nf* town, built-up area.

aggraver /agʁave/ **1** *vt* aggravate, make worse. □ **s'**~ *vpr* get worse.

agile /aʒil/ *adj* agile, nimble.

agir /aʒiʁ/ **2** *vi* act; (se comporter) behave; (avoir un effet) work, take effect. □ **s'**~ **de** *vpr* (être nécessaire) il s'agit de faire we/you *etc.* must do; (être question de) il s'agit de faire it is a matter of doing; dans ce livre il s'agit de this book is about; dont il s'agit in question; il s'agit de ton fils it's about your son; de quoi s'agit-il? what is it about?

agitation /aʒitasjɔ̃/ *nf* bustle; (trouble) agitation; (malaise social) unrest.

agité, ~e /aʒite/ *adj* restless, fidgety; (troublé) agitated; (mer) rough.

agiter /aʒite/ **1** *vt* (bras, mouchoir) wave; (liquide, boîte) shake; (troubler) agitate; (discuter) debate. □ **s'**~ *vpr* bustle about; (enfant) fidget; (foule, pensées) stir.

agneau (*pl* ~x) /aɲo/ *nm* lamb.

agrafe /agʁaf/ *nf* hook; (pour papiers) staple. **agrafeuse** *nf* stapler.

agrandir /agʁɑ̃diʁ/ **2** *vt* enlarge; (maison) extend. □ **s'**~ *vpr* expand, grow. **agrandissement** *nm* extension; (de photo) enlargement.

agréable /agʁeabl/ *adj* pleasant.

agréé, ~e /agʁee/ *adj* (agence) authorized; (nourrice, médecin) registered; (matériel) approved.

agréer /agʁee/ **15** *vt* accept; ~ à

please; veuillez ~, Monsieur, mes salutations distinguées (personne non nommée) yours faithfully; (personne nommée) yours sincerely.

agrégation /agʁegasjɔ̃/ *nf* highest examination for recruitment of teachers. **agrégé**, ~e *nm, f* teacher (who has passed the agrégation).

agrément /agʁemɑ̃/ *nm* charm; (plaisir) pleasure; (accord) approval.

agresser /agʁese/ **1** *vt* attack; (pour voler) mug.

agressif, -ive /agʁesif, -v/ *adj* aggressive. **agression** *nf* attack; (pour voler) mugging; (Mil) aggression.

agricole /agʁikɔl/ *adj* agricultural; (ouvrier, produit) farm. **agriculteur**, -trice *nm, f* farmer. **agriculture** *nf* agriculture, farming.

agripper /agʁipe/ **1** *vt* grab. □ **s'**~ *vpr* cling (à to).

agroalimentaire /agʁoalimɑ̃tɛʁ/ *nm* food industry.

agrumes /agʁym/ *nmpl* citrus fruit(s).

ai /e/ ➡**avoir** **5**.

aide /ɛd/ *nf* help, assistance; (en argent) aid; **à l'**~ **de** with the help of; **venir en** ~ **à** help; ~ **à domicile** carer, home help; ~ **familiale** mother's help; ~ **sociale** social security; (US) welfare. ● *nmf* assistant. **aide-éducateur**, -trice *nm, f* classroom assistant. **aide-mémoire** *nm inv* handbook of key facts.

aider /ede/ **1** *vt/i* help, assist; (subventionner) aid, give aid to; ~ **à faire** help to do. □ **s'**~ **de** *vpr* use.

aïeul, ~e /ajœl/ *nm, f* grandparent.

aigle /ɛgl/ *nm* eagle.

aigre /ɛgʁ/ *adj* sour, sharp; (fig) sharp.

aigrir /egʁiʁ/ **2** *vt* embitter. □ **s'**~ *vpr* turn sour; (personne) become embittered.

aigu, ~ĕ /egy/ *adj* (douleur, problème) acute; (objet) sharp; (voix) shrill; (Mus) high(-pitched); (accent) acute.

aiguille /egɥij/ *nf* needle; (de montre) hand; (de balance) pointer; ~ à tricoter knitting needle.

aiguilleur /egɥijœʀ/ *nm* pointsman; ~ du ciel air traffic controller.

aiguiser /eg(ɥ)ize/ **1** *vt* sharpen; (fig) stimulate.

ail (*pl* ~s *ou* aulx) /aj, o/ *nm* garlic.

aile /ɛl/ *nf* wing.

ailier /elje/ *nm* winger; (US) end.

aille /aj/ ➡ ALLER **8**.

ailleurs /ajœʀ/ *adv* elsewhere, somewhere else; d'~ besides, moreover; nulle part ~ nowhere else; par ~ moreover, furthermore; partout ~ everywhere else.

aimable /ɛmabl/ *adj* kind.

aimant /ɛmɑ̃/ *nm* magnet.

aimer /eme/ **1** *vt* like; (d'amour) love; j'aimerais faire I'd like to do; ~ bien quite like; ~ mieux *ou* autant prefer.

aîné, ~e /ene/ *adj* eldest; (de deux) elder. ● *nm, f* eldest (child); (premier de deux) elder (child); ~s elders; il est mon ~ he is older than me *ou* my senior.

ainsi /ɛ̃si/ *adv* like this, thus; (donc) so; et ~ de suite and so on; pour ~ dire so to speak, as-it were; ~ que as well as; (comme) as.

air /ɛʀ/ *nm* air; (mine) look, air; (mélodie) tune; ~ conditionné airconditioning; avoir l'~ look, appear; avoir l'~ de look like; avoir l'~ de faire appear to be doing; en l'~ (up) in the air; (promesses) empty; prendre l'~ get some fresh air.

aire /ɛʀ/ *nf* area; ~ d'atterrissage landing-strip; ~ de pique-nique picnic area; ~ de repas rest area; ~ de services (motorway) services.

aisance /ɛzɑ̃s/ *nf* ease; (richesse) affluence.

aise /ɛz/ *nf* joy; à l'~ (sur un siège) comfortable; (pas gêné) at ease; (fortuné) comfortably off; mal à l'~ uncomfortable; ill at ease; aimer ses ~s like one's creature comforts; mettre qn à l'~ put sb at ease; se mettre à l'~ make oneself comfortable.

aisé, ~e /eze/ *adj* easy; (fortuné) well-off.

aisselle /ɛsɛl/ *nf* armpit.

ait /ɛ/ ➡ AVOIR **5**.

ajourner /aʒuʀne/ **1** *vt* postpone; (débat, procès) adjourn.

ajout /aʒu/ *nm* addition.

ajouter /aʒute/ **1** *vt* add (à to); ~ foi à lend credence to. □ s'~ *vpr* be added.

ajuster /aʒyste/ **1** *vt* adjust; (cible) aim at; (adapter) fit; ~ son coup adjust one's aim.

alarme /alaʀm/ *nf* alarm; donner l'~ raise the alarm.

alarmer /alaʀme/ **1** *vt* alarm. □ s'~ *vpr* become alarmed (de at).

Albanie /albani/ *nf* Albania.

alcool /alkɔl/ *nm* alcohol; (eau de vie) brandy; ~ à brûler methylated spirit. **alcoolique** *adj* & *nmf* alcoholic. **alcoolisé,** ~e *adj* (boisson) alcoholic. **alcoolisme** *nm* alcoholism.

alcootest /alkɔtɛst/ *nm* breath test; (appareil) Breathalyser®.

aléa /alea/ *nm* hazard. **aléatoire** *adj* unpredictable, uncertain; (Ordinat) random.

alentours /alɑ̃tuʀ/ *nmpl* surroundings; aux ~ de (de lieu) around; (de chiffre, date) about, around.

alerte /alɛʀt/ *adj* (personne) alert;

a (vif) lively. ● *nf* alert; ~ **à la bombe** bomb scare. **alerter** **1** *vt* alert.

algèbre /alʒɛbʀ/ *nf* algebra.

Algérie /alʒeʀi/ *nf* Algeria.

algue /alg/ *nf* seaweed; **les** ~**s** (Bot) algae.

aliéné, ~e /aljene/ *nm, f* insane person.

aliéner /aljene/ **14** *vt* alienate; (céder) give up. □ **s'**~ *vpr* alienate.

aligner /aliɲe/ **1** *vt* (objets) line up, make lines of; (chiffres) string together; ~ **sur** bring into line with. □ **s'**~ *vpr* line up; **s'**~ **sur** align oneself on.

aliment /alimɑ̃/ *nm* food.

alimentaire /alimɑ̃tɛʀ/ *adj* (industrie) food; (habitudes) dietary; **produits** ~**s** foodstuffs.

alimentation /alimɑ̃tasjɔ̃/ *nf* feeding, supply(ing); (régime) diet; (aliments) food; **magasin d'**~ grocery shop ou store.

alimenter /alimɑ̃te/ **1** *vt* feed; (fournir) supply; (fig) sustain. □ **s'**~ *vpr* eat.

allaiter /alete/ **1** *vt* (bébé) breastfeed; (US) nurse; (animal) suckle.

allée /ale/ *nf* path, lane; (menant à une maison) drive(way); (dans un cinéma, magasin) aisle; (rue) road; ~**s et venues** comings and goings.

allégé, ~e /aleʒe/ *adj* diet; (beurre, yaourt) low-fat.

alléger /aleʒe/ **14 40** *vt* make lighter; (fardeau, chargement) lighten; (fig) (souffrance) alleviate.

allégresse /alegʀɛs/ *nf* gaiety, joy.

alléguer /alege/ **14** *vt* (exemple) invoke; (prétexter) allege.

Allemagne /almaɲ/ *nf* Germany.

allemand, ~e /almɑ̃, -d/ *adj* German. ● *nm* (Ling) German. **A**~**, ~e** *nm, f* German.

aller /ale/ **8**
● *verbe auxiliaire*
••••▶ **je vais l'appeler** I'm going to call him; **j'allais partir** I was about to leave; **va savoir! va savoir! qui sait?**; ~ **en s'améliorant** to be improving.
● *verbe intransitif*
••••▶ (se déplacer) go; **allons-y!** let's go!; **allez! come on!**
••••▶ (se porter) **comment allez-vous?, comment ça va?** how are you?; **ça va (bien)** I'm fine; **qu'est-ce qui ne va pas?** what's the matter?; **ça ne va pas la tête?** **1** are you mad? **1**.
••••▶ (mettre en valeur) ~ **à** **suit sb**; **ça te va bien** it really suits you.
••••▶ (convenir) **ça va ma coiffure?** is my hair OK?; **ça ne va pas du tout** that's no good at all.
□ **s'en aller** *verbe pronominal*
••••▶ go; **va-t'en!** go away!; **ça ne s'en va pas** (tache) it won't come out.
● *nom masculin*
••••▶ outward journey; ~ **(simple)** single (ticket); (US) one-way (ticket); ~ **retour** return (ticket); (US) round trip (ticket); **à l'**~ on the way out.

allergie /alɛʀʒi/ *nf* allergy. **allergique** *adj* allergic (**à** to).

alliance /aljɑ̃s/ *nf* alliance; (bague) wedding-ring; (mariage) marriage.

allier /alje/ **45** *vt* combine; (Pol) ally. □ **s'**~ *vpr* combine; (Pol) form an alliance; (famille) become related (**à** to).

allô /alo/ *interj* hallo, hello.

allocation /alɔkasjɔ̃/ *nf* allowance; ~ **chômage** unemployment benefit; ~s **familiales** family allowance.

allonger /alɔ̃ʒe/ 40 vt lengthen; (bras, jambe) stretch (out); (coucher) lay down. □ s'~ vpr get longer; (s'étendre) lie down; (s'étirer) stretch (oneself) out.

allouer /alwe/ 1 vt allocate; (prêt) grant.

allumer /alyme/ 1 vt (bougie, gaz) light; (lampe, appareil) turn on; (pièce) switch the light(s) on in; (fig) arouse. □ s'~ vpr (lumière, appareil) come on.

allumette /alymɛt/ nf match.

allure /alyr/ nf speed, pace; (démarche) walk; (apparence) appearance; à **toute** ~ at full speed; **avoir de l'**~ have style; **avoir des** ~s **de** look like; **avoir une drôle d'**~ be funny-looking.

allusion /alyzjɔ̃/ nf allusion (à to); (implicite) hint (à at); **faire** ~ à allude to; hint at.

alors /alɔr/ adv (à ce moment-là) then; (de ce fait) so; (dans ce cas-là) then; **ça** ~! welll; **et** ~? so what? ● conj ~ **que** (pendant que) while; (tandis que) when, whereas.

alouette /alwɛt/ nf lark.

alourdir /alurdir/ 2 vt weigh down; (rendre plus important) increase.

aloyau (pl ~x) /alwajo/ nm sirloin.

Alpes /alp/ nfpl **les** ~ the Alps.

alphabet /alfabɛ/ nm alphabet. **alphabétique** adj alphabetical.

alphabétiser /alfabetize/ 1 vt teach to read and write.

alpiniste /alpinist/ nmf mountaineer.

altérer /altere/ 14 vt (fait, texte) distort; (abîmer) spoil; (donner soif à) make thirsty. □ s'~ vpr de-

teriorate.

alternance /alternɑ̃s/ nf alternation; **en** ~ alternately.

altitude /altityd/ nf altitude, height.

amabilité /amabilite/ nf kindness.

amaigrir /amegrir/ 2 vt make thin(ner).

amande /amɑ̃d/ nf almond; (d'un fruit à noyau) kernel.

amant /amɑ̃/ nm lover.

amarre /amar/ nf (mooring) rope; ~s moorings.

amas /ama/ nm heap, pile.

amasser /amase/ 1 vt amass, gather; (empiler) pile up. □ s'~ vpr pile up; (gens) gather.

amateur /amatœr/ nm amateur; ~ **de** lover of; **d'**~ amateur; (péj) amateurish.

ambassade /ɑ̃basad/ nf embassy. **ambassadeur, -drice** nm, f ambassador.

ambiance /ɑ̃bjɑ̃s/ nf atmosphere. **ambiant,** ~e adj surrounding.

ambigu, ~ë /ɑ̃bigy/ adj ambiguous.

ambitieux, -ieuse /ɑ̃bisjø, -z/ adj ambitious. **ambition** nf ambition.

ambulance /ɑ̃bylɑ̃s/ nf ambulance.

ambulant, ~e /ɑ̃bylɑ̃, -t/ adj itinerant, travelling.

âme /am/ nf soul; ~ **sœur** soul mate.

amélioration /ameljɔrasjɔ̃/ nf improvement.

améliorer /ameljɔre/ 1 vt improve. □ s'~ vpr improve.

aménagement /amenaʒmɑ̃/ nm (de magasin) fitting out; (de grenier) conversion; (de territoire) development; (de cuisine) equipping.

a

aménager /amenaʒe/ 40 vt (*magasin*) fit out; (*transformer*) convert; (*territoire*) develop; (*cuisine*) equip.

amende /amɑ̃d/ nf fine; faire ~ honorable make amends.

amener /am(ə)ne/ 6 vt bring; (*causer*) bring about; ~ qn à faire cause sb to do. □ s'~ vpr 1 turn up.

amer, -ère /amɛR/ adj bitter.

américain, ~e /ameʀikɛ̃, -ɛn/ adj American. A~, ~e nm, f American.

Amérique /ameʀik/ nf America; ~ centrale/latine Central/Latin America; ~ du Nord/Sud North/ South America.

amertume /amɛʀtym/ nf bitterness.

ami, ~e /ami/ nm, f friend; (*amateur*) lover; un ~ des bêtes an animal lover. ● adj friendly.

amiable /amjabl/ adj amicable; à l'~ (*divorcer*) by mutual consent; (*se séparer*) on friendly terms; (*séparation*) amicable.

amical, ~e (*mpl* -aux) /amikal, -o./ adj friendly.

amiral (*pl* -aux) /amiʀal, -o/ nm admiral.

amitié /amitje/ nf friendship; ~s (en fin de lettre) kind regards; prendre qn en ~ take a liking to sb.

amnistie /amnisti/ nf amnesty.

amoindrir /amwɛ̃dʀiʀ/ 2 vt reduce.

amont: en ~ /ɑ̃mɔ̃/ loc upstream.

amorcer /amɔʀse/ 10 vt start; (*hameçon*) bait; (*pompe*) prime; (*arme à feu*) arm.

amortir /amɔʀtiʀ/ 2 vt (*choc*) cushion; (*bruit*) deaden; (*dette*) pay off; ~ un achat make a purchase pay for itself.

amortisseur /amɔʀtisœʀ/ nm shock absorber.

amour /amuʀ/ nm love; pour l'~ de for the sake of.

amoureux, -euse /amuʀø, -z/ adj (*personne*) in love; (*relation, regard*) loving; (*vie*) love; ~ de qn in love with sb. ● nm, f lover.

amour-propre /amuʀpʀɔpʀ/ nm self-esteem.

amphithéâtre /ɑ̃fiteatʀ/ nm amphitheatre; (d'université) lecture hall.

ampleur /ɑ̃plœʀ/ nf extent, size; (de *vêtement*) fullness; prendre de l'~ spread, grow.

amplifier /ɑ̃plifje/ 45 vt amplify; (fig) expand, develop. □ s'~ vpr (son) grow; (scandale) intensify.

ampoule /ɑ̃pul/ nf (électrique) bulb; (sur la peau) blister; (Méd) phial, ampoule.

amusant, ~e /amyzɑ̃, -t/ adj (*blague*) funny; (*soirée*) enjoyable, entertaining.

amuse-gueule /amyzɡœl/ nm inv cocktail snack.

amusement /amyzmɑ̃/ nm amusement; (passe-temps) entertainment.

amuser /amyze/ 1 vt amuse; (détourner l'attention de) distract. □ s'~ vpr enjoy oneself; (jouer) play.

amygdale /amidal/ nf tonsil.

an /ɑ̃/ nm year; avoir dix ~s be ten years old; un garçon de deux ~s a two-year-old boy; à soixante ~s at the age of sixty; les moins de dix-huit ~s under eighteens.

analogie /analɔʒi/ nf analogy.

analogue /analɔg/ adj similar, analogous (à to).

analphabète /analfabɛt/ adj & nmf illiterate.

analyse /analiz/ *nf* analysis; (Méd) test. **analyser** ◼ *vt* analyse; (Méd) test.

ananas /anana(s)/ *nm* pineapple.

anarchie /anaʀʃi/ *nf* anarchy.

anatomie /anatɔmi/ *nf* anatomy.

ancêtre /ɑ̃sɛtʀ/ *nm* ancestor.

anchois /ɑ̃ʃwa/ *nm* anchovy.

ancien, ~ne /ɑ̃sjɛ̃, -jɛn/ *adj* old; (de jadis) ancient; (meuble) antique; (précédent) former, ex-, old; (dans une fonction) senior; ~ **combattant** veteran. ● *nm, f* senior; (par l'âge) elder. **anciennement** *adv* formerly. **ancienneté** *nf* age, seniority.

ancre /ɑ̃kʀ/ *nf* anchor; jeter/lever l'~ cast/weigh anchor.

andouille /ɑ̃duj/ *nf* sausage (*filled with chitterlings*); (idiot ◼) fool; faire l'~ fool around.

âne /ɑn/ *nm* donkey, ass; (imbécile ◼) dimwit ◼.

anéantir /aneɑ̃tiʀ/ ◼ *vt* destroy; (exterminer) annihilate; (accabler) overwhelm.

anémie /anemi/ *nf* anaemia.

ânerie /ɑnʀi/ *nf* stupid remark.

anesthésie /anɛstezi/ *nf* (opération) anaesthetic.

ange /ɑ̃ʒ/ *nm* angel; aux ~s in seventh heaven.

angine /ɑ̃ʒin/ *nf* throat infection.

anglais, ~e /ɑ̃glɛ, -z/ *adj* English. ● *nm* (Ling) English. A~, ~e *nm, f* Englishman, Englishwoman.

angle /ɑ̃gl/ *nm* angle; (coin) corner.

Angleterre /ɑ̃glətɛʀ/ *nf* England.

anglophone /ɑ̃glɔfɔn/ *adj* English-speaking. ● *nmf* English speaker.

angoissant, ~e /ɑ̃gwasɑ̃, -t/ *adj* alarming; (effrayant) harrowing.

angoisse /ɑ̃gwas/ *nf* anxiety. **angoissé, ~e** *adj* anxious. **angoisser**

◼ *vi* worry.

animal (*pl* **-aux**) /animal, -o/ *nm* animal; ~ **familier**, ~ **de compagnie** pet. ● *adj* (*pl* **-aux**) animal.

animateur, -trice /animatœʀ, -tʀis/ *nm, f* organizer, leader; (TV) host, hostess.

animation /animasjɔ̃/ *nf* liveliness; (affairement) activity; (au cinéma) animation; (activité dirigée) organized activity.

animé, ~e /anime/ *adj* lively; (affairé) busy; (être) animate.

animer /anime/ ◼ *vt* liven up; (débat, atelier) lead; (spectacle) host; (pousser) drive; (encourager) spur on. □ s'~ *vpr* liven up.

anis /ani(s)/ *nm* (Culin) aniseed; (Bot) anise.

anneau (*pl* ~**x**) /ano/ *nm* ring; (de chaîne) link.

année /ane/ *nf* year; ~ **bissextile** leap year; ~ **civile** calendar year.

annexe /anɛks/ *adj* (document) attached; (question) related; (bâtiment) adjoining. ● *nf* (bâtiment) annexe; (US) annex; (document) appendix; (électronique) attachment. **annexer** ◼ *vt* annex; (document) attach.

anniversaire /anivɛʀsɛʀ/ *nm* birthday; (d'un événement) anniversary. ● *adj* anniversary.

annonce /anɔ̃s/ *nf* announcement; (publicitaire) advertisement; (indice) sign.

annoncer /anɔ̃se/ ◼ *vt* announce; (prédire) forecast; (être l'indice de) herald. □ s'~ *vpr* (crise, tempête) be brewing; s'~ **bien/mal** look good/ bad. **annonceur** *nm* advertiser.

annuaire /anɥɛʀ/ *nm* year-book; ~ (**téléphonique**) (telephone) directory.

annuel, ~le /anɥɛl/ *adj* annual,

a

yearly.

annulation /anylasjɔ̃/ nf cancellation; (de sanction, loi) repeal; (de mesure) abolition.

annuler /anyle/ **1** vt cancel; (contrat) nullify; (jugement) quash; (loi) repeal. □ s'~ vpr cancel each other out.

anodin, ~e /anɔdɛ̃, -in/ adj insignificant; (sans risques) harmless, safe.

anonymat /anɔnima/ nm anonymity; garder l'~ remain anonymous. **anonyme** adj anonymous.

anorexie /anɔʀɛksi/ nf anorexia.

anormal, ~e (mpl **-aux**) /anɔʀmal, -o/ adj abnormal.

anse /ɑ̃s/ nf handle; (baie) cove.

Antarctique /ɑ̃taʀktik/ nm Antarctic.

antenne /ɑ̃tɛn/ nf aerial; (US) antenna; (d'insecte) antenna; (succursale) agency; (Mil) outpost; à l'~ on the air; ~ chirurgicale mobile emergency unit; ~ parabolique satellite dish.

antérieur, ~e /ɑ̃teʀjœʀ/ adj previous, earlier; (placé devant) front; ~ à prior to.

antiaérien, ~ne /ɑ̃tiaeʀjɛ̃, -ɛn/ adj anti-aircraft; abri ~ air-raid shelter.

antiatomique /ɑ̃tiatɔmik/ adj abri ~ nuclear fall-out shelter.

antibiotique /ɑ̃tibjɔtik/ nm antibiotic.

anticipation /ɑ̃tisipasjɔ̃/ nf d'~ (livre, film) science fiction; par ~ in advance.

anticiper /ɑ̃tisipe/ **1** vt ~ (sur) anticipate; (effectuer à l'avance) bring forward.

anticorps /ɑ̃tikɔʀ/ nm antibody.

antidater /ɑ̃tidate/ **1** vt back-

date, antedate.

antigel /ɑ̃tiʒɛl/ nm antifreeze.

Antilles /ɑ̃tij/ nfpl les ~ the West Indies.

antipathique /ɑ̃tipatik/ adj unpleasant.

antiquaire /ɑ̃tikɛʀ/ nmf antique dealer.

antiquité /ɑ̃tikite/ nf (objet) antique; l'A~ antiquity.

antisémite /ɑ̃tisemit/ adj antiSemitic.

antiseptique /ɑ̃tisɛptik/ adj & nm antiseptic.

antivirus /ɑ̃tiviʀys/ nm inv (Ordinat) antivirus software.

antivol /ɑ̃tivɔl/ nm anti-theft device; (Auto) steering lock.

anxiété /ɑ̃ksjete/ nf anxiety.

anxieux, -ieuse /ɑ̃ksjø, -z/ adj anxious. ● nm, f worrier.

août /u(t)/ nm August.

apaiser /apeze/ **1** vt calm down; (colère, militant) appease; (douleur) soothe; (faim) satisfy. □ s'~ vpr (tempête) die down.

apathie /apati/ nf apathy. **apathique** adj apathetic.

apercevoir /apɛʀsəvwaʀ/ **52** vt see. □ s'~ de vpr notice; s'~ que notice ou realize that.

aperçu /apɛʀsy/ nm (échantillon) glimpse, taste; (intuition) insight.

apéritif /apeʀitif/ nm aperitif, drink.

aphte /aft/ nm mouth ulcer.

apitoyer /apitwaje/ **31** vt move (to pity). □ s'~ vpr s'~ sur (le sort de) qn feel sorry for sb.

aplanir /aplaniʀ/ **2** vt level; (fig) iron out.

aplatir /aplatiʀ/ **2** vt flatten (out). □ s'~ vpr (s'immobiliser) flatten oneself.

aplomb /aplɔ̃/ nm balance; (fig) self-confidence; **d'~** (en équilibre) steady; **je ne suis pas bien d'~** I don't feel very well.

apogée /apɔʒe/ nm peak.

apologie /apɔlɔʒi/ nf panegyric.

apostrophe /apɔstʀɔf/ nf apostrophe; (remarque) remark.

apothéose /apɔteoz/ nf high point; (d'événement) grand finale.

apparaître /apaʀɛtʀ/ [18] vi appear; **il apparaît que** it appears that.

appareil /apaʀɛj/ nm device; (électrique) appliance; (Anat) system; (téléphone) phone; (avion) plane; (Culin) mixture; (système administratif) apparatus; **~ (dentaire)** brace; (dentier) dentures; **~ (photo)** camera; **c'est Gabriel à l'~** it's Gabriel on the phone; **~ auditif** hearing aid; **~ électroménager** household electrical appliance.

appareiller /apaʀeje/ [1] vi (navire) cast off, put to sea.

apparemment /apaʀamɑ̃/ adv apparently.

apparence /apaʀɑ̃s/ nf appearance; **en ~** outwardly; (apparemment) apparently.

apparent, ~e /apaʀɑ̃, -t/ adj apparent; (visible) conspicuous.

apparenté, ~e /apaʀɑ̃te/ adj related; (semblable) similar.

apparition /apaʀisjɔ̃/ nf appearance; (spectre) apparition.

appartement /apaʀtəmɑ̃/ nm flat; (US) apartment.

appartenir /apaʀtəniʀ/ [58] vi belong (à to); **il lui appartient de** it is up to him to.

appât /apa/ nm bait; (fig) lure.

appauvrir /apovʀiʀ/ [2] vt impoverish. □ **s'~** vpr become impoverished.

appel /apɛl/ nm call; (Jur) appeal; (supplique) appeal, plea; (Mil) call-up; (US) draft; **faire ~** appeal; **faire ~ à** (recourir à) call on; (invoquer) appeal to; (évoquer) call up; (exiger) call for; **faire l'~** (Scol) call the register; (Mil) take a roll-call; **~ d'offres** (Comm) invitation to tender; **faire un ~ de phares** flash one's headlights.

appeler /aple/ [8] vt call; (téléphoner) phone, call; (nécessiter) call for; **en ~ à** appeal to; (destiné) destined for. □ **s'~** vpr be called; **il s'appelle Tim** his name is Tim ou he is called Tim.

appellation /apɛlasjɔ̃/ nf name, designation.

appendice /apɛ̃dis/ nm appendix.

appendicite nf appendicitis.

appesantir /apəzɑ̃tiʀ/ [2] vt weigh down. □ **s'~** vpr grow heavier; **s'~ sur** dwell upon.

appétissant, ~e /apetisɑ̃, -t/ adj appetizing.

appétit /apeti/ nm appetite; **bon ~!** enjoy your meal!

applaudir /aplodiʀ/ [2] vt/i applaud. **applaudissements** nmpl applause.

application /aplikasjɔ̃/ nf (soin) care; (de loi) (respect) application; (mise en œuvre) implementation; (Ordinat) application program.

appliqué, ~e /aplike/ adj (travail) painstaking; (sciences) applied; (élève) hard-working.

appliquer /aplike/ [1] vt apply; (loi) enforce. □ **s'~** vpr apply oneself (à to), take great care (à faire to do); **s'~ à** (concerner) apply to.

appoint /apwɛ̃/ nm support; **d'~** extra; **faire l'~** give the correct money.

a **apport** /apɔʀ/ nm contribution.

apporter /apɔʀte/ **1** vt bring; (aide, précision) give; (causer) bring about.

appréciation /apʀesjasjɔ̃/ nf estimate, evaluation; (de monnaie) appreciation; (jugement) assessment.

apprécier /apʀesje/ **45** vt appreciate; (évaluer) assess; (objet) value, appraise.

appréhender /apʀeɑ̃de/ **1** vt dread, fear; (arrêter) apprehend.

apprendre /apʀɑ̃dʀ/ **50** vt learn; (être informé de) hear, learn; (de façon indirecte) hear of; ~ qch à qn teach sb sth; (informer) tell sb sth; ~ à faire learn to do; ~ à qn à faire teach sb to do; ~ que learn that; (être informé) hear that.

apprenti, ~e /apʀɑ̃ti/ nm, f apprentice. **apprentissage** nm apprenticeship; (d'un sujet) learning.

apprêter /apʀete/ **1** vt prepare; (bois) prime; (mur) size. □ s'~ à vpr prepare to.

apprivoiser /apʀivwaze/ **1** vt tame.

approbation /apʀɔbasjɔ̃/ nf approval.

approchant, ~e /apʀɔʃɑ̃, -t/ adj close, similar.

approche /apʀɔʃ/ **1** vt (objet) move near(er) (de to); (personne) approach; ~ de get nearer or closer to. ● vi approach. □ s'~ de vpr approach, move near(er) to.

approfondir /apʀɔfɔ̃diʀ/ **2** vt deepen; (fig) (sujet) go into sth in depth; (connaissances) improve.

approprié, ~e /apʀɔpʀije/ adj appropriate.

approprier (s') /(s)apʀɔpʀije/ **45** vpr appropriate.

approuver /apʀuve/ **1** vt approve; (trouver louable) approve of;

(soutenir) agree with.

approvisionner /apʀɔvizjɔne/ **1** vt supply (en with); (compte en banque) pay money into. □ s'~ vpr stock up.

approximatif, -ive /apʀɔksimatif, -v/ adj approximate.

appui /apɥi/ nm support; (de fenêtre) sill; (pour objet) rest; à l'~ de in support of; prendre ~ sur lean on.

appui-tête (pl **appuis-tête**) /apɥitɛt/ nm headrest.

appuyer /apɥije/ **31** vt lean, rest; (presser) press; (soutenir) support, back. ● vi ~ sur press (on); (fig) stress. □ s'~ sur vpr lean on; (compter sur) rely on.

après /apʀɛ/ prép after; (au-delà de) after, beyond; ~ avoir fait after doing; ~ tout after all; ~ coup after the event; d'~ (selon) according to; (en imitant) from; (adapté de) based on. ● adv after (wards); (plus tard) later; le bus d'~ the next bus. ● conj ~ qu'il est parti after he left. **après-demain** adv the day after tomorrow. **après-guerre** (pl ~s) nm ou f postwar period. **après-midi** nm ou f inv afternoon. **après-rasage** (pl ~s) nm aftershave. **après-shampooing** nm conditioner. **après-ski** nm inv moon boot. **après-vente** adj inv aftersales.

a priori /apʀijɔʀi/ adv (à première vue) offhand, on the face of it; (sans réfléchir) out of hand. ● nm preconception.

à-propos /apʀopo/ nm timing, timeliness; (fig) presence of mind.

apte /apt/ adj capable (à of); (ayant les qualités requises) suitable (à for); (en état) fit (à for).

aptitude /aptityd/ nf aptitude,

ability.

aquarelle /akwaʀɛl/ nf water-colour.

aquatique /akwatik/ adj aquatic; (Sport) water.

arabe /aʀab/ adj Arab; (Ling) Arabic; (désert) Arabian. ● nm (Ling) Arabic. **A~** nmf Arab.

Arabie /aʀabi/ nf ~ Saoudite Saudi Arabia.

arachide /aʀaʃid/ nf groundnut; huile d'~ groundnut oil.

araignée /aʀeɲe/ nf spider.

arbitraire /aʀbitʀɛʀ/ adj arbitrary.

arbitre /aʀbitʀ/ nm referee; (au cricket, tennis) umpire; (expert) arbiter; (Jur) arbitrator. **arbitrer** 1 vt (match) referee, umpire; (Jur) arbitrate in.

arbre /aʀbʀ/ nm tree; (Tech) shaft.

arbuste /aʀbyst/ nm shrub.

arc /aʀk/ nm (arme) bow; (courbe) curve; (voûte) arch; ~ de cercle arc of a circle.

arc-en-ciel (pl **arcs-en-ciel**) /aʀkɑ̃sjɛl/ nm rainbow.

arche /aʀʃ/ nf arch; ~ de Noé Noah's ark.

archéologie /aʀkeɔlɔʒi/ nf archaeology.

archevêque /aʀʃəvɛk/ nm arch-bishop.

architecte /aʀʃitɛkt/ nmf architect. **architecture** nf architecture.

Arctique /aʀktik/ nm Arctic.

ardent, ~e /aʀdɑ̃, -t/ adj burning; (passionné) ardent; (foi) fervent. **ardeur** nf (passion) ardour; (chaleur) heat.

ardoise /aʀdwaz/ nf slate; ~ électronique notepad computer.

arène /aʀɛn/ nf arena; ~s amphitheatre; (pour corridas) bullring.

arête /aʀɛt/ nf (de poisson) bone; (bord) ridge.

argent /aʀʒɑ̃/ nm money; (métal) silver; ~ comptant cash; prendre pour ~ comptant take at face value; ~ de poche pocket money. **a**

argenté, ~e /aʀʒɑ̃te/ adj silver(y); (métal) (silver-)plated.

argenterie /aʀʒɑ̃tʀi/ nf silverware.

Argentine /aʀʒɑ̃tin/ nf Argentina.

argile /aʀʒil/ nf clay.

argot /aʀgo/ nm slang.

argument /aʀgymɑ̃/ nm argument; ~ de vente selling point. **argumenter** 1 vi argue.

aristocratie /aʀistɔkʀasi/ nf aristocracy.

arithmétique /aʀitmetik/ nf arithmetic. ● adj arithmetical.

armature /aʀmatyʀ/ nf framework; (de tente) frame.

arme /aʀm/ nf arm, weapon; ~ à feu firearm; ~s (blason) coat of arms; ~s de destruction massive weapons of mass destruction.

armée /aʀme/ nf army; ~ de l'air Air Force; ~ de terre Army.

armer /aʀme/ 1 vt arm; (fusil) cock; (navire) equip; (renforcer) reinforce; (Photo) wind on. □ s'~ de vpr arm oneself with.

armoire /aʀmwaʀ/ nf cupboard; (penderie) wardrobe; (US) closet; ~ à pharmacie medicine cabinet.

armure /aʀmyʀ/ nf armour.

arnaque /aʀnak/ nf 🟦 swindling; c'est de l'~ it's a swindle🟦.

arobas(e) /aʀɔbas, aʀɔbaz/ nm at sign.

aromate /aʀɔmat/ nm herb, spice.

aromatisé, ~e /aʀɔmatize/ adj flavoured.

arôme /aʀom/ nm aroma; (additif) flavouring.

arpenter /aʀpɑ̃te/ 1 vt pace up and down; (terrain) survey.

a **arqué**, ~e /aʀke/ adj arched; (jambes) bandy.

arrache-pied: d'~ /daʀaʃpje/ loc relentlessly.

arracher /aʀaʃe/ **1** vt pull out ou off; (plante) pull ou dig up; (cheveux, page) tear ou pull out; (par une explosion) blow off; ~ à (enlever à) snatch from; (fig) force ou wrest from. □ **s'~ qch** vpr fight over sth.

arrangement /aʀɑ̃ʒmɑ̃/ nm arrangement.

arranger /aʀɑ̃ʒe/ **40** vt arrange, fix up; (réparer) put right; (régler) sort out; (convenir à) suit. □ **s'~** vpr (se mettre d'accord) come to an arrangement; (se débrouiller) manage (pour to).

arrestation /aʀɛstɑsjɔ̃/ nf arrest.

arrêt /aʀɛ/ nm stopping; (de combats) cessation; (de production) halt; (lieu) stop; (pause) pause; (Jur) ruling; **aux ~s** (Mil) under arrest; à l'~ (véhicule) stationary; (machine) idle; **faire un ~** (make a) stop; **sans ~** (sans escale) nonstop; (sans interruption) constantly; ~ **maladie** sick leave; ~ **de travail** (grève) stoppage; (Méd) sick leave.

arrêté /aʀete/ nm order; ~ **municipal** bylaw.

arrêter /aʀete/ **1** vt stop; (date) fix; (appareil) turn off; (renoncer à) give up; (appréhender) arrest. ● vi stop. □ **s'~** vpr stop; **s'~ de faire** stop doing.

arrhes /aʀ/ nfpl deposit; **verser des ~** pay a deposit.

arrière /aʀjɛʀ/ adj inv back, rear. ● nm back, rear; (football) back; à l'~ in ou at the back; **en ~** behind; (marcher, tomber) backwards; ~ **de** behind. **arrière-boutique** (pl ~s) nf back room (of the shop). **arrière-garde** (pl ~s) nf rearguard. **arrière-goût** (pl ~s) nm aftertaste. **arrière-grand-mère** (pl arrière-

grands-mères) nf great-grandmother. **arrière-grand-père** (pl arrière-grands-pères) nm great-grandfather. **arrière-pays** nm inv backcountry. **arrière-pensée** (pl ~s) nf ulterior motive. **arrière-plan** nm (pl ~s) background.

arrimer /aʀime/ **1** vt secure; (cargaison) stow.

arrivage /aʀivaʒ/ nm consignment.

arrivée /aʀive/ nf arrival; (Sport) finish.

arriver /aʀive/ **1** vi (aux être) arrive, come; (réussir) succeed; (se produire) happen; ~ **à** (atteindre) reach; ~ **à faire** manage to do; je n'arrive pas à faire I can't do; **en ~ à faire** get to the stage of doing; **il arrive que** it happens that; **il lui arrive de faire** he (sometimes) does.

arriviste /aʀivist/ nmf go-getter, self-seeker.

arrondir /aʀɔ̃diʀ/ **2** vt (make) round; (somme) round off. □ **s'~** vpr become round(ed).

arrondissement /aʀɔ̃dismɑ̃/ nm district.

> **Arrondissement** A subdivision of a *département*. Each *arrondissement* has a *sous-préfet* representing the state administration at local level. In Paris, Lyons and Marseilles, an *arrondissement* is a sub-division of the commune, and has its own *maire* and local council.

arroser /aʀoze/ **1** vt water; (repas) wash down (with a drink); (rôti) baste; (victoire) drink to. **arrosoir** nm watering can.

art /aʀ/ nm art; (don) knack (de faire of doing); ~**s et métiers** arts and crafts; ~s ménagers home economics (+ *sg*).

artère /aʀtɛʀ/ *nf* artery; (grande) ~ main road.

arthrite /aʀtʀit/ *nf* arthritis.

arthrose /aʀtʀoz/ *nf* osteoarthritis.

artichaut /aʀtiʃo/ *nm* artichoke.

article /aʀtikl/ *nm* article; (Comm) item, article; à l'~ de la mort at death's door; ~ de fond feature (article); ~s de voyage travel goods.

articulation /aʀtikylasjɔ̃/ *nf* articulation; (Anat) joint.

articuler /aʀtikyle/ **1** *vt* articulate; (structurer) structure; (assembler) connect (sur to).

artificiel, ~le /aʀtifisjɛl/ *adj* artificial.

artisan /aʀtizɑ̃/ *nm* artisan, craftsman; l'~ de (fig) the architect of.

artisanal, ~e (*mpl* ~aux) /aʀtizanal/ *adj* craft; (méthode) traditional; (amateur) home-made; de fabrication ~e hand-made, hand-crafted.

artiste /aʀtist/ *nmf* artist. **artistique** *adj* artistic.

as¹ /a/ ►AVOIR **5**.

as² /ɑs/ *nm* ace.

ascenseur /asɑ̃sœʀ/ *nm* lift; (US) elevator.

ascension /asɑ̃sjɔ̃/ *nf* ascent; l'A~ Ascension.

aseptiser /asɛptize/ **1** *vt* disinfect; (stériliser) sterilize; aseptisé (péj) sanitized.

asiatique /azjatik/ *adj* Asian. A~ *nmf* Asian.

Asie /azi/ *nf* Asia.

asile /azil/ *nm* refuge; (Pol) asylum; (pour malades, vieillards) home; ~ de nuit night shelter.

aspect /aspɛ/ *nm* appearance; (fa-

cettes) aspect; (perspective) side; à l'~ de at the sight of.

asperge /aspɛʀʒ/ *nf* asparagus.

asperger /aspɛʀʒe/ **40** *vt* spray.

asphyxier /asfiksje/ **45** *vt* (*personne*) asphyxiate; (*entreprise, réseau*) paralyse. □ s'~ *vpr* suffocate; gas oneself; (*entreprise, réseau*) become paralysed.

aspirateur /aspiʀatœʀ/ *nm* vacuum cleaner.

aspirer /aspiʀe/ **1** *vt* inhale; (*liquide*) suck up. ● *vi* ~ à aspire to.

aspirine® /aspiʀin/ *nf* aspirin.

assainir /aseniʀ/ **2** *vt* clean up.

assaisonnement /asɛzɔnmɑ̃/ *nm* seasoning.

assassin /asasɛ̃/ *nm* murderer; (Pol) assassin. **assassiner** **1** *vt* murder; (Pol) assassinate.

assaut /aso/ *nm* assault, onslaught; donner l'~ à, prendre d'~ storm.

assemblage /asɑ̃blaʒ/ *nm* assembly; (combinaison) collection; (Tech) joint.

assemblée /asɑ̃ble/ *nf* meeting; (gens réunis) gathering; (Pol) assembly.

> **Assemblée nationale** The lower house of the French parliament, in which 577 *députés* are elected for a five-year term. *Députés* sit in parties in the semi-circular chamber, with the most left-wing to the extreme left and the most right-wing to the extreme right. The *Assemblée nationale* passes laws, votes on the Budget, and questions ministers. ***i***

assembler /asɑ̃ble/ **1** *vt* assemble, put together; (réunir) gather. □ s'~ *vpr* gather, assemble.

asseoir /aswaʀ/ **9** *vt* sit (down),

seat; (*bébé, malade*) sit up; (affermir) establish; (baser) base. □ **s'~** *vpr* sit (down).

assez /ase/ *adv* (suffisamment) enough; (plutôt) quite, fairly; ~ **grand/rapide** big/fast enough (pour to); ~ **de** enough; **j'en ai** (~ **de**) I've had enough (of).

assidu, ~**e** /asidy/ *adj* (zélé) assiduous; (régulier) regular; ~ **auprès de** attentive to. **assiduité** *nf* assiduousness, regularity.

assiéger /asjeʒe/ 14 40 *vt* besiege.

assiette /asjɛt/ *nf* plate; (équilibre) seat; ~ **anglaise** assorted cold meats; ~ **creuse/plate** soup-/dinner-plate; **ne pas être dans son** ~ feel out of sorts.

assigner /asiɲe/ 1 *vt* assign; (limite) fix.

assimilation /asimilasjɔ̃/ *nf* assimilation; (comparaison) likening, comparison.

assimiler /asimile/ 1 *vt* ~ **à** liken to; (classer) class as. □ **s'~** *vpr* assimilate; (être comparable) be comparable (à to).

assis, ~**e** /asi, -z/ *adj* sitting (down), seated. ● ⇒ASSEOIR 9.

assise /asiz/ *nf* (base) foundation; ~**s** (tribunal) assizes; (congrès) conference, congress.

assistance /asistɑ̃s/ *nf* audience; (aide) assistance; **l'A~** (publique) welfare services.

assistant, ~**e** /asistɑ̃, -t/ *nm, f* assistant; (Scol) foreign language assistant; **~s** (spectateurs) members of the audience; ~**e sociale** social worker; ~ **numérique** personal digital assistant, PDA.

assister /asiste/ 1 *vt* assist; ~ **à** attend, be (present) at; (accident) witness; **assisté par ordinateur** computer-assisted.

association /asɔsjasjɔ̃/ *nf* association.

associé, ~**e** /asɔsje/ *nm, f* partner, associate. ● *adj* associate.

associer /asɔsje/ 45 *vt* associate; (mêler) combine (à with); ~ **qn à** (*projet*) involve sb in; (*bénéfices*) give sb a share of. □ **s'~** *vpr* (sociétés, personnes) become associated, join forces (à with); (s'harmoniser) combine (à with); **s'~ à** (joie, opinion de qn) share; (projet) take part in.

assommer /asɔme/ 1 *vt* knock out; (animal) stun; (fig) overwhelm; (ennuyer 11) bore.

Assomption /asɔ̃psjɔ̃/ *nf* Assumption.

assortiment /asɔrtimɑ̃/ *nm* assortment.

assortir /asɔrtir/ 2 *vt* match (à with, to); ~ **de** accompany with. □ **s'~** *vpr* match; **s'~ à qch** match sth.

assoupir (**s'**) /(s)asupir/ 2 *vpr* doze off; (s'apaiser) subside.

assouplir /asuplir/ 2 *vt* make supple; (fig) make flexible.

assourdir /asurdir/ 2 *vt* (personne) deafen; (bruit) muffle.

assouvir /asuvir/ 2 *vt* satisfy.

assujettir /asyʒetir/ 2 *vt* subjugate, subdue; ~ **à** subject to.

assumer /asyme/ 1 *vt* assume; (coût) meet; (accepter) come to terms with, accept.

assurance /asyrɑ̃s/ *nf* (self-) assurance; (garantie) assurance; (contrat) insurance; ~**s sociales** social insurance; ~ **automobile/maladie** car/health insurance.

assuré, ~**e** /asyre/ *adj* certain, assured; (sûr de soi) confident, assured. ● *nm, f* insured party.

assurer /asyre/ 1 *vt* ensure;

(fournir) provide; (exécuter) carry out; (Comm) insure; (stabiliser) steady; (frontières) make secure; ~ à qn que assure sb that; ~ qn de assure sb of; ~ la gestion/défense de manage/defend. □ s'~ vpr take out insurance; s'~ de/que make sure of/that; s'~ qch (se procurer) secure sth. **assureur** nm insurer.

astérisque /asteʀisk/ nm asterisk.

asthmatique /asmatik/ adj & nmf asthmatic.

asthme /asm/ nm asthma.

asticot /astiko/ nm maggot.

astreindre /astʀɛ̃dʀ/ [22] vt ~ qn à qch force sth on sb; ~ qn à faire force sb to do.

astrologie /astʀɔlɔʒi/ nf astrology. **astrologue** nmf astrologer.

astronaute /astʀonot/ nmf astronaut.

astronomie /astʀonɔmi/ nf astronomy. **astronome** nmf astronomer.

astuce /astys/ nf smartness; (truc) trick; (plaisanterie) wisecrack.

astucieux, -ieuse /astysjø, -z/ adj smart, clever.

atelier /atalje/ nm (local) workshop; (de peintre) studio; (séance de travail) workshop.

athée /ate/ nmf atheist. ● adj atheistic.

athlète /atlɛt/ nmf athlete. **athlétisme** nm athletics.

Atlantique /atlɑ̃tik/ nm Atlantic (Ocean).

atmosphère /atmosfɛʀ/ nf atmosphere.

atomique /atɔmik/ adj atomic; (énergie, centrale) nuclear.

atomiseur /atɔmizœʀ/ nm spray.

atout /atu/ nm trump (card); (avantage) asset.

atroce /atʀɔs/ adj atrocious.

attabler (s') /(s)atable/ [1] vpr sit down at table.

attachant, ~e /ataʃɑ̃, -t/ adj charming.

attache /ataʃ/ nf (agrafe) fastener; (lien) tie.

attaché, ~e /ataʃe/ adj être ~ à (aimer) be attached to. ● nm, f (Pol) attaché.

attacher /ataʃe/ [1] vt tie (up); (ceinture, robe) fasten; (bicyclette) lock; ~ à (attribuer à) attach to. ● vi (Culin) stick. □ s'~ vpr fasten, do up; s'~ à become attached to; (se consacrer à) apply oneself to.

attaquant, ~e /atakɑ̃, -t/ nm, f attacker; (au football) striker; (au football américain) forward.

attaque /atak/ nf attack; ~ (cérébrale) stroke; il va en faire une ~ he'll have a fit; ~ à main armée armed attack.

attaquer /atake/ [1] vt attack; (banque) raid. ● vi attack. □ s'~ à vpr attack; (problème, sujet) tackle.

attardé, ~e /ataʀde/ adj backward; (idées) outdated; (en retard) late.

attarder (s') /(s)ataʀde/ [1] vpr linger.

atteindre /atɛ̃dʀ/ [22] vt reach; (blesser) hit; (affecter) affect.

atteint, ~e /atɛ̃, -t/ adj ~ de suffering from.

atteinte /atɛ̃t/ nf attack (à on); porter ~ à attack; (droit) infringe.

atteler /atle/ [38] vt (cheval) harness; (remorque) couple. □ s'~ à vpr get down to.

attelle /atɛl/ nf splint.

attenant, ~e /atnɑ̃, -t/ adj ~ (à) adjoining.

attendant: en ~ /ɑ̃natɑ̃dɑ̃/ loc meanwhile.

attendre /atɑ̃dʀ/ **3** vt wait for; (bébé) expect; (être le sort de) await; (escompter) expect; ~ que qn fasse wait for sb to do. ● vi wait; (au téléphone) hold. □ s'~ à vpr expect.

attendrir /atɑ̃dʀiʀ/ **2** vt move (to pity). □ s'~ vpr be moved to pity.

attendu /atɑ̃dy/ prép given, considering; ~ que considering that.

attendu², ~e /atɑ̃dy/ adj (escompté) expected; (espéré) long-awaited.

attentat /atɑ̃ta/ nm assassination attempt; ~ (à la bombe) (bomb) attack.

attente /atɑ̃t/ nf wait(ing); (espoir) expectations (+ pl).

attenter /atɑ̃te/ **1** vi ~ à make an attempt on; (fig) violate.

attentif, -ive /atɑ̃tif, -v/ adj attentive; (scrupuleux) careful; ~ à mindful of; (soucieux) careful of.

attention /atɑ̃sjɔ̃/ nf attention; (soin) care; ~ (à)! watch out (for)!; faire ~ à (écouter) pay attention to; (prendre garde à) watch out for; (prendre soin de) take care of; faire ~ à faire be careful to do. **attentionné**, ~e adj considerate.

attentisme /atɑ̃tism/ nm wait-and-see policy.

atténuer /atenɥe/ **1** vt (violence) reduce; (critique) tone down; (douleur) ease; (faute) mitigate. □ s'~ vpr subside.

atterrir /ateʀiʀ/ **2** vi land. **atterrissage** nm landing.

attestation /atɛstasjɔ̃/ nf certificate.

attester /atɛste/ **1** vt testify to; ~ que testify that.

attirant, ~e /atiʀɑ̃, -t/ adj attractive.

attirer /atiʀe/ **1** vt draw, attract;

(causer) bring. □ s'~ vpr bring upon oneself; (amis) win.

attiser /atize/ **1** vt (feu) poke; (sentiment) stir up.

attitré, ~e /atitʀe/ adj accredited; (habituel) usual, regular.

attitude /atityd/ nf attitude; (maintien) bearing.

attraction /atʀaksjɔ̃/ nf attraction.

attrait /atʀɛ/ nm attraction.

attraper /atʀape/ **1** vt catch; (corde, maladie) catch hold of; (habitude, accent) pick up; (maladie) catch; se faire ~ **1** get told off.

attrayant, ~e /atʀɛjɑ̃, -t/ adj attractive.

attribuer /atʀibɥe/ **1** vt allocate; (prix) award; (imputer) attribute. □ s'~ vpr claim (for oneself). **attribution** nf awarding, allocation.

attrouper (s') /(s)atʀupe/ **1** vpr gather.

au /o/ ➡À.

aubaine /obɛn/ nf godsend, opportunity.

aube /ob/ nf dawn, daybreak.

auberge /obɛʀʒ/ nf inn; ~ de jeunesse youth hostel.

aubergine /obɛʀʒin/ nf aubergine; (US) eggplant.

aucun, ~e /okœ̃, okyn/ adj (dans une phrase négative) no, not any; (positif) any. ● pron (dans une phrase négative) none, not any; (positif) any; ~ des deux neither of the two; d'~s some. **aucunement** adv not at all, in no way.

audace /odas/ nf daring; (impudence) audacity.

audacieux, -ieuse /odasjø, -z/ adj daring.

au-delà /od(ə)la/ adv beyond. ● prép ~ de beyond.

au-dessous /od(ə)su/ adv below.
● prép ~ de below; (couvert par) under.

au-dessus /od(ə)sy/ adv above.
● prép ~ de above.

au-devant /od(ə)vã/ prép aller ~ de qn go to meet sb; aller ~ des désirs de qn anticipate sb's wishes.

audience /odjãs/ nf audience; (d'un tribunal) hearing; (succès, attention) success.

audimat® /odimat/ nm l'~ the TV ratings.

audiovisuel, ~le /odjovizɥɛl/ adj audio-visual.

auditeur, -trice /oditœr, -tris/ nm, f listener.

audition /odisjõ/ nf hearing; (Théât, Mus) audition.

auditoire /oditwar/ nm audience.

augmentation /ogmãtasjõ/ nf increase; ~ (de salaire) (pay) rise; (US) raise.

augmenter /ogmãte/ **1** vt/i increase; (employé) give a pay rise ou raise to.

augure /ogyr/ nm (devin) oracle; être de bon/mauvais ~ be a good/ bad sign.

aujourd'hui /oʒurdɥi/ adv today.

auparavant /oparavã/ adv (avant) before; (précédemment) previously; (en premier lieu) beforehand.

auprès /oprɛ/ prép ~ de (à côté de) beside, next to; (comparé à) compared with; s'excuser/se plaindre ~ de apologize/complain to.

auquel /okɛl/ ⇒LEQUEL.

aura, aurait /ora, orɛ/ ⇒AVOIR **5**.

aurore /oror/ nf dawn.

aussi /osi/ adv (également) too, also, as well; (dans une comparaison) as; (si, tellement) so; ~ bien que as well as. ● conj (donc) so, consequently.

aussitôt /osito/ adv immediately; ~ que as soon as, the moment; ~ arrivé as soon as he arrived.

austère /ostɛr/ adj austere.

Australie /ostrali/ nf Australia.

australien, ~ne /ostraljɛ̃, -ɛn/ adj Australian. A~, ~ne nm, f Australian.

autant /otã/ adv (travailler, manger) as much (que as); ~ (de) (quantité) as much (que as); (nombre) as many (que as); (tant) so much, so many; ~ faire one had better do; d'~ plus que all the more than; en faire ~ do the same; pour ~ for all that.

autel /otɛl/ nm altar.

auteur /otœr/ nm author; l'~ du crime the perpetrator of the crime.

authentifier /otãtifje/ **45** vt authenticate.

authentique /otãtik/ adj authentic.

auto /oto/ nf car; ~ tamponneuse dodgem, bumper car.

autobus /otobys/ nm bus.

autocar /otokar/ nm coach.

autochtone /otokton/ nmf native.

autocollant, ~e /otokolã, -t/ adj self-adhesive. ● nm sticker.

autodidacte /otodidakt/ nmf self-taught person.

auto-école (pl ~s) /otoekol/ nf driving school.

automate /otomat/ nm automaton, robot.

automatique /otomatik/ adj automatic.

automatisation /otomatizasjõ/ nf automation.

automne /oton/ nm autumn; (US) fall.

automobile /otomobil/ adj

a

motor, car; (US) automobile. ● *nf* (motor) car; **l'~** the motor industry; (Sport) motoring. **automobiliste** *nmf* motorist.

autonome /otɔnɔm/ *adj* autonomous; (Ordinat) stand-alone.

autoradio /otɔʀadjo/ *nm* car radio.

autorisation /otɔʀizasjɔ̃/ *nf* permission, authorization; (permis) permit.

autorisé, ~e /otɔʀize/ *adj* (opinions) authoritative; (approuvé) authorized.

autoriser /otɔʀize/ **1** *vt* authorize, permit; (rendre possible) allow (of); (donner un droit) **~ qn à faire** entitle sb to do.

autoritaire /otɔʀitɛʀ/ *adj* authoritarian.

autorité /otɔʀite/ *nf* authority; **faire ~** be authoritative.

autoroute /otɔʀut/ *nf* motorway; (US) highway; **~ de l'information** (Ordinat) information superhighway.

auto-stop /otostɔp/ *nm* hitchhiking; **faire de l'~** hitch-hike; **prendre qn en ~** give a lift to sb.

autour /otuʀ/ *adv* around; **tout ~** all around. ● *prép* **~ de** around.

autre /otʀ/ *adj* other; **un ~ jour/ livre** another day/book; **~ chose/ part** something/somewhere else; **quelqu'un/rien d'~** somebody/ nothing else; **quoi d'~?** what else?; **d'~ part** on the other hand; (de plus) moreover, besides; **vous ~s Anglais** you English. ● *pron* **un ~, une ~** another (one); **l'~** the other (one); **les ~s** the others; (autrui) others; **d'~s** (some) others; **l'un l'~s** each other; **l'un et l'~** both of them; **d'un jour à l'~** (bientôt) any day now; **entre ~s** among other things.

autrefois /otʀəfwa/ *adv* in the past; (précédemment) formerly.

autrement /otʀəmɑ̃/ *adv* differently; (sinon) otherwise; (plus 🔢) far more; **~ dit** in other words.

Autriche /otʀiʃ/ *nf* Austria.

autrichien, ~ne /otʀiʃjɛ̃, -jɛn/ *adj* Austrian. **A~, ~ne** *nm, f* Austrian.

autruche /otʀyʃ/ *nf* ostrich.

autrui /otʀɥi/ *pron* others, other people.

aux /o/ ⇒**À**.

auxiliaire /oksiljɛʀ/ *adj* auxiliary. ● *nmf* (assistant) auxiliary. ● *nm* (Gram) auxiliary.

auxquels, -quelles /okɛl/ ⇒**LEQUEL**.

aval: **en ~** /ɑ̃naval/ *loc* downstream.

avaler /avale/ **1** *vt* swallow.

avance /avɑ̃s/ *nf* advance; (sur un concurrent) lead; **~ (de fonds)** advance; **à l'~** in advance; **d'~** already; **en ~** early; (montre) fast; **en ~ (sur)** (menant) ahead (of).

avancement /avɑ̃smɑ̃/ *nm* promotion.

avancé, ~e /avɑ̃se/ *adj* advanced.

avancer /avɑ̃se/ **10** *vi* move forward, advance; (travail) make progress; (montre) be fast; (faire saillie) jut out. ● *vt* move forward; (dans le temps) bring forward; (argent) advance; (montre) put forward. □ **s'~** *vpr* move forward, advance; (se hasarder) commit oneself.

avant /avɑ̃/ *nm* front; (Sport) forward. ● *adj inv* front. ● *prép* before; **~ de faire** before doing; **en ~ de** in front of; **~ peu** shortly; **~ tout** above all. ● *adv* (dans le temps) before, beforehand; (d'abord) first; **en ~** (dans l'espace) forward(s); (dans le temps) ahead; **le bus d'~** the previous bus. ● *conj* ~ que before; ~ qu'il (ne) fasse before he does.

avantage /avɑ̃taʒ/ *nm* advantage; (Comm) benefit.

avantager /avɑ̃taʒe/ 🔟 *vt* favour; (embellir) show off to advantage.

avantageux, -euse /avɑ̃taʒø, -z/ *adj* advantageous, favourable; (*prix*) attractive.

avant-bras /avɑ̃bra/ *nm inv* forearm.

avant-centre (*pl* **avants-centres**) /avɑ̃sɑ̃tr/ *nm* centre forward.

avant-coureur (*pl* ~s) /avɑ̃kurœr/ *adj* precursory, foreshadowing.

avant-dernier, -ière (*pl* ~s) /avɑ̃dɛrnje, -jɛr/ *adj & nm, f* last but one.

avant-goût (*pl* ~s) /avɑ̃gu/ *nm* foretaste.

avant-hier /avɑ̃tjɛr/ *adv* the day before yesterday.

avant-poste (*pl* ~s) /avɑ̃pɔst/ *nm* outpost.

avant-première (*pl* ~s) /avɑ̃prəmjɛr/ *nf* preview.

avant-propos /avɑ̃prɔpo/ *nm inv* foreword.

avare /avar/ *adj* miserly; ~ de sparing with. ● *nmf* miser.

avarié, ~e /avarje/ *adj* (*aliment*) spoiled.

avatar /avatar/ *nm* misfortune.

avec /avɛk/ *prép* with. ● *adv* 🔟 with it *ou* them.

avènement /avɛnmɑ̃/ *nm* advent; (d'un roi) accession.

avenir /avnir/ *nm* future; à l'~ in future; d'~ with (future) prospects.

aventure /avɑ̃tyr/ *nf* adventure; (sentimentale) affair. **aventureux, -euse** *adj* adventurous; (hasardeux)

risky.

avérer (s') /(s)avere/ 🔟 *vpr* prove (to be).

averse /avɛrs/ *nf* shower.

avertir /avɛrtir/ 🔟 *vt* inform; (mettre en garde, menacer) warn. **avertissement** *nm* warning.

avertisseur /avɛrtisœr/ *nm* alarm; (Auto) horn; ~ d'incendie fire-alarm; ~ lumineux warning light.

aveu (*pl* ~x) /avø/ *nm* confession; de l'~ de by the admission of.

aveugle /avœgl/ *adj* blind. ● *nmf* blind man, blind woman.

aviateur, -trice /avjatœr, -tris/ *nm, f* aviator.

aviation /avjasjɔ̃/ *nf* flying; (industrie) aviation; (Mil) air force.

avide /avid/ *adj* greedy (de for); (anxieux) eager (de for); ~ de faire eager to do.

avion /avjɔ̃/ *nm* plane, aeroplane, aircraft; (US) airplane; ~ à réaction jet.

aviron /avirɔ̃/ *nm* oar; l'~ (Sport) rowing.

avis /avi/ *nm* opinion; (conseil) advice; (renseignement) notification; (Comm) advice; à mon ~ in my opinion; changer d'~ change one's mind; être d'~ que be of the opinion that; ~ au lecteur foreword.

avisé, ~e /avize/ *adj* sensible; être bien/mal ~ de be well-/ill-advised to.

aviser /avize/ 🔟 *vt* advise, notify. ● *vi* decide what to do. □ s'~ de *vpr* suddenly realize; s'~ de faire take it into one's head to do.

avocat, ~e /avɔka, -t/ *nm, f* barrister; (US) attorney; (fig) advocate; ~ de la défense counsel for the defence. ● *nm* (fruit) avocado (pear).

avoine /avwan/ *nf* oats (+ *pl*).

a

b

avoir /avwar/ 5

● *verbe auxiliaire*

••••▸ have; **il nous a appelés hier** he called us yesterday.

● *verbe transitif*

••••▸ (possession) have (got).

••••▸ (obtenir) get; (au téléphone) get through to.

••••▸ (duper) ① have; **on m'a eu!** I've been had!

••••▸ ~ **chaud/faim** be hot/hungry.

••••▸ ~ **dix ans** be ten years old.

● **avoir à** *verbe + préposition*

••••▸ to have to; **j'ai beaucoup à faire** I have a lot to do; **tu n'as qu'à leur écrire** all you have to do is write to them.

● **en avoir pour** *verbe + préposition*

••••▸ **j'en ai pour une minute** I will only be a minute; **j'en ai eu pour 100 euros** it cost me 100 euros.

● **il y a** *verbe impersonnel*

••••▸ there is; (pluriel) there are; **qu'est-ce qu'il y a?** what's the matter?; **il est venu il y a cinq ans** he came here five years ago; **il y a au moins 5 km jusqu'à la gare** it's at least 5 km to the station.

● *nom masculin*

••••▸ (dans un magasin) credit note.

••••▸ (biens) asset (+ *pl*).

avortement /avɔrtəmɑ̃/ *nm* (Méd) abortion.

avorter /avɔrte/ 1 *vi* (*projet*) abort; (**se faire**) ~ have an abortion.

avoué, ~**e** /avwe/ *adj* avowed. ● *nm* solicitor; (US) attorney.

avouer /avwe/ 1 *vt* (*amour, ignorance*) confess; (*crime*) confess to, admit. ● *vi* confess.

avril /avril/ *nm* April.

axe /aks/ *nm* axis; (essieu) axle; (d'une politique) main line(s), basis; ~ (**routier**) main road.

ayant /ɛjɑ̃/ ➡**AVOIR** 5.

azote /azɔt/ *nm* nitrogen.

azur /azyr/ *nm* sky-blue.

Bb

baba /baba/ *nm* ~ (**au rhum**) (rum) baba; **en rester** ① be flabbergasted.

babillard /babijar/ *nm* ~ **électronique** (Internet) bulletin board system, BBS.

babines /babin/ *nfpl* **se lécher les** ~ lick one's chops.

babiole /babjɔl/ *nf* trinket.

bâbord /babɔr/ *nm* port (side).

baby-foot /babifut/ *nm inv* table football.

bac /bak/ *nm* (Scol) ➡**BACCALAURÉAT**; (bateau) ferry; (récipient) tub; (plus petit) tray.

baccalauréat /bakalɔrea/ *nm* school leaving certificate.

> **Baccalauréat** Known informally as *le bac*, the *Baccalauréat* is an examination taken in the final year of the *lycée* (*la terminale*). Students sit exams in a broad range of subjects in a

particular category: the *bac S* emphasises science subjects, for example, while the *bac L* has a literary bias.

bâche /baʃ/ *nf* tarpaulin.

bachelier, -ière /baʃəlje, -jɛʀ/ *nm, f* holder of the *baccalauréat*.

bachoter /baʃɔte/ **1** *vi* cram (for an exam).

bâcler /bakle/ **1** *vt* botch (up).

bactérie /bakteʀi/ *nf* bacterium; **~s** bacteria.

badaud, ~e /bado, -d/ *nm, f* onlooker.

badigeonner /badiʒɔne/ **1** *vt* whitewash; (barbouiller) daub.

badiner /badine/ **1** *vi* banter.

baffe /baf/ *nf* **1** slap.

baffle /bafl/ *nm* speaker.

bafouiller /bafuje/ **1** *vt/i* stammer.

bagage /bagaʒ/ *nm* bag; (connaissances) knowledge; **~s** luggage; **~ à main** hand luggage.

bagarre /bagaʀ/ *nf* fight.

bagatelle /bagatɛl/ *nf* trifle; (somme) trifling amount.

bagnard /baɲaʀ/ *nm* convict.

bagnole /baɲɔl/ *nf* **1** car.

bague /bag/ *nf* (bijou) ring.

baguette /bagɛt/ *nf* stick; (de chef d'orchestre) baton; (chinoise) chopstick; (pain) baguette; **~ magique** magic wand; **~ de tambour** drumstick.

baie /bɛ/ *nf* (Géog) bay; (fruit) berry; **~ (vitrée)** picture window; (Ordinat) bay.

baignade /bɛɲad/ *nf* swimming.

baigner /beɲe/ **1** *vt* bathe; (enfant) bath. ● *vi* **~ dans l'huile** swim in grease. □ se **~** *vpr* have a swim. **baigneur, -euse** *nm, f*

swimmer.

baignoire /bɛɲwaʀ/ *nf* bath(tub).

bail (*pl* **baux**) /baj, bo/ *nm* lease.

bâiller /baje/ **1** *vi* yawn; (être ouvert) gape.

bailleur /bajœʀ/ *nm* **~ de fonds** (Comm) sleeping partner.

bain /bɛ̃/ *nm* bath; (baignade) swim; prendre un **~ de soleil** sunbathe; **~ de bouche** mouthwash; être dans le **~** (fig) be in the swing of things; se remettre dans le **~** get back into the swing of things; prendre un **~ de foule** mingle with the crowd.

bain-marie (*pl* **bains-marie**) /bɛ̃maʀi/ *nm* double boiler.

baiser /beze/ **1** *vt* (main) kiss; ⊠ screw ⊠. ● *nm* kiss.

baisse /bɛs/ *nf* fall, drop; être en **~** be going down.

baisser /bese/ **1** *vt* lower; (radio, lampe) turn down. ● *vi* (niveau) go down, fall; (santé, forces) fail. □ se **~** *vpr* bend down.

bal (*pl* **~s**) /bal/ *nm* dance; (habillé) ball; (lieu) dance-hall; **~ costumé** fancy-dress ball.

balade /balad/ *nf* stroll; (en auto) drive.

balader /balade/ **1** *vt* take for a stroll. □ se **~** *vpr* (à pied) (go for a) stroll; (en voiture) go for a drive; (voyager) travel.

baladeur /baladœʀ/ *nm* personal stereo.

balafre /balafʀ/ *nf* gash; (cicatrice) scar.

balai /balɛ/ *nm* broom.

balance /balɑ̃s/ *nf* scales (+ *pl*); la **B~** Libra.

balancer /balɑ̃se/ **10** *vt* swing; (doucement) sway; (lancer **1**) chuck! (se débarrasser de **1**) chuck out **1**. ● *vi* sway. □ se **~** *vpr* swing;

sway; **s'en ~ 🔟** not to give a damn 🔟.

balancier /balɑ̃sje/ nm (d'horloge) pendulum; (d'équilibriste) pole.

balançoire /balɑ̃swaR/ nf swing.

balayage /baleja3/ nm sweeping; (cheveux) highlights.

balayer /baleje/ 🔢 vt sweep (up); (vent) sweep away; (se débarrasser de) sweep aside.

balbutiement /balbysimɑ̃/ nm stammering; les ~s (fig) the first steps.

balcon /balkɔ̃/ nm balcony; (Théât) dress circle.

baleine /balɛn/ nf whale.

balise /baliz/ nf beacon; (bouée) buoy; (Auto) (road) sign. **baliser** 🔟 vt mark out (with beacons); (route) signpost; (sentier) mark out.

balivernes /balivɛRn/ nfpl nonsense.

ballant, ~e /balɑ̃, -t/ adj dangling.

balle /bal/ nf (projectile) bullet; (Sport) ball; (paquet) bale.

ballerine /balRin/ nf (danseuse) ballerina; (chaussure) ballet pump.

ballet /balɛ/ nm ballet.

ballon /balɔ̃/ nm (Sport) ball; ~ (de baudruche) balloon; ~ de football football.

ballonné, ~e /balɔne/ adj bloated.

balnéaire /balneɛR/ adj seaside.

balourd, ~e /baluR, -d/ nm, f oaf. ● adj uncouth.

balustrade /balystRad/ nf railing.

ban /bɑ̃/ nm round of applause; ~s (de mariage) banns; mettre au ~ de cast out from.

banal, ~e (mpl ~s) /banal/ adj commonplace, banal.

banane /banan/ nf banana.

banc /bɑ̃/ nm bench; (de poissons)

shoal; ~ des accusés dock; ~ d'essai (test) testing ground.

bancaire /bɑ̃kɛR/ adj (secteur) banking; (chèque) bank.

bancal, ~e (mpl ~s) /bɑ̃kal/ adj wobbly; (solution) shaky.

bande /bɑ̃d/ nf (groupe) gang; (de papier) strip; (rayure) stripe; (de film) reel; (pansement) bandage; ~ dessinée comic strip; ~ (magnétique) tape; ~ sonore sound-track.

Bande dessinée More than just a comic book, this form of popular literature (known as the *neuvième art*) plays a significant cultural role in France and is celebrated annually at the Festival d'Angoulême. Cartoon characters such as *Astérix*, *Lucky Luke* and *Tintin* are household names, and older *BD* are often collectors' items.

---

bande-annonce (pl **bandes-annonces**) /bɑ̃danɔ̃s/ nf trailer.

bandeau (pl ~x) /bɑ̃do/ nm headband; (sur les yeux) blindfold; ~ publicitaire (Ordinat) banner.

bander /bɑ̃de/ 🔟 vt bandage; (arc) bend; (muscle) tense; ~ les yeux à blindfold.

banderole /bɑ̃dRɔl/ nf banner.

bandit /bɑ̃di/ nm bandit. **banditisme** nm crime.

bandoulière: en ~ /ɑ̃buduljɛR/ loc across one's shoulder.

banlieue /bɑ̃ljø/ nf suburbs; de ~ suburban. **banlieusard, ~e** nm, f (suburban) commuter.

bannir /baniR/ 🔢 vt banish.

banque /bɑ̃k/ nf bank; (activité) banking; ~ de données databank.

banqueroute /bɑ̃kRut/ nf bankruptcy.

banquet /bɑ̃kɛ/ nm banquet.

banquette /bɑ̃kɛt/ nf seat.

banquier, -ière /bɑ̃kje, -jɛʀ/ nm, f banker.

baptême /batɛm/ nm baptism, christening. **baptiser** 1 vt baptize, christen; (nommer) call.

bar /baʀ/ nm (lieu) bar.

baragouiner /baʀagwine/ 1 vt/i gabble; (langue) speak a few words of.

baraque /baʀak/ nf hut, shed; (maison 1) house.

baratin /baʀatɛ̃/ nm 1 sweet ou smooth talk.

barbare /baʀbaʀ/ adj barbaric. ● nmf barbarian.

barbe /baʀb/ nf beard; ~ à papa candy-floss; (US) cotton candy; quelle ~! 1 what a drag! 1.

barbelé /baʀbəle/ adj fil ~ barbed wire.

barber /baʀbe/ 1 vt 1 bore.

barboter /baʀbɔte/ 1 vi (dans l'eau) paddle, splash. ● vt (voler 1) pinch.

barbouiller /baʀbuje/ 1 vt (souiller) smear (de with); tu es tout barbouillé your face is all dirty; être barbouillé feel queazy.

barbu, ~e /baʀby/ adj bearded.

barème /baʀɛm/ nm list, table; (échelle) scale.

baril /baʀil/ nm barrel.

bariolé, ~e /baʀjɔle/ adj multicoloured.

baromètre /baʀɔmɛtʀ/ nm barometer.

baron, ~ne /baʀɔ̃, -ɔn/ nm, f baron, baroness.

barque /baʀk/ nf (small) boat.

barrage /baʀaʒ/ nm dam; (sur route) roadblock.

barre /baʀ/ nf bar; (trait) line;

stroke; (Naut) helm; ~ de boutons (Ordinat) toolbar.

barreau (pl ~x) /baʀo/ nm bar; (d'échelle) rung; le ~ (Jur) the bar.

barrer /baʀe/ 1 vt block; (porte) bar; (rayer) cross out; (Naut) steer. □ se ~ vpr 1 leave.

barrette /baʀɛt/ nf (hair) slide.

barrière /baʀjɛʀ/ nf (porte) gate; (clôture) fence; (obstacle) barrier.

bar-tabac (pl **bars-tabac**) /baʀtaba/ nm café (selling stamps and cigarettes).

bas, basse /ba, bas/ adj (niveau, table) low; (action) base; au ~ mot at the lowest estimate; en ~ âge young; ~ morceaux (viande) cheap cuts. ● nm bottom; (chaussette) stocking; ~ de laine (fig) nest-egg. ● adv low; en ~ down below; (dans une maison) downstairs; en ~ de la page at the bottom of the page; plus ~ further ou lower down; mettre ~ give birth (to). **bas de casse** nm inv lower case. **bas-côté** (pl ~s) nm (de route) verge; (US) shoulder.

bascule /baskyl/ nf (balance) scales (+ pl); cheval/fauteuil à ~ rocking-horse/-chair.

basculer /baskyle/ 1 vi topple over; (benne) tip up.

base /bɑz/ nf base; (fondement) basis; (Pol) rank and file; de ~ basic. **base de données** nf database.

baser /bɑze/ 1 vt base. □ se ~ sur vpr go by.

bas-fonds /bafɔ̃/ nmpl (eau) shallows; (fig) dregs.

basilic /bazilik/ nm basil.

basilique /bazilik/ nf basilica.

basque /bask/ adj Basque. B~ nmf Basque.

basse /bas/ ➡BAS.

basse-cour (pl **basses-cours**) /baskuR/ nf farmyard.

bassesse /bases/ nf baseness; (action) base act.

bassin /basɛ̃/ nm (pièce d'eau) pond; (de piscine) pool; (Géog) basin; (Anat) pelvis; (plat) bowl; ~ houiller coalfield.

bassine /basin/ nf bowl.

basson /basɔ̃/ nm bassoon.

bas-ventre (pl ~s) /bavɑ̃tR/ nm lower abdomen.

bat /ba/ ➞BATTRE **11**.

bataille /bataj/ nf battle; (fig) fight.

bâtard, ~e /batar, -d/ adj (solution) hybrid. ● nm, f bastard.

bateau (pl ~x) /bato/ nm boat; ~ pneumatique rubber dinghy. **bateau-mouche** (pl **bateaux-mouches**) nm sightseeing boat.

bâti, ~e /bati/ adj bien ~ well-built.

bâtiment /batimɑ̃/ nm building; (industrie) building trade; (navire) vessel.

bâtir /batiR/ **2** vt build.

bâton /batɔ̃/ nm stick; conversation à ~s rompus rambling conversation; ~ de rouge lipstick.

battant /batɑ̃/ nm (vantail) flap; porte à deux ~s double door.

battement /batmɑ̃/ nm (de cœur) beat(ing); (temps) interval; (Mus) beat.

batterie /batRi/ nf (Mil, Électr) battery; (Mus) drums; ~ de cuisine pots and pans.

batteur /batœR/ nm (Mus) drummer; (Culin) whisk.

battre /batR/ **11** vt/i beat; (cartes) shuffle; (Culin) whisk; (l'emporter sur) beat; ~ des ailes flap its wings; ~ des mains clap; ~ des paupières blink; ~ en retraite beat a retreat; ~ la semelle stamp one's feet; ~ son plein be in full swing. □ se ~ vpr fight.

baume /bom/ nm balm.

bavard, ~e /bavar, -d/ adj talkative. ● nm, f chatterbox.

bavardage /bavardaʒ/ nm chatter, gossip. **bavarder 11** vi chat; (jacasser) chatter, gossip.

bave /bav/ nf dribble, slobber; (de limace) slime. **baver 11** vi dribble, slobber. **baveux**, **-euse** adj dribbling; (omelette) runny.

bavoir /bavwaR/ nm bib.

bavure /bavyR/ nf smudge; (erreur) blunder; ~ policière police blunder.

bazar /bazar/ nm bazaar; (objets **11**) clutter.

BCBG abrév mf (**bon chic bon genre**) posh.

BD abrév f (**bande dessinée**) comic strip.

béant, ~e /beɑ̃, -t/ adj gaping.

béat, ~e /bea, -t/ adj (hum) blissful; ~ d'admiration wide-eyed with admiration.

beau (**bel** before vowel or mute h), **belle** (mpl ~x) /bo, bɛl/ adj beautiful; (femme) beautiful; (homme) handsome; (temps) fine, nice. ● nm beauty. ● adv il fait ~ the weather is nice; au ~ milieu right in the middle; bel et bien well and truly; de plus belle more than ever; faire le ~ sit up and beg; on a ~ essayer/insister however much one tries/insists.

beaucoup /boku/ adv a lot, very much; ~ de (nombre) many; (quantité) a lot of; pas ~ (de) not many; (quantité) much; ~ plus/mieux much more/better; ~ trop far too much; de ~ by far.

beau-fils (pl **beaux-fils**) /bofis/

nm (remariage) stepson.

beau-frère (*pl* **beaux-frères**) /boﬀɛʀ/ *nm* brother-in-law.

beau-père (*pl* **beaux-pères**) /bopɛʀ/ *nm* father-in-law; (remariage) stepfather.

beauté /bote/ *nf* beauty; finir en ~ end magnificently.

beaux-arts /bozaʀ/ *nmpl* fine arts.

beaux-parents /bopaʀɑ̃/ *nmpl* parents-in-law.

bébé /bebe/ *nm* baby. **bébé-éprouvette** (*pl* **bébés-éprouvette**) *nm* test-tube baby.

bec /bɛk/ *nm* beak; (de théière) spout; (de casserole) lip; (bouche 🗊) mouth; ~ de gaz gas street-lamp.

bécane /bekan/ *nf* 🗊 bike.

bêche /bɛʃ/ *nf* spade.

bégayer /begeje/ 🗊 *vt*/i stammer.

bègue /bɛg/ *nmf* stammerer. ● *adj* être ~ stammer.

bégueule /begœl/ *adj* prudish.

beige /bɛʒ/ *adj & nm* beige.

beignet /bɛɲɛ/ *nm* fritter.

bel /bɛl/ ⇒BEAU.

bêler /bele/ 🗊 *vi* bleat.

belette /bəlɛt/ *nf* weasel.

belge /bɛlʒ/ *adj* Belgian. B~ *nmf* Belgian.

Belgique /bɛlʒik/ *nf* Belgium.

bélier /belje/ *nm* ram; le B~ Aries.

belle /bɛl/ ⇒BEAU.

belle-fille (*pl* **belles-filles**) /bɛlfij/ *nf* daughter-in-law; (remariage) stepdaughter.

belle-mère (*pl* **belles-mères**) /bɛlmɛʀ/ *nf* mother-in-law; (remariage) stepmother.

belle-sœur (*pl* **belles-sœurs**) /bɛlsœʀ/ *nf* sister-in-law.

belliqueux, -euse /belikø, -z/ *adj*

warlike.

bémol /bemol/ *nm* (Mus) flat.

bénédiction /benediksjɔ̃/ *nf* blessing.

bénéfice /benefis/ *nm* (gain) profit; (avantage) benefit.

bénéficiaire /benefisjɛʀ/ *nmf* beneficiary.

bénéficier /benefisje/ 45 *vi* ~ de benefit from; (jouir de) enjoy, have.

bénéfique /benefik/ *adj* beneficial.

Bénélux /benelyks/ *nm* Benelux.

bénévole /benevɔl/ *adj* voluntary.

bénin, -igne /benɛ̃, -iɲ/ *adj* minor; (tumeur) benign.

bénir /beniʀ/ 🗊 *vt* bless. **bénit, ~e** *adj* (eau) holy; (pain) consecrated.

benjamin, ~e /bɛ̃ʒamɛ̃, -in/ *nm, f* youngest child.

benne /bɛn/ *nf* (de grue) scoop; ~ à ordures (camion) waste disposal truck; (conteneur) skip; ~ (basculante) dump truck.

béquille /bekij/ *nf* crutch; (de moto) stand.

berceau (*pl* ~x) /bɛʀso/ *nm* (de bébé, civilisation) cradle.

bercer /bɛʀse/ 🗊 *vt* (balancer) rock; (apaiser) lull; (leurrer) delude.

béret /beʀɛ/ *nm* beret.

berge /bɛʀʒ/ *nf* (bord) bank.

berger, -ère /bɛʀʒe, -ɛʀ/ *nm, f* shepherd, shepherdess.

berne: en ~ /ɑ̃bɛʀn/ *loc* at halfmast.

berner /bɛʀne/ 🗊 *vt* fool.

besogne /bəzɔɲ/ *nf* task, job.

besoin /bəzwɛ̃/ *nm* need; avoir ~ de need; au ~ if need be; dans le ~ in need.

bestiole /bɛstjɔl/ *nf* 🗊 bug.

bétail /betaj/ *nm* livestock.

bête /bɛt/ *adj* stupid. ● *nf* animal;

~ noire pet hate; ~ sauvage wild beast; chercher la petite ~ be overfussy.

bêtise /betiz/ nf stupidity; (action) stupid thing.

béton /betɔ̃/ nm concrete; ~ armé reinforced concrete; en ~ (mur) concrete; (argument 🗓) watertight. **bétonnière** nf concrete mixer.

betterave /bɛtʀav/ nf beet; ~ rouge beetroot.

beugler /bøgle/ **1** vi bellow; (radio) blare out.

beur /bœʀ/ nmf & adj 🗓 second-generation North African living in France.

beurre /bœʀ/ nm butter. **beurré, ~e** adj buttered; 🗓 drunk. **beurrier** nm butter-dish.

bévue /bevy/ nf blunder.

biais /bjɛ/ nm (moyen) way; par le ~ de by means of; de ~, en ~ at an angle.

bibelot /biblo/ nm ornament.

biberon /bibʀɔ̃/ nm (feeding) bottle; nourrir au ~ bottle-feed.

bible /bibl/ nf bible; la B~ the Bible.

bibliographie /biblijɔgʀafi/ nf bibliography.

bibliothécaire /biblijotekɛʀ/ nmf librarian.

bibliothèque /biblijotɛk/ nf library; (meuble) bookcase.

bic® /bik/ nm biro®.

bicarbonate /bikaʀbɔnat/ nm ~ (de soude) bicarbonate (of soda).

biceps /bisɛps/ nm biceps.

biche /biʃ/ nf doe; ma ~ darling.

bichonner /biʃɔne/ **1** vt pamper.

bicyclette /bisiklɛt/ nf bicycle.

bide /bid/ nm (ventre 🗓) paunch; (échec 🗓) flop.

bidet /bidɛ/ nm bidet.

bidon /bidɔ̃/ nm can; (plus grand) drum; (ventre 🗓) belly; c'est du ~ it's a load of hogwash 🗓. ● adj inv 🗓 phoney.

bidonville /bidɔ̃vil/ nm shanty town.

bidule /bidyl/ nm 🗓 thing.

Biélorussie /bjelɔʀysi/ nf Byelorussia.

bien /bjɛ̃/ adv well; (très) quite, very; ~ des (nombre) many; tu as ~ de la chance you are very lucky; j'aimerais ~ I would like to; ce n'est pas ~ de it is not nice to; ~ sûr of course. ● nm good; (patrimoine) possession; ~s de consommation consumer goods. ● adj inv good; (passable) all right; (en forme) well; (à l'aise) comfortable; (beau) attractive; (respectable) nice, respectable. ● conj ~ que (al-)though; ~ que ce soit although it is. **bien-aimé, ~e** adj & nm, f beloved. **bien-être** nm wellbeing.

bienfaisance /bjɛ̃fəzɑ̃s/ nf charity; fête de ~ charity event. **bienfaisant, ~e** adj beneficial.

bienfait /bjɛ̃fɛ/ nm (faveur) favour; (avantage) beneficial effect. **bienfaiteur, -trice** nm, f benefactor.

bien-pensant, ~e /bjɛ̃pɑ̃sɑ̃, -t/ adj right-thinking.

bienséance /bjɛ̃seɑ̃s/ nf propriety.

bientôt /bjɛ̃to/ adv soon; à ~ see you soon.

bienveillance /bjɛ̃vɛjɑ̃s/ nf kind-(li)ness.

bienvenu, ~e /bjɛ̃vny/ adj welcome. ● nm, f être le ~, être la ~e be welcome.

bienvenue /bjɛ̃vny/ nf welcome; souhaiter la ~ à welcome.

bière /bjɛʀ/ nf beer; (cercueil) coffin; ~ blonde lager; ~ brune ≈

stout; ~ **pression** draught beer.

bifteck /biftɛk/ nm steak.

bifurquer /bifyʀke/ **1** vi branch off, fork.

bigarré, ~e /bigaʀe/ adj motley.

bigoudi /bigudi/ nm curler.

bijou (pl ~x) /biʒu/ nm jewel; ~ en or gold jewellery. **bijouterie** nf (boutique) jewellery shop; (Comm) jewellery. **bijoutier, -ière** nm, f jeweller.

bilan /bilɑ̃/ nm outcome; (d'une catastrophe) (casualty) toll; (Comm) balance sheet; **faire le** ~ **de** assess; ~ **de santé** check-up.

bile /bil/ nf bile; **se faire de la** ~ 🆘 worry.

bilingue /bilɛ̃g/ adj bilingual.

billard /bijaʀ/ nm billiards (+ pl); (table) billiard-table.

bille /bij/ nf (d'enfant) marble; (de billard) billiard-ball.

billet /bijɛ/ nm ticket; (lettre) note; (article) column; ~ **(de banque)** (bank) note; ~ **de 50 euros** 50-euro note.

billetterie /bijetʀi/ nf cash dispenser.

billion /biljɔ̃/ nm billion; (US) trillion.

bimensuel, ~le /bimɑ̃sɥɛl/ adj fortnightly, bimonthly.

binette /binɛt/ nf hoe; (visage) face; (Internet) smiley.

biochimie /bjoʃimi/ nf biochemistry.

biodégradable /bjodegʀadabl/ adj biodegradable.

biographie /bjɔgʀafi/ nf biography.

biologie /bjɔlɔʒi/ nf biology. **biologique** adj biological; (produit) organic.

bioterrorisme /bjotɛʀɔʀism/ nm bioterrorism.

bis /bis/ nm & interj encore.

biscornu, ~e /biskɔʀny/ adj crooked; (bizarre) cranky 🆘.

biscotte /biskɔt/ nf continental toast.

biscuit /biskɥi/ nm biscuit; (US) cookie; ~ **salé** cracker; ~ **de Savoie** sponge-cake.

bise /biz/ nf 🆘 kiss; (vent) north wind.

bison /bizɔ̃/ nm buffalo.

>
> **Bison Futé** Devised by the French traffic information service, *Bison Futé* reports on travel conditions nationally and recommends alternative routes (*les itinéraires 'bis'*) for travellers wishing to avoid traffic jams. *Bison Futé* traffic tips are made known through the media and appear on road signs in yellow on a green background.

bisou /bizu/ nm 🆘 kiss.

bistro(t) /bistʀo/ nm 🆘 café, bar.

bit /bit/ nm (Ordinat) bit.

bitume /bitym/ nm asphalt.

bizarre /bizaʀ/ adj odd, strange. **bizzarerie** nf peculiarity.

blafard, ~e /blafaʀ, -d/ adj pale.

blague /blag/ nf 🆘 joke; **sans** ~! no kidding! 🆘.

blaguer /blage/ **1** 🆘 vi joke.

blaireau (pl ~x) /blɛʀo/ nm shaving-brush; (animal) badger.

blâmer /blame/ **1** vt criticize.

blanc, blanche /blɑ̃, blɑ̃ʃ/ adj white; (papier, page) blank; ● nm white; (espace) blank; ~ **d'œuf** egg white; ~ **de poireau** white part of the leek; ~ **(de poulet)** chicken breast; **le** ~ **(linge)** whites; **laisser en** ~ leave blank 🆘. **B~, Blanche** nm,

blanchiment /blɑ̃ʃimɑ̃/ *nm* (d'argent) laundering.

blanchir /blɑ̃ʃiʀ/ **2** *vt* whiten; (*personne*: fig) clear; (*argent*) launder; (Culin) blanch; ~ (à la chaux) whitewash. ● *vi* turn white.

blanchisserie /blɑ̃ʃisʀi/ *nf* laundry.

blason /blazɔ̃/ *nm* coat of arms.

blasphème /blasfɛm/ *nm* blasphemy.

blé /ble/ *nm* wheat.

blême /blɛm/ *adj* pallid.

blessant, ~e /blesɑ̃, -t/ *adj* hurtful.

blessé, ~e /blese/ *nm, f* casualty, injured person.

blesser /blese/ **1** *vt* injure, hurt; (*par balle*) wound; (*offenser*) hurt. □ **se** ~ *vpr* injure ou hurt oneself. **blessure** *nf* wound.

bleu, ~e /blø/ *adj* blue; (Culin) very rare; ~ marine/turquoise navy blue/turquoise; **avoir une peur** ~**e** be scared stiff. ● *nm* blue; (*contusion*) bruise; ~ (de travail) overalls (+ *pl*).

bleuet /bløɛ/ *nm* cornflower.

blindé, ~e /blɛ̃de/ *adj* armoured; (fig) immune (contre to); **porte** ~**e** security car. ● *nm* armoured car, tank.

blinder /blɛ̃de/ **1** *vt* armour; (fig) harden.

bloc /blɔk/ *nm* block; (de papier) pad; **serrer à** ~ tighten hard; **en** ~ (*matériau*) in a block; (*nier*) outright.

blocage /blɔkaʒ/ *nm* (des prix) freeze, freezing; (des roues) locking; (Psych) block.

bloc-notes (*pl* **blocs-notes**) /blɔknɔt/ *nm* note-pad.

blocus /blɔkys/ *nm* blockade.

blond, ~e /blɔ̃, -d/ *adj* fair, blond. ● *nm, f* fair-haired man, fair-haired woman.

bloquer /blɔke/ **1** *vt* block; (*porte, machine*) jam; (*roues*) lock; (*prix, crédits*) freeze. □ **se** ~ *vpr* jam; (*roues*) lock; (*freins*) jam; (*ordinateur*) crash; **bloqué par la neige** snowbound.

blottir (se) /(sə)blɔtiʀ/ **2** *vpr* snuggle, huddle (contre against).

blouse /bluz/ *nf* overall. **blouse blanche** *nf* white coat.

blouson /bluzɔ̃/ *nm* jacket, blouson.

bluffer /blœfe/ **1** *vt/i* bluff.

bobine /bɔbin/ *nf* (de fil, film) reel; (Électr) coil.

bobo /bɔbo/ *nm* **1** sore, cut; **avoir** ~ have a pain.

bocal (*pl* **-aux**) /bɔkal, -o/ *nm* jar.

bœuf (*pl* **~s**) /bœf, bø/ *nm* bullock; (US) steer; (*viande*) beef; ~**s** oxen.

bogue /bɔg/ *nm* (Ordinat) bug.

bohème /bɔɛm/ *adj & nmf* bohemian.

boire /bwaʀ/ **12** *vt/i* (*personne, plante*) drink; (*argile*) soak up; ~ **un coup** **1** have a drink.

bois /bwa/ →**BOIRE 12**. ● *nm* (*matériau, forêt*) wood; **de** ~, **en** ~ wooden. ● *nmpl* (de cerf) antlers.

boiseries /bwazʀi/ *nfpl* panelling.

boisson /bwasɔ̃/ *nf* drink.

boit /bwa/ →**BOIRE 12**.

boîte /bwat/ *nf* box; (de conserves) tin, can; (entreprise **1**) firm; **en** ~ tinned, canned; ~ **à gants** glove compartment; ~ **aux lettres** letter-box; ~ **aux lettres électronique** mailbox; ~ **de nuit** night-club; ~ **postale** post-office box; ~ **de vitesses** gear box.

f white man, white woman. **blanche** *nf* (Mus) minim.

boiter /bwate/ **1** vi limp. **boiteux, -euse** adj lame; (raisonnement) shaky.

boîtier /bwatje/ nm case.

bol /bɔl/ nm bowl; ~ d'air a breath of fresh air; **avoir du** ~! be lucky.

bolide /bɔlid/ nm racing car.

Bolivie /bɔlivi/ nf Bolivia.

bombardement /bɔ̃bardəmɑ̃/ nm bombing; shelling.

bombarder /bɔ̃barde/ **1** vt bomb; (par obus) shell; ~ qn de (fig) bombard sb with. **bombardier** nm (Aviat) bomber.

bombe /bɔ̃b/ nf bomb; (atomiseur) spray, aerosol.

bombé, ~e /bɔ̃be/ adj rounded; (route) cambered.

bon, bonne /bɔ̃, bɔn/ adj good; (qui convient) right; ~ à/pour (approprié) it to/for; **bonne année** happy New Year; ~ anniversaire happy birthday; ~ appétit/voyage enjoy your meal/trip; **bonne chance/nuit** good luck/night; ~ **sens** common sense; **bonne femme** (péj) woman; **de bonne heure** early; **à quoi** ~? what's the point? ● adv **sentir** ~ smell nice; **tenir** ~ stand firm; **il fait** ~ the weather is mild. ● interj right, well. ● nm (billet) voucher, coupon; ~ **de commande** order form; **pour de** ~ for good. **bonne** nf (domestique) maid.

bonbon /bɔ̃bɔ̃/ nm sweet; (US) candy.

bonbonne /bɔ̃bɔn/ nf demijohn; (de gaz) cylinder.

bond /bɔ̃/ nm leap; **faire un** ~ (de surprise) jump.

bonde /bɔ̃d/ nf plug; (trou) plughole.

bondé, ~e /bɔ̃de/ adj packed.

bondir /bɔ̃diʀ/ **2** vi leap; (de surprise) jump.

bonheur /bɔnœʀ/ nm happiness; (chance) (good) luck; **au petit** ~ haphazardly; **par** ~ luckily.

bonhomme /bɔnɔm, bɔzɔm/ nm fellow; ~ **de neige** snowman. ● adj inv good hearted.

bonifier (se) /(sə)bɔnifje/ **45** vpr improve.

bonjour /bɔ̃ʒuʀ/ nm & interj hallo, hello, good morning or afternoon.

bon marché /bɔ̃maʀʃe/ adj inv cheap. ● adv cheap (ly)

bonne /bɔn/ →**BON**.

bonne-maman (pl **bonnes-mamans**) /bɔnmamɑ̃/ nf **1** granny.

bonnement /bɔnmɑ̃/ adv **tout** ~ quite simply.

bonnet /bɔnɛ/ nm hat; (de soutien-gorge) cup; ~ **de bain** swimming cap. **bonneterie** nf hosiery.

bonsoir /bɔ̃swaʀ/ nm good evening; (en se couchant) good night.

bonté /bɔ̃te/ nf kindness.

bonus /bɔnys/ nm (Auto) no-claims bonus.

boots /buts/ nmpl ankle boots.

bord /bɔʀ/ nm edge; (rive) bank; **à** (~ **de**) on board; **au** ~ **de la mer** at the seaside; **au** ~ **des larmes** on the verge of tears; ~ **de la route** road-side.

bordeaux /bɔʀdo/ adj inv maroon. ● nm inv Bordeaux.

bordel /bɔʀdɛl/ nm brothel; (désordre **1**) shambles.

border /bɔʀde/ **1** vt line, border; (tissu) edge; (personne, lit) tuck in.

bordereau (pl ~**x**) /bɔʀdəʀo/ nm (document) slip.

bordure /bɔʀdyʀ/ nf border; **en** ~

de on the edge of.

borgne /bɔʀɲ/ adj one-eyed.

borne /bɔʀn/ nf boundary marker; (pour barrer le passage) bollard; ~ (kilométrique) ≈ milestone; ~s limits.

borné, ~e /bɔʀne/ adj (esprit) narrow; (personne) narrow minded.

borner (se) /(sə)bɔʀne/ **1** vpr confine oneself (à to).

bosniak /bɔsnjak/ adj Bosnian. **B**~ nmf Bosnian.

Bosnie /bɔsni/ nf Bosnia.

bosse /bɔs/ nf bump; (de chameau) hump; avoir la ~ de **1** have a gift for; avoir roulé sa ~ have been around. **bosselé,** ~e adj dented; (terrain) bumpy.

bosser /bose/ **1** vi **1** work (hard).

bossu, ~e /bɔsy/ adj hunchbacked. ● nm, f hunchback.

botanique /bɔtanik/ nf botany. ● adj botanical.

botte /bɔt/ nf boot; (de fleurs, légumes) bunch; (de paille) bundle, bale; ~s de caoutchouc wellingtons.

botter /bote/ **1** vt **1** ça me botte I like the idea.

bottin® /bɔtɛ̃/ nm phone book.

bouc /buk/ nm (billy-goat); (barbe) goatee; ~ émissaire scapegoat.

boucan /bukɑ̃/ nm **1** din.

bouche /buʃ/ nf mouth; (lèvres) lips; ~ bée open-mouthed; ~ d'égout manhole; ~ d'incendie (fire)hydrant; ~ de métro entrance to the underground ou subway (US). **bouche-à-bouche** nm inv mouth-to-mouth resuscitation. **bouche-à-oreille** nm inv word of mouth.

bouché, ~e /buʃe/ adj (profession, avenir) oversubscribed; (stupide, péj) stupid.

bouchée /buʃe/ nf mouthful.

boucher¹ /buʃe/ **1** vt block; (bouteille) cork. □ se ~ vpr get blocked; se ~ le nez hold one's nose.

boucher², -ère /buʃe, -ɛʀ/ nm, f butcher. **boucherie** nf butcher's (shop); (carnage) butchery.

bouchon /buʃɔ̃/ nm stopper; (en liège) cork; (de stylo, tube) cap; (de pêcheur) float; (embouteillage) traffic jam; ~ de cérumen plug of earwax.

boucle /bukl/ nf (de ceinture) buckle; (de cheveux) curl; (forme) loop; ~ d'oreille earring. **bouclé,** ~e adj (cheveux) curly.

boucler /bukle/ **1** vt fasten; (enfermer **1**) shut up; (encercler) seal off; (budget) balance; (terminer) finish off. ● vi curl.

bouclier /buklije/ nm shield.

bouddhiste /budist/ adj & nmf Buddhist.

bouder /bude/ **1** vi sulk. ● vt stay away from.

boudin /budɛ̃/ nm black pudding.

boue /bu/ nf mud.

bouée /bwe/ nf buoy; ~ de sauvetage lifebuoy.

boueux, -euse /buø, -z/ adj muddy.

bouffe /buf/ nf **1** food, grub.

bouffée /bufe/ nf puff, whiff; (d'orgueil) fit; ~ de chaleur (Méd) hot flush.

bouffi, ~e /bufi/ adj bloated.

bouffon, ~ne /bufɔ̃, -ɔn/ adj farcical. ● nm buffoon.

bougeoir /buʒwaʀ/ nm candlestick.

bougeotte /buʒɔt/ nf avoir la ~ **1** have the fidgets.

bouger /buʒe/ **40** vt/i move. □ se ~ vpr **1** move.

bougie /buʒi/ nf candle; (Auto)

spark(ing)-plug.

bouillant, ~e /bujɑ̃, -t/ *adj* boiling; (très chaud) boiling hot.

bouillie /buji/ *nf* (pour bébé) baby cereal; (péj) mush; **en** ~ crushed, mushy.

bouillir /bujiʀ/ **13** *vi* boil; (fig) seethe; **faire** ~ boil.

bouilloire /bujwaʀ/ *nf* kettle.

bouillon /bujɔ̃/ *nm* (de cuisson) stock; (potage) broth.

bouillonner /bujɔne/ **1** *vi* bubble.

bouillotte /bujɔt/ *nf* hot-water bottle.

boulanger, -ère /bulɑ̃ʒe, -ɛʀ/ *nm, f* baker. **boulangerie** *nf* bakery. **boulangerie-pâtisserie** *nf* bakery (selling cakes and pastries).

boule /bul/ *nf* ball; ~s (jeu) boules; **jouer aux** ~s play boules; **une** ~ **dans la gorge** a lump in one's throat; ~ **de neige** snowball.

> **Boules** A form of bowls, played on rough, dry ground with metal balls. The aim is to throw the balls to land as near as possible to a smaller target ball called the co-chonnet. In the South of France, *boules* is often called *pétanque*.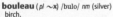

bouleau (*pl* ~x) /bulo/ *nm* (silver) birch.

boulet /bulɛ/ *nm* (de forçat) ball and chain; ~ (de canon) cannonball; ~ **de charbon** coal nut.

boulette /bulɛt/ *nf* (de pain, papier) pellet; (bévue) blunder; ~ **de viande** meat ball.

boulevard /bulvaʀ/ *nm* boulevard.

bouleversant, ~e /bulvɛʀsɑ̃, -t/ *adj* deeply moving. **bouleverse-**

ment *nm* upheaval. **bouleverser** **1** *vt* turn upside down; (*pays, plans*) disrupt; (émouvoir) upset.

boulimie /bulimi/ *nf* bulimia.

boulon /bulɔ̃/ *nm* bolt.

boulot, ~te /bulo, -ɔt/ *adj* (rond **1**) dumpy. ●*nm* (travail **1**) work.

boum /bum/ *nm & interj* bang. ●*nf* (fête **1**) party.

bouquet /bukɛ/ *nm* (de fleurs) bunch, bouquet; (d'arbres) clump; **c'est le** ~! **1** that's the last straw!

bouquin /bukɛ̃/ *nm* **1** book. **bouquiner** **1** *vt/i* **1** read. **bouquiniste** *nmf* second-hand bookseller.

bourbier /buʀbje/ *nm* mire; (fig) tangle.

bourde /buʀd/ *nf* blunder.

bourdon /buʀdɔ̃/ *nm* bumble bee. **bourdonnement** *nm* buzzing.

bourg /buʀ/ *nm* (market) town (centre), village centre.

bourgeois, ~e /buʀʒwa, -z/ *adj & nm,f* middle-class (person); (péj) bourgeois. **bourgeoisie** *nf* middle class(es).

bourgeon /buʀʒɔ̃/ *nm* bud.

bourgogne /buʀgɔɲ/ *nm* Burgundy.

bourlinguer /buʀlɛ̃ge/ **1** *vi* **1** travel about.

bourrage /buʀaʒ/ *nm* ~ **de crâne** brainwashing.

bourratif, -ive /buʀatif, -v/ *adj* stodgy.

bourreau (*pl* ~x) /buʀo/ *nm* executioner; ~ **de travail** (fig) workaholic.

bourrelet /buʀlɛ/ *nm* weather strip, draught excluder; (de chair) roll of fat.

bourrer /buʀe/ **1** *vt* cram (de with); (*pipe*) fill; ~ **de** (nourriture) stuff with; ~ **de coups** thrash; ~

le crâne à qn brainwash sb.

bourrique /buʁik/ nf donkey; 🔲 pig-headed person.

bourru, ~e /buʁy/ adj gruff.

bourse /buʁs/ nf purse; (subvention) grant; la B~ the Stock Exchange.

boursier, -ière /buʁsje, -jɛʁ/ adj (valeurs) Stock Exchange. ● nm, f grant holder.

boursoufler /buʁsufle/ 🔲 vt (visage) cause to swell; (peinture) blister.

bousculade /buskylad/ nf crush; (précipitation) rush. **bousculer** 🔲 vt (pousser) jostle; (presser) rush; (renverser) knock over.

bousiller /buzije/ 🔲 vt 🔲 wreck.

boussole /busɔl/ nf compass.

bout /bu/ nm end; (de langue, bâton) piece; (morceau) bit; à ~ exhausted; à ~ de souffle out of breath; à ~ portant point-blank; au ~ de (après) after; venir à ~ de (finir) manage to finish; d'un ~ à l'autre throughout; au ~ du compte in the end; ~ filtre filtertip.

bouteille /butɛj/ nf bottle; ~ d'oxygène oxygen cylinder.

boutique /butik/ nf shop; (de mode) boutique.

bouton /butɔ̃/ nm button; (sur la peau) spot, pimple; (pousse) bud; (de porte, radio) knob; ~ de manchette cuff-link. **boutonner** 🔲 vt button (up). **boutonnière** nf buttonhole. **bouton-pression** (pl **boutons-pression**) nm press-stud; (US) snap.

bouture /butyʁ/ nf cutting.

bovin, ~e /bɔvɛ̃, -in/ adj bovine. **bovins** nmpl cattle pl.

box (pl ~ ou **boxes**) /bɔks/ nm lock-up garage; (de dortoir) cubicle;

(d'écurie) (loose) box; (Jur) dock.

boxe /bɔks/ nf boxing.

boyau (pl ~x) /bwajo/ nm gut; (corde) catgut; (galerie) gallery; (de bicyclette) tyre; (US) tire.

boycotter /bɔjkɔte/ 🔲 vt boycott.

BP abrév f (**boîte postale**) PO Box.

bracelet /bʁaslɛ/ nm bracelet; (de montre) watchstrap.

braconnier /bʁakɔnje/ nm poacher.

brader /bʁade/ 🔲 vt sell off. **braderie** nf clearance sale.

braguette /bʁagɛt/ nf fly.

braille /bʁaj/ nm & adj Braille.

brailler /bʁaje/ 🔲 vt/i bawl.

braise /bʁɛz/ nf embers (+ pl).

braiser /bʁeze/ 🔲 vt (Culin) braise.

brancard /bʁɑ̃kaʁ/ nm stretcher; (de charrette) shaft.

branche /bʁɑ̃ʃ/ nf branch.

branché, ~e /bʁɑ̃ʃe/ adj 🔲 trendy.

branchement /bʁɑ̃ʃmɑ̃/ nm connection. **brancher** 🔲 vt (prise) plug in; (à un réseau) connect.

brandir /bʁɑ̃diʁ/ 🗷 vt brandish.

branler /bʁɑ̃le/ 🔲 vi be shaky.

braquer /bʁake/ 🔲 vt (arme) aim; (regard) fix; (roue) turn; (banque: 🔲) hold up; ~ qn contre turn sb against. ● vt (Auto) turn (the wheel). ☐ se ~ vpr dig one's heels in.

bras /bʁa/ nm arm; (de rivière) branch; (Tech) arm; ~ dessus ~ dessous arm in arm; ~ droit (fig) right hand man; ~ de mer sound; en ~ de chemise in one's shirtsleeves. ● nmpl (fig) labour, hands.

brasier /bʁazje/ nm blaze.

brassard /bʁasaʁ/ nm armband.

brasse /bʁas/ nf breast-stroke; ~ papillon butterfly (stroke).

brasser /brase/ ◆ *vt* mix; (*bière*) brew; (*affaires*) handle a lot of.
brasserie *nf* brewery; (*café*) brasserie.

brave /brav/ *adj* (*bon*) good; (*valeureux*) brave. **braver** ◆ *vt* defy.

bravo /bravo/ *interj* bravo. ● *nm* cheer.

bravoure /bravur/ *nf* bravery.

break /brɛk/ *nm* estate car; (US) station-wagon.

brebis /brəbi/ *nf* ewe.

brèche /brɛʃ/ *nf* gap, breach; être sur la ~ be on the go.

bredouille /brəduj/ *adj* empty-handed.

bredouiller /brəduje/ ◆ *vt/i* mumble.

bref, brève /brɛf, -v/ *adj* short, brief. ● *adv* in short; en ~ in short.

Brésil /brezil/ *nm* Brazil.

Bretagne /brətaɲ/ *nf* Brittany.

bretelle /brətɛl/ *nf* (de sac, maillot) strap; (d'autoroute) access road; ~s (pour pantalon) braces; (US) suspenders.

breton, ~ne /brətɔ̃, -ɔn/ *adj & nm* (Ling) Breton. **B~, ~ne** *nm, f* Breton.

breuvage /brœvaʒ/ *nm* beverage.

brève /brɛv/ ➔ **BREF.**

brevet /brəvɛ/ *nm* ~ (d'invention) patent; (diplôme) diploma. **breveté, ~e** /brəvte/ *adj* patented.

bribes /brib/ *nfpl* scraps.

bricolage /brikɔlaʒ/ *nm* do-it yourself (jobs).

bricole /brikɔl/ *nf* trifle.

bricoler /brikɔle/ ◆ *vi* do DIY; (US) fix things, tinker with. **bricoleur, -euse** /brikɔlœr, -øz/ *nm, f* handyman, handywoman.

bride /brid/ *nf* bridle.

bridé, ~e /bride/ *adj* yeux ~s slanting eyes.

brider /bride/ ◆ *vt* (*cheval*) bridle; (fig) keep in check.

brièvement /brijɛvmɑ̃/ *adv* briefly.

brigade /brigad/ *nf* (de police) squad; (Mil) brigade; (fig) team. **brigadier** *nm* (de gendarmerie) sergeant.

brigand /brigɑ̃/ *nm* robber.

brillant, ~e /brijɑ̃, -t/ *adj* (*couleur*) bright; (*luisant*) shiny; (*remarquable*) brilliant. ● *nm* (*éclat*) shine; (*diamant*) diamond.

briller /brije/ ◆ *vi* shine.

brimade /brimad/ *nf* vexation.

brimer ◆ *vt* bully, harass; se sentir brimé feel put down.

brin /brɛ̃/ *nm* (de muguet) sprig; (d'herbe) blade; (de paille) wisp; un ~ de (un peu) a bit of.

brindille /brɛ̃dij/ *nf* twig.

brioche /brijɔʃ/ *nf* brioche, sweet bun; (ventre ◼) paunch.

brique /brik/ *nf* brick.

briquet /brikɛ/ *nm* (cigarette-)lighter.

brise /briz/ *nf* breeze.

briser /brize/ ◆ *vt* break. □ se ~ *vpr* break.

britannique /britanik/ *adj* British. **B~** *nmf* Briton; les B~s the British.

brocante /brɔkɑ̃t/ *nf* bric-à-brac trade; (marché) flea market.

broche /brɔʃ/ *nf* brooch; (Culin) spit; à la ~ spit-roasted.

broché, ~e /brɔʃe/ *adj* paperback.

brochet /brɔʃɛ/ *nm* pike.

brochette /brɔʃɛt/ *nf* skewer.

brochure /brɔʃyr/ *nf* brochure, booklet.

broder /brɔde/ ◆ *vt/i* embroider.

broderie /bʀɔdʀi/ nf embroidery.

broncher /bʀɔ̃ʃe/ **1** vi sans ~ without turning a hair.

bronchite /bʀɔ̃ʃit/ nf bronchitis.

bronze /bʀɔ̃z/ nm bronze.

bronzé, ~e /bʀɔ̃ze/ adj (sun-)tanned.

bronzer /bʀɔ̃ze/ **1** vi (personne) get a (sun-)tan.

brosse /bʀɔs/ nf brush; ~ à dents toothbrush; ~ à habits clothes brush; en ~ (coiffure) in a crew cut.

brosser /bʀɔse/ **1** vt brush; (fig) paint. □ se ~ vpr se ~ les dents; les cheveux brush one's teeth/hair.

brouette /bʀuɛt/ nf wheelbarrow.

brouhaha /bʀuaa/ nm hubbub.

brouillard /bʀujaʀ/ nm fog.

brouille /bʀuj/ nf quarrel.

brouiller /bʀuje/ **1** vt (vue) blur; (œufs) scramble; (amis) set at odds; ~ les pistes cloud the issue. □ se ~ vpr (ciel) cloud over; (amis) fall out.

brouillon, ~ne /bʀujɔ̃, -ɔn/ adj untidy. ● nm (rough) draft.

brousse /bʀus/ nf la ~ the bush.

brouter /bʀute/ **1** vt/i graze.

broyer /bʀwaje/ **31** vt crush; (moudre) grind.

bru /bʀy/ nf daughter-in-law.

bruine /bʀɥin/ nf drizzle.

bruissement /bʀɥismɑ̃/ nm rustling.

bruit /bʀɥi/ nm noise; ~ de couloir (fig) rumour.

bruitage /bʀɥitaʒ/ nm sound effects.

brûlant, ~e /bʀylɑ̃, -t/ adj burning (hot); (sujet) red-hot; (passion) fiery.

brûlé /bʀyle/ nm burning; ça sent le ~ I can smell something burning. ● →BRÛLER **1**.

brûler /bʀyle/ **1** vt/i burn; (es-sence) use (up); (cierge) light (à to); ~ un feu (rouge) jump the lights; ~ d'envie de faire be longing to do. □ se ~ vpr burn oneself.

brûlure /bʀylyʀ/ nf burn; ~s d'es-tomac heartburn.

brume /bʀym/ nf mist. **brumeux**, -euse adj misty; (esprit) hazy.

brun, ~e /bʀœ̃, -yn/ adj brown, dark. ● nm brown. ● nm, f dark haired person. **brunir** **2** vi turn brown; (bronzer) get a tan.

brushing /bʀœʃiŋ/ nm blow-dry.

brusque /bʀysk/ adj (personne) abrupt; (geste) violent; (soudain) sudden.

brusquer /bʀyske/ **1** vt be abrupt with; (précipiter) rush.

brut, ~e /bʀyt/ adj (diamant) rough; (champagne) dry; (pétrole) crude; (Comm) gross.

brutal, ~e (mpl -aux) /bʀytal, -o/ adj brutal. **brutalité** nf brutality.

brute /bʀyt/ nf brute.

Bruxelles /bʀysɛl/ npr Brussels.

bruyant, ~e /bʀɥijɑ̃, -t/ adj noisy.

bruyère /bʀyjɛʀ/ nf heather.

bu /by/ →BOIRE **12**.

bûche /byʃ/ nf log; ~ de Noël Christmas log; ramasser une ~ **1** fall.

bûcher /byʃe/ **1** vt/i **1** slog away (at) **1**. ● nm (supplice) stake.

bûcheron /byʃʀɔ̃/ nm lumberjack.

budget /bydʒɛ/ nm budget. **bud-gétaire** adj budgetary.

buée /bɥe/ nf condensation.

buffet /byfɛ/ nm sideboard; (table garnie) buffet.

buffle /byfl/ nm buffalo.

buisson /bɥisɔ̃/ nm bush.

buissonnière /bɥisɔnjɛʀ/ adj faire l'école ~ play truant.

bulbe /bylb/ nm bulb.

bulgare /bylgaʀ/ *adj & nm* Bulgarian. **B~** *nmf* Bulgarian.

Bulgarie /bylgaʀi/ *nf* Bulgaria.

bulldozer /buldozɛʀ/ *nm* bulldozer.

bulle /byl/ *nf* bubble.

bulletin /byltɛ̃/ *nm* bulletin, report; (Scol) report; ~ d'information news bulletin; ~ météorologique weather report; ~ de vote ballot-paper; ~ de salaire pay-slip.

buraliste /byʀalist/ *nmf* tobacconist.

bureau (*pl* ~x) /byʀo/ *nm* office; (meuble) desk; (comité) board; ~ d'études design office; ~ de poste post office; ~ de tabac tobacconist's (shop); ~ de vote polling station.

bureaucrate /byʀokʀat/ *nmf* bureaucrat. **bureaucratie** *nf* bureaucracy. **bureaucratique** *adj* bureaucratic.

bureautique /byʀotik/ *nf* office automation.

burlesque /byʀlɛsk/ *adj* (*histoire*) ludicrous; (*film*) farcical.

bus /bys/ *nm* bus.

business /biznɛs/ *nm inv* (affaires commerciales) business; (affaires privées) affairs.

buste /byst/ *nm* bust.

but /by(t)/ *nm* target; (*dessein*) aim, goal; (football) goal; avoir pour ~ de aim to; de ~ en blanc point-blank; dans le ~ de with the intention of; aller droit au ~ go straight to the point.

butane /bytan/ *nm* butane, Calor gas®.

buté, **~e** /byte/ *adj* obstinate.

buter /byte/ **1** *vi* ~ contre knock against; (*problème*) come up against. ● *vt* antagonize. □ se ~ *vpr* (s'entêter) become obstinate.

buteur /bytœʀ/ *nm* (au football) striker.

butin /bytɛ̃/ *nm* booty, loot.

butte /byt/ *nf* mound; en ~ à exposed to.

buvard /byvaʀ/ *nm* blotting-paper.

buvette /byvɛt/ *nf* (refreshment) bar.

buveur, **-euse** /byvœʀ, -øz/ *nm, f* drinker.

Cc

c' /s/ ➡CE.

ça /sa/

● *pronom démonstratif*

····▸ (sujet) it; that; ~ flotte it floats; ~ suffit! that's enough!; ~ y est! that's it!; ~ sent le brûlé there's a smell of burning; ~ va? how are things?

····▸ (objet) (proche) this; (plus éloigné) that; c'est ~ that's right.

····▸ (dans expressions) où ~? where?; quand ~? when?; et avec ~? anything else?

çà /sa/ *adv* ~ et là here and there.

cabane /kaban/ *nf* hut; (à outils) shed.

cabaret /kabaʀɛ/ *nm* cabaret.

cabillaud /kabijo/ *nm* cod.

cabine /kabin/ *nf* (à la piscine) cubicle; (de bateau) cabin; (de camion) cab; (d'ascenseur) cage; ~ d'essayage fitting room; ~ de pilotage cockpit; ~ de plage beach hut; ~ (téléphonique) phone booth, phone box.

cabinet /kabinε/ nm (de médecin) surgery; (US) office; (d'avocat) office; (clientèle) practice; (cabinet collectif) firm; (Pol) Cabinet; (pièce) room; ~s (toilettes) toilet; (US) bathroom; ~ de toilette bathroom.

câble /kɑbl/ nm (cordage) (corde) rope; (TV) cable TV. **câbler** vt **1** cable; (TV) install cable television in.

cabosser /kabose/ **1** vt dent.

cabotage /kabotaʒ/ nm coastal navigation.

cabrer (se) /(sə)kabʀe/ **1** vpr (cheval) rear; se ~ contre rebel against.

cabriole /kabʀijɔl/ nf faire des ~s caper about.

cacahuète /kakawεt/ nf peanut.

cacao /kakao/ nm cocoa.

cachalot /kaʃalo/ nm sperm whale.

cache /kaʃ/ nm mask. ● nf hiding place; ~ d'armes arms cache.

cache-cache /kaʃkaʃ/ nm inv hide-and-seek.

cache-nez /kaʃne/ nm inv scarf.

cacher /kaʃe/ **1** vt hide, conceal (à from). □ se ~ vpr hide; (se trouver caché) be hidden.

cachet /kaʃε/ nm (de cire) seal; (à l'encre) stamp; (de la poste) postmark; (comprimé) tablet; (d'artiste) fee; (chic) style, cachet.

cachette /kaʃεt/ nf hiding-place; en ~ in secret.

cachot /kaʃo/ nm dungeon.

cachottier, -ière /kaʃɔtje, -jεʀ/ adj secretive.

cacophonie /kakɔfɔni/ nf cacophony.

cactus /kaktys/ nm cactus.

cadavérique /kadaveʀik/ adj (teint) deathly pale.

cadavre /kadavʀ/ nm corpse; (de victime) body.

caddie /kadi/ nm (de supermarché®) trolley; (au golf) caddie.

cadeau (pl ~x) /kado/ nm present, gift; faire un ~ à qn give sb a present.

cadenas /kadna/ nm padlock.

cadence /kadɑ̃s/ nf rhythm, cadence; (de travail) rate; en ~ in time; (marcher) in step.

cadet, -te /kadε, -t/ adj youngest; (entre deux) younger. ● nm, f youngest (child); younger (child).

cadran /kadʀɑ̃/ nm dial; ~ solaire sundial.

cadre /kadʀ/ nm frame; (lieu) setting; (milieu) surroundings; (limites) scope; (contexte) framework; dans le ~ de (à l'occasion de) on the occasion of; (dans le contexte de) in the framework of. ● nm (personne) executive; les ~s the managerial staff.

cadrer /kadʀe/ **1** vi ~ avec tally with. ● vt (photo) centre.

cafard /kafaʀ/ nm (insecte) cockroach; avoir le ~ **1** be down in the dumps.

café /kafe/ nm coffee; (bar) café; ~ crème espresso with milk; ~ en grains coffee beans; ~ au lait white coffee.

cafetière /kaftjεʀ/ nf coffee-pot; ~ électrique coffee machine.

cage /kaʒ/ nf cage; ~ d'ascenseur lift shaft; ~ d'escalier stairwell; ~ thoracique rib cage.

cageot /kaʒo/ nm crate.

cagibi /kaʒibi/ nm storage room.

cagneux, -euse /kaɲø, -z/ adj avoir les genoux ~ be knock-kneed.

cagnotte | cambrioler

cagnotte /kaɲɔt/ nf kitty.

cagoule /kagul/ nf hood; (passe-montagne) balaclava.

cahier /kaje/ nm notebook; (Scol) exercise book; ~ de textes homework notebook; ~ des charges (Tech) specifications (+ pl).

cahot /kao/ nm bump, jolt. **cahoteux, -euse** adj bumpy.

caïd /kaid/ nm 🔟 big shot.

caille /kaj/ nf quail.

cailler /kaje/ 🔟 vt curdle; ça caille 🔟 it's freezing. □ **se** ~ vpr (sang) clot; (lait) curdle. **caillot** nm (blood) clot.

caillou (pl ~x) /kaju/ nm stone; (galet) pebble.

caisse /kɛs/ nf crate, case; (tiroir, machine) till; (guichet) cash desk; (au supermarché) check-out; (bureau) office; (Mus) drum; ~ enregistreuse cash register; ~ d'épargne savings bank; ~ de.retraite pension fund. **caissier, -ière** nm, f cashier.

cajoler /kaʒɔle/ 🔟 vt coax.

calcaire /kalkɛʀ/ adj (sol) chalky; (eau) hard.

calciné, ~e /kalsine/ adj charred.

calcul /kalkyl/ nm calculation; (Scol) arithmetic; (différentiel) calculus; ~ biliaire gallstone.

calculatrice /kalkylatʀis/ nf calculator. **calculer** 🔟 vt calculate. **calculette** nf (pocket) calculator.

cale /kal/ nf wedge; (pour roue) chock; (de navire) hold; ~ sèche dry dock.

calé, ~e /kale/ adj 🔟 clever.

caleçon /kalsɔ̃/ nm boxer shorts (+ pl); underpants (+ pl); (de femme) leggings.

calembour /kalɑ̃buʀ/ nm pun.

calendrier /kalɑ̃dʀije/ nm calendar; (fig) schedule, timetable.

calepin /kalpɛ̃/ nm notebook.

caler /kale/ 🔟 vt wedge. ● vi stall; (abandonner 🔟) give up.

calfeutrer /kalføtʀe/ 🔟 vt (fissure) stop up; (porte) draught proof.

calibre /kalibʀ/ nm calibre; (d'un œuf, fruit) grade.

calice /kalis/ nm (Relig) chalice; (Bot) calyx.

californfuchon: à ~ /akalifuʀʃɔ̃/ loc astride.

câlin, ~e /kɑlɛ̃, -in/ adj (regard, ton) affectionate; (personne) cuddly.

calmant /kalmɑ̃/ nm sedative.

calme /kalm/ adj calm. ● nm peace; calm; (maîtrise de soi) composure; du ~! calm down!

calmer /kalme/ 🔟 vt (personne) calm down; (situation) defuse; (douleur) ease; (soif) quench. □ **se** ~ vpr (personne, situation) calm down; (agitation, tempête) calm down; (douleur) ease.

calomnie /kalɔmni/ nf (orale) slander; (écrite) libel. **calomnier** 45 vt slander; libel. **calomnieux, -ieuse** adj slanderous; libellous.

calorie /kalɔʀi/ nf calorie.

calque /kalk/ nm tracing; (papier) ~ tracing paper; (fig) exact copy. **calquer** 🔟 vt trace; (fig) copy; ~ qch sur model sth on.

calvaire /kalvɛʀ/ nm (croix) Calvary; (fig) suffering.

calvitie /kalvisi/ nf baldness.

camarade /kamaʀad/ nmf friend; (Pol) comrade; ~ de jeu playmate. **camaraderie** nf friendship.

cambouis /kɑ̃bwi/ nm dirty oil.

cambrer /kɑ̃bʀe/ 🔟 vt arch. □ **se** ~ vpr arch one's back.

cambriolage /kɑ̃bʀijɔlaʒ/ nm burglary. **cambrioler** 🔟 vt burgle.

cambrioleur, -euse nm, f burglar.

camelot /kamlo/ nm ① street vendor.

camelote /kamlɔt/ nf ① junk.

caméra /kamera/ nf (cinéma, télévision) camera.

caméscope® /kameskɔp/ nm camcorder.

camion /kamjõ/ nm lorry, truck. **camion-citerne** (pl **camions-citernes**) nm tanker. **camionnage** nm haulage. **camionnette** nf van. **camionneur** nm lorry ou truck driver; (entrepreneur) haulage contractor.

camisole /kamizɔl/ nf ∼ (de force) straitjacket.

camoufler /kamufle/ **1** vt camouflage.

camp /kã/ nm camp; (Sport, Pol) side.

campagnard, ∼e /kãpaɲar, -d/ adj country. ● nm, f countryman, countrywoman.

campagne /kãpaɲ/ nf country; countryside; (Mil, Pol) campaign.

campement /kãpmã/ nm camp, encampment.

camper /kãpe/ **1** vi camp. ● vt (esquisser) sketch. □ se ∼ vpr plant oneself. **campeur, -euse** nm, f camper.

camping /kãpiŋ/ nm camping; faire du ∼ go camping; (terrain de) ∼ campsite. **camping-car** (pl ∼s) nm camper-van; (US) motorhome. **camping-gaz**® nm inv (réchaud) camping stove.

Canada /kanada/ nm Canada.

canadien, ∼ne /kanadjẽ, -ɛn/ adj Canadian. **C∼, ∼ne** nm, f Canadian. **canadienne** nf (veste) fur-lined jacket; (tente) ridge tent.

canaille /kanɑj/ nf rogue.

canal (pl **-aux**) /kanal, -o/ nm (artificiel) canal; (bras de mer) channel; (Tech, TV) channel; (moyen) channel; par le ∼ de through. **canalisation** nf (tuyaux) mains (+ pl). **canaliser** vt (eau) canalize; (fig) channel.

canapé /kanape/ nm sofa.

canard /kanar/ nm duck; (journal ①) rag.

canari /kanari/ nm canary.

cancans /kãkã/ nmpl ① gossip.

cancer /kãsɛr/ nm cancer; le C∼ Cancer. **cancéreux, -euse** adj cancerous. **cancérigène** adj carcinogenic.

cancre /kãkr/ nm dunce.

candeur /kãdœr/ nf ingenuousness.

candidat, ∼e /kãdida, -t/ nm, f (à un examen, Pol) candidate; (à un poste) applicant, candidate (à for).

candidature /kãdidatyr/ nf application; (Pol) candidacy; poser sa ∼ à un poste apply for a job.

candide /kãdid/ adj ingenuous.

cane /kan/ nf (female) duck. **caneton** nm duckling.

canette /kanɛt/ nf (bouteille) bottle; (boîte) can.

canevas /kanva/ nm canvas; (ouvrage) tapestry; (plan) framework, outline.

caniche /kaniʃ/ nm poodle.

canicule /kanikyl/ nf scorching heat; (vague de chaleur) heatwave.

canif /kanif/ nm penknife.

canine /kanin/ nf canine (tooth).

caniveau (pl ∼x) /kanivo/ nm gutter.

cannabis /kanabis/ nm cannabis.

canne /kan/ nf (walking) stick; ∼ à pêche fishing rod; ∼ à sucre sugar cane.

cannelle /kanɛl/ nf cinnamon.

cannibale /kanibal/ *adj & nmf* cannibal.

canoë /kanɔe/ *nm* canoe; (Sport) canoeing.

canon /kanɔ̃/ *nm* (big) gun; (ancien) cannon; (d'une arme) barrel; (principe, règle) canon.

canot /kano/ *nm* dinghy, (small) boat; ~ de sauvetage lifeboat; ~ pneumatique rubber dinghy. **canotier** *nm* boater.

cantatrice /kɑ̃tatris/ *nf* opera singer.

cantine /kɑ̃tin/ *nf* canteen.

cantique /kɑ̃tik/ *nm* hymn.

cantonner /kɑ̃tɔne/ **1** *vt* (Mil) billet. □ se ~ dans *vpr* confine oneself to.

canular /kanylar/ *nm* hoax.

caoutchouc /kautʃu/ *nm* rubber; (élastique) rubber band; ~ mousse foam rubber.

cap /kap/ *nm* cape, headland; (direction) course; (obstacle) hurdle; franchir le ~ de la cinquantaine pass the fifty mark; mettre le ~ sur steer a course for.

capable /kapabl/ *adj* capable (de of); ~ de faire able to do, capable of doing.

capacité /kapasite/ *nf* ability; (contenance, potentiel) capacity.

cape /kap/ *nf* cape; rire sous ~ laugh up one's sleeve.

capillaire /kapilɛr/ *adj* (lotion, soins) hair; (vaisseau) capillary.

capitaine /kapitɛn/ *nm* captain.

capital, ~e (*mpl* -aux) /kapital,-o/ *adj* key, crucial, fundamental; (peine, lettre) capital. ●*nm* (*pl* -aux) (Comm) capital; (fig) stock; capitaux (Comm) capital; ~ risque venture capital; ~-risqueur venture capitalist. **capitale** *nf* (ville, lettre) capital.

capitalisme /kapitalism/ *nm* capitalism.

capitonné, ~e /kapitɔne/ *adj* padded.

capituler /kapityle/ **1** *vi* capitulate.

caporal (*pl* -aux) /kapɔral, -o/ *nm* corporal.

capot /kapo/ *nm* (Auto) bonnet; (US) hood.

capote /kapɔt/ *nf* (Auto) hood; (US) top; (préservatif 🛈) condom.

capoter /kapɔte/ **1** *vi* overturn; (fig) collapse.

câpre /kɑpr/ *nf* (Culin) caper.

caprice /kapris/ *nm* whim; (colère) tantrum; faire un ~ throw a tantrum. **capricieux**, **-ieuse** *adj* capricious; (appareil) temperamental.

Capricorne /kaprikɔrn/ *nm* le ~ Capricorn.

capsule /kapsyl/ *nf* capsule; (de bouteille) cap.

capter /kapte/ **1** *vt* (eau) collect; (émission) get; (signal) pick up; (fig) win, capture.

captif, **-ive** /kaptif, -v/ *adj & nm, f* captive.

captiver /kaptive/ **1** *vt* captivate.

capturer /kaptyre/ **1** *vt* capture.

capuche /kapyʃ/ *nf* hood. **capuchon** *nm* hood; (de stylo) cap.

car /kar/ *conj* because, for. ●*nm* coach; (US) bus.

carabine /karabin/ *nf* rifle.

caractère /karaktɛr/ *nm* (lettre) character; (nature) nature; ~s d'imprimerie block letters; avoir bon/mauvais ~ be good-natured/bad-tempered; avoir du ~ have character.

caractériel, ~le /karakterjɛl/ *adj* (trait) character; (enfant) disturbed.

caractériser /karakterize/ **1** *vt*

characterize. □ **se ~ par** *vpr* be characterized by. **caractéristique** *adj & nf* characteristic.

carafe /kaʀaf/ *nf* carafe.

Caraïbes /kaʀaib/ *nfpl* **les ~** the Caribbean.

carambolage /kaʀɑ̃bɔlaʒ/ *nm* pile-up.

caramel /kaʀamɛl/ *nm* caramel; (bonbon) toffee.

carapace /kaʀapas/ *nf* shell.

caravane /kaʀavan/ *nf* (Auto) caravan; (US) trailer; (convoi) caravan.

carbone /kaʀbɔn/ *nm* carbon; (papier) ~ carbon (paper). **carboniser** 1 *vt* burn (to ashes).

carburant /kaʀbyʀɑ̃/ *nm* (motor) fuel.

carburateur /kaʀbyʀatœʀ/ *nm* carburettor; (US) carburetor.

carcan /kaʀkɑ̃/ *nm* constraints (+ *pl*).

carcasse /kaʀkas/ *nf* (squelette) carcass; (armature) frame; (de voiture) shell.

cardiaque /kaʀdjak/ *adj* heart.
● *nmf* heart patient.

cardinal, ~e (*mpl* -aux) /kaʀdinal, -o/ *adj & nm* cardinal.

Carême /kaʀɛm/ *nm* **le ~** Lent.

carence /kaʀɑ̃s/ *nf* shortcomings (+ *pl*); inadequacy; (Méd) deficiency; (absence) lack.

caresse /kaʀɛs/ *nf* caress; (à un animal) stroke. **caresser** 1 *vt* caress, stroke; (espoir) cherish.

cargaison /kaʀɡɛzɔ̃/ *nf* cargo.

cargo /kaʀɡo/ *nm* cargo boat.

caricature /kaʀikatyʀ/ *nf* caricature.

carie /kaʀi/ *nf* (trou) cavity; **la ~** (dentaire) tooth decay.

carillon /kaʀijɔ̃/ *nm* chimes (+ *pl*);

(horloge) chiming clock.

caritatif, -ive /kaʀitatif, -v/ *adj* association caritative charity.

carnage /kaʀnaʒ/ *nm* carnage.

carnassier, -ière /kaʀnasje, -jɛʀ/ *adj* carnivorous.

carnaval (*pl* ~s) /kaʀnaval/ *nm* carnival.

carnet /kaʀnɛ/ *nm* notebook; (de tickets, timbres) book; ~ d'adresses address book; ~ de chèques chequebook.

carotte /kaʀɔt/ *nf* carrot.

carpe /kaʀp/ *nf* carp.

carré, ~e /kaʀe/ *adj* (forme, mesure) quare; (fig) straightforward; **un mètre ~** one square metre.
● *nm* square; (de terrain) patch.

carreau (*pl* ~x) /kaʀo/ *nm* (window) pane; (par terre, au mur) tile; (dessin) check; (aux cartes) diamonds (+ *pl*); **à ~x** (tissu) check(ed); (papier) squared.

carrefour /kaʀfuʀ/ *nm* crossroads (+ *sg*).

carrelage /kaʀlaʒ/ *nm* tiling; (sol) tiles.

carrément /kaʀemɑ̃/ *adv* (complètement) completely; (stupide, dangereux) downright; (dire) straight out; **elle a ~ démissionné** she went straight ahead and resigned.

carrière /kaʀjɛʀ/ *nf* career; (terrain) quarry.

carrossable /kaʀɔsabl/ *adj* suitable for vehicles.

carrosse /kaʀɔs/ *nm* (horse-drawn) coach.

carrosserie /kaʀɔsʀi/ *nf* (Auto) body(work).

carrure /kaʀyʀ/ *nf* shoulders; (fig) necessary qualities, calibre.

cartable /kaʀtabl/ *nm* satchel.

carte /kaʀt/ *nf* card; (Géog) map;

(Naut) chart; (au restaurant) menu; ~s (jeu) cards; à la ~ (manger) à la carte; (horaire) personalized; donner ~ blanche à qn a give a free hand to; ~ bleue® credit card; ~ de crédit credit card; ~ de fidélité loyalty card; ~ grise (car) registration document; ~ d'identité identity card; ~ magnétique swipe card; ~ de paiement debit card; ~ postale postcard; ~ à puce smart card; ~ de séjour resident's permit; ~ SIM SIM card; ~ des vins wine list; ~ de visite (business) card; ~ vitale social insurance smart card.

Carte d'identité Not to be confused with a passport, this is a proof of identity carried by French citizens. It is issued by the préfecture and is valid for ten years. Though not compulsory, it is used to guarantee payments by cheque and is accepted as a travel document within the EU.

cartilage /kartilaʒ/ nm cartilage.

carton /kartõ/ nm cardboard; (boîte) (cardboard) box; ~ à dessin portfolio; faire un ~ 🔲 do well.

cartonné, ~e /kartɔne/ adj livre ~ hardback.

cartouche /kartuʃ/ nf cartridge; (de cigarettes) carton. **cartouchière** nf cartridge-belt.

cas /kɑ/ nm case; au ~ où in case; ~ urgent emergency; en aucun ~ on no account; en ~ de in the event of, in case of; en tout ~ in any case; (du moins) at least; faire ~ de set great store by; ~ de conscience moral dilemma.

casanier, -ière /kazanje, -jɛʀ/ adj home-loving.

cascade /kaskad/ nf waterfall; (au cinéma) stunt; (fig) spate, series (+ sg).

cascadeur, -euse /kaskadœr, -øz/ nm, f stuntman, stuntwoman.

case /kɑz/ nf hut; (de damier) square; (compartiment) pigeon-hole; (sur un formulaire) box.

caser /kaze/ 🔲 vt 🔲 (mettre) put; (loger) put up; (dans un travail) find a job for; (marier: péj) marry off.

caserne /kazɛʀn/ nf barracks; ~ de sapeurs-pompiers fire station.

casier /kazje/ nm pigeon-hole, compartment; (à chaussures) rack; ~ judiciaire criminal record.

casque /kask/ nm (de motard) crash helmet; (de cycliste) cycle helmet; (chez le coiffeur) (hair-)drier; ~ (à écouteurs) headphones; ~ anti-bruit ear defenders; ~ de protection safety helmet.

casquette /kaskɛt/ nf cap.

cassant, ~e /kasɑ̃, -t/ adj brittle; (brusque) curt.

cassation /kasasjõ/ nf cour de ~ appeal court.

casse /kas/ nf (objets) breakages; (lieu) breaker's yard; mettre à la ~ scrap.

casse-cou /kasku/ nmf inv daredevil.

casse-croûte /kaskrut/ nm inv snack.

casse-noix /kasnwa/ nm inv nutcrackers (+ pl).

casse-pieds /kaspje/ nmf inv 🔲 pain (in the neck) 🔲.

casser /kase/ 🔲 vt break; (annuler) annul; ~ les pieds à qn 🔲 annoy sb. ● vi break. □ se ~ vpr break; (partir) 🔲 be off 🔲.

casserole /kasrɔl/ nf saucepan.

casse-tête /kastɛt/ nm inv (problème) headache; (jeu) brain teaser.

cassette /kasɛt/ nf casket; (de magnétophone) cassette, tape; (de vidéo) video tape; ~ audio numérique ~ digital audio tape.

cassis /kasi(s)/ nm inv blackcurrant.

cassure /kasyʀ/ nf break.

castor /kastɔʀ/ nm beaver.

castration /kastʀasjɔ̃/ nf castration.

catalogue /katalɔg/ nm catalogue.

catalyseur /katalizœʀ/ nm catalyst; (Auto) catalytic convertor.

catastrophe /katastʀɔf/ nf disaster, catastrophe. **catastrophique** adj catastrophic.

catch /katʃ/ nm (all-in) wrestling.

catéchisme /kateʃism/ nm catechism.

catégorie /kategɔʀi/ nf category. **catégorique** adj categorical.

cathédrale /katedʀal/ nf cathedral.

catholique /katɔlik/ adj Catholic; pas très ~ a bit fishy.

catimini: en ~ /ɑ̃katimini/ loc on the sly.

cauchemar /koʃmaʀ/ nm nightmare.

cause /koz/ nf cause; (raison) reason; (Jur) case; à ~ de because of; en ~ (en jeu, concerné) involved; pour ~ de on account of; mettre en ~ implicate; remettre en ~ call into question.

causer /koze/ **1** vt cause; (discuter de 🄸) ~ travail talk shop; ~ de talk about. • vi chat. **causerie** nf talk.

causette /kozɛt/ nf (Internet) chat; faire la ~ have a chat.

caution /kosjɔ̃/ nf surety; (Jur) bail; (appui) backing; (garantie) deposit; libéré sous ~ released on bail. **cautionner** **1** vt guarantee; (soutenir) back.

cavalcade /kavalkad/ nf stampede, rush.

cavalier, -ière /kavalje, -jɛʀ/ adj offhand; allée cavalière bridle path. • nm, f rider; (pour danser) partner. • nm (aux échecs) knight.

cave /kav/ nf cellar. • adj sunken.

caveau (pl ~x) /kavo/ nm vault.

caverne /kavɛʀn/ nf cave.

CCP abrév m (compte chèque postal) post office account.

CD abrév m (compact disc) CD.

CD-ROM abrév m inv (compact disc read only memory) CD-ROM.

---

ce, c', cet, cette (pl ces)
/sə, s, sɛt, se/

c' before e. cet before vowel or mute h.

● **ce, cet, cette** (pl ces) adjectif démonstratif

····▸ this; (plus éloigné) that; ces these; (plus éloigné) those; cette nuit (passée) last night; (à venir) tonight.

● **ce, c'** pronom démonstratif

····▸ c'est it's ou it is; c'est un policier he's a policeman; ~ sont eux qui l'ont fait they did it; qui est ~? who is it?

····▸ ce que/qui what; ~ que je ne comprends pas what I don't understand; elle est venue, ~ qui est étonnant she came, which is surprising; ~ que tu as de la chance! how lucky you are! tout ~ qu'elle trouve/peut everything she finds/can

---

CE abrév f (Communauté européenne) EC.

CEAM abrév f (Carte européenne d'assurance maladie) EHIC.

ceci /səsi/ pron this.

cécité /sesite/ *nf* blindness.

céder /sede/ 14 *vt* give up; ~ le passage give way; (vendre) sell. • *vi* (se rompre) give way; (se soumettre) give in.

cédérom /sederɔm/ *nm* CD-ROM.

cédille /sedij/ *nf* cedilla.

cèdre /sɛdʀ/ *nm* cedar.

CEI *abrév f* (**Communauté des États indépendants**) CIS.

ceinture /sɛ̃tyʀ/ *nf* belt; (taille) waist; ~ de sauvetage lifebelt; ~ de sécurité seatbelt.

cela /səla/ *pron* it, that; (pour désigner) that; ~ va de soi it is obvious; ~ dit/fait having said/done that.

célèbre /selɛbʀ/ *adj* famous. **célébrer** 14 *vt* celebrate. **célébrité** *nf* fame; (personne) celebrity.

céleri /sɛlʀi/ *nm* (en branches) celery. **céleri-rave** (*pl* céleris-raves) *nm* celeriac.

célibat /seliba/ *nm* celibacy; (état) single status.

célibataire /selibatɛʀ/ *adj* single. • *nm* bachelor. • *nf* single woman.

celle, celles /sɛl/ ➡CELUI.

cellulaire /selylɛʀ/ *adj* cell; emprisonnement ~ solitary confinement; fourgon ou voiture ~ prison van; téléphone ~ cellular phone.

cellule /selyl/ *nf* cell; ~ souche stem cell.

celui, celle, celle (*pl* ceux, celles) /səlɥi, sɛl, sø/ *pron* the one; ~ de mon ami my friend's; ~-ci this (one); ~-là that (one); ceux-ci these (ones); ceux-là those (ones).

cendre /sɑ̃dʀ/ *nf* ash.

cendrier /sɑ̃dʀije/ *nm* ashtray.

censé, ~e /sɑ̃se/ *adj* être ~ faire be supposed to do.

censeur /sɑ̃sœʀ/ *nm* censor; (Scol)

administrator in charge of discipline.

censure /sɑ̃syʀ/ *nf* censorship.

censurer 1 *vt* censor; (critiquer) censure.

cent /sɑ̃/ *adj* (a) hundred; 20 pour ~ 20 per cent. • *n* (quantité) hundred; ~ un a hundred and one;)centième (*d'euro*) cent.

centaine /sɑ̃tɛn/ *nf* hundred; une ~ (de) (about) a hundred.

centenaire /sɑ̃tnɛʀ/ *nm* (anniversaire) centenary.

centième /sɑ̃tjɛm/ *adj & nmf* hundredth.

centimètre /sɑ̃timɛtʀ/ *nm* centimetre; (ruban) tape-measure.

central, ~e (*mpl* -aux) /sɑ̃tʀal,-o/ *adj* central. • *nm* (*pl* -aux) ~ (téléphonique) (telephone) exchange. **centrale** *nf* power-station.

centre /sɑ̃tʀ/ *nm* centre; ~ commercial shopping centre; (US) mall; ~ d'appels call centre; ~ de formation training centre; ~ hospitalier hospital. **centrer** 1 *vt* centre. **centre-ville** (*pl* centres-villes) *nm* town centre.

centuple /sɑ̃typl/ *nm* le ~ de a hundred times; au ~ a hundredfold.

cep /sep/ *nm* vine stock.

cépage /sepaʒ/ *nm* grape variety.

cèpe /sep/ *nm* cep.

cependant /səpɑ̃dɑ̃/ *adv* however.

céramique /seʀamik/ *nf* ceramic; (art) ceramics (+ *sg*).

cercle /sɛʀkl/ *nm* circle; (cerceau) hoop; (association) society, club; ~ vicieux vicious circle.

cercueil /sɛʀkœj/ *nm* coffin.

céréale /seʀeal/ *nf* cereal; ~s (Culin) (breakfast) cereal.

cérébral, ~e (*mpl* -aux) /seʀebʀal, -o/ *adj* cerebral.

cérémonie /seʀemɔni/ nf ceremony; sans ~s (repas) informal; (recevoir) informally.

cerf /sɛʀ/ nm stag.

cerfeuil /sɛʀfœj/ nm chervil.

cerf-volant (pl cerfs-volants) /sɛʀvɔlɑ̃/ nm kite.

cerise /s(ə)ʀiz/ nf cherry. **cerisier** nm cherry tree.

cerner /sɛʀne/ **1** vt surround; (question) define; avoir les yeux cernés have rings under one's eyes.

certain, ~e /sɛʀtɛ̃, -ɛn/ adj certain; (sûr) certain, sure (de of; que that); d'un ~ âge no longer young; un ~ temps some time. **certainement** adv (probablement) most probably; (avec certitude) certainly. **certains**, **-es** pron some people.

certes /sɛʀt/ adv (sans doute) admittedly; (bien sûr) of course.

certificat /sɛʀtifika/ nm certificate.

certifier /sɛʀtifje/ **45** vt certify; ~ qch à qn assure sb of sth; copie certifiée conforme certified true copy.

certitude /sɛʀtityd/ nf certainty.

cerveau (pl ~x) /sɛʀvo/ nm brain.

cervelle /sɛʀvɛl/ nf (Anat) brain; (Culin) brains.

ces /se/ ➡CE.

césarienne /sezaʀjɛn/ nf Caesarean (section).

cesse /sɛs/ nf n'avoir de ~ que have no rest until; sans ~ constantly, incessantly.

cesser /sese/ **1** vt stop; ~ de faire stop doing. ● vi cease; faire ~ put an end to.

cessez-le-feu /seselfœ/ nm inv ceasefire.

cession /sesjɔ̃/ nf transfer.

c'est-à-dire /setadiʀ/ conj that

is (to say).

cet, **cette** /sɛt /set/ ➡CE.

ceux /sø/ ➡CELUI.

chacun, ~e /ʃakœ̃, -yn/ pron each (one), every one; (tout le monde) everyone; ~ d'entre nous each (one) of us.

chagrin /ʃagʀɛ̃/ nm sorrow; avoir du ~ be sad.

chahut /ʃay/ nm row, din.

chahuter /ʃayte/ **1** vi make a row. ● vt (enseignant) be rowdy with; (orateur) heckle.

chaîne /ʃɛn/ nf chain; (de télévision) channel; ~ (d'assemblage) assembly line; ~s (Auto) snow chains; ~ de montagnes mountain range; ~ de montage/fabrication assembly/production line; ~ hi-fi hi-fi system; ~ laser CD player; en ~ (accidents) multiple; (réaction) chain. **chaînette** nf (small) chain. **chaînon** nm link.

chair /ʃɛʀ/ nf flesh; bien en ~ plump; en ~ et en os in the flesh; ~ à saucisses sausage meat; la ~ de poule goose pimples. ● adj inv (couleur) ~ flesh-coloured.

chaire /ʃɛʀ/ nf (d'église) pulpit; (Univ) chair.

chaise /ʃɛz/ nf chair; ~ longue deckchair.

châle /ʃɑl/ nm shawl.

chaleur /ʃalœʀ/ nf heat; (moins intense) warmth; (d'un accueil, d'une couleur) warmth. **chaleureux**, **-euse** adj warm.

chalumeau (pl ~x) /ʃalymo/ nm blowtorch.

chalutier /ʃalytje/ nm trawler.

chamailler (se) /(sə)ʃamɑje/ **1** vpr squabble.

chambre /ʃɑ̃bʀ/ nf (bed) room; (Pol, Jur) chamber; faire ~ à part sleep in separate rooms; ~ à air inner tube; ∼ **d'amis** spare ou guest room; ∼ **de commerce (et d'industrie)** Chamber of Commerce; ∼ **à coucher bedroom**; ∼ **à un lit/deux lits** single/twinroom; ∼ **pour deux personnes** ∼ **double room**; ∼ **forte** strong-room; ∼ **d'hôte** bed and breakfast. **chambrer** 🔳 vt (vin) bring to room temperature.

chameau (pl ∼x) /ʃamo/ nm camel.

chamois /ʃamwa/ nm chamois.

champ /ʃɑ̃/ nm field; ∼ **de bataille** battlefield; ∼ **de courses** racecourse; ∼ **de tir** firing range.

champêtre /ʃɑ̃pɛtʀ/ adj rural.

champignon /ʃɑ̃piɲɔ̃/ nm mushroom; (moisissure) fungus; ∼ **de Paris** button mushroom.

champion, ∼**ne** /ʃɑ̃pjɔ̃, -ɔn/ nm, f champion. **championnat** nm championship.

chance /ʃɑ̃s/ nf (good) luck; (possibilité) chance; **avoir de la** ∼ be lucky; **quelle** ∼! what luck!

chanceler /ʃɑ̃sle/ 🔢 vi stagger; (fig) falter, waver.

chancelier /ʃɑ̃səlje/ nm chancellor.

chanceux, -euse /ʃɑ̃sø, -z/ adj lucky.

chandail /ʃɑ̃daj/ nm sweater.

chandelier /ʃɑ̃dəlje/ nm candlestick.

chandelle /ʃɑ̃dɛl/ nf candle; **dîner aux** ∼**s** candlelight dinner.

change /ʃɑ̃ʒ/ nm (foreign) exchange; (taux) exchange rate.

changement /ʃɑ̃ʒmɑ̃/ nm change; ∼ **climatique** climate change; ∼ **de vitesse** (dispositif) ears.

changer /ʃɑ̃ʒe/ 🔢 vt change; ∼ **qch de place** move sth; (échanger) change (**pour, contre** for); ∼ **de**

nom/voiture change one's name/car; ∼ **de place/train** change places/trains; ∼ **de direction** change direction; ∼ **d'avis** ou **d'idée** change one's mind; ∼ **de vitesse** change gear. □ **se** ∼ vpr change, get changed.

chanson /ʃɑ̃sɔ̃/ nf song.

chant /ʃɑ̃/ nm singing; (chanson) song; (Relig) hymn.

chantage /ʃɑ̃taʒ/ nm blackmail.

chanter /ʃɑ̃te/ 🔳 vt sing; **si cela vous chante** 🔢 if you feel like it. ● vi sing; **faire** ∼ (délit) blackmail. **chanteur, -euse** nm, f singer.

chantier /ʃɑ̃tje/ nm building site; ∼ **naval** shipyard; **mettre en** ∼ get under way, start.

chaos /kao/ nm chaos.

chaparder /ʃapaʀde/ 🔳 vt 🔢 pinch 🔢, filch.

chapeau (pl ∼x) /ʃapo/ nm hat; ∼**!** well done!

chapelet /ʃaplɛ/ nm rosary; (fig) string.

chapelle /ʃapɛl/ nf chapel.

chapelure /ʃaplyʀ/ nf (Culin) breadcrumbs.

chaperonner /ʃapʀɔne/ 🔳 vt chaperone.

chapiteau (pl ∼x) /ʃapito/ nm marquee; (de cirque) big top; (de colonne) capital.

chapitre /ʃapitʀ/ nm chapter; (fig) subject.

chaque /ʃak/ adj every, each.

char /ʃaʀ/ nm (Mil) tank; (de carnaval) float; (charrette) cart; (dans l'antiquité) chariot.

charabia /ʃaʀabja/ nm 🔢 gibberish.

charade /ʃaʀad/ nf riddle.

charbon /ʃaʀbɔ̃/ nm coal; (Méd) anthrax; ∼ **de bois** charcoal.

charcuterie /ʃaʀkytʀi/ nf pork

butcher's shop; (aliments) (cooked) pork meats. **charcutier, -ière** nm, f pork butcher.

chardon /ʃaʁdɔ̃/ nm thistle.

charge /ʃaʁʒ/ nf load, burden; (Mil, Électr, Jur) charge; (responsabilité) responsibility; avoir qn à ~ be responsible for; ~s expenses; (de locataire) service charges; être à la ~ de (personne) be the responsibility of; (frais) be payable by; ~s sociales social security contributions; prendre en ~ take charge of.

chargé, ~e /ʃaʁʒe/ adj (véhicule) loaded; (journée, emploi du temps) busy; (langue) coated. ● nm, f ~ de mission head of mission; ~ d'affaires chargé d'affaires; ~ de cours lecturer.

chargement /ʃaʁʒəmɑ̃/ nm loading; (objets) load.

charger /ʃaʁʒe/ [40] vt load; (Ordinat, Photo) load; (attaquer) charge; (batterie) charge; ~ qn de (fardeau) weigh sb down with; (tâche) entrust sb with; ~ qn de faire make sb responsible for doing. ● vi (attaquer) charge. □ **se ~ de** vpr take charge ou care of.

chariot /ʃaʁjo/ nm (à roulettes) rolley; (US) cart; (pour bagages) cart. trolley cart.

charitable /ʃaʁitabl/ adj charitable.

charité /ʃaʁite/ nf charity; faire la ~ à give (money) to.

charlatan /ʃaʁlatɑ̃/ nm charlatan.

charmant, ~e /ʃaʁmɑ̃, -t/ adj charming.

charme /ʃaʁm/ nm charm; (qui envoûte) spell. **charmer** [1] vt charm. **charmeur, -euse** nm, f charmer.

charnel, ~le /ʃaʁnɛl/ adj carnal.

charnière /ʃaʁnjɛʁ/ nf hinge; à la ~ de at the meeting point between.

charnu, ~e /ʃaʁny/ adj plump, fleshy.

charpente /ʃaʁpɑ̃t/ nf framework; (carrure) build.

charpentier /ʃaʁpɑ̃tje/ nm carpenter.

charrette /ʃaʁɛt/ nf cart.

charrue /ʃaʁy/ nf plough.

chasse /ʃas/ nf hunting; (au fusil) shooting; (poursuite) chase; (recherche) hunt(ing); ~ (d'eau) (toilet) flush; ~ sous-marine harpoon fishing.

chasse-neige /ʃasnɛʒ/ nm inv snowplough.

chasser /ʃase/ [1] vt hunt; (au fusil) shoot; (faire partir) chase away; (odeur, employé) get rid of. ● vi go hunting; (au fusil) go shooting.

chasseur, -euse /ʃasœʁ, -øz/ nm, f hunter. ● nm bellboy; (US) bellhop; (avion) fighter plane.

châssis /ʃasi/ nm frame; (Auto) chassis.

chasteté /ʃastəte/ nf chastity.

chat¹ /ʃa/ nm cat; (mâle) tomcat.

chat² /tʃat/ nm (Internet) chat.

châtaigne /ʃatɛɲ/ nf chestnut. **châtaignier** nm chestnut tree. **châtain** adj inv chestnut (brown).

château (pl ~x) /ʃato/ nm castle; (manoir) manor; ~ d'eau water tower; ~ fort fortified castle.

châtiment /ʃatimɑ̃/ nm punishment.

chaton /ʃatɔ̃/ nm (chat) kitten.

chatouillement /ʃatujmɑ̃/ nm tickling. **chatouiller** [1] vt tickle. **chatouilleux, -euse** adj ticklish; (susceptible) touchy.

châtrer /ʃatʁe/ [1] vt castrate; (chat) neuter.

chatte /ʃat/ nf female cat.

chaud, ~e /ʃo, -d/ *adj* warm; (brûlant) hot; (vif: fig) warm. ● *nm* heat; au ~ in the warm(th); avoir ~ be warm; be hot; il fait ~ it is warm; it is hot; pour te tenir ~ to keep you warm. **chaudement** *adv* warmly; (disputé) hotly.

chaudière /ʃodjɛr/ *nf* boiler.

chaudron /ʃodrɔ̃/ *nm* cauldron.

chauffage /ʃofaʒ/ *nm* heating; ~ central central heating.

chauffard /ʃofar/ *nm* (péj) reckless driver.

chauffer /ʃofe/ **1** *vt/i* heat (up); (moteur, appareil) overheat. □ **se** ~ *vpr* warm oneself (up).

chauffeur /ʃofœr/ *nm* driver; (aux gages de qn) chauffeur.

chaume /ʃom/ *nm* (de toit) thatch.

chaussée /ʃose/ *nf* road (way).

chausse-pied /ʃospje/ (*pl* ~s) /ʃospje/ *nm* shoehorn.

chausser /ʃose/ **1** *vt* (chaussures) put on; (enfant) put shoes on (to). ● *vi* ~ bien (aller) fit well; ~ du 35 take a size 35 shoe. □ **se** ~ *vpr* put one's shoes on.

chaussette /ʃosɛt/ *nf* sock.

chausson /ʃosɔ̃/ *nm* slipper; (de bébé) bootee; ~ de danse ballet shoe; ~ aux pommes apple turnover.

chaussure /ʃosyr/ *nf* shoe; ~ de ski ski boot; ~ de marche hiking boot.

chauve /ʃov/ *adj* bald.

chauve-souris (*pl* **chauves-souris**) /ʃovsuri/ *nf* bat.

chauvin, ~e /ʃovɛ̃, -in/ *adj* chauvinistic. ● *nm, f* chauvinist.

chavirer /ʃavire/ **1** *vt* (bateau) capsize; (objets) tip over.

chef /ʃɛf/ *nm* leader, head; (supérieur) boss, superior; (Culin) chef; (de tribu) chief; architecte en ~

chief *ou* head architect; ~ d'accusation (Jur) charge; ~ d'équipe foreman; (Sport) captain; ~ d'État head of State; ~ de famille head of the family; ~ de file (Pol) leader; ~ de gare stationmaster; ~ d'orchestre conductor; ~ de service department head; ~ de train guard; (US) conductor.

chef-d'œuvre (*pl* **chefs-d'œuvre**) /ʃedœvr/ *nm* masterpiece.

chef-lieu (*pl* **chefs-lieux**) /ʃɛfljø/ *nm* county town, administrative centre.

chemin /ʃəmɛ̃/ *nm* road; (étroit) lane; (de terre) track; (pour piétons) path; (passage) way; (direction, trajet) way; avoir du ~ à faire have a long way to go; ~ de fer railway; par ~ de fer by rail; ~ de halage towpath; ~ vicinal country lane.

cheminée /ʃəmine/ *nf* chimney; (intérieure) fireplace; (encadrement) mantelpiece; (de bateau) funnel.

cheminot /ʃəmino/ *nm* railwayman; (US) railroad man.

chemise /ʃəmiz/ *nf* shirt; (dossier) folder; (de livre) jacket; ~ de nuit nightdress. **chemisette** *nf* short-sleeved shirt. **chemisier** *nm* blouse.

chêne /ʃɛn/ *nm* oak.

chenil /ʃəni(l)/ *nm* (pension) kennels (+ *sg*).

chenille /ʃənij/ *nf* caterpillar; véhicule à ~s tracked vehicle.

cheptel /ʃɛptɛl/ *nm* livestock.

chèque /ʃɛk/ *nm* cheque; ~ sans provision bad cheque; ~ de voyage traveller's cheque. **chéquier** *nm* chequebook.

cher, ~ère /ʃɛr/ *adj* (coûteux) dear, expensive; (aimé) dear; (dans la correspondance) dear. ● *adv* (coûter, payer) a lot (of money); (en importance) dearly. ● *nm, f* mon ∼, ma chère my dear.

chercher /ʃɛʀʃe/ **1** *vt* look for; (*aide, paix, gloire*) seek; aller ∼ go and get ou fetch, go for; ∼ à faire attempt to do; ∼ la petite bête to be finicky.

chercheur, -euse /ʃɛʀʃœʀ, -øz/ *nm, f* research worker.

chèrement /ʃɛʀmɑ̃/ *adv* dearly.

chéri, ∼e /ʃeʀi/ *adj* beloved. ● *nm, f* darling.

chérir /ʃeʀiʀ/ **2** *vt* cherish.

chétif, -ive /ʃetif, -v/ *adj* puny.

cheval (*pl* **-aux**) /ʃəval, -o/ *nm* horse; à ∼ on horseback; à ∼ sur astride, straddling; faire du ∼ ride, go horse-riding.

chevalerie /ʃəvalʀi/ *nf* chivalry.

chevalet /ʃəvalɛ/ *nm* easel; (de menuisier) trestle.

chevalier /ʃəvalje/ *nm* knight.

chevalière /ʃəvaljɛʀ/ *nf* signet ring.

cheval-vapeur (*pl* **chevaux-vapeur**) /ʃəvalvapœʀ/ *nm* horsepower.

chevaucher /ʃəvoʃe/ **1** *vt* sit astride. □ **se ∼** *vpr* overlap.

chevelu, ∼e /ʃəvly/ *adj* (*péj*) long-haired; (Bot) hairy.

chevelure /ʃəvlyʀ/ *nf* hair.

chevet /ʃəvɛ/ *nm* au ∼ de at the bedside of; livre de ∼ bedside book.

cheveu (*pl* **∼x**) /ʃəvø/ *nm* (poil) air; ∼x (chevelure) hair; avoir les ∼x longs have long hair.

cheville /ʃəvij/ *nf* ankle; (fiche) peg, pin; (pour mur) (wall) plug.

chèvre /ʃɛvʀ/ *nf* goat.

chevreuil /ʃəvʀœj/ *nm* roe (deer); (Culin) venison.

chevron /ʃəvʀɔ̃/ *nm* (poutre) rafter; à ∼s herringbone.

chez /ʃe/ *prép* (au domicile de) at the house of; (parmi) among; (dans le caractère ou l'œuvre de) in; aller ∼ qn go to sb's house; ∼ le boucher at ou to the butcher's; ∼ soi at home; rentrer ∼ soi go home. **chez-soi** *nm inv* home.

chic /ʃik/ *adj inv* smart; (gentil) kind. ● *nm* style; avoir le ∼ pour have a knack for; ∼ (alors)! great!

chicane /ʃikan/ *nf* double bend; chercher ∼ à qn pick a quarrel with sb.

chiche /ʃiʃ/ *adj* mean (de with); ∼ que je le fais! **1** I bet you I can do it.

chichis /ʃiʃi/ *nmpl* **1** fuss.

chicorée /ʃikɔʀe/ *nf* (frisée) endive; (à café) chicory.

chien /ʃjɛ̃/ *nm* dog; ∼ d'aveugle guide dog; ∼ de garde watch-dog. **chienne** *nf* dog, bitch.

chiffon /ʃifɔ̃/ *nm* rag; (pour nettoyer) duster; ∼ humide damp cloth. **chiffonner** **1** *vt* crumple; (préoccuper **1**) bother.

chiffre /ʃifʀ/ *nm* figure; (numéro) number; (code) code; ∼s arabes/romains Arabic/Roman numerals; ∼s (statistiques) statistics; ∼ d'affaires turnover.

chiffrer /ʃifʀe/ **1** *vt* put a figure on, assess; (texte) encode. □ **se ∼** *vpr* come to.

chignon /ʃiɲɔ̃/ *nm* bun, chignon.

Chili /ʃili/ *nm* Chile.

chimère /ʃimɛʀ/ *nf* fantasy.

chimie /ʃimi/ *nf* chemistry. **chimique** *adj* chemical. **chimiste** *nmf* chemist.

chimpanzé /ʃɛ̃pɑ̃ze/ *nm* chimpanzee.

Chine /ʃin/ *nf* China.

chinois /ʃinwa, -z/ adj Chinese. ● nm (Ling) Chinese. C~, ~e nm, f Chinese.

chiot /ʃjo/ nm pup(py).

chipoter /ʃipɔte/ 🗌 vi (manger) pick at one's food; (discuter) quibble.

chips /ʃips/ nf inv crisp; (US) chip.

chirurgie /ʃiryʁʒi/ nf surgery; ~ esthétique plastic surgery. **chirurgien** nm surgeon.

chlore /klɔʁ/ nm chlorine.

choc /ʃɔk/ nm (heurt) impact, shock; (émotion) shock; (collision) crash; (affrontement) clash; (Méd) shock; sous le ~ in shock.

chocolat /ʃɔkɔla/ nm chocolate; (à boire) drinking chocolate; ~ au lait milk chocolate; ~ chaud hot chocolate; ~ noir plain ou dark chocolate.

chœur /kœʁ/ nm (antique) chorus; (chanteurs, nef) choir; en ~ in chorus.

choisir /ʃwaziʁ/ 🗌 vt choose, select.

choix /ʃwa/ nm choice, selection; fromage ou dessert au ~ a choice of cheese or dessert; de ~ choice; de premier ~ top quality.

chômage /ʃomaʒ/ nm unemployment; au ~, en ~ unemployed; mettre en ~ technique lay off.

chômeur, -euse /ʃomœʁ, -øz/ nm, f unemployed person; les ~s the unemployed.

choquer /ʃɔke/ 🗌 vt shock; (commotionner) shake.

choral, ~e (mpl ~s) /kɔʁal/ adj choral. **chorale** nf choir, choral society.

chorégraphie /kɔʁeɡʁafi/ nf choreography.

choriste /kɔʁist/ nmf (à l'église) chorister; (à l'opéra) member of the chorus ou choir.

chose /ʃoz/ nf thing; (très) peu de ~ nothing much; pas grand ~ not much.

chou (pl ~x) /ʃu/ nm cabbage; (à la crème) cream puff; ~ de Bruxelles Brussels sprout; mon petit ~ 🗌 my dear.

chouchou, ~te /ʃuʃu, -t/ nm, f (de professeur) pet; (du public) darling.

choucroute /ʃukʁut/ nf sauerkraut.

chouette /ʃwɛt/ nf owl. ● adj 🗌 super.

chou-fleur (pl choux-fleurs) /ʃuflœʁ/ nm cauliflower.

choyer /ʃwaje/ 🗌 vt pamper.

chrétien, ~ne /kʁetjɛ̃, -jɛn/ adj & nm, f Christian.

Christ /kʁist/ nm le ~ Christ.

chrome /kʁom/ nm chromium, chrome.

chromosome /kʁomozom/ nm chromosome.

chronique /kʁonik/ adj chronic. ● nf (rubrique) column; (nouvelles) news; (annales) chronicle.

chronologique /kʁonolɔʒik/ adj chronological.

chronomètre /kʁonomɛtʁ/ nm stopwatch. **chronométrer** 🗌 vt time.

chrysanthème /kʁizɑ̃tɛm/ nm chrysanthemum.

chuchoter /ʃyʃɔte/ 🗌 vt/i whisper.

chut /ʃyt/ interj shh, hush.

chute /ʃyt/ nf fall; (déchet) offcut; ~ (d'eau) waterfall; ~ de pluie rainfall; ~ des cheveux hair loss; ~ des ventes ~ drop in sales; ~ de 5% 5% drop. **chuter** 🗌 vi fall.

Chypre /ʃipʀ/ nf Cyprus.

ci /si/ adv here; ~-gît here lies; cet homme-~ this man; ces maisons-~ these houses.

ci-après /siapʀe/ adv below.

cible /sibl/ nf target.

ciboulette /sibulɛt/ nf (Culin) chives (+ pl).

cicatrice /sikatʀis/ nf scar.

cicatriser /sikatʀize/ **1** vt heal.
□ se ~ vpr heal.

ci-dessous /sidəsu/ adv below.

ci-dessus /sidəsy/ adv above.

cidre /sidʀ/ nm cider.

ciel (pl cieux, ciels) /sjɛl, sjø/ nm sky; (Relig) heaven; cieux (Relig) heaven.

cierge /sjɛʀʒ/ nm (church) candle.

cigale /sigal/ nf cicada.

cigare /sigaʀ/ nm cigar.

cigarette /sigaʀɛt/ nf cigarette.

cigogne /sigɔɲ/ nf stork.

ci-joint /sijwɛ̃/ adv enclosed.

cil /sil/ nm eyelash.

cime /sim/ nf peak, tip.

ciment /simɑ̃/ nm cement.

cimetière /simtjɛʀ/ nm cemetery, graveyard; ~ de voitures breaker's yard.

cinéaste /sineast/ nmf film-maker.

cinéma /sinema/ nm cinema; (US) movie theater. **cinémathèque** nf film archive; (salle) film theatre. **cinématographique** adj cinema.

cinéphile /sinefil/ nmf film lover.

cinglant, ~e /sɛ̃glɑ̃, -t/ adj (vent) biting; (remarque) scathing.

cinglé, ~e /sɛ̃gle/ adj **1** crazy.

cinq /sɛ̃k/ adj & nm five.

cinquante /sɛ̃kɑ̃t/ adj & nm fifty.

cinquième /sɛ̃kjɛm/ adj & nmf fifth.

Cinquième République
As established by the constitution of 1958 and still in force today, the *Cinquième République* refers to the system of government established by Charles de Gaulle, enshrining a strong executive and institutions to guarantee stability.

cintre /sɛ̃tʀ/ nm coat-hanger; (Archit) curve.

cirage /siʀaʒ/ nm polish.

circoncision /siʀkɔ̃sizjɔ̃/ nf circumcision.

circonflexe /siʀkɔ̃flɛks/ adj circumflex.

circonscription /siʀkɔ̃skʀipsjɔ̃/ nf district; ~ électorale constituency; (US) district; (de conseiller, maire) ward.

circonscrire /siʀkɔ̃skʀiʀ/ **30** vt (incendie, épidémie) contain; (sujet) define.

circonspect, ~e /siʀkɔ̃spɛkt/ adj circumspect.

circonstance /siʀkɔ̃stɑ̃s/ nf circumstance; (situation) situation; (occasion) occasion; ~s atténuantes mitigating circumstances.

circuit /siʀkɥi/ nm circuit; (trajet) tour, trip.

circulaire /siʀkylɛʀ/ adj & nf circular.

circulation /siʀkylasjɔ̃/ nf circulation; (de véhicules) traffic.

circuler /siʀkyle/ **1** vi (se répandre, être distribué) circulate; (aller d'un lieu à un autre) get around; (en voiture) travel; (piéton) walk; (être en service) (bus, train) run; faire ~ (badauds) move on; (rumeur) spread.

cire /siʀ/ nf wax.

ciré /siʀe/ nm oilskin.

cirer /siʀe/ **1** vt polish.

cirque /siʀk/ nm circus; (arène) amphitheatre; (désordre: fig) chaos; faire le ~! make a racket **1**.

ciseau (pl ~x) /sizo/ nm chisel; ~x scissors.

ciseler /sizle/ **6** vt chisel.

citadelle /sitadɛl/ nf citadel.

citadin, ~e /sitadɛ̃, -in/ nm, f city-dweller. ● adj city.

citation /sitasjɔ̃/ nf quotation; (Jur) summons.

cité /site/ nf city; (logements) housing estate; ~ universitaire (university) halls of residence.

citer /site/ **1** vt quote, cite; (Jur) summon.

citerne /sitɛʀn/ nf tank.

citoyen, ~ne /sitwajɛ̃, -ɛn/ nm, f citizen.

citron /sitʀɔ̃/ nm lemon; ~ vert lime. **citronnade** nf lemon squash, (still) lemonade.

citrouille /sitʀuj/ nf pumpkin.

civet /sivɛ/ nm stew; ~ de lièvre jugged hare.

civière /sivjɛʀ/ nf stretcher.

civil, ~e /sivil/ adj civil; (non militaire) civilian; (poli) civil. ● nm civilian; dans le ~ in civilian life; en ~ in plain clothes.

civilisation /sivilizasjɔ̃/ nf civilization.

civiliser /sivilize/ **1** vt civilize. □ se ~ vpr become civilized.

civique /sivik/ adj civic.

clair, ~e /klɛʀ/ adj clear; (éclairé) light, bright; (couleur) light; le plus ~ de most of. ● adv clearly; il faisait ~ it was already light. ● nm ~ de lune moonlight; tirer une histoire au ~ get to the bottom of things. **clairement** adv clearly.

clairière /klɛʀjɛʀ/ nf clearing.

clairsemé, ~e /klɛʀsəme/ adj sparse.

clamer /klame/ **1** vt proclaim.

clameur /klamœʀ/ nf clamour.

clan /klɑ̃/ nm clan.

clandestin, ~e /klɑ̃dɛstɛ̃, -in/ adj secret; (journal) underground; (immigration, travail) illegal; passager ~ stowaway.

clapier /klapje/ nm (rabbit) utch.

clapoter /klapɔte/ **1** vi lap.

claquage /klakaʒ/ nm strained muscle; se faire un ~ pull a muscle.

claque /klak/ nf slap.

claquer /klake/ **1** vi bang; (porte) slam, bang; (fouet) crack; (se casser **1**) conk out; (mourir **1**) snuff it!; ~ des doigts snap one's fingers; ~ des mains clap one's hands; il claque des dents his teeth are chattering. ● vt (porte) slam, bang; (dépenser **1**) blow; (fatiguer **1**) tire out.

claquettes /klakɛt/ nfpl tap-dancing.

clarifier /klaʀifje/ **45** vt clarify.

clarinette /klaʀinɛt/ nf clarinet.

clarté /klaʀte/ nf light, brightness; (netteté) clarity.

classe /klas/ nf class; (salle: Scol) classroom; (cours) class, lesson; aller en ~ go to school; faire la ~ teach; ~ ouvrière/moyenne working/middle class.

classement /klasmɑ̃/ nm classification; (d'élèves) grading; (de documents) filing; (rang) place, grade; (de coureur) placing.

classer /klase/ **1** vt classify; (par mérite) grade; (papiers) file; (Jur) (affaire) close. □ se ~ vpr rank.

classeur /klasœʀ/ nm (meuble) filing cabinet; (chemise) file; (à anneaux) ring binder.

classification /klasifikasjɔ̃/ nf

classification.

classique /klasik/ adj classical; (de qualité) classic; (habituel) classic, standard. ● nm classic; (auteur) classical author.

clavecin /klavsɛ̃/ nm harpsichord.

clavicule /klavikyl/ nf collarbone.

clavier /klavje/ nm keyboard; ~ numérique keypad.

clé, clef /kle/ nf key; (outil) spanner; (Mus) clef; ~ anglaise (monkey-)wrench; ~ de contact ignition key; ~ à molette adjustable spanner; ~ de voûte keystone. ● adj inv key.

clémence /klemɑ̃s/ nf (de climat) mildness; (indulgence) leniency.

clergé /klɛʀʒe/ nm clergy.

clérical, ~e (mpl -aux) /klerikal, -o/ adj clerical.

clic /klik/ nm (Ordinat) click.

cliché /kliʃe/ nm cliché; (Photo) negative.

client, ~e /klijɑ̃, -t/ nm, f customer; (d'un avocat) client; (d'un médecin) patient; (d'hôtel) guest; (de taxi) passenger.

clientèle /klijɑ̃tɛl/ nf customers, clientele; (d'un avocat) clients, practice; (d'un médecin) patients, practice; (soutien) custom.

cligner /kliɲe/ **1** vi ~ des yeux blink; ~ de l'œil wink.

clignotant /kliɲɔtɑ̃/ nm (Auto) indicator, turn.

clignoter /kliɲɔte/ **1** vi blink; (lumière) flicker; (comme signal) flash.

climat /klima/ nm climate.

climatisation /klimatizasjɔ̃/ nf air-conditioning.

clin d'œil /klɛ̃dœj/ nm wink; en un ~ in a flash.

clinique /klinik/ adj clinical. ● nf (private) clinic.

clinquant, ~e /klɛ̃kɑ̃, -t/ adj showy.

clip /klip/ nm video.

cliquer /klike/ **1** vi (Ordinat) click (sur on).

cliqueter /klikte/ **38** vi (couverts) clink; (clés, monnaie) jingle; (ferraille) rattle. **cliquetis** nm clink(ing), jingle, rattle.

clivage /klivaʒ/ nm divide.

clochard, ~e /klɔʃaʀ, -d/ nm, f tramp.

cloche /klɔʃ/ nf bell; (imbécile [!]) idiot; ~ à fromage cheese-cover.

cloche-pied: à ~ /akloʃpje/ loc sauter à ~ hop on one leg.

clocher /klɔʃe/ nm bell-tower; (pointu) steeple; de ~ parochial.

cloison /klwazɔ̃/ nf partition; (fig) barrier.

cloître /klwatʀ/ nm cloister. **cloîtrer (se)** **1** vpr shut oneself away.

clonage /klonaʒ/ nm clonage.

cloner /klone/ **1** vt clone.

cloque /klɔk/ nf blister.

clos, ~e /klo, -z/ adj closed.

clôture /klotyʀ/ nf fence; (fermeture) closure; (de magasin, bureau) closing; (de débat, liste) close; (en Bourse) close of trading. **clôturer** **1** vt enclose, fence in; (festival, séance) close.

clou /klu/ nm nail; (furoncle) boil; (de spectacle) star attraction; les ~s (passage) pedestrian crossing; (US) crosswalk.

clouer /klue/ **1** vt nail down; (fig) pin down; être cloué au lit be confined to one's bed; ~ le bec à qn shut sb up.

clouté, ~e /klute/ adj studded; passage ~ pedestrian crossing; (US) crosswalk.

CMU abrév f free health care for

people on low incomes.
coaliser (se) /(sə)kɔalize/ **1** *vpr* join forces.
coalition /kɔalisjɔ̃/ *nf* coalition.
cobaye /kɔbaj/ *nm* guinea-pig.
cocaïne /kɔkain/ *nf* cocaine.
cocasse /kɔkas/ *adj* comical.
coccinelle /kɔksinɛl/ *nf* ladybird; (US) ladybug.
cocher /kɔʃe/ **1** *vt* tick (off), check. ● *nm* coachman.
cochon, ~e /kɔʃɔ̃, -ɔn/ *nm, f* (personne 1) pig. ● *adj* 1 filthy. ● *nm* pig. **cochonnerie** *nf* (saleté 1) filth; (marchandise 1) rubbish, junk.
cocon /kɔkɔ̃/ *nm* cocoon.
cocorico /kɔkɔʀiko/ *nm* cock-a-doodle-doo.
cocotier /kɔkɔtje/ *nm* coconut palm.
cocotte /kɔkɔt/ *nf* (marmite 1) casserole; ~ **minute**® pressure-cooker; **ma** ~ 1 my dear.
cocu, ~e /kɔky/ *nm,f* 1 deceived husband, deceived wife.
code /kɔd/ *nm* code; ~**s** dipped headlights; **se mettre en** ~**s** dip one's headlights; ~ **(à) barres** bar code; ~ **confidentiel (d'identification)** PIN number; ~ **postal** post code; (US) **zip code;** ~ **de la route** Highway Code. **coder 1** *vt* code, encode.
coéquipier, -ière /kɔekipje, -jɛʀ/ *nm, f* team mate.
cœur /kœʀ/ *nm* heart; (aux cartes) hearts (+ *pl*); ~ **d'artichaut** artichoke heart; ~ **de palmier** palm heart; **à** ~ **ouvert** (*opération*) open-heart; (*parler*) freely; **avoir bon** ~ be kind-hearted; **de bon** ~ willingly; (*rire*) heartily; **par** ~ by heart; **avoir mal au** ~ feel sick *ou* nauseous; **je veux en avoir le** ~

net I want to be clear in my own mind (about it).
coffre /kɔfʀ/ *nm* chest; (pour argent) safe; (Auto) boot; (US) trunk. **coffre-fort** (*pl* **coffres-forts**) *nm* safe.
coffret /kɔfʀɛ/ *nm* casket, box; (de livres, cassettes) boxed set.
cogner /kɔɲe/ **1** *vt/i* knock. □ **se** ~ *vpr* knock oneself; **se** ~ **la tête** bump one's head.
cohabiter /kɔabite/ **1** *vi* live together.
cohérent, ~e /kɔeʀɑ̃, -t/ *adj* coherent; (homogène) consistent.
cohue /kɔy/ *nf* crowd.
coi, ~te /kwa, -t/ *adj* silent.
coiffe /kwaf/ *nf* headgear.
coiffer /kwafe/ **1** *vt* do the hair of; (*chapeau*) put on; (surmonter) cap; ~ **qn d'un chapeau** put a hat on sb; **coiffé de** wearing; **être bien/ mal coiffé** have tidy/untidy hair. □ **se** ~ *vpr* do one's hair.
coiffeur, -euse /kwafœʀ, -øz/ *nm, f* hairdresser. **coiffeuse** *nf* dressing-table.
coiffure /kwafyʀ/ *nf* hairstyle; (métier) hairdressing; (chapeau) hat.
coin /kwɛ̃/ *nm* corner; (endroit) spot; (cale) wedge; **au** ~ **du feu** by the fireside; **dans le** ~ locally; **du** ~ local.
coincer /kwɛ̃se/ **10** *vt* jam; (caler) wedge; (attraper 1) catch. □ **se** ~ *vpr* get jammed.
coïncidence /kɔɛ̃sidɑ̃s/ *nf* coincidence.
coing /kwɛ̃/ *nm* quince.
coït /kɔit/ *nm* intercourse.
col /kɔl/ *nm* collar; (de bouteille) neck; (de montagne) pass; ~ **blanc** white-collar worker; ~ **roulé** polo-neck; (US) turtle-neck; ~ **de l'utérus** cervix; **se casser le** ~ **du**

fémur break one's hip.

colère /kɔlɛʀ/ *nf* anger; (*accès*) fit of anger; **en** ∼ angry; **se mettre en** ∼ lose one's temper; **faire une** ∼ throw a tantrum.

coléreux, -euse /kɔleʀø, -z/ *adj* quick-tempered.

colin /kɔlɛ̃/ *nm* (merlu) hake; (lieu noir) coley.

colique /kɔlik/ *nf* diarrhoea; (Méd) colic.

colis /kɔli/ *nm* parcel.

collaborateur, -trice /kɔlabɔʀatœʀ, -tʀis/ *nm, f* collaborator; (journaliste) contributor; (collègue) colleague.

collaboration /kɔlabɔʀasjɔ̃/ *nf* collaboration (à on); (à ouvrage, projet) contribution (à to).

collaborer /kɔlabɔʀe/ **1** *vi* collaborate (à on); ∼ **à** (journal) contribute to.

collant, ∼e /kɔlɑ̃, -t/ *adj* (moulant) kin-tight; (poisseux) sticky.
● *nm* (bas) tights; (US) panty hose.

colle /kɔl/ *nf* glue; (en pâte) paste; (problème 🄸) poser; (Scol 🄸) detention.

collecter /kɔlɛkte/ **1** *vt* collect.

collectif, -ive /kɔlɛktif, -v/ *adj* collective; (billet, voyage) group.

collection /kɔlɛksjɔ̃/ *nf* collection; (ouvrages) series (+ sg); (du même auteur) set. **collectionner** **1** *vt* collect. **collectionneur, -euse** *nm, f* collector.

collectivité /kɔlɛktivite/ *nf* community; ∼ **locale** local authority.

collège /kɔlɛʒ/ *nm* secondary school (up to age 15); (US) junior high school; (assemblée) college. **collégien, ∼ne** *nm, f* schoolboy, schoolgirl.

collègue /kɔlɛg/ *nmf* colleague.

coller /kɔle/ **1** *vt* stick; (avec colle liquide) glue; (affiche) stick up; (mettre 🄸) stick; (par une question 🄸) stump; (Scol 🄸) **se faire** ∼ get a detention; **je me suis fait** ∼ **en maths** I failed *ou* flunked maths.
● *vi* stick (à to); (être collant) be sticky; ∼ **à** (convenir à) fit, correspond to.

collet /kɔlɛ/ *nm* (piège) snare; ∼ **monté** prim and proper; **mettre la main au** ∼ **de qn** collar sb.

collier /kɔlje/ *nm* necklace; (de chien) collar.

colline /kɔlin/ *nf* hill.

collision /kɔlizjɔ̃/ *nf* (choc) collision; (lutte) clash; **entrer en** ∼ (avec) collide (with).

collyre /kɔliʀ/ *nm* eye drops (+ pl).

colmater /kɔlmate/ **1** *vt* plug, seal.

colombe /kɔlɔ̃b/ *nf* dove.

Colombie /kɔlɔ̃bi/ *nf* Colombia.

colon /kɔlɔ̃/ *nm* settler.

colonel /kɔlɔnɛl/ *nm* colonel.

colonie /kɔlɔni/ *nf* colony; ∼ **de vacances** children's holiday camp.

Colonie de vacances A holiday village or summer camp where children take part in a variety of outdoor activities. Originally set up to give poorer children a means of getting out into the countryside, they are still largely state-subsidized. Colloquially they are referred to as *la/une* colo.

---

colonne /kɔlɔn/ *nf* column; ∼ **vertébrale** spine; **en** ∼ **par deux** in double file.

colorant /kɔlɔʀɑ̃/ *nm* colouring.

colorier /kɔlɔʀje/ **45** *vt* colour (in).

colosse /kɔlɔs/ *nm* giant.

colza /kɔlza/ *nm* rape(-seed).

coma /kɔma/ *nm* coma; dans le ~ in a coma.

combat /kɔba/ *nm* fight; (Sport) match; ~s fighting. **combatif, -ive** *adj* eager to fight; (*esprit*) fighting.

combattre /kɔbatʁ/ 🔟 *vt/i* fight.

combien /kɔbjɛ̃/ *adv* ~ (de) quantité) how much; (nombre) how many; (temps) how long; ~ il a changé! (comme) how he has changed!; ~ y a-t-il d'ici à...? how far is it to...?; on est le ~ aujourd'hui? what's the date today?

combinaison /kɔbinɛzɔ̃/ *nf* combination; (de femme) slip; (bleu de travail) boiler suit; (US) overalls; ~ d'aviateur flying-suit; ~ de plongée wetsuit.

combine /kɔbin/ *nf* trick; (fraude) fiddle; (intrigue) scheme.

combiné /kɔbine/ *nm* (de téléphone) receiver, handset.

combiner /kɔbine/ 🔟 *vt* (réunir) combine; (calculer) devise; ~ de faire plan to do.

comble /kɔbl/ *adj* packed. ● *nm* height; ~s (mansarde) attic, loft; c'est le ~! that's the (absolute) limit!

combler /kɔble/ 🔟 *vt* fill; (*perte, déficit*) make good; (désir) fulfil; ~ qn de cadeaux lavish gifts on sb.

combustible /kɔbystibl/ *nm* fuel.

comédie /kɔmedi/ *nf* comedy; (histoire 🔟) fuss; ~ musicale musical; jouer la ~ put on an act. **comédien, ~ne** *nm, f* actor, actress.

comestible /kɔmɛstibl/ *adj* edible.

comète /kɔmɛt/ *nf* comet.

comique /kɔmik/ *adj* comical, funny; (genre) comic. ● *nm* (acteur) comic; (comédie) comedy; (côté drôle) comical aspect.

commandant /kɔmɑ̃dɑ̃/ *nm* commander; (dans l'armée de terre) major; ~ (de bord) captain; ~ en chef Commander-in-Chief.

commande /kɔmɑ̃d/ *nf* (Comm) order; (Tech) control; ~s (d'avion) controls.

commandement /kɔmɑ̃dmɑ̃/ *nm* command; (Relig) commandment.

commander /kɔmɑ̃de/ 🔟 *vt* command; (acheter) order; (étude, œuvre d'art) commission; ~ à (maîtriser) control; ~ à qn de command sb to. ● *vi* be in command.

comme /kɔm/ *adv* ~ c'est bon! it's so good!; ~ il est mignon! isn't he sweet! ● *conj* (dans une comparaison) as; (dans une équivalence, illustration) like; (en tant que) as; (puisque) as, since; (au moment où) as; vif ~ l'éclair as quick as a flash; travailler ~ sage-femme work as a midwife; ~ ci ~ ça so-so; ~ il faut properly; ~ pour faire as if to do; jolie ~ tout as pretty as anything; qu'est-ce qu'il y a ~ légumes? what is there in the way of vegetables?

commencer /kɔmɑ̃se/ 🔟 *vt/i* begin, start; ~ à faire begin ou start to do.

comment /kɔmɑ̃/ *adv* how; ~? (répétition) pardon?; (surprise) what?; ~ est-il? what is he like?; le ~ et le pourquoi the whys and wherefores.

commentaire /kɔmɑ̃tɛʁ/ *nm* comment; (d'un texte, événement) commentary. **commentateur, -trice** *nm, f* commentator.

commenter /kɔmɑ̃te/ 🔟 *vt* comment on; (film, visite) provide a commentary for; (radio, TV) commentate.

commérages /kɔmeʁaʒ/ *nmpl*

gossip.

commerçant, ~e /kɔmɛʀsɑ̃, -t/
adj (rue) shopping; (personne)
business-minded. ● nm, f shop-
keeper.

commerce /kɔmɛʀs/ nm trade,
commerce; (magasin) business;
faire du ~ be in business; ~ électrique e-commerce; ~ équitable
fair trade.

commercial, ~e (mpl -iaux) kɔ-
mɛʀsjal, -jo/ adj commercial. **commercialiser** 1 vt market.

commettre /kɔmɛtʀ/ 42 vt
commit.

commis /kɔmi/ nm (de magasin)
assistant; (de bureau) clerk.

commissaire /kɔmisɛʀ/ nm
missioner; (Sport) steward; ~ (de
police) superintendent.
commissaire-priseur (pl commis-
saires-priseurs) nm auctioneer.

commissariat /kɔmisaʀja/ nm ~
(de police) police station.

commission /kɔmisjɔ̃/ nf commission; (course) errand; (message)
message; ~s shopping.

commode /kɔmɔd/ adj handy; (facile) easy; il n'est pas ~ he's a difficult customer. ● nf chest of
(drawers). **commodité** nf convenience.

commotion /kɔmosjɔ̃/ nf ~ (cérébrale) concussion.

commun, ~e /kɔmœ̃, -yn/ adj
common; (effort, action) joint;
(frais, pièce) shared; en ~ jointly;
avoir ou mettre en ~ share; le ~
des mortels ordinary mortals.
communal, ~e (mpl -aux) adj of
the commune, local.

communauté /kɔmynote/ nf
community.

commune /kɔmyn/ nf (circonscription, collectivité) commune.

communicatif, -ive
/kɔmynikatif, -v/ adj (personne)
talkative; (gaieté) infectious.

communication /kɔmynikasjɔ̃/
nf communication; (téléphonique)
call; ~s (relations) communications
(+ pl); voies ou moyens de ~ communications (+ pl).

communier /kɔmynje/ 45 vi
(Relig) receive communion; (fig)
commune.

communiqué /kɔmynike/ nm
statement; (de presse) communiqué.

communiquer /kɔmynike/ 1 vt
pass on, communicate; (date, décision) announce. ● vi communicate.
□ se ~ à vpr spread to.

communiste /kɔmynist/ adj &
nmf communist.

commutateur /kɔmytatœʀ/ nm
(Électr) switch.

compagne /kɔ̃paɲ/ nf companion.

compagnie /kɔ̃paɲi/ nf company;
tenir ~ à keep company; en ~ de
together with; ~ aérienne airline.

compagnon /kɔ̃paɲɔ̃/ nm companion.

comparable /kɔ̃paʀabl/ adj comparable (à to). **comparaison** nf
comparison; (littéraire) simile.

comparaître /kɔ̃paʀɛtʀ/ 18 vi
(Jur) appear (devant before).

comparatif, -ive /kɔ̃paʀatif, -v/
adj & nm comparative.

comparer /kɔ̃paʀe/ 1 vt compare (à with). □ se ~ vpr compare oneself; (être comparable) be comparable.

compartiment /kɔ̃paRtimɑ̃/ nm compartment.

comparution /kɔ̃paRysjɔ̃/ nf (Jur) appearance.

compas /kɔ̃pa/ nm (pair of) compasses; (boussole) compass.

compassion /kɔ̃pasjɔ̃/ nf compassion.

compatible /kɔ̃patibl/ adj compatible.

compatir /kɔ̃patiR/ **2** vi sympathize; ~ à share in.

compatriote /kɔ̃patRijɔt/ nmf compatriot.

compensation /kɔ̃pɑ̃sasjɔ̃/ nf compensation. **compenser** **1** vt compensate for, make up for.

compère /kɔ̃pɛR/ nm accomplice.

compétence /kɔ̃petɑ̃s/ nf competence; (fonction) domain, sphere; entrer dans les ~s de qn be in sb's domain. **compétent, ~e** adj competent.

compétition /kɔ̃petisjɔ̃/ nf competition; (sportive) event; de ~ competitive.

complaire (se) /(sə)kɔ̃plɛR/ **47** vpr se ~ dans take delight in.

complaisance /kɔ̃plɛzɑ̃s/ nf kindness; (indulgence) indulgence.

complément /kɔ̃plemɑ̃/ nm supplement; (Gram) complement; ~ (d'objet) (Gram) object; ~ d'information further information. **complémentaire** adj complementary; (renseignements) supplementary.

complet, -ète /kɔ̃plɛ, -t/ adj complete; (train, hôtel) full. ● nm suit.

compléter /kɔ̃plete/ **14** vt complete; (agrémenter) complement. □ se ~ vpr complement each other.

complexe /kɔ̃plɛks/ adj com-

plex. ● nm (sentiment, bâtiments) complex.

complexé, ~e /kɔ̃plekse/ adj être ~ have a lot of hang-ups.

complice /kɔ̃plis/ nm accomplice.

compliment /kɔ̃plimɑ̃/ nm compliment; ~s (félicitations) compliments, congratulations.

compliquer /kɔ̃plike/ **1** vt complicate. □ se ~ vpr become complicated.

complot /kɔ̃plo/ nm plot.

comportement /kɔ̃pɔRtəmɑ̃/ nm behaviour; (de joueur, voiture) performance.

comporter /kɔ̃pɔRte/ **1** vt (être composé de) comprise; (inclure) include; (risque) entail. □ se ~ vpr behave; (joueur, voiture) perform.

composant /kɔ̃pozɑ̃/ nm component.

composé, ~e /kɔ̃poze/ adj composite; (salade) mixed; (guindé) affected. ● nm compound.

composer /kɔ̃poze/ **1** vt make up, compose; (chanson, visage) compose; (numéro) dial; (page) typeset. ● vi (transiger) compromise. □ se ~ de vpr be made up ou composed of. **compositeur, -trice** nm, f (Mus) composer.

composter /kɔ̃pɔste/ **1** vt (billet) punch.

compote /kɔ̃pɔt/ nf stewed fruit; ~ de pommes stewed apples.

compréhensible /kɔ̃pReɑ̃sibl/ adj understandable; (intelligible) comprehensible.

compréhensif, -ive /kɔ̃pReɑ̃sif, -v/ adj understanding.

compréhension /kɔ̃pReɑ̃sjɔ̃/ nf understanding, comprehension.

comprendre /kɔ̃pRɑ̃dR/ **50** vt understand; (comporter) comprise, be made up of. □ se ~

c

vpr (*personnes*) understand each other; ça se comprend that is understandable.

compresse /kɔ̃pʀɛs/ *nf* compress.

comprimé /kɔ̃pʀime/ *nm* tablet.

comprimer /kɔ̃pʀime/ ➊ *vt* compress; (réduire) reduce.

compris, ~e /kɔ̃pʀi, -z/ *adj* included; (d'accord) agreed; ~ (contained) between; service (non) ~ service (not) included; tout ~ (all) inclusive; y ~ including.

compromettre /kɔ̃pʀɔmɛtʀ/ ➋ *vt* compromise. **compromis** *nm* compromise.

comptabilité /kɔ̃ptabilite/ *nf* accountancy; (comptes) accounts; (service) accounts department.

comptable /kɔ̃tabl/ *adj* accounting. ● *nmf* accountant.

comptant /kɔ̃tɑ̃/ *adv* (payer) (in) cash; (acheter) for cash.

compte /kɔ̃t/ *nm* count; (facture, comptabilité) account; (nombre exact) right number; ~ bancaire, ~ en banque bank account; prendre qch en ~, tenir ~ de qch take sth into account; se rendre ~ de realize; demander/rendre des ~s ask for/give an explanation; à bon ~ cheaply; s'en tirer à bon ~ get off lightly; travailler à son ~ be self-employed; faire le ~ de count; pour le ~ de on behalf of; sur le ~ de about; au bout du ~ all things considered; ~ à rebours countdown.

compte-gouttes /kɔ̃tgut/ *nm inv* (Méd) dropper; au ~ (fig) in dribs and drabs.

compter /kɔ̃te/ ➊ *vt* count; (prévoir) allow, reckon on; (facturer) charge for; (avoir) have; (classer) consider; ~ faire intend to do. ● *vi* (calculer, importer) count; ~ avec reckon with; ~ parmi (figurer) be

considered among; ~ sur rely on, count on.

compte(-)rendu /kɔ̃tʀɑ̃dy/ *nm* report; (de film, livre) review.

compteur /kɔ̃tœʀ/ *nm* meter; ~ de vitesse speedometer.

comptine /kɔ̃tin/ *nf* nursery rhyme.

comptoir /kɔ̃twaʀ/ *nm* counter; (de café) bar.

comte /kɔ̃t/ *nm* count.

comté /kɔ̃te/ *nm* county.

comtesse /kɔ̃tɛs/ *nf* countess.

con, ~ne /kɔ̃, kɔn/ *adj* 🟥 bloody stupid 🟥. ● *nm, f* 🟥 bloody fool 🟥.

concentrer /kɔ̃sɑ̃tʀe/ ➊ *vt* concentrate. □ **se** ~ *vpr* be concentrated.

concept /kɔ̃sɛpt/ *nm* concept.

concerner /kɔ̃sɛʀne/ ➊ *vt* concern; en ce qui me concerne as far as I am concerned.

concert /kɔ̃sɛʀ/ *nm* concert; de ~ in unison.

concerter /kɔ̃sɛʀte/ ➊ *vt* organize, prepare. □ **se** ~ *vpr* confer.

concession /kɔ̃sesjɔ̃/ *nf* concession; (terrain) plot.

concevoir /kɔ̃svwaʀ/ ➋ *vt* (imaginer, engendrer) conceive; (comprendre) understand; (élaborer) design.

concierge /kɔ̃sjɛʀʒ/ *nmf* caretaker.

concilier /kɔ̃silje/ ➍ *vt* reconcile. □ **se** ~ *vpr* (s'attirer) win (over).

concis, ~e /kɔ̃si, -z/ *adj* concise.

conclure /kɔ̃klyʀ/ ➓ *vt* conclude; ~ à conclude in favour of. ● *vi* ~ en faveur de/contre find in favour of/against. **conclusion** *nf* conclusion.

concombre /kɔ̃kɔ̃bʀ/ *nm* cucumber.

concordance /kɔ̃kɔʀdɑ̃s/ *nf* agreement.

concourir /kɔ̃kuRiR/ 20 vi compete. ● vt ~ à contribute towards.

concours /kɔ̃kuR/ nm competition; (examen) competitive examination; (aide) help; (de circonstances) combination.

concret, -ète /kɔ̃kRɛ, -t/ adj concrete.

concrétiser /kɔ̃kRetize/ 1 vt give concrete form to. □ se ~ vpr materialize.

conçu, ~e /kɔ̃sy/ adj bien/mal ~ well/badly designed.

concubinage /kɔ̃kybinaʒ/ nm cohabitation; vivre en ~ live together, cohabit.

concurrence /kɔ̃kyRɑ̃s/ nf competition; faire ~ à compete with; jusqu'à ~ de up to a limit of.

concurrencer /kɔ̃kyRɑ̃se/ 10 vt compete with.

concurrent, ~e /kɔ̃kyRɑ̃, -t/ nm, f competitor; (Scol) candidate. ● adj rival.

condamnation /kɔ̃danasjɔ̃/ nf condemnation; (peine) sentence; ~ centralisée des portières central locking. **condamné, ~e** nm, f condemned man, condemned woman. **condamner** 1 vt (censurer, obliger) condemn; (Jur) sentence; (porte) block up.

condition /kɔ̃disjɔ̃/ nf condition; ~s (prix) terms; à ~ de ou que provided (that); sans ~ unconditional(ly); sous ~ conditional(ly). **conditionnel, ~le** /kɔ̃disjɔnɛl/ adj conditional. ● nm conditional (tense).

conditionnement /kɔ̃disjɔnmɑ̃/ nm conditioning; (emballage) packaging.

condoléances /kɔ̃dɔleɑ̃s/ nfpl condolences.

conducteur, -trice /kɔ̃dyktœR,

-tRis/ nm, f driver.

conduire /kɔ̃dɥiR/ 17 vt take (à to); (guider) lead; (Auto) drive; (affaire) conduct; ~ à (faire aboutir) lead to. ● vi drive. □ se ~ vpr behave.

conduit /kɔ̃dɥi/ nm duct.

conduite /kɔ̃dɥit/ nf conduct, behaviour; (Auto) driving; (tuyau) pipe; voiture avec ~ à droite right-hand drive car.

confection /kɔ̃fɛksjɔ̃/ nf making; de ~ ready-made; la ~ the clothing industry.

conférence /kɔ̃feRɑ̃s/ nf conference; (exposé) lecture; ~ au sommet summit meeting. **conférencier, -ière** nm, f lecturer.

confesser /kɔ̃fese/ 1 vt confess. □ se ~ vpr go to confession.

confiance /kɔ̃fjɑ̃s/ nf trust; avoir ~ en trust.

confiant, ~e /kɔ̃fjɑ̃, -t/ adj (assuré) confident; (sans défiance) trusting.

confidence /kɔ̃fidɑ̃s/ nf confidence.

confidentiel, ~le /kɔ̃fidɑ̃sjɛl/ adj confidential.

confier /kɔ̃fje/ 45 vt ~ à qn entrust sb with; ~ un secret à qn tell sb a secret. □ se ~ à vpr confide in.

configuration /kɔ̃figyRasjɔ̃/ nf configuration.

configurer /kɔ̃figyRe/ vt configure.

confiner /kɔ̃fine/ 1 vt confine; ~ à border on. □ se ~ vpr confine oneself (à, dans to).

confirmation /kɔ̃fiRmasjɔ̃/ nf confirmation. **confirmer** 1 vt confirm.

confiserie /kɔ̃fizRi/ nf sweet shop; ~s confectionery.

confisquer /kɔ̃fiske/ 1 vt confiscate.

confit, ~e /kɔ̃fi, -t/ adj candied; (fruits) crystallized. ● nm ~ de canard confit of duck.

confiture /kɔ̃fityʀ/ nf jam.

conflit /kɔ̃fli/ nm conflict.

confondre /kɔ̃fɔ̃dʀ/ [3] vt confuse, mix up; (étonner) confound. □ se ~ vpr merge; se ~ en excuses apologize profusely.

conforme /kɔ̃fɔʀm/ adj être ~ à comply with; (être en accord) be in keeping with.

conformer /kɔ̃fɔʀme/ [1] vt adapt. □ se ~ à vpr conform to.

conformité /kɔ̃fɔʀmite/ nf compliance, conformity; agir en ~ avec act in accordance with.

confort /kɔ̃fɔʀ/ nm comfort; tout ~ with all mod cons. **confortable** adj comfortable.

confrère /kɔ̃fʀɛʀ/ nm colleague.

confronter /kɔ̃fʀɔ̃te/ [1] vt confront; (textes) compare. □ se ~ à vpr be confronted with.

confus, ~e /kɔ̃fy, -z/ adj confused; (gêné) embarrassed.

congé /kɔ̃ʒe/ nm holiday; (arrêt momentané) time off, leave; (avis de départ) notice; en ~ on holiday ou leave; ~ de maladie/maternité sick/maternity leave; jour de ~ day off; prendre ~ de take one's leave of.

congédier /kɔ̃ʒedje/ [45] vt dismiss.

congélateur /kɔ̃ʒelatœʀ/ nm freezer.

congeler /kɔ̃ʒle/ [6] vt freeze.

congère /kɔ̃ʒɛʀ/ nf snowdrift.

congrès /kɔ̃gʀɛ/ nm conference; (Pol) congress.

conjoint, ~e /kɔ̃ʒwɛ̃, -t/ nm, f spouse. ● adj joint.

conjonctivite /kɔ̃ʒɔ̃ktivit/ nf conjunctivitis.

conjoncture /kɔ̃ʒɔ̃ktyʀ/ nf situation; (économique) economic climate.

conjugaison /kɔ̃ʒygɛzɔ̃/ nf conjugation.

conjugal, ~e (mpl -aux) /kɔ̃ʒygal, -o/ adj conjugal, married.

conjuguer /kɔ̃ʒyge/ [1] vt (Gram) conjugate; (efforts) combine. □ se ~ vpr (Gram) be conjugated; (facteurs) be combined.

conjurer /kɔ̃ʒyʀe/ [1] vt (éviter) avert; (implorer) beg.

connaissance /kɔnɛsɑ̃s/ nf knowledge; (personne) acquaintance; ~s (science) knowledge; faire la ~ de meet; (apprécier une personne) get to know; perdre/reprendre ~ lose/regain consciousness; sans ~ unconscious.

connaisseur /kɔnɛsœʀ/ nm expert, connoisseur.

connaître /kɔnɛtʀ/ [18] vt know; (difficultés, faim, succès) experience; faire ~ make known. □ se ~ vpr (se rencontrer) meet; s'y ~ en know (all) about.

connecter /kɔnɛkte/ [1] vt connect; être/ne pas être connecté be on-/off-line. □ se ~ à vpr (Ordinat) log on to.

connerie /kɔnʀi/ nf ✗ faire une ~ do something stupid; dire des ~s talk rubbish.

connexion /kɔnɛksjɔ̃/ nf (Ordinat) connection.

connu, ~e /kɔny/ adj well-known.

conquérant, ~e /kɔ̃keʀɑ̃, -t/ nm, f conqueror.

conquête /kɔ̃kɛt/ nf conquest.

consacrer /kɔ̃sakʀe/ [1] vt devote; (Relig) consecrate; (sanctionner) sanction. □ se ~ à vpr devote oneself to.

conscience /kɔ̃sjɑ̃s/ nf conscience; (perception) awareness; (de collectivité) consciousness; avoir/prendre ~ de be/become aware of; perdre/reprendre ~ lose/regain consciousness; avoir bonne/mauvaise ~ have a clear/guilty conscience.

conscient, ~e /kɔ̃sjɑ̃, -t/ adj conscious; ~ de aware ou conscious of.

conseil /kɔ̃sɛj/ nm (piece of) advice; (assemblée) council, committee; (séance) meeting; (personne) consultant; ~ d'administration board of directors; ~ en gestion management consultant; ~ des ministres Cabinet; ~ municipal town council.

conseiller[1] /kɔ̃seje/ **1** vt advise; ~ à qn de advise sb to; ~ qch à qn recommend sth to sb.

conseiller,[2] **-ère** /kɔ̃seje, -jɛʀ/ nm, f adviser, counsellor; ~ municipal town councillor; ~ d'orientation careers adviser.

consentement /kɔ̃sɑ̃tmɑ̃/ nm consent.

conséquence /kɔ̃sekɑ̃s/ nf consequence; en ~ (comme il convient) accordingly; en ~ (de quoi) as a result of which.

conséquent, ~e /kɔ̃sekɑ̃, -t/ adj consistent, logical; (important) substantial; par ~ consequently, therefore.

conservateur, -trice /kɔ̃sɛʀvatœʀ, -tʀis/ adj conservative. ● nm, f (Pol) conservative; (de musée) curator. ● nm preservative.

conservation /kɔ̃sɛʀvasjɔ̃/ nf preservation; (d'espèce, patrimoine) conservation.

conservatoire /kɔ̃sɛʀvatwaʀ/ nm academy.

conserve /kɔ̃sɛʀv/ nf tinned ou canned food; en ~ tinned, canned; boîte de ~ tin, can.

conserver /kɔ̃sɛʀve/ **1** vt keep; (en bon état) preserve; (Culin) preserve. □ se ~ vpr (Culin) keep.

considérer /kɔ̃sideʀe/ **14** vt consider; (respecter) esteem; ~ comme consider to be.

consigne /kɔ̃siɲ/ nf (de gare) left-luggage office; (US) baggage checkroom; (somme) deposit; (ordres) orders; ~ automatique left-luggage lockers; (US) baggage lockers.

consistance /kɔ̃sistɑ̃s/ nf consistency; (fig) substance, weight. **consistant,** ~e adj solid; (épais) thick.

consister /kɔ̃siste/ **1** vi ~ en/dans consist of/in; ~ à faire consist in doing.

consoler /kɔ̃sɔle/ **1** vt console. □ se ~ vpr find consolation; se ~ de qch get over sth.

consolider /kɔ̃sɔlide/ **1** vt strengthen; (fig) consolidate.

consommateur, -trice /kɔ̃sɔmatœʀ, -tʀis/ nm, f (Comm) consumer; (dans un café) customer.

consommation /kɔ̃sɔmasjɔ̃/ nf consumption; (accomplissement) consummation; (boisson) drink; de ~ (Comm) consumer.

consommer /kɔ̃sɔme/ **1** vt consume, use; (manger) eat; (boire) drink; (mariage) consummate. □ se ~ vpr (être mangé) be eaten; (être utilisé) be used.

consonne /kɔ̃sɔn/ nf consonant.

constat /kɔ̃sta/ nm (official) report; ~ (à l')amiable accident report drawn up by those involved.

constatation /kɔ̃statasjɔ̃/ nf observation, statement of fact. **constater** **1** vt note, notice; (certifier) certify.

consternation /kɔ̃stɛʀnasjɔ̃/ nf dismay.

constipé, ~e /kɔ̃stipe/ adj constipated; (fig) uptight.

constituer /kɔ̃stitɥe/ **1** vt (composer) make up, constitute; (organiser) form; (être) constitute; constitué de made up of. □ **se** ~ **prisonnier** give oneself up.

constitution /kɔ̃stitysjɔ̃/ nf formation, setting up; (Pol, Méd) constitution.

constructeur /kɔ̃stryktœR/ nm manufacturer, builder.

construction /kɔ̃stryksjɔ̃/ nf building; (structure, secteur) construction; (fabrication) manufacture.

construire /kɔ̃strɥiR/ **17** vt build; (système, phrase) construct.

consulat /kɔ̃syla/ nm consulate.

consultation /kɔ̃syltasjɔ̃/ nf consultation; (réception: Méd) surgery; (US) office; **heures de** ~ surgery ou office (US) hours.

consulter /kɔ̃sylte/ **1** vt consult. ● vi (médecin) hold surgery, see patients. □ **se** ~ vpr consult together.

contact /kɔ̃takt/ nm contact; (toucher) touch; **au** ~ **de** on contact with; (personne) by contact with, by seeing; **mettre/couper le** ~ (Auto) switch on/off the ignition; **prendre** ~ **avec** get in touch with. **contacter** **1** vt contact.

contagieux, -ieuse /kɔ̃taʒjø, -z/ adj contagious.

conte /kɔ̃t/ nm tale; ~ **de fées** fairy tale.

contempler /kɔ̃tɑ̃ple/ **1** vt contemplate.

contemporain, ~e /kɔ̃tɑ̃pɔRɛ̃, -ɛn/ adj & nm,f contemporary.

contenance /kɔ̃t(ə)nɑ̃s/ nf (volume) capacity; (allure) bearing; **perdre** ~ lose one's composure.

contenir /kɔ̃t(ə)niR/ **58** vt contain; (avoir une capacité de) hold. □ **se**

~ vpr contain oneself.

content, ~e /kɔ̃tɑ̃, -t/ adj pleased, happy (de with); ~ **de faire** pleased ou happy to do.

contenter /kɔ̃tɑ̃te/ **1** vt satisfy. □ **se** ~ **de** vpr content oneself with.

contenu /kɔ̃t(ə)ny/ nm (de récipient) contents (+ pl); (de texte) content.

conter /kɔ̃te/ **1** vt tell, relate.

contestation /kɔ̃testasjɔ̃/ nf dispute; (opposition) protest.

contester /kɔ̃teste/ **1** vt question, dispute; (s'opposer) protest against. ● vi protest.

conteur, -euse /kɔ̃tœR, -øz/ nm, f storyteller.

contigu, -ë /kɔ̃tigy/ adj adjacent (à to).

continent /kɔ̃tinɑ̃/ nm continent.

continu, ~e /kɔ̃tiny/ adj continuous.

continuer /kɔ̃tinɥe/ **1** vt continue. ● vi continue, go on; ~ **à** ou **de faire** carry on ou go on ou continue doing.

contorsionner (se) /(sə) kɔ̃tɔRsjɔne/ **1** vpr wriggle.

contour /kɔ̃tuR/ nm outline, contour; ~**s** (d'une route) twists and turns, bends.

contourner /kɔ̃tuRne/ **1** vt go round, by-pass; (difficulté) get round.

contraceptif, -ive /kɔ̃tRasɛptif, -v/ adj contraceptive. ● nm contraceptive. **contraception** nf contraception.

contracter /kɔ̃tRakte/ **1** vt (maladie) contract; (dette) incur; (muscle) tense; (assurance) take out. □ **se** ~ vpr contract.

contractuel, ~**le** /kɔ̃tRaktɥel/ nm, f (agent) traffic warden.

contradictoire /kɔ̃tRadiktwaR/

adj contradictory; (*débat*) open.

contraignant, ~e /kɔ̃trɛɲɑ̃, -t/ *adj* restricting.

contraindre /kɔ̃trɛ̃dʀ/ 22 *vt* force, compel (à faire to do).

contrainte /kɔ̃trɛ̃t/ *nf* constraint.

contraire /kɔ̃trɛʀ/ *adj* opposite; ~ à contrary to. ● *nm* opposite; au ~ on the contrary; au ~ de unlike.

contrarier /kɔ̃traʀje/ 45 *vt* annoy; (*projet, volonté*) frustrate; (chagriner) upset.

contraste /kɔ̃trast/ *nm* contrast.

contrat /kɔ̃tra/ *nm* contract.

contravention /kɔ̃travɑ̃sjɔ̃/ *nf* (parking) ticket; en ~ in breach (à of).

contre /kɔ̃tr(ə)/ *prép* against; (en échange de) for; par ~ on the other hand; tout ~ close by. **contreattaque** (*pl* ~s) *nf* counterattack. **contre-attaquer** 1 *vt* counter-attack. **contre-balancer** 10 *vt* counterbalance.

contrebande /kɔ̃trəbɑ̃d/ *nf* contraband; faire la ~ de smuggle.

contrebas: en ~ /ɑ̃kɔ̃trəba/ *loc* below.

contrebasse /kɔ̃trəbas/ *nf* double bass.

contrecœur: à ~ /akɔ̃trəkœr/ *loc* reluctantly.

contrecoup /kɔ̃trəku/ *nm* effects, repercussions.

contredire /kɔ̃trədir/ 37 *vt* contradict. □ **se** ~ *vpr* contradict oneself.

contrée /kɔ̃tre/ *nf* region; (pays) land.

contrefaçon /kɔ̃trəfasɔ̃/ *nf* (objet imité, action) forgery.

contre-indiqué, ~e /kɔ̃trɛ̃dike/ *adj* (Méd) contra-indicated; (déconseillé) not recommended.

contre-jour: à ~ /akɔ̃trəʒur/ *loc* against the light.

contrepartie /kɔ̃trəparti/ *nf* compensation; en ~ in exchange, in return.

contreplaqué /kɔ̃trəplake/ *nm* plywood.

contresens /kɔ̃trəsɑ̃s/ *nm* misinterpretation; (absurdité) nonsense; à ~ the wrong way.

contretemps /kɔ̃trətɑ̃/ *nm* hitch; à ~ (fig) at the wrong time.

contribuable /kɔ̃tribɥabl/ *nmf* taxpayer.

contribuer /kɔ̃tribɥe/ 1 *vt* contribute (à to, towards).

contrôle /kɔ̃trol/ *nm* (maîtrise) control; (vérification) check; (des prix) control; (poinçon) hallmark; (Scol) test; ~ continu continuous assessment; ~ des changes exchange control; ~ des naissances birth control; ~ de soi-même self-control; ~ technique (des véhicules) MOT (test).

contrôler /kɔ̃trole/ 1 *vt* (vérifier) check; (surveiller, maîtriser) control. □ **se** ~ *vpr* control oneself.

contrôleur, -euse /kɔ̃trolœr, -øz/ *nm, f* inspector.

convaincre /kɔ̃vɛ̃kr/ 59 *vt* convince; ~ qn de faire persuade sb to do.

convalescence /kɔ̃valesɑ̃s/ *nf* convalescence; être en ~ be convalescing.

convenable /kɔ̃vnabl/ *adj* (correct) decent, proper; (approprié) suitable; (acceptable) reasonable, acceptable.

convenance /kɔ̃vnɑ̃s/ *nf* à ma ~ to my satisfaction; les ~s convention.

convenir /kɔ̃vnir/ 58 *vt/i* be suitable; ~ à suit; ~ que admit that;

~ de qch (avouer) admit sth; (s'accorder sur) agree on sth; ~ de faire agree to do; il convient de it is advisable to; (selon les bienséances) it would be right to.

convention /kɔ̃vɑ̃sjɔ̃/ nf agreement, convention; (clause) article, clause; ~s (convenances) convention; de ~ conventional; ~ collective industrial agreement.

convenu, ~e /kɔ̃vny/ adj agreed.

conversation /kɔ̃vɛʀsasjɔ̃/ nf conversation.

convertir /kɔ̃vɛʀtiʀ/ [2] vt convert (à to; en into). □ se ~ vpr be converted, convert.

conviction /kɔ̃viksjɔ̃/ nf conviction; avoir la ~ que be convinced that.

convivial, ~e /kɔ̃vivjal, -jo/ adj convivial; (Ordinat) user-friendly.

convocation /kɔ̃vɔkasjɔ̃/ nf (Jur) summons; (d'une assemblée) convening; (document) notification to attend.

convoi /kɔ̃vwa/ nm convoy; (train) train; ~ (funèbre) funeral procession.

convoquer /kɔ̃vɔke/ [1] vt (assemblée) convene; (personne) summon; être convoqué pour un entretien be called for interview.

coopération /kɔɔpeʀasjɔ̃/ nf cooperation; (Mil) civilian national service abroad.

coordination /kɔɔʀdinasjɔ̃/ nf coordination. **coordonnées** nfpl coordinates; (adresse) address and telephone number.

copain /kɔpɛ̃/ nm friend; (petit ami) boyfriend.

copie /kɔpi/ nf copy; (Scol) paper; ~ d'examen exam paper ou script; ~ de sauvegarde back-up copy.

copier /kɔpje/ [45] vt/i copy; ~ sur (Scol) copy ou crib from.

copieux, -ieuse /kɔpjø, -z/ adj copious.

copine /kɔpin/ nf friend; (petite amie) girlfriend.

coq /kɔk/ nm cockerel.

coque /kɔk/ nf shell; (de bateau) hull.

coquelicot /kɔkliko/ nm poppy.

coqueluche /kɔklyʃ/ nf whooping cough.

coquet, ~te /kɔkɛ, -t/ adj flirtatious; (élégant) pretty; (somme 🗊) tidy.

coquetier /kɔktje/ nm eggcup.

coquillage /kɔkijaʒ/ nm shellfish; (coquille) shell.

coquille /kɔkij/ nf shell; (faute) misprint; ~ Saint-Jacques scallop.

coquin, ~e /kɔkɛ̃, -in/ adj mischievous. ● nm, f rascal.

cor /kɔʀ/ nm (Mus) horn; (au pied) corn.

corail (pl -aux) /kɔʀaj, -o/ nm coral.

corbeau (pl ~x) /kɔʀbo/ nm (oiseau) crow.

corbeille /kɔʀbɛj/ nf basket; ~ à papier waste-paper basket.

corbillard /kɔʀbijaʀ/ nm hearse.

cordage /kɔʀdaʒ/ nm rope; ~s (Naut) rigging.

corde /kɔʀd/ nf rope; (d'arc, de violon) string; ~ à linge washing line; ~ à sauter skipping-rope; ~ raide tightrope; ~s vocales vocal cords.

cordon /kɔʀdɔ̃/ nm string, cord; ~ de police police cordon.

cordonnier /kɔʀdɔnje/ nm cobbler.

Corée /kɔʀe/ nf Korea.

coriace /kɔʀjas/ adj tough.

corne /kɔrn/ nf horn.

corneille /kɔrnɛj/ nf crow.

cornemuse /kɔrnəmyz/ nf bag-pipes (+ pl).

corner /kɔrne/ **1** vt (page) turn down the corner of; (page cornée dog-eared page. ● vi (Auto) hoot, honk.

cornet /kɔrnɛ/ nm (paper) cone; (crème glacée) cornet, cone.

corniche /kɔrniʃ/ nf cornice; (route) cliff road.

cornichon /kɔrniʃɔ̃/ nm gherkin.

corporel, ~le /kɔrpɔrɛl/ adj bod-ily; (châtiment) corporal.

corps /kɔr/ nm body; (Mil) corps; combat ~ à ~ hand-to-hand com-bat; ~ électoral electorate; ~ en-seignant teaching profession.

correct, ~e /kɔrɛkt/ adj proper, correct; (exact) correct.

correcteur, -trice /kɔrɛktœr, -tris/ nm, f (d'épreuves) proof-reader; (Scol) examiner; ~ liquide correction fluid; ~ d'orthographe spell-checker.

correction /kɔrɛksjɔ̃/ nf correc-tion; (d'examen) marking, grading; (punition) beating.

correspondance /kɔrɛspɔ̃dɑ̃s/ nf correspondence; (de train, d'auto-bus) connection; vente par ~ mail order; faire des études par ~ do a correspondence course.

correspondant, ~e /kɔrɛspɔ̃dɑ̃, -t/ adj corresponding. ● nm, f correspondent; penfriend; (au téléphone) votre ~ the person you are calling.

correspondre /kɔrɛspɔ̃dr/ **3** vi (s'accorder, écrire) correspond; (chambres) communicate. ● v + prép ~ à (être approprié à) match, suit; (équivaloir à) correspond to. □ se ~ vpr correspond.

corrida /kɔrida/ nf bullfight.

corriger /kɔriʒe/ **40** vt correct; (devoir) mark, grade, correct; (punir) beat; (guérir) cure.

corsage /kɔrsaʒ/ nm bodice; (che-misier) blouse.

corsaire /kɔrsɛr/ nm pirate.

Corse /kɔrs/ nf Corsica. ● nmf Cor-sican. **corse** adj Corsican.

corsé, ~e /kɔrse/ adj (vin) full-bodied; (café) strong; (scabreux) racy; (problème) tough.

cortège /kɔrtɛʒ/ nm procession; ~ funèbre funeral procession.

corvée /kɔrve/ nf chore.

cosmonaute /kɔsmɔnot/ nmf cosmonaut.

cosmopolite /kɔsmɔpɔlit/ adj cosmopolitan.

cosse /kɔs/ nf (de pois) pod.

cossu, ~e /kɔsy/ adj (gens) well-to-do; (demeure) opulent.

costaud, ~e /kɔsto, -d/ **1** adj strong. ● nm strong man.

costume /kɔstym/ nm suit; (Théât) costume.

cote /kɔt/ nf (classification) mark; (en Bourse) quotation; (de cheval) odds (de on); (de candidat, acteur) rating; ~ d'alerte danger level; avoir la ~ be popular.

côte /kot/ nf (littoral) coast; (pente) hill; (Anat) rib; (Culin) chop; ~ à ~ side by side; la C~ d'Azur the (French) Riviera.

côté /kote/ nm side; (direction) way; ~ nearby; voisin d'à ~ next-door neighbour; à ~ next to; (comparé à) compared to; à ~ de la cible wide of the target; aux ~s de by the side of; de ~ (regar-der) sideways; (sauter) to one side; mettre de ~ put aside; de ce ~ this way; de chaque ~ on each side; de tous les ~s on every side;

(partout) everywhere; **du ~ de** (vers) towards; (proche de) near.
côtelette /kotlɛt/ nf chop.
coter /kɔte/ **1** vt (Comm) quote; **coté en Bourse** listed on the Stock Exchange; **très coté** highly rated.
cotiser /kɔtize/ **1** vi pay one's contributions (**à** to); (**à un club**) pay one's subscription. □ **se ~** vpr club together.
coton /kɔtɔ̃/ nm cotton; **~ hydrophile** cotton wool.
cou /ku/ nm neck.
couchant /kuʃɑ̃/ nm sunset.
couche /kuʃ/ nf layer; (de peinture) coat; (de bébé) nappy; (US) diaper; **~s** (Méd) childbirth; **~s sociales** social strata.
coucher /kuʃe/ **1** vt put to bed; (loger) put up; (étendre) lay down; **~ (par écrit)** set down. ● vi sleep. □ **se ~** vpr go to bed; (s'étendre) lie down; (soleil) set. ● nm **~ de soleil** sunset.
couchette /kuʃɛt/ nf (de train) couchette; (Naut) berth.
coude /kud/ nm elbow; (de rivière, chemin) bend; **~ à ~** side by side.
cou-de-pied /kudpje/ nm (pl **cous-de-pied**) instep.
coudre /kudʀ/ **19** vt/i sew.
couette /kwɛt/ nf duvet, quilt.
couler /kule/ **1** vi flow, run; (fromage, nez) run; (fuir) leak; (bateau) sink; (entreprise) go under; **faire ~ un bain** run a bath. ● vt (bateau) sink; (sculpture, métal) cast. □ **se ~** vpr slip (dans into).
couleur /kulœʀ/ nf colour; (peinture) paint; (aux cartes) suit; **~s** (teint) colour; **de ~** (homme, femme) coloured; **en ~s** (télévision, film) colour.
couleuvre /kulœvʀ/ nf grass snake.

coulisse /kulis/ nf (de tiroir) runner; **à ~** (porte, fenêtre) sliding; **~s** (Théât) wings; **dans les ~s** (fig) behind the scenes.
couloir /kulwaʀ/ nm corridor; (Sport) lane; **~ de bus** bus lane.
coup /ku/ nm blow; (choc) knock; (Sport) stroke; (de crayon, chance, cloche) stroke; (de fusil, pistolet) shot; (fois) time; (aux échecs) move; **donner un ~ de pied/poing** a kick/punch; **à ~ sûr** definitely; **après ~** after the event; **boire un ~** ⊞ have a drink; **~ sur ~** in rapid succession; **du ~** as a result; **d'un seul ~** in one go; **du premier ~** first go; **sale ~** dirty trick; **sous le ~ de** la fatigue/colère out of tiredness/anger; **sur le ~** instantly; **tenir le ~** hold out; **manquer son ~** ⊞ blow it!; **~ de chiffon** wipe (with a rag); **~ de coude** nudge; **~ de couteau** stab; **~ d'envoi** kickoff; **~ d'État** (Pol) coup; **~ franc** free kick; **~ de main** helping hand; **~ d'œil** glance; **~ de soleil** sunburn; **~ de téléphone** telephone call; **~ de vent** gust of wind.
coupable /kupabl/ adj guilty.
coupe /kup/ nf cup; (de champagne) goblet; (à fruits) dish; (de vêtement) cut; (dessin) section; **~ de cheveux** haircut.
couper /kupe/ **1** vt cut; (arbre) cut down; (arrêter) cut off; (voyage) break up; (appétit) take away; (vin) water down; **~ par** take a short cut via; **~ la parole à qn** cut sb short. ● vi cut. □ **se ~** vpr cut oneself; **~ le doigt** cut one's finger; (routes) intersect; **se ~ de** cut oneself off from.
couple /kupl/ nm couple; (d'animaux) pair.
coupure /kupyʀ/ nf cut; (billet de banque) note; (de presse) cutting;

**(pause, rupture) break; (~ de courant) power cut.

cour /kur/ *nf* (court) yard; (du roi) court; (tribunal) court; (de récréation) playground; ~ martiale court-martial; faire la ~ à court.

courageux, -euse /kuraʒø, -z/ *adj* courageous.

couramment /kuramɑ̃/ *adv* frequently; (parler) fluently.

courant, ~e /kurɑ̃, -t/ *adj* standard, ordinary; (en cours) current. ● *nm* current; (de mode, d'idées) trend; ~ d'air draught; dans le ~ de in the course of; être/mettre au ~ de know/tell about; (à jour) be/bring up to date on.

courbature /kurbatyr/ *nf* ache; avoir des ~s be stiff, ache.

courber /kurbe/ **1** *vt* bend.

coureur, -euse /kurœr, -øz/ *nm, f* (Sport) runner; ~ automobile racing driver; ~ cycliste racing cyclist. ● *nm* womanizer.

courgette /kurʒɛt/ *nf* courgette; (US) zucchini.

courir /kurir/ **20** *vi* run; (se hâter) rush; (nouvelles) go round; ~ après qn/qch chase after sth. ● *vt* (risque) run; (danger) face; (épreuve sportive) run ou compete in; (fréquenter) do the rounds of; (filles) chase (after).

couronne /kurɔn/ *nf* crown; (de fleurs) wreath.

couronnement /kurɔnmɑ̃/ *nm* coronation, crowning; (fig) crowning achievement.

courriel /kurjɛl/ *nm* email.

courrier /kurje/ *nm* post, mail; (à écrire) letters; (à **du cœur** problem page; ~ électronique email.

cours /kur/ *nm* (leçon) class; (série de leçons) course; (prix) price; (cote) (de valeur, denrée) price; (de

devises) exchange rate; (déroulement, d'une rivière) course; (allée) avenue; au ~ de in the course of; avoir ~ (monnaie) be legal tender; (fig) be current; (Scol) have a lesson; ~ d'eau river, stream; ~ du soir evening class; ~ particulier private lesson; ~ magistral (Univ) lecture; en ~ current; (travail) in progress; en ~ de route along the way.

course /kurs/ *nf* running; (épreuve de vitesse) race; (activité) racing; (entre rivaux: fig) race; (de projectile) flight; (voyage) journey; (commission) errand; (achats) shopping; (de chevaux) races; faire la ~ avec qn race sb.

coursier, -ière /kursje, -jɛr/ *nm, f* messenger.

court, ~e /kur, -t/ *adj* short. ● *adv* short; à ~ de short of; pris de ~ caught unawares. ● *nm* ~ (de tennis) (tennis) court.

courtier, -ière /kurtje, -jɛr/ *nm, f* broker.

courtiser /kurtize/ **1** *vt* woo, court.

courtois, ~e /kurtwa, -z/ *adj* courteous. **courtoisie** *nf* courtesy.

cousin, ~e /kuzɛ̃, -in/ *nm, f* cousin; ~ germain first cousin.

coussin /kusɛ̃/ *nm* cushion.

coût /ku/ *nm* cost; le ~ de la vie the cost of living.

couteau (*pl* ~x) /kuto/ *nm* knife; ~ à cran d'arrêt flick knife.

coûter /kute/ **1** *vt/i* cost; coûte que coûte at all costs; au prix coûtant at cost (price).

coutume /kutym/ *nf* custom.

couture /kutyr/ *nf* sewing; (métier) dressmaking; (points) seam. **couturier** *nm* fashion designer. **couturière** *nf* dressmaker.

couvée /kuve/ nf brood.

couvent /kuvɑ̃/ nm convent.

couver /kuve/ **1** vt (œufs) hatch; (personne) overprotect, pamper; (maladie) be coming down with, be sickening for; (mal) be brewing. ● vi (feu) smoulder; (fig) be brewing.

couvercle /kuvɛʀkl/ nm (de marmite, boîte) lid; (qui se visse) screwtop.

couvert, ~e /kuvɛʀ, -t/ adj covered (de with); (habillé) covered up; (ciel) overcast. ● nm (à table) place setting; (prix) cover charge; ~s (couteaux etc.) cutlery; mettre le ~ lay the table; (abri) cover; à ~ (Mil) under cover; à ~ de (fig) safe from.

couverture /kuvɛʀtyʀ/ nf cover; (de lit) blanket; (toit) roofing; (dans la presse) coverage; ~ chauffante electric blanket.

couvre-feu (pl ~x) /kuvʀəfø/ nm curfew.

couvre-lit (pl ~s) /kuvʀəli/ nm bedspread.

couvrir /kuvʀiʀ/ **21** vt cover. □ se ~ vpr (s'habiller) wrap up; (se coiffer) put one's hat on; (ciel) become overcast.

covoiturage /kɔvwatyʀaʒ/ nm car sharing.

cracher /kʀaʃe/ **1** vi spit; (radio) crackle. ● vt spit (out); (fumée) belch out.

crachin /kʀaʃɛ̃/ nm drizzle.

craie /kʀɛ/ nf chalk.

craindre /kʀɛ̃dʀ/ **22** vt be afraid of, fear; (être sensible à) be easily damaged by.

crainte /kʀɛ̃t/ nf fear (pour for); de ~ de/que for fear of/that. **craintif, -ive** adj timid.

crampon /kʀɑ̃pɔ̃/ nm (de chaussure) stud.

cramponner (se) /(sə)kʀɑ̃pɔne/ **1** vpr se ~ à cling to.

cran /kʀɑ̃/ nm (entaille) notch; (trou) hole; (courage **1**) guts **1**, courage; ~ de sûreté safety catch.

crâne /kʀɑn/ nm skull.

crapaud /kʀapo/ nm toad.

craquer /kʀake/ **1** vi crack, snap; (plancher) creak; (couture) split; (fig) (personne) break down; (céder) give in. ● vt (allumette) strike; (vêtement) split.

crasse /kʀas/ nf grime.

cravache /kʀavaʃ/ nf (horse) whip.

cravate /kʀavat/ nf tie.

crayon /kʀɛjɔ̃/ nm pencil; ~ de couleur coloured pencil; ~ à bille ballpoint pen; ~ optique light pen.

créateur, -trice /kʀeatœʀ, -tʀis/ adj creative. ● nm, f creator, designer.

crèche /kʀɛʃ/ nf day nursery, crèche; (Relig) crib.

crédit /kʀedi/ nm credit; (somme allouée) funds; à ~ on credit; faire ~ give credit (à to).

créer /kʀee/ **15** vt create; (produit) design; (société) set up.

crémaillère /kʀemajɛʀ/ nf pendre la ~ have a housewarming party.

crème /kʀɛm/ adj inv cream. ● nm (café) ~ espresso with milk. ● nf cream; (dessert) cream dessert; ~ anglaise egg custard; ~ fouettée whipped cream; ~ pâtissière confectioner's custard. **crémerie** nf dairy. **crémeux, -euse** adj creamy. **crémier, -lère** nm, f dairyman, dairywoman.

créneau (pl ~x) /kʀeno/ nm (trou, moment) slot, window; (dans le marché) gap; faire un ~ to parallel-park.

crêpe /kʀɛp/ nf (galette) pancake. ●nm (tissu) crêpe; (matière) crêpe (rubber).

crépitement /kʀepitmɑ̃/ nm crackling; (d'huile) sizzling.

crépuscule /kʀepyskyl/ nm twilight, dusk.

cresson /kʀəsɔ̃/ nm (water) cress.

crête /kʀɛt/ nf crest; (de coq) comb.

crétin, ~e /kʀetɛ̃, -in/ nm, f 🟥 moron 🟥.

creuser /kʀøze/ 🟥 vt dig; (évider) hollow out; (fig) go into in depth. □ se ~ vpr (écart) widen; se ~ (la cervelle) 🟥 rack one's brains.

creux, -euse /kʀø, -z/ adj hollow; (heures) off-peak. ●nm hollow; (de l'estomac) pit; dans le ~ de la main in the palm of the hand.

crevaison /kʀəvɛzɔ̃/ nf puncture.

crevasse /kʀəvas/ nf crack; (de glacier) crevasse; (de la peau) crack.

crevé, ~e /kʀəve/ adj 🟥 worn out.

crever /kʀəve/ 🟥 vt burst; (pneu) puncture, burst; (exténuer 🟥) exhaust; (œil) put out. ●vi (pneu, sac) burst; (mourir 🟥) die.

crevette /kʀəvɛt/ nf ~ grise shrimp; ~ rose prawn.

cri /kʀi/ nm cry; (de douleur) scream, cry; **pousser un ~** cry out, scream.

criard, ~e /kʀijaʀ, -d/ adj (couleur) garish; (voix) shrill.

crier /kʀije/ 🟥 vi (fort) shout, cry (out); (de douleur) scream; (grincer) creak. ●vt (ordre) shout (out).

crime /kʀim/ nm crime; (meurtre) murder.

criminel, ~le /kʀiminɛl/ adj criminal. ●nm, f criminal; (assassin) murderer.

crinière /kʀinjɛʀ/ nf mane.

crise /kʀiz/ nf crisis; (Méd) attack; (de colère) fit; ~ **cardiaque** heart attack; ~ **de foie** bilious attack; ~ **de nerfs** hysterics (+ pl).

crisper /kʀispe/ 🟥 vt tense; (énerver 🟥) irritate. □ se ~ vpr tense; (mains) clench.

critère /kʀitɛʀ/ nm criterion.

critique /kʀitik/ adj critical. ●nf criticism; (article) review; (commentateur) critic; **la** ~ (personnes) the critics. **critiquer** 🟥 vt criticize.

Croate /kʀɔat/ adj Croatian. **C**~ nmf Croatian.

Croatie /kʀɔasi/ nf Croatia.

croche /kʀɔʃ/ nf quaver.

croche-pied (pl ~s) /kʀɔʃpje/ nm 🟥 **faire un** ~ à trip up.

crochet /kʀɔʃɛ/ nm hook; (détour) detour; (signe) (square) bracket; (tricot) crochet; **faire au** ~ crochet.

crochu, ~e /kʀɔʃy/ adj hooked.

crocodile /kʀɔkɔdil/ nm crocodile.

croire /kʀwaʀ/ 🟥 vt believe (à, en in); (estimer) think, believe (que that). ●vi believe.

croisade /kʀwazad/ nf crusade.

croisement /kʀwazmɑ̃/ nm crossing; (fait de passer à côté de) passing; (carrefour) crossroads.

croiser /kʀwaze/ 🟥 vi (bateau) cruise. ●vt cross; (passant, véhicule) pass; ~ **les bras** fold one's arms; ~ **les jambes** cross one's legs; (animaux) crossbreed. □ se ~ vpr (véhicules, piétons) pass each other; (lignes) cross. **croisière** nf cruise.

croissance /kʀwasɑ̃s/ nf growth.

croissant, ~e /kʀwasɑ̃, -t/ adj growing. ●nm crescent; (pâtisserie) croissant.

croix /kʀwa/ nf cross; ~ **gammée** swastika; **C**~-**Rouge** Red Cross.

croquant, ~e /kʀɔkɑ̃, -t/ adj crunchy.

croque-monsieur /krɔkməsjø/ *nm inv* toasted ham and cheese sandwich.

croque-mort (*pl* ~s) /krɔkmɔr/ *nm* ⊡ undertaker.

croquer /krɔke/ 🗄 *vt* crunch; (dessiner) sketch; chocolat à ~ plain chocolate. ● *vi* be crunchy.

croquis /krɔki/ *nm* sketch.

crotte /krɔt/ *nf* dropping.

crotté, ~e /krɔte/ *adj* muddy.

crottin /krɔtɛ̃/ *nm* (horse) dropping.

croupir /krupir/ 🗄 *vi* stagnate.

croustillant, ~e /krustijɑ̃, -t/ *adj* crispy; (*pain*) crusty; (fig) spicy.

croûte /krut/ *nf* crust; (de fromage) rind; (de plaie) scab; en ~ (Culin) in pastry.

croûton /krutɔ̃/ *nm* (bout de pain) crust; (avec potage) croûton.

CRS *abrév m* (Compagnie républicaine de sécurité) French riot police; un ~ a member of the French riot police.

cru[1] /kry/ ⇒CROIRE 🗄.

cru[2], ~e /kry/ *adj* raw; (*lumière*) harsh; (*propos*) crude. ● *nm* vineyard; (vin) vintage wine.

crû /kry/ ⇒CROÎTRE 🗄.

cruauté /kryote/ *nf* cruelty.

cruche /kryʃ/ *nf* jug, pitcher.

crucial, ~e (*mpl* -iaux) /krysjal, -jo/ *adj* crucial.

crudité /krydite/ *nf* (de langage) crudeness; ~s (Culin) raw vegetables.

crue /kry/ *nf* rise in water level; en ~ in spate.

crustacé /krystase/ *nm* shellfish.

cube /kyb/ *nm* cube. ● *adj* (*mètre*) cubic.

cueillir /kœjir/ 🗄 *vt* pick, gather; (*personne* ⊡) pick up.

cuiller, cuillère /kɥijɛr/ *nf* spoon; ~ à soupe soup spoon; (mesure) tablespoonful.

cuir /kɥir/ *nm* leather; ~ chevelu scalp.

cuire /kɥir/ 🗄 *vt* cook; ~ (au four) bake. ● *vi* cook; faire ~ cook.

cuisine /kɥizin/ *nf* kitchen; (art) cookery, cooking; (aliments) food; faire la ~ cook.

cuisiner /kɥizine/ 🗄 *vt* cook; (interroger ⊡) grill. ● *vi* cook.

cuisinier, -ière /kɥizinje, -jɛr/ *nm, f* cook. **cuisinière** *nf* (appareil) cooker, stove.

cuisse /kɥis/ *nf* thigh; (de poulet) thigh; (de grenouille) leg.

cuisson /kɥisɔ̃/ *nf* cooking.

cuit, ~e /kɥi, -t/ *adj* cooked; bien ~ well done *ou* cooked; trop ~ overdone.

cuivre /kɥivr/ *nm* copper; (jaune) brass; ~s (Mus) brass.

cul /ky/ *nm* (derrière ⊠) backside, bottom, arse ⊠.

culbuter /kylbyte/ 🗄 *vi* (*personne*) tumble; (*objet*) topple (over). ● *vt* knock over.

culminer /kylmine/ 🗄 *vi* reach its highest point *ou* peak.

culot /kylo/ *nm* (audace ⊡) nerve, cheek; (Tech) base.

culotte /kylɔt/ *nf* (de femme) pants (+ *pl*), knickers (+ *pl*); (US) panties (+ *pl*); ~ de cheval riding breeches; en ~ courte in short trousers.

culpabilité /kylpabilite/ *nf* guilt.

culte /kylt/ *nm* cult, worship; (religion) religion; (office protestant) service.

cultivateur, -trice /kyltivatœr, -tris/ *nm, f* farmer.

cultiver /kyltive/ 🗄 *vt* cultivate; (*plantes*) grow.

culture /kyltyʀ/ nf cultivation; (de plantes) growing; (agriculture) farming; (éducation) culture; (connaissances) knowledge; ~s (terrains) lands under cultivation; ~ physique physical training.

culturel, ~le /kyltyʀɛl/ adj cultural.

cumuler /kymyle/ **1** vt accumulate; (fonctions) hold concurrently.

cure /kyʀ/ nf (course of) treatment.

curé /kyʀe/ nm (parish) priest.

cure-dent (pl ~s) /kyʀdã/ nm toothpick.

curer /kyʀe/ **1** vt clean. □ se ~ vpr se ~ les dents/ongles clean one's teeth/nails.

curieux, -ieuse /kyʀjø, -z/ adj curious. ● nm, f (badaud) onlooker.

curiosité /kyʀjozite/ nf curiosity; (objet) curio; (spectacle) unusual sight.

curriculum vitae /kyʀikylɔm vite/ nm inv curriculum vitae; (US) résumé.

curseur /kyʀsœʀ/ nm cursor.

cutané, ~e /kytane/ adj skin.

cuve /kyv/ nf vat; (à mazout, eau) tank.

cuvée /kyve/ nf (de vin) vintage.

cuvette /kyvɛt/ nf bowl; (de lavabo) (wash) basin; (des cabinets) pan, bowl.

CV abrév m (**curriculum vitae**) CV.

cyberbranché, ~e /siberbrãʃe/ adj cyberwired.

cybercafé /siberkafe/ nm cybercafe.

cyberespace /sibersepas/ nm cyberspace.

cybernaute /sibernot/ nmf Netsurfer.

cybernétique /sibernetik/ nf cybernetics (+ pl).

cyclisme /siklism/ nm cycling.

cycliste /siklist/ nmf cyclist. ● nm cycling shorts. ● adj cycle.

cyclone /siklon/ nm cyclone.

cygne /siɲ/ nm swan.

cynique /sinik/ adj cynical. ● nm cynic.

Dd

d' /d/ ⇒DE.

d'abord /dabɔʀ/ adv first; (au début) at first.

dactylo /daktilo/ nf typist. **dactylographier** **45** vt type.

dada /dada/ nm hobby-horse.

daim /dɛ̃/ nm (fallow) deer; (cuir) suede.

dallage /dalaʒ/ nm paving. **dalle** nf slab.

daltonien, ~ne /daltɔnjɛ̃, -ɛn/ adj colour-blind.

dame /dam/ nf lady; (cartes, échecs) queen; ~s (jeu) draughts; (US) checkers.

damier /damje/ nm draught board; (US) checker-board; à ~ chequered.

damner /dane/ **1** vt damn.

dandiner (se) /(sə)dãdine/ **1** vpr waddle.

Danemark /danmaʀk/ nm Denmark.

danger /dãʒe/ nm danger; en ~ in danger; mettre en ~ endanger.

dangereux, -euse /dãʒ(ə)ʀø, -z/ adj dangerous.

danois, ~e /danwa, -z/ adj Danish. ● nm (Ling) Danish. **D~**, ~e nm, f Dane.

dans /dɑ̃/ *prép* in; (mouvement) into; (à l'intérieur de) inside, in; être ~ un avion be on a plane; ~ dix jours in ten days' time; boire ~ un verre drink out of a glass; ~ les 10 euros about 10 euros.

danse /dɑ̃s/ *nf* dance; (art) dancing.

danser /dɑ̃se/ **1** *vt/i* dance. **danseur, -euse** *nm, f* dancer.

darne /daʀn/ *nf* steak (of fish).

date /dat/ *nf* date; ~ limite deadline; ~ limite de vente sell-by date; ~ de péremption useby date.

dater /date/ **1** *vt/i* date; à ~ de as from.

datte /dat/ *nf* (fruit) date.

daube /dob/ *nf* casserole.

dauphin /dofɛ̃/ *nm* (animal) dolphin.

davantage /davɑ̃taʒ/ *adv* more; (plus longtemps) longer; ~ de more; je n'en sais pas ~ that's as much as I know.

---

de, d' /də, d/

d' before vowel or mute h.

● *préposition*
····▸ of; le livre ~ mon ami my friend's book; un pont ~ fer an iron bridge.

····▸ (provenance) from.

····▸ (temporel) from; ~ 8 heures à 10 heures from 8 till 10.

····▸ (mesure, manière) dix mètres ~ haut ten metres high; pleurer ~ rage cry with rage.

····▸ (agent) by; un livre ~ Marcel Aymé a book by Marcel Aymé.

● **de, de l', de la, du,** (*pl* **des**) *déterminant*

····▸ some; du pain (some) bread; des fleurs (some) flowers; je ne bois jamais ~ vin I never drink wine.

de + le = du
de + les = des

---

dé /de/ *nm* (à jouer) dice; (à coudre) thimble; ~s (jeu) dice.

débâcle /debɑkl/ *nf* (Géog) breaking up; (Mil) rout.

déballer /debale/ **1** *vt* unpack; (révéler) spill out.

débarbouiller /debaʀbuje/ *vt* wash the face of. □ **se** ~ *vpr* wash one's face.

débarcadère /debaʀkadɛʀ/ *nm* landing-stage.

débardeur /debaʀdœʀ/ *nm* (vêtement) tank top.

débarquement /debaʀkəmɑ̃/ *nm* disembarkation. **débarquer** **1** *vt/i* disembark, land; (arriver **I**) turn up.

débarras /debaʀa/ *nm* junk room; bon ~! good riddance!

débarrasser /debaʀase/ **1** *vt* clear (de of); ~ qn de relieve sb of; (défaut, ennemi) rid sb of. □ **se** ~ **de** *vpr* get rid of.

débat /deba/ *nm* debate.

débattre /debatʀ/ **11** *vt* debate. ● *vi* ~ de discuss. □ **se** ~ *vpr* struggle (to get free).

débauche /deboʃ/ *nf* debauchery; (fig) profusion.

débaucher /deboʃe/ **1** *vt* (licencier) lay off; (distraire) tempt away.

débile /debil/ *adj* weak; **I** stupid. ● *nmf* moron **I**.

débit /debi/ *nm* (rate of) flow; (élocution) delivery; (de compte) debit; ~ de tabac tobacconist's shop; ~ de boissons bar; haut ~

broadband.

débiter /debite/ **1** vt (compte) debit; (fournir) produce; (vendre) sell; (dire: péj) spout; (couper) cut up.

débiteur, -trice /debitœr, -tris/ nm, f debtor. ● adj (compte) in debit.

déblayer /debleje/ **31** vt clear.

déblocage /deblɔkaʒ/ nm (de prix) deregulating. **débloquer** **1** vt (prix, salaires) unfreeze.

déboiser /debwaze/ **1** vt clear (of trees).

déboîter /debwate/ **1** vi (véhicule) pull out. ● vt (membre) dislocate.

débordement /debɔrdəmɑ̃/ nm (de joie) excess.

déborder /debɔrde/ **1** vi overflow. ● vt (dépasser) extend beyond; ~ de (joie etc.) be brimming over with.

débouché /debuʃe/ nm opening; (carrière) prospect; (Comm) outlet; (sortie) end, exit.

déboucher /debuʃe/ **1** vt (bouteille) uncork; (évier) unblock. ● vi come out (de from); ~ **sur** (rue) lead into.

débourser /deburse/ **1** vt pay out.

debout /dəbu/ adv standing; (levé, éveillé) up; être ~, se tenir ~ be standing, stand; se mettre ~ stand up.

déboutonner /debutɔne/ **1** vt unbutton. □ se ~ vpr unbutton oneself; (vêtement) come undone.

débrancher /debrɑ̃ʃe/ **1** vt (prise) unplug; (système) disconnect.

débrayer /debreje/ **31** vi (Auto) declutch; (faire grève) stop work.

débris /debri/ nmpl fragments; (détritus) rubbish (+ sg); debris.

débrouillard, ~e /debrujar, -d/ adj [1] resourceful.

débrouiller /debruje/ **1** vt disentangle; (problème) solve. □ se ~ vpr manage.

début /deby/ nm beginning; faire ses ~s (en public) make one's début; à mes ~s when I started out. **débutant, ~e** nm, f beginner. **débuter** **1** vi begin; (dans un métier etc.) start out.

déca /deka/ nm [1] decaf.

deçà: en ~ /ɑ̃dəsa/ loc this side. ● prép en ~ de this side of.

décacheter /dekaʃte/ **6** vt open.

décade /dekad/ nf ten days; (décennie) decade.

décadent, ~e /dekadɑ̃, -t/ adj decadent.

décalage /dekalaʒ/ nm (écart) gap; ~ **horaire** time difference. **décaler** **1** vt shift.

décalquer /dekalke/ **1** vt trace.

décamper /dekɑ̃pe/ **1** vi clear off.

décanter /dekɑ̃te/ **1** vt allow to settle. □ se ~ vpr settle.

décapant /dekapɑ̃/ nm chemical agent; (pour peinture) paint stripper. ● adj (humour) caustic.

décapotable /dekapotabl/ adj convertible.

décapsuleur /dekapsylœr/ nm bottle-opener.

décédé, ~e /desede/ adj deceased. **décéder** **14** vi die.

déceler /desle/ **6** vt detect; (montrer) reveal.

décembre /desɑ̃br/ nm December.

décemment /desamɑ̃/ adv decently. **décence** nf decency. **décent, ~e** adj decent.

décennie /deseni/ nf decade.

décentralisation /desɑ̃tralizasjɔ̃/ nf decentralization. **décentraliser** **1** vt decentralize.

déception /desɛpsjɔ̃/ nf disappointment.

décerner /desɛʀne/ **1** vt award.

décès /desɛ/ nm death.

décevant, ~e /des(ə)vɑ̃, -t/ adj disappointing. **décevoir** 52 vt disappoint.

déchaîner /deʃene/ **1** vt (enthousiasme) rouse. □ se ~ vpr go wild.

décharge /deʃaʀʒ/ nf (de fusil) discharge; ~ électrique electric shock; ~ publique municipal dump.

décharger /deʃaʀʒe/ 40 vt unload; ~ qn de relieve sb from. □ se ~ vpr (batterie, pile) go flat.

déchausser (se) /(sə)deʃose/ **1** vpr take off one's shoes; (dent) work loose.

dèche /dɛʃ/ nf 🛈 dans la ~ broke.

déchéance /deʃeɑ̃s/ nf decay.

déchet /deʃɛ/ nm (reste) scrap; (perte) waste; ~s (ordures) refuse.

déchiffrer /deʃifʀe/ **1** vt decipher.

déchiqueter /deʃikte/ 38 vt tear to shreds.

déchirement /deʃiʀmɑ̃/ nm heartbreak; (conflit) split.

déchirer /deʃiʀe/ **1** vt (par accident) tear; (lacérer) tear up; (arracher) tear off ou out; (diviser) tear apart. □ se ~ vpr tear. **déchirure** nf tear.

décibel /desibɛl/ nm decibel.

décidément /desidemɑ̃/ adv really.

décider /deside/ **1** vt decide on; (persuader) persuade; ~ que/de decide that/to; ~ de qch decide on sth. □ se ~ vpr make up one's mind (à to).

décimal, ~e /desimal/ (mpl ~aux) /desimal, -o/ adj & nf decimal.

décisif, -ive /desizif, -v/ adj decisive.

décision /desizjɔ̃/ nf decision.

déclaration /deklaʀasjɔ̃/ nf declaration; (commentaire politique) statement; ~ d'impôts tax return.

déclarer /deklaʀe/ **1** vt declare; (naissance) register; déclaré coupable found guilty; ~ forfait (Sport) withdraw. □ se ~ vpr (feu) break out.

déclencher /deklɑ̃ʃe/ **1** vt (Tech) set off; (conflit) spark off; (avalanche) start; (rire) provoke. □ se ~ vpr (Tech) go off. **déclencheur** nm (Photo) shutter release.

déclic /deklik/ nm click.

déclin /deklɛ̃/ nm decline.

déclinaison /deklinɛzɔ̃/ nf (Ling) declension.

décliner /dekline/ **1** vt (refuser) decline; (dire) state; (Ling) decline.

décocher /dekɔʃe/ **1** vt (coup) fling; (regard) shoot.

décollage /dekɔlaʒ/ nm take-off.

décoller /dekɔle/ **1** vt unstick. ● vi (avion) take off. □ se ~ vpr come off.

décolleté, ~e /dekɔlte/ adj low-cut. ● nm low neckline.

décolorer /dekɔlɔʀe/ **1** vt fade; (cheveux) bleach. □ se ~ vpr fade.

décombres /dekɔ̃bʀ/ nmpl rubble.

décommander /dekɔmɑ̃de/ **1** vt cancel.

décomposer /dekɔ̃poze/ **1** vt break up; (substance) decompose. □ se ~ vpr (pourrir) decompose.

décompte /dekɔ̃t/ nm deduction; (détail) breakdown.

décongeler /dekɔ̃ʒle/ 6 vt thaw.

déconseillé, ~e /dekɔ̃seje/ adj not recommended, inadvisable.

déconseiller /dekɔ̃seje/ **1** vt ~

qch à qn advise sb against sth.

décontracté, ~e /dekɔ̃trakte/
adj relaxed.

déconvenue /dekɔ̃vny/ *nf* disappointment.

décor /dekɔʀ/ *nm* (paysage) scenery; (de cinéma, théâtre) set; (cadre) setting; (de maison) décor.

décoratif, -ive /dekɔʀatif, -v/ *adj* decorative.

décorateur, -trice /dekɔʀatœʀ, -tʀis/ *nm, f* (de cinéma) set designer. **décoration** *nf* decoration. **décorer** **1** *vt* decorate.

décortiquer /dekɔʀtike/ **1** *vt* shell; (fig) dissect.

découdre (se) /(sə)dekudʀ/ **19** *vpr* come unstitched.

découler /dekule/ **1** *vi* ~ de follow from.

découper /dekupe/ **1** *vt* cut up; (viande) carve; (détacher) cut out.

découragement /dekuʀaʒmɑ̃/ *nm* discouragement.

décourager /dekuʀaʒe/ **40** *vt* discourage. □ **se** ~ *vpr* become discouraged.

décousu, ~e /dekuzy/ *adj* (vêtement) which has come unstitched; (idées) disjointed.

découvert, ~e /dekuvɛʀ, -t/ *adj* (tête) bare; (terrain) open. • *nm* (de compte) overdraft; à ~ exposed; (fig) openly.

découverte /dekuvɛʀt/ *nf* discovery; à la ~ de in search of.

découvrir /dekuvʀiʀ/ **21** *vt* discover; (voir) see; (montrer) reveal. □ **se** ~ *vpr* (se décoiffer) take one's hat off; (ciel) clear.

décrasser /dekʀase/ **1** *vt* clean.

décrépit, ~e /dekʀepi, -t/ *adj* decrepit. **décrépitude** *nf* decay.

décret /dekʀɛ/ *nm* decree. **décréter** **14** *vt* order; (dire) declare.

décrié, ~e /dekʀije/ *adj* criticized.

décrire /dekʀiʀ/ **30** *vt* describe.

décroché, ~e /dekʀɔʃe/ *adj* (téléphone) off the hook.

décrocher /dekʀɔʃe/ **1** *vt* unhook; (obtenir ①) get. • *vi* (abandonner ①) give up; ~ (le téléphone) pick up the phone.

décroître /dekʀwatʀ/ **24** *vi* decrease.

déçu, ~e /desy/ *adj* disappointed.

décupler /dekyple/ **1** *vt/i* increase tenfold.

dédaigner /dedeɲe/ **1** *vt* scorn.

dédain /dedɛ̃/ *nm* scorn.

dédale /dedal/ *nm* maze.

dedans /dədɑ̃/ *adv & nm* inside; en ~ on the inside.

dédicacer /dedikase/ **10** *vt* dedicate; (signer) sign.

dédier /dedje/ **45** *vt* dedicate.

dédommagement
/dedɔmaʒmɑ̃/ *nm* compensation.

dédommager **40** *vt* compensate (de for).

déduction /dedyksjɔ̃/ *nf* deduction; ~ d'impôts tax deduction.

déduire /deduiʀ/ **17** *vt* deduct; (conclure) deduce.

déesse /deɛs/ *nf* goddess.

défaillance /defajɑ̃s/ *nf* (panne) failure; (évanouissement) blackout. **défaillant**, ~e *adj* (système) faulty; (personne) faint.

défaire /defɛʀ/ **33** *vt* undo; (valise) unpack; (démonter) take down. □ **se** ~ *vpr* come undone; se ~ de rid oneself of.

défait, ~e /defɛ, -t/ *adj* (cheveux) ruffled; (visage) haggard; (nœud) undone. **défaite** *nf* defeat.

défaitiste /defetist/ *adj & nmf* defeatist.

défalquer /defalke/ **1** *vt* (somme)

deduct.

défaut /defo/ nm fault, defect; (d'un verre, diamant, etc.) flaw; (pénurie) shortage; à ~ de for lack of; pris en ~ caught out; faire ~ (argent etc.) be lacking; par ~ (Jur) in one's absence; ~ de paiement non-payment.

défavorable /defavɔʀabl/ adj unfavourable.

défavoriser /defavɔʀize/ **1** vt discriminate against.

défectueux, -euse /defɛktɥø, -z/ adj faulty, defective.

défendre /defɑ̃dʀ/ **3** vt defend; (interdire) forbid; ~ à qn de forbid sb to. □ se ~ vpr defend oneself; (se protéger) protect oneself; (se débrouiller) manage; se ~ de (refuser) refrain from.

défense /defɑ̃s/ nf defence; ~ de fumer no smoking; (d'éléphant) tusk. **défenseur** nm defender. **défensif, -ive** adj defensive.

déferler /defɛʀle/ **1** vi (vagues) break; (violence) erupt.

défi /defi/ nm challenge; (provocation) defiance; mettre au ~ challenge.

déficience /defisjɑ̃s/ nf deficiency. **déficient, ~e** adj deficient.

déficit /defisit/ nm deficit. **déficitaire** adj in deficit.

défier /defje/ **45** vt challenge; (braver) defy.

défilé /defile/ nm procession; (Mil) parade; (fig) (continual) stream; (Géog) gorge; ~ de mode fashion parade.

défiler /defile/ **1** vi march; (visiteurs) stream; (images) flash by; (chiffres, minutes) add up. □ se ~ vpr **1** sneak off.

défini, ~e /defini/ adj (Ling) definite.

définir /definiʀ/ **2** vt define.

définitif, -ive /definitif, -v/ adj final, definitive; en définitive in the end.

définition /definisjɔ̃/ nf definition; (de mots croisés) clue.

définitivement /definitivmɑ̃/ adv definitively, permanently.

déflagration /deflagʀasjɔ̃/ nf explosion.

déflation /deflasjɔ̃/ nf deflation. **déflationniste** adj deflationary.

défoncé, ~e /defɔ̃se/ adj (terrain) full of potholes; (siège) broken; (drogué: **1**) high.

défoncer /defɔ̃se/ **10** vt (porte) break down; (mâchoire) break. □ se ~ vpr **1** to give one's all.

déformation /defɔʀmasjɔ̃/ nf distortion. **déformer** **1** vt put out of shape; (faits, pensée) distort.

défouler (se) /(sə)defule/ **1** vpr let off steam.

défrayer /defʀeje/ **31** vt (payer) pay the expenses of; ~ la chronique be the talk of the town.

défricher /defʀiʃe/ **1** vt clear.

défroisser /defʀwase/ **1** vt smooth out.

défunt, ~e /defɛ̃, -t/ adj (mort) late. ● nm, f deceased.

dégagé, ~e /degaʒe/ adj (ciel) clear; (front) bare; d'un ton ~ casually.

dégagement /degaʒmɑ̃/ nm clearing; (football) clearance.

dégager /degaʒe/ **40** vt (exhaler) give off; (désencombrer) clear; (faire ressortir) bring out; (ballon) clear. □ se ~ vpr free oneself; (ciel, rue) clear; (odeur) emanate.

dégarnir (se) /(sə)degaʀniʀ/ **2** vpr clear, empty; (personne) be going bald.

dégâts /dega/ nmpl damage (+ sg).

dégel /deʒɛl/ *nm* thaw. **dégeler** 6 *vi* thaw (out).

dégénéré, ~e /deʒenere/ *adj & nm,f* degenerate.

dégivrer /deʒivre/ 1 *vt* (Auto) de-ice; (*réfrigérateur*) defrost.

déglinguer /deglɛ̃ge/ 1 *vt* bust. □ **se ~** *vpr* break down.

dégonflé, ~e /degɔ̃fle/ *adj* (*pneu*) flat; (*lâche* 1) yellow.

dégonfler /degɔ̃fle/ 1 *vt* deflate. ● *vi* (*blessure*) go down. □ **se ~** *vpr* 1 chicken out.

dégouliner /deguline/ 1 *vi* trickle.

dégourdi, ~e /degurdi/ *adj* smart.

dégourdir /degurdir/ 2 *vt* (*membre, liquide*) warm up. □ **se ~** *vpr* **se ~ les jambes** stretch one's legs.

dégoût /degu/ *nm* disgust.

dégoûtant, ~e /degutɑ̃, -t/ *adj* disgusting.

dégoûter /degute/ 1 *vt* disgust; **~ qn de qch** put sb off sth.

dégradant, ~e /degradɑ̃, -t/ *adj* degrading.

dégradation /degradasjɔ̃/ *nf* damage; **commettre des ~s** cause damage.

dégrader /degrade/ 1 *vt* (*abîmer*) damage. □ **se ~** *vpr* (*se détériorer*) deteriorate.

dégrafer /degrafe/ 1 *vt* unhook.

degré /dəgre/ *nm* degree; (*d'escalier*) step.

dégressif, -ive /degresif, -v/ *adj* graded; **tarif ~** tapering charge.

dégrèvement /degrɛvmɑ̃/ *nm* **~ fiscal ou d'impôts** tax reduction.

dégringolade /degrɛ̃gɔlad/ *nf* tumble.

dégrossir /degrosir/ 2 *vt* (*bois*)

trim; (*projet*) rough out.

déguerpir /degɛrpir/ 2 *vi* clear off.

dégueulasse /degœlas/ *adj* 🗷 disgusting, lousy.

dégueuler /degœle/ 1 *vt* 🗷 throw up.

déguisement /degizmɑ̃/ *nm* (de carnaval) fancy dress; (pour duper) disguise.

déguiser /degize/ 1 *vt* dress up; (pour duper) disguise. □ **se ~** (au carnaval etc.) dress up; (pour duper) disguise oneself.

déguster /degyste/ 1 *vt* taste, sample; (savourer) enjoy.

dehors /dəɔr/ *adv* **en ~** outside; (hormis) apart from; **jeter/mettre ~** throw/put out. ● *nm* outside. ● *nmpl* (aspect de qn) exterior.

déjà /deʒa/ *adv* already; (avant) before, already.

déjeuner /deʒœne/ 1 *vi* have lunch; (le matin) have breakfast. ● *nm* lunch; **petit ~** breakfast.

delà /dəla/ *adv & prép* **au ~ (de) par ~** beyond.

délai /delɛ/ *nm* time-limit; (attente) wait; (sursis) extension of time; **sans ~** immediately; **dans un ~ de 2 jours** within 2 days; **finir dans les ~s** finish within the deadline; **dans les plus brefs ~s** as soon as possible.

délaisser /delese/ 1 *vt* (négliger) neglect.

délassement /delasmɑ̃/ *nm* relaxation.

délation /delasjɔ̃/ *nf* informing.

délavé, ~e /delave/ *adj* faded.

délayer /deleje/ 31 *vt* mix (with liquid); (idée) drag out.

délecter (se) /(sə)delɛkte/ 1 *vpr* **se ~ de** delight in.

délégué, ~e /delege/ *nm, f*

delegate.

délibéré, ~e /delibere/ adj deliberate; (résolu) resolute.

délicat, ~e /delika, -t/ adj delicate; (plein de tact) tactful. **délicatesse** nf delicacy; (tact) tact. **délicatesses** nfpl (kind) attentions.

délice /delis/ nm delight. **délicieux, -ieuse** adj (au goût) delicious; (charmant) delightful.

délier /delje/ vt untie; (délivrer) free. □ **se** ~ vpr come untied.

délimiter /delimite/ vt determine, demarcate.

délinquance /delɛ̃kɑ̃s/ nf delinquency. **délinquant,** ~e adj & nm, f delinquent.

délirant, ~e /deliʀɑ̃, -t/ adj delirious; (frénétique) frenzied; wild.

délire /deliʀ/ nm delirium; (fig) frenzy. **délirer** vi be delirious (de with); be off one's rocker.

délit /deli/ nm offence.

délivrance /delivʀɑ̃s/ nf release; (soulagement) relief; (remise) issue. **délivrer** vt free, release; (pays) liberate; (remettre) issue.

déloyal, ~e (mpl -aux) /delwajal, -jo/ adj disloyal; (procédé) unfair.

deltaplane /dɛltaplan/ nm hang-glider.

déluge /delyʒ/ nm downpour; le D~ the Flood.

démagogie /demagɔʒi/ nf demagogy. **démagogue** nmf demagogue.

demain /dəmɛ̃/ adv tomorrow.

demande /dəmɑ̃d/ nf request; ~ d'emploi job application; ~ en mariage marriage proposal.

demander /dəmɑ̃de/ vt ask for; (chemin, heure) ask; (nécessiter) require; ~ qch à qn ask sb sth; ~ à qn de ask sb to; ~ en mariage propose to. □ **se** ~ vpr se ~ si/où wonder if/where.

demandeur, -euse /dəmɑ̃dœʀ, -øz/ nm, f ~ d'emploi job seeker; ~ d'asile asylum-seeker.

démangeaison /demɑ̃ʒɛzɔ̃/ nf itch(ing).

démaquillant /demakijɑ̃/ nm make-up remover. **démaquiller (se)** vpr remove one's make-up.

démarchage /demaʀʃaʒ/ nm door-to-door selling.

démarche /demaʀʃ/ nf walk, gait; (procédé) step.

démarcheur, -euse /demaʀʃœʀ, -øz/ nm, f (door-to-door) canvasser.

démarrage /demaʀaʒ/ nm start.

démarrer /demaʀe/ vi (moteur) start (up); (partir) move off; (fig) get moving. ● vt get moving.

démarreur /demaʀœʀ/ nm starter.

démêlant /demelɑ̃/ nm conditioner. **démêler** vt disentangle.

déménagement /demenaʒmɑ̃/ nm move; (transport) removal.

déménager /demenaʒe/ vi move (house). ● vt (meubles) remove.

déménageur /demenaʒœʀ/ nm removal man.

démence /demɑ̃s/ nf insanity.

démener (se) /(sə)demne/ vt move about wildly; (fig) put oneself out.

dément, ~e /demɑ̃, -t/ adj insane. ● nm, f lunatic.

démenti /demɑ̃ti/ nm denial.

démentir /demɑ̃tiʀ/ vt deny; (contredire) refute; ~ que deny that.

démerder (se) /(sə)demɛʀde/ vpr manage.

démettre /demɛtʀ/ 42 vt (poignet etc.) dislocate; ∼ qn de relieve sb of. □ se ∼ vpr resign (from).

demeure /dəmœʀ/ nf residence; mettre en ∼ de order to.

demeurer /dəmœʀe/ 1 vi live; (rester) remain.

demi, ∼e /dəmi/ adj half(-). ● nm, f half. ● nm (bière) (half-pint) glass of beer; (football) half-back. ● adv à ∼ half; (ouvrir, fermer) halfway; à la ∼e at half past; une heure et ∼e an hour and a half; (à l'horloge) half past one; une ∼-journée/-livre half a day/pound. **demi-cercle** (pl ∼s) nm semicircle. **demi-finale** (pl ∼s) nf semifinal. **demi-frère** (pl ∼s) nm half-brother, stepbrother. **demi-heure** nf half-hour, half an hour. **demi-litre** (pl ∼s) nm half a litre. **demi-mesure** (pl ∼s) nf half-measure. à demi mot adv without having to express every word. **demi-pension** nf half-board. **demi-queue** nm boudoir grand piano.

demi-sel adj inv slightly salted.

demi-sœur (pl ∼s) nf half-sister, stepsister.

démission /demisjɔ̃/ nf resignation.

demi-tarif (pl ∼s) /dəmitaʀif/ nm half-fare.

demi-tour (pl ∼s) /dəmituʀ/ nm about turn; (Auto) U-turn; faire ∼ turn back.

démocrate /demɔkʀat/ nmf democrat. ● adj democratic. **démocratie** nf democracy.

démodé, ∼e /demɔde/ adj old-fashioned.

demoiselle /dəmwazɛl/ nf young lady; (célibataire) single lady; ∼ d'honneur bridesmaid.

démolir /demɔliʀ/ 2 vt demolish.

démon /demɔ̃/ nm demon; le D∼

the Devil. **démoniaque** adj fiendish.

démonstration /demɔ̃stʀasjɔ̃/ nf demonstration; (de force) show.

démonter /demɔ̃te/ 1 vt take apart, dismantle; (installation) take down; (fig) disconcert. □ se ∼ vpr come apart.

démontrer /demɔ̃tʀe/ 1 vt demonstrate; (indiquer) show.

démoraliser /demɔʀalize/ 1 vt demoralize.

démuni, ∼e /demyni/ adj impoverished; ∼ de without.

démunir /demyniʀ/ 2 vt ∼ de deprive of. □ se ∼ de vpr part with.

dénaturer /denatyʀe/ 1 vt (faits) distort.

dénigrement /denigʀəmɑ̃/ nm denigration.

dénivellation /denivɛlasjɔ̃/ nf (pente) slope.

dénombrer /denɔ̃bʀe/ 1 vt count.

dénomination /denɔminasjɔ̃/ nf designation.

dénommé, ∼e /denɔme/ nm, f le ∼ X the said X.

dénoncer /denɔ̃se/ 10 vt denounce. □ se ∼ vpr give oneself up. **dénonciateur, -trice** nm, f informer.

dénouement /denumɑ̃/ nm outcome; (Théât) dénouement.

dénouer /denwe/ 1 vt undo. □ se ∼ vpr (nœud) come undone.

dénoyauter /denwajote/ 1 vt stone.

denrée /dɑ̃ʀe/ nf ∼ alimentaire foodstuff.

dense /dɑ̃s/ adj dense. **densité** nf density.

dent /dɑ̃/ nf tooth; faire ses ∼s teethe; ∼ de lait milk tooth; ∼ de sagesse wisdom tooth; (de roue) cog. **dentaire** adj dental.

denté, ~e /dɑ̃te/ adj (roue) toothed.

dentelé, ~e /dɑ̃tle/ adj jagged.

dentelle /dɑ̃tɛl/ nf lace.

dentier /dɑ̃tje/ nm dentures (+ pl), false teeth (+ pl).

dentifrice /dɑ̃tifʁis/ nm toothpaste.

dentiste /dɑ̃tist/ nmf dentist.

dentition /dɑ̃tisjɔ̃/ nf teeth, dentition.

dénudé, ~e /denyde/ adj bare.

dénué, ~e /denɥe/ adj ~ de devoid of.

dénuement /denymɑ̃/ nm destitution.

déodorant /deodorɑ̃/ nm deodorant.

dépannage /depanaʒ/ nm repair; (Ordinat) troubleshooting. **dépanner** 🚹 vt repair; (fig) help out. **dépanneuse** nf breakdown lorry.

dépareillé, ~e /depareje/ adj odd, not matching.

départ /depar/ nm departure; (Sport) start; **au ~ de Nice** from Nice; **au ~** (d'abord) at first.

département /departəmɑ̃/ nm department.

> **Département** An administrative unit, of which there are 96 in Metropolitan France, most are named after rivers or mountains within their borders. Each *département* has a number which appears as the first two digits in postcodes for addresses within the *département* and as the final two-digit number in vehicle registration numbers. See ▷ RÉGION. *i*

dépassé, ~e /depɑse/ adj

outdated.

dépasser /depɑse/ 🚹 vt go past, pass; (véhicule) overtake; (excéder) exceed; (rival) surpass; **ça me dépasse** 🔢 it's beyond me. ● vi stick out.

dépaysement /depeizmɑ̃/ nm change of scenery; (désagréable) disorientation.

dépêche /depɛʃ/ nf dispatch.

dépêcher /depeʃe/ 🚹 vt dispatch. □ **se ~** vpr hurry (up).

dépendance /depɑ̃dɑ̃s/ nf dependence; (à une drogue) dependency; (bâtiment) outbuilding.

dépendre /depɑ̃dr/ 🔢 vt take down. ● vi depend (~ **de on**); ~ **de** (appartenir à) belong to.

dépens /depɑ̃/ nmpl **aux ~ de** at the expense of.

dépense /depɑ̃s/ nf expense; expenditure.

dépenser /depɑ̃se/ 🚹 vt/i spend; (énergie etc.) use up. □ **se ~** vpr get some exercise.

dépérir /deperir/ 🔢 vi wither.

dépêtrer (se) /(sə)depetre/ 🚹 vpr get oneself out (de of).

dépeupler /depœple/ 🚹 vt depopulate. □ **se ~** vpr become depopulated.

déphasé, ~e /defɑze/ adj 🔢 out of step.

dépilatoire /depilatwar/ adj & nm depilatory.

dépistage /depistaʒ/ nm screening. **dépister** 🚹 vt detect; (criminel) track down.

dépit /depi/ nm resentment; **par ~** out of pique; **en ~ de** despite; **en ~ du bon sens** in a very illogical way. **dépité**, ~e adj vexed.

déplacé, ~e /deplase/ adj (remarque) uncalled for.

déplacement /deplasmɑ̃/ nm

(voyage) trip.

déplacer /deplase/ **10** vt move.
□ se ~ vpr move; (voyager) travel.

déplaire /deplɛʀ/ **47** vi ~ à (irriter) displease; ça me déplaît I don't like it.

déplaisant, ~e /deplɛzɑ̃, -t/ adj unpleasant, disagreeable.

dépliant /deplijɑ̃/ nm leaflet.

déplier /deplije/ **45** vt unfold.

déploiement /deplwamɑ̃/ nm (démonstration) display; (militaire) deployment.

déplorable /deplɔʀabl/ adj deplorable. **déplorer** **1** vt (trouver regrettable) deplore; (mort) lament.

déployer /deplwaje/ **31** vt (ailes, carte) spread; (courage) display; (armée) deploy.

déportation /depɔʀtasjɔ̃/ nf (en 1940) internment in a concentration camp.

déposer /depoze/ **1** vt put down; (laisser) leave; (passager) drop; (argent) deposit; (plainte) lodge; (armes) lay down. ● vi (Jur) testify. □ se ~ vpr settle.

dépositaire /depozitɛʀ/ nmf (Comm) agent.

déposition /depozisjɔ̃/ nf (Jur) statement.

dépôt /depo/ nm (entrepôt) warehouse; (d'autobus) depot; (particules) deposit; (garantie) deposit; laisser en ~ give for safe keeping; ~ légal formal deposit of a publication with an institution.

dépouille /depuj/ nf skin, hide; (~ mortelle) mortal remains.

dépouiller /depuje/ **1** vt (courrier) open; (scrutin) count; (écorcher) skin; ~ qn de strip sb of.

dépourvu, ~e /depuʀvy/ adj ~ de devoid of; prendre au ~ catch unawares.

déprécier /depʀesje/ **45** vt depreciate. □ se ~ vpr depreciate.

déprédations /depʀedasjɔ̃/ nfpl damage (+ sg).

dépression /depʀesjɔ̃/ nf depression; ~ nerveuse nervous breakdown.

déprimer /depʀime/ **1** vt depress.

depuis /dəpɥi/

● **préposition**

••••➤ (point de départ) since; ~ quand attendez-vous? how long have you been waiting?

••••➤ (durée) for; ~ toujours always; ~ peu recently.

● **adverbe**

••••➤ since; il a eu une attaque le mois dernier, ~ nous sommes inquiets he had a stroke last month and we've been worried ever since.

● **depuis que** conjonction

••••➤ since, ever since; Sophie a beaucoup changé depuis que Camille est née Sophie has changed a lot since Camille was born.

député /depyte/ nm ≈ Member of Parliament.

déraciné, -e /deʀasine/ nm, f rootless person.

déraillement /deʀajmɑ̃/ nm derailment.

dérailler /deʀaje/ **1** vi be derailed; (fig **II**) be talking nonsense; faire ~ derail. **dérailleur** nm (de vélo) derailleur.

déraisonnable /deʀɛzɔnabl/ adj unreasonable.

dérangement /deʀɑ̃ʒmɑ̃/ nm bother; (désordre) disorder, upset;

en ~ out of order; les ~s the fault reporting service.

déranger /deʁɑ̃ʒe/ 40 vt (gêner) bother, disturb; (déréger) upset, disrupt. ● se ~ vpr (aller) go; (fig) put oneself out; ça te dérangerait de...? would you mind...?

dérapage /deʁapaʒ/ nm skid. **dé-raper** 1 vi skid; (fig) (prix) get out of control.

déréglé, ~e /deʁegle/ adj (vie) dissolute; (estomac) upset; (méca-nisme) (that is) not running properly.

dérégler /deʁegle/ 14 vt make go wrong. □ se ~ vpr go wrong.

dérision /deʁizjɔ̃/ nf mockery; tourner en ~ ridicule.

dérive /deʁiv/ nf aller à la ~ drift.

dérivé /deʁive/ nm by-product.

dériver /deʁive/ 1 vi (bateau) drift; ~ de stem from.

dermatologie /dɛʁmatɔlɔʒi/ nf dermatology.

dernier, -ière /dɛʁnje, -jɛʁ/ adj last; (nouvelles, mode) latest; (étage) top. ● nm, f last (one); ce ~ the latter; le ~ de mes soucis the least of my worries.

dernièrement /dɛʁnjɛʁmɑ̃/ adv recently.

dérober /deʁɔbe/ 1 vt steal. □ se ~ vpr slip away; se ~ à (obligation) shy away from.

dérogation /deʁɔgasjɔ̃/ nf special authorization.

déroger /deʁɔʒe/ 40 vi ~ à depart from.

déroulement /deʁulmɑ̃/ nm (d'une action) development.

dérouler /deʁule/ 1 vt (fil etc.) unwind. □ se ~ vpr unwind; (avoir lieu) take place; (récit, paysage) unfold.

déroute /deʁut/ nf (Mil) rout.

dérouter /deʁute/ 1 vt discon-cert.

derrière /dɛʁjɛʁ/ prép & adv be-hind. ● nm back, rear; (postérieur 11) behind 11; de ~ (fenêtre) back, rear; (pattes) hind.

des /de/ ⇒**DE**.

dès /dɛ/ prép (right) from; ~ lors from then on; ~ que as soon as.

désabusé, ~e /dezabyze/ adj dis-illusioned.

désaccord /dezakɔʁ/ nm dis-agreement.

désaffecté, ~e /dezafɛkte/ adj disused.

désagréable /dezagʁeabl/ adj un-pleasant.

désagrément /dezagʁemɑ̃/ nm annoyance, inconvenience.

désaltérer (se) /(sə)dezaltere/ 14 vpr quench one's thirst.

désamorcer /dezamɔʁse/ 10 vt (situation, bombe) defuse.

désapprobation /dezapʁɔbasjɔ̃/ nf disapproval. **désapprouver** 1 vt disapprove of.

désarçonner /dezaʁsɔne/ 1 vt throw.

désarmement /dezaʁməmɑ̃/ nm (Pol) disarmament.

désarroi /dezaʁwa/ nm distress.

désastre /dezastʁ/ nm disaster. **désastreux, -euse** adj disastrous.

désavantage /dezavɑ̃taʒ/ nm dis-advantage. **désavantager** 40 vt put at a disadvantage.

désaveu (pl ~x) /dezavø/ nm de-nial. **désavouer** 1 vt deny.

descendance /desɑ̃dɑ̃s/ nf des-cent; (enfants) descendants (+ pl). **descendant, ~e** nm, f descendant.

descendre /desɑ̃dʁ/ 3 vi (aux être) go down; (venir) come down; (passager) get off ou out; (nuit) fall;

~ **à pied** walk down; ~ **par l'ascenseur** take the lift down; ~ **de**
(être issu de) be descended from;
~ **à l'hôtel** go to a hotel; ~ **dans
la rue** (Pol) take to the streets. ● *vt*
(aux avoir) (escalier etc.) go ou come
down; (objet) take down; (abattre
①) shoot down.

descente /desɑ̃t/ *nf* descent; (à
ski) downhill; (raid) raid; **dans la** ~
going downhill; ~ **de lit** bedside rug.

descriptif, -ive /dɛskriptif, -v/ *adj*
descriptive. **description** *nf* description.

désemparé, ~**e** /dezɑ̃pare/ *adj*
distraught.

désendettement /dezɑ̃dɛtmɑ̃/
nm reduction of the debt.

déséquilibré, ~**e** /dezekilibre/
adj unbalanced; ① crazy. ● *nm, f* lunatic. **déséquilibrer** ① *vt* throw off
balance.

désert, ~**e** /dezɛʀ, -t/ *adj* deserted. ● *nm* desert.

déserter /dezɛʀte/ ① *vt/i* desert.
déserteur *nm* deserter.

désertique /dezɛʀtik/ *adj* desert.

désespérant, ~**e** /dezɛspeʀɑ̃, -t/
adj utterly disheartening.

désespéré, ~**e** /dezɛspeʀe/ *adj* in
despair; (état, cas) hopeless; (effort)
desperate.

désespérer /dezɛspeʀe/ ⑭ *vt*
drive to despair. ● *vi* despair, lose
hope; ~ **de** despair of. □ **se** ~ *vpr*
despair.

désespoir /dezɛspwaʀ/ *nm* despair; **en** ~ **de cause** as a last
resort.

déshabillé, ~**e** /dezabije/ *adj* undressed. ● *nm* négligée.

déshabiller /dezabije/ ① *vt* undress. □ **se** ~ *vpr* get undressed.

désherbant /dezɛʀbɑ̃/ *nm*

weedkiller.

déshérité, ~**e** /dezeʀite/ *adj* (région) deprived; (personne) the
underprivileged.

déshériter /dezeʀite/ ① *vt* dis-
inherit.

déshonneur /dezɔnœʀ/ *nm*
disgrace.

déshonorer /dezɔnɔʀe/ ① *vt* dishonour.

déshydrater /dezidʀate/ ① *vt*
dehydrate. □ **se** ~ *vpr* get dehy-
drated.

désigner /dezine/ ① *vt* (montrer)
point to ou out; (élire) appoint; (signifier) designate.

désillusion /dezilyzjɔ̃/ *nf* disillusionment.

désinence /dezinɑ̃s/ *nf* (Gram)
ending.

désinfectant /dezɛ̃fɛktɑ̃/ *nm* disinfectant. **désinfecter** ① *vt* disinfect.

désintéressé, ~**e** /dezɛ̃teʀese/
adj (personne, acte) selfless.

désintéresser (se)
/(sə)dezɛ̃teʀese/ *vpr* **se** ~ **de**
lose interest in.

désintoxiquer /dezɛ̃tɔksike/ ①
vt detoxify; **se faire** ~ to undergo
detoxification.

désinvolte /dezɛ̃vɔlt/ *adj* casual.
désinvolture *nf* casualness.

désir /deziʀ/ *nm* wish, desire; (con-
voitise) desire.

désirer /deziʀe/ ① *vt* want;
(sexuellement) desire; **vous dési-
rez?** what would you like?

désireux, -euse /deziʀø, -z/ *adj* ~
de faire anxious to do.

désistement /dezistəmɑ̃/ *nm*
withdrawal.

désobéir /dezɔbeiʀ/ ② *vi* (~ **à**)
disobey. **désobéissant,** ~**e** *adj* disobedient.

d

désobligeant, ~e /dezɔbliʒɑ̃, -t/ adj disagreeable, unkind.

désodorisant /dezɔdɔrizɑ̃/ nm air freshener.

désodoriser /dezɔdɔrize/ 1 vt freshen up.

désœuvré, ~e /dezœvre/ adj at a loose end. **désœuvrement** nm lack of anything to do.

désolation /dezɔlasjɔ̃/ nf distress.

désolé, ~e /dezɔle/ adj (au regret) sorry; (région) desolate.

désoler /dezɔle/ 1 vt distress. □ se ~ vpr be upset (de qch about sth).

désopilant, ~e /dezɔpilɑ̃, -t/ adj hilarious.

désordonné, ~e /dezɔrdɔne/ adj untidy; (mouvements) uncoordinated.

désordre /dezɔrdr/ nm untidiness; (Pol) disorder; en ~ untidy.

désorganiser /dezɔrganize/ 1 vt disorganize.

désorienter /dezɔrjɑ̃te/ 1 vt disorient.

désormais /dezɔrmɛ/ adv from now on.

desquels, desquelles /dekɛl/ ⇒LEQUEL.

dessécher /deseʃe/ 1 vt dry out. □ se ~ vpr dry out, become dry; (plante) wither.

dessein /desɛ̃/ nm intention; à ~ intentionally.

desserrer /desere/ 1 vt loosen; il n'a pas desserré les dents he never once opened his mouth. □ se ~ vpr come loose.

dessert /desɛr/ nm dessert; en ~ for dessert.

desservir /deservir/ 46 vt/i (débarrasser) clear away; (autobus) serve.

dessin /desɛ̃/ nm drawing; (motif) design; (discipline) art; (contour) outline; professeur de ~ art teacher; ~ animé (cinéma) cartoon; ~ humoristique cartoon.

dessinateur, -trice /desinatœr, -tris/ nm, f artist; (industriel) draughtsman.

dessiner /desine/ 1 vt/i draw; (fig) outline. □ se ~ vpr appear, take shape.

dessoûler /desule/ 1 vt/i sober up.

dessous /dəsu/ adv underneath. ● nm underside, underneath. ● nmpl underwear; les ~ d'une histoire what is behind a story; du ~ bottom; (voisins) downstairs; en ~, par-~ underneath. **dessous-de-plat** nm inv (heat resistant) table-mat. **dessous-de-table** nm inv backhander. **dessous-de-verre** nm inv coaster.

dessus /dəsy/ adv on top (of it), on it. ● nm top; du ~ top; (voisins) upstairs; avoir le ~ get the upper hand. **dessus-de-lit** nm inv bedspread.

déstabiliser /destabilize/ 1 vt destabilize, unsettle.

destin /destɛ̃/ nm (sort) fate; (avenir) destiny.

destinataire /destinatɛr/ nmf addressee.

destination /destinasjɔ̃/ nf destination; (fonction) purpose; vol à ~ de flight to.

destinée /destine/ nf destiny.

destiner /destine/ 1 vt ~ à intend for; (vouer) destine for; le commentaire m'est destiné this comment is aimed at me; être destiné à faire be intended to do; (obligé) be destined to do. □ se ~ à vpr (carrière) intend to take up.

destituer /destitye/ 1 vt discharge.

destructeur, -trice /dɛstryktœr, -tris/ adj destructive. **destruction** nf destruction.

désuet, -ète /dezɥɛ, -t/ adj outdated.

détachant /detaʃɑ̃/ nm stain remover.

détacher /detaʃe/ **1** vt untie; (ôter) remove, detach; (déléguer) second. □ se ~ vpr come off, break away; (nœud etc.) come undone; (ressortir) stand out.

détail /detaj/ nm detail; (de compte) breakdown; (Comm) retail; au ~ (vendre etc.) retail; de ~ (prix etc.) retail; en ~ in detail; entrer dans les ~s go into detail.

détaillant, -e /detajɑ̃, -t/ nm, f retailer.

détaillé, ~e /detaje/ adj detailed.

détailler /detaje/ **1** vt (rapport) detail; ~ ce que qn fait scrutinize what sb does.

détaler /detale/ **1** vi bolt.

détartrant /detartrɑ̃/ nm descaler.

détecter /detɛkte/ **1** vt detect. **détecteur** nm detector.

détective /detɛktiv/ nm detective.

déteindre /detɛ̃dr/ **22** vi (dans l'eau) run (sur on to); (au soleil) fade; ~ sur (fig) rub off on.

détendre /detɑ̃dr/ **3** vt slacken; (ressort) release; (personne) relax. □ se ~ vpr (ressort) slacken; (personne) relax. **détendu,** ~e adj (calme) relaxed.

détenir /det(ə)niR/ **58** vt hold; (secret, fortune) possess.

détente /detɑ̃t/ nf relaxation; (Pol) détente; (saut) spring; (gâchette) trigger; être lent à la ~ **①** be slow on the uptake.

détenteur, -trice /detɑ̃tœr, -tris/ nm, f holder.

détention /detɑ̃sjɔ̃/ nf detention; ~ provisoire custody.

détenu, ~e /detny/ nm, f prisoner.

détergent /detɛrʒɑ̃/ nm detergent.

détérioration /deterjɔrasjɔ̃/ nf deterioration; (dégât) damage.

détériorer /deterjɔre/ **1** vt damage. □ se ~ vpr deteriorate.

détermination /detɛrminasjɔ̃/ nf determination. **déterminé,** ~e adj (résolu) determined; (précis) definite. **déterminer** **1** vt determine.

déterrer /detere/ **1** vt dig up.

détestable /detɛstabl/ adj (caractère, temps) foul.

détester /detɛste/ **1** vt hate. □ se ~ vpr hate each other.

détonation /detɔnasjɔ̃/ nf explosion, detonation.

détour /detur/ nm (crochet) detour; (fig) roundabout means; (virage) bend.

détournement /deturnəmɑ̃/ nm hijack(ing); (de fonds) embezzlement.

détourner /deturne/ **1** vt (attention) divert; (tête, yeux) turn away; (avion) hijack; (argent) embezzle. □ se ~ de vpr stray from.

détraquer /detrake/ **1** vt make go wrong; (estomac) upset. □ se ~ vpr (machine) go wrong.

détresse /detrɛs/ nf distress; dans la ~, en ~ in distress.

détritus /detrity(s)/ nmpl rubbish (+ sg).

détroit /detrwa/ nm strait.

détromper /detrɔ̃pe/ **1** vt set straight. □ se ~ vpr détrompe-toi! you'd better think again!

détruire /detrɥir/ **17** vt destroy.

dette /dɛt/ nf debt.

deuil /dœj/ nm (période) mourning; (décès) bereavement; porter le ~

be in mourning; **faire son** ∼ **de qch** give sth up as past.

deux /dø/ adj & nm two; ∼ **fois** twice; **tous (les** ∼**)** both.

deuxième adj & nmf second. **deux-pièces** nm inv (maillot de bain) two-piece; (logement) two-room flat.

deux-points nm inv (Gram) colon.

deux-roues nm inv two-wheeled vehicle.

dévaliser /devalize/ **1** vt rob, clean out.

dévalorisant, ∼**e** /devalɔʀizɑ̃, -t/ adj demeaning.

dévaloriser /devalɔʀize/ **1** vt (monnaie) devalue. □ **se** ∼ vpr (personne) put oneself down.

dévaluation /devalɥasjɔ̃/ nf devaluation.

dévaluer /devalɥe/ **1** vt devalue. □ **se** ∼ vpr devalue.

devancer /dəvɑ̃se/ **10** vt be ou go ahead of; (arriver) arrive ahead of; (prévenir) anticipate.

devant /d(ə)vɑ̃/ prép in front of; (distance) ahead of; (avec mouvement) past; (en présence de) in front of; (face à) in the face of; **avoir du temps** ∼ **soi** have plenty of time. ● adv in front; (à distance) ahead; **de** ∼ front. ● nm front; **prendre les** ∼**s** take the initiative.

devanture /dəvɑ̃tyʀ/ nf shop front; (vitrine) shop window.

développement /devlɔpmɑ̃/ nm development; (de photos) developing.

développer /devlɔpe/ **1** vt develop. □ **se** ∼ vpr (corps, talent) develop; (entreprise) grow, expand.

devenir /dəvniʀ/ **58** vi (aux être) become; **qu'est-il devenu?** what has become of him?

dévergondé, ∼**e** /devɛʀgɔ̃de/ adj & nm,f shameless (person).

déverser /devɛʀse/ **1** vt (liquide)

pour; (ordures, pétrole) dump. □ **se** ∼ vpr (rivière) flow; (égout, foule) pour.

dévêtir /devetiʀ/ **61** vt undress. □ **se** ∼ vpr get undressed.

déviation /devjasjɔ̃/ nf diversion.

dévier /devje/ **45** vt divert; (coup) deflect. ● vi (ballon, balle) veer; (personne) deviate.

devin /dəvɛ̃/ nm soothsayer.

deviner /dəvine/ **1** vt guess; (apercevoir) distinguish.

devinette /dəvinɛt/ nf riddle.

devis /dəvi/ nm estimate, quote.

dévisager /devizaʒe/ **40** vt stare at.

devise /dəviz/ nf motto; ∼**s** (monnaie) (foreign) currency.

dévisser /devise/ **1** vt unscrew.

dévitaliser /devitalize/ **1** vt (dent) carry out root canal treatment on.

dévoiler /devwale/ **1** vt reveal.

---

devoir /dəvwaʀ/ **26**

● verbe auxiliaire

····▸ ∼ **faire** (obligation, hypothèse) must do; (nécessité) have got to do; **je dois dire que...** I have to say that...; **il a dû partir** (nécessité) he had to leave; (hypothèse) he must have left.

····▸ (prévision) **je devais lui dire** I was to tell her; **elle doit rentrer bientôt** she's due back soon.

····▸ (conseil) **tu devrais y aller** you should.

● verbe transitif

····▸ (argent, excuses) owe; **combien je vous dois?** (en achetant) how much is it?

□ **se devoir** verbe pronominal

····▸ je me dois de le faire it's my duty to do it. **● nom masculin ····▸** duty; **faire son ~ do** one's duty. **····▸ (Scol) ~ (surveillé)** test; **les ~s homework** (+ *sg*); **faire ses ~s** do one's homework.

dévorer /devɔʀe/ **1** vt devour.

dévot, ~e /devo, -ɔt/ adj devout.

dévoué, ~e /devwe/ adj devoted. **dévouement** nm devotion.

dévouer (se) /(sə)devwe/ **1** vpr devote oneself (à to); (se sacrifier) sacrifice oneself.

dextérité /dɛksteʀite/ nf skill.

diabète /djabɛt/ nm diabetes. **diabétique** adj & nmf diabetic.

diable /djɑbl/ nm devil.

diagnostic /djagnɔstik/ nm diagnosis. **diagnostiquer** **1** vt diagnose.

diagonal, ~e (*mpl* **-aux**) /djagɔnal, -o/ adj diagonal. **diagonale** nf diagonal; **en ~e** diagonally.

diagramme /djagʀam/ nm diagram; (graphique) graph.

dialecte /djalɛkt/ nm dialect.

dialogue /djalɔg/ nm dialogue. **dialoguer** **1** vi have talks, enter into a dialogue.

diamant /djamɑ̃/ nm diamond.

diamètre /djamɛtʀ/ nm diameter.

diapositive /djapozitiv/ nf slide.

diarrhée /djaʀe/ nf diarrhoea.

dictateur /diktatœʀ/ nm dictator.

dicter /dikte/ **1** vt dictate. **dictée** nf dictation.

dictionnaire /diksjɔnɛʀ/ nm dictionary.

dicton /diktɔ̃/ nm saying.

dièse /djɛz/ nm (Mus) sharp.

diesel /djezɛl/ nm & adj inv diesel.

diète /djɛt/ nf restricted diet.

diététicien, ~ne /djetetisjɛ̃, -ɛn/ nm, f dietician.

diététique /djetetik/ nf dietetics. **● adj produit** ou **aliment ~** dietary product; **magasin ~** health food shop ou store.

dieu (*pl* **~x**) /djø/ nm god; **D~** God.

diffamation /difamasjɔ̃/ nf slander; (par écrit) libel. **diffamer 1** vt slander; (par écrit) libel.

différé: en ~ /ɑ̃difeʀe/ loc (émission) pre-recorded.

différemment /difeʀamɑ̃/ adv differently.

différence /difeʀɑ̃s/ nf difference; **à la ~ de** unlike.

différencier /difeʀɑ̃sje/ **45** vt differentiate. □ **se ~** vpr differentiate oneself; **se ~ de** (différer de) differ from.

différend /difeʀɑ̃/ nm difference (of opinion).

différent, ~e /difeʀɑ̃, -t/ adj different (de from).

différer /difeʀe/ **14** vt postpone. **● vi** differ (de from).

difficile /difisil/ adj difficult; (exigeant) fussy. **difficilement** adv with difficulty.

difficulté /difikylte/ nf difficulty; **faire des ~s** raise objections.

diffus, ~e /dify, -z/ adj diffuse.

diffuser /difyze/ **1** vt (émission) broadcast; (nouvelle) spread; (lumière, chaleur) diffuse; (Comm) distribute. **diffusion** nf broadcasting; diffusion; distribution.

digérer /diʒeʀe/ **14** vt digest; (endurer [I]) stomach. **digeste** adj digestible.

digestif, -ive /diʒɛstif, -v/ adj digestive. **● nm** after-dinner liqueur.

digital, ~e (*mpl* **-aux**) /diʒital, -o/

adj digital.

digne /diɲ/ *adj* (noble) dignified; (approprié) worthy; ~ de worthy of; ~ de foi trustworthy.

digue /dig/ *nf* dyke; (US) dike.

dilater /dilate/ **1** *vt* dilate. □ se ~ *vpr* dilate; (estomac) distend.

dilemme /dilɛm/ *nm* dilemma.

dilettante /diletɑ̃t/ *nmf* amateur.

diluant /dilɥɑ̃/ *nm* thinner.

diluer /dilɥe/ **1** *vt* dilute.

dimanche /dimɑ̃ʃ/ *nm* Sunday.

dimension /dimɑ̃sjɔ̃/ *nf* (taille) size; (mesure) dimension; (aspect) dimension.

diminuer /diminɥe/ **1** *vt* reduce, decrease; (plaisir, courage) dampen; (dénigrer) diminish. ● *vi* (se réduire) decrease; (faiblir) (bruit, flamme) die down; (ardeur) cool. **diminutif** *nm* diminutive; (surnom) pet name. **diminution** *nf* decrease (de in); (réduction) reduction; (affaiblissement) diminishing.

dinde /dɛ̃d/ *nf* turkey.

dîner /dine/ **1** *vi* have dinner. ● *nm* dinner.

dingue /dɛ̃g/ *adj* 𝕋 crazy.

dinosaure /dinozɔʀ/ *nm* dinosaur.

diphtongue /diftɔ̃g/ *nf* diphthong.

diplomate /diplɔmat/ *nmf* diplomat. ● *adj* diplomatic. **diplomatique** *adj* diplomatic.

diplôme /diplom/ *nm* certificate, diploma; (Univ) degree. **diplômé, ~e** *adj* qualified.

dire /diʀ/ 27 *vt* say; (secret, vérité, heure) tell; (penser) think; ~ que say that; ~ à qn que tell sb that; ~ à qn de tell sb to; ça me dit de faire I feel like doing; on dirait que it would seem that, it seems that; dis/dites donc! hey! □ se ~ *vpr* (mot) be said; (penser) tell oneself;

(se prétendre) claim to be. ● *nm* au ~ de, selon les ~s de according to.

direct, ~e /diʀɛkt/ *adj* direct. ● *nm* (train) express train; en ~ (émission) live.

directeur, -trice /diʀɛktœʀ, -tʀis/ *nm, f* director; (chef de service) manager, manageress; (de journal) editor; (d'école) headteacher; (US) principal; ~ de banque bank manager; ~ commercial sales manager; ~ des ressources humaines human resources manager.

direction /diʀɛksjɔ̃/ *nf* (sens) direction; (de société) management; (Auto) steering; en ~ de (going) to.

dirigeant, ~e /diʀiʒɑ̃, -t/ *nm, f* (Pol) leader; (Comm) manager. ● *adj* (classe) ruling.

diriger /diʀiʒe/ 40 *vt* (service, école, parti, pays) run; (entreprise, usine) manage; (travaux) supervise; (véhicule) steer; (orchestre) conduct; (braquer) aim; (tourner) turn. □ se ~ *vpr* (s'orienter) find one's way; se ~ vers head for, make for.

dis /di/ →DIRE 27.

discernement /disɛʀnəmɑ̃/ *nm* discernment.

disciplinaire /disiplineʀ/ *adj* disciplinary. **discipline** *nf* discipline.

discontinu, ~e /diskɔ̃tiny/ *adj* intermittent.

discordant, ~e /diskɔʀdɑ̃, -t/ *adj* discordant.

discothèque /diskɔtɛk/ *nf* record library; (boîte de nuit) disco(thèque).

discours /diskuʀ/ *nm* speech; (propos) views.

discret, -ète /diskʀɛ, -t/ *adj* discreet.

discrétion /diskʀesjɔ̃/ *nf* discretion; à ~ (vin) unlimited; (manger, boire) as much as one desires.

discrimination /diskʀiminasjɔ̃/ nf discrimination. **discriminatoire** adj discriminatory.

disculper /diskylpe/ **1** vt exonerate. □ **se** ~ vpr vindicate oneself.

discussion /diskysjɔ̃/ nf discussion; (querelle) argument.

discutable /diskytabl/ adj debatable; (critiquable) questionable.

discuter /diskyte/ **1** vt discuss; (contester) question. ● vi (parler) talk; (répliquer) argue; ~ **de** discuss.

disette /dizɛt/ nf food shortage.

disgrâce /disɡʀɑs/ nf disgrace.

disgracieux, -ieuse /disɡʀasjø, -z/ adj ugly, unsightly.

disjoindre /disʒwɛ̃dʀ/ **22** vt take apart. □ **se** ~ vpr come apart.

disloquer /disloke/ **1** vt (membre) dislocate; (machine) break (apart). □ **se** ~ vpr (parti, cortège) break up; (meuble) come apart.

disparaître /dispaʀɛtʀ/ **19** vi disappear; (mourir) die; **faire** ~ get rid of. **disparition** nf disappearance; (mort) death.

disparate /dispaʀat/ adj ill-assorted.

disparu, ~e /dispaʀy/ adj missing. ● nm, f missing person; (mort) dead person.

dispensaire /dispɑ̃sɛʀ/ nm clinic.

dispense /dispɑ̃s/ nf exemption.

dispenser /dispɑ̃se/ **1** vt exempt (de from). □ **se** ~ **de** vpr avoid.

disperser /dispɛʀse/ **1** vt (éparpiller) scatter; (répartir) disperse. □ **se** ~ vpr disperse.

disponibilité /disponibilite/ nf availability. **disponible** adj available.

dispos, ~e /dispo, -z/ adj frais et

~ fresh and alert.

disposé, ~e /dispoze/ adj **bien/ mal** ~ in a good/bad mood; ~ **à** prepared to; ~ **envers** disposed towards.

disposer /dispoze/ **1** vt arrange; ~ **à** (engager à) incline to. ● vi ~ **de** have at one's disposal. □ **se** ~ **à** vpr prepare to.

dispositif /dispozitif/ nm device; (ensemble de mesures) operation.

disposition /dispozisjɔ̃/ nf arrangement, layout; (tendance) tendency; ~**s** (humeur) mood; (préparatifs) arrangements; (mesures) measures; (aptitude) aptitude; **mettre à la** ~ **de** place ou put at the disposal of.

disproportionné, ~e /dispʀɔpɔʀsjɔne/ adj disproportionate; ~ **à** out of proportion with.

dispute /dispyt/ nf quarrel.

disputer /dispyte/ **1** vt (match) play; (course) run in; (prix) fight for; (gronder **1**) tell off. □ **se** ~ vpr quarrel; (se battre pour) fight over; (match) be played.

disquaire /diskɛʀ/ nmf record dealer.

disque /disk/ nm (Mus) record; (Sport) discus; (cercle) disc, disk; (Ordinat) disk; ~ **compact** compact disc; ~ **dur** hard disk; ~ **optique compact** CD-ROM; ~ **souple** floppy disk.

disquette /diskɛt/ nf floppy disk, diskette; ~ **de sauvegarde** back-up disk.

disséminer /disemine/ **1** vt spread, scatter.

dissertation /disɛʀtasjɔ̃/ nf essay, paper.

disserter /disɛʀte/ **1** vi ~ **sur** speak about; (par écrit) write about.

dissident, ~e /disidɑ̃, -t/ adj &

d

nm, f dissident.

dissimulation /disimylasjɔ̃/ *nf* concealment; (fig) deceit.

dissimuler /disimyle/ **1** *vt* conceal (à from). □ se ~ *vpr* conceal oneself.

dissipé, ~e /disipe/ *adj* (*élève*) unruly.

dissiper /disipe/ **1** *vt* (*fumée*, *crainte*) dispel; (*fortune*) squander; (*personne*) distract. □ se ~ *vpr* disappear; (*élève*) grow restless.

dissolvant /disɔlvɑ̃/ *nm* solvent; (*pour ongles*) nail polish remover.

dissoudre /disudʀ/ **53** *vt* dissolve. □ se ~ *vpr* dissolve.

dissuader /disɥade/ **1** *vt* dissuade (de from).

dissuasion /disɥazjɔ̃/ *nf* dissuasion; force de ~ deterrent force.

distance /distɑ̃s/ *nf* distance; (*écart*) gap; à ~ at ou from a distance.

distancer /distɑ̃se/ **10** *vt* outdistance.

distendre /distɑ̃dʀ/ **3** *vt* (*estomac*) distend; (*corde*) stretch.

distinct, ~e /distɛ̃(kt)/, -ɛkt/ *adj* distinct.

distinctif, -ive /distɛ̃ktif, -v/ *adj* (*trait*) distinctive; (*signe*, *caractère*) distinguishing.

distinction /distɛ̃ksjɔ̃/ *nf* distinction; (*récompense*) honour.

distinguer /distɛ̃ge/ **1** *vt* distinguish.

distraction /distraksjɔ̃/ *nf* absent-mindedness; (*passe-temps*) entertainment, leisure; (*détente*) recreation.

distraire /distʀɛʀ/ **29** *vt* amuse; (*rendre inattentif*) distract; ~ qn de qch take sb's mind off sth. □ se ~ *vpr* amuse oneself.

distrait, ~e /distʀɛ, -t/ *adj* absent-minded; (*élève*) inattentive.

distrayant, ~e /distʀɛjɑ̃, -t/ *adj* entertaining.

distribuer /distʀibɥe/ **1** *vt* hand out, distribute; (*répartir*) distribute; (*tâches*, *rôles*) allocate; (*cartes*) deal; (*courrier*) deliver.

distributeur /distʀibytœʀ/ *nm* (Auto, Comm) distributor; ~ (automatique) vending-machine; ~ de billets (de banque) cash dispenser.

distribution /distʀibysjɔ̃/ *nf* distribution; (*du courrier*) delivery; (*acteurs*) cast; (*secteur*) retailing.

district /distʀikt/ *nm* district.

dit¹, dites /di, dit/ →DIRE **27**.

dit², ~e /di, dit/ *adj* (*décidé*) agreed; (*surnommé*) known as.

diurne /djyʀn/ *adj* diurnal; (*activité*) daytime.

divagations /divagasjɔ̃/ *nfpl* ravings.

divergence /divɛʀʒɑ̃s/ *nf* divergence. **divergent**, ~e *adj* divergent. **diverger** **40** *vi* diverge.

divers, ~e /divɛʀ, -s/ *adj* (*varié*) diverse; (*différent*) various; (*frais*) miscellaneous; dépenses ~es sundries. **diversifier** **45** *vt* diversify.

diversité /divɛʀsite/ *nf* diversity, variety.

divertir /divɛʀtiʀ/ **2** *vt* amuse, entertain. □ se ~ *vpr* amuse oneself; (*passer du bon temps*) enjoy oneself. **divertissement** *nm* amusement, entertainment.

dividende /dividɑ̃d/ *nm* dividend.

divin, ~e /divɛ̃, -in/ *adj* divine. **divinité** *nf* divinity.

diviser /divize/ **1** *vt* divide. □ se ~ *vpr* become divided; se ~ par sept be divisible by seven. **division** *nf* division.

divorce /divɔʀs/ *nm* divorce.

divorcé, ~e /divɔʀse/ *adj*

divorcer | donner

divorced. ● *nm, f* divorcee.

divorcer /divɔʀse/ **10** *vi* (d'avec) divorce.

dix /dis/ (/di/ *before consonant,* /diz/ *before vowel*) *adj & nm* ten.

dix-huit /dizɥit/ *adj & nm* eighteen.

dixième /dizjɛm/ *adj & nmf* tenth.

dix-neuf /diznœf/ *adj & nm* nineteen.

dix-sept /disɛt/ *adj & nm* seventeen.

docile /dɔsil/ *adj* docile.

docteur /dɔktœʀ/ *nm* doctor.

doctorat /dɔktɔʀa/ *nm* doctorate, PhD.

document /dɔkymɑ̃/ *nm* document. **documentaire** *adj & nm* documentary.

documentaliste /dɔkymɑ̃talist/ *nmf* information officer; (Scol) librarian.

documentation /dɔkymɑ̃tasjɔ̃/ *nf* information, literature; centre de ~ resource centre.

documenté, -e /dɔkymɑ̃te/ *adj* well-documented.

documenter /dɔkymɑ̃te/ **1** *vt* provide with information. □ se ~ *vpr* collect information.

dodo /dodo/ *nm* faire ~ (langage enfantin) sleep.

dodu, ~e /dɔdy/ *adj* plump.

dogmatique /dɔgmatik/ *adj* dogmatic. **dogme** *nm* dogma.

doigt /dwa/ *nm* finger; un ~ de a drop of; montrer qch du ~ point at sth; à deux ~s de a hair's breadth away from; ~ de pied toe. **doigté** *nm* (Mus) fingering; touch; (diplomatie) tact.

dois, doit /dwa/ →DEVOIR 28.

doléances /dɔleɑ̃s/ *nfpl* grievances.

dollar /dɔlaʀ/ *nm* dollar.

domaine /dɔmɛn/ *nm* estate, domain; (fig) domain, field.

domestique /dɔmɛstik/ *adj* domestic. ● *nmf* servant. **domestiquer** **1** *vt* domesticate.

domicile /dɔmisil/ *nm* home; à ~ at home; (livrer) to the home. **domicilié,** ~e /dɔmisilje/ *adj* resident; être ~ à Paris live ou be resident in Paris.

dominant, ~e /dɔminɑ̃, -t/ *adj* dominant. **dominante** *nf* dominant feature.

dominer /dɔmine/ **1** *vt* dominate; (surplomber) tower over, dominate; (sujet) master; (peur) overcome. ● *vi* dominate; (équipe) be in the lead; (prévaloir) stand out.

domino /dɔmino/ *nm* domino.

dommage /dɔmaʒ/ *nm* (tort) harm; (~s) (dégâts) damage; c'est ~ it's a pity ou shame; quel ~ what a pity ou shame. **dommages-intérêts** *nmpl* (Jur) damages.

dompter /dɔ̃te/ **1** *vt* tame. **dompteur, -euse** *nm, f* tamer.

DOM-TOM /dɔmtɔm/ *abrév mpl* (départements et territoires d'outre-mer) French overseas departments and territories.

don /dɔ̃/ *nm* (cadeau, aptitude) gift. **donateur, -trice** *nm, f* donor. **donation** *nf* donation.

donc /dɔ̃k/ *conj* so, then; (par conséquent) so, therefore; quoi ~? what did you say?; tiens ~! fancy that!

donjon /dɔ̃ʒɔ̃/ *nm* (tour) keep.

donné, ~e /dɔne/ *adj* (fixé) given; (pas cher **1**) dirt cheap; étant ~ que given that.

donnée /dɔne/ *nf* (élément d'information) fact; ~s data.

donner /dɔne/ **1** *vt* give; (vieilles

affaires) give away; (distribuer) give
up; (fruits, résultats) produce;
(film) show; (pièce) put on; ça
donne **soif/faim** it makes one
thirsty/hungry; ~ **qch à réparer**
take sth to be repaired; ~ **lieu à**
give rise to. ● vi ~ **sur** look out on
to; ~ **dans** tend towards. □ **se** ~ **à**
vpr devote oneself to; **se** ~ **du mal**
go to a lot of trouble (**pour faire**
to do).

---

dont /dɔ̃/

● *pronom*

····▶ (personne) **la fille** ~ **je te**
parlais the girl I was telling you
about; **l'homme** ~ **la fille a**
dit... the man whose daughter
said...

····▶ (chose) **which, l'affaire** ~ **il**
parle the matter which he is referring to; **la manière** ~ **elle**
parle the way she speaks; **ce**
~ **il parle** what he's talking about

····▶ (provenance) from which.

····▶ (parmi lesquels) **deux per-**
sonnes ~ **toi** two people, one
of whom is you; **plusieurs thè-**
mes ~ **l'identité et le racisme**
several topics including identity
and racism.

---

dopage /dɔpaʒ/ *nm* (de cheval)
doping; (d'athlète) illegal drug-use.
doper /dɔpe/ 1 *vt* dope. □ **se** ~
vpr take drugs.
doré, ~**e** /dɔʀe/ *adj* (couleur d'or)
golden; (qui rappelle de l'or) gold;
(avec de l'or) gilt; **la jeunesse** ~**e**
gilded youth.
dorénavant /dɔʀenavɑ̃/ *adv*
henceforth.
dorer /dɔʀe/ 1 *vt* gild; (Culin)
brown.

dormir /dɔʀmiʀ/ 46 *vi* sleep; (être
endormi) be asleep; ~ **debout** be
asleep on one's feet; **une histoire à**
~ **debout** a cock-and-bull story.
dortoir /dɔʀtwaʀ/ *nm* dormitory.
dorure /dɔʀyʀ/ *nf* gilding.
dos /do/ *nm* back; (de livre) spine; **à**
~ **de** riding on; **au** ~ **de** (chèque)
on the back of; **de** ~ from behind;
~ **crawlé** backstroke.
dosage /dozaʒ/ *nm* (mélange) mixture; (quantité) amount, proportions. **dose** *nf* dose. **doser** 1 *vt*
measure out; (contrôler) use in a
controlled way.
dossier /dɔsje/ *nm* (documents)
file; (Jur) case; (de chaise) back; (TV,
presse) special feature.
dot /dɔt/ *nf* dowry.
douane /dwan/ *nf* customs.
douanier, -ière /dwanje, -jɛʀ/ *adj*
customs. ● *nm* customs officer.
double /dubl/ *adj* & *adv* double.
● *nm* (copie) duplicate; (sosie)
double; **le** ~ **(de)** twice as much *ou*
as many (as); **le** ~ **messieurs** the
men's doubles.
double-cliquer /dublklike/ 1 *vt*
double-click.
doubler /duble/ 1 *vt* double; (dépasser) overtake; (vêtement) line;
(film) dub; (classe) repeat; (cap)
round. ● *vi* double.
doublure /dublyʀ/ *nf* (étoffe) lining; (acteur) understudy.
douce /dus/ ⇒**DOUX**.
doucement /dusmɑ̃/ *adv* gently;
(sans bruit) quietly; (lentement)
slowly.
douceur /dusœʀ/ *nf* (mollesse)
softness; (de climat) mildness; (de
personne) gentleness; (friandise)
sweet; (US) candy; **en** ~ smoothly.
douche /duʃ/ *nf* shower.
doucher (se) /(sə)duʃe/ 1 *vpr* have

ou take a shower.

doudoune /dudun/ *nf* 🔢 down jacket.

doué, ~e /dwe/ *adj* gifted; ~ de endowed with.

douille /duj/ *nf* (Électr) socket.

douillet, ~te /duj, -t/ *adj* cosy, comfortable; (*personne*: péj) soft.

douleur /dulœʀ/ *nf* pain; (chagrin) sorrow, grief. **douloureux, -euse** *adj* painful.

doute /dut/ *nm* doubt; sans ~ no doubt; sans aucun ~ without doubt.

douter /dute/ 🔢 *vt* ~ de doubt; ~ que doubt that. ● *vi* doubt. ☐ se ~ de *vpr* suspect; je m'en doutais I thought so.

douteux, -euse /dutø, -z/ *adj* dubious, doubtful.

Douvres /duvʀ/ *npr* Dover.

doux, douce /du, dus/ *adj* (moelleux) soft; (sucré) sweet; (clément, pas fort) mild; (pas brusque, bienveillant) gentle.

douzaine /duzɛn/ *nf* about twelve; (douze) dozen; une ~ d'œufs a dozen eggs.

douze /duz/ *adj & nm* twelve. **douzième** *adj & nmf* twelfth.

doyen, ~ne /dwajɛ̃, -ɛn/ *nm, f* dean; (en âge) most senior person.

dragée /dʀaʒe/ *nf* sugared almond.

draguer /dʀage/ 🔢 *vt* (rivière) dredge; (filles 🔢) chat up.

drainer /dʀene/ 🔢 *vt* drain.

dramatique /dʀamatik/ *adj* dramatic; (tragique) tragic. ● *nf* (television) drama.

dramatiser /dʀamatize/ 🔢 *vt* dramatize.

dramaturge /dʀamatyʀʒ/ *nmf* dramatist.

drame /dʀam/ *nm* (genre) drama;

(pièce) play; (événement tragique) tragedy.

drap /dʀa/ *nm* sheet; (tissu) (woollen) cloth.

drapeau (*pl* ~x) /dʀapo/ *nm* flag.

drap-housse (*pl* **draps-housses**) /dʀaus/ *nm* fitted sheet.

dressage /dʀesaʒ/ *nm* training; (compétition équestre) dressage.

dresser /dʀese/ 🔢 *vt* put up, erect; (tête) raise; (animal) train; (liste, plan) draw up; ~ l'oreille prick up one's ears. ☐ se ~ *vpr* (bâtiment) stand; (personne) draw oneself up. **dresseur, -euse** *nm, f* trainer.

dribbler /dʀible/ 🔢 *vi* (Sport) dribble.

drive /dʀajv/ *nm* (Ordinat) drive.

drogue /dʀɔg/ *nf* drug; la ~ drugs.

drogué, ~e /dʀɔge/ *nm, f* drug addict.

droguer /dʀɔge/ 🔢 *vt* (malade) drug heavily; (victime) drug. ☐ se ~ *vpr* take drugs.

droguerie /dʀɔgʀi/ *nf* hardware shop. **droguiste** *nmf* owner of a hardware shop.

droit, ~e /dʀwa, -t/ *adj* (contraire de gauche) right; (non courbe) straight; (loyal) upright; angle ~ right angle. ● *adv* straight. ● *nm* right; ~(s) (taxe) duty; le ~ (Jur) law; avoir ~ à be entitled to; avoir le ~ de be allowed to; être dans son ~ be in the right; ~ d'auteur copyright; ~ d'inscription registration fee; ~s d'auteur royalties.

droite /dʀwat/ *nf* (contraire de gauche) right; à ~ on the right; (direction) (to the) right; la ~ the right (side); (Pol) the right (wing); (ligne) straight line. **droitier, -ière** *adj* right-handed.

drôle /dʀol/ *adj* (amusant) funny; (bizarre) funny, odd. **drôlement** *adv* funnily; (très 🎲) really.

dru, ~e /dʀy/ *adj* thick; tomber ~ fall thick and fast.

drugstore /dʀœgstoʀ/ *nm* drugstore.

DTD *abrév m* (**document type definition**) DTD.

du /dy/ →DE.

dû, due /dy/ *adj* due. ● *nm* due; (argent) dues; ~ à due to. ● →DEVOIR 🎲.

duc, duchesse /dyk, dyʃɛs/ *nm, f* duke, duchess.

duo /dɥo/ *nm* (Mus) duet; (fig) duo.

dupe /dyp/ *nf* dupe.

duplex /dyplɛks/ *nm* split-level apartment; (US) duplex; (émission) link-up.

duplicata /dyplikata/ *nm inv* duplicate.

duquel /dykɛl/ →LEQUEL.

dur, ~e /dyʀ/ *adj* hard; (sévère) harsh, hard; (viande) tough; (col, brosse) stiff; ~ d'oreille hard of hearing. ● *adv* hard. ● *nm, f* tough nut 🎲; (Pol) hardliner.

durable /dyʀabl/ *adj* lasting.

durant /dyʀɑ̃/ *prép* (au cours de) during; (avec mesure de temps) for; ~ des heures for hours; des heures ~ for hours and hours.

durcir /dyʀsiʀ/ 🎲 *vt* harden. ● *vi* (terre) harden; (ciment) set; (pain) go hard. ☐ **se** ~ *vpr* harden.

durée /dyʀe/ *nf* length; (période) duration; de courte ~ short-lived; pile longue ~ long-life battery.

durer /dyʀe/ 🎲 *vi* last.

dureté /dyʀte/ *nf* hardness; (sévérité) harshness.

duvet /dyvɛ/ *nm* down; (sac) sleeping-bag.

DVD *abrév m* (**digital versatile disc**) DVD.

dynamique /dinamik/ *adj* dynamic.

dynamite /dinamit/ *nf* dynamite.

dynamo /dinamo/ *nf* dynamo.

Ee

eau (*pl* ~x) /o/ *nf* water; ~ courante running water; ~ de mer seawater; ~ de source spring water; ~ douce/salée fresh/salt water; ~ de pluie rainwater; ~ potable drinking water; ~ de Javel bleach; ~ minérale mineral water; ~ gazeuse sparkling water; ~ plate still water; ~ de toilette eau de toilette; ~x usées dirty water; ~x et forêts forestry commission (+ *sg*); tomber à l'~ (fig) fall through; prendre l'~ take in water. **eau-de-vie** (*pl* **eaux-de-vie**) *nf* brandy.

ébahi, ~e /ebai/ *adj* dumbfounded.

ébauche /eboʃ/ *nf* (dessin) sketch; (fig) attempt.

ébéniste /ebenist/ *nm* cabinetmaker.

éblouir /ebluiʀ/ 🎲 *vt* dazzle.

éboueur /ebwœʀ/ *nm* dustman.

ébouillanter /ebujɑ̃te/ 🎲 *vt* scald.

éboulement /ebulmɑ̃/ *nm* landslide.

ébouriffé, ~e /eburife/ *adj* dishevelled.

ébrécher /ebʀeʃe/ 🎲 *vt* chip.

ébruiter /ebʀɥite/ 🎲 *vt* spread

about. □ s'∼ vpr get out.

ébullition /ebylisjɔ̃/ nf boiling; en ∼ boiling.

écaille /ekaj/ nf (de poisson) scale; (de peinture, roc) flake; (matière) tortoiseshell.

écarlate /ekarlat/ adj scarlet.

écarquiller /ekarkije/ **1** vt ∼ les yeux open one's eyes wide.

écart /ekar/ nm gap; (de prix) difference; (embardée) swerve; ∼ de conduite lapse in behaviour; être à l'∼ be isolated; se tenir à l'∼ de stand apart from; (fig) keep out of the way of.

écarté, ∼e /ekarte/ adj (lieu) remote; les jambes ∼es (with) legs apart; les bras ∼s with one's arms out.

écarter /ekarte/ **1** vt (séparer) move apart; (membres) spread; (branches) part; (éliminer) dismiss; ∼ qch de move sth away from; ∼ qn de keep sb away from. □ s'∼ vpr (s'éloigner) move away; (quitter son chemin) move aside; ∼ de stray from.

ecchymose /ekimoz/ nf bruise.

écervelé, ∼e /eservəle/ adj scatterbrained. ● nm, f scatterbrain.

échafaudage /eʃafodaʒ/ nm scaffolding; (amas) heap.

échalote /eʃalɔt/ nf shallot.

échancré, ∼e /eʃɑ̃kre/ adj lowcut.

échange /eʃɑ̃ʒ/ nm exchange; en ∼ (de) in exchange (for). **échanger** **40** vt exchange (contre for).

échangeur /eʃɑ̃ʒœr/ nm (Auto) interchange.

échantillon /eʃɑ̃tijɔ̃/ nm sample.

échappatoire /eʃapatwar/ nf way out.

échappement /eʃapmɑ̃/ nm exhaust.

échapper /eʃape/ **1** vi ∼ à escape; (en fuyant) escape (from); ∼ des mains de slip out of the hands of; ça m'a échappé (fig) it just slipped out; l'∼ belle have a narrow ou lucky escape. □ s'∼ vpr escape.

écharde /eʃard/ nf splinter.

écharpe /eʃarp/ nf scarf; (de maire) sash; en ∼ (bras) in a sling.

échasse /eʃas/ nf stilt.

échauffement /eʃofmɑ̃/ nm (Sport) warm-up.

échauffer /eʃofe/ **1** vt heat; (fig) excite. □ s'∼ vpr warm up.

échéance /eʃeɑ̃s/ nf due date (for payment); (délai) deadline; (obligation) (financial) commitment.

échéant: le cas ∼ /ləkazeʃeɑ̃/ loc if need be.

échec /eʃɛk/ nm failure; ∼s (jeu) chess; ∼ et mat checkmate.

échelle /eʃɛl/ nf ladder; (dimension) scale.

échelon /eʃlɔ̃/ nm rung; (hiérarchique) grade; (niveau) level.

échevelé, ∼e /eʃəvle/ adj dishevelled.

écho /eko/ nm echo; ∼s (dans la presse) gossip.

échographie /ekografi/ nf (ultrasound) scan.

échouer /eʃwe/ **1** vi (bateau) run aground; (ne pas réussir) fail; ∼ à un examen fail an exam. ● vt (bateau) ground. □ s'∼ vpr run aground.

échu, ∼e /eʃy/ adj (délai) expired.

éclabousser /eklabuse/ **1** vt splash.

éclair /eklɛr/ nm (flash of) lightning; (fig) flash; (gâteau) éclair. ● adj inv (visite) brief.

éclairage /eklɛraʒ/ nm lighting.

e

éclaircie /eklɛʀsi/ nf sunny interval.

éclaircir /eklɛʀsiʀ/ **2** vt lighten; (mystère) clear up. □ **s'~** vpr (ciel) clear; (mystère) become clearer. **éclaircissement** nm clarification.

éclairer /ekleʀe/ **1** vt light (up); (personne) (fig) enlighten; (situation) throw light on. ● vi give light. □ **s'~** vpr become clearer.

éclaireur, -euse /eklɛʀœʀ, -øz/ nm, f (boy) scout, (girl) guide.

éclat /ekla/ nm fragment; (de lumière) brightness; (splendeur) brilliance; ~ de rire burst of laughter.

éclatant, ~e /eklatɑ̃, -t/ adj brilliant; (soleil) dazzling.

éclater /eklate/ **1** vi burst; (exploser) go off; (verre) shatter; (guerre) break out; (groupe) split up; ~ de rire burst out laughing.

éclipse /eklips/ nf eclipse.

éclosion /eklozjɔ̃/ nf hatching, opening.

écluse /eklyz/ nf (de canal) lock.

écœurant, ~e /ekœʀɑ̃, -t/ adj (gâteau) sickly; (fig) disgusting. **écœurer** **1** vt sicken.

éco-guerrier, -ière /ekogeʀje, jɛʀ/ nmf eco-warrior.

école /ekɔl/ nf school; ~ maternelle/primaire/secondaire nursery/primary/secondary school; ~ normale teachers' training college. **écolier, -ière** nm, f schoolboy, schoolgirl.

écologie /ekɔlɔʒi/ nf ecology. **écologique** adj ecological, green. **écologiste** nmf (chercheur) ecologist; (dans l'âme) environmentalist; (Pol) Green.

économie /ekɔnɔmi/ nf economy; (discipline) economics; ~s (argent) savings; une ~ de (gain) a saving of. **économique** adj (Pol) economic;

(bon marché) economical.

économiser /ekɔnɔmize/ **1** vt/i save.

écorce /ekɔʀs/ nf bark; (de fruit) peel.

écorcher /ekɔʀʃe/ **1** vt (genou) graze; (animal) skin. □ **s'~** vpr graze oneself. **écorchure** nf graze.

écossais, ~e /ekɔsɛ, -z/ adj Scottish. **É~, ~e** nm, f Scot.

Écosse /ekɔs/ nf Scotland.

écoulement /ekulmɑ̃/ nm flow.

écouler /ekule/ **1** vt dispose of, sell. □ **s'~** vpr (liquide) flow; (temps) pass.

écourter /ekuʀte/ **1** vt shorten.

écoute /ekut/ nf listening; à l'~ (de) listening in (to); heures de grande ~ prime time; ~s téléphoniques phone tapping.

écouter /ekute/ **1** vt listen to. ● vi listen; ~ aux portes eavesdrop. **écouteur** nm earphones (+ pl); (de téléphone) receiver.

écran /ekʀɑ̃/ nm screen; ~ total sun-block.

écraser /ekʀaze/ **1** vt crush; (piéton) run over; (cigarette) stub out. □ **s'~** vpr crash (contre into).

écrémé, ~e /ekʀeme/ adj skimmed; demi-~ semi-skimmed.

écrevisse /ekʀəvis/ nf crayfish.

écrier (s') /(s)ekʀije/ **45** vpr exclaim.

écrin /ekʀɛ̃/ nm case.

écrire /ekʀiʀ/ **30** vt/i write; (orthographier) spell. □ **s'~** vpr (mot) be spelt.

écrit /ekʀi/ nm document; (examen) written paper; par ~ in writing.

écriteau (pl ~x) /ekʀito/ nm notice.

écriture /ekʀityʀ/ nf writing; ~s

(Comm) accounts.

écrivain /ekʀivɛ̃/ nm writer.

écrou /ekʀu/ nm (Tech) nut.

écrouler (s') /(s)ekʀule/ **1** vpr collapse.

écru, ~e /ekʀy/ adj (couleur) natural; (tissu) raw.

écueil /ekœj/ nm reef; (fig) danger.

éculé, ~e /ekyle/ adj (soulier) worn at the heel; (fig) well-worn.

écume /ekym/ nf foam; (Culin) scum.

écumer /ekyme/ **1** vt skim.
● vi foam.

écureuil /ekyʀœj/ nm squirrel.

écurie /ekyʀi/ nf stable.

écuyer, -ère /ekɥije, -jɛʀ/ nm, f (horse) rider.

eczéma /ɛgzema/ nm eczema.

EDF abrév f (**Électricité de France**) French electricity board.

édifice /edifis/ nm building.

édifier /edifje/ **45** vt construct; (porter à la vertu) edify.

Édimbourg /edɛ̃buʀ/ npr Edinburgh.

édit /edi/ nm edict.

éditer /edite/ **1** vt publish; (annoter) edit. **éditeur, -trice** nm, f publisher; (réviseur) editor.

édition /edisjɔ̃/ nf (activité) publishing; (livre, disque) edition.

éditique /editik/ nf electronic publishing.

éditorial, ~e (pl -iaux) /editɔʀjal, -jo/ adj & nm editorial.

édredon /edʀedɔ̃/ nm eiderdown.

éducateur, -trice /edykatœʀ, -tʀis/ nm, f youth worker.

éducatif, -ive /edykatif, -v/ adj educational.

éducation /edykasjɔ̃/ nf (façon d'élever) upbringing; (enseignement, manières) education; (manières) man-

ners; ~ **physique** physical education.

éduquer /edyke/ **1** vt (élever) bring up; (former) educate.

effacé, ~e /efase/ adj (modeste) unassuming.

effacer /efase/ **10** vt (gommer) rub out; (à l'écran) delete; (souvenir) erase. □ **s'~** vpr fade; (s'écarter) step aside.

effarer /efaʀe/ **1** vt alarm; **être effaré** be astounded.

effaroucher /efaʀuʃe/ **1** vt scare away.

effectif, -ive /efɛktif, -v/ adj effective. ● nm (d'école) number of pupils; ~**s** numbers. **effectivement** adv effectively; (en effet) indeed.

effectuer /efɛktɥe/ **1** vt carry out, make.

efféminé, ~e /efemine/ adj feminate.

effervescent, ~e /efɛʀvesɑ̃, -t/ adj **comprimé ~** effervescent tablet.

effet /efɛ/ nm effect; (impression) impression; ~**s** (habits) clothes, things; **sous l'~ d'une drogue** under the influence of drugs; **en ~** indeed; **faire de l'~** have an effect, be effective; **faire bon/ mauvais ~** make a good/bad impression; **ça fait un drôle d'~** it feels strange.

efficace /efikas/ adj effective; (personne) efficient. **efficacité** nf effectiveness; (de personne) efficiency.

effleurer /eflœʀe/ **1** vt touch lightly; (sujet) touch on; **ça ne m'a pas effleuré** it did not cross my mind.

effondrement /efɔ̃dʀemɑ̃/ nm collapse. **effondrer (s')** **1** vpr collapse.

efforcer (s') /(s)efɔʀse/ **10** vpr try (hard) (de to).

effort /efɔʀ/ nm effort.

effraction /efʀaksjɔ̃/ nf entrer par ~ break in.

effrayant, ~e /efʀɛjɑ̃, -t/ adj frightening; (fig) frightful.

effrayer /efʀeje/ **31** vt frighten; (décourager) put off. □ s'~ vpr be frightened.

effréné, ~e /efʀene/ adj wild.

effriter (s') /(s)efʀite/ **1** vpr crumble.

effroi /efʀwa/ nm dread.

effronté, ~e /efʀɔ̃te/ adj cheeky. ●nm, f cheeky boy, cheeky girl.

effroyable /efʀwajabl/ adj dreadful.

égal, ~e /egal/ (mpl -aux) adj equal; (surface, vitesse) even. ●nm, f equal; ça m'est/lui est ~ it is all the same to me/him; sans ~ matchless; d'~ à ~ between equals. **également** adv equally; (aussi) as well. **égaler** **1** vt equal.

égaliser /egalize/ **1** vt/i (Sport) equalize; (niveler) level out; (cheveux) trim.

égalitaire /egalitɛʀ/ adj egalitarian.

égalité /egalite/ nf equality; (de surface) evenness; être à ~ be level.

égard /egaʀ/ nm consideration; ~s respect (+ sg); par ~ pour out of consideration for; à cet ~ in this respect; à l'~ de with regard to; (envers) towards.

égarer /egaʀe/ **1** vt mislay; (tromper) lead astray. □ s'~ vpr get lost; (se tromper) go astray.

égayer /egeje/ **31** vt (personne) cheer up; (pièce) brighten up.

église /egliz/ nf church.

égoïsme /egoism/ nm selfishness, egoism.

égoïste /egoist/ adj selfish. ●nmf

egoist.

égorger /egɔʀʒe/ **40** vt slit the throat of.

égout /egu/ nm sewer.

égoutter /egute/ **1** vt drain. □ s'~ vpr (vaisselle) drain; (lessive) drip dry. **égouttoir** nm draining-board.

égratigner /egʀatiɲe/ **1** vt scratch. **égratignure** nf scratch.

Égypte /eʒipt/ nf Egypt.

éjecter /eʒɛkte/ **1** vt eject.

élaboration /elabɔʀasjɔ̃/ nf elaboration. **élaborer** **1** vt elaborate.

élan /elɑ̃/ nm (animal) moose; (Sport) run-up; (vitesse) momentum; (fig) surge.

élancé, ~e /elɑ̃se/ adj slender.

élancement /elɑ̃smɑ̃/ nm twinge.

élancer (s') /(s)elɑ̃se/ **10** vpr leap forward, dash; (arbre, édifice) soar.

élargir /elaʀʒiʀ/ **2** vt (route) widen; (connaissances) broaden. □ s'~ vpr (famille) expand; (route) widen; (écart) increase; (vêtement) stretch.

élastique /elastik/ adj elastic. ●nm elastic band; (tissu) elastic.

électeur, -trice /elɛktœʀ, -tʀis/ nm, f voter. **élection** nf election. **électoral, ~e** (mpl -aux) adj (réunion) election. **électorat** nm electorate, voters (+ pl).

électricien, ~ne /elɛktʀisjɛ̃, ɛn/ nm, f electrician. **électricité** nf electricity.

électrifier /elɛktʀifje/ **45** vt electrify.

électrique /elɛktʀik/ adj electric; (installation) electrical.

électrocuter /elɛktʀɔkyte/ **1** vt electrocute.

électroménager /elɛktʀɔmenaʒe/ nm l'~ household

appliances (+ *pl*).

électron /elɛktʁɔ̃/ *nm* electron.

électronicien, **~ne** *nm, f* electronics engineer.

électronique /elɛktʁɔnik/ *adj* electronic. ● *nf* electronics.

élégance /elegɑ̃s/ *nf* elegance. **élégant**, **~e** *adj* elegant.

élément /elemɑ̃/ *nm* element; (*meuble*) unit. **élémentaire** *adj* elementary.

éléphant /elefɑ̃/ *nm* elephant.

élevage /ɛlvaʒ/ *nm* (stock-) breeding.

élévation /elevasjɔ̃/ *nf* rise; (*hausse*) rise; (*plan*) elevation; **~ de terrain** rise in the ground.

élève /elɛv/ *nmf* pupil.

élevé, **~e** /ɛlve/ *adj* high; (*noble*) elevated; **bien ~** well-mannered.

élever /ɛlve/ [6] *vt* (*lever*) raise; (*enfants*) bring up; (*animal*) breed. □ **s'~** *vpr* rise; (*dans le ciel*) soar up; **s'~ à** amount to. **éleveur**, **-euse** *nm, f* (stock-)breeder.

éligible /eliʒibl/ *adj* eligible.

élimination /eliminasjɔ̃/ *nf* elimination.

éliminatoire /eliminatwaʁ/ *adj* qualifying. ● *nf* (Sport) heat.

éliminer /elimine/ [1] *vt* eliminate.

élire /eliʁ/ [39] *vt* elect.

elle /ɛl/ *pron* she; (*complément*) her; (*chose*) it. **elle-même** *pron* herself; itself. **elles** *pron* they; (*complément*) them. **elles-mêmes** *pron* themselves.

élocution /elɔkysjɔ̃/ *nf* diction.

éloge /elɔʒ/ *nm* praise; **faire l'~ de** praise; **~s** praise (+ *sg*).

éloigné, **~e** /elwaɲe/ *adj* distant; **~ de** far away from; **parent ~** distant relative.

éloigner /elwaɲe/ [1] *vt* take away

ou remove (de from); (*danger*) ward off; (*visite*) put off. □ **s'~** *vpr* go ou move away (de from); (*affectivement*) become estranged (de from).

élongation /elɔ̃gasjɔ̃/ *nf* strained muscle.

éloquent, **~e** /elɔkɑ̃, -t/ *adj* eloquent.

élu, **~e** /ely/ *adj* elected. ● *nm, f* (Pol) elected representative.

élucider /elyside/ [1] *vt* elucidate.

éluder /elyde/ [1] *vt* evade.

> **Élysée** Le *palais de l'Élysée* is the official residence of the *Président de la République*, not far from the *Champs Élysées* in central Paris. The word *Élysée* is often used to refer to the president's office. See ▶**MATIGNON**.

émacié, **~e** /emasje/ *adj* emaciated.

e-mail /imɛl/ *nm* email; **envoyer un ~ à qn** email sb.

émail (*pl* -**aux**) /emaj, -o/ *nm* enamel.

émanciper /emɑ̃sipe/ [1] *vt* emancipate. □ **s'~** *vpr* become emancipated.

émaner /emane/ [1] *vi* emanate.

emballage /ɑ̃balaʒ/ *nm* (dur) packaging; (souple) wrapping.

emballer /ɑ̃bale/ [1] *vt* pack; (en papier) wrap; **ça ne m'emballe pas** [1] I'm not really taken by it. □ **s'~** *vpr* (moteur) race; (cheval) bolt; (personne) get carried away; (prices) shoot up.

embarcadère /ɑ̃baʁkadɛʁ/ *nm* landing-stage.

embarcation /ɑ̃baʁkasjɔ̃/ *nf* boat.

embardée /ɑ̃baʁde/ *nf* swerve.

embarquement /ãbaʁkəmã/ nm (de passagers) boarding; (de fret) loading.

embarquer /ãbaʁke/ **1** vt take on board; (frêt) load; (emporter **1**) cart off. ● vi board. □ s'~ vpr board; s'~ dans embark upon.

embarras /ãbaʁa/ nm (gêne) embarrassment; (difficulté) difficulty.

embarrasser /ãbaʁase/ **1** vt (encombrer) clutter (up); (fig) embarrass. □ s'~ de burden oneself with.

embauche /ãboʃ/ nf hiring. **embaucher** **1** vt hire, take on.

embaumer /ãbome/ **1** vt (pièce) fill; (cadavre) embalm. ● vi be fragrant.

embellir /ãbeliʁ/ **2** vt make more attractive; (récit) embellish.

embêtant, ~e /ãbɛtã, -t/ adj **1** annoying.

embêter /ãbɛte/ **1** vt bother. □ s'~ vpr be bored.

emblée: d'~ /dãble/ loc right away.

emblème /ãblɛm/ nm emblem.

emboîter /ãbwate/ **1** vt fit together; ~ le pas à qn (imiter) follow suit. □ s'~ vpr fit together; (s')~ dans fit into.

embonpoint /ãbõpwɛ̃/ nm stoutness.

embourber (s') /(s)ãbuʁbe/ **1** vpr get stuck in the mud; (fig) become bogged down.

embouteillage /ãbutɛjaʒ/ nm traffic jam.

emboutir /ãbutiʁ/ **2** vt (Auto) crash into.

embraser (s') /(s)ãbʁaze/ **1** vpr catch fire.

embrasser /ãbʁase/ **1** vt kiss; (adopter, contenir) embrace. □ s'~ vpr kiss.

embrayage /ãbʁɛjaʒ/ nm clutch. **embrayer** **31** vi engage the clutch.

embrouiller /ãbʁuje/ **1** vt confuse; (fils) tangle. □ s'~ vpr become confused.

embryon /ãbʁijõ/ nm embryo.

embûches /ãbyʃ/ nfpl traps.

embuer (s') /(s)ãbɥe/ **1** vpr mist up.

embuscade /ãbyskad/ nf ambush.

émeraude /ɛmʁod/ nf emerald.

émerger /emɛʁʒe/ **40** vi emerge; (fig) stand out.

émeri /ɛmʁi/ nm emery.

émerveillement /emɛʁvɛjmã/ nm amazement, wonder.

émerveiller /emɛʁveje/ **1** vt fill with wonder. □ s'~ vpr marvel at.

émetteur /emɛtœʁ/ nm transmitter.

émettre /emɛtʁ/ **42** vt (son) produce; (message) send out; (timbre, billet) issue; (opinion) express.

émeute /emøt/ nf riot.

émietter /emjete/ **1** vt crumble. □ s'~ vpr crumble.

émigrant, ~e /e/emigʁã, -t/ nm, f emigrant. **émigration** nf emigration. **émigrer** **1** vi emigrate.

émincer /emɛ̃se/ **10** vt cut into thin slices.

éminent, ~e /eminã, -t/ adj eminent.

émissaire /emisɛʁ/ nm emissary.

émission /emisjõ/ nf (programme) programme; (de chaleur, gaz) emission; (de timbre) issue.

emmagasiner /ãmagazine/ **1** vt store.

emmanchure /ãmãʃyʁ/ nf armhole.

emmêler /ãmele/ **1** vt tangle. □ s'~ vpr get mixed up.

emménager /ãmenaʒe/ 40 vi move in; ~ dans move into.

emmener /ãmne/ 6 vt take; (comme prisonnier) take away.

emmerder /ãmɛʀde/ 1 ⊠ vt ~ qn get on sb's nerves. □ s'~ vpr be bored.

emmitoufler /ãmitufle/ 1 vt wrap up warmly. □ s'~ vpr wrap oneself up warmly.

émoi /emwa/ nm turmoil; (plaisir) excitement.

émotif, **-ive** /emotif, -v/ adj emotional. **émotion** nf emotion; (peur) fright. **émotionnel**, **~le** adj emotional.

émousser /emuse/ 1 vt blunt.

émouvant, **~e** /emuvã, -t/ adj moving.

empailler /ãpaje/ 1 vt stuff.

empaqueter /ãpakte/ 38 vt package.

emparer (s') /(s)ãpaʀe/ 1 vpr s'~ de get hold of.

empêchement /ãpɛʃmã/ nm avoir un ~ to be held up.

empêcher /ãpeʃe/ 1 vt prevent; ~ de faire prevent ou stop (from) doing; (il) n'empêche que still. □ s'~ vpr il ne peut pas s'en ~ he cannot help it.

empereur /ãpʀœʀ/ nm emperor.

empester /ãpɛste/ 1 vt stink out; (essence) stink of. ● vi stink.

empêtrer (s') /(s)ãpetʀe/ 1 vpr become entangled.

empiéter /ãpjete/ 14 vi ~ sur encroach upon.

empiffrer (s') /(s)ãpifʀe/ 1 ⊞ stuff oneself.

empiler /ãpile/ 1 vt pile up. □ s'~ vpr pile up.

empire /ãpiʀ/ nm empire.

emplacement /ãplasmã/ nm site.

emplâtre /ãplɑtʀ/ nm (Méd) plaster.

emploi /ãplwa/ nm (travail) job; (embauche) employment; (utilisation) use; un ~ de chauffeur a job as a driver; ~ du temps timetable. **employé**, **~e** nm, f employee. **employer** /ãplwaje/ 31 vt (personne) employ; (utiliser) use. □ s'~ vpr be used; s'~ à devote oneself to. **employeur**, **-euse** nm, f employer.

empoigner /ãpwaɲe/ 1 vt grab. □ s'~ vpr come to blows.

empoisonnement /ãpwazɔnmã/ nm poisoning.

empoisonner /ãpwazɔne/ 1 vt poison; (embêter ⊞) annoy. □ s'~ vpr to poison oneself.

emporter /ãpɔʀte/ 1 vt take (away); (entraîner) sweep away; (arracher) tear off. □ s'~ vpr lose one's temper; l'~ get the upper hand (sur of); plat à ~ take-away.

empoté, **~e** /ãpote/ adj clumsy.

empreinte /ãpʀɛ̃t/ nf mark; ~ (digitale) fingerprint; ~ écologique carbon footprint; ~ de pas footprint.

empressé, **~e** /ãpʀese/ adj attentive.

empresser (s') /(s)ãpʀese/ 1 vpr s'~ de hasten to; s'~ auprès de be attentive to.

emprise /ãpʀiz/ nf influence.

emprisonnement /ãpʀizɔnmã/ nm imprisonment. **emprisonner** 1 vt imprison.

emprunt /ãpʀœ̃/ nm loan; faire un ~ take out a loan.

emprunté, **~e** /ãpʀœ̃te/ adj awkward.

emprunter /ãpʀœ̃te/ 1 vt borrow (à from); (route) take; (fig) assume. **emprunteur**, **-euse** nm, f borrower.

e

ému, ~e /emy/ *adj* moved; (intimidé) nervous.

émule /emyl/ *nmf* imitator.

en /ã/

➡️ Pour les expressions comme en principe, en train de, s'en aller, etc. ➡️principe, train, aller, etc.

● *préposition*

····▸ (lieu) in.

····▸ (avec mouvement) to.

····▸ (temps) in.

····▸ (manière, état) in; ~ faisant by du while doing; je t'appelle ~ rentrant I will call you when I get back.

····▸ (en qualité de) as.

····▸ (transport) by.

····▸ (composition) made of; table ~ bois wooden table.

● *pronom*

····▸ en avoir/vouloir have/want some; ne pas ~ avoir/vouloir not have/want any; j'~ ai deux I've got two; prends-~ plusieurs take several; il m'~ reste un I have one left; j'~ suis content I am pleased with him/her/it/them; je m'~ souviens I remember it.

····▸ ~ êtes-vous sûr? are you sure?

encadrement /ãkadʀəmã/ *nm* framing; (de porte) frame. **encadrer** 🔟 *vt* frame; (entourer d'un trait) circle; (superviser) supervise.

encaisser /ãkese/ 🔟 *vt* (argent) collect; (chèque) cash; (coups 🔟) take.

encart /ãkaʀ/ *nm* ~ publicitaire (advertising) insert.

en-cas /ãka/ *nm* (stand-by) snack.

encastré, ~e /ãkastʀe/ *adj* built-in.

encaustique /ãkɔstik/ *nf* wax polish.

enceinte /ãsɛ̃t/ *adj f* pregnant; ~ de 3 mois 3 months pregnant. ● *nf* enclosure; ~ (acoustique) speaker.

encens /ãsã/ *nm* incense.

encercler /ãseʀkle/ 🔟 *vt* surround.

enchaînement /ãʃenmã/ *nm* (suite) chain; (d'idées) sequence.

enchaîner /ãʃene/ 🔟 *vt* chain (up); (phrases) link (up). ● *vi* continue. □ s'~ *vpr* follow on.

enchanté, ~e /ãʃãte/ *adj* (ravi) delighted. **enchanter** 🔟 *vt* delight; (ensorceler) enchant.

enchère /ãʃeʀ/ *nf* bid; mettre *ou* vendre aux ~s sell by auction.

enchevêtrer /ãʃəvetʀe/ 🔟 *vt* tangle. □ s'~ *vpr* become tangled.

enclave /ãklav/ *nf* enclave.

enclencher /ãklãʃe/ 🔟 *vt* engage.

enclin, ~e /ãklɛ̃, -in/ *adj* ~ à inclined to.

enclos /ãklo/ *nm* enclosure.

enclume /ãklym/ *nf* anvil.

encoche /ãkɔʃ/ *nf* notch.

encolure /ãkɔlyʀ/ *nf* neck.

encombrant, ~e /ãkõbʀã, -t/ *adj* cumbersome.

encombre /ãkõbʀ/ *nm* sans ~ without any problems.

encombrement /ãkõbʀəmã/ *nm* (Auto) traffic congestion; (volume) bulk.

encombrer /ãkõbʀe/ 🔟 *vt* clutter (up); (obstruer) obstruct. □ s'~ de *vpr* burden oneself with.

encontre: à l'~ de /alãkõtʀədə/ *loc* against.

encore /ãkɔʀ/ *adv* (toujours) still; (de nouveau) again; (de plus) more;

(aussi) also; ~ plus grand even larger; ~ un café another coffee; pas ~ not yet; si ~ if only; et puis quoi ~? ① what next?

encouragement /ākuraʒmā/ nm encouragement. **encourager** 40 vt encourage.

encourir /ākurir/ 20 vt incur.

encrasser /ākrase/ ① vt clog up (with dirt).

encre /ākr/ nf ink. **encrier** nm ink-well.

encyclopédie /āsiklɔpedi/ nf encyclopaedia.

endettement /ādɛtmā/ nm debt.

endetter /ādete/ ① vt put into debt. □ s'~ vpr get into debt.

endiguer /ādige/ ① vt dam; (fig) curb.

endimanché, ~e /ādimāʃe/ adj in one's Sunday best.

endive /ādiv/ nf chicory.

endoctriner /ādɔktrine/ ① vt indoctrinate.

endommager /ādɔmaʒe/ 40 vt damage.

endormi, ~e /ādɔrmi/ adj asleep; (apathique) sleepy.

endormir /ādɔrmir/ 46 vt send to sleep; (médicalement) put to sleep; (duper) dupe (avec with). □ s'~ vpr fall asleep.

endosser /ādɔse/ ① vt (vêtement) put on; (assumer) take on; (Comm) endorse.

endroit /ādrwa/ nm place; (de tissu) right side; à l'~ the right way round; par ~s in places.

enduire /āduir/ 17 vt coat. **enduit** nm coating.

endurance /ādyrās/ nf endurance. **endurant**, ~e adj tough.

endurcir /ādyrsir/ ② vt strengthen. □ s'~ vpr become

hard (hardened).

endurer /ādyre/ ① vt endure.

énergétique /enerʒetik/ adj energy; (food) high-calorie. **énergie** nf energy; (Tech) power. **énergique** adj energetic.

énervant, ~e /enervā, -t/ adj irritating, annoying.

énerver /enerve/ ① vt irritate. □ s'~ vpr get worked up.

enfance /āfās/ nf childhood; la petite ~ infancy.

enfant /āfā/ nmf child. **enfantillage** nm childishness. **enfantin**, ~e adj simple, easy; (puéril) childish; (jeu, langage) children's.

enfer /āfer/ nm (Relig) Hell; (fig) hell.

enfermer /āferme/ ① vt shut up. □ s'~ vpr shut oneself up.

enfiler /āfile/ ① vt (aiguille) thread; (vêtement) slip on; (rue) take.

enfin /āfē/ adv (de soulagement) at last; (en dernier lieu) finally; (résignation, conclusion) well; ~ presque well nearly.

enflammé, ~e /āflame/ adj (Méd) inflamed; (discours) fiery; (lettre) passionate.

enflammer /āflame/ ① vt set fire to. □ s'~ vpr catch fire.

enfler /āfle/ ① vt (histoire) exaggerate. ● vi (partie du corps) swell (up); (mer) swell; (rumeur, colère) spread. □ s'~ vpr (colère) mount; (rumeur) grow.

enfoncer /āfɔse/ 10 vt (épingle) push ou drive in; (chapeau) push down; (porte) break down. ● vi sink. □ s'~ vpr sink (dans into).

enfouir /āfwir/ ② vt bury.

enfourcher /āfurʃe/ ① vt mount.

enfreindre /āfrēdr/ 22 vt infringe, break.

enfuir (s') /ɑ̃fɥiʀ/ 38 vpr run away.

enfumé, ~e /ɑ̃fyme/ adj filled with smoke.

engagé, ~e /ɑ̃ɡaʒe/ adj committed.

engagement /ɑ̃ɡaʒmɑ̃/ nm (promesse) promise; (Pol, Comm) commitment.

engager /ɑ̃ɡaʒe/ 40 vt (lier) bind, commit; (embaucher) take on; (commencer) start; (introduire) insert; (investir) invest. □ s'~ vpr (promettre) commit oneself; (commencer) start; (soldat) enlist; (concurrent) enter; s'~ à faire undertake to do; s'~ dans (voie) enter.

engelure /ɑ̃ʒlyʀ/ nf chilblain.

engendrer /ɑ̃ʒɑ̃dʀe/ 1 vt (causer) generate.

engin /ɑ̃ʒɛ̃/ nm device; (véhicule) vehicle; (missile) missile.

engloutir /ɑ̃ɡlutiʀ/ 2 vt swallow (up).

engouement /ɑ̃ɡumɑ̃/ nm passion.

engouffrer /ɑ̃ɡufʀe/ 1 vt 🗌 gobble up. □ s'~ dans vpr rush in.

engourdir /ɑ̃ɡuʀdiʀ/ 2 vt numb. □ s'~ vpr go numb.

engrais /ɑ̃ɡʀɛ/ nm manure; (chimique) fertilizer.

engrenage /ɑ̃ɡʀənaʒ/ nm gears (pl); (fig) spiral.

engueuler /ɑ̃ɡœle/ 1 🗷 vt shout at. □ s'~ vpr have a row.

enhardir (s') /(s)ɑ̃aʀdiʀ/ 2 vpr become bolder.

énième /enjɛm/ adj umpteenth.

énigmatique /enigmatik/ adj enigmatic. énigme nf enigma; (devinette) riddle.

enivrer /ɑ̃nivʀe/ 1 vt intoxicate. □ s'~ vpr get intoxicated.

enjambée /ɑ̃ʒɑ̃be/ nf stride. enjamber 1 vt step over; (pont) span.

enjeu (pl ~x) /ɑ̃ʒø/ nm stake.

enjoué, ~e /ɑ̃ʒwe/ adj cheerful.

enlacer /ɑ̃lase/ 10 vt entwine.

enlèvement /ɑ̃lɛvmɑ̃/ nm (de colis) removal; (d'ordures) collection; (rapt) kidnapping.

enlever /ɑ̃lve/ 6 vt remove (à from); (vêtement) take off; (tache, organe) take out, remove; (kidnapper) kidnap; (gagner) win.

enliser (s') /(s)ɑ̃lize/ 1 vpr get bogged down.

enneigé, ~e /ɑ̃neʒe/ adj snow-covered.

ennemi, ~e /ɛnmi/ adj & nm enemy; ~ de (fig) hostile to.

ennui /ɑ̃nɥi/ nm problem; (tracas) boredom; s'attirer des ~s run into trouble.

ennuyer /ɑ̃nɥije/ 31 vt bore; (irriter) annoy; (préoccuper) worry; si cela ne t'ennuie pas if you don't mind. □ s'~ vpr get bored.

ennuyeux, -euse /ɑ̃nɥijø, -z/ adj boring; (fâcheux) annoying.

énoncé /enɔ̃se/ nm wording, text; (Gram) utterance.

énoncer /enɔ̃se/ 10 vt express, state.

enorgueillir (s') /(s)ɑ̃nɔʀɡœjiʀ/ 2 vpr s'~ de pride oneself on.

énorme /enɔʀm/ adj enormous.

enquête /ɑ̃kɛt/ nf (Jur) investigation, inquiry; (sondage) survey; mener l'~ lead the inquiry. enquêter 1 vi ~ (sur) investigate. enquêteur, -euse nm, f investigator.

enquiquinant, ~e /ɑ̃kikinɑ̃, -t/ adj 🗌 irritating.

enraciné, ~e /ɑ̃ʀasine/ adj deep rooted.

enragé, ~e /ɑ̃ʀaʒe/ adj furious; (chien) rabid; (fig) fanatical.

enrager /ɑ̃ʀaʒe/ 40 vi be furious; faire ~ qn annoy sb.

enregistrement /ɑ̃ʀ(ə)ʒistʀəmɑ̃/ nm recording; (des bagages) check-in. **enregistrer** 1 vt (Mus, TV) record; (mémoriser) take in; (bagages) check in.

enrhumer (s') /(s)ɑ̃ʀyme/ 1 vpr catch a cold.

enrichir /ɑ̃ʀiʃiʀ/ 2 vt enrich. □ s'~ vpr grow rich(er). **enrichissant**, ~e adj (expérience) rewarding.

enrober /ɑ̃ʀɔbe/ 1 vt coat (de with).

enrôler /ɑ̃ʀole/ 1 vt recruit. □ s'~ vpr enlist, enrol.

enroué, ~e /ɑ̃ʀwe/ adj hoarse.

enrouler /ɑ̃ʀule/ 1 vt wind, wrap. □ s'~ vpr wind; s'~ dans une couverture roll oneself up in a blanket.

ensanglanté, ~e /ɑ̃sɑ̃glɑ̃te/ adj bloodstained.

enseignant, ~e /ɑ̃sɛɲɑ̃, -t/ nm, f teacher. ●adj teaching.

enseigne /ɑ̃sɛɲ/ nf sign.

enseignement /ɑ̃sɛɲəmɑ̃/ nm (profession) teaching; (instruction) education.

enseigner /ɑ̃sɛɲe/ 1 vt/i teach; ~ qch à qn teach sb sth.

ensemble /ɑ̃sɑ̃bl/ adv together. ●nm group; (Mus) ensemble; (vêtements) outfit; (cohésion) unity; (maths) set; dans l'~ on the whole; d'~ (idée) general; l'~ de (totalité) all of, the whole of.

ensevelir /ɑ̃səvliʀ/ 2 vt bury.

ensoleillé, ~e /ɑ̃sɔleje/ adj sunny.

ensorceler /ɑ̃sɔʀsəle/ 38 vt bewitch.

ensuite /ɑ̃sɥit/ adv next, then; (plus tard) later.

ensuivre (s') /(s)ɑ̃sɥivʀ/ 57 vpr follow; et tout ce qui s'ensuit and all the rest of it.

entaille /ɑ̃taj/ nf cut; (profonde) gash; (encoche) notch.

entamer /ɑ̃tame/ 1 vt start; (inciser) cut into; (ébranler) shake.

entasser /ɑ̃tase/ 1 vt (livres) pile; (argent) hoard; (personnes) cram (dans into). □ s'~ vpr (objets) pile up (dans into); (personnes) squeeze (dans into).

entendement /ɑ̃tɑ̃dmɑ̃/ nm understanding; ça dépasse l'~ it's beyond belief.

entendre /ɑ̃tɑ̃dʀ/ 3 vt hear; (comprendre) understand; (vouloir dire) mean; ~ parler de hear of; ~ dire que hear that. □ s'~ vpr (être d'accord) agree; s'~ (bien) get on (avec with); cela s'entend of course.

entendu, ~e /ɑ̃tɑ̃dy/ adj (convenu) agreed; (sourire, air) knowing; bien ~ of course; (c'est) ~! all right!

entente /ɑ̃tɑ̃t/ nf understanding; bonne ~ good relationship.

enterrement /ɑ̃teʀmɑ̃/ nm funeral.

enterrer /ɑ̃teʀe/ 1 vt bury.

en-tête /ɑ̃tɛt/ nm heading; à ~ headed.

entêté, ~e /ɑ̃tete/ adj stubborn. **entêtement** nm stubbornness. **entêter (s')** 1 vpr persist (à, dans in).

enthousiasme /ɑ̃tuzjasm/ nm enthusiasm. **enthousiasmer** 1 vt fill with enthusiasm. **enthousiaste** adj enthusiastic.

enticher (s') /(s)ɑ̃tiʃe/ 1 vpr s'~ de become infatuated with.

entier, -ière /ɑ̃tje, -jɛʀ/ adj whole; (absolu) absolute; (entêté) unyielding. ●nm whole; en ~ entirely.

entonnoir /ɑ̃tɔnwaʀ/ nm funnel; (trou) crater.

entorse /ɑ̃tɔʀs/ nf sprain; (fig) ~ à (loi) infringement of.

entortiller /ɑ̃tɔʀtije/ **1** vt wind, wrap (autour around); (duper 1) get round.

entourage /ɑ̃tuʀaʒ/ nm circle of family and friends; (bordure) surround.

entouré, ~e /ɑ̃tuʀe/ adj (personne) supported.

entourer /ɑ̃tuʀe/ **1** vt surround (de with); (réconforter) rally round; ~ qch de mystère shroud sth in mystery.

entracte /ɑ̃tʀakt/ nm interval.

entraide /ɑ̃tʀɛd/ nf mutual aid. **entraider (s')** **1** vpr help each other.

entrain /ɑ̃tʀɛ̃/ nm zest, spirit.

entraînement /ɑ̃tʀɛnmɑ̃/ nm (Sport) training.

entraîner /ɑ̃tʀene/ **1** vt (emporter) carry away; (provoquer) lead to; (Sport) train; (actionner) drive. □ s'~ vpr train. **entraîneur** nm trainer.

entrave /ɑ̃tʀav/ nf hindrance. en**traver** **1** vt hinder.

entre /ɑ̃tʀ(ə)/ prép between; (parmi) among(st); ~ autres among other things; l'un d'~ nous/eux one of us/them.

entrebâillé, ~e /ɑ̃tʀəbaje/ adj ajar, half-open.

entrechoquer (s') /(s)ɑ̃tʀə ʃɔke/ **1** vpr knock against each other.

entrecôte /ɑ̃tʀəkot/ nf rib steak.

entrecouper /ɑ̃tʀəkupe/ **1** vt ~ de intersperse with.

entrecroiser (s') /(s)ɑ̃tʀə kʀwaze/ **1** vpr (routes) intertwine.

entrée /ɑ̃tʀe/ nf entrance; (vesti-bule) hall; (accès) admission, entry; (billet) ticket; (Culin) starter; (Ordi-nat) tapez sur E~ press Enter; '~ interdite' 'no entry'.

entrejambes /ɑ̃tʀəʒɑ̃b/ nm crotch.

entremets /ɑ̃tʀəmɛ/ nm dessert.

entremise /ɑ̃tʀəmiz/ nf interven-tion; par l'~ de through.

entreposer /ɑ̃tʀəpoze/ **1** vt store.

entrepôt /ɑ̃tʀəpo/ nm warehouse.

entreprenant, ~e /ɑ̃tʀəpʀənɑ̃, -t/ adj (actif) enterprising; (séduc-teur) forward.

entreprendre /ɑ̃tʀəpʀɑ̃dʀ/ **50** vt start on, undertake; (personne) but-tonhole; ~ de faire undertake to do.

entrepreneur /ɑ̃tʀəpʀənœʀ/ nm (de bâtiment) contractor; (chef d'entreprise) firm manager.

entreprise /ɑ̃tʀəpʀiz/ nf (projet) undertaking; (société) firm, busi-ness, company.

entrer /ɑ̃tʀe/ **1** vi (aux être) go in, enter; (venir) come in, enter; ~ dans go ou come into, enter; (club) join; ~ en collision collide (avec with); faire ~ (personne) show in; laisser ~ let in; ~ en guerre go to war. ● vt (données) enter.

entre-temps /ɑ̃tʀətɑ̃/ adv meanwhile.

entretenir /ɑ̃tʀət(ə)niʀ/ **58** vt (ap-pareil) maintain; (vêtement) look after; (alimenter) (feu) keep going; (amitié) keep alive; ~ qn de con-verse with sb about. □ s'~ vpr speak (de about; avec to). **entre-tien** nm maintenance; (discussion) talk; (pour un emploi) interview.

entrevoir /ɑ̃tʀəvwaʀ/ **63** vt make out; (brièvement) glimpse.

entrevue /ɑ̃tʀəvy/ nf meeting.

entrouvert, ~e /ɑ̃truvɛr, -t/ *adj* ajar, half-open.

énumération /enymerasjɔ̃/ *nf* enumeration. **énumérer** 14 *vt* enumerate.

envahir /ɑ̃vair/ 2 *vt* invade, overrun; (*douleur, peur*) overcome.

enveloppe /ɑ̃vlɔp/ *nf* envelope; (*emballage*) wrapping; ~ budgetaire budget. **envelopper** 1 *vt* wrap (up); (fig) envelop.

envergure /ɑ̃vɛrgyr/ *nf* wingspan; (*importance*) scope; (*qualité*) calibre.

envers /ɑ̃vɛr/ *prép* toward(s), to.
● *nm* (de tissu) wrong side; à l'~ (*tableau*) upside down; (*devant derrière*) back to front; (*chaussette*) inside out.

envie /ɑ̃vi/ *nf* urge; (*jalousie*) envy; avoir ~ de qch feel like sth; avoir ~ de faire want to do; (*moins urgent*) feel like doing; faire ~ à qn make sb envious.

envier /ɑ̃vje/ 45 *vt* envy. **envieux, -leuse** *adj* envious.

environ /ɑ̃virɔ̃/ *adv* about.

environnant, ~e /ɑ̃virɔnɑ̃, -t/ *adj* surrounding.

environnement /ɑ̃virɔnmɑ̃/ *nm* environment.

environs /ɑ̃virɔ̃/ *nmpl* vicinity; aux ~ de (*lieu*) in the vicinity of; (*heure*) round about.

envisager /ɑ̃vizaʒe/ 40 *vt* consider; (*imaginer*) envisage; ~ de faire consider doing.

envoi /ɑ̃vwa/ *nm* dispatch; (*paquet*) consignment; faire un ~ send; coup d'~ (Sport) kick-off.

envoler (s') /(s)ɑ̃vɔle/ 1 *vpr* fly away; (*avion*) take off; (*papiers*) blow away.

envoyé, ~e /ɑ̃vwaje/ *nm, f* envoy; ~ spécial special correspondent.

envoyer /ɑ̃vwaje/ 32 *vt* send; (lancer) throw.

éolienne /eɔljɛn/ *nf* windmill; ferme d'~s wind farm.

épais, ~se /epɛ, -s/ *adj* thick.
épaisseur *nf* thickness.

épaissir /epesir/ 2 *vt/i* thicken.
□ s'~ *vpr* thicken; (*mystère*) deepen.

épanoui, ~e /epanwi/ *adj* (*personne*) beaming, radiant.

épanouir (s') /(s)epanwir/ 2 *vpr* (*fleur*) open out; (*visage*) beam; (*personne*) blossom. **épanouissement** *nm* (*éclat*) blossoming, full bloom.

épargne /eparɲ/ *nf* savings.

épargner /eparɲe/ 1 *vt/i* save; (ne pas tuer) spare; ~ qch à qn spare sb sth.

éparpiller /eparpije/ 1 *vt* scatter.
□ s'~ *vpr* scatter; (fig) dissipate one's efforts.

épars, ~e /epar, -s/ *adj* scattered.

épatant, ~e /epatɑ̃, -t/ *adj* 1 amazing.

épaule /epol/ *nf* shoulder.

épave /epav/ *nf* wreck.

épée /epe/ *nf* sword.

épeler /eple/ 6 *vt* spell.

éperdu, ~e /eperdy/ *adj* wild, frantic.

éperon /eprɔ̃/ *nm* spur.

éphémère /efemɛr/ *adj* ephemeral.

épi /epi/ *nm* (de blé) ear; (*mèche*) tuft of hair; ~ de maïs corn cob.

épice /epis/ *nf* spice. **épicé,** ~e *adj* spicy.

épicerie /episri/ *nf* grocery shop; (produits) groceries. **épicier, -lère** *nm, f* grocer.

épidémie /epidemi/ *nf* epidemic.

épiderme /epidɛrm/ *nm* skin.

épier /epje/ 45 *vt* spy on.

épilepsie /epilɛpsi/ nf epilepsy. **épileptique** adj & nmf epileptic.

épiler /epile/ **1** vt remove unwanted hair from; (sourcils) pluck.

épilogue /epilɔg/ nm epilogue; (fig) outcome.

épinard /epinaʀ/ nm ∼s spinach (+ sg).

épine /epin/ nf thorn, prickle; (d'animal) prickle, spine; ∼ dorsale backbone. **épineux, -euse** adj thorny.

épingle /epɛ̃gl/ nf pin; ∼ de nourrice, ∼ de sûreté safety-pin.

épisode /epizɔd/ nm episode; à ∼s serialized.

épitaphe /epitaf/ nf epitaph.

épluche-légumes /eplyʃlegym/ nm inv (potato) peeler.

éplucher /eplyʃe/ **1** vt peel; (examiner: fig) scrutinize.

épluchure /eplyʃyʀ/ nf ∼s peelings.

éponge /epɔ̃ʒ/ nf sponge. **éponger** **40** vt (liquide) mop up; (surface, front) mop; (fig) (dettes) wipe out.

épopée /epɔpe/ nf epic.

époque /epɔk/ nf time, period; à l'∼ at the time; d'∼ period.

épouse /epuz/ nf wife.

épouser /epuze/ **1** vt marry; (forme, idée) adopt.

épousseter /epuste/ **38** vt dust.

épouvantable /epuvɑ̃tabl/ adj appalling.

épouvantail /epuvɑ̃taj/ nm scarecrow.

épouvante /epuvɑ̃t/ nf terror. **épouvanter** **1** vt terrify.

époux /epu/ nm husband; les ∼ the married couple.

éprendre (s') /(s)epʀɑ̃dʀ/ **50** vpr s'∼ de fall in love with.

épreuve /epʀœv/ nf test; (Sport)

event; (malheur) ordeal; (Photo, d'imprimerie) proof; mettre à l'∼ put to the test.

éprouver /epʀuve/ **1** vt (ressentir) experience; (affliger) distress; (tester) test.

éprouvette /epʀuvɛt/ nf test tube.

EPS abrév f (**éducation physique et sportive**) PE.

épuisé, ∼e /epɥize/ adj exhausted; (livre) out of print. **épuisement** nm exhaustion.

épuiser /epɥize/ **1** vt (fatiguer, user) exhaust. □ **s'∼** vpr become exhausted.

épuration /epyʀasjɔ̃/ nf purification; (Pol) purge. **épurer** **1** vt purify; (Pol) purge.

équateur /ekwatœʀ/ nm equator.

équilibre /ekilibʀ/ nm balance; être ou se tenir en ∼ (personne) balance; (objet) be balanced. **équilibré, ∼e** adj well-balanced.

équilibrer /ekilibʀe/ **1** vt balance. □ **s'∼** vpr balance each other.

équilibriste /ekilibʀist/ nmf acrobat.

équipage /ekipaʒ/ nm crew.

équipe /ekip/ nf team; ∼ de nuit/ jour night/day shift.

équipé, ∼e /ekipe/ adj equipped; cuisine ∼e fitted kitchen.

équipement /ekipmɑ̃/ nm equipment; ∼s (installations) amenities, facilities.

équiper /ekipe/ **1** vt equip (de with). □ **s'∼** vpr equip oneself.

équipier, -ière /ekipje, -jɛʀ/ nm, f team member.

équitable /ekitabl/ adj fair.

équitation /ekitasjɔ̃/ nf (horse-) riding.

équivalence /ekivalɑ̃s/ nf equivalence. **équivalent**, ∼e *adj* equivalent.

équivaloir /ekivalwaʀ/ 60 *vi* ∼ à be equivalent to.

équivoque /ekivɔk/ *adj* equivocal; (louche) questionable. ● *nf* ambiguity.

érable /eʀabl/ *nm* maple.

érafler /eʀafle/ 1 *vt* scratch. **éraflure** *nf* scratch.

éraillé, ∼e /eʀɑje/ *adj* (voix) raucous.

ère /ɛʀ/ *nf* era.

éreintant, ∼e /eʀɛ̃tɑ̃, -t/ *adj* exhausting. **éreinter (s')** 1 *vpr* wear oneself out.

ériger 40 *vt* erect. □ **s'**∼ **en** *vpr* set (oneself) up as.

éroder /eʀɔde/ 1 *vt* erode. **érosion** *nf* erosion.

errer /eʀe/ 1 *vi* wander.

erreur /eʀœʀ/ *nf* mistake, error; **dans l'**∼ mistaken; **par** ∼ by mistake; ∼ **judiciaire** miscarriage of justice.

erroné, ∼e /eʀɔne/ *adj* erroneous.

érudit, ∼e /eʀydi, -t/ *adj* scholarly. ● *nm, f* scholar.

éruption /eʀypsjɔ̃/ *nf* eruption; (Méd) rash.

es /ɛ/ →**ÊTRE** 4.

escabeau (*pl* ∼**x**) /ɛskabo/ *nm* step-ladder.

escadron /ɛskadʀɔ̃/ *nm* (Mil) company.

escalade /ɛskalad/ *nf* climbing; (Pol, Comm) escalation. **escalader** 1 *vt* climb.

escale /ɛskal/ *nf* (d'avion) stopover; (port) port of call; **faire** ∼ à (avion, passager) stop over at; (navire, passager) put in at.

escalier /ɛskalje/ *nm* stairs (+ *pl*); ∼ **mécanique** *ou* **roulant** escalator.

escalope /ɛskalɔp/ *nf* escalope.

escargot /ɛskaʀɡo/ *nm* snail.

escarpé, ∼e /ɛskaʀpe/ *adj* steep.

escarpin /ɛskaʀpɛ̃/ *nm* court shoe; (US) pump.

escient: **à bon** ∼ /abɔnesjɑ̃/ *loc* wisely.

esclandre /ɛsklɑ̃dʀ/ *nm* scene.

esclavage /ɛsklavaʒ/ *nm* slavery. **esclave** *nmf* slave.

escompte /ɛskɔ̃t/ *nm* discount. **escompter** 1 *vt* expect; (Comm) discount.

escorte /ɛskɔʀt/ *nf* escort.

escrime /ɛskʀim/ *nf* fencing.

escroc /ɛskʀo/ *nm* swindler.

escroquer /ɛskʀoke/ 1 *vt* swindle; ∼ **qch** à **qn** swindle sb out of sth. **escroquerie** *nf* swindle.

espace /ɛspas/ *nm* space; ∼s **verts** gardens and parks.

espacer /ɛspase/ 10 *vt* space out. □ **s'**∼ *vpr* become less frequent.

espadrille /ɛspadʀij/ *nf* rope sandal.

Espagne /ɛspaɲ/ *nf* Spain.

espagnol, ∼e /ɛspaɲɔl/ *adj* Spanish. ● *nm* (Ling) Spanish. **E**∼, ∼e *nm, f* Spaniard.

espèce /ɛspɛs/ *nf* kind, sort; (race) species; **en** ∼s (*argent*) in cash; ∼ **d'idiot!** 1 you idiot! 1.

espérance /ɛspeʀɑ̃s/ *nf* hope.

espérer /ɛspeʀe/ 14 *vt* hope for; ∼ **faire/que** hope to do/that. ● *vi* hope.

espiègle /ɛspjɛɡl/ *adj* mischievous.

espion, ∼e /ɛspjɔ̃, -ɔn/ *nm, f* spy. **espionnage** *nm* espionage, spying. **espionner** 1 *vt* spy (on).

espoir /ɛspwaʀ/ *nm* hope; **reprendre** ∼ feel hopeful again.

esprit /ɛspʀi/ *nm* (intellect) mind; (humour) wit; (fantôme) spirit; (ambiance) atmosphere; **perdre l'~** lose one's mind; **reprendre ses ~s** come to; **faire de l'~** try to be witty.

esquimau, **~de** (mpl **~x**) /ɛskimo, -d/ nm, f Eskimo.

esquinter /ɛskɛ̃te/ **1** vt **1** ruin.

esquisse /ɛskis/ nf sketch; (fig) outline.

esquiver /ɛskive/ **1** vt dodge. □ **s'~** vpr slip away.

essai /esɛ/ nm (épreuve) test, trial; (tentative) try; (article) essay; (au rugby) try; **~s** (Auto) qualifying round (+ sg); **à l'~** on trial.

essaim /esɛ̃/ nm swarm.

essayage /esɛjaʒ/ nm fitting; **salon d'~** fitting room.

essayer /eseje/ **31** vt/i try; (vêtement) try (on); (voiture) try (out); **~ de faire** try to do.

essence /esɑ̃s/ nf (carburant) petrol; (nature, extrait) essence; **~ sans plomb** unleaded petrol.

essentiel, **~le** /esɑ̃sjɛl/ adj essential. ● nm **l'~** the main thing; (quantité) the main part.

essieu (pl **~x**) /esjø/ nm axle.

essor /esɔr/ nm expansion; **prendre son ~** expand.

essorage /esɔraʒ/ nm spin drying.

essorer /esɔre/ **1** vt (linge) spin-dry; (en tordant) wring.

essoreuse /esɔrøz/ nf spin-drier; **~ à salade** salad spinner.

essoufflé, **~e** /esufle/ adj out of breath.

essuie-glace /esɥiglas/ nm inv windscreen wiper.

essuie-mains /esɥimɛ̃/ nm inv hand-towel.

essuie-tout /esɥitu/ nm inv kitchen paper.

essuyer /esɥije/ **31** vt wipe; (subir)

suffer. □ **s'~** vpr dry ou wipe oneself.

est[1] /ɛ/ ➡ÊTRE **4**.

est[2] /ɛst/ nm east. ● adj inv east; (partie) eastern; (direction) easterly.

estampe /ɛstɑ̃p/ nf print.

esthète /ɛstɛt/ nmf aesthete.

esthéticienne /ɛstetisjɛn/ nf beautician.

esthétique /ɛstetik/ adj aesthetic.

estimation /ɛstimasjɔ̃/ nf (de coûts) estimate; (valeur) valuation.

estime /ɛstim/ nf esteem.

estimer /ɛstime/ **1** vt (tableau) value; (calculer) estimate; (respecter) esteem; (considérer) consider (que that).

estival, **~e** (mpl **-aux**) /ɛstival, -o/ adj summer. **estivant**, **~e** nm, f summer visitor.

estomac /ɛstɔma/ nm stomach.

estomaqué, **~e** /ɛstɔmake/ adj **1** stunned.

Estonie /ɛstɔni/ nf Estonia.

estrade /ɛstrad/ nf platform.

estragon /ɛstragɔ̃/ nm tarragon.

estropié, **~e** /ɛstrɔpje/ nm, f cripple. ● adj crippled.

estuaire /ɛstɥɛr/ nm estuary.

et /e/ conj and; **~ moi?** what about me?; **~ alors?** so what?

étable /etabl/ nf cow-shed.

établi, **~e** /etabli/ adj established; **un fait bien ~** a well-established fact. ● nm work-bench.

établir /etablir/ **2** vt establish; (liste, facture) draw up; (personne, camp, record) set up. □ **s'~** vpr (personne) settle; **s'~ à son compte** set up on one's own.

établissement /etablismɑ̃/ nm (entreprise) organization; (institution) establishment; **~ scolaire** school.

étage /etaʒ/ *nm* floor, storey; (de fusée) stage; à l'∼ upstairs; au premier ∼ on the first floor.

étagère /etaʒεʀ/ *nf* shelf; (meuble) shelving unit.

étain /etɛ̃/ *nm* pewter.

étais, était /etε/ ➡ÊTRE ◢.

étalage /etalaʒ/ *nm* display; (vitrine) shop-window; faire ∼ de flaunt. **étalagiste** *nmf* window-dresser.

étaler /etale/ ◢ *vt* spread; (journal) spread (out); (pâte) roll out; (exposer) display; (richesse) flaunt. □ s'∼ *vpr* (prendre de la place) spread out; (tomber ⓵) fall flat; s'∼ sur (paiement) be spread over.

étalon /etalɔ̃/ *nm* (cheval) stallion; (modèle) standard.

étanche /etɑ̃ʃ/ *adj* watertight; (montre) waterproof.

étancher /etɑ̃ʃe/ ◢ *vt* (soif) quench.

étang /etɑ̃/ *nm* pond.

étant /etɑ̃/ ➡ÊTRE ◢.

étape /etap/ *nf* stage; (lieu d'arrêt) stopover; (fig) stage.

état /eta/ *nm* state; (liste) statement; (métier) profession; en bon/mauvais ∼ in good/bad condition; en ∼ de in a position to; en ∼ de marche in working order; faire ∼ de (citer) mention; être dans tous ses ∼s be in a state; ∼ civil civil status; ∼ des lieux inventory of fixtures. **État** *nm* State.

état-major (*pl* états-majors) /etamaʒɔʀ/ *nm* (officiers) staff (+ *pl*).

États-Unis /etazyni/ *nmpl* ∼ (d'Amérique) United States (of America).

étau (*pl* ∼x) /eto/ *nm* vice.

étayer /eteje/ ⾼ *vt* prop up.

été¹ /ete/ ➡ÊTRE ◢.

été² /ete/ *nm* summer.

éteindre /etɛ̃dʀ/ ㉒ *vt* (feu) put out; (lumière, radio) turn off. □ s'∼ *vpr* (feu, lumière) go out; (appareil) go off; (mourir) die. **éteint, ∼e** *adj* (feu) out; (volcan) extinct.

étendard /etɑ̃daʀ/ *nm* standard.

étendre /etɑ̃dʀ/ 🟦 *vt* (nappe) spread (out); (bras, jambes) stretch (out); (linge) hang out; (agrandir) extend. □ s'∼ *vpr* (s'allonger) lie down; (se propager) spread; (plaine) stretch; s'∼ sur (sujet) dwell on.

étendu, ∼e /etɑ̃dy/ *adj* extensive. **étendue** *nf* area; (d'eau) stretch; (importance) extent.

éternel, ∼le /etεʀnεl/ *adj* (vie) eternal; (fig) endless.

éterniser (s') /(s)etεʀnize/ ◢ *vpr* (durer) drag on.

éternité /etεʀnite/ *nf* eternity.

éternuement /etεʀnymɑ̃/ *nm* sneeze. **éternuer** ◢ *vi* sneeze.

êtes /εt/ ➡ÊTRE ◢.

éthique /etik/ *adj* ethical. ●*nf* ethics (+ *sg*).

ethnie /εtni/ *nf* ethnic group. **ethnique** *adj* ethnic.

étincelant, ∼e /etɛ̃slɑ̃, -t/ *adj* sparkling. **étinceler** ㊳ *vi* sparkle. **étincelle** *nf* spark.

étiqueter /etikte/ ㊳ *vt* label. **étiquette** *nf* label; (protocole) etiquette.

étirer /etire/ ◢ *vt* stretch. □ s'∼ *vpr* stretch.

étoffe /etɔf/ *nf* fabric.

étoffer /etɔfe/ ◢ *vt* expand. □ s'∼ *vpr* fill out.

étoile /etwal/ *nf* star; à la belle ∼ in the open; ∼ filante shooting star; ∼ de mer starfish.

étonnant, ∼e /etɔnɑ̃, -t/ *adj* (curieux) surprising; (formidable) amazing. **étonnement** *nm* surprise; (plus fort) amazement.

étonner /etɔne/ **1** vt amaze. □ s'~ vpr be amazed de (de at).

étouffant, ~e /etufɑ̃, -t/ adj stifling.

étouffer /etufe/ **1** vt/i suffocate; (sentiment, révolte) stifle; (feu) smother; (bruit) muffle; on étouffe it is stifling. □ s'~ vpr suffocate; (en mangeant) choke.

étourderie /eturdəri/ nf thoughtlessness; (acte) careless mistake.

étourdi, ~e /eturdi/ adj absent-minded. ● nm, f scatterbrain.

étourdir /eturdir/ **2** vt stun; (fatiguer) make sb's head spin. **étourdissant**, ~e adj stunning.

étourneau (pl ~x) /eturno/ nm starling.

étrange /etrɑ̃ʒ/ adj strange.

étranger, -ère /etrɑ̃ʒe, -ɛʀ/ adj (inconnu) strange, unfamiliar; (d'un autre pays) foreign. ● nm, f foreigner; (inconnu) stranger; à l'~ abroad; de l'~ from abroad.

étrangler /etrɑ̃gle/ **1** vt strangle; (col) throttle. □ s'~ vpr choke.

être /ɛtr/ **4**
● verbe auxiliaire
····▸ (du passé) have; elle est partie/venue hier she left/came yesterday.
····▸ (de la voix passive) be.
● verbe intransitif (aux avoir)
····▸ be; ~ médecin be a doctor; je suis à vous I'm all yours; j'en suis à me demander si... I'm beginning to wonder whether...; qu'en est-il de...? what's the news about...?
····▸ (appartenance) be, belong to.
····▸ (heure, date) be; nous sommes le 3 mars it's March 3.

····▸ (aller) be; je n'y ai jamais été I've never been; il a été le voir he went to see him.
····▸ c'est it is or it's; c'est moi qui l'ai fait I did it; est-ce que tu veux du thé? do you want some tea?
● nom masculin
····▸ being; ~ humain human being.
····▸ (personne) person; un ~ cher a loved one.

étreindre /etrɛ̃dr/ **22** vt embrace.

étreinte nf embrace.

étrennes /etrɛn/ nfpl (New Year's) gift (+ sg); (argent) money.

étrier /etrije/ nm stirrup.

étriqué, ~e /etrike/ adj tight.

étroit, ~e /etrwa, -t/ adj narrow; (vêtement) tight; (liens, surveillance) close; à l'~ cramped. **étroitement** adv closely. **étroitesse** nf narrowness.

étude /etyd/ nf study; (enquête) survey; (bureau) office; (salle d')~ (Scol) prep room; à l'~ under consideration; faire des ~s (de) study; il n'a pas fait d'~s he didn't go to university; ~ de marché market research.

étudiant, ~e /etydjɑ̃, -t/ nm, f student.

étudier /etydje/ **45** vt/i study.

étui /etɥi/ nm case.

étuve /etyv/ nf steam room.

eu, ~e /y/ →AVOIR **5**.

euro /øro/ nm euro.

Europe /ørɔp/ nf Europe.

européen, ~ne /ørɔpeɛ̃, -ɛɛn/ adj European. **E~**, ~ne nm, f European.

euthanasie /øtanazi/ nf euthanasia.

eux /ø/ pron they; (complément) them. **eux-mêmes** pron themselves.

évacuation /evakyasjɔ̃/ nf evacuation; (d'eaux usées) discharge. **évacuer** ◨ vt evacuate.

évadé, ~e /evade/ adj escaped. ●nm, f escaped prisoner. **évader (s')** ◨ vpr escape.

évaluation /evalyasjɔ̃/ nf assessment. **évaluer** ◨ vt assess.

évangile /evãʒil/ nm gospel; l'É~ the Gospel.

évanouir (s') /(s)evanwir/ ◨ vpr faint; (disparaître) vanish.

évaporation /evapɔrasjɔ̃/ nf evaporation. **évaporer (s')** ◨ vpr evaporate.

évasif, -ive /evazif, -v/ adj evasive.

évasion /evazjɔ̃/ nf escape.

éveil /evɛj/ nm awakening; en ~ alert.

éveillé, ~e /eveje/ adj awake; (intelligent) alert.

éveiller /eveje/ ◨ vt awake(n); (susciter) arouse. □ s'~ vpr awake.

événement /evenmã/ nm event.

éventail /evãtaj/ nm fan; (gamme) range.

éventrer /evãtre/ ◨ vt (sac) rip open.

éventualité /evãtyalite/ nf possibility; dans cette ~ in that event.

éventuel, ~le /evãtɥɛl/ adj possible. **éventuellement** adv possibly.

évêque /evɛk/ nm bishop.

évertuer (s') /(s)evertɥe/ ◨ vpr s'~ à struggle hard to.

éviction /eviksjɔ̃/ nf eviction.

évidemment /evidamã/ adv obviously; (bien sûr) of course.

évidence /evidãs/ nf obviousness; (fait) obvious fact; être en ~ be conspicuous; mettre en ~ (fait) highlight. **évident, ~e** adj obvious, evident.

évier /evje/ nm sink.

évincer /evɛ̃se/ ◨ vt oust.

éviter /evite/ ◨ vt avoid (de faire doing); ~ qch à qn (dérangement) save sb sth.

évocateur, -trice /evokatœr, -tris/ adj evocative. **évocation** nf evocation.

évolué, ~e /evolɥe/ adj highly developed.

évoluer /evolɥe/ ◨ vi evolve; (situation) develop; (se déplacer) glide. **évolution** nf evolution; (d'une situation) development.

évoquer /evoke/ ◨ vt call to mind, evoke.

exacerber /ɛgzaserbe/ ◨ vt exacerbate.

exact, ~e /ɛgza(kt), -akt/ adj (précis) exact, accurate; (juste) correct; (personne) punctual. **exactement** adv exactly. **exactitude** nf exactness; punctuality.

ex æquo /ɛgzeko/ adv être ~ tie (avec qn with sb).

exagération /ɛgzaʒerasjɔ̃/ nf exaggeration. **exagéré, ~e** adj excessive.

exagérer /ɛgzaʒere/ ⒁ vt/i exaggerate; (abuser) go too far.

exalté, ~e /ɛgzalte/ nm, f fanatic. **exalter** ◨ vt excite; (glorifier) exalt.

examen /ɛgzamɛ̃/ nm examination; (Scol) exam. **examinateur, -trice** nm, f examiner. **examiner** ◨ vt examine.

exaspération /ɛgzasperasjɔ̃/ nf exasperation. **exaspérer** ⒁ vt exasperate.

exaucer /ɛgzose/ ⒑ vt grant; (personne) grant the wish(es) of.

excédent /ɛksedã/ nm surplus; ~ de bagages excess luggage; ~ de la balance commerciale trade surplus. **excédentaire** adj excess, surplus.

excéder /ɛksede/ 14 vt (dépasser) exceed; (agacer) irritate.

excellence /ɛksɛlɑ̃s/ nf excellence. **excellent, ~e** adj excellent. **exceller** 1 vi excel (dans in).

excentricité /ɛksɑ̃trisite/ nf eccentricity. **excentrique** adj & nmf eccentric.

excepté, ~e /ɛksɛpte/ adj & prép except.

excepter /ɛksɛpte/ 1 vt except.

exception /ɛksɛpsjɔ̃/ nf exception; à l'~ de except for; d'~ exceptional; faire ~ be an exception. **exceptionnel, ~le** adj exceptional. **exceptionnellement** adv exceptionally.

excès /ɛksɛ/ nm excess; ~ de vitesse speeding.

excessif, -ive /ɛksesif, -v/ adj excessive.

excitant, ~e /ɛksitɑ̃, -t/ adj stimulating; (palpitant) exciting. ● nm stimulant.

exciter /ɛksite/ 1 vt excite; (irriter) get excited. □ s'~ vpr get excited.

exclamer (s') /(s)ɛksklame/ 1 vpr exclaim.

exclure /ɛksklyʀ/ 16 vt exclude; (expulser) expel; (empêcher) preclude.

exclusif, -ive /ɛksklyzif, -v/ adj exclusive.

exclusion /ɛksklyzjɔ̃/ nf exclusion.

exclusivité /ɛksklyzivite/ nf (Comm) exclusive rights (+ pl); projeter en ~ show exclusively.

excursion /ɛkskyʀsjɔ̃/ nf excursion; (à pied) hike.

excuse /ɛkskyz/ nf excuse; ~s apology (+ sg); faire des ~s apologize.

excuser /ɛkskyze/ 1 vt excuse; excusez-moi excuse me. □ s'~ vpr

apologize (de for).

exécrable /ɛgzekʀabl/ adj dreadful. **exécrer** 14 vt loathe.

exécuter /ɛgzekyte/ 1 vt carry out, execute; (Mus) perform; (tuer) execute.

exécutif, -ive /ɛgzekytif, -v/ adj & nm (Pol) executive.

exécution /ɛgzekysjɔ̃/ nf execution; (Mus) performance.

exemplaire /ɛgzɑ̃plɛʀ/ adj exemplary. ● nm copy.

exemple /ɛgzɑ̃pl/ nm example; par ~ for example; donner l'~ set an example.

exempt, ~e /ɛgzɑ̃, -t/ adj ~ de exempt (de from).

exempter /ɛgzɑ̃te/ 1 vt exempt (de from). **exemption** nf exemption.

exercer /ɛgzɛʀse/ 10 vt exercise; (influence, contrôle) exert; (former) train, exercise; ~ un métier have a job; ~ le métier de... work as a... □ s'~ vpr practise.

exercice /ɛgzɛʀsis/ nm exercise; (de métier) practice; en ~ in office; (médecin) in practice.

exhaler /ɛgzale/ 1 vt emit.

exhaustif, -ive /ɛgzostif, -v/ adj exhaustive.

exhiber /ɛgzibe/ 1 vt exhibit.

exhorter /ɛgzɔʀte/ 1 vt exhort (à to).

exigeant, ~e /ɛgziʒɑ̃, -t/ adj demanding; être ~ avec qn demand a lot of sb. **exigence** nf demand. **exiger** 40 vt demand.

exigu, ~ë /ɛgzigy/ adj tiny.

exil /ɛgzil/ nm exile. **exilé, ~e** nm, f exile.

exiler /ɛgzile/ 1 vt exile. □ s'~ vpr go into exile.

existence /ɛgzistɑ̃s/ nf existence.

exister ◼ *vi* exist.

exode /ɛgzɔd/ *nm* exodus.

exonérer /ɛgzɔnere/ ◼ *vt* exempt (de from).

exorbitant, ~e /ɛgzɔrbitɑ̃, -t/ *adj* exorbitant.

exorciser /ɛgzɔrsize/ ◼ *vt* exorcize.

exotique /ɛgzɔtik/ *adj* exotic.

expansé, ~e /ɛkspɑ̃se/ *adj* (Tech) expanded.

expansif, -ive /ɛkspɑ̃sif, -v/ *adj* expansive. **expansion** *nf* expansion.

expatrié, ~e /ɛkspatrije/ *nm, f* expatriate.

expectative /ɛkspɛktativ/ *nf* être dans l'~ wait and see.

expédient /ɛkspedjɑ̃/ *nm* expedient; vivre d'~s live by one's wits; user d'~s resort to expedients.

expédier /ɛkspedje/ ◼ *vt* send, dispatch; (*tâche* ◼) polish off. **expéditeur, -trice** *nm, f* sender.

expéditif, -ive /ɛkspeditif, -v/ *adj* quick.

expédition /ɛkspedisjɔ̃/ *nf* (envoi) dispatching; (voyage) expedition.

expérience /ɛksperjɑ̃s/ *nf* experience; (scientifique) experiment.

expérimental, ~e *(mpl* -aux) /ɛksperimɑ̃tal, o/ *adj* experimental. **expérimentation** *nf* experimentation. **expérimenté, ~e** *adj* experienced. **expérimenter** ◼ *vt* test, experiment with.

expert, ~e /ɛkspɛr, -t/ *adj* expert. ● *nm* expert; (d'assurances) adjuster. **expert-comptable** (*pl* experts-comptables) *nm* accountant.

expertise /ɛkspɛrtiz/ *nf* valuation; (de dégâts) assessment. **expertiser** ◼ *vt* value; (dégâts) assess.

expier /ɛkspje/ ◼ *vt* atone for.

expiration /ɛkspirasjɔ̃/ *nf* expiry.

expirer /ɛkspire/ ◼ *vi* breathe out; (finir, mourir) expire.

explicatif, -ive /ɛksplikatif, -v/ *adj* explanatory.

explication /ɛksplikasjɔ̃/ *nf* explanation; (fig) discussion; ~ de texte (Scol) literary commentary.

explicite /ɛksplisit/ *adj* explicit.

expliquer /ɛksplike/ ◼ *vt* explain. □ s'~ *vpr* explain oneself; (discuter) discuss things; (être explicable) be understandable.

exploit /ɛksplwa/ *nm* exploit.

exploitant, ~e /ɛksplwatɑ̃, -t/ *nm, f* ~ (agricole) farmer.

exploitation /ɛksplwatasjɔ̃/ *nf* exploitation; (d'entreprise) running; (ferme) farm.

exploiter /ɛksplwate/ ◼ *vt* exploit; (*ferme*) run; (*mine*) work.

explorateur, -trice /ɛksplɔratœr, -tris/ *nm, f* explorer. **exploration** *nf* exploration. **explorer** ◼ *vt* explore.

exploser /ɛksploze/ ◼ *vi* explode; faire ~ explode; (*bâtiment*) blow up.

explosif, -ive /ɛksplozif, -v/ *adj & nm* explosive. **explosion** *nf* explosion.

exportateur, -trice /ɛkspɔrtatœr, -tris/ *nm, f* exporter. ● *adj* exporting. **exportation** *nf* export. **exporter** ◼ *vt* export.

exposant, ~e /ɛkspozɑ̃, -t/ *nm, f* exhibitor.

exposé, ~e /ɛkspoze/ *nm* talk (sur on); (d'une action) account; faire l'~ de la situation give an account of the situation. ● *adj* ~ au nord facing north.

exposer /ɛkspoze/ ◼ *vt* display, show; (expliquer) explain; (soumettre, mettre en danger) expose (à

e

to); (*vie*) endanger. □ **s'~ à** *vpr* expose oneself to.

exposition /ɛkspozisjɔ̃/ *nf* (d'art) exhibition; (de faits) exposition; (géographique) aspect.

exprès¹ /ɛkspRɛ/ *adv* specially; (délibérément) on purpose.

exprès², **-esse** /ɛkspRɛs/ *adj* express.

express /ɛkspRɛs/ *adj & nm inv* (café) ~ espresso; (train) ~ fast train.

expressif, **-ive** /ɛkspResif, -v/ *adj* expressive. **expression** *nf* expression.

exprimer /ɛkspRime/ **1** *vt* express. □ **s'~** *vpr* express oneself.

expulser /ɛkspylse/ **1** *vt* expel; (*locataire*) evict; (*joueur*) send off. **expulsion** *nf* (d'élève) expulsion; (de locataire) eviction; (d'immigré) deportation.

exquis, **~e** /ɛkski, -z/ *adj* exquisite.

extase /ɛkstaz/ *nf* ecstasy.

extasier (s') /(s)ɛkstazje/ **45** *vpr* **s'~ sur** be ecstatic about.

extensible /ɛkstɑ̃sibl/ *adj* (tissu) stretch.

extension /ɛkstɑ̃sjɔ̃/ *nf* extension; (expansion) expansion.

exténuer /ɛkstenɥe/ **1** *vt* exhaust.

extérieur, **~e** /ɛksteRjœR/ *adj* outside; (*signe*, *gaieté*) outward; (*politique*) foreign. ● *nm* outside, exterior; (de personne) exterior; à l'~ (de) outside. **extérioriser** **1** *vt* show, externalize.

extermination /ɛkstɛRminasjɔ̃/ *nf* extermination. **exterminer** **1** *vt* exterminate.

externe /ɛkstɛRn/ *adj* external. ● *nmf* (Scol) day pupil.

extincteur /ɛkstɛ̃ktœR/ *nm* fire extinguisher.

extinction /ɛkstɛ̃ksjɔ̃/ *nf* extinction; avoir une ~ de voix have lost one's voice.

extorquer /ɛkstɔRke/ **1** *vt* extort.

extra /ɛkstRa/ *adj inv* first-rate. ● *nm inv* (repas) (special) treat.

extraction /ɛkstRaksjɔ̃/ *nf* extraction.

extrader /ɛkstRade/ **1** *vt* extradite.

extraire /ɛkstRɛR/ **29** *vt* extract. **extrait** *nm* extract.

extraordinaire /ɛkstRaɔRdineR/ *adj* extraordinary.

extravagance /ɛkstRavagɑ̃s/ *nf* extravagance. **extravagant**, **~e** *adj* extravagant.

extraverti, **~e** /ɛkstRavɛRti/ *nm*, *f* extrovert.

extrême /ɛkstRɛm/ *adj & nm* extreme. **extrêmement** *adv* extremely.

Extrême-Orient /ɛkstRɛmɔRjɑ̃/ *nm* Far East.

extrémiste /ɛkstRemist/ *nmf* extremist.

extrémité /ɛkstRemite/ *nf* end; (mains, pieds) extremity.

exubérance /ɛgzybeRɑ̃s/ *nf* exuberance. **exubérant**, **~e** *adj* exuberant.

Ff

F *abrév* f (**franc, francs**) franc, francs.

fabricant, **~e** /fabRikɑ̃, -t/ *nm, f* manufacturer. **fabrication** *nf* making; manufacture.

fabrique /fabRik/ *nf* factory. **fabriquer** **1** *vt* make; (industriellement) manufacture; (fig) make up.

fabuler /fabyle/ **1** vi fantasize.

fabuleux, -euse /fabylø, -z/ adj fabulous.

fac /fak/ nf **1** university.

façade /fasad/ nf front; (fig) façade.

face /fas/ nf face; (d'un objet) side; en (~ de), d'en ~ opposite; en ~ de (fig) faced with; ~ à facing; (fig) faced with; **faire** ~ à face. **face-à-face** nm inv (débat) one-to-one debate.

fâcher /faʃe/ **1** vt anger; (désolé) sorry. □ **se** ~ vpr get angry; (se brouiller) fall out.

facile /fasil/ adj easy; (caractère) easygoing.

facilité /fasilite/ nf easiness; (aisance) ease; (aptitude) ability; ~s (possibilités) facilities, opportunities; ~s d'importation import opportunities; ~s de paiement easy terms.

faciliter /fasilite/ **1** vt facilitate, make easier.

façon /fasɔ̃/ nf way; (de vêtement) cut; de cette ~ in this way; de ~ à so as to; de toute ~ anyway; ~s (chichis) fuss; **faire des** ~s stand on ceremony; **sans** ~s (repas) informal; (personne) unpretentious. **façonner** **1** vt shape; (faire) make.

fac-similé (pl ~s) /faksimile/ nm facsimile.

facteur, -trice /faktœr, -tʁis/ nm, f postman, postwoman. ● nm (élément) factor.

facture /faktyʁ/ nf bill; (Comm) invoice; ~ détaillée itemized bill. **facturer** **1** vt invoice. **facturette** nf credit card slip.

facultatif, -ive /fakyltatif, -v/ adj optional.

faculté /fakylte/ nf faculty; (possi-

bilité) power; (Univ) faculty.

fade /fad/ adj insipid.

faible /fɛbl/ adj weak; (espoir, quantité, écart) slight; (revenu, intensité) low; ~ d'esprit feeble-minded. ● nm (personne) weakling; (penchant) weakness. **faiblesse** nf weakness. **faiblir** **2** vi weaken.

faïence /fajɑ̃s/ nf earthenware.

faillir /fajiʁ/ **2** vi j'ai failli acheter I almost bought.

faillite /fajit/ nf bankruptcy; (fig) collapse.

faim /fɛ̃/ nf hunger; **avoir** ~ be hungry; **rester sur sa** ~ (fig) be left wanting more.

fainéant, ~e /feneɑ̃, -t/ adj idle. ● nm, f idler.

> **faire** /fɛʁ/ **33**

➡ Pour les expressions comme faire attention, faire la cuisine, etc. ➡ attention, cuisine etc.

● verbe transitif

····▸ (préparer, créer) make; ~ une tarte/une erreur make a tart/a mistake.

····▸ (se livrer à une activité) do; ~ du droit do law; ~ du foot/ du violon play football/the violin; qu'est-ce qu'elle fait? (dans la vie) what does she do?; (en ce moment précis) what is she doing?

····▸ (dans les calculs, mesures, etc.) 10 et 10 font 20 10 and 10 make 20; ça fait 25 euros that's 25 euros; ~ 60 kilos weigh 60 kilos; **il fait 1,75 m** he's 1.75 m tall.

····▸ (dans les expressions de temps) ça fait une heure que

j'attends I have been waiting for an hour.

····▸ (imiter) ~ le clown act the clown; faire le malade pretend to be ill.

····▸ (parcourir) ~ 10 km do ou cover 10 km; ~ les musées go round the museums.

····▸ (entraîner, causer) ça ne fait rien it doesn't matter; l'accident a fait 8 morts 8 people died in the accident.

····▸ (dire) say; 'excusez-moi', fit-elle 'excuse me', she said.

● **verbe auxiliaire**

····▸ (faire + infinitif + qn) make; ~ pleurer qn make sb cry.

····▸ (faire + infinitif + qch) have, get; ~ réparer sa voiture have ou get one's car mended.

····▸ (ne faire que + infinitif) (continuellement) ne ~ que pleurer do nothing but cry; (seulement) je ne fais qu'obéir I'm only following orders.

● **verbe intransitif**

····▸ (agir) do, act; ~ vite act quickly; fais comme tu veux do as you please; fais comme chez toi make yourself at home.

····▸ (paraître) look; ~ joli look pretty; ça fait cher it's expensive.

····▸ (en parlant du temps) il fait chaud/gris it's hot/overcast.

□ **se faire** verbe pronominal

····▸ (obtenir, confectionner) make; se ~ des amis make friends; se ~ un thé make (oneself) a cup of tea.

····▸ (se faire + infinitif) se ~ gronder be scolded; se ~ couper les cheveux have one's hair cut.

····▸ (devenir) il se fait tard it's getting late.

····▸ (être d'usage) ça ne se fait pas it's not the done thing.

····▸ (emploi impersonnel) comment se fait-il que tu sois ici? how come you're here?

····▸ □ se faire à get used to; je ne m'y fais pas I can't get used to it.

····▸ □ s'en faire worry; ne t'en fais pas don't worry.

① Lorsque faire remplace un verbe plus précis, on traduira quelquefois par ce dernier: faire une visite pay a visit, faire un nid build a nest.

faire-part /fɛʀpaʀ/ nm inv announcement.

fais /fɛ/ →FAIRE ᴣᴣ.

faisan /fəzɑ̃/ nm pheasant.

faisceau (pl ~x) /fɛso/ nm (rayon) beam; (fagot) bundle.

fait, ~e /fɛ, fɛt/ adj done; (fromage) ripe; ~ pour made for; tout ~ ready-made; c'est bien ~ pour toi it serves you right. ● nm fact; (événement) event; au ~ (de) informed (of); de ce ~ therefore; du ~ de on account of; ~ divers (trivial) news item; ~ nouveau new development; prendre qn sur le ~ catch sb in the act. ● →FAIRE ᴣᴣ.

faîte /fɛt/ nm top; (fig) peak.

faites /fɛt/ →FAIRE ᴣᴣ.

falaise /falɛz/ nf cliff.

falloir /falwaʀ/ ᴣ4 vi il faut qch/qn we/you etc. need sth/sb; il lui faut du pain he needs bread; il faut rester we/you etc. have to ou must stay; il faut que j'y aille I have to ou must go; il faudrait que tu partes you should leave; il aurait fallu le faire we/you etc. should have done it; comme il faut (*manger, se tenir*) properly; (*personne*) respectable, proper. □ **s'en** ~ *vpr* il s'en est fallu de peu qu'il gagne he nearly won; il s'en faut de beaucoup que je sois I am far from being.

falsifier /falsifje/ 45 *vt* falsify; (*signature, monnaie*) forge.

famé, ~e /fame/ *adj* mal ~ disreputable, seedy.

fameux, -euse /famø, -z/ *adj* famous; (*excellent* 1) first-rate.

familial, ~e (*mpl* -iaux) /familjal, -jo/ *adj* family.

familiale /familjal/ *nf* estate car; (US) station wagon.

familiariser /familjarize/ 1 *vt* familiarize (avec with). □ **se** ~ *vpr* familiarize oneself.

familier, -ière /familje, -jɛʀ/ *adj* familiar; (*amical*) informal.

famille /famij/ *nf* family; en ~ with one's family.

famine /famin/ *nf* famine.

fanatique /fanatik/ *adj* fanatical. ● *nmf* fanatic.

fanfare /fãfaʀ/ *nf* brass band; (*musique*) fanfare.

fantaisie /fãtezi/ *nf* imagination, fantasy; (*caprice*) whim; (de) ~ (*boutons etc.*) fancy. **fantaisiste** *adj* unorthodox; (*personne*) eccentric.

fantasme /fãtasm/ *nm* fantasy.

fantastique /fãtastik/ *adj* fantastic.

fantôme /fãtom/ *nm* ghost; cabinet(-)~ (Pol) shadow cabinet.

faon /fã/ *nm* fawn.

FAQ *abrév f* (**Foire aux questions**) (Internet) FAQ, Frequently Asked Questions.

farce /faʀs/ *nf* (practical) joke; (Théât) farce; (hachis) stuffing.

farcir /faʀsiʀ/ 2 *vt* stuff.

fard /faʀ/ *nm* make-up; ~ à paupières eye-shadow; piquer un ~ blush.

fardeau (*pl* ~x) /faʀdo/ *nm* burden.

farfelu, ~e /faʀfǝly/ *adj & nm,f* eccentric.

farine /faʀin/ *nf* flour. **farineux**, -euse *adj* floury. **farineux** *nmpl* starchy food.

farouche /faʀuʃ/ *adj* shy; (peu sociable) unsociable; (*violent*) fierce.

fascicule /fasikyl/ *nm* (brochure) booklet; (partie d'un ouvrage) fascicule.

fasciner /fasine/ 1 *vt* fascinate.

fascisme /faʃism/ *nm* fascism.

fasse /fas/ →FAIRE 33.

fast-food /fastfud/ *nm* fast-food place.

fastidieux, -ieuse /fastidjø, -z/ *adj* tedious.

fatal, ~e (*mpl* ~s) /fatal/ *adj* inevitable; (*mortel*) fatal. **fatalité** *nf* (*destin*) fate.

fatigant, ~e /fatigã, -t/ *adj* tiring; (*ennuyeux*) tiresome.

fatigue /fatig/ *nf* fatigue, tiredness.

fatigué, ~e /fatige/ *adj* tired.

fatiguer /fatige/ 1 *vt* tire; (*yeux, moteur*) strain. ● *vi* (*moteur*) labour. □ **se** ~ *vpr* get tired, tire (de of).

faubourg /fobuʀ/ *nm* suburb.

faucher /foʃe/ 1 *vt* (*herbe*) mow; (voler 1) pinch; ~ qn (*véhicule, tir*) mow sb down.

faucon /fokõ/ *nm* falcon, hawk.

faudra, faudrait /fodʀa, fodʀɛ/ →FALLOIR 34.

faufiler (se) /(sa)fofile/ 1 *vpr* edge one's way, squeeze.

faune /fon/ *nf* wildlife, fauna.

faussaire /fosɛʀ/ *nmf* forger.

fausse /fos/ →**FAUX**².

fausser /fose/ **1** *vt* buckle; (fig) distort; ~ **compagnie à qn** give sb the slip.

faut /fo/ →**FALLOIR** 34.

faute /fot/ *nf* mistake; (responsabilité) fault; (délit) offence; (péché) sin; **en** ~ at fault; ~ **de** for want of; ~ **de quoi** failing which; **sans** ~ without fail; ~ **de frappe** typing error; ~ **de goût** bad taste; ~ **professionnelle** professional misconduct.

fauteuil /fotœj/ *nm* armchair; (de président) chair; (Théât) seat; ~ **roulant** wheelchair.

fautif, -ive /fotif, -v/ *adj* guilty; (faux) faulty. ● *nm, f* guilty party.

fauve /fov/ *adj* (couleur) fawn, tawny. ● *nm* wild cat.

faux¹ /fo/ *nf* scythe.

faux², fausse /fo, fos/ *adj* false; (falsifié) fake, forged; (numéro, calcul) wrong; (voix) out of tune; **c'est** ~! that is wrong!; ~ **témoignage** perjury; **faire** ~ **bond à qn** stand sb up; **fausse couche** miscarriage; ~ **frais** incidental expenses. ● *adv* (chanter) out of tune. ● *nm* forgery. **faux-filet** (*pl* ~**s**) *nm* sirloin.

faveur /favœʀ/ *nf* favour; **de** ~ (régime) preferential; **en** ~ **de** in favour of.

favorable /favɔʀabl/ *adj* favourable.

favori, ~te /favɔʀi, -t/ *adj & nm.f* favourite. **favoriser** **1** *vt* favour.

fax /faks/ *nm* fax. **faxer** **1** *vt* fax.

fébrile /febʀil/ *adj* feverish.

fécond, ~e /fekɔ̃, -d/ *adj* fertile. **féconder** **1** *vt* fertilize. **fécondité** *nf* fertility.

fédéral, ~e (*mpl* -**aux**) /federal, -o/ *adj* federal. **fédération** *nf* federation.

fée /fe/ *nf* fairy. **féerie** *nf* magical spectacle. **féerique** *adj* magical.

feindre /fɛ̃dʀ/ 22 *vt* feign; ~ **de** pretend to.

fêler /fele/ **1** *vt* crack. □ **se** ~ *vpr* crack.

félicitations /felisitasjɔ̃/ *nfpl* congratulations (**pour** on). **féliciter** **1** *vt* congratulate (**de** on).

félin, ~e /felɛ̃, -in/ *adj & nm* feline.

femelle /fəmɛl/ *adj & nf* female.

féminin, ~e /feminɛ̃, -in/ *adj* feminine; (sexe) female; (mode, équipe) women's. ● *nm* feminine. **féministe** *nmf* feminist.

femme /fam/ *nf* woman; (épouse) wife; ~ **au foyer** housewife; ~ **de chambre** chambermaid; ~ **de ménage** cleaning lady.

fémur /femyʀ/ *nm* thigh-bone.

fendre /fɑ̃dʀ/ **3** *vt* (couper) split; (fissurer) crack. □ **se** ~ *vpr* crack.

fenêtre /fənɛtʀ/ *nf* window.

fenouil /fənuj/ *nm* fennel.

fente /fɑ̃t/ *nf* (ouverture) slit, slot; (fissure) crack.

féodal, ~e (*mpl* -**aux**) /feodal, -o/ *adj* feudal.

fer /fɛʀ/ *nm* iron; ~ (**à repasser**) iron; ~ **à cheval** horseshoe; ~ **de lance** spearhead; ~ **forgé** wrought iron.

fera, ferait /fəʀa, fəʀɛ/ →**FAIRE** 33.

férié, ~e /feʀje/ *adj* **jour** ~ public holiday.

ferme /fɛʀm/ *nf* farm; (maison) farm(house); ~ **éolienne** wind farm. ● *adj* firm. ● *adv* (travailler) hard.

fermé, ~e /fɛʀme/ *adj* closed; (gaz, radio) off.

fermenter /fɛʀmɑ̃te/ **1** *vi* ferment.

fermer /fɛʀme/ **1** *vt/i* close, shut;

(cesser d'exploiter) close ou shut down; (gaz, robinet) turn off. □ se ~ vpr close, shut.

fermeté /fɛʀməte/ nf firmness.

fermeture /fɛʀmətyʀ/ nf closing; (dispositif) catch; ~ **annuelle** annual closure; ~ **éclair**® zip(-fastener); (US) zipper.

fermier, **-ière** /fɛʀmje, -jɛʀ/ nm farm. ● nm farmer. **fermière** nf farmer's wife.

féroce /feʀɔs/ adj ferocious.

ferraille /feʀɑj/ nf scrap-iron.

ferrer /feʀe/ **1** vt (cheval) shoe.

ferroviaire /feʀɔvjɛʀ/ adj rail(way).

ferry /feʀi/ nm ferry.

fertile /fɛʀtil/ adj fertile; ~ **en** (fig) rich in. **fertiliser** **1** vt fertilize. **fertilité** nf fertility.

fervent, ~**e** /fɛʀvɑ̃, -t/ adj fervent. ● nm, f enthusiast (de of).

fesse /fɛs/ nf buttock. **fessée** nf spanking, smack.

festin /fɛstɛ̃/ nm feast.

festival (pl ~**s**) /fɛstival/ nm festival.

fêtard, ~**e** /fɛtaʀ, -d/ nm, f 🅴 party animal.

fête /fɛt/ nf holiday; (religieuse) feast; (du nom) name-day; (réception) party; (en famille) celebration; (foire) fair; (folklorique) festival; ~ **des Mères** Mother's Day; ~ **foraine** fun-fair; **faire la** ~ live it up; **les** ~**s** (de fin d'année) the Christmas season. **fêter** **1** vt celebrate; (personne) give a celebration for.

fétiche /fetiʃ/ nm fetish; (fig) mascot.

feu¹ (pl ~**x**) /fø/ nm fire; (lumière) light; (de réchaud) burner; à ~ **doux/vif** on a low/high heat; ~ **rouge/vert/orange** red/green/amber light; **aux** ~**x, tournez à**

droite turn right at the traffic lights; **avez-vous du** ~? (pour cigarette) have you got a light?; **au** ~! fire!; **mettre le** ~ **à** set fire to; **prendre** ~ catch fire; **jouer avec le** ~ play with fire; **ne pas faire long** ~ not last; ~ **d'artifice** firework display; ~ **de joie** bonfire; ~ **de position** sidelight.

feu² /fø/ adj inv (mort) late.

feuillage /fœjaʒ/ nm foliage.

feuille /fœj/ nf leaf; (de papier) sheet; (formulaire) form; ~ **d'impôts** tax return; ~ **de paie** payslip.

feuilleté, ~**e** /fœjte/ adj **pâte** ~ puff pastry. ● nm savoury pasty.

feuilleter /fœjte/ **1** vt leaf through.

feuilleton /fœjtɔ̃/ nm (à suivre) serial; (histoire complète) series.

feutre /føtʀ/ nm felt; (chapeau) felt hat; (crayon) felt-tip (pen).

fève /fɛv/ nf broad bean.

février /fevʀije/ nm February.

fiable /fjabl/ adj reliable.

fiançailles /fjɑ̃sɑj/ nfpl engagement.

fiancé, ~**e** /fjɑ̃se/ adj engaged. ● nm fiancé. **fiancée** nf fiancée.

fiancer (se) **10** vpr become engaged (avec to).

fibre /fibʀ/ nf fibre; ~ **de verre** fibreglass.

ficeler /fisle/ **38** vt tie up.

ficelle /fisɛl/ nf string.

fiche /fiʃ/ nf (index) card; (formulaire) form, slip; (Électr) plug.

ficher¹ /fiʃe/ **1** vt (enfoncer) drive (dans into).

ficher² /fiʃe/ **1** 🅸 vt (faire) do; (donner) give; (mettre) put; ~ **le camp** clear off. □ se ~ **de** vpr make fun of; **il s'en fiche** he couldn't care less.

f

fichier /fiʃje/ nm file.

fichu, ~e /fiʃy/ adj 🔢 (mauvais) rotten; (raté) done for; mal ~ terrible.

fictif, -ive /fiktif, -v/ adj fictitious. **fiction** nf fiction.

fidèle /fidɛl/ adj faithful. ● nmf (client) regular; (Relig) believer; ~s (à l'église) congregation. **fidélité** nf fidelity.

fier¹, **fière** /fjɛʀ/ adj proud (de of).

fier²(se) /(sə)fje/ 🔢 vpr se ~ à trust.

fierté /fjɛʀte/ nf pride.

fièvre /fjɛvʀ/ nf fever; avoir de la ~ have a temperature; ~ aphteuse foot-and-mouth disease. **fiévreux, -euse** adj feverish.

figer /fiʒe/ 🔢 vi (graisse) congeal; (sang) clot; figé sur place frozen to the spot. □ se ~ vpr (personne, sourire) freeze; (graisse) congeal; (sang) clot.

figue /fig/ nf fig.

figurant, ~e /figyʀɑ̃, -t/ nm, f (au cinéma) extra.

figure /figyʀ/ nf face; (forme, personnage) figure; (illustration) picture.

figuré, ~e /figyʀe/ adj (sens) figurative.

figurer /figyʀe/ 🔢 vi appear. ● vt represent. □ se ~ vpr imagine.

fil /fil/ nm thread; (métallique, électrique) wire; (de couteau) edge; (à coudre) cotton; au ~ de with the passing of; au ~ de l'eau with the current; ~ de fer wire; au bout du ~ 🔢 on the phone.

file /fil/ nf line; (voie: Auto) lane; ~ (d'attente) queue; (US) line; en ~ indienne in single file.

filer /file/ 🔢 vt spin; (suivre) shadow; ~ qch à qn 🔢 slip sb sth. ● vi (bas) ladder, run; (liquide) run;

(aller vite 🔢) speed along, fly by; (partir 🔢) dash off; (disparaître 🔢) ~ entre les mains slip through one's fingers; ~ doux do as one's told.

filet /filɛ/ nm net; (d'eau) trickle; (de viande) fillet; ~ (à bagages) (luggage) rack; ~ à provisions string bag (for shopping).

filiale /filjal/ nf subsidiary (company).

filière /filjɛʀ/ nf (official) channels; (de trafiquants) network; passer par ou suivre la ~ (employé) work one's way up.

fille /fij/ nf girl; (opposé à fils) daughter. **fillette** nf little girl.

filleul /fijœl/ nm godson.

filleule /fijœl/ nf god-daughter.

film /film/ nm film; ~ d'épouvante/muet/parlant horror/silent/talking film; ~ dramatique drama. **filmer** 🔢 vt film.

filon /filɔ̃/ nm (Géol) seam; (travail lucratif 🔢) money spinner; avoir trouvé le bon ~ be onto a good thing.

fils /fis/ nm son.

filtre /filtʀ/ nm filter. **filtrer** 🔢 vt/i filter; (personne) screen.

fin¹ /fɛ̃/ nf end; à la ~ finally; en ~ de compte all things considered; ~ de semaine weekend; mettre ~ à put an end to; prendre ~ come to an end.

fin², ~e /fɛ̃, fin/ adj fine; (tranche, couche) slim; (taille) slim; (plat) exquisite; (esprit, vue) sharp; ~es herbes mixed herbs. ● adv (couper) finely.

final, ~e (mpl -aux) /final, -o/ adj final.

finale /final/ nm (Mus) finale. ● nf (Sport) final; (Gram) final syllable.

finalement adv finally; (somme

toute) after all. **finaliste** *nmf* finalist.

finance /finɑ̃s/ *nf* finance. **financer** [10] *vt* finance.

financier, -ière /finɑ̃sje, -jɛʀ/ *adj* financial. ● *nm* financier.

finesse /fines/ *nf* fineness; (de taille) slimness; (acuité) sharpness; ~s (de langue) niceties.

finir /finiʀ/ [2] *vt/i* finish, end; (arrêter) stop; (manger) finish (up); en ~ avec have done with; ~ par faire end up doing; ça va mal ~ it will turn out badly.

finlandais, ~e /fɛ̃lɑ̃dɛ, -z/ *adj* Finnish. F~, ~e *nm, f* Finn.

Finlande /fɛ̃lɑ̃d/ *nf* Finland.

finnois, ~e /finwa/ *adj* Finnish. ● *nm* (Ling) Finnish.

firme /fiʀm/ *nf* firm.

fisc /fisk/ *nm* tax authorities. **~e** /-z/ (*mpl* -**aux**) *adj* tax, fiscal. **fiscalité** *nf* tax system.

fissure /fisyʀ/ *nf* crack.

FIV *abrév f* (**fécondation in vitro**) IVF.

fixe /fiks/ *adj* fixed; (stable) steady; à heure ~ at a set time; menu à prix ~ set menu. ● *nm* basic pay.

fixer /fikse/ [1] *vt* fix; (du regard) stare at; être fixé (*personne*) have made up one's mind. □ **se** ~ *vpr* (s'attacher) be attached; (s'installer) settle down.

flacon /flakɔ̃/ *nm* bottle.

flagrant, ~e /flagʀɑ̃, -t/ *adj* flagrant, blatant; en ~ délit in the act.

flair /flɛʀ/ *nm* (sense of) smell; (fig) intuition.

flamand, ~e /flamɑ̃, -d/ *adj* Flemish. ● *nm* (Ling) Flemish. F~, ~e *nm, f* Fleming.

flamant /flamɑ̃/ *nm* flamingo.

flambeau (*pl* ~x) /flɑ̃bo/ *nm* torch.

flambée /flɑ̃be/ *nf* blaze; (fig) explosion.

flamber /flɑ̃be/ [1] *vi* blaze; (*prix*) shoot up. ● *vt* (*aiguille*) sterilize; (*volaille*) singe.

flamme /flam/ *nf* flame; (fig) ardour; en ~s ablaze.

flan /flɑ̃/ *nm* custard tart.

flanc /flɑ̃/ *nm* side; (d'animal, d'armée) flank.

flâner /flɑne/ [1] *vi* stroll. **flânerie** *nf* stroll.

flanquer /flɑ̃ke/ [1] *vt* flank; (jeter [1]) chuck; (donner [1]) give; ~ à la porte kick out.

flaque /flak/ *nf* (d'eau) puddle; (de sang) pool.

flash (*pl* ~**es**) /flaʃ/ *nm* (Photo) flash; (information) news flash; ~ publicitaire commercial.

flatter /flate/ [1] *vt* flatter. □ **se** ~ **de** *vpr* pride oneself on.

flatteur, -euse /flatœʀ, -øz/ *adj* flattering. ● *nm, f* flatterer.

fléau (*pl* ~x) /fleo/ *nm* (désastre) scourge; (personne) pest.

flèche /flɛʃ/ *nf* arrow; (de clocher) spire; monter en ~ spiral; partir en ~ shoot off.

flécher /fleʃe/ [14] *vt* mark *ou* signpost (with arrows). **fléchette** *nf* dart.

fléchir /fleʃiʀ/ [2] *vt* bend; (*personne*) move, sway. ● *vi* (faiblir) weaken; (*prix*) fall; (*poutre*) sag, bend.

flemme /flɛm/ *nf* [1] laziness; j'ai la ~ de faire I can't be bothered doing.

flétrir (se) /(sə)fletʀiʀ/ [2] *vpr* (*plante*) wither; (*fruit*) shrivel; (*beauté*) fade.

fleur /flœʀ/ *nf* flower; à ~ de terre/d'eau just above the ground/

water; à ~s flowery; ~ de l'âge prime of life; en ~s in flower.

fleurir /flœʀiʀ/ **②** vi flower; (arbre) blossom; (fig) flourish. ● vt decorate with flowers. **fleuriste** nmf florist.

fleuve /flœv/ nm river.

flic /flik/ nm **□** cop.

flipper /flipœʀ/ nm pinball (machine).

flirter /flœʀte/ **①** vi flirt.

flocon /flɔkɔ̃/ nm flake.

flore /flɔʀ/ nf flora.

florissant, ~e /flɔʀisɑ̃, -t/ adj flourishing.

flot /flo/ nm flood, stream; être à ~ be afloat; les ~s the waves.

flottant, ~e /flɔtɑ̃, -t/ adj (vêtement) loose; (indécis) indecisive.

flotte /flɔt/ nf fleet; (pluie **□**) rain; (eau **□**) water.

flottement /flɔtmɑ̃/ nm (incertitude) indecision.

flotter /flɔte/ **①** vi float; (drapeau) flutter; (nuage, parfum, pensées) drift; (pleuvoir **□**) rain. **flotteur** nm float.

flou, ~e /flu/ adj out of focus; (fig) vague.

fluctuer /flyktɥe/ **①** vi fluctuate.

fluet, ~te /flɥɛ, -t/ adj thin.

fluide /flɥid/ adj & nm fluid.

fluor /flyɔʀ/ nm (pour les dents) fluoride.

fluorescent, ~e /flyɔʀesɑ̃, -t/ adj fluorescent.

flûte /flyt/ nf flute; (verre) champagne glass.

fluvial, ~e (mpl -iaux) /flyvjal, -jo/ adj river.

flux /fly/ nm flow; ~ et reflux ebb and flow.

FM abrév f (**frequency modulation**) FM.

fœtus /fetys/ nm foetus.

foi /fwa/ nf faith; être de bonne/ mauvaise ~ be acting in good/bad faith; ma ~! well (indeed)!

foie /fwa/ nm liver.

foin /fwɛ̃/ nm hay.

foire /fwaʀ/ nf fair; faire la ~ **□** live it up.

fois /fwa/ nf time; une ~ once; deux ~ twice; à la ~ at the same time; des ~ (parfois) sometimes; une ~ pour toutes once and for all.

fol /fɔl/ ➡FOU.

folie /fɔli/ nf madness; (bêtise) foolish thing, folly; faire une ~, faire des ~s be extravagant.

folklore /fɔlklɔʀ/ nm folklore. **folklorique** adj folk; **□** eccentric.

folle /fɔl/ ➡FOU.

foncé, ~e /fɔ̃se/ adj dark.

foncer /fɔ̃se/ **⑩** vt darken. ● vi (s'assombrir) darken; (aller vite **□**) dash away; ~ sur **□** charge at.

foncier, -ière /fɔ̃sje, -jɛʀ/ adj fundamental; (Comm) real estate.

fonction /fɔ̃ksjɔ̃/ nf function; (emploi) position; ~s (obligations) duties; en ~ de according to; ~ publique civil service; voiture de ~ company car. **fonctionnaire** nmf civil servant. **fonctionnement** nm working.

fonctionner /fɔ̃ksjɔne/ **①** vi work; faire ~ work.

fond /fɔ̃/ nm bottom; (de salle, magasin, etc.) back; (essentiel) basis; (contenu) content; (plan) background; (Sport) long-distance running; à ~ thoroughly; au ~ basically; de ~ (bruit) background; de ~ en comble from top to bottom; au ou dans le ~ really; ~ de teint foundation, make-up base.

fondamental, ~e (mpl -aux) /fɔ̃damɑ̃tal, -o/ adj fundamental.

fondateur, -trice /fɔ̃datœʀ, -tʀis/ nm, f founder. **fondation** nf foundation.

fonder /fɔ̃de/ **1** vt found; (baser) base (**sur** on); (**bien**) **fondé** wellfounded. □ **se ~ sur** vpr be guided by, be based on.

fonderie /fɔ̃dʀi/ nf foundry.

fondre /fɔ̃dʀ/ **3** vt/i melt; (dans l'eau) dissolve; (mélanger) merge; **faire ~** melt; dissolve; **~ en larmes** burst into tears; **~ sur** swoop on. □ **se ~** vpr merge.

fonds /fɔ̃/ nm fund; **~ de commerce** business. ● nmpl (capitaux) funds.

fondu, **~e** /fɔ̃dy/ adj melted; (métal) molten.

font /fɔ̃/ ➡FAIRE **33**.

fontaine /fɔ̃tɛn/ nf fountain; (source) spring.

fonte /fɔ̃t/ nf melting; (fer) cast iron; **~ des neiges** thaw.

foot /fut/ nm **1** football.

football /futbɔl/ nm football.

footing /futiŋ/ nm jogging.

forain /fɔʀɛ̃/ nm fairground entertainer; **marchand ~** stallholder.

forçat /fɔʀsa/ nm convict.

force /fɔʀs/ nf force; (physique) strength; (hydraulique etc.) power; **~s** (physiques) strength; **à ~ de** by sheer force of; **de ~, par la ~** by force; **~ de dissuasion** deterrent; **~ de frappe** strike force, deterrent; **~ de l'âge** prime of life; **~s de l'ordre** police (force) ; **~s de marché** market forces.

forcé, **~e** /fɔʀse/ adj forced; (inévitable) inevitable; **c'est ~ qu'il fasse 1** he's bound to do. **forcément** adv necessarily; (évidemment) obviously.

forcené, **~e** /fɔʀsəne/ adj frenzied. ● nm, f maniac.

forcer /fɔʀse/ **10** vt force (à faire to do); (voix) strain; **~ la dose 1** overdo it. ● vi force; (exagérer) overdo it. □ **se ~** vpr force oneself.

forer /fɔʀe/ **1** vt drill.

forestier, -ière /fɔʀɛstje, -jɛʀ/ adj forest. ● nm, f forestry worker.

forêt /fɔʀɛ/ nf forest.

forfait /fɔʀfɛ/ nm (Comm) (prix fixe) fixed price; (offre promotionnelle) package. **forfaitaire** adj (prix) fixed.

forger /fɔʀʒe/ **40** vt forge; (inventer) make up.

forgeron /fɔʀʒəʀɔ̃/ nm blacksmith.

formaliser (se) /(sə)fɔʀmalize/ **1** vpr take offence (de at).

formalité /fɔʀmalite/ nf formality.

format /fɔʀma/ nm format. **formater 1** vt (Ordinat) format.

formation /fɔʀmasjɔ̃/ nf formation; (professionnelle) training; (culture) education; **~ permanente** ou **continue** continuing education.

forme /fɔʀm/ nf form; (contour) shape, form; **~s** (de femme) figure; **être en ~** be in good shape, be on form; **en ~ de** in the shape of; **en bonne et due ~** in due form.

formel, **~le** /fɔʀmɛl/ adj formal; (catégorique) positive.

former /fɔʀme/ **1** vt form; (instruire) train. □ **se ~** vpr form.

formidable /fɔʀmidabl/ adj fantastic.

formulaire /fɔʀmylɛʀ/ nm form.

formule /fɔʀmyl/ nf formula; (expression) expression; (feuille) form; **~ de politesse** polite phrase, letter ending. **formuler 1** vt formulate.

fort, **~e** /fɔʀ, -t/ adj strong; (grand) big; (pluie) heavy; (bruit) loud; (pente) steep; (élève) clever; **au plus ~ de** at the height of; **c'est une ~e tête** she/he's headstrong. ● adv (*frapper*) hard; (*parler*) loud; (*très*) very; (*beaucoup*) very much. ● *nm* (*atout*) strong point; (Mil) fort.

fortifiant /fɔʀtifjɑ̃/ *nm* tonic. **fortifier** 45 *vt* fortify.

fortune /fɔʀtyn/ *nf* fortune; de ∼ (*improvisé*) makeshift; faire ∼ make one's fortune.

forum /fɔʀɔm/ *nm* forum; ∼ de discussion (Internet) newsgroup.

fosse /fos/ *nf* pit; (*tombe*) grave; ∼ d'orchestre orchestra pit; ∼ septique septic tank.

fossé /fose/ *nm* ditch; (fig) gulf; ∼ numérique digital divide.

fossette /fosɛt/ *nf* dimple.

fossile /fosil/ *nm* fossil.

fou (**fol** before vowel or mute h), **folle** /fu, fɔl/ *adj* mad; (*course, regard*) wild; (*énorme* 🔢) tremendous; ∼ de crazy about; le ∼ rire the giggles. ● *nm* madman; (*bouffon*) jester. **folle** *nf* madwoman.

foudre /fudʀ/ *nf* lightning.

foudroyant, ∼e /fudʀwajɑ̃, -t/ *adj* (*mort, maladie*) violent.

foudroyer /fudʀwaje/ 31 *vt* (*orage*) strike; (*maladie etc.*) strike down; ∼ qn du regard look daggers at sb.

fouet /fwɛ/ *nm* whip; (Culin) whisk.

fougère /fuʒɛʀ/ *nf* fern.

fougue /fug/ *nf* ardour. **fougueux, -euse** *adj* ardent.

fouille /fuj/ *nf* search; (Archéol) excavation.

fouiller /fuje/ 1 *vt/i* search; (*creuser*) dig; ∼ dans (*tiroir*) rummage through.

fouillis /fuji/ *nm* jumble.

foulard /fulaʀ/ *nm* scarf.

foule /ful/ *nf* crowd; une ∼ de (fig) a mass of.

foulée /fule/ *nf* stride; il l'a fait dans la ∼ he did it while he was at ou about it.

fouler /fule/ 1 *vt* (*raisin*) press; (*sol*) set foot on; ∼ qch aux pieds trample sth underfoot; (fig) ride roughshod over sth. □ se ∼ *vpr* se ∼ le poignet/le pied sprain one's wrist/foot; ne pas se 🔢 not strain oneself.

four /fuʀ/ *nm* oven; (*de potier*) kiln; (Théât) flop; ∼ à micro-ondes microwave oven; ∼ crématoire crematorium.

fourbe /fuʀb/ *adj* deceitful.

fourche /fuʀʃ/ *nf* fork; (à foin) pitchfork. **fourchette** *nf* fork; (Comm) bracket, range.

fourgon /fuʀgɔ̃/ *nm* van.

fourmi /fuʀmi/ *nf* ant; avoir des ∼s have pins and needles.

fourmiller /fuʀmije/ 1 *vi* swarm (with).

fourneau (*pl* ∼x) /fuʀno/ *nm* stove.

fourni, ∼e /fuʀni/ *adj* (*épais*) thick.

fournir /fuʀniʀ/ 2 *vt* supply, provide; (*client*) supply; (*effort*) put in; ∼ à qn supply sb with. □ se ∼ chez *vpr* shop at.

fournisseur /fuʀnisœʀ/ *nm* supplier; ∼ d'accès à l'Internet Internet service provider.

fourniture /fuʀnityʀ/ *nf* supply.

fourrage /fuʀaʒ/ *nm* fodder.

fourré, ∼e /fuʀe/ *adj* (*vêtement*) fur-lined; (*gâteau etc.*) filled (*with* jam, cream, etc.). ● *nm* thicket.

fourre-tout /fuʀtu/ *nm inv* (*sac*) holdall.

fourreur /fuʀœʀ/ *nm* furrier.

fourrière /fuʀjɛʀ/ *nf* (*lieu*) pound.

fourrure /fuʀyʀ/ *nf* fur.

foutre /futʀ/ 3 *vt* ☒= ficher² 1.

foutu, ~e /futy/ adj 🅇 = fichu.

foyer /fwaje/ nm home; (âtre) hearth; (club) club; (d'étudiants) hostel; (Théât) foyer; (Photo) focus; (centre) centre.

fracas /fraka/ nm din; (de train) roar; (d'objet qui tombe) crash. **fracassant,** ~e adj (bruyant) deafening; (violent) shattering.

fraction /fraksjɔ̃/ nf fraction.

fracture /fraktyʀ/ nf fracture; ~ du poignet fractured wrist.

fragile /fraʒil/ adj fragile; (peau) sensitive; (cœur) weak. **fragilité** nf fragility.

fragment /fragmã/ nm bit, fragment. **fragmenter** 🛈 vt split, fragment.

fraîchement /fʀɛʃmã/ adv (récemment) freshly; (avec froideur) coolly. **fraîcheur** nf coolness; (nouveauté) freshness. **fraîchir** 🛾 vi freshen, become colder.

frais¹, fraîche /fʀɛ, -ʃ/ adj fresh; (temps, accueil) cool; (peinture) wet; ~ et dispos fresh; il fait ~ it is cool. ● adv (récemment) newly, freshly. ● nm mettre au ~ put in a cool place; prendre le ~ get some fresh air.

frais² /fʀɛ/ nmpl expenses; (droits) fees; aux ~ de at the expense of; faire des ~ spend a lot of money; ~ généraux (Comm) overheads, running expenses; ~ de scolarité school fees.

fraise /fʀɛz/ nf strawberry. **fraisier** nm strawberry plant; (gâteau) strawberry gateau.

framboise /fʀɑ̃bwaz/ nf raspberry. **framboisier** nm raspberry bush.

franc, franche /fʀɑ̃, -ʃ/ adj frank; (regard) frank, candid; (cassure) clean; (net) clear; (libre) free; (véritable) downright. ● nm franc.

français, ~e /fʀɑ̃sɛ, -z/ adj French. ● nm (Ling) French. F~, ~e nm, f Frenchman, Frenchwoman.

France /fʀɑ̃s/ nf France.

franchement /fʀɑ̃ʃmã/ adv frankly; (nettement) clearly; (tout à fait) really.

franchir /fʀɑ̃ʃiʀ/ 🛾 vt (obstacle) get over; (distance) cover; (limite) exceed; (traverser) cross.

franchise /fʀɑ̃ʃiz/ nf (qualité) frankness; (Comm) franchise; (exemption) exemption; ~ douanière exemption from duties.

franc-maçon (pl francs-maçons) /fʀɑ̃maʃɔ̃/ nm Freemason. **franc-maçonnerie** nf Freemasonry.

franco /fʀɑ̃ko/ adv postage paid.

francophone /fʀɑ̃kɔfɔn/ adj French-speaking. ● nmf French speaker.

franc-parler /fʀɑ̃paʀle/ nm inv outspokenness.

frange /fʀɑ̃ʒ/ nf fringe.

frappe /fʀap/ nf (de texte) typing.

frappé, ~e /fʀape/ adj chilled.

frapper /fʀape/ 🛈 vt/i strike; (battre) hit, strike; (monnaie) mint; (à la porte) knock, bang; frappé de panique panic-stricken.

fraternel, ~le /fʀatɛʀnɛl/ adj brotherly. **fraternité** nf brotherhood.

fraude /fʀod/ nf fraud; (à un examen) cheating; passer qch en ~ smuggle sth in. **frauder** vt/i cheat. **frauduleux, -euse** adj fraudulent.

frayer /fʀeje/ 🛨 vt open up. □ se ~ vpr se ~ un passage force one's way (à travers, dans through).

frayeur /fʀejœʀ/ nf fright.

fredonner /fʀadɔne/ 🛈 vt hum.

free-lance /fʀilɑ̃s/ adj & nmf freelance.

freezer /fʁizœʁ/ *nm* freezer.

frein /fʁɛ̃/ *nm* brake; mettre un ~ à curb; ~ à main hand brake.

freiner /fʁene/ **1** *vt* slow down; (modérer, enrayer) curb. ● *vi* (Auto) brake.

frêle /fʁɛl/ *adj* frail.

frelon /fʁəlɔ̃/ *nm* hornet.

frémir /fʁemiʁ/ **2** *vi* shudder, shake; (feuille, eau) quiver.

frêne /fʁɛn/ *nm* ash.

frénésie /fʁenezi/ *nf* frenzy. **frénétique** *adj* frenzied.

fréquemment /fʁekamɑ̃/ *adv* frequently. **fréquence** *nf* frequency. **fréquent, ~e** *adj* frequent. **fréquentation** *nf* frequenting.

fréquentations /fʁekɑ̃tasjɔ̃/ *nfpl* acquaintances; avoir de mauvaises ~ keep bad company.

fréquenter /fʁekɑ̃te/ **1** *vt* frequent; (école) attend; (personne) see.

frère /fʁɛʁ/ *nm* brother.

fret /fʁɛt/ *nm* freight.

friand, ~e /fʁijɑ̃, -d/ *adj* ~ de very fond of. **friandise** /fʁijɑ̃diz/ *nf* sweet; (US) candy; (gâteau) cake.

fric /fʁik/ *nm* 🔟 money.

friction /fʁiksjɔ̃/ *nf* friction; (massage) rub-down.

frigidaire ® /fʁiʒidɛʁ/ *nm* refrigerator.

frigo /fʁigo/ *nm* 🔟 fridge. **frigorifique** *adj* (vitrine etc.) refrigerated.

frileux, -euse /fʁilø, -z/ *adj* sensitive to cold.

frime /fʁim/ *nf* 🔟 c'est de la ~ it's all pretence; pour la ~ for show.

frimousse /fʁimus/ *nf* face.

fringale /fʁɛ̃gal/ *nf* 🔟 ravenous appetite.

fringant, ~e /fʁɛ̃gɑ̃, -t/ *adj* dashing.

fringues /fʁɛ̃g/ *nfpl* 🔟 gear.

friper /fʁipe/ **1** *vt* crumple, crease. □ se ~ *vpr* crumple, crease.

fripon, ~ne /fʁipɔ̃, -ɔn/ *nm, f* rascal. ● *adj* mischievous.

fripouille /fʁipuj/ *nf* rogue.

frire /fʁiʁ/ 🔢 *vt/i* fry; faire ~ fry.

frise /fʁiz/ *nf* frieze.

friser /fʁize/ **1** *vt/i* (cheveux) curl; (personne) curl the hair of; frisé curly.

frisson /fʁisɔ̃/ *nm* (de froid) shiver; (de peur) shudder. **frissonner** **1** *vi* shiver; shudder.

frit, ~e /fʁi, -t/ *adj* fried.

frite /fʁit/ *nf* chip; avoir la ~ 🔟 feel good.

friteuse /fʁitøz/ *nf* chip pan; (électrique) (deep) fryer.

friture /fʁityʁ/ *nf* fried fish; (huile) (frying) oil ou fat.

frivole /fʁivɔl/ *adj* frivolous.

froid, ~e /fʁwa, -d/ *adj & nm* cold; avoir/prendre ~ be/catch cold; il fait ~ it is cold. **froidement** *adv* coldly; (calculer) coolly. **froideur** *nf* coldness.

froisser /fʁwase/ **1** *vt* crumple; (fig) offend. □ se ~ *vpr* crumple; (fig) take offence; se ~ un muscle strain a muscle.

frôler /fʁole/ **1** *vt* brush against, skim; (fig) come close to.

fromage /fʁɔmaʒ/ *nm* cheese.

fromager, -ère /fʁɔmaʒe, -ɛʁ/ *adj* cheese. ● *nm, f* (fabricant) cheesemaker; (marchand) cheesemonger.

froment /fʁɔmɑ̃/ *nm* wheat.

froncer /fʁɔ̃se/ 🔟 *vt* gather; ~ les sourcils frown.

front /fʁɔ̃/ *nm* forehead; (Mil, Pol) front; de ~ at the same time; (de face) head-on; (côte à côte) abreast; faire ~ à face up to. **frontal, ~e** (mpl **-aux**) adj frontal; (Ordinat) front-end.

frontalier, -ière /frɔ̃talje, -jɛʀ/ adj border; travailleur ~ commuter from across the border.

frontière /frɔ̃tjɛʀ/ nf border, frontier.

frottement /frɔtmɑ̃/ nm rubbing; (Tech) friction. **frotter** [1] vt/i rub; (allumette) strike.

frottis /frɔti/ nm ~ vaginal cervical smear.

frousse /frus/ nf [1] fear; avoir la ~ [1] be scared.

fructifier /fryktifje/ [45] vi faire ~ put to work.

fructueux, -euse /fryktɥø, -z/ adj fruitful.

frugal, ~e (mpl **-aux**) /frygal, -o/ adj frugal.

fruit /frɥi/ nm fruit; des ~s (some) fruit; ~s de mer seafood. **fruité, ~e** adj fruity.

frustrant, ~e /frystrɑ̃, -t / adj frustrating. **frustrer** [1] vt frustrate.

fuel /fjul/ nm fuel oil.

fugitif, -ive /fyʒitif, -v/ adj (passager) fleeting. ● nm, f fugitive.

fugue /fyg/ nf (Mus) fugue; faire une ~ run away.

fuir /fɥiʀ/ [35] vi flee, run away; (eau, robinet, etc.) leak. ● vt (quitter) flee; (éviter) shun.

fuite /fɥit/ nf flight; (de liquide, d'une nouvelle) leak; en ~ on the run; mettre en ~ put to flight; prendre la ~ take flight.

fulgurant, ~e /fylgyrɑ̃, -t / adj (vitesse) lightning.

fumé, ~e /fyme/ adj (poisson, verre) smoked.

fumée /fyme/ nf smoke; (vapeur) steam.

fumer /fyme/ [1] vt/i smoke.

fumeur, -euse /fymœr, -øz/ nm, f smoker; zone non-~s no smoking area.

fumier /fymje/ nm manure.

funambule /fynɑ̃byl/ nmf tightrope walker.

funèbre /fynɛbʀ/ adj funeral; (fig) gloomy.

funérailles /fyneʀaj/ nfpl funeral.

funéraire /fyneʀɛʀ/ adj funeral.

funeste /fynɛst/ adj fatal.

fur: au ~ et à mesure /ofyʀeamøzyʀ/ loc as one goes along, progressively; **au ~ et à mesure que** as.

furet /fyʀɛ/ nm ferret.

fureur /fyʀœʀ/ nf fury; (passion) passion; avec ~ furiously; passionately; mettre en ~ infuriate; faire ~ be all the rage.

furieux, -ieuse /fyʀjø, -z/ adj furious.

furoncle /fyʀɔ̃kl/ nm boil.

furtif, -ive /fyʀtif, -v/ adj furtive.

fuseau (pl **~x**) /fyzo/ nm ski trousers; (pour filer) spindle; ~ horaire time zone.

fusée /fyze/ nf rocket.

fusible /fyzibl/ nm fuse.

fusil /fyzi/ nm rifle, gun; (de chasse) shotgun; ~ mitrailleur machine-gun.

fusion /fyzjɔ̃/ nf fusion; (Comm) merger. **fusionner** [1] vt/i merge.

fut /fy/ ⇒ÊTRE [5].

fût /fy/ nm (tonneau) barrel; (d'arbre) trunk.

futé, ~e /fyte/ adj cunning.

futile /fytil/ adj futile.

futur, ~e /fytyʀ/ adj future; ~e femme/maman wife-/mother-to-be. ● nm future.

fuyant, ~e /fɥijɑ̃, -t / adj (front,

ligne) receding; (*personne*) evasive.
fuyard, ~e /fɥijaʀ, -d/ *nm, f* runaway.

Gg

gabardine /gabaʀdin/ *nf* raincoat.
gabarit /gabaʀi/ *nm* size; (*patron*) template; (*fig*) calibre.
gâcher /gɑʃe/ **1** *vt* (*gâter*) spoil; (*gaspiller*) waste.
gâchette /gɑʃɛt/ *nf* trigger.
gâchis /gɑʃi/ *nm* waste.
gaffe /gaf/ *nf* **T** blunder; faire ~ be careful (à of).
gage /gaʒ/ *nm* security; (*de bonne foi*) pledge; (*de jeu*) forfeit; ~s (*salaire*) wages; en ~ de as a token of; mettre en ~ pawn; tueur à ~s hired killer.
gageure /gaʒyʀ/ *nf* challenge.
gagnant, ~e /gaɲɑ̃, -t/ *adj* winning. ● *nm, f* winner.
gagne-pain /gaɲpɛ̃/ *nm inv* job.
gagner /gaɲe/ **1** *vt* (*match, prix*) win; (*argent, pain*) earn; (*terrain*) gain; (*temps*) save; (*atteindre*) reach; (*convaincre*) win over; ~ sa vie earn one's living. ● *vi* win; (*fig*) gain.
gai, ~e /ge/ *adj* cheerful; (*ivre*) merry. **gaiement** *adv* cheerfully.
gaieté *nf* cheerfulness.
gain /gɛ̃/ *nm* (*salaire*) earnings; (*avantage*) gain; (*économie*) saving; ~s (*Comm*) profits; (*au jeu*) winnings.
gaine /gɛn/ *nf* (*corset*) girdle; (*étui*) sheath.
galant, ~e /galɑ̃, -t/ *adj* courte-

ous; (*amoureux*) romantic.
galaxie /galaksi/ *nf* galaxy.
gale /gal/ *nf* (*de chat etc.*) mange.
galère /galɛʀ/ *nf* (*navire*) galley; c'est la ~! **T** what an ordeal!
galérer /galeʀe/ **14** *vi* **T** (*peiner*) have a hard time.
galerie /galʀi/ *nf* gallery; (*Théât*) circle; (*de voiture*) roof-rack; ~ marchande shopping arcade.
galet /galɛ/ *nm* pebble.
galette /galɛt/ *nf* flat cake; ~ des Rois Twelfth Night cake.
Galles /gal/ *nfpl* le pays de ~ Wales.
gallois, ~e /galwa, -z/ *adj* Welsh. ● *nm* (*Ling*) Welsh. **G**~, ~e *nm, f* Welshman, Welshwoman.
galon /galɔ̃/ *nm* braid; (*Mil*) stripe; prendre du ~ to be promoted.
galop /galo/ *nm* canter; aller au ~ canter; grand ~ gallop; ~ d'essai trial run. **galoper** **1** *vi* (*cheval*) canter; (*au grand galop*) gallop; (*personne*) run.
galopin /galopɛ̃/ *nm* **T** rascal.
gambader /gɑ̃bade/ **1** *vi* leap about.
gamelle /gamɛl/ *nf* (*de soldat*) mess kit; (*d'ouvrier*) lunch-box.
gamin, ~e /gamɛ̃, -in/ *adj* childish; (*air*) youthful. ● *nm, f* **T** kid.
gamme /gam/ *nf* (*Mus*) scale; (*série*) range; haut de ~ up-market, top of the range; bas de ~ down-market, bottom of the range.
gang /gɑ̃g/ *nm* **T** gang.
ganglion /gɑ̃glijɔ̃/ *nm* ganglion.
gangster /gɑ̃gstɛʀ/ *nm* gangster; (*escroc*) crook.
gant /gɑ̃/ *nm* glove; ~ de ménage rubber glove; ~ de toilette face-flannel, face-cloth.

garage /ɡaʀaʒ/ nm garage. **gara-giste** nmf garage owner; (employé) car mechanic.

garant, ~e /ɡaʀã, -t/ nm, f guarantor. ● adj se porter ~ de vouch for.

garanti, ~e /ɡaʀãti/ adj guaranteed.

garantie /ɡaʀãti/ nf guarantee; ~s (de police d'assurance) cover. **garantir** ② vt guarantee; (protéger) protect (de from).

garçon /ɡaʀsɔ̃/ nm boy; (jeune homme) young man; (célibataire) bachelor; ~ (de café) waiter; ~ d'honneur best man. **garçonnière** nf bachelor flat.

garde[1] /ɡaʀd/ nf guard; (d'enfants, de bagages) care; (service) guard (duty); (infirmière) nurse; de ~ on duty; ~ à vue (police) custody; mettre en ~ warn; prendre ~ be careful (à of); (droit de ~ custody (de of).

garde[2] /ɡaʀd/ nm guard; (de propriété, parc) warden; ~ champêtre village policeman; ~ du corps bodyguard.

garde-à-vous /ɡaʀdavu/ nm inv (Mil) se mettre au ~ stand to attention.

garde-chasse (pl ~s) /ɡaʀdə-ʃas/ nm gamekeeper.

garde-manger /ɡaʀdmãʒe/ nm inv meat safe; (placard) larder.

garder /ɡaʀde/ ① vt (conserver, maintenir) keep; (vêtement) keep on; (surveiller) look after; (défendre) guard; ~ le lit stay in bed. □ se ~ vpr (denrée) keep; se ~ de faire be careful not to do.

garderie /ɡaʀdəʀi/ nf day nursery.

garde-robe (pl ~s) /ɡaʀdəʀɔb/ nf wardrobe.

gardien, ~ne /ɡaʀdjɛ̃, -ɛn/ nm, f (de locaux) security guard; (de pri-son, réserve) warden; (d'immeuble) caretaker; (de musée) attendant; (de zoo) keeper; (de traditions) guardian; ~ de but goalkeeper; ~ de la paix policeman; ~ de nuit night watchman; gardienne d'enfants childminder.

gare /ɡaʀ/ nf (Rail) station; ~ routière coach station; (US) bus station. ● interj ~ (à toi) watch out!

garer /ɡaʀe/ ① vt park. □ se ~ vpr park; (s'écarter) move out of the way.

gargouille /ɡaʀɡuj/ nf waterspout; (sculptée) gargoyle. **gargouiller** ① vi gurgle; (stomach) rumble.

garni, ~e /ɡaʀni/ adj (plat) served with vegetables; bien ~ (rempli) well-filled.

garnir /ɡaʀniʀ/ ② vt (remplir) fill; (décorer) decorate; (couvrir) cover; (doubler) line; (Culin) garnish. **garniture** nf (légumes) vegetables; (ornement) trimming; (de voiture) trim.

gars /ɡɑ/ nm [1] lad; (adulte) guy, bloke.

gas-oil /ɡazwal/ nm diesel (oil).

gaspillage /ɡaspijaʒ/ nm waste. **gaspiller** ① vt waste.

gastrique /ɡastʀik/ adj gastric.

gastronome /ɡastʀɔnɔm/ nmf gourmet.

gâteau (pl ~x) /ɡɑto/ nm cake; ~ sec biscuit; (US) cookie; un papa ~ a doting dad.

gâter /ɡɑte/ ① vt spoil. □ se ~ vpr (viande) go bad; (dent) rot; (temps) get worse.

gâterie /ɡɑtʀi/ nf little treat.

gâteux, -euse /ɡɑtø, -z/ adj senile.

gauche /ɡoʃ/ adj left; (maladroit) awkward. ● nf left; à ~ on the left; (direction) (to the) left; la ~ the

g

left (side); (Pol) the left (wing).

gaucher, -ère /goʃe, -ɛʀ/ *adj* left handed.

gaufre /gofʀ/ *nf* waffle. **gaufrette** *nf* wafer.

gaulois, ~e /golwa, -z/ *adj* Gallic; (fig) bawdy. **G~, ~e** *nm, f* Gaul.

gaver /gave/ **1** *vt* force-feed; (fig) cram. □ **se ~ de** *vpr* gorge oneself with; (fig) devour.

gaz /gɑz/ *nm inv* gas; ~ **d'échappement** exhaust fumes; ~ **lacrymogène** tear-gas.

gaze /gɑz/ *nf* gauze.

gazer /gaze/ **1** *vi* **1** **ça gaze?** how's things?

gazette /gazɛt/ *nf* newspaper.

gazeux, -euse /gɑzø, -z/ *adj* (boisson) fizzy; (eau) sparkling.

gazoduc /gazɔdyk/ *nm* gas pipeline.

gazon /gɑzɔ̃/ *nm* lawn, grass.

gazouiller /gazuje/ **1** *vi* (oiseau) chirp; (bébé) babble.

GDF *abrév m* (**Gaz de France**) French gas board.

géant, ~e /ʒeɑ̃, -t/ *adj* giant. ● *nm* giant. **géante** *nf* giantess.

geindre /ʒɛ̃dʀ/ **22** *vi* groan, moan.

gel /ʒɛl/ *nm* frost; (produit) gel; (Comm) freeze; ~ **coiffant** hair gel.

gelée /ʒ(ə)le/ *nf* frost; (Culin) jelly; ~ **blanche** hoarfrost.

geler /ʒale/ **6** *vt/i* freeze; **on gèle** (on a froid) it's freezing; **il ou ça gèle** (il fait froid) it's freezing.

gélule /ʒelyl/ *nf* (Méd) capsule.

Gémeaux /ʒemo/ *nmpl* Gemini.

gémir /ʒemiʀ/ **2** *vi* groan.

gênant, ~e /ʒenɑ̃, -t/ *adj* embarrassing; (irritant) annoying; (incommode) cumbersome.

gencive /ʒɑ̃siv/ *nf* gum.

gendarme /ʒɑ̃daʀm/ *nm* police-

man, gendarme. **gendarmerie** *nf* police force; (local) police station.

> **Gendarmerie nationale** A section of the military, which provides the police service outside major towns.

gendre /ʒɑ̃dʀ/ *nm* son-in-law.

gène /ʒɛn/ *nm* gene.

gêne /ʒɛn/ *nf* discomfort; (confusion) embarrassment; (dérangement) trouble, inconvenience; (pauvreté) poverty.

gêné, ~e /ʒene/ *adj* embarrassed; (désargenté) short of money.

généalogie /ʒenealɔʒi/ *nf* genealogy.

gêner /ʒene/ **1** *vt* bother, disturb; (troubler) embarrass; (entraver) block; (faire mal) hurt.

général, ~e /ʒeneʀal, -o/ *adj* general; **en ~** in general. ● *nm* (*pl* **-aux**) general.

généralement /ʒeneʀalmɑ̃/ *adv* generally.

généraliser /ʒeneʀalize/ **1** *vt* make general. ● *vi* generalize. □ **se ~** *vpr* become widespread ou general.

généraliste /ʒeneʀalist/ *nmf* general practitioner, GP.

généralité /ʒeneʀalite/ *nf* general point.

génération /ʒeneʀasjɔ̃/ *nf* generation.

généreux, -euse /ʒeneʀø, -z/ *adj* generous.

générique /ʒeneʀik/ *nm* (au cinéma) credits. ● *adj* generic.

générosité /ʒeneʀozite/ *nf* generosity.

génétique /ʒenetik/ *adj* genetic. ● *nf* genetics.

Genève /ʒənɛv/ *npr* Geneva.

génial, ~e (*mpl* -iaux) /ʒenjal, -jo/ *adj* brilliant; (fantastique 🗊) fantastic.

génie /ʒeni/ *nm* genius; ~ **civil** civil engineering.

génital, ~e (*mpl* -aux) /ʒenital, -o/ *adj* genital.

génocide /ʒenɔsid/ *nm* genocide.

génoise /ʒenwaz/ *nf* sponge (cake).

génome /ʒenom/ *nm* genome.

génothèque /ʒenotɛk/ *nf* gene bank.

genou (*pl* ~x) /ʒənu/ *nm* knee; **être à** ~x be kneeling.

genre /ʒɑ̃R/ *nm* sort, kind; (Gram) gender; (allure) look; **bon/mauvais** ~ to look nice/disreputable; (comportement) **c'est bien son** ~ it's just like him/her.

gens /ʒɑ̃/ *nmpl* people.

gentil, ~le /ʒɑ̃ti, -j/ *adj* kind, nice; (sage) good. **gentillesse** *nf* kindness. **gentiment** *adv* kindly.

géographie /ʒeɔgʀafi/ *nf* geography.

geôlier, -ière /ʒolje, -jɛʀ/ *nm, f* gaoler, jailer.

géologie /ʒeɔlɔʒi/ *nf* geology.

géomètre /ʒeɔmɛtʀ/ *nm* surveyor.

géométrie /ʒeɔmetʀi/ *nf* geometry. **géométrique** *adj* geometric.

gérance /ʒeʀɑ̃s/ *nf* management.

gérant, ~e /ʒeʀɑ̃, -t/ *nm, f* manager, manageress; ~ **d'immeuble** landlord's agent.

gerbe /ʒɛʀb/ *nf* (de fleurs) bunch, bouquet; (d'eau) spray; (de blé) sheaf.

gercer /ʒɛʀse/ 🔟 *vt* chap; **avoir les lèvres gercées** have chapped lips. ● *vi* become chapped. **gerçure** *nf* crack, chap.

gérer /ʒeʀe/ 🔢 *vt* manage; run; (traiter: fig) (crise, situation) handle.

germe /ʒɛʀm/ *nm* germ; ~**s de soja** bean sprouts.

germer /ʒɛʀme/ 🔟 *vi* germinate.

gestation /ʒɛstasjɔ̃/ *nf* gestation.

geste /ʒɛst/ *nm* gesture.

gesticuler /ʒɛstikyle/ 🔟 *vi* gesticulate.

gestion /ʒɛstjɔ̃/ *nf* management. **gestionnaire** *nmf* administrator.

ghetto /ɡeto/ *nm* ghetto.

gibier /ʒibje/ *nm* (animaux) game.

giboulée /ʒibule/ *nf* shower.

gicler /ʒikle/ 🔟 *vi* squirt; **faire** ~ squirt.

gifle /ʒifl/ *nf* slap in the face. **gifler** 🔟 *vt* slap.

gigantesque /ʒigɑ̃tɛsk/ *adj* gigantic.

gigot /ʒigo/ *nm* leg (of lamb).

gigoter /ʒigote/ 🔟 *vi* wriggle; (nerveusement) fidget.

gilet /ʒile/ *nm* waistcoat; (cardigan) cardigan; ~ **de sauvetage** life jacket.

gingembre /ʒɛ̃ʒɑ̃bʀ/ *nm* ginger.

girafe /ʒiʀaf/ *nf* giraffe.

giratoire /ʒiʀatwaʀ/ *adj* sens ~ roundabout.

girofle /ʒiʀɔfl/ *nm* clou de ~ clove.

girouette /ʒiʀwɛt/ *nf* weathercock, weathervane.

gisement /ʒizmɑ̃/ *nm* deposit.

gitan, ~e /ʒitɑ̃, -an/ *nm, f* gypsy.

gîte /ʒit/ *nm* (maison) home; (abri) shelter; ~ **rural** holiday cottage.

givre /ʒivʀ/ *nm* frost; (sur pare-brise) ice.

givré, ~e /ʒivʀe/ *adj* 🗊 crazy.

glace /ɡlas/ *nf* ice; (crème) icecream; (vitre) window; (miroir) mirror; (verre) glass.

g

glacé, ~e /glase/ *adj* (*vent, accueil*) icy; (*hands*) frozen; (*gâteau*) iced.

glacer /glase/ [10] *vt* freeze; (*gâteau, boisson*) chill; (*pétrifier*) chill. □ **~ vpr** freeze.

glacier /glasje/ *nm* (Géog) glacier; (*vendeur*) ice-cream seller. **glacière** *nf* coolbox. **glaçon** *nm* ice-cube.

glaïeul /glajœl/ *nm* gladiolus.

glaise /glɛz/ *nf* clay.

gland /glɑ̃/ *nm* acorn; (*ornement*) tassel.

glande /glɑ̃d/ *nf* gland.

glander /glɑ̃de/ [1] *vi* [1] laze around.

glaner /glane/ [1] *vt* glean.

glauque /glok/ *adj* (fig) murky; (*street*) squalid.

glissade /glisad/ *nf* (*jeu*) slide; (*dérapage*) skid.

glissant, ~e /glisɑ̃, -t/ *adj* slippery.

glissement /glismɑ̃/ *nm* sliding; gliding; (fig) shift; **~ de terrain** landslide.

glisser /glise/ [1] *vi* slide; (*être glissant*) be slippery; (*sur l'eau*) glide; (*déraper*) slip; (*véhicule*) skid. ● *vt* (*objet*) slip (*dans into*); (*remarque*) slip in. □ **se ~ vpr** slip (*dans into*).

glissière /glisjɛʀ/ *nf* slide; **porte à ~** sliding door; **~ de sécurité** (Auto) crash-barrier; **fermeture à ~** zip.

global, ~e (*mpl* **-aux**) /global, -o/ *adj* (*entier, général*) overall. **globalement** *adv* as a whole.

globe /glɔb/ *nm* globe; **~ oculaire** eyeball; **~ terrestre** globe.

globule /glɔbyl/ *nm* (*du sang*) corpuscle.

gloire /glwaʀ/ *nf* glory, fame. **glorieux, -ieuse** *adj* glorious. **glorifier** [45] *vt* glorify.

glose /gloz/ *nf* gloss.

glossaire /glɔsɛʀ/ *nm* glossary.

gloussement /glusmɑ̃/ *nm* chuckle; (*de poule*) cluck.

glouton, ~ne /glutɔ̃, -ɔn/ *adj* gluttonous. ● *nm, f* glutton.

gluant, ~e /glyɑ̃, -t/ *adj* sticky.

glucose /glykoz/ *nm* glucose.

glycérine /gliseʀin/ *nf* glycerin(e).

GO *abrév fpl* (**grandes ondes**) long wave.

goal /gol/ *nm* [1] goalkeeper.

gobelet /gɔblɛ/ *nm* cup; (*en verre*) tumbler.

gober /gɔbe/ [1] *vt* swallow (whole); **je ne peux pas le ~** [1] I can't stand him.

goéland /gɔelɑ̃/ *nm* (sea)gull.

gogo: à ~ /agɔgo/ *loc* [1] galore, in abundance.

goinfre /gwɛ̃fʀ/ *nm* (glouton [1]) pig. **goinfrer (se)** [1] *vpr* [1] stuff oneself (*de with*).

golf /gɔlf/ *nm* golf; (*terrain*) golf course.

golfe /gɔlf/ *nm* gulf.

gomme /gɔm/ *nf* rubber; (US) eraser; (*résine*) gum. **gommer** [1] *vt* rub out.

gond /gɔ̃/ *nm* hinge; **sortir de ses ~s** [1] go mad.

gondoler (se) /(sa)gɔ̃dɔle/ [1] *vpr* (*bois*) warp; (*métal*) buckle.

gonflé, ~e /gɔ̃fle/ *adj* swollen; **il est ~** [1] he's got a nerve.

gonflement /gɔ̃flǝmɑ̃/ *nm* swelling.

gonfler /gɔ̃fle/ [1] *vt* (*ballon, pneu*) pump up, blow up; (*augmenter*) increase; (*exagérer*) inflate. ● *vi* swell.

gorge /gɔʀʒ/ *nf* throat; (*poitrine*) breast; (*vallée*) gorge.

gorgée /gɔʀʒe/ *nf* sip, gulp.

gorger /gɔʀʒe/ 🔟 vt fill (de with); **gorgé de** full of. □ **se ~** vpr gorge oneself (de with).

gorille /gɔʀij/ nm gorilla; (garde 🔟) bodyguard.

gosier /gozje/ nm throat.

gosse /gɔs/ nmf 🔟 kid.

gothique /gɔtik/ adj Gothic.

goudron /gudʀɔ̃/ nm tar. **goudronner** 🔟 vt tarmac.

gouffre /gufʀ/ nm abyss, gulf.

goujat /guʒa/ nm lout, boor.

goulot /gulo/ nm neck; **boire au ~** drink from the bottle.

goulu, ~e /guly/ adj gluttonous.
● nm, f glutton.

gourde /guʀd/ nf (à eau) flask; (idiot 🔟) fool.

gourer (se) /(sə)guʀe/ 🔟 vpr 🔟 make a mistake.

gourmand, ~e /guʀmã, -d/ adj greedy. ● nm, f glutton.

gourmandise /guʀmãdiz/ nf greed; **~s** sweets.

gourmet /guʀmɛ/ nm gourmet.

gourmette /guʀmɛt/ nf chain bracelet.

gousse /gus/ nf **~ d'ail** clove of garlic.

goût /gu/ nm taste; (gré) liking; **prendre ~ à** develop a taste for; **avoir bon ~** (aliment) taste nice; (personne) have good taste; **donner du ~ à** give flavour.

goûter /gute/ 🔟 vt taste; (apprécier) enjoy; **~ à** ou **de** taste. ● vi have tea. ● nm tea, snack.

goutte /gut/ nf drop; (Méd) gout. **goutte-à-goutte** nm inv drip. **goutter** 🔟 vi drip.

gouttière /gutjɛʀ/ nf gutter.

gouvernail /guvɛʀnaj/ nm rudder; (barre) helm.

gouvernement /guvɛʀnəmã/ nm government.

gouverner /guvɛʀne/ 🔟 vt/i govern; (dominer) control. **gouverneur** nm governor.

GPS abrév m (**global positioning system**) GPS.

grâce /gʀɑs/ nf (charme) grace; (faveur) favour; (volonté) grace; (Jur) pardon; (Relig) grace; **~ à** thanks to; **rendre (~s)** à give thanks to.

gracier /gʀasje/ 🔟 vt pardon.

gracieusement /gʀasjøzmã/ adv gracefully; (gratuitement) free (of charge).

gracieux, -ieuse /gʀasjø, -z/ adj graceful.

grade /gʀad/ nm rank; **monter en ~** be promoted.

gradin /gʀadɛ̃/ nm tier, step; **en ~s** terraced; **les ~s** terraces.

gradué, ~e /gʀadɥe/ adj graded, graduated; **verre ~** measuring jug.

graffiti /gʀafiti/ nmpl graffiti.

grain /gʀɛ̃/ nm grain; (Naut) squall; **~ de beauté** beauty spot; **~ de café** coffee bean; **~ de poivre** pepper corn; **~ de raisin** grape.

graine /gʀɛn/ nf seed.

graisse /gʀɛs/ nf fat; (lubrifiant) grease. **graisser** 🔟 vt grease. **graisseux, -euse** adj greasy.

grammaire /gʀam(m)ɛʀ/ nf grammar.

gramme /gʀam/ nm gram.

grand, ~e /gʀã, -d/ adj big, large; (haut) tall; (intense, fort) great; (brillant) great; (principal) main; (plus âgé) big, elder; (adulte) grown-up; **au ~ air** in the open air; **au ~ jour** in broad daylight; (fig) in the open; **en ~e partie** largely; **~e banlieue** outer suburbs; **~s ensemble** housing estate; **~es lignes** (Rail) main lines; **~ magasin** department store; **~e personne**

grown-up; ~ public general public; ~e surface hypermarket; ~es vacances summer holidays. ● adv (ouvrir) wide; ~ ouvert wide open; voir ~ think big. ● nm, f (adulte) grown-up; (enfant) big boy, big girl; (Scol) senior.

grand-chose /gʁɑ̃ʃoz/ pron pas ~ not much, not a lot.

Grande-Bretagne /gʁɑ̃dbʁətaɲ/ nf Great Britain.

Grande école A prestigious tertiary education institution to which admission is usually by competitive examination or concours. Places are much sought after as they generally guarantee more promising career prospects than the standard universities. Many grandes écoles specialize in particular disciplines or fields of study, e.g. ENA (public administration), Sciences Po (political science), etc.

grandeur /gʁɑ̃dœʁ/ nf greatness; (dimension) size; folie des ~s delusions of grandeur.

grandir /gʁɑ̃diʁ/ ② vi grow; (bruit) grow louder. ● vt (talons) make taller; (loupe) magnify.

grand-mère (pl grands-mères) /gʁɑ̃mɛʁ/ nf grandmother.

grand-père (pl grands-pères) /gʁɑ̃pɛʁ/ nm grandfather.

grands-parents /gʁɑ̃paʁɑ̃/ nmpl grandparents.

grange /gʁɑ̃ʒ/ nf barn.

granulé /gʁanyle/ nm granule.

graphique /gʁafik/ adj graphic; (Ordinat) graphics; informatique ~ computer graphics. ● nm graph.

graphologie /gʁafɔlɔʒi/ nf graphology.

grappe /gʁap/ nf cluster; ~ de

raisin bunch of grapes.

gras, ~se /gʁa, -s/ adj (gros) fat; (aliment) fatty; (surface, peau, cheveux) greasy; (épais) thick; (caractères) bold; faire la ~se matinée sleep late. ● nm (Culin) fat.

gratifiant, ~e /gʁatifjɑ̃, -t/ adj gratifying; (travail) rewarding.

gratifier /gʁatifje/ 45 vt favour, reward (de with).

gratin /gʁatɛ̃/ nm gratin (baked dish with cheese topping); (élite 🗓) upper crust.

gratis /gʁatis/ adv free.

gratitude /gʁatityd/ nf gratitude.

gratte-ciel /gʁatsjɛl/ nm inv skyscraper.

gratter /gʁate/ ① vt/i scratch; (avec un outil) scrape; ça me gratte 🗓 it itches. □ se ~ vpr scratch oneself; se ~ la tête scratch one's head.

gratuiciel /gʁatɥisjɛl/ nm (Internet) freeware.

gratuit, ~e /gʁatɥi, -t/ adj free; (acte) gratuitous. **gratuitement** adv free (of charge).

grave /gʁav/ adj (maladie, accident, problème) serious; (solennel) grave; (voix) deep; (accent) grave. **gravement** adv seriously; gravely.

graver /gʁave/ ① vt engrave; (sur bois) carve; (Ordinat) burn.

graveur /gʁavœʁ/ nm (Ordinat) burner.

gravier /gʁavje/ nm du ~ gravel.

gravité /gʁavite/ nf gravity.

graviter /gʁavite/ ① vi revolve.

gravure /gʁavyʁ/ nf engraving; (de tableau, photo) print, plate.

gré /gʁe/ nm (volonté) will; (goût) taste; à son ~ (agir) as one likes; de bon ~ willingly; bon ~ mal ~ like it or not; je vous en saurais ~ I'd be grateful for that.

grec, ~**que** /grɛk/ adj Greek. ● nm (Ling) Greek. **G**~, ~**que** nm, f Greek.

Grèce nf /grɛs/ Greece.

greffe /grɛf/ nf graft; (d'organe) transplant. **greffer** 🗓 vt graft; transplant.

greffier, -ière /grefje, -jɛr/ nm, f clerk of the court.

grêle /grɛl/ adj (maigre) spindly; (voix) shrill. ● nf hail.

grêler /grɛle/ 🗓 vi hail; il grêle it's hailing. **grêlon** nm hailstone.

grelot /grəlo/ nm (little) bell.

grelotter /grəlote/ 🗓 vi shiver.

grenade /grənad/ nf (fruit) pomegranate; (explosif) grenade.

grenat /grəna/ adj inv dark red.

grenier /grənje/ nm attic; (pour grain) loft.

grenouille /grənuj/ nf frog.

grès /grɛ/ nm sandstone; (poterie) stoneware.

grésiller /grezije/ 🗓 vi sizzle; (radio) crackle.

grève /grɛv/ nf (rivage) shore; (cessation de travail) strike; faire ~, être en ~ be on strike; se mettre en ~ go on strike. **gréviste** nm striker.

gribouiller /gribuje/ 🗓 vt/i scribble.

grief /grijɛf/ nm grievance.

grièvement /grijɛvmɑ̃/ adv seriously.

griffe /grif/ nf claw; (de couturier) label; coup de ~ scratch.

griffé, ~**e** /grife/ adj (vêtement, article) designer.

griffer /grife/ 🗓 vt scratch, claw.

grignoter /griɲote/ 🗓 vt/i nibble.

gril /gril/ nm (de cuisinière) grill; (plaque) grill pan.

grillade /grijad/ nf (viande) grill.

grillage /grijaʒ/ nm wire netting.

grille /grij/ nf railings; (portail) (metal) gate; (de fenêtre) bars; (de cheminée) grate; (fig) grid. **grille-pain** nm inv toaster.

griller /grije/ 🗓 vt (pain) toast; (viande) grill; (ampoule) blow; (feu rouge) go through; (appareil) burn out. ● vi (ampoule) blow; (Culin) faire ~ (viande) grill; (pain) toast.

grillon /grijɔ̃/ nm cricket.

grimace /grimas/ nf (funny) face; (de douleur, dégoût) grimace; faire des ~s make faces; faire la ~ pull a face, grimace.

grimper /grɛ̃pe/ 🗓 vt climb. ● vi climb; ~ sur ou dans un arbre climb a tree.

grincement /grɛ̃smɑ̃/ nm creak(ing).

grincer /grɛ̃se/ 🔟 vi creak; ~ des dents grind one's teeth.

grincheux, -euse /grɛ̃ʃø, -z/ adj grumpy.

grippe /grip/ nf influenza, flu.

grippé, ~**e** /gripe/ adj être ~ have (the) flu; (mécanisme) be seized up ou jammed.

gris, ~**e** /gri, -z/ adj grey; (saoul) tipsy.

grivois, ~**e** /grivwa, -z/ adj bawdy.

grog /grog/ nm hot toddy.

grogner /groɲe/ 🗓 vi (animal) growl; (personne) grumble.

grognon /groɲɔ̃/ adj grumpy.

groin /grwɛ̃/ nm snout.

gronder /grɔ̃de/ 🗓 vi (tonnerre, volcan) rumble; (chien) growl; (conflit) be brewing. ● vt scold.

groom /grum/ nm bellboy.

gros, ~**se** /gro, -s/ adj big, large; (gras) fat; (important) big; (épais) thick; (lourd) heavy; (buveur, fu-

meur) heavy; ~ bonnet 🔲 bigwig; ~ lot jackpot; ~ mot swear word; ~ plan close-up; ~se caisse bass drum; ~ titre headline. ● *nm, f* fat man, fat woman. ● *adv* (*écrire*) big; (*risquer, gagner*) a lot. ● *nm* le ~ de the bulk of; de ~ (Comm) wholesale; en ~ roughly; (Comm) wholesale.

groseille /gʀɔzɛj/ *nf* redcurrant; ~ à maquereau gooseberry.

grossesse /gʀosɛs/ *nf* pregnancy.

grosseur /gʀosœʀ/ *nf* (volume) size; (enflure) lump.

grossier, -ière /gʀosje, -jɛʀ/ *adj* (sans finesse) coarse, rough; (rudimentaire) crude; (vulgaire) coarse; (impoli) rude; (erreur) gross. **grossièrement** *adv* (sommairement) roughly; (vulgairement) coarsely.

grossièreté *nf* coarseness; crudeness; rudeness; (mot) rude word.

grossir /gʀosiʀ/ 🔲 *vt* (faire augmenter) increase, boost; (agrandir) enlarge; (exagérer) exaggerate; ~ les rangs *ou* la foule swell the ranks. ● *vi* (personne) put on weight; (augmenter) grow.

grossiste /gʀosist/ *nmf* wholesaler.

grosso modo /gʀosomodo/ *adv* roughly.

grotesque /gʀɔtɛsk/ *adj* grotesque; (ridicule) ludicrous.

grotte /gʀɔt/ *nf* cave; grotto.

grouiller /gʀuje/ 🔲 *vi* swarm; ~ de be swarming with.

groupe /gʀup/ *nm* group; (Mus) group, band; ~ électrogène generating set; ~ scolaire school; ~ de travail working party.

groupement /gʀupmɑ̃/ *nm* grouping.

grouper /gʀupe/ 🔲 *vt* put together. □ se ~ *vpr* group (together).

grue /gʀy/ *nf* (machine, oiseau) crane.

gruyère /gʀyjɛʀ/ *nm* gruyère (cheese).

gué /ge/ *nm* ford; passer *ou* traverser à ~ ford.

guenon /gənɔ̃/ *nf* female monkey.

guépard /gepaʀ/ *nm* cheetah.

guêpe /gɛp/ *nf* wasp.

guère /gɛʀ/ *adv* ne ~ hardly; il n'y a ~ d'espoir there is no hope; elle n'a ~ dormi she didn't sleep much, she hardly slept.

guérilla /geʀija/ *nf* guerrilla warfare; (groupe) guerillas.

guérir /geʀiʀ/ 🔲 *vt* (personne, maladie, mal) cure (de of); (plaie, membre) heal. ● *vi* get better; (blessure) heal; ~ de recover from. **guérison** *nf* curing; healing; (de personne) recovery.

guerre /gɛʀ/ *nf* war; en ~ at war; faire la ~ wage war (à against); ~ civile civil war; ~ mondiale world war.

guerrier, -ière /geʀje, -jɛʀ/ *adj* warlike. ● *nm, f* warrior.

guet /gɛ/ *nm* watch; faire le ~ be on the watch. **guet-apens** (*pl* **guets-apens**) *nm* ambush.

guetter /gete/ 🔲 *vt* watch; (attendre) watch out for.

gueule /gœl/ *nf* mouth; (figure 🔲) face; ta ~! shut up!; ~ de bois 🔲 hangover.

gueuleton /gœltɔ̃/ *nm* 🔲 blowout, slap-up meal.

gui /gi/ *nm* mistletoe.

guichet /giʃɛ/ *nm* window, counter; (de gare) ticket-office; (Théât) box-office; jouer à ~s fermés (pièce) be sold out; ~ automatique cash dispenser.

guide /gid/ *nm* guide. ● *nf* (fille scout) girl guide.

guider /ɡide/ **1** *vt* guide.

guidon /ɡidɔ̃/ *nm* handlebars.

guignol /ɡiɲɔl/ *nm* puppet; (personne) clown; (spectacle) puppet-show.

guillemets /ɡijmɛ/ *nmpl* quotation marks, inverted commas; entre ∼ in inverted commas.

guillotine /ɡijɔtin/ *nf* guillotine.

guimauve /ɡimov/ *nf* marshmallow; c'est de la ∼ 🄵 it's slushy *ou* schmaltzy 🄵.

guindé, ∼e /ɡɛ̃de/ *adj* stiff, formal; (style) stilted.

guirlande /ɡiʀlɑ̃d/ *nf* garland; tinsel.

guitare /ɡitaʀ/ *nf* guitar.

gym /ʒim/ *nf* gymnastics; (Scol) physical education, PE.

gymnase /ʒimnaz/ *nm* gym(nasium). **gymnastique** *nf* gymnastics.

gynécologie /ʒinekɔlɔʒi/ *nf* gynaecology.

•••••••••••••••••••

Hh

•••••••••••••••••••

habile /abil/ *adj* skilful, clever.

habillé, ∼e /abije/ *adj* (vêtement) smart; (soirée) formal.

habillement /abijmɑ̃/ *nm* clothing.

habiller /abije/ **1** *vt* dress (de in); (équiper) clothe; (recouvrir) cover (de with). □ s'∼ *vpr* get dressed; (élégamment) dress up.

habit /abi/ *nm* (de personnage) outfit; (de cérémonie) tails; ∼s clothes.

habitant, ∼e /abitɑ̃, -t/ *nm, f* (de maison, quartier) resident; (de pays) inhabitant.

habitat /abita/ *nm* (mode de peuplement) settlement; (conditions) housing.

habitation /abitasjɔ̃/ *nf* (logement) house.

habité, ∼e /abite/ *adj* (terre) inhabited.

habiter /abite/ **1** *vi* live. • *vt* live in.

habitude /abityd/ *nf* habit; avoir l'∼ de be used to; d'∼ usually; comme d'∼ as usual.

habitué, ∼e /abitɥe/ *nm, f* (client) regular.

habituel, ∼le /abitɥɛl/ *adj* usual. **habituellement** *adv* usually.

habituer /abitɥe/ **1** *vt* ∼ qn à get sb used to. □ s'∼ à *vpr* get used to.

hache /ʾaʃ/ *nf* axe.

haché, ∼e /ʾaʃe/ *adj* (viande) minced; (phrases) jerky.

hacher /ʾaʃe/ **1** *vt* mince; (au couteau) chop.

hachis /ʾaʃi/ *nm* minced meat; (US) ground meat; ∼ Parmentier ≈ *shepherd's pie.*

hachisch /ʾaʃiʃ/ *nm* hashish.

hachoir /ʾaʃwaʀ/ *nm* (appareil) mincer; (couteau) chopper; (planche) chopping board.

haie /ʾɛ/ *nf* hedge; course de ∼s hurdle race.

haillon /ʾajɔ̃/ *nm* rag.

haine /ʾɛn/ *nf* hatred.

haïr /ʾaiʀ/ **36** *vt* hate.

hâlé, ∼e /ʾɑle/ *adj* (sun-)tanned.

haleine /ʾalɛn/ *nf* breath; travail de longue ∼ long job.

haleter /ʾalte/ **6** *vi* pant.

hall /ʾol/ *nm* hall; (de gare) concourse.

g
h

halle /'al/ nf market hall; ~s covered market.

halte /'alt/ nf stop; faire ~ stop. ● interj stop; (Mil) halt.

haltère /altɛʀ/ nm dumbbell; faire des ~s to do weightlifting.

hameau (pl ~x) /'amo/ nm hamlet.

hameçon /amsɔ̃/ nm hook.

hanche /'ɑ̃ʃ/ nf hip.

handicap /'ɑ̃dikap/ nm handicap. **handicapé, ~e** adj & nm, f disabled (person).

hangar /'ɑ̃gaʀ/ nm shed; (pour avions) hangar.

hanter /'ɑ̃te/ ▧ vt haunt.

hantise /'ɑ̃tiz/ nf dread; avoir la ~ de dread.

haras /'aʀɑ/ nm stud-farm.

harasser /'aʀase/ ▧ vt exhaust.

harcèlement /'aʀsɛlmɑ̃/ nm ~ sexuel sexual harassment.

harceler /'aʀsəle/ ▧ vt harass.

hardi, ~e /'aʀdi/ adj bold.

hareng /'aʀɑ̃/ nm herring.

hargne /'aʀɲ/ nf (aggressive) bad temper.

haricot /'aʀiko/ nm bean; ~ vert French bean; (US) green bean.

harmonie /aʀmɔni/ nf harmony. **harmonieux, -ieuse** adj harmonious.

harmoniser /aʀmɔnize/ ▧ vt harmonize. □ s'~ vpr harmonize.

harnacher /'aʀnaʃe/ ▧ vt harness.

harnais /'aʀnɛ/ nm harness.

harpe /'aʀp/ nf harp.

harpon /'aʀpɔ̃/ nm harpoon.

hasard /'azaʀ/ nm chance; (coïncidence) coincidence; les ~s de the fortunes of; au ~ (choisir etc.) at random; (flâner) aimlessly. **hasardeux, -euse** adj risky.

hasarder /'azaʀde/ vt risk; (remarque) venture.

hâte /'ɑt/ nf haste; à la ~, en ~ hurriedly; avoir ~ de look forward to.

hâter /'ɑte/ ▧ vt hasten. □ se ~ vpr hurry (de to).

hâtif, -ive /'atif, -v/ adj hasty; (précoce) early.

hausse /'os/ nf rise (de in); ~ des prix price rise; en ~ rising.

hausser /'ose/ ▧ vt raise; (épaules) shrug.

haut, ~e /'o, 'ot/ adj high; (de taille) tall; à voix ~e aloud; ~ en couleur colourful; plus ~ higher up; (dans un texte) above; en ~ lieu in high places. ● adv high; tout ~ out loud. ● nm top; des ~s et des bas ups and downs; en ~ (regarder) up; (à l'étage) upstairs; en ~ de) at the top (of).

hautbois /'obwa/ nm oboe.

haut-de-forme /'odfɔʀm/ (pl **hauts-de-forme**) nm top hat.

hauteur /'otœʀ/ nf height; (colline) hill; (arrogance) haughtiness; être à la ~ be up to it; à la ~ de (ville) near; être à la ~ de la situation be equal to the situation.

haut-le-cœur /'olkœʀ/ nm inv nausea.

haut-parleur (pl ~s) /'oparlœʀ/ nm loudspeaker.

havre /'ɑvʀ/ nm haven (de of).

hayon /'ajɔ̃/ nm (Auto) hatchback.

hebdomadaire /ɛbdɔmadɛʀ/ adj & nm weekly.

hébergement /ebɛʀʒəmɑ̃/ nm accommodation.

héberger /ebɛʀʒe/ ▧ vt (ami) put up; (réfugiés) take in.

hébreu (pl ~x) /ebʀø/ am Hebrew. ● nm (Ling) Hebrew; c'est de l'~! it's all Greek to me!

Hébreu (pl ~x) /ebʀœ/ nm Hebrew; **les ~x** the Hebrews.

hécatombe /ekatɔ̃b/ nf slaughter.

hectare /ɛktaʀ/ nm hectare (= 10,000 square metres).

hélas /'elɑs/ interj alas. ● adv sadly.

hélice /elis/ nf propeller.

hélicoptère /elikɔptɛʀ/ nm helicopter.

helvétique /ɛlvetik/ adj Swiss.

hématome /ematom/ nm bruise.

hémorragie /emɔʀaʒi/ nf haemorrhage.

hémorroïdes /emɔʀoid/ nfpl piles, haemorrhoids.

hennir /'eniʀ/ ② vi neigh.

hépatite /epatit/ nf hepatitis.

herbe /ɛʀb/ nf grass; (Méd, Culin) herb; **en ~** in the blade; (fig) budding.

héréditaire /eʀeditɛʀ/ adj hereditary.

hérédité /eʀedite/ nf heredity.

hérisser /'eʀise/ ❶ vt bristle; **~ qn** ruffle sb. □ **se ~** vpr bristle.

hérisson /'eʀisɔ̃/ nm hedgehog.

héritage /eʀitaʒ/ nm inheritance; (spirituel) heritage.

hériter /eʀite/ ❶ vt/i inherit (de from); **~ de qch** inherit sth. **héritier, -ière** nm, f heir, heiress.

hermétique /ɛʀmetik/ adj airtight; (fig) unfathomable.

hernie /'ɛʀni/ nf hernia.

héroïne /eʀɔin/ nf (femme) heroine; (drogue) heroin.

héroïque /eʀɔik/ adj heroic.

héros /'eʀo/ nm hero.

hésiter /ezite/ ❶ vi hesitate (à to); **j'hésite** I'm not sure.

hétérogène /eteʀɔʒɛn/ adj heterogeneous.

hétérosexuel, ~le /eteʀɔsɛksɥɛl/ nm/f & adj heterosexual.

hêtre /'ɛtʀ/ nm beech.

heure /œʀ/ nf time; (soixante minutes) hour; **quelle ~ est-il?** what time is it?; **il est dix ~s** it is ten o'clock; **à l'~** (venir, être) on time; **d'~ en ~** by the hour; **toutes les deux ~s** every two hours; **~ de pointe** rush-hour; **~ de cours** (Scol) period; **~ indue** ungodly hour; **~s creuses** off peak periods; **~s supplémentaires** overtime.

heureusement /œʀøzmɑ̃/ adv fortunately, luckily.

heureux, -euse /œʀø, -z/ adj happy; (chanceux) lucky, fortunate.

heurt /'œʀ/ nm collision; (conflit) clash; **sans ~** smoothly.

heurter /'œʀte/ ❶ vt (cogner) hit; (mur) bump into, hit; (choquer) offend. □ **se ~ à** vpr bump into, hit; (fig) come up against.

hexagone /ɛgzagon/ nm hexagon; **l'~** France.

hiberner /ibɛʀne/ ❶ vi hibernate.

hibou (pl ~x) /'ibu/ nm owl.

hier /jɛʀ/ adv yesterday; **~ soir** last night, yesterday evening.

hiérarchie /jeʀaʀʃi/ nf hierarchy.

hilare /ilaʀ/ adj (visage) merry; **être ~** be laughing.

hindou, ~e /ɛ̃du/ adj & nm, f Hindu. **H~, ~e** nm, f Hindu.

hippique /ipik/ adj equestrian; **le concours ~** showjumping.

hippodrome /ipodʀom/ nm racecourse.

hippopotame /ipopotam/ nm hippopotamus.

hirondelle /iʀɔ̃dɛl/ nf swallow.

hisser /'ise/ ❶ vt hoist, haul. □ **se ~** vpr heave oneself up.

histoire /istwaʀ/ nf (récit) story; (étude) history; (affaire) business;

h

~(s) (chichis) fuss; (ennuis) trouble. **historique** adj historical.

hiver /ivɛʀ/ nm winter. **hivernal**, ~e (mpl -aux) adj winter; (glacial) wintry.

H.L.M. abbrév m ou f (**habitation à loyer modéré**) block of council flats; (US) low-rent apartment building.

hocher /ɔʃe/ **1** vt ~ la tête (pour dire oui) nod; (pour dire non) shake one's head.

hochet /ɔʃɛ/ nm rattle.

hockey /ɔkɛ/ nm hockey; ~ sur glace ice hockey.

hollandais, ~e /ɔlɑ̃dɛ, -z/ adj Dutch. ● nm (Ling) Dutch. H~, ~e nm, f Dutchman, Dutchwoman.

Hollande /ɔlɑ̃d/ nf Holland.

homard /ɔmaʀ/ nm lobster.

homéopathie /ɔmeopati/ nf homoeopathy.

homicide /ɔmisid/ nm homicide; ~ **involontaire** manslaughter.

hommage /ɔmaʒ/ nm tribute; ~s (salutations) respects; **rendre ~ à** pay tribute to.

homme /ɔm/ nm man; (espèce) man (kind); ~ **d'affaires** businessman; ~ **de la rue** man in the street; ~ **d'État** statesman; ~ **politique** politician.

homogène /ɔmɔʒɛn/ adj homogeneous.

homonyme /ɔmɔnim/ nm (personne) namesake.

homosexualité /ɔmɔsɛksɥalite/ nf homosexuality.

homosexuel, ~le /ɔmɔsɛksɥɛl/ adj & nm, f homosexual.

Hongrie /ˈɔ̃gʀi/ nf Hungary.

hongrois, ~e /ˈɔ̃gʀwa, -z/ adj Hungarian. ● nm (Ling) Hungarian. H~, ~e nm, f Hungarian.

honnête /ɔnɛt/ adj honest; (juste) fair. **honnêteté** nf honesty.

honneur /ɔnœʀ/ nm honour; (mérite) credit; **d'~** (invité, place) of honour; **en l'~ de** in honour of; **en quel ~?** ⚏ why?; **faire ~ à** (équipe, famille) bring credit to.

honorable /ɔnɔʀabl/ adj honourable; (convenable) respectable.

honoraire /ɔnɔʀɛʀ/ adj honorary. **honoraires** nmpl fees.

honorer /ɔnɔʀe/ **1** vt honour; (faire honneur à) do credit to.

honte /ˈɔ̃t/ nf shame; **avoir ~** be ashamed (de of); **faire ~ à** make ashamed. **honteux, -euse** adj (personne) ashamed (de of); (action) shameful.

hôpital (pl -aux) /ɔpital, -o/ nm hospital.

hoquet /ˈɔkɛ/ nm **le ~** (the) hiccups.

horaire /ɔʀɛʀ/ adj hourly. ● nm timetable; ~s **libres** flexitime.

horizon /ɔʀizɔ̃/ nm horizon; (Fig) outlook.

horizontal, ~e (mpl -aux) /ɔʀizɔ̃tal, -o/ adj horizontal.

horloge /ɔʀlɔʒ/ nf clock.

hormis /ˈɔʀmi/ prép save.

hormonal, ~e (mpl -aux) /ɔʀmɔnal, -o/ adj hormonal. **hormone** /ɔʀmɔn/ nf hormone.

horreur /ɔʀœʀ/ nf horror; **avoir ~ de** hate.

horrible /ɔʀibl/ adj horrible.

horrifier /ɔʀifje/ **45** vt horrify.

hors /ˈɔʀ/ prép ~ **de** outside, (avec mouvement) out of; ~ **d'atteinte** out of reach; ~ **d'haleine** out of breath; ~ **de prix** extremely expensive; ~ **pair** outstanding; ~ **de soi** beside oneself. **hors-bord** nm inv speedboat. **hors-d'œuvre** nm inv

h

hors-d'œuvre. **hors-jeu** *adj inv* offside. **hors-la-loi** *nm inv* outlaw. **hors-piste** *nm* off-piste skiing. **hors-taxe** *adj inv* duty-free.

horticulteur, -trice /ɔʀtikyltœʀ, -tʀis/ *nm, f* horticulturist.

hospice /ɔspis/ *nm* home.

hospitalier, -ière /ɔspitalje, -jɛʀ/ *adj* hospitable; (Méd) hospital. **hospitaliser** 1 *vt* take to hospital. **hospitalité** *nf* hospitality.

hostile /ɔstil/ *adj* hostile. **hostilité** *nf* hostility.

hôte /ot/ *nm* (maître) host; (invité) guest.

hôtel /otɛl/ *nm* hotel; ∼ (particulier) (private) mansion; ∼ de ville town hall.

hôtelier, -ière /otalje, -jɛʀ/ *adj* hotel. ●*nm, f* hotel keeper. **hôtellerie** *nf* hotel business.

hôtesse /otɛs/ *nf* hostess; ∼ de l'air stewardess.

hotte /ɔt/ *nf* basket; ∼ aspirante extractor (hood), (US) ventilator.

houblon /ublõ/ *nm* le ∼ hops.

houille /uj/ *nf* coal; ∼ blanche hydroelectric power.

houle /ul/ *nf* swell. **houleux, -euse** *adj* (mer) rough; (débat) stormy.

housse /us/ *nf* cover; ∼ de siège seat cover.

houx /u/ *nm* holly.

huées /'ɥe/ *nfpl* boos. **huer** 1 *vt* boo.

huile /ɥil/ *nf* oil; (personne 1) bigwig. **huiler** 1 *vt* oil. **huileux, -euse** *adj* oily.

huis /ɥi/ *nm* à ∼ clos in camera.

huissier /ɥisje/ *nm* (Jur) bailiff; (portier) usher.

huit /'ɥi(t) / *adj* eight; ∼ jours a week; lundi en ∼ a week on Monday. ●*nm* eight. **huitième** *adj & nmf* eighth.

huître /ɥitʀ/ *nf* oyster.

humain, -e /ymɛ̃, -ɛn/ *adj* human; (compatissant) humane. **humanitaire** *adj* humanitarian. **humanité** *nf* humanity.

humble /œ̃bl/ *adj* humble.

humeur /ymœʀ/ *nf* mood; (tempérament) temper; de bonne/mauvaise ∼ in a good/bad mood.

humide /ymid/ *adj* damp; (chaleur, climat) humid; (lèvres, yeux) moist. **humidité** *nf* humidity.

humilier /ymilje/ 45 *vt* humiliate.

humoristique /ymɔʀistik/ *adj* humorous.

humour /ymuʀ/ *nm* humour; avoir de l'∼ have a sense of humour.

hurlement /yʀləmɑ̃/ *nm* howl (ing). **hurler** 1 *vt/i* howl.

hutte /'yt/ *nf* hut.

hydratant, -e /idʀatɑ̃, -t/ *adj* (lotion) moisturizing.

hydravion /idʀavjõ/ *nm* seaplane.

hydroélectrique /idʀoelɛktʀik/ *adj* hydroelectric.

hydrogène /idʀɔʒɛn/ *nm* hydrogen.

hygiène /iʒjɛn/ *nf* hygiene. **hygiénique** *adj* hygienic.

hymne /imn/ *nm* hymn; ∼ national national anthem.

hyperlien /ipɛʀljɛ̃/ *nm* (Internet) hyperlink.

hypermarché /ipɛʀmaʀʃe/ *nm* (supermarché) hypermarket.

hypertension /ipɛʀtɑ̃sjõ/ *nf* high blood-pressure.

hypertexte /ipɛʀtɛkst/ *nm* (Internet) hypertext.

hypnotiser /ipnotize/ 1 *vt* hypnotize.

hypocrisie /ipɔkrizi/ nf hypocrisy.
hypocrite /ipɔkrit/ adj hypocritical. ● nmf hypocrite.
hypothèque /ipɔtɛk/ nf mortgage.
hypothèse /ipɔtɛz/ nf hypothesis.
hystérie /isteri/ nf hysteria.

....

Ii

....

ici /isi/ adv (dans l'espace) here; (dans le temps) now; d'~ demain by tomorrow; d'~ là in the meantime; d'~ peu shortly; ~ même in this very place; jusqu'~ until now; (dans le passé) until then.

idéal, ~e (mpl -aux) /ideal, -o/ adj & nm ideal. **idéaliser** 🗓 vt idealize.

idée /ide/ nf idea; (esprit) mind; avoir dans l'~ de faire plan to do; il ne me viendrait jamais à l'~ de faire it would never occur to me to do; ~ fixe obsession; ~ reçue conventional opinion.

identification /idɑtifikasjɔ̃/ nf identification. **identifier** 🗓 vt, s'identifier vpr identify (à with).

identique /idɑtik/ adj identical.

identité /idɑtite/ nf identity.

idéologie /ideɔlɔʒi/ nf ideology.

idiome /idjom/ nm idiom.

idiot, ~e /idjo, -ɔt/ adj idiotic. ● nm, f idiot. **idiotie** /idjɔsi/ nf idiocy; (acte, parole) idiotic thing.

idole /idɔl/ nf idol.

if /if/ nm yew.

ignare /iɲar/ adj ignorant. ● nmf ignoramus.

ignoble /iɲɔbl/ adj vile.

ignorance /iɲɔrɑ̃s/ nf ignorance.

ignorant, ~e /iɲɔrɑ̃, -t/ adj ignorant. ● nm, f ignoramus.

ignorer /iɲɔre/ 🗓 vt not know; je l'ignore I don't know; (personne) ignore.

il /il/ pron (personne, animal familier) he; (chose, animal) it; (impersonnel) it; ~ est vrai que it is true that; ~ neige/pleut it is snowing/raining; ~ y a there is; (pluriel) there are; (temps) ago; (durée) for; ~ y a 2 ans 2 years ago; ~ y a plus d'une heure que j'attends I've been waiting for over an hour.

île /il/ nf island; ~ déserte desert island; ~s anglo-normandes Channel Islands; ~s Britanniques British Isles.

illégal, ~e (mpl ~aux) /ilegal, -o/ adj illegal.

illégitime /ileʒitim/ adj illegitimate.

illettré, ~e /iletre/ adj & nm, f illiterate.

illicite /ilisit/ adj illicit; (Jur) unlawful.

illimité, ~e /ilimite/ adj unlimited.

illisible /ilizibl/ adj illegible; (livre) unreadable.

illogique /ilɔʒik/ adj illogical.

illuminé, ~e /ilymine/ adj lit up; (monument) floodlit.

illusion /ilyzjɔ̃/ nf illusion; se faire des ~s delude oneself. **illusoire** adj illusory.

illustre /ilystr/ adj illustrious.

illustré, ~e /ilystre/ adj illustrated. ● nm comic.

illustrer /ilystre/ 🗓 vt illustrate. □ s'~ vpr become famous.

îlot /ilo/ nm islet; (de maisons) block.

ils /il/ pron they.

image /imaʒ/ nf picture; (méta-

imaginaire | impensable

phore) image; (reflet) reflection.
imagé, ~e adj full of imagery.
imaginaire /imaʒinɛʀ/ adj imaginary. **imaginatif, -ive** adj imaginative. **imagination** nf imagination.
imaginer /imaʒine/ **1** vt imagine; (inventer) think up. □ **s'~** vpr (se représenter) imagine (que that); (croire) think (que that).
imbécile /ɛ̃besil/ adj idiotic. ● nmf idiot.
imbiber /ɛ̃bibe/ **1** vt soak (de with). □ **s'~** vpr become soaked (de with).
imbriqué, ~e /ɛ̃bʀike/ adj (lié) interlinked; (tuiles) overlapping.
imbu, ~e /ɛ̃by/ adj ~ de full of.
IMC abrév m (**indice de masse corporelle**) BMI.
imitateur, -trice /imitatœʀ, -tʀis/ nm, f imitator; (comédien) impersonator. **imiter** **1** vt imitate; (personnage) impersonate; (signature) forge; (faire comme) do the same as.
immatriculation /imatʀikylasjɔ̃/ nf registration.
immatriculer /imatʀikyle/ **1** vt register; se faire ~ register; faire ~ une voiture have a car registered.
immédiat, ~e /imedja, -t/ adj immediate. ● nm dans l'~ for the time being.
immense /imɑ̃s/ adj huge.
immerger /imɛʀʒe/ **40** vt immerse. □ **s'~** vpr immerse oneself (dans in).
immeuble /imœbl/ nm block of flats, building; ~ de bureaux office building ou block.
immigrant, ~e /imigʀɑ̃, -t/ adj & nm, f immigrant. **immigration** nf immigration. **immigré, ~e** adj &

nm, f immigrant. **immigrer** **1** vi immigrate.
imminent, ~e /iminɑ̃, -t/ adj imminent.
immobile /imɔbil/ adj still, motionless.
immobilier, -ière /imɔbilje, -jɛʀ/ adj property; agence immobilière estate agent's office; (US) real estate office; agent ~ estate agent; (US) real estate agent. ● nm l'~ property; (US) real estate.
immobiliser /imɔbilize/ **1** vt immobilize; (stopper) stop. □ **s'~** vpr stop.
immonde /imɔ̃d/ adj filthy.
immoral, ~e (mpl **-aux**) /imɔʀal, -o/ adj immoral.
immortel, ~le /imɔʀtɛl/ adj immortal.
immuable /imɥabl/ adj unchanging.
immuniser /imynize/ **1** vt immunize; immunisé contre (à l'abri de) immune to. **immunité** nf immunity.
impact /ɛ̃pakt/ nm impact.
impair, ~e /ɛ̃pɛʀ/ adj (numéro) odd. ● nm blunder, faux pas.
imparfait, ~e /ɛ̃paʀfɛ, -t/ adj & nm imperfect.
impasse /ɛ̃pɑs/ nf (rue) dead end; (situation) deadlock.
impatient, ~e /ɛ̃pasjɑ̃, -t/ adj impatient.
impatienter /ɛ̃pasjɑ̃te/ **1** vt annoy. □ **s'~** vpr get impatient (contre qn with sb).
impayé, ~e /ɛ̃peje/ adj unpaid.
impeccable /ɛ̃pekabl/ adj (propre) impeccable, spotless; (soigné) perfect.
impensable /ɛ̃pɑ̃sabl/ adj unthinkable.

impératif, -ive /ɛpeʀatif, -v/ adj imperative. ● nm (Gram) imperative; (contrainte) imperative; ~s (exigences) requirements, demands (de of).

impératrice /ɛpeʀatʀis/ nf empress.

impérial, ~e (mpl -iaux) /ɛpeʀjal, -jo/ adj imperial.

impérieux, -ieuse /ɛpeʀjø, -z/ adj imperious; (pressant) pressing.

imperméable /ɛpeʀmeabl/ adj impervious (à to); (manteau, tissu) waterproof. ● nm raincoat.

impersonnel, ~le /ɛpeʀsɔnɛl/ adj impersonal.

impertinent, ~e /ɛpeʀtinɑ̃, -t/ adj impertinent.

imperturbable /ɛpeʀtyʀbabl/ adj unshakeable, unruffled.

impétueux, -euse /ɛpetɥø, -z/ adj impetuous.

impitoyable /ɛpitwajabl/ adj merciless.

implant /ɛplɑ̃/ nm implant.

implanter /ɛplɑ̃te/ **1** vt establish, set up. □ s'~ vpr become established.

implication /ɛplikasjɔ̃/ nf (conséquence) implication; (participation) involvement.

impliquer /ɛplike/ **1** vt (mêler) implicate (dans in); (signifier) imply, mean (que that); (nécessiter) involve (de faire doing).

implorer /ɛplɔʀe/ **1** vt implore, beg for.

impoli, ~e /ɛpɔli/ adj impolite, rude.

importance /ɛpɔʀtɑ̃s/ nf importance; (taille) size; (ampleur) extent; sans ~ unimportant.

important, ~e /ɛpɔʀtɑ̃, -t/ adj important; (en quantité) considerable, sizeable, big; (air) self-important. ● nm l'~ the important thing.

importateur, -trice /ɛpɔʀtatœʀ, -tʀis/ nm, f importer. ● adj importing. **importation** nf import.

importer /ɛpɔʀte/ **1** vt (Comm) import. ● vi matter, be important (à to); il importe que it is important that; n'importe, peu importe it does not matter; n'importe comment anyhow; n'importe où anywhere; n'importe qui anybody; n'importe quoi anything.

importun, ~e /ɛpɔʀtœ̃, -yn/ adj troublesome. ● nm, f nuisance.

imposer /ɛpoze/ **1** vt impose (à on); (taxer) tax; en ~ à qn impress sb. □ s'~ vpr (action) be essential; (se faire reconnaître) stand out; (s'astreindre à) s'~ de faire force oneself to do.

imposition /ɛpozisjɔ̃/ nf taxation; ~ des mains laying-on of hands.

impossible /ɛposibl/ adj impossible. ● nm faire l'~ do one's utmost.

impôt /ɛpo/ nm tax; ~s (contributions) tax(ation), taxes; ~ sur le revenu income tax.

impotent, ~e /ɛpɔtɑ̃, -t/ adj disabled.

imprécis, ~e /ɛpʀesi, -z/ adj imprecise.

imprégner /ɛpʀeɲe/ **14** vt fill (de with); (imbiber) impregnate (de with). □ s'~ de vpr (fig) immerse oneself in.

impression /ɛpʀesjɔ̃/ nf impression; (de livre) printing. **impressionnant**, ~e adj impressive; (choquant) disturbing. **impressionner** **1** vt impress; (choquer) disturb.

imprévisible /ɛpʀevizibl/ adj unpredictable.

imprévu, ~e /ɛpʀevy/ adj unex-

pected. ● *nm* unexpected incident;
sauf ~ unless anything unexpected
happens.
imprimante /ɛ̃pʀimɑ̃t/ *nf* (Ordinat) printer; **~ à jet d'encre** ink-jet
printer; **~ (à) laser** laser printer.
imprimé, ~e /ɛ̃pʀime/ *adj*
printed. ● *nm* printed form.
imprimer /ɛ̃pʀime/ **1** *vt* print;
(*marquer*) imprint. **imprimerie** *nf*
(*art*) printing; (*lieu*) printing works.
imprimeur *nm* printer.
improbable /ɛ̃pʀɔbabl/ *adj* unlikely, improbable.
impropre /ɛ̃pʀɔpʀ/ *adj* incorrect;
~ à unfit for.
improviste: à l'~ /alɛ̃pʀɔvist/
loc unexpectedly.
imprudence /ɛ̃pʀydɑ̃s/ *nf* carelessness; (*acte*) careless action.
imprudent, ~e /ɛ̃pʀydɑ̃, -t/ *adj*
careless; **il est ~ de** it is unwise to.
impudent, ~e /ɛ̃pydɑ̃, -t/ *adj* impudent.
impuissant, ~e /ɛ̃pɥisɑ̃, -t/ *adj*
helpless; (*Méd*) impotent; **~ à faire**
powerless to do.
impulsif, -ive /ɛ̃pylsif, -v/ *adj* impulsive. **impulsion** *nf* (*poussée, influence*) impetus; (*instinct, mouvement*) impulse.
impur, ~e /ɛ̃pyʀ/ *adj* impure.
imputer /ɛ̃pyte/ **1** *vt* **~ à** attribute to, impute to.
inabordable /inabɔʀdabl/ *adj*
(*prix*) prohibitive.
inacceptable /inaksɛptabl/ *adj*
unacceptable.
inactif, -ive /inaktif, -v/ *adj* inactive.
inadapté, ~e /inadapte/ *adj* mal-
adjusted. ● *nm, f* (Psych) mal-
adjusted person.
inadmissible /inadmisibl/ *adj*
unacceptable.

inadvertance /inadvɛʀtɑ̃s/ *nf*
par ~ by mistake.
inanimé, ~e /inanime/ *adj* (*éva-
noui*) unconscious; (*mort*) lifeless;
(*matière*) inanimate.
inaperçu, ~e /inapɛʀsy/ *adj* unnoticed.
inapte /inapt/ *adj* unsuited (à to);
~ à faire incapable of doing; **~ au
service militaire** unfit for military
service.
inattendu, ~e /inatɑ̃dy/ *adj* unexpected.
inaugurer /inogyʀe/ **1** *vt* inaugurate.
incapable /ɛ̃kapabl/ *adj* incapable
(de qch of sth); **~ de faire** unable
to do, incapable of doing. ● *nmf* incompetent.
incapacité /ɛ̃kapasite/ *nf* inability,
incapacity; **être dans l'~ de faire**
be unable to do.
incarcérer /ɛ̃kaʀseʀe/ **14** *vt* imprison, incarcerate.
incarnation /ɛ̃kaʀnasjɔ̃/ *nf* embodiment, incarnation. **incarné, ~e**
adj (*ongle*) ingrowing.
incassable /ɛ̃kasabl/ *adj* un-
breakable.
incendiaire /ɛ̃sɑ̃djɛʀ/ *adj* incendi-
ary; (*propos*) inflammatory. ● *nmf*
arsonist.
incendie /ɛ̃sɑ̃di/ *nm* fire; **~ criminel** arson. **incendier** **45** *vt* set
fire to.
incertain, ~e /ɛ̃sɛʀtɛ̃, -ɛn/ *adj* uncertain; (*contour*) vague; (*temps*) unsettled. **incertitude** *nf* uncertainty.
inceste /ɛ̃sɛst/ *nm* incest.
incidence /ɛ̃sidɑ̃s/ *nf* effect.
incident /ɛ̃sidɑ̃/ *nm* incident; **~
technique** technical hitch.
incinérer /ɛ̃sineʀe/ **14** *vt* incinerate; (*mort*) cremate.
inciser /ɛ̃size/ **1** *vt* make an inci-

sion in; (abcès) lance. **incisif, -ive**
adj incisive. **incision** nf incision;
(d'abcès) lancing.

incitation /ɛ̃sitasjɔ̃/ nf (Jur) incite-
ment (à to); (encouragement) incentive. **inciter** 1 vt incite (à to);
(encourager) encourage.

inclinaison /ɛ̃klinɛzɔ̃/ nf incline;
(de la tête) tilt.

inclination /ɛ̃klinasjɔ̃/ nf (penchant) inclination; (geste) (du
buste) bow; (de la tête) nod.

incliner /ɛ̃kline/ 1 vt tilt, lean;
(courber) bend; (inciter) encourage
(à to); ~ la tête (approuver) nod;
(révérence) bow. □ s'~ vpr be inclined to. □ s'~ vpr lean forward;
(se courber) bow down (devant before); (céder) give in, yield (devant
to); (chemin) slope.

inclure /ɛ̃klyʁ/ 16 vt include; (enfermer) enclose; jusqu'au lundi inclus up to and including Monday.

incohérence /ɛ̃koeʁɑ̃s/ nf inco-
herence; (contradiction) discrepancy. **incohérent, ~e** adj incoher-
ent, inconsistent.

incolore /ɛ̃kɔlɔʁ/ adj colourless;
(verre) clear.

incommoder /ɛ̃kɔmɔde/ 1 vt inconvenience, bother.

incompatible /ɛ̃kɔ̃patibl/ adj incompatible.

incompétent, ~e /ɛ̃kɔ̃petɑ̃, -t/
adj incompetent.

incomplet, -ète /ɛ̃kɔ̃plɛ, -t/ adj incomplete.

incompréhension /ɛ̃kɔ̃pʁeɑ̃sjɔ̃/
nf lack of understanding.

incompris, ~e /ɛ̃kɔ̃pʁi, -z/ adj
misunderstood.

inconcevable /ɛ̃kɔ̃svabl/ adj inconceivable.

incongru, ~e /ɛ̃kɔ̃gʁy/ adj unseemly.

inconnu, ~e /ɛ̃kɔny/ adj unknown (à to). ● nm, f stranger. ● nm
l'~ the unknown.

inconscience /ɛ̃kɔ̃sjɑ̃s/ nf uncon-
sciousness; (folie) madness.

inconscient, ~e /ɛ̃kɔ̃sjɑ̃, -t/ adj
unconscious (de of); (fou) mad.
● nm (Psych) subconscious.

incontestable /ɛ̃kɔ̃tɛstabl/ adj
indisputable.

incontrôlable /ɛ̃kɔ̃tʁolabl/ adj
unverifiable; (non maîtrisé) uncon-
trollable.

inconvenant, ~e /ɛ̃kɔ̃vnɑ̃, -t/ adj
improper.

inconvénient /ɛ̃kɔ̃venjɑ̃/ nm dis-
advantage, drawback; (objection)
objection.

incorporer /ɛ̃kɔʁpɔʁe/ 1 vt incorporate; (Culin) blend (à into);
(Mil) enlist.

incorrect, ~e /ɛ̃kɔʁɛkt/ adj (faux)
incorrect; (malséant) improper; (impoli) impolite; (déloyal) unfair.

incrédule /ɛ̃kʁedyl/ adj in-
credulous.

incriminer /ɛ̃kʁimine/ 1 vt (personne) incriminate; (conduite, action)
attack.

incroyable /ɛ̃kʁwajabl/ adj incredible.

incruster /ɛ̃kʁyste/ 1 vt inlay (de
with).

incubateur /ɛ̃kybatœʁ/ nm incubator.

inculpation /ɛ̃kylpasjɔ̃/ nf charge
(de, pour of). **inculpé, ~e** nm, f accused. **inculper** 1 vt charge (de
with).

inculquer /ɛ̃kylke/ 1 vt instil (à
into).

inculte /ɛ̃kylt/ adj uncultivated;
(personne) uneducated.

incurver /ɛ̃kyʁve/ 1 vt curve,
bend. □ s'~ vpr curve, bend.

Inde /ɛ̃d/ nf India.

indécent, ~e /ɛ̃desɑ̃, -t/ adj indecent.

indécis, ~e /ɛ̃desi, -z/ adj (de nature) indecisive; (temporairement) undecided.

indéfini, ~e /ɛ̃defini/ adj (Gram) indefinite; (vague) undefined; (sans limites) indeterminate.

indemne /ɛ̃dɛmn/ adj unharmed.

indemniser /ɛ̃dɛmnize/ **1** vt compensate (for).

indemnité /ɛ̃dɛmnite/ nf indemnity, compensation; (allocation) allowance; ~s de licenciement redundancy payment.

indépendance /ɛ̃depɑ̃dɑ̃s/ nf independence. **indépendant, ~e** adj independent.

indéterminé, ~e /ɛ̃detɛrmine/ adj unspecified.

index /ɛ̃dɛks/ nm forefinger; (liste) index.

indicateur, -trice /ɛ̃dikatœr, -tris/ nm, f (police) informer. ● nm (livre) guide; (Tech) indicator.

indicatif, -ve /ɛ̃dikatif, -v/ adj indicative (de of). ● nm (à la radio) signature tune; (téléphonique) dialling code; (Gram) indicative.

indication /ɛ̃dikasjɔ̃/ nf indication; (renseignement) information; (directive) instruction.

indice /ɛ̃dis/ nm sign; (dans une enquête) clue; (des prix) index; (évaluation) rating; ~ d'écoute audience ratings.

indifférence /ɛ̃diferɑ̃s/ nf indifference.

indifférent, ~e /ɛ̃diferɑ̃, -t/ adj indifferent (à to); ça m'est ~ it makes no difference to me.

indigène /ɛ̃diʒɛn/ adj & nmf native, indigenous; (du pays) local. ● nmf native.

indigent, ~e /ɛ̃diʒɑ̃, -t/ adj destitute.

indigeste /ɛ̃diʒɛst/ adj indigestible. **indigestion** nf indigestion.

indigne /ɛ̃diɲ/ adj unworthy (de of); (acte) vile. **indigner (s')** **1** vpr become indignant (de at).

indiqué, ~e /ɛ̃dike/ adj (heure) appointed; (opportun) appropriate; (conseillé) recommended.

indiquer /ɛ̃dike/ **1** vt (montrer) show, indicate; (renseigner sur) point out, tell; (déterminer) give, state, appoint; ~ du doigt point to ou out ou at.

indirect, ~e /ɛ̃dirɛkt/ adj indirect.

indiscipliné, ~e /ɛ̃disipline/ adj unruly.

indiscret, -ète /ɛ̃diskrɛ, -t/ adj (personne) inquisitive; (question) indiscreet.

indiscutable /ɛ̃diskytabl/ adj unquestionable.

indispensable /ɛ̃dispɑ̃sabl/ adj indispensable; il est ~ qu'il vienne it is essential that he comes.

individu /ɛ̃dividy/ nm individual.

individuel, ~le /ɛ̃dividɥɛl/ adj (pour une personne) individual; (qui concerne l'individu) personal; chambre ~le single room; maison ~le detached house.

indolore /ɛ̃dɔlɔr/ adj painless.

Indonésie /ɛ̃dɔnezi/ nf Indonesia.

indu, ~e /ɛ̃dy/ adj à une heure ~e at some ungodly hour.

induire /ɛ̃dɥir/ **17** vt infer (de from); (inciter) induce (à faire to do); ~ en erreur mislead.

indulgence /ɛ̃dylʒɑ̃s/ nf indulgence; (de jury) leniency. **indulgent, ~e** adj indulgent; (clément) lenient.

industrialisé, ~e /ɛ̃dystrijalize/

adj industrialized.

industrie /ɛ̃dystʀi/ *nf* industry.

industriel, ~le /ɛ̃dystʀijɛl/ *adj* industrial. ● *nm* industrialist.

inédit, ~e /inedi, -t/ *adj* unpublished; (fig) original.

inefficace /inefikas/ *adj* (remède, mesure) ineffective; (appareil, système) inefficient.

inégal, ~e (*mpl* **-aux**) /inegal, -o/ *adj* unequal; (irrégulier) uneven. **inégalable** *adj* matchless. **inégalité** *nf* (injustice) inequality; (irrégularité) unevenness; (disproportion) disparity.

inéluctable /inelyktabl/ *adj* inescapable.

inepte /inɛpt/ *adj* inept, absurd.

inerte /inɛʀt/ *adj* inert; (immobile) lifeless; (sans énergie) apathetic. **inertie** *nf* inertia; (fig) apathy.

inespéré, ~e /inɛspeʀe/ *adj* unhoped for.

inestimable /inɛstimabl/ *adj* priceless; (aide) invaluable.

inexact, ~e /inɛgza(kt) , -kt/ *adj* (imprécis) inaccurate; (incorrect) incorrect.

in extremis /inɛkstʀemis/ *adv* (par nécessité) as a last resort; (au dernier moment) at the last minute. ● *adj* last-minute.

infaillible /ɛ̃fajibl/ *adj* infallible.

infâme /ɛ̃fɑm/ *adj* vile.

infantile /ɛ̃fɑ̃til/ *adj* (puéril) infantile; (maladie) childhood; (mortalité) infant.

infarctus /ɛ̃faʀktys/ *nm* coronary, heart attack.

infatigable /ɛ̃fatigabl/ *adj* tireless.

infect, ~e /ɛ̃fɛkt/ *adj* revolting.

infecter /ɛ̃fɛkte/ **1** *vt* infect. □ **s'~** *vpr* become infected. **infectieux, -ieuse** *adj* infectious.

infection *nf* infection.

inférieur, ~e /ɛ̃feʀjœʀ/ *adj* (plus bas) lower; (moins bon) inferior (à to); **~ à** (plus petit que) smaller than; (plus bas que) lower than. ● *nm,f* inferior. **infériorité** *nf* inferiority.

infernal, ~e (*mpl* **-aux**) /ɛ̃fɛʀnal, -o/ *adj* infernal.

infester /ɛ̃fɛste/ **1** *vt* infest.

infidèle /ɛ̃fidɛl/ *adj* unfaithful (à to). **infidélité** *nf* unfaithfulness; (acte) infidelity.

infiltrer (s') /sɛ̃filtʀe/ **1** *vpr* **~** (dans) (personnes, idées) infiltrate; (liquide) seep through.

infime /ɛ̃fim/ *adj* tiny, minute.

infini, ~e /ɛ̃fini/ *adj* infinite. ● *nm* infinity; **à l'~** endlessly. **infinité** *nf* **l'~** infinity; **une ~** an endless number of.

infinitif /ɛ̃finitif/ *nm* infinitive.

infirme /ɛ̃fiʀm/ *adj* disabled. ● *nmf* disabled person. **infirmerie** *nf* sickbay, infirmary. **infirmier** *nm* (male) nurse. **infirmière** *nf* nurse. **infirmité** *nf* disability.

inflammable /ɛ̃flamabl/ *adj* inflammable.

inflation /ɛ̃flasjɔ̃/ *nf* inflation.

infliger /ɛ̃fliʒe/ **40** *vt* inflict; (sanction) impose.

influence /ɛ̃flyɑ̃s/ *nf* influence. **influencer** **10** *vt* influence. **influent, ~e** *adj* influential.

influer /ɛ̃flye/ **1** *vi* **~ sur** influence.

informateur, -trice /ɛ̃fɔʀmatœʀ, -tʀis/ *nm,f* informant; (pour la police) informer.

informaticien, ~ne /ɛ̃fɔʀmatisjɛ̃, -ɛn/ *nm,f* computer scientist.

information /ɛ̃fɔʀmasjɔ̃/ *nf* information; (Jur) inquiry; **une ~** (some) information; (nouvelle) (some) news; les ~s the news.

informatique /ɛ̃fɔrmatik/ nf computer science; (techniques) information technology. **informatiser** ❶ vt computerize.

informer /ɛ̃fɔrme/ ❶ vt inform (de about, of). □ s'~ vpr enquire (de about).

inforoute /ɛ̃fɔrut/ nf (Ordinat) information highway.

infortune /ɛ̃fɔrtyn/ nf misfortune.

infraction /ɛ̃fraksjɔ̃/ nf offence; ~ à (loi, règlement) breach of.

infrastructure /ɛ̃frastryktyr/ nf infrastructure; (équipements) facilities.

infructueux, -euse /ɛ̃fryktɥø, -z/ adj fruitless.

infuser /ɛ̃fyze/ ❶ vt/i infuse, brew. **infusion** nf herbal tea, infusion.

ingénier (s') /(s)ɛ̃ʒenje/ 45 vpr s'~ à strive to.

ingénieur /ɛ̃ʒenjœr/ nm engineer.

ingénieux, -ieuse /ɛ̃ʒenjø, -z/ adj ingenious. **ingéniosité** nf ingenuity.

ingénu, ~e /ɛ̃ʒeny/ adj naïve.

ingérence /ɛ̃ʒerɑ̃s/ nf interference.

ingérer (s') /sɛ̃ʒere/ 14 vpr s'~ dans interfere in.

ingrat, ~e /ɛ̃gra, -t/ adj (personne) ungrateful; (travail) unrewarding, thankless; (visage) unattractive.

ingrédient /ɛ̃gredjɑ̃/ nm ingredient.

ingurgiter /ɛ̃gyrʒite/ ❶ vt swallow.

inhabité, ~e /inabite/ adj uninhabited.

inhabituel, ~le /inabitɥɛl/ adj unusual.

inhumain, ~e /inymɛ̃, -ɛn/ adj inhuman.

inhumation /inymasjɔ̃/ nf burial.

initial, ~e (mpl -iaux) /inisjal, -jo/ adj initial. **initiale** nf initial.

initialisation /inisjalizasjɔ̃/ nf (Ordinat) formatting. **initialiser** ❶ vt format.

initiation /inisjasjɔ̃/ nf initiation; (formation) introduction (à to); cours d'~ introductory course.

initiative /inisjativ/ nf initiative.

initier /inisje/ 45 vt initiate (à into); (faire découvrir) introduce (à to). □ s'~ vpr s'~ à qch learn sth.

injecter /ɛ̃ʒekte/ ❶ vt inject; injecté de sang bloodshot. **injection** nf injection.

injure /ɛ̃ʒyr/ nf insult. **injurier** 45 vt insult. **injurieux, -ieuse** adj insulting.

injuste /ɛ̃ʒyst/ adj unjust, unfair. **injustice** nf injustice.

inné, ~e /inne/ adj innate, inborn.

innocence /inosɑ̃s/ nf innocence. **innocent, ~e** adj & nm, f innocent. **innocenter** ❶ vt clear, prove innocent.

innombrable /inɔ̃brabl/ adj countless.

innovateur, -trice /inovatœr, -tris/ nm, f innovator. **innovation** nf innovation. **innover** ❶ vi innovate.

inodore /inodɔr/ adj odourless.

inoffensif, -ive /inofɑ̃sif, -v/ adj harmless.

inondation /inɔ̃dasjɔ̃/ nf flood; (action) flooding.

inonder /inɔ̃de/ ❶ vt flood; (mouiller) soak; (envahir) inundate (de with); inondé de soleil bathed in sunlight.

inopiné, ~e /inopine/ adj unexpected; (mort) sudden.

inopportun, ~e /inɔpɔrtœ̃, -yn/ adj inopportune, ill-timed.

inoubliable /inublijabl/ *adj* unforgettable.

inouï, ~e /inwi/ *adj* incredible; (*événement*) unprecedented.

inox® /inɔks/ *nm* stainless steel.

inoxydable /inɔksidabl/ *adj* acier ~ stainless steel.

inqualifiable /ɛ̃kalifjabl/ *adj* unspeakable.

inquiet, -iète /ɛ̃kjɛ, -t/ *adj* worried. **inquiétant, ~e** *adj* worrying.

inquiéter /ɛ̃kjete/ [14] *vt* worry. □ **s'~** *vpr* worry (de about). **inquiétude** *nf* anxiety, worry.

insaisissable /ɛ̃sezisabl/ *adj* (*personne*) elusive; (*nuance*) indefinable.

insalubre /ɛ̃salybʀ/ *adj* unhealthy.

insatisfaisant, ~e /ɛ̃satisfəzɑ̃, -t/ *adj* unsatisfactory. **insatisfait, ~e** *adj* (*mécontent*) dissatisfied; (*frustré*) unfulfilled.

inscription /ɛ̃skʀipsjɔ̃/ *nf* inscription; (*immatriculation*) enrolment.

inscrire /ɛ̃skʀiʀ/ [30] *vt* write (down); (*graver, tracer*) inscribe; (*personne*) enrol; (*sur une liste*) put down. □ **s'~** *vpr* put one's name down; **s'~ à** (*école*) enrol at; (*club, parti*) join; (*examen*) enter for.

insecte /ɛ̃sɛkt/ *nm* insect.

insécurité /ɛ̃sekyʀite/ *nf* insecurity.

insensé, ~e /ɛ̃sɑ̃se/ *adj* mad.

insensibilité /ɛ̃sɑ̃sibilite/ *nf* insensitivity. **insensible** *adj* insensitive (à to); (*graduel*) imperceptible.

insérer /ɛ̃seʀe/ [14] *vt* insert. □ **s'~** *vpr* be inserted; **s'~ dans** be part of.

insigne /ɛ̃siɲ/ *nm* badge; **~s** (d'une fonction) insignia.

insignifiant, ~e /ɛ̃siɲifjɑ̃, -t/ *adj* insignificant.

insinuation /ɛ̃sinɥasjɔ̃/ *nf* insinuation.

insinuer /ɛ̃sinɥe/ [1] *vt* insinuate. □ **s'~** *vpr* (socialement) ingratiate oneself (auprès de qn with sb); **s'~ dans** (se glisser) slip into; (*idée, nuance*) creep into.

insipide /ɛ̃sipid/ *adj* insipid.

insistance /ɛ̃sistɑ̃s/ *nf* insistence. **insistant, ~e** *adj* insistent.

insister /ɛ̃siste/ [1] *vi* insist (pour faire on doing); ~ **sur** stress.

insolation /ɛ̃sɔlasjɔ̃/ *nf* (Méd) sunstroke.

insolent, ~e /ɛ̃sɔlɑ̃, -t/ *adj* insolent.

insolite /ɛ̃sɔlit/ *adj* unusual.

insolvable /ɛ̃sɔlvabl/ *adj* insolvent.

insomnie /ɛ̃sɔmni/ *nf* insomnia.

insonoriser /ɛ̃sɔnɔʀize/ [1] *vt* soundproof.

insouciance /ɛ̃susjɑ̃s/ *nf* lack of concern. **insouciant, ~e** *adj* carefree.

insoutenable /ɛ̃sutnabl/ *adj* unbearable; (*argument*) untenable.

inspecter /ɛ̃spɛkte/ [1] *vt* inspect. **inspecteur, -trice** *nm, f* inspector. **inspection** *nf* inspection.

inspiration /ɛ̃spiʀasjɔ̃/ *nf* inspiration; (*respiration*) breath.

inspirer /ɛ̃spiʀe/ [1] *vt* inspire; ~ **la méfiance à qn** inspire distrust in sb. ● *vi* breathe in. □ **s'~ de** *vpr* be inspired by.

instabilité /ɛ̃stabilite/ *nf* instability; unsteadiness. **instable** *adj* unstable; (*temps*) unsettled.

installation /ɛ̃stalasjɔ̃/ *nf* installation; (de local) fitting out; (de locataire) settling in. **installations** *nfpl* facilities.

installer /ɛ̃stale/ [1] *vt* install; (meuble) put in; (étagère) put up; (gaz, téléphone) connect; (équiper) fit out. □ s'~ vpr settle (down); (emménager) settle in; s'~ comme set oneself up as.

instance /ɛ̃stɑ̃s/ nf authority; (prière) entreaty; avec ~ with insistence; en ~ pending; en ~ de in the course of, on the point of.

instant /ɛ̃stɑ̃/ nm moment, instant; à l'~ this instant.

instantané, ~e /ɛ̃stɑ̃tane/ adj instantaneous; (café) instant.

instar: à l'~ de /alɛstaʀdə/ loc like.

instaurer /ɛ̃stoʀe/ **1** vt institute.

instigateur, -trice /ɛ̃stigatœʀ, -tʀis/ nm, f instigator.

instinct /ɛ̃stɛ̃/ nm instinct; d'~ instinctively. **instinctif, -ive** adj instinctive.

instituer /ɛ̃stitɥe/ **1** vt establish.

institut /ɛ̃stity/ nm institute; ~ de beauté beauty parlour.

instituteur, -trice /ɛ̃stitytœʀ, -tʀis/ nm, f primary-school teacher.

institution /ɛ̃stitysjɔ̃/ nf institution; (école) private school.

instructif, -ive /ɛ̃stʀyktif, -v/ adj instructive.

instruction /ɛ̃stʀyksjɔ̃/ nf (formation) education; (Mil) training; (document) directive; ~s (ordres, mode d'emploi) instructions; (Ordinat) (énoncé) instruction; (pas de séquence) statement.

instruire /ɛ̃stʀɥiʀ/ **17** vt teach, educate; ~ de inform of. □ s'~ vpr learn, educate oneself; s'~ de enquire about. **instruit, ~e** adj educated.

instrument /ɛ̃stʀymɑ̃/ nm instrument; (outil) tool; (moyen, fig) instrument; ~ de gestion management tool; ~s de bord (Aviat) controls.

insu: à l'~ de /alɛ̃syda/ loc without the knowledge of.

insuffisance /ɛ̃syfizɑ̃s/ nf (pénurie) shortage; (médiocrité) inadequacy. **insuffisant, ~e** adj inadequate; (en nombre) insufficient.

insulaire /ɛ̃sylɛʀ/ adj island. ● nmf islander.

insuline /ɛ̃sylin/ nf insulin.

insulte /ɛ̃sylt/ nf insult. **insulter** **1** vt insult.

insupportable /ɛ̃sypɔʀtabl/ adj unbearable.

insurger (s') /(s)ɛ̃syʀʒe/ **40** vpr rebel.

intact, ~e /ɛ̃takt/ adj intact.

intangible /ɛ̃tɑ̃ʒibl/ adj intangible; (principe) inviolable.

intarissable /ɛ̃taʀisabl/ adj inexhaustible.

intégral, ~e (mpl -aux) /ɛ̃tegʀal, -o/ adj complete; (texte, édition) unabridged; (paiement) full, in full. **intégralement** adv in full. **intégralité** nf whole.

intègre /ɛ̃tɛgʀ/ adj upright.

intégrer /ɛ̃tegʀe/ **14** vt integrate. □ s'~ vpr (personne) integrate; (maison) fit in.

intégriste /ɛ̃tegʀist/ nmf fundamentalist.

intégrité /ɛ̃tegʀite/ nf integrity.

intellect /ɛ̃telɛkt/ nm intellect. **intellectuel, ~le** adj & nm, f intellectual.

intelligence /ɛ̃teliʒɑ̃s/ nf intelligence; (compréhension) understanding; (complicité) agreement; agir d'~ avec qn act in agreement with sb. **intelligent, ~e** adj intelligent.

intempéries /ɛ̃tɑ̃peʀi/ nfpl severe weather.

intempestif, -ive /ɛ̃tɑ̃pɛstif, -v/ adj untimely.

intenable /ɛ̃tnabl/ *adj* unbearable; (*enfant*) impossible.

intendance /ɛ̃tɑ̃dɑ̃s/ *nf* (Scol) bursar's office.

intendant, ~e /ɛ̃tɑ̃dɑ̃, -t/ *nm* (Mil) quartermaster. ● *nm, f* (Scol) bursar.

intense /ɛ̃tɑ̃s/ *adj* intense; (*circulation*) heavy. **intensif, -ive** *adj* intensive. **intensité** *nf* intensity.

intenter /ɛ̃tɑ̃te/ **1** *vt* ~ un procès ou une action institute proceedings (à, contre against).

intention /ɛ̃tɑ̃sjɔ̃/ *nf* intention (de faire of doing); à l'~ de qn for sb. **intentionnel, ~le** *adj* intentional.

interactif, -ive /ɛ̃tɛʀaktif, -v/ *adj* (TV, vidéo) interactive.

interaction /ɛ̃tɛʀaksjɔ̃/ *nf* interaction.

intercaler /ɛ̃tɛʀkale/ **1** *vt* insert.

intercéder /ɛ̃tɛʀsede/ **14** *vi* intercede (en faveur de on behalf of).

intercepter /ɛ̃tɛʀsɛpte/ **1** *vt* intercept.

interdiction /ɛ̃tɛʀdiksjɔ̃/ *nf* ban; ~ de fumer no smoking.

interdire /ɛ̃tɛʀdir/ **37** *vt* forbid; (*officiellement*) ban, prohibit; ~ à qn de faire forbid sb to do.

interdit, ~e /ɛ̃tɛʀdi, -t/ *adj* prohibited, forbidden; (*étonné*) dumbfounded.

intéressant, ~e /ɛ̃teʀesɑ̃, -t/ *adj* interesting; (*avantageux*) attractive.

intéressé, ~e /ɛ̃teʀese/ *adj* (en cause) concerned; (pour profiter) self-interested. ● *nm, f* person concerned.

intéresser /ɛ̃teʀese/ **1** *vt* interest; (*concerner*) concern. □ s'~ à *vpr* be interested in.

intérêt /ɛ̃teʀɛ/ *nm* interest; (*égoïsme*) self-interest; (~s) (Comm) interest; vous avez ~ à it is in your interest to.

interface /ɛ̃tɛʀfas/ *nf* (Ordinat) interface.

intérieur, ~e /ɛ̃teʀjœʀ/ *adj* inner, inside; (*mur, escalier*) internal; (*vol, politique*) domestic; (*vie, calme*) inner. ● *nm* interior; (de boîte, tiroir) inside; à l'~ (de) inside; (fig) within. **intérieurement** *adv* inwardly.

intérim /ɛ̃teʀim/ *nm* interim; assurer l'~ deputize (de for); par ~ on an interim basis; président par ~ acting president; faire de l'~ temp.

intérimaire /ɛ̃teʀimɛʀ/ *adj* temporary, interim. ● *nmf* (secrétaire) temp; (médecin) locum.

interjection /ɛ̃tɛʀʒɛksjɔ̃/ *nf* interjection.

interlocuteur, -trice /ɛ̃tɛʀlɔkytœʀ, -tʀis/ *nm, f* son ~ the person one is speaking to.

interloqué, ~e /ɛ̃tɛʀlɔke/ *adj* être ~ be taken aback.

intermède /ɛ̃tɛʀmɛd/ *nm* interlude.

intermédiaire /ɛ̃tɛʀmedjɛʀ/ *adj* intermediate. ● *nmf* intermediary. ● *nm* sans ~ without an intermediary, direct; par l'~ de through.

interminable /ɛ̃tɛʀminabl/ *adj* endless.

intermittence /ɛ̃tɛʀmitɑ̃s/ *nf* par ~ intermittently.

internat /ɛ̃tɛʀna/ *nm* boarding-school.

international, ~e (*mpl* **-aux**) /ɛ̃tɛʀnasjɔnal, -o/ *adj* international.

internaute /ɛ̃tɛʀnot/ *nmf* (Ordinat) Netsurfer, Internet user.

interne /ɛ̃tɛʀn/ *adj* internal; (*cours, formation*) in-house. ● *nmf* (Scol) boarder; (Méd) house officer; (US) intern.

internement /ɛ̃tɛʀnəmɑ̃/ *nm* (Pol) internment. **interner 1** *vt*

(Pol) intern; (Méd) commit.
Internet /ɛtɛʀnɛt/ nm Internet; **sur**
~ **on** the Internet.
interpellation /ɛtɛʀpelasjɔ̃/ nf
(Pol) questioning. **interpeller** 🔟 vt
shout to; (apostropher) shout at;
(interroger) question.
interphone /ɛtɛʀfɔn/ nm intercom; (d'immeuble) entry phone.
interposer (s') /(s)ɛtɛʀpoze/ 🔟
vpr intervene.
interprétariat /ɛtɛʀpʀetaʀja/ nm
interpreting. **interprétation** nf interpretation; (d'artiste) performance. **interprète** nmf interpreter;
(artiste) performer. **interpréter** 🔢
vt interpret; (jouer) play; (chanter) sing.
interrogateur, -trice
/ɛtɛʀɔgatœʀ, -tʀis/ adj questioning.
interrogatif, -ive adj interrogative.
interrogation nf question; (action)
questioning; (épreuve) test. **inter-
rogatoire** nm interrogation. **interroger** 🔢 vt question; (élève) test.
interrompre /ɛtɛʀɔ̃pʀ/ 🔢 vt
break off, interrupt; (personne)
interrupt. □ **s'~** vpr break off. **interrupteur** nm switch. **interruption** nf interruption; (arrêt) break.
interurbain, ~e /ɛtɛʀyʀbɛ̃, -ɛn/
adj long-distance, trunk.
intervalle /ɛtɛʀval/ nm space;
(temps) interval; **dans l'~** in the
meantime.
intervenir /ɛtɛʀvəniʀ/ 🔢 vi (agir)
intervene (auprès de qn with sb);
(survenir) occur, take place; (Méd)
operate. **intervention** nf interven-
tion; (Méd) operation.
intervertir /ɛtɛʀvɛʀtiʀ/ 🔢 vt invert; (rôles) reverse.
interview /ɛtɛʀvju/ nf interview.
interviewer 🔟 vt interview.
intestin /ɛtɛstɛ̃/ nm intestine.

intime /ɛtim/ adj intimate; (fête,
vie) private; (dîner) quiet. ● nmf intimate friend.
intimider /ɛtimide/ 🔟 vt intimidate.
intimité /ɛtimite/ nf intimacy; (vie
privée) privacy.
intituler /ɛtityle/ 🔟 vt call, entitle. □ **s'~** vpr be called ou entitled.
intolérable /ɛtɔleʀabl/ adj intoler-
able. **intolérance** nf intolerance. **intolérant, ~e** adj intolerant.
intonation /ɛtɔnasjɔ̃/ nf intonation.
intox /ɛtɔks/ nf 🔟 brainwashing.
intoxication /ɛtɔksikasjɔ̃/ nf poisoning; (fig) brainwashing; ~ **alimentaire** food poisoning. **intoxi-
quer** 🔟 vt poison; (fig) brainwash.
intraitable /ɛtʀetabl/ adj in-
flexible.
Intranet /ɛtʀanɛt/ nm Intranet.
intransigeant, ~e /ɛtʀɑ̃ziʒɑ̃, -t/
adj intransigent.
intransitif, -ive /ɛtʀɑ̃zitif, -v/ adj
intransitive.
intraveineux, -euse /ɛtʀavɛnø,
-z/ adj intravenous.
intrépide /ɛtʀepid/ adj fearless.
intrigue /ɛtʀig/ nf intrigue; (scénario) plot.
intrinsèque /ɛtʀɛ̃sɛk/ adj intrinsic.
introduction /ɛtʀɔdyksjɔ̃/ nf
introduction; (insertion) insertion.
introduire /ɛtʀɔdɥiʀ/ 🔢 vt introduce, bring in; (insérer) put in, insert; ~ **qn** show sb in. □ **s'~** vpr
get in; **s'~ dans** get into, enter.
introuvable /ɛtʀuvabl/ adj that
cannot be found.
introverti, ~e /ɛtʀɔvɛʀti/ nm, f
introvert. ● adj introverted.

i

intrus, ~e /ɛ̃tʀy, -z/ nm, f intruder. **intrusion** nf intrusion.

intuitif, -ive /ɛ̃tyitif, -iv/ adj intuitive. **intuition** nf intuition.

inusable /inyzabl/ adj hard-wearing.

inusité, ~e /inyzite/ adj little used.

inutile /inytil/ adj useless; (vain) needless. **inutilement** adv needlessly. **inutilisable** adj unusable.

invalide /ɛ̃valid/ adj & nmf disabled (person).

invariable /ɛ̃vaʀjabl/ adj invariable.

invasion /ɛ̃vazjɔ̃/ nf invasion.

invectiver /ɛ̃vɛktive/ **1** vt abuse.

inventaire /ɛ̃vɑ̃tɛʀ/ nm inventory; (Comm) stocklist; faire l'~ draw up an inventory; (Comm) do a stocktake.

inventer /ɛ̃vɑ̃te/ **1** vt invent. **inventeur**, -trice nm, f inventor. **inventif**, -ive adj inventive. **invention** nf invention.

inverse /ɛ̃vɛʀs/ adj opposite; (ordre) reverse; en sens ~ in ou from the opposite direction. ● nm reverse; c'est l'~ it's the other way round. **inversement** adv conversely. **inverser** **1** vt reverse, invert.

investir /ɛ̃vɛstiʀ/ **2** vt invest. **investissement** nm investment.

investiture /ɛ̃vɛstityʀ/ nf (de candidat) nomination; (de président) investiture.

invétéré, ~e /ɛ̃vetere/ adj inveterate; (menteur) compulsive; (enraciné) deep-rooted.

invisible /ɛ̃vizibl/ adj invisible.

invitation /ɛ̃vitasjɔ̃/ nf invitation. **invité**, ~e nm, f guest. **inviter** **1** vt invite (à to).

involontaire /ɛ̃vɔlɔ̃tɛʀ/ adj involuntary; (témoin, héros) unwitting.

invoquer /ɛ̃vɔke/ **1** vt call upon, invoke.

invraisemblable /ɛ̃vʀɛsɑ̃blabl/ adj improbable, unlikely; (incroyable) incredible. **invraisemblance** nf improbability.

iode /jɔd/ nm iodine.

ira, irait /iʀa, iʀɛ/ ➡ALLER **8**.

Irak /iʀak/ nm Iraq.

Iran /iʀɑ̃/ nm Iran.

iris /iʀis/ nm iris.

irlandais, ~e /iʀlɑ̃dɛ, -z/ adj Irish. l~, ~e nm, f Irishman, Irishwoman.

Irlande /iʀlɑ̃d/ nf Ireland.

IRM abrév nf (imagerie par résonance magnétique) magnetic resonance imaging.

ironie /iʀɔni/ nf irony. **ironique** adj ironic.

irrationnel, ~le /iʀasjɔnɛl/ adj irrational.

irréalisable /iʀealizabl/ adj (idée, rêve) unachievable; (projet) unworkable.

irrécupérable /iʀekypeʀabl/ adj irretrievable; (capital) irrecoverable.

irréel, ~le /iʀeɛl/ adj unreal.

irréfléchi, ~e /iʀefleʃi/ adj thoughtless.

irrégulier, -ière /iʀegylje, -jɛʀ/ adj irregular.

irrémédiable /iʀemedjabl/ adj irreparable.

irremplaçable /iʀɑ̃plasabl/ adj irreplaceable.

irréparable /iʀepaʀabl/ adj (objet) beyond repair; (tort, dégâts) irreparable.

irréprochable /iʀepʀɔʃabl/ adj flawless.

irrésistible /iʀezistibl/ adj irresistible; (drôle) hilarious.

irrésolu, ~e /iʀezɔly/ adj indecisive; (problème) unsolved.

irrespirable /iʀɛspiʀabl/ adj stifling.

irresponsable /iʀɛspɔ̃sabl/ adj irresponsible.

irrigation /iʀigasjɔ̃/ nf irrigation. **irriguer** 🔟 vt irrigate.

irritable /iʀitabl/ adj irritable.

irriter /iʀite/ 🔟 vt irritate. □ **s'~** vpr get annoyed (de at).

irruption /iʀypsjɔ̃/ nf **faire ~ dans** burst into.

Islam /islam/ nm Islam. **islamique** adj Islamic.

islamiste /islamist/ adj Islamist, Islamic; n m,f Islamist.

islandais, ~e /islɑ̃dɛ, -z/ adj Icelandic. ● nm (Ling) Icelandic. **I~, ~e** nm, f Icelander.

Islande /islɑ̃d/ nf Iceland.

isolant /izɔlɑ̃/ nm insulating material. **isolation** nf insulation.

isolé, ~e /izɔle/ adj isolated. **isolement** nm isolation.

isoler /izɔle/ 🔟 vt isolate; (Électr) insulate. □ **s'~** vpr isolate oneself.

isoloir /izɔlwaʀ/ nm polling booth.

Isorel ® /izɔʀɛl/ nm hardboard.

Israël /isʀaɛl/ nm Israel. **israélien, ~ne** adj Israeli.

israélite /isʀaelit/ adj Jewish. ● nmf Jew.

issu, ~e /isy/ adj **être ~ de** (personne) come from; (résulter de) result ou stem from.

issue /isy/ nf (sortie) exit; (résultat) outcome; (fig) solution; **à l'~ de** at the conclusion of; **~ de secours** emergency exit; **rue** ou **voie sans ~** dead end.

Italie /itali/ nf Italy.

italien, ~ne /italjɛ̃, -ɛn/ adj Italian. ● nm (Ling) Italian. **I~, ~ne** nm, f Italian.

italique /italik/ nm italics.

itinéraire /itineʀɛʀ/ nm itinerary, route.

I.U.T. abrév m (**Institut universitaire de technologie**) university institute of technology.

I.V.G. abrév f (**interruption volontaire de grossesse**) abortion.

ivoire /ivwaʀ/ nm ivory.

ivre /ivʀ/ adj drunk. **ivresse** nf drunkenness; (fig) exhilaration. **ivrogne** nmf drunk(ard).

Jj

j' /ʒ/ ➡JE.

jacinthe /ʒasɛ̃t/ nf hyacinth.

jadis /ʒadis/ adv long ago.

jaillir /ʒajiʀ/ 🔁 vi (liquide) spurt (out); (lumière) stream out; (apparaître) burst forth, spring out.

jalonner /ʒalɔne/ 🔟 vt mark (out).

jalousie /ʒaluzi/ nf jealousy; (store) (venetian) blind. **jaloux, -ouse** adj jealous.

jamais /ʒamɛ/ adv ever; **ne ~** never; **il ne boit ~** he never drinks; **à ~** for ever; **si ~** if ever.

jambe /ʒɑ̃b/ nf leg.

jambon /ʒɑ̃bɔ̃/ nm ham. **jambonneau** (pl **~x**) nm knuckle of ham.

janvier /ʒɑ̃vje/ nm january.

japon /ʒapɔ̃/ nm Japan.

japonais, ~e /ʒapɔnɛ, -z/ adj Japanese. ● nm (Ling) Japanese. **J~, ~e** nm, f Japanese.

japper /ʒape/ 🔟 vi yap.

jaquette /ʒakɛt/ nf (de livre, femme) jacket; (d'homme) morning coat.

jardin /ʒaʀdɛ̃/ nm garden; ~ d'enfants nursery (school); ~ public public park. **jardinage** nm gardening. **jardiner** **1** vi do some gardening, garden. **jardinier, -ière** nm, f gardener.

jardinière /ʒaʀdinjɛʀ/ nf (meuble) plant-stand; ~ de légumes mixed vegetables.

jarretelle /ʒaʀtɛl/ nf suspender; (US) garter.

jarretière /ʒaʀtjɛʀ/ nf garter.

jatte /ʒat/ nf bowl.

jauge /ʒoʒ/ nf capacity; (de navire) tonnage; (compteur) gauge; ~ d'huile dipstick.

jaune /ʒon/ adj & nm yellow; (péj) scab; ~ d'œuf (egg) yolk; rire ~ give a forced laugh. **jaunir** **2** vt/i turn yellow. **jaunisse** nf jaundice.

javelot /ʒavlo/ nm javelin.

jazz /dʒaz/ nm jazz.

J.C. abrév m (**Jésus-Christ**) 500 avant/après ~ 500 B.C./A.D.

je, j' /ʒə, ʒ/ pron I.

jean /dʒin/ nm jeans; un ~ a pair of jeans.

jet¹ /ʒɛ/ nm throw; (de liquide, vapeur) jet; ~ d'eau fountain.

jet² /dʒɛt/ nm (avion) jet.

jetable /ʒətabl/ adj disposable.

jetée /ʒəte/ nf pier.

jeter /ʒəte/ **38** vt throw; (au rebut) throw away; (regard, ancre, lumière) cast; (cri) utter; (bases) lay; ~ un coup d'œil have ou take a look (à at). □ se ~ vpr se ~ contre crash ou bash into; se ~ dans (fleuve) flow into; se ~ sur (se ruer sur) rush at.

jeton /ʒətɔ̃/ nm token; (pour compter) counter; (au casino) chip.

jeu (pl ~x) /ʒø/ nm game; (amusement) play; (au casino) gambling; (Théât) acting; (série) set; (de lu-

mière, ressort) play; en ~ (honneur) at stake; (forces) at work; ~ de cartes (paquet) pack of cards; ~d'échecs (boîte) chess set; ~ de mots pun; ~ télévisé tv game show; ~ vidéo video game; ~x de grattage scratch cards; les ~x olympiques/paralympiques the Olympic Games/Paralympic Games.

jeudi /ʒødi/ nm Thursday.

jeun: à ~ /aʒœ̃/ loc on an empty stomach.

jeune /ʒœn/ adj young; ~ fille girl; ~ pousse (Comm) start-up; ~s mariés newlyweds. ● nmf young person; les ~s young people.

jeûne /ʒøn/ nm fast.

jeunesse /ʒœnɛs/ nf youth; (apparence) youthfulness; la ~ (jeunes) the young.

joaillerie /ʒoajʀi/ nf jewellery; (magasin) jeweller's shop.

joie /ʒwa/ nf joy.

joindre /ʒwɛ̃dʀ/ **22** vt join (à to); (mains, pieds) put together; (efforts) combine; (contacter) contact; (dans une enveloppe) enclose. □ se ~ à vpr join.

joint, ~e /ʒwɛ̃, -t/ adj (efforts) joint; (pieds) together. ● nm joint; (de robinet) washer.

joli, ~e /ʒoli/ adj pretty, nice; (somme, profit) nice; c'est du ~! (ironique) charming! c'est bien ~ mais that is all very well but.

joncher /ʒɔ̃ʃe/ **1** vt litter, be strewn over; jonché de littered with.

jonction /ʒɔ̃ksjɔ̃/ nf junction.

jongleur, -euse /ʒɔ̃glœʀ, øz/ nm, f juggler.

jonquille /ʒɔ̃kij/ nf daffodil.

joue /ʒu/ nf cheek.

jouer /ʒwe/ **1** vt/i play; (Théât) act; (au casino) gamble; (fonctionner) work; (*film, pièce*) put on; (*cheval*) back; (être important) count; ~ à (*jeu*, Sport) play; ~ de (Mus) play; ~ la comédie put on an act; bien joué! well done!

jouet /ʒwɛ/ *nm* toy; (*personne*: fig) plaything; (*victime*) victim.

joueur, -euse /ʒwœʀ, -øz/ *nm, f* player; (*parieur*) gambler.

joufflu, -e /ʒufly/ *adj* chubby-cheeked; (*visage*) chubby.

jouir /ʒwiʀ/ **②** *vi* (sexe) come; ~ de (*droit, avantage*) enjoy; (*bien, concession*) enjoy the use of. **jouissance** *nf* pleasure; (*usage*) use (de qch of sth).

joujou (*pl* ~x) /ʒuʒu/ *nm* **①** toy.

jour /ʒuʀ/ *nm* day; (*opposé à nuit*) day (time); (*lumière*) daylight; (*aspect*) light; (*ouverture*) gap; de nos ~s nowadays; du ~ au lendemain overnight; il fait ~ it is daylight; ~ chômé ou férié public holiday; ~ de fête holiday; ~ ouvrable, ~ de travail working day; mettre à ~ update; mettre au ~ uncover; au grand ~ in the open; donner le ~ give birth; voir le ~ be born; vivre au ~ le jour live from day to day.

journal (*pl* -aux) /ʒuʀnal, -o/ *nm* (news)paper; (*spécialisé*) journal; (*intime*) diary; (à la radio) news; ~ de bord log-book.

journalier, -ière /ʒuʀnalje, -jɛʀ/ *adj* daily.

journalisme /ʒuʀnalism/ *nm* journalism. **journaliste** *nmf* journalist.

journée /ʒuʀne/ *nf* day.

jovial, -e (*mpl* -iaux) /ʒɔvjal, -jo/ *adj* jovial.

joyau (*pl* ~x) /ʒwajo/ *nm* gem.

joyeux, -euse /ʒwajø, -z/ *adj* merry, joyful; ~ anniversaire happy birthday.

jubiler /ʒybile/ **①** *vi* be jubilant.

jucher /ʒyʃe/ **①** *vt* perch. □ se ~ *vpr* perch.

judaïsme /ʒydaism/ *nm* Judaism.

judiciaire /ʒydisjɛʀ/ *adj* judicial.

judicieux, -ieuse /ʒydisjø, -z/ *adj* judicious.

judo /ʒydo/ *nm* judo.

juge /ʒyʒ/ *nm* judge; (*arbitre*) referee; ~ de paix Justice of the Peace; ~ de touche linesman.

jugé: au ~ /oʒyʒe/ *loc* by guesswork.

jugement /ʒyʒmɑ̃/ *nm* judgement; (*criminel*) sentence.

juger /ʒyʒe/ **40** *vt/i* judge; (*estimer*) consider (que that); ~ de judge.

juguler /ʒygyle/ **①** *vt* stamp out; curb.

juif, -ive /ʒɥif, -v/ *adj* Jewish. ● *nm, f* Jew.

juillet /ʒɥijɛ/ *nm* July.

juin /ʒɥɛ̃/ *nm* June.

jumeau, -elle (*mpl* ~x) /ʒymo, -ɛl/ *adj et nm, f* twin. **jumeler** **38** *vt* (*villes*) twin.

jumelles /ʒymɛl/ *nfpl* binoculars.

jument /ʒymɑ̃/ *nf* mare.

junior /ʒynjɔʀ/ *adj et nmf* junior.

jupe /ʒyp/ *nf* skirt.

jupon /ʒypõ/ *nm* slip, petticoat.

juré, -e /ʒyʀe/ *nm, f* juror. ● *adj* sworn.

jurer /ʒyʀe/ **①** *vt* swear (que that). ● *vi* (*pester*) swear; (*contraster*) clash (avec with).

juridiction /ʒyʀidiksjõ/ *nf* jurisdiction; (*tribunal*) court of law.

juridique /ʒyʀidik/ *adj* legal.

juriste /ʒyʀist/ *nmf* legal expert.

juron /ʒyʀõ/ *nm* swearword.

jury /ʒyʀi/ *nm* (Jur) jury; (examinateurs) panel of judges.

jus /ʒy/ nm juice; (de viande) gravy; ~ de fruit fruit juice.

jusque /ʒysk(ə)/ prép jusqu'à (up) to, as far as; (temps) until, till; (limite) up to; (y compris) even; jusqu'à ce que until; jusqu'à présent until now; jusqu'en until; jusqu'où? how far?; ~ dans, ~ sur as far as.

juste /ʒyst/ adj fair, just; (légitime) just; (correct, exact) right; (vrai) true; (vêtement) tight; (quantité) on the short side; le ~ milieu the happy medium. ● adv rightly, correctly; (chanter) in tune; (seulement, exactement) just; (un peu) a bit fine or close; au ~ exactly; c'était ~ (presque raté) it was a close thing. **justement** adv (précisément) precisely; (à l'instant) just; (avec justesse) correctly; (légitimement) justifiably.

justesse /ʒystɛs/ nf accuracy; de ~ just, narrowly.

justice /ʒystis/ nf justice; (autorités) law; (tribunal) court.

justifier /ʒystifje/ [45] vt justify. ● vi ~ de prove. □ se ~ vpr justify oneself.

juteux, -euse /ʒytø, -z/ adj juicy.

juvénile /ʒyvenil/ adj youthful; (délinquance, mortalité) juvenile.

. . . .

Kk

. . . .

kaki /kaki/ adj inv & nm khaki.

kangourou /kãguʁu/ nm kangaroo.

karaté /kaʁate/ nm karate.

kart /kaʁt/ nm go-cart.

kascher /kaʃɛʁ/ adj inv kosher.

kayak /kajak/ nm kayak.

képi /kepi/ nm kepi.

kermesse /kɛʁmɛs/ nf fête.

kidnapper /kidnape/ [1] vt kidnap.

kilo /kilo/ nm kilo.

kilogramme /kilogʁam/ nm kilogram.

kilométrage /kilometʁaʒ/ nm ≈ mileage. **kilomètre** nm kilometre.

kinésithérapeute /kineziteʁapøt/ nmf physiotherapist. **kinésithérapie** nf physiotherapy.

kiosque /kjɔsk/ nm kiosk; ~ à musique bandstand.

kit /kit/ nm kit; ~ mains libres conducteur hands-free kit.

klaxon® /klaksɔn/ nm (Auto) horn. **klaxonner** [1] vi sound one's horn.

Ko abrév m (kilo-octet) (Ordinat) KB.

KO abrév m (knock-out) KO [1].

K-way® /kawɛ/ nm inv windcheater.

kyste /kist/ nm cyst.

. . . .

Ll

. . . .

l', la /l, la/ ➡le.

là /la/

● adverbe

••••▸ (dans ce lieu) there; (ici) here; (chez soi) in; c'est ~ que this is where; ~ où where; par ~ (dans cette direction) this

way; (dans cette zone) around there; de ~ hence.
····➤ (à ce moment) then; c'est ~ que that's when.
····➤ cet homme-~ that man; ces maisons-~ those houses.
● interjection
····➤ ~ 🗓 c'est fini there (now), it's all over!

là-bas /laba/ adv there; (à l'endroit que l'on indique) over there.

label /label/ nm seal, label.

laboratoire /labɔʀatwaʀ/ nm laboratory.

laborieux, -ieuse /labɔʀjø, -z/ adj laborious; (personne) industrious; classes laborieuses working classes.

labour /labuʀ/ nm ploughing; (US) plowing. **labourer** 🗓 vt plough; (US) plow; (déchirer) rip at.

labyrinthe /labiʀɛ̃t/ nm maze, labyrinth.

lac /lak/ nm lake.

lacer /lase/ 🔟 vt lace up.

lacet /lase/ nm (de chaussure) (shoe-)lace; (de route) sharp bend.

lâche /lɑʃ/ adj cowardly; (détendu) loose; (sans rigueur) lax. ● nmf coward.

lâcher /lɑʃe/ 🗓 vt let go of; (laisser tomber) drop; (abandonner) give up; (laisser) leave; (libérer) release; (flèche, balle) fire; (juron, phrase) come out with; (desserrer) loosen; ~ prise let go. ● vi give way.

lâcheté /lɑʃte/ nf cowardice.

lacrymogène /lakʀimɔʒɛn/ adj gaz ~ tear gas.

lacune /lakyn/ nf gap.

là-dedans /lad(ə)dɑ̃/ adv (près) in here; (plus loin) in there.

là-dessous /lad(ə)su/ adv (près)

under here; (plus loin) under there.

là-dessus /lad(ə)sy/ adv (sur une surface) on here; (plus loin) on there; (sur ce) with that; (quelque temps après) after that; qu'avez-vous à dire ~? what have you got to say about it?

ladite /ladit/ ⇒**ledit**.

lagune /lagyn/ nf lagoon.

là-haut /lao/ adv (en hauteur) up here; (plus loin) up there; (à l'étage) upstairs.

laïc /laik/ nm layman.

laid, ~e /lɛ, lɛd/ adj ugly; (action) vile. **laideur** nf ugliness.

lainage /lɛnaʒ/ nm woollen garment.

laine /lɛn/ nf wool; de ~ woollen.

laïque /laik/ adj (état, loi) secular; (habit, personne) lay; (école) nondenominational. ● nmf layman, laywoman.

laisse /lɛs/ nf lead, leash; tenir en ~ keep on a lead.

laisser /lese/ 🗓 vt (déposer) leave, drop off; (confier) leave (à qn with sb); (abandonner) leave; (rendre) ~ qn perplexe/froid leave sb puzzled/cold; ~ qch à qn (céder, prêter) let sb have sth; (donner) (choix, temps) give sb sth. □ se ~ vpr se ~ persuader/insulter let oneself be persuaded/insulted; elle ne se laisse pas faire she won't be pushed around; laisse-toi faire leave it to me/him/her etc.; se ~ aller let oneself go. ● vt laisser qn/qch faire let sb/sth do; laisse-moi faire let me do it; (je m'en occupe) leave it to me; laisse faire! so what! **laisser-aller** nm inv carelessness; (dans la tenue) scruffiness; **laissez-passer** nm inv pass.

lait /lɛ/ nm milk; ~ longue conservation long-life *ou* UHT milk; **frère/- sœur de** ~ foster-brother/-sister. **laitage** *nm* milk product. **laiterie** *nf* dairy. **laiteux, -euse** *adj* milky.

laitier, -ière /letje, -jɛʀ/ *adj* dairy.
● *nm, f* (livreur) milkman, milkwoman.

laiton /letɔ̃/ *nm* brass.

laitue /lety/ *nf* lettuce.

lama /lama/ *nm* llama.

lambeau (*pl* ~x) /lɑ̃bo/ *nm* shred; **en** ~x in shreds.

lame /lam/ *nf* blade; (lamelle) strip; (vague) wave; ~ **de fond** ground swell; ~ **de rasoir** razor blade.

lamentable /lamɑ̃tabl/ *adj* deplorable. **lamenter (se)** 🔟 *vpr* moan (*sur* about, over).

lampadaire /lɑ̃padɛʀ/ *nm* standard lamp; (de rue) street lamp.

lampe /lɑ̃p/ *nf* lamp; (ampoule) bulb; (de radio) valve; ~ **(de poche)** torch; (US) flashlight; ~ **à souder** blowlamp; ~ **de chevet** bedside lamp; ~ **solaire**, ~ **à bronzer** sunlamp.

lance /lɑ̃s/ *nf* spear; (de tournoi) lance; (tuyau) hose; ~ **d'incendie** fire hose.

lancement /lɑ̃smɑ̃/ *nm* throwing; (de navire, de missile, mise sur le marché) launch.

lance-missiles /lɑ̃smisil/ *nm inv* missile launcher.

lance-pierres /lɑ̃spjɛʀ/ *nm inv* catapult.

lancer /lɑ̃se/ 🔟 *vt* throw; (avec force) hurl; (navire, idée, artiste) launch; (émettre) give out; (regard) cast; (moteur) start. □ **se** ~ *vpr* (Sport) gain momentum; (se précipiter) rush; **se** ~ **dans** (explication) launch into; (passetemps) take up. ● *nm* throw; (action) throwing.

lancinant, -e /lɑ̃sinɑ̃, -t/ *adj*

(douleur) shooting; (problème) nagging.

landau /lɑ̃do/ *nm* pram; (US) baby carriage.

lande /lɑ̃d/ *nf* heath, moor.

langage /lɑ̃gaʒ/ *nm* language; ~ **machine/de programmation** machine/programming language.

langouste /lɑ̃gust/ *nf* spiny lobster. **langoustine** *nf* Dublin Bay prawn.

langue /lɑ̃g/ *nf* (Anat) tongue; (Ling) language; **il m'a tiré la** ~ he stuck his tongue out at me; **de** ~ **anglaise** (personne) English-speaking; (journal) English-language; ~ **maternelle** mother tongue; ~ **vivante** modern language.

lanière /lanjɛʀ/ *nf* strap.

lanterne /lɑ̃tɛʀn/ *nf* lantern; (électrique) lamp; (de voiture) sidelight.

lapin /lapɛ̃/ *nm* rabbit; **poser un** ~ **à qn** 🔟 stand sb up; **le coup du** ~ rabbit punch; (en voiture) whiplash injury.

lapsus /lapsys/ *nm* slip of the tongue.

laque /lak/ *nf* lacquer; (pour cheveux) hairspray; (peinture) gloss paint.

laquelle /lakɛl/ ➡LEQUEL.

lard /laʀ/ *nm* streaky bacon.

large /laʀʒ/ *adj* wide, broad; (grand) large; (généreux) generous; **avoir les idées** ~**s** be broad-minded; ~ **d'esprit** broad-minded. ● *adv* (calculer, mesurer) on the generous side; **voir** ~ think big. ● *nm* **faire 10 cm de** ~ be 10 cm wide; **le** ~ (mer) the open sea; **au** ~ **de** (Naut) off. **largement** *adv* widely; (ouvrir) wide; (amplement) amply; (généreusement) generously; (au moins) easily.

largesse /laʀʒɛs/ *nf* generous gift.

largeur /laʀʒœʀ/ nf width, breadth; ~ **d'esprit** broad-mindedness.

larguer /laʀge/ **1** vt drop; ~ **les amarres** cast off.

larme /laʀm/ nf tear; (goutte **1**) drop; **en** ~**s** in tears.

larmoyant, ~**e** /laʀmwajɑ̃, -t/ adj full of tears. **larmoyer 31** vi (yeux) water; (pleurnicher) whine.

larynx /laʀɛ̃ks/ nm larynx.

las, ~**se** /lɑ, lɑs/ adj weary.

lasagnes /lazaɲ/ nfpl lasagna.

laser /lazɛʀ/ nm laser.

lasser /lase/ **1** vt weary. □ **se** ~ vpr grow tired, get weary (**de** of).

latéral, ~**e** (mpl -**aux**) /lateʀal, -o/ adj lateral.

latin, ~**e** /latɛ̃, -in/ adj Latin. ● nm (Ling) Latin.

latte /lat/ nf lath; (de plancher) board; (de siège) slat; (de mur, plafond) lath.

lauréat, ~**e** /lɔʀea, -t/ adj prize-winning. ● nm, f prize-winner.

laurier /lɔʀje/ nm (Bot) laurel; (Culin) bay-leaves.

lavable /lavabl/ adj washable.

lavabo /lavabo/ nm wash-basin; ~**s** toilet(s).

lavage /lavaʒ/ nm washing; ~ **de cerveau** brainwashing.

lavande /lavɑ̃d/ nf lavender.

lave /lav/ nf lava.

lave-glace (pl ~**s**) /lavglas/ nm windscreen washer.

lave-linge /lavlɛ̃ʒ/ nm inv washing machine.

laver /lave/ **1** vt wash; ~ **qn de** (fig) clear sb of. □ **se** ~ vpr wash (oneself); **se** ~ **les mains** wash one's hands.

laverie /lavʀi/ nf ~ (**automatique**) launderette; (US) laundromat.

lave-vaisselle /lavvɛsɛl/ nm inv dishwasher.

laxatif, -ive /laksatif, -v/ adj & nm laxative.

layette /lɛjɛt/ nf baby clothes.

---

le, la, l' (pl **les**) /lə, la, l, le/

l' before vowel or mute h.

● déterminant

····▸ the.

····▸ (notion générale) **aimer la musique** like music; **l'amour** love.

····▸ (possession) **avoir les yeux verts** have green eyes; **il s'est cassé la jambe** he broke his leg.

····▸ (prix) **10 euros** ~ **kilo** 10 euros a kilo.

····▸ (temps) ~ **lundi** on Mondays; **tous les mardis** every Tuesday.

····▸ (avec nom propre) **les Dury** the Durys; **la reine Margot** Queen Margot; **la Belgique** Belgium.

····▸ (avec adjectif) the; **je veux la rouge** I want the red one; **les riches** the rich.

● pronom

····▸ (homme) him; (femme) her; (chose, animal) it; (au pluriel) them.

····▸ (remplaçant une phrase) **je te l'avais bien dit** I told you so; **je** ~ **croyais aussi** I thought so too.

---

lécher /leʃe/ **14** vt lick; (flamme) lick; (mer) lap.

lèche-vitrines /lɛʃvitʀin/ nm inv **faire du** ~ go window-shopping.

leçon /ləsɔ̃/ nf lesson; **faire la** ~ **à** lecture sb; ~ **particulière** private lesson; ~**s de conduite**

driving lessons.

lecteur, -trice /lɛktœʀ, -tʀis/ *nm, f* reader; (Univ) foreign language assistant; ~ **de cassettes** cassette player; ~ **de disquettes** (disk) drive; ~ **laser CD** player; ~ **optique** optical scanner.

lecture /lɛktyʀ/ *nf* reading.

ledit, ladite (*mpl* **lesdit(e)s**) /lədi, ladit, ledi(t)/ *adj* the aforementioned.

légal, ~e (*mpl* **-aux**) /legal, -o/ *adj* legal. **légaliser** 1 *vt* legalize. **légalité** *nf* legality; (loi) law.

légendaire /leʒɑ̃dɛʀ/ *adj* legendary. **légende** *nf* (histoire, inscription) legend; (de carte) key; (d'illustration) caption.

léger, -ère /leʒe, -ɛʀ/ *adj* light; (bruit, faute, maladie) slight; (café, argument) weak; (imprudent) thoughtless; (frivole) fickle; **à la légère** thoughtlessly. **légèrement** *adv* lightly; (agir) thoughtlessly; (un peu) slightly. **légèreté** *nf* lightness; thoughtlessness.

légion /leʒjɔ̃/ *nf* legion.

> **Légion d'honneur** The system of honours awarded by the state for meritorious achievement. The *Président de la République* is the *Grand maître*. The basic rank is *Chevalier*. Holders of the *Légion d'honneur* are entitled to wear *une rosette* (a small red lapel ribbon). **i**

légionellose /leʒjɔneloz/ *nf* (Méd) legionnaire's disease.

législatif, -ive /leʒislatif, -v/ *adj* legislative; **élections législatives** general election.

législature /leʒislatyʀ/ *nf* term of office.

légitime /leʒitim/ *adj* (Jur) legitim-

ate; (fig) rightful; **agir en état de** ~ **défense** act in self-defence. **légitimité** *nf* legitimacy.

legs /lɛɡ/ *nm* legacy; (d'effets personnels) bequest.

léguer /lege/ 14 *vt* bequeath.

légume /leɡym/ *nm* vegetable.

lendemain /lɑ̃dmɛ̃/ *nm* le ~ the next day; (fig) the future; **le** ~ **de** the day after; **le** ~ **matin/soir** the next morning/evening; **du jour au** ~ from one day to the next.

lent, ~e /lɑ̃, -t/ *adj* slow. **lentement** *adv* slowly. **lenteur** *nf* slowness.

lentille /lɑ̃tij/ *nf* (Culin) lentil; (verre) lens; **~s de contact** contact lenses.

léopard /leɔpaʀ/ *nm* leopard.

lèpre /lɛpʀ/ *nf* leprosy.

---

lequel, laquelle (*pl* **lesquel(le)s**), **auquel** (*pl* **auxquel(le)s**), **duquel** (*pl* **desquel(le)s**) /ləkɛl, lakɛl, lekɛl, ɔkɛl, dykɛl, dekɛl/

à + lequel = auquel,
à + lesquel(le)s = auxquel(le)s;
de + lequel = duquel,
de + lesquel(le)s = desquel(le)s

● *pronom*
····▸ (relatif) (personne) who; (complément indirect) whom; (autres cas) which; **l'ami auquel tu as écrit** the friend to whom you wrote; **les voisins chez lesquels Sophie est allée** the neighbours whose house Sophie went to.

····▸ (interrogatif) which; ~ **tu veux?** which one do you want?

● *adjectif*
····▸ **auquel cas** in which case.

les /le/ ➞le.

lesbienne /lɛsbjɛn/ nf lesbian.

léser /leze/ 14 vt wrong.

lésiner /lezine/ 1 vi ne pas ~ sur not stint on.

lesquels, lesquelles /lekɛl/ ➞lequel.

lessive /lesiv/ nf (poudre) washing-powder; (liquide) washing liquid; (linge, action) washing.

leste /lɛst/ adj agile, nimble; (grivois) coarse.

Lettonie /letoni/ nf Latvia.

lettre /lɛtʀ/ nf letter; à la ~, au pied de la ~ literally; en toutes ~s in full; les ~s (Univ) (the) arts.

leucémie /løsemi/ nf leukaemia.

<hr>

leur (pl ~s) /lœʀ/

● pronom personnel invariable

····➤ them; donne-le ~ give it to them; je ~ fais confiance I trust them.

● adjectif possessif

····➤ their; ~s enfants their children; à ~ arrivée when they arrived.

● le leur, la leur, (pl les leurs) pronom possessif

····➤ theirs; chacun le ~ one each; je suis de ~s I am one of them.

<hr>

levain /ləvɛ̃/ nm leaven.

levé, ~e /ləve/ adj (debout) up.

levée /ləve/ nf (de peine, de sanctions) lifting; (de courrier) collection; (de troupes, d'impôts) levying.

lever /ləve/ 6 vt lift (up), raise; (interdiction) lift; (séance) close; (armée, impôts) levy. ● vi (pâte) rise. □ se ~ vpr get up; (soleil, rideau) rise; (jour) break. ● nm au ~ on getting up; ~ du jour daybreak; ~

de rideau (Théât) curtain (up); ~ du soleil sunrise.

levier /ləvje/ nm lever; ~ de changement de vitesse gear lever.

lèvre /lɛvʀ/ nf lip.

lévrier /levʀije/ nm greyhound.

levure /ləvyʀ/ nf yeast; ~ chimique baking powder.

lexique /lɛksik/ nm vocabulary; (glossaire) lexicon.

lézard /lezaʀ/ nm lizard.

lézarde /lezaʀd/ nf crack.

liaison /ljɛzɔ̃/ nf connection; (transport, Ordinat) link; (contact) contact; (Gram, Mil) liaison; (amoureuse) affair; être en ~ avec be in contact with; assurer la ~ entre liaise between.

liane /ljan/ nf creeper.

Liban /libɑ̃/ nm Lebanon.

libeller /libele/ 1 vt (chèque) write; (contrat) draw up; libellé à l'ordre de made out to.

libellule /libelyl/ nf dragonfly.

libéral, ~e (mpl -aux) /liberal, -o/ adj liberal; les professions ~es the professions.

libérateur, -trice /liberatœʀ, -tʀis/ adj liberating. ● nm, f liberator.

libération /liberasjɔ̃/ nf release; (de pays) liberation.

libérer /libere/ 14 vt (personne) free, release; (pays) liberate, free; (bureau, lieux) vacate; (gaz) release. □ se ~ vpr free oneself.

liberté /libɛʀte/ nf freedom, liberty; (loisir) free time; être/mettre en ~ be/set free; ~ conditionnelle parole; ~ provisoire provisional release (pending trial); ~ surveillée probation; ~s publiques civil liberties.

Libertel /libɛʀtɛl/ nm (Internet) Freenet.

libraire /libʀɛʀ/ nmf bookseller.

librairie *nf* bookshop.

libre /libʀ/ *adj* free; (*place, pièce*) vacant, free; (*passage*) clear; (*école*) private (*usually religious*); ~ **de qch/ de faire** free from sth/to do.

libre-échange *nm* free trade. **libre-service** (*pl* **libres-services**) *nm* (*magasin*) self-service shop; (*restaurant*) self-service restaurant.

licence /lisãs/ *nf* licence; (Univ) degree.

licencié, **-e** /lisãsje/ *nm, f* graduate; ~ **ès lettres/sciences** Bachelor of Arts/Science.

licenciements /lisãsimã/ *nm* redundancy; (*pour faute*) dismissal. **licencier** [45] *vt* make redundant; (*pour faute*) dismiss.

licorne /likɔʀn/ *nf* unicorn.

liège /ljɛʒ/ *nm* cork.

lien /ljɛ̃/ *nm* (*rapport*) link; (*attache*) bond, tie; (*corde*) rope; ~**s affectifs/de parenté** emotional/ family ties.

lier /lje/ [45] *vt* tie (up), bind; (*relier*) link; (*engager, unir*) bind; ~ **conversation** strike up a conversation; **ils sont très liés** they are very close. □ **se** ~ **avec** *vpr* make friends with.

lierre /ljɛʀ/ *nm* ivy.

lieu (*pl* ~**x**) /ljø/ *nm* place; ~**x** (*locaux*) premises; (*d'un accident*) scene; **sur les** ~**x** at the scene; **au** ~ **de** instead of; **avoir** ~ take place; **donner** ~ **à** give rise to; **tenir** ~ **de** serve as; **s'il y a** ~ if necessary; **en premier** ~ firstly; **en dernier** ~ lastly; ~ **commun** commonplace; ~ **de rencontre** meeting place.

lièvre /ljɛvʀ/ *nm* hare.

lifting /liftiŋ/ *nm* face-lift.

ligne /liɲ/ *nf* line; (*trajet*) route; (*de métro, train*) line; (*formes*) lines;

(*de femme*) figure; **en** ~ (*joueurs*) lined up; (*au téléphone*) on the phone; (Ordinat) on line; ~ **spécialisée** (Internet) dedicated line.

ligoter /ligɔte/ [1] *vt* tie up.

ligue /lig/ *nf* league. **liguer (se)** [1] *vpr* join forces (**contre** against).

lilas /lila/ *nm & a inv* lilac.

limace /limas/ *nf* slug.

limande /limãd/ *nf* (*poisson*) dab.

lime /lim/ *nf* file; ~ **à ongles** nail file.

limitation /limitasjɔ̃/ *nf* limitation; ~ **de vitesse** speed limit.

limite /limit/ *nf* limit; (*de jardin, champ*) boundary; **à la** ~ (*fig*) verging on, bordering on; **à la** ~ if it comes to it, at a pinch; **dans une certaine** ~ up to a point; **dans la** ~ **du possible** as far as possible. ● *adj* (*vitesse, âge*) maximum; **cas** ~ borderline case; **date** ~ deadline; **date** ~ **de vente** sell-by date.

limiter /limite/ [1] *vt* limit; (*délimiter*) form the border of. □ **se** ~ *vpr* limit oneself (**à** to).

limonade /limɔnad/ *nf* lemonade.

limpide /lɛ̃pid/ *adj* limpid, clear.

lin /lɛ̃/ *nm* (*tissu*) linen.

linge /lɛ̃ʒ/ *nm* linen; (*lessive*) washing; (*torchon*) cloth; ~ (**de corps**) underwear. **lingerie** *nf* underwear. **lingette** *nf* wipe.

lingot /lɛ̃go/ *nm* ingot.

linguistique /lɛ̃gɥistik/ *adj* linguistic. ● *nf* linguistics.

lion /ljɔ̃/ *nm* lion; **le L**~ Leo. **lionceau** (*pl* ~**x**) *nm* lion cub. **lionne** *nf* lioness.

liquidation /likidasjɔ̃/ *nf* liquidation; (*vente*) (*clearance*) sale; **entrer en** ~ go into liquidation.

liquide /likid/ *adj* liquid. ● *nm* (*argent*) ~ ready money; **payer en** ~ pay cash; ~ **de frein** brake fluid.

liquider /likide/ **1** *vt* liquidate; (*vendre*) sell.

lire /lir/ **39** *vt/i* read. ● *nf* lira.

lis[1] /li/ ➡LIRE **39**.

lis[2] /lis/ *nm* (fleur) lily.

lisible /lizibl/ *adj* legible; (*roman*) readable.

lisière /lizjɛr/ *nf* edge.

lisse /lis/ *adj* smooth.

liste /list/ *nf* list; ~ d'attente waiting list; ~ électorale register of voters; être sur (la) ~ rouge be ex-directory.

listing /listiŋ/ *nm* printout.

lit /li/ *nm* bed; se mettre au ~ get into bed; ~ de camp camp-bed; ~ d'enfant cot; ~ d'une personne single bed; ~ de deux personnes, grand ~ double bed.

literie /litri/ *nf* bedding.

litière /litjɛr/ *nf* litter.

litige /litiʒ/ *nm* dispute.

litre /litr/ *nm* litre.

littéraire /literɛr/ *adj* literary; (*études, formation*) arts.

littéral, ~e (*mpl* **-aux**) /literal, -o/ *adj* literal.

littérature /literatyr/ *nf* literature.

littoral (*pl* **-aux**) /litoral, -o/ *nm* coast.

Lituanie /lituani/ *nf* Lithuania.

livide /livid/ *adj* deathly pale.

livraison /livrɛzõ/ *nf* delivery.

livre /livr/ *nf* (monnaie, poids) pound. ● *nm* book; ~ de bord logbook; ~ de compte books; ~ de poche paperback.

livrer /livre/ **1** *vt* (Comm) deliver; (*abandonner*) give over (à to); (*remettre*) (*coupable, document*) hand over (à to); livré à soi-même left to oneself. □ se ~ *vpr* (se rendre)

give oneself up (à to); se ~ à (*boisson, actes*) indulge in; (*ami*) confide in.

livret /livrɛ/ *nm* book; (Mus) libretto; ~ de caisse d'épargne savings book; ~ scolaire school report (book).

livreur, -euse /livrœr, -øz/ *nm, f* delivery man, delivery woman.

local[1], **~e** (*mpl* **-aux**) /lokal, -o/ *adj* local.

local[2] (*pl* **-aux**) /lokal, -o/ *nm* premises; locaux premises.

localement /lokalmã/ *adv* locally.

localisation /lokalizasjõ/ *nf* localization.

localiser /lokalize/ **1** *vt* (repérer) locate; (circonscrire) localize.

locataire /lokatɛr/ *nmf* tenant; (de chambre) lodger.

location /lokasjõ/ *nf* (de maison) renting; (de voiture, de matériel) hire, rental; (de place) booking, reservation; (par propriétaire) renting out; hiring out; en ~ (*voiture*) on hire, rented; (*habiter*) in rented accommodation.

locomotive /lokomotiv/ *nf* engine, locomotive.

locution /lokysjõ/ *nf* phrase.

loft /loft/ *nm* loft (apartment).

loge /loʒ/ *nf* (de concierge, de franc-maçons) lodge; (d'acteur) dressing-room; (de spectateur) box.

logement /loʒmã/ *nm* accommodation; (appartement) flat; (habitat) housing.

loger /loʒe/ **40** *vt* (réfugié, famille) house; (ami) put up; (client) accommodate. ● *vi* live. □ se ~ *vpr* live; trouver à se ~ find accommodation; se ~ dans (*balle*) lodge itself in.

logiciel /loʒisjɛl/ *nm* software; ~

contributif shareware; ~ d'application application software; ~ de groupe groupware; ~ de jeux games software; ~ de navigation browser; ~ public freeware.

logique /lɔʒik/ adj logical. ● nf logic.

logis /lɔʒi/ nm dwelling.

logistique /lɔʒistik/ nf logistics.

loi /lwa/ nf law.

loin /lwɛ̃/ adv far (away); au ~ far away; de ~ from far away; (de beaucoup) by far; ~ de là far from it; plus ~ further; il revient de ~ (fig) he had a close shave.

lointain, ~e /lwɛ̃tɛ̃, -ɛn/ adj distant. ● nm distance; dans le ~ in the distance.

loisir /lwazir/ nm (spare) time; ~s (temps libre) leisure, spare time; (distractions) leisure activities; à ~ at one's leisure; avoir le ~ de faire have time to do.

londonien, ~ne /lɔ̃dɔnjɛ̃, -ɛn/ adj London. L~, ~ne nm, f Londoner.

Londres /lɔ̃dR/ npr London.

long, longue /lɔ̃, lɔ̃g/ adj long; à ~ terme long-term; être ~ à faire be a long time doing. ● nm de ~ (mesure) long; de ~ en large back and forth; (tout) le ~ de (all) along. ● adv en dire ~ sur qn/qch say a lot about sb/sth; en savoir plus ~ sur know more about.

longer /lɔ̃ʒe/ [40] vt go along; (limiter) border.

longitude /lɔ̃ʒityd/ nf longitude.

longtemps /lɔ̃tɑ̃/ adv a long time; avant ~ before long; trop ~ too long; ça prendra ~ it will take a long time; prendre plus ~ que prévu take longer than anticipated.

longuement /lɔ̃gmɑ̃/ adv (longtemps) for a long time; (en détail) at length.

longueur /lɔ̃gœR/ nf length; ~s (de texte) over-long parts; à ~ de journée all day long; en ~ lengthwise; ~ d'onde wavelength.

lopin /lɔpɛ̃/ nm ~ de terre patch of land.

loque /lɔk/ nf ~s rags; ~ (humaine) (human) wreck.

loquet /lɔkɛ/ nm latch.

lors de /lɔRdə/ prép (au moment de) at the time of; (pendant) during.

lorsque /lɔRsk(ə)/ conj when.

losange /lɔzɑ̃ʒ/ nm diamond.

lot /lo/ nm (portion) share; (aux enchères) lot; (Ordinat) batch; (destin) lot; gagner le gros ~ hit the jackpot.

loterie /lɔtRi/ nf lottery.

lotion /lɔsjɔ̃/ nf lotion.

lotissement /lɔtismɑ̃/ nm (à construire) building plot; (construit) (housing) development.

louable /luabl/ adj praiseworthy. **louange** nf praise.

louche /luʃ/ adj shady, dubious. ● nf ladle.

loucher /luʃe/ [1] vi squint.

louer /lwe/ [1] vt (approuver) praise (de for); (prendre en location) (maison) rent; (voiture, matériel) hire, rent; (place) book, reserve; (donner en location) (maison) rent out; (matériel) rent out, hire out; à ~ to let, for rent (US).

loufoque /lufɔk/ adj [1] crazy.

loup /lu/ nm wolf.

loupe /lup/ nf magnifying glass.

louper /lupe/ [1] vt [1] miss; (examen) flunk [1].

lourd, ~e /luR, -d/ adj heavy; (faute) serious; ~ de dangers fraught with danger; **il fait ~** it's close ou muggy.

loutre /lutʀ/ nf otter.

louveteau (pl ~x) /luvto/ nm wolf cub; (scout) Cub (Scout).

loyal, ~e (mpl -aux) /lwajal, -o/ adj loyal, faithful; (honnête) fair.

loyauté /lwajote/ nf loyalty; fairness.

loyer /lwaje/ nm rent.

lu /ly/ →LIRE 39.

lubrifiant /lybʀifjã/ nm lubricant.

lucide /lysid/ adj lucid. **lucidité** nf lucidity.

lucratif, -ive /lykʀatif, -v/ adj lucrative; **à but non ~** non-profitmaking.

ludiciel /lydisjɛl/ nm (Ordinat) games software.

lueur /lɥœʀ/ nf (faint) light, glimmer; (fig) glimmer, gleam.

luge /lyʒ/ nf toboggan.

lugubre /lygybʀ/ adj gloomy.

---

lui /lɥi/

● pronom

····▸ (masculin) (sujet) he; **~, il est à l'étranger** he's abroad; **c'est ~!** it's him!; (objet) him; (animal) it; **c'est à ~** it's his; **elle conduit mieux que ~** she's a better driver than he is.

····▸ (féminin) her; **je ~ ai annoncé** I told her.

····▸ (masculin/féminin) **donne-le-~** give it to him/her.

---

lui-même /lɥimɛm/ pron himself; (animal) itself.

luire /lɥiʀ/ 17 vi shine; (reflet humide) glisten; (reflet chaud, faible) glow.

lumière /lymjɛʀ/ nf light; **~s** (connaissances) knowledge; **faire**

(toute) la **~** sur une affaire clear a matter up.

luminaire /lyminɛʀ/ nm lamp.

lumineux, -euse /lyminø, -z/ adj luminous; (éclairé) illuminated; (rayon) of light; (radieux) radiant; **source lumineuse** light source.

lunaire /lynɛʀ/ adj lunar.

lunatique /lynatik/ adj temperamental.

lunch /lœnʃ/ nm buffet lunch.

lundi /lœdi/ nm Monday.

lune /lyn/ nf moon; **~ de miel** honeymoon.

lunettes /lynɛt/ nfpl glasses; (de protection) goggles; **~ de ski/natation** ski/swimming goggles; **~ noires** dark glasses; **~ de soleil** sun-glasses.

lustre /lystʀ/ nm (éclat) lustre; (objet) chandelier.

lutin /lytɛ̃/ nm goblin.

lutte /lyt/ nf fight, struggle; (Sport) wrestling. **lutter** 1 vi fight, struggle; (Sport) wrestle. **lutteur**, -euse nm, f fighter; (Sport) wrestler.

luxe /lyks/ nm luxury; **de ~** luxury; (produit) de luxe.

Luxembourg /lyksãbuʀ/ nm Luxemburg.

luxer (se) /(sə)lykse/ 1 vpr **se ~ le genou** dislocate one's knee.

luxueux, -euse /lyksɥø, -z/ adj luxurious.

lycée /lise/ nm (secondary) school. **lycéen**, ~ne nm, f pupil (at secondary school).

lyophilisé, ~e /ljofilize/ adj freeze-dried.

lyrique /liʀik/ adj (poésie) lyric; (passionné) lyrical; **artiste/théâtre ~** opera singer/house.

lys /lis/ nm lily.

Mm

m' /m/ ➡ME.

ma /ma/ ➡MON.

macabre /makabʀ/ adj macabre.

macadam /makadam/ nm Tarmac®.

macaron /makaʀɔ̃/ nm (gâteau) macaroon; (insigne) badge.

macédoine /masedwan/ nf mixed diced vegetables; ~ de fruits fruit salad.

macérer /maseʀe/ 14 vt/i soak; (dans du vinaigre) pickle.

mâcher /maʃe/ 1 vt chew; ne pas ~ ses mots not mince one's words.

machin /maʃɛ̃/ nm 1 (chose) thing; (dont on ne trouve pas le nom) whatsit 1.

machinal, ~e (mpl **-aux**) /maʃinal, -o/ adj automatic. **machinalement** adv mechanically, automatically.

machination /maʃinasjɔ̃/ nf plot; des ~s machinations.

machine /maʃin/ nf machine; (d'un train, navire) engine; ~ à écrire typewriter; ~ à laver/coudre washing-/sewing-machine; ~ à sous fruit machine; (US) slot machine. **machine-outil** (pl **machines-outils**) nf machine tool. **machinerie** nf machinery.

machiniste /maʃinist/ nm (Théât) stage-hand; (conducteur) driver.

mâchoire /maʃwaʀ/ nf jaw.

mâchonner /maʃɔne/ 1 vt chew.

maçon /masɔ̃/ nm (entrepreneur) builder; (poseur de briques) bricklayer; (qui construit en pierre) mason. **maçonnerie** nf (briques) brickwork; (pierres) stonework, masonry; (travaux) building.

madame (pl **mesdames**) /madam, medam/ nf (à une inconnue) (dans une lettre) M~ Dear Madam; **bonjour, ~** good morning; **mesdames et messieurs** ladies and gentlemen; (à une femme dont on connaît le nom) (dans une lettre) **Chère M~** Dear Mrs ou Ms X; **bonjour, ~** good morning Mrs ou Ms X; **oui M ~ le Ministre** yes Minister; (formule de respect) **oui M~** yes madam.

mademoiselle (pl **mesdemoiselles**) /madmwazɛl, medmwazɛl/ nf (à une inconnue) (dans une lettre) M~ Dear Madam; **bonjour, ~** good morning; **entrez mesdemoiselles** come in (ladies); (à une jeune fille dont on connaît le nom) (dans une lettre) **Chère M~** Dear Ms ou Miss X; **bonjour, ~** good morning Miss ou Ms X.

magasin /magazɛ̃/ nm shop, store; (entrepôt) warehouse; (d'une arme) magazine; **en ~** in stock.

magazine /magazin/ nm magazine; (émission) programme.

Maghreb /magʀɛb/ nm North Africa.

magicien, ~ne /maʒisjɛ̃, -ɛn/ nm, f magician.

magie /maʒi/ nf magic. **magique** adj magic; (mystérieux) magical.

magistral, ~e (mpl **-aux**) /maʒistʀal, -o/ adj masterly; (grand: hum) tremendous; **cours ~** lecture.

magistrat /maʒistʀa/ nm magistrate.

magistrature /maʒistʀatyʀ/ nf judiciary; (fonction) public office.

magner (se) /(sə)maɲe/ 1 vpr ⊠ get a move on.

magnétique /maɲetik/ *adj* magnetic. **magnétiser** ▮ *vt* magnetize. **magnétisme** *nm* magnetism.

magnétophone /maɲetɔfɔn/ *nm* tape recorder; (à cassettes) cassette recorder.

magnétoscope /maɲetɔskɔp/ *nm* video recorder.

magnificence /maɲifisɑ̃s/ *nf* magnificence. **magnifique** *adj* magnificent.

magot /mago/ *nm* ▮ hoard (of money).

magouille /maguj/ *nf* ▮ scheming, skulduggery.

magret /magʀɛ/ *nm* ~ de canard duck breast.

mai /mɛ/ *nm* May.

maigre /mɛgʀ/ *adj* thin; (viande) lean; (yaourt) low-fat; (fig) poor, meagre; **faire** ~ abstain from meat. **maigreur** *nf* thinness; leanness; (fig) meagreness.

maigrir /megʀiʀ/ ▮ *vi* get thin(ner); (en suivant un régime) slim. ● *vt* make thin(ner).

maille /maj/ *nf* stitch; (de filet) mesh; ~ **qui file** ladder, run; **avoir** ~ **à partir avec qn** have a brush with sb.

maillet /majɛ/ *nm* mallet.

maillon /majɔ̃/ *nm* link.

maillot /majo/ *nm* (Sport) shirt, jersey; (~ de corps) vest; (US) undershirt; (~ de bain) (swimming) costume.

main /mɛ̃/ *nf* hand; **donner la** ~ **à qn** hold sb's hand; **se donner la** ~ hold hands; **en** ~**s propres** in person; **en bonnes** ~**s** in good hands; ~ **courante** handrail; **se faire la** ~ get the hang of it; **perdre la** ~ lose one's touch; **sous la** ~ to hand; **vol à** ~ **armée** armed robbery; **fait (à la)** ~ handmade; **haut**

les ~**s!** hands up! **main-d'œuvre** (pl **mains-d'œuvre**) *nf* labour; (ouvriers) labour force.

main-forte /mɛ̃fɔʀt/ *nf inv* **prêter** ~ **à qn** come to sb's aid.

maint, ~**e** /mɛ̃, mɛ̃t/ *adj* many a (+ sg); ~**s** many; **à** ~**es reprises** many times.

maintenant /mɛ̃t(ə)nɑ̃/ *adv* now; (de nos jours) nowadays; (l'époque actuelle) today.

maintenir /mɛ̃t(ə)niʀ/ 59 *vt* keep, maintain; (soutenir) support, hold up; (affirmer) maintain; (decision) stand by. □ **se** ~ *vpr* (tendance) persist; (prix, malade) remain stable.

maintien /mɛ̃tjɛ̃/ *nm* (attitude) bearing; (conservation) maintenance.

maire /mɛʀ/ *nm* mayor.

mairie /meʀi/ *nf* town hall; (administration) town council.

mais /mɛ/ *conj* but; ~ **oui** of course; ~ **non** of course not.

maïs /mais/ *nm* maize, corn; (Culin) sweetcorn.

maison /mɛzɔ̃/ *nf* house; (foyer) home; (immeuble) building; (~ de commerce) firm; **à la** ~ at home; **rentrer** ou **aller à la** ~ go home; ~ **des jeunes (et de la culture)** youth club; ~ **de repos** rest home; ~ **de convalescence** convalescent home; ~ **de retraite** old people's home; ~ **mère** parent company. ● *adj inv* (Culin) home-made.

m

Maison des jeunes et de la culture The *Maison des jeunes et de la culture* (MJC) is an organization which provides community arts, sports and leisure activities for young people. Attached to the Ministry of Sport, the MJC was founded in 1964 to enable young people in rural communities to take part in cultural activities in winter.

maître, -esse /mɛtʀ, -ɛs/ adj (qui contrôle) être ~ **de soi** be one's own master; ~ **de la situation** in control of the situation; (principal) (idée, qualité) key, main. ● nm, f (Scol) teacher; (d'animal) owner, master. ● nm (expert, guide) master; (dirigeant) leader; ~ **de conférences** senior lecturer; ~ **d'hôtel** head waiter; (domestique) butler. **maître-assistant, ~ e** (pl **maîtres-assistants**) nm, f lecturer. **maître-chanteur** (pl **maîtres-chanteurs**) nm blackmailer. **maître-nageur** (pl **maîtres-nageurs**) nm swimming instructor. **maîtresse** nf (amante) mistress.

maîtrise /mɛtʀiz/ nf mastery; (contrôle) control; (Mil) supremacy; (Univ) master's degree; (~ **de soi**) self-control.

maîtriser /mɛtʀize/ **1** vt (sujet, technique) master; (incendie, sentiment, personne) control. □ **se** ~ vpr have self-control.

maïzena® /maizena/ nf cornflour.

majesté /maʒɛste/ nf majesty.

majestueux, -euse /maʒɛstɥø, z/ adj majestic.

majeur, ~e /maʒœʀ/ adj major, main; (Jur) of age; en ~e **partie** mostly; **la** ~e **partie de** most of. ● nm middle finger.

majoration /maʒɔʀasjɔ̃/ nf increase (de in). **majorer 1** vt increase.

majoritaire /maʒɔʀitɛʀ/ adj majority; être ~ be in the majority. **majorité** nf majority; en ~ chiefly.

Majorque /maʒɔʀk/ nf Majorca.

majuscule /maʒyskyl/ adj capital.
● nf capital letter.

mal¹ /mal/ adv badly; (incorrectement) wrong(ly); **aller** ~ (personne) be unwell; (affaires) go badly; ~ **entendre/comprendre** not hear/understand properly; ~ **en point** in a bad state; **pas** ~ quite a lot. ● adj inv bad, wrong; **c'est** ~ **de** it is wrong ou bad to; **ce n'est pas** ~ 🅸 it's not bad; **Nick n'est pas** ~ 🅸 Nick is not bad-looking.

mal² (pl **maux**) /mal, mo/ nm evil; (douleur) pain, ache; (maladie) disease; (effort) trouble; (dommage) harm; (malheur) misfortune; **avoir** ~ **à la tête/à la gorge** have a headache/a sore throat; **avoir le** ~ **de mer/du pays** be seasick/ homesick; **faire** ~ hurt; **se faire** ~ hurt oneself; **j'ai** ~ it hurts; **faire du** ~ **à** hurt, harm; **se donner du** ~ **pour faire qch** go to a lot of trouble to do sth.

malade /malad/ adj sick, ill; (bras, œil) bad; (plante, poumons, côlon) diseased; **tomber** ~ fall ill; (fou 🅸) mad. ● nmf sick person; (d'un médecin) patient; ~ **mental** mentally ill person.

maladie /maladi/ nf illness, disease; (manie 🅸) mania.

maladif, -ive /maladif, -v/ adj sickly; (jalousie, peur) pathological.

maladresse /maladʀɛs/ nf clumsiness; (erreur) blunder.

maladroit, ~e /maladʀwa, -t/ adj clumsy; (sans tact) tactless.

malaise /malɛz/ nm feeling of faintness; (gêne) uneasiness; (état de crise) unrest.

malaisé, ~e /maleze/ adj difficult.

Malaisie /malɛzi/ nf Malaysia.

malaria /malaʀja/ nf malaria.

malaxer /malakse/ **1** vt (pétrir) knead; (mêler) mix.

malchance /malʃɑ̃s/ nf misfortune. **malchanceux, -euse** adj unlucky.

mâle /mɑl/ adj male; (viril) manly. ● nm male.

malédiction /malediksjɔ̃/ nf curse.

maléfice /malefis/ nm evil spell. **maléfique** adj evil.

malentendant, ~e /malɑ̃tɑ̃dɑ̃, -t/ adj hard of hearing.

malentendu /malɑ̃tɑ̃dy/ nm misunderstanding.

malfaçon /malfasɔ̃/ nf defect.

malfaisant, ~e /malfəzɑ̃, -t/ adj harmful; (personne) evil.

malfaiteur /malfɛtœr/ nm criminal.

malformation /malfɔrmasjɔ̃/ nf malformation.

malgré /malgre/ prép in spite of, despite; ~ tout nevertheless.

malheur /malœr/ nm misfortune; (accident) accident; par ~ unfortunately; faire un ~ 🛈 be a big hit; porter ~ be ou bring bad luck.

malheureusement /malœrøzmɑ̃/ adv unfortunately.

malheureux, -euse /malœrø, -z/ adj unhappy; (regrettable) unfortunate; (sans succès) unlucky; (insignifiant) paltry, pathetic. ● nm, f (poor) wretch.

malhonnête /malɔnɛt/ adj dishonest. **malhonnêteté** nf dishonesty.

malice /malis/ nf mischief; sans ~ harmless; avec ~ mischievously. **malicieux, -ieuse** adj mischievous.

malignité /maliɲite/ nf malignancy. **malin, -igne** adj clever, smart; (méchant) malicious; (tumeur) malignant; (difficile 🛈) difficult.

malingre /malɛ̃gr/ adj puny.

malle /mal/ nf (valise) trunk; (Auto) boot; (US) trunk.

mallette /malɛt/ nf (small) suitcase; (pour le bureau) briefcase.

malmener /malməne/ 6 vt manhandle; (fig) give a rough ride to.

malnutrition /malnytrisjɔ̃/ nf malnutrition.

malodorant, ~e /malodorɑ̃, -t/ adj smelly, foul-smelling.

malpoli, ~e /malpoli/ adj rude, impolite.

malpropre /malprɔpr/ adj dirty.

malsain, ~e /malsɛ̃, -ɛn/ adj unhealthy.

malt /malt/ nm malt.

Malte /malt/ nf Malta.

maltraiter /maltrete/ 1 vt illtreat.

malveillance /malvejɑ̃s/ nf malice. **malveillant, ~e** adj malicious.

maman /mamɑ̃/ nf mum(my), mother; (US) mom(my).

mamelle /mamɛl/ nf teat.

mamelon /mamlɔ̃/ nm (Anat) nipple; (colline) hillock.

mamie /mami/ nf 🛈 granny.

mammifère /mamifɛr/ nm mammal.

manche /mɑ̃ʃ/ nf sleeve; (Sport, Pol) round. ● nm (d'un instrument) handle; ~ à balai broomstick; (Aviat) joystick. **M~** (of) la M~ the Channel; le tunnel sous la M~ the Channel tunnel.

manchette /mɑ̃ʃɛt/ nf cuff; (de journal) headline.

manchot, ~te /mɑ̃ʃo, -ot/ nm, f one-armed person; (sans bras) armless person. ● nm (oiseau) penguin.

mandarine /mɑ̃darin/ nf tangerine, mandarin (orange).

mandat /mɑ̃da/ nm (postal) money order; (Pol) mandate; (pro-

m

curation) proxy; (de police) warrant; ~ d'arrêt arrest warrant.

mandataire /mɑ̃datɛʀ/ nm representative; (Jul) proxy.

manège /manɛʒ/ nm riding school; (à la foire) merry-go-round; (manœuvre) trick.

manette /manɛt/ nf lever; (de jeu) joystick.

mangeable /mɑ̃ʒabl/ adj edible.

mangeoire /mɑ̃ʒwaʀ/ nf trough; (pour oiseaux) feeder.

manger /mɑ̃ʒe/ 40 vt eat; (fortune) go through; (profits) eat away at; (économies) use up; (ronger) eat into. ● vi eat; donner à ~ a feed. ● nm food.

mangue /mɑ̃g/ nf mango.

maniable /manjabl/ adj easy to handle.

maniaque /manjak/ adj fussy. ● nmf fusspot; (fou) maniac; (fanatique) fanatic; un ~ de l'ordre a stickler for tidiness.

manie /mani/ nf habit; (marotte) obsession.

maniement /manimɑ̃/ nm handling. **manier** 45 vt handle.

manière /manjɛʀ/ nf way, manner; ~s (politesse) manners; (chichis) fuss; à la ~ de in the style of; de ~ à so as to; de toute ~ anyway, in any case.

maniéré, ~e /manjeʀe/ adj affected.

manif /manif/ nf 1 demo.

manifestant, ~e /manifɛstɑ̃, -t/ nm, f demonstrator.

manifestation /manifɛstasjɔ̃/ nf expression, manifestation; (de maladie, phénomène) appearance; (Pol) demonstration; (événement) event; ~ culturelle cultural event.

manifeste /manifɛst/ adj obvious. ● nm manifesto.

manifester /manifɛste/ 1 vt show, manifest; (désir, crainte) express. ● vi (Pol) demonstrate. □ se ~ vpr (sentiment) show itself; (apparaître) appear; (répondre à un appel) come forward.

manigance /manigɑ̃s/ nf little plot. **manigancer** 10 vt plot.

manipulation /manipylasjɔ̃/ nf handling; (péj) manipulation.

manivelle /manivɛl/ nf handle, crank.

mannequin /mankɛ̃/ nm (personne) model; (statue) dummy.

manœuvrer /manœvʀe/ 1 vt manoeuvre; (machine) operate. ● vi manoeuvre.

manoir /manwaʀ/ nm manor.

manque /mɑ̃k/ nm lack (de of); (lacune) gap; ~ à gagner loss of earnings; en (état de) ~ having withdrawal symptoms.

manqué, ~e /mɑ̃ke/ adj (écrivain) failed; garçon ~ tomboy.

manquement /mɑ̃kmɑ̃/ nm ~ à breach of.

manquer /mɑ̃ke/ 1 vt miss; (gâcher) spoil; ~ à (devoir) fail in; ~ de be short of, lack; il/ça lui manque he misses him/it; ~ (de) faire (faillir) nearly do; ne manquez pas de be sure to; ~ à sa parole break one's word. ● vi be short ou lacking; (être absent) be absent; (en moins, disparu) be missing; il me manque 20 euros I'm 20 euros short.

mansarde /mɑ̃saʀd/ nf attic (room).

manteau (pl ~x) /mɑ̃to/ nm coat.

manucure /manykyʀ/ nmf manicurist. ● nf (soins) manicure.

manuel, ~le /manɥɛl/ adj manual. ● nm (livre) manual; (Scol) textbook.

manufacture | marié

manufacture /manyfaktyʀ/ nf factory; (fabrication) manufacture. **manufacturer 1** vt manufacture.

manuscrit, ~e /manyskʀi, -t/ adj handwritten. ● nm manuscript.

mappemonde /mapmɔ̃d/ nf world map; (sphère) globe.

maquereau (pl ~x) /makʀo/ nm (poisson) mackerel; ⊞ pimp.

maquette /makɛt/ nf (scale) model; ~ (de mise en page) paste-up.

maquillage /makijaʒ/ nm make-up.

maquiller /makije/ 1 vt make up; (truquer) doctor, fake. □ **se ~** vpr make (oneself) up.

maquis /maki/ nm (paysage) scrub; (Mil) Maquis, underground.

maraîcher, -ère /maʀeʃe, -ɛʀ/ ant, f market gardener; (US) truck farmer.

marais /maʀɛ/ nm marsh.

marasme /maʀasm/ nm slump, stagnation; **dans le ~** in the doldrums.

marbre /maʀbʀ/ nm marble.

marc /maʀ/ nm (eau-de-vie) marc; ~ **de café** coffee grounds.

marchand, ~e /maʀʃɑ̃, -d/ adj (valeur) market. ● nm, f trader; (de charbon, vins) merchant; ~ **de couleurs** ironmonger; (US) hardware merchant; ~ **de journaux** newsagent; ~ **de légumes** greengrocer; ~ **de poissons** fishmonger.

marchander /maʀʃɑ̃de/ 1 vt haggle over. ● vi haggle.

marchandise /maʀʃɑ̃diz/ nf goods.

marche /maʀʃ/ nf (démarche, trajet) walk; (rythme) pace; (Mil, Mus, Pol) march; (d'escalier) step; (Sport) walking; (de machine) operation, working; (de véhicule) running; en ~ (train) moving; (moteur, machine) running; **faire ~ arrière** (véhicule) reverse; **mettre en ~** start (up); **se mettre en ~** start moving.

marché /maʀʃe/ nm market; (contrat) deal; **faire son ~** do one's shopping; ~ **aux puces** flea market; ~ **noir** black market.

marchepied /maʀʃəpje/ nm (de train, camion) step.

marcher /maʀʃe/ 1 vi walk; (poser le pied) tread (**sur** on); (aller) go; (fonctionner) work, run; (prospérer) go well; (film, livre) do well; (consentir ⊞) agree; **faire ~ qn** ⊞ pull sb's leg.

mardi /maʀdi/ nm Tuesday; **M ~ gras** Shrove Tuesday.

mare /maʀ/ nf (étang) pond; (flaque) pool.

marécage /maʀekaʒ/ nm marsh; (sous les tropiques) swamp.

maréchal (pl -aux) /maʀeʃal, -o/ nm field marshal.

maréchal-ferrant (pl -aux-ferrants /maʀeʃalfeʀɑ̃/) nm blacksmith.

marée /maʀe/ nf tide; (poissons) fresh fish; ~ **haute/basse** high/ low tide; ~ **noire** oil slick.

marelle /maʀɛl/ nf hopscotch.

margarine /maʀgaʀin/ nf margarine.

marge /maʀʒ/ nf margin; **en ~ de** (à l'écart de) on the fringe(s) of; ~ **bénéficiaire** profit margin.

marginal, ~e (mpl -aux /maʀʒinal, -o/ adj marginal. ● nm, f drop-out.

marguerite /maʀgəʀit/ nf daisy; (qui imprime) daisy-wheel.

mari /maʀi/ nm husband.

mariage /maʀjaʒ/ nm marriage; (cérémonie) wedding.

marié, ~e /maʀje/ adj married.

● *nm, f* (bride) groom, bride; les ~s the bride and groom.

Marianne The symbolic female figure often used to represent the French Republic. There are statues of her in public places all over France, always wearing the Phrygian bonnet, a pointed cap which became a symbol of liberty as represented by the 1789 Revolution. She also appears on the standard French postage stamp.

marier /marje/ 45 *vt* marry. □ **se ~** *vpr* get married, marry; **se ~ avec** marry, get married to.

marin, ~e /marɛ̃, -in/ *adj* sea. ● *nm* sailor.

marine /marin/ *nf* navy; **~ marchande** merchant navy. ● *adj inv* navy (blue).

marionnette /marjɔnɛt/ *nf* puppet; (à fils) marionette.

maritalement /maritalmɑ̃/ *adv* (vivre) as husband and wife.

maritime /maritim/ *adj* maritime, coastal; (agent, compagnie) shipping.

marmaille /marmaj/ *nf* [1] brats.

marmelade /marmǝlad/ *nf* stewed fruit; **~ d'oranges** (orange) marmalade.

marmite /marmit/ *nf* (cooking-)pot.

marmonner /marmɔne/ 1 *vt* mumble.

marmot /marmo/ *nm* [1] kid.

Maroc /marɔk/ *nm* Morocco.

maroquinerie /marɔkinri/ *nf* (magasin) leather goods shop.

marquant, ~e /markɑ̃, -t/ *adj* (remarquable) outstanding; (qu'on n'oublie pas) memorable.

marque /mark/ *nf* mark; (de produits) brand, make; (décompte) score; **à vos ~s!** (Sport) on your marks!; **de ~** (Comm) brand name; (fig) important; **~ de fabrique** trademark; **~ déposée** registered trademark.

marquer /marke/ 1 *vt* mark; (indiquer) show, say; (écrire) note down; (point, but) score; (joueur) mark; (influencer) leave its mark on; (exprimer) (volonté, sentiment) show. ● *vi* (laisser une trace) leave a mark; (événement) stand out; (Sport) score.

marquis, ~e /marki, -z/ *nm, f* marquis, marchioness.

marraine /marɛn/ *nf* godmother.

marrant, ~e /marɑ̃, -t/ *adj* [1] funny.

marre /mar/ *adv* **en avoir ~** [1] be fed up (de with).

marrer (se) /(sǝ)mare/ 1 *vpr* [1] laugh, have a (good) laugh.

marron /marɔ̃/ *nm* chestnut; (couleur) brown; (coup [1]) thump; **~ d'Inde** horse chestnut. ● *adj inv* brown.

mars /mars/ *nm* March.

Marseillaise, la The popular name of the French national anthem, composed by Claude-Joseph Rouget de Lisle in 1792. It was adopted as a marching song by a group of Republican volunteers from Marseilles and became famous as they sang it on entering Paris.

marteau /pl ~x/ /marto/ *nm* hammer; **~ (de porte)** (door) knocker; **~ piqueur** *ou* **pneumatique** pneumatic drill; **être ~** [1] be mad.

marteler /martǝle/ 6 *vt* hammer;

martial, ~e (*mpl* **-iaux**) /maʀsjal, -jo/ *adj* military; (*art*) martial.

martien, ~ne /maʀsjɛ̃, -ɛn/ *adj* & *nm*, *f* Martian.

martyr, ~e /maʀtiʀ/ *nm*, *f* martyr. ● *adj* martyred; (*enfant*) battered.

martyre /maʀtiʀ/ *nm* (Relig) martyrdom; (fig) agony, suffering.

martyriser /maʀtiʀize/ **1** *vt* (Relig) martyr; (*torturer*) torture; (*enfant*) batter.

marxisme /maʀksism/ *nm* Marxism. **marxiste** *adj* & *nmf* Marxist.

masculin, ~e /maskylɛ̃, -in/ *adj* masculine; (*sexe*) male; (*mode, équipe*) men's. ● *nm* masculine.

masochisme /mazoʃism/ *nm* masochism.

masochiste /mazoʃist/ *nmf* masochist. ● *adj* masochistic.

masque /mask/ *nm* mask; ~ de beauté face pack. **masquer** **1** *vt* (*cacher*) hide, conceal (à from); (*lumière*) block (off).

massacre /masakʀ/ *nm* massacre. **massacrer** **1** *vt* massacre; (*abîmer* ⊞) ruin.

massage /masaʒ/ *nm* massage.

masse /mas/ *nf* (*volume*) mass; (*gros morceau*) lump, mass; (*outil*) sledge-hammer; **en** ~ (*vendre*) in bulk; (*venir*) in force; **produire en** ~ mass-produce; **la** ~ the masses; **une** ~ **de** ⊞ masses of; **la** ~ **de** the majority of.

masser /mase/ **1** *vt* (*assembler*) assemble; (*pétrir*) massage. □ **se** ~ *vpr* (*gens, foule*) mass.

massif, **-ive** /masif, -v/ *adj* massive; (*or, argent*) solid. ● *nm* (*de fleurs*) clump; (*parterre*) bed; (Géog) massif. **massivement** *adv* (*en masse*) in large numbers.

massue /masy/ *nf* club, bludgeon.

mastic /mastik/ *nm* putty; (*pour trous*) filler.

mastiquer /mastike/ **1** *vt* (*mâcher*) chew.

mat /mat/ *adj* (*couleur*) matt; (*bruit*) dull; (*teint*) olive; **être** ~ (*aux échecs*) be in checkmate.

mât /ma/ *nm* mast; (*pylône*) pole; ~ **de drapeau** flagpole.

match /matʃ/ *nm* match; (US) game; **faire** ~ **nul** tie, draw; ~ **aller** first leg; ~ **retour** return match.

matelas /matla/ *nm* mattress; ~ **pneumatique** air bed.

matelassé, ~e /matlase/ *adj* padded; (*tissu*) quilted.

matelot /matlo/ *nm* sailor.

mater /mate/ **1** *vt* (*révolte*) put down; (*personne*) bring into line.

matérialiser (se) /(sa)mateʀjalize/ *vpr* materialize.

matérialiste /mateʀjalist/ *adj* materialistic. ● *nmf* materialist.

matériau (*pl* ~x) /mateʀjo/ *nm* material.

matériel, ~le /mateʀjɛl/ *adj* material. ● *nm* equipment, materials; ~ **informatique** hardware.

maternel, ~le /mateʀnɛl/ *adj* maternal; (*comme d'une mère*) motherly. **maternelle** *nf* nursery school.

maternité /mateʀnite/ *nf* maternity hospital; (*état de mère*) motherhood; **de** ~ maternity.

mathématicien, ~ne /matematisjɛ̃, -ɛn/ *nm*, *f* mathematician.

mathématique /matematik/ *adj* mathematical. **mathématiques** *nfpl* mathematics (+ *sg*).

maths /mat/ *nfpl* ⊞ maths (+ *sg*).

m

Matignon The *Hôtel Matignon* is the official residence and office of the French prime minister, situated in the *rue de Varenne*, Paris. The word *Matignon* is often used to refer to the prime minister's office. See ▷ **ÉLYSÉE**

matière /matjɛʀ/ nf matter; (produit) material; (sujet) subject; en ~ de as regards; ~ plastique plastic; ~s grasses fat content; ~s premières raw materials.

matin /matɛ̃/ nm morning; de bon ~ early in the morning.

matinal, ~e (mpl -aux) /matinal, -o/ adj morning; (de bonne heure) early; être ~ be up early; (d'habitude) be an early riser.

matinée /matine/ nf morning; (spectacle) matinée.

matou /matu/ nm tomcat.

matraque /matʀak/ nf (de police) truncheon; (US) billy (club). **matraquer** 🔟 vt club, beat; (produit, chanson) plug.

matrimonial, ~e (mpl -iaux) /matʀimɔnjal, -jo/ adj matrimonial; agence ~e marriage bureau.

maturité /matyʀite/ nf maturity.

maudire /modiʀ/ 🚯 vt curse.

maudit, ~e /modi, -t/ adj 🔟 blasted, damned.

maugréer /mogʀee/ 🔢 vi grumble.

mausolée /mozɔle/ nm mausoleum.

maussade /mosad/ adj gloomy.

mauvais, ~e /mɔvɛ, -z/ adj bad; (erroné) wrong; (malveillant) evil; (désagréable) nasty, bad; (mer) rough; le ~ moment the wrong time; ~e herbe weed; ~e langue gossip; ~e passe tight spot; ~

traitements ill-treatment. ● adv (sentir) bad; il fait ~ the weather is bad. ● nm le bon et le ~ the good and the bad.

mauve /mov/ adj & nm mauve.

mauviette /movjɛt/ nf weakling, wimp.

maux /mo/ →MAL².

maximal, ~e (mpl -aux) /maksimal, -o/ adj maximum.

maxime /maksim/ nf maxim.

maximum /maksimɔm/ adj maximum. ● nm maximum; au ~ as much as possible; (tout au plus) at most; faire le ~ do one's utmost.

mazout /mazut/ nm (fuel) oil.

me, m' /ma, m/ pron me; (indirect) (to) me; (réfléchi) myself.

méandre /meɑ̃dʀ/ nm meander.

mec /mɛk/ nm 🔟 bloke, guy.

mécanicien, ~ne /mekanisjɛ̃, -jɛn/ nm, f mechanic. ● nm train driver.

mécanique /mekanik/ adj mechanical; (jouet) clockwork; problème ~ engine trouble. ● nf mechanics (+ sg); (mécanisme) mechanism. **mécaniser** 🔟 vt mechanize.

mécanisme /mekanism/ nm mechanism.

méchamment /meʃamɑ̃/ adv spitefully. **méchanceté** nf nastiness; (action) wicked action.

méchant, ~e /meʃɑ̃, -t/ adj (cruel) wicked; (désagréable, grave) nasty; (enfant) naughty; (chien) vicious; (sensationnel 🔟) terrific. ● nm, f (enfant) naughty child.

mèche /mɛʃ/ nf (de cheveux) lock; (de bougie) wick; (d'explosif) fuse; (outil) drill bit; de ~ avec in league with.

méconnaissable /mekɔnɛsabl/ adj unrecognizable.

méconnaître /mekɔnɛtʀ/ 🔟 vt

misunderstand, misread; (mésestimer) underestimate.

méconnu, ~e /mekɔny/ adj unrecognized; (artiste) neglected.

mécontent, ~e /mekɔ̃tã, -t/ adj dissatisfied (de with); (irrité) annoyed (de at, with). **mécontentement** nm dissatisfaction; annoyance. **mécontenter ❶** vt dissatisfy; (irriter) annoy.

médaille /medaj/ nf medal; (insigne) badge; (bijou) medallion. **médaillé**, ~e nm, f medallist.

médaillon /medajɔ̃/ nm medallion; (bijou) locket.

médecin /medsɛ̃/ nm doctor.

médecine /medsin/ nf medicine.

média /medja/ nm medium; les ~s the media.

médiateur, -trice /medjatœʀ, -tʀis/ nm, f mediator.

médiatique /medjatik/ adj (événement, personnalité) media.

médical, ~e (mpl -aux) /medikal, -o/ adj medical.

médicament /medikamã/ nm medicine, drug.

médico-légal, ~e (mpl -aux) /medikolegal, -o/ adj forensic.

médiéval, ~e (mpl -aux) /medjeval, -o/ adj medieval.

médiocre /medjɔkʀ/ adj mediocre, poor. **médiocrité** nf mediocrity.

médire /mediʀ/ ❸❼ vi ~ de speak ill of, malign.

médisance /medizãs/ nf ~(s) malicious gossip.

méditer /medite/ ❶ vi meditate (sur on). ● vt contemplate; (paroles, conseils) mull over; ~ de plan to.

Méditerranée /mediteʀane/ nf la ~ the Mediterranean.

méditerranéen, ~ne

/mediteʀaneɛ̃, -ɛn/ adj Mediterranean.

médium /medjɔm/ nm (personne) medium.

méduse /medyz/ nf jellyfish.

meeting /mitiŋ/ nm meeting.

méfait /mefɛ/ nm misdeed; les ~s de (conséquences) the ravages of.

méfiance /mefjɑ̃s/ nf suspicion, distrust. **méfiant**, ~e adj suspicious, distrustful.

méfier (se) /(sə)mefje/ ❹❺ vpr be wary or careful; se ~ de distrust, be wary of.

mégaoctet /megaɔkte/ nm (Ordinat) megabyte.

mégère /meʒɛʀ/ nf (femme) shrew.

mégot /mego/ nm cigarette end.

meilleur, ~e /mejœʀ/ adj (comparatif) better (que than); (superlatif) best; le ~ livre the best book; mon ~ ami my best friend; ~ marché cheaper. ● nm, f le ~, la ~e the best (one). ● adv (sentir) better; il fait ~ the weather is better.

mél /mel/ nm email; envoyer un ~ send an email.

mélancolie /melɑ̃kɔli/ nf melancholy.

mélange /melɑ̃ʒ/ nm mixture, blend.

mélanger /melɑ̃ʒe/ ❹❶ vt mix; (thés, parfums) blend. □ se ~ vpr mix; (thés, parfums) blend; (idées) get mixed up.

mélasse /melas/ nf black treacle; (US) molasses.

mêlée /mele/ nf free for all; (au rugby) scrum.

mêler /mele/ ❶ vt mix (à with); (qualités) combine; (embrouiller) mix up; ~ qn à (impliquer dans) involve sb in. □ se ~ vpr mix; combine; se ~ à (se joindre à) mingle with; (participer à) join in; se ~ de meddle in; **mêle-toi de ce qui te regarde** mind your own business.

méli-mélo /pl mélis-mélos/ /melimelo/ nm jumble.

mélo /melo/ ① nm melodrama. ● adj inv slushy, schmaltzy ①.

mélodie /melɔdi/ nf melody. **mélodieux, -ieuse** adj melodious. **mélodique** adj melodic.

mélodramatique /melɔdramatik/ adj melodramatic. **mélodrame** nm melodrama.

mélomane /melɔman/ nmf music lover.

melon /məlɔ̃/ nm melon; (chapeau) ~ bowler (hat).

membrane /mɑ̃bran/ nf membrane.

membre /mɑ̃br/ nm (Anat) limb; (adhérent) member.

même /mɛm/ adj same; ce livre ~ this very book; la bonté ~ kindness itself; en ~ temps at the same time. ● pron le ~, la ~ the same (one). ● adv even; ici ~ directly on; à ~ de in a position to; de ~ (aussi) too; (de la même façon) likewise; de ~ que just as; ~ si even if.

mémé /meme/ nf ① granny.

mémo /memo/ nm note, memo.

mémoire /memwar/ nm (rapport) memorandum; (Univ) dissertation; ~s (souvenirs écrits) memoirs. ● nf memory; à la ~ de to the memory of; de ~ from memory; ~ morte/vive (Ordinat) ROM/RAM.

mémorable /memɔrabl/ adj memorable.

menace /manas/ nf threat. **menacer** ⑩ vt threaten (de faire to do).

ménage /menaʒ/ nm (couple) couple; (travail) housework; (fa-

mille) household; se mettre en ~ set up house.

ménagement /menaʒmɑ̃/ nm avec ~s gently; sans ~s (dire) bluntly; (jeter, pousser) roughly.

ménager¹, **-ère** /menaʒe, -ɛr/ adj household, domestic; travaux ~s housework.

ménager² /menaʒe/ ④⓪ vt be gentle with, handle carefully; (utiliser) be careful with; (organiser) prepare (carefully); ne pas ~ ses efforts spare no effort.

ménagère /menaʒɛr/ nf housewife.

ménagerie /menaʒri/ nf menagerie.

mendiant, ~e /mɑ̃djɑ̃, -t/ nm, f beggar.

mendier /mɑ̃dje/ ④⑤ vt beg for. ● vi beg.

mener /mane/ ⑥ vt lead; (entreprise, pays) run; (étude, enquête) carry out; (politique) pursue; ~ à (accompagner à) take to; (faire aboutir) lead to; ~ à bien see through. ● vi lead.

méningite /menɛ̃ʒit/ nf meningitis.

menotte /manɔt/ nf ① hand; ~s handcuffs.

mensonge /mɑ̃sɔ̃ʒ/ nm lie; (action) lying. **mensonger, -ère** adj untrue, false.

mensualité /mɑ̃sɥalite/ nf monthly payment.

mensuel, -le /mɑ̃sɥel/ adj monthly. ● nm monthly (magazine). **mensuellement** adv monthly.

mensurations /mɑ̃syrasjɔ̃/ nfpl measurements.

mental, ~e /mɑ̃tal, -o/ (mpl -aux) adj mental; malade ~ mentally ill person; handicapé ~ mentally handicapped person.

mentalité /mɑ̃talite/ nf mentality.

menteur, -euse /mɑ̃tœr, -øz/ nm, f liar. ● adj untruthful.

menthe /mɑ̃t/ nf mint.

mention /mɑ̃sjɔ̃/ nf mention; (annotation) note; (Scol) grade; rayer la ~ inutile delete as appropriate. **mentionner** 1 vt mention.

mentir /mɑ̃tir/ 46 vi lie.

menton /mɑ̃tɔ̃/ nm chin.

menu, ~e /məny/ adj (petit) tiny; (fin) fine; (insignifiant) minor. ● adv (couper) fine. ● nm (carte) menu; (repas) meal; (Ordinat) menu; ~ déroulant pull-down menu.

menuiserie /mənɥizri/ nf carpentry, joinery. **menuisier** nm carpenter, joiner.

méprendre (se) /(sə)meprɑ̃dr/ 50 vpr se ~ sur be mistaken about.

mépris /mepri/ nm contempt, scorn (de for); au ~ de regardless of.

méprisable /meprizabl/ adj contemptible, despicable.

méprise /mepriz/ nf mistake.

méprisant, ~e /meprizɑ̃, -t/ adj scornful. **mépriser** 1 vt scorn, despise.

mer /mɛr/ nf sea; (marée) tide; en pleine ~ out at sea.

mercenaire /mɛrsənɛr/ nm & a mercenary.

mercerie /mɛrs(ə)ri/ nf haberdashery; (US) notions store. **mercier, -ière** nm, f haberdasher; (US) notions seller.

merci /mɛrsi/ interj thank you, thanks (de, pour for); ~ beaucoup, ~ bien thank you very much. ● nm thank you. ● nf mercy.

mercredi /mɛrkrədi/ nm Wednesday; ~ des Cendres Ash Wednesday.

merde /mɛrd/ nf ✗ shit ✗.

mère /mɛr/ nf mother; ~ de famille mother.

méridional, ~e (mpl -aux) /meridjɔnal, -o/ adj southern. ● nm, f Southerner.

mérite /merit/ nm merit; avoir du ~ à faire deserve credit for doing.

mériter /merite/ 1 vt deserve; ~ d'être lu be worth reading.

méritoire /meritwar/ adj commendable.

merlan /mɛrlɑ̃/ nm whiting.

merle /mɛrl/ nm blackbird.

merveille /mɛrvɛj/ nf wonder, marvel; à ~ wonderfully; faire des ~s work wonders.

merveilleux, -euse /mɛrvɛjø, -z/ adj wonderful, marvellous.

mes /me/ ➡MON.

mésange /mezɑ̃ʒ/ nf tit(mouse).

mésaventure /mezavɑ̃tyr/ nf misadventure; par ~ by some misfortune.

mesdames /medam/ ➡MADAME.

mesdemoiselles /medmwazel/ ➡MADEMOISELLE.

mésentente /mezɑ̃tɑ̃t/ nf disagreement.

mesquin, ~e /mɛskɛ̃, -in/ adj mean-minded, petty; (chiche) mean. **mesquinerie** nf meanness.

message /mesaʒ/ nm message; un ~ électronique an email; ~ texte text message.

messager, -ère /mesaʒe, -ɛr/ nm, f messenger. ● nm ~ de poche pager.

messagerie /mesaʒri/ nf (transports) freight forwarding; (télécommunications) messaging; ~ électronique electronic mail; ~ vocale voice mail.

messe /mɛs/ nf (Relig) mass.

messieurs /mesjø/ ➡MONSIEUR.

mesure /məzyʀ/ nf measurement; (quantité, unité) measure; (disposition) measure, step; (cadence) time; en ~ in time; (modération) moderation; à ~ que as; dans la ~ où in so far as; dans une certaine ~ to some extent; en ~ de in a position to; sans ~ to excess; (fait) sur ~ made-to-measure.

mesuré, ~e /məzyʀe/ adj measured; (atttitude) moderate.

mesurer /məzyʀe/ **1** vt measure; (juger) assess; (argent, temps) ration. ● vi ~ 15 mètres de long be 15 metres long. □ **se** ~ **avec** vpr pit oneself against.

met /mɛ/ ➡ METTRE **42**.

métal (pl **-aux**) /metal, -o/ nm metal. **métallique** adj (objet) metal; (éclat) metallic.

métallurgie /metalyʀʒi/ nf (industrie) metalworking industry.

métamorphoser /metamɔʀfoze/ **1** vt transform. □ **se** ~ vpr be transformed; se ~ en metamorphose into.

métaphore /metafɔʀ/ nf metaphor.

météo /meteo/ nf (bulletin) weather forecast.

météore /meteɔʀ/ nm meteor.

météorologie /meteɔʀɔlɔʒi/ nf meteorology.

météorologique /meteɔʀɔlɔʒik/ adj meteorological; conditions ~s weather conditions.

méthode /metɔd/ nf method; (ouvrage) course, manual. **méthodique** adj methodical.

méticuleux, -euse /metikylø, -z/ adj meticulous.

métier /metje/ nm job; (manuel) trade; (intellectuel) profession; (expérience) experience, skill; ~ (à tisser) loom; remettre qch sur le ~ rework sth.

métis, ~se /metis/ adj mixed race. ● nm, f person of mixed race.

métrage /metʀaʒ/ nm length; court ~ short (film); long ~ feature-length film.

mètre /mɛtʀ/ nm metre; (règle) rule; ~ ruban tape-measure.

métreur, -euse /metʀœʀ, -øz/ nm, f quantity surveyor.

métrique /metʀik/ adj metric.

métro /metʀo/ nm underground; (US) subway.

métropole /metʀopɔl/ nf metropolis; (pays) mother country. **métropolitain, ~e** adj metropolitan.

mets /mɛ/ nm dish. ● ➡ METTRE **42**.

mettable /metabl/ adj wearable.

metteur /metœʀ/ nm ~ en scène director.

mettre /mɛtʀ/ **42** vt put; (radio, chauffage) put ou switch on; (réveil) set; (installer) put in; (revêtir) put on; (porter habituellement) (vêtement, lunettes) wear; (prendre) take; (investir, dépenser) put; (écrire) write, say; elle a mis deux heures it took her two hours; ~ la table lay the table; ~ en question question; ~ en valeur highlight; (terrain) develop; mettons que suppose that. ● vi ~ bas (animal) give birth. □ **se** ~ vpr (vêtement, maquillage) put on; (se placer) (objet) go; (personne) stand; (assis) sit; (couché) lie; se ~ en short put shorts on; se ~ debout stand up; se ~ au lit go to bed; se ~ à table sit down at table; se ~ en ligne line up; se ~ du sable dans les yeux get sand in one's eyes; se ~ au chinois/tennis take up Chinese/tennis; se ~ au travail set to work; se ~ à faire start to do.

meuble /mœbl/ *nm* piece of furniture; ~s furniture.

meublé /møble/ *nm* furnished flat.

meubler /møble/ **1** *vt* furnish; (fig) fill. □ se ~ *vpr* buy furniture.

meugler /møgle/ **1** *vi* moo.

meule /møl/ *nf* millstone; ~ de foin haystack.

meunier, -ière /mønje, -jɛʀ/ *nm, f* miller.

meurs, meurt /mœʀ/ ➡**MOURIR** 48.

meurtre /mœʀtʀ/ *nm* murder.

meurtrier, -ière /mœʀtʀije, -jɛʀ/ *adj* deadly. ● *nm, f* murderer.

meurtrir /mœʀtʀiʀ/ **2** *vt* bruise.

meute /møt/ *nf* pack of hounds.

Mexique /mɛksik/ *nm* Mexico.

mi- /mi/ *préf* mid-, half-; à mi-chemin half-way; à mi-pente half-way up the hill; à la mi-juin in mid-June.

miauler /mjole/ **1** *vi* miaow.

micro /mikʀo/ *nm* microphone, mike; (Ordinat) micro.

microbe /mikʀob/ *nm* germ.

microfilm /mikʀofilm/ *nm* microfilm.

micro-onde /mikʀoɔ̃d/ *nf* microwave; un four à ~s microwave (oven). **micro-ondes** *nm inv* microwave (oven).

micro-ordinateur (*pl* ~s) /mikʀoɔʀdinatœʀ/ *nm* personal computer.

microphone /mikʀofɔn/ *nm* microphone.

microprocesseur /mikʀopʀosesœʀ/ *nm* microprocessor.

microscope /mikʀoskop/ *nm* microscope.

midi /midi/ *nm* twelve o'clock, midday, noon; (déjeuner) lunch-time;

(sud) south. **Midi** *nm* le M~ the South of France.

mie /mi/ *nf* soft part (of the loaf); un pain de ~ a sandwich loaf.

miel /mjɛl/ *nm* honey.

mielleux, -euse /mjɛlø, -z/ *adj* unctuous.

mien, ~ne /mjɛ̃, -ɛn/ *pron* le ~, la ~ne, les ~(ne)s mine.

miette /mjɛt/ *nf* crumb; (fig) scrap; en ~s in pieces.

mieux /mjø/ *adj inv* better (que than); le ou la ou les ~ (the) best. ● *nm* best; (progrès) improvement; faire de son ~ do one's best; le ~ serait de the best thing would be to. ● *adv* better; le ou la ou les ~ (de deux) the better; (de plusieurs) the best; elle va ~ she is better; j'aime ~ rester I'd rather stay; il vaudrait ~ partir it would be best to leave; tu ferais ~ de faire you would be best to do.

mièvre /mjɛvʀ/ *adj* insipid.

mignon, ~ne /miɲɔ̃, -ɔn/ *adj* cute; (gentil) kind.

migraine /migʀɛn/ *nf* headache; (plus fort) migraine.

migrant /migʀɑ̃/ *nm, f* migrant.

migration /migʀasjɔ̃/ *nf* migration.

mijoter /miʒote/ **1** *vt/i* simmer; (tramer 1) cook up.

mil /mil/ *nm* a thousand.

milice /milis/ *nf* militia.

milieu (*pl* ~x) /miljø/ *nm* middle; (environnement) environment; (appartenance sociale) background; (groupe) circle; (voie) middle way; (criminel) underworld; au ~ de in the middle of; en plein ou au beau ~ de right in the middle (of).

militaire /militɛʀ/ *adj* military. ● *nm* soldier, serviceman.

militant, ~e /militã, -t/ *nm, f*

militant.

militer /milite/ **1** *vi* be a militant; ~ **pour** militate in favour of.

mille¹ /mil/ *adj & nm inv* a thousand; **deux** ~ two thousand; **mettre dans le** ~ (fig) hit the nail on the head.

mille² /mil/ *nm* ~ (**marin**) (nautical) mile.

millénaire /milenɛʀ/ *nm* millennium. ● *adj* a thousand years old.

mille-pattes /milpat/ *nm inv* centipede.

millésime /milezim/ *nm* date; (de vin) vintage.

millet /mijɛ/ *nm* millet.

milliard /miljaʀ/ *nm* thousand million, billion. **milliardaire** *nmf* multi-millionaire.

millième /miljɛm/ *adj & nmf* thousandth.

millier /milje/ *nm* thousand; **un** ~ (**de**) about a thousand.

millimètre /milimɛtʀ/ *nm* millimetre.

million /miljɔ̃/ *nm* million; **deux** ~**s** (**de**) two million. **millionnaire** *nmf* millionaire.

mime /mim/ *nmf* mime-artist. ● *nm* (art) mime. **mimer** **1** *vt* mime; (imiter) mimic.

mimique /mimik/ *nf* expressions and gestures.

minable /minabl/ *adj* **1** (logement) shabby; (médiocre) pathetic, crummy.

minauder /minode/ **1** *vi* simper.

mince /mɛ̃s/ *adj* thin; (svelte) slim; (faible) (espoir, majorité) slim. ● *interj* **1** blast **1**, darn it **1**. **minceur** *nf* thinness; slimness.

mincir /mɛ̃siʀ/ **2** *vi* get slimmer; **ça te mincit** it makes you look slimmer.

mine /min/ *nf* expression; (allure) appearance; **avoir bonne** ~ look well; **faire** ~ **de** make as if to; (exploitation, explosif) mine; (de crayon) lead; ~ **de charbon** coalmine.

miner /mine/ **1** *vt* (saper) undermine; (garnir d'explosifs) mine.

minerai /minʀɛ/ *nm* ore.

minéral, ~e (*mpl* **-aux**) /mineʀal, -o/ *adj* mineral. ● *nm* (*pl* **-aux**) mineral.

minéralogique /mineʀalɔʒik/ *adj* **plaque** ~ numberplate; (US) license plate.

minet, ~te /minɛ, -t/ *nm, f* (chat **1**) pussy(cat).

mineur, ~e /minœʀ/ *adj* minor; (Jur) under age. ● *nm, f* (Jur) minor. ● *nm* (ouvrier) miner.

miniature /minjatyʀ/ *nf & adj* miniature.

minier, -ière /minje, -jɛʀ/ *adj* mining.

minimal, ~e (*mpl* **-aux**) /minimal, o/ *adj* minimal, minimum.

minime /minim/ *adj* minimal, minor. ● *nmf* (Sport) junior.

minimum /minimɔm/ *adj* minimum. ● *nm* minimum; **au** ~ (**pour le moins**) at the very least; **en faire un** ~ do as little as possible.

ministère /ministɛʀ/ *nm* ministry; (gouvernement) government; ~ **public** public prosecutor's office. **ministériel, ~le** *adj* ministerial, government.

ministre /ministʀ/ *nm* minister; (au Royaume-Uni) Secretary of State; (US) Secretary.

Minitel® /minitɛl/ *nm* Minitel (telephone videotext system).

minorer /minɔʀe/ **1** *vt* reduce.

minoritaire /minɔʀitɛʀ/ *adj* minority; être ∼ be in the minority. **minorité** *nf* minority.

minuit /minɥi/ *nm* midnight.

minuscule /minyskyl/ *adj* minute. ●*nf* (lettre) ∼ lower case.

minute /minyt/ *nf* minute; 'talons ∼' 'heels repaired while you wait'.

minuterie /minytʀi/ *nf* timeswitch.

minutie /minysi/ *nf* meticulousness.

minutieux, -ieuse /minysjø, -z/ *adj* meticulous.

mioche /mjɔʃ/ *nm, f* ① kid.

mirabelle /miʀabɛl/ *nf* (mirabelle) plum.

miracle /miʀakl/ *nm* miracle; par ∼ miraculously.

miraculeux, -euse /miʀakylø, -z/ *adj* miraculous.

mirage /miʀaʒ/ *nm* mirage.

mire /miʀ/ *nf* (fig) centre of attraction; (TV) test card.

mirobolant, ∼e /miʀɔbɔlɑ̃, -t/ *adj* ① marvellous.

miroir /miʀwaʀ/ *nm* mirror.

miroiter /miʀwate/ ① *vi* shimmer, sparkle.

mis, ∼e /mi, miz/ *adj* bien ∼ well-dressed. ●—▶METTRE ⚏.

mise /miz/ *nf* (argent) stake; (tenue) attire; ∼ à feu blast-off; ∼ au point adjustment; (fig) clarification; ∼ de fonds capital outlay; ∼ en garde warning; ∼ en plis set; ∼ en scène direction.

miser /mize/ ① *vt* (argent) bet, stake (sur on). ●*vi* ∼ sur (parier) place a bet on; (compter sur) bank on.

misérable /mizeʀabl/ *adj* miserable, wretched; (indigent) destitute; (minable) seedy, squalid.

misère /mizɛʀ/ *nf* destitution.

(malheur) trouble, woe. **miséreux, -euse** *nm, f* destitute person.

miséricorde /mizeʀikɔʀd/ *nf* mercy.

missel /misɛl/ *nm* missal.

missile /misil/ *nm* missile.

mission /misjɔ̃/ *nf* mission. **missionnaire** *nmf* missionary.

missive /misiv/ *nf* missive.

mistral /mistʀal/ *nm* (vent) mistral.

mitaine /mitɛn/ *nf* fingerless mitt.

mite /mit/ *nf* (clothes-)moth.

mi-temps /mitɑ̃/ *nf inv* (arrêt) half-time; (période) half. ●*nm inv* part-time work; à ∼ part-time.

miteux, -euse /mitø, -z/ *adj* shabby.

mitigé, ∼e /mitiʒe/ *adj* (modéré) lukewarm; (succès) qualified.

mitonner /mitɔne/ ① *vt* cook slowly with care; (fig) cook up.

mitoyen, ∼ne /mitwajɛ̃, -ɛn/ *adj* mur ∼ party wall.

mitrailler /mitʀaje/ ① *vt* machine-gun; (fig) bombard.

mitraillette /mitʀajɛt/ *nf* submachine gun. **mitrailleuse** *nf* machine gun.

mi-voix : à ∼ /amivwa/ *loc* in a low voice.

mixeur /miksœʀ/ *nm* liquidizer, blender; (batteur) mixer.

mixte /mikst/ *adj* mixed; (commission) joint; (école) coeducational; (peau) combination.

mobile /mɔbil/ *adj* mobile; (pièce) moving; (feuillet) loose. ●*nm* (art) mobile; (raison) motive.

mobilier /mɔbilje/ *nm* furniture.

mobilisation /mɔbilizasjɔ̃/ *nf* mobilization. **mobiliser** ① *vt* mobilize.

mobilité /mɔbilite/ *nf* mobility.

m

mobylette® /mɔbilɛt/ nf moped.

moche /mɔʃ/ adj 🗓 (laid) ugly; (mauvais) lousy.

modalités /mɔdalite/ nfpl (conditions) terms; (façon de fonctionner) practical details.

mode /mɔd/ nf fashion; (coutume) custom; à la ~ fashionable. ● nm method, mode; (genre) way; ~ d'emploi directions (for use).

modèle /mɔdɛl/ adj model. ● nm model; (exemple) example; (Comm) (type) model; (taille) size; (style) style; ~ familial family size; ~ réduit (small-scale) model.

modeler /mɔdle/ 🖸 vt model (sur on). □ se ~ sur vpr model oneself on.

modem /mɔdɛm/ nm modem.

modérateur, -trice /mɔderatœr, -tris/ adj moderating. **modération** nf moderation.

modéré, -e /mɔdere/ adj & nm, f moderate.

modérer /mɔdere/ 🗓 vt (propos) moderate; (désirs, sentiments) curb. □ se ~ vpr restrain oneself.

moderne /mɔdɛrn/ adj modern. **moderniser** 🚹 vt modernize.

modeste /mɔdɛst/ adj modest. **modestie** nf modesty.

modification /mɔdifikasjɔ̃/ nf modification.

modifier /mɔdifje/ 🗓 vt change, modify. □ se ~ vpr change, alter.

modique /mɔdik/ adj modest.

modiste /mɔdist/ nf milliner.

moduler /mɔdyle/ 🚹 vt modulate; (adapter) adjust.

moelle /mwal/ nf marrow; ~ épinière spinal cord; ~ osseuse bone marrow.

moelleux, -euse /mwalø, -z/ adj soft; (onctueux) smooth.

mœurs /mœr(s)/ nfpl (morale) morals; (usages) customs; (manières) habits, ways.

moi /mwa/ pron me; (indirect) (to) me; (sujet) I. ● nm self.

moignon /mwaɲɔ̃/ nm stump.

moi-même /mwamɛm/ pron myself.

moindre /mwɛ̃dr/ adj (moins grand) lesser; le ou la ~, les ~s the slightest, the least.

moine /mwan/ nm monk.

moineau (pl ~x) /mwano/ nm sparrow.

moins /mwɛ̃/ prép minus; (pour dire l'heure) to; une heure ~ dix ten to one. ● adv less (que than); le ou la ou les ~ the least; le ~ grand/haut the smallest/lowest; ~ de (avec un nom non dénombrable) less (que than); ~ de dix euros less than ten euros; ~ de livres fewer books; au ~, du ~ at least; à ~ que unless; de ~ less; de ~ en ~ less and less; en ~ less; (manquant) missing.

mois /mwa/ nm month.

moisi, -e /mwazi/ adj mouldy. ● nm mould; de ~ (odeur) musty.

moisir 🗓 vi go mouldy. **moisissure** nf mould.

moisson /mwasɔ̃/ nf harvest.

moissonner /mwasɔne/ 🚹 vt harvest, reap. **moissonneur, -euse** nm, f harvester.

moite /mwat/ adj sticky, clammy.

moitié /mwatje/ nf half; (milieu) halfway mark; s'arrêter à la ~ stop halfway through; à ~ vide half empty; à ~ prix (at) half-price; la ~ de half (of). **moitié-moitié** adv half-and-half.

mol /mɔl/ →MOU.

molaire /mɔlɛr/ nf molar.

molécule /mɔlekyl/ nf molecule.

molester /mɔlɛste/ **1** vt manhandle, rough up.

molle /mɔl/ ➞MOU.

mollement /mɔlmɑ̃/ adv softly; (faiblement) feebly. **mollesse** nf softness; (faiblesse) feebleness; (apathie) listlessness.

mollet /mɔlɛ/ nm (de jambe) calf.

mollir /mɔliʀ/ **2** vi soften; (céder) yield.

môme /mom/ nmf **1** kid.

moment /mɔmɑ̃/ nm moment; (période) time; (petit) ~ short while; au ~ où when; par ~s now and then; du ~ où ou que (pourvu que) as long as, provided that; (puisque) since; en ce ~ at the moment.

momentané, ~e /mɔmɑ̃tane/ adj momentary. **momentanément** adv momentarily; (en ce moment) at present.

momie /mɔmi/ nf mummy.

mon, ma (**mon** before vowel or mute h) (pl **mes**) /mɔ̃, ma, mɔ̃, me/ adj my.

Monaco /mɔnako/ npr Monaco.

monarchie /mɔnaʀʃi/ nf monarchy.

monarque /mɔnaʀk/ nm monarch.

monastère /mɔnastɛʀ/ nm monastery.

monceau (pl ~x) /mɔ̃so/ nm heap, pile.

mondain, ~e /mɔ̃dɛ̃, -ɛn/ adj society, social.

monde /mɔ̃d/ nm world; du ~ (a lot of) people; (quelqu'un) somebody; le (grand) ~ (high) society; se faire (tout) un ~ de qch make a great deal of fuss about sth; pas le moins du ~ not in the least.

mondial, ~e (mpl -iaux) /mɔ̃djal, -jo/ adj world; (influence) worldwide.

mondialement adv the world over.

mondialisation /mɔ̃djalizasjɔ̃/ nf globalisation.

monétaire /mɔnetɛʀ/ adj monetary.

moniteur, -trice /mɔnitœʀ, -tʀis/ nm, f instructor; (de colonie de vacances) group leader; (US) (camp) counselor.

monnaie /mɔnɛ/ nf currency; (pièce) coin; (appoint) change; faire la ~ de get change for; faire de la ~ à qn give sb change; menue ou petite ~ small change.

monnayer /mɔneje/ **31** vt convert into cash.

monologue /mɔnɔlɔg/ nm monologue.

monoparental, ~e /mɔnɔpaʀɑ̃tal/ adj famille ~e single-parent family.

monopole /mɔnɔpɔl/ nm monopoly. **monopoliser** **1** vt monopolize.

monospace /mɔnɔspas/ nm (Auto) people carrier.

monotone /mɔnɔtɔn/ adj monotonous. **monotonie** nf monotony.

Monseigneur (pl **Messeigneurs**) /mɔ̃sɛɲœʀ/ nm (à un duc, archevêque) Your Grace; (à un prince) Your Highness.

monsieur (pl **messieurs**) /məsjø, mesjø/ nm (à un inconnu) (dans une lettre) M~ Dear Sir; bonjour, ~ good morning; mesdames et messieurs ladies and gentlemen; (à un homme dont on connaît le nom) (dans une lettre) Cher M~ Dear Mr X; bonjour, ~ good morning Mr X; M~ le curé Father X; oui M~ le ministre yes Minister; (homme) man; (formule de respect) sir.

monstre /mɔ̃stʀ/ nm monster.
● adj **1** colossal.

monstrueux, -euse /mɔ̃stʀyø, -z/

adj monstrous. **monstruosité** *nf* monstrosity.

mont /mɔ̃/ *nm* mountain; le ~ Everest Mount Everest; être toujours par ~s et par vaux be always on the move.

montage /mɔ̃taʒ/ *nm* (assemblage) assembly; (au cinéma) editing.

montagne /mɔ̃taɲ/ *nf* mountain; (région) mountains; ~s russes roller-coaster. **montagneux, -euse** *adj* mountainous.

montant, ~e /mɔ̃tɑ̃, -t/ *adj* rising; (col) high; (chemin) uphill. ● *nm* amount; (pièce de bois) upright.

mont-de-piété (*pl* **monts-de-piété**) /mɔ̃dpjete/ *nm* pawnshop.

monte-charge /mɔ̃tʃaʀʒ/ *nm inv* goods lift.

montée /mɔ̃te/ *nf* ascent, climb; (de prix) rise; (de coûts, risques) increase; (côte) hill.

monter /mɔ̃te/ **1** *vt* (aux. avoir) take up; (à l'étage) take upstairs; (escalier, rue, pente) go up; (assembler) assemble; (tente, échafaudage) put up; (col, manche) let in; (organiser) (pièce) stage; (société) set up; (attaque, garde) mount. ● *vi* (aux. être) go ou come up; (à l'étage) go ou come upstairs; (avion) climb; (route) go uphill, climb; (augmenter) rise; (marée) come up; ~ sur (trottoir, toit) get up on; (cheval, bicyclette) get on; ~ à l'échelle/ l'arbre climb the ladder/tree; ~ dans (voiture) get in; (train, bus, avion) get on; ~ à bord climb on board; ~ (à cheval) ride; ~ à bicyclette/moto ride a bike/ motorbike.

monteur, -euse /mɔ̃tœʀ, -øz/ *nm, f* (Tech) fitter; (au cinéma) editor.

montre /mɔ̃tʀ/ *nf* watch; faire ~ de show.

montrer /mɔ̃tʀe/ **1** *vt* show (à to); ~ du doigt point to. □ **se ~** *vpr* du oneself; (être) be; (s'avérer) prove to be.

monture /mɔ̃tyʀ/ *nf* (cheval) mount; (de lunettes) frames (+ *pl*); (de bijou) setting.

monument /mɔnymɑ̃/ *nm* monument; ~ aux morts war memorial. **monumental** (*pl* **-aux**) *adj* monumental.

moquer (se) /(sə)mɔke/ **1** *vpr* se ~ de make fun of; je m'en moque **1** I couldn't care less. **moquerie** *nf* mockery. **moqueur, -euse** *adj* mocking.

moquette /mɔkɛt/ *nf* fitted carpet; (US) wall-to-wall carpeting.

moral, ~e (*mpl* **-aux**) /mɔʀal, -o/ *adj* moral. ● *nm* (*pl* **-aux**) morale; ne pas avoir le ~ feel down; avoir le ~ be in good spirits; ça m'a remonté le ~ it gave me a boost. **morale** /mɔʀal/ *nf* moral code; (mœurs) morals; (de fable) moral; faire la ~ à lecture. **moralité** *nf* (de personne) morals (+ *pl*); (d'action, œuvre) morality; (de fable) moral.

moralisateur, -trice /mɔʀalizatœʀ, -tʀis/ *adj* moralizing.

morbide /mɔʀbid/ *adj* morbid.

morceau (*pl* **~x**) /mɔʀso/ *nm* piece, bit; (de sucre) lump; (de viande) cut; (passage) passage; manger un ~ **1** have a bite to eat; mettre en ~x smash *ou* tear to bits.

morceler /mɔʀsəle/ **6** *vt* divide up.

mordant, ~e /mɔʀdɑ̃, -t/ *adj* scathing; (froid) biting. ● *nm* vigour, energy.

mordiller /mɔʀdije/ **1** *vt* nibble at.

mordre /mɔʀdʀ/ **3** *vi* bite (**dans** into); ~ **sur** (*ligne*) go over; (*territoire*) encroach on; ~ **à l'hameçon** bite. ● *vt* bite.

mordu, ~**e** /mɔʀdy/ **1** *nm, f* fan. ● *adj* smitten; ~ **de** crazy about.

morfondre (se) /(sə)mɔʀfɔ̃dʀ/ **3** *vpr* wait anxiously; (*languir*) mope.

morgue /mɔʀg/ *nf* morgue, mortuary; (*attitude*) arrogance.

moribond, ~**e** /mɔʀibɔ̃, -d/ *adj* dying.

morne /mɔʀn/ *adj* dull.

morphine /mɔʀfin/ *nf* morphine.

mors /mɔʀ/ *nm* (*de cheval*) bit.

morse /mɔʀs/ *nm* (*animal*) walrus; (*code*) Morse code.

morsure /mɔʀsyʀ/ *nf* bite.

mort[1] /mɔʀ/ *nf* death.

mort[2], ~**e** /mɔʀ, -t/ *adj* dead; ~ **de fatigue** dead tired. ● *nm, f* dead man, dead woman; **les** ~**s** the dead.

mortalité /mɔʀtalite/ *nf* mortality; (**taux de**) ~ death rate.

mortel, ~**le** /mɔʀtɛl/ *adj* mortal; (*accident*) fatal; (*poison, silence*) deadly. ● *nm, f* mortal. **mortellement** *adv* mortally.

mortifié, ~**e** /mɔʀtifje/ *adj* mortified.

mort-né, ~**e** /mɔʀne/ *adj* stillborn.

mortuaire /mɔʀtɥɛʀ/ *adj* (*cérémonie*) funeral.

morue /mɔʀy/ *nf* cod.

mosaïque /mozaik/ *nf* mosaic.

mosquée /mɔske/ *nf* mosque.

mot /mo/ *nm* word; (*lettre, message*) note; ~ **d'ordre** watchword; ~ **de passe** password; ~**s croisés** crossword (puzzle).

motard /mɔtaʀ/ *nm* biker; (*policier*) police motorcyclist.

moteur, -**trice** /mɔtœʀ, -tʀis/ *adj* (*Méd*) motor; (*force*) driving; **à 4 roues motrices** 4-wheel drive. ● *nm* engine, motor; **barque à** ~ motor launch; ~ **de recherche** (Internet) search engine.

motif /mɔtif/ *nm* (*raisons*) grounds (+ *pl*); (*cause*) reason; (*Jur*) motive; (*dessin*) pattern.

motion /mosjɔ̃/ *nf* motion.

motivation /mɔtivasjɔ̃/ *nf* motivation. **motiver** **1** *vt* motivate.

moto /mɔto/ *nf* motor cycle. **motocycliste** *nmf* motorcyclist.

motorisé, ~**e** /mɔtɔʀize/ *adj* motorized.

motrice /mɔtʀis/ ➡**MOTEUR.**

motte /mɔt/ *nf* lump; (*de beurre*) slab; (*de terre*) clod; ~ **de gazon** turf.

mou (**mol** *before vowel or mute h*), **molle** /mu, mɔl/ *adj* soft; (*ventre*) flabby; (*sans conviction*) feeble; (*apathique*) sluggish, listless. ● *nm* slack; **avoir du** ~ be slack.

mouchard, ~**e** /muʃaʀ, -d/ *nm, f* informer; (*Scol*) sneak.

mouche /muʃ/ *nf* fly; (*de cible*) bull's-eye.

moucher (se) /(sə)muʃe/ **1** *vpr* blow one's nose.

moucheron /muʃʀɔ̃/ *nm* midge.

moucheté, ~**e** /muʃte/ *adj* speckled.

mouchoir /muʃwaʀ/ *nm* handkerchief, hanky; ~ **en papier** tissue.

moue /mu/ *nf* pout; **faire la** ~ pout.

mouette /mwɛt/ *nf* (sea)gull.

moufle /mufl/ *nf* (*gant*) mitten.

mouillé, ~**e** /muje/ *adj* wet.

mouiller /muje/ **1** *vt* wet, make wet; ~ **l'ancre** drop anchor.

m

□ se ~ *vpr* get (oneself) wet.

moulage /mulaʒ/ *nm* cast.

moule /mul/ *nf* (coquillage) mussel. ●*nm* mould; ~ à gâteau cake tin; ~ à tarte flan dish. **mouler** ◻ *vt* mould; (statue) cast.

moulin /mulɛ̃/ *nm* mill; ~ à café coffee grinder; ~ à poivre pepper mill; ~ à vent windmill.

moulinet /mulinɛ/ *nm* (de canne à pêche) reel; faire des ~s avec qch twirl sth around.

moulinette® /mulinɛt/ *nf* vegetable mill.

moulu, ~e /muly/ *adj* ground; (fatigué ◻) worn out.

moulure, ~e /mulyʀ/ *nf* moulding.

mourant, ~e /muʀɑ̃, -t/ *adj* dying. ●*nm, f* dying person.

mourir /muʀiʀ/ ◻ *vi* (aux. être) die; ~ d'envie de be dying to; ~ de faim be starving; ~ d'ennui be dead bored.

mousquetaire /muskətɛʀ/ *nm* musketeer.

mousse /mus/ *nf* moss; (écume) froth, foam; (de savon) lather; (dessert) mousse; ~ à raser shaving foam. ●*nm* ship's boy.

mousseline /muslin/ *nf* muslin; (de soie) chiffon.

mousser /muse/ ◻ *vi* froth, foam; (savon) lather.

mousseux, -euse /musø, -z/ *adj* frothy. ●*nm* sparkling wine.

mousson /musɔ̃/ *nf* monsoon.

moustache /mustaʃ/ *nf* moustache; ~s (d'animal) whiskers.

moustique /mustik/ *nm* mosquito.

moutarde /mutaʀd/ *nf* mustard.

mouton /mutɔ̃/ *nm* sheep; (peau) sheepskin; (viande) mutton.

mouvant, ~e /muvɑ̃, -t/ *adj* changing; (terrain) shifting, unstable.

mouvement /muvmɑ̃/ *nm* movement; (agitation) bustle; (en gymnastique) exercise; (impulsion) impulse; (tendance) tend, tendency; en ~ in motion.

mouvementé, ~e /muvmɑ̃te/ *adj* eventful.

moyen, ~ne /mwajɛ̃, -ɛn/ *adj* average; (médiocre) poor; de taille moyenne medium-sized. ●*nm* means, way; ~s means; (dons) ability; au ~ de by means of; il n'y a pas ~ de it is not possible to. **Moyen Âge** *nm* Middle Ages (+ *pl*).

moyennant /mwajɛnɑ̃/ *prép* (pour) for; (grâce à) with.

moyenne /mwajɛn/ *nf* average; (Scol) pass-mark; en ~ on average; ~ d'âge average age. **moyennement** *adv* moderately.

Moyen-Orient /mwajɛnɔʀjɑ̃/ *nm* Middle East.

moyeu (*pl* ~x) /mwajø/ *nm* hub.

mû, **mue** /my/ *adj* driven (par by).

mucoviscidose /mykɔvisidoz/ *nf* cystic fibrosis.

mue /my/ *nf* moulting; (de voix) breaking of the voice.

muer /mɥe/ ◻ *vi* moult; (voix) break. □ se ~ en *vpr* change into.

muet, ~te /mɥe, -t/ *adj* (Méd) dumb; (fig) speechless (de with); (silencieux) silent. ●*nm, f* mute.

mufle /myfl/ *nm* nose, muzzle; (personne ◻) boor, lout.

mugir /myʒiʀ/ ◻ *vi* (vache) moo; (bœuf) bellow; (fig) howl.

muguet /mygɛ/ *nm* lily of the valley.

mule /myl/ *nf* (female) mule; (pantoufle) mule.

mulet /mylɛ/ *nm* (male) mule.

multicolore /myltikɔlɔʀ/ *adj* multicoloured.

multimédia /myltimedja/ adj &
nm multimedia.

multinational, ~e (mpl -aux)
/myltinasjɔnal, -o/ adj multinational. **multinationale** nf multinational (company).

multiple /myltipl/ nm multiple.
●adj numerous, many; (naissances)
multiple.

multiplication /myltiplikasjɔ̃/ nf
multiplication.

multiplicité /myltiplisite/ nf
multiplicity.

multiplier /myltiplije/ 45 vt
multiply; (risques) increase. □ se ~
vpr multiply; (accidents) be on the
increase; (difficultés) increase.

multitude /myltityd/ nf multitude, mass.

municipal, ~e (mpl -aux)
/mynisipal, -o/ adj municipal; conseil ~ town council. **municipalité**
nf (ville) municipality; (conseil) town
council.

munir /mynir/ 2 vt ~ de provide
with. □ se ~ de vpr (apporter)
bring; (emporter) take.

munitions /mynisjɔ̃/ nfpl ammunition.

mur /myr/ nm wall; ~ du son
sound barrier.

mûr, ~e /myr/ adj ripe; (personne)
mature.

muraille /myrɑj/ nf (high) wall.

mural, ~e (mpl -aux) /myral, -o/
adj wall; peinture ~e mural.

mûre /myr/ nf blackberry.

mûrir /myrir/ 2 vi ripen; (abcès)
come to a head; (personne, projet)
mature. ●vt (fruit) ripen; (personne)
mature.

murmure /myrmyr/ nm murmur.

muscade /myskad/ nf noix ~
nutmeg.

muscle /myskl/ nm muscle. **mus-**

clé, ~e adj muscular. **musculaire**
adj muscular.

musculation /myskylasjɔ̃/ nf
bodybuilding.

musculature /myskylatyr/ nf
muscles (+ pl).

museau (pl ~x) /myzo/ nm muzzle; (de porc) snout.

musée /myze/ nm museum; (de
peinture) art gallery.

muselière /myzəljɛr/ nf muzzle.

musette /myzɛt/ nf haversack.

muséum /myzeɔm/ nm natural
history museum.

musical, ~e (mpl -aux) /myzikal,
-o/ adj musical.

musicien, ~ne /myzisjɛ̃, -ɛn/ adj
musical. ●nm, f musician.

musique /myzik/ nf music; (orchestre) band.

must /myst/ nm Ⅰ must.

musulman, ~e /myzylmã, -an/
adj & nm, f Muslim.

mutation /mytasjɔ̃/ nf change;
(biologique) mutation; (d'un employé) transfer.

muter /myte/ 1 vt transfer. ●vi
mutate.

mutilation /mytilasjɔ̃/ nf mutilation. **mutiler** 1 vt mutilate. **mu-**
tilé, ~e nm, f disabled person.

mutin, ~e /mytɛ̃, -in/ adj mischievous. ●nm mutineer; (prisonnier) rioter.

mutinerie /mytinri/ nf mutiny;
(de prisonniers) riot.

mutisme /mytism/ nm silence.

mutuel, ~le /mytɥɛl/ adj mutual.
mutuelle nf mutual insurance company. **mutuellement** adv mutually;
(l'un l'autre) each other.

myope /mjɔp/ adj short-sighted.
myopie nf short-sightedness.

myosotis /mjozotis/ nm

m

forget-me-not.

myrtille /miʀtij/ nf bilberry, blueberry.

mystère /mistɛʀ/ nm mystery.

mystérieux, -ieuse /misterjø, -z/ adj mysterious.

mystification /mistifikasjɔ̃/ nf hoax.

mysticisme /mistisism/ nm mysticism.

mystique /mistik/ adj mystic(al). ● nmf mystic. ● nf mystique.

mythe /mit/ nm myth. **mythique** adj mythical.

mythologie /mitɔlɔʒi/ nf mythology.

. . . .

Nn

. . . .

n' /n/ ➡NE.

nacre /nakʀ/ nf mother-of-pearl.

nage /naʒ/ nf swimming; (manière) stroke; traverser à la ~ swim across; en ~ sweating.

nageoire /naʒwaʀ/ nf fin; (de mammifère) flipper.

nager /naʒe/ 40 vt/i swim. **nageur, -euse** nm, f swimmer.

naguère /nagɛʀ/ adv (autrefois) formerly.

naïf, -ïve /naif, -v/ adj naïve.

nain, ~e /nɛ̃, nɛn/ nm, f & adj dwarf.

naissance /nɛsɑ̃s/ nf birth; donner ~ à give birth to; (fig) give rise to.

naître /nɛtʀ/ 44 vi be born; (résulter) arise (de from); faire ~ (susciter) give rise to.

naïveté /naivte/ nf naïvety.

nappe /nap/ nf tablecloth; (de pétrole, gaz) layer; ~ phréatique ground water.

napperon /napʀɔ̃/ nm (cloth) tablemat.

narco-dollars /naʀkodɔlaʀ/ nmpl drug money.

narcotique /naʀkɔtik/ adj & nm narcotic. **narco(-)trafiquant, ~e** (pl ~s) nm, f drug trafficker.

narguer /naʀge/ 1 vt taunt; (autorité) flout.

narine /naʀin/ nf nostril.

nasal, ~e (mpl -aux) /nazal, -o/ adj nasal.

naseau (pl ~x) /nazo/ nm nostril.

natal, ~e (mpl ~s) /natal/ adj native.

natalité /natalite/ nf birth rate.

natation /natasjɔ̃/ nf swimming.

natif, -ive /natif, -v/ adj native.

nation /nasjɔ̃/ nf nation.

national, ~e (mpl -aux) /nasjonal, -o/ adj national. **nationale** nf A road; (US) highway. **nationaliser** 1 vt nationalize.

nationalité /nasjonalite/ nf nationality.

natte /nat/ nf (de cheveux) plait; (US) braid; (tapis de paille) mat.

nature /natyʀ/ nf nature; ~ morte still life; de ~ à likely to; payer en ~ pay in kind. ● adj inv plain; (yaourt) natural; (thé) black.

naturel, ~le /natyʀɛl/ adj natural. ● nm nature; (simplicité) naturalness; (Culin) au ~ plain; (thon) in brine. **naturellement** adv naturally; (bien sûr) of course.

naufrage /nofʀaʒ/ nm shipwreck; faire ~ be shipwrecked; (bateau) be wrecked.

nauséabond, ~e /nozeabɔ̃, -d/ adj nauseating.

nausée /noze/ *nf* nausea.

nautique /notik/ *adj* nautical; sports ~s water sports.

naval, ~e (*mpl* ~s) /naval/ *adj* naval; chantier ~ shipyard.

navet /navɛ/ *nm* turnip; (film: péj) flop; (US) turkey.

navette /navɛt/ *nf* shuttle (service); faire la ~ shuttle back and forth.

navigateur, -trice /navigatœʀ, -tʀis/ *nm, f* sailor; (qui guide) navigator; (Internet) browser. **navigation** *nf* navigation; (trafic) shipping; (Internet) browsing.

naviguer /navige/ **1** *vi* sail; (piloter) navigate; (Internet) browse; ~ dans l'Internet surf the Internet.

navire /naviʀ/ *nm* ship.

navré, ~e /navʀe/ *adj* sorry (de to).

---

ne, n' /nə, n/

n' before vowel or mute h.

● *adverbe*

····▸ je n'ai que 10 euros I've only got 10 euros.

····▸ tu n'avais qu'à le dire! you only had to say so!

····▸ je crains qu'il ~ parte I am afraid he will leave.

➡ Pour les expressions comme ne... guère, ne... jamais, ne... pas, ne... plus, etc. ➡guère, jamais, pas, plus, etc.

---

né, ~e /ne/ *adj* born; ~e Martin née Martin; (dans composés) dernier-~ last-born. ●➡NAÎTRE 44.

néanmoins /neɑ̃mwɛ̃/ *adv* nevertheless.

néant /neɑ̃/ *nm* nothingness; réduire à ~ (*effet, efforts*) negate, nullify; (*espoir*) dash; 'revenus: ~' 'income: nil'.

nécessaire /neseseʀ/ *adj* necessary. ●*nm* (sac) bag; (trousse) kit; le ~ (l'indispensable) the necessities *ou* essentials; faire le ~ do what is necessary.

nécessité /nesesite/ *nf* necessity; de première ~ vital.

nécessiter /nesesite/ **1** *vt* necessitate.

néerlandais, ~e /neeʀlɑ̃dɛ, -z/ *adj* Dutch. ●*nm* (Ling) Dutch. N~, ~e *nm, f* Dutchman, Dutchwoman.

néfaste /nefast/ *adj* harmful (à to).

négatif, -ive /negatif, -v/ *adj & nm* negative.

négligé, ~e /neglize/ *adj* (*travail*) careless; (*tenue*) scruffy. ●*nm* (tenue) negligee.

négligent, ~e /negliʒɑ̃, -t/ *adj* careless, negligent.

négliger /neglize/ **40** *vt* neglect; (ne pas tenir compte de) ignore, disregard; ~ de faire fail to do. □ se ~ *vpr* neglect oneself.

négoce /negɔs/ *nm* business, trade. **négociant, ~e** *nm, f* merchant.

négociation /negɔsjasjɔ̃/ *nf* negotiation. **négocier** 45 *vt/i* negotiate.

nègre /nɛgʀ/ *adj* (*musique, art*) Negro. ●*nm* (écrivain) ghost writer.

neige /nɛʒ/ *nf* snow. **neiger** 40 *vi* snow.

nénuphar /nenyfaʀ/ *nm* waterlily.

nerf /nɛʀ/ *nm* nerve; (vigueur) stamina; être sur les ~s be on edge.

nerveux, -euse /nɛʀvø, -z/ *adj* nervous; (irritable) nervy; (*centre, cellule*) nerve; (*voiture*) responsive. **nervosité** *nf* nervousness; (irritabilité] touchiness.

net, **~te** /nɛt/ adj (clair, distinct) clear; (propre) clean; (notable) marked; (soigné) neat; (prix, poids) net. ● **N~** nm (Ordinat) net. ● adv (s'arrêter) dead; (refuser) flatly; (parler) plainly; (se casser) cleanly; (tuer) outright. **nettement** adv (expliquer) clearly; (augmenter, se détériorer) markedly; (indiscutablement) distinctly, decidedly. **netteté** nf clearness.

netéconomie /nɛtekɔnɔmi/ nf e-economy.

nétiquette /netikɛt/ nf netiquette.

nettoyage /nɛtwajaʒ/ nm cleaning; **~ à sec** dry-cleaning; **produit de ~** cleaner; **~ ethnique** ethnic cleansing.

nettoyer /nɛtwaje/ **31** vt clean.

neuf[1] /nœf/ (/nœv/ before vowels and mute h) adj inv & nm nine.

neuf[2], **-euve** /nœf, -v/ adj new; **tout ~** brand new. ● nm new; remettre à **~** brighten up; du **~** a new development; **quoi de ~?** what's new?

neutre /nøtʀ/ adj neutral; (Gram) neuter. ● nm (Gram) neuter.

neuve /nœv/ ➡NEUF[2].

neuvième /nœvjɛm/ adj & nm, f ninth.

neveu (pl **~x**) /nəvø/ nm nephew.

névrose /nevʀoz/ nf neurosis. **névrosé**, **~e** adj & nm, f neurotic.

nez /ne/ nm nose; **~ à ~** face to face; **retroussé** turned-up nose.

ni /ni/ conj neither, nor; **~ grand ~ petit** neither big nor small; **~ l'un ~ l'autre ne fument** neither (one nor the other) smokes; **sortir sans manteau ~ chapeau** go without a coat or hat; **elle n'a dit ~ oui ~ non** she didn't say either yes or no.

niais, **~e** /njɛ, -z/ adj silly.

niche /niʃ/ nf (de chien) kennel; (cavité) niche.

nicher /niʃe/ **1** vi nest. □ **se ~** vpr nest; (se cacher) hide.

nicotine /nikɔtin/ nf nicotine.

nid /ni/ nm nest; **faire un ~** build a nest. **nid-de-poule** (pl **nids-de-poule**) nm pot-hole.

nièce /njɛs/ nf niece.

nier /nje/ **45** vt deny.

nigaud, **~e** /nigo, -d/ nm, f fool.

nippon, **~ne** /nipɔ̃, -ɔn/ adj Japanese. **N~**, **~ne** nm, f Japanese.

niveau (pl **~x**) /nivo/ nm level; (compétence) standard; (étage) storey; (US) story; **au ~** up to standard; **mettre à ~** (Ordinat) upgrade; **~ à bulle (d'air)** spirit level; **~ de vie** standard of living.

niveler /nivle/ **6** vt level.

noble /nɔbl/ adj noble. ● nm, f nobleman, noblewoman. **noblesse** nf nobility.

noce /nɔs/ nf (fête ☐) party; (invités) wedding guests; **~s** wedding; **faire la ~** ☐ live it up.

nocif, **-ive** /nɔsif, -v/ adj harmful.

nocturne /nɔktyʀn/ adj nocturnal. ● nm (Mus) nocturne. ● nf (Sport) evening fixture; (de magasin) late-night opening.

Noël /nɔɛl/ nm Christmas.

nœud /nø/ nm (Naut) knot; (pour lier) knot; (pour orner) bow; **~s** (fig) ties; **~ coulant** slipknot, noose; **~ papillon** bow-tie.

noir, **~e** /nwaʀ/ adj black; (obscur, sombre) dark; (triste) gloomy. ● nm black; (obscurité) dark; **travail au ~** moonlighting. ● nf (personne) Black.

noircir /nwaʀsiʀ/ **2** vt blacken; **~ la situation** paint a black picture of the situation. ● vi (banane) go black; (*mur*) get dirty; (*métal*) tarnish. □ **se ~** *vpr* (*ciel*) darken.

noire /nwaʀ/ *nf* (Mus) crotchet.

noisette /nwazɛt/ *nf* hazelnut; (*de beurre*) knob.

noix /nwa/ *nf* nut; (*du noyer*) walnut; (*de beurre*) knob; **~ de cajou** cashew nut; **~ de coco** coconut; **à la ~** ① useless.

nom /nɔ̃/ *nm* name; (Gram) noun; **au ~ de** on behalf of; **~ et prénom** full name; **~ déposé** registered trademark; **~ de famille** surname; **~ de jeune fille** maiden name; **~ de plume** pen name; **~ propre** proper noun; **~ d'utilisateur** username.

nomade /nɔmad/ *adj* nomadic; (*worker*) mobile. ● *nmf* nomad.

nombre /nɔ̃bʀ/ *nm* number; **au ~ de** (*parmi*) among; (*l'un de*) one of; **en (grand) ~** in large numbers; **sans ~** countless.

nombreux, -euse /nɔ̃bʀø, -z/ *adj* (*en grand nombre*) many, numerous; (*important*) large; **de ~ enfants** many children; **nous étions très ~** there were a great many of us.

nombril /nɔ̃bʀil/ *nm* navel.

nomination /nɔminasjɔ̃/ *nf* appointment.

nommer /nɔme/ ① *vt* name; (*élire*) (à un poste) appoint; (à un lieu) post. □ **se ~** *vpr* (s'appeler) be called.

non /nɔ̃/ *adv* no; (*pas*) not; **~ (pas) que** not that; **il vient, ~?** he is coming, isn't he?; **~** plus neither am/do/can/*etc.* I. ● *nm inv* no.

non- /nɔ̃/ *préf* non-; **~-fumeur** non-smoker.

nonante /nɔnɑ̃t/ *adj & nm* ninety.

non-sens /nɔ̃sɑ̃s/ *nm inv* absurdity.

nord /nɔʀ/ *adj inv* (*façade, côte*)

north; (*frontière, zone*) northern. ● *nm* north; **le ~ de l'Europe** northern Europe; **vent de ~** northerly (wind); **aller vers le ~** go north; **le Nord** the North; **du Nord** northern. **nord-est** *nm* north-east.

nordique /nɔʀdik/ *adj* Scandinavian.

nord-ouest /nɔʀwɛst/ *nm* north-west.

normal, -e (*mpl* -**aux**) /nɔʀmal, -o/ *adj* normal. **normale** *nf* normality; (*norme*) norm; (*moyenne*) average.

normand, ~e /nɔʀmɑ̃, -d/ *adj* Norman. **N~, ~e** *nm, f* Norman.

Normandie /nɔʀmɑ̃di/ *nf* Normandy.

norme /nɔʀm/ *nf* norm; (*de production*) standard; **~s de sécurité** safety standards.

Norvège /nɔʀvɛʒ/ *nf* Norway.

norvégien, ~ne /nɔʀveʒjɛ̃, -ɛn/ *adj* Norwegian. **N~, ~ne** *nm, f* Norwegian.

nos /no/ ➡**NOTRE.**

nostalgie /nɔstalʒi/ *nf* nostalgia; **avoir la ~ de son pays** be homesick. **nostalgique** *adj* nostalgic.

notaire /nɔtɛʀ/ *nm* notary public.

notamment /nɔtamɑ̃/ *adv* notably.

note /nɔt/ *nf* (*remarque*) note; (*chiffrée*) mark, grade; (*facture*) bill; (Mus) note; **~ (de service)** memorandum.

noter /nɔte/ ① *vt* note, notice; (*écrire*) note (down); (*devoir*) mark; (US) grade; **bien/mal noté** (*employé*) highly/poorly rated.

notice /nɔtis/ *nf* note; (*mode d'emploi*) instructions, directions.

notifier /nɔtifje/ ⁴⁵ *vt* notify (à to).

notion /nosjɔ̃/ *nf* notion; **avoir des**

n

~s de have a basic knowledge of.
notoire /nɔtwaʀ/ *adj* well-known;
(*criminel*) notorious.

notre (*pl* **nos**) /nɔtʀ, no/ *adj* our.

nôtre /notʀ/ *pron* le ou la ~, les
~s ours.

nouer /nwe/ **1** *vt* tie, knot; (*relations*) strike up.

nouille /nuj/ *nf* (Culin) noodle; des
~s noodles, pasta; (idiot 1) idiot.

nounours /nunuʀs/ *nm* 1
teddy bear.

nourri, ~e /nuʀi/ *adj* être logé ~
have bed and board; ~ au sein
breastfed.

nourrice /nuʀis/ *nf* childminder.

nourrir /nuʀiʀ/ **2** *vt* feed; (*espoir,
crainte*) harbour; (*projet*) nurture;
(*passion*) fuel. ● *vi* be nourishing.
□ **se** ~ *vpr* eat; **se** ~ **de** feed on.

nourrissant, ~e /nuʀisɑ̃/ *adj* nourishing.

nourrisson /nuʀisɔ̃/ *nm* infant.

nourriture /nuʀityʀ/ *nf* food.

nous /nu/ *pron* (*sujet*) we; (*complément*) us; (*indirect*) (to) us; (*réfléchi*) ourselves; (*l'un l'autre*) each
other; **la voiture est à** ~ the car is
ours. **nous-mêmes** *pron* ourselves.

nouveau (**nouvel** *before vowel or
mute h*), **nouvelle** (*mpl* ~**x**) /nuvo,
nuvɛl/ *adj* new; **nouvel an** new
year; ~**x mariés** newly-weds; ~
venu, **nouvelle venue** newcomer.
● *nm, f* (*élève*) new boy, new girl.
● *nm* **du** ~ (*fait nouveau*) a new
development; **de** ~, **à** ~ again.
nouveau-né (*pl* ~**s**) *nm* new-
born baby.

nouveauté /nuvote/ *nf* novelty;
(*chose*) new thing; (*livre*) new publication; (*disque*) new release.

nouvelle /nuvɛl/ *nf* (piece) of
news; (*récit*) short story; ~**s** news.

Nouvelle-Zélande /nuvɛlzelɑ̃d/
nf New Zealand.

novembre /nɔvɑ̃bʀ/ *nm* November.

noyade /nwajad/ *nf* drowning.

noyau (*pl* ~**x**) /nwajo/ *nm* (de
fruit) stone; (US) pit; (de *cellule*)
nucleus; (*groupe*) group; (*centre:
fig*) core.

noyer /nwaje/ **31** *vt* drown; (*inonder*) flood. □ **se** ~ *vpr* drown; (*volontairement*) drown oneself; **se** ~
dans un verre d'eau make a
mountain out of a molehill. ● *nm*
walnut-tree.

nu, ~**e** /ny/ *adj* (*corps, personne*)
naked; (*mains, mur, fil*) bare; **à l'œil**
~ to the naked eye. ● *nm* nude;
mettre à ~ expose.

nuage /nyaʒ/ *nm* cloud.

nuance /nyɑ̃s/ *nf* shade; (de *sens*)
nuance; (*différence*) difference.
nuancer 10 *vt* (*opinion*) qualify.

nucléaire /nykleɛʀ/ *adj* nuclear.
● *nm* **le** ~ nuclear energy.

nudisme /nydism/ *nm* nudism.

nudité /nydite/ *nf* nudity; (de *lieu*)
bareness.

nuée /nɥe/ *nf* swarm, host.

nues /ny/ *nfpl* **tomber des** ~ **be**
amazed; **porter qn aux** ~ praise sb
to the skies.

nuire /nɥiʀ/ **17** *vi* ~ **à** harm.

nuisible /nɥizibl/ *adj* harmful
(à to).

nuit /nɥi/ *nf* night; **cette** ~ tonight; (*hier*) last night; **il fait** ~ it is
dark; ~ **blanche** sleepless night; **la**
~, **de** ~ at night; ~ **de noces**
wedding night.

nul, ~**le** /nyl/ *adj* (*aucun*) no;
(*zéro*) nil; (*qui ne vaut rien*) useless;
(*non valable*) null; (*contrat*) void;
(*testament*) invalid; **match** ~ draw;
~ **en sciences** no good at science;
nulle part nowhere; ~ **autre** no
one else. ● *pron* no one. **nullement**

adv not at all. **nullité** *nf* uselessness; (personne) nonentity.

numérique /nymeʀik/ *adj* numerical; (montre, horloge) digital.

numériser /nymeʀize/ *vt* digitize.

numéro /nymeʀo/ *nm* number; (de journal) issue; (spectacle) act; ~ **de téléphone** telephone number; ~ **vert** freephone number. **numéroter 1** *vt* number.

nuque /nyk/ *nf* nape (of the neck).

nurse /nœʀs/ *nf* nanny.

nutritif, -ive /nytʀitif, -v/ *adj* nutritious; (valeur) nutritional.

....

Oo

....

oasis /ɔazis/ *nf* oasis.

obéir /ɔbeiʀ/ **2** *vt* ~ **à** obey. ● *vi* obey. **obéissance** *nf* obedience. **obéissant, ~e** *adj* obedient.

obèse /ɔbɛz/ *adj* obese.

objecter /ɔbʒɛkte/ **1** *vt* object.

objectif, -ive /ɔbʒɛktif, -v/ *adj* objective. ● *nm* objective; (Photo) lens.

objection /ɔbʒɛksjɔ̃/ *nf* objection; soulever des ~ raise objections.

objet /ɔbʒɛ/ *nm* (chose) object; (sujet) subject; (but) purpose, object; être ou faire l'~ de be the subject of; ~ **d'art** objet d'art; ~s **trouvés** lost property; (US) lost and found.

obligation /ɔbligasjɔ̃/ *nf* obligation; (Comm) bond; être dans l'~ **de** be under obligation to.

obligatoire /ɔbligatwaʀ/ *adj* compulsory. **obligatoirement** *adv* (par règlement) of necessity; (inévitablement) inevitably.

obligeance /ɔbliʒɑ̃s/ *nf* avoir l'~ **de faire** be kind enough to do.

obliger /ɔbliʒe/ **40** *vt* compel, force (à faire to do); (aider) oblige; être obligé de have to (de for).

oblique /ɔblik/ *adj* oblique; regard ~ sidelong glance; en ~ at an angle.

oblitérer /ɔblitere/ **14** *vt* (timbre) cancel.

obnubilé, ~e /ɔbnybile/ *adj* obsessed.

obscène /ɔpsɛn/ *adj* obscene.

obscur, ~e /ɔpskyʀ/ *adj* dark; (confus, humble) obscure; (vague) vague.

obscurcir /ɔpskyʀsiʀ/ **2** *vt* make dark; (fig) obscure. □ **s'~** *vpr* (ciel) darken.

obscurité /ɔpskyʀite/ *nf* dark(-ness); (de passage, situation) obscurity.

obsédant, ~e /ɔpsedɑ̃, -t/ *adj* (problème) nagging; (musique, souvenir) haunting.

obsédé, ~e /ɔpsede/ *nm, f* ~ (sexuel) sex maniac; ~ **du ski/jazz** ski/jazz freak.

obséder /ɔpsede/ **14** *vt* obsess.

obsèques /ɔpsɛk/ *nfpl* funeral.

observateur, -trice /ɔpsɛʀvatœʀ, -tʀis/ *adj* observant. ● *nm, f* observer.

observation /ɔpsɛʀvasjɔ̃/ *nf* observation; (remarque) remark, comment; (reproche) criticism; (obéissance) observance; en ~ under observation.

observer /ɔpsɛʀve/ **1** *vt* (regarder) observe; (surveiller) watch, observe; (remarquer) notice, observe; faire ~ **qch** point sth out (à to).

obsession /ɔpsesjɔ̃/ *nf* obsession.

obstacle /ɔpstakl/ *nm* obstacle; (pour cheval) fence, jump; (pour

n
o

athlète) hurdle; **faire ~ à** stand in the way of, obstruct.

obstétrique /ɔpstetrik/ *nf* obstetrics (+ *sg*).

obstiné, ~e /ɔpstine/ *adj* obstinate.

obstiner (s') /(s)ɔpstine/ **1** *vpr* persist (à in).

obstruction /ɔpstryksjɔ̃/ *nf* obstruction; (de conduit) blockage.

obstruer /ɔpstrye/ **1** *vt* obstruct.

obtenir /ɔptənir/ **58** *vt* get, obtain. **obtention** *nf* obtaining.

obus /ɔby/ *nm* shell.

occasion /ɔkazjɔ̃/ *nf* opportunity (de faire of doing); (circonstance) occasion; (achat) bargain; (article non neuf) second-hand buy; **à l'~** sometimes; **d'~** second-hand. **occasionnel,** ~le *adj* occasional.

occasionner /ɔkazjɔne/ **1** *vt* cause.

occident /ɔksidɑ̃/ *nm* (direction) west; **l'O~** the West.

occidental, ~e (*mpl* **-aux**) /ɔksidɑtal, -o/ *adj* western. **O~,** ~e (*mpl* **-aux**) *nm, f* westerner.

occulte /ɔkylt/ *adj* occult.

occupant, ~e /ɔkypɑ̃, -t/ *nm, f* occupant. ● *nm* (Mil) forces of occupation.

occupation /ɔkypasjɔ̃/ *nf* occupation.

occupé, ~e /ɔkype/ *adj* busy; (place, pays) occupied; (téléphone) engaged, busy; (toilettes) engaged.

occuper /ɔkype/ **1** *vt* occupy; (poste) hold; (espace, temps) take up. □ **s'~** *vpr* (s'affairer) keep busy (à faire doing); **s'~ de** (personne, problème) take care of; (bureau, firme) be in charge of; (se méler) **occupe-toi de tes affaires** mind your own business.

occurrence: en l'~ /ɑ̃lɔkyrɑ̃s/

loc in this case.

océan /ɔseɑ̃/ *nm* ocean.

Océanie /ɔseani/ *nf* Oceania.

ocre /ɔkr/ *adj inv* ochre.

octante /ɔktɑ̃t/ *adj* eighty.

octet /ɔktɛ/ *nm* byte.

octobre /ɔktɔbr/ *nm* October.

octogone /ɔktɔgɔn/ *nm* octagon.

octroyer /ɔktrwaje/ **31** *vt* grant.

oculaire /ɔkylɛr/ *adj* **témoin ~** eye-witness; **troubles ~s** eye trouble.

oculiste /ɔkylist/ *nmf* ophthalmologist.

odeur /ɔdœr/ *nf* smell.

odieux, -ieuse /ɔdjø, -z/ *adj* odious.

odorant, ~e /ɔdɔrɑ̃, -t/ *adj* sweet-smelling.

odorat /ɔdɔra/ *nm* sense of smell.

œil (*pl* **~s yeux**) /œj, jø/ *nm* eye; **à l'~** **1** for free; **à mes yeux** in my view; **faire de l'~ à** make eyes at; **faire les gros yeux à** glare at; **ouvrir l'~** keep one's eyes open; **~ poché** black eye; **fermer les yeux** shut one's eyes; (fig) turn a blind eye.

œillères /œjɛr/ *nfpl* blinkers.

œillet /œjɛ/ *nm* (plante) carnation; (trou) eyelet.

œuf (*pl* **~s**) /œf, ø/ *nm* egg; **~ à la coque/dur/sur le plat** boiled/hard-boiled/fried egg.

œuvre /œvr/ *nf* (ouvrage, travail) work; **~ d'art** work of art; (**~ de** bienfaisance) charity; **être à l'~** be at work; **mettre en ~** (réforme, moyens) implement; **mise en ~** implementation. ● *nm* (ensemble spécifié) **l'~ entier de Beethoven** the complete works of Beethoven.

œuvrer /œvre/ **1** *vi* work.

offense /ɔfɑ̃s/ *nf* insult.

offenser /ɔfɑ̃se/ **1** *vt* offend.

□ **s'~** *vpr* take offence (de at).

offensive /ɔfɑ̃siv/ *nf* offensive.

offert, ~e /ɔfɛʀ, -t/ ➡OFFRIR 21.

office /ɔfis/ *nm* office; (Relig) service; (de cuisine) pantry; faire ~ de act as; d'~ without consultation, automatically; ~ du tourisme tourist information office.

officiel, ~le /ɔfisjɛl/ *adj* official.
● *nm* official.

officier /ɔfisje/ 45 *vi* (Relig) officiate. ● *nm* officer.

officieux, -ieuse /ɔfisjø, -z/ *adj* unofficial.

offre /ɔfʀ/ *nf* offer; (aux enchères) bid; l'~ et la demande supply and demand; '~s d'emploi' 'situations vacant'.

offrir /ɔfʀiʀ/ 21 *vt* offer (de faire to do); (cadeau) give; (acheter) buy; ~ à boire à (chez soi) give a drink to; (au café) buy a drink for. □ **s'~** *vpr* (se proposer) offer oneself (comme as); (solution) present itself; (s'acheter) treat oneself to.

ogive /ɔʒiv/ *nf* ~ nucléaire nuclear warhead.

OGM (organisation génétiquement modifié) genetically modified organism.

oie /wa/ *nf* goose.

oignon /ɔɲɔ̃/ *nm* (légume) onion; (de fleur) bulb.

oiseau (*pl* ~x) /wazo/ *nm* bird.

oisif, -ive /wazif, -v/ *adj* idle.

olive /ɔliv/ *nf* & *adj* olive. **olivier** *nm* olive tree.

olympique /ɔlɛ̃pik/ *adj* Olympic.

ombrage /ɔ̃bʀaʒ/ *nm* shade; prendre ~ de take offence at. **ombragé, ~e** *adj* shady.

ombre /ɔ̃bʀ/ *nf* (pénombre) shade; (contour) shadow; (soupçon: fig) hint, shadow; dans l'~ (agir, rester) behind the scenes; faire de l'~ à

qn be in sb's light.

ombrelle /ɔ̃bʀɛl/ *nf* parasol.

omelette /ɔmlɛt/ *nf* omelette.

omettre /ɔmɛtʀ/ 42 *vt* omit, leave out.

omnibus /ɔmnibys/ *nm* stopping *ou* local train.

omoplate /ɔmoplat/ *nf* shoulder blade.

on /ɔ̃/ *pron* (tu, vous) you; (nous) we; (ils, elles) they; (les gens) people, they; (quelqu'un) someone; (indéterminé) one, you; ~ dit people say, they say, it's said; ~ m'a demandé mon avis I was asked for my opinion.

oncle /ɔ̃kl/ *nm* uncle.

onctueux, -euse /ɔktɥø, -z/ *adj* smooth.

onde /ɔ̃d/ *nf* wave; ~s courtes/longues short/long wave; sur les ~s on the air.

on-dit /ɔ̃di/ *nm inv* les ~ hearsay.

onduler /ɔ̃dyle/ 1 *vi* undulate; (cheveux) be wavy.

onéreux, -euse /ɔneʀø, -z/ *adj* costly.

ONG (organisation non gouvernementale) NGO, non-governmental organization.

ongle /ɔ̃gl/ *nm* (finger) nail; ~ de pied toenail; se faire les ~s do one's nails.

ont /ɔ̃/ ➡AVOIR 5.

ONU *abrév f* (**Organisation des Nations unies**) UN.

onze /ɔ̃z/ *adj* & *nm* eleven. **onzième** *adj* & *nmf* eleventh.

OPA *abrév f* (**offre publique d'achat**) takeover bid.

opéra /ɔpeʀa/ *nm* opera; (édifice) opera house. **opéra-comique** (*pl* **opéras-comiques**) *nm* light opera.

opérateur, -trice /ɔpeʀatœʀ,

o

-tris/ *nm, f* operator.

opération /ɔpeʀasjɔ̃/ *nf* operation; (Comm) deal; (calcul) calculation; ~ escargot slow-moving protest convoy.

opératoire /ɔpeʀatwaʀ/ *adj* (Méd) surgical; **bloc** ~ operating suite.

opérer /ɔpeʀe/ [14] *vt* (*personne*) operate on; (*exécuter*) carry out, make; ~ **qn d'une tumeur** operate on sb to remove a tumour; **se faire** ~ have surgery *ou* an operation. ● *vi* (Méd) operate; (*faire effet*) work. □ **s'~** *vpr* (*se produire*) occur.

opiniâtre /ɔpinjɑtʀ/ *adj* tenacious.

opinion /ɔpinjɔ̃/ *nf* opinion.

opportuniste /ɔpɔʀtynist/ *nmf* opportunist.

opposant, ~e /ɔpozɑ̃, -t/ *nm, f* opponent.

opposé, ~e /ɔpoze/ *adj* (*sens, angle, avis*) opposite; (*factions*) opposing; (*intérêts*) conflicting; **être** ~ **à** be opposed to. ● *nm* opposite; **à l'~ de** (*contrairement à*) contrary to, unlike.

opposer /ɔpoze/ [1] *vt* (*objets*) place opposite each other; (*personnes*) match, oppose; (*contraster*) contrast; (*résistance, argument*) put up. □ **s'~** *vpr* (*personnes*) confront each other; (*styles*) contrast; **s'~ à** oppose.

opposition /ɔpozisjɔ̃/ *nf* opposition; **par** ~ **à** in contrast with; **entrer en** ~ **avec** come into conflict with; **faire** ~ **à un chèque** stop a cheque.

oppressant, ~e /ɔpʀesɑ̃, -t/ *adj* oppressive.

opprimer /ɔpʀime/ [1] *vt* oppress.

opter /ɔpte/ [1] *vi* ~ **pour** opt for.

opticien, ~ne /ɔptisjɛ̃, -ɛn/ *nm, f* optician.

optimisme /ɔptimism/ *nm*

optimism.

optimiste /ɔptimist/ *nmf* optimist. ● *adj* optimistic.

option /ɔpsjɔ̃/ *nf* option.

optique /ɔptik/ *adj* (*verre*) optical. ● *nf* (*science*) optics (+ *sg*); (*perspective*) perspective.

or ¹ /ɔʀ/ *nm* gold; **d'~** golden; **en** ~ gold; (*occasion*) golden.

or ² /ɔʀ/ *conj* now, well; (*indiquant une opposition*) and yet.

orage /ɔʀaʒ/ *nm* (thunder)storm.

orageux, -euse *adj* stormy.

oral, ~e (*mpl* -**aux**) /ɔʀal, -o/ *adj* oral. ● *nm* (*pl* -**aux**) oral.

orange /ɔʀɑ̃ʒ/ *adj inv* orange; (Aut) (*feu*) amber; (US) yellow. ● *nf* orange. **orangeade** *nf* orangeade. **oranger** *nm* orange tree.

orateur, -trice /ɔʀatœʀ, -tʀis/ *nm, f* speaker.

orbite /ɔʀbit/ *nf* orbit; (*d'œil*) socket.

orchestre /ɔʀkɛstʀ/ *nm* orchestra; (*de jazz*) band; (parterre) stalls.

ordinaire /ɔʀdinɛʀ/ *adj* ordinary; (*habituel*) usual; (*qualité*) standard; (*médiocre*) very average. ● *nm* **l'~** the ordinary; (*nourriture*) the standard fare; **d'~**, **à l'~** usually. **ordinairement** *adv* usually.

ordinateur /ɔʀdinatœʀ/ *nm* computer; ~ **personnel/de bureau** personal/desktop computer; ~ **portable** laptop (computer); ~ **hôte** (Internet) host.

ordonnance /ɔʀdɔnɑ̃s/ *nf* (*ordre, décret*) order; (*de médecin*) prescription.

ordonné, ~e /ɔʀdɔne/ *adj* tidy.

ordonner /ɔʀdɔne/ [1] *vt* order (**à qn de sb** to); (*agencer*) arrange; (Méd) prescribe; (*prêtre*) ordain.

ordre /ɔʀdʀ/ *nm* order; (*propreté*) tidiness; **aux** ~**s de qn** at sb's disposal; **avoir de l'~** be tidy; **en ~** tidy, in order; **de premier ~** first-rate; **d'~ officiel** of an official nature; **l'~ du jour** (programme) agenda; **mettre de l'~ dans** tidy up; **jusqu'à nouvel ~** until further notice; **un ~ de grandeur** an approximate idea.

ordure /ɔʀdyʀ/ nf filth; **~s** (détritus) rubbish; (US) garbage; **~s ménagères** household refuse.

oreille /ɔʀɛj/ nf ear.

oreiller /ɔʀeje/ nm pillow.

oreillons /ɔʀejɔ̃/ nmpl mumps.

orfèvre /ɔʀfɛvʀ/ nm goldsmith.

organe /ɔʀgan/ nm organ.

organigramme /ɔʀganigʀam/ nm organization chart; (Ordinat) flowchart.

organique /ɔʀganik/ adj organic.

organisateur, -trice /ɔʀganizatœʀ, -tʀis/ nm, f organizer.

organisation /ɔʀganizasjɔ̃/ nf organization.

organiser /ɔʀganize/ **1** vt organize. □ **s'~** vpr organize oneself, get organized.

organisme /ɔʀganism/ nm body, organism.

orge /ɔʀʒ/ nf barley.

orgelet /ɔʀʒəlɛ/ nm sty.

orgue /ɔʀg/ nm organ; **~ de Barbarie** barrel-organ. **orgues** nfpl organ.

orgueil /ɔʀgœj/ nm pride. **orgueilleux, -euse** adj proud.

orient /ɔʀjɑ̃/ nm (direction) east; **l'O~** the Orient.

oriental, ~e (mpl **-aux**) /ɔʀjɑ̃tal, -o/ adj eastern; (de l'Orient) oriental. **O~, ~e** (mpl **-aux**) nm, f Asian.

orientation /ɔʀjɑ̃tasjɔ̃/ nf direction; (tendance politique) leanings (+ pl); (de maison) aspect; (Sport)

orienteering; **~ professionnelle** careers advice; **~ scolaire** curriculum counselling.

orienter /ɔʀjɑ̃te/ **1** vt position; (personne) direct. □ **s'~** vpr (se repérer) find one's bearings; **s'~ vers** turn towards.

origan /ɔʀigɑ̃/ nm oregano.

originaire /ɔʀiʒinɛʀ/ adj **être ~ de** be a native of.

original, ~e (mpl **-aux**) /ɔʀiʒinal, -o/ adj original; (curieux) eccentric. ● nm (œuvre) original. ● nm, f eccentric. **originalité** nf originality; eccentricity.

origine /ɔʀiʒin/ nf origin; **à l'~** originally; **d'~** (pièce, pneu) original; **être d'~ noble** come from a noble background.

originel, ~le /ɔʀiʒinɛl/ adj original.

orme /ɔʀm/ nm elm.

ornement /ɔʀnəmɑ̃/ nm ornament.

orner /ɔʀne/ **1** vt decorate.

orphelin, ~e /ɔʀfəlɛ̃, -in/ nm, f orphan. ● adj orphaned. **orphelinat** nm orphanage.

orteil /ɔʀtɛj/ nm toe.

orthodoxe /ɔʀtɔdɔks/ adj orthodox.

orthographe /ɔʀtɔgʀaf/ nf spelling.

ortie /ɔʀti/ nf nettle.

os /ɔs, o/ nm inv bone.

OS abrév m ⇒**OUVRIER SPÉCIALISÉ**.

osciller /ɔsile/ **1** vi sway; (Tech) oscillate; (hésiter) waver; (fluctuer) fluctuate.

osé, ~e /oze/ adj daring.

oseille /ozɛj/ nf (plante) sorrel.

oser /oze/ **1** vi dare.

osier /ozje/ nm wicker.

ossature /ɔsatyʀ/ nf skeleton,

frame.

ossements /ɔsmã/ *nmpl* bones, remains.

osseux, -euse /ɔsø, -z/ *adj* bony; (Méd) bone.

otage /ɔtaʒ/ *nm* hostage.

OTAN /ɔtã/ *abrév f* (Organisation du traité de l'Atlantique Nord) NATO.

otarie /ɔtaʀi/ *nf* eared seal.

ôter /ote/ **1** *vt* remove (à qn from sb); (déduire) take away.

otite /ɔtit/ *nf* ear infection.

ou /u/ *conj* or; ∼ bien or else; ∼ (bien)... ∼ (bien)... either... or...; vous ∼ moi either you or me.

où /u/ *pron* where; (dans lequel) in which; (sur lequel) on which; (auquel) at which; d'∼ from which; (pour cette raison) hence; par ∼ through which; ∼ qu'il soit wherever he may be; juste au moment ∼ just as; le jour ∼ the day when. ● *adv* where; d'∼? where?

ouate /wat/ *nf* cotton wool; (US) absorbent cotton.

oubli /ubli/ *nm* forgetfulness; (trou de mémoire) lapse of memory; (négligence) oversight; tomber dans l'∼ sink into oblivion.

oublier /ublije/ **45** *vt* forget; (omettre) leave out, forget. □ s'∼ *vpr* (chose) be forgotten.

ouest /wɛst/ *adj inv* (façade, côte) west; (frontière, zone) western. ● *nm* west; l'∼ de l'Europe western Europe; vent d'∼ westerly (wind); aller vers l'∼ go west; l'O∼ the West; de l'O∼ western.

oui /wi/ *adv & nm inv* yes.

ouï-dire : par ∼ /paʀwidiʀ/ *loc* by hearsay.

ouïe /wi/ *nf* hearing; (de poisson) gill.

ouragan /uʀagã/ *nm* hurricane.

ourlet /uʀlɛ/ *nm* hem.

ours /uʀs/ *nm* bear; ∼ blanc polar bear; ∼ en peluche teddy bear.

outil /uti/ *nm* tool. **outillage** *nm* tools (+ *pl*). **outiller** **1** *vt* equip.

outrage /utʀaʒ/ *nm* (grave) insult.

outrance /utʀãs/ *nf* à ∼ excessively. **outrancier, -ière** *adj* extreme.

outre /utʀ/ *prép* besides. ● *adv* passer ∼ pay no heed; ∼ mesure unduly; en ∼ in addition. **outre-mer** *adv* overseas.

outrepasser /utʀəpase/ **1** *vt* exceed.

outrer /utʀe/ **1** *vt* exaggerate; (indigner) incense.

ouvert, -e /uvɛʀ, -t/ *adj* open; (gaz, radio) on. ●➡OUVRIR **21**.

ouverture /uvɛʀtyʀ/ *nf* opening; (Mus) overture; (Photo) aperture; ∼s (offres) overtures; ∼ d'esprit open-mindedness.

ouvrable /uvʀabl/ *adj* jour ∼ working day; aux heures ∼s during business hours.

ouvrage /uvʀaʒ/ *nm* (travail, livre) work; (couture) (piece of) needlework.

ouvre-boîtes /uvʀəbwat/ *nm inv* tin-opener.

ouvre-bouteilles /uvʀəbutɛj/ *nm inv* bottle-opener.

ouvreur, -euse /uvʀœʀ, -øz/ *nm, f* usherette.

ouvrier, -ière /uvʀije, -jɛʀ/ *nm, f* worker; ∼ qualifié/spécialisé skilled/unskilled worker. ● *adj* working-class; (conflit) industrial; syndicat ∼ trade union.

ouvrir /uvʀiʀ/ **21** *vt* open (up); (gaz, robinet) turn on. ● *vi* open (up). □ s'∼ *vpr* open (up); s'∼ à qn open one's heart to sb.

ovaire /ɔvɛʀ/ *nm* ovary.

ovale /ɔval/ adj & nm oval.

ovni /ɔvni/ abrév m (**objet volant non-identifié**) UFO.

ovule /ɔvyl/ nm (à féconder) ovum; (gynécologique) pessary.

oxygène /ɔksiʒɛn/ nm oxygen.

oxygéner (s') /(s)ɔksiʒene/ [14] vpr get some fresh air.

ozone /ozon/ nf ozone; la couche d'~ the ozone layer.

Pp

pacifique /pasifik/ adj peaceful; (personne) peaceable; (Géog) Pacific. P~ nm le P~ the Pacific.

pacotille /pakɔtij/ nf junk, rubbish.

PACS abrév nm (**pacte de solidarité**) contract of civil union.

pacser (se) /sapakse/ [1] vpr sign a contract of civil union (PACS).

pagaie /pagɛ/ nf paddle.

pagaille /pagaj/ nf [1] mess, shambles (+ sg).

page /paʒ/ nf page; mise en ~ layout; tourner la ~ turn over a new leaf; être à la ~ be up to date; ~ d'accueil (Internet) home page.

paie /pɛ/ nf pay.

paiement /pɛmã/ nm payment.

païen, ~ne /pajɛ̃, -ɛn/ adj & nm, f pagan.

paillasson /pajasɔ̃/ nm doormat.

paille /pɑj/ nf straw. ● adj (cheveux) straw-coloured.

paillette /pajɛt/ nf (sur robe) sequin; (de savon) flake.

pain /pɛ̃/ nm bread; (miche) loaf (of bread); (de savon, cire) bar; ~ d'é-

pices gingerbread; ~ grillé toast.

pair, ~e /pɛR/ adj (nombre) even. ● nm (personne) peer; aller de ~ go together (avec with); au ~ (jeune fille) au pair. **paire** nf pair.

paisible /pezibl/ adj peaceful.

paître /pɛtR/ [44] vi graze.

paix /pɛ/ nf peace; fiche-moi la ~! [1] leave me alone!

Pakistan /pakistã/ nm Pakistan.

palace /palas/ nm luxury hotel.

palais /palɛ/ nm palace; (Anat) palate; ~ de justice law courts; ~ des sports sports stadium.

pâle /pɑl/ adj pale.

Palestine /palɛstin/ nf Palestine.

palier /palje/ nm (d'escalier) landing; (étape) stage.

pâlir /pɑliR/ [2] vt/i (turn) pale.

palissade /palisad/ nf fence.

pallier /palje/ [45] vt compensate for.

palmarès /palmaRɛs/ nm list of prize-winners.

palme /palm/ nf palm leaf; (de nageur) flipper. **palmé**, ~e adj (patte) webbed.

palmier /palmje/ nm palm (tree).

palper /palpe/ [1] vt feel.

palpiter /palpite/ [1] vi (battre) pound; (frémir) quiver.

paludisme /palydism/ nm malaria.

pamplemousse /pɑ̃pləmus/ nm grapefruit.

panaché, ~e /panaʃe/ adj (bariolé, mélangé) motley; glace ~e mixed-flavour ice cream. ● nm shandy.

pancarte /pɑ̃kaRt/ nf sign; (de manifestant) placard.

pané, ~e /pane/ adj breaded.

panier /panje/ nm basket; (de basket-ball) basket; mettre au ~ [1]

o
p

throw out; ~ à salade salad shaker; (fourgon 🅣) police van.

panique /panik/ *nf* panic. **paniquer** 🅵 *vi* panic.

panne /pan/ *nf* breakdown; être en ~ have broken down; être en ~ sèche have run out of petrol; ~ d'électricité *ou* de courant power failure.

panneau (*pl* ~x) /pano/ *nm* sign; (publicitaire) hoarding; (de porte) panel; (~ d'affichage) notice board; (~ de signalisation) road sign.

panoplie /panɔpli/ *nf* (jouet) outfit; (gamme) range.

pansement /pɑ̃smɑ̃/ *nm* dressing; ~ adhésif plaster. **panser** 🅵 *vt* (*plaie*) dress; (*personne*) dress the wound(s) of; (*cheval*) groom.

pantalon /pɑ̃talɔ̃/ *nm* trousers (+ *pl*).

panthère /pɑ̃tɛʀ/ *nf* panther.

pantin /pɑ̃tɛ̃/ *nm* puppet.

pantomime /pɑ̃tɔmim/ *nf* mime; (spectacle) mime show.

pantoufle /pɑ̃tufl/ *nf* slipper.

paon /pɑ̃/ *nm* peacock.

papa /papa/ *nm* dad(dy).

pape /pap/ *nm* pope.

paperasse /papʀas/ *nf* (péj) bumf.

papeterie /papetʀi/ *nf* (magasin) stationer's shop.

papier /papje/ *nm* paper; (formulaire) form; ~s (d'identité) (identity) papers; ~ absorbant kitchen paper; ~ aluminium tin foil; ~ buvard blotting paper; ~ cadeau wrapping paper; ~ calque tracing paper; ~ carbone carbon paper; ~ collant adhesive tape; ~ hygiénique toilet paper; ~ journal newspaper; ~ à lettres writing paper; ~ mâché papier mâché; ~ peint wallpaper; ~ de verre sandpaper.

papillon /papijɔ̃/ *nm* butterfly; (contravention 🅣) parking-ticket; ~ de nuit moth.

papoter /papɔte/ 🅵 *vi* chatter.

paquebot /pakbo/ *nm* liner.

pâquerette /pakʀɛt/ *nf* daisy.

Pâques /pak/ *nfpl* & *nm* Easter.

paquet /pakɛ/ *nm* packet; (de cartes) pack; (colis) parcel; un ~ de (beaucoup 🅣) a mass of.

par /paʀ/ *prép* by; (à travers) through; (motif) out of, from; (provenance) from; commencer/finir ~ qch begin/end with sth; commencer/finir ~ faire begin by/end up (by) doing; ~ an/mois a *ou* per year/month; ~ jour a day; ~ personne each, per person; ~ avion (lettre) (by) airmail; ~-ci, ~-là here and there; ~ contre on the other hand; ~ ici/là this/that way.

parachute /paʀaʃyt/ *nm* parachute. **parachutiste** *nmf* parachutist; (Mil) paratrooper.

parader /paʀade/ 🅵 *vi* show off.

paradis /paʀadi/ *nm* (Relig) heaven; (lieu idéal) paradise; ~ fiscal tax haven.

paradoxal, ~e (*mpl* -aux) /paʀadɔksal, -o/ *adj* paradoxical.

paraffine /paʀafin/ *nf* paraffin wax.

parages /paʀaʒ/ *nmpl* dans les ~ around.

paragraphe /paʀagʀaf/ *nm* paragraph.

paraître /paʀɛtʀ/ 🔟 *vi* (se montrer) appear; (sembler) seem, appear; (*ouvrage*) be published, come out; faire ~ (*ouvrage*) bring out; il paraît que... apparently they...; oui, il paraît so I hear.

parallèle /paʀalɛl/ *adj* parallel; (illégal) unofficial. ● *nm* parallel; faire le ~ make a connection. ● nf parallel (line).

paralyser /paralize/ **1** vt paralyse. **paralysie** nf paralysis.

paramètre /paramεtr/ nm parameter.

parapente /parapɑ̃t/ nm paraglider; (activité) paragliding.

parapharmacie /parafarmasi/ nf toiletries and vitamins (pl.).

parapher /parafe/ **1** vt initial; (signer) sign.

parapluie /paraplɥi/ nm umbrella.

parasite /parazit/ nm parasite; ~s (radio) interference (+ sg).

parasol /parasɔl/ nm sunshade.

paratonnerre /paratɔnεr/ nm lightning conductor ou rod.

paravent /paravɑ̃/ nm screen.

parc /park/ nm park; (de bétail) pen; (de bébé) play-pen; (entrepôt) depot; ~ **de loisirs** theme park; ~ **relais** park and ride; ~ **de stationnement** car park.

parce que /pars(ə)/ conj because.

parchemin /parʃəmɛ̃/ nm parchment.

parcmètre /parkmεtr/ nm parking meter.

parcourir /parkurir/ **20** vt travel ou go through; (distance) cover; (des yeux) glance at ou over.

parcours /parkur/ nm route; (voyage) journey.

par-delà /pardəla/ prép beyond.

par-derrière /pardεrjεr/ adv (attaquer) from behind; (critiquer) behind sb's back.

par-dessous /pardəsu/ prép & adv under (neath).

pardessus /pardəsy/ nm overcoat.

par-dessus /pardəsy/ prép & adv

over; ~ **bord** overboard; ~ **le marché** into the bargain; ~ **tout** above all.

par-devant /pardəvɑ̃/ adv (passer) by the front.

pardon /pardɔ̃/ nm forgiveness; (je vous demande) ~! (I am) sorry!; (pour demander qch) excuse me.

pardonner /pardɔne/ **1** vt forgive; ~ **qch à qn** forgive sb for sth.

pare-brise /parbriz/ nm inv windscreen.

pare-chocs /parʃɔk/ nm inv bumper.

pareil, ~le /parεj/ adj similar (à to); (tel) such (a); c'est ~ it's the same; ce n'est pas ~ it's not the same thing. ● nm, f equal. ● adv **1** the same.

parent, ~e /parɑ̃, -t/ adj related (de to). ● nm, f relative, relation; ~s (père et mère) parents; ~ **isolé** single parent; réunion de ~s d'élèves parents' evening.

parenté /parɑ̃te/ nf relationship.

parenthèse /parɑ̃tεz/ nf bracket, parenthesis; (fig) digression.

parer /pare/ **1** vt (esquiver) parry; (orner) adorn. ● vi ~ **à** deal with; ~ **au plus pressé** tackle the most urgent things first.

paresse /parεs/ nf laziness.

paresseux, -euse /parεsø, -z/ adj lazy. ● nm, f lazy person.

parfait, ~e /parfε, -t/ adj perfect. **parfaitement** adv perfectly; (bien sûr) absolutely.

parfois /parfwa/ adv sometimes.

parfum /parfœ̃/ nm (senteur) scent; (substance) perfume, scent; (goût) flavour. **parfumé, ~e** adj fragrant; (savon) scented; (thé) flavoured.

parfumer /parfyme/ **1** vt (embaumer) scent; (gâteau) flavour.

□ se ~ vpr put on one's perfume.
parfumerie nf (produits) perfumes;
(boutique) perfume shop.
pari /paʀi/ nm bet.
Paris /paʀi/ npr Paris.
parisien, ~ne /paʀizjɛ̃, -ɛn/ adj
Parisian; (banlieue) Paris. P~,
~ne nm, f Parisian.
parking /paʀkiŋ/ nm car park.
parlement /paʀləmɑ̃/ nm parliament.
parlementaire /paʀləmɑ̃tɛʀ/ adj
parliamentary. ● nmf Member of
Parliament.
parlementer /paʀləmɑ̃te/ **1** vi
negotiate.
parler /paʀle/ **1** vi talk (à to); ~
de talk about; tu parles d'un avantage! call that a benefit!; de quoi
ça parle? what is it about? ● vt
(langue) speak; (politique, affaires)
talk. □ se ~ vpr (personnes) talk (to
each other); (langue) be spoken.
● nm speech; (dialecte) dialect.
parmi /paʀmi/ prép among(st).
paroi /paʀwa/ nf wall; ~ rocheuse
rock face.
paroisse /paʀwas/ nf parish.
parole /paʀɔl/ nf (mot, promesse)
word; (langage) speech; demander
la ~ ask to speak; prendre la ~
(begin to) speak; tenir ~ keep
one's word; croire qn sur ~ take
sb's word for it.
parquet /paʀkɛ/ nm (parquet)
floor; lame de ~ floorboard; le ~
(Jur) prosecution.
parrain /paʀɛ̃/ nm godfather; (fig)
sponsor.
parsemer /paʀsəme/ **6** vt strew
(de with).
part /paʀ/ nf share, part; à ~ de
côté) aside; (séparément) separate;
(excepté) apart from; d'une ~ on
the one hand; d'autre ~ on the

other hand; (de plus) moreover; de
la ~ de from; de toutes ~s from
all sides; de ~ et d'autre on both
sides; faire ~ à qn inform sb (de
of); faire ~ des choses make al-
lowances for; prendre ~ à take part
in; (joie, douleur) share; pour ma ~
as for me.
partage /paʀtaʒ/ nm (division) divi-
ding; (répartition) sharing out; recevoir qch en ~ be left sth in
a will.
partager /paʀtaʒe/ **40** vt divide;
(distribuer) share out; (avoir en
commun) share. □ se ~ qch vpr
share sth.
partenaire /paʀtənɛʀ/ nmf
partner.
parterre /paʀtɛʀ/ nm flower bed;
(Théât) stalls.
parti /paʀti/ nm (Pol) party; (décision) decision; (en mariage) match;
~ pris bias; prendre ~ get involved; prendre ~ pour qn side
with sb; j'en ai pris mon ~ I've
come to terms with that.
partial, ~e (mpl -iaux) /paʀsjal,
-jo/ adj biased.
participe /paʀtisip/ nm (Gram)
participle.
participant, ~e /paʀtisipɑ̃, -t/
nm, f participant (à in).
participation /paʀtisipasjɔ̃/ nf
participation; (financière) contribution; (d'un artiste) appearance.
participer /paʀtisipe/ **1** vi ~ à
take part in, participate in; (profits,
frais) share.
particule /paʀtikyl/ nf particle.
particulier, -ière /paʀtikylje,
-jɛʀ/ adj (spécifique) particular; (bizarre) unusual; (privé) private; rien
de ~ nothing special. ● nm private
individual; en ~ in particular, particularly. **particulièrement** adv

particularly.

partie /paʀti/ nf part; (cartes, Sport) game; (Jur) party; une ~ de pêche a fishing trip; en ~ partly, in part; en grande ~ largely; faire ~ de be part of; (adhérer à) be a member of; faire ~ intégrante de be an integral part of.

partiel, ~le /paʀsjɛl/ adj partial. ●nm (Univ) exam based on a module.

partir /paʀtiʀ/ 46 vi (aux être) go; (quitter un lieu) leave, go; (tache) come out; (bouton) come off; (coup de feu) go off; (commencer) start; ~ pour le Brésil leave for Brazil; ~ du principe que work on the assumption that; à ~ de from; à ~ de maintenant from now on.

partisan, ~e /paʀtizã, -an/ nm, f supporter. ●nm (Mil) partisan; être ~ de be in favour of.

partition /paʀtisjɔ̃/ nf (Mus) score.

partout /paʀtu/ adv everywhere; ~ où wherever.

paru /paʀy/ ➡PARAÎTRE 18.

parure /paʀyʀ/ nf finery; (bijoux) set of jewels; (de draps) set.

parution /paʀysjɔ̃/ nf publication.

parvenir /paʀvəniʀ/ 58 vi (aux être) ~ à reach; ~ à faire manage to do; faire ~ send.

parvenu, ~e /paʀvəny/ nm, f upstart.

pas¹ /pɑ/

➡ Pour les expressions comme pas encore, pas mal, etc. ➡encore, mal etc.

●adverbe

····➤ not; ne ~ not; je ne sais ~ I don't know; je ne pense ~ I

don't think so; il a aimé, moi ~ he liked it, I didn't; ~ cher/poli cheap/impolite.

····➤ du tout not at all; ~ de chance! tough luck!

····➤ on a bien ri, ~ vrai? 🔹 we had a good laugh, didn't we?

! In spoken colloquial French ! ne... pas is often shortened to pas. You will hear j'ai pas compris instead of je n'ai pas compris (I didn't understand). NB This is not correct written French.

pas² /pɑ/ nm step; (bruit) footstep; (trace) footprint; (vitesse) pace; à deux ~ (de) a step away (from); marcher au ~ march; rouler au ~ move very slowly; à ~ de loup stealthily; faire les cent ~ walk up and down; faire le premier ~ make the first move; ~ de porte doorstep; ~ de vis (Tech) thread.

passage /pasaʒ/ nm (traversée) crossing; (visite) visit; (chemin) way, passage; (d'une œuvre) passage; de ~ (voyageur) visiting; (amant) casual; la tempête a tout emporté sur son ~ the storm swept everything away; ~ clouté pedestrian crossing; ~ interdit (panneau) no thoroughfare; ~ à niveau level crossing; ~ souterrain subway.

passager, -ère /pasaʒe, -ɛʀ/ adj temporary. ●nm, f passenger; ~ clandestin stowaway.

passant, ~e /pasã, -t/ adj (rue) busy. ●nm, f passer-by. ●nm (anneau) loop.

passe /pas/ nf pass; bonne/ mauvaise ~ good/bad patch; en ~ de on the road to.

passé, ~e /pase/ adj (révolu) past; (dernier) last; (fané) faded; ~ de

mode out of fashion. ● nm past.
● prép after.

passe-partout /pɑspartu/ nm inv master-key. ● adj inv for all occasions.

passeport /pɑspɔʀ/ nm passport.

passer /pɑse/ **1** vi (aux être ou avoir) go past, pass; (aller) go; (venir) come; (temps, douleur) pass; (film) be on; (couleur) fade; laisser ~ let through; (occasion) miss; ~ devant (à pied) walk past; (en voiture) drive past; ~ par go through; où est-il passé? where did he get to?; ~ outre take no notice; passons! let's forget about it!; passons aux choses sérieuses let's turn to serious matters; ~ dans la classe supérieure go up a year; ~ pour un idiot look a fool. ● vt (aux avoir) (franchir) cross, (donner) pass, hand; (temps) spend; (enfiler) slip on; (vidéo, disque) put on; (examen) take, sit; (commande) place; (faire) ~ le temps while away the time; ~ l'aspirateur hoover; ~ un coup de fil à qn give sb a ring; je vous passe Mme X (par le standard) I'll put you through to Mrs X; (en donnant l'appareil) I'll pass you over to Mrs X; ~ qch en fraude smuggle sth. □ se ~ vpr happen, take place; (s'écouler) go by; se ~ de go ou do without.

passerelle /pɑsʀɛl/ nf footbridge; (de navire) gangway; (d'avion) (passenger) footbridge; (Internet) gateway.

passe-temps /pɑstɑ̃/ nm inv pastime.

passif, -ive /pɑsif, -v/ adj passive. ● nm (Comm) liabilities.

passion /pɑsjɔ̃/ nf passion. **passionnant, ~e** adj fascinating.

passionné, ~e /pɑsjɔne/ adj passionate; être ~ de have a

passion for.

passionner /pɑsjɔne/ **1** vt fascinate. □ se ~ pour vpr have a passion for.

passoire /pɑswaʀ/ nf (à thé) strainer; (à légumes) colander.

pastèque /pɑstɛk/ nf watermelon.

pasteur /pɑstœʀ/ nm (Relig) minister.

pastille /pɑstij/ nf (médicament) pastille, lozenge.

patate /patat/ nf **1** spud; ~ (douce) sweet potato.

patauger /patoʒe/ **40** vi splash about.

pâte /pɑt/ nf paste; (à gâteau) dough; (à tarte) pastry; (à frire) batter; ~s (alimentaires) pasta (+ sg.) ~ à modeler Plasticine®; ~ d'amandes marzipan.

pâté /pɑte/ nm (Culin) pâté; (d'encre) blot; (de sable) sandpie; ~ en croûte ≈ pie; ~ de maisons block (of houses).

pâtée /pɑte/ nf feed, mash.

patente /patɑ̃t/ nf trade licence.

paternel, ~le /patɛʀnɛl/ adj paternal. **paternité** nf paternity.

pathétique /patetik/ adj moving.

patience /pɑsjɑ̃s/ nf patience. **patient, ~e** adj & nm, f patient. **patienter** **1** vi wait.

patin /patɛ̃/ nm skate; ~ à roulettes roller-skate.

patinage /patinaʒ/ nm skating. **patiner** **1** vi skate; (roue) spin. **patinoire** nf ice rink.

pâtisserie /pɑtisʀi/ nf cake shop; (gâteau) pastry; (secteur) cake making. **pâtissier, -ière** nm, f confectioner, pastry-cook.

patrie /patʀi/ nf homeland.

patrimoine /patʀimwan/ nm heritage.

patriote /patʀijɔt/ *adj* patriotic.
● *nmf* patriot.

patron, ~ne /patʀɔ̃, -ɔn/ *nm, f* employer, boss; (propriétaire) owner, boss; (saint) patron saint.
● *nm* (couture) pattern. **patronal, ~e** (*mpl* **-aux**) *adj* employers'. **patronat** *nm* employers (+ *pl*).

patrouille /patʀuj/ *nf* patrol.

patte /pat/ *nf* leg; (pied) foot; (de chat) paw; ~s (favoris) sideburns; marcher à quatre ~s walk on all fours; (bébé) crawl; ~s de derrière hind legs.

paume /pom/ *nf* (de main) palm.

paumé, ~e /pome/ *nm, f* misfit.

paupière /popjɛʀ/ *nf* eyelid.

pause /poz/ *nf* pause; (halte) break.

pauvre /povʀ/ *adj* poor. ● *nmf* poor man, poor woman. **pauvreté** *nf* poverty.

pavé /pave/ *nm* cobblestone.

pavillon /pavijɔ̃/ *nm* (maison) house; (drapeau) flag.

payant, ~e /pɛjɑ̃, -t/ *adj* (hôte) paying; c'est ~ you have to pay to get in.

payer /peje/ [31] *vt/i* pay; (service, travail) pay for; ~ qch à qn buy sb sth; faire ~ qn charge sb; il me le paiera! he'll pay for this. □ se ~ *vpr* se ~ qch buy oneself sth; se ~ la tête de make fun of.

pays /pei/ *nm* country; (région) region; du ~ local.

paysage /peizaʒ/ *nm* landscape.

paysan, ~ne /peizɑ̃, -an/ *nm, f* farmer, country person; (péj) peasant. ● *adj* (agricole) farming; (rural) country.

Pays-Bas /peiba/ *nmpl* les ~ the Netherlands.

PCV *abrév m* (**paiement contre vérification**) téléphoner en ~ reverse the charges.

PDG *abrév m* (**président-directeur général**) chairman and managing director.

péage /peaʒ/ *nm* toll; (lieu) tollgate.

peau /po/ (*pl* ~x) /po/ *nf* skin; (cuir) hide; ~ de chamois shammy (leather); ~ de mouton sheepskin; être bien/mal dans sa ~ be/not be at ease with oneself.

pêche /pɛʃ/ *nf* (fruit) peach; (activité) fishing; (poissons) catch; ~ à la ligne angling.

péché /peʃe/ *nm* sin.

pêcher /peʃe/ *vt* (poisson) catch; (dénicher 🔟) dig up. ● *vi* fish. **pêcheur** *nm* fisherman; (à la ligne) angler.

pécuniaire /pekynjɛʀ/ *adj* financial.

pédagogie /pedagɔʒi/ *nf* education.

pédale /pedal/ *nf* pedal.

pédalo ® /pedalo/ *nm* pedal boat.

pédant, ~e /pedɑ̃, -t/ *adj* pedantic.

pédestre /pedɛstʀ/ *adj* faire de la randonnée ~ go walking *ou* hiking.

pédiatre /pedjatʀ/ *nmf* paediatrician.

pédicure /pedikyʀ/ *nmf* chiropodist.

peigne /pɛɲ/ *nm* comb.

peigner /peɲe/ 🔟 *vt* comb; (personne) comb the hair of. □ se ~ *vpr* comb one's hair.

peignoir /pɛɲwaʀ/ *nm* dressing gown.

peindre /pɛ̃dʀ/ [22] *vt* paint.

peine /pɛn/ *nf* sadness, sorrow; (effort, difficulté) trouble; (Jur) sentence; avoir de la ~ feel sad; faire de la ~ à hurt; ce n'est pas la ~ de sonner you don't need to ring the bell; j'ai de la ~ à le croire I find it hard to believe; se donner ou prendre la ~ de faire go to the trouble of doing; ~ de mort death penalty. ● adv à ~ hardly.

peiner /pene/ **1** vi struggle. ● vt sadden.

peintre /pɛ̃tʀ/ nm painter; ~ en bâtiment house painter.

peinture /pɛ̃tyʀ/ nf painting; (matière) paint; ~ à l'huile oil painting.

péjoratif, -ive /peʒɔʀatif, -v/ adj pejorative.

pelage /pəlaʒ/ nm coat, fur.

pêle-mêle /pɛlmɛl/ adv in a jumble.

peler /pəle/ **6** vt/i peel.

pèlerinage /pɛlʀinaʒ/ nm pilgrimage.

pelle /pɛl/ nf shovel; (d'enfant) spade.

pellicule /pelikyl/ nf film; ~s (cheveux) dandruff.

pelote /pəlɔt/ nf (of wool) ball.

peloton /p(ə)lɔtɔ̃/ nm platoon; (Sport) pack; ~ d'exécution firing squad.

pelotonner (se) /(sə)plɔtɔne/ **1** vpr curl up.

pelouse /p(ə)luz/ nf lawn.

peluche /p(ə)lyʃ/ nf (matière) plush; (jouet) cuddly toy; en ~ (lapin, chien) fluffy.

pénal, ~e (mpl -aux) /penal, -o/ adj penal. **pénaliser 1** vt penalize. **pénalité** nf penalty.

penchant /pɑ̃ʃɑ̃/ nm inclination; (goût) liking (pour for).

pencher /pɑ̃ʃe/ **1** vt tilt; ~ pour favour. ● vi lean (over), tilt. □ se ~ vpr lean (forward); se ~ sur (problème) examine.

pendaison /pɑ̃dɛzɔ̃/ nf hanging.

pendant¹ /pɑ̃dɑ̃/ prép (au cours de) during; (durée) for; ~ que while.

pendant², ~e /pɑ̃dɑ̃, -t/ adj hanging; jambes ~es with one's legs dangling. ● nm (contrepartie) matching piece (de to); ~ d'oreille drop earring.

pendentif /pɑ̃dɑ̃tif/ nm pendant.

penderie /pɑ̃dʀi/ nf wardrobe.

pendre /pɑ̃dʀ/ **3** vt/i hang. □ se ~ vpr hang (à from); (se tuer) hang oneself.

pendule /pɑ̃dyl/ nf clock. ● nm pendulum.

pénétrer /penetʀe/ **14** vi ~ (dans) enter; (balle) ~ une crème rub a cream in. ● vt penetrate.

pénible /penibl/ adj (travail) hard; (nouvelle) painful; (enfant) tiresome.

péniche /peniʃ/ nf barge.

pénitence /penitɑ̃s/ nf (Relig) penance; (punition) punishment; faire ~ repent.

pénitentiaire /penitɑ̃sjɛʀ/ adj (établissement) penal.

pénombre /penɔ̃bʀ/ nf half-light.

pensée /pɑ̃se/ nf (idée) thought; (fleur) pansy.

penser /pɑ̃se/ **1** vt/i think; ~ à (réfléchir à) think about; (se souvenir de, prévoir) think of; ~ faire think of doing; faire ~ à remind one of.

pensif, -ive /pɑ̃sif, -v/ adj pensive.

pension /pɑ̃sjɔ̃/ nf (Scol) boarding school; (repas, somme) board; (allocation) pension; (~ de famille) guest house; ~ alimentaire (Jur) alimony. **pensionnaire** nmf (Scol) boarder; (d'hôtel) guest. **pensionnat** nm boarding school.

pente /pɑ̃t/ nf slope; en ~ sloping.

Pentecôte /pɑ̃tkot/ nf la ~ Whitsun.

pénurie /penyʀi/ nf shortage.

pépin /pepɛ̃/ nm (graine) pip; (ennui 🔢) hitch.

pépinière /pepinjɛr/ nf (tree) nursery.

perçant, **~e** /pɛrsɑ̃, -t/ adj (cri) shrill; (regard) piercing.

perce-neige /pɛrsənɛʒ/ nm or f inv snowdrop.

percepteur /pɛrsɛptœr/ nm tax inspector.

percer /pɛrse/ 🔟 vt pierce; (avec perceuse) drill; (mystère) penetrate. ● vi break through; (dent) come through. **perceuse** nf drill.

percevoir /pɛrsəvwar/ 🗹 vt perceive; (impôt) collect.

perche /pɛrʃ/ nf (bâton) pole.

percher (se) /(sə)pɛrʃe/ 🔝 vpr perch.

percolateur /pɛrkɔlatœr/ nm coffee machine.

percuter /pɛrkyte/ 🔝 vt (véhicule) crash into.

perdant, **~e** /pɛrdɑ̃, -t/ adj losing. ● nm, f loser.

perdre /pɛrdr/ 🔢 vt/i lose; (gaspiller) waste; **~ ses poils** (chat) moult. □ **se ~** vpr get lost; (rester inutilisé) go to waste.

perdrix /pɛrdri/ nf partridge.

perdu, **~e** /pɛrdy/ adj lost; (endroit) isolated; (balle) stray; **c'est du temps ~** it's a waste of time.

père /pɛr/ nm father; **~ de famille** father, family man; **~ spirituel** father figure; **le ~ Noël** Santa Claus.

perfection /pɛrfɛksjɔ̃/ nf perfection.

perfectionner /pɛrfɛksjɔne/ 🔝 vt (technique) perfect; (art) refine. □ **se ~** vpr improve; **se ~ en anglais** improve one's English.

perforer /pɛrfɔre/ 🔝 vt perforate; (billet, bande) punch.

performance /pɛrfɔrmɑ̃s/ nf performance.

perfusion /pɛrfyzjɔ̃/ nf drip; **sous ~ on** a drip.

péridurale /peridyral/ nf epidural.

péril /peril/ nm peril; **à tes risques et ~s** at your own risk.

périlleux, **-euse** /perijø, -z/ adj perilous.

périmé, **~e** /perime/ adj (produit) past its use-by date; (désuet) outdated.

période /perjɔd/ nf period.

périodique /perjɔdik/ adj periodic(al). ● nm (journal) periodical.

péripétie /peripesi/ nf (unexpected) event, adventure.

périphérique /periferik/ adj peripheral. ● nm (boulevard) ring road.

périple /peripl/ nm journey.

périr /perir/ 🔢 vi perish, die.

perle /pɛrl/ nf (d'huître) pearl; (de verre) bead.

permanence /pɛrmanɑ̃s/ nf permanence; (Scol) study room; **de ~ on** duty; **en ~** permanently; **assurer une ~** keep the office open.

permanent, **~e** /pɛrmanɑ̃, -t/ adj permanent; (constant) constant; **formation ~e** continuous education. **permanente** nf (coiffure) perm.

permettre /pɛrmɛtr/ 🔢 vt allow; **~ à qn de** allow sb to. □ **se ~** vpr (achat) afford; **se ~ de faire** take the liberty of doing.

permis, **~e** /pɛrmi, -z/ adj allowed. ● nm licence, permit; **~ (de conduire)** driving licence.

permission /pɛrmisjɔ̃/ nf permission; **en ~** (Mil) on leave.

Pérou /peru/ nm Peru.

perpendiculaire /pɛʀpɑ̃dikylɛʀ/ *adj & nf* perpendicular.

perpétuité /pɛʀpetɥite/ *nf* à ∼ for life.

perplexe /pɛʀplɛks/ *adj* perplexed.

perquisition /pɛʀkizisjɔ̃/ *nf* (police) search.

perron /peʀɔ̃/ *nm* (front) steps.

perroquet /peʀɔkɛ/ *nm* parrot.

perruche /peʀyʃ/ *nf* budgerigar.

perruque /peʀyk/ *nf* wig.

persécuter /pɛʀsekyte/ **1** *vt* persecute.

persévérance /pɛʀseveʀɑ̃s/ *nf* perseverance. **persévérer** **14** *vi* persevere.

persienne /pɛʀsjɛn/ *nf* (outside) shutter.

persil /pɛʀsi/ *nm* parsley.

persistance /pɛʀsistɑ̃s/ *nf* persistence. **persistant, ∼e** *adj* persistent; (*feuillage*) evergreen.

persister /pɛʀsiste/ **1** *vi* persist (à faire in doing).

personnage /pɛʀsɔnaʒ/ *nm* character; (personne célèbre) personality.

personnalité /pɛʀsɔnalite/ *nf* personality.

personne /pɛʀsɔn/ *nf* person; ∼s people. ● *pron* nobody, no-one; je n'ai vu ∼ I didn't see anybody.

personnel, ∼le /pɛʀsɔnɛl/ *adj* personal; (égoïste) selfish. ● *nm* staff.

perspective /pɛʀspɛktiv/ *nf* (art, point de vue) perspective; (vue) view; (éventualité) prospect.

perspicace /pɛʀspikas/ *adj* shrewd. **perspicacité** *nf* shrewdness.

persuader /pɛʀsɥade/ **1** *vt* persuade (de faire to do).

persuasif, -ive /pɛʀsɥazif, -v/ *adj* persuasive.

perte /pɛʀt/ *nf* loss; (ruine) ruin; à ∼ de vue as far as the eye can see; ∼ de (temps, argent) waste of; ∼ sèche total loss; ∼s (Méd) discharge.

pertinent, ∼e /pɛʀtinɑ̃, -t/ *adj* pertinent.

perturbateur, -trice /pɛʀtyʀbatœʀ, -tʀis/ *adj, m, f* disruptive element. **perturbation** *nf* disruption. **perturber** **1** *vt* disrupt; (personne) perturb.

pervers, ∼e /pɛʀvɛʀ, -s/ *adj* (dépravé) perverted; (méchant) wicked.

pervertir /pɛʀvɛʀtiʀ/ **2** *vt* pervert.

pesant, ∼e /pəzɑ̃, -t/ *adj* heavy. **pesanteur** /pəzɑ̃tœʀ/ *nf* heaviness; la ∼ (force) gravity.

pesée /pəze/ *nf* weighing; (effort) pressure.

pèse-personne (*pl* ∼s) /pɛzpɛʀsɔn/ *nm* (bathroom) scales.

peser /pəze/ **6** *vt/i* weigh; ∼ sur bear upon.

pessimiste /pesimist/ *adj* pessimistic. ● *nmf* pessimist.

peste /pɛst/ *nf* plague; (personne **1**) pest.

pet /pe/ *nm* **1** fart **1**.

pétale /petal/ *nm* petal.

Pétanque See ▸**Boules**.

---

pétard /petaʀ/ *nm* banger.

péter /pete/ **14** *vi* **1** fart **1**, go bang; (casser) snap.

pétillant, ∼e /petijɑ̃, -t/ *adj* (boisson) sparkling; (personne) bubbly.

pétiller /petije/ **1** *vi* (feu) crackle; (champagne, yeux) sparkle; ∼ d'intelligence sparkle with intelligence.

petit, ∼e /p(ə)ti, -t/ *adj* small;

(avec nuance affective) little; (jeune) young, small; (défaut) minor; (mesquin) petty; en ~ in miniature; ~ à ~ little by little; un ~ peu a little bit; ~ ami boyfriend; ~e amie girlfriend; ~es annonces small ads; ~e cuillère teaspoon; ~ déjeuner breakfast; ~ pois garden pea. ● nm, f little child; (Scol) junior; ~s (de chat) kittens; (de chien) pups. **petite-fille** (pl **petites-filles**) nf granddaughter. **petit-fils** (pl **petits-fils**) nm grandson.

pétition /petisjɔ̃/ nf petition.

petits-enfants /pətizɑ̃fɑ̃/ nmpl grandchildren.

pétrin /petʀɛ̃/ nm dans le ~ 1 in a fix 1.

pétrir /petʀiʀ/ 2 vt knead.

pétrole /petʀɔl/ nm oil; ~ brut crude oil.

pétrolier, -ière /petʀɔlje, -jɛʀ/ adj oil. ● nm (navire) oil-tanker.

peu /pø/ adv (~ de) (quantité) little, not much; (nombre) few, not many; ~ intéressant not very interesting; **il mange** ~ he doesn't eat very much. ● pron few. ● nm little; **un** ~ **(de)** a little; **à** ~ **près** more or less; **de** ~ only just; **à** ~ ~ gradually; ~ **après/avant** shortly after/before; ~ **de chose** not much; ~ **nombreux** few; ~ **souvent** seldom; **pour** ~ **que** if.

peuple /pœpl/ nm people. **peupler** 1 vt populate.

peuplier /pøplije/ nm poplar.

peur /pœʀ/ nf fear; **avoir** ~ be afraid (**de**) (of); **de** ~ **de** for fear of; **faire** ~ **à** frighten. **peureux, -euse** adj fearful.

peut /pø/ ➡POUVOIR 49.

peut-être /pøtɛtʀ/ adv perhaps, maybe; ~ **qu'il viendra** he might come.

peux /pø/ ➡POUVOIR 49.

phare /faʀ/ nm (tour) lighthouse; (de véhicule) headlight; ~ anti-brouillard fog lamp.

pharmacie /faʀmasi/ nf (magasin) chemist's (shop), pharmacy; (science) pharmacy; (armoire) medicine cabinet. **pharmacien, ~ne** nm, f chemist, pharmacist.

phénomène /fenɔmɛn/ nm phenomenon; (personne) 1 eccentric.

philosophe /filɔzɔf/ nmf philosopher. ● adj philosophical. **philosophie** nf philosophy. **philosophique** adj philosophical.

phobie /fɔbi/ nf phobia.

phonétique /fɔnetik/ adj phonetic. ● nf phonetics.

phoque /fɔk/ nm (animal) seal.

photo /fɔto/ nf photo; (art) photography; **prendre en** ~ take a photo of; ~ **d'identité** passport photograph.

photocopie /fɔtokɔpi/ nf photocopy. **photocopier** 45 vt photocopy.

photographe /fɔtɔgʀaf/ nmf photographer. **photographie** nf photograph; (art) photography. **photographier** 45 vt take a photo of.

phrase /fʀɑz/ nf sentence.

physicien, ~ne /fizisjɛ̃, -ɛn/ nm, f physicist.

physique /fizik/ adj physical. ● nm physique; **au** ~ physically. ● nf physics (+ sg.)

piano /pjano/ nm piano.

pianoter /pjanote/ 1 vi tinkle; ~ **sur** (ordinateur) tap at.

PIB abrév m (**produit intérieur brut**) GDP.

pic /pik/ nm (outil) pickaxe; (sommet) peak; (oiseau) woodpecker; **à** ~ (falaise) sheer; (couler) straight to the bottom; **tomber à** ~ 1 come just at the right time.

P

pichet /piʃɛ/ nm jug.

picorer /pikɔʀe/ **1** vt/i peck.

picotement /pikɔtmɑ̃/ nm tingling. **picoter** **1** vt sting; (yeux) sting.

pie /pi/ nf magpie.

pièce /pjɛs/ nf (d'habitation) room; (de monnaie) coin; (Théât) play; (pour raccommoder) patch; (écrit) document; (morceau) piece; (~ de théâtre) play; deux euros (la ~) ten euros each; ~ **détachée** part; ~ **d'identité** identity paper; ~s **jointes** enclosures; (courrier électronique) attachments; ~s **justificatives** written proof; ~ **montée** tiered cake; ~ **de rechange** spare part; un deux-~s a tworoom flat.

pied /pje/ nm foot; (de meuble) leg; (de lampe) base; (de verre) stem; (d'appareil photo) stand; être ~s nus be barefoot; à ~ on foot; au ~ **de la lettre** literally; avoir ~ be able to touch the bottom; jouer au tennis comme un ~ **1** be hopeless at tennis; mettre les ~s dans le plat **1** put one's foot in it; c'est le ~ **1** it's great. **pied-bot** (pl **pieds-bots**) nm club-foot.

piédestal /pjedɛstal/ nm pedestal.

piège /pjɛʒ/ nm trap.

piéger /pjeʒe/ **14 40** vt trap; lettre/voiture piégée letter/car bomb.

piercing /pirsiŋ/ nm body piercing.

pierre /pjɛʀ/ nf stone; ~ **précieuse** precious stone; ~ **tombale** tombstone.

piétiner /pjetine/ **1** vi (avancer lentement) shuffle along; (fig) make no headway; ~ **d'impatience** hop up and down with impatience. ● vt trample (on).

piéton /pjetɔ̃/ nm pedestrian.

pieu (pl ~x) /pjø/ nm post, stake.

pieuvre /pjœvʀ/ nf octopus.

pieux, -ieuse /pjø, -z/ adj pious.

pigeon /piʒɔ̃/ nm pigeon.

piger /piʒe/ **40** vt/i **1** understand, get (it).

pile /pil/ nf (tas) pile; (Électr) battery; ~ **ou face?** heads or tails? ● adv (s'arrêter **1**) dead; à dix heures ~ **1** at ten on the dot.

pilier /pilje/ nm pillar.

pillage /pijaʒ/ nm looting. **pillard**, ~e nm, f looter. **piller** **1** vt loot.

pilote /pilɔt/ nm (Aviat, Naut) pilot; (Auto) driver. ● adj pilot. **piloter** **1** vt (Aviat, Naut) pilot; (Auto) drive.

pilule /pilyl/ nf pill; la ~ **the pill**.

piment /pimɑ̃/ nm hot pepper; (fig) spice. **pimenté**, ~e adj spicy.

pin /pɛ̃/ nm pine.

pinard /pinaʀ/ nm **1** plonk **1**, cheap wine.

pince /pɛ̃s/ nf (outil) pliers (+ pl); (levier) crowbar; (de crabe) pincer; (à sucre) tongs (+ pl); ~ **à épiler** tweezers (+ pl); ~ **à linge** clothes peg.

pinceau (pl ~x) /pɛ̃so/ nm paintbrush.

pincée /pɛ̃se/ nf pinch (de of).

pincer /pɛ̃se/ **10** vt pinch; (attraper **1**) catch. □ **se** ~ vpr catch oneself; se ~ **le doigt** catch one's finger.

pince-sans-rire /pɛ̃ssɑ̃ʀiʀ/ nmf inv c'est un ~ he has a deadpan sense of humour.

pingouin /pɛ̃gwɛ̃/ nm penguin.

pingre /pɛ̃gʀ/ adj **1** stingy.

pintade /pɛ̃tad/ nf guinea fowl.

piocher /pjɔʃe/ **1** vt/i dig; (étudier **1**) study hard, slog away (at).

pion /pjɔ̃/ nm (de jeu) counter; (aux échecs) pawn; (Scol) supervisor.

pipe /pip/ *nf* pipe; fumer la ~ smoke a pipe.

piquant, ~e /pikã, -t/ *adj* (*barbe*) prickly; (*goût*) pungent; (*remarque*) cutting. ●*nm* prickle.

pique /pik/ *nm* (*aux cartes*) spades.

pique-nique (*pl* ~s) /piknik/ *nm* picnic.

piquer /pike/ **1** *vt* (*épine*) prick; (*épice*) burn, sting; (*abeille, ortie*) sting; (*serpent, moustique*) bite; (*enfoncer*) stick; (*coudre*) (*machine-*) stitch; (*curiosité*) excite; (*voler* [I]) pinch. ●*vi* (*avion*) dive; (*goût*) be hot. □ **se** ~ *vpr* prick oneself.

piquet /pike/ *nm* stake; (*de tente*) peg; (*de parasol*) pole; ~ **de grève** (*strike*) picket.

piqûre /pikyʀ/ *nf* prick; (*d'abeille*) sting; (*de serpent*) bite; (*point*) stitch; (*Méd*) injection, jab; **faire une ~ à qn** give sb an injection.

pirate /piʀat/ *nm* pirate; ~ **informatique** computer hacker; ~ **de l'air** hijacker.

pire /piʀ/ *adj* worse (**que** than); **les** ~**s mensonges** the most wicked lies. ●*nm* **le** ~ the worst; **au** ~ at worst.

pis /pi/ *nm* (*de vache*) udder. ●*adj inv* & *adv* worse; **aller de mal en** ~ go from bad to worse.

piscine /pisin/ *nf* swimming pool; ~ **couverte** indoor swimming-pool.

pissenlit /pisãli/ *nm* dandelion.

pistache /pistaʃ/ *nf* pistachio.

piste /pist/ *nf* track; (*de personne, d'animal*) track, trail; (*Aviat*) runway; (*de cirque*) ring; (*de ski*) slope; (*de danse*) floor; (*Sport*) racetrack; ~ **cyclable** cycle lane.

pistolet /pistɔle/ *nm* gun, pistol; (*de peintre*) spray-gun.

piteux, -euse /pitø, -z/ *adj* pitiful.

pitié /pitje/ *nf* pity; **il me fait ~ I** feel sorry for him.

piton /pitɔ̃/ *nm* (*à crochet*) hook; (*sommet pointu*) peak.

pitoyable /pitwajabl/ *adj* pitiful.

pitre /pitʀ/ *nm* clown; **faire le** ~ clown around.

pittoresque /pitɔʀɛsk/ *adj* picturesque.

pivot /pivo/ *nm* pivot. **pivoter** **1** *vi* revolve; (*personne*) swing round.

placard /plakaʀ/ *nm* cupboard; (*affiche*) poster. **placarder** **1** *vt* (*affiche*) post up; (*mur*) cover with posters.

place /plas/ *nf* place; (*espace libre*) room, space; (*siège*) seat, place; (*prix d'un trajet*) fare; (*esplanade*) square; (*emploi*) position; (*de parking*) space; **à la** ~ **de** instead of; **en** ~, **à sa** ~ in its place; **faire** ~ **à** give way to; **sur** ~ on the spot; **remettre qn à sa** ~ put sb in his place; **ça prend de la** ~ it takes up a lot of room; **se mettre à la** ~ **de qn** put oneself in sb's shoes *ou* place.

placement /plasmã/ *nm* (*d'argent*) investment.

placer /plase/ **10** *vt* place; (*invité, spectateur*) seat; (*argent*) invest. □ **se** ~ *vpr* (*personne*) take up a position.

plafond /plafɔ̃/ *nm* ceiling.

plage /plaʒ/ *nf* beach; ~ **horaire** time slot.

plagiat /plaʒja/ *nm* plagiarism.

plaider /plede/ **1** *vt/i* plead. **plaidoirie** *nf* (*defence*) speech. **plaidoyer** *nm* plea.

plaie /plɛ/ *nf* wound; (*personne* [I]) nuisance.

plaignant, ~e /plɛɲã, -t/ *nm, f* plaintiff.

plaindre /plɛ̃dʀ/ **22** *vt* pity. □ **se** ~ *vpr* complain (**de** about); **se** ~

p

de (souffrir de) complain of.

plaine /plɛn/ nf plain.

plainte /plɛ̃t/ nf complaint; (gémissement) groan. **plaintif, -ive** adj plaintive.

plaire /plɛʀ/ [47] vi à please; ça lui plaît he likes it; elle lui plaît he likes her; ça me plaît de faire I like ou enjoy doing; s'il vous plaît please. □ se ~ vpr il se plaît ici he likes it here.

plaisance /plɛzɑ̃s/ nf la (navigation de) ~ boating.

plaisant, ~e /plɛzɑ̃, -t/ adj pleasant; (drôle) amusing.

plaisanter /plɛzɑ̃te/ [1] vi joke. **plaisanterie** nf joke. **plaisantin** nm joker.

plaisir /plɛziʀ/ nm pleasure; faire ~ à please; pour le ~ for fun ou pleasure.

plan /plɑ̃/ nm plan; (de ville) map; (de livre) outline; ~ d'eau artificial lake; ~ social planned redundancy programme; premier ~ foreground.

planche /plɑ̃ʃ/ nf board, plank; (gravure) plate; ~ à repasser ironing-board; ~ à voile windsurfing board; (Sport) windsurfing.

plancher /plɑ̃ʃe/ nm floor.

planer /plane/ [1] vi glide; ~ sur (mystère, danger) hang over.

planète /planɛt/ nf planet.

planeur /planœʀ/ nm glider.

planifier /planifje/ [45] vt plan.

plant /plɑ̃/ nm seedling; (de légumes) patch.

plante /plɑ̃t/ nf plant; ~ d'appartement houseplant; ~ des pieds sole (of the foot).

planter /plɑ̃te/ [1] vt (plante) plant; (enfoncer) drive in; (tente) put up; rester planté [1] stand still.

plaque /plak/ nf plate; (de marbre) slab; (insigne) badge; ~ chauffante hotplate; ~ commémorative plaque; ~ minéralogique numberplate; ~ de verglas patch of ice.

plaquer /plake/ [1] vt (bois) veneer; (aplatir) flatten; (rugby) tackle; (abandonner [1]) ditch [1]; tout ~ chuck it all.

plastique /plastik/ adj & nm plastic; en ~ plastic.

plastiquer /plastike/ [1] vt blow up.

plat, ~e /pla, -t/ adj flat. ● nm (Culin) dish; (partie de repas) course; (de la main) flat. ● à plat adv (poser) flat; (batterie, pneu) flat; à ~ ventre flat on one's face.

platane /platan/ nm plane tree.

plateau (pl ~x) /plato/ nm tray; (de cinéma) set; (de balance) pan; (Géog) plateau; ~ de fromages cheeseboard; ~ de fruits de mer seafood platter. **plate-bande** (pl **plates-bandes**) nf flower bed.

platine /platin/ nm platinum. ● nf (tourne-disque) turntable; ~ laser compact disc player.

plâtre /plɑtʀ/ nm plaster; (Méd) (plaster) cast.

plein, ~e /plɛ̃, -ɛn/ adj full (de of); (total) complete. ● nm faire le ~ (d'essence) fill up (the tank); à ~ fully; à ~ temps full-time; en ~ air in the open air; en ~ milieu/ visage right in the middle/the face; en ~e nuit in the middle of the night. ● adv avoir des idées ~ la tête to be full of ideas. **pleinement** adv fully.

pleurer /plœʀe/ [1] vi cry, weep (sur over); (yeux) water. ● vt mourn.

pleurnicher /plœʀniʃe/ [1] [1] vi snivel.

pleurs | plus

pleurs /plœʀ/ *nmpl* tears; **en ~** in tears.

pleuvoir /plœvwaʀ/ 48 *vi* rain; (fig) rain *ou* shower down; **il pleut** it is raining; **il pleut à verse** *ou* **des cordes** it is pouring.

pli /pli/ *nm* fold; (de jupe) pleat; (de pantalon) crease; (lettre) letter; (habitude) habit; (faux ~) crease.

pliant, ~e /plijɑ̃, -t/ *adj* folding. ● *nm* folding stool, camp-stool.

plier /plije/ 45 *vt* fold; (courber) bend; (soumettre) submit (à to). ● *vi* bend. □ **se ~** *vpr* fold; **se ~ à** submit to.

plinthe /plɛ̃t/ *nf* skirting-board.

plissé, ~e /plise/ *adj* (jupe) pleated.

plisser /plise/ 1 *vt* crease; (yeux) screw up.

plomb /plɔ̃/ *nm* lead; (fusible) fuse; **~s** (de chasse) lead shot; **de** *ou* **en ~** lead. **plombage** *nm* filling.

plomberie /plɔ̃bʀi/ *nf* plumbing. **plombier** *nm* plumber.

plongée /plɔ̃ʒe/ *nf* diving; **en ~** (sous-marin) submerged.

plongeoir /plɔ̃ʒwaʀ/ *nm* diving board.

plonger /plɔ̃ʒe/ 40 *vi* dive; (route) plunge. ● *vt* plunge. □ **se ~** *vpr* plunge into; **se ~ dans** (fig) (lecture) bury oneself in. **plongeur, -euse** *nm, f* diver; (de restaurant) dishwasher.

plu /ply/ ➡PLAIRE 47, PLEUVOIR 48.

pluie /plɥi/ *nf* rain; (averse) shower; **~ battante/diluvienne** driving/torrential rain.

plume /plym/ *nf* feather; (pointe) nib.

plumeau (*pl* **~x**) /plymo/ *nm* feather duster.

plumier /plymje/ *nm* pencil box.

plupart: **la ~** /laplypaʀ/ *loc* **la ~**

des (gens, cas) most; **la ~ du temps** most of the time; **pour la ~** for the most part.

pluriel, ~le /plyʀjɛl/ *adj & nm* plural.

---

plus /ply, plys, plyz/

● *adverbe de comparaison*
····▸ more (que than); **~ âgé/tard** older/later; **~ beau** more beautiful; **~ j'y pense...** the more I think about it...; **deux fois ~** twice as much; **deux fois ~ cher** twice as expensive.

····▸ **le ~** the most; **le ~ grand** the biggest; (de deux) the bigger.

····▸ **~ de** (pain) more; (dix jours) more than; **il est ~ de 8 heures** it is after 8 o'clock.

····▸ **de ~** more (que than); (en outre) moreover; **les enfants de ~ de 10 ans** children over 10 years old; **de ~ en ~** more and more.

····▸ **en ~** on top of that; **c'est en ~** it's extra; **en ~ de** in addition to.

····▸ **~ ou moins** more or less.

····▸ **au ~ tard** at the latest.

● *adverbe de négation*
····▸ **ne ~** (temps) no longer, not any more; **je n'y vais ~** I don't go there any longer *ou* any more.

····▸ **ne ~ de** (quantité) no more; **il n'y a ~ de pain** there is no more bread.

····▸ **~ que deux jours!** only two days left!

● *préposition & nom masculin*
····▸ (maths) plus.

---

plusieurs /plyzjœr/ *adj & pron* several.

plus-value (*pl* ~s) /plyvaly/ *nf* (bénéfice) profit.

plutôt /plyto/ *adv* rather (que than).

pluvieux, -ieuse /plyvjø, -z/ *adj* rainy.

PME *abrév f* (petites et moyennes entreprises) SME.

PNB *abrév m* (produit national brut) GNP.

pneu (*pl* ~s) /pnø/ *nm* tyre. **pneumatique** *adj* inflatable.

pneumonie /pnømɔni/ *nf* pneumonia; ~ atypique severe acute respiratory syndrome.

poche /pɔʃ/ *nf* (de vêtement) pocket; (sac) bag; ~s (sous les yeux) bags.

pocher /pɔʃe/ **1** *vt* (œuf) poach.

pochette /pɔʃɛt/ *nf* (de documents) folder; (sac) bag, pouch; (d'allumettes) book; (de disque) sleeve; (mouchoir) pocket handkerchief.

poêle /pwal/ *nf* (~ à frire) frying-pan. ● *nm* stove.

poème /pɔɛm/ *nm* poem. **poésie** *nf* poetry; (poème) poem. **poète** *nm* poet. **poétique** *adj* poetic.

poids /pwa/ *nm* weight; ~ coq/lourd/plume bantamweight/heavyweight/featherweight; ~ lourd (camion) lorry, juggernaut; (US) truck.

poignard /pwaɲar/ *nm* dagger. **poignarder** **1** *vt* stab.

poigne /pwaɲ/ *nf* avoir de la ~ have a strong grip.

poignée /pwaɲe/ *nf* (de porte) handle; (quantité) handful; ~ de main handshake.

poignet /pwaɲɛ/ *nm* wrist; (de chemise) cuff.

poil /pwal/ *nm* hair; (pelage) fur; (de brosse) bristle; ~s (de tapis) pile; à ~ 🄸 naked; ~ à gratter itching powder. **poilu**, -e *adj* hairy.

poinçon /pwɛ̃sɔ̃/ *nm* awl; (marque) hallmark. **poinçonner** **1** *vt* (billet) punch.

poing /pwɛ̃/ *nm* fist.

point /pwɛ̃/ *nm* (endroit, Sport) point; (marque visible) spot, dot; (de couture) stitch; (pour évaluer) mark; enlever un ~ par faute take a mark off for each mistake; à ~ (Culin) medium; (arriver) at the right time; faire le ~ take stock; mettre au ~ (photo) focus; (technique) develop; mettre les choses au ~ get things clear; Camille n'est pas encore au ~ pour ses examens Camille is not ready for her exams; sur le ~ de about to; au ~ que to the extent that; (~ final) full stop, period; deux ~s colon; ~ d'interrogation/d'exclamation question/exclamation mark; ~s de suspension suspension points; ~ virgule semicolon; ~ culminant peak; ~ du jour daybreak; ~ mort (Auto) neutral; ~ de repère landmark; ~ de suture (Méd) stitch; ~ de vente point of sale; ~ de vue point of view. ● *adv* (ne) ~ not.

pointe /pwɛ̃t/ *nf* point, tip; (clou) tack; (de grille) spike; (fig) touch (de of); de ~ (industrie) high-tech; en ~ pointed; heure de ~ peak hour; sur la ~ des pieds on tiptoe.

pointer /pwɛ̃te/ **1** *vt* (cocher) tick off; (diriger) point, aim. ● *vi* (employé) (en arrivant) clock in; (en sortant) clock out. □ **se** ~ *vpr* 🄸 turn up.

pointillé /pwɛ̃tije/ *nm* dotted line.

pointilleux, -euse /pwɛ̃tijø, -z/ *adj* fastidious, particular.

pointu, -e /pwɛ̃ty/ *adj* pointed; (aiguisé) sharp.

pointure /pwɛtyʀ/ nf size.

poire /pwaʀ/ nf pear.

poireau (pl ~x) /pwaʀo/ nm leek.

poirier /pwaʀje/ nm pear tree.

pois /pwa/ nm pea; (motif) dot; robe à ~ polka dot dress.

poison /pwazɔ̃/ nm poison.

poisseux, -euse /pwasø, -z/ adj sticky.

poisson /pwasɔ̃/ nm fish; ~ rouge goldfish; ~ d'avril April fool; les P~s Pisces. **poissonnerie** nf fish shop. **poissonnier, -ière** nm, f fishmonger.

poitrine /pwatʀin/ nf chest; (seins) bosom.

poivre /pwavʀ/ nm pepper. **poivré, ~e** adj peppery. **poivrière** nf pepper-pot.

poivron /pwavʀɔ̃/ nm sweet pepper.

polaire /pɔlɛʀ/ adj polar. ● nf (veste) fleece.

pôle /pol/ nm pole.

polémique /pɔlemik/ nf debate. ● adj controversial.

poli, ~e /pɔli/ adj (personne) polite.

police /pɔlis/ nf (force) police (+ pl); (discipline) (law and) order; (d'assurance) policy.

policier, -ière /pɔlisje, -jɛʀ/ adj police; (roman) detective. ● nm policeman.

polir /pɔliʀ/ 2 vt polish.

politesse /pɔlitɛs/ nf politeness; (parole) polite remark.

politicien, ~ne /pɔlitisjɛ̃, -ɛn/ nm, f (péj) politician.

politique /pɔlitik/ adj political; homme ~ politician. ● nf politics; (ligne de conduite) policy.

pollen /pɔlɛn/ nm pollen.

polluant, ~e /pɔlɥɑ̃, -t/ adj polluting. ● nm pollutant.

polluer /pɔlɥe/ 1 vt pollute. **pollution** nf pollution.

polo /pɔlo/ nm (Sport) polo; (vêtement) polo shirt.

Pologne /pɔlɔɲ/ nf Poland.

polonais, ~e /pɔlɔnɛ, -z/ adj Polish. ● nm (Ling) Polish. P~, ~e nm, f Pole.

poltron, ~ne /pɔltʀɔ̃, -ɔn/ adj cowardly. ● nm, f coward.

polygame /pɔligam/ nmf polygamist.

polyvalent, ~e /pɔlivalɑ̃, -t/ adj varied; (personne) versatile.

pommade /pɔmad/ nf ointment.

pomme /pɔm/ nf apple; (d'arrosoir) rose; ~ d'Adam Adam's apple; ~ de pin pine cone; ~ de terre potato; ~s frites chips; (US) French fries; tomber dans les ~s 1 pass out.

pommette /pɔmɛt/ nf cheekbone.

pommier /pɔmje/ nm apple tree.

pompe /pɔ̃p/ nf pump; (splendeur) pomp; ~ à incendie fire engine; ~s funèbres undertaker's (+ sg).

pomper /pɔ̃pe/ 1 vt pump; (copier 1) copy, crib; ~ l'air à qn 1 get on sb's nerves.

pompier /pɔ̃pje/ nm fireman.

pomponner (se) /(sə)pɔ̃pɔne/ 1 vpr get dolled up.

poncer /pɔ̃se/ 10 vt sand.

ponctuation /pɔ̃ktɥasjɔ̃/ nf punctuation.

ponctuel, ~le /pɔ̃ktɥɛl/ adj punctual.

pondre /pɔ̃dʀ/ 3 vt/i lay.

poney /pɔnɛ/ nm pony.

pont /pɔ̃/ nm bridge; (de navire) deck; (de graissage) ramp; faire le ~ get an extended weekend; ~ aérien airlift. **pont-levis** (pl ponts-levis) *nm* drawbridge.

populaire /pɔpylɛʀ/ *adj* popular; (*expression*) colloquial; (*quartier, origine*) working-class. **popularité** *nf* popularity.

population /pɔpylasjɔ̃/ *nf* population.

porc /pɔʀ/ *nm* pig; (*viande*) pork.

porcelaine /pɔʀsəlɛn/ *nf* china, porcelain.

porc-épic (*pl* **porcs-épics**) /pɔʀkepik/ *nm* porcupine.

porcherie /pɔʀʃəʀi/ *nf* pigsty.

pornographie /pɔʀnɔɡʀafi/ *nf* pornography.

port /pɔʀ/ *nm* port, harbour; à bon ~ safely; ~ maritime seaport; (*transport*) carriage; (*d'armes*) carrying; (*de barbe*) wearing.

portable /pɔʀtabl/ *adj* (*Ordinat*) laptop (computer); (*telephone*) mobile (phone).

portail /pɔʀtaj/ *nm* gate.

portatif, -ive /pɔʀtatif, -v/ *adj* portable.

porte /pɔʀt/ *nf* door; (*passage*) doorway; (*de jardin, d'embarquement*) gate; mettre à la ~ throw out; ~ d'entrée front door.

porté, ~e /pɔʀte/ *adj* ~ à inclined to; ~ sur keen on.

porte-avions /pɔʀtavjɔ̃/ *nm inv* aircraft carrier.

porte-bagages /pɔʀtbagaʒ/ *nm inv* (*de vélo*) carrier.

porte-bonheur /pɔʀtbɔnœʀ/ *nm inv* lucky charm.

porte-clefs /pɔʀtəkle/ *nm inv* key ring.

porte-documents /pɔʀtdɔkymã/ *nm inv* briefcase.

portée, ~e /pɔʀte/ *nf* (*d'une arme*) range; (*de voûte*) span; (*d'animaux*) litter; (*impact*) significance; (*Mus*)

stave; à ~ de (la) main within (arm's) reach; hors de ~ (de) out of reach (of); à la ~ de qn at sb's level.

porte-fenêtre (*pl* **portes-fenêtres**) /pɔʀtfənɛtʀ/ *nf* French window.

portefeuille /pɔʀtəfœj/ *nm* wallet; (*de ministre*) portfolio.

porte-jarretelles /pɔʀtʒaʀtɛl/ *nm inv* suspender belt.

portemanteau (*pl* ~x) /pɔʀtmãto/ *nm* coat ou hat stand.

porte-monnaie /pɔʀtmɔne/ *nm inv* purse.

porte-parole /pɔʀtpaʀɔl/ *nm inv* spokesperson.

porter /pɔʀte/ **1** *vt* carry; (*vêtement, bague*) wear; (*fruits, responsabilité, nom*) bear; (*coup*) strike; (*amener*) bring; (*inscrire*) enter. • *vi* (*bruit*) carry; (*coup*) hit home; (*concerner*) be about; ~ sur rest on; (*concerner*) be about. □ **se** ~ *vpr* bien se ~ be ou feel well; se ~ candidat stand as a candidate.

porteur, -euse /pɔʀtœʀ, -øz/ *nm, f* (*de nouvelles*) bearer; (*Méd*) carrier. • *nm* (*Rail*) porter.

portier /pɔʀtje/ *nm* doorman.

portière /pɔʀtjɛʀ/ *nf* door.

porto /pɔʀto/ *nm* port (wine).

portrait /pɔʀtʀe/ *nm* portrait. **portrait-robot** (*pl* **portraits-robots**) *nm* identikit®, photofit®.

portuaire /pɔʀtɥɛʀ/ *adj* port.

portugais, ~e /pɔʀtygɛ, -z/ *adj* Portuguese. • *nm* (*Ling*) Portuguese. P~, ~e *nm, f* Portuguese.

Portugal /pɔʀtygal/ *nm* Portugal.

pose /poz/ *nf* installation; (*attitude*) pose; (*Photo*) exposure.

posé, ~e /poze/ *adj* calm, serious.

poser /poze/ **1** *vt* put (down); (*installer*) install, put in; (*fondations*)

lay; (*question*) ask; (*problème*) pose; ∼ sa candidature apply (à for).
● *vi* (*modèle*) pose. □ se ∼ *vpr* (*avion*, *oiseau*) land; (*regard*) fall; (*se présenter*) arise.

positif, -ive /pozitif, -v/ *adj* positive.

position /pozisjɔ̃/ *nf* position; prendre ∼ take a stand.

posologie /pozɔlɔʒi/ *nf* dosage.

posséder /posede/ [14] *vt* (*propriété*) own, possess; (*diplôme*) have.

possessif, -ive /posesif, -v/ *adj* possessive.

possession /posesjɔ̃/ *nf* possession; prendre ∼ de take possession of.

possibilité /posibilite/ *nf* possibility.

possible /posibl/ *adj* possible; dès que ∼ as soon as possible; le plus tard ∼ as late as possible. ● *nm* le ∼ what is possible; faire son ∼ do one's utmost.

postal, ∼e (*mpl* **-aux**) /postal, -o/ *adj* postal.

poste /post/ *nf* (*service*) post; (*bureau*) post office; ∼ aérienne airmail; mettre à la ∼ post; ∼ restante poste restante. ● *nm* (*lieu*, *emploi*) post; (*de radio*, *télévision*) set; (*téléphone*) extension (number); ∼ d'essence petrol station; ∼ d'incendie fire point; ∼ de pilotage cockpit; ∼ de police police station; ∼ de secours first-aid post.

poster[1] /poste/ [1] *vt* (*lettre*, *personne*) post.

poster[2] /poster/ *nm* poster.

postérieur, ∼e /posterjœr/ *adj* later; (*partie*) back; ∼ à after. ● *nm* [1] posterior.

posthume /postym/ *adj* posthumous.

postiche /postiʃ/ *adj* false.

postier, -ière /postje, -jɛr/ *nm, f* postal worker.

post-scriptum /postskriptom/ *nm inv* postscript.

postuler /postyle/ [1] *vt/i* apply (à for); (*principe*) postulate.

pot /po/ *nm* pot; (en plastique) carton; (en verre) jar; (*chance* [1]) luck; (*boisson* [1]) drink; ∼ catalytique catalytic converter; ∼ d'échappement exhaust pipe.

potable /potabl/ *adj* eau ∼ drinking water.

potage /potaʒ/ *nm* soup.

potager, -ère /potaʒe, -ɛr/ *adj* vegetable. ● *nm* vegetable garden.

pot-au-feu /potofø/ *nm inv* (plat) stew.

pot-de-vin (*pl* **pots-de-vin**) /podvɛ̃/ *nm* bribe.

poteau (*pl* ∼**x**) /poto/ *nm* post; (*télégraphique*) pole; ∼ indicateur signpost.

potelé, ∼e /potle/ *adj* plump.

potentiel, ∼le /potɑ̃sjɛl/ *adj & nm* potential.

poterie /potri/ *nf* pottery; (objet) piece of pottery. **potier** *nm* potter.

potins /potɛ̃/ *nmpl* gossip (+ *sg*).

potiron /potirɔ̃/ *nm* pumpkin.

pou (*pl* ∼**x**) /pu/ *nm* louse.

poubelle /pubɛl/ *nf* dustbin.

pouce /pus/ *nm* thumb; (de pied) big toe; (*mesure*) inch.

poudre /pudr/ *nf* powder; (∼ à canon) gunpowder; en ∼ (*lait*) powdered; (*chocolat*) drinking.

poudrier /pudrije/ *nm* (powder) compact.

pouf /puf/ *nm* pouffe.

poulailler /pulaje/ *nm* henhouse.

poulain /pulɛ̃/ *nm* foal; (*protégé*) protégé.

poule /pul/ *nf* hen; (Culin) fowl;

P

poulet | pratique

(femme ⊠) tart.

poulet /pulɛ/ nm chicken.

pouliche /puliʃ/ nf filly.

poulie /puli/ nf pulley.

pouls /pu/ nm pulse.

poumon /pumɔ̃/ nm lung.

poupe /pup/ nf stern.

poupée /pupe/ nf doll.

pour /puʀ/ prép for; (envers) to; (à la place de) on behalf of; (comme) as; ~ cela for that reason; ~ cent per cent; ~ de bon for good; ~ faire (in order) to do; ~ que so that; ~ moi (à mon avis) as for me; trop poli ~ too polite to; ~ ce qui est de as for; être ~ in favour. ● nm inv le ~ et le contre the pros and cons.

pourboire /puʀbwaʀ/ nm tip.

pourcentage /puʀsɑ̃taʒ/ nm percentage.

pourparlers /puʀpaʀle/ nmpl talks.

pourpre /puʀpʀ/ adj & nm crimson; (violet) purple.

pourquoi /puʀkwa/ conj & adv why. ● nm inv le ~ et le comment the why and the wherefore.

pourra, pourrait /puʀa, puʀɛ/ →POUVOIR 49.

pourri, ~e /puʀi/ adj rotten.

pourrir 2 vt/i rot. **pourriture** nf rot.

poursuite /puʀsɥit/ nf pursuit (de of); ~s (Jur) legal action (+ sg).

poursuivre /puʀsɥivʀ/ 57 vt pursue; (continuer) continue (with); ~ (en justice) take to court; (droit civil) sue. ● vi continue. □ se ~ vpr continue.

pourtant /puʀtɑ̃/ adv yet.

pourvoir /puʀvwaʀ/ 63 vi ~ à provide for; **pourvu de** supplied with.

pourvu que /puʀvy(ə)/ conj (condition) provided (that); (souhait) let us hope (that).

pousse /pus/ nf growth; (bourgeon) shoot.

poussé, ~e /puse/ adj (études) advanced; (enquête) thorough.

poussée /puse/ nf pressure; (coup) push; (de prix) upsurge; (Méd) attack.

pousser /puse/ **1** vt push; (cri) let out; (soupir) heave; (continuer) continue; (exhorter) urge (à to); (forcer) drive (à to). ● vi push; (grandir) grow; faire ~ (cheveux) let grow; (plante) grow. □ se ~ vpr move over ou up; **pousse-toi!** move over!

poussette /pusɛt/ nf pushchair.

poussière /pusjɛʀ/ nf dust. **poussiéreux, -euse** adj dusty.

poussin /pusɛ̃/ nm chick.

poutre /putʀ/ nf beam; (en métal) girder.

pouvoir /puvwaʀ/ 49 v aux (possibilité) can, be able; (permission, éventualité) may, can; **il peut/pouvait/pourrait venir** he can/could/might come; **je n'ai pas pu** I couldn't; **j'ai pu faire** (réussi à) I managed to do; **je n'en peux plus** I am exhausted; **il se peut que** it may be that. ● nm power; (gouvernement) government; **au ~** in power; **~s publics** authorities.

prairie /pʀeʀi/ nf meadow.

praticien, ~ne /pʀatisjɛ̃, -ɛn/ nm, f practitioner.

pratiquant, ~e /pʀatikɑ̃, -t/ adj practising. ● nm, f churchgoer.

pratique /pʀatik/ adj practical. ● nf practice; (expérience) experience; **la ~ du golf/du cheval** golfing/riding. **pratiquement** adv (en pratique) in practice; (presque) practically.

pratiquer /pratike/ **1** vt/i practise; (Sport) play; (faire) make.

pré /pre/ nm meadow.

pré-affranchi, ~e /preafrɑ̃ʃi/ adj postage-paid.

préalable /prealabl/ adj preliminary, prior. ●nm precondition; au ~ first.

préambule /preɑ̃byl/ nm preamble.

préavis /preavi/ nm notice.

précaire /preker/ adj precarious. **précarité** nf (d'emploi) insecurity.

précaution /prekosjɔ̃/ nf (mesure) precaution; (prudence) caution.

précédent, ~e /presedɑ̃, -t/ adj previous. ●nm precedent.

précéder /presede/ **14** vt/i precede.

précepteur, -trice /preseptœr, -tris/ nm, f (private) tutor.

prêcher /preʃe/ **1** vt/i preach.

précieux, -ieuse /presjø, -z/ adj precious.

précipitamment /presipitamɑ̃/ adv hastily. **précipitation** nf haste.

précipiter /presipite/ **1** vt throw, precipitate; (hâter) hasten. □ se ~ vpr (se dépêcher) rush (sur at, on to); (se jeter) throw oneself; (s'accélérer) speed up.

précis, ~e /presi, -z/ adj precise, specific; (mécanisme) accurate; dix heures ~es ten o'clock sharp. ●nm summary.

préciser /presize/ **1** vt specify; précisez votre pensée could you be more specific. □ se ~ vpr become clear(er). **précision** nf precision; (détail) detail.

précoce /prekɔs/ adj (enfant) precocious.

préconiser /prekɔnize/ **1** vt advocate.

précurseur /prekyrsœr/ nm forerunner.

prédicateur /predikatœr/ nm preacher.

prédilection /predileksjɔ̃/ nf preference.

prédire /predir/ **37** vt predict.

prédominer /predɔmine/ **1** vi predominate.

préface /prefas/ nf preface.

préfecture /prefektyr/ nf prefecture; ~ de police police headquarters.

préféré, ~e /prefere/ adj & nm, f favourite.

préférence /preferɑ̃s/ nf preference; de ~ preferably.

préférentiel, ~le /preferɑ̃sjɛl/ adj preferential.

préférer /prefere/ **14** vt prefer (à to); ~ faire prefer to do; je ne préfère pas I'd rather not; j'aurais préféré ne pas savoir I wish I hadn't found out.

préfet /prefɛ/ nm prefect; ~ de police prefect ou chief of police.

préfixe /prefiks/ nm prefix.

préhistorique /preistɔrik/ adj prehistoric.

préjudice /preʒydis/ nm harm, prejudice; porter ~ à harm.

préjugé /preʒyʒe/ nm prejudice; être plein de ~s be very prejudiced.

prélasser (se) /(sə)prelase/ **1** vpr loll (about).

prélèvement /prelɛvmɑ̃/ nm deduction; (de sang) sample. **prélever** **6** vt deduct (sur from); (sang) take.

préliminaire /preliminɛr/ adj & nm preliminary; ~s (sexuels) foreplay.

prématuré, ~e /prematyre/ adj

premature. ● *nm* premature baby.

premier, -ière /prəmje, -jɛr/ *adj*
first; (*rang*) front, first; (*enfance*)
early; (*nécessité, souci*) prime; (*qualité*) top, prime; de ~ ordre first-
rate; ~ ministre Prime Minister.
● *nm, f* first (one). ● *nm* (date) first;
(*étage*) first floor; *en* ~ first. **première** *nf* (Rail) first class; (*exploit jamais vu*) first; (cinéma, Théât)
première; (Aut) (*vitesse*) first (gear).
premièrement *adv* firstly.

prémunir /premynir/ **2** *vt* protect (contre against).

prenant, -e /prənɑ̃, -t/ *adj* (*activité*) engrossing; (*enfant*) demanding.

prénatal, -e /prenatal/ *adj* antenatal.

prendre /prɑ̃dr/ **50** *vt* take; (*attraper*) catch, get; (*acheter*) get;
(*repas*) have; (*engager, adopter*)
take on; (*poids*) put on; (*chercher*)
pick up; qu'est-ce qui te prend?
what's the matter with you? ● *vi* (*liquide*) set; (*feu*) catch; (*vaccin*) take.
□ **se** ~ *vpr* **se** ~ **pour** think one is;
s'en ~ à attack; (*rendre responsa-
ble*) blame; s'y ~ set about (it).

preneur, -euse /prənœr, -øz/ *nm,
f* buyer; **être** ~ be willing to buy;
trouver ~ find a buyer.

prénom /prenɔ̃/ *nm* first name.

prénommer /prenɔme/ **1** *vt*
call. □ **se** ~ *vpr* be called.

préoccupation /preɔkypasjɔ̃/ *nf*
(*souci*) worry; (*idée fixe*) preoccu-
pation.

préoccuper /preɔkype/ **1** *vt*
worry; (*absorber*) preoccupy. □ **se**
~ **de** *vpr* think about.

préparation /preparasjɔ̃/ *nf*
preparation. **préparatoire** *adj* preparatory.

préparer /prepare/ **1** *vt* prepare;

(*repas, café*) make; **plats préparés**
ready-cooked meals. □ **se** ~ *vpr*
prepare oneself (à for); (*s'apprêter*)
get ready; (*être proche*) be
brewing.

préposé, -e /prepoze/ *nm, f* employee; (*des postes*) postman,
postwoman.

préposition /prepozisjɔ̃/ *nf* preposition.

préretraite /prerətrɛt/ *nf* early
retirement.

près /prɛ/ *adv* near, close; ~ **de**
near (to), close to; (*presque*) nearly;
à cela ~ except that; **de** ~ closely.

présage /prezaʒ/ *nm* omen.

presbyte /prɛsbit/ *adj* long-
sighted, far-sighted.

prescrire /prɛskrir/ **30** *vt* prescribe.

préséance /preseɑ̃s/ *nf* precedence.

présence /prezɑ̃s/ *nf* presence;
(Scol) attendance.

présent, -e /prezɑ̃, -t/ *adj* present. ● *nm* (temps, cadeau) present;
à ~ now.

présentateur, -trice /prezɑ̃ta-
tœr, -tris/ *nm, f* presenter.

présentation /prezɑ̃tasjɔ̃/ *nf* (de
personne) introduction; (*exposé*)
presentation.

présenter /prezɑ̃te/ **1** *vt* present;
(*personne*) introduce (à to); (*montrer*) show. ● *vi* ~ **bien** have a
pleasing appearance. □ **se** ~ *vpr*
introduce oneself (à to); (*aller*) go;
(*apparaître*) appear; (*candidat*) come
forward; (*occasion*) arise; **se** ~ **à**
(*examen*) sit for; (*élection*) stand for;
se ~ **bien** look good.

préservatif /prezɛrvatif/ *nm*
condom.

préserver /prezɛrve/ **1** *vt*
protect.

présidence /prezidãs/ *nf* (d'État) presidency; (de société) chairmanship.

président, ~e /prezidã, -t/ *nm, f* president; (de société, comité) chairman, chairwoman; ~-**directeur général** managing director.

présidentiel, ~le /prezidãsjɛl/ *adj* presidential.

présider /prezide/ **1** *vt* preside.

présomptueux, -euse /prezõptɥø, -z/ *adj* presumptuous.

presque /prɛsk(ə)/ *adv* almost, nearly; ~ **jamais** hardly ever; ~ **rien** hardly anything; ~ **pas (de)** hardly any.

presqu'île /prɛskil/ *nf* peninsula.

pressant, ~e /prɛsã, -t/ *adj* pressing, urgent.

presse /prɛs/ *nf* (journaux, appareil) press.

pressentiment /prɛsãtimã/ *nm* premonition. **pressentir** **46** *vt* have a premonition of.

pressé, ~e /prɛse/ *adj* in a hurry; (orange, citron) freshly squeezed.

presser /prɛse/ **1** *vt* squeeze, press; (appuyer sur, harceler) press; (hâter) hasten; (inciter) urge (de to). ● *vi* (temps) press; (affaire) be pressing. □ se ~ *vpr* (se hâter) hurry; (se grouper) crowd.

pressing /prɛsiŋ/ *nm* (teinturerie) dry-cleaner's.

pression /prɛsjõ/ *nf* pressure; (bouton) press-stud.

prestance /prɛstãs/ *nf* (imposing) presence.

prestation /prɛstasjõ/ *nf* allowance; (d'artiste) performance.

prestidigitation /prɛstidiʒitasjõ/ *nf* conjuring.

prestige /prɛstiʒ/ *nm* prestige.

prestigieux, -ieuse *adj* prestigious.

présumé, e /prezyme/ *adj* alleged.

présumer /prezyme/ **1** *vt* presume; ~ **que** assume that; ~ **de** overrate.

prêt, ~e /prɛ, -t/ *adj* ready (à qch for sth, à faire to do). ● *nm* loan.

prêt-à-porter *nm inv* ready-to-wear clothes.

prétendre /pretãdʀ/ **3** *vt* claim (que that); (vouloir) intend; on le prétend riche he is said to be very rich. **prétendu,** ~e *adj* so-called. **prétendument** *adv* supposedly, allegedly.

prétentieux, -ieuse /pretãsjø, -z/ *adj* pretentious.

prêter /pʀete/ **1** *vt* lend (à to); (attribuer) attribute; ~ **son aide à qn** give sb some help; ~ **attention** pay attention; ~ **serment** take an oath. ● *vi* ~ **à** lead to.

prêteur, -euse /pʀetœʀ, -øz/ *nm, f* (money-)lender; ~ **sur gages** pawnbroker.

prétexte /pʀetɛkst/ *nm* pretext, excuse.

prêtre /pʀɛtʀ/ *nm* priest.

preuve /pʀœv/ *nf* proof; des ~s evidence (+ *sg*); faire ~ de show; faire ses ~s prove oneself.

prévaloir /pʀevalwaʀ/ **60** *vi* prevail.

prévenant, ~e /pʀevnã, -t/ *adj* thoughtful.

prévenir /pʀevniʀ/ **58** *vt* (menacer) warn; (informer) tell; (médecin) call; (éviter, anticiper) prevent.

préventif, -ive /pʀevãtif, -v/ *adj* preventive.

prévention /pʀevãsjõ/ *nf* prevention; faire de la ~ take preventive action; ~ **routière** road safety.

prévenu, ~e /pʀevny/ *nm, f* defendant.

p

prévisible /previzibl/ adj predictable. **prévision** nf prediction; (météorologique) forecast.

prévoir /prevwar/ 39 vt foresee; (temps) forecast; (organiser) plan (for), provide for; (envisager) allow (for); **prévu pour** (jouet) designed for; **comme prévu** as planned.

prévoyance /prevwajãs/ nf foresight. **prévoyant, ~e** adj farsighted.

prier /prije/ 45 vi pray. ● vt pray to; (demander à) ask (de to); **je vous en prie** please; (il n'y a pas de quoi) don't mention it.

prière /prijer/ nf prayer; (demande) request; **~ de** (vous êtes prié de) will you please.

primaire /primer/ adj primary.

prime /prim/ nf free gift; (d'employé) bonus; (subvention) subsidy; (d'assurance) premium.

primé, ~e /prime/ adj prizewinning.

primeurs /primœr/ nfpl early fruit and vegetables.

primevère /primver/ nf primrose.

primitif, -ive /primitif, -v/ adj primitive; (d'origine) original. ● nm, f primitive.

primordial, ~e (mpl **-iaux**) /primordjal, -jo/ adj essential.

prince /prɛ̃s/ nm prince. **princesse** nf princess.

principal, ~e (mpl **-aux**) /prɛ̃sipal, -o/ adj main, principal. ● nm headmaster; (chose) main thing.

principe /prɛ̃sip/ nm principle; **en ~** in theory; (d'habitude) as a rule.

printanier, -ière /prɛ̃tanje, -jɛr/ adj spring(-like).

printemps /prɛ̃tɑ̃/ nm spring.

prioritaire /prijoriter/ adj prior-

ity; **être ~** have priority. **priorité** nf priority; (Auto) right of way.

Priorité à droite Except at roundabouts, and unless there are other indications or regulations in force, French drivers must always give way to traffic approaching from the right. *i*

pris, ~e /pri, -z/ adj (place) taken; (personne, journée) busy; (nez) stuffed up; **~ de** (peur, fièvre) stricken with; **~ de panique** panic-stricken. ● **➜PRENDRE** 50.

prise /priz/ nf hold, grip; (animal attrapé) catch; (Mil) capture; (~ de courant) (mâle) plug; (femelle) socket; **~ multiple** multiplug adapter; **avoir ~ sur qn** have a hold over sb; **aux ~s avec** to grapple with; **~ de conscience** awareness; **~ de contact** first contact; **~ de position** stand; **~ de sang** blood test.

prisé, ~e /prize/ adj popular.

prison /prizɔ̃/ nf prison, jail; (réclusion) imprisonment. **prisonnier, -ière** nm, f prisoner.

privation /privasjɔ̃/ nf deprivation; (sacrifice) hardship.

privatiser /privatize/ 1 vt privatize.

privé /prive/ adj private. ● nm (Comm) private sector; (Scol) private schools (+ pl); **en ~** in private.

priver /prive/ 1 vt **~ de** deprive of. □ **se ~** (de) vpr go without.

privilège /privileʒ/ nm privilege. **privilégié, ~e** nm, f privileged person.

prix /pri/ nm price; (récompense) prize; **à tout ~** at all costs; **au ~ de** (fig) at the expense of; **~ coûtant, ~ de revient** cost price; **à ~ fixe** set price.

probabilité /pRɔbabilite/ nf probability. **probable** adj probable, likely. **probablement** adv probably.

probant, ~e /pRɔbɑ̃, -t/ adj convincing, conclusive.

problème /pRɔblɛm/ nm problem.

procédé /pRɔsede/ nm process; (manière d'agir) practice.

procéder /pRɔsede/ **14** vi proceed; ~ à carry out.

procès /pRɔsɛ/ nm (criminel) trial; (civil) lawsuit, proceedings (+ pl).

processus /pRɔsesys/ nm process; ~ de paix peace process.

procès-verbal (pl procès-verbaux) /pRɔsɛvɛRbal, -o/ nm minutes (+ pl); (contravention) ticket.

prochain, ~e /pRɔʃɛ̃, -ɛn/ adj (suivant) next; (proche) imminent; (avenir) near. ● nm fellow man. **prochainement** adv soon.

proche /pRɔʃ/ adj near, close; (avoisinant) neighbouring; (parent, ami) close; ~ de close ou near to; de ~ en ~ gradually; dans un ~ avenir in the near future; être ~ (imminent) be approaching. ● nm close relative; (ami) close friend.

Proche-Orient /pRɔʃɔRjɑ̃/ nm Near East.

proclamation /pRɔklamasjɔ̃/ nf declaration, proclamation. **proclamer** **1** vt declare, proclaim.

procuration /pRɔkyRasjɔ̃/ nf proxy.

procurer /pRɔkyRe/ **1** vt bring (à to). □ se ~ vpr obtain.

procureur /pRɔkyRœR/ nm public prosecutor.

prodige /pRɔdiʒ/ nm (fait) marvel; (personne) prodigy; enfant/ musicien ~ child/musical prodigy. **prodigieux**, **-ieuse** adj tremendous, prodigious.

prodigue /pRɔdig/ adj wasteful; fils ~ prodigal son.

producteur, **-trice** /pRɔdyktœR, -tRis/ adj producing. ● nm, f producer. **productif**, **-ive** adj productive. **production** nf production; (produit) product. **productivité** nf productivity.

produire /pRɔdɥiR/ **17** vt produce. □ se ~ vpr (survenir) happen; (acteur) perform.

produit /pRɔdɥi/ nm product; ~s (de la terre) produce (+ sg) ; ~ chimique chemical; ~s alimentaires foodstuffs; ~ de consommation consumer goods; ~ intérieur brut gross domestic product; ~ national brut gross national product.

proéminent, ~e /pRɔeminɑ̃, -t/ adj prominent.

profane /pRɔfan/ adj secular. ● nmf lay person.

proférer /pRɔfeRe/ **14** vt utter.

professeur /pRɔfesœR/ nm teacher; (Univ) lecturer; (avec chaire) professor.

profession /pRɔfesjɔ̃/ nf occupation; ~ libérale profession. **professionnel**, **-le** /pRɔfesjɔnɛl/ adj professional; (école) vocational. ● nm, f professional.

profil /pRɔfil/ nm profile.

profit /pRɔfi/ nm profit; au ~ de in aid of. **profitable** adj profitable.

profiter /pRɔfite/ **1** vi ~ à benefit; ~ de take advantage of.

profond, ~e /pRɔfɔ̃, -d/ adj deep; (sentiment, intérêt) profound; (causes) underlying; au plus ~ de in the depths of. **profondément** adv deeply; (différent, triste) profoundly; (dormir) soundly. **profondeur** nf depth.

progéniture /pRɔʒenityR/ nf offspring.

progiciel /pRɔʒisjɛl/ nm (Ordinat)

package.

programmation /prɔgramasjɔ̃/ nf programming.

programme /prɔgram/ nm programme; (Scol) (d'une matière) syllabus; (général) curriculum; (Ordinat) program. **programmer 1** vt (ordinateur, appareil) program; (émission) schedule. **programmeur, -euse** nm, f computer programmer.

progrès /prɔgrɛ/ nm & nmpl progress; faire des ~ make progress. **progresser 1** vi progress. **progressif, -ive** adj progressive. **progression** nf progression.

prohibitif, -ive /prɔibitif, -v/ adj prohibitive.

proie /prwa/ nf prey; en ~ à tormented by.

projecteur /prɔʒɛktœr/ nm floodlight; (Mil) searchlight; (cinéma) projector.

projectile /prɔʒɛktil/ nm missile.

projection /prɔʒɛksjɔ̃/ nf projection; (séance) show.

projet /prɔʒɛ/ nm plan; (ébauche) draft; ~ de loi bill.

projeter /prɔʒte/ 38 vt (prévoir) plan (de to); (film) project, show; (jeter) hurl, project.

prolétaire /prɔletɛr/ nmf proletarian.

prologue /prɔlɔg/ nm prologue.

prolongation /prɔlɔ̃gasjɔ̃/ nf extension; ~s (football) extra time.

prolonger /prɔlɔ̃ʒe/ 40 vt extend. □ se ~ vpr go on.

promenade /prɔmnad/ nf walk; (à bicyclette, à cheval) ride; (en auto) drive, ride; faire une ~ go for a walk.

promener /prɔmne/ 6 vt take for a walk; ~ son regard sur cast an eye over. □ se ~ vpr walk; (aller) go for a walk. **prome-**

neur, -euse nm, f walker.

promesse /prɔmɛs/ nf promise.

prometteur, -euse /prɔmɛtœr, -øz/ adj promising.

promettre /prɔmɛtr/ 42 vt/i promise. ● vi be promising. □ se ~ de vpr resolve to.

promoteur /prɔmɔtœr/ nm (immobilier) property developer.

promotion /prɔmɔsjɔ̃/ nf promotion; (Univ) year; (Comm) special offer.

prompt, ~e /prɔ̃, -t/ adj swift.

promu, ~e /prɔmy/ adj être ~ be promoted.

prôner /prone/ 1 vt extol.

pronom /prɔnɔ̃/ nm pronoun. **pronominal, ~e** (mpl -aux) adj pronominal.

prononcé, ~e /prɔnɔ̃se/ adj strong.

prononcer /prɔnɔ̃se/ 10 vt pronounce; (discours) make. □ se ~ vpr (mot) be pronounced; (personne) make a decision (pour in favour of). **prononciation** nf pronunciation.

pronostic /prɔnɔstik/ nm forecast; (Méd) prognosis.

propagande /prɔpagɑ̃d/ nf propaganda.

propager /prɔpaʒe/ 40 vt spread. □ se ~ vpr spread.

prophète /prɔfɛt/ nm prophet. **prophétie, ~e** nf prophecy.

propice /prɔpis/ adj favourable.

proportion /prɔpɔrsjɔ̃/ nf proportion; (en mathématiques) ratio; toutes ~s gardées relatively speaking. **proportionné, ~e** adj proportionate (à to). **proportionnel, ~le** adj proportional. **proportionnellement** adv proportionately.

propos /prɔpo/ nm intention; (sujet) subject; à ~ at the right time; (dans un dialogue) by the way; à ~ de about; à tout ~ at every possible occasion. ● nmpl (paroles) remarks.

proposer /prɔpoze/ 1 vt suggest, propose; (offrir) offer. □ se ~ vpr volunteer (pour to). **proposition** nf proposal; (affirmation) proposition; (Gram) clause.

propre /prɔpr/ adj (non sali) clean; (soigné) neat; (honnête) decent; (à soi) own; (sens) literal; ~ à (qui convient) suited to; (spécifique) particular to. ● nm mettre au ~ write out again neatly; c'est du ~! (ironique) well done!

proprement /prɔprəmɑ̃/ adv (avec soin) neatly; (au sens strict) strictly; le bureau ~ dit the office itself.

propreté /prɔprəte/ nf cleanliness.

propriétaire /prɔprijetɛr/ nmf owner; (Comm) proprietor; (qui loue) landlord, landlady.

propriété /prɔprijete/ nf property; (droit) ownership.

propulser /prɔpylse/ 1 vt propel.

proroger /prɔrɔʒe/ 40 vt (contrat) defer; (passeport) extend.

proscrire /prɔskrir/ 30 vt proscribe.

proscrit, ~e /prɔskri, -t/ adj proscribed. ● nm, f (exilé) exile.

prose /proz/ nf prose.

prospectus /prɔspɛktys/ nm leaflet.

prospère /prɔspɛr/ adj flourishing, thriving. **prospérer** 14 vi thrive, prosper. **prospérité** nf prosperity.

prosterner (se) /(sə)prɔstɛrne/ 1 vpr prostrate oneself; prosterné devant prostrate before.

prostituée /prɔstitɥe/ nf prostitute. **prostitution** nf prostitution.

protecteur, -trice /prɔtɛktœr,

-tris/ nm, f protector. ● adj protective.

protection /prɔtɛksjɔ̃/ nf protection.

protégé, ~e /prɔteʒe/ nm, f protégé.

protéger /prɔteʒe/ 40 vt protect. □ se ~ vpr protect oneself.

protéine /prɔtein/ nf protein.

protestant, ~e /prɔtɛstɑ̃, -t/ adj & nm, f Protestant.

protestation /prɔtɛstasjɔ̃/ nf protest. **protester** 1 vt/i protest.

protocole /prɔtɔkɔl/ nm protocol.

protubérant, ~e /prɔtyberɑ̃/ adj protruding.

proue /pru/ nf bow, prow.

prouesse /prues/ nf feat, exploit.

prouver /pruve/ 1 vt prove.

provenance /prɔvnɑ̃s/ nf origin; en ~ de from.

provençal, ~e (mpl -aux) /prɔvɑ̃sal, -o/ adj & nm, f Provençal.

provenir /prɔvnir/ 58 vi ~ de come from.

proverbe /prɔvɛrb/ nm proverb.

province /prɔvɛ̃s/ nf province; de ~ provincial; la ~ the provinces (+ pl). **provincial, ~e** (mpl -iaux) adj & nm, f provincial.

proviseur /prɔvizœr/ nm headmaster, principal.

provision /prɔvizjɔ̃/ nf supply, store; (sur un compte) credit (balance); (acompte) deposit; ~s (vivres) food shopping.

provisoire /prɔvizwar/ adj provisional.

provocant, ~e /prɔvɔkɑ̃, -t/ adj provocative. **provocation** nf provocation. **provoquer** 1 vt cause; (sexuellement) arouse; (défier) provoke.

p

proxénète /pRɔksenɛt/ nm pimp, procurer.

proximité /pRɔksimite/ nf proximity; à ~ de close to.

prude /pRyd/ adj prudish.

prudemment /pRydamɑ̃/ adv (conduire) carefully; (attendre) cautiously. **prudence** nf caution. **prudent,** ~e adj (au volant) careful; (à agir) cautious; (sage) wise.

prune /pRyn/ nf plum.

pruneau (pl ~x) /pRyno/ nm prune.

prunelle /pRynɛl/ nf (pupille) pupil; (fruit) sloe.

prunier /pRynje/ nm plum tree.

psaume /psom/ nm psalm.

pseudonyme /psødɔnim/ nm pseudonym.

psychanalyse /psikanaliz/ nf psychoanalysis. **psychanalyste** nmf psychoanalyst.

psychiatre /psikjatR/ nmf psychiatrist. **psychiatrie** nf psychiatry. **psychiatrique** adj psychiatric.

psychique /psiʃik/ adj mental, psychological.

psychologie /psikɔlɔʒi/ nf psychology. **psychologique** adj psychological. **psychologue** nmf psychologist.

pu /py/ ➡POUVOIR 49.

puant, ~e /pɥɑ̃, -t/ adj stinking.

pub /pyb/ nf 🔟 la ~ advertising; une ~ an advert.

puberté /pybɛRte/ nf puberty.

public, -que /pyblik/ adj public. ● nm public; (assistance) audience; (Scol) state schools (+ pl); en ~ in public.

publication /pyblikasjɔ̃/ nf publication.

publicitaire /pyblisitɛR/ adj pub-

licity. **publicité** nf publicity, advertising; (annonce) advertisement.

publier /pyblije/ 45 vt publish.

publiquement /pyblikmɑ̃/ adv publicly.

puce /pys/ nf flea; (électronique) chip; marché aux ~s flea market.

pudeur /pydœR/ nf modesty.

pudibond, ~e /pydibɔ̃, -d/ adj prudish.

pudique /pydik/ adj modest.

puer /pɥe/ 🔟 vi stink. ● vt stink of.

puéricultrice /pɥeRikyltRis/ nf pediatric nurse.

puéril, ~e /pɥeRil/ adj puerile.

puis /pɥi/ adv then.

puiser /pɥize/ 🔟 vt draw (dans from). ● vi ~ dans qch dip into sth.

puisque /pɥisk(ə)/ conj since, as.

puissance /pɥisɑ̃s/ nf power; en ~ potential.

puissant, ~e /pɥisɑ̃, -t/ adj powerful.

puits /pɥi/ nm well; (de mine) shaft.

pull(-over) /pyl(ɔvɛR)/ nm pullover, jumper.

pulpe /pylp/ nf pulp.

pulsation /pylsasjɔ̃/ nf (heart-) beat.

pulvériser /pylveRize/ 🔟 vt pulverize; (liquide) spray.

punaise /pynɛz/ nf (insecte) bug; (clou) drawing pin.

punch¹ /pɔ̃ʃ/ nm (boisson) punch.

punch² /pœnʃ/ nm avoir du ~ have drive.

punir /pyniR/ 🛽 vt punish. **punition** nf punishment.

pupille /pypij/ nf (de l'œil) pupil. ● nmf (enfant) ward.

pupitre /pypitʀ/ nm (Scol) desk; ~ à musique music stand.

pur /pyʀ/ adj pure; (whisky) neat.

purée /pyʀe/ nf purée; (de pommes de terre) mashed potatoes (+ pl).

pureté /pyʀte/ nf purity.

purgatoire /pyʀɡatwaʀ/ nm purgatory.

purge /pyʀʒ/ nf purge. **purger** 40 vt (Pol, Méd) purge; (peine; jur) serve.

purifier /pyʀifje/ 45 vt purify.

puritain, ~e /pyʀitɛ̃, -ɛn/ nm, f puritan. ● adj puritanical.

pur-sang /pyʀsɑ̃/ nm inv (cheval) thoroughbred.

pus /py/ nm pus.

putain /pytɛ̃/ nf p whore.

puzzle /pœzl/ nm jigsaw (puzzle).

P-V abrév m (procès-verbal) ticket, traffic fine.

pyjama /piʒama/ nm pyjamas (+ pl); un ~ a pair of pyjamas.

pylône /pilon/ nm pylon.

Pyrénées /piʀene/ nfpl les ~ the Pyrenees.

pyromane /piʀɔman/ nmf arsonist.

Qq

QG abrév m (**quartier général**) HQ.

QI abrév m (**quotient intellectuel**) IQ.

qu' /k/ ⇒QUE.

quadriller /kadʀije/ 1 vt (armée) take control of; (police) spread one's net over; papier quadrillé squared paper.

quadrupède /kadʀyped/ nm quadruped.

quadruple /kadʀypl/ adj quadruple. ● nm le ~ de four times. **quadrupler** 1 vt/i quadruple.

quai /ke/ nm (de gare) platform; (de port) quay; (de rivière) bank.

qualification /kalifikasjɔ̃/ nf qualification; (compétence pratique) skills (+ pl).

qualifié, ~e /kalifje/ adj (diplômé) qualified; (main-d'œuvre) skilled.

qualifier /kalifje/ 45 vt qualify; (décrire) describe (de as). □ se ~ vpr qualify (pour for).

qualité /kalite/ nf quality; (titre) occupation; (fonction) position; en sa ~ de in his ou her capacity as.

quand /kɑ̃/ adv when; ~ même all the same. ● conj when; (toutes les fois que) whenever; ~ bien même even if.

quant à /kɑ̃ta/ prép as for.

quantité /kɑ̃tite/ nf quantity; une ~ de a lot of; des ~s (de) masses ou lots (of).

quarantaine /kaʀɑ̃tɛn/ nf (Méd) quarantine; une ~ (de) about forty; avoir la ~ be in one's forties.

quarante /kaʀɑ̃t/ adj & nm forty.

quart /kaʀ/ nm quarter; (Naut) watch; onze heures moins le ~ quarter to eleven; ~ (de litre) quarter litre; ~ de finale quarter-final; ~ d'heure quarter of an hour; ~ de tour ninety-degree turn.

quartier /kaʀtje/ nm area, district; (zone ethnique) quarter; (de lune, pomme, bœuf) quarter; (d'une orange) segment; ~s (Mil) quarters; de ~, du ~ local; ~ général headquarters; avoir ~

P
q

libre be free.

quasiment /kazimɑ̃/ *adv* almost, practically.

quatorze /katɔʀz/ *adj & nm* fourteen.

quatre /katʀ(ə)/ *adj & nm* four.
quatre-vingt(s) *adj & nm* eighty.
quatre-vingt-dix *adj & nm* ninety.

quatre-quatre /katʀkatʀ/ *nm* four-wheel drive.

quatrième /katʀijɛm/ *adj & nmf* fourth. ● *nf* (Auto) fourth gear.

quatuor /kwatɥɔʀ/ *nm* quartet.

---

que, qu' /kə, k/

qu' before vowel or mute h.

● *conjonction*
····▸ that; je crains ~... I'm worried that...
····▸ (souhait, volonté) je veux ~ tu viennes I want you to come; ~ tu viennes ou non whether you come or not; qu'il entre let him come in.
····▸ (comparaison) than; plus grand ~ toi taller than you.

● *pronom interrogatif*
····▸ what; ~ voulez-vous manger? what would you like to eat?

● *pronom relatif*
····▸ (personne) whom, that; l'homme ~ j'ai rencontré the man (whom) I met.
····▸ (chose) that, which; le cheval ~ Nick m'a offert the horse (which) Nick gave me.

● *adverbe*
····▸ que c'est joli! it's so pretty!; ~ de monde! what a lot of people!

Québec /kebɛk/ *nm* Quebec.

---

quel, quelle (*pl* quel(le)s) /kɛl/

● *adjectif interrogatif*
····▸ which, what; ~ auteur a écrit...? which writer wrote...?; ~ jour sommes-nous? what day is it today?

● *adjectif exclamatif*
····▸ what; ~ idiot! what an idiot!; quelle horreur! that's horrible!

● *adjectif relatif*
····▸ ~ que soit son âge whatever his age; quelles que soient tes raisons whatever your reasons; ~ que soit le gagnant whoever the winner is.

quelconque /kɛlkɔ̃k/ *adj* any, some; (banal) ordinary; (médiocre) poor, second rate.

quelque /kɛlkə/ *adj* some; ~s a few, some. ● *adv* (environ) about, some; et ~ 1 and a bit; ~ chose something; (dans les phrases interrogatives) anything; ~ part somewhere; ~ peu somewhat.

quelquefois /kɛlkəfwa/ *adv* sometimes.

quelques-uns, -unes /kɛlkəzœ̃, -yn/ *pron* some, a few.

quelqu'un /kɛlkœ̃/ *pron* someone, somebody; (dans les phrases interrogatives) anyone, anybody.

querelle /kəʀɛl/ *nf* quarrel. **quereller (se)** 1 *vpr* quarrel. **querelleur, -euse** *adj* quarrelsome.

question /kɛstjɔ̃/ *nf* question; (affaire) matter, question; poser une ~ ask a question; en ~ in question; il est ~ de (cela concerne) it is about; (on parle de) there is talk of; il n'en est pas ~ it is out of the question; pas ~! no way!

questionnaire /kɛstjɔnɛʀ/ *nm* questionnaire.

questionner /kɛstjɔne/ **1** *vt* question.

quête /kɛt/ *nf* (Relig) collection; (recherche) search; **en ~ de** in search of.

queue /kø/ *nf* tail; (de poêle) handle; (de fruit) stalk; (de fleur) stem; (file) queue; (US) line; (de train) rear; **faire la ~** queue (up); (US) line up; **~ de cheval** ponytail; **faire une ~ de poisson à qn** (Auto) cut in front of sb.

---

qui /ki/

● *pronom interrogatif*

····▸ (sujet) who; **~ a fait ça?** who did that?

····▸ (complément) whom; **à ~ est ce livre?** whose book is this?

● *pronom relatif*

····▸ (personne sujet) who; **c'est Isabelle qui vient d'appeler** it's Isabelle who's just called.

····▸ (autres cas) that, which; **qu'est-ce ~ te prend?** what is the matter with you?; **invite ~ tu veux** invite whoever you want; **~ que ce soit** whoever it is, anybody.

---

quiche /kiʃ/ *nf* quiche.

quiconque /kikɔ̃k/ *pron* whoever; (n'importe qui) anyone.

quille /kij/ *nf* (de bateau) keel; (jouet) skittle.

quincaillerie /kɛ̃kajʀi/ *nf* hardware; (magasin) hardware shop. **quincaillier, -ière** *nm, f* hardware dealer.

quintal (*pl* **-aux**) /kɛ̃tal, -o/ *nm* quintal, one hundred kilos.

quinte /kɛ̃t/ *nf* **~ de toux** coughing fit.

quintuple /kɛ̃typl/ *adj* quintuple. ● *nm* **le ~ de** five times. **quintupler** **1** *vt/i* quintuple, increase fivefold.

quinzaine /kɛ̃zɛn/ *nf* **une ~ (de)** about fifteen.

quinze /kɛ̃z/ *adj & nm inv* fifteen; **~ jours** two weeks.

quiproquo /kipʀɔko/ *nm* misunderstanding.

quittance /kitɑ̃s/ *nf* receipt.

quitte /kit/ *adj* quits (envers with); **~ à faire** even if it means doing.

quitter /kite/ **1** *vt* leave; (vêtement) take off; **ne quittez pas!** hold the line, please! □ **se ~** *vpr* part.

qui-vive /kiviv/ *nm inv* **être sur le ~** be alert.

quoi /kwa/ *pron* what; (après une préposition) which; **de ~ vivre** (assez) enough to live on; **de ~ écrire** something to write with; **~ qu'il dise** whatever he says; **~ que ce soit** anything; **il n'y a pas de ~** my pleasure; **il n'y a pas de ~ s'inquiéter** there's nothing to worry about.

quoique /kwak(ə)/ *conj* although, though.

quota /kɔta/ *nm* quota.

quote-part (*pl* **quotes-parts**) /kɔtpaʀ/ *nf* share.

quotidien, -ne /kɔtidjɛ̃, -ɛn/ *adj* daily; (banal) everyday. ● *nm* daily (paper); (vie quotidienne) everyday life. **quotidiennement** *adv* daily.

q

Rr

rabâcher /ʀabaʃe/ **1** vt keep repeating.

rabais /ʀabɛ/ nm reduction, discount. **rabaisser 1** vt (déprécier) belittle; (réduire) reduce.

rabat-joie /ʀabaʒwa/ nm inv killjoy.

rabattre /ʀabatʀ/ **1** vt (chapeau, visière) pull down; (refermer) shut; (diminuer) reduce; (déduire) take off; (col, drap) turn down. □ se ∼ vpr (se refermer) close; (véhicule) cut back in; se ∼ sur make do with.

rabot /ʀabo/ nm plane.

rabougri, ∼e /ʀabugʀi/ adj stunted.

racaille /ʀakɑj/ nf rabble.

raccommoder /ʀakɔmɔde/ **1** vt mend; (personnes 🗐) reconcile.

raccompagner /ʀakɔ̃paɲe/ **1** vt see ou take back (home).

raccord /ʀakɔʀ/ nm link; (de papier peint) join; (retouche) touch-up. **raccorder 1** vt connect, join.

raccourci /ʀakuʀsi/ nm short cut; en ∼ in short.

raccourcir /ʀakuʀsiʀ/ **2** vt shorten. ● vi get shorter.

raccrocher /ʀakʀɔʃe/ **1** vt hang back up; (passant) grab hold of; (relier) connect; ∼ le combiné ou le téléphone hang up. ● vi hang up. □ se ∼ à vpr cling to; (se relier à) be connected to ou with.

race /ʀas/ nf race; (animale) breed; de ∼ (chien) pedigree; (cheval) thoroughbred.

racheter /ʀaʃte/ **6** vt buy (back); (acheter encore) buy more; (nouvel objet) buy another; (société) buy

out; ∼ des chaussettes buy new socks. □ se ∼ vpr make amends.

racial, ∼e (mpl **-iaux**) /ʀasjal, -o/ adj racial.

racine /ʀasin/ nf root; ∼ carrée/ cubique square/cube root.

racisme /ʀasism/ nm racism. **raciste** adj & nmf racist.

racket /ʀakɛt/ nm racketeering.

raclée /ʀɑkle/ nf 🗐 thrashing.

racler /ʀɑkle/ **1** vt scrape. □ se ∼ vpr se ∼ la gorge clear one's throat.

racolage /ʀakɔlaʒ/ nm soliciting.

raconter /ʀakɔ̃te/ **1** vt (histoire) tell; (vacances) tell about; (vie, épisode) describe; ∼ à qn que tell sb that, say to sb that; qu'est-ce que tu racontes? what are you talking about?

radar /ʀadaʀ/ nm radar; (automatique) speed camera.

radeau (pl ∼x) /ʀado/ nm raft.

radiateur /ʀadjatœʀ/ nm radiator; (électrique) heater.

radiation /ʀadjasjɔ̃/ nf radiation.

radical, ∼e (mpl **-aux**) /ʀadikal, -o/ adj radical. ● nm (pl **-aux**) radical.

radieux, -ieuse /ʀadjø, -z/ adj radiant.

radin, ∼e /ʀadɛ̃, -in/ adj 🗐 stingy.

radio /ʀadjo/ nf radio; à la ∼ on the radio; (radiographie) X-ray.

radioactif, -ive /ʀadjoaktif, -v/ adj radioactive. **radioactivité** nf radioactivity.

radiocassette /ʀadjokasɛt/ nf radio cassette player.

radiodiffuser /ʀadjodifyze/ **1** vt broadcast.

radiographie /ʀadjoɡʀafi/ nf (photographie) X-ray.

radiomessageur /ʀadjɔmesa-ʒœʀ/ nm pager.

radis /ʀadi/ nm radish; **ne pas avoir un ~** ① be broke.

radoter /ʀadɔte/ ① vi ① talk drivel.

radoucir (se) /(sə)ʀadusiʀ/ ② vpr (humeur) improve; (temps) become milder.

rafale /ʀafal/ nf (de vent) gust; (de mitraillette) burst.

raffermir /ʀafɛʀmiʀ/ ② vt strengthen. □ **se ~** vpr become stronger.

raffiné, **~e** /ʀafine/ adj refined. **raffinement** nm refinement.

raffiner /ʀafine/ ① vt refine. **raffinerie** nf refinery.

raffoler /ʀafɔle/ ① vt ① **~ de** be crazy about.

raffut /ʀafy/ nm ① din.

rafle /ʀafl/ nf (police) raid.

rafraîchir /ʀafʀeʃiʀ/ ② vt cool (down); (mur) give a fresh coat of paint to; (personne, mémoire) refresh. □ **se ~** vpr (boire) refresh oneself; (temps) get cooler. **rafraîchissant**, **~e** adj refreshing.

rafraîchissement /ʀafʀeʃismã/ nm (boisson) cold drink; **~s** refreshments.

ragaillardir /ʀagajaʀdiʀ/ ② vt ① cheer up.

rage /ʀaʒ/ nf rage; (maladie) rabies; **faire ~** (bataille, incendie) rage; (maladie) be rife; **~ de dents** raging toothache. **rageant**, **~e** adj infuriating.

ragots /ʀago/ nmpl ① gossip.

ragoût /ʀagu/ nm stew.

raid /ʀɛd/ nm (Mil) raid; (Sport) trek.

raide /ʀɛd/ adj stiff; (côte) steep; (corde) tight; (cheveux) straight. ● adv (monter, descendre) steeply.

raideur nf stiffness; steepness.

raidir /ʀediʀ/ ② vt (corps) tense. □ **se ~** vpr tense up; (position) harden; (corde) tighten.

raie /ʀɛ/ nf (ligne) line; (bande) strip; (de cheveux) parting; (poisson) skate.

raifort /ʀɛfɔʀ/ nm horseradish.

rail /ʀaj/ nm rail, track; **le ~** (transport) rail.

raisin /ʀezɛ̃/ nm **le ~** grapes; **~ sec** raisin; **un grain de ~** a grape.

raison /ʀezɔ̃/ nf reason; **à ~ de** at the rate of; **avec ~** rightly; **avoir ~** be right (de faire to do); **avoir ~ de qn** get the better of sb; **donner ~ à** prove right; **en ~ de** because of; **~ de plus** all the more reason; **perdre la ~** lose one's mind.

raisonnable /ʀezɔnabl/ adj reasonable, sensible.

raisonnement /ʀezɔnmã/ nm reasoning; (propositions) argument.

raisonner /ʀezɔne/ ① vi think. ● vt (personne) reason with.

rajeunir /ʀaʒœniʀ/ ② vt **~ qn** make sb (look) younger; (moderniser) modernize; (Méd) rejuvenate. ● vi (personne) look younger.

rajuster /ʀaʒyste/ ① vt straighten; (salaires) (re)adjust.

ralenti, **~e** /ʀalãti/ adj slow. ● nm (au cinéma) slow motion; **tourner au ~** tick over, idle.

ralentir /ʀalãtiʀ/ ② vt/i slow down. □ **se ~** vpr slow down.

ralentisseur /ʀalãtisœʀ/ nm speed ramp.

râler /ʀɑle/ ① vi groan; (protester ①) moan.

rallier /ʀalje/ 45 vt rally; (rejoindre) rejoin. □ **se ~** vpr rally; **se ~ à** (avis) come round to; (parti) join.

rallonge /ʀalɔ̃ʒ/ nf (de table) leaf; (de fil électrique) extension lead.

r

rallonger 40 vt lengthen; (*séjour, fil, table*) extend.

rallumer /ralyme/ 1 vt (*feu*) relight; (*lampe*) switch on again; (*ranimer*: fig) revive.

rallye /rali/ nm rally.

ramassage /ramasaʒ/ nm (*cueillette*) gathering; (*d'ordures*) collection; ∼ scolaire school bus service.

ramasser /ramase/ 1 vt pick up; (*récolter*) gather; (*recueillir, rassembler*) collect. □ se ∼ vpr huddle up, curl up.

rame /ram/ nf (*aviron*) oar; (*train*) train.

ramener /ramne/ 1 vt (*rapporter, faire revenir*) bring back; (*reconduire*) take back; (*réduire à*) reduce to. □ se ∼ vpr turn up; se ∼ à (*problème*) come down to.

ramer /rame/ 1 vi row.

ramollir /ramɔlir/ 2 vt soften. □ se ∼ vpr become soft.

ramoneur /ramɔnœr/ nm (chimney) sweep.

rampe /rɑ̃p/ nf banisters; (*pente*) ramp; ∼ d'accès (Auto) slip road; ∼ de lancement launching pad.

ramper /rɑ̃pe/ 1 vi crawl.

rancard /rɑ̃kar/ nm 1 date.

rancart /rɑ̃kar/ nm mettre ou jeter au ∼ 1 scrap.

rance /rɑ̃s/ adj rancid.

rancœur /rɑ̃kœr/ nf resentment.

rançon /rɑ̃sɔ̃/ nf ransom. **rançonner** 1 vt rob, extort money from.

rancune /rɑ̃kyn/ nf grudge; sans ∼! no hard feelings! **rancunier, -ière** adj vindictive.

randonnée /rɑ̃dɔne/ nf walk, ramble; la ∼ à cheval pony trekking; faire une ∼ go walking ou rambling.

rang /rɑ̃/ nm row; (*hiérarchie, condition*) rank; se mettre en ∼ line up; au premier ∼ in the first row; (*fig*) at the forefront; de second ∼ (*péj*) second-rate.

rangée /rɑ̃ʒe/ nf row.

rangement /rɑ̃ʒmɑ̃/ nm (*de pièce*) tidying (up); (*espace*) storage space.

ranger /rɑ̃ʒe/ 40 vt put away; (*chambre*) tidy (up); (*disposer*) place. □ se ∼ vpr (*véhicule*) park; (*s'écarter*) stand aside; (*conducteur*) pull over; (*s'assagir*) settle down; se ∼ à (*avis*) accept.

ranimer /ranime/ 1 vt revive; (Méd) resuscitate. □ se ∼ vpr come round.

rapace /rapas/ nm bird of prey. ● adj grasping.

rapatriement /rapatrimɑ̃/ nm repatriation. **rapatrier** 45 vt repatriate.

rap /rap/ nm rap (music).

râpe /rɑp/ nf (Culin) grater; (*lime*) rasp.

râpé, ∼e /rɑpe/ adj (*vêtement*) threadbare; (*fromage*) grated.

râper /rɑpe/ 1 vt grate; (*bois*) rasp.

rapide /rapid/ adj fast, rapid. ● nm (*train*) express (train); (*cours d'eau*) rapids (+ pl). **rapidement** adv fast, rapidly. **rapidité** nf speed.

rappel /rapɛl/ nm recall; (*deuxième avis*) reminder; (*de salaire*) back pay; (Méd) booster; (*de diplomate*) recall; (*de réservistes*) call-up; (Théât) curtain call.

rappeler /raple/ 38 vt (*par téléphone*) call back; (*réserviste*) call up; (*diplomate*) recall; (*évoquer*) recall; ∼ qch à qn remind sb of sth. □ se ∼ vpr remember, recall.

rappeur, -euse /rapœːr, -øz/

nmf rapper.

rapport /ʀapɔʀ/ *nm* connection; (compte-rendu) report; (profit) yield; ~s (relations) relations; en ~ avec (accord) in keeping with; mettre/se mettre en ~ avec put/ get in touch with; par ~ à (comparé à) compared with; (vis-à-vis de) with regard to; ~s (sexuels) intercourse.

rapporter /ʀapɔʀte/ **1** *vt* (ici) bring back; (là-bas) take back, return; (profit) bring in; (dire, répéter) report. ● *vi* (Comm) bring in a good return; (moucharder 🖵) tell tales. □ se ~ à *vpr* relate to.

rapporteur, -euse /ʀapɔʀtœʀ, -øz/ *nm, f* (mouchard) tell-tale. ● *nm* protractor.

rapprochement /ʀapʀɔʃmɑ̃/ *nm* reconciliation; (Pol) rapprochement; (rapport) connection; (comparaison) parallel.

rapprocher /ʀapʀɔʃe/ *vt* move closer (de to); (réconcilier) bring together; (comparer) compare; (date, rendez-vous) bring forward. □ se ~ *vpr* get ou come closer (de to); (personnes, pays) come together; (s'apparenter) be close (de to).

rapt /ʀapt/ *nm* abduction.

raquette /ʀakɛt/ *nf* (de tennis) racket; (de ping-pong) bat.

rare /ʀaʀ/ *adj* rare; (insuffisant) scarce. **rarement** *adv* rarely, seldom. **rareté** *nf* rarity; scarcity.

ras, ~e /ʀɑ, ʀɑz/ *adj* coupé ~ cut short. ● *adj* (herbe, poil) short; à ~ de terre very close to the ground; en avoir ~ le bol 🖵 be really fed up; ~e campagne open country; à ~ bord to the brim.

raser /ʀɑze/ **1** *vt* shave; (cheveux, barbe) shave off; (frôler) skim; (abattre) raze. □ se ~ *vpr* shave.

rasoir /ʀɑzwaʀ/ *nm* razor. ● *adj inv* 🖵 boring.

rassasier /ʀasazje/ **45** *vt* satisfy, fill up; être rassasié de have had enough of.

rassemblement /ʀasɑ̃bləmɑ̃/ *nm* gathering; (manifestation) rally.

rassembler /ʀasɑ̃ble/ **1** *vt* gather; (forces, courage) summon up; (idées) collect. □ se ~ *vpr* gather.

rassis, ~e /ʀasi, -z/ *adj* (pain) stale.

rassurer /ʀasyʀe/ **1** *vt* reassure. □ se ~ *vpr* reassure oneself; rassure-toi don't worry.

rat /ʀa/ *nm* rat.

rate /ʀat/ *nf* spleen.

raté, ~e /ʀate/ *nm, f* (personne) failure. ● *nm* avoir des ~s (voiture) backfire.

râteau (*pl* ~x) /ʀɑto/ *nm* rake.

râtelier /ʀɑtəlje/ *nm* hayrack; (dentier 🖵) dentures.

rater /ʀate/ **1** *vt* (train, rendez-vous, cible) miss; (gâcher) make a mess of, spoil; (examen) fail. ● *vi* fail.

ratio /ʀasjo/ *nm* ratio.

rationaliser /ʀasjonalize/ **1** *vt* rationalize.

rationnel, ~le /ʀasjonɛl/ *adj* rational.

rationnement /ʀasjonmɑ̃/ *nm* rationing.

ratisser /ʀatise/ **1** *vt* rake; (fouiller) comb.

rattacher /ʀataʃe/ **1** *vt* (lacets) tie up again; (ceinture de sécurité, collier) refasten; (relier) link; (incorporer) join.

rattrapage /ʀatʀapaʒ/ *nm* (Comm) adjustment; cours de ~ remedial lesson.

rattraper /ʀatʀape/ **1** *vt* catch;

r

(rejoindre) catch up with; (retard, erreur) make up for. □ se ~ vpr catch up; (se dédommager) make up for it; se ~ à catch hold of.

rature /ʀatyʀ/ nf deletion.

rauque /ʀok/ adj raucous, harsh.

ravager /ʀavaʒe/ [40] vt devastate, ravage.

ravages /ʀavaʒ/ nmpl faire des ~ wreak havoc.

ravaler /ʀavale/ [1] vt (façade) clean; (colère) swallow.

ravi, ~e /ʀavi/ adj delighted (que that).

ravin /ʀavɛ̃/ nm ravine.

ravir /ʀaviʀ/ [2] vt delight; ~ qch à qn rob sb of sth.

ravissant, ~e /ʀavisɑ̃, -t/ adj beautiful.

ravisseur, -euse /ʀavisœʀ, -øz/ nm, f kidnapper.

ravitaillement /ʀavitajmɑ̃/ nm provision of supplies (de to); (denrées) supplies; ~ en essence refuelling.

ravitailler /ʀavitaje/ [1] vt provide with supplies; (avion) refuel. □ se ~ vpr stock up.

raviver /ʀavive/ [1] vt revive; (feu, colère) rekindle.

rayé, ~e /ʀeje/ adj striped.

rayer /ʀeje/ [31] vt cross out; (biffer) cross out; '~ la mention inutile' 'delete as appropriate'.

rayon /ʀejɔ̃/ nm ray; (étagère) shelf; (de magasin) department; (de roue) spoke; (de cercle) radius; ~ d'action range; ~ de miel honeycomb; ~ X X-ray; en connaître un ~ [I] know one's stuff [I].

rayonnement /ʀejɔnmɑ̃/ nm (éclat) radiance; (influence) influence; (radiations) radiation. **rayonner** [1] vi radiate; (de joie) beam; (se déplacer) tour around (from a

central point).

rayure /ʀejyʀ/ nf scratch; (dessin) stripe; à ~s striped.

raz-de-marée /ʀɑdmaʀe/ nm inv tidal wave; ~ électoral electoral landslide.

réacteur /ʀeaktœʀ/ nm jet engine; (nucléaire) reactor.

réaction /ʀeaksjɔ̃/ nf reaction; ~ en chaîne chain reaction; moteur à ~ jet engine.

réagir /ʀeaʒiʀ/ [2] vi react; ~ sur have an effect on.

réalisateur, -trice /ʀealizatœʀ, -tʀis/ nm, f (au cinéma) director; (TV) producer.

réalisation /ʀealizasjɔ̃/ nf (de rêve) fulfilment; (œuvre) achievement; (TV, cinéma) production; projet en ~ project in progress.

réaliser /ʀealize/ [1] vt carry out; (effort, bénéfice, achat) make; (rêve) fulfil; (film) direct; (capital) realize; (se rendre compte de) realize. □ se ~ vpr be fulfilled.

réalisme /ʀealism/ nm realism.

réaliste /ʀealist/ adj realistic. ● nmf realist.

réalité /ʀealite/ nf reality.

réanimation /ʀeanimasjɔ̃/ nf resuscitation; service de ~ intensive care. **réanimer** [1] vt resuscitate.

réarmement /ʀeaʀməmɑ̃/ nm rearmament.

rébarbatif, -ive /ʀebaʀbatif, -v/ adj forbidding, off-putting.

rebelle /ʀəbɛl/ adj rebellious; (soldat) rebel; ~ à resistant to. ● nmf rebel.

rébellion /ʀebeljɔ̃/ nf rebellion.

rebondir /ʀəbɔ̃diʀ/ [2] vi bounce; rebound; (fig) get moving again.

rebondissement /ʀəbɔ̃dismɑ̃/ nm (new) development.

rebord /RəbɔR/ nm edge; ~ de la fenêtre window ledge ou sill.

rebours: à ~ /aRabuR/ loc (compter, marcher) backwards.

rebrousse-poil: à ~ /aRəbRuspwal/ loc the wrong way; (fig) prendre qn à ~ rub sb up the wrong way.

rebrousser /RəbRuse/ **1** vt ~ chemin turn back.

rebut /Rəby/ nm mettre ou jeter au ~ scrap.

rebutant, ~e /Rəbytɑ̃, -t/ adj off-putting.

recaler /Rəkale/ **1** vt **1** fail; se faire ~, être recalé fail.

recel /Rəsɛl/ nm receiving. **receler** **6** vt (objet volé) receive; (cacher) conceal.

récemment /Resamɑ̃/ adv recently.

recensement /Rəsɑ̃smɑ̃/ nm census; (inventaire) inventory. **recenser** **1** vt (population) take a census of; (objets) list.

récent, ~e /Resɑ̃, -t/ adj recent.

récépissé /Resepise/ nm receipt.

récepteur /ReseptœR/ nm receiver.

réception /Resepsjɔ̃/ nf reception; (de courrier) receipt. **réceptionniste** nmf receptionist.

récession /Resesjɔ̃/ nf recession.

recette /Rəsɛt/ nf (Culin) recipe; (argent) takings; ~s (Comm) receipts.

receveur, -euse /Rəs(ə)vœR, -øz/ nm, f (de bus) conductor; ~ des contributions tax collector.

recevoir /Rəs(ə)vwaR/ **52** vt receive, get; (client, malade) see; (invités) welcome, receive; être reçu à un examen pass an exam.

rechange: de ~ /dəRəʃɑ̃ʒ/ loc (roue, vêtements) spare; (solution) alternative.

réchapper /Reʃape/ **1** vt/i ~ de come through, survive.

recharge /RəʃaRʒ/ nf (de stylo) refill.

réchaud /Reʃo/ nm stove.

réchauffement /Reʃofmɑ̃/ nm (de température) rise (de in); le ~ de la planète global warming.

réchauffer /Reʃofe/ **1** vt warm up. □ se ~ vpr warm oneself up; (temps) get warmer.

rêche /Rɛʃ/ adj rough.

recherche /RəʃɛRʃ/ nf search (de for); (raffinement) meticulousness; ~(s) (Univ) research; ~s (enquête) investigations; ~ d'emploi job-hunting.

recherché, ~e /RəʃɛRʃe/ adj in great demand; (style) original, recherché (péj); ~ pour meurtre wanted for murder.

rechercher /RəʃɛRʃe/ **1** vt search for.

rechute /Rəʃyt/ nf (Méd) relapse; faire une ~ have a relapse.

récidiver /Residive/ **1** vi commit a second offence.

récif /Resif/ nm reef.

récipient /Resipjɑ̃/ nm container.

réciproque /ResipRɔk/ adj mutual, reciprocal.

réciproquement /ResipRɔkmɑ̃/ adv each other; et ~ and vice versa.

récit /Resi/ nm (compte-rendu) account, story; (histoire) story.

réciter /Resite/ **1** vt recite.

réclamation /Reklamasjɔ̃/ nf complaint; (demande) claim.

réclame /Reklam/ nf advertisement; faire de la ~ advertise; en ~ on offer.

réclamer /Reklame/ **1** vt call for, demand. ● vi complain.

reclus, ~e /Rəkly, -z/ nm, f recluse.

● *adj* reclusive.

réclusion /reklyzjɔ̃/ *nf* imprisonment.

récolte /rekɔlt/ *nf* (action) harvest; (produits) crop, harvest; (fig) crop. **récolter** ⓵ *vt* harvest, gather; (fig) collect, get.

recommandation /rəkɔmɑ̃dasjɔ̃/ *nf* recommendation.

recommandé /rəkɔmɑ̃de/ *nm* registered letter; envoyer en ∼ send by registered post.

recommander /rəkɔmɑ̃de/ ⓵ *vt* recommend.

recommencer /rəkɔmɑ̃se/ ⓾ *vt* (reprendre) begin ou start again; (refaire) repeat. ● *vi* start ou begin again; ne recommence pas don't do it again.

récompense /rekɔ̃pɑ̃s/ *nf* reward; (prix) award. **récompenser** ⓵ *vt* reward (de for).

réconcilier /rekɔ̃silje/ ⑭ *vt* reconcile. □ **se** ∼ *vpr* become reconciled (avec with).

reconduire /rəkɔ̃dɥir/ ⑰ *vt* see home; (à la porte) show out; (renouveler) renew.

réconfort /rekɔ̃fɔr/ *nm* comfort.

reconnaissance /rəkɔnɛsɑ̃s/ *nf* gratitude; (fait de reconnaître) recognition; (Mil) reconnaissance. **reconnaissant**, ∼e *adj* grateful (de for).

reconnaître /rəkɔnɛtr/ ⑱ *vt* recognize; (admettre) admit (que that); (Mil) reconnoitre; (enfant, tort) acknowledge. □ **se** ∼ *vpr* (s'orienter) know where one is; (l'un l'autre) recognize each other.

reconstituer /rəkɔ̃stitɥe/ ⓵ *vt* reconstitute; (crime) reconstruct; (époque) recreate.

reconversion /rəkɔ̃vɛrsjɔ̃/ *nf* (de main-d'œuvre) redeployment.

recopier /rəkɔpje/ ⑮ *vt* copy out.

record /rəkɔr/ *nm & a inv* record.

recouper /rəkupe/ ⓵ *vt* confirm. □ **se** ∼ *vpr* check, tally, match up.

recourbé, ∼e /rəkurbe/ *adj* curved; (nez) hooked.

recourir /rəkurir/ ⓴ *vi* ∼ à (expédient, violence) resort to; (remède, méthode) have recourse to.

recours /rəkur/ *nm* resort; avoir ∼ à have recourse to, resort to; avoir ∼ à qn turn to sb.

recouvrer /rəkuvre/ ⓵ *vt* recover.

recouvrir /rəkuvrir/ ㉑ *vt* cover.

récréation /rekreasjɔ̃/ *nf* recreation; (Scol) break; (US) recess.

recroqueviller (se) /(sə)rəkrɔkvije/ ⓵ *vpr* curl up.

recrudescence /rəkrydesɑ̃s/ *nf* new outbreak.

recrue /rəkry/ *nf* recruit.

recrutement /rəkrytmɑ̃/ *nm* recruitment. **recruter** ⓵ *vt* recruit.

rectangle /rɛktɑ̃gl/ *nm* rectangle. **rectangulaire** *adj* rectangular.

rectifier /rɛktifje/ ⑮ *vt* correct, rectify.

recto /rɛkto/ *nm* au ∼ on the front of the page.

reçu, ∼e /rəsy/ *adj* accepted; (candidat) successful. ● *nm* receipt.

● →**RECEVOIR** ㊾.

recueil /rəkœj/ *nm* collection.

recueillement /rəkœjmɑ̃/ *nm* meditation.

recueillir /rəkœjir/ ㉕ *vt* collect; (prendre chez soi) take in. □ **se** ∼ *vpr* meditate.

recul /rəkyl/ *nm* retreat; (éloignement) distance; (déclin) decline; avoir un mouvement de ∼ recoil; être en ∼ be on the decline; avec le ∼ with hindsight.

reculé, ∼e /Rəkyle/ *adj* (*région*) remote.

reculer /Rəkyle/ **1** *vt* move back; (*véhicule*) reverse; (*différer*) postpone. ● *vi* move back; (*voiture*) reverse; (*armée*) retreat; (*régresser*) fall; (*céder*) back down; ∼ **devant** (fig) shrink from. □ **se** ∼ *vpr* move back.

récupération /Rekyperasjɔ̃/ *nf* (de l'organisme, de dette) recovery; (d'objets) salvage.

récupérer /Rekypere/ **14** *vt* recover; (*vieux objets*) salvage. ● *vi* recover.

récurer /Rekyre/ **1** *vt* scour; **poudre à** ∼ scouring powder.

récuser /Rekyze/ **1** *vt* challenge. □ **se** ∼ *vpr* state that one is not qualified to judge.

recyclage /Rəsiklaʒ/ *nm* (de personnel) retraining; (de matériau) recycling.

recycler /Rəsikle/ **1** *vt* (*personne*) retrain; (*chose*) recycle. □ **se** ∼ *vpr* retrain.

rédacteur, **-trice** /RedaktœR, -tRis/ *nm, f* author, writer; (de journal, magazine) editor.

rédaction /Redaksjɔ̃/ *nf* writing; (Scol) essay, composition; (personnel) editorial staff.

redevable /Rədvabl/ *adj* **être** ∼ **à qn de** (*argent*) owe sb; (fig) be indebted to sb for.

redevance /Rədvɑ̃s/ *nf* (de télévision) licence fee; (de téléphone) rental charge.

rédiger /Rediʒe/ **40** *vt* write; (*contrat*) draw up.

redire /RədiR/ **27** *vt* repeat; **avoir ou trouver à** ∼ **à** find fault with.

redondant, ∼e /Rədɔ̃dɑ̃, -t/ *adj* superfluous.

redonner /Rədɔne/ **1** *vt* (*rendre*) give back; (*donner davantage*) give more; (*donner de nouveau*) give again.

redoubler /Rəduble/ **1** *vt* increase; (*classe*) repeat; ∼ **de prudence** be even more careful. ● *vi* (Scol) repeat a year; (s'intensifier) intensify.

redoutable /Rədutabl/ *adj* formidable.

redouter /Rədute/ **1** *vt* dread.

redressement /RədRεsmɑ̃/ *nm* (reprise) recovery; ∼ **judiciaire** receivership.

redresser /RədRese/ **1** *vt* straighten (out ou up); (*situation*) right, redress; (*économie, entreprise*) turn around. □ **se** ∼ *vpr* (*personne*) straighten (oneself) up; (se remettre debout) stand up; (*pays, économie*) recover.

réduction /Redyksjɔ̃/ *nf* reduction.

réduire /RedɥiR/ **17** *vt* reduce (**à** to). □ **se** ∼ *vpr* be reduced ou cut; **se** ∼ **à** (revenir à) come down to.

réduit, ∼e /Redɥi, -t/ *adj* (*objet*) small-scale; (*limité*) limited. ● *nm* cubbyhole.

rééducation /Reedykasjɔ̃/ *nf* (de handicapé) rehabilitation; (Méd) physiotherapy. **rééduquer** **1** *vt* (*personne*) rehabilitate; (*membre*) restore normal movement to.

réel, ∼le /Reεl/ *adj* real. ● *nm* reality. **réellement** *adv* really.

réexpédier /Reεkspedje/ **45** *vt* forward; (*retourner*) send back.

refaire /RəfεR/ **33** *vt* do again; (*erreur, voyage*) make again; (*réparer*) do up, redo.

réfectoire /Refεktwar/ *nm* refectory.

référence /ʀefeʀɑ̃s/ nf reference.

référendum /ʀefeʀɛ̃dɔm/ nm referendum.

référer /ʀefeʀe/ nm à ~ à consult. □ **se ~ à** vpr refer to, consult.

refermer /ʀəfɛʀme/ 1 vt close (again). □ **se ~** vpr close (again).

réfléchi, ~**e** /ʀefleʃi/ adj (personne) thoughtful; (verbe) reflexive.

réfléchir /ʀefleʃiʀ/ 2 vi think (à, sur about). ● vt reflect. □ **se ~** vpr be reflected.

reflet /ʀəflɛ/ nm reflection; (nuance) sheen.

refléter /ʀəflete/ 14 vt reflect. □ **se ~** vpr be reflected.

réflexe /ʀeflɛks/ adj reflex. ● nm reflex; (réaction) reaction.

réflexion /ʀeflɛksjɔ̃/ nf (pensée) thought, reflection; (remarque) remark, comment; **à la ~** on second thoughts.

refluer /ʀəflye/ 1 vi flow back; (foule) retreat; (inflation) go down.

reflux /ʀəfly/ nm (marée) ebb, tide.

réforme /ʀefɔʀm/ nf reform. **réformer** /ʀefɔʀme/ 1 vt reform; (soldat) invalid out.

refouler /ʀəfule/ 1 vt (larmes) hold back; (désir) repress; (souvenir) suppress.

refrain /ʀəfʀɛ̃/ nm chorus; le même ~ the same old story.

refréner /ʀəfʀene/ 14 vt curb, check.

réfrigérateur /ʀefʀiʒeʀatœʀ/ nm refrigerator.

refroidir /ʀəfʀwadiʀ/ 2 vt/i cool (down). □ **se ~** vpr (personne, temps) get cold. **refroidissement** nm cooling; (rhume) chill.

refuge /ʀəfyʒ/ nm refuge; (chalet) mountain hut.

réfugié, ~**e** /ʀefyʒje/ nm, f refugee. **réfugier (se)** 45 vpr take refuge.

refus /ʀəfy/ nm refusal; ce n'est pas de ~ 1 I wouldn't say no.

refuser /ʀəfyze/ 1 vt refuse (de to); (client, spectateur) turn away; (recaler) fail; (à un poste) turn down. □ **se ~ à** vpr (évidence) reject; **se ~ à faire** refuse to do.

regain /ʀəgɛ̃/ nm ~ de renewal ou revival of; (Comm) rise.

régal (pl ~**s**) /ʀegal/ nm treat, delight.

régaler /ʀegale/ 1 vt ~ qn de treat sb to. □ **se ~** vpr (de nourriture) je me régale it's delicious.

regard /ʀəgaʀ/ nm (expression, coup d'œil) look; (vue) eye; (yeux) eyes; ~ fixe stare; au ~ de with regard to; en ~ de compared with.

regardant, ~**e** /ʀəgaʀdɑ̃, -t/ adj ~ avec son argent careful with money; peu ~ (sur) not fussy (about).

regarder /ʀəgaʀde/ 1 vt look at; (observer) watch; (considérer) consider; (concerner) concern; ~ fixement stare at; ~ à think about, pay attention to. ● vi look. □ **se ~** vpr (soi-même) look at oneself; (personnes) look at each other.

régate /ʀegat/ nf regatta.

régie /ʀeʒi/ nf ~ d'État public corporation; (radio, TV) control room; (au cinéma) production; (Théât) stage management.

régime /ʀeʒim/ nm (organisation) system; (Pol) regime; (Méd) diet; (de moteur) speed; (de bananes) bunch; se mettre au ~ go on a diet; à ce ~ at this rate.

régiment /ʀeʒimɑ̃/ nm regiment.

région /ʀeʒjɔ̃/ nf region. **régional**, ~**e** (mpl -**aux**) adj regional.

> **Région** The largest admin- *i*
> istrative unit in France,
> consisting of a number of
> *départements*. Each has its own
> *Conseil régional* (regional council)
> which has responsibilities in edu-
> cation and economic planning.
> ▷ **DÉPARTEMENT**.

régir /ʀeʒiʀ/ [2] vt govern.

régisseur /ʀeʒisœʀ/ nm (Théât)
stage manager; ~ **de plateau** (TV)
floor manager; (au cinéma) studio
manager.

registre /ʀəʒistʀ/ nm register.

réglage /ʀeɡlaʒ/ nm adjustment;
(de moteur) tuning.

règle /ʀɛɡl/ nf rule; (instrument)
ruler; ~**s** (de femme) period; **en** ~
in order.

réglé, ~**e** /ʀeɡle/ adj (vie) ordered;
(arrangé) settled; (papier) ruled.

règlement /ʀɛɡləmɑ̃/ nm (règles)
regulations; (solution) settlement;
(paiement) payment. **réglemen-
taire** adj (uniforme) regulation. **réglementation** nf regulation, rules.
réglementer [1] vt regulate,
control.

régler /ʀeɡle/ [14] vt settle; (machine) adjust; (programmer) set;
(facture) settle; (personne) settle up
with; ~ **son compte à** [1] settle a
score with.

réglisse /ʀeɡlis/ nf liquorice.

règne /ʀɛɲ/ nm reign; (végétal, animal, minéral) kingdom.

regret /ʀəɡʀɛ/ nm regret; **à** ~ with
regret.

regretter /ʀəɡʀete/ [1] vt regret;
(personne) miss; (pour s'excuser) be
sorry.

regrouper /ʀəɡʀupe/ [1] vt group
ou bring together. □ **se** ~ vpr
gather ou group together.

régularité /ʀeɡylaʀite/ nf regularity; (de rythme, progrès) steadiness;
(de surface, écriture) evenness.

régulier, -**ière** /ʀeɡylje, -jɛʀ/ adj
regular; (qualité, vitesse) steady,
even; (ligne, paysage) even; (légal)
legal; (honnête) honest.

rehausser /ʀaose/ [1] vt raise;
(faire valoir) enhance.

rein /ʀɛ̃/ nm kidney; ~**s** (dos) small
of the back.

reine /ʀɛn/ nf queen.

réinsertion /ʀeɛ̃sɛʀsjɔ̃/ nf reinte-
gration.

réintégrer /ʀeɛ̃teɡʀe/ [14] vt (lieu)
return to; (Jur) reinstate; (personne)
reintegrate.

réitérer /ʀeiteʀe/ [14] vt repeat.

rejaillir /ʀəʒajiʀ/ [2] vi ~ **sur**
splash back onto; ~ **sur qn** (succès)
reflect on sb.

rejet /ʀəʒɛ/ nm rejection; ~**s** (déchets) waste.

rejeter /ʀəʒte/ [38] vt throw back;
(refuser) reject; (déverser) discharge; ~ **une faute sur qn** shift
the blame for a mistake onto sb.

rejoindre /ʀəʒwɛ̃dʀ/ [22] vt go back
to, rejoin; (rattraper) catch up with;
(rencontrer) join, meet up with.
□ **se** ~ vpr (personnes) meet up;
(routes) join, meet.

réjoui, ~**e** /ʀeʒwi/ adj joyful.

réjouir /ʀeʒwiʀ/ [2] vt delight. □ **se**
~ vpr be delighted (de at). **réjouissances** nfpl festivities. **réjouissant**,
~**e** adj cheering.

relâche /ʀəlɑʃ/ nm (repos) break,
rest; **faire** ~ (Théât) be closed.

relâcher /ʀəlɑʃe/ [1] vt slacken;
(personne) release; (discipline) relax.
□ **se** ~ vpr slacken.

relais /ʀəlɛ/ nm (Sport) relay;
(hôtel) hotel; (intermédiaire) inter-

r

mediary; **prendre le ~ de** take over from.

relancer /rəlãse/ 10 vt boost, revive; (renvoyer) throw back.

relatif, -ive /rəlatif, -v/ adj relative; **~ à** relating to.

relation /rəlasjõ/ nf relationship; (ami) acquaintance; (personne puissante) connection; **~s** relations; **~s extérieures** foreign affairs; **en ~ avec qn** in touch with sb.

relativement /rəlativmã/ adv relatively; **~ à** in relation to.

relativité /rəlativite/ nf relativity.

relax /rəlaks/ adj inv 🔟 laid-back.

relaxer (se) /(sə)rəlakse/ 🔟 vpr relax.

relayer /rəleje/ 31 vt relieve; (émission) relay. □ **se ~** vpr take over from one another.

reléguer /rəlege/ 14 vt relegate.

relent /rəlã/ nm stink; (fig) whiff.

relève /rəlɛv/ nf relief; **prendre ou assurer la ~** take over (de from).

relevé, ~e /rəlve/ adj spicy. ● nm (de compteur) reading; (facture) bill; **~ bancaire, ~ de compte** bank statement; **faire le ~ de** list.

relever /rəlve/ 6 vt pick up; (personne tombée) help up; (remonter) raise; (col) turn up; (compteur) read; (défi) accept; (relayer) relieve; (remarquer, noter) note; (plat) spice up; (rebâtir) rebuild; **~ de** come within the competence of; (Méd) recover from. □ **se ~** vpr (personne) get up (again); (pays, économie) recover.

relief /rəljɛf/ nm relief; **mettre en ~** highlight.

relier /rəlje/ 45 vt link (up) (à to); (livre) bind.

religieux, -ieuse /rəliʒjø, -z/ adj religious. ● nm, f monk, nun.

religion /rəliʒjõ/ nf religion.

reliure /rəljyr/ nf binding.

reluire /rəlɥir/ 17 vi shine.

remaniement /rəmanimã/ nm revision; **~ ministériel** cabinet reshuffle.

remarquable /rəmarkabl/ adj remarkable.

remarque /rəmark/ nf remark; (par écrit) comment.

remarquer /rəmarke/ 🔟 vt notice; (dire) say; **faire ~** point out (à to); **se faire ~** draw attention to oneself; **remarque(z)** mind you.

remblai /rãblɛ/ nm embankment.

remboursement /rãbursəmã/ nm (d'emprunt, dette) repayment; (Comm) refund.

rembourser /rãburse/ 🔟 vt (dette, emprunt) repay; (billet, frais) refund; (client) give a refund to; (ami) pay back.

remède /rəmɛd/ nm remedy; (médicament) medicine.

remédier /rəmedje/ 45 vi **~ à** remedy.

remerciements /rəmɛrsimã/ nmpl thanks. **remercier** 45 vt thank (de for); (licencier) dismiss.

remettre /rəmɛtr/ 42 vt put back; (vêtement) put back on; (donner) hand over; (devoir, démission) hand in; (faire fonctionner) switch back on; (restituer) give back; (différer) put off; (ajouter) add; (se rappeler) remember; **~ en cause ou en question** call into question. □ **se ~** vpr (guérir) recover; **se ~ au tennis** take up tennis again; **se ~ au travail** get back to work; **se ~ à faire** start doing again; **s'en ~ à** leave it to.

remise /rəmiz/ nf (abri) shed; (rabais) discount; (transmission) handing over; (ajournement) postponement; **~ en cause ou en question**

calling into question; ∼ des prix prizegiving; ∼ des médailles medals ceremony; ∼ de peine remission.

remontant /ʀəmɔ̃tɑ̃/ nm tonic.

remontée /ʀəmɔ̃te/ nf ascent; (d'eau, de prix) rise; ∼ mécanique ski lift.

remonte-pente (pl ∼s) /ʀəmɔ̃tpɑ̃t/ nm ski tow.

remonter /ʀəmɔ̃te/ **1** vi go ou come (back) up; (prix, niveau) rise (again); (revenir) go back (à to); ∼ dans le temps go back in time. ● vt (rue, escalier) go ou come (back) up; (relever) raise; (montre) wind up; (objet démonté) put together again; (personne) buck up.

remontoir /ʀəmɔ̃twaʀ/ nm winder.

remords /ʀəmɔʀ/ nm remorse; avoir du ou des ∼s feel remorse.

remorque /ʀəmɔʀk/ nf trailer; en ∼ on tow. **remorquer 1** vt tow.

remous /ʀəmu/ nm eddy; (de bateau) backwash; (fig) turmoil.

rempart /ʀɑ̃paʀ/ nm rampart.

remplaçant, ∼e /ʀɑ̃plasɑ̃, -t/ nm, f replacement; (joueur) reserve, substitute.

remplacement /ʀɑ̃plasmɑ̃/ nm replacement; faire des ∼s do supply teaching. **remplacer 10** vt replace.

rempli, ∼e /ʀɑ̃pli/ adj full (de of); (journée) busy.

remplir /ʀɑ̃pliʀ/ **2** vt fill (up); (formulaire) fill in ou out; (condition) fulfil; (devoir, tâche, rôle) carry out. □ se ∼ vpr fill (up). **remplissage** nm filling; (de texte) padding.

remporter /ʀɑ̃pɔʀte/ **1** vt take back; (victoire) win.

remuant, ∼e /ʀəmɥɑ̃, -t/ adj boisterous.

remue-ménage /ʀəmymenaʒ/ nm inv commotion, bustle.

remuer /ʀəmɥe/ **1** vt move; (thé, café) stir; (passé) rake up. ● vi move; (gigoter) fidget. □ se ∼ vpr move.

rémunération /ʀemyneʀasjɔ̃/ nf payment.

renaissance /ʀənɛsɑ̃s/ nf rebirth.

renard /ʀənaʀ/ nm fox.

renchérir /ʀɑ̃ʃeʀiʀ/ **2** vi (dans une vente) raise the bidding; ∼ sur go one better than. ● vt increase, put up.

rencontre /ʀɑ̃kɔ̃tʀ/ nf meeting; (de routes) junction; (Mil) encounter; (match) match; (US) game.

rencontrer /ʀɑ̃kɔ̃tʀe/ **1** vt meet; (heurter) hit; (trouver) find. □ se ∼ vpr meet.

rendement /ʀɑ̃dmɑ̃/ nm yield; (travail) output.

rendez-vous /ʀɑ̃devu/ nm appointment; (d'amoureux) date; (lieu) meeting-place; prendre ∼ (avec) make an appointment (with).

rendormir (se) /(sə)ʀɑ̃dɔʀmiʀ/ **46** vpr go back to sleep.

rendre /ʀɑ̃dʀ/ **3** vt give back, return; (donner en retour) return; (monnaie) give; (justice) dispense; (jugement) pronounce; ∼ heureux/possible make happy/possible; (vomir **1**) vomit; ∼ compte de report on; ∼ service (à) help; ∼ visite à visit. ● vi (terres) yield; (activité) be profitable. □ se ∼ vpr (capituler) surrender; (aller) go (à to); se ∼ utile make oneself useful.

rêne /ʀɛn/ nf rein.

renfermé, ∼e /ʀɑ̃fɛʀme/ adj withdrawn. ● nm sentir le ∼ smell musty.

renflé, ∼e /ʀɑ̃fle/ adj bulging.

renforcer /ʀɑ̃fɔʀse/ **10** vt

renfort /ʀɑ̃fɔʀ/ nm reinforcement; **à grand ~ de** with a great deal of.

renier /ʀənje/ 45 vt (personne, œuvre) disown; (foi) renounce.

renifler /ʀənifle/ 1 vt/i sniff.

renne /ʀɛn/ nm reindeer.

renom /ʀənɔ̃/ nm renown; (réputation) reputation. **renommé, ~e** adj famous. **renommée** nf (célébrité) fame; (réputation) reputation.

renoncement /ʀənɔ̃smã/ nm renunciation.

renoncer /ʀənɔ̃se/ 10 vi **~ à** (habitude, ami) give up, renounce; (projet) abandon; **~ à faire** abandon the idea of doing.

renouer /ʀənwe/ 1 vt tie up (again); (amitié) renew; **~ avec qn** get back in touch with sb; (après une dispute) make up with sb.

renouveau (pl ~x) /ʀənuvo/ nm revival.

renouveler /ʀənuvle/ 38 vt renew; (réitérer) repeat; (remplacer) replace. □ **se ~** vpr be renewed; (incident) recur, happen again.

renouvellement /ʀənuvɛlmɑ̃/ nm renewal.

rénovation /ʀenɔvasjɔ̃/ nf (d'édifice) renovation; (d'institution) reform.

renseignement /ʀɑ̃sɛɲ(ə)mɑ̃/ nm ~(s) information; (bureau des) ~s information desk; (service des) ~s téléphoniques directory enquiries.

renseigner /ʀɑ̃seɲe/ 1 vt inform, give information to. □ **se ~** vpr enquire, make enquiries, find out.

rentabilité /ʀɑ̃tabilite/ nf profitability. **rentable** adj profitable.

rente /ʀɑ̃t/ nf (private) income; (pension) annuity. **rentier, -ière** nm, f person of private means.

rentrée /ʀɑ̃tʀe/ nf return; (revenu) income; **la ~ (des classes)** the start of the new school year; **faire sa ~** make a comeback.

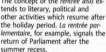

Rentrée The start of the new school year at the beginning of September, used as a major marketing opportunity by stores and supermarkets. The concept of the *rentrée* also extends to literary, political and other activities which resume after the holiday period. *La rentrée parlementaire*, for example, signals the return of Parliament after the summer recess.

rentrer /ʀɑ̃tʀe/ 1 vi (aux être) go ou come back home, return home; (entrer) go ou come in; (entrer à nouveau) go ou come back in; (revenu) come in; (élèves) go back (to school); **~ dans** (heurter) smash into; **tout est rentré dans l'ordre** everything is back to normal; **~ dans ses frais** break even. ● vt (aux avoir) bring in; (griffes) draw in; (vêtement) tuck in.

renverser /ʀɑ̃vɛʀse/ 1 vt knock over ou down; (piéton) knock down; (liquide) upset, spill; (mettre à l'envers) turn upside down; (gouvernement) overthrow; (inverser) reverse. □ **se ~** vpr (véhicule) overturn; (verre, vase) fall over.

renvoi /ʀɑ̃vwa/ nm return; (d'employé) dismissal; (d'élève) expulsion; (report) postponement; (dans un livre, fichier) cross-reference; (rot) burp.

renvoyer /ʀɑ̃vwaje/ 32 vt send back, return; (employé) dismiss; (élève) expel; (ajourner) postpone; (référer) refer; (réfléchir) reflect.

repaire /ʀəpɛʀ/ nm den.

répandre /Repɑ̃dʀ/ 🔞 vt (liquide) spill; (étendre, diffuser) spread; (odeur) give off. ☐ se ~ vpr spread; (liquide) spill; se ~ **en injures** let out a stream of abuse.

répandu, ~e /Repɑ̃dy/ adj widespread.

réparateur, -trice /ʀepaʀatœʀ, -tʀis/ nm engineer. **réparation** nf repair; (compensation) compensation. **réparer** 🔳 vt repair, mend; (faute) make amends for; (remédier à) put right.

repartie /Rəpaʀti/ nf retort; **avoir de la** ~ always have a ready reply.

repartir /Rəpaʀtiʀ/ 🔞 vi start again; (voyageur) set off again; (s'en retourner) go back; (secteur économique) pick up again.

répartir /Repaʀtiʀ/ 🔳 vt distribute; (partager) share out; (étaler) spread. **répartition** nf distribution.

repas /Rəpɑ/ nm meal.

repassage /Rəpasaʒ/ nm ironing.

repasser /Rəpase/ 🔳 vi come ou go back; ~ **devant qch** go past sth again. ● vt (linge) iron; (examen) retake, resit; (film) show again.

repêcher /Rəpeʃe/ 🔳 vt recover, fish out; (candidat) allow to pass.

repentir[1] /Rəpɑ̃tiʀ/ nm repentance.

repentir[2] **(se)** /(sə)Rəpɑ̃tiʀ/ 🔢 vpr (Relig) repent (de of); **se** ~ **de** (regretter) regret.

répercuter /ʀepɛʀkyte/ 🔳 vt (bruit) send back. ☐ **se** ~ vpr echo; **se** ~ **sur** have repercussions on.

repère /Rəpɛʀ/ nm mark; (jalon) marker; (événement) landmark; (référence) reference point.

repérer /Rəpeʀe/ 🔟 vt locate, spot. ☐ **se** ~ vpr get one's bearings.

répertoire /Repɛʀtwaʀ/ nm (artistique) repertoire; (liste) directory;

~ **téléphonique** telephone directory; (personnel) telephone book. **répertorier** 🔢 vt index.

répéter /Repete/ 🔢 vt repeat; (Théât) rehearse. ● vi rehearse. ☐ **se** ~ vpr be repeated; (personne) repeat oneself.

répétition /Repetisjɔ̃/ nf repetition; (Théât) rehearsal.

répit /Repi/ nm respite, break.

replier /Rəplije/ 🔢 vt fold (up); (ailes, jambes) tuck in. ☐ **se** ~ vpr withdraw (sur soi-même into oneself).

réplique /Replik/ nf reply; (riposte) retort; (objection) objection; (Théât) line; (copie) replica. **répliquer** 🔳 vt/i reply; (riposter) retort; (objecter) answer back.

répondeur /Repɔ̃dœʀ/ nm answering machine.

répondre /Repɔ̃dʀ/ 🔞 vt (injure, bêtise) reply with; ~ **que** answer ou reply that; ~ **à** (être conforme à) answer; (affection, sourire) return; (avances, appel, critique) respond to; ~ **de** answer for. ● vi answer, reply; (être insolent) answer back; (réagir) respond (à to).

réponse /Repɔ̃s/ nf answer, reply; (fig) response.

report /Rəpɔʀ/ nm (transcription) transfer; (renvoi) postponement.

reportage /Rəpɔʀtaʒ/ nm reportage; (par écrit) article.

reporter[1] /Rəpɔʀte/ 🔳 vt take back; (ajourner) put off; (transcrire) transfer. ☐ **se** ~ **à** vpr refer to.

reporter[2] /Rəpɔʀtɛʀ/ nm reporter.

repos /Rəpo/ nm rest; (paix) peace. **reposant,** ~e adj restful.

reposer /Rəpoze/ 🔳 vt put down again; (délasser) rest. ● vi rest (sur on); **laisser** ~ (pâte) leave to stand. ☐ **se** ~ vpr rest;

se ~ sur rely on.

repousser /ʀəpuse/ **1** vt push back; (écarter) push away; (dégoûter) repel; (décliner) reject; (ajourner) postpone, put back. ● vi grow again.

reprendre /ʀəpʀɑ̃dʀ/ **50** vt take back; (confiance, conscience) regain; (souffle) get back; (évadé) recapture; (recommencer) resume; (redire) repeat; (modifier) alter; (blâmer) reprimand; ~ du pain take some more bread; on ne m'y reprendra pas I won't be caught out again. ● vi (recommencer) resume; (affaires) pick up. □ se ~ vpr (se ressaisir) pull oneself together; (se corriger) correct oneself.

représailles /ʀəpʀezaj/ nfpl reprisals.

représentant, ~e /ʀəpʀezɑ̃tɑ̃, -t/ nm, f representative.

représentation /ʀəpʀezɑ̃tasjɔ̃/ nf representation; (Théât) performance.

représenter /ʀəpʀezɑ̃te/ **1** vt represent; (figures) depict, show; (pièce de théâtre) perform. □ se ~ vpr (s'imaginer) imagine.

répression /ʀepʀesjɔ̃/ nf repression; (d'élan) suppression.

réprimande /ʀepʀimɑ̃d/ nf reprimand.

réprimer /ʀepʀime/ **1** vt (peuple) repress; (sentiment) suppress; (fraude) crack down on.

reprise /ʀəpʀiz/ nf resumption; (Théât) revival; (TV) repeat; (de tissu) darn, mend; (essor) recovery; (Comm) part-exchange, trade-in; à plusieurs ~s on several occasions.

repriser /ʀəpʀize/ **1** vt darn, mend.

reproche /ʀəpʀɔʃ/ nm reproach; faire des ~s à find fault with.

reprocher /ʀəpʀɔʃe/ **1** vt ~ qch à qn reproach ou criticize sb for sth.

reproducteur, -trice /ʀəpʀɔdyktœʀ, -tʀis/ adj reproductive.

reproduire /ʀəpʀɔdɥiʀ/ **17** vt reproduce; (répéter) repeat. □ se ~ vpr reproduce; (se répéter) recur.

reptile /ʀɛptil/ nm reptile.

repu, ~e /ʀəpy/ adj satiated, replete.

républicain, ~e /ʀepyblikɛ̃, -ɛn/ adj & nm, f republican.

république /ʀepyblik/ nf republic; ~ populaire people's republic.

répudier /ʀepydje/ **45** vt repudiate; (droit) renounce.

répugnance /ʀepyɲɑ̃s/ nf repugnance; (hésitation) reluctance; avoir de la ~ pour loathe. **répugnant, ~e** adj repulsive.

répugner /ʀepyɲe/ **1** vt be repugnant to, disgust; ~ à (effort, violence) be averse to; ~ à faire be reluctant to do.

répulsion /ʀepylsjɔ̃/ nf repulsion.

réputation /ʀepytasjɔ̃/ nf reputation.

réputé, ~e /ʀepyte/ adj renowned (pour for); (école, compagnie) reputable; ~ pour être reputed to be.

requérir /ʀəkeʀiʀ/ **7** vt require, demand.

requête /ʀəkɛt/ nf request; (Jur) petition.

requin /ʀəkɛ̃/ nm shark.

requis, ~e /ʀəki, -z/ adj (exigé) required; (nécessaire) necessary.

RER abrév m (réseau express régional) Parisian rapid transit rail system.

rescapé, ~e /ʀɛskape/ nm, f survivor. ● adj surviving.

rescousse /ʀɛskus/ nf à la ~ to

the rescue.

réseau /pl ~x/ /Rezo/ nm network; ~ **local** local area network, LAN; **le des ~x** (Ordinat) Internet.

réservation /RezeRvasjɔ̃/ nf reservation, booking.

réserve /RezeRv/ nf reserve; (restriction) reservation, reserve; (indienne) reservation; (entrepôt) store-room; **en ~** in reserve; **les ~s** (Mil) the reserves.

réserver /RezeRve/ **1** vt reserve; (place) book, reserve. □ **se ~** vpr ~ **qch** save sth for oneself; **se ~ pour** save oneself for; **se ~ le droit de** reserve the right to.

réservoir /RezeRvwaR/ nm tank; (lac) reservoir.

résidence /Rezidãs/ nf residence; ~ **secondaire** second home; ~ **universitaire** hall of residence.

résident, ~e /Rezidã, -t/ nm, f resident; (étranger) foreign resident.

résider /Rezide/ **1** vi reside; ~ **dans qch** (difficulté) lie in.

résigner (se) /(sə)Rezine/ **1** vpr **se ~ à faire** resign oneself to doing.

résilier /Rezilje/ 45 vt terminate.

résine /Rezin/ nf resin.

résistance /Rezistãs/ nf resistance; (fil électrique) element. **résistant, ~e** adj tough.

résister /Reziste/ **1** vi resist; ~ **à** (agresseur, assaut, influence, tentation) resist; (corrosion, chaleur) withstand.

résolu, ~e /Rezɔly/ adj resolute; ~ **à faire** determined to do.
  ● ⇒RÉSOUDRE 59.

résolution /Rezɔlysjɔ̃/ nf (fermeté) resolution; (d'un problème) solving.

résonner /Rezɔne/ **1** vi resound.

résorber /RezɔRbe/ **1** vt reduce.

□ **se ~** vpr be reduced.

résoudre 59 vt solve; (crise, conflit) resolve. □ **se ~ à** vpr (se décider) resolve to; (se résigner) resign oneself to.

respect /Respɛ/ nm respect. **respectabilité** nf respectability.

respecter /Respɛkte/ **1** vt respect; **faire ~** (loi, décision) enforce.

respectueux, -euse /Respɛktɥø, -z/ adj respectful; ~ **de l'environnement** environmentally friendly.

respiration /RespiRasjɔ̃/ nf breathing; (haleine) breath. **respiratoire** adj respiratory, breathing.

respirer /RespiRe/ **1** vi breathe; (se reposer) catch one's breath. ● vt breathe (in); (exprimer) radiate.

resplendir /RɛsplãdiR/ **2** vi shine (de with). **resplendissant, ~e** adj brilliant, radiant.

responsabilité /Rɛspɔ̃sabilite/ nf responsibility; (légale) liability.

responsable /Rɛspɔ̃sabl/ adj responsible (de for); ~ **de** (chargé de) in charge of. ● nmf person in charge; (coupable) person responsible.

resquiller /Rɛskije/ **1** vi 🔢 (dans le train) fare-dodge; (au spectacle) get in without paying; (dans la queue) jump the queue.

ressaisir (se) /(sə)RəseziR/ **2** vpr pull oneself together; (équipe sportive, valeurs boursières) make a recovery.

ressemblance /Rəsãblãs/ nf resemblance.

ressemblant, ~e /Rəsãblã, -t/ adj **être ~** (portrait) be a good likeness.

ressembler /Rəsãble/ **1** vi ~ **à** resemble, look like. □ **se ~** vpr be alike; (physiquement) look alike.

ressentiment /Rəsɑ̃timɑ̃/ nm resentment.

ressentir /RəsɑtiR/ 46 vt feel. □ se ~ de vpr feel the effects of.

resserrer /RəseRe/ 1 vt tighten; (contracter) compress; (vêtement) take in. □ se ~ vpr tighten; (route) narrow; (se regrouper) move closer together.

ressort /RəsɔR/ nm (objet) spring; (fig) energy; être du ~ de be the province of; (Jur) be within the jurisdiction of; en dernier ~ as a last resort.

ressortir /RəsɔRtiR/ 46 vi go ou come back out; (se voir) stand out; (film, disque) be re-released; faire ~ bring out; il ressort que it emerges that. ● vt take out again; (redire) come out with again; (disque, film) re-release.

ressortissant, ~e /RəsɔRtisɑ̃, -t/ nm, f national.

ressource /RəsuRs/ nf resource; ~s resources; à bout de ~ at one's wits' end.

ressusciter /Resysite/ 1 vi come back to life. ● vt bring back to life; (fig) revive.

restant, ~e /Restɑ̃, -t/ adj remaining. ● nm remainder.

restaurant /RɛstɔRɑ̃/ nm restaurant.

restauration /RɛstɔRasjɔ̃/ nf restoration; (hôtellerie) catering.

restaurer /RɛstɔRe/ 1 vt restore. □ se ~ vpr eat.

reste /Rɛst/ nm rest; (d'une soustraction) remainder; ~s remains (de of); (nourriture) leftovers; un ~ de poulet some left-over chicken; au ~, du ~ moreover, besides.

rester /Rɛste/ 1 vi (aux être) stay, remain; (subsister) be left, remain; il reste du pain there is some

bread left (over); il me reste du pain I have some bread left (over); il me reste à it remains for me to; en ~ à go no further than; en ~ là stop there.

restituer /Rɛstitɥe/ 1 vt (rendre) return; (recréer) reproduce; (rétablir) reconstruct.

restreindre /RɛstRɛ̃dR/ 22 vt restrict. □ se ~ vpr (dans les dépenses) cut back.

restriction /Rɛstriksjɔ̃/ nf restriction.

résultat /Rezylta/ nm result.

résulter /Rezylte/ 1 vi ~ de result from, be the result of.

résumé /Rezyme/ nm summary; en ~ in short; (pour finir) to sum up.

résumer /Rezyme/ 1 vt summarize.

résurrection /RezyRɛksjɔ̃/ nf resurrection; (renouveau) revival.

rétablir /Retablir/ 2 vt restore; (personne) restore to health. □ se ~ vpr (ordre, silence) be restored; (guérir) recover. **rétablissement** nm restoration; (de malade, monnaie) recovery.

retard /RətaR/ nm lateness; (sur un programme) delay; (infériorité) backwardness; avoir du ~ be late; (montre) be slow; en ~ late; (retardé) behind; en ~ sur l'emploi du temps behind schedule; rattraper ou combler son ~ catch up; prendre du ~ fall behind.

retardataire /RətaRdatɛR/ nmf latecomer. ● adj late.

retarder /RətaRde/ 1 vt ~ qn/ qch delay sb/sth, hold sb/sth up; (par rapport à une heure convenue) make sb/sth late; (montre) put back. ● vi be slow; (personne) be out of touch.

retenir /RətniR/ 58 vt hold back; (souffle, attention, prisonnier) hold;

(*eau, chaleur*) retain, hold; (*larmes*) hold back; (*garder*) (retarder) detain, hold up; (*réserver*) book; (*se rappeler*) remember; (*déduire*) deduct; (*accepter*) accept. □ se ~ vpr (se contenir) restrain oneself; se ~ à hold on to; se ~ de faire stop oneself from doing.

rétention /retɑ̃sjɔ̃/ nf retention.

retentir /rətɑ̃tiːr/ ② vi ring out, resound; ~ sur have an impact on. **retentissant, ~e** adj resounding. **retentissement** nm (effet) effect.

retenue /rətny/ nf restraint; (*somme*) deduction; (Scol) detention.

réticent, ~e /retisɑ̃, -t/ adj (hésitant) hesitant; (qui rechigne) reluctant; (réservé) reticent.

rétine /retin/ nf retina.

retiré, ~e /rətiːre/ adj (vie) secluded; (*lieu*) remote.

retirer /rətiːre/ ① vt (sortir) take out; (ôter) take off; (*argent, offre, candidature*) withdraw; (écarter) (*main, pied*) withdraw; (*billet, bagages*) collect, pick up; (*avantage*) derive; ~ à qn take away from sb. □ se ~ vpr withdraw, retire.

retombées /rətɔ̃be/ nfpl (conséquences) effects; ~ radioactives nuclear fall-out.

retomber /rətɔ̃be/ ① vi (faire une chute) fall again; (retourner au sol) land, come down; ~ dans (*erreur*) fall back into.

retouche /rətuʃ/ nf alteration; (de photo, tableau) retouch.

retour /rətuːr/ nm return; être de ~ be back (de from); ~ en arrière flashback; par ~ du courrier by return of post; en ~ in return.

retourner /rəturne/ ① vt (aux avoir) turn over; (*vêtement*) turn inside out; (*maison*) turn upside

down; (*lettre, compliment*) return; (émouvoir ①) shake, upset. ● vi (aux être) go back, return. □ se ~ vpr turn round, turn back; (tourner) turn and turn; s'en ~ go back; se ~ contre turn against.

retrait /rətrɛ/ nm withdrawal; (des eaux) receding; être (situé) en ~ (de) be set back (from).

retraite /rətrɛt/ nf retirement; (pension) (retirement) pension; (fuite, refuge) retreat; mettre à la ~ pension off; prendre sa ~ retire. **retraité, ~e** /rətrete/ adj retired. ● nm, f (old-age) pensioner.

retrancher /rətrɑ̃ʃe/ ① vt remove; (soustraire) deduct, subtract. □ se ~ vpr (Mil) entrench oneself; se ~ derrière take refuge behind.

retransmettre /rətrɑ̃smɛtr/ ④② vt broadcast.

rétrécir /retresiːr/ ② vt make narrower; (*vêtement*) take in. ● vi (*tissu*) shrink. □ se ~ vpr (*rue*) narrow.

rétribution /retribysjɔ̃/ nf payment.

rétroactif, -ive /retroaktif, -v/ adj retrospective; augmentation à effet ~ backdated pay rise.

retrousser /rətruse/ ① vt pull up; (*manche*) roll up.

retrouvailles /rətruvaj/ nfpl reunion.

retrouver /rətruve/ ① vt find (again); (rejoindre) meet (again); (*forces, calme*) regain; (*lieu*) be back in; (se rappeler) remember. □ se ~ vpr find oneself (back); (se réunir) meet (again); (être présent) be found; s'y ~ (s'orienter, comprendre) find one's way; (rentrer dans ses frais ①) break even.

rétroviseur /retrovizœr/ nm (Auto) (rear-view) mirror.

réunion /reynjɔ̃/ nf meeting; (rencontre) gathering; (après une séparation) réunion; (d'objets) collection.

réunir /ʁeyniʁ/ **2** vt gather, collect; (rapprocher) bring together; (convoquer) call together; (raccorder) join; (qualités) combine. □ se ~ vpr meet.

réussi, ~e /ʁeysi/ adj successful.

réussir /ʁeysiʁ/ **2** vi succeed, be successful; ~ à faire succeed in doing, manage to do; ~ à un examen pass an exam; ~ à qn (méthode) work well for sb.; (climat, mode de vie) agree with sb. ● vt (vie) make a success of.

réussite /ʁeysit/ nf success; (jeu) patience.

revaloir /ʁəvalwaʁ/ **60** vt je vous revaudrai cela (en mal) I'll pay you back for this; (en bien) I'll repay you some day.

revanche /ʁəvɑ̃ʃ/ nf revenge; (Sport) return ou revenge match; en ~ on the other hand.

rêvasser /ʁevase/ **1** vi daydream.

rêve /ʁɛv/ nm dream; faire un ~ have a dream.

réveil /ʁevɛj/ nm waking up, (fig) awakening; (pendule) alarm clock.

réveillé, ~e /ʁeveje/ adj awake.

réveille-matin /ʁevɛjmatɛ̃/ nm inv alarm clock.

réveiller /ʁeveje/ **1** vt wake (up); (sentiment, souvenir) awaken; (curiosité) arouse. □ se ~ vpr wake up.

réveillon /ʁevɛjɔ̃/ nm (Noël) Christmas Eve; (nouvel an) New Year's Eve. **réveillonner** **1** vi see Christmas ou the New Year in.

révéler /ʁevele/ **14** vt reveal. □ se ~ vpr be revealed; se ~ facile turn out to be easy, prove easy.

revendeur, -euse /ʁəvɑ̃dœʁ, -øz/ nm, f dealer, stockist; ~ de drogue

drug dealer.

revendication /ʁəvɑ̃dikasjɔ̃/ nf claim. **revendiquer** **1** vt claim.

revendre /ʁəvɑ̃dʁ/ **3** vt sell (again); avoir de l'énergie à ~ have energy to spare.

revenir /ʁəvniʁ/ **58** vi (aux être) come back, return (à to); ~ à (activité) go back to; (se résumer à) come down to; (échoir à) fall to; ~ à 100 euros cost 100 euros; ~ de (maladie, surprise) get over; ~ sur ses pas retrace one's steps; faire ~ (Culin) brown; ça me revient! now I remember!; je n'en reviens pas! ⚠ I can't get over it!

revenu /ʁəvny/ nm income; (de l'État) revenue.

rêver /ʁeve/ **1** vt/i dream (à de; faire of doing).

réverbère /ʁeveʁbɛʁ/ nm street lamp.

révérence /ʁeveʁɑ̃s/ nf reverence; (salut d'homme) bow; (salut de femme) curtsy.

rêverie /ʁevʁi/ nf daydream; (activité) daydreaming.

revers /ʁəvɛʁ/ nm reverse; (de main) back; (d'étoffe) wrong side; (de veste) lapel; (de pantalon) turn-up; (de manche) cuff; (tennis) backhand; (fig) set-back.

revêtement /ʁəvɛtmɑ̃/ nm covering; (de route) surface; ~ de sol floor covering. **revêtir** **61** vt cover; (habit) put on; (prendre, avoir) assume.

rêveur, -euse /ʁevœʁ, -øz/ adj dreamy. ● nm, f dreamer.

réviser /ʁevize/ **1** vt revise; (machine, véhicule) service. **révision** nf revision; service.

revivre /ʁəvivʁ/ **62** vi come alive again. ● vt relive.

révocation /ʁevɔkasjɔ̃/ nf repeal;

(d'un fonctionnaire) dismissal.

revoir¹ /ʀəvwaʀ/ [58] *vt* see (again); (réviser) revise.

revoir² /ʀəvwaʀ/ *nm* au ∼ goodbye.

révolte /ʀevɔlt/ *nf* revolt. **révolté, ∼e** *nm, f* rebel.

révolter /ʀevɔlte/ [1] *vt* appal, revolt. □ **se ∼** *vpr* revolt.

révolu, ∼e /ʀevɔly/ *adj* past; avoir 21 ans ∼s be over 21 years of age.

révolution /ʀevɔlysjɔ̃/ *nf* revolution. **révolutionnaire** *adj & nmf* revolutionary. **révolutionner** [1] *vt* revolutionize.

revolver /ʀevɔlvɛʀ/ *nm* revolver, gun.

révoquer /ʀevɔke/ [1] *vt* repeal; (*fonctionnaire*) dismiss.

revue /ʀəvy/ *nf* (examen, défilé) review; (magazine) magazine; (spectacle) variety show.

rez-de-chaussée /ʀedʃose/ *nm inv* ground floor; (US) first floor.

RF *abrév f* (**République Française**) French Republic.

rhinocéros /ʀinɔseʀos/ *nm* rhinoceros.

rhubarbe /ʀybaʀb/ *nf* rhubarb.

rhum /ʀɔm/ *nm* rum.

rhumatisme /ʀymatism/ *nm* rheumatism.

rhume /ʀym/ *nm* cold; ∼ des foins hay fever.

ri /ʀi/ ➔**RIRE** [54].

ricaner /ʀikane/ [1] *vi* snigger.

riche /ʀiʃ/ *adj* rich (en *in*). ● *nmf* rich man, rich woman.

richesse /ʀiʃes/ *nf* wealth; (de sol, décor) richness; ∼s wealth; (ressources) resources.

ride /ʀid/ *nf* wrinkle; (sur l'eau) ripple.

rideau (*pl* ∼x) /ʀido/ *nm* curtain;

(métallique) shutter; (fig) screen.

ridicule /ʀidikyl/ *adj* ridiculous. ● *nm* (d'une situation) absurdity; (le grotesque) le ∼ ridicule. **ridiculiser** [1] *vt* ridicule.

rien /ʀjɛ̃/ *pron* nothing; (quoi que ce soit) anything; de ∼! I don't mention it!; ∼ de bon nothing good; elle n'a ∼ dit she didn't say anything; ∼ d'autre/de plus nothing else/more; ∼ du tout nothing at all; ∼ que (seulement) just, only; trois fois ∼ next to nothing; il n'y est pour ∼ he has nothing to do with it; ∼ à faire! (c'est impossible) it's no good!; (refus) no way! [1]. ● *nm* un ∼ de a touch of; être puni pour un ∼ be punished for the slightest thing; se disputer pour un ∼ fight over nothing; en un ∼ de temps in next to no time.

rieur, -euse /ʀijœʀ, -øz/ *adj* cheerful; (*yeux*) laughing.

rigide /ʀiʒid/ *adj* rigid.

rigolade /ʀigɔlad/ *nf* fun.

rigoler /ʀigɔle/ [1] *vi* laugh; (s'amuser) have some fun; (plaisanter) joke.

rigolo, -te /ʀigɔlo, -ɔt/ *adj* [1] funny. ● *nm, f* [1] joker.

rigoureux, -euse /ʀiguʀø, -z/ *adj* rigorous; (*hiver*) harsh; (sévère) strict; (*travail, recherches*) meticulous.

rigueur /ʀigœʀ/ *nf* rigour; à la ∼ at a pinch; être de ∼ be obligatory; tenir ∼ à qn de qch bear sb a grudge for sth.

rime /ʀim/ *nf* rhyme.

rimer /ʀime/ [1] *vi* rhyme (avec *with*); cela ne rime à rien it makes no sense.

rinçage /ʀɛ̃saʒ/ *nm* rinse; (action) rinsing.

rincer /ʀɛ̃se/ [10] *vt* rinse.

r

riposte /Ripɔst/ nf retort.

riposter /Ripɔste/ **1** vi retaliate; ~ à (attaque) counter; (insulte) reply to. ● vt retort (que that).

rire /RiR/ **54** vi laugh (de at); (plaisanter) joke; (s'amuser) have fun; c'était pour ~ it was a joke. ● nm laugh; des ~s laughter.

risée /Rize/ nf la ~ de the laughing stock of.

risque /Risk/ nm risk. **risqué, ~e** adj risky; (osé) daring.

risquer /Riske/ **1** vt risk (de faire de doing); (être passible de) face; il risque de pleuvoir it might rain; tu risques de te faire mal you might hurt yourself. □ se ~ à/ dans vpr venture to/into.

ristourne /Risturn/ nf discount.

rite /Rit/ nm rite; (habitude) ritual. **rituel, ~le** adj & nm ritual.

rivage /Rivaʒ/ nm shore.

rival, ~e /Rival, -o/ adj (mpl -aux) rival. & nm, f rival. **rivaliser** **1** vi compete (avec with). **rivalité** nf rivalry.

rive /Riv/ nf (de fleuve) bank; (de lac) shore.

riverain, ~e /RivRɛ̃, -ɛn/ adj riverside. ● nm, f riverside resident; (d'une rue) resident.

rivière /RivjɛR/ nf river.

riz /Ri/ nm rice. **rizière** nf paddy field.

robe /Rɔb/ nf (de femme) dress; (de juge) robe; (de cheval) coat; ~ de chambre dressing-gown.

robinet /Rɔbinɛ/ nm tap; (US) faucet.

robot /Rɔbo/ nm robot; ~ ménager food processor.

robuste /Rɔbyst/ adj robust.

roche /Rɔʃ/ nf rock.

rocher /Rɔʃe/ nm rock.

rock /Rɔk/ nm (Mus) rock.

rodage /Rɔdaʒ/ nm en ~ (Auto) running in.

roder /Rɔde/ **1** vt (Auto) run in; être rodé (personne) have got the hang of things.

rôder /Rɔde/ **1** vi roam; (suspect) prowl.

rogne /Rɔɲ/ nf **①** anger; en ~ in a temper.

rogner /Rɔɲe/ **1** vt trim; ~ sur cut down on.

rognon /Rɔɲɔ̃/ nm (Culin) kidney.

roi /Rwa/ nm king; les R ~ mages the Magi; la fête des R~ Twelfth Night.

rôle /Rol/ nm role, part.

roller /RɔlɛR/ nm (patin) rollerblade®; (activité) rollerblading.

romain, ~e /Rɔmɛ̃, -ɛn/ adj Roman. R~, ~e nm, f Roman. **romaine** nf (laitue) cos.

roman /Rɔmɑ̃/ nm novel; (genre) fiction.

romance /Rɔmɑ̃s/ nf ballad.

romancier, -ière /Rɔmɑ̃sje, -jɛR/ nm, f novelist.

romanesque /Rɔmanɛsk/ adj romantic; (fantastique) fantastic; (récit) fictional; œuvres ~s novels, fiction.

romantique /Rɔmɑ̃tik/ adj & nmf romantic. **romantisme** nm romanticism.

rompre /RɔpR/ **3** vt break; (relations) break off. ● vi (se séparer) break up; ~ avec (fiancé) break up with; (parti) break away from; (tradition) break with. □ se ~ vpr break.

ronce /Rɔs/ nf bramble.

rond, ~e /Rɔ̃, -d/ adj round; (gras) plump; (ivre) **①** drunk. ● nm (cercle) ring; (tranche) slice; en ~ in a circle; il n'a pas un ~ **①** he hasn't got a penny.

ronde /ʀɔ̃d/ *nf* (de policier) beat; (de soldat, gardien) watch; (Mus) semibreve.

rondelle /ʀɔ̃dɛl/ *nf* (Tech) washer; (tranche) slice.

rondement /ʀɔ̃dmɑ̃/ *adv* promptly; (franchement) frankly.

rondeur /ʀɔ̃dœʀ/ *nf* roundness; (franchise) frankness; (embonpoint) plumpness.

rondin /ʀɔ̃dɛ̃/ *nm* log.

rond-point (*pl* ronds-points) /ʀɔ̃pwɛ̃/ *nm* roundabout; (US) traffic circle.

ronfler /ʀɔ̃fle/ **1** *vi* snore; (moteur) purr.

ronger /ʀɔ̃ʒe/ **40** *vt* gnaw (at); (vers, acide) eat into. □ **se ~** *vpr* **~ les ongles** bite one's nails.

rongeur /ʀɔ̃ʒœʀ/ *nm* rodent.

ronronner /ʀɔ̃ʀɔne/ **1** *vi* purr.

rosbif /ʀɔsbif/ *nm* roast beef.

rose /ʀoz/ *nf* rose. ● *adj* & *nm* pink.

rosé, ~e /ʀoze/ *adj* pinkish. ● *nm* rosé.

roseau (*pl* ~x) /ʀozo/ *nm* reed.

rosée /ʀoze/ *nf* dew.

rosier /ʀozje/ *nm* rose bush.

rossignol /ʀɔsiɲɔl/ *nm* nightingale.

rotatif, -ive /ʀɔtatif, -v/ *adj* rotary.

roter /ʀɔte/ **1** *vi* **1** burp.

rôti /ʀoti/ *nm* joint; (cuit) roast; **~ de porc** roast pork.

rotin /ʀɔtɛ̃/ *nm* (rattan) cane.

rôtir /ʀotiʀ/ **2** *vi* roast.

rôtissoire /ʀotiswaʀ/ *nf* roasting spit.

rotule /ʀɔtyl/ *nf* kneecap.

rouage /ʀwaʒ/ *nm* (Tech) wheel; **les ~s** the works; (d'une organisation: fig) wheels.

roucouler /ʀukule/ **1** *vi* coo.

roue /ʀu/ *nf* wheel; **~ dentée** cog

(wheel); **~ de secours** spare wheel.

rouer /ʀwe/ **1** *vt* **~ de coups** thrash.

rouge /ʀuʒ/ *adj* red; (fer) red-hot. ● *nm* red; (vin) red wine; (fard) blusher; **~ à lèvres** lipstick. ● *nmf* (Pol) red. **rouge-gorge** (*pl* rouges-gorges) *nm* robin.

rougeole /ʀuʒɔl/ *nf* measles (+ *sg*). **rouget** /ʀuʒɛ/ *nm* red mullet.

rougeur /ʀuʒœʀ/ *nf* redness; (tache) red blotch.

rougir /ʀuʒiʀ/ **2** *vi* turn red; (de honte) blush.

rouille /ʀuj/ *nf* rust. **rouillé, ~e** *adj* rusty.

rouiller /ʀuje/ **1** *vi* rust. □ **se ~** *vpr* get rusty.

rouleau (*pl* ~x) /ʀulo/ *nm* roll; (outil, vague) roller; **~ à pâtisserie** rolling pin; **~ compresseur** steamroller.

roulement /ʀulmɑ̃/ *nm* rotation; (bruit) rumble; (alternance) rotation; (de tambour) roll; **~ à billes** ballbearing; **travailler par ~** work in shifts.

rouler /ʀule/ **1** *vt* roll; (ficelle, manches) roll up; (pâte) roll out; (duper **1**) cheat. ● *vi* (véhicule, train) go, travel; (conducteur) drive. □ **se ~ dans** *vpr* (herbe) roll in; (couverture) roll oneself up in.

roulette /ʀulɛt/ *nf* (de meuble) castor; (de dentiste) drill; (jeu) roulette; **comme sur des ~s** very smoothly.

roulotte /ʀulɔt/ *nf* caravan.

roumain, ~e /ʀumɛ̃, -ɛn/ *adj* Romanian. **R~, ~e** *nm, f* Romanian.

Roumanie /ʀumani/ *nf* Romania.

rouquin, ~e /ʀukɛ̃, -in/ **1** *adj* redhaired. ● *nm, f* redhead.

rouspéter /ʀuspete/ **14** *vi* **1** grumble, moan.

rousse /ʀus/ →ROUX.

roussir /ʀusiʀ/ ② *vt* scorch. ● *vi* turn brown.

route /ʀut/ *nf* road; (Naut, Aviat) route; (direction) way; (voyage) journey; (chemin: fig) path; en ∼ on the way; en ∼! let's go!; mettre en ∼ start; ∼ nationale trunk road, main road; se mettre en ∼ set out.

routier, -ière /ʀutje, -jɛʀ/ *adj* road. ● *nm* long-distance lorry *ou* truck driver; (restaurant) transport café; (US) truck stop.

routine /ʀutin/ *nf* routine.

roux, rousse /ʀu, ʀus/ *adj* red, russet; (*personne*) red-haired; (*chat*) ginger. ● *nm, f* redhead.

royal, ∼e (*mpl* -**aux**) /ʀwajal, -jo/ *adj* royal; (*cadeau*) fit for a king.

royaume /ʀwajom/ *nm* kingdom.

Royaume-Uni /ʀwajomyni/ *nm* United Kingdom.

royauté /ʀwajote/ *nf* royalty.

RTT *abrév f* (**réduction du temps de travail**) reduction in working hours.

ruban /ʀybɑ̃/ *nm* ribbon; (de chapeau) band; ∼ adhésif sticky tape; ∼ magnétique magnetic tape.

rubéole /ʀybeɔl/ *nf* German measles (+ *sg*).

rubis /ʀybi/ *nm* ruby.

rubrique /ʀybʀik/ *nf* heading; (article) column.

ruche /ʀyʃ/ *nf* beehive.

rude /ʀyd/ *adj* (au toucher) rough; (pénible) tough; (grossier) coarse; (fameux 🔝) tremendous.

rudement /ʀydmɑ̃/ *adv* (frapper) hard; (traiter) harshly; (très 🔝) really.

rudimentaire /ʀydimɑ̃tɛʀ/ *adj* rudimentary.

rue /ʀy/ *nf* street.

ruée /ʀɥe/ *nf* rush.

ruer /ʀɥe/ ① *vi* (cheval) buck. □ se ∼ *vpr* rush (dans into; vers towards); se ∼ sur pounce on.

rugby /ʀygbi/ *nm* rugby.

rugir /ʀyʒiʀ/ ② *vi* roar.

rugueux, -euse /ʀygø, -z/ *adj* rough.

ruine /ʀɥin/ *nf* ruin; en (∼s) in ruins. **ruiner** ① *vt* ruin.

ruisseau (*pl* ∼**x**) /ʀɥiso/ *nm* stream; (rigole) gutter.

rumeur /ʀymœʀ/ *nf* (nouvelle) rumour; (son) murmur, hum.

ruminer /ʀymine/ ① *vi* (animal) ruminate; (méditer) meditate.

rupture /ʀyptyʀ/ *nf* break; (action) breaking; (de contrat) breach; (de pourparlers) breakdown; (de relations) breaking off; (de couple, coalition) break-up.

rural, ∼e (*mpl* -**aux**) /ʀyʀal, -o/ *adj* rural.

ruse /ʀyz/ *nf* cunning; une ∼ a trick, a ruse. **rusé, ∼e** *adj* cunning.

russe /ʀys/ *adj* Russian. ● *nm* (Ling) Russian. **R∼** *nmf* Russian.

Russie /ʀysi/ *nf* Russia.

rustique /ʀystik/ *adj* rustic.

rythme /ʀitm/ *nm* rhythm; (vitesse) rate; (de la vie) pace. **rythmique** *adj* rhythmical.

················

Ss

s' /s/ →SE.

sa /sa/ →SON¹.

SA *abrév f* (**société anonyme**) PLC.

sabbatique /sabatik/ *adj* (année) sabbatical year.

sable /sabl/ nm sand; ~s mouvants quicksands. **sabler** vt **1** grit.

sablier /sablije/ nm (Culin) eggtimer.

sablonneux, -euse /sablonø, -z/ adj sandy.

sabot /sabo/ nm (de cheval) hoof; (chaussure) clog; (de frein) shoe; ~ de Denver® (wheel) clamp.

saboter /sabote/ **1** vt sabotage; (bâcler) botch.

sac /sak/ nm bag; (grand, en toile) sack; mettre à ~ (maison) ransack; (ville) sack; ~ à dos rucksack; ~ à main handbag; ~ de couchage sleeping-bag; mettre dans le même ~ lump together.

saccadé, ~e /sakade/ adj jerky.

saccager /sakaʒe/ **40** vt (abîmer) wreck; (maison) ransack; (ville, pays) sack.

saccharine /sakaʀin/ nf saccharin.

sachet /saʃɛ/ nm (small) bag; (d'aromates) sachet; ~ de thé teabag.

sacoche /sakɔʃ/ nf bag; (de vélo) saddlebag.

sacre /sakʀ/ nm (de roi) coronation; (d'évêque) consecration.

sacré, ~e adj sacred; (maudit **1**) damned. **sacrement** nm sacrament. **sacrer** **1** vt crown; consecrate.

sacrifice /sakʀifis/ nm sacrifice.

sacrifier /sakʀifje/ **45** vt sacrifice; ~ à conform to. □ **se ~** vpr sacrifice oneself.

sacrilège /sakʀilɛʒ/ nm sacrilege. ● adj sacrilegious.

sadique /sadik/ adj sadistic. ● nmf sadist.

sage /saʒ/ adj wise; (docile) good, well behaved. ● nm wise man.

sage-femme (pl **sages-femmes**) /saʒfam/ nf midwife.

sagesse /saʒɛs/ nf wisdom.

Sagittaire /saʒitɛʀ/ nm le ~ Sagittarius.

saignant, ~e /sɛɲɑ̃, -t/ adj (Culin) rare.

saigner /seɲe/ **1** vt/i bleed; ~ du nez have a nosebleed.

saillant, ~e /sajɑ̃, -t/ adj prominent.

sain, ~e /sɛ̃, sɛn/ adj healthy; (moralement) sane; ~ et sauf safe and sound.

saindoux /sɛ̃du/ nm lard.

saint, ~e /sɛ̃, -t/ adj holy; (bon, juste) saintly. ● nm, f saint. **Saint-Esprit** nm Holy Spirit. **sainteté** nf holiness; (d'un lieu) sanctity. **Sainte Vierge** nf Blessed Virgin. **Saint-Sylvestre** nf New Year's Eve.

sais /sɛ/ →SAVOIR **55**.

saisie /sezi/ nf (Jur) seizure; (Comput) keyboarding; ~ de données data capture.

saisir /seziʀ/ **2** vt grab (hold of); (proie) seize; (occasion, biens) seize; (comprendre) grasp; (frapper) strike; (Ordinat) keyboard, capture; saisi de (peur) stricken by, overcome by. □ **se ~ de** vpr seize. **saisissant, ~e** adj (spectacle) gripping.

saison /sezɔ̃/ nf season; la morte ~ the off season. **saisonnier, -ière** adj seasonal.

sait /sɛ/ →SAVOIR **55**.

salade /salad/ nf (plat) salad; (plante) lettuce. **saladier** nm salad bowl.

salaire /salɛʀ/ nm wages (+ pl), salary.

salarié, ~e /salaʀje/ adj wage-earning. ● nm, f wage earner.

sale /sal/ adj dirty; (mauvais) nasty.

salé, ~e /sale/ adj (goût) salty; (plat) salted; (opposé à sucré) savoury; (grivois **1**) spicy; (excessif

Ⅱ) steep. **saler** ❶ vt salt.

saleté /salte/ nf dirtiness; (crasse) dirt; (obscénité) obscenity; ~(s) (camelote) rubbish; (détritus) mess.

salir /saliʀ/ ❷ vt (make) dirty; (réputation) tarnish. □ se ~ vpr get dirty. **salissant**, ~e adj dirty; (étoffe) easily dirtied.

salive /saliv/ nf saliva.

salle /sal/ nf room; (grande, publique) hall; (de restaurant) dining room; (Théât, cinéma) auditorium; cinéma à trois ~s three-screen cinema; ~ à manger dining room; ~ d'attente waiting room; ~ de bains bathroom;~ de causette chatroom; ~ de séjour living room; ~ de classe classroom; ~ d'embarquement departure lounge; ~ d'opération operating theatre; ~ des ventes saleroom.

salon /salɔ̃/ nm lounge; (de coiffure, beauté) salon; (exposition) show; ~ de thé tea-room; ~ virtuel chatroom.

salopette /salɔpɛt/ nf dungarees (+ pl); (d'ouvrier) overalls (+ pl).

saltimbanque /saltɛ̃bɑ̃k/ nmf (street) acrobat.

salubre /salybʀ/ adj healthy.

saluer /salɥe/ ❶ vt greet; (en partant) take one's leave of; (de la tête) nod to; (de la main) wave to; (Mil) salute; (accueillir favorablement) welcome.

salut /saly/ nm greeting; (de la tête) nod; (de la main) wave; (Mil) salute; (rachat) salvation. ●interj (bonjour Ⅱ) hello; (au revoir Ⅱ) bye.

salutation /salytasjɔ̃/ nf greeting.

samedi /samdi/ nm Saturday.

SAMU /samy/ abrév m (**Service d'assistance médicale d'urgence**) ≈ mobile accident unit.

sanction /sɑ̃ksjɔ̃/ nf sanction. **sanctionner** ❶ vt sanction; (punir) punish.

sandale /sɑ̃dal/ nf sandal.

sang /sɑ̃/ nm blood; se faire du mauvais ~ ou un ~ d'encre be worried stiff. **sang-froid** nm inv self-control. **sanglant**, ~e adj bloody.

sangle /sɑ̃gl/ nf strap.

sanglier /sɑ̃glije/ nm wild boar.

sanglot /sɑ̃glo/ nm sob. **sangloter** ❶ vi sob.

sanguin, ~e /sɑ̃gɛ̃, -in/ adj (groupe) blood.

sanguinaire /sɑ̃ginɛʀ/ adj bloodthirsty.

sanitaire /sanitɛʀ/ adj (directives) health; (conditions) sanitary; (appareils, installations) bathroom, sanitary. **sanitaires** nmpl bathroom.

sans /sɑ̃/ prép without; ~ ça, ~ quoi otherwise; ~ arrêt nonstop; ~ encombre/faute/tarder without incident/fail/delay; ~ fin/goût/limite endless/tasteless/limitless; ~ importance/pareil/précédent/travail unimportant/unparalleled/unprecedented/unemployed; j'ai aimé mais ~ plus it was good, it wasn't great.

sans-abri /sɑ̃zabri/ nmf inv homeless person.

sans-gêne /sɑ̃ʒɛn/ adj inv inconsiderate, thoughtless. ●nm inv thoughtlessness.

sans-papiers /sɑ̃papje/ nm inv illegal immigrant.

santé /sɑ̃te/ nf health; à ta ou

votre ∼! cheers!

saoul, ∼**e** /su, sul/ ➡SOUL.

sapin /sapɛ̃/ *nm* fir (tree); ∼ **de Noël** Christmas tree.

sarcasme /saRkasm/ *nm* sarcasm. **sarcastique** *adj* sarcastic.

sardine /saRdin/ *nf* sardine.

sas /sɑs/ *nm* (Naut, Aviat) airlock.

satané, ∼**e** /satane/ *adj* ⓵ damned.

satellite /satelit/ *nm* satellite.

satin /satɛ̃/ *nm* satin.

satire /satiR/ *nf* satire.

satisfaction /satisfaksjɔ̃/ *nf* satisfaction.

satisfaire /satisfɛR/ 53 *vt* satisfy. ● *vi* ∼ **à** fulfil. **satisfaisant**, ∼**e** *adj* (acceptable) satisfactory. **satisfait**, ∼**e** *adj* satisfied (**de** with).

saturer /satyRe/ ⓵ *vt* saturate.

sauce /sos/ *nf* sauce; ∼ **tartare** tartar sauce. **saucière** *nf* sauceboat.

saucisse /sosis/ *nf* sausage.

saucisson /sosisɔ̃/ *nm* (slicing) sausage.

sauf¹ /sof/ *prép* except; ∼ **erreur** if I'm not mistaken; ∼ **imprévu** unless anything unforeseen happens; ∼ **avis contraire** unless otherwise stated.

sauf², **-ve** /sof, sov/ *adj* safe, unharmed.

sauge /soʒ/ *nf* (Culin) sage.

saule /sol/ *nm* willow; ∼ **pleureur** weeping willow.

saumon /somɔ̃/ *nm* salmon. ● *adj inv* salmon-(pink).

sauna /sona/ *nm* sauna.

saupoudrer /sopudRe/ ⓵ *vt* sprinkle (**de** with).

saut /so/ *nm* jump; **faire un** ∼ **chez qn** pop round to sb's (place); **le** ∼ (Sport) jumping; ∼ **en hauteur/longueur** high/long jump;

∼ **périlleux** somersault; **au** ∼ **du lit** on getting up.

sauté, ∼**e** /sote/ *adj* & *nm* (Culin) sauté.

saute-mouton /sotmutɔ̃/ *nm inv* leap-frog.

sauter /sote/ ⓵ *vi* jump; (exploser) blow up; (*fusible*) blow; (se détacher) come off; **faire** ∼ (détruire) blow up; (*fusible*) blow; (casser) break; ∼ **à la corde** skip; ∼ **aux yeux** be obvious; ∼ **au cou de qn** fling one's arms round sb; ∼ **sur une occasion** jump at an opportunity. ● *vt* jump (over); (page, classe) skip.

sauterelle /sotRɛl/ *nf* grasshopper.

sautiller /sotije/ ⓵ *vi* hop.

sauvage /sovaʒ/ *adj* wild; (primitif, cruel) savage; (farouche) unsociable; (illégal) unauthorized. ● *nmf* unsociable person; (brute) savage.

sauve /sov/ ➡SAUF.²

sauvegarder /sovgaRde/ ⓵ *vt* safeguard; (Ordinat) back up.

sauver /sove/ ⓵ *vt* save; (d'un danger) rescue, save; (matériel) salvage. □ **se** ∼ *vpr* (fuir) run away; (partir) be off. **sauvetage** *nm* rescue. **sauveteur** *nm* rescuer. **sauveur** *nm* saviour.

savant, ∼**e** /savɑ̃, -t/ *adj* learned; (habile) skilful. ● *nm* scientist.

saveur /savœR/ *nf* flavour; (fig) savour.

savoir /savwaR/ 55 *vt* know; **elle sait conduire/nager** she can drive/ swim; **faire** ∼ **à qn que** inform sb that; **(pas) que je sache** (not) as far as I know; **à** ∼ namely. ● *nm* learning.

savon /savɔ̃/ *nm* soap; **passer un** ∼ **à qn** ⓵ give sb a telling-off. **savonnette** *nf* bar of soap.

savourer /savuRe/ ⓵ *vt* savour. **savoureux**, **-euse** *adj* tasty;

scandale | se

(fig) spicy.
scandale /skɑ̃dal/ *nm* scandal; (tapage) uproar; (en public) noisy scene; faire ~ shock people; faire un ~ make a scene. **scandaleux, -euse** *adj* scandalous. **scandaliser** **1** *vt* scandalize, shock.

scander /skɑ̃de/ **1** *vt* (vers) scan; (slogan) chant.

scandinave /skɑ̃dinav/ *adj* Scandinavian. **S~** *nmf* Scandinavian.

Scandinavie /skɑ̃dinavi/ *nf* Scandinavia.

scarabée /skaʁabe/ *nm* beetle.

sceau (*pl* ~**x**) /so/ *nm* seal.

scélérat /selera/ *nm* scoundrel.

sceller /sele/ **1** *vt* seal.

scène /sɛn/ *nf* scene; (estrade, art dramatique) stage; mettre en ~ (pièce) stage; (film) direct; mise en ~ direction; ~ de ménage domestic dispute.

scepticisme /sɛptisism/ *nm* scepticism.

sceptique /sɛptik/ *adj* sceptical. ● *nmf* sceptic.

schéma /ʃema/ *nm* diagram. **schématique** *adj* schematic; (sommaire) sketchy. **schématiser** **1** *vt* simplify.

schizophrène /skizɔfʁɛn/ *adj & nmf* schizophrenic.

sciatique /sjatik/ *adj* (nerf) sciatic. ● *nf* sciatica.

scie /si/ *nf* saw.

sciemment /sjamɑ̃/ *adv* knowingly.

science /sjɑ̃s/ *nf* science; (savoir) knowledge.

science-fiction /sjɑ̃sfiksjɔ̃/ *nf* science fiction.

scientifique /sjɑ̃tifik/ *adj* scientific. ● *nmf* scientist.

scier /sje/ **45** *vt* saw.

scintiller /sɛ̃tije/ **1** *vi* glitter; (étoile) twinkle.

scission /sisjɔ̃/ *nf* split.

sclérose /skleʁoz/ *nf* sclerosis; ~ en plaques multiple sclerosis.

scolaire /skɔlɛʁ/ *adj* school. **scolarisé, -e** *adj* going to school. **scolarité** *nf* schooling.

score /skɔʁ/ *nm* score.

scorpion /skɔʁpjɔ̃/ *nm* scorpion; le S~ Scorpio.

scotch /skɔtʃ/ *nm* (boisson) Scotch (whisky); (ruban adhésif)® Sellotape®.

scout, -e /skut/ *nm & adj* scout.

scrupule /skʁypyl/ *nm* scruple. **scrupuleux, -euse** *adj* scrupulous.

scruter /skʁyte/ **1** *vt* examine, scrutinize.

scrutin /skʁytɛ̃/ *nm* (vote) ballot; (élections) polls (+ *pl*).

sculpter /skylte/ **1** *vt* sculpt, carve. **sculpteur** *nm* sculptor. **sculpture** *nf* sculpture.

SDF *abrév m* (sans domicile fixe) homeless person.

---

se, s' /sə, s/

s' before vowel or mute h.

● *pronom*
···▸ himself, (féminin) herself; (indéfini) oneself; (non humain) itself; (au pluriel) themselves; ~ laver les mains wash one's hands; (réciproque) each other, one another; ils se détestent they hate each other.

❗ The translation of se will vary according to which verb it is associated with. You should therefore refer to the verb to find it. For example, se promener, se taire will be treated respectively under promener and taire.

séance /seɑ̃s/ *nf* session; (Théât, cinéma) show; ~ **de pose** sitting; ~ **tenante** forthwith.

seau (*pl* ~**x**) /so/ *nm* bucket, pail.

sec, sèche /sɛk, sɛʃ/ *adj* dry; (*fruits*) dried; (*coup, bruit*) sharp; (*cœur*) hard; (*whisky*) neat. ● *nm* à ~ (sans eau) dry; (sans argent) broke; **au** ~ in a dry place.

sèche-cheveux /sɛʃʃəvø/ *nm inv* hairdrier.

sèchement /sɛʃmɑ̃/ *adv* drily.

sécher /seʃe/ **4** *vt/i* dry; (*cours*: 1) skip; (ne pas savoir 1) be stumped. □ **se** ~ *vpr* dry oneself. **sécheresse** *nf* (de climat) dryness; (temps sec) drought. **séchoir** *nm* drier.

second, ~e /səgɔ̃, -d/ *adj & nm, f* second. ● *nm* (adjoint) second in command; (étage) second floor. **secondaire** *adj* secondary. **seconde** *nf* (instant) second; (vitesse) second gear.

seconder /səgɔ̃de/ **1** *vt* assist.

secouer /səkwe/ **1** *vt* shake; (*poussière, torpeur*) shake off. □ **se** ~ *vpr* 1 (se dépêcher) get a move on; (réagir) shake oneself up.

secourir /səkuʀiʀ/ **20** *vt* assist, help. **secouriste** *nmf* first-aid worker.

secours /səkuʀ/ *nm* assistance, help; **au** ~**!** help!; **de** ~ (sortie) emergency; (équipe, opération) rescue. ● *nmpl* (Méd) first aid.

secousse /səkus/ *nf* jolt, jerk; (séisme) tremor.

secret, -ète /səkʀɛ, -t/ *adj* secret. ● *nm* secret; (discrétion) secrecy; le ~ **professionnel** professional confidentiality; ~ **de Polichinelle** open secret; **en** ~ in secret, secretly.

secrétaire /səkʀetɛʀ/ *nmf* secretary; ~ **de direction** personal as-

sistant. ● *nm* (meuble) writing desk; ~ **d'État** junior minister.

secrétariat /səkʀetaʀja/ *nm* secretarial work; (bureau) secretariat.

sectaire /sɛktɛʀ/ *adj* sectarian.

secte /sɛkt/ *nf* sect.

secteur /sɛktœʀ/ *nm* area; (Comm) sector; (circuit: Électr) mains (+ *pl*).

section /sɛksjɔ̃/ *nf* section; (Scol) stream; (Mil) platoon. **sectionner** **1** *vt* sever.

sécuriser /sekyʀize/ **1** *vt* reassure.

sécurisé, e /sekyʀize/ *adj* (Ordinat) secure; **une ligne** ~**e** a secure line.

sécurité /sekyʀite/ *nf* security; (absence de danger) safety; **en** ~ safe, secure; **Sécurité sociale** *nf* social services, social security services; ~ **des frontières** homeland security.

sédatif /sedatif/ *nm* sedative.

sédentaire /sedɑ̃tɛʀ/ *adj* sedentary.

séducteur, -trice /sedyktœʀ, -tʀis/ *adj* seductive. ● *nm, f* seducer. **séduction** *nf* seduction; (charme) charm.

séduire /seduiʀ/ **17** *vt* charm; (plaire à) appeal to; (sexuellement) seduce. **séduisant, ~e** *adj* attractive.

ségrégation /segʀegasjɔ̃/ *nf* segregation.

seigle /sɛɡl/ *nm* rye.

seigneur /sɛɲœʀ/ *nm* lord; **le S**~ the Lord.

sein /sɛ̃/ *nm* breast; **au** ~ **de** within.

séisme /seism/ *nm* earthquake.

seize /sɛz/ *adj & nm* sixteen.

séjour /seʒuʀ/ *nm* stay; (pièce) living room. **séjourner** **1** *vi* stay.

s

sel /sɛl/ nm salt; (piquant) spice.

sélectif, -ive /selɛktif, -v/ adj selective.

sélection /selɛksjɔ̃/ nf selection. **sélectionner** 🔳 vt select.

selle /sɛl/ nf saddle; ~s (Méd) stools.

sellette /selɛt/ nf sur la ~ (personne) in the hot seat.

selon /səlɔ̃/ prép according to; ~ que depending on whether.

semaine /səmɛn/ nf week; en ~ during the week.

sémantique /semãtik/ adj semantic. ● nf semantics.

semblable /sãblabl/ adj similar (à to). ● nm fellow (creature).

semblant /sãblã/ nm faire ~ de pretend to; un ~ de a semblance of.

sembler /sãble/ 🔳 vi seem (à to; que that); il me semble que it seems to me that.

semelle /səmɛl/ nf sole; ~ compensée wedge heel.

semence /s(ə)mãs/ nf seed.

semer /s(ə)me/ 🔳 vt (graine, doute) sow; (jeter, parsemer) strew; (personne 🔳) lose; ~ la panique spread panic.

semestre /səmɛstr/ nm half year; (Univ) semester. **semestriel, ~le** adj (revue) biannual; (examen) end-of-semester.

séminaire /seminɛr/ nm (Relig) seminary; (Univ) seminar.

semi-remorque /s(ə)mirəmɔrk/ nm articulated lorry.

semis /s(ə)mi/ nm seedling.

semoule /s(ə)mul/ nf semolina.

sénat /sena/ nm senate. **sénateur** nm senator.

sénile /senil/ adj senile.

senior /senjɔr/ adj (âgé) senior; (mode, publication) for senior citizens. ● nmf senior citizen.

sens /sãs/ nm (Méd) sense; (signification) meaning, sense; (direction) direction; à mon ~ to my mind; à ~ unique (rue) one-way; ça n'a pas de ~ it doesn't make sense; ~ commun common sense; ~ giratoire roundabout; ~ interdit no-entry sign; (rue) one-way street; dans le ~ des aiguilles d'une montre clockwise; dans le ~ inverse des aiguilles d'une montre anticlockwise; ~ dessus dessous upside down; ~ devant derrière back to front.

sensation /sãsasjɔ̃/ nf feeling, sensation; faire ~ create a sensation. **sensationnel, ~le** adj sensational.

sensé, ~e /sãse/ adj sensible.

sensibiliser /sãsibilize/ 🔳 vt ~ l'opinion increase people's awareness (à qch to sth).

sensibilité /sãsibilite/ nf sensitivity. **sensible** adj sensitive (à to); (appréciable) noticeable. **sensiblement** adv noticeably.

sensoriel, ~le /sãsɔrjɛl/ adj sensory.

sensualité /sãsɥalite/ nf sensuousness; sensuality. **sensuel, ~le** adj sensual.

sentence /sãtãs/ nf sentence.

senteur /sãtœr/ nf scent.

sentier /sãtje/ nm path.

sentiment /sãtimã/ nm feeling; faire du ~ sentimentalize; j'ai le ~ que... I get the feeling that... **sentimental, ~e** (mpl -aux) adj sentimental.

sentir /sãtir/ 🔟 vt feel; (odeur) smell; (pressentir) sense; ~ la lavande smell of lavender; je ne

peux pas le ~ 🔢 I can't stand him.
● vi smell. □ se ~ vpr se ~ fier/
mieux feel proud/better.

séparation /sepaʀasjɔ̃/ nf separation.

séparatiste /sepaʀatist/ adj & nmf separatist.

séparé, ~e /sepaʀe/ adj separate; (conjoints) separated.

séparer /sepaʀe/ 🔢 vt separate; (en deux) split. □ se ~ vpr separate, part (de from); (se détacher) split; se ~ de (se défaire de) part with.

sept /sɛt/ adj & nm seven.

septante /sɛptɑ̃t/ adj & nm seventy.

septembre /sɛptɑ̃bʀ/ nm September.

septentrional, ~e (mpl -aux) /sɛptɑ̃tʀijɔnal, -o/ adj northern.

septième /sɛtjɛm/ adj & nmf seventh.

sépulture /sepyltyʀ/ nf burial; (lieu) burial place.

séquelles /sekɛl/ nfpl (maladie) after-effects; (fig) aftermath.

séquence /sekɑ̃s/ nf sequence.

séquestrer /sekɛstʀe/ 🔢 vt confine (illegally).

sera, serait /səʀa, səʀɛ/ ➡ÊTRE 🔢.

serbe /sɛʀb/ adj Serbian. S~ nmf Serbian.

Serbie /sɛʀbi/ nf Serbia.

serein, ~e /səʀɛ̃, -ɛn/ adj serene.

sérénité /seʀenite/ nf serenity.

sergent /sɛʀʒɑ̃/ nm sergeant.

série /seʀi/ nf series (+ sg); (d'objets) set; de ~ (véhicule etc.) standard; fabrication ou production en ~ mass production.

sérieusement /seʀjøzmɑ̃/ adv seriously.

sérieux, -ieuse /seʀjø, -z/ adj serious; (digne de confiance) reliable;

(chances, raison) good. ● nm seriousness; garder son ~ keep a straight face; prendre au ~ take seriously.

serin /səʀɛ̃/ nm canary.

seringue /səʀɛ̃g/ nf syringe.

serment /sɛʀmɑ̃/ nm oath; (promesse) vow.

sermon /sɛʀmɔ̃/ nm sermon. **sermonner** 🔢 vt lecture.

séropositif, -ive /seʀopozitif, -v/ adj HIV positive.

serpent /sɛʀpɑ̃/ nm snake; ~ à sonnettes rattlesnake.

serpillière /sɛʀpijɛʀ/ nf floorcloth.

serre /sɛʀ/ nf (de jardin) greenhouse; (griffe) claw.

serré, ~e /seʀe/ adj (habit, nœud, écrou) tight; (personnes) packed, crowded; (lutte, mailles) close; (écriture) cramped; (cœur) heavy.

serrer /seʀe/ 🔢 vt (saisir) grip; (presser) squeeze; (vis, corde, ceinture) tighten; (poing, dents) clench; ~ qn dans ses bras hug sb; ~ les rangs close ranks; ~ qn (vêtement) be tight on sb; ~ qn de près follow sb closely; ~ la main à shake hands with. ● vi ~ à droite keep over to the right. □ se ~ vpr (se rapprocher) squeeze (up).

serrure /seʀyʀ/ nf lock. **serrurier** nm locksmith.

servante /sɛʀvɑ̃t/ nf (maid) servant.

serveur, -euse /sɛʀvœʀ, -øz/ nm, f (homme) waiter; (femme) waitress. ● nm (Ordinat) server.

serviable /sɛʀvjabl/ adj helpful.

service /sɛʀvis/ nm service; (fonction, temps de travail) duty; (pourboire) service (charge); (dans une société) department; (~ non) compris service (not) included; être de ~ be on duty; pendant le ~

s

(when) on duty; rendre ~ à qn be a help to sb; ~ à thé tea set; ~ d'ordre stewards (+ pl); ~ après-vente after-sales service; ~ militaire military service; les ~s secrets the secret service (+ sg).

serviette /sɛrvjɛt/ nf (de toilette) towel; (cartable) briefcase; (~ de table) serviette, napkin; ~ hygiénique sanitary towel.

servir /sɛrviʁ/ 46 vt/i serve; (être utile) be of use, serve; ~ qn (à table) wait on sb; ça sert à (outil, récipient) it is used for; ça me sert à/de I use it to/as; ça ne sert à rien (action) it's pointless; ~ de serve as, be used as; ~ à qn de guide act as a guide for sb. □ se ~ vpr (à table) help oneself (to); se ~ de use. **serviteur** nm servant.

ses /se/ ⟶SON¹.

session /sesjɔ̃/ nf session.

seuil /sœj/ nm doorstep; (entrée) doorway; (fig) threshold.

seul, ~e /sœl/ adj alone, on one's own; (unique) only; un ~ exemple only one example; pas un ~ ami not a single friend; lui ~ le sait only he knows; dans le ~ but de with the sole aim of; parler tout ~ talk to oneself; faire qch tout ~ do sth on one's own. ● nm, f le ~ la ~e the only one. **seulement** adv only.

sève /sɛv/ nf sap.

sévère /sevɛʁ/ adj severe. **sévérité** nf severity.

sévices /sevis/ nmpl physical abuse.

sévir /seviʁ/ 2 vi (fléau) rage; ~ contre punish.

sevrer /səvʁe/ 6 vt wean.

sexe /sɛks/ nm sex; (organes génitals (+ pl). **sexiste** adj sexist. **sexualité** nf sexuality. **sexuel**, ~le adj sexual.

shampooing /ʃɑ̃pwɛ̃/ nm

shampoo.

shérif /ʃeʁif/ nm sheriff.

short /ʃɔʁt/ nm shorts (+ pl).

si (s' before il, ils) /si, s/ conj if; (interrogation indirecte) if, whether; ~ on allait se promener? what about a walk?; s'il vous ou te plaît please; ~ oui if so; ~ seulement if only. ● adv (tellement) so; (oui) yes; un ~ bon repas such a good meal; ~ habile qu'il soit however skilful he may be; ~ bien que with the result that.

sida /sida/ nm (Méd) Aids.

sidérurgie /sideʁyʁʒi/ nf steel industry.

siècle /sjɛkl/ nm century; (époque) age.

siège /sjɛʒ/ nm seat; (Mil) siege; ~ éjectable ejector seat; ~ social head office, headquarters (+ pl). **siéger** 14 40 vi (assemblée) sit.

sien, ~ne /sjɛ̃, -ɛn/ pron le ~, la ~ne, les (~ne)s (homme) his; (femme) hers; (chose) its; les ~s (famille) one's family.

sieste /sjɛst/ nf nap, siesta.

sifflement /siflamɑ̃/ nm whistling; un ~ a whistle.

siffler /sifle/ 1 vi whistle; (avec un sifflet) blow one's whistle; (serpent, gaz) hiss. ● vt (air) whistle to ou for; (acteur) hiss; (chien) whistle to ou for; (acteur) hiss.

sifflet /siflɛ/ nm whistle; ~s (huées) boos.

sigle /sigl/ nm acronym.

signal (pl -aux) /siɲal, -o/ nm signal; ~ sonore (de répondeur) tone.

signalement /siɲalmɑ̃/ nm description.

signaler /siɲale/ 1 vt indicate; (par une sonnerie, un écriteau) signal; (dénoncer, mentionner) report; (faire remarquer) point out.

signalisation /siɲalizasjɔ̃/ nf sig-

nalling, signposting; (signaux) signals (+ pl).

signataire /siɲatɛʀ/ nmf signatory.

signature /siɲatyʀ/ nf signature;
(action) signing; ~ électronique
digital signature.

signe /siɲ/ nm sign; (de ponctuation) mark; faire ~ à qn wave at
sb; (contacter) contact; faire ~ à
qn de beckon sb to; faire ~ que
non shake one's head; faire ~ que
oui nod.

signer /siɲe/ **1** vt sign. □ se ~ vpr
(Relig) cross oneself.

signet /siɲɛ/ nm (pour livre, Internet) bookmark; ~s favoris (Internet) hotlist.

significatif, **-ive** /siɲifikatif, -v/
adj significant.

signification /siɲifikasjɔ̃/ nf
meaning. **signifier** **45** vt mean, signify; (faire connaître) make known
(à to).

silence /silɑ̃s/ nm silence; (Mus)
rest; garder le ~ keep silent.

silencieux, **-ieuse** /silɑ̃sjø, -z/ adj
silent. ●nm silencer.

silex /silɛks/ nm inv flint.

silhouette /silwɛt/ nf outline, silhouette.

sillon /sijɔ̃/ nm furrow; (de disque)
groove.

sillonner /sijone/ **1** vt crisscross.

similaire /similɛʀ/ adj similar. **si-
militude** nf similarity.

simple /sɛ̃pl/ adj simple; (non double) single. ●nm ~ dames/
messieurs ladies'/men's singles (+
pl). **simple d'esprit** nmf simpleton.
simplement adv simply. **simplicité**
nf simplicity; (naïveté) simpleness.

simplification /sɛ̃plifikasjɔ̃/ nf
simplification. **simplifier** **45** vt
simplify.

simpliste /sɛ̃plist/ adj simplistic.

simulacre /simylakʀ/ nm pretence, sham.

simulation /simylasjɔ̃/ nf simulation. **simuler** **1** vt simulate.

simultané, **-e** /simyltane/ adj
simultaneous.

sincère /sɛ̃sɛʀ/ adj sincere. **sincérité** nf sincerity.

singe /sɛ̃ʒ/ nm monkey; (grand)
ape. **singer** **40** vt mimic, ape.

singulier, **-ière** /sɛ̃gylje, -jɛʀ/ adj
peculiar, remarkable; (Gram) singular. ●nm (Gram) singular.

sinistre /sinistʀ/ adj sinister. ●nm
disaster; (incendie) blaze; (domma-
ges) damage.

sinistré, **-e** /sinistʀe/ adj
stricken. ●nm, f disaster victim.

sinon /sinɔ̃/ conj (autrement)
otherwise; (sauf) except (que that);
difficile ~ impossible difficult if
not impossible.

sinueux, **-euse** /sinɥø, -z/ adj
winding; (fig) tortuous.

sirène /siʀɛn/ nf (appareil) siren;
(femme) mermaid.

sirop /siʀo/ nm (de fruits, Méd)
syrup; (boisson) cordial.

sismique /sismik/ adj seismic.

site /sit/ nm site; ~ touristique
place of interest; ~ Internet or
Web Web site.

sitôt /sito/ adv ~ entré immediately after coming in; ~ que as
soon as; pas de ~ not for a while.

situation /sitɥasjɔ̃/ nf situation;
(emploi) job, position; ~ de famille
marital status.

situé, **-e** /sitɥe/ adj situated.

situer /sitɥe/ **1** vt situate, locate.
□ se ~ vpr (se trouver) be situated.

six /sis/ (/si/ before consonant, /siz/
before vowel) adj & nm six. **sixième**

s

adj & nmf sixth.

sketch (*pl* ~es) /skɛtʃ/ *nm* (Théât) sketch.

ski /ski/ *nm* (matériel) ski; (Sport) skiing; faire du ~ ski; ~ de fond cross-country skiing; ~ nautique water skiing. **skier 45** *vi* ski.

slave /slav/ *adj* Slav; (Ling) Slavonic.

slip /slip/ *nm* (d'homme) underpants (+ *pl*); (de femme) knickers (+ *pl*); ~ de bain (swimming) trunks (+ *pl*); (du bikini) bikini bottom.

slogan /slɔgɑ̃/ *nm* slogan.

Slovaquie /slɔvaki/ *nf* Slovakia.

Slovénie /slɔveni/ *nf* Slovenia.

smoking /smɔkiŋ/ *nm* dinner jacket.

SNCF *abrév f* (**Société nationale des Chemins de fer français**) *French national railway company.*

snob /snɔb/ *nmf* snob. ● *adj* snobbish. **snobisme** *nm* snobbery.

sobre /sɔbʀ/ *adj* sober.

social, ~e (*mpl* -iaux) /sɔsjal, -jo/ *adj* social.

socialisme /sɔsjalism/ *nm* socialism. **socialiste** *nmf & a* socialist.

société /sɔsjete/ *nf* society; (entreprise) company; ~ point com dot-com.

socle /sɔkl/ *nm* (de colonne, statue) plinth; (de lampe) base.

socquette /sɔkɛt/ *nf* ankle sock.

soda /sɔda/ *nm* fizzy drink.

sœur /sœʀ/ *nf* sister.

soi /swa/ *pron* oneself; derrière ~ behind one; en ~ in itself; aller de ~ be obvious.

soi-disant /swadizɑ̃/ *adj inv* so-called. ● *adv* supposedly.

soie /swa/ *nf* silk.

soif /swaf/ *nf* thirst; avoir ~ be thirsty; donner ~ make one thirsty.

soigné, ~e /swaɲe/ *adj* (apparence) tidy, neat; (travail) carefully done.

soigner /swaɲe/ **1** *vt* (s'occuper de) look after, take care of; (tenue, style) take care over; (maladie) treat. □ **se** ~ *vpr* look after oneself.

soigneusement /swaɲøzmɑ̃/ *adv* carefully. **soigneux**, **-euse** *adj* careful (de about); (ordonné) tidy.

soi-même /swamɛm/ *pron* oneself.

soin /swɛ̃/ *nm* care; (ordre) tidiness; ~s care; (Méd) treatment; avec ~ carefully; avoir ou prendre ~ de qn/de faire take care of sb/to do; premiers ~s first aid (+ *sg*).

soir /swaʀ/ *nm* evening; à ce ~ see you tonight.

soirée /swaʀe/ *nf* evening; (réception) party.

soit /swa/ *conj* (à savoir) that is to say; ~... ~ either... or.
● →ÊTRE **4**.

soixante /swasɑ̃t/ *adj & nm* sixty. **soixante-dix** *adj & nm* seventy.

soja /sɔʒa/ *nm* (graines) soya beans (+ *pl*); (plante) soya.

sol /sɔl/ *nm* ground; (de maison) floor; (terrain agricole) soil.

solaire /sɔlɛʀ/ *adj* solar; (huile, filtre) sun.

soldat /sɔlda/ *nm* soldier.

solde¹ /sɔld/ *nf* (salaire) pay.

solde² /sɔld/ *nm* (Comm) balance; les ~s the sales; ~s (écrit en vitrine) sale; en ~ (acheter) at sale price.

solder /sɔlde/ **1** *vt* sell off at sale price; (compte) settle. □ **se** ~ **par** *vpr* (aboutir à) end in.

sole /sɔl/ *nf* (poisson) sole.

soleil /sɔlɛj/ *nm* sun; (fleur) sunflower; il y a du ~ it's sunny.

solennel, ~**le** /sɔlanɛl/ adj
solemn.

solfège /sɔlfɛʒ/ nm musical theory.

solidaire /sɔlidɛʀ/ adj (mécanismes) interdependent; (collègues)
(mutually) supportive; **être ~ de
qn** support sb. **solidarité** nf solidarity.

solide /sɔlid/ adj solid; (personne)
strong. ● nm solid.

solidifier /sɔlidifje/ 45 vt solidify.
□ **se ~** vpr solidify.

solitaire /sɔlitɛʀ/ adj solitary.
● nmf (personne) loner. **solitude** nf
solitude.

solliciter /sɔlisite/ 1 vt seek;
(faire appel à) call upon; **être très
sollicité** be very much in demand.

sollicitude /sɔlisityd/ nf concern.

solo /sɔlo/ nm & a inv (Mus) solo.

solution /sɔlysjɔ̃/ nf solution.

solvable /sɔlvabl/ adj solvent.

solvant /sɔlvɑ̃/ nm solvent.

sombre /sɔ̃bʀ/ adj dark; (triste)
sombre.

sombrer /sɔ̃bʀe/ 1 vi sink (dans
into).

sommaire /sɔmɛʀ/ adj (exécution)
summary; (description) rough. ● nm
contents (+ pl); **au ~** on the programme.

sommation /sɔmasjɔ̃/ nf (Mil)
warning; (Jur) notice.

somme /sɔm/ nf sum; **en ~**, ~
toute in short; **faire la ~ de** add
(up), total (up). ● nm nap.

sommeil /sɔmɛj/ nm sleep; **avoir
~ be** ou feel sleepy; **en ~** (projet)
put on ice. **sommeiller** 1 vi doze;
(fig) lie dormant.

sommelier /sɔməlje/ nm wine
steward.

sommer /sɔme/ 1 vt summon.

sommes /sɔm/ ➜ÊTRE 4.

sommet /sɔmɛ/ nm top; (de montagne) summit; (de triangle) apex;
(gloire) height.

sommier /sɔmje/ nm bed base.

somnambule /sɔmnɑ̃byl/ nm
sleepwalker.

somnifère /sɔmnifɛʀ/ nm sleeping pill.

somnolent, ~**e** /sɔmnɔlɑ̃, -t/ adj
drowsy. **somnoler** 1 vi doze.

somptueux, -**euse** /sɔ̃ptɥø, -z/
adj sumptuous.

son[1], **sa** (**son** before vowel or
mute h) (pl **ses**) /sɔ̃, sa, sɔ̃, se/ adj
(homme) his; (femme) her; (chose)
its; (indéfini) one's.

son[2] /sɔ̃/ nm (bruit) sound; (de blé)
bran; **baisser le ~** turn the volume down.

sondage /sɔ̃daʒ/ nm ~ (**d'opinion**) (opinion) poll.

sonde /sɔ̃d/ nf (de forage) drill;
(Méd) (d'évacuation) catheter;
(d'examen) probe.

sonder /sɔ̃de/ 1 vt (population)
poll; (explorer) sound; (terrain) drill;
(intentions) sound out.

songe /sɔ̃ʒ/ nm dream.

songer /sɔ̃ʒe/ 40 vt ~ **que** think
that; ~ **à** think about. **songeur,
-euse** adj pensive.

sonné, ~**e** /sɔne/ adj (étourdi)
groggy; 1 crazy.

sonner /sɔne/ 1 vt/i ring; (clairon,
glas) sound; (heure) strike; (domestique) ring for; **midi sonné** well past
noon; ~ **de** (clairon) sound, blow.

sonnerie /sɔnʀi/ nf ringing; (de
clairon) sounding; (sonnette) bell;
(téléphone portable) ringtone.

sonnette /sɔnɛt/ nf bell.

sonore /sɔnɔʀ/ adj resonant; (onde,
effets) sound; (rire) resounding.

sonorisation /sɔnɔʀizasjɔ̃/ nf

s

(matériel) public address system.

sonorité /sɔnɔʀite/ nf resonance; (d'un instrument) tone.

sont /sɔ̃/ ⇒ÊTRE 4.

sophistiqué, ~e /sɔfistike/ adj sophisticated.

sorcellerie /sɔʀsɛlʀi/ nf witchcraft. **sorcier** nm (guérisseur) witch doctor; (maléfique) sorcerer. **sorcière** nf witch.

sordide /sɔʀdid/ adj sordid; (lieu) squalid.

sort /sɔʀ/ nm (destin, hasard) fate; (condition) lot; (maléfice) spell; **tirer** (qch) **au ~** draw lots (for sth).

sortant, ~e /sɔʀtɑ̃, -t/ adj (président etc.) outgoing.

sorte /sɔʀt/ nf sort, kind; **de ~ que** so that; **en quelque ~** in a way; **de la ~** in this way; **faire en ~ que** make sure that.

sortie /sɔʀti/ nf exit; (promenade, dîner) outing; (déclaration 🏠) remark; (parution) publication; (de disque, film) release; (d'un ordinateur) output; **~s** (argent) outgoings.

sortilège /sɔʀtilɛʒ/ nm (magic) spell.

sortir /sɔʀtiʀ/ 46 vi (aux être) go out, leave; (venir) come out; (aller au spectacle) go out; (livre, film) come out; (plante) come up; **de** (pièce) leave; (milieu social) come from; (limites) go beyond; **~ du commun ou de l'ordinaire** be out of the ordinary. ● vt (aux avoir) take out; (livre, modèle) bring out; (dire 🏠) come out with; **~ qn de** get sb out of; **être sorti d'affaire** be in the clear. □ **s'en ~** vpr cope, manage.

sosie /sɔzi/ nm double.

sot, ~te /so, sɔt/ adj silly.

sottise /sɔtiz/ nf silliness; (action,

remarque) foolish thing; **faire des ~s** be naughty.

sou /su/ nm 🧡 **~s** money; **sans le ~** without a penny; **près de ses ~s** tight-fisted.

soubresaut /subʀəso/ nm (sudden) start.

souche /suʃ/ nf (d'arbre) stump; (de famille) stock; (de carnet) counterfoil.

souci /susi/ nm (inquiétude) worry; (préoccupation) concern; (plante) marigold; **se faire du ~** worry.

soucier (se) /(sə)susje/ 45 vpr se **~ de** care about. **soucieux, -ieuse** adj concerned (de about).

soucoupe /sukup/ nf saucer; **~ volante** flying saucer.

soudain, ~e /sudɛ̃, -ɛn/ adj sudden. ● adv suddenly.

soude /sud/ nf soda.

souder /sude/ 🚹 vt weld, solder; **famille très soudée** close-knit family. □ **se ~** vpr (os) knit (together).

soudoyer /sudwaje/ 🗎 vt bribe.

souffle /sufl/ nm (haleine) breath; (respiration) breathing; (explosion) blast; (vent) breath of air; **le ~ coupé** out of breath; **à couper le ~** breathtaking.

souffler /sufle/ 🚹 vi blow; (haleter) puff. ● vt (bougie) blow out; (poussière, fumée) blow; (verre) blow; (par explosion) destroy; (chuchoter) whisper; **~ la réplique à** prompt. **souffleur, -euse** nm, f (Théât) prompter.

souffrance /sufʀɑ̃s/ nf suffering; **en ~** (affaire) pending. **souffrant, ~e** adj unwell.

souffrir /sufʀiʀ/ 21 vi suffer (de from). ● vt (endurer) suffer; **il ne peut pas le ~** he cannot stand ou bear him.

soufre /sufʀ/ nm sulphur.

souhait /swɛ/ nm wish; à tes ~s! bless you!; **possible à** ~ incredibly peaceful. **souhaitable** adj desirable.

souhaiter /swete/ **1** vt ~ qch à qn wish sb sth; ~ que/faire hope that/to do; ~ la bienvenue à qn welcome sb.

soûl, ~e /su, sul/ adj drunk. ● nm tout son ~ as much as one can.

soulagement /sulaʒmɑ̃/ nm relief. **soulager** 40 vt relieve.

soûler /sule/ **1** vt make drunk. □ **se** ~ vpr get drunk.

soulèvement /sulɛvmɑ̃/ nm uprising.

soulever /sulve/ **6** vt lift, raise; (question, poussière) raise; (enthousiasme) arouse; (foule) stir up. □ **se** ~ vpr lift ou raise oneself up; (se révolter) rise up.

soulier /sulje/ nm shoe.

souligner /suliɲe/ **1** vt underline; (yeux) outline; (taille) emphasize.

soumettre /sumɛtr/ 42 vt (assujettir) subject (à to); (présenter) submit (à to). □ **se** ~ vpr submit (à to). **soumis**, ~e adj submissive. **soumission** nf submission.

soupape /supap/ nf valve.

soupçon /supsɔ̃/ nm suspicion; un ~ de (un peu de) a touch of. **soupçonner** **1** vt suspect. **soupçonneux**, **-euse** adj suspicious.

soupe /sup/ nf soup.

souper /supe/ **6** vi have supper. ● nm supper.

soupeser /supəze/ **1** vt judge the weight of; (fig) weigh up.

soupière /supjɛr/ nf (soup) tureen.

soupir /supir/ nm sigh; pousser un ~ heave a sigh.

soupirer /supire/ **1** vi sigh.

souple /supl/ adj supple; (règlement, caractère) flexible. **souplesse** nf suppleness; (de règlement) flexibility.

source /surs/ nf (de rivière, origine) source; (eau) spring; prendre sa ~ à rise in; de ~ sûre from a reliable source; ~ thermale hot spring.

sourcil /sursi/ nm eyebrow.

sourciller /sursije/ **1** vi sans ~ without batting an eyelid.

sourd, ~e /sur, -d/ adj deaf; (bruit, douleur) dull; faire la ~e oreille turn a deaf ear. ● nm, f deaf person.

sourd-muet (pl **sourds-muets**), **sourde-muette** (pl **sourdes-muettes**) /surmyɛ, surdmyɛt/ adj deaf and dumb. ● nm, f deafmute.

souricière /surisjɛr/ nf mousetrap; (fig) trap.

sourire /surir/ 54 vi smile (à at); ~ à (fortune) smile on. ● nm smile; garder le ~ keep smiling.

souris /suri/ nf mouse; des ~ mice.

sournois, ~e /surnwa, -z/ adj sly, underhand.

sous /su/ prép under, beneath; ~ la main handy; ~ la pluie in the rain; ~ peu shortly; ~ terre underground.

sous-alimenté, ~e /suzalimɑ̃te/ adj undernourished.

souscription /suskripsjɔ̃/ nf subscription. **souscrire** 30 vi ~ à subscribe to.

sous-entendre /suzɑ̃tɑ̃dr/ 3 vt imply. **sous-entendu** nm innuendo, insinuation.

sous-estimer /suzɛstime/ **1** vt underestimate.

sous-jacent, ~e /suʒasɑ̃, -t/ adj underlying.

sous-marin, ~e /sumarɛ̃, -in/ adj underwater; (plongée) deep-sea. ● nm submarine.

s

soussigné, ~e /susiɲe/ adj & nm, f undersigned.

sous-sol /susɔl/ nm (cave) basement.

sous-titre /sutitʁ/ nm subtitle.

soustraction /sustʁaksjɔ̃/ nf (déduction) subtraction.

soustraire /sustʁɛʁ/ 29 vt (déduire) subtract; (retirer) take away (à from). □ se ~ à vpr escape from.

sous-traitant /sutʁɛtɑ̃/ nm subcontractor.

sous-verre /suvɛʁ/ nm inv glass mount.

sous-vêtement /suvɛtmɑ̃/ nm underwear.

soute /sut/ nf (de bateau) hold; ~ à charbon coal-bunker.

soutenir /sutniʁ/ 59 vt support; (effort, rythme) sustain; (résister à) withstand; ~ que maintain that.

soutenu, ~e /sutny/ adj (constant) sustained; (style) formal.

souterrain, ~e /suteʁɛ̃, -ɛn/ adj underground. ● nm underground passage.

soutien /sutjɛ̃/ nm support.

soutien-gorge /pl soutiens-gorge/ /sutjɛ̃gɔʁʒ/ nm bra.

soutirer /sutiʁe/ 1 vt ~ à qn extract from sb.

souvenir[1] /suvniʁ/ nm memory, recollection; (objet) memento; (cadeau) souvenir; en ~ de in memory of.

souvenir[2] (se) /(sə)suvniʁ/ 59 vpr se ~ de remember; se ~ que remember that.

souvent /suvɑ̃/ adv often.

souverain, ~e /suvʁɛ̃, -ɛn/ adj sovereign. ● nm, f sovereign.

soviétique /sɔvjetik/ adj Soviet.

soyeux, -euse /swajø, -z/ adj silky.

spacieux, -ieuse /spasjø, -z/ adj spacious.

sparadrap /spaʁadʁa/ nm (sticking) plaster.

spatial, ~e (mpl -iaux) /spasjal, -jo/ adj space.

speaker, ~ine /spikœʁ, -kʁin/ nm, f announcer.

spécial, ~e (mpl -iaux) /spesjal, -jo/ adj special; (bizarre) odd. **spécialement** adv (exprès) specially; (très) especially.

spécialiser (se) /səspesjalize/ 1 vpr specialize (dans in). **spécialiste** nmf specialist. **spécialité** nf speciality; (US) specialty.

spécifier /spesifje/ 45 vt specify.

spécifique /spesifik/ adj specific.

spécimen /spesimɛn/ nm specimen.

spectacle /spɛktakl/ nm show; (vue) sight, spectacle.

spectaculaire /spɛktakylɛʁ/ adj spectacular.

spectateur, -trice /spɛktatœʁ, -tʁis/ nm, f (Sport) spectator; (témoin oculaire) onlooker; les ~s (Théât) the audience (+ sg).

spectre /spɛktʁ/ nm (revenant) spectre; (images) spectrum.

spéculateur, -trice /spekylatœʁ, -tʁis/ nm, f speculator. **spéculation** nf speculation. **spéculer** 1 vi speculate.

spéléologie /speleolɔʒi/ nf cave exploration, pot-holing.

spermatozoïde /spɛʁmatozoid/ nm spermatozoon. **sperme** nm sperm.

sphère /sfɛʁ/ nf sphere.

spirale /spiʁal/ nf spiral.

spirituel, ~le /spiʁitɥɛl/ adj spiritual; (amusant) witty.

spiritueux /spiʁitɥø/ nm (alcool) spirit.

splendeur /splɑ̃dœʀ/ nf splendour. **splendide** adj splendid.

sponsoriser /spɔ̃sɔʀize/ **1** vt sponsor.

spontané, ~e /spɔ̃tane/ adj spontaneous. **spontanéité** nf spontaneity.

sport /spɔʀ/ adj inv (vêtements) casual. ●nm sport; veste/voiture de ~ sports jacket/car.

sportif, -ive /spɔʀtif, -v/ adj (personne) sporty; (physique) athletic; (résultats) sports. ●nm, f sportsman, sportswoman.

spot /spɔt/ nm spotlight; (~ publicitaire) ad.

square /skwaʀ/ nm small public garden.

squatter /skwate/ **1** vt squat in.

squelette /skəlɛt/ nm skeleton. **squelettique** adj skeletal.

SRAS abrév m (**syndrome respiratoire aigu sévère**) SARS.

SSII abrév f (**société de services et d'ingénierie informatiques**) computer services company

stabiliser /stabilize/ **1** vt stabilize. **stable** adj stable.

stade /stad/ nm (Sport) stadium; (phase) stage.

stage /staʒ/ nm (cours) course; (professionnel) placement. **stagiaire** nmf course member; (apprenti) trainee.

stagner /stagne/ **1** vi stagnate.

stand /stɑ̃d/ nm stand; (de fête foraine) stall.

standard /stɑ̃daʀ/ nm switchboard. ●adj inv standard. **standardiser** **1** vt standardize.

standardiste /stɑ̃daʀdist/ nmf switchboard operator.

standing /stɑ̃diŋ/ nm status, standing; de ~ (hôtel) luxury.

starter /staʀtɛʀ/ nm (Auto) choke.

station /stasjɔ̃/ nf station; (halte) stop; ~ **debout** standing position; ~ **de taxis** taxi rank; ~ **balnéaire/ de ski** seaside/ski resort; ~ **thermale** spa.

stationnaire /stasjɔnɛʀ/ adj stationary.

stationnement /stasjɔnmɑ̃/ nm parking. **stationner** **1** vi park.

station-service (pl **stations-service**) /stasjɔ̃sɛʀvis/ nf service station.

statique /statik/ adj static.

statistique /statistik/ nf statistic; (science) statistics (+ sg.) ●adj statistical.

statue /staty/ nf statue.

statuer /statɥe/ **1** vi ~ **sur** give a ruling on.

statut /staty/ nm status. **statutaire** adj statutory.

sténo /steno/ nf (sténographie) shorthand. **sténodactylo** nf shorthand typist. **sténographie** nf shorthand.

stéréo /steʀeo/ nf & adj inv stereo.

stéréotype /steʀeotip/ nm stereotype.

stérile /steʀil/ adj sterile.

stérilet /steʀilɛ/ nm coil, IUD.

stérilisation /steʀilizasjɔ̃/ nf sterilization. **stériliser** **1** vt sterilize.

stéroïde /steʀɔid/ adj & nm steroid.

stimulant /stimylɑ̃/ nm stimulus; (médicament) stimulant.

stimulateur /stimylatœʀ/ nm ~ **cardiaque** (Méd) pacemaker.

stimuler /stimyle/ **1** vt stimulate.

stipuler /stipyle/ **1** vt stipulate.

stock /stɔk/ nm stock. **stocker** **1** vt stock.

stoïque /stɔik/ adj stoical. ●nmf stoic.

S

stop /stɔp/ interj stop. ● nm stop sign; (feu arrière) brake light; faire du ~ 🄸 hitch-hike. **stopper** 🄵 vt/i stop.

store /stɔʀ/ nm blind; (de magasin) awning.

strapontin /stʀapɔ̃tɛ̃/ nm folding seat, jump seat.

stratégie /stʀateʒi/ nf strategy. **stratégique** adj strategic.

stress /stʀɛs/ nm stress. **stressant**, ~e adj stressful. **stressé**, ~e adj stressed. **stresser** 🄵 vt put under stress.

strict /stʀikt/ adj strict; (tenue, vérité) plain; le ~ minimum the bare minimum. **strictement** adv strictly.

strident, ~e /stʀidɑ̃, -t/ adj shrill.

strophe /stʀɔf/ nf stanza, verse.

structure /stʀyktyʀ/ nf structure.

studieux, -ieuse /stydjø, -z/ adj studious.

studio /stydjo/ nm (d'artiste, de télévision) studio; (logement) studio flat.

stupéfaction /stypefaksjɔ̃/ nf amazement. **stupéfait**, ~e adj amazed.

stupéfiant, ~e /stypefjɑ̃, -t/ adj astounding. ● nm drug, narcotic.

stupéfier /stypefje/ 🄴🄵 vt amaze.

stupeur /stypœʀ/ nf amazement; (Méd) stupor.

stupide /stypid/ adj stupid. **stupidité** nf stupidity.

style /stil/ nm style.

styliste /stilist/ nmf fashion designer.

stylo /stilo/ nm pen; ~ (à) bille ballpoint pen; ~ (à) encre fountain pen.

su /sy/ ➡SAVOIR 🄸🄸.

suave /sɥav/ adj sweet.

subalterne /sybaltɛʀn/ adj & nmf subordinate.

subconscient /sypkɔ̃sjɑ̃/ nm subconscious.

subir /sybiʀ/ 🄶 vt be subjected to; (traitement, expériences) undergo.

subit, ~e /sybi, -t/ adj sudden.

subjectif, -ive /sybʒɛktif, -v/ adj subjective.

subjonctif /sybʒɔ̃ktif/ nm subjunctive.

subjuguer /sybʒyge/ 🄵 vt (charmer) captivate.

sublime /syblim/ adj sublime.

submerger /sybmɛʀʒe/ 🄴🄾 vt submerge; (fig) overwhelm.

subordonné, ~e /sybɔʀdɔne/ adj & nm, f subordinate.

subside /sybzid/ nm grant.

subsidiaire /sybzidjɛʀ/ adj subsidiary; question ~ tiebreaker.

subsistance /sybzistɑ̃s/ nf subsistence. **subsister** 🄸 vi subsist; (durer, persister) exist.

substance /sypstɑ̃s/ nf substance.

substantiel, ~le /sypstɑ̃sjɛl/ adj substantial.

substantif /sypstɑ̃tif/ nm noun.

substituer /sypstitɥe/ 🄵 vt substitute (à for). □ **se** ~ **à** vpr (remplacer) substitute for. **substitut** nm substitute; (Jur) deputy public prosecutor.

subtil, ~e /syptil/ adj subtle.

subtiliser /syptilize/ 🄵 vt ~ qch (à qn) steal sth (from sb).

subvenir /sybvaniʀ/ 🄵🄼 vi ~ à provide for.

subvention /sybvɑ̃sjɔ̃/ nf subsidy. **subventionner** 🄸 vt subsidize.

subversif, -ive /sybvɛʀsif, -v/ adj subversive.

suc /syk/ nm juice.

succédané /syksedane/ nm substitute (de for).

succéder | suivi

succéder /syksede/ [14] vi ~ à succeed. □ se ~ vpr succeed one another.

succès /sykse/ nm success; à ~ (film, livre) successful; avoir du ~ be a success.

successeur /syksesœʀ/ nm successor. **successif, -ive** adj successive. **succession** nf succession; (Jur) inheritance.

succinct, ~e /syksɛ̃, -t/ adj succinct.

succomber /sykɔ̃be/ [1] vi die; ~ à succumb to.

succulent, ~e /sykylɑ̃, -t/ adj delicious.

succursale /sykyʀsal/ nf (Comm) branch.

sucer /syse/ [10] vt suck.

sucette /syset/ nf (bonbon) lollipop; (tétine) dummy; (US) pacifier.

sucre /sykʀ/ nm sugar; ~ d'orge barley sugar; ~ en poudre caster sugar; ~ glace icing sugar; ~ roux brown sugar.

sucré /sykʀe/ adj sweet; (additionné de sucre) sweetened. **sucrer** [1] vt sugar, sweeten. **sucreries** nfpl sweets.

sucrier, -ière /sykʀije, -jɛʀ/ adj sugar. ● nm (récipient) sugar-bowl.

sud /syd/ nm south. ● adj inv south; (partie) southern.

sud-est /sydɛst/ nm south-east.

sud-ouest /sydwɛst/ nm southwest.

Suède /sɥɛd/ nf Sweden.

suédois, ~e /sɥedwa, -z/ adj Swedish. ● nm (Ling) Swedish. S~, ~e nm, f Swede.

suer /sɥe/ [1] vt/i sweat; faire ~ qn [1] get on sb's nerves.

sueur /sɥœʀ/ nf sweat; en ~ covered in sweat.

suffire /syfiʀ/ [57] vi be enough (à qn for sb); il suffit de compter all you have to do is count; une goutte suffit a drop is enough; ~ à (besoin) satisfy. □ se ~ vpr se ~ à soi-même be self-sufficient.

suffisamment /syfizamɑ̃/ adv sufficiently; ~ de qch enough of sth. **suffisance** nf (vanité) conceit. **suffisant, ~e** adj sufficient; (vaniteux) conceited.

suffixe /syfiks/ nm suffix.

suffoquer /syfɔke/ [1] vt/i choke, suffocate.

suffrage /syfʀaʒ/ nm (voix: Pol) vote; (système) suffrage.

suggérer /sygʒeʀe/ [14] vt suggest. **suggestion** nf suggestion.

suicidaire /sɥisidɛʀ/ adj suicidal. **suicide** nm suicide. **suicider (se)** [1] vpr commit suicide.

suinter /sɥɛ̃te/ [1] vi ooze.

suis /sɥi/ →ÊTRE [4], →SUIVRE [57].

Suisse /sɥis/ nf Switzerland. ● nmf Swiss. **suisse** adj Swiss.

suite /sɥit/ nf continuation, rest; (d'un film) sequel; (série) series; (appartement, escorte) suite; (résultat) consequence; à la ~, de ~ (successivement) in a row; à la ~ de (derrière) behind; à la ~ de, par ~ de (en conséquence) as a result of; faire ~ (à) follow; par la ~ afterwards; ~ à votre lettre du further to your letter of the; des ~s de as a result of.

suivant¹, ~e /sɥivɑ̃, -t/ adj following, next. ● nm, f following ou next person.

suivant² /sɥivɑ̃/ prép (selon) according to.

suivi, ~e /sɥivi/ adj (effort) steady, sustained; (cohérent) consistent; peu/très ~ (cours) poorly/well attended.

suivre /sɥivʀ/ *vt/i* follow; (comprendre) follow; faire ~ (courrier) forward. □ se ~ *vpr* follow each other.

sujet, ~te /syʒɛ, -t/ *adj* ~ à liable *ou* subject to. ● *nm* (d'un royaume) subject; (question) subject; (motif) cause; (Gram) subject; au ~ de about.

super /sypɛʀ/ *nm* (essence) fourstar. ● *adj inv* ① (très) great. ● *adv* ① ultra, really.

superbe /sypɛʀb/ *adj* superb.

supérette /sypeʀɛt/ *nf* minimarket.

superficie /sypɛʀfisi/ *nf* area.

superficiel, ~le /sypɛʀfisjɛl/ *adj* superficial.

superflu /sypɛʀfly/ *adj* superfluous. ● *nm* (excédent) surplus.

supérieur, ~e /sypeʀjœʀ/ *adj* (plus haut) upper; (quantité, nombre) greater (à than); (études, principe) higher (à than); (meilleur, hautain) superior (à to). ● *nm, f* superior. **supériorité** *nf* superiority.

superlatif, -ive /sypɛʀlatif, -v/ *adj & nm* superlative.

supermarché /sypɛʀmaʀʃe/ *nm* supermarket.

superposer /sypɛʀpoze/ ① *vt* superimpose; lits superposés bunk beds.

superproduction /sypɛʀpʀɔdyksjɔ̃/ *nf* (film) blockbuster.

superpuissance /sypɛʀpɥisãs/ *nf* superpower.

superstitieux, -ieuse /sypɛʀstisjø, -z/ *adj* superstitious.

superviser /sypɛʀvize/ ① *vt* supervise.

suppléant, ~e /sypleã, -t/ *nmf & adj* (professeur ~) supply teacher; (juge) ~ deputy (judge).

suppléer /syplee/ ⑮ *vt* (rempla-

cer) fill in for. ● *vi* ~ à (compenser) make up for.

supplément /syplemã/ *nm* (argent) extra charge; (de frites, légumes) extra portion; en ~ extra; un ~ de (travail) additional; payer un ~ pay a supplement. **supplémentaire** *adj* extra, additional.

supplice /syplis/ *nm* torture.

supplier /syplije/ ⑮ *vt* beg, beseech (de to).

support /sypɔʀ/ *nm* support; (Ordinat) medium.

supportable /sypɔʀtabl/ *adj* bearable.

supporter[1] /sypɔʀte/ ① *vt* (privations) bear; (personne) put up with; (structure; Ordinat) support; il ne supporte pas les enfants/de perdre he can't stand children/losing.

supporter[2] /sypɔʀtɛʀ/ *nm* (Sport) supporter.

supposer /sypoze/ ① *vt* suppose; (impliquer) imply; à ~ que supposing that.

suppression /sypʀesjɔ̃/ *nf* (de taxe) abolition; (de sanction) lifting; (de mot) deletion. **supprimer** ① *vt* (allocation) withdraw; (contrôle) lift; (train) cancel; (preuve) suppress.

suprématie /sypʀemasi/ *nf* supremacy.

suprême /sypʀɛm/ *adj* supreme.

sur /syʀ/ *prép* on, upon; (pardessus) over; (au sujet de) about, on; (proportion) out of; (mesure) by; ~ la photo in the photograph; mettre/jeter ~ put/throw on to; ~ mesure made to measure; ~ place on the spot; ~ ce, je pars with that, I must go; ~ le moment at the time.

sûr /syʀ/ *adj* certain, sure; (sans danger) safe; (digne de confiance) reliable; (main) steady; (jugement)

sound; être ~ de soi be self-confident; **j'en étais ~!** I knew it!

surabondance /syʀabɔ̃dɑ̃s/ *nf* overabundance.

surcharge /syʀʃaʀʒ/ *nf* overloading; (poids) excess load. **surcharger 1** *vt* overload; (texte) alter.

surchauffer /syʀʃofe/ **1** *vt* overheat.

surcroît /syʀkʀwa/ *nm* increase (de in); **de ~** in addition.

surdité /syʀdite/ *nf* deafness.

surélever /syʀelve/ **6** *vt* raise.

sûrement /syʀmɑ̃/ *adv* certainly; (sans danger) safely; **il a ~ oublié** he must have forgotten.

surenchère /syʀɑ̃ʃɛʀ/ *nf* higher bid. **surenchérir 2** *vi* bid higher (sur than).

surestimer /syʀɛstime/ **1** *vt* overestimate.

sûreté /syʀte/ *nf* safety; (de pays) security; (d'un geste) steadiness; **être en ~** be safe; **S~ (nationale)** police (+ *pl*).

surexcité, ~e /syʀɛksite/ *adj* very excited.

surf /sœʀf/ *nm* surfing.

surface /syʀfas/ *nf* surface; **faire ~** (sous-marin, fig) surface; **en ~** on the surface.

surfait, ~e /syʀfɛ, -t/ *adj* overrated.

surfer /sœʀfe/ **1** *vi* go surfing; **~ sur l'Internet** surf the Internet.

surgelé, ~e /syʀʒəle/ *adj* (deep-) frozen; **aliments ~s** frozen food.

surgir /syʀʒiʀ/ **2** *vi* appear (suddenly); (difficulté) crop up.

sur-le-champ /syʀləʃɑ̃/ *adv* right away.

surlendemain /syʀlɑ̃dmɛ̃/ *nm* le **~** two days later; **le ~ de** two days after.

surligneur /syʀliɲœʀ/ *nm* highlighter (pen).

surmenage /syʀmənaʒ/ *nm* overwork.

surmonter /syʀmɔ̃te/ **1** *vt* (vaincre) overcome, surmount; (être au-dessus de) surmount, top.

surnaturel, ~le /syʀnatyʀɛl/ *adj* supernatural.

surnom /syʀnɔ̃/ *nm* nickname. **surnommer 1** *vt* nickname.

surpeuplé, ~e /syʀpœple/ *adj* overpopulated.

surplomber /syʀplɔ̃be/ **1** *vt/i* overhang.

surplus /syʀply/ *nm* surplus.

suprenant, ~e /sypʀənɑ̃, -t/ *adj* surprising. **surprendre 50** *vt* (étonner) surprise; (prendre au dépourvu) catch, surprise; (entendre) overhear. **surpris, ~e** *adj* surprised (de at).

surprise /syʀpʀiz/ *nf* surprise.

surréaliste /syʀʀealist/ *adj & nmf* surrealist.

sursaut /syʀso/ *nm* start, jump; **en ~** with a start; **~ de** (regain) burst of. **sursauter 1** *vi* start, jump.

sursis /syʀsi/ *nm* reprieve; (Mil) deferment; **deux ans (de prison) avec ~** a two-year suspended sentence.

surtaxe /syʀtaks/ *nf* surcharge.

surtout /syʀtu/ *adv* especially; (avant tout) above all; **~ pas** certainly not.

surveillance /syʀvejɑ̃s/ *nf* watch; (d'examen) supervision; (de la police) surveillance. **surveillant, ~e** *nm, f* (de prison) warder; (au lycée) supervisor (in charge of discipline). **surveiller 1** *vt* watch; (travaux, élèves) supervise.

survenir /syʀvəniʀ/ **59** *vi* occur, take place; (personne) turn up.

survêtement /syʀvɛtmɑ̃/ nm (Sport) tracksuit.

survie /syʀvi/ nf survival.

survivant, ~e /syʀvivɑ̃, -t/ adj surviving. ● nm, f survivor.

survivre /syʀvivʀ/ 58 vi survive; ~ à (conflit) survive; (personne) outlive.

survoler /syʀvɔle/ 1 vt fly over; (livre) skim through.

sus: en ~ /ɑ̃sys/ loc in addition.

susceptible /sysɛptibl/ adj touchy; ~ de faire likely to do.

susciter /sysite/ 1 vt (éveiller) arouse; (occasionner) create.

suspect, ~e /syspɛ, -ɛkt/ adj (individu, faits) suspicious; (témoignage) suspect; ~ de suspected of. ● nm, f suspect. **suspecter** 1 vt suspect.

suspendre /syspɑ̃dʀ/ 3 vt (accrocher) hang (up); (interrompre, destituer) suspend; suspendu à hanging from. □ se ~ à vpr hang from.

suspens: en ~ /ɑ̃syspɑ̃/ loc (affaire) outstanding; (dans l'indécision) in suspense.

suspense /syspɛns/ nm suspense.

suture /sytyʀ/ nf point de ~ stitch.

svelte /svɛlt/ adj slender.

S.V.P. abrév (s'il vous plaît) please.

syllabe /silab/ nf syllable.

symbole /sɛ̃bɔl/ nm symbol. **symboliser** 1 vt symbolize.

symétrie /simetʀi/ nf symmetry.

sympa /sɛ̃pa/ adj inv 🗓 nice; sois ~ be a pal.

sympathie /sɛ̃pati/ nf (goût) liking; (compassion) sympathy; avoir de la ~ pour like. **sympathique** adj nice, pleasant. **sympathisant**, ~e nm, f sympathizer. **sympathiser** 1 vi get on well (avec with).

symphonie /sɛ̃fɔni/ nf symphony.

symptôme /sɛ̃ptom/ nm symptom.

synagogue /sinagɔg/ nf synagogue.

synchroniser /sɛ̃kʀɔnize/ 1 vt synchronize.

syncope /sɛ̃kɔp/ nf (Méd) blackout.

syndic /sɛ̃dik/ nm ~ (d'immeuble) property manager.

syndicaliste /sɛ̃dikalist/ nmf (trade-)unionist. ● adj (trade-) union.

syndicat /sɛ̃dika/ nm (trade) union; ~ d'initiative tourist office.

syndiqué, ~e /sɛ̃dike/ adj être ~ be a (trade-)union member.

synonyme /sinɔnim/ adj synonymous. ● nm synonym.

syntaxe /sɛ̃taks/ nf syntax.

synthèse /sɛ̃tɛz/ nf synthesis. **synthétique** adj synthetic.

synthé(tiseur) /sɛ̃te(tizœʀ)/ nm synthesizer.

systématique /sistematik/ adj systematic.

système /sistɛm/ nm system; le D 🗓 resourcefulness.

• •

Tt

t' /t/ ➙TE.

ta /ta/ ➙TON ¹.

tabac /taba/ nm tobacco; (magasin) tobacconist's shop.

table /tabl/ nf table; à ~! dinner is ready!; ~ de nuit bedside table; ~ des matières table of contents; ~ à repasser ironing board; ~ roulante (tea-)trolley; (US) (serving) cart.

tableau (pl ∼x) /tablo/ nm picture; (peinture) painting; (panneau) board; (graphique) chart; (Scol) blackboard; ∼ d'affichage noticeboard; ∼ de bord dashboard.

tablette /tablɛt/ nf shelf; ∼ de chocolat bar of chocolate.

tableur /tablœʀ/ nm spreadsheet.

tablier /tablije/ nm apron; (de pont) platform; (de magasin) shutter.

tabou /tabu/ nm & adj taboo.

tabouret /tabuʀɛ/ nm stool.

tache /taʃ/ nf mark, spot; (salissure) stain; faire ∼ d'huile spread; ∼ de rousseur freckle.

tâche /tɑʃ/ nf task, job.

tacher /taʃe/ ① vt stain. □ se ∼ vpr (personne) get oneself dirty.

tâcher /tɑʃe/ ① vi ∼ de faire try to do.

tacheté, ∼e /taʃte/ adj spotted.

tact /takt/ nm tact.

tactique /taktik/ adj tactical. ● nf (Mil) tactics; une ∼ a tactic.

taie /tɛ/ nf ∼ (d'oreiller) pillowcase.

taille /taj/ nf (milieu du corps) waist; (hauteur) height; (grandeur) size; de ∼ sizeable; être de ∼ à faire be up to doing.

taille-crayons /tajkʀɛjɔ̃/ nm inv pencil-sharpener.

tailler /taje/ ① vt cut; (barbe) prune; (crayon) sharpen; (vêtement) cut out. □ se ∼ vpr 🄸 clear off.

tailleur /tajœʀ/ nm (costume) woman's suit; (couturier) tailor; en ∼ cross-legged; ∼ de pierre stonecutter.

taire /tɛʀ/ ⁴⁷ vt not to reveal; faire ∼ silence. □ se ∼ vpr be silent ou quiet; (devenir silencieux) fall silent.

talc /talk/ nm talcum powder.

talent /talɑ̃/ nm talent. **talentueux, -euse** adj talented, gifted.

talon /talɔ̃/ nm heel; (de chèque) stub.

tambour /tɑ̃buʀ/ nm drum; (d'église) vestibule.

Tamise /tamiz/ nf Thames.

tampon /tɑ̃pɔ̃/ nm (de bureau) stamp; (ouate) wad, pad; (∼ hygiénique) tampon.

tamponner /tɑ̃pɔne/ ① vt (document) stamp; (véhicule) crash into; (plaie) swab.

tandem /tɑ̃dɛm/ nm (vélo) tandem; (personnes) fig) duo.

tandis que /tɑ̃di(k)ə/ conj while.

tanière /tanjɛʀ/ nf den.

tant /tɑ̃/ adv (travailler, manger) so much; ∼ de (quantité) so much; (nombre) so many; ∼ que as long as; en ∼ que as; ∼ mieux! all the better!; ∼ pis! too bad!

tante /tɑ̃t/ nf aunt.

tantôt /tɑ̃to/ adv sometimes.

tapage /tapaʒ/ nm din.

tape /tap/ nf slap. **tape-à-l'œil** adj inv flashy, tawdry.

taper /tape/ ① vt hit; (prendre 🄸) scrounge; ∼ (à la machine) type. ● vi (cogner) bang; (soleil) beat down; ∼ dans (puiser dans) dig into; ∼ sur hit; ∼ sur l'épaule de qn tap qn on the shoulder. □ se ∼ vpr (corvée 🄸) get stuck with 🄸.

tapis /tapi/ nm carpet; (petit) rug; ∼ de bain bathmat; (∼ roulant (pour objets) conveyor belt; (pour piétons) moving walkway.

tapisser /tapise/ ① vt (wall) paper; (fig) cover (de with). **tapisserie** nf tapestry; (papier peint) wallpaper.

taquin, ∼e /takɛ̃, -in/ adj fond of teasing. ● nm, f tease(r).

t

tard /taʀ/ adv late; au plus ~ at the latest; plus ~ later; sur le ~ late in life.

tarder /taʀde/ **1** vi (être lent à venir) be a long time coming; ~ (à faire) take a long time (doing), delay (doing); sans (plus) ~ without (further) delay; il me tarde de I'm longing to.

tardif, -ive /taʀdif, -v/ adj late.

tare /taʀ/ nf (défaut) defect.

tarif /taʀif/ nm rate; (de train, taxi) fare; plein ~ full price.

tarir /taʀiʀ/ **2** vt/i dry up. □ **se** ~ vpr dry up.

tarte /taʀt/ nf tart. ● adj inv (ridicule 🗌) ridiculous.

tartine /taʀtin/ nf slice of bread; ~ de beurre slice of bread and butter. **tartiner** **1** vt spread.

tartre /taʀtʀ/ nm (de bouilloire) fur, scale; (sur les dents) tartar.

tas /tɑ/ nm pile, heap; un ou des ~ de 🗌 lots of.

tasse /tɑs/ nf cup; ~ à thé teacup.

tasser /tɑse/ **1** vt pack, squeeze; (terre) pack (down). □ **se** ~ vpr (terrain) sink; (se serrer) squeeze up.

tâter /tɑte/ **1** vt feel; (opinion: fig) sound out. ● vi ~ de try out.

tatillon, -ne /tatijɔ̃, -jɔn/ adj finicky.

tâtonnements /tɑtɔnmɑ̃/ nmpl (essais) trial and error (+ sg). **tâtons: à** ~ /atatɔ̃/ loc avancer à ~ grope one's way along.

tatouage /tatwaʒ/ nm (dessin) tattoo.

taupe /top/ nf mole.

taureau (pl ~x) /tɔʀo/ nm bull; le T~ Taurus.

taux /to/ nm rate.

taxe /taks/ nf tax.

taxi /taksi/ nm taxi(-cab); (personne 🗌) taxi driver.

taxiphone ® /taksifɔn/ nm pay phone.

Tchécoslovaquie /tʃekɔslɔvaki/ nf Czechoslovakia.

tchèque /tʃɛk/ adj Czech; République ~ Czech Republic. **T~** nmf Czech.

te, t' /tə, t/ pron you; (indirect) (to) you; (réfléchi) yourself.

technicien, -ne /tɛknisjɛ̃, -ɛn/ nm, f technician.

technique /tɛknik/ adj technical. ● nf technique.

techno /tɛkno/ nf (Mus) techno.

technologie /tɛknɔlɔʒi/ nf technology.

teindre /tɛ̃dʀ/ **22** vt dye. □ **se** ~ vpr se ~ les cheveux dye one's hair.

teint /tɛ̃/ nm complexion.

teinte /tɛ̃t/ nf shade. **teinter** **1** vt (verre) tint; (bois) stain.

teinture /tɛ̃tyʀ/ nf (produit) dye.

teinturier, -ière /tɛ̃tyʀje, -jɛʀ/ nm, f dry-cleaner.

tel, ~le /tɛl/ adj such; un ~ livre such a book; ~ que such as, like; (ainsi que) (just) as; ~ ou ~ such-and-such; ~ quel (just) as it is.

télé /tele/ nf 🗌 TV; ~ réalité nf reality TV.

télécharger /teleʃaʀʒe/ **40** vt (Ordinat) download.

télécommande /telekɔmɑ̃d/ nf remote control.

télécommunications /telekɔmynikasjɔ̃/ nfpl telecommunications.

téléconférence /telekɔ̃feʀɑ̃s/ nf teleconferencing.

télécopie /telekɔpi/ nf fax. **télécopieur** nm fax machine.

téléfilm /telefilm/ nm TV film.

télégramme /telegram/ nm telegram.

télégraphier /telegrafje/ [45] vt/i ~ (à) cable.

téléguidé, ~e /telegide/ adj radiocontrolled.

télématique /telematik/ nf telematics (+ sg).

téléphérique /teleferik/ nm cable car.

téléphone /telefɔn/ nm (tele-) phone; ~ à carte cardphone. **téléphoner** /telefɔne/ vt/i ~ (à) (tele)phone.

téléphonie /telefɔni/ nf telephony; ~ mobile mobile telephony. **téléphonique** adj (tele)phone.

télé-réalité /telerealite/ nf reality TV.

téléserveur /teleservœr/ nm (Internet) remote server.

télésiège /telesjɛʒ/ nm chairlift.

téléski /teleski/ nm ski tow.

téléspectateur, -trice /telespɛktatœr, -tris/ nm, f (tv) viewer.

télévente /televãt/ nf telesales (+ pl).

télévisé, ~e /televize/ adj (débat) televised; émission ~e television programme. **télévision** nf television.

télex /telɛks/ nm telex.

tellement /tɛlmã/ adv (tant) so much; (si) so; ~ de (quantité) so much; (nombre) so many.

téméraire /temerer/ adj (personne) reckless.

témoignage /temwaɲaʒ/ nm testimony, evidence; (récit) account; ~ de (marque) token of.

témoigner /temwaɲe/ [1] vi testify (de to). ●vt (montrer) show; ~ que testify that.

témoin /temwɛ̃/ nm witness; (Sport) baton; être ~ de witness;

~ oculaire eyewitness.

tempe /tɑ̃p/ nf (Anat) temple.

tempérament /tɑ̃peramɑ̃/ nm temperament, disposition.

température /tɑ̃peratyr/ nf temperature.

tempête /tɑ̃pɛt/ nf storm; ~ de neige snowstorm.

temple /tɑ̃pl/ nm temple; (protestant) church.

temporaire /tɑ̃pɔrɛr/ adj temporary.

temps /tɑ̃/ nm (notion) time; (Gram) tense; (étape) stage; à ~ partiel/plein part-/full-time; ces derniers ~ lately; dans le ~ at one time; dans quelque ~ in a while; de ~ en ~ from time to time; ~ d'arrêt pause; avoir tout son ~ have plenty of time; (météo) weather; ~ de chien filthy weather; quel ~ fait-il? what's the weather like?

tenace /tanas/ adj stubborn.

tenaille /tanaj/ nf pincers (+ pl).

tendance /tɑ̃dɑ̃s/ nf tendency; (évolution) trend; avoir ~ à tend to.

tendon /tɑ̃dɔ̃/ nm tendon.

tendre[1] /tɑ̃dr/ [3] vt stretch; (piège) set; (bras) stretch out; (main) hold out; (cou) crane; ~ qch à qn hold sth out to sb; ~ l'oreille prick up one's ears. ●vi ~ à tend to.

tendre[2] /tɑ̃dr/ adj tender; (couleur, bois) soft. **tendresse** nf tenderness.

tendu, ~e /tɑ̃dy/ adj (corde) tight; (personne, situation) tense.

ténèbres /tenɛbr/ nfpl darkness.

teneur /tanœr/ nf content.

tenir /tanir/ [58] vt hold; (pari, promesse, hôtel) keep; (place) take up; (propos) utter; (rôle) play; ~ de (avoir reçu de) have got from;

t

pour regard as; ~ chaud keep warm; ~ compte de take into account; ~ le coup hold out; ~ tête à stand up to. ● *vi* hold; ~ à be attached to; ~ à faire be anxious to do; ~ bon stand firm; ~ dans fit into; ~ de qn take after sb; tiens! (surprise) hey! □ se ~ *vpr* (debout) stand; (avoir lieu) be held; se ~ à hold on to; s'en ~ à (se limiter à) confine oneself to.

tennis /tenis/ *nm* tennis; ~ de table table tennis. ● *nmpl* (chaussures) sneakers.

ténor /tenɔʁ/ *nm* tenor.

tension /tɑ̃sjɔ̃/ *nf* tension; avoir de la ~ have high blood pressure.

tentation /tɑ̃tasjɔ̃/ *nf* temptation.

tentative /tɑ̃tativ/ *nf* attempt.

tente /tɑ̃t/ *nf* tent.

tenter /tɑ̃te/ **1** *vt* (allécher) tempt; (essayer) try (de faire to do).

tenture /tɑ̃tyʁ/ *nf* curtain; ~s draperies.

tenu, ~e /təny/ *adj* bien ~ well kept; ~ de required. ● →TENIR 58.

tenue /təny/ *nf* (habillement) dress; (de maison) upkeep; (conduite) (good) behaviour; (maintien) posture; ~ de soirée evening dress.

Tergal ® /tɛʁgal/ *nm* Terylene®.

terme /tɛʁm/ *nm* (mot) term; (date limite) time-limit; (fin) end; né avant ~ premature; à long/court ~ long-/short-term; en bons ~s on good terms (avec with).

terminaison /tɛʁminɛzɔ̃/ *nf* (Gram) ending.

terminal, ~e *m* (*mpl* -aux) /tɛʁminal, -o/ *adj* terminal. ● *nm* terminal.

terminale *nf* (Scol) ≈ sixth form; (US) twelfth grade.

terminer /tɛʁmine/ **1** *vt/i* finish; (discours) end, finish. □ se ~ *vpr* end (par with).

terne /tɛʁn/ *adj* dull, drab.

ternir /tɛʁniʁ/ **2** *vt/i* tarnish. □ se ~ *vpr* tarnish.

terrain /teʁɛ̃/ *nm* ground; (parcelle) piece of land; (à bâtir) plot; ~ d'aviation airfield; ~ de camping campsite; ~ de golf golf course; ~ de jeu playground; ~ vague waste ground.

terrasse /teʁas/ *nf* terrace; à la ~ (d'un café) outside (a café).

terrasser /teʁase/ **1** *vt* (adversaire) knock down; (maladie) strike down.

terre /tɛʁ/ *nf* (planète, matière) earth; (étendue, pays) land; (sol) ground; (à ~ (Naut) ashore; par ~ (dehors) on the ground; (dedans) on the floor; ~ (cuite) terracotta; la ~ ferme dry land; ~ glaise clay. ● *pl* ~s *nm* compost.

terreau (*pl* ~x) *nm* compost.

terre-plein (*pl* **terres-pleins**) *nm* platform; (de route) central reservation.

terrestre /teʁɛstʁ/ *adj* (animaux) land; (de notre planète) of the Earth.

terreur /teʁœʁ/ *nf* terror.

terrible /teʁibl/ *adj* terrible; (formidable 🔢) terrific.

terrier /teʁje/ *nm* (trou) burrow; (chien) terrier.

terrifier /teʁifje/ 45 *vt* terrify.

territoire /teʁitwaʁ/ *nm* territory.

terroir /teʁwaʁ/ *nm* land; du ~ local.

terroriser /teʁɔʁize/ **1** *vt* terrorize.

terrorisme /teʁɔʁism/ *nm* terrorism. **terroriste** *nmf* terrorist.

tertiaire /tɛʁsjɛʁ/ *adj* (secteur) service.

tes /te/ →TON¹.

test /tɛst/ *nm* test.

testament /tɛstamɑ̃/ *nm* (Jur) will;

(politique, artistique) testament; **Ancien/Nouveau T~** Old/New Testament.

tétanos /tetanos/ nm tetanus.

têtard /tɛtaʀ/ nm tadpole.

tête /tɛt/ nf head; (visage) face; (cheveux) hair; **à la ~ de** at the head of; **à ~ reposée** at one's leisure; **de ~** (calculer) in one's head; **faire la ~** sulk; **tenir ~ à qn** stand up to sb; **il n'en fait qu'à sa ~** he does just as he pleases; **en ~** (Sport) in the lead; **faire une ~** (au football) head the ball; **une forte ~** a rebel; **la ~** la première head first; **de la ~ aux pieds** from head to toe.

tête-à-tête /tɛtatɛt/ nm inv tête-à-tête; **en ~** in private.

tétée /tete/ nf feed.

tétine /tetin/ nf (de biberon) teat; (sucette) dummy; (US) pacifier.

têtu, ~e /tety/ adj stubborn.

texte /tɛkst/ nm text; (de leçon) subject; (morceau choisi) passage.

texteur /tɛkstœʀ/ nm (Ordinat) word-processor.

textile /tɛkstil/ nm & adj textile.

texto /tɛksto/ nm ⓵ text message.

TGV abrév m (**train à grande vitesse**) TGV, high-speed train.

> *i*
> **TGV** Abbreviation of *Train à grande vitesse*, the high-speed electric passenger train operated by the SNCF. It runs on special track and can reach speeds of up to 300 km/h (180 mph). Marseilles, for example, is now only three hours from Paris by *TGV*.

thé /te/ nm tea.

théâtre /teatʀ/ nm theatre; (d'un crime) scene; **faire du ~** act.

théière /tejɛʀ/ nf teapot.

thème /tɛm/ nm theme; (traduction: Scol) prose.

théorie /teɔʀi/ nf theory. **théorique** adj theoretical.

thérapie /teʀapi/ nf therapy.

thermique /tɛʀmik/ adj thermal.

thermomètre /tɛʀmɔmɛtʀ/ nm thermometer.

thermos® /tɛʀmos/ nm ou f Thermos® (flask).

thermostat /tɛʀmɔsta/ nm thermostat.

thèse /tɛz/ nf thesis.

thon /tɔ̃/ nm tuna.

thym /tɛ̃/ nm thyme.

tibia /tibja/ nm shinbone.

tic /tik/ nm (contraction) tic, twitch; (manie) habit.

ticket /tikɛ/ nm ticket.

tiède /tjɛd/ adj lukewarm; (nuit) warm.

tiédir /tjediʀ/ ② vt/i (faire) ~ warm up.

tien, ~ne /tjɛ̃, -ɛn/ pron **le ~, la ~ne, les ~(ne)s** yours; **à la ~ne!** cheers!

tiens, tient /tjɛ̃/ ➜ TENIR 59.

tiercé /tjɛʀse/ nm place-betting.

tiers, tierce /tjɛʀ, tjɛʀs/ adj third. ● nm (fraction) third; (personne) third party. **tiers-monde** nm Third World.

tige /tiʒ/ nf (Bot) stem, stalk; (en métal) shaft, rod.

tigre /tigʀ/ nm tiger.

tigresse /tigʀɛs/ nf tigress.

tilleul /tijœl/ nm lime tree.

timbre /tɛ̃bʀ/ nm stamp; (sonnette) bell; (de voix) tone. **~ poste** (pl **~s poste**) nm postage stamp. **timbrer** ① vt stamp.

timide /timid/ adj shy, timid. **timidité** nf shyness.

timoré, ~e /timɔʀe/ adj timorous.

tintement /tɛ̃tmɑ̃/ nm (de sonnette) ringing; (de clés) jingling.

tique /tik/ nf tick.

tir /tiʀ/ nm (Sport) shooting; (action de tirer) firing; (feu, rafale) fire; ~ à l'arc archery; ~ au pigeon clay pigeon shooting.

tirage /tiʀaʒ/ nm (de photo) printing; (de journal) circulation; (de livre) edition; (Ordinat) hard copy; (de cheminée) draught; ~ au sort draw.

tire-bouchon (pl ~s) /tiʀbuʃɔ̃/ nm corkscrew.

tirelire /tiʀliʀ/ nf piggy bank.

tirer /tiʀe/ **1** vt pull; (langue) stick out; (conclusion, trait, rideaux) draw; (coup de feu) fire; (gibier) shoot; (photo) print; ~ de (sortir) take ou get out of; (extraire) extract from; (plaisir, nom) derive from; ~ parti de take advantage of; ~ profit de profit from; se faire ~ l'oreille get told off. ● vi shoot, fire (sur at); ~ sur (corde) pull at; (couleur) verge on; ~ à sa fin be drawing to a close; ~ au clair clarify; ~ au sort draw lots (pour). □ se ~ clear off; se ~ de get out of; s'en ~ (en réchapper) pull through; (réussir **1**) cope.

tiret /tiʀɛ/ nm dash.

tireur /tiʀœʀ/ nm gunman; ~ d'élite marksman; ~ isolé sniper.

tiroir /tiʀwaʀ/ nm drawer. **tiroir-caisse** (pl tiroirs-caisses) nm till, cash register.

tisane /tizan/ nf herbal tea.

tissage /tisaʒ/ nm weaving. **tisser** **1** vt weave. **tisserand** nm weaver.

tissu /tisy/ nm fabric, material; (biologique) tissue; un ~ de mensonges (fig) a pack of lies.

tissu-éponge (pl tissus-éponge)

nm towelling.

titre /titʀ/ nm title; (diplôme) qualification; (Comm) bond; ~s (droits) claims; (gros) ~s headlines; à ~ d'exemple as an example; à juste ~ rightly; à ~ privé in a private capacity; à double ~ on two accounts; ~ de propriété title deed.

tituber /titybe/ **1** vi stagger.

titulaire /titylɛʀ/ adj être ~ be a permanent staff member; être ~ de hold. ● nmf (de permis) holder. **titulariser** **1** vt give permanent status to.

toast /tost/ nm (pain) piece of toast; (canapé, allocution) toast.

toboggan /tɔbɔgɑ̃/ nm (de jeu) slide; (Auto) flyover.

toi /twa/ pron you; (réfléchi) yourself; dépêche-~ hurry up.

toile /twal/ nf cloth; (tableau) canvas; ~ d'araignée cobweb; ~ de fond (fig) backdrop; la ~ (Internet) the Web.

toilette /twalɛt/ nf (habillement) outfit; ~s (cabinets) toilet(s); de ~ (articles, savon) toilet; faire sa ~ have a wash.

toi-même /twamɛm/ pron yourself.

toit /twa/ nm roof; ~ ouvrant (Auto) sunroof.

toiture /twatyʀ/ nf roof.

tôle /tol/ nf (plaque) iron sheet; ~ ondulée corrugated iron.

tolérant, ~e /tɔleʀɑ̃, -t/ adj tolerant. **tolérer** **14** vt tolerate.

tomate /tɔmat/ nf tomato.

tombe /tɔ̃b/ nf grave; (pierre) gravestone.

tombeau (pl ~x) /tɔ̃bo/ nm tomb.

tomber /tɔ̃be/ **1** vi (aux être) fall; (fièvre, vent) drop; faire ~ knock over; (gouvernement) bring down; laisser ~ (objet, amoureux) drop;

(*collègue*) let down; (*activité*) give up; laisse ~l 1 forget it!; ~ à l'eau (*projet*) fall through; ~ bien ou à point come at the right time; ~ en panne break down; ~ en syncope faint; ~ sur (*trouver*) run across.

tombola /tɔ̃bɔla/ *nf* tombola; (US) lottery.

tome /tɔm/ *nm* volume.

ton¹, ta (**ton** before vowel or mute *h*) (*pl* **tes**) /tɔ̃, ta, tɔ̃, te/ *adj* your.

ton² /tɔ̃/ *nm* (hauteur de voix) pitch; d'un ~ sec drily; de bon ~ in good taste.

tonalité /tɔnalite/ *nf* (Mus) key; (de téléphone) dialling tone; (US) dial tone.

tondeuse /tɔ̃døz/ *nf* (à moutons) shears (+ *pl*); (à cheveux) clippers (+ *pl*); ~ à gazon lawn-mower. **tondre** 3 *vt* (*herbe*) mow; (*mouton*) shear; (*cheveux*) clip.

tonne /tɔn/ *nf* tonne.

tonneau (*pl* ~x) /tɔno/ *nm* barrel; (en voiture) somersault.

tonnerre /tɔnɛʀ/ *nm* thunder.

tonton /tɔ̃tɔ̃/ *nm* 1 uncle.

tonus /tɔnys/ *nm* energy.

torche /tɔʀʃ/ *nf* torch.

torchon /tɔʀʃɔ̃/ *nm* (pour la vaisselle) tea towel.

tordre /tɔʀdʀ/ 3 *vt* twist. □ se ~ *vpr* se ~ la cheville twist one's ankle; se ~ de douleur writhe in pain; se ~ (de rire) split one's sides.

tordu, ~e /tɔʀdy/ *adj* twisted, bent; (*esprit*) warped, twisted.

torpille /tɔʀpij/ *nf* torpedo.

torrent /tɔʀɑ̃/ *nm* torrent.

torride /tɔʀid/ *adj* torrid; (*chaleur*) scorching.

torse /tɔʀs/ *nm* chest; (Anat) torso.

tort /tɔʀ/ *nm* wrong; avoir ~ be wrong (de faire to do); donner ~ à prove wrong; être dans son ~ be in the wrong; faire (du) ~ à harm; à ~ wrongly; à ~ et à travers without thinking.

torticolis /tɔʀtikɔli/ *nm* stiff neck.

tortiller /tɔʀtije/ 1 *vt* twist, twirl. □ se ~ *vpr* wriggle.

tortionnaire /tɔʀsjɔnɛʀ/ *nm* torturer.

tortue /tɔʀty/ *nf* tortoise; (d'eau) turtle.

tortueux, -euse /tɔʀtɥø, -z/ *adj* (*chemin*) twisting; (*explication*) tortuous.

torture /tɔʀtyʀ/ *nf* torture. **torturer** 1 *vt* torture.

tôt /to/ *adv* early; au plus ~ at the earliest; le plus ~ possible as soon as possible; ~ ou tard sooner or later; ce n'est pas trop ~! it's about time!

total, ~e (*mpl* -aux) /tɔtal, -o/ *adj* total. ● *nm* (*pl* -aux) total; au ~ all in all. **totalement** *adv* totally. **totaliser** 1 *vt* total. **totalitaire** *adj* totalitarian.

totalité /tɔtalite/ *nf* la ~ de all of.

touche /tuʃ/ *nf* (de piano) key; (de peinture) touch; (ligne de) ~ (Sport) touchline.

toucher /tuʃe/ 1 *vt* touch; (*émouvoir*) move, touch; (contacter) get in touch with; (*cible*) hit; (*argent*) draw; (*chèque*) cash; (concerner) affect. ● *vi* ~ à touch; (*question*) touch on; (*fin, but*) approach; je vais lui en ~ deux mots I'll talk to him about it. □ se ~ *vpr* (*lignes*) touch. ● *nm* sense) touch.

touffe /tuf/ *nf* (de poils, d'herbe) tuft; (de plantes) clump.

toujours /tuʒuʀ/ *adv* always; (encore) still; (de toute façon) anyway;

t

pour ∼ for ever; ∼ est-il que the fact remains that.

toupet /tupɛ/ nm (culot 🆒) cheek, nerve.

tour /tur/ nf tower; (immeuble) tower block; (échecs) rook; ∼ de contrôle control tower. ● nm (mouvement, succession, tournure) turn; (excursion) trip; (à pied) walk; (en auto) drive; (artifice) trick; (circonférence) circumference; (Tech) lathe; ∼ (de piste) lap; à ∼ de rôle in turn; à mon ∼ when it is my turn; c'est mon ∼ de it is my turn to; faire le ∼ de go round; (question) survey; ∼ d'horizon overview; ∼ de potier potter's wheel; ∼ de taille waist measurement; (ligne) waistline.

Tour de France The race for professional cyclists held annually in July since 1903, when it was created by Henri Desgrange (1865-1940). Renowned for its mountain stages, it covers approximately 4,800 km (3,000 miles) over a three-week period, finishing triumphantly on the Champs Élysées. Throughout the *Tour*, the previous day's leader wears the coveted *maillot jaune* (yellow jersey).

---

tourbillon /turbijɔ̃/ nm whirlwind; (d'eau) whirlpool; (fig) swirl.

tourisme /turism/ nm tourism; faire du ∼ do some sightseeing.

touriste /turist/ nmf tourist. **touristique** adj tourist; (route) scenic.

tourmenter /turmɑ̃te/ vt torment. ▢ se ∼ vpr worry.

tournant, ∼e /turnɑ̃, -t/ adj (qui pivote) revolving. ● nm bend; (fig) turning-point.

tourne-disque (pl ∼s)

/turnədisk/ nm record-player.

tournée /turne/ nf (de facteur, au café) round; c'est ma ∼ I'll buy this round; (d'artiste) tour.

tourner /turne/ 🆒 vt turn; (film) shoot, make; ∼ le dos à turn one's back on; ∼ en dérision mock. ● vi turn; (toupie, tête) spin; (moteur, usine) run; ∼ autour de go round; (personne, maison) hang around; (terre) revolve round; (question) centre on; ∼ de l'œil 🆒 faint; mal ∼ (affaire) turn out badly. ▢ se ∼ vpr turn.

tournesol /turnəsɔl/ nm sunflower.

tournevis /turnəvis/ nm screwdriver.

tournoi /turnwa/ nm tournament.

tourte /turt/ nf pie.

tourterelle /turtərɛl/ nf turtle dove.

Toussaint /tusɛ̃/ nf la ∼ All Saints' Day.

tousser /tuse/ 🆒 vi cough.

tout, ∼e (pl **tous, toutes**) /tu, tu̯/ nm (ensemble) whole; en ∼ in all; pas du ∼! not at all! ● adj all; (n'importe quel) any; ∼ le pays the whole country, all the country; ∼e la nuit/journée the whole night/day; ∼ un paquet a whole pack; tous les jours every day; tous les deux ans every two years; ∼ le monde everyone; tous les deux, toutes les deux both of them; tous les trois all three (of them). ● pron everything; anything; tous /tus/, toutes all; tous ensemble all together; prends ∼ take everything; ∼ ce que tu veux everything you want. ● adv (très) very; (entièrement) all; ∼ au bout/début right at the end/beginning; ∼ en marchant while walking; ∼ à coup all of a sudden; ∼ à fait quite,

completely; ~ à l'heure in a moment; (passé) a moment ago; ~ au ou le long de throughout; ~ au plus/moins at most/least; ~ de même all the same; ~ de suite straight away; ~ entier whole; ~ neuf brand new; ~ nu stark naked.
tout-à-l'égout *nm inv* main drainage.

toutefois /tutfwa/ *adv* however.

tout(-)terrain /tuteRɛ̃/ *adj inv* all terrain.

toux /tu/ *nf* cough.

toxicomane /tɔksikɔman/ *nmf* drug addict.

toxique /tɔksik/ *adj* toxic.

trac /tRak/ *nm* le ~ nerves; (Théât) stage fright.

tracas /tRaka/ *nm* worry.

trace /tRas/ *nf* (traînée, piste) trail; (d'animal, de pneu) tracks; ~s de pas footprints.

tracer /tRase/ [10] *vt* draw; (écrire) write; (route) open up.

trachée-artère /tRaʃeaRtɛR/ *nf* windpipe.

tracteur /tRaktœR/ *nm* tractor.

tradition /tRadisjɔ̃/ *nf* tradition. **traditionnel**, ~**le** *adj* traditional.

traducteur, **-trice** /tRadyktœR, -tRis/ *nm*, *f* translator. **traduction** *nf* translation.

traduire /tRadɥiR/ [17] *vt* translate; ~ en justice take to court.

trafic /tRafik/ *nm* (commerce, circulation) traffic.

trafiquant, ~**e** /tRafikɑ̃, -t/ *nm*, *f* trafficker; (d'armes, de drogues) dealer.

trafiquer /tRafike/ [1] *vi* traffic. ● *vt* [1] (moteur) fiddle with.

tragédie /tRaʒedi/ *nf* tragedy. **tragique** *adj* tragic.

trahir /tRaiR/ [2] *vt* betray. **trahi-**

son *nf* betrayal; (Mil) treason.

train /tRɛ̃/ *nm* (Rail) train; (allure) pace; aller bon ~ walk briskly; en ~ de faire (busy) doing; ~ d'atterrissage undercarriage; ~ électrique (jouet) electric train set; ~ de vie lifestyle.

traîne /tRɛn/ *nf* (de robe) train; à la ~ a lagging behind.

traîneau (*pl* ~x) /tRɛno/ *nm* sleigh.

traînée /tRɛne/ *nf* (trace) trail; (longue) streak; (femme: péj) slut.

traîner /tRɛne/ [1] *vt* drag (along); ~ les pieds drag one's feet. ● *vi* (pendre) trail; (rester en arrière) trail behind; (flâner) hang about; (papiers, affaires) lie around; ~ (en longueur) drag on. □ se ~ *vpr* (par terre) crawl.

traire /tRɛR/ [29] *vt* milk.

trait /tRɛ/ *nm* line; (en dessinant) stroke; (caractéristique) feature, trait; ~s (du visage) features; avoir ~ à relate to; d'un ~ (boire) in one gulp; ~ d'union hyphen; (fig) link.

traite /tRɛt/ *nf* (de vache) milking; (Comm) draft; d'une (seule) ~ in one go, at a stretch.

traité /tRɛte/ *nm* (pacte) treaty; (ouvrage) treatise.

traitement /tRɛtmɑ̃/ *nm* treatment; (salaire) salary; ~ de données data processing; ~ de texte word processing.

traiter /tRɛte/ [1] *vt* treat; (affaire) deal with; (données, produit) process; ~ qn de lâche call sb a coward. ● *vi* deal (avec with); ~ de (sujet) deal with.

traiteur /tRɛtœR/ *nm* caterer; (boutique) delicatessen.

traître, **-esse** /tRɛtR, -ɛs/ *adj* treacherous. ● *nm*, *f* traitor.

trajectoire /tRaʒɛktwaR/ *nf* path.

trajet /tʀaʒɛ/ nm (voyage) journey; (itinéraire) route.

trame /tʀam/ nf (de tissu) weft.

tramway /tʀamwɛ/ nm tram; (US) streetcar.

tranchant, **~e** /tʀɑ̃ʃɑ̃, -t/ adj sharp; (fig) cutting. ● nm cutting edge; à double ~ two-edged.

tranche /tʀɑ̃ʃ/ nf (rondelle) slice; (bord) edge; (d'âge, de revenu) bracket.

tranchée /tʀɑ̃ʃe/ nf trench.

trancher /tʀɑ̃ʃe/ **1** vt cut; (question) decide; (contraster) contrast (sur with).

tranquille /tʀɑ̃kil/ adj quiet; (esprit) at rest; (conscience) clear; être/laisser ~ be/leave in peace; tiens-toi ~! be quiet! **tranquillisant** nm tranquillizer. **tranquilliser** **1** vt reassure. **tranquillité** nf (peace and) quiet; (d'esprit) peace of mind.

transcription /tʀɑ̃skʀipsjɔ̃/ nf transcription; (copie) transcript. **transcrire** **30** vt transcribe.

transe /tʀɑ̃s/ nf en ~ in a trance.

transférer /tʀɑ̃sfeʀe/ **14** vt transfer.

transfert /tʀɑ̃sfɛʀ/ nm transfer; ~ d'appel (au téléphone) call diversion.

transformation /tʀɑ̃sfɔʀmasjɔ̃/ nf change; transformation.

transformer /tʀɑ̃sfɔʀme/ **1** vt change; (radicalement) transform; (vêtement) alter. □ se ~ vpr change; (radicalement) be transformed; (se) ~ en turn into.

transgénique /tʀɑ̃sʒenik/ adj genetically modified.

transiger /tʀɑ̃siʒe/ **40** vi compromise.

transiter /tʀɑ̃zite/ **1** vt/i ~ par pass through.

transitif, -ive /tʀɑ̃zitif, -v/ adj transitive.

translucide /tʀɑ̃slysid/ adj translucent.

transmettre /tʀɑ̃smɛtʀ/ **42** vt (savoir, maladie) pass on; (ondes) transmit; (à la radio) broadcast. **transmission** nf transmission; (radio) broadcasting.

transparence /tʀɑ̃spaʀɑ̃s/ nf transparency. **transparent**, **~e** adj transparent.

transpercer /tʀɑ̃spɛʀse/ **10** vt pierce.

transpiration /tʀɑ̃spiʀasjɔ̃/ nf perspiration. **transpirer** **1** vi perspire.

transplanter /tʀɑ̃splɑ̃te/ **1** vt (Bot, Méd) transplant.

transport /tʀɑ̃spɔʀ/ nm transport(ation); durant le ~ in transit; les ~s transport (+ sg); les ~s en commun public transport (+ sg). **transporter** /tʀɑ̃spɔʀte/ **1** vt transport; (à la main) carry. **transporteur** nm haulier; (US) trucker.

transversal, **~e** (mpl **-aux**) /tʀɑ̃svɛʀsal, -o/ adj cross, transverse.

trapu, **~e** /tʀapy/ adj stocky.

traumatisant, **~e** /tʀomatizɑ̃, -t/ adj traumatic. **traumatiser** vt **1** traumatize. **traumatisme** nm trauma.

travail (pl **-aux**) /tʀavaj, -o/ nm work; (emploi, tâche) job; (façonnage) working; **travaux** work (+ sg); (routiers) roadworks; ~ à la chaîne production line work; **travaux dirigés** (Scol) practical; **travaux forcés** hard labour; **travaux manuels** handicrafts; **travaux ménagers** housework.

travailler /tʀavaje/ **1** vi work; (se déformer) warp. ● vt (façonner) work; (étudier) work at ou on.

travailleur, -euse /travajœr, -øz/ *nm, f* worker. ● *adj* hardworking.

travailliste /travajist/ *adj* Labour. ● *nmf* Labour party member.

travers /travɛr/ *nm* (défaut) failing; à ~ through; au ~ (de) through; de ~ (chapeau, nez) crooked; (regarder) askance; j'ai avalé de ~ it went down the wrong way; en ~ (de) across.

traversée /travɛrse/ *nf* crossing.

traverser /travɛrse/ **1** *vt* cross; (transpercer) go (right) through; (période, forêt) go ou pass through.

traversin /travɛrsɛ̃/ *nm* bolster.

travesti /travɛsti/ *nm* transvestite.

trébucher /trebyʃe/ **1** *vi* stumble, trip (over); faire ~ trip (up).

trèfle /trɛfl/ *nm* (plante) clover; (cartes) clubs.

treillis /trɛji/ *nm* trellis; (en métal) wire mesh; (tenue militaire) combat uniform.

treize /trɛz/ *adj & nm* thirteen.

> **Treizième mois** An addition to an employee's salary, equal to his/her usual monthly payment, which some employees receive at the end of the calendar year. *i*

tréma /trema/ *nm* diaeresis.

tremblement /trɑ̃bləmɑ̃/ *nm* shaking; ~ de terre earthquake. **trembler** **1** *vi* shake, tremble; (lumière, voix) quiver.

tremper /trɑ̃pe/ **1** *vt/i* soak; (plonger) dip; (acier) temper; faire ~ soak; ~ dans (fig) be mixed up. □ **se** ~ *vpr* (se baigner) have a dip.

tremplin /trɑ̃plɛ̃/ *nm* springboard.

trente /trɑ̃t/ *adj & nm* thirty; se mettre sur son ~ et un dress up;

tous les ~-six du mois once in a blue moon.

trépied /trepje/ *nm* tripod.

très /trɛ/ *adv* very; ~ aimé/estimé much liked/esteemed.

trésor /trezɔr/ *nm* treasure; le T~ public the revenue department.

trésorerie /trezɔrri/ *nf* (bureaux) accounts department; (du Trésor public) revenue office; (argent) funds (+ *pl*); (gestion) accounts (+ *pl*). **trésorier, -ière** *nm, f* treasurer.

tressaillement /tresajmɑ̃/ *nm* quiver; start.

tresse /trɛs/ *nf* braid, plait.

trêve /trɛv/ *nf* truce; (fig) respite; ~ de plaisanteries that's enough joking.

tri /tri/ *nm* (classement) sorting; (sélection) selection; faire le ~ de (classer) sort; (choisir) select; centre de ~ sorting office.

triangle /trijɑ̃gl/ *nm* triangle.

tribal, ~e (*mpl* **-aux**) /tribal, -o/ *adj* tribal.

tribord /tribɔr/ *nm* starboard.

tribu /triby/ *nf* tribe.

tribunal (*mpl* **-aux**) /tribynal, -o/ *nm* court.

tribune /tribyn/ *nf* (de stade) grandstand; (d'orateur) rostrum; (débat) forum; (d'église) gallery.

tribut /triby/ *nm* tribute.

tributaire /tribytɛr/ *adj* ~ de dependent on.

tricher /triʃe/ **1** *vi* cheat. **tricheur, -euse** *nm, f* cheat.

tricolore /trikɔlɔr/ *adj* three-coloured; (français) red, white and blue; (équipe) French.

tricot /triko/ *nm* (activité) knitting; (pull) sweater; en ~ knitted; ~ de corps vest; (US) undershirt. **tricoter** 🔟 vt/i knit.

trier /tʀije/ 45 vt (classer) sort; (choisir) select.

trimestre /tʀimɛstʀ/ nm quarter; (Scol) term. **trimestriel, ~le** adj quarterly; (bulletin) end-of-term.

tringle /tʀɛ̃gl/ nf rail.

trinquer /tʀɛ̃ke/ 🔟 vi clink glasses.

triomphant, ~e /tʀijɔ̃fɑ̃, -t/ adj triumphant. **triomphe** nm triumph. **triompher** 🔟 vi triumph (de over); (jubiler) be triumphant.

tripes /tʀip/ nfpl (mets) tripe (+ sg); (entrailles 🔟) guts.

triple /tʀipl/ adj triple, treble. ● nm le ~ three times as much (de as). **triplés, -es** nm, fpl triplets.

tripot /tʀipo/ nm gambling den.

tripoter /tʀipɔte/ 🔟 vt 🔟 (personne) grope; (objet) fiddle with.

trisomique /tʀizɔmik/ adj être ~ have Down's syndrome.

triste /tʀist/ adj sad; (rue, temps, couleur) dreary; (lamentable) dreadful. **tristesse** nf sadness; dreariness.

trivial, ~e (mpl -iaux) /tʀivjal, -jo/ adj coarse.

troc /tʀɔk/ nm exchange; (Comm) barter.

trognon /tʀɔɲɔ̃/ nm (de fruit) core.

trois /tʀwa/ adj & nm three; hôtel ~ étoiles three-star hotel. **troisième** adj & nmf third.

trombone /tʀɔ̃bɔn/ nm (Mus) trombone; (agrafe) paperclip.

trompe /tʀɔ̃p/ nf (d'éléphant) trunk; (Mus) horn.

tromper /tʀɔ̃pe/ 🔟 vt deceive, mislead; (déjouer) elude. □ se ~ vpr be mistaken; se ~ de route/ d'heure take the wrong road/get the time wrong.

trompette /tʀɔ̃pɛt/ nf trumpet.

trompeur, -euse /tʀɔ̃pœʀ, -øz/ adj (apparence) deceptive.

tronc /tʀɔ̃/ nm trunk; (boîte) collection box.

tronçon /tʀɔ̃sɔ̃/ nm section.

tronçonneuse /tʀɔ̃sɔnøz/ nf chain saw.

trône /tʀon/ nm throne. **trôner** 🔟 vi (vase) have pride of place (sur on).

trop /tʀo/ adv (grand, loin) too; (boire, marcher) too much; ~ (de) (quantité) too much; (nombre) too many; ce serait ~ beau une should be so lucky; de ~ en ~ too much; too many; il a bu un verre de ~ he's had one too many; se sentir de ~ feel one is in the way.

trophée /tʀɔfe/ nm trophy.

tropical, ~e (mpl -aux) /tʀɔpikal, -o/ adj tropical. **tropique** nm tropic.

trop-plein (pl ~s) /tʀɔplɛ̃/ nm excess; (dispositif) overflow.

troquer /tʀɔke/ 🔟 vt exchange; (Comm) barter (contre for).

trot /tʀo/ nm trot; aller au ~ trot. **trotter** 🔟 vi trot.

trotteuse /tʀɔtøz/ nf (de montre) second hand.

trottoir /tʀɔtwaʀ/ nm pavement; (US) sidewalk; ~ roulant moving walkway.

trou /tʀu/ nm hole; (moment) gap; (lieu: péj) dump; ~ (de mémoire) memory lapse; ~ de serrure keyhole; faire son ~ carve one's niche.

trouble /tʀubl/ adj (eau, image) unclear; (louche) shady. ● nm (émoi) emotion; ~s (Pol) disturbances; (Méd) disorder (+ sg). **troubler** /tʀuble/ 🔟 vt disturb; (eau) make cloudy; (inquiéter) trouble.

□ se ~ vpr (personne) become flustered.

trouer /tʁue/ **1** vt make a hole ou holes in; mes chaussures sont trouées my shoes have got holes in them.

troupe /tʁup/ nf troop; (d'acteurs) company.

troupeau (pl ~x) /tʁupo/ nm herd; (de moutons) flock.

trousse /tʁus/ nf case, bag; aux ~s de hot on sb's heels; ~ de toilette toilet bag.

trousseau (pl ~x) /tʁuso/ nm (de clefs) bunch; (de mariée) trousseau.

trouver /tʁuve/ **1** vt find; (penser) think; il est venu me ~ he came to see me. □ se ~ vpr (être) be; (se sentir) feel; il se trouve que it happens that; si ça se trouve maybe; se ~ mal faint.

truand /tʁyɑ̃/ nm gangster.

truc /tʁyk/ nm (moyen) way; (artifice) trick; (chose ⊞) thing. **trucage** nm (cinéma) special effect.

truffe /tʁyf/ nf (champignon, chocolat) truffle; (de chien) nose.

truffer /tʁyfe/ **1** vt (fig) fill, pack (de with).

truie /tʁyi/ nf (animal) sow.

truite /tʁyit/ nf trout.

truquer /tʁyke/ **1** vt fix, rig; (photo) fake; (résultats) fiddle.

tsar /tsaʁ/ nm tsar, czar.

tu /ty/ pron (parent, ami, enfant) you. ➔**TAIRE 47**.

tuba /tyba/ nm (Mus) tuba; (Sport) snorkel.

tube /tyb/ nm tube.

tuberculose /tybɛʁkyloz/ nf tuberculosis.

tuer /tɥe/ **1** vt kill; (d'une balle) shoot, kill; (épuiser) exhaust; ~ par

balles shoot dead. □ se ~ vpr kill oneself; (accident) be killed.

tuerie /tyʁi/ nf killing.

tue-tête: à ~ /atytɛt/ loc at the top of one's voice.

tuile /tɥil/ nf tile; (malchance ⊞) (stroke of) bad luck.

tulipe /tylip/ nf tulip.

tumeur /tymœʁ/ nf tumour.

tumulte /tymylt/ nm commotion; (désordre) turmoil.

tunique /tynik/ nf tunic.

Tunisie /tynizi/ nf Tunisia.

tunnel /tynɛl/ nm tunnel.

turbo /tyʁbo/ adj turbo. ● nf (voiture) turbo.

turbulent, ~e /tyʁbylɑ̃, -t/ adj boisterous, turbulent.

turc, -que /tyʁk/ adj Turkish. ● nm (Ling) Turkish. **T~, -que** Turk.

turfiste /tyʁfist/ nmf racegoer.

Turquie /tyʁki/ nf Turkey.

tutelle /tytɛl/ nf (Jur) guardianship; (fig) protection.

tuteur, -trice /tytœʁ, -tʁis/ nm, f (Jur) guardian. ● nm (bâton) stake.

tutoiement /tytwamɑ̃/ nm use of the 'tu' form. **tutoyer 31** vt address using the 'tu' form.

tuyau (pl ~x) /tɥijo/ nm pipe; (conseil ⊞) tip; ~ d'arrosage hosepipe.

TVA abrév f (taxe à la valeur ajoutée) VAT.

tympan /tɛ̃pɑ̃/ nm ear-drum.

type /tip/ nm (genre, traits) type; (individu ⊞) bloke, guy; le ~ même de a classic example of. ● adj inv typical.

typique /tipik/ adj typical.

tyran /tiʁɑ̃/ nm tyrant. **tyrannie** nf tyranny. **tyranniser 1** vt oppress, tyrannize.

t

Uu

UE *abrév f* (**Union européenne**) European Union.

Ukraine /ykʀɛn/ *nf* Ukraine.

ulcère /ylsɛʀ/ *nm* (Méd) ulcer.

ULM *abrév m* (**ultraléger motorisé**) microlight.

ultérieur, ~e /ylteʀjœʀ/ *adj* later. **ultérieurement** *adv* later.

ultime /yltim/ *adj* final.

---

un, une /œ̃, yn/
- **déterminant**
  - ⋯▸ a; (devant voyelle) an; ~ animal an animal; ~ jour one day; pas ~arbre not a single tree; il fait ~froid! it's so cold!
- **pronom**
  - ⋯▸ one; l'~ d'entre nous one of us; les ~s croient que... some believe...
  - ⋯▸ la une the front page.
  - ⋯▸ j'en veux une I want one.
- **adjectif**
  - ⋯▸ one, a, an; j'ai ~ garçon et deux filles I have a one boy and two girls; il est une heure it is one o'clock.
- **nom masculin & féminin**
  - ⋯▸ ~ par ~ one by one.

---

unanime /ynanim/ *adj* unanimous.

unanimité /ynanimite/ *nf* unanimity; à l'~ unanimously.

uni, ~e /yni/ *adj* united; (couple) close; (surface) smooth; (tissu) plain.

unième /ynjɛm/ *adj* -first; vingt et ~ twenty-first; cent ~ one

hundred and first.

unifier /ynifje/ **45** *vt* unify.

uniforme /ynifɔʀm/ *nm* uniform.
- *adj* uniform. **uniformiser** **1** *vt* standardize. **uniformité** *nf* uniformity.

unilatéral, ~e (*mpl* -aux) /ynilateʀal, -o/ *adj* unilateral.

union /ynjɔ̃/ *nf* union; l'U ~ européenne the European Union.

unique /ynik/ *adj* (seul) only; (prix, voie) one; (incomparable) unique; enfant ~ only child; sens ~ one-way street. **uniquement** *adv* only, solely.

unir /yniʀ/ **2** *vt* unite. □ **s'~** *vpr* unite, join.

unité /ynite/ *nf* unit; (harmonie) unity; ~ **centrale** (Ordinat) processor.

univers /ynivɛʀ/ *nm* universe.

universel, ~le /ynivɛʀsɛl/ *adj* universal.

universitaire /ynivɛʀsitɛʀ/ *adj* (résidence) university; (niveau) academic. *nmf* academic.

université /ynivɛʀsite/ *nf* university.

uranium /yʀanjɔm/ *nm* uranium.

urbain, ~e /yʀbɛ̃, -ɛn/ *adj* urban. **urbanisme** *nm* town planning.

urgence /yʀʒɑ̃s/ *nf* (cas) emergency; (de situation, tâche) urgency; d'~ (mesure) emergency; (transporter) urgently; les ~s casualty (+ sg). **urgent**, ~e *adj* urgent.

urine /yʀin/ *nf* urine. **urinoir** *nm* urinal.

urne /yʀn/ *nf* (électorale) ballot box; (vase) urn; aller aux ~s go to the polls.

urticaire /yʀtikɛʀ/ *nf* hives (+ pl), urticar.

us /ys/ *nmpl* les ~ et coutumes habits and customs.

usage /yzaʒ/ nm use; (coutume) custom; (de langage) usage; à l'~ de for; d'~ (habituel) customary; faire ~ de make use of.

usagé, ~e /yzaʒe/ adj worn.

usager /yzaʒe/ nm user.

usé, ~e /yze/ adj worn (out); (banal) trite.

user /yze/ **1** vt wear (out). ● vi ~ de use. □ s'~ vpr (tissu) wear (out).

usine /yzin/ nf factory, plant; ~ sidérurgique ironworks (+ pl).

usité, ~e /yzite/ adj common.

ustensile /ystɑ̃sil/ nm utensil.

usuel, ~le /yzɥɛl/ adj ordinary, everyday.

usure /yzyR/ nf (détérioration) wear (and tear).

utérus /yteRys/ nm womb, uterus.

utile /ytil/ adj useful.

utilisable /ytilizabl/ adj usable.

utilisation nf use. **utiliser** **1** vt use.

utopie /ytɔpi/ nf Utopia; (idée) Utopian idea. **utopique** adj Utopian.

UV¹ abrév f (**unité de valeur**) course unit.

UV² abrév mpl (**ultraviolets**) ultraviolet rays; faire des ~ use a sunbed.

Vv

va /va/ ⟶**ALLER** 🔟.

vacance /vakɑ̃s/ nf (poste) vacancy.

vacances /vakɑ̃s/ nfpl holiday(s); (US) vacation; en ~ on holiday; ~ d'été, grandes ~ summer holidays. **vacancier, -ière** nm, f holidaymaker; (US) vacationer.

vacant, ~e /vakɑ̃, -t/ adj vacant.

vacarme /vakaRm/ nm din.

vaccin /vaksɛ̃/ nm vaccine. **vacciner** 🔟 vt vaccinate.

vache /vaʃ/ nf cow. ● adj (méchant 🆃) nasty.

vaciller /vasije/ **1** vi sway, wobble; (lumière) flicker; (hésiter) falter; (santé, mémoire) fail.

vadrouiller /vadRuje/ **1** vi 🆃 wander about.

va-et-vient /vaevjɛ̃/ nm inv toing and froing; (de personnes) comings and goings; faire le ~ go to and fro; (interrupteur) two-way switch.

vagabond, ~e /vagabɔ̃, -d/ nm, f vagrant.

vagin /vaʒɛ̃/ nm vagina.

vague /vag/ adj vague. ● nm regarder dans le ~ stare into space; il est resté dans le ~ he was vague about it. ● nf wave; ~ de fond ground swell; ~ de froid cold spell; ~ de chaleur heatwave.

vaillant, ~e /vajɑ̃, -t/ adj brave; (vigoureux) strong.

vaille /vaj/ ⟶**VALOIR** 🔟.

vain, ~e /vɛ̃, vɛn/ adj vain, futile; en ~ in vain.

vaincre /vɛ̃kR/ 🗔 vt defeat; (surmonter) overcome. **vaincu, ~e** nm, f (Sport) loser. **vainqueur** nm victor; (Sport) winner.

vais /vɛ/ ⟶**ALLER** 🔟.

vaisseau (pl ~x) /veso/ nm ship; (veine) vessel; ~ spatial spaceship.

vaisselle /vɛsɛl/ nf crockery; (à laver) dishes; faire la ~ do the washing-up, wash the dishes; liquide ~ washing-up liquid.

valable /valabl/ adj valid; (de qualité) worthwhile.

valet /valɛ/ nm (aux cartes) jack; (~ de chambre) manservant.

valeur /valœR/ nf value; (mérite)
worth, value; ~s (Comm) stocks
and shares; avoir de la ~ be valuable; prendre/perdre de la ~ go
up/down in value; objets de ~
valuables; sans ~ worthless.

valide /valid/ adj (personne) fit;
(billet) valid. **valider** 1 vt validate.

valise /valiz/ nf (suit) case; faire
ses ~s pack (one's bags).

vallée /vale/ nf valley.

valoir /valwaR/ 60 vi (mériter) be
worth; (égaler) be as good as; (être
valable) apply; faire ~ (mé-
rite, qualité) emphasize; (terrain) cultivate; (droit) assert; se faire ~ put
oneself forward; ~ cher/100 euros
be worth a lot/100 euros; que vaut
ce vin? what's this wine like?; ne
rien ~ be useless ou no good; ça
ne me dit rien qui vaille I don't
like the sound of that; ~ la peine
or le coup 1 be worth it; il vaut
vaudrait mieux faire it is/would be
better to do. ● vt ~ qch à qn (éloges, critiques) earn sb sth; (admiration) win sb sth. □ se ~ vpr (être
équivalents) be as good as each
other; ça se vaut it's all the same.

valoriser /valoRize/ 1 vt add
value to; (produit) promote; (profession) make attractive; (région, ressources) develop.

valse /vals/ nf waltz.

vandale /vãdal/ nmf vandal.

vanille /vanij/ nf vanilla.

vanité /vanite/ nf vanity. **vaniteux, -euse** /-tø, -z/ adj vain, conceited.

vanne /van/ nf (d'écluse) sluice-
gate; (propos 1) dig 1

vantard, -e /vãtaR, -d/ adj boast-
ful. ● nm, f boaster.

vanter /vãte/ 1 vt praise. □ se ~
vpr boast (de about); se ~ de faire
pride oneself on doing.

vapeur /vapœR/ nf (eau) steam;
(brume, émanation) vapour; ~s
fumes; à ~ (bateau, locomotive)
steam; faire cuire à la ~ steam.

vaporisateur /vapoRizatœR/ nm
spray, atomizer. **vaporiser** 1 vt
spray.

varappe /vaRap/ nf rock-climbing.

variable /vaRjabl/ adj variable;
(temps) changeable.

varicelle /vaRisɛl/ nf chickenpox.

varié, -e /vaRje/ adj (non monotone, étendu) varied; (divers) various; sandwichs ~s a selection of
sandwiches.

varier /vaRje/ 45 vt/i vary.

variété /vaRjete/ nf variety; spectacle de ~s variety show.

vase /vaz/ nm vase. ● nf silt, mud.

vaseux, -euse /vazø, -z/ adj (confus 1) woolly, hazy.

vaste /vast/ adj vast, huge.

vaurien, -ne /voRjɛ̃, -ɛn/ nm, f
good-for-nothing.

vautour /votuR/ nm vulture.

vautrer (se) /(sə)votRe/ 1 vpr
sprawl; se ~ dans (vice, boue) wal-
low in.

veau (pl ~x) /vo/ nm calf; (viande)
veal; (cuir) calfskin.

vécu, -e /veky/ adj (réel) true,
real. ⇒ VIVRE 62.

vedette /vədɛt/ nf (artiste) star; en
~ (objet) in a prominent position;
(personne) in the limelight; joueur
~ star player; (bateau) launch.

végétal, -aux /veʒetal, -o/ adj
plant. ● nm (pl -aux) plant.

végétalien, ~ne /veʒetaljɛ̃, -ɛn/
adj & nm, f vegan.

végétarien, ~ne /veʒetaRjɛ̃, -ɛn/
adj & nm, f vegetarian.

végétation /veʒetasjɔ̃/ nf vegetation; ~s (Méd) adenoids.

véhicule /veikyl/ nm vehicle.

veille /vɛj/ nf (état) wakefulness; (jour précédent) la ~ (de) the day before; la ~ de Noël Christmas Eve; à la ~ de on the eve of; la ~ au soir the previous evening.

veillée /veje/ nf evening (gathering).

veiller /veje/ **1** vi stay up; (monter la garde) be on watch. ● vt (malade) watch over; ~ à attend to; ~ sur watch over.

veilleur /vejœʀ/ nm ~ de nuit night-watchman.

veilleuse /vejøz/ nf night light; (de véhicule) sidelight; (de réchaud) pilot light; mettre qch en ~ put sth on the back burner.

veine /vɛn/ nf (Anat) vein; (nervure, filon) vein; (chance 🔢) luck; avoir de la ~ 🔢 be lucky.

véliplanchiste /veliplɑ̃ʃist/ nmf windsurfer.

vélo /velo/ nm bike; (activité) cycling; faire du ~ go cycling; ~ tout terrain mountain bike.

vélomoteur /velomotœʀ/ nm moped.

velours /v(ə)luʀ/ nm velvet; ~ côtelé corduroy.

velouté, ~e /vəlute/ adj smooth. ● nm (Culin) ~ d'asperges cream of asparagus soup.

vendanges /vɑ̃dɑ̃ʒ/ nfpl grape harvest.

vendeur, -euse /vɑ̃dœʀ, -øz/ nm, f shop assistant; (marchand) salesman, saleswoman; (Jur) vendor, seller.

vendre /vɑ̃dʀ/ **3** vt sell; à ~ for sale. □ se ~ vpr (être vendu) be sold; (trouver acquéreur) sell; se ~ bien sell well.

vendredi /vɑ̃dʀədi/ nm Friday; V~ saint Good Friday.

vénéneux, -euse /venenø, -z/ adj poisonous.

vénérer /venere/ **14** vt revere.

vénérien, ~ne /veneʀjɛ̃, -ɛn/ adj maladie ~ne venereal disease.

vengeance /vɑ̃ʒɑ̃s/ nf revenge, vengeance.

venger /vɑ̃ʒe/ **40** vt avenge. □ se ~ vpr take ou get one's revenge (de qch for sth; de qn on sb).

vengeur, -eresse /vɑ̃ʒœʀ, -əʀɛs/ adj vengeful. ● nm, f avenger.

venimeux, -euse /vənimø, -z/ adj poisonous, venomous.

venin /vənɛ̃/ nm venom.

venir /vəniʀ/ **58** vi (aux être) come (de from); faire ~ qn send for sb, call sb; en ~ à come to; en ~ aux mains come to blows; où veut-elle en ~? what is she driving at?; il m'est venu à l'esprit ou à l'idée que it occurred to me that; s'il venait à pleuvoir if it should rain; dans les jours à ~ in the next few days. ● v aux ~ de faire have just done; il vient/venait d'arriver he has/had just arrived; en ~ à faire come to do; viens voir come and see.

vent /vɑ̃/ nm wind; il fait du ~ it is windy; être dans le ~ 🔢 be trendy.

vente /vɑ̃t/ nf sale; ~ (aux enchères) auction; en ~ on ou for sale; mettre qch en ~ put sth up for sale; ~ de charité (charity) bazaar; ~ au détail ou en gros retailing; wholesaling; équipe de ~ sales team.

ventilateur /vɑ̃tilatœʀ/ nm fan, ventilator. **ventiler** **1** vt ventilate.

ventouse /vɑ̃tuz/ nf suction pad; (pour déboucher) plunger.

ventre /vɑ̃tʀ/ nm stomach; (d'animal) belly; (utérus) womb; avoir du ~ have a paunch.

v

venu, ~e /vəny/ adj bien ~ (à propos) apt, timely; mal ~ badly timed; il serait mal ~ de faire it wouldn't be a good idea to do.
● →VENIR 59

venue /vəny/ nf coming.

ver /vɛʀ/ nm worm; (dans la nourriture) maggot; (du bois) woodworm; ~ luisant glow-worm; ~ à soie silkworm; ~ solitaire tapeworm; ~ de terre earthworm.

verbal, ~e (mpl -aux) /vɛʀbal, -o/ adj verbal.

verbe /vɛʀb/ nm verb.

verdir /vɛʀdiʀ/ 2 vi turn green.

véreux, -euse /veʀø, -z/ adj wormy; (malhonnête) shady.

verger /vɛʀʒe/ nm orchard.

verglas /vɛʀɡla/ nm black ice.

véridique /veʀidik/ adj true.

vérification /veʀifikasjɔ̃/ nf check(ing), verification.

vérifier /veʀifje/ 45 vt check, verify; (confirmer) confirm.

véritable /veʀitabl/ adj true, real; (authentique) real.

vérité /veʀite/ nf truth; (de tableau, roman) realism; en ~ in fact, actually.

Verlan A form of French slang which reverses the order of syllables in many common words. The term itself is derived from the word l'envers the syllables of which are reversed to create vers-l'en (verlan). Single syllable words are also converted so femme becomes meuf, mec becomes keum, etc.

vermine /vɛʀmin/ nf vermin.

verni, ~e /vɛʀni/ adj (chaussures) patent (leather); (chanceux 🗓) lucky.

vernir /vɛʀniʀ/ 2 vt varnish. □ se ~ vpr se ~ les ongles apply nail polish.

vernis /vɛʀni/ nm varnish; (de poterie) glaze; ~ à ongles nail polish.

verra, verrait /vɛʀa, vɛʀɛ/ →VOIR 64.

verre /vɛʀ/ nm glass; (de lunettes) lens; ~ à vin wine glass; prendre ou boire un ~ have a drink; ~ de contact contact lens; ~ dépoli frosted glass.

verrière /vɛʀjɛʀ/ nf (toit) glass roof; (paroi) glass wall.

verrou /veʀu/ nm bolt; sous les ~s behind bars.

verrouillage /veʀujaʒ/ nm ~ central or centralisé (des portes) central locking.

verrue /veʀy/ nf wart; ~ plantaire verruca.

vers¹ /vɛʀ/ prép towards; (aux environs de) (temps) about; (lieu) near, around; (période) towards; ~ le soir towards evening.

vers² /vɛʀ/ nm (poésie) line of verse.

versatile /vɛʀsatil/ adj unpredictable, volatile.

verse: à ~ /avɛʀs/ loc in torrents.

Verseau /vɛʀso/ nm le ~ Aquarius.

versement /vɛʀsəmɑ̃/ nm payment; (échelonné) instalment.

verser /vɛʀse/ 1 vt/i pour; (larmes, sang) shed; (payer) pay. ● vi pour; (voiture) overturn; ~ dans (fig) lapse into.

version /vɛʀsjɔ̃/ nf version; (traduction) translation.

verso /vɛʀso/ nm back (of the page); voir au ~ see overleaf.

vert, ~e /vɛʀ, -t/ adj green; (vieillard) sprightly. ● nm green; les ~s the Greens.

vertèbre /vɛʀtɛbʀ/ nf vertebra; se déplacer une ~ slip a disc.

vertical, ~e (mpl -aux) /vɛʀtikal, -o/ adj vertical.

vertige /vɛʀtiʒ/ nm dizziness; ~s dizzy spells; avoir le ~ feel dizzy. **vertigineux**, -euse adj dizzy; (très grand) staggering.

vertu /vɛʀty/ nf virtue; en ~ de in accordance with. **vertueux**, -euse adj virtuous.

verveine /vɛʀvɛn/ nf verbena.

vessie /vesi/ nf bladder.

veste /vɛst/ nf jacket.

vestiaire /vɛstjɛʀ/ nm cloakroom; (Sport) changing-room; (US) locker-room.

vestibule /vɛstibyl/ nm hall; (Théât, d'hôtel) foyer.

vestige /vɛstiʒ/ nm (objet) relic; (trace) vestige.

veston /vɛstɔ̃/ nm jacket.

vêtement /vɛtmɑ̃/ nm article of clothing; ~s clothes, clothing.

vétéran /veteʀɑ̃/ nm veteran.

vétérinaire /veteʀinɛʀ/ nmf vet, veterinary surgeon, (US) veterinarian.

vêtir /vetiʀ/ **61** vt dress. □ se ~ vpr dress.

veto /veto/ nm inv veto.

vêtu, ~e /vety/ adj dressed (de in).

veuf, veuve /vœf, -vœf/ adj widowed. ● nm, f widower, widow.

veuille /vœj/ →VOULOIR **64**.

veut, veux /vø/ →VOULOIR **64**.

vexation /vɛksasjɔ̃/ nf humiliation.

vexer /vɛkse/ **1** vt upset, hurt. □ se ~ vpr be upset, be hurt.

viable /vjabl/ adj viable; (projet) feasible.

viande /vjɑ̃d/ nf meat.

vibrer /vibʀe/ **1** vi vibrate; faire ~ (âme, foules) stir.

vicaire /vikɛʀ/ nm curate.

vice /vis/ nm (moral) vice; (physique) defect.

vicier /visje/ **45** vt contaminate; (air) pollute.

vicieux, -ieuse /visjø, -z/ adj depraved. ● nm, f pervert.

victime /viktim/ nf victim; (d'un accident) casualty.

victoire /viktwaʀ/ nf victory; (Sport) win. **victorieux**, -ieuse adj victorious; (équipe) winning.

vidange /vidɑ̃ʒ/ nf emptying; (Auto) oil change; (tuyau) waste pipe ou outlet.

vide /vid/ adj empty. ● nm (absence, manque) vacuum, void; (espace) space; (trou) gap; (sans air) vacuum; à ~ empty; emballé sous ~ vacuum packed; suspendu dans le ~ dangling in space.

vide-greniers /vidgʀənje/ nm inv bric-a-brac sale.

vidéo /video/ adj inv video; jeu ~ video game. ● nf video.

vidéocassette nf video (tape).

vidéoclip nm music video.

vidéoconférence nf videoconferencing; (séance) videoconference. **vidéodisque** nm videodisc. **vidéophone** nm videophone.

vide-ordures /vidɔʀdyʀ/ nm inv rubbish chute.

vidéothèque /videotɛk/ nf video library.

vider /vide/ **1** vt empty; (poisson) gut; (expulser 🗊) throw out. □ se ~ vpr empty.

vie /vi/ nf life; (durée) lifetime; à ~, pour la ~ for life; donner la ~ à give birth to; en ~ alive; la ~ est chère the cost of living is high.

vieil /vjɛj/ →VIEUX.

vieillard /vjɛjaʀ/ nm old man.

vieille /vjɛj/ →VIEUX.

vieillesse /vjɛjɛs/ nf old age.

vieillir /vjejiʀ/ 2 vi grow old, age; (mot, idée) become old-fashioned. ● vt age. **vieillissement** nm ageing.

viens, vient /vjɛ̃/ →VENIR 59.

vierge /vjɛʀʒ/ nf virgin; la V~ Virgo. ● adj virgin; (feuille, cassette) blank; (cahier, pellicule) unused, new.

vieux (**vieil** before vowel or mute h) , **vieille** (mpl **vieux**) /vjø, vjɛj/ adj old. ● nm, f old man, old woman; petit ~ little old man; les ~ old people; vieille fille (péj) spinster; ~ garçon old bachelor. **vieux jeu** adj inv old-fashioned.

vif, vive /vif, viv/ adj (animé) lively; (émotion, vent) keen; (froid) biting; (lumière) bright; (douleur, contraste, parole) sharp; (souvenir, style, teint) vivid; (succès, impatience) great; brûler/enterrer ~ burn/bury alive; de vive voix voix personally. ● nm à ~ (plaie) open; avoir les nerfs à ~ be on edge; blessé au ~ cut to the quick.

vigie /viʒi/ nf lookout.

vigilant, ~e /viʒilɑ̃, -t/ adj vigilant.

Vigipirate /viʒipiʀat/ nm government public security measures.

vigne /viɲ/ nf (plante) vine; (vignoble) vineyard. **vigneron, ~ne** nm, f wine-grower.

vignette /viɲɛt/ nf (étiquette) label; (Auto) road tax disc.

vignoble /viɲɔbl/ nm vineyard.

vigoureux, -euse /viguʀø, -z/ adj vigorous, sturdy.

vigueur /vigœʀ/ nf vigour; être; entrer en ~ (loi) be/come into force; en ~ current.

VIH abrév m (virus immuno-

déficitaire humain) HIV.

vilain, ~e /vilɛ̃, -ɛn/ adj (mauvais) nasty; (laid) ugly. ● nm, f naughty boy, naughty girl.

villa /villa/ nf detached house.

village /vilaʒ/ nm village.

villageois, ~e /vilaʒwa, -z/ adj village. ● nm, f villager.

ville /vil/ nf town; (importante) city; ~ d'eaux spa.

vin /vɛ̃/ nm wine; ~ d'honneur reception.

vinaigre /vinɛgʀ/ nm vinegar. **vinaigrette** nf oil and vinegar dressing, vinaigrette.

vingt /vɛ̃/ (/vɛ̃t/ before vowel and in numbers 22-29) adj & nm twenty.

vingtaine /vɛ̃tɛn/ nf une ~ (de) about twenty.

vingtième /vɛ̃tjɛm/ adj & nmf twentieth.

vinicole /vinikɔl/ adj wine(-producing).

viol /vjɔl/ nm (de femme) rape; (de lieu, loi) violation.

violemment /vjɔlamã/ adv violently.

violence /vjɔlɑ̃s/ nf violence; (acte) act of violence. **violent, ~e** adj violent.

violer /vjɔle/ 1 vt rape; (lieu, loi) violate.

violet, ~te /vjɔlɛ, -t/ adj purple. ● nm purple. **violette** nf violet.

violon /vjɔlɔ̃/ nm violin; ~ d'Ingres hobby.

violoncelle /vjɔlɔ̃sɛl/ nm cello.

vipère /vipɛʀ/ nf viper, adder.

virage /viʀaʒ/ nm bend; (en ski) turn; (changement d'attitude: fig) change of course.

virée /viʀe/ nf 1 trip, tour; (en voiture) drive; (à vélo) ride.

virement /viʀmã/ nm (Comm)

(credit) transfer; ~ automatique standing order.

virer /vire/ **1** vi turn; ~ de bord tack; (fig) do a U-turn; ~ au rouge turn red. ● vt (argent) transfer; (expulser **1**) throw out; (élève) expel; (licencier **1**) fire.

virgule /virgyl/ nf comma; (dans un nombre) (decimal) point.

viril, ~e /viril/ adj virile.

virtuel, ~le /virtɥɛl/ adj (potentiel) potential; (mémoire, réalité) virtual.

virulent, ~e /virylɑ̃, -t/ adj virulent.

virus /virys/ nm virus.

vis¹ /vi/ ⇒VIVRE **62**, ⇒VOIR **63**.

vis² /vis/ nf screw.

visa /viza/ nm visa.

visage /vizaʒ/ nm face.

vis-à-vis /vizavi/ prép ~ de (en face de) opposite; (à l'égard de) in relation to; (comparé à) compared to, beside. ● nm (personne) person opposite; en ~ opposite each other.

visée /vize/ nf aim; avoir des ~s sur have designs on.

viser /vize/ **1** vt (cible, centre) aim at; (poste, résultats) aim for; (concerner) be aimed at; (document) stamp; ~ à aim at; (mesure, propos) be aimed at; ~ à faire aim to do. ● vi aim.

viseur /vizœr/ nm (d'arme) sights (+ pl); (Photo) viewfinder.

visière /vizjɛr/ nf (de casquette) peak; (de casque) visor.

vision /vizjɔ̃/ nf vision.

visite /vizit/ nf visit; (pour inspecter) inspection; (personne) visitor; heures de ~ visiting hours; ~ guidée guided tour; ~ médicale medical; rendre ~ à, faire une ~ à pay a visit; être en ~ (chez qn) be

visiting (sb); avoir de la ~ have visitors.

visiter /vizite/ **1** vt visit; (appartement) view. **visiteur, -euse** nm, f visitor.

visser /vise/ vt screw (on).

visuel, ~le /vizɥɛl/ adj visual. ● nm (Ordinat) visual display unit, VDU.

vit /vi/ ⇒VIVRE **62**, ⇒VOIR **63**.

vital, ~e (mpl -aux) /vital, -o/ adj vital.

vitamine /vitamin/ nf vitamin.

vite /vit/ adv fast, quickly; (tôt) soon; ~! quick!; faire ~ be quick; au plus ~, le plus ~ possible as quickly as possible.

vitesse /vites/ nf speed; (régime: Auto) gear; à toute ~ at top speed; en ~ in a hurry, quickly; boîte à cinq ~s five-speed gearbox.

viticole /vitikol/ adj (industrie) wine; (région) wine-producing. **viticulteur** nm wine-grower.

vitrage /vitraʒ/ nm (vitres) windows; double ~ double glazing.

vitrail (pl -aux) /vitraj, -o/ nm stained-glass window.

vitre /vitr/ nf (window) pane; (de véhicule) window.

vitrine /vitrin/ nf (shop) window; (meuble) display cabinet.

vivace /vivas/ adj (plante) perennial; (durable) enduring.

vivacité /vivasite/ nf liveliness; (en vie) alive, living; (agilité) quickness; (d'émotion, d'intelligence) keenness; (de souvenir, style, teint) vividness.

vivant, ~e /vivɑ̃, -t/ adj (example, symbole) living; (en vie) alive, living; (actif, vif) lively. ● nm un bon ~ a bon viveur; de son ~ in his lifetime; les ~s the living.

vive¹ /viv/ ⇒VIF.

vive² /viv/ *interj* ~ le roi! long live the king!

vivement /vivmã/ *adv* (fortement) strongly; (vite, sèchement) sharply; (avec éclat) vividly; (beaucoup) greatly; ~ la fin! I'll be glad when it's the end!

vivier /vivje/ *nm* fish pond; (artificiel) fish tank.

vivifier /vivifje/ 45 *vt* invigorate.

vivre /vivʀ/ 83 *vi* live; ~ de (nourriture) live on; ~ encore be still alive; faire ~ (famille) support. ● *vt* (vie) live; (période, aventure) live through.

vivres /vivʀ/ *nmpl* supplies.

VO *abrév f* (version originale) en ~ in the original language.

vocabulaire /vɔkabylɛʀ/ *nm* vocabulary.

vocal, ~**e** (*mpl* -**aux**) /vɔkal, -o/ *adj* vocal.

vœu (*pl* ~**x**) /vø/ *nm* (souhait) wish; (promesse) vow; meilleurs ~x best wishes.

vogue /vɔg/ *nf* fashion, vogue; en ~ in fashion ou vogue.

voguer /vɔge/ 1 *vi* sail.

voici /vwasi/ *prép* here is, this is; (au pluriel) here are, these are; me ~ here I am; ~ un an (temps passé) a year ago; ~ un an que it is a year since.

voie /vwa/ *nf* (route) road; (partie de route) lane; (chemin) way; (moyen) means, way; (rails) track; (quai) platform; en ~ de in the process of; en ~ de développement (pays) developing; espèce en ~ de disparition endangered species; par la ~ des airs by air; par ~ orale orally; sur la bonne/ mauvaise ~ (fig) on the right/ wrong track; montrer la ~ lead the way; ~ de dégagement slip-

road; ~ ferrée railway; (US) railroad; V ~ lactée Milky Way; ~ navigable waterway; ~ publique public highway; ~ sans issue (sur panneau) no through road; (fig) dead end.

voilà /vwala/ *prép* there is, that is; (au pluriel) there are, those are; (voici) here is, here are; le ~ there he is; ~! right!; (en offrant qch) there you are!; ~ un an (temps passé) a year ago; ~ un an que it is a year since; tu en veux? ~ do you want some? here you are; en ~ des histoires! what a fuss!; et ~ que and then.

voilage /vwalaʒ/ *nm* net curtain.

voile /vwal/ *nf* (de bateau) sail; (Sport) sailing. ● *nm* veil; (tissu léger) sail.

voilé, ~**e** /vwale/ *adj* (allusion, femme) veiled; (flou) hazy.

voiler /vwale/ 1 *vt* (dissimuler) veil; (déformer) buckle. □ se ~ *vpr* (devenir flou) become hazy; (se déformer) (roue) buckle.

voilier /vwalje/ *nm* sailing ship.

voir /vwaʀ/ 64 *vt* see; faire ~ qch à qn show sth to sb; laisser ~ show; avoir quelque chose à ~ avec have something to do with; ça n'a rien à ~ that's got nothing to do with it; je ne peux pas le ~ 1 I can't stand him. ● *vi* y ~ be able to see; je n'y vois rien I cannot see; ~ trouble have blurred vision; voyons let's see now; voyons, soyez sages! come on now, behave yourselves! □ se ~ *vpr* (dans la glace) see oneself; (être visible) show; (se produire) be seen; (se trouver) find oneself; (se fréquenter, se rencontrer) see each other; (être vu) be seen.

voire /vwaʀ/ *adv* or even, not to say.

voirie | voter

voirie /vwaʀi/ nf (service) highway maintenance.

voisin, ~e /vwazɛ̃, -in/ adj (de voisinage) neighbouring; (proche) nearby; (adjacent) next (de to); (semblable) similar (de to). ● nm, f neighbour; le ~ the man next door, the neighbour. **voisinage** nm neighbourhood; (proximité) proximity.

voiture /vwatyʀ/ nf (motor) car; (wagon) coach, carriage; en ~! all aboard!; ~ bélier ramraiding car; ~ à cheval horse-drawn carriage; ~ de course racing car; ~ école driving school car; ~ d'enfant pram; (US) baby carriage; ~ de tourisme saloon car.

voix /vwa/ nf voice; (suffrage) vote; à ~ basse in a whisper.

vol /vɔl/ nm (d'avion, d'oiseau) flight; (groupe d'oiseaux) flock, flight; (délit) theft; (hold-up) robbery; ~ à l'étalage shoplifting; ~ à la tire pickpocketing; à ~ d'oiseau as the crow flies; de haut ~ high-ranking; ~ libre hang-gliding; ~ à voile gliding.

volaille /vɔlɑj/ nf la ~ (poules) poultry; une ~ a fowl.

volant /vɔlɑ̃/ nm (steering-)wheel; (de jupe) flounce; (de badminton) shuttlecock; **donner un coup de ~** turn the wheel sharply.

volcan /vɔlkɑ̃/ nm volcano.

volée /vɔle/ nf flight; (oiseaux) flight, flock; (de coups, d'obus, au tennis) volley; à toute ~ hard; à la ~ in flight, in mid-air.

voler /vɔle/ 1 vi (oiseau) fly; (dérober) steal (à from). ● vt steal; ~ qn rob sb; il ne l'a pas volé he deserved it.

volet /vɔlɛ/ nm (de fenêtre) shutter; (de document) (folded ou tear-off) section; **trié sur le ~**

hand-picked.

voleur, -euse /vɔlœʀ, -øz/ nm, f thief; au ~! stop thief! ● adj thieving.

volley-ball /vɔlebol/ nm volleyball.

volontaire /vɔlɔ̃tɛʀ/ adj (délibéré) voluntary; (opiniâtre) determined. ● nmf volunteer. **volontairement** adv voluntarily; (exprès) intentionally.

volonté /vɔlɔ̃te/ nf (faculté, intention) will; (souhait) wish; (énergie) willpower; à ~ (comme on veut) as required; du vin à ~ unlimited wine; bonne ~ goodwill; mauvaise ~ ill will.

volontiers /vɔlɔ̃tje/ adv (de bon gré) with pleasure, willingly, gladly; (admettre) readily.

volt /vɔlt/ nm volt.

volte-face /vɔltəfas/ nf inv (fig) U-turn; faire ~ do a U-turn.

voltige /vɔltiʒ/ nf acrobatics (+ pl).

volume /vɔlym/ nm volume.

volumineux, -euse /vɔlyminø, -z/ adj bulky; (livre, dossier) thick.

volupté /vɔlypte/ nf voluptuousness.

vomi /vɔmi/ nm vomit.

vomir /vɔmiʀ/ 2 vt vomit; (fig) belch out. ● vi be sick, vomit.

vomissement /vɔmismɑ̃/ nm vomiting; ~s du matin morning sickness.

vont /vɔ̃/ →ALLER 8.

vorace /vɔʀas/ adj voracious.

vos /vo/ →VOTRE.

votant, -e /vɔtɑ̃, -t/ nm, f voter.

vote /vɔt/ nm (action) voting; (suffrage) vote; ~ d'une loi passing of a bill; ~ par correspondance/ procuration postal/proxy vote.

voter /vɔte/ 1 vi vote. ● vt vote

for; (adopter) pass; (crédits) vote.

votre (pl **vos**) /vɔtʀ, vo/ adj your.

vôtre /votʀ/ pron le ou la ~, les ~s yours.

vouer /vwe/ **1** vt (vie, temps) dedicate (à to); **voué à l'échec** doomed to failure.

vouloir /vulwaʀ/ **64** vt (exiger) want (faire to do); (souhaiter) want; **que veux-tu boire?** what would you like to drink?; **je voudrais bien y aller** I'd really like to go; **je veux bien venir** I'm happy to come; **comme tu voudras** as you wish; (accepter) **veuillez vous asseoir** please sit down; **veuillez patienter (au téléphone)** please hold the line; (signifier) ~ **dire** mean; **qu'est-ce que cela veut dire?** what does that mean?; **en** ~ **à qn** bear a grudge against sb. □ **se** ~ vpr regret; **je m'en veux de lui avoir dit** I really regret having told her.

voulu, ~**e** /vuly/ adj (délibéré) intentional; (requis) required.

vous /vu/ pron (sujet, complément) you; (indirect) (to) you; (réfléchi) yourself; (pluriel) yourselves; (l'un l'autre) each other. **vous-même** pron yourself. **vous-mêmes** pron yourselves.

voûte /vut/ nf (plafond) vault; (porche) archway.

vouvoiement /vuvwamɑ̃/ nm use of the 'vous' form. **vouvoyer** **31** vt address using the 'vous' form.

voyage /vwajaʒ/ nm trip; (déplacement) journey; (par mer) voyage; ~**(s)** (action) travelling; ~ **d'affaires** business trip; ~ **d'études** study trip; ~ **de noces** honeymoon; ~ **organisé** (package) tour.

voyager /vwajaʒe/ **40** vi travel.

voyageur, -euse /vwajaʒœʀ, -øz/ nm, f traveller; (passager) passenger;

~ **de commerce** travelling salesman.

voyant, ~**e** /vwajɑ̃, -t/ adj gaudy. ● nm (signal) (warning) light.

voyelle /vwajɛl/ nf vowel.

voyou /vwaju/ nm hooligan.

vrac: **en** ~ /āvʀak/ loc (pêle-mêle) haphazardly; (sans emballage) loose; (en gros) in bulk.

vrai, ~**e** /vʀɛ/ adj true; (authentique) real. ● nm truth; **à** ~ **dire** to tell the truth; **pour de** ~ for real. **vraiment** adv really.

vraisemblable /vʀɛsɑ̃blabl/ adj (probable) likely; (excuse, histoire) plausible. **vraisemblablement** adv probably. **vraisemblance** nf likelihood, plausibility.

vrombir /vʀɔ̃biʀ/ vi roar.

VRP abrév m (**voyageur représentant placier**) rep, representative.

VTC abrév m (**vélo tous chemins**) hybrid bike.

VTT abrév m (**vélo tout terrain**) mountain bike.

vu, ~**e** /vy/ adj **bien** ~ well thought of; **ce serait plutôt mal** ~ it wouldn't go down well; **bien** ~**!** good point! ● prép in view of; **que seeing that.** ● →**VOIR** **64**.

vue /vy/ nf (spectacle) sight; (vision) (eye) sight; (panorama, idée, image, photo) view; **avoir en** ~ have in mind; **à** ~ (tirer) on sight; (payable) at sight; **de** ~ by sight; **perdre de** ~ lose sight of; **en** ~ (proche) in sight; (célèbre) in the public eye; **en** ~ **de faire** with a view to doing; **à** ~ **d'œil** visibly; **avoir des** ~**s sur** have designs on.

vulgaire /vylgɛʀ/ adj (grossier) vulgar; (ordinaire) common.

vulnérable /vylneʀabl/ adj vulnerable.

Ww

wagon /vagɔ̃/ *nm* (de voyageurs) carriage; (de marchandises) wagon. **wagon-lit** (*pl* **wagons-lits**) *nm* sleeper. **wagon-restaurant** (*pl* **wagons-restaurants**) *nm* restaurant car.

walkman® /wokman/ *nm* personal stereo, walkman®.

Wallon A regional Romance language spoken in southern Belgium (*Wallonie*) by approximately 600,000 *Wallons*. It belongs to the same linguistic family as the French language, and is sometimes considered a French dialect. *Wallon* should not be confused with Belgian French, which differs from the French of France in pronunciation and vocabulary only.

waters /watɛʀ/ *nmpl* toilets.

watt /wat/ *nm* watt.

wc /(dublə)vese/ *nmpl* toilet (+ *sg*).

Web /wɛb/ *nm* Web; **un site** ~ a website; **une page** ~ web page.

webcam /wɛbkam/ *nf* webcam.

webmestre /wɛbmɛstʀ/ *nm* webmaster.

week-end /wikɛnd/ *nm* weekend.

whisky (*pl* **-ies**) /wiski/ *nm* whisky.

Xx

xénophobe /gzenɔfɔb/ *adj* xenophobic. ● *nmf* xenophobe.

xérès /gzeʀɛs/ *nm* sherry.

xylophone /ksilɔfon/ *nm* xylophone.

Yy

y /i/
● *adverbe*
···▸ there; (dessus) on it; (pluriel) on them; (dedans) in it; (pluriel) in them; **j'~ vais** I'm on my way; **n'~ va pas** don't go; **du lait? il n'~ en a pas** milk? there's none; **tu n'~ arriveras jamais** you'll never manage it.

● *pronom*
···▸ **s'~ habituer** get used to it.
···▸ **s'~ attendre** expect it.
···▸ ~ **penser** think about it.
···▸ ~ **être pour qch** have sth to do with it.

yaourt /'jauʀ(t)/ *nm* yoghurt. **yaourtière** *nf* yoghurt-maker.

yard /'jaʀd/ *nm* yard (= 91,44 *cm*).

yen /'jɛn/ *nm* yen.

yeux /jø/ →**ŒIL**.

yoga /'jɔga/ *nm* yoga.

yougoslave /'jugɔslav/ *adj* Yugoslav. **Y~** *nmf* Yugoslav.

Yougoslavie /'jugɔslavi/ *nf*

Yugoslavia.

yo-yo® /'jojo/ *nm inv* yo-yo®.

....

Zz

....

zapper /zape/ **1** *vi* (à la télévision)
channel-hop.

zèbre /zɛbʀ/ *nm* zebra.

zèle /zɛl/ *nm* zeal.

zéro /zeʀo/ *nm* nought, zero; (température) zero; (Sport) nil; (tennis)
love; (personne) nonentity; **partir
de ~** start from scratch; **repartir à
~** start all over again.

zeste /zɛst/ *nm* peel; **un ~ de** (fig)

a touch of.

zézayer /zezeje/ **31** *vi* lisp.

zigzag /zigzag/ *nm* zigzag; **en ~**
winding.

zinc /zɛ̃g/ *nm* (métal) zinc; (comptoir **1**) bar.

zizanie /zizani/ *nf* discord; **semer
la ~** put the cat among the
pigeons.

zizi /zizi/ *nm* **1** willy.

zodiaque /zɔdjak/ *nm* zodiac.

zona /zona/ *nm* (Méd) shingles
(+ *sg*).

zone /zon/ *nf* zone, area; (banlieue
pauvre) slums; **~ bleue** restricted
parking zone; **~ euro** eurozone; **~
de saisie** input box.

zoo /zo(o) / *nm* zoo.

zoom /zum/ *nm* zoom lens.

zut /zyt/ *interj* **1** damn **1**.

Phrasefinder/Phrases utiles

Key phrases	1	Phrases-clés
Going Places	3	Se déplacer
Keeping in touch	10	Rester en contact
Food and Drink	15	Boire et manger
Places to stay	20	Où dormir
Shopping and money	22	Achats et argent
Sport and leisure	25	Sports et loisirs
Good timing	28	En temps et en heure
Health and Beauty	30	Santé et beauté
Weights and measures	34	Poids et mesures

Key phrases — Phrases-clés

yes, please	oui, s'il vous plaît
no, thank you	non, merci
sorry!	désolé/-e!
you're welcome	de rien

Meeting people — Rencontres

hello/goodbye	bonjour/au revoir
how are you?	comment allez-vous?
nice to meet you!	enchanté/-e!

1

Asking questions	**Poser des questions**
do you speak English/French?	parlez-vous anglais/français?
what's your name?	comment vous appelez-vous?
where are you from?	d'où venez-vous?
how much is it?	combien ça coûte?
is it far?	c'est loin d'ici?
where is...?	où est...?
can I have...?	est-ce que je peux avoir...?
would you like...?	voulez-vous...?

About you	**Parler de soi**
my name is...	je m'appelle...
I'm English/French/American	je suis anglais/-e/français/-e/américain/-e
I don't speak French/English very well	je ne parle pas très bien français/anglais
I'm here on holiday	je suis en vacances ici
I live near Sheffield/Bordeaux	j'habite près de Sheffield/Bordeaux
I'm a student	je suis étudiant/-e

Emergencies	**Urgences**
can you help me?	pouvez-vous m'aider?
I'm lost	je me suis perdu/-e
I'm ill	je suis malade
call an ambulance	appelez une ambulance
watch out!	attention!

Reading signs	**Les pancartes**
no entry	défense d'entrer
no smoking	défense de fumer
fire exit	sortie de secours
for sale	à vendre
push	pousser
pull	tirer
press	appuyer

Going Places/Se déplacer

By rail and underground En train et en métro

where can I buy a ticket?	où est-ce que je peux acheter un billet?
what time is the next train to Paris/New York?	à quelle heure est le prochain train pour Paris/New York?
do I have to change?	est-ce qu'il y a un changement?
can I take my bike on the train?	est-ce que je peux prendre mon vélo dans le train?
which platform for the train to Marseilles/Bath?	de quel quai part le train pour Marseille/Bath?
a single/return, (Amer) round trip to Baltimore/Nice, please	un aller/aller-retour pour Baltimore/Nice, s'il vous plaît
I'd like an all-day ticket	je voudrais un billet valable toute la journée
I'd like to reserve a seat	je voudrais réserver une place
is there a student/senior citizen discount?	est-ce qu'il y a une réduction pour les étudiants/les personnes âgées?
is this the train for Lyons/Manchester?	est-ce que c'est bien le train pour Lyon/Manchester?
what time does the train arrive in Paris/London?	à quelle heure le train arrive-t-il à Paris/Londres?
have I missed the train?	est-ce que j'ai raté le train?
which line do I need to take for the Eiffel Tower/London Eye?	quelle ligne dois-je prendre pour aller à la tour Eiffel/au London Eye?

YOU WILL HEAR:	VOUS ENTENDREZ:
le train entre en gare au quai numéro 2	the train is arriving at platform 2
il y a un train pour Paris à 10 heures	there's a train to Paris at 10 o'clock
le train est en retard/à l'heure	the train is delayed/on time
prochain arrêt : ...	the next stop is...
votre ticket n'est pas valable	your ticket isn't valid

MORE USEFUL WORDS:	D'AUTRES MOTS UTILES:
underground station, (*Amer*) subway station	la station de métro
timetable	l'horaire
connection	la correspondance, le changement
express train	le train express
local train	le train régional
high-speed train	le TGV

DID YOU KNOW...?	LE SAVIEZ-VOUS...?
In a French train station, before you get on the train you must *composter* your ticket, i.e. have it stamped in the special machine positioned at the entrance of the platform to make it valid for your journey. You risk a fine if you forget to do this.	En Angleterre, l'aéroport de Londres–Heathrow est relié au centre de la capitale par le train Heathrow Express qui met moins de vingt minutes à parcourir ce trajet.

At the airport   En avion

when's the next flight to Paris/Rome?	quand part le prochain vol pour Paris/Rome?
what time do I have to check in?	à quelle heure est-ce que je dois me présenter à l'enregistrement?
where do I check in?	où est le comptoir d'enregistrement?
I'd like to confirm my flight	je voudrais confirmer mon vol
I'd like a window seat/an aisle seat	je voudrais une place côté fenêtre/côté couloir
I want to change/cancel my reservation	je voudrais modifier/annuler ma réservation
can I carry this in my hand, (Amer) carry-on luggage?	puis-je prendre ce sac en bagage à main?
my luggage hasn't arrived	mes bagages ne sont pas arrivés

YOU WILL HEAR: VOUS ENTENDREZ:

le vol BA7057 est retardé/annulé	flight BA7057 is delayed/cancelled
veuillez vous rendre à la porte d'embarquement numéro 29	please go to gate 29
votre carte d'embarquement, s'il vous plaît	your boarding card, please

MORE USEFUL WORDS: D'AUTRES MOTS UTILES:

arrivals	arrivées
departures	départs
baggage claim	réception des bagages

Asking how to get there · Trouver son chemin

how do I get to the airport?	comment est-ce que je fais pour aller à l'aéroport?
how long will it take to get there?	combien de temps est-ce qu'il faut pour y arriver?
how far is it from here?	combien y a-t-il d'ici?
which bus do I take for the cathedral?	quel bus est-ce que je dois prendre pour aller à la cathédrale?
where does this bus go?	où va ce bus?
does this bus/train go to...?	est-ce que ce bus/train va à ... ?
where do I get off?	pouvez-vous me dire où je dois descendre?
how much is it to the town centre?	quel est le prix d'un billet pour le centre-ville?...?
what time is the last bus?	à quelle heure est le dernier bus?
where's the nearest underground station, (*Amer*) subway station?	où est la station de métro la plus proche?
is this the turning for...?	est-ce que c'est là qu'il faut tourner pour aller à ... ?
can you call me a taxi?	pouvez-vous m'appeler un taxi, s'il vous plaît ?

YOU WILL HEAR: · VOUS ENTENDREZ:

prenez la première rue à droite	take the first turning on the right
prenez à gauche aux feux/juste après l'église	turn left at the traffic lights/just past the church

Disabled travellers · Les voyageurs handicapés

I'm disabled	je suis handicapé/-e
is there wheelchair access?	y a-t-il un accès pour les fauteuils roulants?
are guide dogs permitted?	les chiens d'aveugle sont-ils autorisés?

On the road　Par la route

where's the nearest petrol station, (*Amer*) gas station?	où se trouve la station d'essence la plus proche?
what's the best way to get there?	quel est le meilleur chemin pour y aller?
I've got a puncture, (*Amer*) flat tire	j'ai crevé
I'd like to hire, (*Amer*) rent a bike/car	je voudrais louer un vélo/une voiture
where can I park around here?	où peut-on se garer par ici?
there's been an accident	il y a eu un accident
my car's broken down	ma voiture est en panne
the car won't start	la voiture ne démarre pas
where's the nearest garage?	où se trouve le garage le plus proche?
pump number six, please	la pompe numéro 6, s'il vous plaît
fill it up, please	le plein, s'il vous plaît
can I get my car washed here?	est-ce que je peux utiliser le lavage automatique?
can I park here?	puis-je me garer ici?
there's a problem with the brakes/lights	il y a un problème de freins/phares
the clutch/gearstick isn't working	l'embrayage/le levier de vitesse ne fonctionne pas
take the third exit off the roundabout, (*Amer*) traffic circle	prenez la troisième sortie au rond-point
turn right at the next junction	tournez à droite au prochain carrefour
slow down	ralentissez
I can't drink – I'm driving	je ne peux pas boire d'alcool, je conduis
can I buy a road map here?	est-ce que vous vendez des cartes routières?

YOU WILL HEAR:	VOUS ENTENDREZ:
votre permis de conduire, s'il vous plaît?	can I see your driving licence?
vous devez remplir un constat d'accident	you need to fill out an accident report
c'est un sens unique	this road is one-way
il est interdit de se garer ici	you can't park here

MORE USEFUL WORDS:	D'AUTRES MOTS UTILES:
diesel	le diesel, le gazole
unleaded	sans plomb
motorway, (*Amer*) expressway	l'autoroute
toll	le péage
satnav, (*Amer*) GPS	le GPS
speed camera	le radar
roundabout	le rond-point
crossroads	l'intersection, le carrefour
dual carriageway, (*Amer*) divided highway	la route à quatre voies
traffic lights	les feux de circulation
driver	le conducteur/la conductrice

DID YOU KNOW...?	LE SAVIEZ-VOUS...?
The speed limits on French roads are as follows: motorway 130 km/h (80 m/h), 110 km/h (74 m/h) when it rains, open roads 90 km/h (56 m/h), towns and villages 50 km/h (31 mph).	Pour circuler dans le centre de Londres, les motoristes doivent payer une taxe appelée *congestion charge*.

COMMON FRENCH ROAD SIGNS

Aire de Lavallière : 2000 m	Lavallière rest area in two kilometres
Allumez vos feux	Switch on dipped headlights
Chaussée déformée	Uneven road surface
Circulation alternée, circulation à sens alterné	Contraflow
Déviation	Diverted traffic, Diversion
Halte péage/douanes/gendarmerie	Stop: Toll/ Customs/ Police
Interdiction de tourner à droite/ gauche	No right/left turn
Interdit sauf de 19h à 9h	No entry except between 7pm and 9am
Prochaine sortie : gendarmerie	Next exit: Police
Sauf riverains	Local residents only
Sens interdit	No entry
SOS *(on motorway)*	Emergency stopping area
Travaux sur 15 kms	Roadworks for 15 kms

PANNEAUX DE SIGNALISATION EN PAYS ANGLOPHONES

Cattle	Bétail
Contraflow	Circulation à sens alterné, circulation alternée
Ford	Passage à gué
Get in lane	Mettez-vous dans la bonne file
Give way	Cédez le passage
Keep clear	Arrêt et stationnement interdits
No overtaking, *(Amer)* Do not pass	Interdiction de dépasser
Pedestrians crossing	Passage pour piétons
Red route – no stopping	Axe rouge – arrêt et stationnement interdits
Reduce speed now	Ralentir
Stop	Stop

Keeping in touch/Rester en contact

On the phone   Au téléphone

where can I buy a phone card?	où est-ce que je peux acheter une carte de téléphone?
may I use your phone?	est-ce que je peux utiliser votre téléphone?
do you have a mobile, (Amer) cell phone?	avez-vous un portable?
what is your phone number?	quel est votre numéro de téléphone?
what is the area code for Lyons/St Albans?	quel est l'indicatif pour Lyon/St Albans?
I want to make a phone call	je veux téléphoner
I'd like to reverse the charges, (Amer) call collect	je voudrais appeler en PCV
the line's engaged/busy	la ligne est occupée
there's no answer	ça ne répond pas
hello, this is Natalie	allô, c'est Natalie
is Jean there, please?	est-ce que Jean est là, s'il vous plaît?
who's calling?	qui est à l'appareil?
sorry, wrong number	désolé/-e, vous faites erreur
just a moment, please	un instant, s'il vous plaît
would you like to hold?	vous patientez?
it's a business/personal call	c'est un appel professionnel/privé
I'll put you through to him/her	je vous le/la passe
s/he cannot come to the phone at the moment	il/elle n'est pas disponible pour l'instant
please tell him/her I called	pourriez-vous lui dire que j'ai appelé?
I'd like to leave a message for him/her	j'aimerais lui laisser un message
I'll try again later	je réessaierai plus tard

please tell him/her that Marie called	pourriez-vous lui dire que Marie a appelé, s'il vous plaît
can he/she ring me back?	est-ce qu'il/elle peut me rappeler?
my home number is...	mon numéro personnel est...
my business number is...	mon numéro professionnel est...
my fax number is...	mon numéro de télécopie est...
we were cut off	on a été coupé
I'll call you later	je vous rappelle plus tard
I need to top up my phone	j'ai besoin de recharger mon portable
the battery's run out	il n'y a plus de batterie
I'm running low on credit	je n'ai presque plus de crédit sur mon portable
send me a text	envoie-moi un texto/message
there's no signal here	il n'y a pas de réception ici
you're breaking up	la ligne est mauvaise
could you speak a little louder?	pouvez-vous parler un peu plus fort?

YOU WILL HEAR:	VOUS ENTENDREZ:
allô	hello
appelez-moi sur mon portable	call me on my mobile, (*Amer*) cell phone
vous voulez laisser un message?	would you like to leave a message?

MORE USEFUL WORDS:	D'AUTRES MOTS UTILES:
text message	le texto, le message
top-up card	la carte de recharge, la carte prépayée
phone box, (*Amer*) phone booth	la cabine téléphonique
dial 3615	composez le 3615
directory enquiries	les renseignements

Writing Écrire

what's your address?	quelle est votre adresse?
where is the nearest post office?	où est le bureau de poste le plus proche?
could I have a stamp for France/Italy, please?	je voudrais un timbre pour la France/l'Italie, s'il vous plaît
I'd like to send a parcel	je voudrais envoyer un paquet
where is the nearest postbox, (Amer) mailbox?	où se trouve la boîte aux lettres la plus proche?
dear Isabelle/Fred	Chère Isabelle/Cher Fred
dear Sir or Madam	Monsieur/Madame
yours sincerely	veuillez agréer, Monsieur/Madame, mes/nos sincères salutations
yours faithfully	veuillez agréer, Monsieur/Madame, mes/nos sincères salutations
best wishes	(letter) meilleurs vœux; (e-mail) bien amicalement

YOU WILL HEAR:	VOUS ENTENDREZ:
vous voulez l'envoyer en tarif normal?	would you like to send it first class?
c'est un objet de valeur?	is it valuable?

MORE USEFUL WORDS:	D'AUTRES MOTS UTILES:
letter	la lettre
postcode, (Amer) ZIP code	le code postal
airmail	par avion
fragile	fragile
urgent	urgent
registered post, (Amer) mail	le courrier recommandé

On line   En ligne

are you on the Internet?	êtes-vous sur Internet?
what's your e-mail address?	quelle est votre adresse électronique?
I'll e-mail it to you on Tuesday	je vous l'enverrai par courrier électronique mardi
I looked it up on the Internet	j'ai vérifié sur Internet
the information is on their website	l'information se trouve sur leur site Internet
my e-mail address is jane dot smith at new99 dot com	mon adresse électronique est jane point smith arobase new99 point com
can I check my e-mail here?	puis-je vérifier mon courrier électronique ici?
I have broadband/dial-up	j'ai une connexion Internet haut-débit/par ligne téléphonique
do you have wireless Internet access?	avez-vous un accès sans fil à Internet?
I'll send you the file as an attachment	je vous enverrai le fichier en pièce jointe

YOU WILL SEE: VOUS VERREZ:

rechercher	search
double-cliquer sur l'icône	double-click on the icon
ouvrir l'application	open (up) the application
télécharger le fichier	download file

MORE USEFUL WORDS: D'AUTRES MOTS UTILES:

subject (of an email)	le sujet
password	le mot de passe
social networking site	le site de réseau social
search engine	le moteur de recherche
mouse	la souris
keyboard	le clavier

13

Meeting up Se retrouver

what shall we do this evening?	qu'est-ce qu'on fait ce soir?
do you want to go out tonight?	tu veux sortir ce soir?
where shall we meet?	où est-ce qu'on se retrouve?
I'll see you outside the café at 6 o'clock	on se retrouve à 6 heures devant le café
see you later	à tout à l'heure
I can't today, I'm busy	je ne peux pas aujourd'hui, je suis occupé/-e
I'm sorry, I've got something planned	je suis désolé/-e, j'ai déjà quelque chose de prévu
let's meet for a coffee in town	allons prendre un café en ville
would you like to see a show/film, (Amer) movie?	est-ce que tu voudrais aller voir un spectacle/un film?
what about next week instead?	la semaine prochaine alors?
shall we go for something to eat?	si on allait manger quelque part?

YOU WILL HEAR:	VOUS ENTENDREZ
enchanté/-e (de faire votre connaissance)	nice to meet you
puis-je vous offrir un verre?	can I buy you a drink?

MORE USEFUL WORDS:	D'AUTRES MOTS UTILES:
bar	le bar
bar (serving counter in a bar/pub)	le comptoir, le bar
meal	le repas
snack	le repas léger, le casse-croûte
date	le rendez-vous
cigarette	la cigarette

Food and Drink/Boire et manger

Booking a table — Réserver une table

can you recommend a good restaurant?	pouvez-vous me recommander un bon restaurant?
I'd like to reserve a table for four	je voudrais réserver une table pour quatre personnes
a reservation for tomorrow evening at eight o'clock	une réservation pour demain soir à huit heures
I booked a table for two	j'ai réservé une table pour deux

Ordering — Passer commande

could we see the menu/wine list, please?	est-ce qu'on pourrait voir la carte/la carte des vins?
do you have a vegetarian/children's menu?	est-ce que vous avez un menu végétarien/enfant?
what would you recommend?	que (nous) conseillez-vous?
I'd like a white/black coffee	j'aimerais un café/un café noir
... an espresso	... un express
... a decaffeinated coffee	... un café décaféiné
... a tea/a herbal tea	... un thé/une infusion
the bill, (*Amer*) check, please	l'addition, s'il vous plaît
we'd like to pay separately	on voudrait payer séparément

YOU WILL HEAR: ON VOUS DIRA:

Désirez-vous un apéritif?	Would you like an aperitif?
Souhaitez-vous commander?	Are you ready to order?
Désirez-vous une entrée?	Would you like a starter?
Quel plat avez-vous choisi?	What will you have for the main course?
Je (vous) conseille le/la...	I can recommend the ...
Souhaitez-vous prendre un dessert?	Would you like a dessert?
Désirez-vous un café/un digestif?	Would you like coffee?/a liqueur?
Désirez-vous autre chose?	Anything else?
Bon appétit	Enjoy your meal!

··

The menu Le Menu

starters	entrées		entrées	starters
hors d'oeuvres	hors d'œuvres		hors d'œuvres	hors d'oeuvres
omelette	omelette		omelette	omelette
soup	soupe		soupe	soup

fish	poisson		poisson	fish
bass	perche		anguille	eel
cod	cabillaud		cabillaud	cod
eel	anguille		cal(a)mar	squid
hake	colin		crevettes grises	shrimps
herring	hareng		crevettes roses	prawns
monkfish	lotte		colin	hake
mullet	mulet		hareng	herring
mussels	moules		huîtres	oysters
oysters	huîtres		lotte	monkfish
prawns	crevettes roses		moules	mussels
salmon	saumon		mulet	mullet
sardines	sardines		perche	bass
shrimps	crevettes grises		sardines	sardines
sole	sole		saumon	salmon
squid	cal(a)mar		sole	sole
trout	truite		thon	tuna
tuna	thon		truite	trout
turbot	turbot		turbot	turbot

meat	viande		viande	meat
beef	bœuf		agneau	lamb
chicken	poulet		bifteck	steak
duck	canard		bœuf	beef
goose	oie		canard	duck
guinea fowl	pintade		foie	liver

hare	lièvre
kidneys	rognons
lamb	agneau
liver	foie
pork	porc
rabbit	lapin
steak	bifteck
veal	veau
wild boar	sanglier

lapin	rabbit
lièvre	hare
oie	goose
poulet	chicken
pintade	guinea fowl
porc	pork
rognons	kidneys
sanglier	wild boar
veau	veal

vegetables | légumes

artichokes	artichaut
asparagus	asperges
aubergine	aubergine
cabbage	chou
carrots	carrottes
cauliflower	chou-fleur
celery	céleri
courgettes	courgettes
endive	endives
green beans	haricots verts
mushrooms	champignons
onions	oignons
peas	petits pois
peppers	poivron
potatoes	pommes de terre
spinach	épinards

légumes | vegetables

artichaut	artichokes
asperges	asparagus
aubergine	aubergine
carrottes	carrots
céleri	celery
champignons	mushrooms
chou	cabbage
chou-fleur	cauliflower
courgettes	courgettes
endives	endive
épinards	spinach
haricots verts	green beans
oignons	onions
petits pois	peas
poivron	peppers
pommes de terre	potatoes

the way it's cooked | la cuisson

fried	poêlé
grilled	grillé

la cuisson | the way it's cooked

à la vapeur	steamed
à point	medium rare

medium rare	à point		bien cuit	well done
puréed	mixé		bleu	very rare
rare	saignant		cuit à l'étouffée	stewed
roast	rôti		grillé	grilled
steamed	à la vapeur		mixé	puréed
stewed	cuit à l'étouffée		poêlé	fried
very rare	bleu		rôti	roast
well done	bien cuit		saignant	rare

desserts	**fromages et desserts**		**fromages et desserts**	**desserts**
cheeseboard	plateau de fromages		fruit	fruit
fruit	fruit		glace	ice cream
ice cream	glace		plateau de fromages	cheeseboard
pie	tarte (recouverte de pâte)		sorbet	sorbet
sorbet	sorbet		tarte	tart
tart	tarte		tarte (recouverte de pâte)	pie

sundries	**divers**		**divers**	**sundries**
bread	pain		assaisonnement	seasoning
butter	beurre		beurre	butter
green salad	salade verte		herbes	herbs
herbs	herbes		huile d'olive	olive oil
mayonnaise	mayonnaise		mayonnaise	mayonnaise
mustard	moutarde		moutarde	mustard
olive oil	huile d'olive		pain	bread
pepper	poivre		poivre	pepper
salt	sel		salade verte	green salad
sauce	sauce		sauce	sauce
seasoning	assaisonnement		sel	salt
vinegar	vinaigre		vinaigre	vinegar

drinks	boissons		boissons	drinks
beer	bière		bière	beer
bottle	bouteille		boissons non alcoolisées	soft drinks
carbonated	gazeux		bouteille	bottle
half-bottle	demi-bouteille		demi-bouteille	half-bottle
liqueur	digestif		digestif	liqueur
mineral water	eau minérale		eau minérale	mineral water
red wine	vin rouge		gazeux	carbonated
rosé	rosé		plat	still
soft drinks	boissons non alcoolisées		rosé	rosé
still	plat, non gazeux		vin	wine
table wine	vin de table		vin blanc	white wine
white wine	vin blanc		vin de table	table wine
wine	vin		vin rouge	red wine

Places to stay/Où dormir

Camping Camper

can we pitch our tent here?	est-ce qu'on peut planter notre tente ici?
can we park our caravan here?	est-ce qu'on peut mettre notre caravane ici?
what are the facilities like?	le camping est-il bien équipé?
how much is it per night?	c'est combien par nuit?
where do we park the car?	où est-ce qu'on peut garer la voiture?
we're looking for a campsite	on cherche un camping
this is a list of local campsites	c'est une liste des campings de la région
we go on a camping holiday every year	nous partons camper chaque année pour les vacances

At the hotel À l'hôtel

I'd like a double/single room with bath	je voudrais une chambre double/simple avec bain
we have a reservation in the name of Milne	nous avons une réservation au nom de Milne
we'll be staying three nights, from Friday to Sunday	nous resterons trois nuits, de vendredi à dimanche
how much does the room cost?	combien coûte la chambre?
I'd like to see the room, please	je voudrais voir la chambre, s'il vous plaît
what time is breakfast?	à quelle heure est le petit déjeuner?
bed and breakfast	chambres d'hôtes
we'd like to stay another night	on voudrait rester une nuit de plus
please call me at 7:30	réveillez-moi à 7h30
are there any messages for me?	est-ce qu'il y a des messages pour moi?

Hostels	Auberges de jeunesse
could you tell me where the youth hostel is?	pourriez-vous me dire où se trouve l'auberge de jeunesse?
what time does the hostel close?	à quelle heure ferme l'auberge de jeunesse?
I'm staying in a hostel	je loge à l'auberge de jeunesse
I know a really good hostel in Dublin	je connais une très bonne auberge de jeunesse à Dublin
I'd like to go backpacking in Australia	j'aimerais bien aller faire de la randonnée en Australie

Rooms to let	Locations
I'm looking for a room with a reasonable rent	je cherche une chambre à louer avec un loyer raisonnable
I'd like to rent an apartment for a few weeks	je voudrais louer un appartement pendant quelques semaines
where do I find out about rooms to let?	où est-ce que je peux me renseigner sur des chambres à louer?
what's the weekly rent?	quel est le montant du loyer pour la semaine?
I'm staying with friends at the moment	je loge chez des amis pour le moment
I rent an apartment on the outskirts of town	je loue un appartement en banlieue
the room's fine – I'll take it	la chambre est bien – je la prends
the deposit is one month's rent in advance	l'acompte correspond à un mois de loyer payable d'avance

Shopping and money/Achats et argent

At the bank À la banque

I'd like to change some money	je voudrais changer de l'argent
I want to change some euros into pounds	je veux changer des euros en livres
do you take Eurocheques?	acceptez-vous les Eurochèques?
what's the exchange rate today?	quel est le taux de change aujourd'hui?
I prefer traveller's cheques, (Amer) traveler's checks to cash	je préfère les chèques de voyage à l'argent liquide
I'd like to transfer some money from my account	je voudrais retirer de l'argent sur mon compte
I'll get some money from the cash machine	je vais retirer de l'argent au distributeur
I usually pay by direct debit	d'habitude, je paye par prélèvement automatique

Finding the right shop Trouver le bon magasin

where's the main shopping district?	où se trouve le principal quartier commerçant?
where's a good place to buy sunglasses?	quel est le meilleur endroit pour acheter des lunettes de soleil?
where can I buy batteries/postcards?	où est-ce que je peux acheter des piles/cartes postales?
where's the nearest chemist/bookshop?	où est la pharmacie/librairie la plus proche?
is there a good food shop around here?	est-ce qu'il y a une bonne épicerie près d'ici?
what time do the shops open/close?	à quelle heure ouvrent/ferment les magasins?
where did you get those?	où les avez-vous trouvés?
I'm looking for presents for my family	je cherche des cadeaux pour ma famille
we'll do all our shopping on Saturday	nous ferons toutes nos courses samedi

Are you being served? On s'occupe de vous?

how much does that cost?	combien ça coûte?
can I try it on?	est-ce que je peux l'essayer?
can you keep it for me?	pouvez-vous me le/la garder?
do you have this in another colour, (Amer) color?	est-ce que vous avez ce modèle-ci dans une autre couleur?
I'm just looking	je regarde
I'll think about it	je vais réfléchir
I need a bigger/smaller size	il me faut une taille au-dessus/au-dessous
I take a size 10/a medium	je fais du 38/il me faut une taille moyenne
it doesn't suit me	ça ne me va pas
could you wrap it for me, please?	pourriez-vous l'emballer, s'il vous plaît?
do you take credit cards?	est-ce que vous acceptez les cartes de crédit?
can I pay by cheque, (Amer) check?	est-ce que je peux payer par chèque?
I'm sorry, I don't have any change	je suis désolé/-e mais je n'ai pas de monnaie
I'd like a receipt, please	je voudrais un reçu, s'il vous plaît

Changing things Faire un échange

can I have a refund?	j'aimerais être remboursé/-e
can you mend it for me?	est-ce que vous pouvez me le/la réparer?
can I speak to the manager?	je voudrais parler au responsable
it doesn't work	ça ne marche pas
I'd like to change it, please	je voudrais l'échanger, s'il vous plaît
I bought this here yesterday	je l'ai acheté/-e ici hier

23

Currency Convertor Convertisseur de devises

€/$	£/$	£/$	€/$
0.25		0.25	
0.50		0.50	
0.75		0.75	
1		1	
1.5		1.5	
2		2	
3		3	
5		5	
10		10	
20		20	
30		30	
40		40	
50		50	
100		100	
200		200	
1000		1000	

Sport and leisure/Sports et loisirs

Keeping fit · Rester en bonne santé

where can we play football/squash?	où est-ce qu'on peut jouer au football/squash?
where is the local sports centre, (Amer) center?	où se trouve le centre sportif?
what's the charge per day?	quel est le prix pour la journée?
is there a reduction for children/a student discount?	est-ce qu'il y a des réductions enfants/étudiants?
I'm looking for a swimming pool/tennis court	je cherche une piscine/un court de tennis
are there any yoga/pilates classes here?	est-ce qu'on donne des cours de yoga/Pilates ici?
I want to do aerobics	je veux faire de l'aérobic
is there a hotel gym?	est-ce qu'il y a une salle de gym dans l'hôtel?
you have to be a member	vous devez être membre
I would like to go fishing/riding	je voudrais aller à la pêche/monter à cheval
I love swimming	j'adore nager

Watching sport · Le sport en spectateur

is there a match, (Amer) game on Saturday?	est-ce qu'il y a un match samedi?
which teams are playing?	quelles sont les équipes qui jouent?
where can I get tickets?	où est-ce que je peux acheter des billets?
I'd like to see the match, (Amer) game	j'aimerais voir le match
my favourite, (Amer) favorite team is...	mon équipe préférée est...
who's winning?	qui gagne?
the reds are winning 3-1	ce sont les rouges qui gagnent 3 à 1

25

SPORTS AND PASTIMES

American football/football	le football américain/le football
badminton	le badminton
cycling	la course cycliste
football/soccer	le football
golf	le golf
hiking	la grande randonnée
horse-riding	l'équitation
rollerblading	le patinage en ligne
rugby	le rugby
running	la course à pied
sailing	la voile
surfing	le surf
swimming	la natation

SPORTS ET PASSE-TEMPS

le basket-ball	basketball
la belote	belote (card game)
la pétanque	boules
les échecs	chess
les dames	draughts
le handball	handball
le patinage à glace	ice-skating
le jogging	jogging
la randonnée à cheval	pony-trekking
le ski	skiing

Movies/theatres/clubs Aller au cinéma/théâtre/ en boîte

what's on?	qu'est-ce qu'il y a au programme?
when does the box office open/ close?	à quelle heure ouvre/ferme le guichet?
what time does the concert/ performance start?	à quelle heure commence le concert/la représentation?
when does it finish?	à quelle heure ça finit?
are there any seats left for tonight?	est-ce qu'il y a encore des places pour ce soir?
how much are the tickets?	combien coûtent les billets?
where can I get a programme, (*Amer*) program?	où est-ce que je peux me procurer un programme?
I want to book tickets for tonight's performance	je veux réserver des places pour la représentation de ce soir
I'll book seats in the circle	je vais réserver des places au balcon
I'd rather have seats in the stalls, (*Amer*) orchestra	je préfère avoir des places à l'orchestre
somewhere in the middle, but not too far back	au milieu, mais pas trop loin de la scène
four, please	quatre, s'il vous plaît
we'd like to go to a club	on voudrait aller en boîte

Hobbies Passe-temps

what do you do at, (*Amer*) on weekends?	que faites-vous les week-ends?
I like reading/listening to music/ going out	j'aime lire/écouter de la musique/ sortir
do you like watching TV/shopping/ travelling, (*Amer*) traveling?	est-ce que tu aimes regarder la télé/faire du shopping/voyager?
I read a lot	je lis beaucoup
I collect comic books	je collectionne les bandes dessinées

Good timing/En temps et en heure

Telling the time Exprimer l'heure

could you tell me the time?	pourriez-vous me dire l'heure?
what time is it?	quelle heure est-il?
it's 2 o'clock	il est 2 heures
at about 8 o'clock	vers 8 heures
at 9 o'clock tomorrow	à 9 heures demain
from 10 o'clock onwards	à partir de 10 heures
it starts at 8 p.m.	ça commence à 20 heures
at 5 o'clock in the morning/afternoon	à 5 heures du matin/de l'après-midi
it's five past/quarter past/half past one	il est une heure cinq/et quart/et demie
it's twenty-five to/quarter to/five to one	il est une heure moins vingt-cinq/le quart/cinq
a quarter of an hour	un quart d'heure

Days and dates Jours et dates

Sunday, Monday, Tuesday, Wednesday, Thursday, Friday, Saturday	dimanche, lundi, mardi, mercredi, jeudi, vendredi, samedi
January, February, March, April, May, June, July, August, September, October, November, December	janvier, février, mars, avril, mai, juin, juillet, août, septembre, octobre, novembre, décembre
what's the date today?	on est le combien aujourd'hui?
it's the second of June	on est le deux juin
what day is it? it's Monday	on est quel jour? on est lundi
we meet up every Monday	on se réunit tous les lundis

she comes on Tuesdays	elle vient le mardi
we're going away in August	nous partons en août
on November 8th	le 8 novembre

Public holidays and special days — Jours fériés

Bank holiday	jour férié
long weekend	week-end prolongé
New Year's Day (1 Jan)	le Jour de l'an
St Valentine's Day (14 Feb)	la Saint-Valentin
Shrove Tuesday/Pancake Day	Mardi gras
Ash Wednesday	le mercredi des Cendres
Mother's Day	la fête des Mères
Palm Sunday	le dimanche des Rameaux
Good Friday	vendredi saint
Easter Day	Pâques
Easter Monday	le lundi de Pâques
Ascension Day	l'Ascension
Pentecost/Whitsun	la Pentecôte
Whit Monday	le lundi de Pentecôte
Father's Day	la fête des Pères
St John the Baptist's Day (24 Jun)	la Saint-Jean
Independence day (4 Jul)	la fête de l'Indépendance (aux États-Unis)
Bastille day (14 July)	le 14 juillet
Halloween (31 Oct)	Halloween (soir des fantômes et des sorcières)
All Saints' Day (1 Nov)	la Toussaint
Guy Fawkes Day/Bonfire Night (5 Nov)	fête de la Conspiration des Poudres avec feux de joie et feux d'artifice
Remembrance Sunday	le jour du Souvenir
Thanksgiving	le jour d'Action de grâces
Christmas Day (25 Dec)	Noël
Boxing Day (26 Dec)	le lendemain de Noël
New Year's Eve (31 Dec)	la Saint-Sylvestre

3

Health and Beauty/Santé et beauté

At the doctor's — Chez le médecin

can I see a doctor?	est-ce que je peux voir un médecin?
I don't feel well	je ne me sens pas bien
it hurts here	j'ai mal là
I have a stomachache/migraine	j'ai mal au ventre/j'ai une migraine
are there any side effects?	est-ce qu'il y a des effets secondaires?
I have a sore ankle/wrist/knee	j'ai mal à la cheville/au poignet/au genou

YOU WILL HEAR: — VOUS ENTENDREZ:

vous devez prendre rendez-vous	you need to make an appointment
asseyez-vous, s'il vous plaît	please take a seat
est-ce que vous avez une carte européenne d'assurance-maladie (CEAM)?	do you have a European Health Insurance Card (EHIC)?
est-ce que vous avez une assurance-maladie?	do you have Health Insurance?
il faut que je prenne votre tension artérielle	I need to take your blood pressure

MORE USEFUL WORDS: — D'AUTRES MOTS UTILES:

nurse	l'infirmier/-ière
antibiotics	les antibiotiques
medicine	le médicament
infection	l'infection
treatment	le traitement
rest	le repos

At the pharmacy Chez le pharmacien

can I have some painkillers?	puis-je avoir quelque chose pour la douleur?
I have asthma/eczema/hay fever	j'ai de l'asthme/de l'eczéma/le rhume des foins
I've been stung by a wasp/bee	j'ai été piqué/-e par une guêpe/une abeille
I've got a cold/the flu	j'ai un rhume/la grippe
I need something for diarrhoea/stomachache	j'ai besoin de quelque chose contre la diarrhée/le mal de ventre
I'm pregnant	je suis enceinte

YOU WILL HEAR: VOUS ENTENDREZ:

avez-vous déjà pris ce médicament?	have you taken this medicine before?
prendre à l'heure du repas/trois fois par jour	take at mealtimes/three times a day
êtes-vous allergique?	are you allergic to anything?
est-ce que vous prenez d'autres médicaments?	are you taking any other medication?

MORE USEFUL WORDS: D'AUTRES MOTS UTILES:

prescription	l'ordonnance
plasters, (Amer) Band-Aid™	le pansement
insect repellent	le produit anti-insecte
contraception	la contraception
sun cream	la crème solaire
aftersun	l'après-soleil
dosage	la posologie

At the hairdresser's/ beauty salon / Chez le coiffeur/ Au salon de beauté

I'd like a cut and blow dry	je voudrais une coupe et un brushing
just a trim, please	juste une coupe d'entretien, s'il vous plaît
a grade 3 back and sides	court derrière et sur les côtés
I'd like my hair washed first, please	je voudrais un shampooing, s'il vous plaît
can I have a manicure/pedicure/ facial?	puis-je avoir une manucure/un soin des pieds/un soin du visage?
how much is a head/back massage?	combien coûte un massage de la tête/du dos?
can I see a price list?	puis-je voir vos tarifs?
do you offer reflexology/ aromatherapy treatments?	est-ce que vous faites des séances de réflexologie/d'aromathérapie?

YOU WILL HEAR: / VOUS ENTENDREZ:

voulez-vous un brushing?	would you like your hair blow-dried?
vous avez la raie au milieu ou sur le côté?	where is your parting?
voulez-vous un dégradé?	would you like your hair layered?

MORE USEFUL WORDS: / D'AUTRES MOTS UTILES:

dry/greasy/fine/flyaway/ frizzy hair	des cheveux secs/gras/fins/ rebels/crépus
highlights	des mèches
extensions	les extensions de cheveux
sunbed	le lit de bronzage
leg/arm/bikini wax	l'épilation à la cire des jambes/des bras/du maillot

At the dentist's   Chez le dentiste

I have toothache	j'ai mal aux dents
I'd like an emergency appointment	il me faut un rendez-vous d'urgence
I have cracked a tooth	je me suis cassé une dent
my gums are bleeding	j'ai les gencives qui saignent

YOU WILL HEAR: VOUS ENTENDREZ:

ouvrez la bouche	open your mouth
vous avez besoin d'un plombage	you need a filling
il faut faire une radio	we need to take an X-ray
rincez-vous la bouche, s'il vous plaît	please rinse

MORE USEFUL WORDS: D'AUTRES MOTS UTILES:

anaesthetic	l'anesthésique
root canal treatment	la dévitalisation
injection	la piqûre
floss	le fil dentaire

DID YOU KNOW...?   LE SAVIEZ-VOUS...?

In France you have to pay for healthcare, and depending on the type of care received a full or partial refund will be obtained. A doctor or dentist's surgery can often be found in a residential house or flat. A plaque at the entrance of the house or block of flats will inform the patient of the doctor's name, specialization, phone number and surgery times.

Le *National Health Service* britannique fournit un service de santé gratuit dans sa grande majorité. Ainsi les consultations généralistes et spécialistes, les hôpitaux, les urgences, la maternité, entre autres, sont gratuits. Par contre, pour la pharmacie ou d'autres soins comme la dentisterie, le patient doit payer une somme forfaitaire.

Weights & measures/ Poids et mesures

Length/Longueur

inches/pouces	0.39	3.9	7.8	11.7	15.6	19.7	39
cm/centimètres	1	10	20	30	40	50	100

Distance/Distance

miles/miles	0.62	6.2	12.4	18.6	24.9	31	62
km/kilomètres	1	10	20	30	40	50	100

Weight/Poids

pounds/livres	2.2	22	44	66	88	110	220
kg/kilogrammes	1	10	20	30	40	50	100

Capacity/Contenance

gallons/gallons	0.22	2.2	4.4	6.6	8.8	11	22
litres/litres	1	10	20	30	40	50	100

Temperature/Température

°C	0	5	10	15	20	25	30	37	38	40
°F	32	41	50	59	68	77	86	98.4	100	104

Clothing and shoe sizes/Tailles et pointures

Women's clothing sizes/Tailles femme

UK	8	10	12	14	16	18
US	6	8	10	12	14	16
Continent	36	38	40	42	44	46

Men's clothing sizes/Tailles homme

UK/US	36	38	40	42	44	46
Continent	46	48	50	52	54	56

Men's and women's shoes/Pointures homme et femme

UK women	4	5	6	7	7.5	8			
UK men			6	7	8	9	10	11	
US		6.5	7.5	8.5	9.5	10.5	11.5	12.5	13.5	14.5
Continent	37	38	39	40	41	42	43	44	45

Aa

a /eɪ, ə/ determiner

an avant voyelle ou h muet.

➡️ For expressions such as make a noise, make a fortune ➡️noise, fortune.

···▸ un/une; ~ tree un arbre; ~ chair une chaise.
···▸ (per) two euros ~ kilo deux euros le kilo; three times ~ day trois fois par jour.

❗ When talking about what people do or are, a is not translated into French: she's a teacher elle est professeur; he's a widower il est veuf.

aback /ə'bæk/ adv taken ~ déconcerté.

abandon /ə'bændən/ vt abandonner. ● n abandon m.

abate /ə'beɪt/ vi (flood, fever) baisser; (storm) se calmer. ● vt diminuer.

abbey /'æbɪ/ n abbaye f.

abbot /'æbət/ n abbé m.

abbreviate /ə'briːvɪeɪt/ vt abréger. **abbreviation** n abréviation f.

abdicate /'æbdɪkeɪt/ vt/i abdiquer.

abdomen /'æbdəmən/ n abdomen m.

abduct /əb'dʌkt/ vt enlever. **abductor** n ravisseur/-euse m/f.

abhor /əb'hɔː(r)/ vt (pt abhorred) exécrer.

abide /ə'baɪd/ vt supporter; ~ by respecter.

ability /ə'bɪlətɪ/ n capacité f (to do à faire); (talent) talent m.

abject /'æbdʒekt/ adj (state) misérable; (coward) abject.

ablaze /ə'bleɪz/ adj en feu.

able /'eɪbl/ adj (skilled) compétent; be ~ to do pouvoir faire; (know how to) savoir faire. **ably** adv avec compétence.

abnormal /æb'nɔːml/ adj anormal. **abnormality** n anomalie f.

aboard /ə'bɔːd/ adv à bord. ● prep à bord de.

abode /ə'bəʊd/ n demeure f; of no fixed ~ sans domicile fixe.

abolish /ə'bɒlɪʃ/ vt abolir.

Aborigine /æbə'rɪdʒənɪ/ n aborigène mf (d'Australie).

abort /ə'bɔːt/ vt faire avorter; (Comput) abandonner. ● vi avorter.

abortion /ə'bɔːʃn/ n avortement m; have an ~ se faire avorter.

abortive /ə'bɔːtɪv/ adj (attempt) avorté; (coup) manqué.

about /ə'baʊt/ adv (approximately) environ; ~ the same à peu près pareil; there was no-one ~ il n'y avait personne. ● prep it's ~ ... il s'agit de ...; what I like ~ her is ce que j'aime chez elle c'est; to wander ~ the streets errer dans les rues; how/what ~ some tea? et si on prenait un thé?; what ~ you? et toi? ● adj be ~ to do être sur le point de faire; be up and ~ être debout. ~-face, ~-turn n (fig) volte-face f inv.

above /ə'bʌv/ prep au-dessus de;

he is not ~ lying il n'est pas incapable de mentir; ~ all surtout.
● *adv* the apartment ~ l'appartement du dessus; see ~ voir ci-dessus. ~**-board** *adj* honnête. ~**-mentioned** *adj* susmentionné.

abrasive /ə'breɪsɪv/ *adj* abrasif; (*manner*) mordant. ● *n* abrasif *m*.

abreast /ə'brest/ *adv* de front; keep ~ of se tenir au courant de.

abroad /ə'brɔːd/ *adv* à l'étranger.

abrupt /ə'brʌpt/ *adj* (*sudden, curt*) brusque; (*steep*) abrupt. **abruptly** *adv* (*suddenly*) brusquement; (*curtly*) avec brusquerie.

abscess /'æbses/ *n* abcès *m*.

abseil /'æbseɪl/ *vi* descendre en rappel.

absence /'æbsəns/ *n* absence *f*; (*lack*) manque *m*; in the ~ of faute de.

absent /'æbsənt/ *adj* absent.

absentee /æbsən'tiː/ *n* absent/-e *m/f*.

absent-minded *adj* distrait.

absolute /'æbsəluːt/ *adj* (*monarch, majority*) absolu; (*chaos, idiot*) véritable. **absolutely** *adv* absolument.

absolve /ab'zɒlv/ *vt* ~ sb of sth décharger qn de qch.

absorb /ab'zɔːb/ *vt* absorber.

abstain /əb'steɪn/ *vi* s'abstenir (from de).

abstract[1] /'æbstrækt/ *adj* abstrait. ● *n* (*summary*) résumé *m*; in the ~ dans l'abstrait.

abstract[2] /əb'strækt/ *vt* tirer.

absurd /əb'sɜːd/ *adj* absurde.

abundance /ə'bʌndəns/ *n* abondance *f*. **abundant** *adj* abondant. **abundantly** *adv* (*entirely*) tout à fait.

abuse[1] /ə'bjuːz/ *vt* (*position*) abuser de; (*person*) maltraiter; (*insult*) injurier.

abuse[2] /ə'bjuːs/ *n* (*misuse*) abus *m* (of de); (*cruelty*) mauvais traitement *m*; (*insults*) injures *fpl*.

abusive /ə'bjuːsɪv/ *adj* (*person*) grossier; (*language*) injurieux.

abysmal /ə'bɪzml/ *adj* épouvantable.

abyss /ə'bɪs/ *n* abîme *m*.

academic /ækə'demɪk/ *adj* (*career*) universitaire; (*year*) académique; (*scholarly*) intellectuel; (*theoretical*) théorique. ● *n* universitaire *mf*.

academy /ə'kædəmɪ/ *n* (*school*) école *f*; (*society*) académie *f*.

accelerate /ək'seləreɪt/ *vi* (*speed up*) s'accélérer; (*Auto*) accélérer. **accelerator** *n* accélérateur *m*.

accent[1] /'æksənt/ *n* accent *m*.

accent[2] /æk'sent/ *vt* accentuer.

accept /ək'sept/ *vt* accepter. **acceptable** *adj* acceptable. **acceptance** *n* (of offer) acceptation *f*; (of proposal) approbation *f*.

access /'ækses/ *n* accès *m*. **accessible** *adj* accessible.

accessory /ək'sesərɪ/ *adj* accessoire. ● *n* (*Jur*) complice *mf* (to de).

accident /'æksɪdənt/ *n* accident *m*; (*chance*) hasard *m*; by ~ par hasard. **accidental** *adj* (*death*) accidentel; (*meeting*) fortuit. **accidentally** *adv* accidentellement; (*by chance*) par hasard.

acclaim /ə'kleɪm/ *vt* applaudir. ● *n* louanges *fpl*.

acclimatize /ə'klaɪmətaɪz/ *vt/i* (s')acclimater (to à).

accommodate /ə'kɒmədeɪt/ *vt* loger; (*adapt to*) s'adapter à; (*satisfy*) satisfaire. **accommodating** *adj* accommodant. **accommodation** *n* logement *m*.

accompaniment /ə'kʌmpənɪmənt/ *n* accompagnement

m. **accompany** *vt* accompagner.

accomplice /əˈkʌmplɪs/ *n* complice *mf* (in, to de).

accomplish /əˈkʌmplɪʃ/ *vt* accomplir; (*objective*) réaliser. **accomplished** *adj* très compétent. **accomplishment** *n* (*feat*) réussite *f*; (*talent*) talent *m*.

accord /əˈkɔːd/ *vi* concorder (with avec). ● *vt* accorder (sb sth qch à qn). ● *n* accord *m*; of my own ~ de moi-même.

accordance /əˈkɔːdəns/ *n* in ~ with conformément à.

according /əˈkɔːdɪŋ/ *adv* ~ to (*principle, law*) selon; (*person, book*) d'après. **accordingly** *adv* en conséquence.

accordion /əˈkɔːdɪən/ *n* accordéon *m*.

accost /əˈkɒst/ *vt* aborder.

account /əˈkaʊnt/ *n* (Comm) compte *m*; (*description*) compte-rendu *m*; on ~ of à cause de; on no ~ en aucun cas; take into ~ tenir compte de; it's of no ~ peu importe. □ ~ for (*explain*) expliquer; (*represent*) représenter. **accountability** *n* responsabilité *f*. **accountable** *adj* responsable (for de; to envers).

accountancy /əˈkaʊntənsɪ/ *n* comptabilité *f*. **accountant** *n* comptable *mf*. **accounts** *npl* comptabilité *f*, comptes *mpl*.

accumulate /əˈkjuːmjʊleɪt/ *vt/i* (s')accumuler.

accuracy /ˈækjərəsɪ/ *n* (of figures) justesse *f*; (of aim) précision *f*; (of forecast) exactitude *f*. **accurate** *adj* juste, précis. **accurately** *adv* exactement, précisément.

accusation /ækjuːˈzeɪʃn/ *n* accusation *f*.

accuse /əˈkjuːz/ *vt* accuser; the ~d

l'accusé/-e *m/f*.

accustomed /əˈkʌstəmd/ *adj* accoutumé; become ~ to s'accoutumer à.

ace /eɪs/ *n* (card, person) as *m*.

ache /eɪk/ *n* douleur *f*. ● *vi* (*person*) avoir mal; my leg ~s ma jambe me fait mal.

achieve /əˈtʃiːv/ *vt* (*aim*) atteindre; (*result*) obtenir; (*ambition*) réaliser. **achievement** *n* (*feat*) réussite *f*; (*fulfilment*) réalisation *f* (of de).

acid /ˈæsɪd/ *adj* & *n* acide (*m*). **acidity** *n* acidité *f*. ~ **rain** *n* pluies *fpl* acides.

acknowledge /əkˈnɒlɪdʒ/ *vt* (*error, authority*) reconnaître. (*letter*) accuser réception de. **acknowledgement** *n* reconnaissance *f*.

acne /ˈæknɪ/ *n* acné *f*.

acorn /ˈeɪkɔːn/ *n* (Bot) gland *m*.

acoustic /əˈkuːstɪk/ *adj* acoustique. **acoustics** *npl* acoustique *f*.

acquaint /əˈkweɪnt/ *vt* ~ sb with sth mettre qn au courant de qch; be ~ed with (*person*) connaître. (*fact*) savoir. **acquaintance** *n* connaissance *f*.

acquire /əˈkwaɪə(r)/ *vt* acquérir; (*habit*) prendre.

acquit /əˈkwɪt/ *vt* (*pt* acquitted) (Jur) acquitter. **acquittal** *n* acquittement *m*.

acre /ˈeɪkə(r)/ *n* acre *f*, ≈ demi-hectare *m*.

acrid /ˈækrɪd/ *adj* âcre.

acrimonious /ækrɪˈməʊnɪəs/ *adj* acrimonieux.

acrobat /ˈækrəbæt/ *n* acrobate *mf*. **acrobatics** *npl* acrobaties *fpl*.

acronym /ˈækrənɪm/ *n* acronyme *m*.

across /əˈkrɒs/ *adv* & *prep* (side to side) d'un côté à l'autre (de); (on other side) de l'autre côté (from de); go or walk ~ traverser; lie ~ the bed se coucher en travers du lit; ~ the world partout dans le monde.

act /ækt/ n acte m; (Jur, Pol) loi f; put on an ~ jouer la comédie. ● vi agir; (Theat) jouer; ~ as servir de. ● vt (part, role) jouer.

acting /ˈæktɪŋ/ n (Theat) jeu m. ● adj (temporary) intérimaire.

action /ˈækʃn/ n action f; (Mil) combat m; out of ~ hors service; take ~ agir.

activate /ˈæktɪveɪt/ vt (machine) faire démarrer; (alarm) déclencher.

active /ˈæktɪv/ adj actif; (volcano) en activité; take an ~ interest in s'intéresser activement à. **activist** n activiste mf; **activity** n activité f.

actor /ˈæktə/ n acteur m. **actress** n actrice f.

actual /ˈæktʃʊəl/ adj réel; the ~ words les mots exacts; in the ~ house (the house itself) dans la maison elle-même. **actuality** n réalité f; **actually** adv (in fact) en fait; (really) vraiment.

acute /əˈkjuːt/ adj (anxiety) vif; (illness) aigu; (shortage) grave; (mind) pénétrant.

ad /æd/ n (TV) pub f 🔲; small ~ petite annonce f.

AD abbr (**Anno Domini**) ap. J.-C.

adamant /ˈædəmənt/ adj catégorique.

adapt /əˈdæpt/ vt/i (s')adapter (to à). **adaptability** n adaptabilité f; **adaptable** adj souple. **adaptation** n adaptation f. **adaptor** n (Electr) adaptateur m.

add /æd/ vt ajouter (to à); (in maths) additionner. □ ~ up (facts, figures) s'accorder; ~ sth up additionner qch; ~ up to s'élever à.

adder /ˈædə(r)/ n vipère f.

addict /ˈædɪkt/ n toxicomane mf; (fig) accro mf 🔲.

addicted /əˈdɪktɪd/ adj be ~ avoir une dépendance (to à); (fig) être accro 🔲 (to à). **addiction** n (Med) dépendance f (to à); passion f (to pour). **addictive** adj qui crée une dépendance.

addition /əˈdɪʃn/ n (item) ajout m; (in maths) addition f; **in** ~ en plus. **additional** adj supplémentaire.

additive /ˈædɪtɪv/ n additif m.

address /əˈdres/ n adresse f; (speech) discours m. ● vt (letter) mettre l'adresse sur; (crowd) s'adresser à; ~ **sth to** adresser qch à. **addressee** n destinataire mf.

adequate /ˈædɪkwət/ adj suffisant; (satisfactory) satisfaisant.

adhere /ədˈhɪə(r)/ vi (lit, fig) adhérer (to à); ~ **to** (policy) observer.

adjacent /əˈdʒeɪsnt/ adj contigu; ~ **to** attenant à.

adjective /ˈædʒɪktɪv/ n adjectif m.

adjoin /əˈdʒɔɪn/ vt être contigu à. **adjoining** adj (room) voisin.

adjourn /əˈdʒɜːn/ vt (trial) ajourner; the session was ~ed la séance a été levée. ● vi s'arrêter; (Parliament) lever la séance; ~ **to** passer à.

adjust /əˈdʒʌst/ vt (level, speed) régler; (price) ajuster; (clothes) rajuster. ● vt/i ~ (oneself) to s'adapter à. **adjustable** adj réglable. **adjustment** n (of rates) rajustement m; (of control) réglage m; (of person) adaptation f.

ad lib /æd ˈlɪb/ vt/i (pt ad libbed) improviser.

administer /ədˈmɪnɪstə(r)/ vt administrer.

administration /ədmɪnɪˈstreɪʃn/ n administration f. **administrative** adj administratif. **administrator** n administrateur/-trice *m/f.*

admiral /ˈædmərəl/ *n* amiral *m.*

admiration /ædməˈreɪʃn/ *n* admiration *f.* **admire** *vt* admirer. **admirer** *n* admirateur/-trice *m/f.*

admission /ədˈmɪʃn/ *n* (to a place) entrée *f;* (confession) aveu *m.*

admit /ədˈmɪt/ *vt* (*pt* **admitted**) (acknowledge) reconnaître, admettre. (*crime*) avouer; (*new member*) admettre; ~ to reconnaître. **admittance** *n* entrée *f.* **admittedly** *adv* il est vrai.

ado /əˈduː/ *n* without more ~ sans plus de cérémonie.

adolescence /ædəˈlesns/ *n* adolescence *f.* **adolescent** *n & a* adolescent/-e *m/f.*

adopt /əˈdɒpt/ *vt* adopter. **adopted** *adj* (*child*) adoptif. **adoption** *n* adoption *f.* **adoptive** *adj* adoptif.

adorable /əˈdɔːrəbl/ *adj* adorable. **adoration** *n* adoration *f.* **adore** *vt* adorer.

adorn /əˈdɔːn/ *vt* orner.

adrift /əˈdrɪft/ *adj & adv* à la dérive.

adult /ˈædʌlt/ *adj & n* adulte (*mf*).

adultery /əˈdʌltərɪ/ *n* adultère *m.*

adulthood /ˈædʌlthʊd/ *n* âge *m* adulte.

advance /ədˈvɑːns/ *vt* (*sum*) avancer; (*tape, career*) faire avancer; (*interests*) servir. ● *vi* (lit) avancer; (*progress*) progresser. ● *n* avance *f;* (*progress*) progrès *m;* in~ à l'avance. **advanced** *adj* avancé; (*studies*) supérieur.

advantage /ədˈvɑːntɪdʒ/ *n* avantage *m;* take ~ of profiter de. (*person*) exploiter. **advantageous** *adj* avantageux.

adventure /ədˈventʃə(r)/ *n* aventure *f.*

adventurer /ədˈventʃərə(r)/ *n* aventurier-ière *m/f.* **adventurous** *adj*

aventureux.

adverb /ˈædvɜːb/ *n* adverbe *m.*

adverse /ˈædvɜːs/ *adj* défavorable.

advert /ˈædvɜːt/ *n* annonce *f;* (TV) pub *f* 🗉.

advertise /ˈædvətaɪz/ *vt* faire de la publicité pour; (*car, house, job*) mettre une annonce pour. ● *vi* faire de la publicité; (for staff) passer une annonce. **advertisement** *n* publicité *f;* (in newspaper) annonce *f.* **advertiser** *n* annonceur *m.* **advertising** *n* publicité *f.*

advice /ədˈvaɪs/ *n* conseils *mpl;* some ~, a piece of ~ un conseil.

advise /ədˈvaɪz/ *vt* conseiller; (inform) aviser; ~ against déconseiller. **adviser** *n* conseiller/-ère *m/f.* **advisory** *adj* consultatif.

advocate[1] /ˈædvəkət/ *n* (jur) avocat *m;* (supporter) partisan *m.*

advocate[2] /ˈædvəkeɪt/ *vt* recommander.

aerial /ˈeərɪəl/ *adj* aérien. ● *n* antenne *f.*

aerobics /eəˈrəʊbɪks/ *n* aérobic *m.*

aeroplane /ˈeərəpleɪn/ *n* avion *m.*

aerosol /ˈeərəsɒl/ *n* bombe *f* aérosol.

aesthetic /iːsˈθetɪk/ *adj* esthétique.

afar /əˈfɑː(r)/ *adv* from ~ de loin.

affair /əˈfeə(r)/ *n* (matter) affaire *f;* (romance) liaison *f.*

affect /əˈfekt/ *vt* affecter.

affection /əˈfekʃn/ *n* affection *f.* **affectionate** *adj* affectueux.

affinity /əˈfɪnətɪ/ *n* affinité *f.*

afflict /əˈflɪkt/ *vt* affliger.

affluence /ˈæflʊəns/ *n* richesse *f.*

afford /əˈfɔːd/ *vt* avoir les moyens d'acheter; (provide) fournir; can you ~ the time? avez-vous le temps?

afloat /əˈfləʊt/ *vt* *adj & adv*

a

(*boat*) à flot.

afoot /ə'fʊt/ *adv* sth is ~ il se prépare qch.

afraid /ə'freɪd/ *adj* be ~ (frightened) avoir peur (of, to de; that que); (worried) craindre (that que); I'm ~ I can't come je suis désolé mais je ne peux pas venir.

Africa /'æfrɪkə/ n Afrique f.

African /'æfrɪkən/ n Africain/-e m/f. ● *adj* africain.

after /'ɑːftə(r)/ *adv* & *prep* après; soon ~ peu après; be ~ sth rechercher qch; ~ all après tout. ● *conj* après que; ~ doing après avoir fait.

aftermath /'ɑːftəmæθ/ n conséquences *fpl* (of de).

afternoon /ɑːftə'nuːn/ n après-midi m or f inv; in the ~ (dans) l'après-midi.

after: ~ **shave** n après-rasage m. ~ **thought** n pensée f après coup.

afterwards /'ɑːftəwədz/ *adv* après, par la suite.

again /ə'geɪn/ *adv* encore; ~ and ~ plusieurs reprises; start ~ recommencer; she never saw him ~ elle ne l'a jamais revu.

against /ə'geɪnst/ *prep* contre; ~ the law illégal.

age /eɪdʒ/ n âge m; (*era*) ère f; époque f; I've been waiting for ~s j'attends depuis des heures. ● *vt/i* (*pres p* **ageing**) vieillir.

aged[1] /'eɪdʒd/ *adj* ~ six âgé de six ans.

aged[2] /'eɪdʒɪd/ *adj* âgé.

ageism /'eɪdʒɪzəm/ n discrimination f en raison de l'âge.

agency /'eɪdʒɪsɪ/ n agence f.

agenda /ə'dʒendə/ n ordre m du jour; (fig) programme m.

agent /'eɪdʒənt/ n agent m.

aggravate /'ægrəveɪt/ *vt* (make worse) aggraver; (annoy) exaspérer.

aggravation n (worsening) aggravation f; (annoyance) ennuis *mpl*.

aggression /ə'greʃn/ n agression f. **aggressive** *adj* agressif. **aggressiveness** n agressivité f. **aggressor** n agresseur m.

agitate /'ædʒɪteɪt/ *vt* agiter.

ago /ə'gəʊ/ *adv* il y a; a month ~ il y a un mois; long ~ il y a longtemps; how long ~? il y a combien de temps?

agonize /'ægənaɪz/ *vi* se tourmenter (over à propos de). **agonized** *adj* angoissé. **agonizing** *adj* déchirant. **agony** n douleur f atroce; (mental) angoisse f.

agree /ə'griː/ *vi* être d'accord (on sur; with avec); ~ to consentir à; ~ with (approve of) approuver. ● *vt* être d'accord (that sur le fait que); (admit) convenir (that que); (*date, solution*) se mettre d'accord sur.

agreeable /ə'griːəbl/ *adj* agréable; be ~ (willing) être d'accord.

agreed /ə'griːd/ *adj* (*time, place*) convenu; we're ~ nous sommes d'accord.

agreement /ə'griːmənt/ n accord m; in ~ d'accord.

agricultural /ægrɪ'kʌltʃərəl/ *adj* agricole. **agriculture** n agriculture f.

aground /ə'graʊnd/ *adv* run ~ (*ship*) s'échouer.

ahead /ə'hed/ *adv* (in front) en avant, devant; (in advance) à l'avance; be 10 points ~ avoir 10 points d'avance; ~ of time en avance; go ~! allez-y!

aid /eɪd/ *vt* aider. ● n aide f; in ~ of au profit de.

aide /eɪd/ n aide *mf*.

Aids /eɪdz/ n (Med) sida m.

aim /eɪm/ vt (gun) braquer (at sur); be ~ ed at sb (campaign, remark) viser qn. ● vi ~ for/at sth viser qch; ~ to do avoir l'intention de faire. ● n but m; take ~ viser. **aimless** adj sans but.

air /eə(r)/ n air m; by ~ par avion; on the ~ à l'antenne. ● vt aérer; (views) exprimer. ● adj (base, disaster) aérien; (pollution, pressure) atmosphérique. ~ **bed** n matelas m pneumatique. ~ **conditioning** n climatisation f. ~**craft** n inv avion m. ~**craft carrier** n porteavions m inv. ~**field** n terrain m d'aviation. ~ **force** n armée f de l'air. ~ **freshener** n désodorisant m d'atmosphère. ~ **hostess** n hôtesse f de l'air. ~**lift** vt transporter par pont aérien. ~**line** n compagnie f aérienne. ~**liner** n avion m de ligne. ~**lock** n (in pipe) bulle f d'air; (chamber) sas m. ~**mail** n (by) ~**mail** par avion. ~**plane** n (US) avion m. ~**port** n aéroport m. ~ **raid** n attaque f aérienne. ~**tight** adj hermétique. ~ **traffic controller** n contrôleur/-euse m/f aérien/-ne. ~**waves** npl ondes fpl.

airy /ˈeərɪ/ adj (-ier, -iest) (room) clair et spacieux.

aisle /aɪl/ n (of church) allée f centrale; (in train) couloir m.

ajar /əˈdʒɑː(r)/ adv & adj entrouvert.

akin /əˈkɪn/ adj ~ to semblable à.

alarm /əˈlɑːm/ n alarme f; (clock) réveil m; (feeling) frayeur f. ● vt inquiéter. ~ **clock** n réveil m.

alas /əˈlæs/ interj hélas.

Albania /ælˈbeɪnɪə/ n Albanie f.

album /ˈælbəm/ n album m.

alcohol /ˈælkəhɒl/ n alcool m.

alcoholic /ælkəˈhɒlɪk/ adj alcoolique; (drink) alcoolisé. ● n alcoolique mf.

ale /eɪl/ n bière f.

alert /əˈlɜːt/ adj alerte; (watchful) vigilant. ● n alerte f; on the ~ sur le qui-vive. ● vt alerter; ~ sb to prévenir qn de. **alertness** n vivacité f; vigilance f.

A-level /ˈeɪlevl/ n ≈ baccalauréat m

algebra /ˈældʒɪbrə/ n algèbre f.

Algeria /ælˈdʒɪərɪə/ n Algérie f.

alias /ˈeɪlɪəs/ n (pl ~es) faux nom m. ● prep alias.

alibi /ˈælɪbaɪ/ n alibi m.

alien /ˈeɪlɪən/ n & a étranger/-ère (m/f) (to à).

alienate /ˈeɪlɪəneɪt/ vt éloigner.

alight /əˈlaɪt/ adj en feu, allumé.

alike /əˈlaɪk/ adj semblable; look ~ de la même façon; look ~ se ressembler.

alive /əˈlaɪv/ adj vivant; ~ to conscient de; ~ with grouillant de.

---

all /ɔːl/

● pronoun

····▶ (everything) tout; is that ~? c'est tout?; that was ~ (that) he said c'est tout ce qu'il a dit; I ate it ~ j'ai tout mangé.

❗ Use the translation tous for a group of masculine or mixed gender people or objects and toutes for a group of feminine gender: we were all delighted nous étions tous ravis; 'where are the cups?'—'they're all in the kitchen' 'où sont les tasses?'-'elles sont toutes dans la cuisine'.

● determiner

····▶ tout/toute/tous/toutes; ~

the time tout le temps; ~ his life toute sa vie; ~ of us nous tous; ~ (the) women toutes les femmes.

● adverb

····▶ (completely) tout; they were ~ alone ils étaient tout seuls; tell me ~ about it raconte-moi tout; ~ for tout à fait pour; not ~ that well pas si bien que ça; ~ too bien trop.

! When the adjective that follows is in the feminine and begins with a consonant, the translation is toute/toutes: she was all alone elle était toute seule.

allege /ə'ledʒ/ vt prétendre. ~d adj présumé; **allegedly** adv prétendument.

allergic /ə'lɜ:dʒɪk/ adj allergique (to à). **allergy** n allergie f.

alleviate /ə'li:vɪeɪt/ vt alléger.

alley /'ælɪ/ n (street) ruelle f.

alliance /ə'laɪəns/ n alliance f.

allied /'ælaɪd/ adj allié.

alligator /'ælɪɡeɪtə(r)/ n alligator m.

allocate /'æləkeɪt/ vt (funds) affecter; (time) accorder; (task) assigner.

allot /ə'lɒt/ vt (pt allotted) (money) attribuer; (task) assigner. **allotment** n attribution f; (land) parcelle f de terre.

all-out /'ɔ:laʊt/ adj (effort) acharné; (strike) total.

allow /ə'laʊ/ vt (authorize) autoriser à; (let) laisser; (enable) permettre; (concede) accorder; ~ for tenir compte de.

allowance /ə'laʊəns/ n allocation f; make ~s for sth tenir compte de

qch; make ~s for sb essayer de comprendre qn.

alloy /'ælɔɪ/ n alliage m.

all right /ɔ:l'raɪt/ adj (not bad) pas mal; are you ~? ça va?; is it ~ if ...? est-ce que ça va si ...? ● adv (see) (function) comme il faut. ● interj d'accord.

ally¹ /'ælaɪ/ n allié/-e m/f.

ally² /ə'laɪ/ vt allier; ~ oneself with s'allier avec.

almighty /ɔ:l'maɪtɪ/ adj tout-puissant; (very great) formidable.

almond /'ɑːmənd/ n amande f. ~ tree n amandier m.

almost /'ɔ:lməʊst/ adv presque; he ~ died il a failli mourir.

alone /ə'ləʊn/ adj & adv seul.

along /ə'lɒŋ/ prep le long de; walk ~ the beach marcher sur la plage. ● adv come ~ venir; walk ~ marcher; push/pull sth ~ pousser/tirer qch; all ~ (time) depuis le début; ~ with avec.

alongside /ə'lɒŋsaɪd/ adv à côté; come ~ (Naut) accoster. ● prep (next to) à côté de; (all along) le long de.

aloof /ə'lu:f/ adj distant.

aloud /ə'laʊd/ adv à haute voix.

alphabet /'ælfəbet/ n alphabet m. **alphabetical** adj alphabétique.

alpine /'ælpaɪn/ adj (landscape) alpestre; (climate) alpin.

already /ɔ:l'redɪ/ adv déjà.

alright /ɔ:l'raɪt/ a & adv ➡ALL RIGHT.

Alsatian /æl'seɪʃn/ n (dog) berger m allemand.

also /'ɔ:lsəʊ/ adv aussi.

altar /'ɔːltə(r)/ n autel m.

alter /'ɔːltə(r)/ vt/i changer; (building) transformer; (garment) retoucher. **alteration** n changement m;

(to building) transformation f; (to garment) retouche f.

alternate¹ /ˈɔːltəneɪt/ vt/i alterner.

alternate² /ɔːlˈtɜːnət/ adj en alternance; on ~ days un jour sur deux. **alternately** adv alternativement.

alternative /ɔːlˈtɜːnətɪv/ adj autre; (solution) de rechange. ● n (specified option) alternative f; (possible option) choix m. **alternatively** adv sinon.

alternator /ˈɔːltəneɪtə(r)/ n alternateur m.

although /ɔːlˈðəʊ/ conj bien que.

altitude /ˈæltɪtjuːd/ n altitude f.

altogether /ɔːltəˈgeðə(r)/ adv (completely) tout à fait; (on the whole) tout compte fait.

aluminium /æljuˈmɪnjəm/ n aluminium m.

always /ˈɔːlweɪz/ adv toujours.

am /æm/ →BE.

a.m. /eɪem/ adv du matin.

amalgamate /əˈmælgəmeɪt/ vt/i (merge) fusionner; (metals) (s')amalgamer.

amateur /ˈæmətə(r)/ n & adj amateur (m).

amaze /əˈmeɪz/ vt stupéfaire. **amazed** adj stupéfait. **amazement** n stupéfaction f. **amazing** adj stupéfiant; (great) exceptionnel.

ambassador /æmˈbæsədə(r)/ n ambassadeur m.

amber /ˈæmbə(r)/ n ambre m; (Auto) orange m.

ambiguity /æmbɪˈgjuːəti/ n ambiguïté f.

ambiguous /æmˈbɪgjʊəs/ adj ambigu.

ambition /æmˈbɪʃn/ n ambition f. **ambitious** adj ambitieux.

ambulance /ˈæmbjʊləns/ n ambulance f.

ambush /ˈæmbʊʃ/ n embuscade f. ● vt tendre une embuscade à.

amenable /əˈmiːnəbl/ adj obligeant; ~ to (responsive) sensible f.

amend /əˈmend/ vt modifier. **amendment** n (to rule) amendement m.

amends /əˈmendz/ npl make ~ réparer son erreur.

amenities /əˈmiːnətiz/ npl équipements mpl.

America /əˈmerɪkə/ n Amérique f.

American /əˈmerɪkən/ n Américain/-e m/f. ● adj américain.

American dream Cette **i** expression désigne un principe américain selon lequel la réussite, en particulier financière et sociale, est accessible à quiconque travaille avec acharnement. Pour les immigrants, s'y ajoute le rêve de liberté et d'égalité.

---

amiable /ˈeɪmɪəbl/ adj aimable.

amicable /ˈæmɪkəbl/ adj amical.

amid(st) /əˈmɪd(st)/ prep au milieu de.

amiss /əˈmɪs/ adj there is something ~ il y a quelque chose qui ne va pas.

ammonia /əˈməʊnɪə/ n (gas) ammoniac m; (solution) ammoniaque f.

ammunition /æmjʊˈnɪʃn/ n munitions fpl.

amnesty /ˈæmnəsti/ n amnistie f.

among(st) /əˈmʌŋ(st)/ prep parmi; (affecting a group) chez; be ~ the poorest être un des plus pauvres; be ~ the first être dans les premiers.

amorous /ˈæmərəs/ adj amoureux.

amount /əˈmaʊnt/ n quantité f; (total) montant m; (sum of money) somme f. ● vi ~ to (add up to) s'élever à; (be equivalent to) revenir à.

amp /æmp/ n ampère m.

amphibian /æm'fɪbɪən/ n amphibie m.

ample /'æmpl/ adj (resources) largement suffisant; (proportions) généreux.

amplifier /'æmplɪfaɪə(r)/ n amplificateur m.

amputate /'æmpjuteɪt/ vt amputer.

amuse /ə'mjuːz/ vt amuser.

amusement /ə'mjuːzmənt/ n (mirth) amusement m; (diversion) distraction f. ~ arcade n salle f de jeux.

an /æn, ən/ ➝A.

anaemia /ə'niːmɪə/ n anémie f.

anaesthetic /ænɪs'θetɪk/ n anesthésique m.

analyse /'ænəlaɪz/ vt analyser. **analysis** n (pl -yses) analyse f. **analyst** n analyste mf.

anarchist /'ænəkɪst/ n anarchiste mf.

anatomical /ænə'tɒmɪkl/ adj anatomique. **anatomy** n anatomie f.

ancestor /'ænsestə(r)/ n ancêtre m.

anchor /'æŋkə(r)/ n ancre f. ● vt mettre à l'ancre. ● vi jeter l'ancre.

anchovy /'æntʃəvɪ/ n anchois m.

ancient /'eɪnʃənt/ adj ancien.

ancillary /æn'sɪlərɪ/ adj auxiliaire.

and /ænd, ənd/ conj et; two hundred ~ sixty deux cent soixante; go ~ see him allez le voir; richer ~ richer de plus en plus riche.

anew /ə'njuː/ adv (once more) encore, de nouveau; (in a new way) à nouveau.

angel /'eɪndʒl/ n ange m.

anger /'æŋgə(r)/ n colère f. ● vt mettre en colère, fâcher.

angle /'æŋgl/ n angle m. ● vi pêcher (à la ligne); ~ for (fig) quêter.
angler n pêcheur/-euse m/f.

Anglo-Saxon /æŋgləʊ'sæksn/ adj anglo-saxon. ● n Anglo-Saxon/-ne m/f.

angry /'æŋgrɪ/ adj (-ier, -iest) fâché, en colère; get ~ se fâcher, se mettre en colère (with contre); make sb ~ mettre qn en colère.

anguish /'æŋgwɪʃ/ n angoisse f.

animal /'ænɪml/ n & adj animal (m).

animate¹ /'ænɪmət/ adj (person) vivant; (object) animé.

animate² /'ænɪmeɪt/ vt animer.

aniseed /'ænɪsiːd/ n anis m.

ankle /'æŋkl/ n cheville f. ~ sock n socquette f.

annex /ə'neks/ vt annexer.

anniversary /ænɪ'vɜːsərɪ/ n anniversaire m.

announce /ə'naʊns/ vt annoncer (that que). **announcement** n (spoken) annonce f; (written) avis m. **announcer** n (radio, TV) speaker/-ine m/f.

annoy /ə'nɔɪ/ vt agacer, ennuyer. **annoyance** n contrariété f. **annoyed** adj fâché (with contre); get ~ed se fâcher. **annoying** adj ennuyeux.

annual /'ænjʊəl/ adj annuel. ● n publication f annuelle. **annually** adv (earn, produce) par an; (do, inspect) tous les ans.

annul /ə'nʌl/ vt (pt annulled) annuler.

anonymity /ænə'nɪmətɪ/ n anonymat m. **anonymous** adj anonyme.

anorak /'ænəræk/ n anorak m.

another /ə'nʌðə(r)/ det & pron un/-e autre; ~ coffee (one more) encore un café; ~ ten minutes encore dix minutes, dix minutes de plus; **can I have ~?** est-ce que je peux en avoir un autre?

answer /'ɑːnsə(r)/ n réponse f; (solution) solution f; (phone) **there's no ~** ça ne répond pas. ● vt répondre à; (prayer) exaucer; **~ the door** ouvrir la porte. ● vi répondre. □ **~ back** répondre; **~ for** répondre de; **~ to** (superior) dépendre de; (description) répondre à. **answerable** adj responsable (for de; to devant). **answering machine** n répondeur m.

ant /ænt/ n fourmi f.

antagonism /æn'tægənɪzəm/ n antagonisme m. **antagonize** vt provoquer l'hostilité de.

Antarctic /æn'tɑːktɪk/ n **the ~** l'Antarctique m. ● adj antarctique.

antenatal /æntɪ'neɪtl/ adj prénatal.

antenna /æn'tenə/ n (pl **-ae**) (of insect) antenne f; (pl **-as**: aerial: US) antenne f.

anthem /'ænθəm/ n (Relig) motet m; (of country) hymne m national.

anthrax /'ænθræks/ n charbon m.

antibiotic /æntɪbaɪ'ɒtɪk/ n & adj antibiotique (m).

antibody /'æntɪbɒdɪ/ n anticorps m.

anticipate /æn'tɪsɪpeɪt/ vt (foresee, expect) prévoir, s'attendre à.

anticipation /æntɪsɪ'peɪʃn/ n attente f; **in ~ of** en prévision or attente de.

anticlimax /æntɪ'klaɪmæks/ n (let-down) déception f.

anticlockwise /æntɪ'klɒkwaɪz/ adv & adj dans le sens inverse des aiguilles d'une montre.

antics /'æntɪks/ npl pitreries fpl.

antifreeze /'æntɪfriːz/ n antigel m.

antiquated /'æntɪkweɪtɪd/ adj

(idea) archaïque; (building) vétuste.

antique /æn'tiːk/ adj (old) ancien; (old-style) à l'ancienne. ● n objet m ancien, antiquité f. **~ dealer** n antiquaire mf. **~ shop** n magasin m d'antiquités.

anti-Semitic /æntɪsɪ'mɪtɪk/ adj antisémite.

antiseptic /æntɪ'septɪk/ adj & n antiseptique (m).

antisocial /æntɪ'səʊʃl/ adj asocial, antisocial; (reclusive) sauvage.

antlers /'æntləz/ npl bois mpl.

anxiety /æŋ'zaɪətɪ/ n (worry) anxiété f; (eagerness) impatience f.

anxious /'æŋkʃəs/ adj (troubled) anxieux; (eager) impatient (de to).

any /'enɪ/ adj (some) du, de l', de la, des; (after negative) de, d'; (every) tout; (no matter which) n'importe quel; **at ~ moment** à tout moment; **have you ~ water?** avez-vous de l'eau? ● pron (no matter which one) n'importe lequel; (any amount of it or them) en; **I do not have ~** je n'en ai pas; **did you see ~ of them?** en avez-vous vu? ● adv (a little) un peu; **do you have ~ more?** en avez-vous encore?; **do you have ~ more tea?** avez-vous encore du thé?; **I don't do it ~ more** je ne le fais plus.

anybody /'enɪbɒdɪ/ pron (no matter who) n'importe qui; (somebody) quelqu'un; (after negative) personne; **he did not see ~** il n'a vu personne.

anyhow /'enɪhaʊ/ adv (anyway) de toute façon; (carelessly) n'importe comment.

anyone /'enɪwʌn/ pron ➡ANYBODY.

anything /'enɪθɪŋ/ pron (no matter what) n'importe quoi; (something) quelque chose; (after negative) rien;

a

he did not see ∼ il n'a rien vu; ∼ but nullement; ∼ you do tout ce que tu fais.

anyway /'enɪweɪ/ adv de toute façon.

anywhere /'enɪweə(r)/ adv (no matter where) n'importe où; (somewhere) quelque part; (after negative) nulle part; he does not go ∼ il ne va nulle part; ∼ you go partout où tu vas, où que tu ailles; ∼ else partout ailleurs.

apart /ə'pɑːt/ adv (on or to one side) à part; (separated) séparé; (into pieces) en pièces; ∼ from à part, excepté; ten metres ∼ à dix mètres l'un de l'autre; come ∼ (break) tomber en morceaux; (machine) se démonter; legs ∼ les jambes écartées; keep ∼ séparer; take ∼ démonter.

apartment /ə'pɑːtmənt/ n (US) appartement m.

ape /eɪp/ n singe m. ● vt singer.

aperitif /ə'perətɪf/ n apéritif m.

apex /'eɪpeks/ n sommet m.

apologetic /əpɒlə'dʒetɪk/ adj (tone) d'excuse; be ∼ s'excuser. **apologetically** adv en s'excusant.

apologize /ə'pɒlədʒaɪz/ vi s'excuser for de; to auprès de).

apology /ə'pɒlədʒɪ/ n excuses fpl.

apostrophe /ə'pɒstrəfɪ/ n apostrophe f.

appal /ə'pɔːl/ vt n appel m; (attractiveness) attrait m, charme m. ● vi (Jur) faire appel; ∼ to sb (beg) faire appel à qn; (attract) plaire à qn; ∼ to sb for sth demander qch à qn.

appealing adj (attractive) attirant.

appear /ə'pɪə(r)/ vi apparaître. (arrive) se présenter; (seem, be published) paraître. (Theat) jouer; on TV passer à la télé. **appearance** n apparition f; (aspect) apparence f.

appease /ə'piːz/ vt apaiser.

appendix /ə'pendɪks/ n (pl -ices) appendice m.

appetite /'æpɪtaɪt/ n appétit m.

appetizer /'æpɪtaɪzə(r)/ n (snack) amuse-gueule m inv; (drink) apéritif m.

appetizing /'æpɪtaɪzɪŋ/ adj appétissant.

applaud /ə'plɔːd/ vt/i applaudir; (decision) applaudir à. **applause** n applaudissements mpl.

apple /'æpl/ n pomme f; ∼-tree n pommier m.

appliance /ə'plaɪəns/ n appareil m.

applicable /'æplɪkəbl/ adj valable; if ∼ le cas échéant.

applicant /'æplɪkənt/ n candidat/-e m/f (for à).

application /æplɪ'keɪʃn/ n application f; (request, form) demande f; (for job) candidature f.

apply /ə'plaɪ/ vt appliquer. ● vi ∼ to (refer) s'appliquer à; (ask) s'adresser à; ∼ for (job) postuler pour; (grant) demander; ∼ oneself to s'appliquer à.

appoint /ə'pɔɪnt/ vt (to post) nommer; (fix) désigner; well-∼ed bien équipé.

appointment /ə'pɔɪntmənt/ n nomination f; (meeting) rendez-vous m inv; (job) poste m; make an ∼ prendre rendez-vous (with avec).

appraisal /ə'preɪzl/ n évaluation f. **appraise** vt évaluer.

appreciate /ə'priːʃɪeɪt/ vt (like) apprécier; (understand) comprendre; (be grateful for) être reconnais-

sant de. ● vi prendre de la valeur.
appreciation n appréciation f;
(gratitude) reconnaissance f; (rise)
augmentation f. **appreciative** adj
reconnaissant; (audience) enthousiaste.

apprehend /æprɪ'hend/ vt (arrest)
appréhender; (understand) comprendre. **apprehension** n (arrest)
appréhension f; (fear) crainte f.

apprehensive /æprɪ'hensɪv/ adj
inquiet; be ~ of craindre.

apprentice /ə'prentɪs/ n apprenti
m. ● vt mettre en apprentissage.

approach /ə'prəʊtʃ/ vt (s')approcher de; (accost) aborder; (with request) s'adresser à. ● vi (s')approcher. ● n approche f; an ~ to (problem) une façon d'aborder; (person) une démarche auprès de.
approachable adj abordable.

appropriate¹ /ə'prəʊprɪeɪt/ vt
s'approprier.

appropriate² /ə'prəʊprɪət/ adj
approprié, propre. **appropriately**
adv à propos.

approval /ə'pruːvl/ n approbation
f; on ~ à or sous condition.

approve /ə'pruːv/ vt approuver.
● vi ~ of approuver. **approving** adj
approbateur.

approximate¹ /ə'prɒksɪmeɪt/ vi
~ to se rapprocher de.

approximate² /ə'prɒksɪmət/ adj
approximatif. **approximately** adv
environ. **approximation** n approximation f.

apricot /'eɪprɪkɒt/ n abricot m.

April /'eɪprɪl/ n avril m. ~ **Fools
Day** n le premier avril.

apron /'eɪprən/ n tablier m.

apt /æpt/ adj (suitable) approprié;
be ~ to avoir tendance à.

aptitude /'æptɪtjuːd/ n aptitude f.

aptly /'æptlɪ/ adv à propos.

Aquarius /ə'kweərɪəs/ n Verseau m.

aquatic /ə'kwætɪk/ adj aquatique;
(Sport) nautique.

Arab /'ærəb/ n Arabe mf. ● adj
arabe.

Arabian /ə'reɪbɪən/ adj d'Arabie.

Arabic /'ærəbɪk/ adj & n (Ling)
arabe (m).

arbitrary /'ɑːbɪtrərɪ/ adj arbitraire.

arbitrate /'ɑːbɪtreɪt/ vi arbitrer. **ar-
bitration** n arbitrage m. **arbitrator**
n médiateur/-trice m/f.

arcade /ɑː'keɪd/ n (shops) galerie f;
(arches) arcades fpl.

arch /ɑːtʃ/ n arche f; (of foot) voûte
f plantaire. ● vt/i (s')arquer. ● adj
(playful) malicieux.

archaeological /ɑːkɪə'lɒdʒɪkl/
adj archéologique. **archaeologist** n
archéologue mf. **archaeology** n archéologie f.

archbishop /ɑːtʃ'bɪʃəp/ n archevêque m.

archery /'ɑːtʃərɪ/ n tir m à l'arc.

architect /'ɑːkɪtekt/ n architecte
mf; (of plan) artisan m. **architectural** adj architectural. **architecture**
n architecture f.

archives /'ɑːkaɪvz/ npl archives fpl.

archway /'ɑːtʃweɪ/ n voûte f.

Arctic /'ɑːktɪk/ n the ~ l'Arctique
m. ● adj (climate) arctique; (expedition) polaire; (conditions) glacial.

ardent /'ɑːdnt/ adj ardent.

are /ɑː(r)/ ⇒BE.

area /'eərɪə/ n (region) région f;
(district) quartier m; (fig) domaine
m; (in geometry) aire f; parking/pic-
nic ~ aire f de parking/de pique-
nique.

arena /ə'riːnə/ n arène f.

aren't /ɑː(r)nt/ ⇒ARE NOT.

Argentina /ɑːdʒən'tiːnə/ n

a

Argentine *f.*

arguable /ˈɑːɡjʊəbl/ *adj* discutable.
arguably *adv* selon certains.

argue /ˈɑːɡjuː/ *vi* (quarrel) se disputer; (reason) argumenter. ● *vt* (debate) discuter; ~ that alléguer que.

argument /ˈɑːɡjʊmənt/ *n* dispute *f;* (reasoning) argument *m;* (discussion) débat *m.* **argumentative** *adj* ergoteur.

Aries /ˈeəriːz/ *n* Bélier *m.*

arise /əˈraɪz/ *vi* (*pt* **arose**; *pp* **arisen**) (problem) survenir; (question) se poser; ~ **from** résulter de.

aristocrat /ˈærɪstəkræt/ *n* aristocrate *mf.*

arithmetic /əˈrɪθmətɪk/ *n* arithmétique *f.*

ark /ɑːk/ *n* (Relig) arche *f.*

arm /ɑːm/ *n* bras *m;* ~ **in arm** bras dessus bras dessous. ● *vt* armer; ~**ed robbery** vol *m* à main armée.

armament /ˈɑːməmənt/ *n* armement *m.*

arm: /ɑːm/ ~**band** *n* brassard *m.*
~**chair** *n* fauteuil *m.*

armour /ˈɑːmə(r)/ *n* armure *f.* **armoured** *adj* blindé. **armoury** *n* arsenal *m.*

armpit /ˈɑːmpɪt/ *n* aisselle *f.*

arms /ɑːmz/ *npl* (weapons) armes *fpl.* ~ **dealer** *n* trafiquant *m* d'armes.

army /ˈɑːmɪ/ *n* armée *f.*

aroma /əˈrəʊmə/ *n* arôme *m.* **aromatic** *adj* aromatique.

arose /əˈrəʊz/ ⇒**ARISE.**

around /əˈraʊnd/ *adv* (tout) autour; (here and there) çà et là.
● *prep* autour de; ~ **here** par ici.

arouse /əˈraʊz/ *vt* (awaken, cause) éveiller; (excite) exciter.

arrange /əˈreɪndʒ/ *vt* arranger; (time, date) fixer; ~ **to**

s'arranger pour.

arrangement /əˈreɪndʒmənt/ *n* arrangement *m;* (agreement) entente *f;* **make** ~**s** prendre des dispositions.

array /əˈreɪ/ *n* **an** ~ **of** (display) un étalage impressionnant (de).

arrears /əˈrɪəz/ *npl* arriéré *m;* **in** ~ (rent) arriéré; **he is in** ~ il a des retards dans ses paiements.

arrest /əˈrest/ *vt* arrêter; (attention) retenir. ● *n* arrestation *f;* **under** ~ en état d'arrestation.

arrival /əˈraɪvl/ *n* arrivée *f;* **new** ~ nouveau venu *m,* nouvelle venue *f.*

arrive /əˈraɪv/ *vi* arriver; ~ **at** (destination) arriver à; (decision) parvenir à.

arrogance /ˈærəɡəns/ *n* arrogance *f.*

arrow /ˈærəʊ/ *n* flèche *f.*

arse /ɑːs/ *n* 🆇 cul *m* 🆇.

arson /ˈɑːsn/ *n* incendie *m* criminel. **arsonist** *n* incendiaire *mf.*

art /ɑːt/ *n* art *m;* (fine arts) beaux-arts *mpl.*

artery /ˈɑːtərɪ/ *n* artère *f.*

art gallery *n* (public) musée *m* (d'art); (private) galerie *f* (d'art).

arthritis /ɑːˈθraɪtɪs/ *n* arthrite *f.*

artichoke /ˈɑːtɪtʃəʊk/ *n* artichaut *m.*

article /ˈɑːtɪkl/ *n* article *m;* ~ **of clothing** vêtement *m.*

articulate /ɑːˈtɪkjʊlət/ *adj* (person) capable de s'exprimer clairement; (speech) distinct.

articulated lorry *n* semiremorque *m.*

artificial /ɑːtɪˈfɪʃl/ *adj* artificiel.

artist /ˈɑːtɪst/ *n* artiste *mf.*

arts /ɑːts/ *npl* **the** ~ les arts *mpl;* (Univ) lettres *fpl.*

artwork /ˈɑːtwɜːk/ *n* (of book)

illustrations fpl.

as /æz/, /əz/ conj comme; (while) pendant que; (over gradual period of time) au fur et à mesure que; ~ she grew older au fur et à mesure qu'elle vieillissait; do ~ I say fais ce que je dis; ~ usual comme d'habitude. ● prep ~ a mother en tant que mère; ~ a gift en cadeau; ~ from Monday à partir de lundi; ~ for, ~ to quant à; ~ if you look ~ if you're tired vous avez l'air (d'être) fatigué. ● adv ~ tall ~ aussi grand que; ~ much ~, ~ many ~ autant que; ~ ~ aussitôt que; ~ well ~ aussi bien que; ~ wide ~ possible aussi large que possible.

asbestos /æz'bestɒs/ n amiante f.

ascend /ə'send/ vt gravir. ● vi monter.

ascertain /æsə'teɪn/ vt établir (that que).

ash /æʃ/ n cendre f; ~(-tree) frêne m.

ashamed /ə'ʃeɪmd/ adj be ~ avoir honte (of de).

ashore /ə'ʃɔː(r)/ adv à terre.

ashtray /'æʃtreɪ/ n cendrier m.

Asia /'eɪʃə/ n Asie f.

Asian /'eɪʃn/ n Asiatique mf. ● adj asiatique.

aside /ə'saɪd/ adv de côté; ~ from à part. ● n aparté m.

ask /ɑːsk/ vt/i demander; (a question) poser; (invite) inviter; ~ sb sth demander qch à qn; ~ sb to do demander à qn de faire; ~ about (thing) se renseigner sur; (person) demander des nouvelles de; ~ for demander.

asleep /ə'sliːp/ adj endormi; (numb) engourdi. ● adv fall ~ s'endormir.

asparagus /ə'spærəgəs/ n (plant)

asperge f. (Culin) asperges fpl.

aspect /'æspekt/ n aspect m; (direction) orientation f.

asphyxiate /əs'fɪksɪeɪt/ vt/i (s')asphyxier.

aspire /ə'spaɪə(r)/ vi aspirer (to à; to do à faire).

aspirin /'æspərɪn/ n aspirine® f.

ass /æs/ n âne m; (person 🄸) idiot/-e mf.

assail /ə'seɪl/ vt attaquer. **assailant** n agresseur m.

assassin /ə'sæsɪn/ n assassin m. **assassinate** vt assassiner. **assassination** n assassinat m.

assault /ə'sɔːlt/ n (Mil) assaut m; (Jur) agression f. ● vt (person: Jur) agresser.

assemble /ə'sembl/ vt(construct) assembler; (gather) rassembler. ● vi se rassembler.

assembly /ə'semblɪ/ n assemblée f. ~ line n chaîne f de montage.

assent /ə'sent/ n assentiment m. ● vi consentir.

assert /ə'sɜːt/ vt affirmer; (rights) revendiquer. **assertion** n affirmation f. **assertive** adj assuré.

assess /ə'ses/ vt évaluer; (payment) déterminer le montant de. **assessment** n évaluation f. **assessor** n (valuer) expert m.

asset /'æset/ n (advantage) atout m; (financial) bien m; ~ s (Comm) actif m.

assign /ə'saɪn/ vt (allot) assigner; ~ sb to (appoint) affecter qn à.

assignment /ə'saɪnmənt/ n (task) mission f; (diplomatic) poste m; (academic) devoir m.

assist /ə'sɪst/ vt/i aider. **assistance** n aide f.

assistant /ə'sɪstənt/ n aide mf; (in shop) vendeur/-euse mf. ● adj (manager) adjoint.

a

associate[1] /əˈsəʊʃɪət/ n & adj associé/-e (m/f).

associate[2] /əˈsəʊʃɪeɪt/ vt associer. ● vi ~ with fréquenter. **association** n association f.

assorted /əˈsɔːtɪd/ adj divers; (foods) assorti.

assortment /əˈsɔːtmənt/ n assortiment m; (of people) mélange m.

assume /əˈsjuːm/ vt supposer; (power, attitude) prendre; (role, burden) assumer.

assurance /əˈʃɔːrəns/ n assurance f.

assure /əˈʃɔː(r)/ vt assurer.

asterisk /ˈæstərɪsk/ n astérisque m.

asthma /ˈæsmə/ n asthme m.

astonish /əˈstɒnɪʃ/ vt étonner.

astound /əˈstaʊnd/ vt stupéfier.

astray /əˈstreɪ/ adv go ~ s'égarer; lead ~ égarer.

astride /əˈstraɪd/ adv & prep à califourchon (sur).

astrologer /əˈstrɒlədʒə(r)/ n astrologue mf. **astrology** n astrologie f.

astronaut /ˈæstrənɔːt/ n astronaute mf.

astronomer /əˈstrɒnəmə(r)/ n astronome m.

asylum /əˈsaɪləm/ n asile m.

at /æt, ət/
● preposition

➡ For expressions such as laugh at, look at →laugh, look.

····▸ (in position or place) à; he's ~ his desk il est à son bureau; she's ~ work/school elle est au travail/à l'école.

····▸ (at someone's house or business) chez; ~Mary's chez the dentist's chez Mary/le dentiste.

····▸ (in times, ages) à; ~ four o'clock à quatre heures; ~ two years of age à l'âge de deux ans.

····▸ (in email addresses) arobase f

ate &/eɪt/ →EAT.

atheist /ˈeɪθɪɪst/ n athée mf.

athlete /ˈæθliːt/ n athlète mf. **athletic** adj athlétique. **athletics** npl athlétisme m; (US) sports mpl.

Atlantic /ətˈlæntɪk/ adj atlantique. ● n the ~ (Ocean) l'Atlantique m.

atlas /ˈætləs/ n atlas m.

atmosphere /ˈætməsfɪə(r)/ n (air) atmosphère f; (mood) ambiance f. **atmospheric** adj atmosphérique; d'ambiance.

atom /ˈætəm/ n atome m.

atrocious /əˈtrəʊʃəs/ adj atroce.

atrocity /əˈtrɒsətɪ/ n atrocité f.

attach /əˈtætʃ/ vt/i (s')attacher; (letter) joindre (to à).

attaché /əˈtæʃeɪ/ n (Pol) attaché/-e m/f. ~ **case** n attaché-case m.

attached /əˈtætʃt/ adj be ~ to (like) être attaché à; the ~ letter la lettre ci-jointe.

attachment /əˈtætʃmənt/ n (accessory) accessoire m; (affection) attachement m; (e-mail) pièces fpl jointes.

attack /əˈtæk/ n attaque f; (Med) crise f. ● vt attaquer.

attain /əˈteɪn/ vt atteindre (à); (gain) acquérir.

attempt /əˈtempt/ vt tenter. ● n tentative f; an ~ on sb's life un attentat contre qn.

attend /əˈtend/ vt assister à; (class) suivre; (school, church) aller à. ● vi assister; ~ (to) (look after) s'occuper de. **attendance** n présence f; (people) assistance f.

attendant /əˈtendənt/ n employé/-e m/f. ● adj associé.

attention /əˈtenʃn/ n attention f; ~! (Mil) garde-à-vous! pay ~ faire or prêter attention (to à).

attentive /əˈtentɪv/ adj attentif; (considerate) attentionné. **attentively** adv attentivement. **attentiveness** n attention f.

attest /əˈtest/ vt/i ~ (to) attester.

attic /ˈætɪk/ n grenier m.

attitude /ˈætɪtjuːd/ n attitude f.

attorney /əˈtɜːnɪ/ n (US) avocat/ -e m/f.

attract /əˈtrækt/ vt attirer. **attraction** n attraction f; (charm) attrait m.

attractive /əˈtræktɪv/ adj trayant, séduisant. **attractively** adv agréablement. **attractiveness** n attrait m, beauté f.

attribute¹ /əˈtrɪbjuːt/ vt ~ to attribuer à.

attribute² /ˈætrɪbjuːt/ n attribut m.

aubergine /ˈəʊbəʒiːn/ n aubergine f.

auction /ˈɔːkʃn/ n vente f aux enchères. ● vt vendre aux enchères. **auctioneer** n commissaire priseur m.

audacious /ɔːˈdeɪʃəs/ adj audacieux.

audience /ˈɔːdɪəns/ n (theatre, radio) public m; (interview) audience f.

audiovisual /ɔːdɪəʊˈvɪʒʊəl/ adj audiovisuel.

audit /ˈɔːdɪt/ n vérification f des comptes. ● vt vérifier.

audition /ɔːˈdɪʃn/ n audition f. ● vt/i auditionner (for pour).

auditor /ˈɔːdɪtə(r)/ n commissaire m aux comptes.

August /ˈɔːgəst/ n août m.

aunt /ɑːnt/ n tante f.

auspicious /ɔːˈspɪʃəs/ adj favorable.

Australia /ɒˈstreɪlɪə/ n Australie f.

Australian /ɒˈstreɪlɪən/ n Australien/-ne m/f. ● adj australien.

Austria /ˈɒstrɪə/ n Autriche f.

Austrian /ˈɒstrɪən/ n Autrichien/-ne m/f. ● adj autrichien.

authentic /ɔːˈθentɪk/ adj authentique.

author /ˈɔːθə(r)/ n auteur m.

authoritarian /ɔːˌθɒrɪˈteərɪən/ adj autoritaire.

authoritative /ɔːˈθɒrətətɪv/ adj (credible) qui fait autorité; (manner) autoritaire.

authority /ɔːˈθɒrətɪ/ n autorité f; (permission) autorisation f.

authorization /ɔːθəraɪˈzeɪʃn/ n autorisation f. **authorize** vt autoriser.

autistic /ɔːˈtɪstɪk/ adj (person) autiste; (response) autistique.

autograph /ˈɔːtəgrɑːf/ n autographe m. ● vt signer, dédicacer.

automate /ˈɔːtəmeɪt/ vt automatiser.

automatic /ɔːtəˈmætɪk/ adj automatique. ● n (Auto) voiture f automatique.

automobile /ˈɔːtəməbiːl/ n (US) auto(mobile) f.

autonomous /ɔːˈtɒnəməs/ adj autonome.

autumn /ˈɔːtəm/ n automne m.

auxiliary /ɔːgˈzɪlɪərɪ/ adj & n auxiliaire (m/f); ~ (verb) auxiliaire m.

avail /əˈveɪl/ vt ~ oneself of profiter de. ● n of no ~ inutile; to no ~ sans résultat.

availability /əveɪləˈbɪlətɪ/ n disponibilité f. **available** adj disponible.

avenge /əˈvendʒ/ vt venger; ~ oneself se venger (on de).

avenue /ˈævənjuː/ n avenue f; (line of approach:fig) voie f.

average /ˈævərɪdʒ/ n moyenne f; on ~ en moyenne. ● adj moyen. ● vt faire la moyenne de; (produce, do) faire en moyenne.

aviary /ˈeɪvɪərɪ/ n volière f.

avocado /ævəˈkɑːdəʊ/ n avocat m.

avoid /əˈvɔɪd/ vt éviter. **avoidance** n (of injuries) prévention f; (of responsibility) refus m.

await /əˈweɪt/ vt attendre.

awake /əˈweɪk/ vt/i (pt awoke; pp awoken) (s')éveiller. ● adj be ~ ne pas dormir, être (r)éveillé.

award /əˈwɔːd/ vt (grant) attribuer; (prize) décerner; (points) accorder. ● n récompense f;prix m; (scholarship) bourse f; pay ~ augmentation f (de salaire).

aware /əˈweə(r)/ adj (well-informed) averti; be ~ of (danger) être conscient de; (fact) savoir; become ~ of prendre conscience de. **awareness** n conscience f.

away /əˈweɪ/ adv (far) au loin; (absent) absent, parti; ~ from loin de; (new home) déménager; six kilometres ~ à six kilomètres (de distance); take ~ emporter; he was snoring ~ il ronflait. ● adj & n ~ (match) match m à l'extérieur.

awe /ɔː/ n crainte f (révérencielle).

awe-inspiring /ˈɔːɪnspaɪərɪŋ/ adj impressionnant.

awesome /ˈɔːsəm/ adj redoutable.

awful /ˈɔːfl/ adj affreux. **awfully** adv (badly) affreusement; (very 🄸) rudement.

awkward /ˈɔːkwəd/ adj difficile; (inconvenient) inopportun; (clumsy)

maladroit; (embarrassing) gênant; (embarrassed) gêné. **awkwardly** adv maladroitement; avec gêne. **awkwardness** n maladresse f; (discomfort) gêne f.

awning /ˈɔːnɪŋ/ n auvent m; (of shop) store m.

awoke, awoken ➡**AWAKE**.

axe /æks/ n hache f. ● vt (pres p **axing**) réduire; (eliminate) supprimer; (employee) renvoyer.

axis /ˈæksɪs/ n (pl **axes**) axe m.

axle /ˈæksl/ n essieu m.

Bb

BA abbr ➡**BACHELOR OF ARTS**.

babble /ˈbæbl/ vi babiller; (stream) gazouiller. ● n babillage m.

baby /ˈbeɪbɪ/ n bébé m. ~ **carriage** n (US) voiture f d'enfant. ~-**sit** vi faire du babysitting, garder des enfants. ~-**sitter** n baby-sitter mf.

bachelor /ˈbætʃələ(r)/ n célibataire m. B~ **of Arts** licencié/-e m/f ès lettres.

back /bæk/ n (of person, hand, page, etc.) dos m; (of house) derrière m; (of vehicle) arrière m; (of room) fond m; (of chair) dossier m; (in football) arrière m; at the ~ of the book à la fin du livre; in ~ of (US) derrière. ● adj (leg, wheel) arrière inv; (door, gate) de derrière; (taxes) arriéré. ● adv en arrière; (returned) de retour, rentré; come ~ revenir; give ~ rendre; take ~ reprendre; I want it ~ je veux le récupérer. ● vt (support) appuyer; (bet on) miser sur; (vehicle) faire reculer. ● vi (of person, vehicle) reculer. ~ **down** céder; ~**out** se désister; (Auto) sortir en marche arrière; ~ **up** (support) appuyer. ~**ache** n mal m de dos. ~**bencher** n (Pol) député m. ~**bone** n colonne f vertébrale. ~**date** vt antidater. ~**fire** vi (Auto) pétarader; (fig) mal tourner. ~**gammon** n trictrac m.

background /'bækgraʊnd/ n fond m, arrièreplan m; (context) contexte m; (environment) milieu m; (experience) formation f. ● adj (music, noise) de fond.

backhand /'bækhænd/ n revers m. **backhander** n (bribe) pot-de-vin m.

backing /'bækɪŋ/ n soutien m.

back: ~**lash** n retour m de bâton; réaction f violente (against contre). ~**log** n retard m. ~ **number** n vieux numéro m. ~**pack** n sac à dos. ~**side** n (buttocks 🗓) derrière m. ~**stage** adj & adv dans les coulisses. ~**stroke** n dos m crawlé. ~**track** vi rebrousser chemin; (change one's opinion) faire marche arrière.

backup /'bækʌp/ n soutien m; (Comput) sauvegarde f. ● adj de secours; (Comput) de sauvegarde.

backward /'bækwəd/ adj (step etc.) en arrière; (retarded) arriéré.

backwards /'bækwəd/ adv en arrière; (walk) à reculons; (read) à l'envers; go ~ and forwards aller et venir.

bacon /'beɪkən/ n lard m; (in rashers) bacon m.

bacteria /bæk'tɪərɪə/ npl bactéries fpl.

bad /bæd/ adj (**worse, worst**) mauvais; (wicked) méchant; (ill) malade; (accident) grave; (food) gâté; feel ~ se sentir mal; go ~ se gâter; ~ language gros mots mpl; too ~! tant pis!; (I'm sorry) dommage!

badge /bædʒ/ n (coat of arms) insigne m.

badger /'bædʒə(r)/ n blaireau m. ● vt harceler.

badly /'bædlɪ/ adv mal; (hurt) gravement; want ~ avoir grande envie de.

badminton /'bædmɪntn/ n badminton m.

bad-tempered adj irritable.

baffle /'bæfl/ vt déconcerter.

bag /bæg/ n sac m; ~ s (luggage) bagages mpl; (under eyes 🗓) valises fpl; ~s of plein de.

baggage /'bægɪdʒ/ n bagages mpl; ~ reclaim réception f des bagages.

baggy /'bægɪ/ adj large.

bagpipes /'bægpaɪps/ npl cornemuse f.

bail /beɪl/ n caution f; on ~ sous caution; (cricket) bâtonnet m. ● vt mettre en liberté provisoire.

bailiff /'beɪlɪf/ n huissier m.

bait /beɪt/ n appât m. ● vt appâter; (fig) tourmenter.

bake /beɪk/ vt faire cuire au four; ~ a cake faire un gâteau. ● vi cuire; (person) faire du pain. **baked beans** n haricots mpl blancs à la tomate. **baked potato** n pomme f de terre en robe des champs. **baker** n boulanger/-ère m/f. **bakery** n boulangerie f.

balance /'bæləns/ n équilibre m; (scales) balance f; (outstanding sum: Comm) solde m; (of payments, of trade) balance f; (remainder) restant m. ● vt mettre en équilibre; (weigh up also Comm) balancer; (budget) équilibrer; (to compensate) contrebalancer. ● vi être en équilibre.

balcony /'bælkənɪ/ n balcon m.

bald /bɔːld/ adj chauve; (tyre) lisse; (fig) simple.

balk /bɔːk/ vt contrecarrer. ● vi ~

at reculer devant.

ball /bɔːl/ n (golf, tennis, etc.) balle f; (football) ballon m; (billiards) bille f; (of wool) pelote f; (sphere) boule f; (dance) bal m.

ballet /'bæleɪ/ n ballet m.

balloon /bə'luːn/ n ballon m.

ballot /'bælət/ n scrutin m. ● vt consulter par vote (on sur). ~ box n urne f. ~ paper n bulletin m de vote.

ballpoint pen n stylo m (à) bille.

ban /bæn/ vt (pt banned) interdire; ~ sb from exclure qn de; ~ sb from doing interdire à qn de faire. ● n interdiction f (on de).

banal /bə'nɑːl/ adj banal.

banana /bə'nɑːnə/ n banane f.

band /bænd/ n (strip, group of people) bande f; (pop group) groupe m; (brass band) fanfare f. ● vi ~ together se réunir.

bandage /'bændɪdʒ/ n bandage m. ● vt bander.

B and B abbr ▸BED AND BREAKFAST.

bandit /'bændɪt/ n bandit m.

bandstand /'bændstænd/ n kiosque m à musique.

bang /bæŋ/ n (blow, noise) coup m; (explosion) détonation f; (of door) claquement m. ● vt/i taper; (door) claquer; ~ one's head se cogner la tête. ● interj vlan. ● adv 🔢 ~ in the middle en plein milieu; ~ on time à l'heure pile.

banger /'bæŋə(r)/ n (firework) pétard m; (Culin) saucisse f; (old) ~ (car 🔢) guimbarde f.

banish /'bænɪʃ/ vt bannir.

banister /'bænɪstə(r)/ n rampe f d'escalier.

bank /bæŋk/ n (Comm) banque f; (of river) rive f; (of sand) banc m. ● vt mettre en banque. ● vi (Aviat)

virer; ~ with avoir un compte à; ~ on compter sur. ~ **account** n compte m en banque. ~ **card** n carte f bancaire. ~ **holiday** n jour m férié.

banking /'bæŋkɪŋ/ n opérations fpl bancaires; (as career) la banque.

> **Bank holiday** jour chômé où les banques sont fermées au Royaume-Uni, en général à l'occasion d'une fête religieuse ou civile (Christmas Day, Easter Monday, May Day, etc.). La plupart tombe un lundi: par exemple, le spring bank holiday, qui coïncide avec la Pentecôte, tombe le dernier lundi de mai ou le premier lundi de juin.

banknote /'bæŋknəʊt/ n billet m de banque.

bankrupt /'bæŋkrʌpt/ adj be ~ être en faillite; go ~ faire faillite. ● n failli/-e m/f. ● vt mettre en faillite. **bankruptcy** n faillite f.

bank statement n relevé m de compte.

banner /'bænə(r)/ n bannière f.

baptism /'bæptɪzəm/ n baptême m. **baptize** vt baptiser.

bar /bɑː(r)/ n (of metal) barre f; (on window, cage) barreau m; (of chocolate) tablette f; (pub) bar m; (counter) comptoir m; (Mus) mesure f; (fig) obstacle m; ~ of soap savonnette f; the ~ (Jur) le barreau. ● vt (pt barred) (obstruct) barrer; (prohibit) interdire; (exclude) exclure. ● prep sauf.

barbecue /'bɑːbɪkjuː/ n barbecue m. ● vt faire au barbecue.

barbed wire n fil m de fer barbelé.

barber /'bɑːbə(r)/ n coiffeur m (pour hommes).

bar code | battle

bar code n code m (à) barres.

bare /beə(r)/ adj nu; (cupboard) vide. ● vt mettre à nu. ~**foot** adj nu-pieds inv, pieds nus. **barely** adv à peine.

bargain /'bɑːgɪn/ n (deal) marché m; (cheap thing) occasion f. ● vi négocier; (haggle) marchander; not ~ for ne pas s'attendre à.

barge /bɑːdʒ/ n péniche f. ● vi ~ in interrompre; (into room) faire irruption.

bark /bɑːk/ n (of tree) écorce f; (of dog) aboiement m. ● vi aboyer.

barley /'bɑːlɪ/ n orge f.

bar: ~**maid** n serveuse f. ~**man** n (pl -**men**) barman m.

barn /bɑːn/ n grange f.

barracks /'bærəks/ npl caserne f.

barrel /'bærəl/ n tonneau m; (of oil) baril m; (of gun) canon m.

barren /'bærən/ adj stérile.

barricade /'bærɪkeɪd/ n barricade f. ● vt barricader.

barrier /'bærɪə(r)/ n barrière f; ticket ~ guichet m.

barrister /'bærɪstə(r)/ n avocat m.

bartender /'bɑːtendə(r)/ n (US) barman m.

barter /'bɑːtə(r)/ n troc m. ● vt troquer (for contre).

base /beɪs/ n base f. ● vt baser (on sur; in à). ● adj ignoble. **baseball** n base-ball m.

basement /'beɪsmənt/ n sous-sol m.

bash /bæʃ/ Ⅰ vt cogner; ~ed in enfoncé. ● n coup m violent; have a ~ at s'essayer à.

basic /'beɪsɪk/ adj fondamental, élémentaire; the ~s l'essentiel m. **basically** adv au fond.

basil /'bæzl/ n basilic m.

basin /'beɪsn/ n (for liquids) cuvette

f; (for food) bol m; (for washing) lavabo m; (of river) bassin m.

basis /'beɪsɪs/ n (pl **bases**) base f.

bask /bɑːsk/ vi se prélasser (in à).

basket /'bɑːskɪt/ n corbeille f; (with handle) panier m. **basketball** n basket(- ball) m.

Basque /bæsk/ n (person) Basque mf; (Ling) basque m. ● adj basque.

bass[1] /beɪs/ adj (voice, part) de basse; (sound, note) grave. ● n (pl **basses**) basse f.

bass[2] /bæs/ n inv (freshwater fish) perche f; (sea) bar m.

bassoon /bə'suːn/ n basson m.

bastard /'bɑːstəd/ n (illegitimate) bâtard/-e m/f; (insult ▨) salaud m ▨.

bat /bæt/ n (cricket etc.) batte f; (table tennis) raquette f; (animal) chauvesouris f. ● vt (pt **batted**) (ball) frapper; not ~ an eyelid ne pas sourciller.

batch /bætʃ/ n (of cakes, people) fournée f; (of goods, text also Comput) lot m.

bath /bɑːθ/ n (pl -**s**) bain m; (tub) baignoire f; have a ~ prendre un bain; (swimming) ~s piscine f. ● vt donner un bain à.

bathe /beɪð/ vt baigner. ● vi se baigner; (US) prendre un bain.

bathing /'beɪðɪŋ/ n baignade f. ~**-costume** n maillot m de bain.

bath: ~**robe** n (US) robe f de chambre. ~**room** n salle f de bains.

baton /'bætn/ n (policeman's) matraque f; (Mus) baguette f.

batter /'bætə(r)/ vt battre. ● n (Culin) pâte f (à frire).

battery /'bætərɪ/ n (Mil, Auto) batterie f; (of torch, radio) pile f.

battle /'bætl/ n bataille f; (fig) lutte

b

f. ● vi se battre. ~**field** n champ m de bataille.

baulk /bɔːk/ vt/i ➡BALK.

bay /beɪ/ n (Bot) laurier m; (Geog, Archit) baie f; (area) aire f; (bark) aboiement m; keep or hold at ~ tenir à distance. ● vi aboyer. ~-**leaf** n feuille f de laurier. ~ **window** n fenêtre f en saillie.

bazaar /bəˈzɑː(r)/ n (shop, market) bazar m; (sale) vente f.

BC abbr (**before Christ**) avant J.-C.

BBS abbr (**Bulletin Board System**) (Internet) babillard m électronique, BBS m.

be /biː/

present am is, are; past was, were; past participle been.

● intransitive verb

····▸ être; I am tired je suis fatigué; it's me c'est moi.

····▸ (feelings) avoir; I am hot j'ai chaud; he is hungry/thirsty il a faim/soif; her hands are cold elle a froid aux mains.

····▸ (age) avoir; I am 15 j'ai 15 ans.

····▸ (weather) faire; it's warm il fait chaud; it's 25° il fait 25°.

····▸ (health) aller; how are you? comment allez-vous or comment vas-tu?

····▸ (visit) aller; I've never been to Italy je ne suis jamais allé en Italie.

● auxiliary verb

····▸ (in tenses) I am working je travaille; he was writing to his mother il écrivait à sa mère; she is to do it at once (obligation) elle doit le faire tout de suite.

····▸ (in passives) he was killed il a été tué; the window has been fixed on a réparé la fenêtre.

····▸ (in tag questions) their house is lovely, isn't it? leur maison est très jolie, n'est-ce pas?

····▸ (in short answers) 'I am a painter'—'are you?' 'je suis peintre'—'ah oui?'; 'are you a doctor?'—'yes, I am' 'êtes-vous médecin?'—'oui'; 'you're not going out'—'yes I am' 'tu ne sors pas'—'si'.

beach /biːtʃ/ n plage f.

beacon /ˈbiːkən/ n (lighthouse) phare m; (marker) balise f.

bead /biːd/ n perle f.

beak /biːk/ n bec m.

beaker /ˈbiːkə(r)/ n gobelet m.

beam /biːm/ n (timber) poutre f; (of light) rayon m; (of torch) faisceau m. ● vi rayonner. ● vt (broadcast) transmettre.

bean /biːn/ n haricot m.

bear /beə(r)/ n ours m. ● vt (pt **bore**; pp **borne**) (carry, show, feel) porter; (endure, sustain) supporter; (child) mettre au monde. ● vi ~ left (go) prendre à gauche; ~ in mind tenir compte de. ~ **out** confirmer; ~ **up** tenir le coup. **bearable** adj supportable.

beard /bɪəd/ n barbe f.

bearer /ˈbeərə(r)/ n porteur/-euse m/f.

bearing /ˈbeərɪŋ/ n (behaviour) maintien m; (relevance) rapport m; get one's ~s s'orienter.

beast /biːst/ n bête f; (person) brute f.

beat /biːt/ vt/i (pt **beat**; pp **beaten**) battre; ~ a retreat battre en re-

beautiful | believe

traite; ~ it! dégage! ⊞; it ~s me ⊞ ça me dépasse. ● n (of drum, heart) battement m; (Mus) mesure f; (of policeman) ronde f. ~ **off** repousser; ~ **up** tabasser. **beating** n raclée f.

beautiful /'bjuːtɪfl/ adj beau.

beauty /'bjuːtɪ/ n beauté f. ~**parlour** n institut m de beauté. ~**spot** n grain m de beauté; (place) site m pittoresque.

beaver /'biːvə(r)/ n castor m.

became /bɪ'keɪm/ →BECOME.

because /bɪ'kɒz/ conj parce que; ~ of à cause de.

become /bɪ'kʌm/ vt/i (pt **became**, pp **become**) devenir; (of) devenir à; what has ~ of her? qu'est-ce qu'elle est devenue?

bed /bed/ n lit m; (layer) couche f; (of sea) fond m; (of flowers) parterre m; go to ~ (aller) se coucher. ● vi (pt **bedded**) ~ **down** se coucher. **bed and breakfast** n chambre f avec petit déjeuner, chambre f d'hôte. ~ **bug** n punaise f. ~**clothes** npl couvertures fpl.

bedding /'bedɪŋ/ n literie f.

bed: ~**ridden** adj cloué au lit. ~**room** n chambre f (à coucher). ~**side** n chevet m. ~**sit**, ~**sitter**, ~**sitting-room** n chambre f meublée, studio m. ~**spread** n dessus m de lit. ~**time** n heure f du coucher.

bee /biː/ n abeille f. make a ~**line** for aller tout droit vers.

beech /biːtʃ/ n hêtre m.

beef /biːf/ n bœuf m. ~**burger** n hamburger m.

beehive /'biːhaɪv/ n ruche f.

been /biːn/ →BE.

beer /bɪə(r)/ n bière f.

beetle /'biːtl/ n scarabée m.

beetroot /'biːtruːt/ n inv betterave f.

before /bɪ'fɔː(r)/ prep (time) avant; (place) devant; the day ~ yesterday avant-hier. ● adv avant; (already) déjà; the ~ la veille. ● conj ~ leaving avant de partir; ~ I forget avant que j'oublie. **beforehand** adv à l'avance.

beg /beg/ vt (pt **begged**) (food, money, favour) demander (from à); ~ sb to do supplier qn de faire. ● vi mendier; it is going ~ging personne n'en veut.

began /bɪ'gæn/ →BEGIN.

beggar /'begə(r)/ n mendiant/-e mf.

begin /bɪ'gɪn/ vt/i (pt **began**, pp **begun**, pres p **beginning**) commencer (to do à faire). **beginner** n débutant/-e mf. **beginning** n commencement m, début m.

begun /bɪ'gʌn/ →BEGIN.

behalf /bɪ'hɑːf/ n on ~ of (act, speak, campaign) pour; (phone, write) de la part de.

behave /bɪ'heɪv/ vi se conduire; (oneself) se conduire bien.

behaviour /bɪ'heɪvjə(r)/, (US) **behavior** n comportement m (towards envers).

behead /bɪ'hed/ vt décapiter.

behind /bɪ'haɪnd/ prep derrière; (in time) en retard sur. ● adv derrière; (late) en retard; leave ~ oublier. ● n (buttocks ⊞) derrière m ⊞.

beige /beɪʒ/ adj & n beige (m).

being /'biːɪŋ/ n (person) être m.

belch /beltʃ/ vi avoir un renvoi. ● vt ~ **out** (smoke) s'échapper. ● n renvoi m.

Belgian /'beldʒən/ n Belge mf. ● adj belge. **Belgium** n Belgique f.

belief /bɪ'liːf/ n conviction f; (trust) confiance f; (faith: Relig) foi f.

believe /bɪ'liːv/ vt/i croire; ~ **in** croire à; (deity) croire en.

believer n croyant/-e m/f.

bell /bel/ n cloche f; (small) clochette f; (on door) sonnette f.

belly /'belɪ/ n ventre m. ~ **button** n nombril m.

belong /bɪ'lɒŋ/ vi ~ **to** appartenir à; (club) être membre de.

belongings /bɪ'lɒŋɪŋz/ npl affaires fpl.

beloved /bɪ'lʌvɪd/ adj & n bien-aimé/-e (m/f).

below /bɪ'ləʊ/ prep sous, au-dessous de; (fig) indigne de. ● adv en dessous; (on page) ci-dessous.

belt /belt/ n ceinture f; (Tech) courroie f; (fig) zone f. ● vt (hit 🔊) rosser. ● vi (rush 🔊) ~ **in/out** entrer/sortir à toute vitesse.

beltway /'beltweɪ/ n (US) périphérique m.

bemused /bɪ'mju:zd/ adj perplexe.

bench /bentʃ/ n banc m; the ~ (Jur) la magistrature (assise).

bend /bend/ vt (pt **bent**) (knee, arm, wire) plier; (head, back) courber. ● vi (road) tourner; (person) ~ **down/over** se pencher. ● n courbe f; (in road) virage m; (of arm, knee) pli m.

beneath /bɪ'ni:θ/ prep sous, au-dessous de; (fig) indigne de. ● adv en dessous.

benefactor /'benɪfæktə(r)/ n bienfaiteur/-trice m/f.

beneficial /benɪ'fɪʃl/ adj bénéfique.

benefit /'benɪfɪt/ n avantage m; (allowance) allocation f. ● vt (be useful to) profiter à; (do good to) faire du bien à. ● vi profiter; ~ **from** tirer profit de.

benign /bɪ'naɪn/ adj (kindly) bienveillant; (Med) bénin.

bent /bent/ n →BEND. ● n (talent) aptitude f; (inclination) penchant m. ● adj tordu; 🔊 corrompu; ~ **on doing** décidé à faire.

bequest /bɪ'kwest/ n legs m.

bereaved /bɪ'ri:vd/ adj endeuillé; the ~ la famille endeuillée. **bereavement** n deuil m.

berry /'berɪ/ n baie f.

berserk /bə'sɜ:k/ adj fou furieux.

berth /bɜ:θ/ n (in train, ship) couchette f; (anchorage) mouillage m; give a wide ~ to éviter. ● vi mouiller.

beside /bɪ'saɪd/ prep à côté de; ~ **oneself** hors de soi; ~ **the point** sans rapport.

besides /bɪ'saɪdz/ prep en plus de. ● adv en plus.

besiege /bɪ'si:dʒ/ vt assiéger.

best /best/ adj meilleur; the ~ **book** le meilleur livre; the ~ **part of** la plus grande partie de; the ~ **thing is to** le mieux est de. ● adv (the) ~ (behave, play) le mieux. ● n the ~ le meilleur, la meilleure; do one's ~ faire de son mieux; make the ~ **of** s'accommoder de. ~ **man** n témoin. ~-**seller** n bestseller m, livre m à succès.

bet /bet/ n pari m. ● vt/i (pt **bet** or **betted**, pres p **betting**) parier (sur).

betray /bɪ'treɪ/ vt trahir.

better /'betə(r)/ adj meilleur; the ~ **part of** la plus grande partie de; get ~ s'améliorer; (recover) se remettre. ● adv mieux; I had ~ **go** je ferais mieux de partir. ● vt (improve) améliorer; (do better than) surpasser. ● n get the ~ **of** l'emporter sur; so much the ~ tant mieux. ~ **off** adj (richer) plus riche; he is/would be ~ **off at home** il est/serait mieux chez lui.

betting shop n bureau m

mixeur n, mixer n.

bless /bles/ vt bénir; be ~ed with jouir de; ~ you! à vos souhaits! **blessed** adj (holy) saint; (damned 🗓) sacré. **blessing** n bénédiction f; (benefit) avantage m; (stroke of luck) chance f.

blew /blu:/ ➡BLOW.

blight /blaɪt/ n (disease: Bot) rouille f; (fig) plaie f.

blind /blaɪnd/ adj aveugle (to à); (corner, bend) sans visibilité. ~ vt aveugler. ● n (on window) store m; the ~ les aveugles mpl.

blindfold /'blaɪndfəʊld/ adj be ~ avoir les yeux bandés. ● adv les yeux bandés. ● n bandeau m. ● vt bander les yeux à.

blindness /'blaɪndnɪs/ n (Med) cécité f; (fig) aveuglement m.

blind spot n (Auto) angle m mort.

blink /blɪŋk/ vi cligner des yeux; (light) clignoter.

bliss /blɪs/ n délice m. **blissful** adj délicieux.

blister /'blɪstə(r)/ n ampoule f; (on paint) cloque f. ● vi cloquer.

blitz /blɪts/ n (Aviat) raid m éclair. ● vt bombarder.

blob /blɒb/ n (drop) (grosse) goutte f; (stain) tache f.

block /blɒk/ n bloc m; (buildings) pâté m de maisons; (in pipe) obstruction f; ~ (of flats) immeuble m; ~ letters majuscules fpl. ● vt bloquer.

blockade /blɒ'keɪd/ n blocus m. ● vt bloquer.

blockage /'blɒkɪdʒ/ n obstruction f.

blockbuster n gros succès m.

bloke /bləʊk/ n 🗓 type m.

blond /blɒnd/ adj & n blond (m).

blonde /blɒnd/ adj & n blonde (f).

blood /blʌd/ n sang m. ● adj (donor, bath) de sang; (bank, poisoning) du sang; (group, vessel) sanguin. ~-**pressure** n tension f artérielle. ~**shed** n effusion f de sang. ~**shot** adj injecté de sang. ~**stream** n sang m. ~ **test** n prise f de sang.

bloody /'blʌdɪ/ adj (-ier, -iest) sanglant; 🗓 sacré. ● adv 🗓 vachement 🗓. ~-**minded** adj 🗓 hargneux, obstiné.

bloom /blu:m/ n fleur f. ● vi fleurir; (person) s'épanouir.

blossom /'blɒsəm/ n fleur(s) f (pl). ● vi fleurir; (person) s'épanouir.

blot /blɒt/ n tache f. ● vt (pt blotted) tacher; (dry) sécher; ~ out effacer.

blotch /blɒtʃ/ n tache f.

blouse /blaʊz/ n chemisier m.

blow /bləʊ/ vt/i (pt blew; pp blown) souffler; (fuse) faire sauter; (squander 🗓) claquer; (opportunity) rater; ~ one's nose se moucher; ~ a whistle siffler. ● n coup m. □ ~ away ou off emporter; ~ out souffler; ~ over passer; ~ up (faire) sauter; (tyre) gonfler; (Photo) agrandir.

blow-dry n brushing m. ● vt faire un brushing à.

blown /bləʊn/ ➡BLOW.

bludgeon /'blʌdʒən/ n matraque f. ● vt matraquer.

blue /blu:/ adj bleu; (movie) porno. ● n bleu m; come out of the ~ être inattendu; have the ~s avoir le cafard. ~**bell** n jacinthe f des bois. ~**print** n projet m.

bluff /blʌf/ vt/i bluffer. ● n bluff m; call sb's ~ dire chiche à qn. ● adj (person) carré.

blunder /'blʌndə(r)/ vi faire une bourde; (move) avancer à tâtons. ● n gaffe f.

blunt /blʌnt/ adj (knife) émoussé; (person) brusque. ● vt émousser. **bluntly** adv carrément.

blur /blɜː(r)/ n image f floue. ● vt (pt blurred) brouiller.

blurb /blɜːb/ n résumé m publicitaire.

blush /blʌʃ/ vi rougir. ● n rougeur f. **blusher** n fard m à joues.

blustery /ˈblʌstərɪ/ adj ~ wind bourrasque f.

BMI abbr (body mass index) IMC m.

boar /bɔː(r)/ n sanglier m.

board /bɔːd/ n planche f; (for notices) tableau m; (food) pension f; full ~ pension f complète; half ~ demipension f; (committee) conseil m; ~ of directors conseil m d'administration; go by the ~ tomber à l'eau; on ~ à bord. ● vt/i (bus, train) monter dans; (Naut) monter à bord (de); ~ with être en pension chez.

boarding-school n école f privée avec internat.

boast /bəʊst/ vi se vanter (about de). ● vt s'enorgueillir de. ● n vantardise f.

boat /bəʊt/ n bateau m; (small) canot m; in the same ~ logé à la même enseigne.

bode /bəʊd/ vi ~ well/ill être de bon/mauvais augure.

bodily /ˈbɒdɪlɪ/ adj (need, well-being) physique; (injury) corporel. ● adv physiquement; (in person) en personne.

body /ˈbɒdɪ/ n corps m; (mass) masse f; (organization) organisme m; ~ part n partie f de corps; ~(work) (Auto) carrosserie f; the main ~ of le gros de. **~-building** n culturisme m. **~guard** n garde m du corps.

bog /bɒg/ n marais m. ● vt (pt bogged) get ~ged down s'enliser dans.

bogus /ˈbəʊgəs/ adj faux.

boil /bɔɪl/ n furoncle m; bring to the ~ porter à ébullition. ● vt/i bouillir. ~ down to se ramener à; ~ over déborder. **boiled** adj (egg) à la coque; (potatoes) à l'eau.

boiler /ˈbɔɪlə(r)/ n chaudière f; ~ suit bleu m (de travail).

boisterous /ˈbɔɪstərəs/ adj tapageur; (child) turbulent.

bold /bəʊld/ adj hardi; (cheeky) effronté; (type) gras.

Bolivia /bəˈlɪvɪə/ n Bolivie f.

bollard /ˈbɒlɑːd/ n (on road) balise f.

bolt /bəʊlt/ n (on door) verrou m; (for nut) boulon m; (lightning) éclair m. ● vt (door) verrouiller; (food) engouffrer. ● vi s'emballer.

bomb /bɒm/ n bombe f; ~ scare alerte f à la bombe. ● vt bombarder.

bomber /ˈbɒmə(r)/ n (aircraft) bombardier m; (person) plastiqueur m.

bond /bɒnd/ n (agreement) engagement m; (link) lien m; (Comm) obligation f, bon m; in ~ (entreposé) en douane.

bone /bəʊn/ n os m; (of fish) arête f. ● vt désosser. **~-dry** adj tout à fait sec.

bonfire /ˈbɒnfaɪə(r)/ n feu m; (for celebration) feu m de joie.

bonnet /ˈbɒnɪt/ n (hat) bonnet m; (of vehicle) capot m.

bonus /ˈbəʊnəs/ n prime f.

bony /ˈbəʊnɪ/ adj (-ier, -iest) (thin) osseux; (fish) plein d'arêtes.

boo /buː/ interj hou. ● vt/i huer. ● n huée f.

booby trap /ˈbuːbɪtræp/ n méca-

book | bounce

nisme *m* piégé. ● *vt* (*pt*) **-trapped**) piéger.

book /bʊk/ *n* livre *m*; (*exercise*) cahier *m*; (*of tickets etc.*) carnet *m*; ~s (Comm) comptes *mpl*. ● *vt* (*reserve*) réserver; (*driver*) dresser un PV à; (*player*) prendre le nom de; (*write down*) inscrire. ● *vi* retenir des places; (**fully**) ~ed complet. ~**case** *n* bibliothèque *f*. **booking-office** *n* guichet *m*. ~**keeping** *n* comptabilité *f*. **booklet** *n* brochure *f*. ~**maker** *n* bookmaker *m*. ~**mark** *n* (for book, Internet) signet *m*. ~**seller** *n* libraire *mf*. ~**shop** *n* librairie *f*. ~**stall** *n* kiosque *m* (à journaux).

boom /buːm/ *vi* (*gun, wind, etc.*) gronder; (*trade*) prospérer. ● *n* grondement *m*; (Comm) boom *m*, prospérité *f*.

boost /buːst/ *vt* stimuler; (*morale*) remonter; (*price*) augmenter; (*publicize*) faire de la réclame pour.

boot /buːt/ *n* (knee-length) botte *f*; (anklelength) chaussure *f* (montante); (for walking) chaussure *f* de marche; (Sport) chaussure *f* de sport; (of vehicle) coffre *m*; get the ~ ⊠ se faire virer. ● *vt/i* ~ **up** (Comput) amorcer.

booth /buːð/ *n* (for telephone) cabine *f*; (at fair) baraque *f*.

booze /buːz/ *vi* ⊞ boire (beaucoup). ● *n* ⊞ alcool *m*.

border /ˈbɔːdə(r)/ *n* (edge) bord *m*; (frontier) frontière *f*; (in garden) bordure *f*. ● *vi* ~ **on** être voisin de, avoisiner.

bore /bɔː(r)/ *vt* ennuyer; be ~d s'ennuyer; ➡BEAR. ● *vi* (Tech) forer. ● *n* raseur/-euse *m/f*; (thing) ennui *m*. **boredom** *n* ennui *m*. **boring** *adj* ennuyeux.

born /bɔːn/ *adj* né; be ~ naître.

borne /bɔːn/ ➡BEAR.

borough /ˈbʌrə/ *n* municipalité *f*.

borrow /ˈbɒrəʊ/ *vt* emprunter (from à).

Bosnia /ˈbɒznɪə/ *n* Bosnie *f*.

Bosnian /ˈbɒznɪən/ *adj* bosniaque. ● *n* Bosniaque.

bosom /ˈbʊzəm/ *n* poitrine *f*; ~ friend ami/-e *m/f* intime.

boss /bɒs/ *n* ⊞ patron/-ne *m/f*. ● *vt* ~(**about**) ⊞ mener par le bout du nez.

bossy /ˈbɒsɪ/ *adj* autoritaire.

botch /bɒtʃ/ *vt* bâcler, saboter.

both /bəʊθ/ *det* les deux; ~ the books les deux. ● *pron* tous/ toutes (les) deux, l'un/-e et l'autre; we ~ agree nous sommes tous les deux d'accord; I bought ~ (of them) j'ai acheté les deux; I saw ~ of you je vous ai vus tous les deux; ~ Paul and Anne (et) Paul et Anne. ● *adv* à la fois.

bother /ˈbɒðə(r)/ *vt* (annoy, worry) ennuyer; (disturb) déranger. ● *vi* se déranger; don't ~ (calling) ce n'est pas la peine (d'appeler); don't ~ about us ne t'inquiète pas pour nous; I can't be ~ed j'ai la flemme ⊞; *n* ennui *m*; (effort) peine *f*; it's no ~ ce n'est rien.

bottle /ˈbɒtl/ *n* bouteille *f*; (for baby) biberon *m*. ● *vt* mettre en bouteille. ~ **up** contenir. ~ **bank** *n* collecteur *m* (de verre usagé). ~**neck** *n* (traffic jam) embouteillage *m*. ~**opener** *n* ouvre-bouteilles *m inv*.

bottom /ˈbɒtəm/ *n* fond *m*; (of hill, page, etc.) bas *m*; (buttocks) derrière *m* ⊞. ● *adj* inférieur, du bas.

bought /bɔːt/ ➡BUY.

bounce /baʊns/ *vi* rebondir; (person) faire des bonds, bondir; (cheques ⊠) être refusé. ● *vt* faire rebondir. ● *n* rebond *m*.

bound /baʊnd/ vi (leap) bondir; **~ed by** limité par; ➡**BIND.** ● n bond m. ● adj **be ~ for** être en route pour, aller vers; **~ to** (obliged) obligé de; (certain) sûr de.

boundary /ˈbaʊndrɪ/ n limite f.

bounds /baʊndz/ npl limites fpl; **out of ~** être interdit d'accès.

bout /baʊt/ n période f; (Med) accès m; (boxing) combat m.

bow¹ /baʊ/ n (weapon) arc m; (of violin) archet m; (knot) nœud m.

bow² /baʊ/ n salut m; (of ship) proue f. ● vt/i (s')incliner.

bowels /ˈbaʊəlz/ npl intestins mpl; (fig) profondeurs fpl.

bowl /bəʊl/ n (for washing) cuvette f; (for food) bol m; (for soup) assiette f creuse. ● vt/i (cricket) lancer; **~ over** bouleverser.

bowler /ˈbəʊlə(r)/ n (cricket) lanceur m; **~ (hat)** (chapeau) melon m.

bowling /ˈbəʊlɪŋ/ n (ten-pin) bowling m; (on grass) jeu m de boules. **~-alley** n bowling m.

bow tie n nœud m papillon.

box /bɒks/ n boîte f; (cardboard) carton m; (Theat) loge f; **the ~** 🔲 la télé. ● vt mettre en boîte; (Sport) boxer; **~ sb's ears** gifler qn; **~ in** enfermer.

boxing /ˈbɒksɪŋ/ n boxe f. ● adj de boxe. **B~ Day** n le lendemain de Noël.

box office n guichet m.

boy /bɔɪ/ n garçon m; **~ band** boys band m.

boycott /ˈbɔɪkɒt/ vt boycotter. ● n boycottage m.

boyfriend /ˈbɔɪfrend/ n (petit) ami m.

bra /brɑː/ n soutien-gorge m.

brace /breɪs/ n (fastener) attache f; (dental) appareil m; (tool) vilbrequin m; **~s** (for trousers) bretelles fpl.

● vt soutenir; **~ oneself** rassembler ses forces.

bracket /ˈbrækɪt/ n (for shelf etc.) tasseau m, support m; (group) tranche f; **in ~s** entre parenthèses. ● vt mettre entre parenthèses or crochets.

braid /breɪd/ n (trimming) galon m; (of hair) tresse f.

brain /breɪn/ n cerveau m; **~s** (fig) intelligence f. ● vt assommer. **brainless** adj stupide. **~wash** vt faire subir un lavage de cerveau à. **~wave** n idée f géniale, trouvaille f. **brainy** adj (**-ier, -iest**) doué.

brake /breɪk/ n (Auto also fig) frein m. ● vt/i freiner. **~ light** n feu m stop.

bran /bræn/ n son m.

branch /brɑːntʃ/ n (of tree) branche f; (of road) embranchement m; (Comm) succursale f; (of bank) agence f. ● vi **~ (off)** bifurquer.

brand /brænd/ n marque f. ● vt **~ sb as sth** désigner qn comme qch.

brand-new /brænd'njuː/ adj tout neuf.

brandy /ˈbrændɪ/ n cognac m.

brass /brɑːs/ n cuivre m; **get down to ~ tacks** en venir aux choses sérieuses; **the ~** (Mus) les cuivres mpl; **top ~** 🔲 galonnés mpl.

brat /bræt/ n 🔲 môme mf 🔲.

brave /breɪv/ adj courageux; (smile) brave. ● n (American Indian) brave m. ● vt braver. **bravery** n courage m.

brawl /brɔːl/ n bagarre f. ● vi se bagarrer.

Brazil /brə'zɪl/ n Brésil m.

breach /briːtʃ/ n (of copyright, privilege) violation f; (in relationship) rupture f; (gap) brèche f. ● vt ouvrir une brèche dans.

bread /bred/ n pain m; **~ and but-**

ter tartine f. ~-**bin**, (US) ~-**box** n boîte f à pain. ~**crumbs** npl chapelure f.

breadth /bretθ/ n largeur f.

bread-winner /'bredwɪnə(r)/ n soutien m de famille.

break /breɪk/ vt (pt **broke**, pp **broken**) casser; (smash into pieces) briser; (vow, silence, rank, etc.) rompre; (law) violer; (a record) battre; (news) révéler; (journey) interrompre; (heart, strike, ice) briser; ~ one's arm se casser le bras. ● vi (se) briser. ● n cassure f, rupture f; (in relationship, continuity) rupture f; (interval) interruption f; (at school) récréation f, récré f; (for coffee) pause f. ~ **away from** se détacher; ~ **down** vi (collapse) s'effondrer; (negotiations) échouer; (machine) tomber en panne; vt (door) enfoncer; (analyse) analyser; ~ **even** rentrer dans ses frais; ~ **into** cambrioler; ~ **off** (se) détacher; (suspend) rompre; (stop talking) s'interrompre; ~ **out** (fire, war, etc.) éclater; ~ **up** (end) (faire) cesser; (couple) rompre; (marriage) (se) briser; (crowd) (se) disperser; (schools) être en vacances. **breakable** adj fragile. **breakage** n casse f.

breakdown /'breɪkdaʊn/ n (Tech) panne f; (Med) dépression f; (of figures) analyse f. ● adj (Auto) de dépannage.

breakfast /'brekfəst/ n petit déjeuner m.

break /breɪk/: ~-**in** n cambriolage m. ~**through** n percée f.

breast /brest/ n sein m; (chest) poitrine f. ~-**feed** vt (pt -**fed**) allaiter. ~-**stroke** n brasse f.

breath /breθ/ n souffle m, haleine f; out of ~ à bout de souffle; under one's ~ tout bas.

breathalyser® /'breθəlaɪzə(r)/ n alcootest m.

breathe /briːð/ vt/i respirer. ~ **in** inspirer; ~ **out** expirer.

breathless /'breθlɪs/ adj à bout de souffle.

breathtaking /'breθteɪkɪŋ/ adj à vous couper le souffle.

bred /bred/ ⇒**BREED**.

breed /briːd/ vt (pt **bred**) élever; (give rise to) engendrer. ● vi se reproduire. ● n race f.

breeze /briːz/ n brise f.

brew /bruː/ vt (beer) brasser; (tea) faire infuser. ● vi (beer) fermenter; (tea) infuser; (fig) se préparer. ● n décoction f. **brewer** n brasseur m. **brewery** n brasserie f.

bribe /braɪb/ n pot-de-vin m. ● vt soudoyer. **bribery** n corruption f.

brick /brɪk/ n brique f. ~**layer** n maçon m.

bridal /'braɪdl/ adj (dress) de mariée; (car, chamber) des mariés.

bride /braɪd/ n mariée f. ~**groom** n marié m. ~**smaid** n demoiselle f d'honneur.

bridge /brɪdʒ/ n pont m; (Naut) passerelle f; (of nose) arête f; (card game) bridge m. ● vt ~ a gap combler une lacune.

bridle /'braɪdl/ n bride f. ● vt brider. ~-**path** n piste f cavalière.

brief /briːf/ adj bref. ● n instructions fpl; (Jur) dossier m. ● vt donner des instructions à.

briefcase /'briːfkeɪs/ n serviette f.

briefs /briːfs/ npl slip m.

bright /braɪt/ adj brillant, vif; (day, room) clair; (cheerful) gai; (clever) intelligent.

brighten /'braɪtn/ vt égayer. ● vi (weather) s'éclaircir; (face) s'éclairer.

brilliant /'brɪlɪənt/ adj (student,

career) brillant; (*light*) éclatant; (*very good* 🔲) super.

brim /brɪm/ n bord m. ● vi (*pt* **brimmed**); ~ **over** déborder (**with** de).

bring /brɪŋ/ vt (*pt* **brought**) (*thing*) apporter; (*person, vehicle*) amener; ~ **to bear** (*pressure etc.*) exercer. ~ **about** provoquer; ~ **back** (return with) rapporter; (*colour, shine*) redonner; ~ **down** faire tomber; (shoot down, knock down) abattre; ~ **forward** avancer; ~ **off** réussir; ~ **out** (take out) sortir; (show) faire ressortir; (book) publier; ~ **round** faire revenir à soi; ~ **up** (*child*) élever; (Med) vomir; (*question*) aborder.

brink /brɪŋk/ n bord m.

brisk /brɪsk/ adj vif.

bristle /ˈbrɪsl/ n poil m. ● vi se hérisser; **bristling with** hérissé de.

Britain /ˈbrɪtn/ n Grande-Bretagne f.

British /ˈbrɪtɪʃ/ adj britannique; the ~ les Britanniques mpl.

Briton /ˈbrɪtn/ n Britannique mf.

Brittany /ˈbrɪtənɪ/ n Bretagne f.

brittle /ˈbrɪtl/ adj fragile.

broad /brɔːd/ adj large; (*choice, range*) grand. ~ **bean** n fève f.

broadband /ˈbrɔːdbænd/adj à haut débit. ● n ADSL m haut débit m.

broadcast /ˈbrɔːdkɑːst/ vt/i (*pt* **broadcast**) diffuser; (person) parler à la television or à la radio. ● n émission f.

broadly /ˈbrɔːdlɪ/ adv en gros.

broad-minded /brɔːdˈmaɪndɪd/ adj large d'esprit.

broccoli /ˈbrɒkəlɪ/ n inv brocoli m.

brochure /ˈbrəʊʃə(r)/ n brochure f.

broke /brəʊk/ →**BREAK**. ● adj

(penniless 🔲) fauché.

broken /ˈbrəʊkən/ →**BREAK**. ● adj ~ **English** mauvais anglais m.

bronchitis /brɒŋˈkaɪtɪs/ n bronchite f.

bronze /brɒnz/ n bronze m.

brooch /brəʊtʃ/ n broche f.

brood /bruːd/ n nichée f, couvée f. ● vi méditer tristement.

broom /bruːm/ n balai m.

broth /brɒθ/ n bouillon m.

brothel /ˈbrɒθl/ n maison f close.

brother /ˈbrʌðə(r)/ n frère m. ~**hood** n fraternité f ~-**in-law** (pl ~**s-in-law**) beau-frère m.

brought /brɔːt/ →**BRING**.

brow /braʊ/ n front m; (of hill) sommet m.

brown /braʊn/ adj (*object*) marron; (*hair*) brun; ~ **bread** pain m complet; ~ **sugar** sucre m roux. ● n marron m; brun m. ● vt/i brunir; (Culin) (faire) dorer.

Brownie /ˈbraʊnɪ/ n jeannette f.

browse /braʊz/ vi flâner; (*animal*) brouter. ● vt (Comput) naviguer.

browser n (Comput) navigateur m.

bruise /bruːz/ n bleu m. ● vt (*knee, arm etc.*) faire un bleu à; (*fruit*) abîmer.

brush /brʌʃ/ n brosse f; (skirmish) accrochage m; (bushes) broussailles fpl. ● vt brosser. ~ **against** frôler; ~ **aside** (dismiss) repousser; (move) écarter; ~ **up (on)** se remettre à.

Brussels /ˈbrʌslz/ n Bruxelles. ~ **sprouts** npl choux mpl de Bruxelles.

brutal /ˈbruːtl/ adj brutal.

brute /bruːt/ n brute f; **by** ~ **force** par la force.

BSE abbr (Bovine Spongiform Encephalopathy) encephalopathie f spongiforme bovine, ESB f.

bubble /'bʌbl/ n bulle f; blow ∼s faire des bulles. ● vi bouillonner; ∼ over déborder. ∼ **bath** n bain m moussant.

buck /bʌk/ n mâle m; (US, ⊠) dollar m; pass the ∼ rejeter la responsabilité (to sur). ● vi (horse) ruer; ∼ **up** ⊠ prendre courage; (hurry ⊠) se grouiller ⊺.

bucket /'bʌkɪt/ n seau m (of de).

buckle /'bʌkl/ n boucle f. ● vt/i (fasten) (se) boucler; (bend) voiler.

bud /bʌd/ n bourgeon m. ● vi (pt budded) bourgeonner.

Buddhism /'bʊdɪzəm/ n bouddhisme m.

budding /'bʌdɪŋ/ adj (talent) naissant; (athlete) en herbe.

budge /bʌdʒ/ vt/i (faire) bouger.

budgerigar /'bʌdʒərɪgɑː(r)/ n perruche f.

budget /'bʌdʒɪt/ n budget m. ● vi ∼ **for** prévoir (dans son budget).

buff /bʌf/ n (colour) chamois m; ⊺ fanatique mf.

buffalo /'bʌfələʊ/ n (pl -oes or -o buffle m; (US) bison m.

buffer /'bʌfə(r)/ n tampon m; ∼ **zone** zone f tampon.

buffet[1] /'bʊfeɪ/ n (meal, counter) buffet m; ∼ **car** buffet m.

buffet[2] /'bʌfɪt/ n (blow) soufflet m. ● vt (pt buffeted) souffleter.

bug /bʌg/ n (bedbug) punaise f; (any small insect) bestiole f; (germ) microbe m; (stomachache ⊺) ennuis mpl gastriques; (device) micro m; (defect) défaut m; (Comput) bogue f, bug m. ● vt (pt bugged) mettre des micros dans; ⊠ embêter.

buggy /'bʌgɪ/ n poussette f.

build /bɪld/ vt/i (pt built) bâtir, construire. ● n carrure f. ∼ **up** (increase) augmenter, monter;

(accumulate) (s')accumuler. **builder** n entrepreneur m en bâtiment; (workman) ouvrier m du bâtiment.

building /'bɪldɪŋ/ n (structure) bâtiment m; (dwelling) immeuble m. ∼ **society** n caisse f d'épargne.

build-up /'bɪldʌp/ n accumulation f; (fig) publicité f.

built /bɪlt/ ➡BUILD.

built-in /bɪlt'ɪn/ adj encastré.

built-up area n agglomération f, zone f urbanisée.

bulb /bʌlb/ n (Bot) bulbe m; (Electr) ampoule f.

Bulgaria /bʌl'georɪə/ n Bulgarie f.

Bulgarian /bʌl'georɪən/ n (person) Bulgare mf; (Ling) bulgare m. ● adj bulgare.

bulge /bʌldʒ/ n renflement m. ● vi se renfler, être renflé; **be bulging with** être gonflé or bourré de.

bulimia /bju:'lɪmɪə/ n boulimie f.

bulk /bʌlk/ n volume m; **in** ∼ (buy, sell) en gros; (transport) en vrac; **the** ∼ **of** la majeure partie de.

bull /bʊl/ n taureau m. ∼**dog** n bouledogue m. ∼**doze** vt raser au bulldozer.

bullet /'bʊlɪt/ n balle f.

bulletin /'bʊlətɪn/ n bulletin m.

bullet-proof /'bʊlɪtpru:f/ adj (vest) pare-balles inv; (vehicle) blindé.

bullfight /'bʊlfaɪt/ n corrida f.

bullion /'bʊlɪən/ n or m or argent m en lingots.

bullring /'bʊlrɪŋ/ n arène f.

bull's-eye /'bʊlzaɪ/ n mille m.

bully /'bʊlɪ/ n (child) petite brute f; (adult) tyran m. ● vt maltraiter.

bum /bʌm/ n ⊠ derrière m ⊺; (US, ⊠) vagabond/-e m/f.

bumble-bee /'bʌmblbi:/ n bourdon m.

bump /bʌmp/ n (swelling) bosse f;

(on road) bosse f. ● vt/i cogner, heurter. ~ along cahoter; ~ **into** (hit) rentrer dans; (meet) tomber sur.

bumper /'bʌmpə(r)/ n pare-chocs m inv. ● adj exceptionnel.

bumpy /'bʌmpɪ/ adj (road) accidenté.

bun /bʌn/ n (cake) petit pain m; (hair) chignon m.

bunch /bʌntʃ/ n (of flowers) bouquet m; (of keys) trousseau m; (of people) groupe m; (of bananas) régime m; ~ of grapes grappe f de raisin.

bundle /'bʌndl/ n paquet m. ● vt mettre en paquet; (push) fourrer.

bung /bʌŋ/ n bouchon m. ● vt (stop up) boucher; (throw 🗙) flanquer 🗓.

bunion /'bʌnjən/ n (Med) oignon m.

bunk /bʌŋk/ n (on ship, train) couchette f. ~-beds npl lits mpl superposés.

buoy /bɔɪ/ n bouée f. ● vt ~ up (hearten) soutenir, encourager.

buoyancy /'bɔɪənsɪ/ n (of floating object) flottabilité f; (cheerfulness) gaieté f.

burden /'bɜ:dn/ n fardeau m. ● vt ennuyer (with de).

bureau /'bjʊərəʊ/ n (pl -eaux bureau m.

bureaucracy /bjʊə'rɒkrəsɪ/ n bureaucratie f.

burglar /'bɜ:glə(r)/ n cambrioleur m; ~ alarm alarme f. burglarize f (US) cambrioler. **burglary** n cambriolage m. **burgle** vt cambrioler.

Burgundy /'bɜ:gəndɪ/ n (wine) bourgogne m.

burial /'berɪəl/ n enterrement m.

burn /bɜ:n/ vt/i (pt burned or burnt) brûler. ● n brûlure f. ~

down être réduit en cendres. **burner** n (on cooker) brûleur m; (on computer) graveur m. **burning** adj en flammes; (fig) brûlant.

burnt /bɜ:nt/ ➡BURN.

burp /bɜ:p/ n 🗓 rot m. ● vi 🗓 roter.

burrow /'bʌrəʊ/ n terrier m. ● vt creuser.

bursar /'bɜ:sə(r)/ n intendant/-e m/f. **bursary** n bourse f.

burst /bɜ:st/ vt/i (pt burst (balloon, bubble) crever; (pipe) (faire) éclater. ● n explosion f; (of laughter) éclat m; (surge) élan m. ~ **into** (room) faire interruption dans; ~ **into** tears fondre en larmes; ~ out ~ out laughing éclater de rire; ~ **with** be ~ing with déborder de.

bury /'berɪ/ vt (person etc.) enterrer; (hide, cover) enfouir; (engross, thrust) plonger.

bus /bʌs/ n (pl buses) (auto)bus m. ● vt transporter en bus. ● vi (pt bussed) prendre l'autobus.

bush /bʊʃ/ n (shrub) buisson m; (land) brousse f.

business /'bɪznɪs/ n (task, concern) affaire f; (commerce) affaires fpl; (line of work) métier m; (shop) commerce m; he has no ~ to il n'a pas le droit de; mean ~ être sérieux; that's none of your ~! ça ne vous regarde pas! ~like adj sérieux. ~man n homme m d'affaires.

busker /'bʌskə(r)/ n musicien/-ne m/f des rues.

bus-stop n arrêt m d'autobus.

bust /bʌst/ n (statue) buste m; (bosom) poitrine f. ● vt/i (pt busted or bust) (burst 🗙) crever; (break 🗙) (se) casser. ● adj (broken, finished 🗙) fichu; go ~ 🗙 faire faillite.

bustle /'bʌsl/ vi s'affairer. ● n affairement *m*, remue-ménage *m*.

busy /'bɪzɪ/ *adj* (**-ier, -iest**) (*person*) occupé; (*street*) animé; (*day*) chargé. ● *vt* ~ oneself with s'occuper à.

but /bʌt/ *conj* mais. ● *prep* sauf; ~ for sans; nobody ~ personne d'autre que; nothing ~ rien que. ● *adv* (only) seulement.

butcher /'bʊtʃə(r)/ *n* boucher *m*. ● *vt* massacrer.

butler /'bʌtlə(r)/ *n* maître *m* d'hôtel.

butt /bʌt/ *n* (of gun) crosse *f*; (of cigarette) mégot *m*; (of joke) cible *f*; (barrel) tonneau *m*; (US, <u>T</u>) derrière *m* <u>T</u>. ● *vi* ~ in interrompre.

butter /'bʌtə(r)/ *n* beurre *m*. ● *vt* beurrer. ~**-bean** *n* haricot *m* blanc. ~**cup** *n* bouton-d'or *m*.

butterfly /'bʌtəflaɪ/ *n* papillon *m*.

buttock /'bʌtək/ *n* fesse *f*.

button /'bʌtn/ *n* bouton *m*. ● *vt*/*i* ~ (up) (se) boutonner.

buttonhole /'bʌtnhəʊl/ *n* boutonnière *f*. ● *vt* accrocher.

buy /baɪ/ *vt* (*pt* **bought**) acheter (from à); ~ sth for sb acheter qch à qn, prendre qch pour qn; (believe <u>✗</u>) croire, avaler.

buzz /bʌz/ *n* bourdonnement *m*. ● *vi* bourdonner. **buzzer** *n* sonnerie *f*.

by /baɪ/ *prep* par, de; (near) à côté de; (before) avant; (means) en, à, par; ~ bike à vélo; ~ car en auto; ~ day de jour; ~ the kilo au kilo; ~ running en courant; ~ sea par mer; ~ that time à ce moment-là; ~ the way à propos; ~ oneself tout seul. ● *adv* close ~ tout près; ~ and large dans l'ensemble.

bye(-bye) /'baɪbaɪ/ *interj* <u>T</u> au revoir, salut <u>T</u>.

by-election *n* élection *f* partielle.

Byelorussia /bjeləʊˈrʊʃə/ *n* Biélo-

russie *f*.

by-law /'baɪlɔː/ *n* arrêté *m* municipal.

bypass /'baɪpɑːs/ *n* (Auto) rocade *f*; (Med) pontage *m*. ● *vt* contourner.

by-product *n* dérivé *m*; (fig) conséquence *f*.

byte /baɪt/ *n* octet *m*.

Cc

cab /kæb/ *n* taxi *m*; (of lorry, train) cabine *f*.

cabbage /'kæbɪdʒ/ *n* chou *m*.

cabin /'kæbɪn/ *n* (hut) cabane *f*; (in ship, aircraft) cabine *f*.

cabinet /'kæbɪnɪt/ *n* petit placard *m*; (glassfronted) vitrine *f*; (Pol) cabinet *m*.

cable /'keɪbl/ *n* câble *m*. ● *vt* câbler. ~**-car** *n* téléphérique *m*. ~ **television** *n* télévision *f* par câble.

cache /kæʃ/ *n* (hoard) cache *f*; (place) cachette *f*.

cackle /'kækl/ *n* (of hen) caquet *m*; (laugh) ricanement *m*. ● *vi* caqueter; (laugh) ricaner.

cactus /'kæktəs/ *n* (*pl* **-ti** or **-es**) cactus *m*.

cadet /kə'det/ *n* élève *m* officier.

Caesarean /sɪ'zeərɪən/ *adj* ~ (section) césarienne *f*.

café /'kæfeɪ/ *n* café *m*, snack-bar *m*.

caffeine /'kæfiːn/ *n* caféine *f*.

cage /keɪdʒ/ *n* cage *f*. ● *vt* mettre en cage.

cagey /'keɪdʒɪ/ *adj* réticent.

cagoule /kə'guːl/ *n* K-way® *m*.

cajole /kə'dʒəʊl/ *vt* ~ sb into doing sth amener qn à faire qch par la cajolerie.

cake /keɪk/ n gâteau m; (of soap) pain m. ● vi former une croûte (on sur).

calculate /ˈkælkjʊleɪt/ vt calculer; (estimate) évaluer. **calculated** adj délibéré; (risk) calculé. **calculating** adj calculateur. **calculation** n calcul m. **calculator** n calculatrice f.

calculus /ˈkælkjʊləs/ n (pl -li or ~es) calcul m.

calendar /ˈkælɪndə(r)/ n calendrier m.

calf /kɑːf/ n (pl **calves**) (young cow or bull) veau m; (of leg) mollet m.

calibre /ˈkælɪbə(r)/ n calibre m.

call /kɔːl/ vt/i appeler; (loudly) crier; he's ~ed John il s'appelle john; ~ sb stupid traiter qn d'imbécile. ● n appel m; (of bird) cri m; (visit) visite f; make/pay a ~ rendre visite à; be on ~ être de garde; ~ box cabine f téléphonique. ~ **centre** n centre m d'appels. ~ **back** rappeler; (visit) repasser; ~ **for** (help) appeler à; (demand) demander; (require) exiger; (collect) passer prendre; ~ **in** passer. ~ **off** annuler. ~ **on** (visit) rendre visite à; (urge) demander à (to de faire). ~ **out (to)** appeler. ~ **round** venir. ~ **up** appeler.

calling /ˈkɔːlɪŋ/ n vocation f.

callous /ˈkæləs/ adj inhumain.

calm /kɑːm/ adj calme. ● n calme m. ● vt/i ~ **(down)** (se) calmer.

calorie /ˈkælərɪ/ n calorie f.

camcorder /ˈkæmkɔːdə(r)/ n caméscope® m.

came /keɪm/ ⇒COME.

camel /ˈkæml/ n chameau m.

camera /ˈkæmərə/ n appareil(-photo) m; (TV, cinema) caméra f; in ~ à huis clos. ~**man** n (pl -**men**) cadreur m, cameraman m.

camouflage /ˈkæməflɑːʒ/ n camouflage m. ● vt camoufler.

camp /kæmp/ n camp m. ● vi camper.

campaign /kæmˈpeɪn/ n campagne f. ● vi faire campagne.

camper /ˈkæmpə(r)/ n campeur/-euse m/f; ~ **(-van)** n camping-car m.

camping /ˈkæmpɪŋ/ n camping m; go ~ faire du camping.

campsite /ˈkæmpsaɪt/ n camping m.

campus /ˈkæmpəs/ n (pl ~**es**) campus m.

---

can¹ /kæn, kən/

infinitive be able to; present can; present negative can't, cannot (formal); past could; past participle been able to

● auxiliary verb

····▸ pouvoir; where ~ I buy stamps? où est-ce que je peux acheter des timbres?; she can't come elle ne peut pas venir.

····▸ (be allowed to) pouvoir; ~ I smoke? est-ce que je peux fumer?

····▸ (know how to) savoir; she ~ swim elle sait nager; he can't drive il ne sait pas conduire.

····▸ (with verbs of perception) ~ hear you je t'entends; ~ they see us? est-ce qu'ils nous voient?

---

can² /kæn/ n (for food) boîte f; (of petrol) bidon m. ● vt (pt canned) mettre en conserve.

Canada /'kænədə/ n Canada m.

Canadian /kə'neɪdɪən/ n Canadien/-ne m/f. ● adj canadien.

canal /kə'næl/ n canal m.

canary /kə'neərɪ/ n canari m.

cancel /'kænsl/ vt/i (pt **cancelled**) (call off, revoke) annuler; (cross out) barrer; (a stamp) oblitérer; ~ **out** (se) neutraliser. **cancellation** n annulation f.

cancer /'kænsə(r)/ n cancer m; **have** ~ avoir un cancer.

Cancer /'kænsə(r)/ n Cancer m.

cancerous /'kænsərəs/ adj cancéreux.

candid /'kændɪd/ adj franc.

candidate /'kændɪdət/ n candidat/-e m/f.

candle /'kændl/ n bougie f; (in church) cierge m. ~**stick** n bougeoir m.

candy /'kændɪ/ n (US) bonbon(s) m(pl). ~**-floss** n barbe f à papa.

cane /keɪn/ n canne f; (for baskets) rotin m; (for punishment) badine f. ● vt donner des coups de badine à.

canister /'kænɪstə(r)/ n boîte f.

cannabis /'kænəbɪs/ n cannabis m.

cannibal /'kænɪbl/ n cannibale mf.

cannon /'kænən/ n (pl ~ or ~s) canon m. ~**-ball** n boulet m de canon.

cannot →CAN NOT.

canoe /kə'nuː/ n canoë m. ● vi faire du canoë. **canoeist** n canoéiste mf.

canon /'kænən/ n (clergyman) chanoine m; (rule) canon m.

can-opener n ouvre-boîtes m inv.

canopy /'kænəpɪ/ n dais m; (for bed) baldaquin m.

can't →CAN NOT.

canteen /kæn'tiːn/ n (restaurant) cantine f; (flask) bidon m.

canter /'kæntə(r)/ n petit galop m.

● vi aller au petit galop.

canvas /'kænvəs/ n toile f.

canvass /'kænvəs/ vt/i (Comm, Pol) faire du démarchage (auprès de); ~ **opinion** sonder l'opinion.

canyon /'kænjən/ n cañon m.

cap /kæp/ n (hat) casquette f; (of bottle, tube) bouchon m; (of beer or milk bottle) capsule f; (of pen) capuchon m; (for toy gun) amorce f. ● vt (pt **capped**) couronner.

capability /keɪpə'bɪlətɪ/ n capacité f.

capable /'keɪpəbl/ adj (person) compétent; ~ **of doing** capable de faire.

capacity /kə'pæsətɪ/ n capacité f; **in my** ~ **as a doctor** en ma qualité de médecin.

cape /keɪp/ n (cloak) cape f; (Geog) cap m.

caper /'keɪpə(r)/ vi gambader. ● n (leap) cabriole f; (funny film) comédie f; (Culin) câpre f.

capital /'kæpɪtl/ adj (letter) majuscule; (offence) capital. ● n (town) capitale f; (money) capital m; ~ (letter) majuscule f.

capitalism /'kæpɪtəlɪzəm/ n capitalisme m.

capitalize /'kæpɪtəlaɪz/ vi ~ **on** tirer parti de.

Capitol Hill Ce quartier historique de Washington D.C. abrite le bâtiment du Capitole, dans lequel se réunit le Congrès depuis 1800, la cour suprême fédérale, plus haute instance judiciaire des États-Unis, et la bibliothèque du Congrès, l'une des plus grandes au monde. Par métonymie, **the Capitol** ou **the Hill** font référence au Congrès.
▷**CONGRESS**

capitulate /kə'pɪtʃʊleɪt/ vi capituler.

Capricorn /'kæprɪkɔːn/ n Capricorne m.

capsize /kæp'saɪz/ vt/i (faire) chavirer.

capsule /'kæpsjuːl/ n capsule f.

captain /'kæptɪn/ n capitaine m.

caption /'kæpʃn/ n (under photo) légende f; (subtitle) sous-titre m.

captivate /'kæptɪveɪt/ vt captiver.

captive /'kæptɪv/ adj & n captif/-ive (m/f) **captivity** n captivité f.

capture /'kæptʃə(r)/ vt (person, animal) capturer; (moment, likeness) saisir. ● n capture f.

car /kɑː(r)/ n voiture f; (industry) automobile f; (accident) de voiture; (journey) en voiture.

caravan /'kærəvæn/ n caravane f.

carbohydrate /kɑːbə'haɪdreɪt/ n hydrate m de carbone.

carbon /'kɑːbən/ n carbone m. ~ **footprint** empreinte f écologique.

carburettor /'kɑːbərettə(r)/ n carburateur m.

card /kɑːd/ n carte f.

cardboard /'kɑːdbɔːd/ n carton m.

cardiac /'kɑːdiæk/ adj cardiaque; ~ **arrest** arrêt m du cœur.

cardigan /'kɑːdɪgən/ n cardigan m.

cardinal /'kɑːdɪnl/ adj (sin) capital; (rule) fondamental; (number) cardinal. ● n cardinal m.

card index n fichier m.

care /keə(r)/ n (attention) soin m, attention f; (worry) souci m; (looking after) soins mpl; take ~ of (deal with) s'occuper de; (be careful with) prendre soin de; take ~ to do sth

faire bien attention à faire qch. ● vi ~ **about** s'intéresser à; ~ **for** s'occuper de; (invalid) soigner; ~ **to do** vouloir faire; I don't ~ ça m'est égal.

career /kə'rɪə(r)/ n carrière f. ● vi ~ **in/out** entrer/sortir à toute vitesse.

carefree /'keəfriː/ adj insouciant.

careful /'keəfl/ adj prudent; (research, study) méticuleux; (be) ~! (fais) attention! **carefully** adv avec soin; (cautiously) prudemment.

careless /'keəlɪs/ adj négligent; (work) bâclé.

caress /kə'res/ n caresse f. ● vt caresser.

caretaker /'keəteɪkə(r)/ n concierge mf. ● adj (president) par intérim.

car ferry n ferry m.

cargo /'kɑːgəʊ/ n (pl ~es) chargement m; (Naut) cargaison f.

Caribbean /kærɪ'biːən/ adj des Caraïbes, des Antilles. ● n the ~ (sea) la mer des Antilles; (islands) les Antilles fpl.

caring /'keərɪŋ/ adj affectueux.

carnation /kɑː'neɪʃn/ n œillet m.

carnival /'kɑːnɪvl/ n carnaval m.

carol /'kærəl/ n chant m de Noël.

carp /kɑːp/ n inv carpe f. ● vi maugréer.

car-park n parc m de stationnement, parking m.

carpenter /'kɑːpəntə(r)/ n (joiner) menuisier m; (builder) charpentier m. **carpentry** n menuiserie f; (structural) charpenterie f.

carpet /'kɑːpɪt/ n (fitted) moquette f; (loose) tapis m. ● vt (pt **carpeted**) mettre de la moquette dans.

carriage /'kærɪdʒ/ n (rail) wagon m; (ceremonial) carrosse m; (of goods) transport m; (cost) port m.

carriageway /ˈkærɪdʒweɪ/ n chaussée f.

carrier /ˈkærɪə(r)/ n transporteur m; (Med) porteur/-euse m/f; ~ (bag) sac m en plastique.

carrot /ˈkærət/ n carotte f.

carry /ˈkærɪ/ vt/i porter; (goods) transporter; (involve) comporter; (motion) voter; **be carried away** s'emballer. □ ~ **off** emporter; (prize) remporter; ~ **on** (continue) continuer; (business) conduire; (conversation) mener; ~ **out** (order, plan) exécuter; (duty) remplir; (experiment, operation, repair) effectuer. **~-cot** n portebébé m.

car sharing n covoiturage m.

cart /kɑːt/ n charrette f. ● vt (heavy bag 🖪) trimballer.

carton /ˈkɑːtn/ n (box) boîte f; (of yoghurt, cream) pot m; (of cigarettes) cartouche f

cartoon /kɑːˈtuːn/ n dessin m humoristique; (cinema) dessin m animé; (strip cartoon) bande f dessinée.

cartridge /ˈkɑːtrɪdʒ/ n cartouche f.

carve /kɑːv/ vt tailler; (meat) découper.

car-wash n lavage m automatique.

cascade /kæˈskeɪd/ n cascade f. ● vi tomber en cascade.

case /keɪs/ n cas m; (Jur) affaire f; (suitcase) valise f; (crate) caisse f; (for spectacles) étui m; **(just) in** ~ au cas où; **in** ~ **he comes** au cas où il viendrait; **in** ~ **of fire** en cas d'incendie; **in any** ~ de toute façon; **the** ~ **for sth** les arguments mpl en faveur de qch; **the** ~ **for the defence** la défense.

cash /kæʃ/ n espèces fpl, argent m; **in** ~ en espèces. ● adj (price) comptant. ● vt encaisser; ~ **in** (on) profiter (de). **~-back** n retrait m

d'argent à la caisse. ~ **desk** n caisse f. ~ **dispenser** n distributeur m de billets.

cashew /ˈkæʃuː/ n cajou m.

cash flow n marge f brute d'autofinancement.

cashier /kæˈʃɪə(r)/ n caissier/-ière m/f.

cashmere /kæʃˈmɪə(r)/ n cachemire m.

cash: ~**point** n distributeur m de billets. ~ **point card** n carte f de retrait. ~ **register** n caisse f enregistreuse.

casino /kəˈsiːnəʊ/ n casino m.

casket /ˈkɑːskɪt/ n (box) coffret m; (coffin) cercueil m.

casserole /ˈkæsərəʊl/ n (pan) daubière f; (food) ragoût m.

cassette /kəˈset/ n cassette f.

cast /kɑːst/ vt (pt cast) (object, glance) jeter; (shadow) projeter; (metal) couler; ~ **(off)** (shed) se dépouiller de; ~ **one's vote** voter; ~ **iron fonte** f ● n (cinema, Theat, TV) distribution f; (Med) plâtre m.

castaway /ˈkɑːstəweɪ/ n naufragé/-e m/f.

cast-iron adj de fonte; (fig) en béton.

castle /ˈkɑːsl/ n château m; (chess) tour f.

cast-offs npl vieux vêtements mpl.

castor /ˈkɑːstə(r)/ n (wheel) roulette f.

castrate /kæˈstreɪt/ vt châtrer.

casual /ˈkæʒʊəl/ adj (informal) décontracté; (remark) désinvolte; (acquaintance) de passage; (work) temporaire. **casually** adv (remark) d'un air détaché; (dress) simplement.

casualty /ˈkæʒʊəltɪ/ n victime f; (part of hospital) urgences fpl.

cat /kæt/ n chat m; (feline) félin m.

catalogue /ˈkætəlɒɡ/ n catalogue m. ● vt dresser un catalogue de.

catalyst /ˈkætəlɪst/ n catalyseur m.

catalytic /kætəˈlɪtɪk/ adj ~ converter pot m catalytique.

catapult /ˈkætəpʌlt/ n lance-pierres m inv. ● vt projeter.

cataract /ˈkætərækt/ n (Med, Geog) cataracte f.

catarrh /kəˈtɑː(r)/ n catarrhe m.

catastrophe /kəˈtæstrəfi/ n catastrophe f.

catch /kætʃ/ vt (pt caught) attraper; (bus, plane) prendre; (understand) saisir; ~ sb doing surprendre qn en train de faire; ~ fire prendre feu; ~ sight of apercevoir; ~ sb's attention/eye attirer l'attention de qn. ● vi (get stuck) se prendre (in dans); (start to burn) prendre. ● n (fastening) fermeture f; (drawback) piège m; (in sport) prise f. ~ on devenir populaire. ~ out prendre de court. ~ up rattraper son retard; ~ up with sb rattraper qn.

catching /ˈkætʃɪŋ/ adj contagieux.

catchment /ˈkætʃmənt/ n ~ area (School) secteur m.

catch-phrase n formule f favorite.

catchy /ˈkætʃi/ adj entraînant.

category /ˈkætəɡəri/ n catégorie f.

cater /ˈkeɪtə(r)/ vi organiser des réceptions; ~ for/to (guests) accueillir; (needs) pourvoir à; (reader) s'adresser à. **caterer** n traiteur m.

caterpillar /ˈkætəpɪlə(r)/ n chenille f.

cathedral /kəˈθiːdrəl/ n cathédrale f.

catholic /ˈkæθəlɪk/ adj éclectique. **Catholic** adj & n catholique (mf). **Catholicism** n catholicisme m.

Catseye® n plot m rétroréfléchissant.

cattle /ˈkætl/ npl bétail m.

caught /kɔːt/ →**CATCH**.

cauliflower /ˈkɒlɪflaʊə(r)/ n chou-fleur m.

cause /kɔːz/ n cause f; (reason) raison f, motif m. ● vt causer; ~ sth to grow/move faire pousser/bouger qch.

causeway /ˈkɔːzweɪ/ n chaussée f.

caution /ˈkɔːʃn/ n prudence f; (warning) avertissement m. ● vt avertir. **cautious** adj prudent. **cautiously** adv prudemment.

cave /keɪv/ n grotte f. ● vi ~ in s'effondrer; (agree) céder. ~**man** n (pl **-men**) homme m des cavernes.

cavern /ˈkævən/ n caverne f.

caviare /ˈkævɪɑː(r)/ n caviar m.

caving /ˈkeɪvɪŋ/ n spéléologie f.

CCTV abbr (closed circuit television) télévision f en circuit fermé.

CD abbr (**compact disc**) disque m compact, CD m.

CD-ROM /siːdiːˈrɒm/ n disque m optique compact, CD-ROM m.

cease /siːs/ vt/i cesser. ~**-fire** n cessez-le-feu m inv.

cedar /ˈsiːdə(r)/ n cèdre m.

cedilla /sɪˈdɪlə/ n cédille f.

ceiling /ˈsiːlɪŋ/ n plafond m.

celebrate /ˈselɪbreɪt/ vt (occasion) fêter; (Easter, mass) célébrer. ● vi faire la fête. **celebrated** adj célèbre. **celebration** n fête f.

celebrity /sɪˈlebrəti/ n célébrité f.

celery /ˈseləri/ n céleri m.

cell /sel/ n cellule f; (Electr) élément m.

cellar /ˈselə(r)/ n cave f.

cellist /ˈtʃelɪst/ n violoncelliste mf.

cello /ˈtʃeləʊ/ n violoncelle m.

cellphone /ˈselfəʊn/ n (téléphone

m) portable.

Celt /kelt/ *n* Celte *mf*.

cement /sɪ'ment/ *n* ciment *m*. ● *vt* cimenter. ~-**mixer** *n* bétonnière *f*.

cemetery /'semətrɪ/ *n* cimetière *m*.

censor /'sensə(r)/ *n* censeur *m*. ● *vt* censurer.

censure /'senʃə(r)/ *n* censure *f*. ● *vt* critiquer.

census /'sensəs/ *n* recensement *m*.

cent /sent/ *n* cent *m*.

centenary /sen'ti:nərɪ/ *n* centenaire *m*.

centigrade /'sentɪɡreɪd/ *adj* centigrade.

centilitre, (US) **centiliter** /'sentɪli:tə(r)/ *n* centilitre *m*.

centimetre, (US) **centimeter** /'sentɪmi:tə(r)/ *n* centimètre *m*.

centipede /'sentɪpi:d/ *n* millepattes *m inv*.

central /'sentrəl/ *adj* central; ~ **heating** chauffage *m* central; ~ **locking** fermeture *f* centralisée des portes. **centralize** *vt* centraliser. **centrally** *adv* (situated) au centre.

centre /'sentə(r)/, (US) **center** *n* centre *m*. ● *vt* (*pt* **centred**) centrer. ● *vi* ~ **on** tourner autour de.

century /'sentʃərɪ/ *n* siècle *m*.

ceramic /sɪ'ræmɪk/ *adj* (*art*) céramique; (*object*) en céramique.

cereal /'sɪərɪəl/ *n* céréale *f*.

ceremonial /serɪ'məʊnɪəl/ *adj* (*dress*) de cérémonie. ● *n* cérémonial *m*. **ceremony** *n* cérémonie *f*.

certain /'sɜ:tn/ *adj* certain; for ~ avec certitude; make ~ **of** s'assurer de. **certainly** *adv* certainement. **certainty** *n* certitude *f*.

certificate /sə'tɪfɪkət/ *n* certificat *m*.

certify /'sɜ:tɪfaɪ/ *vt* certifier.

cesspit, cesspool /'sespɪt, 'sespu:l/ *n* fosse *f* d'aisances.

chafe /tʃeɪf/ *vt/i* frotter (contre).

chagrin /'ʃæɡrɪn/ *n* dépit *m*.

chain /tʃeɪn/ *n* chaîne *f*; ~ **reaction** réaction *f* en chaîne; ~ **store** magasin *m* à succursales multiples. ● *vt* enchaîner. ~-**smoke** *vi* fumer sans arrêt.

chair /tʃeə(r)/ *n* chaise *f*; (armchair) fauteuil *m*; (Univ) chaire *f*; (chairperson) président/-e *m/f*. ● *vt* (preside over) présider. ~**man** *n* (*pl* -**men**) président/-e *m/f*. ~**woman** *n* (*pl* -**women** présidente *f*.

chalk /tʃɔ:k/ *n* craie *f*.

challenge /'tʃælɪndʒ/ *n* défi *m*; (opportunity) challenge *m*. ● *vt* (summon) défier (to do de faire); (question truth of) contester. **challenger** *n* (Sport) challenger *m*. **challenging** *adj* stimulant.

chamber /'tʃeɪmbə(r)/ *n* (old use) chambre *f*. ~**maid** *n* femme *f* de chambre. ~ **music** *n* musique *f* de chambre. ~-**pot** *n* pot *m* de chambre.

champagne /ʃæm'peɪn/ *n* champagne *m*.

champion /'tʃæmpɪən/ *n* champion/-ne *m/f*. ● *vt* défendre. **championship** *n* championnat *m*.

chance /tʃɑ:ns/ *n* (luck) hasard *m*; (opportunity) occasion *f*; (likelihood) chances *fpl*; (risk) risque *m*; **by** ~ par hasard; **by any** ~ par hasard; ~**s are** that il est probable que. ● *adj* fortuit. ● *vt* ~ **doing** prendre le risque de faire; ~ **it** tenter sa chance.

chancellor /'tʃɑ:nsələ(r)/ *n* chancelier *m*; **C~ of the Exchequer** Chancelier de l'échiquier.

chandelier /ʃændə'lɪə(r)/ *n* lustre *m*.

change /tʃeɪndʒ/ vt (alter) changer; (exchange) échanger (for contre). (money) changer; ~ trains/ one's dress changer de train/de robe; ~ one's mind changer d'avis. ● vi changer; (change clothes) se changer; ~ into se transformer en; ~ over passer (to à). ● n changement m; (money) monnaie f; a ~ for the better une amélioration; a ~ for the worse un changement en pire; a ~ of clothes des vêtements de rechange; for a ~ pour changer. changeable adj changeant. changing room n (in shop) cabine f d'essayage; (Sport) vestiaire m.

channel /'tʃænl/ n (for liquid, information) canal m; (TV) chaîne f; (groove) rainure f. ● vt (pt channelled) canaliser. C~ n (the (English) C~ la Manche; the C~ tunnel le tunnel sous la Manche; the C~ Islands les îles fpl Anglo-Normandes

chant /tʃɑːnt/ n (Relig) mélopée f; (of demonstrators) chant m scandé. ● vt/i scander; (Relig) psalmodier.

chaos /'keɪɒs/ n chaos m.

chap /tʃæp/ n (man 🔲) type m 🔲

chapel /'tʃæpl/ n chapelle f.

chaplain /'tʃæplɪn/ n aumônier m.

chapped /tʃæpt/ adj gercé.

chapter /'tʃæptə(r)/ n chapitre m.

char /tʃɑː(r)/ vt (pt charred) carboniser.

character /'kærəktə(r)/ n caractère m; (in novel, play) personnage m; of good ~ de bonne réputation.

characteristic /kærəktə'rɪstɪk/ adj & n caractéristique (f).

charcoal /'tʃɑːkəʊl/ n charbon m de bois; (art) fusain m.

charge /tʃɑːdʒ/ n (fee) frais mpl; (Mil) charge f; (Jur) inculpation f; (task, custody) charge f; in ~ of

responsable de; take ~ of prendre en charge, se charger de. ● vt (customer) faire payer; (enemy, gun) charger; (Jur) inculper (with de); ~ £20 an hour prendre 20 livres de l'heure; ~ card carte f d'achat. ● vi faire payer; (bull) foncer; (person) se précipiter.

charisma /kə'rɪzmə/ n charisme m. charismatic adj charismatique.

charitable /'tʃærɪtəbl/ adj charitable. charity n charité f; (organization) organisation f caritative.

charm /tʃɑːm/ n charme m; (trinket) amulette f. ● vt charmer. charming adj charmant.

chart /tʃɑːt/ n (graph) graphique m; (table) tableau m; (map) carte f. ● vt (route) porter sur la carte.

charter /'tʃɑːtə(r)/ n charte f; ~ (flight) charter m. ● vt affréter; ~ed accountant expert-comptable m.

chase /tʃeɪs/ vt poursuivre; ~ away or off chasser. ● vi courir (after après). ● n chasse f.

chassis /'ʃæsɪ/ n châssis m.

chastise /tʃæ'staɪz/ vt châtier.

chat /tʃæt/ n conversation f; (on Internet) causette f, bavardage m; have a ~ bavarder; ~ show talk-show m. ~room n salle f de causette, salle f de bavardage. ● vi (pt chatted) bavarder. ~ up 🔲 draguer 🔲

chatter /'tʃætə(r)/ n bavardage m. ● vi bavarder; his teeth are ~ing il claque des dents. ~box n bavard/-e m/f.

chatty /'tʃætɪ/ adj bavard.

chauffeur /'ʃəʊfə(r)/ n chauffeur m.

chauvinist /'ʃəʊvɪnɪst/ n chauvin/-e m/f. macho m.

cheap /tʃiːp/ adj bon marché inv;

cheat | chimney

(*fare, rate*) réduit; (*joke, gimmick*) facile; ~**er** meilleur marché *inv.*
cheapen *vt* déprécier. **cheaply** *adv* à bas prix.

cheat /tʃiːt/ *vi* tricher. ● *vt* tromper. ● *n* tricheur/-euse *m/f.*

check /tʃek/ *vt/i* vérifier; (*tickets, rises, inflation*) contrôler; (*stop*) arrêter; (*tick off: US*) cocher. ● *n* contrôle *m*; (*curb*) frein *m*; (*chess*) échec *m*; (*pattern*) carreaux *mpl*; (*bill: US*) addition *f*; (*cheque: US*) chèque *m.* ~ **in** remplir la fiche; (*at airport*) enregistrer; ~ **out** partir; ~ **sth out** vérifier qch. ~ **up** vérifier. ~ **up on** (*story*) vérifier; (*person*) faire une enquête sur.

check: ~**in** *n* enregistrement *m.*
checking account *n* (US) compte *m* courant. ~**list** *n* liste *f* de contrôle. ~**mate** *n* échec *m* et mat. ~**out** *n* caisse *f.* ~**point** *n* contrôle *m.* ~**up** *n* examen *m* médical.

cheek /tʃiːk/ *n* joue *f*; (*impudence*) culot *m* 🄸. **cheeky** *adj* effronté.

cheer /tʃɪə(r)/ *n* ~**s** acclamations *fpl*; (*when drinking*) à la vôtre. ● *vt/i* applaudir; ~ **sb (up)** (*gladden*) remonter le moral à qn; ~ **up** prendre courage. **cheerful** *adj* joyeux. **cheerfulness** *n* gaieté *f.*

cheerio /tʃɪərɪˈəʊ/ *interj* 🄸 salut 🄸.

cheese /tʃiːz/ *n* fromage *m.*

cheetah /tʃiːtə/ *n* guépard *m.*

chef /ʃef/ *n* chef *m.*

chemical /ˈkemɪkl/ *adj* chimique. ● *n* produit *m* chimique.

chemist /ˈkemɪst/ *n* pharmacien/-ne *m/f*; (*scientist*) chimiste *mf*; ~'**s** (*shop*) pharmacie *f.* **chemistry** *n* chimie *f.*

cheque /tʃek/ *n* chèque *m.*
~**-book** *n* chéquier *m.* ~ **card** *n* carte *f* bancaire.

chequered /ˈtʃekəd/ *adj* (*pattern*) à damiers; (*fig*) en dents de scie.

cherish /ˈtʃerɪʃ/ *vt* chérir; (*hope*) caresser.

cherry /ˈtʃerɪ/ *n* cerise *f*; (*tree, wood*) cerisier *m.*

chess /tʃes/ *n* échecs *mpl.* ~**-board** *n* échiquier *m.*

chest /tʃest/ *n* (Anat) poitrine *f*; (*box*) coffre *m*; ~ **of drawers** commode *f.*

chestnut /ˈtʃesnʌt/ *n* (*nut*) marron *m*, châtaigne *f*; (*tree*) marronnier *m*; (*sweet*) châtaignier *m.*

chew /tʃuː/ *vt* mâcher.

chic /ʃiːk/ *adj* chic *inv.*

chick /tʃɪk/ *n* poussin *m.*

chicken /ˈtʃɪkɪn/ *n* poulet *m.* ● *adj* 🄳 froussard. ● *vi* ~ **out** 🄳 se dégonfler. ~**pox** *n* varicelle *f.*

chick-pea /ˈtʃɪkpiː/ *n* pois *m* chiche.

chicory /ˈtʃɪkərɪ/ *n* (*for salad*) endive *f*; (*in coffee*) chicorée *f.*

chief /tʃiːf/ *n* chef *m.* ● *adj* principal. **chiefly** *adv* principalement.

chilblain /ˈtʃɪlbleɪn/ *n* engelure *f.*

child /tʃaɪld/ *n* (*pl* **children**) enfant *mf.* ~**birth** *n* accouchement *m.* **childhood** *n* enfance *f.* **childish** *adj* puéril. **childless** *adj* sans enfants. **childlike** *adj* enfantin. ~**-minder** *n* nourrice *f.*

Chile /ˈtʃɪlɪən/ *n* Chili *m.*

chill /tʃɪl/ *n* froid *m*; (Med) refroidissement *m.* ● *adj* froid. ● *vt* (*person*) faire frissonner; (*wine*) rafraîchir; (*food*) mettre à refroidir.

chilli /ˈtʃɪlɪ/ *n* (*pl* ~**es**) piment *m.*

chilly /ˈtʃɪlɪ/ *adj* froid; **it's** ~ il fait froid.

chime /tʃaɪm/ *n* carillon *m.* ● *vt/i* carillonner.

chimney /ˈtʃɪmnɪ/ *n* cheminée *f.*

~-sweep n ramoneur m.

chimpanzee /tʃɪmpənˈziː/ n chimpanzé m.

chin /tʃɪn/ n menton m.

china /ˈtʃaɪnə/ n porcelaine f.

China /ˈtʃaɪnə/ n Chine f.

Chinese /tʃaɪˈniːz/ n (person) Chinois/-e m/f; (Ling) chinois m. ● adj chinois.

chip /tʃɪp/ n (on plate) ébréchure f; (piece) éclat m; (of wood) copeau m; (Culin) frite f; (Comput) puce f; (potato) ~s (US) chips fpl. ● vt/i (pt chipped) (s')ébrécher; ~ in 🔟 dire son mot; (with money) contribuer.

chiropodist /kɪˈrɒpədɪst/ n pédicure mf.

chirp /tʃɜːp/ n pépiement m. ● vi pépier. **chirpy** adj gai.

chisel /ˈtʃɪzl/ n ciseau m. ● vt (pt chiselled) ciseler.

chit /tʃɪt/ n note f; (voucher) bon m.

chitchat /ˈtʃɪttʃæt/ n 🔟 bavardage m.

chivalrous /ˈʃɪvəlrəs/ adj galant.

chives /tʃaɪvz/ npl ciboulette f.

chlorine /ˈklɔːriːn/ n chlore m.

choc ice /ˈtʃɒkaɪs/ n esquimau m.

chock-a-block /tʃɒkəˈblɒk/ adj plein à craquer.

chocolate /ˈtʃɒklət/ n chocolat m.

choice /tʃɔɪs/ n choix m. ● adj de choix.

choir /ˈkwaɪə(r)/ n chœur m. **~boy** n jeune choriste m.

choke /tʃəʊk/ vt/i (s')étrangler; ~ (up) boucher. ● n starter m.

cholesterol /kəˈlestərɒl/ n cholestérol m.

choose /tʃuːz/ vt/i (pt chose, pp chosen) choisir; ~ to do décider de faire. **choosy** adj difficile.

chop /tʃɒp/ vt/i (pt chopped) (wood) couper; (food) hacher;

chopping board planche f à découper; ~ down abattre. ● n (meat) côtelette f. **chopper** n hachoir m. 🔟 hélico m 🔟.

choppy /ˈtʃɒpɪ/ adj (sea) agité.

chopstick /ˈtʃɒpstɪk/ n baguette f (chinoise).

chord /kɔːd/ n (Mus) accord m.

chore /tʃɔː(r)/ n (routine) tâche f; (unpleasant) corvée f.

chortle /ˈtʃɔːtl/ n gloussement m. ● vi glousser.

chorus /ˈkɔːrəs/ n chœur m; (of song) refrain m.

chose, chosen /tʃəʊz, ˈtʃəʊzən/ ⟶CHOOSE.

Christ /kraɪst/ n le Christ.

christen /ˈkrɪsn/ vt baptiser. **christening** n baptême m.

Christian /ˈkrɪstʃən/ adj & n chrétien/-ne (m/f). ~ **name** nom m de baptême. **Christianity** n christianisme m.

Christmas /ˈkrɪsməs/ n Noël m; ~ **Day/Eve** le jour/la veille de Noël. ● adj (card, tree) de Noël.

chronic /ˈkrɒnɪk/ adj (situation, disease) chronique; (bad 🔟) nul.

chronicle /ˈkrɒnɪkl/ n chronique f.

chronological /krɒnəˈlɒdʒɪkl/ adj chronologique.

chrysanthemum /krɪˈsæn θəməm/ n chrysanthème m.

chubby /ˈtʃʌbɪ/ adj (-ier, -iest) potelé.

chuck /tʃʌk/ vt 🔟 lancer; ~ away or out 🔟 balancer.

chuckle /ˈtʃʌkl/ n gloussement m. ● vi glousser.

chuffed /tʃʌft/ adj 🔟 vachement content f.

chunk /tʃʌŋk/ n morceau m. **chunky** adj (sweater, jewellery) gros; (person) costaud.

church /tʃɜːtʃ/ n église f. ~ **goer** n pratiquant/-e m/f. ~**yard** n cimetière m.

churn /tʃɜːn/ n baratte f; (milk-can) bidon m. ● vt baratter; ~ **out** produire en série.

chute /ʃuːt/ n toboggan m; (for rubbish) vide-ordures m inv.

chutney /ˈtʃʌtnɪ/ n condiment m aigredoux.

cider /ˈsaɪdə(r)/ n cidre m.

cigar /sɪˈgɑː(r)/ n cigare m.

cigarette /sɪgəˈret/ n cigarette f; ~ **end** mégot m.

cinder /ˈsɪndə(r)/ n cendre f.

cinema /ˈsɪnəmə/ n cinéma m.

cinnamon /ˈsɪnəmən/ n cannelle f.

circle /ˈsɜːkl/ n cercle m; (Theat) balcon m. ● vt (go round) tourner autour de; (word, error) encercler. ● vi tourner en rond.

circuit /ˈsɜːkɪt/ n circuit m. ~ **board** n carte f de circuit imprimé. ~**breaker** n disjoncteur m.

circuitous /sɜːˈkjuːɪtəs/ adj indirect.

circular /ˈsɜːkjʊlə(r)/ adj & n circulaire (f).

circulate /ˈsɜːkjʊleɪt/ vt/i (faire) circuler. **circulation** n circulation f; (of newspaper) tirage m.

circumcise /ˈsɜːkəmsaɪz/ vt circoncire.

circumference /səˈkʌmfərəns/ n circonférence f.

circumflex /ˈsɜːkəmfleks/ n circonflexe m.

circumstance /ˈsɜːkəmstəns/ n circonstance f; ~s (financial) situation f; under no ~s en aucun cas.

circus /ˈsɜːkəs/ n cirque m.

cistern /ˈsɪstən/ n réservoir m.

citizen /ˈsɪtɪzn/ n citoyen/-ne m/f; (of town) habitant/-e m/f. **citizen**~**ship** n nationalité f.

citrus /ˈsɪtrəs/ adj ~ **fruit(s)** agrumes mpl; ~ **tree** citrus m.

city /ˈsɪtɪ/ n (grande) ville f.

The City Quartier londonien des affaires et de la finance, la City est le siège des grandes banques, des compagnies d'assurance et de la plupart des sociétés d'agents de change. 500 000 personnes viennent et travailler chaque jour.

civic /ˈsɪvɪk/ adj (official) municipal; (pride, duty) civique.

civil /ˈsɪvl/ adj civil. ~ **disobedience** n résistance f passive. ~ **engineer** n ingénieur m des travaux publics.

civilian /sɪˈvɪlɪən/ adj & n civil/-e (m/f).

civilization /sɪvəlaɪˈzeɪʃn/ n civilisation f. **civilize** vt civiliser.

civil: ~ **law** n droit m civil. ~ **liberties** npl libertés fpl individuelles. ~ **rights** npl droits mpl civils. ~ **servant** n fonctionnaire mf. ~ **service** n fonction f publique. ~ **war** n guerre f civile.

claim /kleɪm/ vt (demand) revendiquer; (assert) prétendre. ● n revendication f; (assertion) affirmation f; (for insurance) réclamation f; (right) droit m. **claimant** n (of benefits) demandeur/-euse m/f.

clairvoyant /kleəˈvɔɪənt/ n voyant/-e m/f.

clam /klæm/ n palourde f.

clamber /ˈklæmbə(r)/ vi grimper.

clammy /ˈklæmɪ/ adj (-ier, -iest) moite.

clamour /ˈklæmə(r)/ n clameur f. ● vi ~ **for** réclamer.

clamp /klæmp/ n valet m; (Med)

pince *f*; (wheel) ∼ sabot *m* de Denver. ● *vt* cramponner; (*jaw*) serrer; (*car*) mettre un sabot de Denver à; ∼ down on faire de la répression contre.

clan /klæn/ *n* clan *m*.

clang /klæŋ/ *n* son *m* métallique.

clap /klæp/ *vt/i* (*pt* **clapped**) applaudir; (put forcibly) mettre; ∼ one's hands frapper dans ses mains. ● *n* applaudissement *m*; (of thunder) coup *m*.

claret /ˈklærət/ *n* bordeaux *m* rouge.

clarification /klærɪfɪˈkeɪʃn/ *n* clarification *f.* **clarify** /ˈklærɪfaɪ/ *vt/i* (se) clarifier.

clarinet /klærəˈnet/ *n* clarinette *f.*

clarity /ˈklærətɪ/ *n* clarté *f.*

clash /klæʃ/ *n* choc *m*; (fig) conflit *m*. ● *vi* (*metal objects*) s'entrechoquer; (*armies*) s'affronter; (*meetings*) avoir lieu en même temps; (*colours*) jurer.

clasp /klɑːsp/ *n* (fastener) fermoir *m*. ● *vt* serrer.

class /klɑːs/ *n* classe *f.* ● *vt* classer; ∼ sb/sth as assimiler qn/qch à.

classic /ˈklæsɪk/ *adj & n* classique (*m*). ∼**s** (Univ) lettres *fpl* classiques. **classical** /ˈklæsɪkl/ *adj* classique.

classified /ˈklæsɪfaɪd/ *adj* (*information*) secret; ∼ (**ad**) petite annonce *f.*

classroom /ˈklɑːsrʊm/ *n* salle *f* de classe.

clatter /ˈklætə(r)/ *n* cliquetis *m.* ● *vi* cliqueter.

clause /klɔːz/ *n* clause *f*; (Gram) proposition *f.*

claw /klɔː/ *n* (of animal, small bird) griffe *f*; (of bird of prey) serre *f*; (of lobster) pince *f.* ● *vt* griffer.

clay /kleɪ/ *n* argile *f.*

clean /kliːn/ *adj* propre; (shape, stroke) net. ● *adv* complètement.

● *vt* nettoyer; ∼ one's teeth se brosser les dents. ● *vi* ∼ **up** faire le nettoyage. **cleaner** *n* (at home) femme *f* de ménage; (industrial) agent *m* de nettoyage; (of clothes) teinturier-/ière *m/f.* **cleanliness** *n* propreté *f.* **cleanly** *adv* proprement; (sharply) nettement.

cleanse /klenz/ *vt* nettoyer; (fig) purifier.

clean-shaven *adj* glabre.

clear /klɪə(r)/ *adj* (explanation) clair; (need, sign) évident; (glass) transparent; (profit) net; (road) dégagé; make sth ∼ être très clair sur qch; ∼ of (away from) à l'écart de. ● *adv* complètement; stand ∼ of s'éloigner de. ● *vt* (free) dégager (of de). (table) débarrasser; (building) évacuer; (cheque) compenser; (jump over) franchir; (debt) liquider; (Jur) disculper. ● *vi* (fog) se dissiper; (cheque) être compensé. ∼ **away** or **off** (remove) enlever. ∼ **off** or **out** 🔲 décamper. ∼ **out** (clean) nettoyer. ∼ **up** (tidy) ranger; (weather) s'éclaircir.

clearance /ˈklɪərəns/ *n* (permission) autorisation *f*; (space) espace *m*; ∼ sale liquidation *f.*

clear-cut *adj* net.

clearing /ˈklɪərɪŋ/ *n* clairière *f.*

clearly /ˈklɪəlɪ/ *adv* clairement.

clef /klef/ *n* (Mus) clé *f.*

cleft /kleft/ *n* fissure *f.*

clench /klentʃ/ *vt* serrer.

clergy /ˈklɜːdʒɪ/ *n* clergé *m.* ∼**man** *n* (*pl* **-men**) ecclésiastique *m.*

cleric /ˈklerɪk/ *n* clerc *m.* **clerical** *adj* (Relig) clérical; (staff, work) de bureau.

clerk /klɑːk/ *n* employé-/e *m/f* de bureau; (US) (sales) ∼ vendeur-/euse *m/f.*

clever | cloud

clever /'klevə(r)/ adj intelligent; (skilful) habile.

click /klɪk/ n déclic m; (Comput) clic m. ● vi faire un déclic; (people ▯) sympathiser; (Comput) cliquer (on sur.) ● vt (heels, tongue) faire claquer.

client /'klaɪənt/ n client/-e m/f.

clientele /kliː.ɑ̃n'tel/ n clientèle f.

cliff /klɪf/ n falaise f.

climate /'klaɪmɪt/ n climat m. ∼ **change** changement m climatique.

climax /'klaɪmæks/ n (of story, contest) point m culminant; (sexual) orgasme m.

climb /klaɪm/ vt grimper; (steps) monter; (tree, ladder) grimper à; (mountain) faire l'ascension de. ● vi grimper; ∼ **into** (car) monter dans; ∼ **into** bed se mettre au lit. ● n (of mountain) escalade f; (steep hill, rise) montée f. ∼ **down** (fig) reculer. **climber** n (Sport) alpiniste mf.

clinch /klɪntʃ/ vt (deal) conclure; (victory, order) décrocher.

cling /klɪŋ/ vi (pt **clung**) se cramponner (to à.); (stick) coller. ∼**film** n scellofrais® m.

clinic /'klɪnɪk/ n centre m médical; (private) clinique f. **clinical** adj clinique.

clink /klɪŋk/ n tintement m. ● vt/i (faire) tinter.

clip /klɪp/ n (for paper) trombone m; (for hair) barrette f; (for tube) collier m; (of film) extrait m. ● vt (pt **clipped**) (fasten) attacher (to à). cut) couper.

clippers /'klɪpəz/ npl tondeuse f; (for nails) coupe-ongles m inv.

clipping /'klɪpɪŋ/ n (from press) coupure f de presse.

cloak /kləʊk/ n cape f; (man's) houppelande f. ∼**room** n vestiaire m; (toilet) toilettes fpl.

clobber /'klɒbə(r)/ n ▯ attirail m. ● vt (hit ▯) tabasser ▯.

clock /klɒk/ n pendule f; (large) horloge f. ● vi on/in or off/out pointer; ∼ **up** (miles) ▯. ∼**-wise** adj & adv dans le sens des aiguilles d'une montre.

clockwork /'klɒkwɜːk/ n mécanisme m. ● adj mécanique.

clog /klɒg/ n sabot m. ● vt/i (pt **clogged**) (se) boucher.

cloister /'klɔɪstə(r)/ n cloître m.

clone /kləʊn/ n clone m. ● vt cloner.

close¹ /kləʊs/ adj (friend) proche (to de). (link) étroit; (examination) minutieux; (match) serré; (weather) lourd; ∼ **together** (crowded) serrés; ∼ **by**, ∼ **at hand** tout près; **have a** ∼ **shave** l'échapper belle; **keep a** ∼ **watch on** surveiller de près. ● adv près. ● n (street) impasse f.

close² /kləʊz/ vt fermer; (meeting, case) mettre fin à. ● vi se fermer; (shop) fermer; (meeting, play) prendre fin. ● n fin f.

closely /'kləʊslɪ/ adv (follow) de près. **closeness** n proximité f.

closet /'klɒzɪt/ n (US) placard m.

close-up n gros plan m.

closure /'kləʊʒə(r)/ n fermeture f.

clot /klɒt/ n (of blood) caillot m; (in sauce) grumeau m. ● vt/i (pt **clot-ted**) se coaguler.

cloth /klɒθ/ n (fabric) tissu m; (duster) chiffon m; (table-cloth) nappe f.

clothe /kləʊð/ vt vêtir.

clothes /kləʊðz/ npl vêtements mpl. ∼**-hanger** n cintre m. ∼**-line** n corde f à linge.

clothing /'kləʊðɪŋ/ n vêtements mpl.

cloud /klaʊd/ n nuage m. ● vi ∼

over se couvrir (de nuages); (face) s'assombrir. **cloudy** adj (sky) couvert; (liquid) trouble.

clout /klaʊt/ n (blow) coup m de poing; (power) influence f. ● vt frapper.

clove /kləʊv/ n clou m de girofle; ~ of garlic gousse f d'ail.

clover /'kləʊvə(r)/ n trèfle m.

clown /klaʊn/ n clown m. ● vi faire le clown.

club /klʌb/ n (group) club m; (weapon) massue f; (golf) ~ club m (de golf); ~s (cards) trèfle m ● vt/i (pt clubbed) matraquer. ~ **together** cotiser.

cluck /klʌk/ vi glousser.

clue /kluː/ n indice m; (in crossword) définition f; I haven't a ~ 🄸 je n'en ai pas la moindre idée.

clump /klʌmp/ n massif m.

clumsy /'klʌmzɪ/ adj (-ier, -iest) maladroit; (tool) peu commode.

clung /klʌŋ/ ➡CLING.

cluster /'klʌstə(r)/ n (of people, islands) groupe m; (of flowers, berries) grappe f. ● vi se grouper.

clutch /klʌtʃ/ vt (hold) serrer fort; (grasp) saisir. ● vi ~ at (try to grasp) essayer de saisir. ● n (Auto) embrayage m; (of eggs) couvée f; (of people) groupe m.

clutter /'klʌtə(r)/ n désordre m. ● vt ~ (up) encombrer.

coach /kəʊtʃ/ n autocar m; (of train) wagon m; (horse-drawn) carrosse m; (Sport) entraîneur-euse m/f. ● vt (team) entraîner; (pupil) donner des leçons particulières à.

coal /kəʊl/ n charbon m. ~**field** n bassin m houiller. ~**mine** n mine f de charbon.

coarse /kɔːs/ adj grossier.

coast /kəʊst/ n côte f. ● vi (car, bicycle) descendre en roue libre.

coastal adj côtier.

coast: ~**guard** n (person) garde-côte m; (organization) gendarmerie f maritime. ~**line** n littoral m.

coat /kəʊt/ n manteau m; (of animal) pelage m; (of paint) couche f; ~ of arms armoiries fpl. ● vt enduire, couvrir; (with chocolate) enrober (with de). **coating** n couche f.

coax /kəʊks/ vt cajoler.

cob /kɒb/ n (of corn) épi m.

cobbler /'kɒblə(r)/ n cordonnier m.

cobblestones /'kɒblstəʊnz/ npl pavés mpl.

cobweb /'kɒbweb/ n toile f d'araignée.

cocaine /kəʊ'keɪn/ n cocaïne f.

cock /kɒk/ n (rooster) coq m. (oiseau) mâle m. ● vt (gun) armer; (ears) dresser.

cockerel /'kɒkrəl/ n jeune coq m.

cockle /'kɒkl/ n (Culin) coque f.

cock: ~**pit** n poste m de pilotage. ~**roach** n cafard m. ~**tail** n cocktail m.

cocky /'kɒkɪ/ adj (-ier, -iest) trop sûr de soi.

cocoa /'kəʊkəʊ/ n cacao m.

coconut /'kəʊkənʌt/ n noix f de coco.

COD abbr (**cash on delivery**) envoi m contre remboursement.

cod /'kɒd/ n inv morue f; ~**-liver oil** huile f de foie de morue.

code /kəʊd/ n code m. ● vt coder.

coerce /kəʊ'ɜːs/ vt contraindre.

coexist /kəʊɪg'zɪst/ vi coexister.

coffee /'kɒfɪ/ n café m. ~ **bar** n café m. ~ **bean** n grain m de café. ~**pot** n cafetière f. ~**table** n table f basse.

coffin /'kɒfɪn/ n cercueil m.

cog /kɒg/ n pignon m; (fig) rouage m.

cognac /ˈkɒnjæk/ *n* cognac *m*.

coil /kɔɪl/ *vt/i* (s')enrouler. ● *n* (of rope) rouleau *m*; (of snake) anneau *m*; (contraceptive) stérilet *m*.

coin /kɔɪn/ *n* pièce *f* (*de monnaie*). ● *vt* (*word*) inventer.

coincide /kəʊɪnˈsaɪd/ *vi* coïncider. **coincidence** *n* coïncidence *f*. **coincidental** *adj* dû à une coïncidence.

colander /ˈkʌləndə(r)/ *n* passoire *f*.

cold /kəʊld/ *adj* froid; (*person*) **be** *or* **feel** ~ avoir froid; **it is** ~ il fait froid; **get** ~ **feet** avoir les jetons [!]; ~**-blooded** (lit) à sang froid; (fig) sans pitié. ● *n* froid *m*; (Med) rhume *m*; ~ **sore** bouton *m* de fièvre. **coldness** *n* froideur *f*.

coleslaw /ˈkəʊlslɔː/ *n* salade *f* de chou cru.

colic /ˈkɒlɪk/ *n* coliques *fpl*.

collaborate /kəˈlæbəreɪt/ *vi* collaborer.

collapse /kəˈlæps/ *vi* s'effondrer; (*person*) s'écrouler; (fold) se plier. ● *n* effondrement *m*.

collar /ˈkɒlə(r)/ *n* col *m*; (of dog) collier *m*. ~**-bone** *n* clavicule *f*.

collateral /kəˈlætərəl/ *n* nantissement *m*.

colleague /ˈkɒliːg/ *n* collègue *mf*.

collect /kəˈlekt/ *vt* rassembler; (pick up) ramasser; (call for) passer prendre; (*money, fare*) encaisser; (*taxes, rent*) percevoir; (as hobby) collectionner. ● *vi* se rassembler; (*dust*) s'amasser. ● *adv* **call** ~ (US) appeler en PCV. **collection** *n* collection *f*; (of money) collecte *f*; (in church) quête *f*; (of mail) levée *f*.

collective /kəˈlektɪv/ *adj* collectif.

collector /kəˈlektə(r)/ *n* (as hobby) collectionneur/-euse *m/f*; (of taxes) percepteur *m*; (of rent, debt) encaisseur *m*.

college /ˈkɒlɪdʒ/ *n* (for higher education) établissement *m* d'enseignement supérieur; (within university) collège *m*; **be at** ~ faire des études supérieures.

collide /kəˈlaɪd/ *vi* entrer en collision (with avec).

colliery /ˈkɒlɪərɪ/ *n* houillère *f*.

collision /kəˈlɪʒn/ *n* collision *f*.

colloquial /kəˈləʊkwɪəl/ *adj* familier. **colloquialism** *n* expression *f* familière.

Colombia /kəˈlɒmbɪə/ *n* Colombie *f*.

colon /ˈkəʊlən/ *n* (Gram) deux-points *m inv*; (Anat) côlon *m*.

colonel /ˈkɜːnl/ *n* colonel *m*.

colonial /kəˈləʊnɪəl/ *adj & n* colonial/-e (*m/f*).

colour, (US) **color** /ˈkʌlə(r)/ *n* couleur *f*; ~**-blind** daltonien. ● *adj* (*photo*) en couleur; (*TV set*) couleur *inv*. ● *vt* colorer; (with crayon) colorier. **coloured** *adj* de couleur. **colourful** *adj* aux couleurs vives; (fig) haut en couleur. **colouring** *n* (of skin) teint *m*; (in food) colorant *m*.

colt /kəʊlt/ *n* poulain *m*.

column /ˈkɒləm/ *n* colonne *f*.

coma /ˈkəʊmə/ *n* coma *m*.

comb /kəʊm/ *n* peigne *m*. ● *vt* peigner; ~ **one's hair** se peigner; ~ **a place** passer un lieu au peigne fin.

combat /ˈkɒmbæt/ *n* combat *m*. ● *vt* (*pt* **combated**) combattre.

combination /kɒmbɪˈneɪʃn/ *n* combinaison *f*.

combine[1] /kəmˈbaɪn/ *vt/i* (se) combiner, (s')unir.

combine[2] /ˈkɒmbaɪn/ *n* (Comm) groupe *m*; ~ **harvester** moissonneuse-batteuse *f*.

come /kʌm/ *vi* (*pt* **came**, *pp* **come**) venir; (*bus, letter*) arriver; (*postman*) passer; ~ **and look!** viens voir!; ~

in (size, colour) exister en; when it ~s to lorsqu'il s'agit de. ~ **about** survenir. ~ **across** (meaning) passer; ~ across sth tomber sur qch. ~ **away** (leave) partir; (come off) se détacher. ~ **back** revenir. ~ **by** obtenir. ~ **down** descendre; (price) baisser; ~ **forward** se présenter. ~ **in** entrer; (be useful) être utile. ~ **in for** recevoir. ~ **into** (money) hériter de. ~ **off** (succeed) réussir; (fare) s'en tirer; (detach) se détacher. ~ **on** (actor) entrer en scène; (light) s'allumer; (improve) faire des progrès; ~ **on!** allez! ~ **out** sortir. ~ **round** reprendre connaissance; (change mind) changer d'avis; ~ **through** s'en tirer. ~ **to** reprendre connaissance; ~ **to sth** (amount) revenir à qch; (decision, conclusion) arriver à qch. ~ **up** (problem) être soulevé; (opportunity) se présenter; (sun) se lever; ~ **up against** heurter à. ~ **up with** trouver.

comedian /kəˈmiːdɪən/ n comique m.

comedy /ˈkɒmədɪ/ n comédie f.

comfort /ˈkʌmfət/ n confort m; (consolation) réconfort m. ● vt consoler. **comfortable** adj (chair, car) confortable; (person) à l'aise; (wealthy) aisé.

comfortably /ˈkʌmftəblɪ/ adv confortablement; ~ **off** aisé.

comfy /ˈkʌmfɪ/ adj ①⇒COM-FORTABLE.

comic /ˈkɒmɪk/ adj comique. ● n (person) comique m. ● n (~ book), ~ **strip** bande f dessinée.

coming /ˈkʌmɪŋ/ n arrivée f; ~**s and goings** allées et venues fpl. ● adj à venir.

comma /ˈkɒmə/ n virgule f.

command /kəˈmɑːnd/ n (authority) commandement m; (order) ordre m; (mastery) maîtrise f. ● vt ordonner à (to do faire); (be able to use) disposer de; (respect) inspirer. **commandeer** vt réquisitionner. **commander** n commandant m. **commanding** adj imposant. **commandment** n commandement m.

commando /kəˈmɑːndəʊ/ n commando m.

commemorate /kəˈmeməreɪt/ vt commémorer.

commence /kəˈmens/ vt/i commencer.

commend /kəˈmend/ vt (praise) louer; (entrust) confier.

commensurate /kəˈmenʃərət/ adj proportionné.

comment /ˈkɒment/ n commentaire m. ● vi faire des commentaires; ~ **on** commenter. **commentary** n commentaire m; (radio, TV) reportage m. **commentate** vi faire un reportage. **commentator** n commentateur/-trice m/f.

commerce /ˈkɒmɜːs/ n commerce m.

commercial /kəˈmɜːʃl/ adj commercial; (traveller) de commerce. ● n publicité f.

commiserate /kəˈmɪzəreɪt/ vi compatir (with avec).

commission /kəˈmɪʃn/ n commission f; (order for work) commande f; out of ~ hors service. ● vt (order) commander; (Mil) nommer officier; ~ **to do** charger de faire. **commissioner** n préfet m (de police); (in EU) membre m de la Commission européenne.

commit /kəˈmɪt/ vt (pt committed) commettre; (entrust) confier; ~ **oneself** s'engager; ~ **perjury** se parjurer; ~ **suicide** se suicider; ~ **to memory** apprendre par cœur. **commitment** n engagement m.

committee /kə'mɪtɪ/ n comité m.

commodity /kə'mɒdətɪ/ n article m.

common /'kɒmən/ adj (shared by all) commun (to à); (usual) courant; (vulgar) vulgaire, commun; in ~ en commun; ~ **people** le peuple; ~ **sense** bon sens m. ● n terrain m communal; the C~s Chambre f des Communes.

commoner /'kɒmənə(r)/ n roturier/-ière m/f.

common law n droit m coutumier.

commonly /'kɒmənlɪ/ adv communément.

commonplace /'kɒmənpleɪs/ adj banal. ● n banalité f.

common-room n salle f de détente.

Commonwealth /'kɒmənwelθ/ n the ~ le Commonwealth m.

Commonwealth of Nations Association de nations ayant pour la plupart fait partie de l'empire britannique et qui maintiennent une coopération avec la Grande-Bretagne en matière d'économie, de culture et d'éducation. Des championnats d'athlétisme, les *Commonwealth Games* ont lieu tous les quatre ans. Le mot *Commonwealth* figure dans le nom officiel de quelques États américains (*Kentucky, Virginia, Pennsylvania, Massachusetts*).

commotion /kə'məʊʃn/ n (noise) vacarme m; (disturbance) agitation f.

communal /'kɒmjʊnl/ adj (shared) commun m; (life) collectif.

commune /'kɒmjuːn/ n (group) communauté f.

communicate /kə'mjuːnɪkeɪt/ vt/i communiquer. **communication**

n communication f. **communicative** adj communicatif.

communion /kə'mjuːnɪən/ n communion f.

Communism /'kɒmjʊnɪzəm/ n communisme m. **Communist** adj & n communiste (mf).

community /kə'mjuːnətɪ/ n communauté f.

commute /kə'mjuːt/ vi faire la navette. ● vt (Jur) commuer. **commuter** n navetteur/-euse m/f.

compact /kəm'pækt/ adj compact; (lady's case) poudrier m.

compact disc n disque m compact. ~ **player** n platine f laser.

companion /kəm'pænɪən/ n compagnon/-agne m/f. **companionship** n camaraderie f.

company /'kʌmpənɪ/ n (companionship, firm) compagnie f; (guests) invités/-es m/fpl.

comparative /kəm'pærətɪv/ adj (study, form) comparatif; (comfort) relatif.

compare /kəm'peə(r)/ vt comparer (with, to à). ~d with par rapport à. ● vi être comparable. **comparison** n comparaison f.

compartment /kəm'pɑːtmənt/ n compartiment m.

compass /'kʌmpəs/ n (for direction) boussole f; (scope) portée f; a pair of ~es un compas.

compassionate /kəm'pæʃənət/ adj compatissant.

compatible /kəm'pætəbl/ adj compatible.

compel /kəm'pel/ vt (pt compelled) contraindre. **compelling** adj irrésistible.

compensate /'kɒmpenseɪt/ vt/i (financially) dédommager (for de). ~ **for sth** compenser qch. **compensation** n compensation f; (financial) dédommagement m.

compete /kəm'pi:t/ vi concourir; ~ with rivaliser avec.

competent /'kɒmpɪtənt/ adj compétent.

competition /kɒmpə'tɪʃn/ n (contest) concours m; (Sport) compétition f; (Comm) concurrence f.

competitive /kəm'petɪtɪv/ adj (prices) compétitif; (person) qui a l'esprit de compétition.

competitor /kəm'petɪtə(r)/ n concurrent/-e m/f.

compile /kəm'paɪl/ vt (list) dresser; (book) rédiger.

complacency /kəm'pleɪsnsɪ/ n suffisance f.

complain /kəm'pleɪn/ vi se plaindre (about, de). **complaint** n plainte f; (official) réclamation f; (illness) maladie f.

complement /'kɒmplɪmənt/ n complément m. ● vt compléter. **complementary** adj complémentaire.

complete /kəm'pli:t/ adj complet; (finished) achevé; (downright) parfait. ● vt achever; (a form) remplir. **completely** adv complètement. **completion** n achèvement m.

complex /'kɒmpleks/ adj complexe. ● n (Psych) complexe m.

complexion /kəm'plekʃn/ n (of face) teint m; (fig) caractère m.

compliance /kəm'plaɪəns/ n (agreement) conformité f.

complicate /'kɒmplɪkeɪt/ vt compliquer. **complicated** adj compliqué. **complication** n complication f.

compliment /'kɒmplɪmənt/ n compliment m. ● vt complimenter. **complimentary** adj (offert) à titre gracieux; (praising) flatteur.

comply /kəm'plaɪ/ vi ~ with se conformer à, obéir à.

component /kəm'pəʊnənt/ n (of machine) pièce f; (chemical substance) composant m; (element: fig) composante f. ● adj constituant.

compose /kəm'pəʊz/ vt composer; ~ oneself se calmer. **composed** adj calme. **composer** n (Mus) compositeur m. **composition** n composition f.

composure /kəm'pəʊʒə(r)/ n calme m.

compound /'kɒmpaʊnd/ n (substance, word) composé m; (enclosure) enclos m. ● adj composé.

comprehend /kɒmprɪ'hend/ vt comprendre. **comprehension** n compréhension f.

comprehensive /kɒmprɪ'hensɪv/ adj étendu, complet; (insurance) tous risques inv. ~ **school** n collège m d'enseignement secondaire.

compress /kəm'pres/ vt comprimer.

comprise /kəm'praɪz/ vt comprendre, inclure.

compromise /'kɒmprəmaɪz/ n compromis m. ● vt compromettre. ● vi transiger, arriver à un compromis.

compulsive /kəm'pʌlsɪv/ adj (Psych) compulsif; (liar, smoker) invétéré.

compulsory /kəm'pʌlsərɪ/ adj obligatoire.

compute /kəm'pju:t/ vt calculer. **computer** /kəm'pju:t/ n ordinateur m; ~ **science** informatique f. **computerize** vt informatiser.

comrade /'kɒmreɪd/ n camarade mf.

con¹ /kɒn/ vt (pt **conned** ▣) rouler ▣, escroquer (out of de.) ● n ▣ escroquerie f.

con² /kɒn/ ➡**PRO**.

conceal /kən'si:l/ vt

dissimuler (from à).

concede /kənˈsiːd/ vt concéder.
● vi céder.

conceited /kənˈsiːtɪd/ adj vaniteux.

conceive /kənˈsiːv/ vt/i concevoir; ~ of concevoir.

concentrate /ˈkɒnsntreɪt/ vt/i (se) concentrer. **concentration** n concentration f.

concept /ˈkɒnsept/ n concept m.

conception /kənˈsepʃn/ n conception f.

concern /kənˈsɜːn/ n (interest, business) affaire f; (worry) inquiétude f; (firm: Comm) entreprise f, affaire f. ● vt concerner; ~ oneself with, be ~ed with s'occuper de. **concerned** adj inquiet. **concerning** prep en ce qui concerne.

concert /ˈkɒnsət/ n concert m.

concession /kənˈseʃn/ n concession f.

conciliation /kənsɪlɪˈeɪʃn/ n conciliation f.

concise /kənˈsaɪs/ adj concis.

conclude /kənˈkluːd/ vt conclure. ● vi se terminer. **conclusion** n conclusion f. **conclusive** adj concluant.

concoct /kənˈkɒkt/ vt confectionner; (invent: fig) fabriquer. **concoction** n mélange m.

concourse /ˈkɒŋkɔːs/ n (Rail) hall m.

concrete /ˈkɒŋkriːt/ n béton m. ● adj de béton; (fig) concret. ● vt bétonner.

concur /kənˈkɜː(r)/ vi (pt concurred) être d'accord.

concurrently /kənˈkʌrəntlɪ/ adv simultanément.

concussion /kənˈkʌʃn/ n commotion f (cérébrale).

condemn /kənˈdem/ vt condamner.

condensation /kɒndenˈseɪʃn/ n (on walls) condensation f; (on windows) buée f. **condense** vt/i (se) condenser.

condition /kənˈdɪʃn/ n condition f; on ~ that à condition que. ● vt conditionner. **conditional** adj conditionnel.

conditioner /kənˈdɪʃənə(r)/ n après-shampooing m.

condolences /kənˈdəʊlənsɪz/ npl condoléances fpl.

condom /ˈkɒndɒm/ n préservatif m.

condone /kənˈdəʊn/ vt pardonner, fermer les yeux sur.

conducive /kənˈdjuːsɪv/ adj ~ to favorable à.

conduct¹ /ˈkɒndʌkt/ n conduite f.

conduct² /kənˈdʌkt/ vt conduire; (orchestra) diriger. **conductor** n chef m d'orchestre; (of bus) receveur m; (on train: US) chef m de train; (Electr) conducteur m. **conductress** n receveuse f.

cone /kəʊn/ n cône m. (of icecream) cornet m.

confectioner /kənˈfekʃənə(r)/ n confiseur/-euse m/f. **confectionery** n confiserie f.

confer /kənˈfɜː(r)/ vt/i (pt conferred) conférer.

conference /ˈkɒnfərəns/ n conférence f.

confess /kənˈfes/ vt/i avouer; (Relig) (se) confesser. **confession** n confession f; (of crime) aveu m.

confide /kənˈfaɪd/ vt confier. ● vi ~ in se confier à.

confidence /ˈkɒnfɪdəns/ n (trust) confiance f. (boldness) confiance f en soi; (secret) confidence f; in ~ en confidence. **confident** adj sûr.

confidential /kɒnfɪ'denʃl/ adj
confidentiel.

configuration /kənfɪɡə'reɪʃn/ n
configuration f. ● **configure** vt configurer.

confine /kən'faɪn/ vt enfermer;
(limit) limiter; ~d **space** espace m
réduit; ~d **to** limité à.

confirm /kən'fɜːm/ vt confirmer.
confirmed adj (bachelor) endurci;
(smoker) invétéré.

confiscate /'kɒnfɪskeɪt/ vt confisquer.

conflict[1] /'kɒnflɪkt/ n conflit m.
conflict[2] /kən'flɪkt/ vi (statements,
views) être en contradiction (with
avec.) (appointments) tomber en
même temps (with que). **conflicting** adj contradictoire.

conform /kən'fɔːm/ vt/i (se) conformer.

confound /kən'faʊnd/ vt confondre.

confront /kən'frʌnt/ vt affronter;
~ **with** confronter avec.

confuse /kən'fjuːz/ vt (bewilder)
troubler; (mistake, confound) confondre; become ~d s'embrouiller; I
am ~d je m'y perds. **confusing** adj
déroutant. **confusion** n confusion f.

congeal /kən'dʒiːl/ vt/i (se) figer.

congested /kən'dʒestɪd/ adj
(road) embouteillé; (passage) encombré; (Med) congestionné. **congestion** n (traffic) embouteillage(s)
m(pl); (Med) congestion f.

congratulate /kən'ɡrætʃʊleɪt/ vt
féliciter (on de). **congratulations**
npl félicitations fpl.

congregate /'kɒnɡrɪɡeɪt/ vi se
rassembler. **congregation** n assemblée f.

congress /'kɒnɡres/ n congrès m.
C ~ (US) le Congrès.

conjugate /'kɒndʒʊɡeɪt/ vt conjuguer. **conjugation** n conjugaison f.

conjunction /kən'dʒʌŋkʃn/ n
(Ling) conjonction f. **in** ~**with** conjointement avec.

conjunctivitis /kəndʒʌŋktɪ
'vaɪtɪs/ n conjonctivite f.

conjure /'kʌndʒə(r)/ vi faire des
tours de passe-passe. ● ~ **up**
faire apparaître. **conjuror** n
prestidigitateur·-trice m/f.

con man 🅇 escroc m.

connect /kə'nekt/ vt/i (se) relier;
(in mind) faire le rapport entre; (install, wire up to mains) brancher; ~
with (of train) assurer la correspondance avec; ~**ed** (idea, event) lié;
be ~**ed with** avoir rapport à.

connection /kə'nekʃn/ n rapport
m. (Rail) correspondance f; (phone
call) communication f; (Electr) contact m; (joining piece) raccord m;
~**s**, (Comm) relations fpl.

connive /kə'naɪv/ vi ~ **at** se faire
le complice de.

conquer /'kɒnkə(r)/ vt vaincre;
(country) conquérir. **conqueror** n
conquérant m.

conquest /'kɒnkwest/ n conquête f.

conscience /'kɒnʃəns/ n conscience f. **conscientious** adj consciencieux.

conscious /ˈkɒnʃəs/ adj conscient; (deliberate) voulu. **consciously** adv consciemment. **consciousness** n conscience f; (Med) connaissance f.

conscript /ˈkɒnskrɪpt/ n appelé m.

consecutive /kənˈsekjʊtɪv/ adj consécutif.

consensus /kənˈsensəs/ n consensus m.

consent /kənˈsent/ vi consentir (to à). ● n consentement m.

consequence /ˈkɒnsɪkwəns/ n conséquence f. **consequently** adv par conséquent.

conservation /kɒnsəˈveɪʃn/ n préservation f. ~ area zone f protégée. **conservationist** n défenseur m de l'environnement.

conservative /kənˈsɜːvətɪv/ adj conservateur; (estimate) minimal.

Conservative Party n parti m conservateur.

conservatory /kənˈsɜːvətrɪ/ n (greenhouse) serre f; (room) véranda f.

conserve /kənˈsɜːv/ vt conserver; (energy) économiser.

consider /kənˈsɪdə(r)/ vt considérer; (allow for) tenir compte de; (possibility) envisager (doing de faire).

considerable /kənˈsɪdərəbl/ adj considérable; (much) beaucoup de.

considerate /kənˈsɪdərət/ adj prévenant, attentionné. **consideration** n considération f. (respect) égard(s) m(pl).

considering /kənˈsɪdərɪŋ/ prep compte tenu de.

consignment /kənˈsaɪnmənt/ n envoi m.

consist /kənˈsɪst/ vi consister (of en; in doing à faire).

consistency /kənˈsɪstənsɪ/ n (of liquids) consistance f. (of argument)

cohérence f.

consistent /kənˈsɪstənt/ adj cohérent; ~ with conforme à.

consolation /kɒnsəˈleɪʃn/ n consolation f.

consolidate /kənˈsɒlɪdeɪt/ vt/i (se) consolider.

consonant /ˈkɒnsənənt/ n consonne f.

conspicuous /kənˈspɪkjʊəs/ adj (easily seen) en évidence; (showy) voyant; (noteworthy) remarquable.

conspiracy /kənˈspɪrəsɪ/ n conspiration f.

constable /ˈkʌnstəbl/ n agent m de police, gendarme m.

constant /ˈkɒnstənt/ adj (questions) incessant; (unchanging) constant; (friend) fidèle. ● n constante f. **constantly** adv constamment.

constellation /kɒnstəˈleɪʃn/ n constellation f.

constipation /kɒnstɪˈpeɪʃn/ n constipation f.

constituency /kənˈstɪtjʊənsɪ/ n circonscription f électorale.

constituent /kənˈstɪtjʊənt/ adj constitutif. ● n élément m constitutif; (Pol) électeur/-trice m/f.

constitution /kɒnstɪˈtjuːʃn/ n constitution f.

constrain /kənˈstreɪn/ vt contraindre. **constraint** n contrainte f.

constrict /kənˈstrɪkt/ vt (flow) comprimer; (movement) gêner.

construct /kənˈstrʌkt/ vt construire. **construction** n construction f. **constructive** adj constructif.

consulate /ˈkɒnsjʊlət/ n consulat m.

consult /kənˈsʌlt/ vt consulter. ● vi ~ with conférer avec. **consultant** n conseiller/-ère m/f. (Med) spécialiste m/f. **consultation** n consultation f.

consume /kən'sju:m/ vt consommer; (destroy) consumer. **consumer** n consommateur/-trice m/f.

consummate /'kɒnsəmeɪt/ vt consommer.

consumption /kən'sʌmpʃn/ n consommation f; (Med) phtisie f.

contact /'kɒntækt/ n contact m; (person) relation f. ● vt contacter. ~ **lenses** npl lentilles fpl (de contact).

contagious /kən'teɪdʒəs/ adj contagieux.

contain /kən'teɪn/ vt contenir; ~ oneself se contenir. **container** n récipient m. (for transport) container m.

contaminate /kən'tæmɪneɪt/ vt contaminer.

contemplate /'kɒntəmpleɪt/ vt (gaze at) contempler; (think about) envisager.

contemporary /kən'temprərɪ/ adj & n contemporain/-e (m/f).

contempt /kən'tempt/ n mépris m. **contemptible** adj méprisable. **contemptuous** adj méprisant.

contend /kən'tend/ vt soutenir. ● vi ~ with (compete) rivaliser avec; (face) faire face à. **contender** n adversaire mf.

content¹ /'kɒntent/ n (of letter) contenu m. (amount) teneur f; ~s contenu m.

content² /kən'tent/ adj satisfait. ● vt contenter. **contented** adj satisfait. **contentment** n contentement m.

contest¹ /'kɒntest/ n (competition) concours m. (struggle) lutte f.

contest² /kən'test/ vt contester; (compete for or in) disputer. **contestant** n concurrent/-e m/f.

context /'kɒntekst/ n contexte m.

continent /'kɒntɪnənt/ n continent m; the C ~ l'Europe f (continentale). **continental** adj continental, européen. **continental quilt** n couette f.

contingency /kən'tɪndʒənsɪ/ n éventualité f. ~ **plan** plan m d'urgence.

continual /kən'tɪnjʊəl/ adj continuel.

continuation /kəntɪnjʊ'eɪʃn/ n continuation f. (after interruption) reprise f; (new episode) suite f.

continue /kən'tɪnju:/ vt/i continuer; (resume) reprendre. **continued** adj continu.

continuous /kən'tɪnjʊəs/ adj continu. **continuously** adv (without a break) sans interruption; (repeatedly) continuellement.

contort /kən'tɔːt/ vt tordre; ~ oneself se contorsionner.

contour /'kɒntʊə(r)/ n contour m.

contraband /'kɒntrəbænd/ n contrebande f.

contraception /kɒntrə'sepʃn/ n contraception f. **contraceptive** adj & n contraceptif (m).

contract¹ /'kɒntrækt/ n contrat m.

contract² /kən'trækt/ vt/i (se) contracter. **contraction** n contraction f.

contractor /kən'træktə(r)/ n entrepreneur/-euse m/f.

contradict /kɒntrə'dɪkt/ vt contredire. **contradictory** adj contradictoire.

contrary¹ /'kɒntrərɪ/ adj contraire (to à). on the ~ au contraire. ● adv ~ to contrairement à.

contrary² /kən'treərɪ/ adj entêté.

contrast¹ /'kɒntrɑːst/ n contraste m.

contrast² /kən'trɑːst/ vt/i contraster.

contravention /kɒntrə'venʃn/ n

infraction *f.*

contribute /kənˈtrɪbjuːt/ *vt* donner. ● *vi* ~ to contribuer à; (take part) participer à; (newspaper) collaborer à. **contribution** *n* contribution *f.* **contributor** *n* collaborateur/-trice *m/f.*

contrive /kənˈtraɪv/ *vt* imaginer; ~ to do trouver moyen de faire.

control /kənˈtrəʊl/ *vt* (*pt* **controlled**) (*firm*) diriger; (check) contrôler; (restrain) maîtriser. ● *n* contrôle *m.* (mastery) maîtrise *f.* ~s commandes *fpl.* (knobs) boutons *mpl*; have under ~ (event) avoir en main; in ~ of maître de. ~ **tower** *n* tour *f* de contrôle.

controversial /kɒntrəˈvɜːʃl/ *adj* discutable, discuté. **controversy** *n* controverse *f.*

conurbation /kɒnɜːˈbeɪʃn/ *n* agglomération *f.* conurbation *f.*

convalesce /kɒnvəˈles/ *vi* être en convalescence.

convene /kənˈviːn/ *vt* convoquer. ● *vi* se réunir.

convenience /kənˈviːnɪəns/ *n* commodité *f.* ~s toilettes *fpl.* all modern ~s tout le confort moderne; at your ~ quand cela vous conviendra, à votre convenance. ~ **foods** *npl* plats *mpl* tout préparés.

convenient /kənˈviːnɪənt/ *adj* commode, pratique; (time) bien choisi; be ~ **for** convenir à.

convent /ˈkɒnvənt/ *n* couvent *m.*

convention /kənˈvenʃn/ *n* (assembly, agreement) convention *f.* (custom) usage *m.* **conventional** *adj* conventionnel.

conversation /kɒnvəˈseɪʃn/ *n* conversation *f.* **conversational** *adj* (tone) de la conversation; (French) de tous les jours.

converse[1] /kənˈvɜːs/ *vi* s'entretenir, converser (with avec).

converse[2] /ˈkɒnvɜːs/ *adj* & *n* inverse (*m*). **conversely** *adv* inversement.

conversion /kənˈvɜːʃn/ *n* conversion *f.*

convert[1] /kənˈvɜːt/ *vt* convertir; (house) aménager. ● *vi* ~ **into** se transformer en.

convert[2] /ˈkɒnvɜːt/ *n* converti/-e *m/f.*

convertible /kənˈvɜːtəbl/ *adj* convertible. ● *n* (car) décapotable *f.*

convey /kənˈveɪ/ *vt* (wishes, order) transmettre; (goods, people) transporter; (idea, feeling) communiquer. **conveyor belt** *n* tapis *m* roulant.

convict[1] /kənˈvɪkt/ *vt* déclarer coupable.

convict[2] /ˈkɒnvɪkt/ *n* prisonnier/-ière *m/f.*

conviction /kənˈvɪkʃn/ *n* (Jur) condamnation *f.* (opinion) conviction *f.*

convince /kənˈvɪns/ *vt* convaincre.

convoke /kənˈvəʊk/ *vt* convoquer.

convoy /ˈkɒnvɔɪ/ *n* convoi *m.*

convulse /kənˈvʌls/ *vt* convulser; (fig) bouleverser; be ~d with laughter se tordre de rire.

cook /kʊk/ *vt/i* (faire) cuire; (of person) faire la cuisine; ~ up 🄸 fabriquer. ● *n* cuisinier/-ière *m/f.* **cooker** *n* (stove) cuisinière *f.* **cookery** *n* cuisine *f.*

cookie /ˈkʊkɪ/ *n* (US) biscuit *m.*

cooking /ˈkʊkɪŋ/ *n* cuisine *f.* ● *adj* de cuisine.

cool /kuːl/ *adj* frais; (calm) calme; (unfriendly) froid. ● *n* fraîcheur *f.* (calmness 🄳) sang-froid *m*; in the ~ au frais. ● *vt/i* rafraîchir. ~ **box** *n* glacière *f.*

coolly /ˈkuːllɪ/ *adv* calmement, froidement.

coop /ku:p/ n poulailler m. ● vt ~ up enfermer.

cooperate /kəʊˈɒpəreɪt/ vi coopérer. **co-operation** n coopération f.

cooperative /kəʊˈɒpərətɪv/ adj coopératif. ● n coopérative f.

coordinate /kəʊˈɔːdɪnət/ vt coordonner.

cop /kɒp/ vt (pt copped) piquer. ● n (policeman) 🄸 flic m. ~ out 🄸 se dérober.

cope /kəʊp/ vi s'en sortir 🄸, se débrouiller; ~ with (problem) faire face à.

copper /ˈkɒpə(r)/ n cuivre m. (coin) sou m; 🄸 flic m. ● adj de cuivre.

copulate /ˈkɒpjʊleɪt/ vi s'accoupler.

copy /ˈkɒpɪ/ n copie f. (of book, newspaper) exemplaire m; (print: Photo) épreuve f. ● vt/i copier.

copyright /ˈkɒpɪraɪt/ n droit m d'auteur, copyright m.

copy-writer n rédacteur-concepteur m, rédactrice-conceptrice f.

cord /kɔːd/ n (petite) corde f; (of curtain, pyjamas) cordon m; (Electr) cordon m électrique; (fabric) velours m côtelé.

cordial /ˈkɔːdɪəl/ adj cordial. ● n (drink) sirop m.

corduroy /ˈkɔːdərɔɪ/ n velours m côtelé.

core /kɔː(r)/ n (of apple) trognon m; (of problem) cœur m; (Tech) noyau m. ● vt (apple) évider.

cork /kɔːk/ n liège m. (for bottle) bouchon m. ● vt boucher. **cork-screw** n tire-bouchon m.

corn /kɔːn/ n blé m. (maize: US) maïs m; (seed) grain m; (hard skin) cor m.

cornea /ˈkɔːnɪə/ n cornée f.

corner /ˈkɔːnə(r)/ n coin m; (bend in road) virage m; (football) corner m. ● vt coincer, acculer; (market) accaparer. ● vi prendre un virage.

cornflour /ˈkɔːnflaʊə(r)/ n farine f de maïs.

cornice /ˈkɔːnɪs/ n corniche f.

corny /ˈkɔːnɪ/ adj (-ier, -iest) (joke) éculé.

corollary /kəˈrɒlərɪ/ n corollaire m.

coronary /ˈkɒrənrɪ/ n infarctus m.

coronation /kɒrəˈneɪʃn/ n couronnement m.

corporal /ˈkɔːpərəl/ n caporal m. ~**punishment** n châtiment m corporel.

corporate /ˈkɔːpərət/ adj (ownership) en commun; (body) constitué.

corporation /kɔːpəˈreɪʃn/ n (Comm) société f.

corpse /kɔːps/ n cadavre m.

corpuscle /ˈkɔːpʌsl/ n globule m.

correct /kəˈrekt/ adj (right) exact, juste, correct; (proper) correct; you are ~ vous avez raison. ● vt corriger.

correction /kəˈrekʃn/ n correction f.

correlate /ˈkɒrəleɪt/ vt/i (faire) correspondre.

correspond /kɒrɪˈspɒnd/ vi correspondre. **correspondence** n correspondance f.

corridor /ˈkɒrɪdɔː(r)/ n couloir m.

corrode /kəˈrəʊd/ vt/i (se) corroder.

corrugated /ˈkɒrəgeɪtɪd/ adj ondulé; ~ iron tôle f ondulée.

corrupt /kəˈrʌpt/ adj corrompu. ● vt corrompre. **corruption** n corruption f.

Corsica /ˈkɔːsɪkə/ n Corse f.

cosh /kɒʃ/ n matraque f. ● vt matraquer.

cosmetic /kɒzˈmetɪk/ n produit m de beauté. ● adj cosmétique; (fig, pej) superficiel. ~ **surgery** n chirurgie f esthétique

cosmopolitan /kɒzməˈpɒlɪtn/ adj & n cosmopolite (mf).

cosmos /ˈkɒzmɒs/ n cosmos m.

cost /kɒst/ vt (pt cost) coûter. (pt costed) établir le prix de. ~s (Jur) dépens mpl. at all ~s à tout prix; to one's ~ à ses dépens; ~ **price** prix m de revient; ~ **of living** coût m de la vie. ~**-effective** adj rentable.

costly /ˈkɒstlɪ/ adj (-ier, -iest) coûteux; (valuable) précieux.

costume /ˈkɒstjuːm/ n costume m. (for swimming) maillot m. ~ **jewellery** npl bijoux mpl de fantaisie.

cosy /ˈkəʊzɪ/ adj (-ier, -iest) confortable, intime.

cot /kɒt/ n lit m d'enfant; (camp-bed: US) lit m de camp.

cottage /ˈkɒtɪdʒ/ n petite maison f de campagne; (thatched) chaumière f. ~ **pie** n hachis m Parmentier.

cotton /ˈkɒtn/ n coton m. (for sewing) fil m (à coudre). ● vi ~ **on** 🅱 piger. ~ **wool** n coton m hydrophile.

couch /kaʊtʃ/ n canapé m. ● vt (express) formuler.

cough /kɒf/ vi tousser. ● n toux f. ~ **up** 🅱 cracher, payer.

could /kʊd/ →CAN¹.

couldn't →COULD NOT.

council /ˈkaʊnsl/ n conseil m. ~ **house** n maison f louée par la municipalité, ≈ H.L.M. m or f.

councillor /ˈkaʊnsələ(r)/ n conseiller/-ère m/f municipal/-e.

counsel /ˈkaʊnsl/ n conseil m. n inv (Jur) avocat/-e m/f. **counsellor** n conseiller/-ère m/f.

count /kaʊnt/ vt/i compter. ● n (numerical record) décompte m. (nobleman) comte m. ~ **on** compter sur.

counter /ˈkaʊntə(r)/ n comptoir m. (in bank) guichet m; (token) jeton m. ● adv ~ **to** à l'encontre de. ● adj opposé. ● vt opposer; (blow) parer. ● vi riposter.

counteract /kaʊntəˈrækt/ vt neutraliser.

counterbalance /ˈkaʊntəbæləns/ n contrepoids m. ● vt contrebalancer.

counterfeit /ˈkaʊntəfɪt/ adj & n faux (m). ● vt contrefaire.

counterfoil /ˈkaʊntəfɔɪl/ n souche f.

counter-productive /kaʊntəprəˈdʌktɪv/ adj qui produit l'effet contraire.

countess /ˈkaʊntɪs/ n comtesse f.

countless /ˈkaʊntlɪs/ adj innombrable.

country /ˈkʌntrɪ/ n (land, region) pays m. (homeland) patrie f; (countryside) campagne f.

countryman /ˈkʌntrɪmən/ n (pl -men) campagnard m; (fellow citizen) compatriote m.

countryside /ˈkʌntrɪsaɪd/ n campagne f.

county /ˈkaʊntɪ/ n comté m.

coup /kuː/ n (achievement) joli coup m. (Pol) coup m d'état.

couple /ˈkʌpl/ n (people, animals) couple m. a ~ **of** (two or three) deux ou trois. ● vt/i (s')accoupler.

coupon /ˈkuːpɒn/ n coupon m; (for shopping) bon m or coupon m de réduction.

courage /ˈkʌrɪdʒ/ n courage m.

courgette /kʊəˈʒet/ n courgette f.

courier /ˈkʊrɪə(r)/ n messager/-ère m/f; (for tourists) guide m.

course /kɔːs/ n course m; (for training) stage m; (series) série f; (Culin) plat m; (for golf) terrain m; (at sea) itinéraire m. change ~ changer de cap; ~ (of action) façon f de faire; during the ~ of pendant; in due ~ en temps utile; of ~ bien sûr.

court /kɔːt/ n cour f; (tennis) court m; go to ~ aller devant les tribunaux. ● vt faire la cour à; (danger) rechercher.

courteous /ˈkɜːtɪəs/ adj courtois.

courtesy /ˈkɜːtəsɪ/ n courtoisie f; by ~ of avec la permission de.

courthouse /ˈkɔːthaʊs/ n (US) palais m de justice.

court-martial vt (pt -martialled) faire passer en conseil de guerre. ● n cour f martiale.

court: ~room n salle f de tribunal. ~shoe n escarpin m. ~yard n cour f.

cousin /ˈkʌzn/ n cousin/-e m/f. first ~ cousin/-e m/f germain/-e.

cove /kəʊv/ n anse f, crique f.

covenant /ˈkʌvənənt/ n convention f.

cover /ˈkʌvə(r)/ vt couvrir. ● n (for bed, book) couverture f. (lid) couvercle m; (for furniture) housse f; (shelter) abri m; take ~ se mettre à l'abri. ~ up cacher; (crime) couvrir; ~up for couvrir.

coverage /ˈkʌvərɪdʒ/ n reportage m.

covering /ˈkʌvərɪŋ/ n enveloppe f. ~ letter lettre f d'accompagnement.

covert /ˈkʌvət/ adj (activity) secret; (threat) voilé; (look) dérobé.

cover-up n opération f de camouflage.

cow /kaʊ/ n vache f.

coward /ˈkaʊəd/ n lâche mf.

cowboy /ˈkaʊbɔɪ/ n cow-boy m.

cowshed /ˈkaʊʃed/ n étable f.

coy /kɔɪ/ adj (faussement) timide, qui fait le or la timide.

cozy US =cosy.

crab /kræb/ n crabe m. ~-apple n pomme f sauvage.

crack /kræk/ n fente f; (in glass) fêlure f; (noise) craquement m; (joke 🟦) plaisanterie f. ● adj 🔢 d'élite. ● vt/i (break partially) (se) fêler; (split) (se) fendre; (nut) casser; (joke) raconter; (problem) résoudre; get ~ing 🔢 s'y mettre. ~ down on 🔢 sévir contre. ~ up 🔢 craquer.

cracker /ˈkrækə(r)/ n (Culin) biscuit m (salé); (for Christmas) diablotin f.

crackle /ˈkrækl/ vi crépiter. ● n crépitement m.

cradle /ˈkreɪdl/ n berceau m. ● vt bercer.

craft /krɑːft/ n métier m artisanal; (technique) art m; (boat) bateau m.

craftsman (n pl -men) artisan m.

craftsmanship n art m.

crafty /ˈkrɑːftɪ/ adj (-ier, -iest) rusé.

crag /kræg/ n rocher m à pic.

cram /kræm/ vt/i (pt crammed). (for an exam) bachoter (for pour;) ~ into (pack) s'entasser dans; ~ with (fill) bourrer de.

cramp /kræmp/ n crampe f.

cramped /kræmpt/ adj à l'étroit.

cranberry /ˈkrænbərɪ/ n canneberge f.

crane /kreɪn/ n grue f. ● vt (neck) tendre.

crank /kræŋk/ n excentrique mf. (Tech) manivelle f.

crap /kræp/ n (nonsense 🟦) conneries fpl 🟦; (faeces 🟦) merde f 🟦.

crash /kræʃ/ n accident m; (noise) fracas m; (of thunder) coup m; (of

crate | crinkle

firm) faillite f. ● vt/i avoir un accident (avec); (of plane) s'écraser; (two vehicles) se percuter; ~ **into** rentrer dans. ~ **course** n cours m intensif. ~**-helmet** n casque m (anti-choc). ~**-land** vi atterrir en catastrophe.

crate /kreɪt/ n cageot m.

cravat /krə'væt/ n foulard m.

crave /kreɪv/ vt/i ~ **for** désirer ardemment. **craving** n envie f irrésistible.

crawl /krɔːl/ vi (insect) ramper; (vehicle) se traîner; be ~**ing with** grouiller de. ● n (pace) pas m; (swimming) crawl m.

crayfish /'kreɪfɪʃ/ n inv écrevisse f.

crayon /'kreɪən/ n craie f grasse.

craze /kreɪz/ n engouement m.

crazy /'kreɪzi/ adj (-ier, -iest) fou; ~ **about** (person) fou de; (thing) fana or fou de.

creak /kriːk/ n grincement m. ● vi grincer.

cream /kriːm/ n crème f. ● adj crème inv. ● vt écrémer.

crease /kriːs/ n pli m. ● vt/i (se) froisser.

create /kriːˈeɪt/ vt créer. **creation** n création f. **creative** adj (person) créatif; (process) créateur. **creator** n créateur/-trice m/f.

creature /'kriːtʃə(r)/ n créature f.

crèche /kreʃ/ n garderie f.

credentials /krɪ'denʃlz/ npl (identity) pièces fpl d'identité; (competence) références fpl.

credibility /kredə'bɪlətɪ/ n crédibilité f.

credit /'kredɪt/ n (credence) crédit m. (honour) honneur m; **in** ~ créditeur; ~**s** (cinema) générique m. ● adj (balance) créditeur. ● vt croire; (Comm) créditer; ~ **sb with** attribuer à qn. ~ **card** n carte f de cré-

dit. ~ **note** n avoir m.

creditor /'kredɪtə(r)/ n créancier/-ière m/f.

creditworthy /'kredɪtwɜːðɪ/ adj solvable.

creed /kriːd/ n credo m.

creek /kriːk/ n (US) ruisseau m. **up the** ~ 🗵 dans le pétrin 🗵.

creep /kriːp/ vi (pt **crept**) (insect, cat) ramper; (fig) se glisser. ● n (person 🗵) pauvre type m 🗓. **give sb the** ~**s** faire frissonner qn. **creeper** n liane f.

cremate /krɪ'meɪt/ vt incinérer. **cremation** n incinération f. **crematorium** n (pl **-ia**) crématorium m.

crêpe /kreɪp/ n crêpe m. ~ **paper** n papier m crêpon.

crept /krept/ ➡CREEP.

crescent /'kresnt/ n croissant m; (of houses) rue f en demi-lune.

cress /kres/ n cresson m.

crest /krest/ n crête f. (coat of arms) armoiries fpl.

cretin /'kretɪn/ n crétin/-e m/f.

crevice /'krevɪs/ n fente f.

crew /kruː/ n (of plane, ship) équipage m; (gang) équipe f. ~ **cut** n coupe f en brosse. ~ **neck** n (col) ras du cou m.

crib /krɪb/ n lit m d'enfant. ● vt/i (pt **cribbed**) copier.

cricket /'krɪkɪt/ n (Sport) cricket m. (insect) grillon m.

crime /kraɪm/ n crime m; (minor) délit m; (acts) criminalité f.

criminal /'krɪmɪnl/ adj & n criminel/-le (m/f).

crimson /'krɪmzn/ adj & n cramoisi (m).

cringe /krɪndʒ/ vi reculer; (fig) s'humilier.

crinkle /'krɪŋkl/ vt/i (cloth) (se)

froisser. ● n pli m.

cripple /'krɪpl/ n infirme mf. ● vt estropier; (fig) paralyser.

crisis /'kraɪsɪs/ n (pl **crises**) crise f.

crisp /krɪsp/ adj (Culin) croquant; (air, reply) vif. **crisps** npl chips fpl.

criss-cross /'krɪskrɒs/ adj entrecroisé. ● vt/i (s')entrecroiser.

criterion /kraɪ'tɪərɪən/ n (pl **-ia**) critère m.

critic /'krɪtɪk/ n critique m. **critical** adj critique. **critically** adv d'une manière critique; (ill) gravement.

criticism /'krɪtɪsɪzəm/ n critique f.

criticize /'krɪtɪsaɪz/ vt/i critiquer.

croak /krəʊk/ n (bird) croassement m; (frog) coassement m. ● vi croasser; coasser.

Croatia /krəʊ'eɪʃə/ n Croatie f.

Croatian /krəʊ'eɪʃn/ n Croate mf. ● adj Croate.

crochet /'krəʊʃeɪ/ n crochet m. ● vt faire du crochet.

crockery /'krɒkərɪ/ n vaisselle f.

crocodile /'krɒkədaɪl/ n crocodile m.

crook /krʊk/ n (criminal 🆃) escroc m; (stick) houlette f.

crooked /'krʊkɪd/ adj tordu; (winding) tortueux; (askew) de travers; (dishonest: fig) malhonnête.

crop /krɒp/ n récolte f; (fig) quantité f. ● vt (pt **cropped**) couper. ● vi ~ up se présenter.

cross /krɒs/ n croix f; (hybrid) hybride m. ● vt/i traverser; (legs, animals) croiser; (cheque) barrer; (paths) se croiser; ~ sb's mind venir à l'esprit de qn. ● adj en colère, fâché (with contre). talk at ~ purposes parler sans se comprendre. □ ~ off ou out rayer. ~-check vt vérifier (pour confirmer). ~-country (running) n cross m.

~-examine vt faire subir un contre-interrogatoire à. ~-eyed adj be ~-eyed loucher. ~fire n feux mpl croisés.

crossing /'krɒsɪŋ/ n (by boat) traversée f; (on road) passage m clouté.

crossly /'krɒslɪ/ adv avec colère.

cross: ~-reference n renvoi m. ~roads n carrefour m. ~word n mots mpl croisés.

crotch /krɒtʃ/ n (of garment) entrejambes m inv.

crouch /kraʊtʃ/ vi s'accroupir.

crow /krəʊ/ n corbeau m; as the ~ flies à vol d'oiseau. ● vi (of cock) chanter; (fig) jubiler. ~bar n pied-de-biche m.

crowd /kraʊd/ n foule f. **crowded** adj plein.

crown /kraʊn/ n couronne f; (top part) sommet m. ● vt couronner.

Crown Court n Cour f d'assises.

crucial /'kruːʃl/ adj crucial.

crucifix /'kruːsɪfɪks/ n crucifix m.

crucify /'kruːsɪfaɪ/ vt crucifier.

crude /kruːd/ adj (raw) brut; (rough, vulgar) grossier.

cruel /'kruːəl/ adj (**crueller, cruellest**) cruel.

cruise /kruːz/ n croisière f. ● vi (ship) croiser; (tourists) faire une croisière; (vehicle) rouler; **cruising speed** vitesse f de croisière.

crumb /krʌm/ n miette f.

crumble /'krʌmbl/ vt/i (s')effriter; (bread) (s')émietter; (collapse) s'écrouler.

crumple /'krʌmpl/ vt/i (se) froisser.

crunch /krʌntʃ/ vt croquer. ● n (event) moment m critique; when it comes to the ~ quand ça devient sérieux.

crusade /kruːˈseɪd/ n croisade f.
crusader n (knight) croisé m; (fig)
militant/-e m/f.

crush /krʌʃ/ vt écraser; (clothes)
froisser. ● n (crowd) presse f; a ~
on ▨ le béguin pour.

crust /krʌst/ n croûte f. **crusty** adj
croustillant.

crutch /krʌtʃ/ n béquille f; (crotch)
entrejambes m inv.

crux /krʌks/ n the ~ of (problem)
le point crucial de.

cry /kraɪ/ n cri m. ● vi (weep) pleurer; (call out) crier. □ ~ **off** se décommander.

crying /ˈkraɪɪŋ/ adj (need) urgent;
a ~ shame une vraie honte. ● n
pleurs mpl.

cryptic /ˈkrɪptɪk/ adj énigmatique.

crystal /ˈkrɪstl/ n cristal m.
~**-clear** adj parfaitement clair.

cub /kʌb/ n petit m; Cub (Scout)
louveteau m.

Cuba /ˈkjuːbə/ n Cuba f.

cube /kjuːb/ n cube m. **cubic** adj
cubique; (metre) cube.

cubicle /ˈkjuːbɪkl/ n (in room,
hospital) box m; (at swimming-pool) cabine f.

cuckoo /ˈkʊkuː/ n coucou m.

cucumber /ˈkjuːkʌmbə(r)/ n concombre m.

cuddle /ˈkʌdl/ vt câliner. ● vi (kiss
and) ~ s'embrasser. ● n caresse f.
cuddly adj câlin; **cuddly toy** peluche f.

cue /kjuː/ n signal m; (Theat) réplique f; (billiards) queue f.

cuff /kʌf/ n manchette f; (US: on
trousers) revers m; off the ~ im-
promptu. ● vt gifler. ~**-link** n bouton m de manchette.

cul-de-sac /ˈkʌldəsæk/ n (pl **culs-**

de-sac) impasse f.

cull /kʌl/ vt (select) choisir; (kill)
massacrer.

culminate /ˈkʌlmɪneɪt/ vi ~ in se
terminer par. **culmination** point
m culminant.

culprit /ˈkʌlprɪt/ n coupable mf.

cult /kʌlt/ n culte m.

cultivate /ˈkʌltɪveɪt/ vt cultiver.
cultivation n culture f.

cultural /ˈkʌltʃərəl/ adj culturel.

culture /ˈkʌltʃə(r)/ n culture f. **cul-
tured** adj cultivé.

cumbersome /ˈkʌmbəsəm/ adj
encombrant.

cunning /ˈkʌnɪŋ/ adj rusé. ● n astuce f, ruse f.

cup /kʌp/ n tasse f; (prize) coupe f;
Cup final finale f de la Coupe.

cupboard /ˈkʌbəd/ n placard m.

cup-tie n match m de coupe.

curate /ˈkjʊərət/ n vicaire m.

curator /kjʊəˈreɪtə(r)/ n (of museum) conservateur m.

curb /kɜːb/ n (restraint) frein m; (of
path) (US) bord m du trottoir. ● vt
(desires) refréner; (price increase)
freiner.

cure /kjʊə(r)/ vt guérir; (fig) éliminer; (Culin) fumer; (in brine) saler.
● n (recovery) guérison f; (remedy)
remède m.

curfew /ˈkɜːfjuː/ n couvre-feu m.

curiosity /kjʊərɪˈɒsɪtɪ/ n curiosité
f. **curious** adj curieux.

curl /kɜːl/ vt/i (hair) boucler. ● n
boucle f. □ ~**up** se pelotonner;
(shrivel) se racornir.

curler /ˈkɜːlə(r)/ n bigoudi m.

curly /ˈkɜːlɪ/ adj (-ier, -iest) bouclé.

currant /ˈkʌrənt/ n raisin m de Co-
rinthe.

currency /ˈkʌrənsɪ/ n (money)

monnaie f; (of word) fréquence f;
foreign ~ devises fpl étrangères.

current /'kʌrənt/ adj (term, word)
usité; (topical) actuel; (year) en
cours. ● n courant m. ~ **account** n
compte m courant. ~ **events** npl
l'actualité f.

currently /'kʌrəntlɪ/ adv actuel-
lement.

curriculum /kə'rɪkjʊləm/ n (pl
-la) programme m scolaire. ~ **vitae**
n curriculum vitae m.

curry /'kʌrɪ/ n curry m. ● vt favour with chercher les bonnes grâces de.

curse /kɜːs/ n (spell) malédiction f;
(swearword) juron m. ● vt maudire.
● vi (swear) jurer.

cursor /'kɜːsə(r)/ n curseur m.

curt /kɜːt/ adj brusque.

curtain /'kɜːtn/ n rideau m.

curve /kɜːv/ n courbe f. ● vi (line)
s'incurver; (edge) se recourber;
(road) faire une courbe. ● vt
courber.

cushion /'kʊʃn/ n coussin m. ● vt
(a blow) amortir; (fig) protéger.

custard /'kʌstəd/ n crème f anglaise; (set) flan m.

custody /'kʌstədɪ/ n (of child)
garde f; (Jur) détention f préventive.

custom /'kʌstəm/ n coutume f;
(patronage: Comm) clientèle f. **customary** adj habituel.

customer /'kʌstəmə(r)/ n client/-e
m/f; (person 🄸) type m.

customize /'kʌstəmaɪz/ vt person-
naliser.

custom-made adj fait sur
mesure.

customs /'kʌstəmz/ npl douane f.
● adj douanier. ~ **officer** n douanier m.

cut /kʌt/ vt/i (pt cut, pres p cutting)

vt couper; (hedge) tailler; (prices) réduire. ● vi couper. ● n (wound) coupure f; (of clothes) coupe f; (in surgery) incision f; (share) part f; (in
prices) réduction f. □ ~ **back** vi
faire des économies. vt réduire. ~
down (on) réduire. ~ **in** (in conversation) intervenir. ~ **off** couper;
(tide, army) isoler; ~ **out** vt découper; (leave out) supprimer; vi (engine) s'arrêter. ~ **short** (visit)
écourter. ~ **up** couper; (carve) découper.

cutback /'kʌtbæk/ n réduction f.

cute /kjuːt/ adj 🄸 mignon.

cutlery /'kʌtlərɪ/ n couverts mpl.

cutlet /'kʌtlɪt/ n côtelette f.

cut-price adj à prix réduit.

cutting /'kʌtɪŋ/ adj cinglant. ● n
(from newspaper) coupure f; (plant)
bouture f.

CV abbr ➞CURRICULUM VITAE.

cyanide /'saɪənaɪd/ n cyanure m.

cyberspace /'saɪbəspeɪs/ n cyberspace m.

cycle /'saɪbəspeɪs/ n cycle m; (bicycle) vélo m. ● vi aller à vélo.

cycling /'saɪklɪŋ/ n cyclisme m. ~
shorts npl cycliste m.

cyclist /'saɪklɪst/ n cycliste mf.

cylinder /'sɪlɪndə(r)/ n cylindre m.

cymbal /'sɪmbl/ n cymbale f.

cynic /'sɪnɪk/ n cynique mf. **cynical**
adj cynique. **cynicism** n cynisme m.

cypress /'saɪprəs/ n cyprès m.

Cypriot /'sɪprɪət/ n Cypriote mf.
● adj cypriote.

Cyprus /'saɪprəs/ n Chypre f.

cyst /sɪst/ n kyste m.

czar /zɑː(r)/ n tsar m.

Czech /tʃek/ n (person) Tchèque mf;
(Ling) tchèque m. ~ **Republic** n République f tchèque.

Dd

dab /dæb/ vt (pt **dabbed**) tamponner; ~ sth on appliquer qch par petites touches. ● n touche f.

dabble /'dæbl/ vi ~ in sth faire qch en amateur.

dad /dæd/ n ① papa m. **daddy** n ① papa m.

daffodil /'dæfədɪl/ n jonquille f.

daft /dɑːft/ adj bête.

dagger /'dægə(r)/ n poignard m.

>
> **Dáil Éireann** Ces mots de gaélique irlandais, que l'on prononce /dɔɪl 'ɜː(ə)n/ désignent la Chambre des représentants au parlement de la République d'Irlande. Les 166 députés qui la composent représentent 42 circonscriptions électorales et sont élus par un système de scrutin à la représentation proportionnelle pour cinq ans.

daily /'deɪlɪ/ adj quotidien. ● adv tous les jours. ● n (newspaper) quotidien m.

dainty /'deɪntɪ/ adj (**-ier, -iest**) (lace, food) délicat; (shoe, hand) mignon.

dairy /'deərɪ/ n (on farm) laiterie f; (shop) crèmerie f. ● adj (farm, cow, product) laitier; (butter) fermier.

daisy /'deɪzɪ/ n pâquerette f.

dam /dæm/ n barrage m.

damage /'dæmɪdʒ/ n (to property) dégâts mpl; (Med) lésions fpl; to do sth ~ (cause, trade) porter atteinte à; ~s (Jur) dommages-intérêts mpl. ● vt (property) endommager; (health) nuire à; (reputation) porter atteinte à. **damaging** adj (to health) nuisible; (to reputation) préjudiciable.

damn /dæm/ vt (Relig) damner; (condemn: fig) condamner. ● interj ① zut ①, merde 图. ● vt not give/care a ~ about se ficher de ①. ● adj fichu ①. ● adv franchement.

damp /dæmp/ n humidité f. ● adj humide. **dampen** vt (lit) humecter; (fig) refroidir. **dampness** n humidité f.

dance /dɑːns/ vt/i danser. ● n danse f; (gathering) bal m; ~ hall dancing m. **dancer** n danseur/-euse m/f.

dandelion /'dændɪlaɪən/ n pissenlit m.

dandruff /'dændrʌf/ n pellicules fpl.

Dane /deɪn/ n Danois/-e m/f.

danger /'deɪndʒə(r)/ n danger m; (risk) risque m; **be in** ~ of risquer de. **dangerous** adj dangereux.

dangle /'dæŋgl/ vt (object) balancer; (legs) laisser pendre. ● vi (object) se balancer (from à).

Danish /'deɪnɪʃ/ n (Ling) danois m. ● adj danois.

dare /deə(r)/ vt oser ((to) do faire). ~ **sb to do** défier qn de faire. ● n défi m. **daring** adj audacieux.

dark /dɑːk/ adj (day, colour, suit, mood, warning) sombre; (hair, eyes, skin) brun; (secret, thought) noir. ● n noir m; (nightfall) tombée f de la nuit; **in the** ~ (fig) dans le noir. **darken** vt/i (sky) (s')obscurcir; (mood) (s')assombrir. **darkness** n obscurité f. ~-**room** n chambre f noire.

darling /'dɑːlɪŋ/ adj & n chéri/-e (m/f).

dart /dɑːt/ n fléchette f; ~**s** (game) fléchettes fpl. ● vi ~ **in/away**

entrer/filer comme une flèche.

dash /dæʃ/ vi se précipiter; ~ off se sauver. ● vt (hope) anéantir; ~ sth against projeter qch contre. ● n course f folle; (of liquid) goutte f; (of colour) touche f; (in punctuation) tiret m.

dashboard /'dæʃbɔːd/ n tableau m de bord.

data /'deɪtə/ npl données fpl. ~base n base f de données. ~ capture n saisie f de données. ~ processing n traitement m des données. ~ protection n protection f de l'information.

date /deɪt/ n date f; (meeting) rendezvous m; (fruit) datte f; out of ~ (old-fashioned) démodé; (passport) périmé; to ~ à ce jour; up to ~ (modern) moderne; (list) à jour. ● vt/i dater; (go out with) sortir avec; ~ from dater de. **dated** adj démodé.

daughter /'dɔːtə(r)/ n fille f. ~-in-law n (pl ~s-in-law) belle-fille f.

daunt /dɔːnt/ vt décourager.

dawdle /'dɔːdl/ vi flâner, traînasser 🛈.

dawn /dɔːn/ n aube f. ● vi (day) se lever; it ~ed on me that je me suis rendu compte que.

day /deɪ/ n jour m; (whole day) journée f; (period) époque f; the ~ before la veille; the following or next ~ le lendemain. ~break n aube f.

daydream /'deɪdriːm/ n rêves mpl. ● vi rêvasser (about de).

day: ~light n jour m. ~time n journée f. ~ trader spéculateur m à la journée, scalpeur m.

daze /deɪz/ n in a ~ (from blow) étourdi; (from drug) hébété. **dazed** adj (by blow) abasourdi; (by news) ahuri.

dazzle /'dæzl/ vt éblouir.

dead /ded/ adj mort; (numb) engourdi. ● adv complètement; in ~ centre au beau milieu; stop ~ s'arrêter net. ● n the ~ of the day au cœur de; the ~ les morts. **deaden** vt (sound, blow) amortir; (pain) calmer. ~ end n impasse f. ~line n date f limite. ~lock n impasse f.

deadly /'dedlɪ/ adj (-ier, -iest) mortel; (weapon) meurtrier.

deaf /def/ adj sourd. **deafen** vt assourdir. **deafness** n surdité f.

deal /diːl/ vt (pt **dealt**) donner; (blow) porter. ● vi (trade) être en activité; ~ in être dans le commerce de. ● n affaire f; (cards) donne f; a great or good ~ beaucoup (of de). □ ~ with (handle, manage) s'occuper de; (be about) traiter de. **dealer** n marchand/-e m/f; (agent) concessionnaire m/f. **dealings** npl relations fpl.

dear /dɪə(r)/ adj cher; ~ Sir/ Madam Monsieur/Madame. ● n (my) ~ mon chéri/ma chérie m/f. ● adv cher. ● interj oh ~! oh mon Dieu!

death /deθ/ n mort f; ~ penalty peine f de mort.

debatable /dɪ'beɪtəbl/ adj discutable.

debate /dɪ'beɪt/ n (formal) débat m; (informal) discussion f. ● vt (formally) débattre de; (informally) discuter.

debit /'debɪt/ n débit m. ● adj (balance) débiteur. ● vt (pt **debited**) débiter.

debris /'debriː/ n débris mpl. (rubbish) déchets mpl.

debt /det/ n dette f; be in ~ avoir des dettes.

debug /diː'bʌg/ vt (Comput) déboguer.

decade /'dekeɪd/ n décennie f.

decadent /'dekədənt/ adj décadent.

decaffeinated /di:'kæfɪneɪtɪd/ adj décaféiné.

decay /dɪ'keɪ/ vi (vegetation) pourrir; (tooth) se carier; (fig) décliner. • n pourriture f; (of tooth) carie f; (fig) déclin m.

deceased /dɪ'si:st/ adj décédé. • n défunt/-e m/f.

deceit /dɪ'si:t/ n tromperie f. **deceitful** adj trompeur.

deceive /dɪ'si:v/ vt tromper.

December /dɪ'sembə(r)/ n décembre m.

decent /'di:snt/ adj (respectable) comme il faut; (adequate) convenable; (good) bon; (kind) gentil; (not indecent) décent. **decently** adv convenablement.

deception /dɪ'sepʃn/ n tromperie f. **deceptive** adj trompeur.

decide /dɪ'saɪd/ vt/i décider (to do de faire); (question) régler; ~ on se décider pour. **decided** adj (firm) résolu; (clear) net. **decidedly** adv nettement.

decimal /'desɪml/ adj décimal. • n décimale f; ~ point virgule f.

decipher /dɪ'saɪfə(r)/ vt déchiffrer.

decision /dɪ'sɪʒn/ n décision f.

decisive /dɪ'saɪsɪv/ adj (conclusive) décisif; (firm) décidé.

deck /dek/ n pont m; (of cards: US) jeu m; (of bus) étage m. ~-chair n chaise f longue.

declaration /deklə'reɪʃn/ n déclaration f. **declare** vt déclarer.

decline /dɪ'klaɪn/ vt/i refuser; (fall) baisser. • n (waning) déclin m; (drop) baisse f; in ~ sur le déclin.

decode /di:'kəʊd/ vt décoder.

decommission /di:kə'mɪʃn/vt (arms) mettre hors service; (reactor) démanteler.

decompose /di:kəm'pəʊz/ vt/i (se) décomposer.

decor /'deɪkɔ:(r)/ n décor m.

decorate /'dekəreɪt/ vt décorer; (room) refaire, peindre. **decoration** n décoration f. **decorative** adj décoratif.

decorator /'dekəreɪtə(r)/ n peintre m; (interior) ~ décorateur/-trice m/f.

decoy /'di:kɔɪ/ n (person, vehicle) leurre m; (for hunting) appeau m.

decrease[1] /dɪ'kri:s/ vt/i diminuer.

decrease[2] /'di:kri:s/ n diminution f.

decree /dɪ'kri:/ n (Pol, Relig) décret m; (Jur) jugement m. • vt (pt **decreed**) décréter.

decrepit /dɪ'krepɪt/ adj (building) délabré; (person) décrépit.

dedicate /'dedɪkeɪt/ vt dédier; ~ oneself to se consacrer à.

dedicated /'dedɪkeɪtɪd/ adj dévoué; ~ line (Internet) ligne f spécialisée.

dedication /dedɪ'keɪʃn/ n dévouement m; (in book) dédicace f.

deduce /dɪ'dju:s/ vt déduire.

deduct /dɪ'dʌkt/ vt déduire; (from wages) retenir.

deed /di:d/ n acte m.

deem /di:m/ vt considérer.

deep /di:p/ adj profond; (mud, carpet) épais. • adv profondément; ~ in thought absorbé dans ses pensées. **deepen** vt/i (admiration, concern) augmenter.

deep-freeze n congélateur m. • vt congeler.

deep vein thrombosis n thrombose f veineuse profonde.

deer /dɪə(r)/ n inv cerf m; (doe) biche f.

deface /dɪ'feɪs/ vt dégrader.

default /dɪˈfɔːlt/ vi (Jur) ~ (on payments) ne pas régler ses échéances. ● n (on payments) non-remboursement m; by ~ par défaut; win by ~ gagner par forfait. ● adj (Comput) par défaut.

defeat /dɪˈfiːt/ vt vaincre; (thwart) faire échouer. ● n défaite f.

defect¹ /ˈdiːfekt/ n défaut m.

defect² /dɪˈfekt/ vi faire défection; ~ to passer à.

defective /dɪˈfektɪv/ adj défectueux.

defector /dɪˈfektə(r)/ n transfuge mf.

defence /dɪˈfens/ n défense f.

defend /dɪˈfend/ vt défendre. **defendant** n (Jur) accusé/-e m/f. **defender** défenseur m.

defensive /dɪˈfensɪv/ adj défensif. ● n défensive f.

defer /dɪˈfɜː(r)/ vt (pt deferred) (postpone) reporter; (judgement) suspendre; (payment) différer.

deference /ˈdefərəns/ n déférence f. **deferential** adj déférent.

defiance /dɪˈfaɪəns/ n défi m; in ~ of contre. **defiant** adj rebelle. **defiantly** adv avec défi.

deficiency /dɪˈfɪʃənsɪ/ n insuffisance f; (fault) défaut m.

deficient /dɪˈfɪʃnt/ adj insuffisant; be ~ in manquer de.

deficit /ˈdefɪsɪt/ n déficit m.

define /dɪˈfaɪn/ vt définir.

definite /ˈdefɪnɪt/ adj (exact) précis; (obvious) net; (firm) ferme; (certain) certain. **definitely** adv certainement; (clearly) nettement.

definition /defɪˈnɪʃn/ n définition f.

deflate /dɪˈfleɪt/ vt dégonfler.

deflect /dɪˈflekt/ vt (missile) dévier; (criticism) détourner.

deforestation /diːfɒrɪˈsteɪʃn/ n déforestation f.

deform /dɪˈfɔːm/ vt déformer.

defraud /dɪˈfrɔːd/ vt (client, employer) escroquer; (state, customs) frauder; ~ sb of sth escroquer qch à qn.

defrost /diːˈfrɒst/ vt dégivrer.

deft /deft/ adj adroit.

defunct /dɪˈfʌŋkt/ adj défunt.

defuse /diːˈfjuːz/ vt désamorcer.

defy /dɪˈfaɪ/ vt défier; (attempts) résister à.

degenerate¹ /dɪˈdʒenəreɪt/ vi dégénérer (into en).

degenerate² /dɪˈdʒenərət/ adj & n dégénéré/-e (m/f).

degrade /dɪˈɡreɪd/ vt (humiliate) humilier; (damage) dégrader.

degree /dɪˈɡriː/ n degré m; (Univ) diplôme m universitaire; (Bachelor's degree) licence f; to such a ~ that à tel point que.

dehydrate /diːˈhaɪdreɪt/ vt/i (se) déshydrater.

deign /deɪn/ vt ~ to do daigner faire.

dejected /dɪˈdʒektɪd/ adj découragé.

delay /dɪˈleɪ/ vt (flight) retarder; (decision) reporter; ~ doing attendre pour faire. ● n (of plane, post) retard m; (time lapse) délai m.

delegate¹ /ˈdelɪɡət/ n délégué /-e m/f.

delegate² /ˈdelɪɡeɪt/ vt déléguer. **delegation** n délégation f.

delete /dɪˈliːt/ vt supprimer; (Comput) effacer; (with pen) barrer. **deletion** n suppression f; (with line) rature f.

deliberate¹ /dɪˈlɪbəreɪt/ vi délibérer.

deliberate² /dɪˈlɪbərət/ adj délibéré; (*steps, manner*) mesuré. **deliberately** *adv* (*do, say*) exprès; (*sarcastically, provocatively*) délibérément.

delicacy /'delɪkəsɪ/ n délicatesse f; (*food*) mets m raffiné.

delicate /'delɪkət/ adj délicat.

delicatessen /delɪkə'tesn/ n épicerie f fine.

delicious /dɪ'lɪʃəs/ adj délicieux.

delight /dɪ'laɪt/ n joie f, plaisir m.
● vt ravir. ● vi ~ in prendre plaisir à. **delighted** adj ravi. **delightful** adj charmant/-e.

delinquent /dɪ'lɪŋkwənt/ adj & n délinquant/-e (m/f).

delirious /dɪ'lɪrɪəs/ adj délirant.

deliver /dɪ'lɪvə(r)/ vt (*message*) remettre; (*goods*) livrer; (*speech*) faire; (*baby*) mettre au monde; (*rescue*) délivrer. **delivery** n (*of goods*) livraison f; (*of mail*) distribution f; (*of baby*) accouchement m.

delude /dɪ'luːd/ vt tromper; ~ oneself se faire des illusions.

deluge /'deljuːdʒ/ n déluge m. ● vt submerger (with de).

delusion /dɪ'luːʒn/ n illusion f.

delve /delv/ vi fouiller.

demand /dɪ'mɑːnd/ vt (*request, require*) demander; (*forcefully*) exiger.
● n (*request*) demande f; (*pressure*) exigence f; in ~ très demandé; on ~ à la demande. **demanding** adj exigeant.

demean /dɪ'miːn/ vt ~ oneself s'abaisser.

demeanour, (US)**demeanor** /dɪ'miːnə(r)/ n comportement m.

demented /dɪ'mentɪd/ adj fou.

demise /dɪ'maɪz/ n disparition f.

demo /'deməʊ/ n (demonstration 🅸) manif f 🅸.

democracy /dɪ'mɒkrəsɪ/ n démocratie f.

democrat /'deməkræt/ n démocrate mf. **democratic** adj démocratique.

demolish /dɪ'mɒlɪʃ/ vt démolir.

demon /'diːmən/ n démon m.

demonstrate /'demənstreɪt/ vt démontrer; (*concern, skill*) manifester. ● vi (Pol) manifester. **demonstration** n démonstration f; (Pol) manifestation f. **demonstrative** adj démonstratif. **demonstrator** n manifestant/-e m/f.

demoralize /dɪ'mɒrəlaɪz/ vt démoraliser.

demote /diː'məʊt/ vt rétrograder.

den /den/ n (of lion) antre m; (room) tanière f.

denial /dɪ'naɪəl/ n (of rumour) démenti m; (of rights) négation f; (of request) rejet m.

denim /'denɪm/ n jean m; ~s (jeans) jean m.

Denmark /'denmɑːk/ n Danemark m.

denomination /dɪnɒmɪ'neɪʃn/ n (Relig) confession f; (money) valeur f.

denounce /dɪ'naʊns/ vt dénoncer.

dense /dens/ adj dense. **densely** adv (packed) très. **density** n densité f.

dent /dent/ n bosse f. ● vt cabosser.

dental /'dentl/ adj dentaire; ~ floss fil m dentaire; ~ surgeon chirurgien-dentiste m.

dentist /'dentɪst/ n dentiste mf. **dentistry** n médecine f dentaire.

dentures /'dentʃəz/ npl dentier m.

deny /dɪ'naɪ/ vt nier (that que); (rumour) démentir; ~ sb sth refuser qch à qn.

deodorant /diː'əʊdərənt/ n déodorant m.

depart /dɪ'pɑːt/ vi partir; ~ from

(deviate) s'éloigner de.

department /dɪˈpɑːtmənt/ n départ m; (in shop) rayon m; (in hospital, office) service m; (Univ) département m; D~ of Health ministère m de la Santé; ~ store grand magasin m.

departure /dɪˈpɑːtʃə(r)/ n départ m; a ~ from (custom, truth) une entorse à.

depend /dɪˈpend/ vi dépendre (on de). ~ on (rely on) compter sur; it (all) ~s ça dépend; ~ing on the season suivant la saison. **dependable** adj (person) digne de confiance. **dependant** n personne f à charge. **dependence** n dépendance f.

dependent /dɪˈpendənt/ adj dépendant; be ~ on dépendre de.

depict /dɪˈpɪkt/ vt (describe) dépeindre; (in picture) représenter.

deplete /dɪˈpliːt/ vt réduire.

deport /dɪˈpɔːt/ vt expulser.

depose /dɪˈpəʊz/ vt déposer.

deposit /dɪˈpɒzɪt/ vt (pt deposited) déposer. ● n (in bank) dépôt m; (on house) versement m initial; (on holiday) acompte m; (against damage) caution f; (on bottle) consigne f; (of mineral) gisement m; ~ account compte m de dépôt. **depositor** n (Comm) déposant/-e m/f.

depot /ˈdepəʊ/ n dépôt m; (US) gare f.

depreciate /dɪˈpriːʃɪeɪt/ vt/i (se) déprécier.

depress /dɪˈpres/ vt déprimer. **depressing** adj déprimant. **depression** n dépression f; (Econ) récession f.

deprivation /deprɪˈveɪʃn/ n privation f.

deprive /dɪˈpraɪv/ vt ~ of priver de. **deprived** adj démuni.

depth /depθ/ n profondeur f; (of

knowledge, ignorance) étendue f; (of colour, emotion) intensité f.

deputize /ˈdepjʊtaɪz/ vi ~ for remplacer.

deputy /ˈdepjʊtɪ/ n adjoint/-e m/f. ● adj adjoint; ~ chairman vice-président m.

derail /dɪˈreɪl/ vt faire dérailler. **derailment** n déraillement m.

deranged /dɪˈreɪndʒd/ adj dérangé.

derelict /ˈderəlɪkt/ adj abandonné.

deride /dɪˈraɪd/ vt ridiculiser. **derision** n moqueries fpl. **derisory** adj dérisoire.

derivative /dəˈrɪvətɪv/ adj & n dérivé (m).

derive /dɪˈraɪv/ vt ~ sth from tirer qch de. ● vi ~ from découler de.

derogatory /dɪˈrɒɡətrɪ/ adj (word) péjoratif; (remark) désobligeant.

descend /dɪˈsend/ vt/i descendre; be ~ed from descendre de. **descendant** n descendant/-e m/f. **descent** n descente f; (lineage) origine f.

describe /dɪˈskraɪb/ vt décrire; ~ sb as sth qualifier qn de qch. **description** n description f. **descriptive** adj descriptif.

desert¹ /ˈdezət/ n désert m.

desert² /dɪˈzɜːt/ vt/i abandonner; (cause) déserter. **deserted** adj désert. **deserter** n déserteur m.

deserts /dɪˈzɜːts/ npl get one's ~ avoir ce qu'on mérite.

deserve /dɪˈzɜːv/ vt mériter (to de). **deservedly** adv à juste titre. **deserving** adj (person) méritant; (action) louable.

design /dɪˈzaɪn/ n (sketch) plan m; (idea) conception f; (pattern) motif m; (art of designing) design m; (aim) dessein m. ● vt (sketch) dessiner;

(devise, intend) concevoir.

designate /'dezɪgneɪt/ vt désigner.

designer /dɪ'zaɪnə(r)/ n concepteur/-trice m/f; (of fashion, furniture) créateur/-trice m/f. ● adj (clothes) de haute couture; (sunglasses, drink) de dernière mode.

desirable /dɪ'zaɪərəbl/ adj (outcome) souhaitable; (person) désirable.

desire /dɪ'zaɪə(r)/ n désir m. ● vt désirer.

desk /desk/ n bureau m; (of pupil) pupitre m; (in hotel) réception f; (in bank) caisse f.

desolate /'desələt/ adj (place) désolé; (person) affligé.

despair /dɪ'speə(r)/ n désespoir m. ● vi désespérer (of de).

desperate /'despərət/ adj désespéré; (criminal) prêt à tout; be ~ for avoir désespérément besoin de. **desperately** adv désespérément; (worried) terriblement; (ill) gravement.

desperation /despə'reɪʃn/ n désespoir m; in ~ en désespoir de cause.

despicable /dɪ'spɪkəbl/ adj méprisable.

despise /dɪ'spaɪz/ vt mépriser.

despite /dɪ'spaɪt/ prep malgré.

despondent /dɪ'spɒndənt/ adj découragé.

dessert /dɪ'zɜːt/ n dessert m. ~spoon n cuillère f à dessert.

destination /destɪ'neɪʃn/ n destination f.

destiny /'destɪnɪ/ n destin m.

destitute /'destɪtjuːt/ adj sans ressources.

destroy /dɪ'strɔɪ/ vt détruire; (animal) abattre. **destroyer** n (warship) contre-torpilleur m.

destruction /dɪ'strʌkʃn/ n destruction f. **destructive** adj destructeur.

detach /dɪ'tætʃ/ vt détacher; ~ed house maison f (individuelle).

detail /'diːteɪl/ n détail m; go into ~ entrer dans les détails. ● vt (plans) exposer en détail.

detain /dɪ'teɪn/ vt retenir; (in prison) placer en détention. **detainee** n détenu/-e m/f.

detect /dɪ'tekt/ vt (error, trace) déceler; (crime, mine, sound) détecter. **detection** n détection f. **detective** n inspecteur/-trice m/f; (private) détective m.

detention /dɪ'tenʃn/ n détention f; (School) retenue f.

deter /dɪ'tɜː(r)/ vt (pt deterred) dissuader (from de).

detergent /dɪ'tɜːdʒənt/ adj & n détergent (m).

deteriorate /dɪ'tɪərɪəreɪt/ vi se détériorer.

determine /dɪ'tɜːmɪn/ vt déterminer; ~ to do résoudre de faire. **determined** adj (person) décidé; (air) résolu.

deterrent /dɪ'terənt/ n moyen m de dissuasion. ● adj (effect) dissuasif.

detest /dɪ'test/ vt détester.

detonate /'detəneɪt/ vt/i (faire) détoner. **detonation** n détonation f. **detonator** n détonateur m.

detour /'diːtʊə(r)/ n détour m.

detract /dɪ'trækt/ vi ~ from (success, value) porter atteinte à; (pleasure) diminuer.

detriment /'detrɪmənt/ n to the ~ of au détriment de. **detrimental** adj nuisible (to à).

devalue /diː'væljuː/ vt dévaluer.

devastate /'devəsteɪt/ vt (place) ravager; (person) accabler.

develop /dɪ'veləp/ vt (plan) élaborer; (*mind, body*) développer; (*land*) mettre en valeur; (*illness*) attraper; (*habit*) prendre. ● vi (*child, country, plot, business*) se développer; (*hole, crack*) se former.

development /dɪ'veləpmənt/ n développement m; (*housing*) ~ lotissement m; (new) ~ fait m nouveau.

deviate /'di:vɪeɪt/ vi dévier; ~ from (*norm*) s'écarter de.

device /dɪ'vaɪs/ n appareil m; (*means*) moyen m; (*bomb*) engin m explosif.

devil /'devl/ n diable m.

devious /'di:vɪəs/ adj (*person*) retors.

devise /dɪ'vaɪz/ vt (*scheme*) concevoir; (*product*) inventer.

devoid /dɪ'vɔɪd/ adj ~ of dépourvu de.

devolution /di:və'lu:ʃn/ n (Pol) régionalisation f.

devote /dɪ'vəʊt/ vt consacrer (to à). **devoted** adj dévoué. **devotion** n dévouement m; (Relig) dévotion f.

devour /dɪ'vaʊə(r)/ vt dévorer.

devout /dɪ'vaʊt/ adj fervent.

dew /dju:/ n rosée f.

diabetes /daɪə'bi:ti:z/ n diabète m. **diabolical** /daɪə'bɒlɪkl/ adj diabolique; (*bad* 🄸) atroce.

diagnose /'daɪəgnəʊz/ vt diagnostiquer. **diagnosis** n (pl -**oses**) diagnostic m.

diagonal /daɪ'ægənl/ adj diagonal. ● n diagonale f.

diagram /'daɪəgræm/ n schéma m.

dial /'daɪəl/ n cadran m. ● vt (pt **dialled**) (*number*) faire; (*person*) appeler; **dialling code** indicatif m; **dialling tone** tonalité f.

dialect /'daɪəlekt/ n dialecte m.

dialogue /'daɪəlɒg/ n dialogue m.

diameter /daɪ'æmɪtə(r)/ n diamètre m.

diamond /'daɪəmənd/ n diamant m; (*shape*) losange m; (*baseball*) terrain m; ~**s** (*cards*) carreau m.

diaper /'daɪəpə(r)/ n (US) couche f.

diaphragm /'daɪəfræm/ n diaphragme m.

diarrhoea, (US) **diarrhea** /daɪə'rɪə/ n diarrhée f.

diary /'daɪərɪ/ n (for appointments) agenda m; (journal) journal m intime.

dice /daɪs/ n inv dé m. ● vt (*food*) couper en dés.

dictate /dɪk'teɪt/ vt/i dicter.

dictation /dɪk'teɪʃn/ n dictée f.

dictator /dɪk'teɪtə(r)/ n dictateur m. **dictatorship** n dictature f.

dictionary /'dɪkʃənrɪ/ n dictionnaire m.

did /dɪd/ →DO.

didn't →DID NOT.

die /daɪ/ vi (pres p **dying**) mourir; (*plant*) crever; **be dying to do** mourir d'envie de faire. □ ~ **down** diminuer. ~ **out** disparaître.

diesel /'di:zl/ n gazole m; ~ **engine** moteur m diesel.

diet /'daɪət/ n (usual food) alimentation f; (restricted) régime m. ● vi être au régime. **dietary** adj alimentaire. **dietician** n diététicien/-ne m/f.

differ /'dɪfə(r)/ vi différer (from de).

difference /'dɪfrəns/ n différence f; (disagreement) différend m. **different** adj différent (from, to de).

differentiate /dɪfə'renʃɪeɪt/ vt différencier. ● vi faire la différence (between entre).

differently /'dɪfrəntlɪ/ adv différemment (from de).

difficult /'dɪfɪkəlt/ adj difficile.

difficulty n difficulté f.

diffuse¹ /dɪˈfjuːs/ adj diffus.

diffuse² /dɪˈfjuːz/ vt diffuser.

dig /dɪg/ vt/i (pt **dug**; pres p **digging**) (excavate) creuser; (in garden) bêcher. ● n (poke) coup m de coude; (remark) pique f 🔢; (Archeol) fouilles fpl. □ ~ **up** déterrer.

digest /daɪˈdʒest/ vt/i digérer. **digestible** adj digestible. **digestion** n digestion f.

digger /ˈdɪgə(r)/ n excavateur m.

digit /ˈdɪdʒɪt/ n chiffre m. ● **digitize** vt numériser.

digital /ˈdɪdʒɪtl/ adj (clock) à affichage numérique; (display, recording) numérique. ~ **audio tape** n cassette f audionumérique. ~ **camera** n appareil m photo numérique.

dignified /ˈdɪgnɪfaɪd/ adj digne.

dignitary /ˈdɪgnɪtərɪ/ n dignitaire m.

dignity /ˈdɪgnətɪ/ n dignité f.

digress /daɪˈgres/ vi faire une digression.

dilapidated /dɪˈlæpɪdeɪtɪd/ adj délabré.

dilate /daɪˈleɪt/ vt/i (se) dilater.

dilemma /daɪˈlemə/ n dilemme m.

diligent /ˈdɪlɪdʒənt/ adj appliqué.

dilute /daɪˈljuːt/ vt diluer.

dim /dɪm/ adj (**dimmer, dimmest**) (weak) faible; (dark) sombre; (indistinct) vague; 🔢 stupide. ● vt/i (pt **dimmed**) (light) baisser.

dime /daɪm/ n (US) (pièce f de) dix cents.

dimension /dɪˈmenʃn/ n dimension f.

diminish /dɪˈmɪnɪʃ/ vt/i diminuer.

dimple /ˈdɪmpl/ n fossette f.

din /dɪn/ n vacarme m.

dine /daɪn/ vi dîner. **diner** n dîneur/-euse m/f; (US) restaurant m

à service rapide.

dinghy /ˈdɪŋgɪ/ n dériveur m.

dingy /ˈdɪndʒɪ/ adj **-ier, -iest**) minable.

dining room /ˈdaɪnɪŋruːm/n salle f à manger.

dinner /ˈdɪnə(r)/ n (evening meal) dîner m; (lunch) déjeuner m; have ~ dîner. ~**jacket** n smoking m. ~ **party** n dîner m.

dinosaur /ˈdaɪnəsɔː(r)/ n dinosaure m.

dip /dɪp/ vt/i (pt **dipped**) plonger; ~ **into** (book) feuilleter; (savings) puiser dans; ~ **one's headlights** se mettre en code. ● n (slope) déclivité f; (in sea) bain m rapide.

diploma /dɪˈpləʊmə/ n diplôme m (in en).

diplomacy /dɪˈpləʊməsɪ/ n diplomatie f. **diplomat** n diplomate mf. **diplomatic** adj (Pol) diplomatique; (tactful) diplomate.

dire /daɪə(r)/ adj affreux; (need, poverty) extrême.

direct /daɪˈrekt/ adj direct. ● adv directement. ● vt diriger; (letter, remark) adresser; (a play) mettre en scène; ~ **sb** to indiquer à qn le chemin de; (order) signifier à qn de.

direction /daɪˈrekʃn/ n direction f; (Theat) mise f en scène; ~s indications fpl; ask ~s demander le chemin; ~s for use mode m d'emploi.

directly /daɪˈrektlɪ/ adv directement; (at once) tout de suite. ● conj dès que.

director /daɪˈrektə(r)/ n directeur/-trice m/f; (Theat) metteur m en scène.

directory /daɪˈrektərɪ/ n (phone book) annuaire m. ~ **enquiries** npl renseignements mpl téléphoniques.

dirt /dɜːt/ n saleté f; (earth) terre f; ~ **cheap** ⚏ très bon marché inv.

~-track n (Sport) cendrée f.

dirty /ˈdɜːtɪ/ adj (-ier, -iest) sale; (word) grossier; get ~ se salir. ● vt/ i (se) salir.

disability /dɪsəˈbɪlətɪ/ n handicap m.

disable /dɪsˈeɪbl/ vt rendre infirme. **disabled** adj handicapé.

disadvantage /dɪsədˈvɑːntɪdʒ/ n désavantage m. **disadvantaged** adj défavorisé.

disagree /dɪsəˈɡriː/ vi ne pas être d'accord (with avec). ~ with sb (food, climate) ne pas convenir à qn. **disagreement** n désaccord m; (quarrel) différend m.

disappear /dɪsəˈpɪə(r)/ vi disparaître. **disappearance** n disparition f (of de).

disappoint /dɪsəˈpɔɪnt/ vt décevoir. **disappointment** n déception f.

disapproval /dɪsəˈpruːvl/ n désapprobation f (of de).

disapprove /dɪsəˈpruːv/ vi ~ (of) désapprouver.

disarm /dɪsˈɑːm/ vt/i désarmer. **disarmament** n désarmement m.

disarray /dɪsəˈreɪ/ n désordre m.

disaster /dɪˈzɑːstə(r)/ n désastre m. **disastrous** adj désastreux.

disband /dɪsˈbænd/ vi disperser. ● vt dissoudre.

disbelief /dɪsbɪˈliːf/ n incrédulité f.

disc /dɪsk/ n disque m; (Comput) →DISK.

discard /dɪsˈkɑːd/ vt se débarrasser de; (beliefs) abandonner.

discharge /dɪsˈtʃɑːdʒ/ vt (unload) décharger; (liquid) déverser; (duty) remplir; (dismiss) renvoyer; (prisoner) libérer. ● vi (of pus) s'écouler.

disciple /dɪˈsaɪpl/ n disciple m.

disciplinary /ˈdɪsɪplɪnərɪ/ adj disciplinaire.

discipline /ˈdɪsɪplɪn/ n discipline f.

● vt discipliner; (punish) punir.

disc jockey n disc-jockey m, animateur m.

disclaimer /dɪsˈkleɪmə(r)/ n démenti m.

disclose /dɪsˈkləʊz/ vt révéler. **disclosure** n révélation f (of de).

disco /ˈdɪskəʊ/ n (club 🔔) discothèque f; (event) soirée f disco.

discolour /dɪsˈkʌlə(r)/ vt/i (se) décolorer.

discomfort /dɪsˈkʌmfət/ n gêne f.

disconcert /dɪskənˈsɜːt/ vt déconcerter.

disconnect /dɪskəˈnekt/ vt détacher; (unplug) débrancher; (cut off) couper.

discontent /dɪskənˈtent/ n mécontentement m.

discontinue /dɪskənˈtɪnjuː/ vt (service) supprimer; (production) arrêter.

discord /ˈdɪskɔːd/ n discorde f; (Mus) discordance f.

discount¹ /ˈdɪskaʊnt/ n remise f; (on minor purchase) rabais m.

discount² /dɪsˈkaʊnt/ vt (advice) ne pas tenir compte de; (possibility) écarter.

discourage /dɪˈskʌrɪdʒ/ vt décourager.

discourse /ˈdɪskɔːs/ n discours m.

discourteous /dɪsˈkɜːtɪəs/ adj peu courtois.

discover /dɪsˈkʌvə(r)/ vt découvrir. **discovery** n découverte f.

discreet /dɪsˈkriːt/ adj discret.

discrepancy /dɪsˈkrepənsɪ/ n divergence f.

discretion /dɪˈskreʃn/ n discrétion f.

discriminate /dɪˈskrɪmɪneɪt/ vt/i distinguer; ~ against faire de la discrimination contre. **discriminat-**

ing adj qui a du discernement. **discrimination** n discernement m; (bias) discrimination f.

discus /'dɪskəs/ n disque m.

discuss /dɪ'skʌs/ vt (talk about) discuter de; (in writing) examiner. **discussion** n discussion f.

disdain /dɪs'deɪn/ n dédain m.

disease /dɪ'ziːz/ n maladie f.

disembark /dɪsɪm'bɑːk/ vt/i débarquer.

disenchanted /dɪsɪn'tʃɑːntɪd/ adj désabusé.

disentangle /dɪsɪn'tæŋgl/ vt démêler.

disfigure /dɪs'fɪgə(r)/ vt défigurer.

disgrace /dɪs'greɪs/ n (shame) honte f; (disfavour) disgrâce f. ● vt déshonorer. **disgraced** adj (in disfavour) disgracié. **disgraceful** adj honteux.

disgruntled /dɪs'grʌntld/ adj mécontent.

disguise /dɪs'gaɪz/ vt déguiser. ● n déguisement m; **in ~** déguisé.

disgust /dɪs'gʌst/ n dégoût m. ● vt dégoûter.

dish /dɪʃ/ n plat m; **the ~es** (crockery) la vaisselle. ● vt ~ **out** 🆃 distribuer; ~ **up** servir.

dishcloth /'dɪʃklɒθ/ n lavette f; (for drying) torchon m.

dishearten /dɪs'hɑːtn/ vt décourager.

dishevelled /dɪ'ʃevld/ adj échevelé.

dishonest /dɪs'ɒnɪst/ adj malhonnête.

dishonour, (US) **dishonor** /dɪs'ɒnə(r)/ n déshonneur m.

dishwasher /'dɪʃwɒʃə(r)/ n lave-vaisselle m inv.

disillusion /dɪsɪ'luːʒn/ vt désabuser. **disillusionment** n désillusion f.

disincentive /dɪsɪn'sentɪv/ n be

a ~ **to** décourager.

disinclined /dɪsɪn'klaɪnd/ adj ~ **to** peu disposé à.

disinfect /dɪsɪn'fekt/ vt désinfecter. **disinfectant** n désinfectant m.

disintegrate /dɪs'ɪntɪgreɪt/ vt/i (se) désintégrer.

disinterested /dɪs'ɪntrəstɪd/ adj désintéressé.

disjointed /dɪs'dʒɔɪntɪd/ adj (talk) décousu.

disk /dɪsk/ n (US) ➡DISC; (Comput) disque m. ~ **drive** n drive m, lecteur m de disquettes.

diskette /dɪs'ket/ n disquette f.

dislike /dɪs'laɪk/ n aversion f. ● vt ne pas aimer.

dislocate /'dɪsləkeɪt/ vt (limb) disloquer.

dislodge /dɪs'lɒdʒ/ vt (move) déplacer; (drive out) déloger.

disloyal /dɪs'lɔɪəl/ adj déloyal (to envers).

dismal /'dɪzməl/ adj morne, triste.

dismantle /dɪs'mæntl/ vt démonter, défaire.

dismay /dɪs'meɪ/ n consternation f (at devant). ● vt consterner.

dismiss /dɪs'mɪs/ vt renvoyer; (appeal) rejeter; (from mind) écarter. **dismissal** n renvoi m.

dismount /dɪs'maʊnt/ vi descendre, mettre pied à terre.

disobedient /dɪsə'biːdɪənt/ adj désobéissant.

disobey /dɪsə'beɪ/ vt désobéir à. ● vi désobéir.

disorder /dɪs'ɔːdə(r)/ n désordre m; (ailment) trouble(s) m(pl). **disorderly** adj désordonné.

disorganized /dɪs'ɔːgənaɪzd/ adj désorganisé.

disown /dɪs'əʊn/ vt renier.

disparaging /dɪ'spærɪdʒɪŋ/ adj

désobligeant.

dispassionate /dɪˈspæʃənət/ adj impartial; (unemotional) calme.

dispatch /dɪˈspætʃ/ vt (send, complete) expédier; (troops) envoyer. ● n expédition f, envoi m; (report) dépêche f.

dispel /dɪˈspel/ vt (pt **dispelled**) dissiper.

dispensary /dɪˈspensərɪ/ n (in hospital) pharmacie f; (in pharmacy) officine f.

dispense /dɪˈspens/ vt distribuer; (medicine) préparer. ● vi ~ with se passer de. **dispenser** n (container) distributeur m.

disperse /dɪˈspɜːs/ vt/i (se) disperser.

display /dɪˈspleɪ/ vt montrer, exposer; (feelings) manifester. ● n exposition f; manifestation f; (Comm) étalage m; (of computer) visuel m.

displeased /dɪsˈpliːzd/ adj mécontent (with de).

disposable /dɪˈspəʊzəbl/ adj jetable.

disposal /dɪˈspəʊzl/ n (of waste) évacuation f; at sb's ~ à la disposition de qn.

dispose /dɪˈspəʊz/ vt disposer. ● vi ~ of se débarrasser de; well ~d to bien disposé envers.

disposition /dɪspəˈzɪʃn/ n disposition f; (character) naturel m.

disprove /dɪsˈpruːv/ vt réfuter.

dispute /dɪˈspjuːt/ vt contester. ● n discussion f; (Pol) conflit m; in ~ contesté.

disqualify /dɪsˈkwɒlɪfaɪ/ vt rendre inapte; (Sport) disqualifier; ~ from driving retirer le permis à.

disquiet /dɪsˈkwaɪət/ n inquiétude f. **disquieting** adj inquiétant.

disregard /dɪsrɪˈɡɑːd/ vt ne pas tenir compte de. ● n

indifférence f (for à).

disrepair /dɪsrɪˈpeə(r)/ n délabrement m.

disreputable /dɪsˈrepjʊtəbl/ adj peu recommandable.

disrepute /dɪsrɪˈpjuːt/ n discrédit m.

disrespect /dɪsrɪˈspekt/ n manque m de respect. **disrespectful** adj irrespectueux.

disrupt /dɪsˈrʌpt/ vt (disturb, break up) perturber; (plans) déranger. **disruption** n perturbation f. **disruptive** adj perturbateur.

dissatisfied /dɪˈsætɪsfaɪd/ adj mécontent.

dissect /dɪˈsekt/ vt disséquer.

disseminate /dɪˈsemɪneɪt/ vt diffuser.

dissent /dɪˈsent/ vi différer (from de). ● n dissentiment m.

dissertation /dɪsəˈteɪʃn/ n mémoire m.

disservice /dɪsˈsɜːvɪs/ n do a ~ to sb rendre un mauvais service à qn.

dissident /ˈdɪsɪdənt/ adj & n dissident/-e (m/f).

dissimilar /dɪˈsɪmɪlə(r)/ adj dissemblable, différent.

dissipate /ˈdɪsɪpeɪt/ vt/i (se) dissiper. **dissipated** adj (person) dissolu.

dissolve /dɪˈzɒlv/ vt/i (se) dissoudre.

dissuade /dɪˈsweɪd/ vt dissuader.

distance /ˈdɪstəns/ n distance f; from a ~ de loin; in the ~ au loin. **distant** adj éloigné, lointain; (relative) éloigné; (aloof) distant.

distaste /dɪsˈteɪst/ n dégoût m. **distasteful** adj désagréable.

distil /dɪsˈtɪl/ vt (pt **distilled**) distiller.

distinct /dɪsˈtɪŋkt/ adj distinct; (definite) net; as ~ from par opposition à. **distinction** n distinction f; (in exam) mention f très bien. **distinctive** adj distinctif.

distinguish /dɪˈstɪŋgwɪʃ/ vt/i distinguer.

distort /dɪˈstɔːt/ vt déformer. **distortion** n distorsion f; (of facts) déformation f.

distract /dɪˈstrækt/ vt distraire. **distracted** adj (distraught) éperdu. **distracting** adj gênant. **distraction** n (lack of attention, entertainment) distraction f.

distraught /dɪˈstrɔːt/ adj éperdu.

distress /dɪˈstres/ n douleur f; (poverty, danger) détresse f. ● vt peiner. **distressing** adj pénible.

distribute /dɪˈstrɪbjuːt/ vt distribuer.

district /ˈdɪstrɪkt/ n région f; (of town) quartier m.

distrust /dɪsˈtrʌst/ n méfiance f. ● vt se méfier de.

disturb /dɪsˈtɜːb/ vt déranger; (alarm, worry) troubler. **disturbance** n dérangement m (of de); (noise) tapage m. **disturbances** npl (Pol) troubles mpl. **disturbed** adj troublé; (psychologically) perturbé. **disturbing** adj troublant.

disused /dɪsˈjuːzd/ adj désaffecté.

ditch /dɪtʃ/ n fossé m. ● vt ⊠ abandonner.

ditto /ˈdɪtəʊ/ adv idem.

dive /daɪv/ vi plonger; (rush) se précipiter. ● n plongeon m; (of plane) piqué m; (place ⊠) bouge m. **diver** n plongeur/-euse m/f.

diverge /daɪˈvɜːdʒ/ vi diverger. **divergent** adj divergent.

diverse /daɪˈvɜːs/ adj divers.

diversion /daɪˈvɜːʃn/ n détournement m; (distraction) diversion f; (of traffic) déviation f. **divert** vt détourner; (traffic) dévier.

divide /dɪˈvaɪd/ vt/i (se) diviser.

dividend /ˈdɪvɪdend/ n dividende m.

divine /dɪˈvaɪn/ adj divin.

diving: ~**board** n plongeoir m. ~**suit** n scaphandre m.

division /dɪˈvɪʒn/ n division f.

divorce /dɪˈvɔːs/ n divorce m (from avec). ● vt divorcer (d'avec).

divulge /daɪˈvʌldʒ/ vt divulguer.

DIY abbr ➡ DO-IT-YOURSELF.

dizziness /ˈdɪzɪnɪs/ n vertige m.

dizzy /ˈdɪzɪ/ adj (-ier, -iest) vertigineux; be or feel ~ avoir le vertige.

---

do /duː/

present do, does; present negative don't, do not; past did; past participle done

● *transitive and intransitive verb*

····▸ faire; she is doing her homework elle fait ses devoirs.

····▸ (progress, be suitable) aller; how are you doing? comment ça va?

····▸ (be enough) suffire; will five dollars ~? cinq dollars, ça suffira?

● *auxiliary verb*

····▸ (in questions) ~ you like Mozart? aimes-tu Mozart?, est-ce que tu aimes Mozart?; did your sister phone? est-ce que ta sœur a téléphoné?, ta sœur a-t-elle téléphoné?

····▸ (in negatives) I don't like Mozart je n'aime pas Mozart.

····▸ (emphatic uses) I ~ like your dress j'aime beaucoup ta robe; I ~ think you should go je pense vraiment que tu devrais y aller.

····▸ (referring back to another verb) I live in Orford and so does Lily j'habite à Orford et Lily aussi; she gets paid more than I ~ elle est payée plus que moi; 'I don't like carrots'—'neither ~ I' 'je n'aime pas les carottes'—'moi non plus'.

····▸ (imperatives) don't shut the door ne ferme pas la porte; ~ be quiet tais-toi!

····▸ (short questions and answers) you like fish, don't you? tu aimes le poisson, n'est-ce pas?; Lola didn't phone, did she? Lola n'a pas téléphoné par hasard?; 'does he play tennis?'—'no he doesn't/yes he does' 'est-ce qu'il joue au tennis?'—'non/oui'; 'Marion didn't say that'—'yes she did' 'Marion n'a pas dit ça'—'si'.

□ **do away with** supprimer. **do up** (fasten) fermer; (house) refaire; **do with it's to ~ with** c'est à propos de; it's nothing to ~ with ça n'a rien à voir avec. **do without** ce passer de.

docile /ˈdəʊsaɪl/ adj docile.

dock /dɒk/ n (Jur) banc m des accusés; dock m. ● vi arriver au port. ● vt mettre à quai; (wages) faire une retenue sur.

doctor /ˈdɒktə(r)/ n médecin m, docteur m; (Univ) docteur m. ● vt (cat) châtrer; (fig) altérer.

doctorate /ˈdɒktərət/ n doctorat m.

document /ˈdɒkjʊmənt/ n docu-

ment m. **documentary** adj & n documentaire (m). **documentation** n documentation f.

dodge /dɒdʒ/ vt esquiver. ● vi faire un saut de côté. ● n mouvement m de côté.

dodgems /ˈdɒdʒəmz/ npl autos fpl tamponneuses.

dodgy /ˈdɒdʒɪ/ adj (-ier, -iest) (🖪: difficult) épineux, délicat; (untrustworthy) louche 🖪.

doe /dəʊ/ n (deer) biche f.

does /dʌz/ ➡DO.

doesn't ➡DOES NOT.

dog /dɒg/ n chien m. ● vt (pt dogged) poursuivre. ~-collar n col m romain. ~-eared adj écorné.

dogged /ˈdɒgɪd/ adj obstiné.

dogma /ˈdɒgmə/ n dogme m. **dogmatic** adj dogmatique.

dogsbody /ˈdɒgzbɒdɪ/ n bonne f à tout faire.

do-it-yourself /duːɪtjɔːˈself/ n bricolage m.

doldrums /ˈdɒldrəmz/ npl be in the ~ (person) avoir le cafard.

dole /dəʊl/ vt ~ out distribuer. ● n 🖪 indemnité f de chômage; on the ~ 🖪 au chômage.

doll /dɒl/ n poupée f. ● vt.~ up 🖪 bichonner.

dollar /ˈdɒlə(r)/ n dollar m.

dollop /ˈdɒləp/ n (of food 🖪) gros morceau m.

dolphin /ˈdɒlfɪn/ n dauphin m.

domain /dəʊˈmeɪn/ n domaine m.

dome /dəʊm/ n dôme m.

domestic /dəˈmestɪk/ adj familial; (trade, flights) intérieur; (animal) domestique. **domesticated** adj (animal) domestique.

domestic science n arts mpl ménagers.

dominant /ˈdɒmɪnənt/ adj

dominant.

dominate /ˈdɒmɪneɪt/ vt/i dominer. **domination** n domination f.

domineering /dɒmɪˈnɪərɪŋ/ adj dominateur.

domino /ˈdɒmɪnəʊ/ n (pl ~es) domino m; ~es (game) dominos mpl.

donate /dəʊˈneɪt/ vt faire don de. **donation** n don m.

done /dʌn/ ⇒DO.

donkey /ˈdɒŋkɪ/ n âne m. ~ work n travail m pénible.

donor /ˈdəʊnə(r)/ n donateur/-trice m/f; (of blood) donneur/-euse m/f.

don't ⇒DO NOT.

doodle /ˈduːdl/ vi griffonner.

doom /duːm/ n (ruin) ruine f; (fate) destin m. ● vt be ~ed to être destiné or condamné à; ~ed (to failure) voué à l'échec.

door /dɔː(r)/ n porte f; (of vehicle) portière f, porte f. ~bell n sonnette f. ~man n (pl -men) portier m. ~mat n paillasson m. ~step n pas m de (la) porte, seuil m. ~way n porte f.

dope /dəʊp/ n 🄚 cannabis m; (idiot 🄚) imbécile mf. ● vt doper. **dopey** adj (foolish 🄚) imbécile.

dormant /ˈdɔːmənt/ adj en sommeil.

dormitory /ˈdɔːmɪtrɪ/ n dortoir m; (Univ, US) résidence f.

dosage /ˈdəʊsɪdʒ/ n dose f; (on label) posologie f.

dose /dəʊs/ n dose f.

dot /dɒt/ n point m; on the ~ à l'heure pile.

dot-com /dɒtˈkɒm/ n (société) point com f. ~ **millionaire** n millionaire mf de l'Internet. ~ **shares** npl actions fpl des sociétés point com.

dote /dəʊt/ vi ~ on adorer.

dotted /ˈdɒtɪd/ adj (fabric) à pois;

~ line pointillé m; ~ with parsemé de.

double /ˈdʌbl/ adj double; (room, bed) pour deux personnes; ~ the size deux fois plus grand. ● adv deux fois; pay ~ payer le double. ● n double m; (stuntman) doublure f; ~s (tennis) double m; at or on the ~ au pas de course. ● vt/i doubler; (fold) plier en deux. ~bass n (Mus) contrebasse f. ~check vt revérifier. ~chin n double menton m. ~cross vt tromper. ~decker n autobus m à impériale.

doubt /daʊt/ n doute m. ● vt douter de; ~ if or that douter que. **doubtful** adj incertain, douteux; (person) qui a des doutes. **doubtless** adv sans doute.

dough /dəʊ/ n pâte f; (money 🄚) fric m 🄚.

doughnut /ˈdəʊnʌt/ n beignet m.

douse /daʊs/ vt arroser; (light, fire) éteindre.

dove /dʌv/ n colombe f.

Dover /ˈdəʊvə(r)/ n Douvres f.

dowdy /ˈdaʊdɪ/ adj (-ier, -iest) (clothes) sans chic, monotone; (person) sans élégance.

down /daʊn/ adv en bas; (of sun) couché; (lower) plus bas; come or go ~ descendre; go ~ to the post office aller à la poste; ~ under aux antipodes; ~ with bas. ● prep en bas de; (along) le long de. ● vt (knock down, shoot down) abattre; (drink) vider. ● n (fluff) duvet m.

down: ~-and-out n clochard/-e m/f. ~cast adj démoralisé. ~fall n chute f. ~grade vt déclasser. ~hearted adj découragé.

downhill /daʊnˈhɪl/ adv go ~ descendre; (pej) baisser.

down: ~load n (Comput) télécharger. ~market adj bas de

gamme. ~ **payment** n acompte m.
~**pour** n grosse averse f.

downright /ˈdaʊnraɪt/ adj (utter)
véritable; (honest) franc. ● adv carrément.

downstairs /daʊnˈsteəz/ adv en
bas. ● adj d'en bas.

down: ~**stream** adv en aval.
~**-to-earth** adj pratique.

Downing Street Célèbre *i*
rue de Londres où se trou-
vent la résidence officielle
du Premier ministre au n°10 et
celle du Chancelier de l'Échiquier
au n°11. Les médias emploient
souvent *Number 10 Downing Street*
ou *Downing Street* pour désigner le
Premier ministre ou le gouvernement britannique.

---

downtown /ˈdaʊntaʊn/ adj (US)
du centre-ville; ~ Boston le centre
de Boston.

downward /ˈdaʊnwəd/ adj & adv,
downwards adv vers le bas.

doze /dəʊz/ vi somnoler; ~ off
s'assoupir. ● n somme m.

dozen /ˈdʌzn/ n douzaine f; a ~
eggs une douzaine d'œufs; ~s of
Ⓣ des dizaines de.

Dr abbr (**Doctor**) Docteur.

drab /dræb/ adj terne.

draft /drɑːft/ n (outline) brouillon
m; (Comm) traite f; the ~ (Mil US)
la conscription; a ~ treaty un projet de traité; (US) ⇒**DRAUGHT**. ● vt
faire le brouillon de; (draw up)
rédiger.

drag /dræg/ vt/i (pt **dragged**) traîner; (river) draguer; (pull away) arracher; ~ on s'éterniser. ● n (task Ⓣ)
corvée f; (person Ⓣ) raseur/-euse
m/f; in ~ en travesti.

dragon /ˈdrægən/ n dragon m.

drain /dreɪn/ vt (land) drainer; (ve-

getables) égoutter; (tank, glass)
vider; (use up) épuiser; ~ (off) (liquid) faire écouler. ● vi ~ (off) (of
liquid) s'écouler. ● n (sewer) égout
m; ~(-pipe) tuyau m d'écoulement;
a ~ on une ponction sur.

draining-board n égouttoir m.

drama /ˈdrɑːmə/ n art m dramatique, théâtre m; (play, event) drame
m. **dramatic** (US) (situation) dramatique; (increase) spectaculaire.

dramatist n dramaturge m. **dramatize** vt adapter pour la scène; (fig)
dramatiser.

drank /dræŋk/ ⇒**DRINK**.

drape /dreɪp/ vt draper. **drapes** npl
(US) rideaux mpl.

drastic /ˈdræstɪk/ adj sévère.

draught /drɑːft/ n courant m d'air;
~s (game) dames fpl. ~ **beer** n
bière f pression.

draughty /ˈdrɑːftɪ/ adj plein de
courants d'air.

draw /drɔː/ vt (pt **drew**; pp
drawn) (picture) dessiner; (line) tracer; (pull) tirer; (attract) attirer. ● vi
dessiner; (Sport) faire match nul;
(come, move) venir. ● n (Sport)
match m nul; (in lottery) tirage m au
sort. □ ~ **back** reculer. ~ **near**
(s')approcher (to de). ~ **out**
(money) retirer. ~ **up** vi (stop) s'arrêter; vt (document) dresser; (chair)
approcher.

drawback /ˈdrɔːbæk/ n inconvénient m.

drawbridge /ˈdrɔːbrɪdʒ/ n pont-
levis m.

drawer /ˈdrɔː(r)/ n tiroir m.

drawing /ˈdrɔːɪŋ/ n dessin m.
~**-board** n planche f à dessin.
~**-pin** n punaise f. ~**-room** n
salon m.

drawl /drɔːl/ n voix f traînante.

drawn /drɔːn/ ⇒**DRAW**. ● adj (fea-

tures) tiré; (*match*) nul.

dread /dred/ *n* terreur *f*, crainte *f*.
● *vt* redouter. **dreadful** *adj* épouvantable, affreux. **dreadfully** *adv*
terriblement.

dream /driːm/ *n* rêve *m*. ● *vt/i* (*pt*
dreamed or **dreamt**) rêver; ~ **up**
imaginer. ● *adj* (ideal) de ses rêves.

dreary /ˈdrɪərɪ/ *adj* (**-ier, -iest**)
triste; (boring) monotone.

dredge /dredʒ/ *vt* (river) draguer;
~ **sth up** (fig) exhumer.

dregs /dregz/ *npl* lie *f*.

drench /drentʃ/ *vt* tremper.

dress /dres/ *n* robe *f*; (clothing)
tenue *f*. ● *vt/i* (s')habiller; (food) assaisonner; (wound) panser; ~ **up** as
se déguiser en; get ~ **ed** s'habiller.
~ **circle** *n* premier balcon *m*.

dresser /ˈdresə(r)/ *n* (furniture)
buffet *m*; be a stylish ~ s'habiller
avec chic.

dressing /ˈdresɪŋ/ *n* (sauce) assaisonnement *m*; (bandage) pansement *m*. ~**-gown** *n* robe *f* de
chambre. ~**-room** *n* (Sport) vestiaire *m*; (Theat) loge *f*. ~**-table** *n*
coiffeuse *f*.

dressmaker /ˈdresmeɪkə(r)/ *n*
couturière *f*. **dressmaking** *n* couture *f*.

dress rehearsal *n* répétition *f*
générale.

dressy /ˈdresɪ/ *adj* (**-ier, -iest**)
chic *inv*.

drew /druː/ ➡**DRAW**.

dribble /ˈdrɪbl/ *vi* (liquid) dégouliner; (person) baver; (football)
dribbler.

dried /draɪd/ *adj* (fruit) sec.

drier /ˈdraɪə(r)/ *n* séchoir *m*.

drift /drɪft/ *vi* aller à la dérive; (pile
up) s'amonceler; ~ **towards** glisser
vers. ● *n* dérive *f*, amoncellement *m*;
(of events) tournure *f*; (meaning)

sens *m*; snow ~ congère *f*. **drift-**
wood *n* bois *m* flotté.

drill /drɪl/ *n* (tool) perceuse *f*; (for
teeth) roulette *f*; (training) exercice
m; (procedure □) marche *f* à suivre;
(pneumatic) marteau *m* piqueur.
● *vt* percer; (train) entraîner. ● *vi*
être à l'exercice.

drink /drɪŋk/ *vt/i* (*pt* **drank**; *pp*
drunk) boire. ● *n* (liquid) boisson *f*;
(glass of alcohol) verre *m*; a ~ of
water un verre d'eau. **drinking**
water *n* eau *f* potable.

drip /drɪp/ *vi* (*pt* **dripped**) (é)gout-
ter; (washing) s'égoutter. ● *n*
goutte *f*; (person □) lavette *f*.

drip-dry *vt* laisser égoutter. ● *adj*
sans essorage.

drive /draɪv/ *vt* (*pt* **drove**; *pp*
driven) (vehicle) conduire; (sb
somewhere) chasser, pousser; (machine) actionner; ~ **mad** rendre
fou. ● *vi* conduire. ● *n* promenade *f*
en voiture; (private road) allée *f*;
(fig) énergie *f*; (Psych) instinct *m*;
(Pol) campagne *f*; (Auto) traction *f*;
(golf, Comput) drive *m*; it's a two-
hour ~ il y a deux heures de route;
lefthand ~ conduite *f* à gauche.
□ ~ **at** en venir à.

drivel /ˈdrɪvl/ *n* bêtises *fpl*.

driver /ˈdraɪvə(r)/ *n* conducteur/-
trice *m/f*, chauffeur *m*. ~**'s license**
n (US) permis *m* de conduire.

driving /ˈdraɪvɪŋ/ *n* conduite *f*;
take one's ~ **test** passer son permis. ● *adj* (rain) battant; (wind) cinglant. ~ **licence** *n* permis *m* de
conduire. ~ **school** *n* auto-école *f*.

drizzle /ˈdrɪzl/ *n* bruine *f*. ● *vi*
bruiner.

drone /drəʊn/ *n* (of engine) ronronnement *m*; (of insects) bourdonnement *m*. ● *vi* ronronner; bourdonner.

drool /druːl/ *vi* baver (over sur).

droop /druːp/ vi pencher, tomber.

drop /drɒp/ n goutte f; (fall, lowering) chute f. ● vt/i (pt **dropped**) (laisser) tomber; (decrease, lower) baisser; ~ (off) (person from car) déposer; ~ a line écrire un mot (to à). □ ~ **in** passer (on chez). ~ **off** (doze) s'assoupir. ~ **out** se retirer (of de); (of student) abandonner.

dropout /ˈdrɒpaʊt/ n marginal/-e m/f, raté/-e m/f.

droppings /ˈdrɒpɪŋz/ npl crottes fpl.

drought /draʊt/ n sécheresse f.

drove /drəʊv/ ⇒DRIVE.

droves /drəʊvz/ npl foules fpl.

drown /draʊn/ vt/i se noyer.

drowsy /ˈdraʊzɪ/ adj somnolent; be or feel ~ avoir envie de dormir.

drug /drʌɡ/ n drogue f; (Med) médicament m. ● vt (pt **drugged**) droguer. ~ **addict** n drogué/-e m/f.

drugstore n (US) drugstore m.

drum /drʌm/ n tambour m; (for oil) bidon m; ~s batterie f. ● vi (pt **drummed**) tambouriner. ● vt ~ **into** sb répéter sans cesse à qn; ~ **up** (support) susciter; (business) créer. **drummer** n tambour m; (in pop group) batteur m.

drumstick /ˈdrʌmstɪk/ n baguette f de tambour; (of chicken) pilon m.

drunk /drʌŋk/ ⇒DRINK. ● adj ivre; get ~ s'enivrer. ● n ivrogne/-esse m/f. **drunkard** n ivrogne/-esse m/f. **drunken** adj ivre. **drunkenness** n ivresse f.

dry /draɪ/ adj (drier, driest) sec; (day) sans pluie; be or feel ~ avoir soif. ● vt/i (faire) sécher; ~ **up** (dry dishes) essuyer la vaisselle; (of supplies) se tarir; (be silent 🗆) se taire. ~**-clean** vt nettoyer à sec. ~**-cleaner** n teinturier m. ~ **run** n galop m d'essai.

DTD abbr (Document Type Definition) DTD f.

dual /ˈdjuːəl/ adj double. ~ **carriageway** n route f à quatre voies. ~**-purpose** adj qui fait double emploi.

dub /dʌb/ vt (pt **dubbed**) (film) doubler (into en); (nickname) surnommer.

dubious /ˈdjuːbɪəs/ adj (pej) douteux; be ~ **about** avoir des doutes sur.

duck /dʌk/ n canard m. ● vi se baisser subitement. ● vt (head) baisser; (person) plonger dans l'eau.

duct /dʌkt/ n conduit m.

dud /dʌd/ adj (tool 🗆) mal fichu; (coin 🗆) faux; (cheque 🗆) sans provision. ● n be a ~ (not work 🗆) ne pas marcher.

due /djuː/ adj (owing) dû; (expected) attendu; (proper) qui convient; ~ **to** à cause de; (caused by) dû à; she's ~ to leave now it is prévu qu'elle parte maintenant; in ~ **course** (at the right time) en temps voulu; (later) plus tard. ● adv ~ **east** droit vers l'est. ● n dû m; ~s droits mpl; (of club) cotisation f.

duel /ˈdjuːəl/ n duel m.

duet /djuːˈet/ n duo m.

dug /dʌɡ/ ⇒DIG.

duke /djuːk/ n duc m.

dull /dʌl/ adj (boring) ennuyeux; (colour) terne; (weather) maussade; (sound) sourd. ● vt (pain) atténuer; (shine) ternir.

duly /ˈdjuːlɪ/ adv comme il convient; (as expected) comme prévu.

dumb /dʌm/ adj muet; (stupid 🗆) bête. □ ~ **down** (course, TV coverage) baisser le niveau intellectuel de.

dumbfound /dʌmˈfaʊnd/ vt sidérer, ahurir.

dummy /'dʌmɪ/ n (of tailor) mannequin m; (of baby) sucette f. ● adj factice. ~ **run** n galop m d'essai.

dump /dʌmp/ vt déposer; (get rid of 🔲) se débarrasser de. ● n tas m d'ordures; (refuse tip) décharge f; (Mil) dépôt m; (dull place 🔲) trou m 🔲; be in the ~s 🔲 avoir le cafard.

dune /djuːn/ n dune f.

dung /dʌŋ/ n (excrement) bouse f, crotte f; (manure) fumier m.

dungarees /dʌŋɡə'riːz/ npl salopette f.

dungeon /'dʌndʒən/ n cachot m.

duplicate¹ /'djuːplɪkət/ n double m. ● adj identique.

duplicate² /'djuːplɪkeɪt/ vt faire un double de; (on machine) polycopier.

durable /'djuərəbl/ adj (tough) résistant; (enduring) durable.

duration /dju'reɪʃn/ n durée f.

during /'djuərɪŋ/ prep pendant.

dusk /dʌsk/ n crépuscule m.

dusky /'dʌskɪ/ adj (-ier, -iest) foncé.

dust /dʌst/ n poussière f. ● vt/i épousseter; (sprinkle) saupoudrer (with de). ~**bin** n poubelle f.

duster /'dʌstə(r)/ n chiffon m.

dust: ~**man** n (pl -men) éboueur m. ~**pan** n pelle f (à poussière).

dusty /'dʌstɪ/ adj (-ier, -iest) poussiéreux.

Dutch /dʌtʃ/ adj néerlandais; go ~ partager les frais. ● n (Ling) néerlandais m. ~**man** n Néerlandais m. ~**woman** n Néerlandaise f.

dutiful /'djuːtɪfl/ adj obéissant.

duty /'djuːtɪ/ n devoir m; (tax) droit m; (of official) fonction f; on ~ de service. ~-**free** adj hors-taxe.

duvet /'duːveɪ/ n couette f.

DVD abbr (**digital versatile disc**) DVD m.

dwarf /dwɔːf/ n nain/-e m/f. ● vt rapetisser.

dwell /dwel/ vi (pt dwelt) demeurer; ~ on s'étendre sur. **dweller** n habitant/-e m/f. **dwelling** n habitation f.

dwindle /'dwɪndl/ vi diminuer.

dye /daɪ/ vt teindre. ● n teinture f.

dying /'daɪɪŋ/ adj mourant; (art) qui se perd.

dynamic /daɪ'næmɪk/ adj dynamique.

dynamite /'daɪnəmaɪt/ n dynamite f.

dysentery /'dɪsəntrɪ/ n dysenterie f.

dyslexia /dɪs'leksɪə/ n dyslexie f. **dyslexic** adj & n dyslexique (mf).

Ee

each /iːtʃ/ det chaque inv; ~ **one** chacun/-e m/f. ● pron chacun/-e m/f; oranges at 30p ~ des oranges à 30 pence pièce.

each other pron l'un/l'une une l'autre, les uns/les unes les autres; know ~ se connaître; love ~ s'aimer.

eager /'iːɡə(r)/ adj impatient (to de); (person, acceptance) enthousiaste; ~ **for** avide de.

eagle /'iːɡl/ n aigle m.

ear /ɪə(r)/ n oreille f; (of corn) épi m. ~**ache** n mal m à l'oreille. ~-**drum** n tympan m.

earl /ɜːl/ n comte m.

early /'ɜːlɪ/ (-ier, -iest) adv tôt, de bonne heure; (ahead of time) en avance; as I said earlier comme je l'ai déjà dit. ● adj (attempt, years) premier; (hour) matinal; (fruit) précoce; (retirement) anticipé; have an ~ dinner dîner tôt; in ~ summer au début de l'été; at the earliest au plus tôt.

earmark /ˈɪəmɑːk/ vt désigner (pour).

earn /ɜːn/ vt gagner; (interest: Comm) rapporter.

earnest /ˈɜːnɪst/ adj sérieux; in ~ sérieusement.

earnings /ˈɜːnɪŋz/ npl salaire m; (profits) gains mpl.

ear: ~phones npl casque m. ~ring n boucle f d'oreille. ~shot n within/in ~shot à portée de voix.

earth /ɜːθ/ n terre f; why/how/where on ~...? pourquoi/comment/où diable...? ● vt (Electr) mettre à la terre. **earthenware** n faïence f. ~quake n tremblement m de terre.

ease /iːz/ n facilité f; (comfort) bien-être m; at ~ à l'aise; (Mil) au repos; with ~ facilement. ● vt (pain, pressure) atténuer; (congestion) réduire; (transition) faciliter. ● vi (pain, pressure) s'atténuer; (congestion, rain) diminuer.

easel /ˈiːzl/ n chevalet m.

east /iːst/ n est m; the E~ (Orient) l'Orient m. ● adj (side, coast) est; (wind) d'est. ● adv à l'est.

Easter /ˈiːstə(r)/ n Pâques m; ~ egg œuf m de Pâques.

easterly /ˈiːstəlɪ/ adj (wind) d'est; (direction) de l'est.

eastern de l'est; ~ France l'est de la France.

eastward /ˈiːstwəd/ adj (side) est inv; (journey) vers l'est.

easy /ˈiːzɪ/ adj (-ier, -lest) facile; go ~ with 🗓 y aller doucement avec; take it ~ ne te fatigue pas. ~going adj accommodant.

eat /iːt/ vt/i (pt ate; pp eaten) manger; ~ into ronger.

eavesdrop /ˈiːvzdrɒp/ vi (pt -dropped) écouter aux portes.

ebb /eb/ n reflux m. ● vi descendre; (fig) décliner.

EC abbr (**European Commission**) CE f.

eccentric /ɪkˈsentrɪk/ adj & n excentrique (mf).

echo /ˈekəʊ/ n (pl -oes) écho m. ● vt répercuter; (idea, opinion) reprendre; ● vi retentir, résonner (to, with de).

eclipse /ɪˈklɪps/ n éclipse f. ● vt éclipser.

ecological /iːkəˈlɒdʒɪkl/ adj écologique.

ecology /ɪˈkɒlədʒɪ/ n écologie f.

e-commerce /ˈiːkɒmɜːs/ n commerce m électronique, commerce m en ligne.

economic /iːkəˈnɒmɪk/ adj économique; (profitable) rentable; ~ refugee réfugié/-e m/f économique. **economical** adj économique; (person) économe. **economics** n économie f, sciences fpl économiques. **economist** n économiste mf.

economize /ɪˈkɒnəmaɪz/ vi ~ (on) économiser.

economy /ɪˈkɒnəmɪ/ n économie f. ~-class syndrome n syndrome m de la classe économique.

ecosystem /ˈiːkəʊsɪstəm/ n écosystème m.

ecstasy /ˈekstəsɪ/ n extase f; (drug) ecstasy m.

edge /edʒ/ n bord m; (of town) abords mpl; (of knife) tranchant m; have the ~ on 🗓 l'emporter sur; on ~ énervé. ● vt (trim) border. ● vi ~ forward avancer doucement.

edgeways /ˈedʒweɪz/ adv I can't

get a word in ∼ je n'arrive pas à placer un mot.

edible /'edɪbl/ adj comestible.

Edinburgh Festival Festival international des Arts qui se déroule tous les étés à Édimbourg (Écosse) depuis 1947. Pendant trois semaines, au programme du festival institutionnel et du festival parallèle (*Fringe festival*), se côtoient les plus grands noms de la musique, de la danse, du théâtre, les artistes d'avant-garde et les nouveaux talents.

---

edit /'edɪt/ vt (pt **edited**) (newspaper, page) être le rédacteur/la rédactrice de; (check) réviser; (cut) couper; (TV, cinema) monter.

edition /ɪ'dɪʃn/ n édition f.

editor /'edɪtə(r)/ n (writer) rédacteur/-trice m/f; (of works, anthology) éditeur/-trice m/f; (TV, cinema) monteur/-teuse m/f; the ∼ (in chief) le rédacteur en chef.

editorial /edɪ'tɔːrɪəl/ adj de la rédaction. ● n éditorial m.

educate /'edʒʊkeɪt/ vt instruire; (mind) éduquer. **educated** adj instruit. **education** n éducation f; (schooling) études fpl. **educational** adj éducatif; (method) d'enseignement.

eel /iːl/ n anguille f.

eerie /'ɪərɪ/ adj (-ier, -iest) sinistre.

effect /ɪ'fekt/ n effet m; come into ∼ entrer en vigueur; in ∼ effectivement; take ∼ agir. ● vt effectuer.

effective /ɪ'fektɪv/ adj (actual) effectif. **effectively** adv efficacement; (in effect) en réalité. **effectiveness** n efficacité f.

effeminate /ɪ'femɪnət/ adj efféminé.

effervescent /efə'vesnt/ adj effer-

vescent.

efficiency /ɪ'fɪʃnsɪ/ n efficacité f; (of machine) rendement m. **efficient** adj efficace. **efficiently** adv efficacement.

effort /'efət/ n efforts mpl; make an ∼ faire un effort; be worth the ∼ en valoir la peine. **effortless** adj facile.

effusive /ɪ'fjuːsɪv/ adj expansif.

e.g. /iː'dʒiː/ abbr par ex.

egg /eg/ n œuf m. ● vt ∼ on pousser. ∼-**cup** n coquetier m. ∼-**plant** n (US) aubergine f. ∼-**shell** n coquille f d'œuf.

ego /'iːgəʊ/ n amour-propre m; (Psych) moi m. **egotism** n égotisme m. **egotist** n égotiste mf.

Egypt /'iːdʒɪpt/ n Égypte f.

EHIC abbr (**European Health Insurance Card**) CEAM f.

eiderdown /'aɪdədaʊn/ n édredon m.

eight /eɪt/ adj & n huit (m). **eighteen** adj & n dix-huit (m). **eighth** adj & n huitième (mf). **eighty** adj & n quatre-vingts (m).

either /'aɪðə(r)/ det & pron l'un/une ou l'autre; (with negative) ni l'un/une ni l'autre; you can take ∼ tu peux prendre n'importe lequel/laquelle. ● adv non plus. ● conj ∼...or ou (bien)...ou (bien); (with negative) ni...ni.

eject /ɪ'dʒekt/ vt (troublemaker) expulser; (waste) rejeter.

elaborate[1] /ɪ'læbərət/ adj compliqué.

elaborate[2] /ɪ'læbəreɪt/ vt élaborer. ● vi préciser; ∼ on s'étendre sur.

elastic /ɪ'læstɪk/ adj & n élastique (m); ∼ band élastique m. **elasticity** n élasticité f.

elated /ɪ'leɪtɪd/ adj transporté de joie.

elbow /'elbəʊ/ n coude m; ~ **room** espace m vital.

elder /'eldə(r)/ adj & n aîné-e (m/f); (tree) sureau m.

elderly /'eldəlɪ/ adj âgé; the ~ les personnes fpl âgées.

eldest /'eldɪst/ adj & n aîné-e (m/f).

elect /ɪ'lekt/ vt élire; ~ **to do** choisir de faire. ● adj (president etc.) futur. **election** n élection f. **elector** n électeur-trice m/f. **electoral** adj électoral. **electorate** n électorat m.

electric /ɪ'lektrɪk/ adj électrique; ~ **blanket** couverture f chauffante. **electrical** adj électrique. **electrician** n électricien-ne m/f. **electricity** n électricité f. **electrify** vt électrifier; (excite) électriser.

electrocute vt électrocuter.

electronic /ɪlek'trɒnɪk/ adj électronique. ~ **publishing** n éditique f. **electronics** n électronique f.

elegance /'elɪɡəns/ n élégance f. **elegant** adj élégant.

element /'elɪmənt/ n élément m; (of heater etc.) résistance f. **elementary** adj élémentaire.

elephant /'elɪfənt/ n éléphant m.

elevate /'elɪveɪt/ vt élever. **elevation** n élévation f. **elevator** n (US) ascenseur m.

eleven /ɪ'levn/ adj & n onze (m). **eleventh** adj & n onzième (m/f).

elicit /ɪ'lɪsɪt/ vt obtenir (from de).

eligible /'elɪdʒəbl/ adj admissible (for à); be ~ **for** (entitled to) avoir droit à.

eliminate /ɪ'lɪmɪneɪt/ vt éliminer.

elm /elm/ n orme m.

elongate /'iːlɒŋɡeɪt/ vt allonger.

elope /ɪ'ləʊp/ vi s'enfuir (with avec). **elopement** n fugue f (amoureuse).

eloquence /'eləkwəns/ n éloquence f.

else /els/ adv d'autre; somebody/ nothing ~ quelqu'un/rien d'autre; everybody ~ tous les autres; somewhere ~ autre part/chose; or ~ ou bien. **elsewhere** adv ailleurs.

elude /ɪ'luːd/ vt échapper à.

elusive /ɪ'luːsɪv/ adj insaisissable.

email /'iːmeɪl/ n (medium) courrier m électronique; (item) e-mail m, mél m; ~ **sb** envoyer un e-mail à qn; ~ **sth** envoyer qch par courrier électronique.

emancipate /ɪ'mænsɪpeɪt/ vt émanciper.

embankment /ɪm'bæŋkmənt/ n (of river) quai m; (of railway) remblai m.

embark /ɪm'bɑːk/ vt embarquer. ● vi (Naut) embarquer; ~ **on** (journey) entreprendre; (campaign, career) se lancer dans.

embarrass /ɪm'bærəs/ vt plonger dans l'embarras; be/feel ~**ed** être, se sentir gêné. **embarrassment** n confusion f, gêne f.

embassy /'embəsɪ/ n ambassade f.

embed /ɪm'bed/ vt (pt embedded) enfoncer (in dans).

embellish /ɪm'belɪʃ/ vt embellir.

embers /'embəz/ npl braises fpl.

embezzle /ɪm'bezl/ vt détourner (from de). **embezzlement** n détournement m de fonds.

emblem /'embləm/ n emblème m.

embodiment /ɪm'bɒdɪmənt/ n incarnation f. **embody** vt incarner; (legally) incorporer.

emboss /ɪm'bɒs/ vt (metal) repousser; (paper) gaufrer.

embrace /ɪm'breɪs/ vt (person) étreindre; (religion) embrasser; (include) comprendre. ● n étreinte f.

embroider /ɪm'brɔɪdə(r)/ vt broder. **embroidery** n broderie f.

embryo /'embriəʊ/ n embryon m.

emerald /'emərəld/ n émeraude f.

emerge /ɪ'mɜːdʒ/ vi (person) sortir (from de); it ~d that il est apparu que. **emergence** n apparition f.

emergency /ɪ'mɜːdʒənsɪ/ n (crisis) crise f; (urgent case: Med) urgence f; in an ~ en cas d'urgence. • adj d'urgence. • **exit** n sortie f de secours; ~ **landing** n atterrissage m forcé. ~ **room** (US) salle f des urgences.

emigrant /'emɪɡrənt/ n émigrant/-e m/f. **emigrate** vi émigrer.

eminence /'emɪnəns/ n éminence f. **eminent** adj éminent.

emission /ɪ'mɪʃn/ n émission f.

emit /ɪ'mɪt/ vt (pt emitted) émettre.

emotion /ɪ'məʊʃn/ n émotion f. **emotional** adj (development) émotif; (reaction) émotionel; (film, scene) émouvant.

emotive /ɪ'məʊtɪv/ adj qui soulève les passions.

emperor /'empərə(r)/ n empereur m.

emphasis /'emfəsɪs/ n accent m; lay ~ on mettre l'accent sur. **emphasize** vt mettre l'accent sur. **emphatic** adj catégorique; (manner) énergique.

empire /'empaɪə(r)/ n empire m.

employ /ɪm'plɔɪ/ vt employer. **employee** n employé/-e m/f. **employer** n employeur/-euse m/f.

employment /ɪm'plɔɪmənt/ n emploi m; find ~ trouver du travail.

empower /ɪm'paʊə(r)/ vt autoriser (to do à faire).

empty /'emptɪ/ adj (-ier, -lest) vide; (street) désert; (promise) vain; on an ~ **stomach** à jeun. • vt/i (se) vider. ~-**handed** adj les mains vides.

emulate /'emjʊleɪt/ vt imiter.

enable /ɪ'neɪbl/ vt ~ sb to permettre à qn de.

enamel /ɪ'næml/ n émail m. • vt (pt enamelled) émailler.

encase /ɪn'keɪs/ vt revêtir, recouvrir (in de).

enchant /ɪn'tʃɑːnt/ vt enchanter.

enclose /ɪn'kləʊz/ vt entourer; (land) clôturer; (with letter) joindre. **enclosed** adj (space) clos; (with letter) ci-joint. **enclosure** n enceinte f; (with letter) pièce f jointe.

encompass /ɪn'kʌmpəs/ vt inclure.

encore /'ɒŋkɔː(r)/ interj & n bis (m).

encounter /ɪn'kaʊntə(r)/ vt rencontrer. • n rencontre f.

encourage /ɪn'kʌrɪdʒ/ vt encourager.

encroach /ɪn'krəʊtʃ/ vi ~ upon empiéter sur.

encyclopedia /ɪnsaɪklə'piːdɪə/ n encyclopédie f. **encyclopaedic** adj encyclopédique.

end /end/ n fin f; (farthest point) bout m; come to an ~ prendre fin f; ~-**product** produit m fini; in the ~ finalement; no ~ of [T] énormément de; on ~ (upright) debout; (in a row) de suite; put an ~ to mettre fin à. • vt (marriage) mettre fin à; ~ one's days finir ses jours. • vi se terminer; ~ up doing finir par faire.

endanger /ɪn'deɪndʒə(r)/ vt mettre en danger.

endearing /ɪn'dɪərɪŋ/ adj attachant.

endeavour, (US) **endeavor** /ɪn'devə(r)/ n (attempt) tentative f; (hard work) effort m. • vi faire tout son possible (to do pour faire).

ending /'endɪŋ/ n fin f.

endive /'endɪv/ n chicorée f.

endless /'endlɪs/ adj interminable; (supply) inépuisable; (patience) infini.

endorse /ɪn'dɔːs/ vt (candidate, decision) appuyer; (product, claim) approuver; (cheque) endosser.

endurance /ɪn'djʊərəns/ n endurance f.

endure /ɪn'djʊə(r)/ vt supporter. ● vi durer. **enduring** adj durable.

enemy /'enəmɪ/ n & adj ennemi/-e (m/f).

energetic /enə'dʒetɪk/ adj énergique. **energy** n énergie f.

enforce /ɪn'fɔːs/ vt (rule, law) appliquer, faire respecter; (silence, discipline) imposer (on à); ~d forcé.

engage /ɪn'geɪdʒ/ vt (staff) engager; (attention) retenir; be ~d in se livrer à. ● vi ~ in se livrer à. **engaged** adj fiancé; (busy) occupé; get ~d se fiancer. **engagement** n fiançailles fpl; (meeting) rendez-vous m; (undertaking) engagement m.

engaging /ɪn'geɪdʒɪŋ/ adj attachant, engageant.

engine /'endʒɪn/ n moteur m; (of train) locomotive f; (of ship) machines fpl. ~-**driver** n mécanicien m.

engineer /endʒɪ'nɪə(r)/ n ingénieur m; (repairman) technicien m; (on ship) mécanicien m. ● vt (contrive) manigancer.

engineering /endʒɪ'nɪərɪŋ/ n ingénierie f; (industry) mécanique f; civil ~ génie m civil.

England /'ɪŋɡlənd/ n Angleterre f.

English /'ɪŋɡlɪʃ/ adj anglais. ● n (Ling) anglais m; the ~ les Anglais mpl. ~**man** n Anglais m. ~-**speaking** adj anglophone. ~**woman** n Anglaise f.

engrave /ɪn'ɡreɪv/ vt graver.

engrossed /ɪn'ɡrəʊst/ adj absorbé (in dans).

engulf /ɪn'ɡʌlf/ vt engouffrer.

enhance /ɪn'hɑːns/ vt (prospects, status) améliorer; (price, value) augmenter.

enjoy /ɪn'dʒɔɪ/ vt aimer (doing faire); (benefit from) jouir de; ~ oneself s'amuser; ~ your meal! bon appétit! **enjoyable** adj agréable. **enjoyment** n plaisir m.

enlarge /ɪn'lɑːdʒ/ vt agrandir. ● vi s'agrandir; (pupil) se dilater; ~ on s'étendre sur. **enlargement** n agrandissement m.

enlighten /ɪn'laɪtn/ vt éclairer (on sur). **enlightenment** n instruction f; (information) éclaircissement m.

enlist /ɪn'lɪst/ vt (person) recruter; (fig) obtenir. ● vi s'engager.

enmity /'enmətɪ/ n inimitié f.

enormous /ɪ'nɔːməs/ adj énorme. **enormously** adv énormément.

enough /ɪ'nʌf/ adv & n assez; have ~ of en avoir assez de. ● det assez de; ~ glasses/time assez de verres/de temps.

enquire ⇒INQUIRE.
enquiry ⇒INQUIRY.

enrage /ɪn'reɪdʒ/ vt mettre en rage, rendre furieux.

enrol /ɪn'rəʊl/ vt/i (pt enrolled) (s')inscrire. **enrolment** n inscription f.

ensure /ɪn'ʃɔː(r)/ vt garantir; ~ that (ascertain) s'assurer que.

entail /ɪn'teɪl/ vt entraîner.

entangle /ɪn'tæŋɡl/ vt emmêler.

enter /'entə(r)/ vt (room, club, phase) entrer dans; (note down, register) inscrire; (data) entrer, saisir. ● vi entrer (into dans); ~ for s'inscrire à.

enterprise /'entəpraɪz/ n entreprise f; (boldness) initiative f. **enterprising** adj entreprenant.

entertain /entəˈteɪn/ vt amuser, divertir; (guests) recevoir; (ideas) considérer. **entertainer** n artiste mf. **entertaining** adj divertissant. **entertainment** n divertissement m; (performance) spectacle m.

enthral /ɪnˈθrɔːl/ vt (pt **enthralled**) captiver.

enthusiasm /ɪnˈθjuːzɪæzəm/ n enthousiasme m (for pour).

enthusiast /ɪnˈθjuːzɪæst/ n passionné/-e m/f (for de). **enthusiastic** adj (supporter) enthousiaste; be ~ic about être enthousiasmé par. **enthusiastically** adv avec enthousiasme.

entice /ɪnˈtaɪs/ vt attirer; ~ sb to do entraîner qn à faire.

entire /ɪnˈtaɪə(r)/ adj entier. **entirely** adv entièrement. **entirety** n in its ~ty en entier.

entitle /ɪnˈtaɪtl/ vt donner droit à (to sth à qch; to do de faire); ~d (book) intitulé; be ~d to sth avoir droit à qch.

entrance[1] /ˈentrəns/ n (entering, way in) entrée f (to de); (right to enter) admission f. ● adj (charge, exam) d'entrée.

entrance[2] /ɪnˈtrɑːns/ vt transporter.

entrant /ˈentrənt/ n (Sport) concurrent/-e m/f; (in exam) candidat/-e m/f.

entrenched /ɪnˈtrentʃt/ adj (opinion) inébranlable; (Mil) retranché.

entrepreneur /ɒntrəprəˈnɜː(r)/ n entrepreneur/-euse m/f.

entrust /ɪnˈtrʌst/ vt confier; ~ sb with sth confier qch à qn.

entry /ˈentrɪ/ n entrée f; ~**form** fiche f d'inscription.

envelop /ɪnˈveləp/ vt (pt **enveloped**) envelopper.

envelope /ˈenvələʊp/ n enveloppe f.

envious /ˈenvɪəs/ adj envieux (of de).

environment /ɪnˈvaɪərənmənt/ n (ecological) environnement m; (social) milieu m. **environmental** adj du milieu; de l'environnement. **environmentalist** n écologiste mf.

envisage /ɪnˈvɪzɪdʒ/ vt prévoir (doing de faire).

envoy /ˈenvɔɪ/ n envoyé/-e m/f.

envy /ˈenvɪ/ n envie f. ● vt envier; ~ sb sth envier qch à qn.

epic /ˈepɪk/ n épopée f. ● adj épique.

epidemic /epɪˈdemɪk/ n épidémie f.

epilepsy /ˈepɪlepsɪ/ n épilepsie f.

episode /ˈepɪsəʊd/ n épisode m.

epitome /ɪˈpɪtəmɪ/ n modèle m. **epitomize** vt incarner.

equal /ˈiːkwəl/ adj & n égal/-e (m/f); ~ opportunities/rights égalité f des chances/droits; ~ to (task) à la hauteur de. ● vt (pt **equalled**) égaler. **equality** n égalité f. **equalize** vt/i égaliser. **equalizer** n (goal) but m égalisateur. **equally** adv (divide) en parts égales; (just as) tout aussi.

equanimity /ekwəˈnɪmɪtɪ/ n sérénité f.

equate /ɪˈkweɪt/ vt assimiler (with à). **equation** n équation f.

equator /ɪˈkweɪtə(r)/ n équateur m.

equilibrium /iːkwɪˈlɪbrɪəm/ n équilibre m.

equip /ɪˈkwɪp/ vt (pt **equipped**) équiper (with de). **equipment** n équipement m.

equity /ˈekwɪtɪ/ n équité f.

equivalence /ɪˈkwɪvələns/ n équivalence f.

era /ˈɪərə/ n ère f, époque f.

eradicate /ɪ'rædɪkeɪt/ vt éliminer; (*disease*) éradiquer.

erase /ɪ'reɪz/ vt effacer. **eraser** n (rubber) gomme f.

erect /ɪ'rekt/ adj droit. ● vt ériger. **erection** n érection f.

erode /ɪ'rəʊd/ vt éroder; (fig) saper. **erosion** n érosion f.

erotic /ɪ'rɒtɪk/ adj érotique.

errand /'erənd/ n commission f, course f.

erratic /ɪ'rætɪk/ adj (behaviour, person) imprévisible; (performance) inégal.

error /'erə(r)/ n erreur f.

erupt /ɪ'rʌpt/ vi (volcano) entrer en éruption; (fig) éclater.

escalate /'eskəleɪt/ vt intensifier. ● vi (conflict) s'intensifier. **escalation** n intensification f. **escalator** n escalier m mécanique, escalator® f.

escapade /'eskəpeɪd/ n frasque f.

escape /ɪ'skeɪp/ vt échapper à. ● vi s'enfuir, s'évader; (gas) fuir. ● n fuite f, évasion f; (of gas etc.) fuite f; **have a lucky or narrow ~** l'échapper belle.

escapism /ɪ'skeɪpɪzəm/ n évasion f (du réel).

escort[1] /'eskɔːt/ n (guard) escorte f; (companion) compagnon/ compagne m/f.

escort[2] /ɪ'skɔːt/ vt escorter.

Eskimo /'eskɪməʊ/ n Esquimau/- de m/f.

especially /ɪ'speʃəlɪ/ adv en particulier.

espionage /'espɪənɑːʒ/ n espionnage m.

espresso /e'spresəʊ/ n (café) express m.

essay /'eseɪ/ n (in literature) essai m; (School) rédaction f; (Univ) dissertation f.

essence /'esns/ n essence f.

essential /ɪ'senʃl/ adj essentiel; **the ~s** l'essentiel m. **essentially** adv essentiellement.

establish /ɪ'stæblɪʃ/ vt établir; (business) fonder.

establishment /ɪ'stæblɪʃmənt/ n (process) instauration f; (institution) établissement m; **the E~** l'ordre m établi.

estate /ɪ'steɪt/ n (house and land) domaine m; (possessions) biens mpl; (housing estate) cité f; **~ agent** n agent m immobilier. **~ car** n break m.

esteem /ɪ'stiːm/ n estime f.

esthetic /es'θetɪk/ adj (US) ➡ AESTHETIC.

estimate[1] /'estɪmət/ n (calculation) estimation f; (Comm) devis m.

estimate[2] /'estɪmeɪt/ vt évaluer; **~ that** estimer que. **estimation** n (esteem) estime f; (judgment) opinion f.

Estonia /ɪ'stəʊnɪə/ n Estonie f.

estuary /'estjʊərɪ/ n estuaire m.

eternal /ɪ'tɜːnl/ adj éternel.

eternity /ɪ'tɜːnətɪ/ n éternité f.

ethic /'eθɪk/ n éthique f; **~s** moralité f. **ethical** adj éthique.

ethnic /'eθnɪk/ adj ethnique. **~ cleansing** nettoyage m ethnique.

EU abbr **European Union** UE f, Union f européenne.

euphoria /juː'fɔːrɪə/ n euphorie f.

euro /'jʊərəʊ/ n euro m. **~ zone** zone f euro.

Europe /'jʊərəp/ n Europe f.

European /jʊərə'pɪən/ adj & n européen/-ne (m/f); **~ Community** Communauté f européenne.

eurosceptic /'jʊərəʊskeptɪk/ n eurosceptique mf.

euthanasia /juːrəʊskeptɪk/ n euthanasie f.

evacuate /ɪˈvækjʊeɪt/ vt évacuer.

evade /ɪˈveɪd/ vt (blow) esquiver; (question) éluder.

evaluation /ɪvæljʊˈeɪʃn/ n évaluation f.

evaporate /ɪˈvæpjuˈeɪʃn/ vi s'évaporer; ~d milk lait m condensé.

evasion /ɪˈveɪʒn/ n fuite f (of devant); (excuse) faux-fuyant m; tax ~ évasion f fiscale. **evasive** adj évasif.

eve /iːv/ n veille f (of de).

even /ˈiːvn/ adj (surface, voice, contest) égal; (teeth, hem) régulier; (number) pair; get ~ with se venger de. ● adv même; ~ better/etc. (still) encore mieux/etc.; ~ so quand même. □ ~ out (differences) s'atténuer; ~ sth out (inequalities) réduire qch; ~ up équilibrer.

evening /ˈiːvnɪŋ/ n soir m; (whole evening, event) soirée f.

evenly /ˈiːvnlɪ/ adv (spread, apply) uniformément; (breathe) régulièrement; (equally) en parts égales.

event /ɪˈvent/ n événement m; (Sport) épreuve f; in the ~ of en cas de. **eventful** adj mouvementé.

eventual /ɪˈventʃʊəl/ adj (outcome, decision) final; (aim) à long terme. **eventuality** n éventualité f. **eventually** adv finalement; (in future) un jour ou l'autre.

ever /ˈevə(r)/ adv jamais; (at all times) toujours.

evergreen /ˈevəgriːn/ n arbre m à feuilles persistantes.

everlasting /evəˈlɑːstɪŋ/ adj éternel.

ever since prep & adv depuis.

every /ˈevrɪ/ adj ~ house/window toutes les maisons/les fenêtres; ~ time/minute chaque fois/minute; ~ day tous les jours; ~ other day

tous les deux jours. **everybody** pron tout le monde. **everyday** adj quotidien. **everyone** pron tout le monde. **everything** pron tout. **everywhere** adv partout; ~where he goes partout où il va.

evict /ɪˈvɪkt/ vt expulser (from de).

evidence /ˈevɪdəns/ n (proof) preuves fpl (that que; of, for de); (testimony) témoignage m; (traces) trace f (of de); give ~ témoigner; be in ~ être visible. **evident** adj manifeste. **evidently** adv (apparently) apparemment; (obviously) manifestement.

evil /ˈiːvl/ adj malfaisant. ● n mal m.

evoke /ɪˈvəʊk/ vt évoquer.

evolution /iːvəˈluːʃn/ n évolution f.

evolve /ɪˈvɒlv/ vi évoluer. ● vt élaborer.

ewe /juː/ n brebis f.

ex- /eks/ pref ex-, ancien.

exact /ɪgˈzækt/ adj exact; the ~ opposite exactement le contraire. ● vt exiger (from de). **exactly** adv exactement.

exaggerate /ɪgˈzædʒəreɪt/ vt/i exagérer.

exalted /ɪgˈzɔːltɪd/ adj élevé.

exam /ɪgˈzæm/ n 🔲 examen m.

examination /ɪgzæmɪˈneɪʃn/ n examen m.

examine /ɪgˈzæmɪn/ vt examiner; (witness) interroger. **examiner** n examinateur/-trice m/f.

example /ɪgˈzɑːmpl/ n exemple m; for ~ par exemple; make an ~ of punir pour l'exemple.

exasperate /ɪgˈzæspəreɪt/ vt exaspérer.

excavate /ˈekskəveɪt/ vt fouiller. **excavations** npl fouilles fpl.

exceed /ɪkˈsiːd/ vt dépasser. **exceedingly** adv extrêmement.

excel /ɪk'sel/ vi (pt **excelled**) exceller (at, in en; at doing à faire). ● vt surpasser.

excellence /'eksələns/ n excellence f. **excellent** adj excellent.

except /ɪk'sept/ prep sauf, excepté; ~ for à part. ● vt excepter. **excepting** prep sauf, excepté.

exception /ɪk'sepʃn/ n exception f; take ~ to s'offusquer de. **exceptional** adj exceptionnel.

excerpt /'eksɜ:pt/ n extrait m.

excess[1] /'ɪk'ses/ n excès m.

excess[2] /'ekses/ adj ~ weight excès m de poids; ~ baggage excédent m de bagages.

excessive /ɪk'sesɪv/ adj excessif.

exchange /ɪks'tʃeɪndʒ/ vt échanger (for contre). ● n échange m; (between currencies) change m; ~ rate taux m de change; telephone ~ central m téléphonique.

Exchequer /ɪks'tʃekə(r)/ n (Pol) ministère m britannique des finances.

excise /'eksaɪz/ n excise f, taxe f.

excite /ɪk'saɪt/ vt exciter; (enthuse) enthousiasmer. **excited** adj excité; get ~d s'exciter. **excitement** n excitation f. **exciting** adj passionnant.

exclaim /ɪk'skleɪm/ vt s'exclamer.

exclamation /eksklə'meɪʃn/ n exclamation f; ~ mark or point (US) point m d'exclamation.

exclude /ɪk'sklu:d/ vt exclure.

exclusive /ɪk'sklu:sɪv/ adj (club) fermé; (rights) exclusif; (news item) en exclusivité; ~ of meals repas non compris. **exclusively** adv exclusivement.

excruciating /ɪk'skru:ʃɪeɪtɪŋ/ adj atroce.

excursion /ɪk'skɜ:ʃn/ n excursion f.

excuse[1] /ɪk'skju:z/ vt excuser; ~

from (exempt) dispenser de; ~ me! excusez-moi, pardon!

excuse[2] /ɪk'skju:s/ n (reason) excuse f; (pretext) prétexte m (for sth à qch; for doing pour faire).

ex-directory /eksdaɪ'rektərɪ/ adj sur liste rouge.

execute /'eksɪkju:t/ vt exécuter. **executioner** n bourreau m.

executive /ɪg'zekjʊtɪv/ n (person) cadre m; (committee) exécutif m. ● adj exécutif.

exemplary /ɪg'zemplərɪ/ adj exemplaire.

exemplify /ɪg'zemplɪfaɪ/ vt illustrer.

exempt /ɪg'zempt/ adj exempt (from de). ● vt exempter.

exercise /'eksəsaɪz/ n exercice m; ~ book cahier m. ● vt exercer; (restraint, patience) faire preuve de. ● vi faire de l'exercice.

exert /ɪg'zɜ:t/ vt exercer; ~ oneself se fatiguer. **exertion** n effort m.

exhaust /ɪg'zɔ:st/ vt épuiser. ● n (Auto) pot m d'échappement. **exhaustive** /ɪg'zɔ:stɪv/ adj exhaustif.

exhibit /ɪg'zɪbɪt/ vt exposer; (fig) manifester. ● n objet m exposé.

exhibition /eksɪ'bɪʃn/ n exposition f; (of skill) démonstration f. **exhibitionist** n exhibitionniste mf.

exhibitor /ɪg'zɪbɪtə(r)/ n exposant/-e m/f.

exhilarate /ɪg'zɪləreɪt/ vt griser.

exile /'eksaɪl/ n exil m; (person) exilé/-e m/f. ● vt exiler.

exist /ɪg'zɪst/ vi exister. **existence** n existence f; be in ~ence exister. **existing** adj actuel.

exit /'eksɪt/ n sortie f. ● vt/i (also Comput) sortir (de).

exodus /'eksədəs/ n exode m.

exonerate /ɪg'zɒnəreɪt/ vt disculper.

exotic /ɪg'zɒtɪk/ adj exotique.

expand /ɪk'spænd/ vt développer; (workforce) accroître. • vi se développer; (population) s'accroître; (metal) se dilater.

expanse /ɪk'spæns/ n étendue f.

expansion /ɪk'spænʃn/ n développement m; (Pol, Comm) expansion f.

expatriate /eks'pætrɪət/ adj & n expatrié/-e (m/f).

expect /ɪk'spekt/ vt s'attendre à; (suppose) supposer; (demand) exiger; (baby) attendre.

expectancy /ɪk'spektənsɪ/ n attente f.

expectant /ɪk'spektənt/ adj ~ mother future maman f.

expectation /ekspek'teɪʃn/ n (assumption) prévision f; (hope) aspiration f; (demand) exigence f.

expedient /ɪk'spiːdɪənt/ adj opportun. • n expédient m.

expedition /ekspɪ'dɪʃn/ n expédition f.

expel /ɪk'spel/ vt (pt expelled) expulser; (pupil) renvoyer.

expend /ɪk'spend/ vt consacrer.

expenditure /ɪk'spendɪtʃə(r)/ n dépenses fpl.

expense /ɪk'spens/ n frais mpl; at sb's ~ aux frais de qn; ~ account frais mpl de représentation. **expensive** adj cher; (tastes) de luxe. **expensively** adv luxueusement.

experience /ɪk'spɪərɪəns/ n expérience f. • vt (undergo) connaître; (feel) éprouver; ~d expérimenté.

experiment /ɪk'sperɪmənt/ n expérience f. • vi expérimenter, faire des essais.

expert /'ekspɜːt/ n spécialiste mf. • adj spécialisé, expert. **expertise** n compétence f. **expertly** adv de

manière experte.

expire /ɪk'spaɪə(r)/ vi expirer; ~d périmé. **expiry** n expiration f.

explain /ɪk'spleɪn/ vt expliquer. **explanation** n explication f. **explanatory** adj explicatif.

explicit /ɪk'splɪsɪt/ adj explicite.

explode /ɪk'spləʊd/ vt/i (faire) exploser.

exploit¹ /'eksplɔɪt/ n exploit m.

exploit² /ɪk'splɔɪt/ vt exploiter.

exploration /eksplə'reɪʃn/ n exploration f; exploratory adj (talks) exploratoire. **explore** vt explorer; (fig) étudier. **explorer** n explorateur/-trice m/f.

explosion /ɪk'spləʊʒn/ n explosion f. **explosive** adj & n explosif (m).

exponent /ɪk'spəʊnənt/ n avocat/-e m/f (of de).

export¹ /ɪk'spɔːt/ vt exporter.

export² /'ekspɔːt/ n (process) exportation f; (product) produit m d'exportation.

expose /ɪk'spəʊz/ vt exposer; (disclose) révéler.

exposure /ɪk'spəʊʒə(r)/ n révélation f; (Photo) pose f; die of ~ mourir de froid.

express /ɪk'spres/ vt exprimer. • adj exprès. • adv send sth ~ envoyer qch en exprès. • n (train) rapide m. **expression** n expression f. **expressive** adj expressif. **expressly** adv expressément.

exquisite /'ekskwɪzɪt/ adj exquis.

extend /ɪk'stend/ vt (visit) prolonger; (house) agrandir; (range) élargir; (arm, leg) étendre. • vi (stretch) s'étendre; (in time) se prolonger. **extension** n (of line, road) prolongement m; (of visa, loan) prorogation f; (building) addition f; (phone number) poste m; (cable) rallonge f.

extensive /ɪk'stensɪv/ adj vaste;

(study) approfondi; (damage) considérable. **extensively** adv (much) beaucoup; (very) très.

extent /ɪkˈstent/ n (size, scope) étendue f; (degree) mesure f; to some ~ dans une certaine mesure; to such an ~ that à tel point que.

extenuating /ɪkˈstenjueɪtɪŋ/ adj atténuant.

exterior /ɪkˈstɪərɪə(r)/ adj & n extérieur (m).

exterminate /ɪkˈstɜːmɪneɪt/ vt exterminer.

external /ɪkˈstɜːnl/ adj extérieur; (cause, medical use) externe.

extinct /ɪkˈstɪŋkt/ adj (species) disparu; (volcano, passion) éteint.

extinguish /ɪkˈstɪŋgwɪʃ/ vt éteindre. **extinguisher** n extincteur m.

extol /ɪkˈstəʊl/ vt (pt extolled) louer, chanter les louanges de.

extort /ɪkˈstɔːt/ vt extorquer (from à). **extortion** n (Jur) extorsion f. **extortionate** adj exorbitant.

extra /ˈekstrə/ adj supplémentaire; ~ charge supplément m; ~ time (football) prolongation f; ~ strong extrafort. ● adv encore; plus. ● n supplément m; (cinema) figurant/-e m/f.

extract[1] /ɪkˈstrækt/ vt sortir (from de); (tooth) extraire; (promise) arracher.

extract[2] /ˈekstrækt/ n extrait m.

extra-curricular /ekstrəkəˈrɪkjʊlə(r)/ adj parascolaire.

extradite /ˈekstrədaɪt/ vt extrader.

extramarital /ekstrəˈmærɪtl/ adj extraconjugal.

extramural /ekstrəˈmjʊərəl/ adj (Univ) hors faculté.

extraordinary /ɪkˈstrɔːdnrɪ/ adj extraordinaire.

extravagance /ɪkˈstrævəgəns/ n prodigalité f. **extravagant** adj (per-

son) dépensier; (claim) extravagant.

extreme /ɪkˈstriːm/ adj & n extrême (m). **extremely** adv extrêmement. **extremist** n extrémiste mf. **extremity** n extrémité f.

extricate /ˈekstrɪkeɪt/ vt dégager.

extrovert /ˈekstrəvɜːt/ n extraverti/-e m/f.

exuberance /ɪgˈzjuːbərəns/ n exubérance f.

exude /ɪgˈzjuːd/ vt (charm) respirer; (smell) exhaler.

eye /aɪ/ n œil m (pl yeux); keep an ~ on surveiller. ● vt (pt eyed; pres p eyeing) regarder. ~**ball** n globe m oculaire. ~**brow** n sourcil m. ~**catching** adj attrayant. ~**lash** n cil m. ~**lid** n paupière f. ~**opener** n révélation f. ~**shadow** n ombre f à paupières. ~**sight** n vue f. ~**sore** n horreur f. ~**witness** n témoin m oculaire.

··

Ff

··

fable /ˈfeɪbl/ n fable f.

fabric /ˈfæbrɪk/ n (cloth) tissu m.

fabulous /ˈfæbjuləs/ adj fabuleux; (marvellous) formidable.

face /feɪs/ n visage m, figure f; (expression) air m; (appearance, dignity) face f; (of clock) cadran m; (Geol) face f; (of rock) paroi f; in the ~ of face à; make a (funny) ~ faire la grimace; ~ to ~ face à face. ● vt être en face de; (risk) devoir affronter; (confront) faire face à; (deal with) I can't ~ him je n'ai pas le courage de le voir. ● vi (person) regarder; (chair) être tourné vers; (window) donner sur; ~ up to faire face à; ~d with face à.

facelift /'feɪslɪft/ n lifting m; give a
~ to donner un coup de neuf à.

face value n valeur f nominale;
take sth at~ prendre qch au pied
de la lettre.

facial /'feɪʃl/ adj (hair) du visage;
(injury) au visage. ● n soin m du
visage.

facility /fə'sɪlətɪ/ n (building) complexe m; (feature) fonction f; facilities (equipment) équipements mpl.

facsimile /fæk'sɪmǝlɪ/ n fac-
similé m.

fact /fækt/ n fait m; as a matter of
~, in ~ en fait; know for a ~
that savoir de source sûre que;
owing/due to the ~ that étant
donné que.

factor /'fæktǝ(r)/ n facteur m.

factory /'fæktǝrɪ/ n usine f.

factual /'fæktʃʊǝl/ adj (account, description) basé sur les faits; (evidence) factuel.

faculty /'fæklti/ n faculté f.

fade /feɪd/ vi (sound) s'affaiblir;
(memory) s'effacer; (flower) se
faner; (material) se décolorer;
(colour) passer.

fail /feɪl/ vi échouer; (grow weak)
(s'af)faiblir; (run short) manquer;
(engine) tomber en panne. ● vt
(exam) échouer à; ~ to do (not do)
ne pas faire; (not be able) ne pas
réussir à faire; without ~ à
coup sûr.

failing /'feɪlɪŋ/ n défaut m; ~ that/
this sinon.

failure /'feɪljǝ(r)/ n échec m; (person) raté/-e m/f; (breakdown) panne
f; ~ to do (inability) incapacité f de
faire.

faint /feɪnt/ adj léger, faible; feel ~
(ill) se sentir mal; I haven't the
~est idea je n'en ai pas la moindre

idée. ● vi s'évanouir. ● n évanouissement m; ~-hearted adj timide.

fair /feǝ(r)/ n foire f. ● adj (hair)
blond; (skin) clair; (weather) beau;
(amount) raisonnable; (just) juste,
équitable. ● adv (play) loyalement.
~ trade commerce m équitable.

fairground n champ m de foire.

fairly /'feǝlɪ/ adv (justly) équitable-
ment; (rather) assez.

fairness /'feǝnɪs/ n justice f.

fairy /'feǝrɪ/ n fée f; ~ story,
~-tale n conte m de fées.

faith /feɪθ/ n (belief) foi f; (confidence) confiance f.

faithful /'feɪθfl/ adj fidèle.

fake /feɪk/ n (forgery) faux m; (person) imposteur m; it is a ~ c'est un
faux. ● adj faux. ● vt (signature)
contrefaire; (results) falsifier; (illness)
feindre.

falcon /'fɔːlkǝn/ n faucon m.

fall /fɔːl/ vi (pt fell; pp fallen) tomber; ~ short être insuffisant. ● n
chute f; (autumn: US) automne m;
Niagara F~s chutes fpl du Niagara.
□ ~ **back on** se rabattre sur; ~
behind prendre du retard. ~
down or **off** tomber. ~ **for** (person
🗊) tomber amoureux de; (a trick
🗊) se laisser prendre à. ~ **in** (Mil)
se mettre en rangs. ~ **off** (decrease) diminuer. ~ **out** se brouiller
(with avec). ~ **over** tomber (par
terre). ~ **through** (plans) tomber à
l'eau.

fallacy /'fælǝsɪ/ n erreur f.

false /fɔːls/ adj faux. ~ **teeth** npl
dentier m.

falter /'fɔːltǝ(r)/ vi (courage) faiblir;
(when speaking) bafouiller 🗊.

fame /feɪm/ n renommée f. **famed**
adj célèbre (for pour).

familiar /fǝ'mɪlɪǝ(r)/ adj familier;
be ~ with connaître.

family /ˈfæməlɪ/ n famille f.

famine /ˈfæmɪn/ n famine f.

famished /ˈfæmɪʃt/ adj affamé.

famous /ˈfeɪməs/ adj célèbre (for pour).

fan /fæn/ n (mechanical) ventilateur m; (hand-held) éventail m; (of person) fan mf 🔲, admirateur/-trice m/f; (enthusiast) fervent/-e m/f, passionné/-e m/f. ● vt (pt fanned) (face) éventer; (fig) attiser. ● vi ~ out se déployer en éventail.

fanatic /fəˈnætɪk/ n fanatique mf.

fan belt n courroie f de ventilateur.

fancy /ˈfænsɪ/ n (whim, fantasy) fantaisie f; take a ~to sb se prendre d'affection pour qn; it took my ~ ça m'a plu. ● adj (buttons etc.) fantaisie inv; (prices) extravagant; (impressive) impressionnant. ● vt s'imaginer; (want 🔲) avoir envie de; (like 🔲) aimer. ~ **dress** n déguisement m.

fang /fæŋ/ n (of dog) croc m; (of snake) crochet m.

fantasize /ˈfæntəsaɪz/ vi fantasmer.

fantastic /fænˈtæstɪk/ adj fantastique.

fantasy /ˈfæntəsɪ/ n fantaisie f; (daydream) fantasme m.

fanzine /ˈfænziːn/ n magazine m des fans, fanzine m.

FAQ abbr (**Frequently Asked Questions**) (Internet) FAQ f, foire f aux questions.

far /fɑː(r)/ adv loin; (much) beaucoup; (very) très; ~ **away**, ~ **off** au loin; as ~ as (up to) jusqu'à à; ~ as I know autant que je sache; by ~ de loin; ~ **from** loin de. ● adj lointain; (end, side) autre. ~**away** adj lointain.

farce /fɑːs/ n farce f.

fare /feə(r)/ n (prix du) billet m;

(food) nourriture f. ● vi (progress) aller; (manage) se débrouiller.

Far East n Extrême-Orient m.

farewell /feəˈwel/ interj & n adieu (m).

farm /fɑːm/ n ferme f. ● vt cultiver; ~ **out** céder en sous-traitance. ● vi être fermier. **farmer** n fermier m. ~**house** n ferme f. **farming** n agriculture f. ~**yard** n basse-cour f.

fart /fɑːt/ 🔲 vi péter 🔲. ● n pet m 🔲.

farther /ˈfɑːðə(r)/ adv plus loin. ● adj plus éloigné.

farthest /ˈfɑːðɪst/ adv le plus loin. ● adj le plus éloigné.

fascinate /ˈfæsɪneɪt/ vt fasciner.

Fascism /ˈfæʃɪzəm/ n fascisme m.

fashion /ˈfæʃn/ n (current style) mode f; (manner) façon f; in ~ à la mode; out of ~ démodé. ● vt façonner. **fashionable** adj à la mode.

fast /fɑːst/ adj rapide; (colour) grand teint inv; (firm) fixe, solide; be ~ (of a clock) avancer. ● adv vite; (firmly) ferme; be ~ **asleep** dormir d'un sommeil profond. ● vi jeûner. ● n jeûne m.

fasten /ˈfɑːsn/ vt/i (s')attacher. **fastener, fastening** n attache f, fermeture f.

fast food n fast-food m, restauration f rapide.

fat /fæt/ n graisse f; (on meat) gras m. ● adj (**fatter, fattest**) gros, gras; (meat) gras; (profit) gros; a ~ **lot** 🔲 bien peu (of de).

fatal /ˈfeɪtl/ adj mortel; (fateful, disastrous) fatal. **fatality** n mort m. **fatally** adv mortellement.

fate /feɪt/ n sort m. **fateful** adj fatidique.

father /ˈfɑːðə(r)/ n père m. ~**hood** n paternité f. ~**-in-law** n (pl ~**s-inlaw**) beau-père m.

fathom | felony

fathom /'fæðəm/ n brasse f (= 1.8 m). ● vt ~(out) comprendre.

fatigue /fə'ti:g/ n épuisement m; (Tech) fatigue f. ● vt fatiguer.

fatten /'fætn/ vt/i engraisser. **fattening** adj qui fait grossir.

fatty /'fætɪ/ adj (food) gras; (tissue) adipeux.

faucet /'fɔ:sɪt/ n (US) robinet m.

fault /fɔ:lt/ n (defect, failing) défaut m; (blame) faute f; (Geol) faille f; at ~ fautif; **find** ~ **with** critiquer. ● vt ~ **sth/sb** prendre en défaut qn/qch. **faulty** adj défectueux.

favour, (US) **favor** /'feɪvə(r)/ n faveur f; **do sb a** ~ rendre service à qn; **in** ~ **of** pour. ● vt favoriser; (support) être en faveur de; (prefer) préférer. **favourable** adj favorable.

favourite /'feɪvərɪt/ adj & n favori/-te (m/f).

fawn /fɔ:n/ n (animal) faon m; (colour) beige m foncé. ● vi ~ **on** flagorner.

fax /fæks/ n fax m, télécopie f. ● vt faxer, envoyer par télécopie. ~ **machine** n fax m, télécopieur m; (for public use) Publifax® m.

FBI abbr (**Federal Bureau of Investigation**) (US) Police f judiciaire fédérale.

fear /fɪə(r)/ n crainte f, peur f; (fig) risque m; **for** ~ **of/that** de peur de/que. ● vt craindre.

feasible /'fi:zəbl/ adj faisable; (likely) plausible.

feast /fi:st/ n festin m; (Relig) fête f. ● vi festoyer. ● vt régaler (**on** de).

feat /fi:t/ n exploit m.

feather /'feðə(r)/ n plume f. ● vt ~ **one's nest** s'enrichir.

feature /'fi:tʃə(r)/ n caractéristique f; (of person, face) trait m; (film) long métrage m; (article) article m de fond. ● vt (advert) représenter;

(give prominence to) mettre en vedette. ● vi figurer (**in** dans).

February /'febrʊərɪ/ n février m.

fed /fed/ ⇒**FEED**. ● adj **be** ~ **up** 🗆 en avoir marre 🗆 (**with** de).

federal /'fedərəl/ adj fédéral.

fee /fi:/ n (for entrance) prix m; ~(s) (of doctor) honoraires mpl; (of actor, artist) cachet m; (for tuition) frais mpl; (for enrolment) droits mpl.

feeble /'fi:bl/ adj faible.

feed /fi:d/ vt (pt **fed**) nourrir, donner à manger à; (suckle) allaiter; (supply) alimenter. ● vi se nourrir (**on** de). ● n nourriture f; (of baby) tétée f.

feedback /'fi:dbæk/ n réaction (s) f(pl); (Med, Tech) feed-back m.

feel /fi:l/ vt (pt **felt**) (touch) tâter; (be conscious of) sentir; (emotion) ressentir; (experience) éprouver; (think) estimer. ● vi (tired, lonely) se sentir; ~ **hot/thirsty** avoir chaud/soif; ~ **as if** avoir l'impression que; ~ **awful** (ill) se sentir malade; ~ **like** (want) 🗆 avoir envie de.

feeler /'fi:lə(r)/ n antenne f; **put out** ~s tâter le terrain.

feeling /'fi:lɪŋ/ n (emotion) sentiment m; (physical) sensation f; (impression) impression f.

feet /fi:t/ ⇒**FOOT**.

feign /feɪn/ vt feindre.

fell /fel/ ⇒**FALL**. ● vt (cut down) abattre.

fellow /'feləʊ/ n compagnon m, camarade m; (of society) membre m; (man 🗆) type m 🗆. ~**-countryman** n compatriote m. ~**-passenger** n compagnon m de voyage.

fellowship /'feləʊʃɪp/ n camaraderie f; (group) association f.

felony /'felənɪ/ n crime m.

felt /felt/ →FEEL. ● n feutre m.
~-tip n feutre m.

female /'fiːmeɪl/ adj (animal) femelle; (voice, sex) féminin. ● n femme f; (animal) femelle f.

feminine /'femɪnɪn/ adj & n féminin (m). **femininity** n féminité f. **feminist** n féministe mf.

fence /fens/ n barrière f; sit on the ~ ne pas prendre position. ● vt (in) clôturer. ● vi (Sport) faire de l'escrime. **fencing** n escrime f.

fend /fend/ vi ~ for oneself se débrouiller tout seul. ● vt ~ off (blow, attack) parer.

fender /'fendə(r)/ n (for fireplace) garde-cendre m; (mudguard: US) garde-boue m inv.

ferment¹ /'fɜːment/ n ferment m; (excitement: fig) agitation f.

ferment² /fə'ment/ vt/i (faire) fermenter.

fern /fɜːn/ n fougère f.

ferocious /fə'rəʊʃəs/ adj féroce.

ferret /'ferɪt/ n (animal) furet m. ● vi ~ about fureter. ● vt ~ out dénicher.

ferry /'ferɪ/ n (long-distance) ferry m; (short-distance) bac m. ● vt transporter.

fertile /'fɜːtaɪl/ adj fertile; (person, animal) fécond. **fertilizer** n engrais m.

festival /'festɪvl/ n festival m; (Relig) fête f.

festive /'festɪv/ adj de fête, gai; ~ season période f des fêtes. **festivity** n réjouissances fpl.

fetch /fetʃ/ vt (go for) aller chercher; (bring person) amener; (bring thing) apporter; (be sold for) rapporter.

fête /feɪt/ n fête f; (church) kermesse f. ● vt fêter.

fetish /'fetɪʃ/ n (object) fétiche m;

(Psych) obsession f.

feud /fjuːd/ n querelle f.

fever /'fiːvə(r)/ n fièvre f. **feverish** adj fiévreux.

few /fjuː/ det peu de; a ~ houses quelques maisons; quite a ~ people un bon nombre de personnes. ● pron quelques-uns/quelques-unes.

fewer /'fjuːə(r)/ det moins de; be ~ être moins nombreux (than que). **fewest** det le moins de.

fiancé /fɪ'ɒseɪ/ n fiancé m. **fiancée** n fiancée f.

fibre, (US) **fiber** /'faɪbə(r)/ n fibre f. **~glass** n fibre f de verre.

fiction /'fɪkʃn/ n fiction f; (works of) ~ romans mpl. **fictional** adj fictif.

fiddle /'fɪdl/ n 🔊 violon m; (swindle 🔊) combine f. ● vi 🔊 frauder. ● vt 🔊 falsifier; ~ with 🔊 tripoter 🔊.

fidget /'fɪdʒɪt/ vi gigoter sans cesse.

field /fiːld/ n champ m; (Sport) terrain m; (fig) domaine m. ● vt (ball: cricket) bloquer.

fierce /fɪəs/ adj féroce; (storm, attack) violent.

fiery /'faɪərɪ/ adj (-ier, -iest) (hot) ardent; (spirited) fougueux.

fifteen /fɪf'tiːn/ adj & n quinze (m).

fifth /fɪfθ/ adj & n cinquième (mf).

fifty /'fɪftɪ/ adj & n cinquante (m).

fig /fɪg/ n figue f.

fight /faɪt/ vi (pt fought) se battre; (struggle: fig) lutter; (quarrel) se disputer. ● vt se battre avec; (evil: fig) lutter contre. ● n (struggle) lutte f; (quarrel) dispute f; (brawl) bagarre f; (Mil) combat m. □ ~ back se défendre (against contre). **~off** surmonter. **~over** se disputer qch. **fighter** n (determined person) lutteur/-euse m/f; (plane) avion m de chasse. **fighting** n combats mpl.

figment /ˈfɪɡmənt/ n a ~ of the imagination un produit de l'imagination.

figure /ˈfɪɡə(r)/ n (number) chiffre m; (diagram) figure f; (shape) forme f; (body) ligne f; ~s arithmétique f. ● vt s'imaginer. ● vi (appear) figurer; that ~s (US, 🈂) c'est logique; ~ out comprendre; ~ of speech ~ façon f de parler.

file /faɪl/ n (tool) lime f; dossier m, classeur m; (Comput) fichier m; (row) file f. ● vt limer; (papers) classer; (Jur) déposer. □ ~ in entrer en file. □ ~ **past** défiler devant.

filing cabinet n classeur m.

fill /fɪl/ vt/i (se) remplir. ● n have had one's ~ en avoir assez. □ ~ **in** (form) remplir. □ ~ **out** prendre du poids. ~ **up** (Auto) faire le plein (de carburant); (bath, theatre) (se) remplir.

fillet /ˈfɪlɪt/ n filet m. ● vt découper en filets.

filling /ˈfɪlɪŋ/ n (of tooth) plombage m; (of sandwich) garniture f. ~ **station** n station-service f.

film /fɪlm/ n film m; (Photo) pellicule f. ● vt filmer. ~**goer** n cinéphile mf. ~**star** n vedette f de cinéma.

filter /ˈfɪltə(r)/ n filtre m; (traffic signal) flèche f. ● vt/i filtrer; (of traffic) suivre la flèche. ~ **coffee** n café m filtre.

filth /fɪlθ/ n crasse f; **filthy** adj crasseux.

fin /fɪn/ n (of fish, seal) nageoire f; (of shark) aileron m.

final /ˈfaɪnl/ adj dernier; (conclusive) définitif. ● n (Sport) finale f.

finale /fɪˈnɑːlɪ/ n (Mus) finale m.

finalize /ˈfaɪnəlaɪz/ vt mettre au point, fixer.

finally /ˈfaɪnəlɪ/ adv (lastly, at last) enfin, finalement; (once and for all) définitivement.

finance /ˈfaɪnæns/ n finance f. ● adj financier. ● vt financer. **financial** adj financier.

find /faɪnd/ vt (pt found) trouver; (sth lost) retrouver. ● n trouvaille f; ~ **out** découvrir; vi se renseigner (about sur). **findings** npl conclusions fpl.

fine /faɪn/ adj fin; (excellent) beau; ~ **arts** beaux-arts mpl. ● n amende f. ● vt condamner à une amende.

finger /ˈfɪŋɡə(r)/ n doigt m. ● vt palper. ~**nail** n ongle m. ~**print** n empreinte f digitale. ~**tip** n bout m du doigt.

finish /ˈfɪnɪʃ/ vt/i finir; ~ **doing** finir de faire; ~ **up doing** finir par faire; ~ **up** se retrouver à. ● n fin f; (of race) arrivée f; (appearance) finition f.

finite /ˈfaɪnaɪt/ adj fini.

Finland /ˈfɪnlənd/ n Finlande f. **Finn** n Finlandais/-e mf.

Finnish /ˈfɪnɪʃ/ adj finlandais. ● n (Ling) finnois m.

fir /fɜː(r)/ n sapin m.

fire /ˈfaɪə(r)/ n (element) feu m; (blaze) incendie m; (heater) radiateur m; set a ~ to mettre le feu à. ● vt (bullet) tirer; (dismiss) renvoyer; (fig) enflammer. ● vi tirer (at sur). ~ **a gun** tirer un coup de revolver/de fusil. ~ **alarm** n alarme f incendie. ~**arm** n arme f à feu. ~ **brigade** n pompiers mpl. ~ **engine** n voiture f de pompiers. ~ **escape** n escalier m de secours. ~ **extinguisher** n extincteur m. ~**man** n (pl -**men**) pompier m. ~**place** n cheminée f. ~ **station** n caserne f de pompiers. ~**wall** n mur m coupe-feu; (Internet) pare-feu m inv. ~**wood** n bois m de chauffage.

~**work** n feu m d'artifice.

firing squad n peloton m d'exécution.

firm /fɜːm/ n entreprise f, société f. ● adj ferme; (belief) solide.

first /fɜːst/ adj premier; at ~ hand de première main; at ~ sight à première vue; ~ of all tout d'abord. ● n premier/-ière m/f. ● adv d'abord, premièrement; (arrive) le premier, la première; at ~ d'abord. ~ **aid** n premiers soins mpl. ~-**class** adj de première classe. ~ **floor** n premier étage m; (US) rez-de-chaussée m inv. ~ **gear** n première (vitesse) f. F~ **Lady** n (US) épouse f du Président.

firstly /ˈfɜːstlɪ/ adv premièrement.

first name n prénom m.

fish /fɪʃ/ n poisson m; ~ **shop** poissonnerie f. ● vi pêcher; ~ **for** (cod) pêcher; ~ **out** (from water) repêcher; (take out 𝔽) sortir. **fisherman** n (pl -**men**) n pêcheur m.

fishing /ˈfɪʃɪŋ/ n pêche f; go ~ aller à la pêche. ~ **rod** n canne f à pêche.

fishmonger /ˈfɪʃmʌŋɡə(r)/ n poissonnier/-ière m/f.

fist /fɪst/ n poing m.

fit /fɪt/ n accès m, crise f; be a good ~ (dress) être à la bonne taille. ● adj (**fitter, fittest**) en bonne santé; (proper) convenable; (good enough) bon; (able) capable; in no ~ **state to do** pas en état de faire. ● vt/i (pt **fitted**) (into space) aller; (install) poser. ~ **in** vt caser; vi (newcomer) s'intégrer. ~ **out**, ~ **up** équiper.

fitness /ˈfɪtnɪs/ n forme f; (of remark) justesse f.

fitted /ˈfɪtɪd/ adj (wardrobe) encastré. ~ **carpet** n moquette f.

fitting /ˈfɪtɪŋ/ adj approprié. ● n essayage m. ~ **room** n cabine f d'essayage.

five /faɪv/ adj & n cinq (m).

fix /fɪks/ vt (make firm, attach, decide) fixer; (mend) réparer; (deal with) arranger; ~ **sb up with sth** trouver qch à qn.

fixture /ˈfɪkstʃə(r)/ n (Sport) match m; ~s (in house) installations fpl.

fizz /fɪz/ vi pétiller. ● n pétillement m. **fizzy** adj gazeux.

flabbergast /ˈflæbəɡɑːst/ vt sidérer.

flabby /ˈflæbɪ/ adj flasque.

flag /flæɡ/ n drapeau m; (Naut) pavillon m. ● vt (pt **flagged**) ~ (**down**) faire signe de s'arrêter à. ● vi (weaken) faiblir; (sick person) s'affaiblir. ~-**pole** n mât m. ~**stone** n dalle f.

flake /fleɪk/ n flocon m; (of paint, metal) écaille f. ● vi s'écailler.

flamboyant /flæmˈbɔɪənt/ adj (colour) éclatant; (manner) extravagant.

flame /fleɪm/ n flamme f; **burst into** ~s exploser; **go up in** ~s brûler. ● vi flamber.

flamingo /fləˈmɪŋɡəʊ/ n flamant m (rose).

flammable /ˈflæməbl/ adj inflammable.

flan /flæn/ n tarte f; (custard tart) flan m.

flank /flæŋk/ n flanc m. ● vt flanquer.

flannel /ˈflænl/ n (material) flannelle f; (for face) gant m de toilette.

flap /flæp/ vi (pt **flapped**) battre. ● vt ~ **its wings** battre des ailes. ● n (of pocket) rabat m; (of table) abattant m.

flare /fleə(r)/ vi ~ **up** (fighting) éclater. ● n flamboiement m; (Mil) fusée f éclairante; (in skirt) évasement m. **flared** adj évasé.

flash /flæʃ/ vi briller; (on and off) clignoter; ~ past passer à toute vitesse. ● vt faire briller; (aim torch) diriger (at sur); (flaunt) étaler; ~ one's headlights faire un appel de phares. ● n (of news, camera) flash m; in a ~ en un éclair. ~**back** n retour m en arrière. ~**light** n lampe f de poche.

flask /flɑːsk/ n (for chemicals) flacon m; (for drinks) thermos® m or f inv.

flat /flæt/ adj (flatter, flattest) plat; (tyre) à plat; (refusal) catégorique. (fare, rate) fixe. ● adv (say) carrément. ● n (rooms) appartement m; (tyre Ⓔ) crevaison f; (Mus) bémol m.

flat out adv (drive) à toute vitesse; (work) d'arrache-pied.

flatten /ˈflætn/ vt/i (s')aplatir.

flatter /ˈflætə(r)/ vt flatter.

flaunt /flɔːnt/ vt étaler, afficher.

flavour, (US) **flavor** /ˈfleɪvə(r)/ n goût m; (of ice-cream) parfum m. ● vt parfumer (with à), assaisonner (with de). **flavouring** n arôme m artificiel.

flaw /flɔː/ n défaut m.

flea /fliː/ n puce f. ~ **market** n marché m aux puces.

fleck /flek/ n petite tache f.

fled /fled/ ➡FLEE.

flee /fliː/ vt/i (pt fled) fuir.

fleece /fliːs/ n toison f; (garment) polaire f. ● vt plumer.

fleet /fliːt/ n (Naut, Aviat) flotte f; a ~ of vehicles (in reserve) parc m; (on road) convoi m.

fleeting /ˈfliːtɪŋ/ adj très bref.

Flemish /ˈflemɪʃ/ adj flamand. ● n (Ling) flamand m.

flesh /fleʃ/ n chair f; one's (own)

~ and blood la chair de sa chair.

flew /fluː/ ➡FLY.

flex /fleks/ vt (knee) fléchir; (muscle) faire jouer. ● n (Electr) fil m.

flexible /ˈfleksəbl/ adj flexible.

flexitime /ˈfleksɪtaɪm/ n horaire m variable.

flick /flɪk/ n petit coup m. ● vt donner un petit coup à; ~ through feuilleter.

flight /flaɪt/ n (of bird, plane) vol m; ~ of stairs escalier m; (fleeing) fuite f; take ~ prendre la fuite. ~**-deck** n poste m de pilotage.

flimsy /ˈflɪmzɪ/ adj (-ier, -iest) (pej) mince, peu solide.

flinch /flɪntʃ/ vi (wince) broncher; (draw back) reculer.

fling /flɪŋ/ vt (pt flung) jeter.

flint /flɪnt/ n (rock) silex m.

flip /flɪp/ vt (pt flipped) donner un petit coup à; ~ through feuilleter. ● n chiquenaude f.

flippant /ˈflɪpənt/ adj désinvolte.

flipper /ˈflɪpə(r)/ n (of seal) nageoire f; (of swimmer) palme f.

flirt /flɜːt/ vi flirter. ● n flirteur/-euse m/f.

float /fləʊt/ vt/i (faire) flotter. ● n flotteur m; (cart) char m.

flock /flɒk/ n (of sheep) troupeau m; (of people) foule f. ● vi affluer.

flog /flɒg/ vt (pt flogged) (beat) fouetter; (sell Ⓔ) vendre.

flood /flʌd/ n inondation f; (fig) flot m. ● vt inonder. ● vi (building) être inondé; (river) déborder; (people; fig) affluer.

floodlight /ˈflʌdlaɪt/ n projecteur m. ● vt (pt floodlit) illuminer.

floor /flɔː(r)/ n sol m, plancher m; (for dancing) piste f; (storey) étage m. ● vt (knock down) terrasser; (baffle) stupéfier. ~**-board** n planche f.

flop /flɒp/ n (pt **flopped**) (drop) s'affaler; (fail 🔲) échouer; (head) tomber. ● n 🔲 échec m, fiasco m.

floppy /'flɒpɪ/ adj lâche, flasque. ● (disk) n disquette f.

florist /'flɒrɪst/ n fleuriste mf.

flounder /'flaʊndə(r)/ n (animal, person) se débattre (in dans); (economy) stagner. ● n flet m; (US) poisson m plat.

flour /'flaʊə(r)/ n farine f.

flourish /'flʌrɪʃ/ vi prospérer. ● vt brandir. ● n geste m élégant.

flout /flaʊt/ vt se moquer de.

flow /fləʊ/ vi couler; (circulate) circuler; (traffic) s'écouler; (hang loosely) flotter; ~ in affluer; ~ into (of river) se jeter dans. ● n (of liquid, traffic) écoulement m; (of tide) flux m; (of orders, words: fig) flot m. ~ **chart** n organigramme m.

flower /'flaʊə(r)/ n fleur f. ● vi fleurir.

flown /fləʊn/ ⇒FLY.

flu /fluː/ n grippe f.

fluctuate /'flʌktjʊeɪt/ vi varier.

fluent /'fluːənt/ adj (style) aisé; be ~ (in a language) parler (une langue) couramment.

fluff /flʌf/ n peluche(s) f(pl). (down) duvet m.

fluid /'fluːɪd/ adj & n fluide (m).

fluke /fluːk/ n coup m de chance.

flung /flʌŋ/ ⇒FLING.

fluoride /'flɔːraɪd/ n fluor m.

flush /flʌʃ/ vi rougir. ● vt nettoyer à grande eau; ~ **the toilet** tirer la chasse d'eau. ● n (blush) rougeur f; (fig) excitation f. ● adj ~ **with** (level with) au ras de. □ ~ **out** chasser.

fluster /'flʌstə(r)/ vt énerver.

flute /fluːt/ n flûte f.

flutter /'flʌtə(r)/ vi voleter; (of wings) battre; (of *wings*) batte-

ment m; (fig) agitation f; (bet 🔲) pari m.

flux /flʌks/ n changement m continuel.

fly /flaɪ/ n mouche f; (of trousers) braguette f. ● vi (pt **flew**; pp **flown**) voler; (passengers) voyager en avion; (flag) flotter; (rush) filer. ● vt (aircraft) piloter; (passengers, goods) transporter par avion; (flag) arborer. □ ~ **off** s'envoler.

flyer /flaɪə(r)/ n (person) aviateur m; (circular) prospectus m.

flying /'flaɪɪŋ/ adj (saucer) volant; **with** ~ **colours** haut la main; ~ **start** commencer départ m; ~ **visit** visite f éclair (adj inv). ● n (activity) aviation f.

flyover /'flaɪəʊvə(r)/ n pont m (routier).

foal /fəʊl/ n poulain m.

foam /fəʊm/ n écume f, mousse f; ~ (rubber) caoutchouc m mousse. ● vi écumer, mousser.

focus /'fəʊkəs/ n (pl ~**es** or -**ci**) foyer m; (fig) centre m; **be in/out of** ~ être/ne pas être au point. ● vt/i (faire) converger; (instrument) mettre au point; (with camera) faire la mise au point (on sur); (fig) (se) concentrer. ~ **group** groupe m de discussion.

fodder /'fɒdə(r)/ n fourrage m.

foe /fəʊ/ n ennemi/-e m/f.

foetus /'fiːtəs/ n fœtus m.

fog /fɒg/ n brouillard m. ● vt/i (pt **fogged**) (window) (s')embuer.

foggy /'fɒgɪ/ adj brumeux; **it is** ~ il fait du brouillard.

foil /fɔɪl/ n (tin foil) papier m d'aluminium; (deterrent) repoussoir m. ● vt (thwart) déjouer.

fold /fəʊld/ vt/i (paper, clothes) (se) plier; (arms) croiser; (fail) s'effondrer. ● n pli m; (for sheep) parc m à moutons; (Relig) bercail m. **folder** n (file) chemise f; (leaflet) dépliant m. **folding** adj pliant.

foliage /ˈfəʊlɪdʒ/ n feuillage m.

folk /fəʊk/ n gens mpl; ~s parents mpl. ● adj (dance) folklorique; (music) folk.

folklore /ˈfəʊklɔː(r)/ n folklore m.

follow /ˈfɒləʊ/ vt/i suivre; it ~s that il s'ensuit que; ~ suit se faire autant; ~ up (letter) donner suite à. **follower** n partisan m.

following /ˈfɒləʊɪŋ/ n partisans mpl. ● adj suivant; ~ day lendemain. ● prep à la suite de.

fond /fɒnd/ adj (loving) affectueux; (hope) cher; be ~ of aimer.

fondle /ˈfɒndl/ vt caresser.

fondness /ˈfɒndnɪs/ n affection f; (for things) attachement m.

food /fuːd/ n nourriture f; French ~ la cuisine française. ● adj alimentaire. ~ **processor** n robot m (ménager).

fool /fuːl/ n idiot/-e m/f. ● vt duper. ● vi ~ around faire l'idiot; **foolish** adj idiot.

foot /fʊt/ n (pl feet) pied m; (measure) pied m (=30.48 cm); (of stairs, page) bas m; on ~ à pied; on or to one's feet debout; under sb's feet dans les jambes de qn. ● vt (bill) payer.

foot-and-mouth disease n fièvre f aphteuse.

football /ˈfʊtbɔːl/ n (ball) ballon m; (game) football m. **footballer** n footballeur m.

foot: ~-**bridge** n passerelle f; ~**hold** n prise f.

footing /ˈfʊtɪŋ/ n on an equal ~ sur un pied d'égalité; be on a friendly ~ with sb avoir des rapports amicaux avec qn; lose one's ~ perdre pied.

foot: ~**note** n note f (en bas de la page). ~**path** n (in countryside) sentier m; (in town) chemin m. ~**print** n empreinte f (de pied). ~**step** n pas m. ~**wear** n chaussures fpl.

for /fɔː(r)/

● preposition

····▸ pour; ~ me pour moi; music ~ dancing de la musique pour danser; what is it ~? ça sert à quoi?

····▸ (with a time period that is still continuing) depuis; I've been waiting ~ two hours j'attends depuis deux heures; I haven't seen him ~ ten years je ne l'ai pas vu depuis dix ans.

····▸ (with a time period that has ended) pendant; I waited ~ two hours j'ai attendu pendant deux heures.

····▸ (with a future time period) pour; I'm going to Paris ~ six weeks je vais à Paris pour six semaines.

····▸ (with distances) pendant; I drove ~ 50 kilometres j'ai roulé pendant 50 kilomètres.

forbid /fəˈbɪd/ vt (pt forbade. pp forbidden) interdire, défendre (sb to do à qn de faire). ~ sb sth interdire or défendre qch à qn; you are forbidden to leave il vous est interdit de partir. **forbidding** adj menaçant.

force /fɔːs/ n force f; come into ~ entrer en vigueur; the ~s les forces fpl armées. ● vt forcer. □ ~ **into** faire entrer de force. ~ **on** imposer à. **forced** adj forcé.

force-feed vt (pt -fed) (person)

nourrir de force; (*animal*) gaver.
forceful /ˈfɔːsfl/ *adj* énergique.
ford /fɔːd/ *n* gué *m.* ● *vt* passer à gué.
forearm /ˈfɔːrɑːm/ *n* avant-bras *m inv.*
forecast /ˈfɔːkɑːst/ *vt* (*pt* forecast) prévoir. ● *n* weather ~ météo *f.*
forecourt /ˈfɔːkɔːt/ *n* (of garage) devant *m;* (of station) cour *f.*
forefinger /ˈfɔːfɪŋɡə(r)/ *n* index *m.*
forefront /ˈfɔːfrʌnt/ *n* at/in the ~ of à la pointe de.
foregone /ˈfɔːɡɒn/ *adj* it's a ~ conclusion c'est couru d'avance.
foreground /ˈfɔːɡraʊnd/ *n* premier plan *m.*
forehead /ˈfɒrɪd/ *n* front *m.*
foreign /ˈfɒrən/ *adj* étranger; (*trade*) extérieur; (*travel*) à l'étranger. **foreigner** *n* étranger/-ère *m/f.*
foreman /ˈfɔːmən/ *n* (*pl* -men) contremaître *m.*
foremost /ˈfɔːməʊst/ *adj* le plus éminent. ● *adv* first and ~ tout d'abord.
forensic /fəˈrensɪk/ *adj* médico-légal; ~ medicine médecine *f* légale.
foresee /fɔːˈsiː/ *vt* (*pt* -saw. pp -seen) prévoir.
forest /ˈfɒrɪst/ *n* forêt *f.* **forestry** *n* sylviculture *f.*
foretaste /ˈfɔːteɪst/ *n* avant-goût *m.*
forever /fəˈgeɪv/ *adv* toujours.
foreword /ˈfɔːwɜːd/ *n* avant-propos *m inv.*
forfeit /ˈfɔːfɪt/ *n* (penalty) peine *f;* (in game) gage *m.* ● *vt* perdre.
forgave /fəˈgeɪv/ →FORGIVE.
forge /fɔːdʒ/ *n* forge *f.* ● *vt* (metal, friendship) forger; (copy) contrefaire, falsifier. ● *vi* ~ ahead aller de l'a-

vant, avancer. **forger** *n* faussaire *m.* **forgery** *n* faux *m,* contrefaçon *f.*
forget /fəˈget/ *vt/i* (*pt* forgot. pp forgotten) oublier; ~ oneself s'oublier. **forgetful** *adj* distrait. ~**-me-not** *n* myosotis *m.*
forgive /fəˈgɪv/ *vt* (*pt* forgave. pp forgiven) pardonner (sb for sth qch à qn).
fork /fɔːk/ *n* fourchette *f;* (for digging) fourche *f;* (in road) bifurcation *f.* ● *vi* (road) bifurquer; ~ out Ⓣ payer. **forked** *adj* fourchu. ~**-lift truck** *n* chariot *m* élévateur.
form /fɔːm/ *n* forme *f;* (document) formulaire *m;* (School) classe *f;* on ~ en forme. ● *vt/i* (se) former.
formal /ˈfɔːml/ *adj* officiel, en bonne et due forme; (*person*) compassé, cérémonieux; (*dress*) de cérémonie; (*denial, grammar*) formel; (*language*) soutenu. **formality** *n* cérémonial *m;* (requirement) formalité *f.*
format /ˈfɔːmæt/ *n* format *m.* ● *vt* (*pt* formatted) (disk) formater.
former /ˈfɔːmə(r)/ *adj* ancien; (first of two) premier. ● *n* the ~ celui-là, celle-là. **formerly** *adv* autrefois.
formula /ˈfɔːmjʊlə/ *n* (*pl* -ae or -as) formule *f.* **formulate** *vt* formuler.
fort /fɔːt/ *n* (Mil) fort *m;* to hold the ~ s'occuper de tout.
forth /fɔːθ/ *adv* from this day ~ à partir d'aujourd'hui; and so ~ et ainsi de suite; go back and ~ aller et venir.
forthcoming /fɔːθˈkʌmɪŋ/ *adj* à venir, prochain; (sociable Ⓣ) communicatif.
forthright /ˈfɔːθraɪt/ *adj* direct.
forthwith /fɔːθˈwɪθ/ *adv* sur-le-champ.
fortnight /ˈfɔːtnaɪt/ *n* quinze jours

mpl, quinzaine f.

fortnightly /'fɔ:tnaɪtlɪ/ adj bimensuel. ● adv tous les quinze jours.

fortunate /'fɔ:tʃənət/ adj heureux; be ~ avoir de la chance. **fortunately** adv heureusement.

fortune /'fɔ:tʃu:n/ n fortune f; make a ~ faire fortune; have the good ~ to avoir la chance de. ~-**teller** n diseur/-euse m/f de bonne aventure.

forty /'fɔ:tɪ/ adj & n quarante (m). ~ winks un petit somme.

forward /'fɔ:wəd/ adj en avant; (advanced) précoce; (bold) effronté. ● n (Sport) avant m. ● adv en avant; come ~ se présenter; go ~ avancer. ● vt (letter, e-mail) faire suivre; (goods) expédier; (fig) favoriser. **forwardness** n précocité f; **forwards** adv en avant.

fossil /'fɒsl/ n & adj fossile (m).

foster /'fɒstə(r)/ vt (promote) encourager; (child) élever. ● adj (child, parent) adoptif; (family, home) de placement.

fought /fɔ:t/ →FIGHT.

foul /faʊl/ adj (smell, weather) infect; (place, action) immonde; (language) ordurier. ● n (football) faute f. ● vt souiller, encrasser; ~ up 🔢 gâcher. ~-**mouthed** adj grossier.

found /faʊnd/ →FIND. ● vt fonder.

foundation n fondation f; (basis) fondement m; (make-up) fond de teint. **founder** n fondateur/-trice m/f.

fountain /'faʊntɪn/ n fontaine f; ~-**pen** n stylo m à encre.

four /fɔ:(r)/ adj & n quatre (m).

fourteen /fɔ:'ti:n/ adj & n quatorze (m).

fourth /fɔ:θ/ adj & n quatrième (mf).

four-wheel drive n (car)

quatre-quatre m.

fowl /faʊl/ n (one bird) poulet m; (group) volaille f.

fox /fɒks/ n renard m. ● vt (baffle) mystifier; (deceive) tromper.

fraction /'frækʃn/ n fraction f.

fracture /'fræktʃə(r)/ n fracture f. ● vt/i (se) fracturer.

fragile /'frædʒaɪl/ adj fragile.

fragment /'frægmənt/ n fragment m.

fragrance /'freɪgrəns/ n parfum m.

frail /freɪl/ adj frêle.

frame /freɪm/ n (of building, boat) charpente f; (of picture) cadre m; (of window) châssis m; (of spectacles) monture f; ~ of mind humeur f. ● vt encadrer; (fig) formuler; (Jur, 🔢) monter un coup contre. ~-**work** n structure f; (context) cadre m.

France /frɑ:ns/ n France f.

franchise /'fræntʃaɪz/ n (Pol) droit m de vote; (Comm) franchise f.

frank /fræŋk/ adj franc. ● vt affranchir. **frankly** adv franchement.

frantic /'fræntɪk/ adj frénétique. ~ with fou de.

fraternity /frə'tɜ:nətɪ/ n (bond) fraternité f; (group, club) confrérie f.

fraud /frɔ:d/ n (deception) fraude f; (person) imposteur m. **fraudulent** adj frauduleux.

fray /freɪ/ n the ~ la bataille. ● vt/i (s')effilocher.

freckle /'frekl/ n tache f de rousseur.

free /fri:/ adj libre; (gratis) gratuit; (lavish) généreux; ~ (of charge) gratuit(ement); a ~ hand carte f blanche. ● vt (pt freed) libérer; (clear) dégager.

freedom /'fri:dəm/ n liberté f

free: ~ **enterprise** n la libre entreprise. ~ **kick** n coup m franc. ~**lance** adj & n free-lance (mf), indépendant/-e (m/f).

freely /ˈfriːlɪ/ adv librement.

Freemason /ˈfriːmeɪsn/ n francmaçon m.

Freenet /ˈfriːnet/ n (Comput) Libertel m.

free: ~**phone**, ~ **number** n numéro m vert. ~**range** adj (eggs) de ferme.

Freeware /ˈfriːweə(r)/ n (Comput) Gratuiciel m.

freeway /ˈfriːweɪ/ n (US) autoroute f.

freeze /friːz/ vt/i (pt **froze**, pp **frozen**) geler; (Culin) (se) congeler; (wages) bloquer. ● n gel m. blocage m; ~-dried adj lyophilisé.

freezer /ˈfriːzə(r)/ n congélateur m.

freezing /ˈfriːzɪŋ/ adj glacial; below ~ au-dessous de zéro.

freight /freɪt/ n fret m.

French /frentʃ/ adj français. ● n (Ling) français m; the ~ les Français mpl; ~ **bean** n haricot m vert; ~ **fries** npl frites fpl; ~**man** n Français m; ~**speaking** adj francophone; ~ **window** n porte-fenêtre f; ~**woman** n Française f.

frenzied /ˈfrenzɪd/ adj frénétique. **frenzy** n frénésie f.

frequent[1] /ˈfriːkwənt/ adj fréquent.

frequent[2] /frɪˈkwent/ vt fréquenter.

fresco /ˈfreskəʊ/ n fresque f.

fresh /freʃ/ adj frais; (different, additional) nouveau; (cheeky 🅸) culotté.

freshen /ˈfreʃn/ vi (weather) fraîchir. ~ **up** (person) se rafraîchir.

freshly /ˈfreʃlɪ/ adv nouvellement.

freshness /ˈfreʃnɪs/ n fraîcheur f.

freshwater /ˈfreʃwɔːtə(r)/ adj d'eau douce.

friction /ˈfrɪkʃn/ n friction f.

Friday /ˈfraɪdɪ/ n vendredi m.

fridge /frɪdʒ/ n frigo m.

fried /fraɪd/ ➡ FRY. ● adj frit; ~ **eggs** œufs mpl sur le plat.

friend /frend/ n ami/-e m/f. **friendly** adj (-ier, -iest) amical, gentil. **friendship** n amitié f.

frieze /friːz/ n frise f.

fright /fraɪt/ n peur f; (person, thing) horreur f.

frighten /ˈfraɪtn/ vt effrayer; ~ **off** faire fuir. **frightened** adj effrayé; be ~**ed** avoir peur (of de). **frightening** adj effrayant.

frill /frɪl/ n (trimming) fanfreluche f; with no ~s très simple.

fringe /frɪndʒ/ n (edging, hair) frange f; (of area) bordure f; (of society) marge f. ~ **benefits** npl avantages mpl sociaux.

frisk /frɪsk/ vt (search) fouiller.

fritter /ˈfrɪtə(r)/ n beignet m. ● vt ~ **away** gaspiller.

frivolity /frɪˈvɒlɪtɪ/ n frivolité f.

frizzy /ˈfrɪzɪ/ adj crépu.

fro ➡ TO AND FRO.

frog /frɒg/ n grenouille f; a ~ in one's throat un chat dans la gorge.

frolic /ˈfrɒlɪk/ vi (pt **frolicked**) s'ébattre. ● n ébats mpl.

from /frɒm/ prep de; (with time, prices) à partir de, de; (habit, conviction) par; (according to) d'après; take ~ sb prendre à qn; take ~ one's pocket prendre dans sa poche.

front /frʌnt/ n (of car, train) avant m; (of garment, building) devant m; (Mil, Pol) front m; (of book, pamphlet) début m; (appearance: fig) façade *f.* ● *adj* de devant, avant *inv*; (first) premier; ~ **door** porte *f* d'entrée; in ~ (of) devant. **frontage** *n* façade *f.*

frontier /'frʌntɪə(r)/ *n* frontière *f.*

frost /frɒst/ *n* gel *m*, gelée *f*; (on glass) givre *m.* ● *vt/i* (se) givrer. ~**-bite** *n* gelure *f.*

frosty /'frɒstɪ/ *adj* (weather, welcome) glacial; (window) givré.

froth /frɒθ/ *n* (on beer) mousse *f*; (on water) écume *f.* ● *vi* mousser, écumer.

frown /fraʊn/ *vi* froncer les sourcils; ~ **on** désapprouver. ● *n* froncement *m* de sourcils.

froze /frəʊz/ →FREEZE.

frozen /'frəʊzn/ →FREEZE. ● *adj* congelé.

fruit /fruːt/ *n* fruit *m*; (collectively) fruits *mpl.* **fruitful** *adj* (discussions) fructueux. ~ **machine** *n* machine *f* à sous.

frustrate /frʌ'streɪt/ *vt* (plan) faire échouer; (person: Psych) frustrer; (upset 𝕋) exaspérer. **frustration** *n* (Psych) frustration *f*; (disappointment) déception *f.*

fry /fraɪ/ *vt/i* (*pt* **fried**) (faire) frire. **frying-pan** *n* poêle *f* (à frire).

FTP *abbr* (File Transfer Protocol) (Internet) protocole *m* FTP.

fudge /fʌdʒ/ *n* caramel *m* mou. ● *vt* (issue) esquiver.

fuel /'fjuːəl/ *n* combustible *m*; (for car engine) carburant *m.* ● *vt* (*pt* **fuelled**) alimenter en combustible.

fugitive /'fjuːdʒətɪv/ *n & a* fugitif/-ive (*m/f*).

fulfil /fʊl'fɪl/ *vt* (*pt* **fulfilled**) accomplir, réaliser; (condition) remplir; ~ **oneself** s'épanouir. **fulfilling** *adj* satisfaisant. **fulfilment** *n* réalisation *f*; épanouissement *m.*

full /fʊl/ *adj* plein (of de); (bus,

hotel) complet; (programme) chargé; (skirt) ample; be ~ (**up**) n'avoir plus faim; at ~ **speed** à toute vitesse. ● *n* in ~ intégralement; to the ~ complètement. ~ **back** *n* (Sport) arrière *m.* ~ **moon** *n* pleine lune *f.* ~ **name** *n* nom *m* et prénom *m.* ~**-scale** *adj* (drawing etc.) grandeur nature *inv*; (fig) de grande envergure. ~ **stop** *n* point *m.* ~**-time** *adj* & *adv* à plein temps.

fully /'fʊlɪ/ *adv* complètement; ~ **fledged** (member, citizen) à part entière.

fume /fjuːm/ *vi* rager. **fumes** *npl* émanations *fpl*, vapeurs *fpl.*

fun /fʌn/ *n* amusement *m*; be ~ être chouette; for ~ pour rire; make ~ of se moquer de.

function /'fʌŋkʃn/ *n* (purpose, duty) fonction *f*; (event) réception *f.* ● *vi* fonctionner.

fund /fʌnd/ *n* fonds *m.* ● *vt* fournir les fonds pour.

fundamental /fʌndə'mentl/ *adj* fondamental. **fundamentalist** *n* intégriste *mf.*

funeral /'fjuːnərəl/ *n* enterrement *m.* ● *adj* funèbre.

funfair /'fʌnfeə(r)/ *n* fête *f* foraine.

fungus /'fʌŋɡəs/ *n* (*pl* -**gi**) (plant) champignon *m*; (mould) moisissure *f.*

funnel /'fʌnl/ *n* (for pouring) entonnoir *m*; (of ship) cheminée *f.*

funny /'fʌnɪ/ *adj* (-**ier**, -**iest**) drôle; (odd) bizarre.

fur /fɜː(r)/ *n* (for garment) fourrure *f*; (on animal) poils *mpl*; (in kettle) tartre *m.*

furious /'fjʊərɪəs/ *adj* furieux.

furnace /'fɜːnɪs/ *n* fourneau *m.*

furnish /'fɜːnɪʃ/ *vt* (room) meubler; (supply) fournir. **furnishings** *npl* ameublement *m.*

f

furniture /'fɜːnɪtʃə(r)/ n meubles mpl, mobilier m.

furry /'fɜːrɪ/ adj (animal) à fourrure; (toy) en peluche.

further /'fɜːðə(r)/ adj plus éloigné; (additional) supplémentaire. ● adv plus loin; (more) davantage. ● vt avancer. ~ **education** n formation f continue.

furthermore /fɜːðə'mɔː(r)/ adv en outre, de plus.

furthest /'fɜːðɪst/ adj le plus éloigné. ● adv le plus loin.

fury /'fjʊərɪ/ n fureur f.

fuse /fjuːz/ vt/i (melt) fondre; (unite; fig) fusionner; ~ **the lights** faire sauter les plombs. ● n (of plug) fusible m; (of bomb) amorce f.

fuss /fʌs/ n (when upset) histoire(s) f(pl); (when excited) agitation f; make a ~ faire des histoires, s'agiter; (about food) faire des chichis; make a ~ of faire grand cas de. ● vi s'agiter. **fussy** adj (finicky) tatillon; (hard to please) difficile.

future /'fjuːtʃə(r)/ adj futur. ● n avenir m; (Gram) futur m; in ~ à l'avenir.

fuzzy /'fʌzɪ/ adj (hair) crépu; (photograph) flou; (person 🗓) à l'esprit confus.

- -

Gg

Gaelic /'geɪlɪk/ n gaélique m.

gag /gæg/ n (on mouth) bâillon m; (joke) blague f. ● vt (pt gagged) bâillonner.

gain /geɪn/ vt (respect, support) gagner; (speed, weight) prendre. ● vi (of clock) avancer. ● n (increase) augmentation f (in de); (profit) gain m.

galaxy /'gæləksɪ/ n galaxie f.

gale /geɪl/ n tempête f.

gallery /'gælərɪ/ n galerie f; (art) ~ musée m.

Gallic /'gælɪk/ adj français.

gallon /'gælən/ n gallon m (imperial = 4.546 litres; Amer. = 3.785 litres).

gallop /'gæləp/ n galop m. ● vi (pt **galloped**) galoper.

galore /gə'lɔː(r)/ adv (prizes, bargains) en abondance; (drinks, sandwiches) à gogo 🗓.

gamble /'gæmbl/ vt/i jouer. ~ **on** miser sur. ● n (venture) entreprise f risquée; (bet) pari m; (risk) risque m. **gambling** n jeu m.

game /geɪm/ n jeu m; (football) match m; (tennis) partie f; (animals, birds) gibier m. ● adj (brave) courageux. ~ **for** prêt à. ~**keeper** n gardechasse m.

gammon /'gæmən/ n jambon m.

gang /gæŋ/ n (of youths) bande f; (of workmen) équipe f. ● vi ~ **up** se liguer (on, against contre).

gangmaster n gangmaster m, chef m d'équipe (d'ouvriers saisonniers).

gangway /'gæŋweɪ/ n passage m; (aisle) allée f; (of ship) passerelle f.

gaol /dʒeɪl/ n & vt ➡JAIL.

gap /gæp/ n trou m, vide m; (in time) intervalle m; (in education) lacune f; (difference) écart m.

gape /geɪp/ vi rester bouche bée. **gaping** adj béant.

garage /'gærɑːʒ/ n garage m. ● vt mettre au garage.

garbage /'gɑːbɪdʒ/ n (US) ordures fpl.

garden /'gɑːdn/ n jardin m. ● vi jardiner. **gardener** n jardinier-ière m/f. **gardening** n jardinage m.

gargle /'gɑːgl/ vi se gargariser.

garish /'geərɪʃ/ adj (clothes) tapeà-l'œil.

garland /'gɑːlənd/ n guirlande f.

garlic /'gɑːlɪk/ n ail m.

garment /'gɑːmənt/ n vêtement m.

garnish /'gɑːnɪʃ/ vt garnir (with de). ● n garniture f.

garter /'gɑːtə(r)/ n jarretière f.

gas /gæs/ n (pl ~es) gaz m; (Med) anesthésie m; (petrol: US) essence f. ● adj (mask, pipe) à gaz. ● vt asphyxier; (Mil) gazer.

gash /gæʃ/ n entaille f. ● vt entailler.

gasoline /'gæsəliːn/ n (petrol: US) essence f.

gasp /gɑːsp/ vi haleter; (in surprise: fig) avoir le souffle coupé. ● n halètement m.

gate /geɪt/ n (in garden, airport) porte f; (of field, level crossing) barrière f. ~**way** n porte f; (Internet) passerelle f.

gather /'gæðə(r)/ vt (people, objects) rassembler; (pick up) ramasser; (flowers) cueillir; (fig) comprendre; ~ speed prendre de la vitesse; (sewing) froncer. ● vi (people) se rassembler; (pile up) s'accumuler. **gathering** n réunion f.

gauge /geɪdʒ/ n jauge f, indicateur m. ● vt (speed, distance) jauger; (reaction, mood) évaluer.

gaunt /gɔːnt/ adj décharné.

gauze /gɔːz/ n gaze f.

gave /geɪv/ ➡GIVE.

gay /geɪ/ adj (joyful) gai; (homosexual) gay inv. ● n gay mf.

gaze /geɪz/ vi ~ (at) regarder (fixement). ● n regard m (fixe).

GB abbr ➡GREAT BRITAIN.

gear /gɪə(r)/ n (equipment) matériel m; (Tech) engrenage m; (Auto) vitesse f; in ~ en prise. out of ~ au point mort. ● vt to be geared to s'adresser à. ~**box** n (Auto) boîte f de vitesses. ~**lever**, (US) ~**shift** n levier m de vitesse.

geese /giːs/ ➡GOOSE.

gel /dʒel/ n (for hair) gel m.

gem /dʒem/ n pierre f précieuse.

Gemini /'dʒemɪnaɪ/ n Gémeaux mpl.

gender /'dʒendə(r)/ n (Ling) genre m; (of person) sexe m.

gene /dʒiːn/ n gène m. ~ **library** n génothèque f.

general /'dʒenrəl/ adj général. ● n général m; in ~ en général.

general election n élections fpl législatives.

generalization /dʒenrəlar'zeɪʃn/ n généralisation f. **generalize** vt/i généraliser.

general practitioner n (Med) généraliste m.

generate /'dʒenəreɪt/ vt produire.

generation /dʒenə'reɪʃn/ n génération f.

generator /'dʒenəreɪtə(r)/ n (Electr) groupe m électrogène.

generosity /dʒenə'rɒsətɪ/ n générosité f. **generous** adj généreux; (plentiful) copieux.

genetics /dʒɪ'netɪks/ n génétique f.

Geneva /dʒɪˈniːvə/ n Genève.

genial /ˈdʒiːnɪəl/ adj affable, sympathique.

genitals /ˈdʒenɪtlz/ npl organes mpl génitaux.

genius /ˈdʒiːnɪəs/ n (pl ~es) génie m.

genome /ˈdʒiːnəʊm/ n génome m.

gentle /ˈdʒentl/ adj (mild, kind) doux; (pressure, breeze) léger; (reminder, hint) discret.

gentleman /ˈdʒentlmən/ n (pl -men) (man) monsieur m; (well-bred) gentleman m.

gently /ˈdʒentlɪ/ adv doucement.

gents /dʒents/ npl (toilets) toilettes fpl; (on sign) 'Messieurs'.

genuine /ˈdʒenjʊɪn/ adj (reason, motive) vrai; (jewel, substance) véritable; (person, belief) sincère.

geography /dʒɪˈɒɡrəfɪ/ n géographie f.

geology /dʒɪˈɒlədʒɪ/ n géologie f.

geometry /dʒɪˈɒmətrɪ/ n géométrie f.

geriatric /dʒerɪˈætrɪk/ adj gériatrique.

germ /dʒɜːm/ n (Med) microbe m.

German /ˈdʒɜːmən/ n (person) Allemand/-e m/f; (Ling) allemand m. ● adj allemand.

German measles n rubéole f.

Germany /ˈdʒɜːmənɪ/ n Allemagne f.

gesture /ˈdʒestʃə(r)/ n geste m.

---

get /get/

past **got**; past participle **got**, **gotten** (US); present participle **getting**

● transitive verb

····▸ recevoir. we got a letter nous avons reçu une lettre.

····▸ (obtain) I got a job in Paris j'ai trouvé un travail à Paris. I'll ~ sth to eat at the airport je mangerai qch à l'aéroport.

····▸ (buy) acheter. ~ sb a present acheter un cadeau à qn.

····▸ (achieve). he got it right il a obtenu le bon résultat. ~ good grades avoir de bonnes notes.

····▸ (fetch) chercher. go and ~ a chair va chercher une chaise.

····▸ (transport) prendre. we can ~ the bus on peut prendre le bus.

····▸ (understand Ⓣ) comprendre. now let me ~ this right alors si je comprends bien...

····▸ (experience) ~ a surprise être surpris. ~ a shock avoir un choc.

····▸ (illness) ~ measles attraper la rougeole. ~ a cold s'enrhumer.

····▸ (ask or persuade) ~ him to call me dis-lui de m'appeler. I'll ~ her to help me je lui demanderai de m'aider.

····▸ (cause to be done) ~ a TV repaired faire réparer une télévision. ~ one's hair cut se faire couper les cheveux.

● intransitive verb

····▸ devenir. he's getting old il vieillit; it's getting late il se fait tard.

····▸ (in passives) ~ married se marier. ~ hurt être blessé.

····▸ (arrive) arriver. ~ to the airport arriver à l'aéroport.

□ ~ **about** (person) se déplacer. ~ **along** (manage) se

débrouiller; (progress) avancer. ~ **along with** s'entendre avec. ~ **at** (reach) atteindre; (imply) vouloir dire. ~ **away** (escape) s'échapper. ~ **back** vi revenir. ● vt récupérer. ~ **by** vi (manage) se débrouiller. ~ **down** vt/i descendre. ● vt (depress) déprimer. ~ **in** entrer. ~ **into** (car) monter dans; (dress) mettre. ~ **off** vt (bus) descendre; (remove) enlever. ● vi (from bus) descendre; (leave) partir; (Jur) être acquitté. ~ **on** vi (to bus) monter; (succeed) réussir. ● vt (bus) monter. ~ **on with** (person) s'entendre avec; (job) attaquer. ~ **out** sortir. ~ **out of** (fig) se soustraire. ~ **over** (illness) se remettre de. ~ **round** (rule) contourner; (person) entortiller. ~ **through** vi passer; (on phone) ~ through to sb avoir qn. ● vt traverser. ~ **up** se lever. ~ **up to** faire.

getaway /ˈɡetəweɪ/ n fuite f.

ghastly /ˈɡɑːstlɪ/ adj (-ier, -iest) affreux.

gherkin /ˈɡɜːkɪn/ n cornichon m.

ghetto /ˈɡetəʊ/ n ghetto m.

ghost /ɡəʊst/ n fantôme m.

giant /ˈdʒaɪənt/ n & adj géant (m).

gibberish /ˈdʒɪbərɪʃ/ n baragouin m, charabia m.

giblets /ˈdʒɪblɪts/ npl abats mpl.

giddy /ˈɡɪdɪ/ adj (-ier, -iest) vertigineux. **be** or **feel** ~ avoir le vertige.

gift /ɡɪft/ n (present) cadeau m; (ability) don m.

gifted /ˈɡɪftɪd/ adj doué.

gift wrap n papier m cadeau.

gigantic /dʒaɪˈɡæntɪk/ adj gigantesque.

giggle /ˈɡɪɡl/ vi ricaner (sottement), glousser. ● n ricanement m; **the** ~s le fou rire.

gimmick /ˈɡɪmɪk/ n truc m.

gin /dʒɪn/ n gin m.

ginger /ˈdʒɪndʒə(r)/ n gingembre m. ● adj (hair) roux. ~ **beer** n boisson f gazeuse au gingembre. ~**bread** n pain m d'épices.

gingerly /ˈdʒɪndʒəlɪ/ adv avec précaution.

giraffe /dʒɪˈrɑːf/ n girafe f.

girl /ɡɜːl/ n (child) (petite) fille f; (young woman) (jeune) fille f. ~ **band** n girls band m. ~**friend** n amie f; (of boy) petite amie f.

giro /ˈdʒaɪrəʊ/ n virement m bancaire; (cheque) mandat m.

gist /dʒɪst/ n essentiel m.

give /ɡɪv/ vt (pt **gave**; pp **given**) donner; (gesture) faire; (laugh, sigh) pousser; ~ **sb sth** donner qch à qn. ● vi donner; (yield) céder; (stretch) se détendre. ● n élasticité f. ~ **away** donner; (secret) trahir; ~ **back** rendre. ~ **in** (yield) céder (to à). ~ **off** (heat, fumes) dégager; (signal, scent) émettre. ~ **out** vt distribuer. ~ **over** (devote) consacrer; (stop ⓘ) cesser; ~ **up** vt/i (renounce) renoncer (à); (yield) céder. ~ **oneself up** se rendre. ~ **way** céder; (collapse) s'effondrer.

given /ˈɡɪvn/ ⇒GIVE. ● adj donné. ~ **name** n prénom m.

glad /ɡlæd/ adj content. **gladly** adv avec plaisir.

glamorous /ˈɡlæmərəs/ adj séduisant, ensorcelant.

glamour, (US) **glamor** /ˈɡlæmə(r)/ n enchantement m, séduction f.

g

glance /glɑːns/ n coup m d'œil. ● vi ~ at jeter un coup d'œil à.

gland /glænd/ n glande f.

glare /gleə(r)/ vi briller très fort. ~ at regarder d'un air furieux. ● n (of lights) éclat m (aveuglant); (stare: fig) regard m furieux. **glaring** adj (dazzling) éblouissant; (obvious) flagrant.

glass /glɑːs/ n verre m. **glasses** npl (spectacles) lunettes fpl.

glaze /gleɪz/ vt (door) vitrer; (pottery) vernisser. ● n vernis m.

gleam /gliːm/ n lueur f. ● vi luire.

glide /glaɪd/ vi glisser; (of plane) planer. **glider** n planeur m.

glimpse /glɪmps/ n (insight) aperçu m; **catch a ~** of entrevoir.

glitter /ˈglɪtə(r)/ vi scintiller. ● n scintillement m.

global /ˈgləʊbl/ adj (world-wide) mondial; (allembracing) global. ~ **warming** n réchauffement m de la planète.

globalization /ˌgləʊbəlaɪˈzeɪʃən/ n globalisation f.

globe /gləʊb/ n globe m.

gloom /gluːm/ n obscurité f; (sadness: fig) tristesse f. **gloomy** adj triste; (pessimistic) pessimiste.

glorious /ˈglɔːrɪəs/ adj splendide; (deed, hero) glorieux.

glory /ˈglɔːrɪ/ n gloire f; (beauty) splendeur f. ● vi ~ **in** être très fier de.

gloss /glɒs/ n lustre m, brillant m. ● adj brillant. ● vi ~ **over** (make light of) glisser sur; (cover up) dissimuler.

glossary /ˈglɒsərɪ/ n glossaire m.

glossy /ˈglɒsɪ/ adj brillant.

glove /glʌv/ n gant m. ~ **compartment** n (Auto) boîte f à gants.

glow /gləʊ/ vi (fire) rougeoyer;

(person, eyes) rayonner. ● n rougeoiement m, éclat m. **glowing** adj (report) enthousiaste.

glucose /ˈgluːkəʊs/ n glucose m.

glue /gluː/ n colle f. ● vt (pres p **gluing**) coller.

GM abbr (genetically modified) transgénique.

gnaw /nɔː/ vt/i ronger.

GNP abbr (**Gross National Product**) produit m national brut, PNB m.

---

go /gəʊ/

present go, goes; past went; past participle gone

● **intransitive verb**

···▸ aller; **~ to school/town/ market** aller à l'école/en ville/ au marché. **~ for a swim/ walk** aller nager/se promener.

···▸ (leave) s'en aller. **I must be ~ing** il faut que je m'en aille.

···▸ (vanish) **the money's gone** il n'y a plus d'argent. **my bike's gone** mon vélo n'est plus là.

···▸ (work, function) marcher. **is the car ~ing?** est-ce que la voiture marche?

···▸ (become) devenir. **~ blind** devenir aveugle. **~ pale/red** pâlir/rougir.

···▸ (turn out, progress) aller. **how's it going?** comment ça va? **how did the exam ~?** comment s'est passé l'examen?

···▸ (in future tenses) be **~ing to do** aller faire.

● **noun**

···▸ (turn) tour m; (try) essai m;

have a ∼! essaie!; full of ∼ 🄸 dynamique.

□ **go across** traverser. **go after** poursuivre. **go away** partir. ∼ away! va-t'en!, allez-vous-en! **go back** retourner. ∼ back in rentrer. ∼ back to work reprendre le travail. **go down** (quality, price) baisser; (person) descendre; (sun) se coucher. **go in** entrer. **go in for** (exam) se présenter à. **go off** (leave) partir; (bomb) exploser; (alarm clock) sonner; (milk) tourner; (light) s'éteindre. **go on** (continue) continuer; (light) s'allumer. ∼ on doing continuer à faire. what's ∼ing on? qu'est-ce qui se passe? **go out** sortir; (light, fire) s'éteindre. **go over** vérifier. **go round** (be enough) être assez. ∼ round to see sb passer voir qn. **go through** (check) examiner; (search) fouiller; ∼ through a difficult time traverser une période difficile. **go together** aller ensemble. **go under** (sink) couler; (fail) échouer. **go up** (person) monter; (price, salary) augmenter. **go without** se passer de.

go-ahead /'gəʊəhed/ n feu m vert. ● adj dynamique.

goal /gəʊl/ n but m. ∼keeper n gardien m de but. ∼post n poteau m de but.

goat /gəʊt/ n chèvre f.

gobble /'gɒbl/ vt engouffrer.

go-between /'gəʊbɪtwiːn/ n intermédiaire mf.

god /gɒd/ n dieu m. ∼child n (pl -children) filleul/-e m/f. ∼daughter n filleule f

goddess /'gɒdɪs/ n déesse f.

god: ∼father n parrain m.

∼mother n marraine f. ∼send n aubaine f. ∼son n filleul m.

goggles /'gɒglz/ npl lunettes fpl (protectrices).

going /'gəʊɪŋ/ n it is slow/hard ∼ c'est lent/difficile. ● adj (price, rate) actuel.

go-kart /'gəʊkɑːt/ n kart m.

gold /gəʊld/ n or m. ● adj en or, d'or.

golden /'gəʊldən/ adj en or, d'or; (in colour) doré; (opportunity) unique.

gold: ∼fish n poisson m rouge. ∼-plated adj plaqué or. ∼smith n orfèvre m

golf /gɒlf/ n golf m. ∼-course n terrain m de golf.

gone /gɒn/ ⇒GO. ● adj parti. ∼ six o'clock six heures passées. the butter's all ∼ il n'y a plus de beurre.

good /gʊd/ adj (better, best) bon; (weather) beau; (well-behaved) sage; as ∼ as (almost) pratiquement. that's ∼ c'est gentil (de ta part). be ∼ with savoir s'y prendre avec. feel ∼ se sentir bien. it is ∼ for you ça vous fait du bien. ● n bien m; do ∼ faire du bien. is it any ∼? est-ce que c'est bien? it's no ∼ ça ne vaut rien. it is no ∼ shouting ça ne sert à rien de crier. for ∼ pour toujours. ∼ afternoon interj bonjour. ∼bye interj & n au revoir (m inv). ∼ evening interj bonsoir. G∼ Friday n Vendredi m saint. ∼-looking adj beau. ∼ morning interj bonjour. ∼-natured adj gentil.

goodness /'gʊdnɪs/ n bonté f; my ∼! mon Dieu!

goodnight interj bonsoir, bonne nuit.

goods /gʊdz/ npl marchandises fpl.

goodwill /gʊd'wɪl/ n bonne volonté f

g

google® /'guːgl/vt/i chercher sur (le moteur de recherche) Google®, googler.

goose /guːs/ n (pl **geese**) oie f. **gooseberry** n groseille f à maquereau. ~**pimples** npl chair f de poule.

gorge /gɔːdʒ/ n (Geog) gorge f. ● vt ~ oneself se gaver (on de).

gorgeous /'gɔːdʒəs/ adj magnifique, splendide, formidable.

gorilla /gə'rɪlə/ n gorille m.

gory /'gɔːrɪ/ adj (-ier, -iest) sanglant; (horrific: fig) horrible.

gospel /'gɒspl/ n évangile m; the G~ l'Évangile m.

gossip /'gɒsɪp/ n bavardages mpl, commérages mpl; (person) bavard/-e m/f. ● vi bavarder.

got /gɒt/ →GET. ● have ~ avoir. have ~ to do devoir faire.

govern /'gʌvn/ vt/i gouverner. **governess** n gouvernante f. **government** n gouvernement m. **governor** n gouverneur m.

gown /gaʊn/ n robe f; (of judge, teacher) toge f.

GP abbr →GENERAL PRACTITIONER.

GPS abbr (Global Positioning System) GPS m.

grab /ɡræb/ vt (pt **grabbed**) saisir.

grace /ɡreɪs/ n grâce f. ● vt (honour) honorer; (adorn) orner. **graceful** adj gracieux.

gracious /'ɡreɪʃəs/ adj (kind) bienveillant; (elegant) élégant.

grade /ɡreɪd/ n catégorie f; (of goods) qualité f; (on scale) grade m; (school mark) note f; (class: US) classe f. ● vt classer; (school work) noter. ~ **school** n (US) école f primaire.

gradual /'ɡrædʒʊəl/ adj progressif, graduel. **gradually** adv progressivement, peu à peu.

graduate¹ /'ɡrædʒʊət/ n (Univ) diplômé/-e m/f.

graduate² /'ɡrædʒʊeɪt/ vi obtenir son diplôme. ● vt graduer. **graduation** n remise f des diplômes.

graffiti /ɡrə'fiːtɪ/ npl graffiti mpl.

graft /ɡrɑːft/ n (Med, Bot) greffe f; (work) boulot m. ● vt greffer (on to sur); (work) trimer.

grain /ɡreɪn/ n (seed, quantity, texture) grain m; (in wood) fibre f.

gram /ɡræm/ n gramme m.

grammar /'ɡræmə(r)/ n grammaire f.

grand /ɡrænd/ adj magnifique; (duke, chorus) grand.

grandad /'ɡrændæd/ n Ⓘ papy m.

grand: ~**child** n (girl) petite-fille f; (boy) petit-fils m; her ~**children** ses petits-enfants mpl. ~**daughter** n petite-fille f. ~**father** n grand-père m. ~**ma** n →GRANNY. ~**mother** n grandmère f. ~**parents** npl grandsparents mpl. ~**piano** n piano m à queue. ~**son** n petit-fils m. ~**stand** n tribune f.

granny /'ɡrænɪ/ n Ⓘ mémé f, mamie f.

grant /ɡrɑːnt/ vt (permission) accorder; (request) accéder à; (admit) admettre (that que); take sth for ~ed considérer qch comme une chose acquise. ● n subvention f; (Univ) bourse f.

granule /'ɡrænjuːl/ n (of sugar, salt) grain m; (of coffee) granulé m.

grape /ɡreɪp/ n grain m de raisin. ~s raisin(s) m (pl).

grapefruit /'ɡreɪpfruːt/ n inv pamplemousse m.

graph /ɡrɑːf/ n graphique m.

graphic /'ɡræfɪk/ adj (arts) graphique; (fig) vivant, explicite. **graphics** npl (Comput) graphiques mpl.

grasp /ɡrɑːsp/ vt saisir. ● n (hold)

prise f; (strength of hand) **poigne** f; (reach) **portée** f; (fig) **compréhension** f.

grass /grɑːs/ n **herbe** f, **~hopper** n **sauterelle** f. **~land** n **prairie** f.

grass roots npl **peuple** m. ● adj (movement) **populaire**; (support) **de base**.

grate /greɪt/ n (hearth) **âtre** m; (fire basket) **grille** f. ● vt **râper**. ● vi **grincer**.

grateful /'greɪtfl/ adj **reconnaissant**.

grater /'greɪtə(r)/ n **râpe** f.

gratified /'grætɪfaɪd/ adj très heureux. **gratify** vt **faire plaisir à**.

grating /'greɪtɪŋ/ n (bars) **grille** f; (noise) **grincement** m.

gratitude /'grætɪtjuːd/ n **reconnaissance** f.

gratuity /grə'tjuːətɪ/ n (tip) **pourboire** m; (bounty: Mil) **prime** f.

grave[1] /greɪv/ n **tombe** f. ● adj (serious) **grave**.

grave[2] /grɑːv/ adj **~ accent** **accent** m **grave**.

gravel /'grævl/ n **graviers** mpl.

grave: ~stone n **pierre** f **tombale**. **~yard** n **cimetière** m.

gravity /'grævətɪ/ n (seriousness) **gravité** f; (force) **pesanteur** f.

gravy /'greɪvɪ/ n **jus** m (de viande).

gray /greɪ/ (US) adj & n ⇒**GREY**.

graze /greɪz/ vi (eat) **paître**. ● vt (touch) **frôler**; (scrape) **écorcher**. ● n **écorchure** f.

grease /griːs/ n **graisse** f. ● vt **graisser**. **greasy** adj **graisseux**.

great /greɪt/ adj **grand**; (very good 🔲) **génial** 🔲, **formidable** 🔲, (grandfather, grandmother) **arrière**.

Great Britain n **Grande-Bretagne** f.

greatly /'greɪtlɪ/ adv (very) **très**;

(much) **beaucoup**.

Greece /griːs/ n **Grèce** f.

greed /griːd/ n **avidité** f; (for food) **gourmandise** f. **greedy** adj **avide**; **gourmand**.

Greek /griːk/ n (person) **Grec/-que** m/f; (Ling) **grec** m. ● adj **grec**.

green /griːn/ adj **vert**; (fig) **naïf**. ● n **vert** m; (grass) **pelouse** f; (golf) **green** m; **~s** **légumes** mpl **verts**. **~grocer** n **marchand/-e** m/f **de fruits et légumes**.

Green Card Document qui permet à un étranger de vivre et de travailler aux États-Unis, et qui lui donne les mêmes droits que ceux d'un citoyen américain, à l'exception du droit de vote. Les services d'immigration américains distribuent 50 000 green cards par an au moyen d'une loterie à laquelle participent des millions de candidats.

greenhouse n **serre** f; **~ effect** **effet** m **de serre**.

greet /griːt/ vt (welcome) **accueillir**; (address politely) **saluer**. **greeting** n **accueil** m.

greetings /'griːtɪŋz/ interj **salutations** 🔲 ● npl (Christmas) **vœux** mpl. **~ card** n **carte** f **de vœux**.

grew /gruː/ ⇒**GROW**.

grey /greɪ/ adj **gris**; (fig) **triste**; **go ~** (hair, person) **grisonner**. ● n **gris** m. **~hound** n **lévrier** m.

grid /grɪd/ n **grille** f; (network: Electr) **réseau** m.

grief /griːf/ n **chagrin** m; **come to ~** (person) **avoir un malheur**; (fail) **tourner mal**.

grievance /'griːvns/ n **griefs** mpl.

grieve /griːv/ vt/i (s')**affliger**; **~ for** **pleurer**.

grill /grɪl/ n (cooking device) gril m; (food) grillade f; (Auto) calandre f. ● vt/i (faire) griller; (interrogate) mettre sur la sellette.

grim /grɪm/ adj sinistre.

grimace /grɪˈmeɪs/ n grimace f. ● vi grimacer.

grime /graɪm/ n crasse f.

grin /grɪn/ vi (pt **grinned**) sourire. ● n (large) sourire m.

grind /graɪnd/ vt (pt **ground**) (grain) écraser; (coffee) moudre; (sharpen) aiguiser; ~ one's teeth grincer des dents. ● vi ~ to a halt s'immobiliser. ● n corvée f.

grip /grɪp/ vt (pt **gripped**) saisir; (interest) passionner. ● n prise f; (strength of hand) poigne f; come to ~s with en venir aux prises avec.

grisly /ˈgrɪzlɪ/ adj (-ier, -iest) (remains) macabre; (sight) horrible.

gristle /ˈgrɪsl/ n cartilage m.

grit /grɪt/ n (for roads) sable m; (fig) courage m. ● vt (pt **gritted**) (road) sabler; (teeth) serrer.

groan /grəʊn/ vi gémir. ● n gémissement m.

grocer /ˈgrəʊsə(r)/ n (person) épicier/-ière m/f; (shop) épicerie f. **groceries** npl (shopping) courses fpl; (goods) épicerie f. **grocery** n (shop) épicerie f.

groin /grɔɪn/ n aine f.

groom /gruːm/ n marié m; (for horses) palefrenier/-ière m/f. ● vt (horse) panser; (fig) préparer.

groove /gruːv/ n (for door etc.) rainure f; (in record) sillon m.

grope /grəʊp/ vi tâtonner. ~ for chercher à tâtons.

gross /grəʊs/ adj (behaviour) vulgaire; (Comm) brut. ● n inv grosse f.

grotto /ˈgrɒtəʊ/ n (pl ~es) grotte f.

grouch /graʊtʃ/ vi (grumble 🛈) rouspéter, râler.

ground[1] /graʊnd/ n terre f, sol m; (area) terrain m; (reason) raison f; (Electr, US) masse f; ~s terres fpl, parc m; (of coffee) marc m; on the ~ par terre. lose ~ perdre du terrain. ● vt/i (Naut) échouer; (aircraft) retenir au sol.

ground[2] /graʊnd/ ⇒**GRIND**. ● adj ~ beef (US) bifteck m haché.

ground-: ~**floor** n rez-de-chaussée m inv. ~**work** n travail m préparatoire.

group /gruːp/ n groupe m. ● vt/i (se) grouper. ~**ware** n (Comput) logiciel m de groupe.

grovel /ˈgrɒvl/ vi (pt **grovelled**) ramper.

grow /grəʊ/ vi (pt **grew**; pp **grown**) (person) grandir; (plant) pousser; (become) devenir; (crime) augmenter. ● vt cultiver. ~ up devenir adulte, grandir. **grower** n cultivateur/-trice m/f.

growl /graʊl/ vi (dog) gronder; (person) grogner. ● n grognement m.

grown /grəʊn/ ⇒**GROW**. ● adj adulte. ~**-up** adj & n adulte (mf).

growth /grəʊθ/ n (of person, plant) croissance f; (in numbers) accroissement m; (of hair, tooth) pousse f; (Med) grosseur f, tumeur f.

grudge /grʌdʒ/ vt ~ doing faire à contrecœur. ~ sb sth (success, wealth) en vouloir à qn de qch. ● n rancune f; have a ~ against en vouloir à.

grumble /ˈgrʌmbl/ vi ronchonner, grogner (at après).

grumpy /ˈgrʌmpɪ/ adj (-ier, -iest) grincheux, grognon.

grunt /grʌnt/ vi grogner. ● n grognement m.

guarantee /gærən'ti:/ n garantie f. ● vt garantir.

guard /gɑːd/ vt protéger; (watch) surveiller. ● vi ~ **against** se protéger contre. ● n (Mil) garde f; (person) garde m; (on train) chef m de train.

guardian /'gɑːdɪən/ n gardien/-ne m/f; (of orphan) tuteur/-trice m/f.

guess /ges/ vt/i deviner; (suppose) penser. ● n conjecture f.

guest /gest/ n invité/-e m/f; (in hotel) client/-e m/f. ~**house** n pension f. ~**room** n chambre f d'amis.

guidance /'gaɪdns/ n (advice) conseils mpl; (information) information f.

guide /gaɪd/ n (person, book) guide m; (girl) guide f. ● vt guider. ~**book** n guide m. ~ **dog** n chien m d'aveugle. ~**line** n indication f; (advice) conseils mpl.

guillotine /'gɪləti:n/ n (for execution) guillotine f; (for paper) massicot m.

guilt /gɪlt/ n culpabilité f. **guilty** adj coupable.

guinea-pig /'gɪnɪpɪg/ n (animal) cochon m d'Inde; (fig) cobaye m.

guitar /gɪ'tɑː(r)/ n guitare f.

gulf /gʌlf/ n (part of sea) golfe m; (hollow) gouffre m.

gull /gʌl/ n mouette f, (larger) goéland m.

gullible /'gʌləbl/ adj crédule.

gully /'gʌlɪ/ n (ravine) ravin m; (drain) rigole f.

gulp /gʌlp/ vt ~ (**down**) avaler en vitesse. ● vi (from fear etc.) avoir la gorge serrée. ● n gorgée f.

gum /gʌm/ n (Anat) gencive f; (glue) colle f; (for chewing) chewing-gum m. ● vt (pt **gummed**) gommer.

gun /gʌn/ n (pistol) revolver m; (rifle) fusil m; (large) canon m. ● vt (pt **gunned**) ~ **down** abattre. ~ **fire** n fusillade f. ~**powder** n poudre f à canon. ~**shot** n coup m de feu.

gurgle /'gɜːgl/ n (of water) gargouillement m; (of baby) gazouillis m. ● vi (water) gargouiller; (baby) gazouiller.

gush /gʌʃ/ vi ~ (**out**) jaillir. ● n jaillissement m.

gust /gʌst/ n rafale f; (of smoke) bouffée f.

gut /gʌt/ n (belly 🄸) ventre m. ● vt (pt **gutted**) (fish) vider; (of fire) dévaster. **gutted** adj 🄸 abattu.

guts /gʌts/ npl 🄸 (insides of human) tripes fpl 🄸; (insides of animal, building) entrailles fpl; (courage) cran m 🄸.

gutter /'gʌtə(r)/ n (on roof) gouttière f; (in street) caniveau m.

guy /gaɪ/ n (man 🄸) type m.

gym /dʒɪm/ n (place) gymnase m; (activity) gym(nastique) f.

gymnasium /dʒɪm'neɪzɪəm/ n gymnase m.

gymnastics /dʒɪm'næstɪks/ npl gymnastique f.

gynaecologist /gaɪnə'kɒlədʒɪst/ n gynécologue mf.

gypsy /'dʒɪpsɪ/ n bohémien/-ne m/f.

g
h

Hh

habit /'hæbɪt/ n habitude f; (costume: Relig) habit m; **be in/get into the** ~ **of** avoir/prendre l'habitude de.

habitual /hə'bɪtʃʊəl/ adj (usual) habituel; (smoker, liar) invétéré.

hack /hæk/ n (writer) écrivaillon m.

hackneyed /ˈhæknɪd/ *adj* rebattu.

had /hæd/ →HAVE.

haddock /ˈhædək/ *n inv* églefin *m*.

haemorrhage /ˈhemərɪdʒ/ *n* hémorragie *f*.

haggard /ˈhægəd/ *adj* (*person*) exténué; (*face, look*) défait.

haggle /ˈhægl/ *vi* marchander; ~ over sth discuter du prix de qch.

hail /heɪl/ *n* grêle *f*; (*greet*) saluer; (*taxi*) héler. ● *vi* grêler; ~ from venir de qch. ~**stone** *n* grêlon *m*.

hair /heə(r)/ *n* (on head) cheveux *mpl*; (on body, of animal) poils *mpl*; (single strand on head) cheveu *m*; (on body) poil *m*. ~**brush** *n* brosse *f* à cheveux. ~**cut** *n* coupe *f* de cheveux. ~**do** *n* ⊞ coiffure *f*. ~**dresser** *n* coiffeur/-euse *m/f*. ~**drier** *n* séchoir *m* (à cheveux). ~**pin** *n* épingle *f* à cheveux. ~**remover** *n* dépilatoire *m*. ~**style** *n* coiffure *f*.

hairy /ˈheərɪ/ *adj* (-**ier**, -**iest**) poilu; (*terrifying*) ⊞ horrifiant.

half /hɑːf/ *n* (*pl* **halves**) (part) moitié *f*; (*fraction*) demi *m*; ~ a dozen une demi-douzaine; ~ an hour une demi-heure; four and a ~ quatre et demi; an hour and a ~ une heure et demie; ~ and half moitié moitié; in ~ en deux. ● *adj* demi; ~ price à moitié prix. ● *adv* à moitié. ~**back** *n* (Sport) demi *m*. ~**hearted** *adj* tiède. ~**mast** *n* at ~ -mast en berne. ~**term** *n* vacances *fpl* de mi-trimestre. ~**time** *n* mi-temps *f*. ~**way** *adv* à mi-chemin. ~**wit** *n* imbécile *mf*.

hall /hɔːl/ *n* (in house) entrée *f*; (corridor) couloir *m*; (in airport) hall *m*; (for events) salle *f*; ~ of residence résidence *f* universitaire.

hallmark /ˈhɔːlmɑːk/ *n* (on gold) poinçon *m*; (fig) caractéristique *f*.

hallo →HELLO.

Hallowe'en /hæləʊˈiːn/ *n* la veille de la Toussaint.

halt /hɔːlt/ *n* arrêt *m*; (*temporary*) suspension *f*; (Mil) halte *f*; (a *proceedings*) interrompre; (*arms sales, experiments*) mettre fin à. ● *vt* (*vehicle*) s'arrêter; (*army*) faire halte.

halve /hɑːv/ *vt* (*time*) réduire de moitié; (*fruit*) couper en deux.

ham /hæm/ *n* jambon *m*.

hamburger /ˈhæmbɜːgə(r)/ *n* hamburger *m*.

hammer /ˈhæmə(r)/ *n* marteau *m*. ● *vt/i* marteler; ~ sth into sth enfoncer qch dans qch; ~ sth out (*agreement*) parvenir à qch.

hammock /ˈhæmək/ *n* hamac *m*.

hamper /ˈhæmpə(r)/ *n* panier *m*. ● *vt* gêner.

hamster /ˈhæmstə(r)/ *n* hamster *m*.

hand /hænd/ *n* main *f*; (of clock) aiguille *f*; (writing) écriture *f*; (worker) ouvrier/-ière *m/f*; (cards) jeu *m*; give sb a ~ donner un coup de main à qn; at ~ proche; on ~ disponible; on the one ~...on the other ~ d'une part...d'autre part; to ~ à portée de la main. ● *vt* ~ sb sth, ~ sth to sb donner qch à qn. □ ~**in** or **over** remettre; ~ **out** distribuer. ~**bag** *n* sac *m* à main. ~**baggage** *n* bagages *mpl* à main. ~**book** *n* manuel *m*. ~**brake** *n* frein *m* à main. ~**cuffs** *npl* menottes *fpl*.

handicap /ˈhændɪkæp/ *n* handicap *m*. ● *vt* (*pt* **handicapped**) handicaper.

handkerchief /ˈhæŋkətʃɪf/ *n* (*pl* ~**s**) mouchoir *m*.

handle /ˈhændl/ *n* (of door, bag) poignée *f*; (of implement) manche *m*; (of cup, bucket) anse *f*; (of frying pan) queue *f*. ● *vt* (manage) manier; (deal with) traiter; (touch) manipuler.

handout /'hændaut/ *n* document *m*; (leaflet) prospectus *m*; (money) aumône *f*.

hands-free kit *n* kit *m* mains libres conducteur.

handshake /'hændʃeɪk/ *n* poignée *f* de main.

handsome /'hænsəm/ *adj* (good looking) beau; (generous) généreux.

handwriting /'hændraɪtɪŋ/ *n* écriture *f*.

handy /'hændɪ/ *adj* (-ier, -iest) (book, skill) utile; (size, shape, tool) pratique; (person) doué. **~man** *n* (*pl* -men) bricoleur *m*.

hang /hæŋ/ *vt* (*pt* hung) (from hook, hanger) accrocher; (from rope) suspendre; (*pt* hanged) (person) pendre. ● *vi* (from hook) être accroché; (from rope) être suspendu; (person) être pendu. ● *n* get the ~ of doing 🔲 piger comment faire 🔲. □ ~ about traîner; ~ on 🔲 hold out) tenir; (wait) attendre; ~ on to sth s'agripper à qch; ~ out *vi* 🔲 (live) crécher 🔲; (spend time) passer son temps; *vt* (washing) étendre; ~ up (telephone) raccrocher.

hanger /'hæŋə(r)/ *n* (for clothes) cintre *m*.

hang-gliding /'hæŋglaɪdɪŋ/ *n* vol *m* libre.

hangover /'hæŋəʊvə(r)/ *n* gueule *f* de bois 🔲.

hang-up /'hæŋʌp/ *n* 🔲 complexe *m*.

haphazard /hæp'hæzəd/ *adj* peu méthodique.

happen /'hæpən/ *vi* arriver, se passer; ~ to sb arriver à qn; it so ~s that il se trouve que.

happily /'hæpɪlɪ/ *adv* joyeusement; (fortunately) heureusement.

happiness /'hæpɪnɪs/ *n* bonheur *m*.

happy /'hæpɪ/ *adj* (-ier, -iest) heureux; I'm not ~ about it je ne suis pas content; ~ with sth satisfait de qch; ~ medium juste milieu *m*.

harass /'hærəs/ *vt* harceler. **harassment** *n* harcèlement *m*.

harbour, (US) **harbor** /'hɑːbə(r)/ *n* port *m*. ● *vt* (shelter) héberger.

hard /hɑːd/ *adj* dur; (difficult) difficile, dur; (evidence, fact) solide; find it ~to do avoir du mal à faire; ~ on sb dur envers qn. ● *adv* (work) dur; (pull, hit, cry) fort; (think, study) sérieusement. **~board** *n* aggloméré *m*. **~ copy** *n* (Comput) tirage *m*. **~ disk** *n* disque *m* dur.

hardly /'hɑːdlɪ/ *adv* à peine; (expect, hope) difficilement; ~ ever presque jamais.

hardship /'hɑːdʃɪp/ *n* (poverty) privations *fpl*; (ordeal) épreuve *f*.

hard: ~ **shoulder** *n* bande *f* d'arrêt d'urgence. ~ **up** *adj* 🔲 fauché 🔲. **~ware** *n* (Comput) matériel *m*, hardware *m*; (goods) quincaillerie *f*. **~working** *adj* travailleur.

hardy /'hɑːdɪ/ *adj* (-ier, -iest) résistant.

hare /heə(r)/ *n* lièvre *m*.

harm /hɑːm/ *n* mal *m*; there is no ~ in it il n'y a pas de mal à. ● *vt* (person) faire du mal à; (object) endommager. **harmful** *adj* nuisible. **harmless** *adj* inoffensif.

harmony /'hɑːmənɪ/ *n* harmonie *f*.

harness /'hɑːnɪs/ *n* harnais *m*. ● *vt* (horse) harnacher; (use) exploiter.

harp /hɑːp/ *n* harpe *f*. ● *vi* ~ on (about) rabâcher.

harrowing /'hærəʊɪŋ/ *adj* (experience) atroce; (story) déchirant.

harsh /hɑːʃ/ *adj* (punishment) sé-

h

vère; (*person*) dur; (*light*) cru; (*voice*) rude; (*chemical*) corrosif. **harshness** n dureté f.

harvest /ˈhɑːvɪst/ n récolte f; the wine ~ les vendanges fpl. ● vt (*corn*) moissonner; (*vegetables*) récolter.

has /hæz/ ➡HAVE.

hassle /ˈhæsl/ n complications fpl. ● vt 🔲 talonner (about à propos de); (*worry*) stresser.

haste /heɪst/ n hâte f; in ~ à la hâte; make ~ se dépêcher.

hasty /ˈheɪstɪ/ adj (-ier, -iest) précipité.

hat /hæt/ n chapeau m.

hatch /hætʃ/ n (Aviat) panneau m mobile; (Naut) écoutille f; (for food) passeplats m inv. ● vt/i (*eggs*) (faire) éclore.

hate /heɪt/ n haine f. ● vt détester; (*violently*) haïr; (*sport, food*) avoir horreur de.

hatred /ˈheɪtrɪd/ n haine f.

haughty /ˈhɔːtɪ/ adj (-ier, -iest) hautain.

haul /hɔːl/ vt tirer. ● n (by thieves) butin m; (by customs) saisie f; it will be a long ~ l'étape sera longue; long/short ~ (*transport*) long/court courrier m. **haulage** n transport m routier. **haulier** n (firm) société f de transports routiers.

haunt /hɔːnt/ vt hanter. ● n lieu m de prédilection.

have /hæv/

● *present* have, has;
● *past* had;
● *past participle* had

● *transitive verb*
⋯▸ (possess) avoir; I ~ (got) a car j'ai une voiture; they ~

(got) **problems** ils ont des problèmes.

⋯▸ (do sth) ~ **a try** essayer; ~ **a bath** prendre un bain.

⋯▸ ~ **sth done** faire faire qch; ~ **your hair cut** se faire couper les cheveux.

● *auxiliary verb*
⋯▸ (in perfect tenses) avoir; être; I ~ **seen him** je l'ai vu; **she had fallen** elle était tombée.

⋯▸ (in tag questions) **you've seen her, haven't you?** tu l'as vue, n'est-ce pas?; **you haven't seen her,** ~**you?** tu ne l'as pas vue, par hasard?

⋯▸ (in short answers) '**you've never met him**'—'**yes I** ~' 'tu ne l'as jamais rencontré'—'mais si!'

⋯▸ (must) ~ **to** devoir; **I** ~ **to go** je dois partir; **you don't** ~ **to do it** tu n'es pas obligé de le faire.

➡ For expressions such as **have a walk**, **have dinner** ➡walk, dinner.

haven /ˈheɪvn/ n refuge m; (fig) havre m.

havoc /ˈhævək/ n dévastation f.

hawk /hɔːk/ n faucon m.

hay /heɪ/ n foin m; ~ **fever** rhume m des foins.

haywire /ˈheɪwaɪə(r)/ adj go ~ (*plans*) dérailler; (*machine*) se détraquer.

hazard /ˈhæzəd/ n risque m; ~ (*warning*) **lights** feux mpl de détresse. ● vt hasarder.

haze /heɪz/ n brume f.

hazel /ˈheɪzl/ n (bush) noisetier m.

~nut n noisette f.

hazy /'heɪzɪ/ adj (**-ier, -iest**) (misty) brumeux; (fig) vague.

he /hiː/ pron il; (emphatic) lui; **here is** le voici.

head /hed/ n tête f; (leader) chef m; (of beer) mousse f; **~s or tails?** pile ou face? ● vt (list) être en tête de; (team) être à la tête de; (chapter) intituler; **~ the ball** faire une tête. ● vi **~ for** se diriger vers.

headache /'hedeɪk/ n mal m de tête; **have a ~** avoir mal à la tête.

heading /'hedɪŋ/ n titre m; (subject category) rubrique f.

head: ~lamp, ~light n phare m. **~line** n gros titre m. **~master** n directeur m. **~mistress** n directrice f. **~ office** n siège m social. **~-on** adj & adv de front. **~phones** npl casque m. **~quarters** npl siège m social; (Mil) quartier m général. **~ rest** n (Auto) repose-tête m inv. **~strong** adj têtu.

heal /hiːl/ vt/i guérir.

health /helθ/ n santé f. **~ centre** n centre m médico-social. **~ food** n produits mpl diététiques. **~ insurance** n assurance f maladie.

healthy /'helθɪ/ adj (person, plant, skin, diet) sain; (air) salutaire.

heap /hiːp/ n tas m; **~s of** 🇬🇧 un tas de. ● vt **~ (up)** entasser.

hear /hɪə(r)/ vt (pt **heard**) entendre; (news, rumour) apprendre; (lecture, broadcast) écouter. ● vi entendre; **~ from** recevoir des nouvelles de; **~ of or about** entendre parler de.

hearing /'hɪərɪŋ/ n ouïe f; (of case) audience f; **give sb a ~** écouter qn. **~-aid** n prothèse f auditive.

hearse /hɜːs/ n corbillard m.

heart /hɑːt/ n cœur m; **~s** (cards) cœur m; **at ~** au fond; **by ~** par

cœur; **be ~-broken** avoir le cœur brisé; **lose ~** perdre courage. **~ attack** n crise f cardiaque. **~burn** n brûlures fpl d'estomac. **~felt** adj sincère.

hearth /hɑːθ/ n foyer m.

heartily /'hɑːtɪlɪ/ adv (greet) chaleureusement; (laugh, eat) de bon cœur.

hearty /'hɑːtɪ/ adj (**-ier, -iest**) (sincere) chaleureux; (meal) solide.

heat /hiːt/ n chaleur f; (contest) épreuve f éliminatoire. ● vt (house) chauffer; **~ (up)** (food) faire chauffer; (reheat) réchauffer. **heated** adj (fig) passionné; (lit) (pool) chauffé. **heater** n appareil m de chauffage.

heather /'heðə(r)/ n bruyère f.

heating /'hiːtɪŋ/ n chauffage m.

heave /hiːv/ vt (lift) hisser; (pull) traîner péniblement; **~ a sigh** pousser un soupir. ● vi (pull) tirer de toutes ses forces; (retch) avoir un haut-le-cœur.

heaven /'hevn/ n ciel m.

heavily /'hevɪlɪ/ adv lourdement; (smoke, drink) beaucoup.

heavy /'hevɪ/ adj (**-ier, -iest**) lourd; (cold, work) gros; (traffic) dense. **~ goods vehicle** n poids m lourd. **~-handed** adj maladroit. **~weight** n poids m lourd.

Hebrew /'hiːbruː/ n (person) Hébreu m; (Ling) hébreu m. ● adj hébreu; (Ling) hébraïque.

hectic /'hektɪk/ adj (activity) intense; (period, day) mouvementé.

hedge /hedʒ/ n haie f. ● vi (in answering) se dérober.

hedgehog /'hedʒhɒg/ n hérisson m.

heel /hiːl/ n talon m.

hefty /'heftɪ/ adj (**-ier, -iest**) (person) costaud 🇬🇧; (object) pesant.

height /haɪt/ n hauteur f; (of person) taille *f*; (of plane, mountain) altitude *f*; (of fame, glory) apogée *m*; (of joy, folly, pain) comble *m*.

heir /eə(r)/ *n* héritier *m*. **heiress** *n* héritière *f*. **heirloom** *n* objet *m* de famille.

held /held/ →HOLD.

helicopter /ˈhelɪkɒptə(r)/ *n* hélicoptère *m*.

hell /hel/ *n* enfer *m*.

hello /həˈləʊ/ *interj* bonjour!; (on phone) allô!

helmet /ˈhelmɪt/ *n* casque *m*.

help /help/ *vt/i* aider (to do *à* faire); ~ (sb) with a bag/the housework aider qn à porter un sac/à faire le ménage; ~ oneself se servir; he can't ~ it ce n'est pas de sa faute. ● *n* aide *f*. ● *interj* au secours! **helper** *n* aide *m*. **helpful** *adj* utile; (person) serviable. **helping** *n* portion *f*. **helpless** *adj* impuissant.

hem /hem/ *n* ourlet *m*. ● *vt* (*pt* **hemmed**) faire un ourlet à; ~ in cerner.

hen /hen/ *n* poule *f*.

hence /hens/ *adv* (for this reason) d'où; (from now on) d'ici. **henceforth** *adv* désormais.

hepatitis /hepəˈtaɪtɪs/ *n* hépatite *f*.

her /hɜː(r)/ *pron* la, l'; (indirect object) lui; (after prep) elle; for ~ pour elle. ● *adj* son, sa; *pl* ses.

herb /hɜːb/ *n* herbe *f*; ~s (Culin) fines herbes *fpl*.

herd /hɜːd/ *n* troupeau *m*.

here /hɪə(r)/ *adv* ici; ~! (take this) tiens!; tenez!; ~ is, ~ are voici; I'm ~ je suis là. **hereabouts** *adv* par ici. **hereafter** *adv* après; (in book) ci-après. **hereby** *adv* par le présent acte; (in letter) par la présente.

herewith /hɪəwɪð/ *adv* ci-joint.

heritage /ˈherɪtɪdʒ/ *n* patrimoine

m. ~ **tourism** *n* tourisme *m* culturel.

hernia /ˈhɜːnɪə/ *n* hernie *f*.

hero /ˈhɪərəʊ/ *n* (*pl* ~es) héros *m*.

heroic /hɪˈrəʊɪk/ *adj* héroïque.

heroin /ˈherəʊɪn/ *n* héroïne *f*.

heroine /ˈherəʊɪn/ *n* héroïne *f*.

heron /ˈherən/ *n* héron *m*.

herring /ˈherɪŋ/ *n* hareng *m*.

hers /hɜːz/ *pron* le sien, la sienne, les sien(ne)s; it is ~ c'est à elle ou le sien ou la sienne.

herself /hɜːˈself/ *pron* (emphatic) elle-même; (reflexive) se; proud of ~ fière d'elle; by ~ toute seule.

hesitate /ˈhezɪteɪt/ *vi* hésiter. **hesitation** *n* hésitation *f*.

heterosexual /hetərəˈsekʃʊəl/ *adj* & *n* hétérosexuel-le (*m/f*).

hexagon /ˈheksəgən/ *n* hexagone *m*.

heyday /ˈheɪdeɪ/ *n* apogée *m*.

HGV *abbr* →HEAVY GOODS VEHICLE.

hi /haɪ/ *interj* 🔲 salut! 🔲.

hiccup /ˈhɪkʌp/ *n* hoquet *m*; (the) ~s le hoquet. ● *vi* hoqueter.

hide /haɪd/ *vt* (*pt* **hid**; *pp* **hidden**) cacher (from *à*). ● *vi* se cacher (from *de*); go into hiding se cacher. ● *n* (skin) peau *f*.

hideous /ˈhɪdɪəs/ *adj* (monster, object) hideux; (noise) affreux.

hiding /ˈhaɪdɪŋ/ *n* go into ~ se cacher; give sb a ~ administrer une correction à qn.

hierarchy /ˈhaɪərɑːkɪ/ *n* hiérarchie *f*.

hi-fi /ˈhaɪfaɪ/ *n* (chaîne *f*) hi-fi *f inv*.

high /haɪ/ *adj* haut; (price, number) élevé; (priest, speed) grand; (voice) aigu; in the ~ season en pleine saison. ● *n* a (new) ~ un niveau record. ● *adv* haut. ~**brow** *adj* & *n* intellectuel-le (*m/f*). ~ **chair**

chaise f haute. **~ court** n cour f suprême. **higher education** n enseignement m supérieur. **~-jump** n saut m en hauteur. **~-level** adj à haut niveau.

highlight /ˈhaɪlaɪt/ n (best moment) point m fort; **~s** (in hair) reflet m; (artificial) mèches fpl; (Sport) résumé m. ● vt (emphasize) souligner.

highly /ˈhaɪlɪ/ adv extrêmement; (paid) très bien; speak/think ~ of dire/penser beaucoup de bien de.

Highness /ˈhaɪnɪs/ n Altesse f.

high: ~-rise (building) n tour f. **~-school** n lycée m. **~-speed** adj (train) à grande vitesse; (film) ultrarapide. **~ street** n rue f principale. **~-tech** adj de pointe.

High School Établissement d'enseignement secondaire aux États-Unis, souvent subdivisé en *Junior high school* (12-14 ans) et *Senior high school* (15-17 ans) où les élèves passent un examen pour être admis dans un *College* (établissement d'enseignement supérieur).

highway /ˈhaɪweɪ/ n route f nationale; (US) autoroute f; **~ code** code m de la route.

hijack /ˈhaɪdʒæk/ vt détourner. ● n détournement m. **hijacker** n pirate m (de l'air).

hike /haɪk/ n randonnée f; price ~ hausse f de prix. ● vi faire de la randonnée.

hilarious /hɪˈleərɪəs/ adj désopilant.

hill /hɪl/ n colline f; (slope) côte f. **hilly** adj vallonné.

him /hɪm/ pron le, l'; (indirect object) lui; it's ~ c'est lui; for ~ pour lui.

himself /hɪmˈself/ pron (emphatic) lui-même; (reflexive) se; proud of ~ fier de lui; by ~ tout seul.

hind /haɪnd/ adj de derrière.

hinder /ˈhɪndə(r)/ vt (hamper) gêner; (prevent) empêcher. **hindrance** n obstacle m, gêne f.

hindsight /ˈhaɪndsaɪt/ n with ~ rétrospectivement.

Hindu /hɪnˈduː/ n Hindou/-e m/f. ● adj hindou.

hinge /hɪndʒ/ n charnière f. ● vi ~ on dépendre de.

hint /hɪnt/ n allusion f; (of spice, accent) pointe f; (of colour) touche f; (advice) conseil m. ● vt laisser entendre. ● vi ~ at faire allusion à.

hip /hɪp/ n hanche f.

hippopotamus /hɪpəˈpɒtəməs/ n (pl **~es**) hippopotame m.

hire /ˈhaɪə(r)/ vt (thing) louer; (person) engager. ● n location f. **~-car** n voiture f de location. **~-purchase** n achat m à crédit.

his /hɪz/ adj son, sa, pl ses. ● pron le sien, la sienne, les sien(ne)s; it is ~ c'est à lui or le sien or à elle.

hiss /hɪs/ n sifflement m. ● vt/i siffler.

history /ˈhɪstrɪ/ n histoire f; make ~ entrer dans l'histoire.

hit /hɪt/ vt (pt hit; pres p hitting) frapper; (collide with) heurter; (find) trouver; (affect, reach) toucher. ● vi ~ on (find) tomber sur; ~ it off s'entendre bien (with avec). ● n (blow) coup m; (fig) succès m; (song) tube m 🔟; (on Internet) (visit) visite f, accès m; (result) page f trouvée, résultat m.

hitch /hɪtʃ/ vt (fasten) accrocher; ~ up remonter. ● n (snag) anicroche f. **~-hike** vi faire du stop 🔟. **~-hiker** n auto-stoppeur/-euse m/f.

hi-tech /ˈhaɪtʃaɪk/ adj

de pointe.

HIV abbr (**human immunodeficiency virus**) VIH m.

hive /haɪv/ n ruche f. ● vt ~ off séparer; (industry) céder.

HIV-positive adj séropositif.

hoard /hɔːd/ vt amasser; (supplies) stocker. ● n trésor m; (of provisions) provisions fpl.

hoarse /hɔːs/ adj enroué.

hoax /həʊks/ n canular m.

hobby /ˈhɒbɪ/ n passe-temps m inv.

hockey /ˈhɒkɪ/ n hockey m.

hog /hɒg/ n cochon m. ● vt (pt hogged) 🔢 monopoliser.

hold /həʊld/ vt (pt held) tenir; (contain) contenir; (conversation, opinion) avoir; (shares, record, person) détenir; ~ (**the line**), please ne quittez pas. ● vi (rope, weather) tenir. ● n prise f; get ~ of attraper; (ticket) se procurer; (person) (by phone) joindre; on ~ en attente. □ ~ **back** (contain) retenir; (hide) cacher; ~ **down** (job) garder; (person) tenir; (costs) limiter; ~ **on** (stand firm) tenir bon; (wait) attendre; ~ **on to** (keep) garder; (cling to) se cramponner à; ~ **out** vt (offer) offrir; vi (resist) tenir le coup; ~ **up** (support) soutenir; (delay) retarder; (rob) attaquer.

holder /ˈhəʊldə(r)/ n détenteur/-trice m/f; (of passport, post) titulaire mf; (for object) support m.

holding /ˈhəʊldɪŋ/ n participation f.

hold-up /ˈhəʊldʌp/ n retard m; (of traffic) embouteillage m; (robbery) hold-up m inv.

hole /həʊl/ n trou m.

holiday /ˈhɒlədeɪ/ n vacances fpl; (public) jour m férié; (time off) congé m. ● vi passer ses vacances. ● adj de vacances. ~**maker** n

vacancier/-ière m/f.

Holland /ˈhɒlənd/ n Hollande f.

hollow /ˈhɒləʊ/ adj creux; (fig) faux. ● n creux m. ● vt creuser.

holly /ˈhɒlɪ/ n houx m.

holy /ˈhəʊlɪ/ adj (-ier, -iest) saint; (water) bénit; H~ Ghost, H~ Spirit Saint-Esprit m.

homage /ˈhɒmɪdʒ/ n hommage m.

home /həʊm/ n (place to live) logement m; maison f; (institution) maison f; (family base) foyer m; (country) pays m. ● adj de la maison, du foyer; (of family) de famille; (Pol) intérieur; (match, visit) à domicile. ● adv (at) ~ à la maison, chez soi; come or go ~ rentrer; (from abroad) rentrer dans son pays; feel at ~ with être à l'aise avec. ~ **computer** n ordinateur m, PC m.

homeland /ˈhəʊmlænd/ n patrie f; ~ **security** n sécurité f des frontières.

homeless /ˈhəʊmlɪs/ adj sans abri. ● n the ~ les sans-abri mpl.

homely /ˈhəʊmlɪ/ adj (-ier, -iest) (cosy) accueillant; (simple) sans prétention; (person: US) sans attraits.

home: ~**-made** adj (fait) maison. H~ **Office** n ministère m de l'Intérieur. ~ **page** n (Internet) page f d'accueil. H~ **Secretary** n Ministre m de l'Intérieur. ~**sick** adj be ~**sick** avoir le mal du pays. ~**work** n devoirs mpl.

homosexual /hɒməˈsekʃʊəl/ adj & n homosexuel/-le (m/f).

honest /ˈɒnɪst/ adj (truthful) intègre; (trustworthy) honnête; (sincere) franc. **honestly** adv honnêtement; franchement. **honesty** n honnêteté f.

honey /ˈhʌnɪ/ n miel m; (person 🔢) chéri-e m/f. ~**moon** n voyage m de noces; (fig) lune f de miel.

honk /hɒŋk/ vi klaxonner.

honorary /'ɒnərərɪ/ adj (person) honoraire; (degree) honorifique.

honour, (US) **honor** /'ɒnə(r)/ n honneur m. ● vt honorer.

hood /hʊd/ n capuchon m; (on car, pram) capote f; (car engine cover: US) capot m.

hoof /huːf/ n (pl ~s) sabot m.

hook /hʊk/ n crochet m; (on garment) agrafe f; (for fishing) hameçon m; **off the** ~ tiré d'affaire; (phone) décroché. ● vt accrocher.

hoot /huːt/ n (of owl) (h)ululement m; (of car) coup m de klaxon. ● vi (owl) (h)ululer; (car) klaxonner; (jeer) huer.

hoover /'huːvə(r)/ vt ~ **a room** passer l'aspirateur dans une pièce.

Hoover® /'huːvə(r)/ n aspirateur m.

hop /hɒp/ vi (pt **hopped**) sauter (à cloche-pied); ~ **in!** 🔲 vas-y, monte! ● n bond m; ~s houblon m.

hope /həʊp/ n espoir m. ● vt/i espérer; ~ **for** espérer avoir; **I** ~ **so** je l'espère.

hopeful /'həʊpfl/ adj (news, sign) encourageant; (person) plein d'espoir; (mood) optimiste. **hopefully** adv (with luck) avec un peu de chance; (with hope) avec optimisme.

hopeless /'həʊplɪs/ adj désespéré; (useless: fig) nul 🔲.

horizon /hə'raɪzn/ n horizon m.

horizontal /hɒrɪ'zɒntl/ adj horizontal.

hormone /ho:'məʊnl/ n hormone f.

horn /hɔːn/ n corne f; (of car) klaxon® m; (Mus) cor m.

horoscope /'hɒrəskəʊp/ n horoscope m.

horrible /'hɒrɪbl/ adj horrible.

horrid /'hɒrɪd/ adj horrible.

horrific /hə'rɪfɪk/ adj horrifiant.

horrify /'hɒrɪfaɪ/ vt horrifier.

horror /'hɒrə(r)/ n horreur f. ● adj (film, story) d'épouvante.

horse /hɔːs/ n cheval m. ~**back** n **on** ~**back** à cheval. ~**chestnut** n marron m (d'Inde). ~**man** n (pl -**men**) cavalier m. ~**power** n puissance f (en chevaux). ~**race** n course f de chevaux. ~**radish** n raifort m. ~**shoe** n fer m à cheval. ~ **show** n concours m hippique.

hose /həʊz/ n tuyau m. ● vt arroser. ~**pipe** n tuyau m.

hospitable /hɒ'spɪtəbl/ adj hospitalier.

hospital /'hɒspɪtl/ n hôpital m.

host /həʊst/ n (to guests) hôte m; (on TV) animateur m; (Internet) ordinateur m hôte; **a** ~ **of** une foule de; (Relig) hostie f.

hostage /'hɒstɪdʒ/ n otage m; **hold sb** ~ garder qn en otage.

hostel /'hɒstl/ n foyer m; (youth) ~ auberge f (de jeunesse).

hostess /'həʊstɪs/ n hôtesse f.

hostile /'hɒstaɪl/ adj hostile.

hot /hɒt/ adj (hotter, hottest) chaud; (Culin) épicé; **be** or **feel** ~ avoir chaud; **it is** ~ il fait chaud; **in** ~ **water** 🔲 dans le pétrin. ● vt/i (pt **hotted**) ~ **up** 🔲 chauffer. ~ **air balloon** n montgolfière f. ~ **dog** n hot-dog m.

hotel /həʊ'tel/ n hôtel m.

hot: ~**headed** adj impétueux. ~ **list** n (Internet) signets mpl favoris. ~**plate** n plaque f chauffante. ~ **water bottle** n bouillotte f.

hound /haʊnd/ n chien m de chasse. ● vt poursuivre.

hour /aʊə(r)/ n heure f.

hourly /'aʊəlɪ/ adj horaire; **on an** ~ **basis** à l'heure. ● adv toutes

h

les heures.

house¹ /haʊs/ *n* maison *f;* (Pol) Chambre *f;* on the ~ aux frais de la maison.

house² /haʊz/ *vt* loger; (of building) abriter.

household /ˈhaʊshəʊld/ *n* (house, family) ménage *m.* ● *adj* ménager.

house: **~keeper** *n* gouvernante *f.* **~-proud** *adj* méticuleux. **~warming** *n* pendaison *f* de crémaillère. **~wife** *n* (*pl* **-wives**) ménagère *f.* **~work** *n* travaux *mpl* ménagers.

housing /ˈhaʊzɪŋ/ *n* logement *m;* ~ **association** service *m* de logement; ~ **development** cité *f;* (smaller) lotissement *m.*

hover /ˈhɒvə(r)/ *vi* (bird) voleter; (vacillate) vaciller. **hovercraft** *n* aéroglisseur *m.*

how /haʊ/ *adv* comment; ~ **are you?** comment allez-vous?; ~ **long it is...?** quelle est la longueur/hauteur de...?; ~ **many?,** ~ **much?** combien?; ~ **pretty!** comme or que c'est joli!; ~ **about a walk?** si on faisait une promenade?; ~ **do you do?** (greeting) enchanté.

however /haʊˈevə(r)/ *adv* (nevertheless) cependant; ~ **hard I try** j'ai beau essayer; ~ **much it costs** quel que soit le prix; ~ **young/poor he is** si jeune/pauvre soit-il; ~ **you like** comme tu veux.

howl /haʊl/ *n* hurlement *m.* ● *vi* hurler.

HP *abbr* ➞**HIRE-PURCHASE.**

hp *abbr* ➞**HORSEPOWER.**

HQ *abbr* ➞**HEADQUARTERS.**

hub /hʌb/ *n* moyeu *m;* (fig) centre *m.*

hug /hʌg/ *vt* (*pt* **hugged**) serrer dans ses bras. ● *n* étreinte *f;* give

sb a ~ serrer qn dans ses bras.

huge /hjuːdʒ/ *adj* énorme.

hull /hʌl/ *n* (of ship) coque *f.*

hum /hʌm/ *vt/i* (*pt* **hummed**) (person) fredonner; (insect) bourdonner; (engine) ronronner. ● *n* bourdonnement *m;* ronronnement *m.*

human /ˈhjuːmən/ *adj* humain. ● *n* humain *m.* ~ **being** *n* être *m* humain.

humane /hjuːˈmeɪn/ *adj* (person) humain; (act) d'humanité; (killing) sans cruauté.

humanitarian /hjuːˌmænɪˈteərɪən/ *adj* humanitaire.

humanity /hjuːˈmænɪtɪ/ *n* humanité *f.*

humble /ˈhʌmbl/ *adj* humble.

humid /ˈhjuːmɪd/ *adj* humide.

humiliate /hjuːˈmɪlɪeɪt/ *vt* humilier.

humorous /ˈhjuːmərəs/ *adj* humoristique; (person) plein d'humour.

humour, (US) **humor** /ˈhjuːmə(r)/ *n* humour *m;* (mood) humeur *f.* ● *vt* amadouer.

hump /hʌmp/ *n* bosse *f.* ● *vt* 🔲 porter.

hunchback /ˈhʌntʃbæk/ *n* bossu/-e *m/f.*

hundred /ˈhʌndrəd/ *adj & n* cent (*m*); **two** ~ and **one** deux cent un; ~s of des centaines de. **hundredth** *adj & n* centième (*mf*).

hung /hʌŋ/ ➞**HANG.**

Hungarian /hʌŋˈgeərɪən/ *n* (person) Hongrois/-e *m/f;* (Ling) hongrois *m.* ● *adj* hongrois. **Hungary** *n* Hongrie *f.*

hunger /ˈhʌŋgə(r)/ *n* faim *f.* ● *vi* ~ **for** avoir faim de.

hungry /ˈhʌŋgrɪ/ *adj* (**-ier, -iest**) affamé; **be** ~ avoir faim.

hunt /hʌnt/ vt/i chasser; ~ for chercher. ● n chasse f. **hunter** n chasseur m. **hunting** n chasse f.

hurdle /'hɜ:dl/ n (Sport) haie f; (fig) obstacle m.

hurricane /'hʌrɪkən/ n ouragan m.

hurry /'hʌrɪ/ vi se dépêcher; ~ out sortir précipitamment. ● vt (work) terminer à la hâte; (person) bousculer. ● n hâte f; in a ~ pressé.

hurt /hɜ:t/ vt/i (pt hurt) faire mal (à); (injure, offend) blesser. ● adj blessé. ● n blessure f.

hurtle /'hɜ:tl/ vi ~ down dévaler; ~ along a road foncer sur une route.

husband /'hʌzbənd/ n mari m.

hush /hʌʃ/ vt faire taire; ~ up (news) étouffer. ● n silence m. ● interj chut!

husky /'hʌskɪ/ adj (-ier, -iest) enroué. ● n husky m.

hustle /'hʌsl/ vt (push, rush) bousculer. ● vi (hurry) se dépêcher; (work: US) se démener. ● n ~ and bustle agitation f.

hut /hʌt/ n cabane f.

hyacinth /'haɪəsɪnθ/ n jacinthe f.

hydrant /'haɪdrənt/ n (fire) ~ bouche f d'incendie.

hydraulic /haɪ'drɔːlɪk/ adj hydraulique.

hydroelectric /haɪdrəʊɪ'lektrɪk/ adj hydroélectrique.

hydrogen /'haɪdrədʒən/ n hydrogène m; ~ bomb bombe f à hydrogène.

hyena /haɪ'iːnə/ n hyène f.

hygiene /'haɪdʒiːn/ n hygiène f. **hygienic** adj hygiénique.

hymn /hɪm/ n cantique m; (fig) hymne m.

hype /haɪp/ n 🔲 battage m publicitaire. ● vt ~ (up) (film, book) faire

du battage pour.

hyperactive /haɪpər'æktɪv/ adj hyperactif.

hyperlink /'haɪpəlɪŋk/ n hyperlien m.

hypermarket /'haɪpəmɑːkɪt/ n hypermarché m.

hypertext /'haɪpətekst/ n hypertexte m.

hyphen /'haɪfn/ n trait m d'union.

hypnosis /hɪp'nəʊsɪs/ n hypnose f.

hypocrisy /hɪ'pɒkrəsɪ/ n hypocrisie f. **hypocrite** n hypocrite mf. **hypocritical** adj hypocrite.

hypothesis /haɪ'pɒθəsɪs/ n (pl -ses) hypothèse f.

hysteria /hɪ'stɪərɪə/ n hystérie f. **hysterical** adj hystérique.

hysterics /hɪ'sterɪks/ npl crise f de nerfs; be in ~ rire aux larmes.

························

I i

························

I /aɪ/ pron je, j'; (stressed) moi.

ice /aɪs/ n glace f; (on road) verglas m. ● vt (cake) glacer. ● vi ~ (up) (window) se givrer; (river) geler. ~box n (US) réfrigérateur m. ~-cream n glace f. ~-cube n glaçon m. ~ hockey n hockey m sur glace.

Iceland /'aɪslənd/ n Islande f. **Icelander** n Islandais/-e m/f. **Icelandic** adj & n islandais (m).

ice: ~ lolly n glace f (sur bâtonnet). ~ rink n patinoire f. ~ skate n patin m à glace.

icicle /'aɪsɪkl/ n stalactite f (de glace).

icing /'aɪsɪŋ/ n (sugar) glaçage m.

icy /'aɪsɪ/ adj (**-ier, -iest**) (hands, wind) glacé; (road) verglacé; (manner, welcome) glacial.

ID /ɪd/ n pièce f d'identité; ~ **card** carte f d'identité.

idea /aɪ'dɪə/ n idée f.

ideal /aɪ'diːəl/ adj idéal. ● n idéal m.

identical /aɪ'dentɪkl/ adj identique.

identification /aɪdentɪfr'keɪʃn/ n identification f; (papers) pièce f d'identité.

identify /aɪ'dentɪfaɪ/ vt identifier. ● vi ~ **with** s'identifier à.

identikit /aɪ'dentɪkɪt/ n ~ **picture** portraitrobot m.

identity /aɪ'dentətɪ/ n identité f; ~ **theft** vol m d'identité.

ideological /aɪdɪə'lɒdʒɪkl/ adj idéologique.

idiom /'ɪdɪəm/ n (phrase) idiome m; (language) parler m, langue f. **idiomatic** /-'mætɪk/ adj idiomatique.

idiosyncrasy /ɪdɪə'sɪŋkrəsɪ/ n particularité f.

idiot /'ɪdɪət/ n idiot/-e m/f. **idiotic** adj idiot.

idle /'aɪdl/ adj (lazy) paresseux; (doing nothing) oisif; (boast, threat) vain. ● vi (engine) tourner au ralenti. ● vt ~ **away** gaspiller.

idol /'aɪdl/ n idole f. **idolize** vt idolâtrer.

idyllic /ɪ'dɪlɪk/ adj idyllique.

i.e. abbr c-à-d, c'est-à-dire.

if /ɪf/ conj si.

ignite /ɪg'naɪt/ vt/i (s')enflammer.

ignition /ɪg'nɪʃn/ n (Auto) allumage m; ~ (**switch**) contact m; ~ **key** clé f de contact.

ignorance /'ɪgnərəns/ n ignorance f. **ignorant** adj ignorant (of de). **ignorantly** adv par ignorance.

ignore /ɪg'nɔː(r)/ vt (person) igno-

rer; (mistake, remark) ne pas relever; (feeling, fact) ne pas tenir compte de.

ill /ɪl/ adj malade. ● adv mal. ● n mal m. ~**-advised** adj malavisé. ~ **at ease** adj mal à l'aise. ~**-bred** adj mal élevé.

illegal /ɪ'liːgl/ adj illégal.

illegible /ɪ'ledʒəbl/ adj illisible.

illegitimate /ɪlɪ'dʒɪtɪmət/ adj illégitime.

ill: ~**-fated** adj malheureux. ~ **feeling** n ressentiment m.

illiterate /ɪ'lɪtərət/ adj & n analphabète (mf).

illness /'ɪlnɪs/ n maladie f.

ill-treat vt maltraiter.

illuminate /ɪ'luːmɪneɪt/ vt éclairer; (decorate with lights) illuminer. **illumination** n éclairage m, illumination f.

illusion /ɪ'luːʒn/ n illusion f.

illustrate /'ɪləstreɪt/ vt illustrer. **illustration** n illustration f. **illustrative** adj qui illustre.

image /'ɪmɪdʒ/ n image f; (of firm, person) image f de marque. **imagery** n images fpl.

imaginable /ɪ'mædʒɪnəbl/ adj imaginable. **imaginary** adj imaginaire. **imagination** n imagination f. **imaginative** adj plein d'imagination.

imagine /ɪ'mædʒɪn/ vt (s')imaginer (that que); ~ **being rich** s'imaginer riche.

imbalance /ɪm'bæləns/ n déséquilibre m.

imitate /'ɪmɪteɪt/ vt imiter.

immaculate /ɪ'mækjʊlət/ adj impeccable.

immaterial /ɪmə'tɪərɪəl/ adj sans importance (to pour; that que).

immature /ɪmə'tjʊə(r)/ adj (person) immature; (*plant*) qui n'est pas arrivé à maturité.

immediate /ɪˈmiːdɪət/ *adj* immédiat.

immediately /ɪˈmiːdɪətlɪ/ *adv* immédiatement. ● *conj* dès que.

immense /ɪˈmens/ *adj* immense. **immensely** *adv* extrêmement, immensément. **immensity** *n* immensité *f*.

immerse /ɪˈmɜːs/ *vt* plonger (in dans). **immersion** *n* immersion *f*; **immersion heater** chauffe-eau *m inv* électrique.

immigrant /ˈɪmɪɡrənt/ *n & adj* immigré/-e (*m/f*). (newly-arrived) immigrant/-e (*m/f*). **immigrate** *vi* immigrer. **immigration** *n* immigration *f*.

imminent /ˈɪmɪnənt/ *adj* imminent.

immobilizer /ɪˈməʊbɪlaɪzə(r)/ *n* système *m* antidémarrage.

immoral /ɪˈmɒrəl/ *adj* immoral.

immortal /ɪˈmɔːtl/ *adj* immortel.

immune /ɪˈmjuːn/ *adj* immunisé (from, to contre); (*reaction, system*) immunitaire. **immunity** *n* immunité *f*. **immunization** *n* immunisation *f*. **immunize** *vt* immuniser.

impact /ˈɪmpækt/ *n* impact *m*.

impair /ɪmˈpeə(r)/ *vt* (*performance*) affecter; (*ability*) affaiblir.

impart /ɪmˈpɑːt/ *vt* communiquer, transmettre.

impartial /ɪmˈpɑːʃl/ *adj* impartial.

impassable /ɪmˈpɑːsəbl/ *adj* (*barrier*) infranchissable; (*road*) impraticable.

impassive /ɪmˈpæsɪv/ *adj* impassible.

impatience /ɪmˈpeɪʃns/ *n* impatience *f*. **impatient** *adj* impatient; **get impatient** s'impatienter. **impa-**

tiently *adv* impatiemment.

impeccable /ɪmˈpekəbl/ *adj* impeccable.

impede /ɪmˈpiːd/ *vt* entraver.

impediment /ɪmˈpedɪmənt/ *n* entrave *f*; **speech ~** défaut *m* d'élocution.

impending /ɪmˈpendɪŋ/ *adj* imminent.

imperative /ɪmˈperətɪv/ *adj* urgent. ● *n* impératif *m*.

imperfect /ɪmˈpɜːfɪkt/ *adj* incomplet; (faulty) défectueux. ● *n* (Gram) imparfait *m*. **imperfection** *n* imperfection *f*.

imperial /ɪmˈpɪərɪəl/ *adj* impérial; (measure) conforme aux normes britanniques. **imperialism** *n* impérialisme *m*.

impersonal /ɪmˈpɜːsənl/ *adj* impersonnel.

impersonate /ɪmˈpɜːsəneɪt/ *vt* se faire passer pour; (mimic) imiter.

impertinent /ɪmˈpɜːtɪnənt/ *adj* impertinent.

impervious /ɪmˈpɜːvɪəs/ *adj* imperméable (to à).

impetuous /ɪmˈpetʃʊəs/ *adj* impétueux.

impetus /ˈɪmpɪtəs/ *n* impulsion *f*.

impinge /ɪmˈpɪndʒ/ *vi* **~ on** affecter; (encroach) empiéter sur.

implement /ˈɪmplɪmənt/ *n* instrument *m*; (tool) outil *m*. ● *vt* exécuter, mettre en application; (*software*) implanter. **implementation** *n* mise *f* en application.

implicit /ɪmˈplɪsɪt/ *adj* (implied) implicite (in dans); (unquestioning) absolu.

imply /ɪmˈplaɪ/ *vt* (assume, mean) impliquer; (insinuate) laisser entendre.

impolite /ɪmpəˈlaɪt/ *adj* impoli.

import[1] /ɪmˈpɔːt/ vt importer.

import[2] /ˈɪmpɔːt/ n (article) importation f; (meaning) signification f.

importance /ɪmˈpɔːtns/ n importance f. **important** adj important.

impose /ɪmˈpəʊz/ vt imposer (on sb à qn; on sth sur qch). ● vi s'imposer; ~ on sb abuser de la bienveillance de qn. **imposing** adj imposant.

impossible /ɪmˈpɒsəbl/ adj impossible. ● n the ~ l'impossible m.

impotent /ˈɪmpətənt/ adj impuissant.

impound /ɪmˈpaʊnd/ vt confisquer, saisir.

impoverish /ɪmˈpɒvərɪʃ/ vt appauvrir.

impractical /ɪmˈpræktɪkl/ adj peu réaliste.

impregnable /ɪmˈpregnəbl/ adj imprenable.

impress /ɪmˈpres/ vt impressionner; ~ sth on sb faire bien comprendre qch à qn. **impression** n impression f. **impressionable** adj impressionnable. **impressive** adj impressionnant.

imprint[1] /ˈɪmprɪnt/ n empreinte f.

imprint[2] /ɪmˈprɪnt/ vt (fix) graver (on dans); (print) imprimer.

imprison /ɪmˈprɪzn/ vt emprisonner.

improbable /ɪmˈprɒbəbl/ adj (not likely) improbable; (incredible) invraisemblable.

improper /ɪmˈprɒpə(r)/ adj (unseemly) malséant; (dishonest) irrégulier.

improve /ɪmˈpruːv/ vt/i (s')améliorer. **improvement** n amélioration f.

improvise /ˈɪmprəvaɪz/ vt/i improviser.

impudent /ˈɪmpjʊdənt/ adj impudent.

impulse /ˈɪmpʌls/ n impulsion f; on ~ sur un coup de tête. **impulsive** adj impulsif. **impulsively** adv par impulsion.

impurity /ɪmˈpjʊərəti/ n impureté f.

in /ɪn/ prep (inside, within) dans; (expressing place, position) à, en; (expressing time) en, dans; ~ the box/garden dans la boîte/le jardin; ~ Paris/school à Paris/l'école; ~ town en ville; ~ the country à la campagne; ~ English en anglais; ~ India en Inde; ~ Japan au Japon; ~ winter en hiver; ~ spring au printemps; ~ an hour (at end of) au bout d'une heure; ~ an hour('s time) dans une heure; ~ (the space of) an hour en une heure; ~ doing en faisant; ~ the evening le soir; one ~ ten un sur dix; ~ between entre les deux; (time) entretemps; ~ a firm voice d'une voix ferme; ~ blue en bleu; ~ ink à l'encre; ~ uniform en uniforme; ~ a skirt en jupe; ~ a whisper en chuchotant; ~ a loud voice d'une voix forte; the best ~ le meilleur de; we are ~ for on a avoir; have it ~ for sb Ⓘ avoir qn dans le collimateur. ● adv (inside) dedans; (at home) là, à la maison; (in fashion) à la mode; come ~ entrer; run ~ entrer en courant.

inability /ɪnəˈbɪləti/ n incapacité f (to do de faire).

inaccessible /ˌɪnækˈsesəbl/ adj inaccessible.

inaccurate /ɪnˈækjʊrət/ adj inexact.

inactive /ɪnˈæktɪv/ adj inactif. **inactivity** n inaction f.

inadequate /ɪnˈædɪkwət/ adj insuffisant.

inadvertently /ˌɪnədˈvɜːtəntli/ adv par mégarde.

inadvisable /ɪnəd'vaɪzəbl/ *adj* inopportun, à déconseiller.

inane /ɪ'neɪn/ *adj* idiot, débile.

inanimate /ɪn'ænɪmət/ *adj* inanimé.

inappropriate /ɪnə'prəʊprɪət/ *adj* inopportun; (*term*) inapproprié.

inarticulate /ɪmɑː'tɪkjʊlət/ *adj* qui a du mal à s'exprimer.

inasmuch as /ɪnəz'mʌtʃəz/ *adv* dans la mesure où; (*because*) vu que.

inaugurate /ɪ'nɔːgjʊreɪt/ *vt* (*open, begin*) inaugurer; (*person*) investir.

inborn /ɪn'bɔːn/ *adj* inné.

inbred /ɪn'bred/ *adj* (*inborn*) inné.

Inc. *abbr* (**Incorporated**) S.A.

incapable /ɪn'keɪpəbl/ *adj* incapable (*of doing* de faire).

incapacitate /ɪnkə'pæsɪteɪt/ *vt* immobiliser.

incense¹ /'ɪnsens/ *n* encens *m*.

incense² /ɪn'sens/ *vt* mettre en fureur.

incentive /ɪn'sentɪv/ *n* motivation *f*; (*payment*) prime *f*.

incessant /ɪn'sesnt/ *adj* incessant. **incessantly** *adv* sans cesse.

incest /'ɪnsest/ *n* inceste *m*. **incestuous** *adj* incestueux.

inch /ɪntʃ/ *n* pouce *m* (=2.54 cm.). ● *vi* ~ **towards** se diriger petit à petit vers.

incidence /'ɪnsɪdəns/ *n* fréquence *f*.

incident /'ɪnsɪdənt/ *n* incident *m*. **incidental** *adj* secondaire. **incidentally** *adv* à propos; (*by chance*) par la même occasion.

incinerate /ɪn'sɪnəreɪt/ *vt* incinérer. **incinerator** *n* incinérateur *m*.

incite /ɪn'saɪt/ *vt* inciter, pousser.

inclination /ɪnklɪ'neɪʃn/ *n* (ten-

dency) tendance *f*; (*desire*) envie *f*.

incline¹ /ɪn'klaɪn/ *vt/i* (s')incliner; **be** ~**d to** avoir tendance à.

incline² /'ɪnklaɪn/ *n* pente *f*.

include /ɪn'kluːd/ *vt* comprendre, inclure. **including** *prep* (y) compris. **inclusion** *n* inclusion *f*.

inclusive /ɪn'kluːsɪv/ *adj & adv* inclus; ~ **of delivery** livraison comprise.

income /'ɪnkʌm/ *n* revenus *mpl*; ~ **tax** impôt *m* sur le revenu.

incoming /'ɪnkʌmɪŋ/ *adj* (*tide*) montant; (*tenant, government*) nouveau; (*call*) qui vient de l'extérieur.

incompatible /ɪnkəm'pætɪbl/ *adj* incompatible.

incompetent /ɪn'kɒmpɪtənt/ *adj* incompétent.

incomplete /ɪnkəm'pliːt/ *adj* incomplet.

incomprehensible /ɪnkɒmprɪ'hensəbl/ *adj* incompréhensible.

inconceivable /ɪnkən'siːvəbl/ *adj* inconcevable.

inconclusive /ɪnkən'kluːsɪv/ *adj* peu concluant.

incongruous /ɪn'kɒŋgrʊəs/ *adj* déconcertant, surprenant.

inconsiderate /ɪnkən'sɪdərət/ *adj* (*person*) peu attentif à autrui; (*act*) maladroit.

inconsistent /ɪnkən'sɪstənt/ *adj* (*argument*) incohérent; (*performance*) inégal; (*behaviour*) changeant; ~ **with** en contradiction avec.

inconspicuous /ɪnkən'spɪkjʊəs/ *adj* qui passe inaperçu.

incontinent /ɪn'kɒntɪnənt/ *adj* incontinent.

inconvenience /ɪnkən'viːnɪəns/ *n* dérangement *m*; (*drawback*) inconvénient *m*. ● *vt* déranger. **inconvenient** *adj* incommode; **if it's not inconvenient for you** si cela ne vous dérange pas.

incorporate /ɪnˈkɔːpəreɪt/ vt incorporer (**into** dans); (contain) comporter.

incorrect /ɪnkəˈrekt/ adj incorrect.

increase[1] /ˈɪŋkriːs/ n augmentation f (**in**, of de). **be on the ~** être en progression.

increase[2] /ɪnˈkriːs/ vt/i augmenter. **increasing** adj croissant. **increasingly** adv de plus en plus.

incredible /ɪnˈkredəbl/ adj incroyable.

incriminate /ɪnˈkrɪmɪneɪt/ vt incriminer. **incriminating** adj compromettant.

incubate /ˈɪŋkjubeɪt/ vt (eggs) couver. **incubation** n incubation f. **incubator** n couveuse f.

incur /ɪnˈkɜː(r)/ vt (pt **incurred**) (penalty, anger) encourir; (debts) contracter.

indebted /ɪnˈdetɪd/ adj ~ **to sb** redevable à qn (**for** de); (grateful) reconnaissant à qn.

indecent /ɪnˈdiːsnt/ adj indécent.

indecisive /ɪndɪˈsaɪsɪv/ adj indécis; (ending) peu concluant.

indeed /ɪnˈdiːd/ adv en effet; (emphatic) vraiment.

indefinite /ɪnˈdefɪnət/ adj vague; (period, delay) illimité. **indefinitely** adv indéfiniment.

indelible /ɪnˈdeləbl/ adj indélébile.

indemnity /ɪnˈdemnəti/ n (protection) assurance f; (payment) indemnité f.

indent /ɪnˈdent/ vt (text) renfoncer. **indentation** n (dent) marque f.

independence /ɪndɪˈpendəns/ n indépendance f. **independent** adj indépendant. **independently** adv de façon indépendante; independently of indépendamment de.

index /ˈɪndeks/ n (pl ~**es**) (in

book) index m; (in library) catalogue m; (in economy) indice m; ~ **card** fiche f; ~ (**finger**) index m. ● vt classer. ~**-linked** adj indexé.

India /ˈɪndɪə/ n Inde f.

Indian /ˈɪndɪən/ n Indien/-ne m/f. ● adj indien.

indicate /ˈɪndɪkeɪt/ vt indiquer. **indication** n indication f.

indicative /ɪnˈdɪkətɪv/ adj & n indicatif (m).

indicator /ˈɪndɪkeɪtə(r)/ n (pointer) aiguille f; (on vehicle) clignotant m; (board) tableau m.

indict /ɪnˈdaɪt/ vt inculper. **indictment** n accusation f.

indifferent /ɪnˈdɪfrənt/ adj indifférent; (not good) médiocre.

indigenous /ɪnˈdɪdʒɪnəs/ adj indigène.

indigestible /ɪndɪˈdʒestəbl/ adj indigeste. **indigestion** n indigestion f.

indignant /ɪnˈdɪgnənt/ adj indigné.

indirect /ɪndɪˈrekt/ adj indirect. **indirectly** adv indirectement.

indiscreet /ɪndɪˈskriːt/ adj indiscret. **indiscretion** n indiscrétion f.

indiscriminate /ɪndɪˈskrɪmɪnət/ adj sans distinction. **indiscriminately** adv sans distinction.

indisputable /ɪndɪˈspjuːtəbl/ adj indiscutable.

individual /ɪndɪˈvɪdʒʊəl/ adj individuel; (tuition) particulier. ● n individu m. **individualist** n individualiste mf. **individuality** n individualité f. **individually** adv individuellement.

indoctrinate /ɪnˈdɒktrɪneɪt/ vt endoctriner. **indoctrination** n endoctrinement m.

indolent /ˈɪndələnt/ adj indolent.

Indonesia /ɪndəʊˈniːzjə/ n Indonésie f.

indoor /ˈɪndɔː(r)/ adj (clothes) d'intérieur; (pool, animal) couvert. **indoors** adv à l'intérieur.

induce /ɪnˈdjuːs/ vt (influence) persuader; (stronger) inciter (to do : faire). **inducement** n (financial) récompense f; (incentive) motivation f.

induction /ɪnˈdʌkʃn/ n (Electr) induction f; (inauguration) installation f.

indulge /ɪnˈdʌldʒ/ vt (person, whim) céder à; (child) gâter. ● vi ~ in se livrer à. **indulgence** n indulgence f; (treat) plaisir m. **indulgent** adj indulgent.

industrial /ɪnˈdʌstriəl/ adj industriel; (accident) du travail; ~ action grève f; ~ dispute conflit m social. **industrialist** n industriel·le m/f. **industrialized** adj industrialisé.

industrious /ɪnˈdʌstriəs/ adj diligent.

industry /ˈɪndəstri/ n industrie f; (zeal) zèle m.

inebriated /ɪˈniːbrieɪtɪd/ adj ivre.

inedible /ɪnˈedɪbl/ adj immangeable.

ineffective /ɪnɪˈfektɪv/ adj inefficace.

inefficient /ɪnɪˈfɪʃnt/ adj inefficace; (person) incompétent.

ineligible /ɪnˈelɪdʒəbl/ adj inéligible; be ~ for ne pas avoir droit à.

inept /ɪˈnept/ adj incompétent; (tactless) maladroit.

inequality /ɪnɪˈkwɒləti/ n inégalité f.

inescapable /ɪnɪˈskeɪpəbl/ adj indéniable.

inevitable /ɪnˈevɪtəbl/ adj inévitable.

inexcusable /ɪnɪkˈskjuːzəbl/ adj inexcusable.

inexhaustible /ɪnɪɡˈzɔːstəbl/ adj inépuisable.

inexpensive /ɪnɪkˈspensɪv/ adj pas cher.

inexperience /ɪnɪkˈspɪəriəns/ n inexpérience f. **inexperienced** adj inexpérimenté.

infallible /ɪnˈfæləbl/ adj infaillible.

infamous /ˈɪnfəməs/ adj (person) tristement célèbre; (deed) infâme.

infancy /ˈɪnfənsi/ n petite enfance f; in its ~ (fig) à ses débuts mpl. **infant** n (baby) bébé m; (at school) enfant m. **infantile** adj infantile.

infatuated /ɪnˈfætʃueɪtɪd/ adj ~ with entiché de. **infatuation** n engouement m.

infect /ɪnˈfekt/ vt contaminer; ~ sb with sth transmettre qch à qn. **infection** n infection f. **infectious** adj contagieux.

infer /ɪnˈfɜː(r)/ vt (pt inferred) (deduce) déduire.

inferior /ɪnˈfɪəriə(r)/ adj inférieur (to à). (work, product) de qualité inférieure. ● n inférieur·e m/f. **inferiority** n infériorité f.

inferno /ɪnˈfɜːnəʊ/ n (hell) enfer m; (blaze) brasier m.

infertile /ɪnˈfɜːtaɪl/ adj infertile.

infest /ɪnˈfest/ vt infester (with de).

infidelity /ɪnfɪˈdeləti/ n infidélité f.

infighting /ˈɪnfaɪtɪŋ/ n conflits mpl internes.

infinite /ˈɪnfɪnət/ adj infini. **infinitely** adv infiniment. **infinitive** n infinitif m. **infinity** n infinité f.

infirm /ɪnˈfɜːm/ adj infirme. **infirmary** n hôpital m; (sick-bay) infirmerie f. **infirmity** n infirmité f.

inflame /ɪnˈfleɪm/ vt enflammer. **inflammable** adj inflammable. **inflammation** n inflammation f. **inflammatory** adj incendiaire.

inflatable /ɪnˈfleɪtəbl/ adj gonflable. **inflate** vt (lit, fig) gonfler.

inflation /ɪnˈfleɪʃn/ n inflation f.

inflection /ɪnˈflekʃn/ n (of word root) flexion f; (of vowel, voice) inflexion f.

inflict /ɪnˈflɪkt/ vt infliger (on à).

influence /ˈɪnfluəns/ n influence f; under the ~ (drunk 🄸) éméché. ● vt (person) influencer; (choice) influer sur. **influential** adj (powerful) influent; (theory, artist) très suivi.

influenza /ɪnfluˈenzə/ n grippe f.

influx /ˈɪnflʌks/ n afflux m.

inform /ɪnˈfɔːm/ vt informer (of de). keep ~ed tenir au courant.

informal /ɪnˈfɔːml/ adj (simple) simple, sans façons; (unofficial) officieux; (colloquial) familier. **informality** n simplicité f. **informally** adv (dress) en tenue décontractée; (speak) en toute simplicité.

informant /ɪnˈfɔːmənt/ n indicateur/-trice m/f.

information /ɪnfəˈmeɪʃn/ n renseignements mpl, informations fpl; some ~ un renseignement. ~ **superhighway** n autoroute f de l'information. ~ **technology** n informatique f.

informative /ɪnˈfɔːmətɪv/ adj (book) riche en renseignements; (visit) instructif.

informer /ɪnˈfɔːmə(r)/ n indicateur/-trice m/f.

infrequent /ɪnˈfriːkwənt/ adj rare.

infringe /ɪnˈfrɪndʒ/ vt (rule) enfreindre; (rights) ne pas respecter. **infringement** n infraction f.

infuriate /ɪnˈfjʊərɪeɪt/ vt exaspérer.

ingenuity /ɪndʒɪˈnjuːətɪ/ n ingéniosité f.

ingot /ˈɪŋgət/ n lingot m.

ingrained /ɪnˈgreɪnd/ adj (hatred) enraciné; (dirt) bien incrusté.

ingratiate /ɪnˈgreɪʃɪeɪt/ vt ~ one-self with se faire bien voir (de).

ingredient /ɪnˈgriːdɪənt/ n ingrédient m.

inhabit /ɪnˈhæbɪt/ vt habiter. **inhabitable** adj habitable. **inhabitant** n habitant/-e m/f.

inhale /ɪnˈheɪl/ vt inhaler; (smoke) avaler. **inhaler** n inhalateur m.

inherent /ɪnˈhɪərənt/ adj inhérent (in à). **inherently** adv en soi, par sa nature.

inherit /ɪnˈherɪt/ vt hériter de; ~ sth from sb hériter qch de qn. **inheritance** n héritage m.

inhibit /ɪnˈhɪbɪt/ vt (restrain) inhiber; (prevent) entraver.

inhospitable /ɪnhɒˈspɪtəbl/ adj inhospitalier.

inhuman /ɪnˈhjuːmən/ adj inhumain.

initial /ɪˈnɪʃl/ n initiale f. ● vt (pt **initialled**) parapher. ● adj initial.

initiate /ɪˈnɪʃɪeɪt/ vt (project) mettre en œuvre; (talks) amorcer; (person) initier (into à). **initiation** n initiation f; (start) amorce f.

initiative /ɪˈnɪʃətɪv/ n initiative f.

inject /ɪnˈdʒekt/ vt injecter (into dans). (new element: fig) insuffler (into à). **injection** n injection f, piqûre f.

injure /ˈɪndʒə(r)/ vt blesser; (damage) nuire à. **injury** n blessure f.

injustice /ɪnˈdʒʌstɪs/ n injustice f.

ink /ɪŋk/ n encre f.

inkling /ˈɪŋklɪŋ/ n petite idée f.

inland /ˈɪnlænd/ adj intérieur; I~ Revenue service m des impôts britannique.

in-laws /ˈɪnlɔːz/ npl (parents) beaux-parents mpl; (family) belle-famille f.

inlay¹ /ɪnˈleɪ/ vt (pt **inlaid**) incruster (with de); (on wood) marqueter.

inlay² /ˈɪnleɪ/ n incrustation f; (on

wood) marqueterie f.

inlet /'ɪnlet/ n bras m de mer;
(Tech) arrivée f.

inmate /'ɪnmeɪt/ n (of asylum)
interné/-e m/f; (of prison) détenu
/-e m/f.

inn /ɪn/ n auberge f.

innate /ɪ'neɪt/ adj inné.

inner /'ɪnə(r)/ adj intérieur; ~ city
quartiers mpl déshérités; ~ tube
chambre f à air.

innocent /'ɪnəsnt/ adj & n
innocent/-e (m/f).

innocuous /ɪ'nɒkjuəs/ adj inoffensif.

innovate /'ɪnəveɪt/ vi innover.

innuendo /ɪnju:'endəʊ/ n (pl
~es) insinuations fpl; (sexual) allu-
sions fpl grivoises.

innumerable /ɪ'nju:mərəbl/ adj
innombrable.

inoculate /ɪ'nɒkjʊleɪt/ vt vacciner
(against contre).

inopportune /ɪn'ɒpətju:n/ adj inopportun.

in-patient /'ɪnpeɪʃnt/ n malade mf
hospitalisé/-e.

input /'ɪnpʊt/ n (of energy) alimentation f (of en); (contribution) contribution f; (data) données fpl; (computer process) saisie f des données.
● vt (data) saisir.

inquest /'ɪnkwest/ n enquête f.

inquire /ɪn'kwaɪə(r)/ vi se renseigner (about, into sur). ● vt demander.

inquiry /ɪn'kwaɪərɪ/ n demande f
de renseignements; (inquest) enquête f.

inquisitive /ɪn'kwɪzətɪv/ adj
curieux.

inroad /'ɪnrəʊd/ n make ~s into
faire une avancée sur.

insane /ɪn'seɪn/ adj fou; (Jur)

aliéné. **insanity** n folie f; (Jur) alié-
nation f mentale.

inscribe /ɪn'skraɪb/ vt inscrire. **inscription** n inscription f.

inscrutable /ɪn'skru:təbl/ adj
énigmatique.

insect /'ɪnsekt/ n insecte m. **insecticide** n insecticide m.

insecure /ɪnsɪ'kjʊə(r)/ adj (person)
qui manque d'assurance; (job) précaire; (lock, property) peu sûr. **insecurity** n (of person) manque m
d'assurance; (of situation) insécurité f.

insensitive /ɪn'sensətɪv/ adj insensible; (remark) indélicat.

inseparable /ɪn'seprəbl/ adj insé-
parable (from de).

insert /ɪn'sɜ:t/ vt insérer (in dans).

in-service /ɪnsɜ:'rvɪs/ adj (training) continu.

inshore /ɪn'ʃɔ:(r)/ adj côtier.

inside /ɪn'saɪd/ n intérieur m; ~s
🄸 entrailles fpl. ● adj intérieur. ● adv
à l'intérieur; go ~ entrer. ● prep à
l'intérieur de; (of time) en moins
de; ~ out à l'envers; (thoroughly)
à fond.

insight /'ɪnsaɪt/ n (perception)
perspicacité f; (idea) aperçu m.

insignia /ɪn'sɪgnɪə/ npl insigne m.

insignificant /ɪnsɪg'nɪfɪkənt/ adj
(cost, difference) négligeable; (person) insignifiant.

insincere /ɪnsɪn'sɪə(r)/ adj peu
sincère.

insinuate /ɪn'sɪnjʊeɪt/ vt insinuer.

insist /ɪn'sɪst/ vt/i insister (that
pour que). ~ on exiger; ~ on
doing vouloir à tout prix faire. **insistence** n insistance f. **insistent** adj
insistant. **insistently** adv avec insistance.

insofar as /ɪnsəʊ'fɑːəz/ adv dans
la mesure où.

insolent /'ɪnsələnt/ adj insolent.

insoluble /ɪn'sɒljʊbl/ adj insolvable.

insomnia /ɪn'sɒmnɪə/ n insomnie f. **insomniac** n insomniaque mf.

inspect /ɪn'spekt/ vt (school, machinery) inspecter; (tickets) contrôler. **inspection** n inspection f; (of passport, ticket) contrôle m. **inspector** n inspecteur-trice m/f; (on bus) contrôleur-euse m/f.

inspiration /ɪnspə'reɪʃn/ n inspiration f. **inspire** vt inspirer.

install /ɪn'stɔːl/ vt installer.

instalment /ɪn'stɔːlmənt/ n (payment) versement m; (of serial) épisode m.

instance /'ɪnstəns/ n exemple m; (case) cas m; for ∼ par exemple; in the first ∼ en premier lieu.

instant /'ɪnstənt/ adj immédiat; (food) instantané. ● n instant m. **instantaneous** adj instantané. **instantly** adv immédiatement.

instead /ɪn'sted/ adv plutôt; ∼ of doing au lieu de faire; ∼ of sb à la place de qn.

instep /'ɪnstep/ n cou-de-pied m.

instigate /'ɪnstɪgeɪt/ vt (attack) lancer; (proceedings) engager.

instil /ɪn'stɪl/ vt (pt instilled) inculquer; (fear) insuffler.

instinct /'ɪnstɪŋkt/ n instinct m. **instinctive** adj instinctif.

institute /'ɪnstɪtjuːt/ n institut m. ● vt instituer; (proceedings) engager. **institution** n institution f; (school, hospital) établissement m.

instruct /ɪn'strʌkt/ vt (teach) instruire; (order) ordonner; ∼ sb in sth enseigner qch à qn; ∼ sb to do donner l'ordre à qn de faire; **instruction** n instruction f. **instructions** npl (for use) mode m d'emploi. **instructive** adj instructif.

instructor n (skiing, driving) moniteur/-trice m/f.

instrument /'ɪnstrəmənt/ n instrument m.

instrumental /ɪnstrʊ'mentl/ adj instrumental; be ∼ in contribuer à. **instrumentalist** n instrumentaliste mf.

insubordinate /ɪnsə'bɔːdɪnət/ adj insubordonné.

insufficient /ɪnsə'fɪʃnt/ adj insuffisant.

insular /'ɪnsjʊlə(r)/ adj (Geog) insulaire; (mind, person: fig) borné.

insulate /'ɪnsjʊleɪt/ vt (room, wire) isoler.

insulin /'ɪnsjʊlɪn/ n insuline f.

insult[1] /ɪn'sʌlt/ vt insulter.

insult[2] /'ɪnsʌlt/ n insulte f.

insurance /ɪn'ʃɔːrəns/ n assurance f (against contre).

insure /ɪn'ʃɔː(r)/ vt assurer; ∼ that (US) s'assurer que.

intact /ɪn'tækt/ adj intact.

intake /'ɪnteɪk/ n (of food) consommation f; (School, Univ) admissions fpl.

integral /'ɪntɪgrəl/ adj intégral (to à).

integrate /'ɪntɪgreɪt/ vt/i (s')intégrer (with à; into dans).

integrity /ɪn'tegrətɪ/ n intégrité f.

intellect /'ɪntəlekt/ n intelligence f. **intellectual** adj & n intellectuel/-le (m/f).

intelligence /ɪn'telɪdʒəns/ n intelligence f; (Mil) renseignements mpl. **intelligent** adj intelligent. **intelligently** adv intelligemment.

intend /ɪn'tend/ vt (outcome) vouloir; ∼ to do avoir l'intention de faire. **intended** adj (result) voulu; (visit) projeté.

intense /ɪn'tens/ adj intense; (per-

son) sérieux. **intensely** adv (very) extrêmement.
intensify /ɪnˈtensɪfaɪ/ vt/i (s')intensifier.
intensive /ɪnˈtensɪv/ adj intensif; in ~ care en réanimation.
intent /ɪnˈtent/ n intention f. ● adj absorbé; ~ on doing résolu à faire.
intention /ɪnˈtenʃn/ n intention f. **intentional** adj intentionnel.
intently /ɪnˈtentlɪ/ adv attentivement.
interact /ɪntərˈækt/ vi (factors) agir l'un sur l'autre; (people) communiquer. **interactive** adj (TV, video) interactif.
intercept /ɪntəˈsept/ vt intercepter.
interchange /ˈɪntətʃeɪndʒ/ n (road junction) échangeur m; (exchange) échange m.
interchangeable /ɪntəˈtʃeɪndʒəbl/ adj interchangeable.
intercom /ˈɪntəkɒm/ n interphone® m.
interconnected /ɪntəkəˈnektɪd/ adj (parts) raccordé; (problems) lié.
intercourse /ˈɪntəkɔːs/ n rapports mpl.
interest /ˈɪntrəst/ n intérêt m; ~ rate taux m d'intérêt. ● vt intéresser (in à). **interested** adj intéressé; be ~ed in s'intéresser à. **interesting** adj intéressant.
interface /ˈɪntəfeɪs/ n interface f.
interfere /ɪntəˈfɪə(r)/ vi se mêler des affaires des autres; ~ in se mêler de; ~ with (freedom) empiéter sur; (tamper with) toucher. **interference** n ingérence f; (sound, light waves) brouillage m; (radio) parasites mpl.
interim /ˈɪntərɪm/ n in the ~ entre-temps. ● adj (government) provisoire; (payment) intermédiaire.
interior /ɪnˈtɪərɪə(r)/ n intérieur m.

● adj intérieur.
interjection /ɪntəˈdʒekʃn/ n interjection f.
interlock /ɪntəˈlɒk/ vt/i (Tech) (s')emboîter, (s')enclencher.
interlude /ˈɪntəluːd/ n intervalle m; (Theat, Mus) intermède m.
intermediary /ɪntəˈmiːdɪərɪ/ adj & n intermédiaire (mf).
intermediate /ɪntəˈmiːdɪət/ adj intermédiaire; (exam, level) moyen.
intermission /ɪntəˈmɪʃn/ n (Theat) entracte m.
intermittent /ɪntəˈmɪtənt/ adj intermittent.
intern[1] /ɪnˈtɜːn/ vt interner.
intern[2] /ˈɪntɜːn/ n (US) stagiaire mf; (Med) interne mf.
internal /ɪnˈtɜːnl/ adj interne; (domestic: Pol) intérieur; I~ Revenue (US) service m des impôts américain.
international /ɪntəˈnæʃnəl/ adj international.
Internet /ˈɪntənet/ n Internet m; on the ~ sur Internet; ~ access accès à Internet; ~ service provider fournisseur m d'accès Internet.
interpret /ɪnˈtɜːprɪt/ vt interpréter (as comme). ● vi faire l'interprète. **interpretation** n interprétation f. **interpreter** n interprète mf.
interrelated /ɪntərɪˈleɪtɪd/ adj interdépendant, lié.
interrogate /ɪnˈterəgeɪt/ vt interroger. **interrogative** adj & n (Ling) interrogatif (m).
interrupt /ɪntəˈrʌpt/ vt/i interrompre. **interruption** n interruption f.
intersect /ɪntəˈsekt/ vt/i (lines, roads) (se) croiser. **intersection** n intersection f.
interspersed /ɪntəˈspɜːst/ adj parsemé (with de).

intertwine /ɪntəˈtwaɪn/ vt/i (s')entrelacer.

interval /ˈɪntəvl/ n intervalle m; (Theat) entracte m.

intervene /ɪntəˈviːn/ vi intervenir; (of time) s'écouler (between entre); (happen) arriver.

interview /ˈɪntəvjuː/ n (for job) entretien m; (by a journalist) interview f. ● vt (candidate) faire passer un entretien à; (celebrity) interviewer.

intestine /ɪnˈtestɪn/ n intestin m.

intimacy /ˈɪntɪməsɪ/ n intimité f.

intimate[1] /ˈɪntɪmeɪt/ vt (state) annoncer; (hint) laisser entendre.

intimate[2] /ˈɪntɪmət/ adj intime. **intimately** adv intimement.

intimidate /ɪnˈtɪmɪdeɪt/ vt intimider.

into /ˈɪntuː/, /ˈɪntə/ prep (put, go, fall) dans; (divide, translate, change) en; be ~ jazz être fana du jazz 🄸; 8 ~ 24 is 3 24 divisé par 8 égale 3.

intolerant /ɪnˈtɒlərənt/ adj intolérant.

intonation /ɪntəˈneɪʃn/ n intonation f.

intoxicate /ɪnˈtɒksɪkeɪt/ vt enivrer. **intoxicated** adj ivre. **intoxication** n ivresse f.

intractable /ɪnˈtræktəbl/ adj (person) intraitable; (problem) rebelle.

intranet /ˈɪntrənet/ n (Comput) intranet m.

intransitive /ɪnˈtrænsətɪv/ adj intransitif.

intravenous /ɪntrəˈviːnəs/ adj (Med) intraveineux.

intricate /ˈɪntrɪkət/ adj complexe.

intrigue /ɪnˈtriːg/ vt intriguer. ● n intrigue f. **intriguing** adj fascinant; (curious) curieux.

intrinsic /ɪnˈtrɪnzɪk/ adj intrinsèque (to à).

introduce /ɪntrəˈdjuːs/ vt (person, idea, programme) présenter; (object, law) introduire (into dans). **introduction** f introduction f; (of person) présentation f. **introductory** adj (words) préliminaire.

introvert /ˈɪntrəvɜːt/ n introverti/-e m/f.

intrude /ɪnˈtruːd/ vi (person) s'imposer (on sb à qn), déranger. **intruder** n intrus/-e m/f. **intrusion** n intrusion f.

intuition /ɪntjuːˈɪʃn/ n intuition f. **intuitive** adj intuitif.

inundate /ˈɪnʌndeɪt/ vt inonder (with de).

invade /ɪnˈveɪd/ vt envahir.

invalid[1] /ˈɪnvəliːd/ n malade mf; (disabled) infirme mf.

invalid[2] /ɪnˈvælɪd/ adj (passport) pas valable; (claim) sans fondement. **invalidate** vt (argument) infirmer; (claim) annuler.

invaluable /ɪnˈvæljʊəbl/ adj inestimable.

invariable /ɪnˈveərɪəbl/ adj invariable. **invariably** adv invariablement.

invasion /ɪnˈveɪʒn/ n invasion f.

invent /ɪnˈvent/ vt inventer. **invention** n invention f. **inventive** adj inventif. **inventor** n inventeur/-trice m/f.

inventory /ˈɪnvəntrɪ/ n inventaire m.

invert /ɪnˈvɜːt/ vt (order) intervertir; (image, values) renverser; ~ed commas guillemets mpl.

invest /ɪnˈvest/ vt investir; (time, effort) consacrer. ● vi faire un investissement; ~ in (buy) s'acheter.

investigate /ɪnˈvestɪgeɪt/ vt examiner; (crime) enquêter sur. **investigation** n investigation f. **Investi-**

gator n (*police*) enquêteur/-euse m/f.

investment /ɪn'vestmənt/ n investissement m; emotional ● engagement m personnel. **investor** n investisseur/-euse m/f; (*in shares*) actionnaire mf.

invigilate /ɪn'vɪdʒɪleɪt/ vi (*exam*) surveiller. **invigilator** n surveillant/-e m/f.

invigorate /ɪn'vɪgəreɪt/ vt revigorer.

invisible /ɪn'vɪzəbl/ adj invisible.

invitation /ɪnvɪ'teɪʃn/ n invitation f. **invite** vt inviter; (*ask for*) demander. **inviting** adj engageant.

invoice /'ɪnvɔɪs/ n facture f. ● vt facturer.

involuntary /ɪn'vɒləntrɪ/ adj involontaire.

involve /ɪn'vɒlv/ vt impliquer; (*person*) faire participer (in à). **involved** adj (*complex*) compliqué; (*at stake*) en jeu; be ~d in (*work*) participer à; (*crime*) être mêlé à. **involvement** n participation f (in à).

inward /'ɪnwəd/ adj (*feeling*) intérieur. **inwardly** adv intérieurement. **inwards** adv vers l'intérieur.

iodine /'aɪədiːn/ n iode m; (*antiseptic*) teinture f d'iode.

iota /aɪ'əʊtə/ n iota m; not one ~ of pas un grain de.

IOU abbr (**I owe you**) reconnaissance f de dette.

IQ abbr (**intelligence quotient**) QI m.

Iran /ɪ'rɑːn/ n Iran m.

Iraq /ɪ'rɑːk/ n Irak m.

irate /aɪ'reɪt/ adj furieux.

IRC abbrev (**Internet Relay Chat**) (*Internet*) conversation f IRC.

Ireland /'aɪələnd/ n Irlande f.

Irish /'aɪərɪʃ/ n & adj irlandais (m).

~**man** n Irlandais m. ~**woman** n Irlandaise f.

iron /'aɪən/ n fer m; (*appliance*) fer m (à repasser). ● adj (*will*) de fer; (*bar*) en fer. ● vt repasser.

ironic /aɪ'rɒnɪk/ adj ironique.

iron: ironing-board n planche f à repasser. ~**monger** n quincaillier m.

irony /'aɪrənɪ/ n ironie f.

irrational /ɪ'ræʃənl/ adj irrationnel; (*person*) pas raisonnable.

irregular /ɪ'regjʊlə(r)/ adj irrégulier.

irrelevant /ɪ'reləvnt/ adj hors de propos.

irreplaceable /ɪrɪ'pleɪsəbl/ adj irremplaçable.

irresistible /ɪrɪ'zɪstəbl/ adj irrésistible.

irrespective /ɪrɪ'spektɪv/ adj ~ of sans tenir compte de.

irresponsible /ɪrɪ'spɒnsəbl/ adj irresponsable.

irreverent /ɪ'revərənt/ adj irrévérencieux.

irrigate /'ɪrɪgeɪt/ vt irriguer.

irritable /'ɪrɪtəbl/ adj irritable.

irritate /'ɪrɪteɪt/ vt irriter. **irritating** adj irritant.

is /ɪz/ ⇒BE.

ISDN abbr (**integrated services digital network**) RNIS n, réseau m numérique à intégration de services.

Islam /ɪz'lɑːm/ n (*faith*) islam m; (*Muslims*) Islam m. **Islamic** adj islamique.

island /'aɪlənd/ n île f.

isle /aɪl/ n île f.

isolate /'aɪsəleɪt/ vt isoler. **isolation** n isolement m.

Israel /'ɪzreɪl/ n Israël m.

Israeli /ɪz'reɪlɪ/ n Israélien/-ne m/f. ● adj israélien.

issue /'ɪsjuː/ n question f; (outcome) résultat m; (of magazine) numéro m; (of stamps) émission f; (offspring) descendance f; **at ~** en cause. ● vt distribuer; (stamps) émettre; (book) publier; (order) délivrer. ● vi **~ from** provenir de.

it /ɪt/

● *pronoun*

····▸ (subject) il, elle; 'where's the book/chair?'— '~'s in the kitchen' 'où est le livre/la chaise?'—'il/elle est dans la cuisine'.

····▸ (object) le, la, l'; **~'s** my book and I want **~** c'est mon livre et je le veux; I liked his shirt, did you notice **~**? sa chemise m'a plu, l'as-tu remarquée?; give **~** to me donne-le-moi.

····▸ (with preposition) we talked a lot about **~** on en a beaucoup parlé; Elliott went to **~** Elliott y est allé.

····▸ (impersonal) il; **~'s** raining il pleut; **~** will snow il va neiger.

IT *abbr* **→INFORMATION TECHNOLOGY.**

Italian /ɪ'tæljən/ n (person) Italien/-ne m/f; (Ling) italien m. ● adj italien.

italics /ɪ'tælɪks/ npl italique m.

Italy /'ɪtəlɪ/ n Italie f.

itch /ɪtʃ/ n démangeaison f. ● vi démanger; my arm **~es** j'ai le bras qui me démange; be **~ing** to do mourir d'envie de faire.

item /'aɪtəm/ n article m; (on agenda) point m.

itemize /'aɪtəmaɪz/ vt détailler; **~d** bill facture f détaillée.

itinerary /aɪ'tɪnərərɪ/ n itinéraire m.

its /ɪts/ det son, sa; pl ses.

it's →IT IS, IT HAS.

itself /ɪt'self/ pron lui-même, elle-même; (reflexive) se.

ivory /'aɪvərɪ/ n ivoire m; **~ tower** tour f d'ivoire.

ivy /'aɪvɪ/ n lierre m.

The Ivy League Ce terme désigne les huit universités les plus prestigieuses de la côte est des États-Unis (Harvard, Yale, Columbia, Cornell, Dartmouth, Brown, Princeton, Pennsylvania). Elles doivent ce nom au lierre qui pousse sur les bâtiments des plus anciennes d'entre elles. Ces universités sont réputées tant dans les domaines académiques que sportifs.

Jj

jab /dʒæb/ vt (pt **jabbed**) **~** sth into sth planter qch dans qch. ● n coup m; (injection) piqûre f.

jack /dʒæk/ n (Auto) cric m; (cards) valet m; (Electr) jack m. ● vt **~ up** soulever avec un cric.

jacket /'dʒækɪt/ n veste f, veston m; (of book) jaquette f.

jackknife /'dʒæknaɪf/ n couteau m pliant. ● vi (lorry) se mettre en portefeuille.

jackpot /'dʒækpɒt/ n gros lot m; hit the **~** gagner le gros lot.

jade /dʒeɪd/ n (stone) jade m.

jaded /'dʒeɪdɪd/ adj (tired) fatigué;

(bored) blasé.

jagged /'dʒægɪd/ adj (rock) déchiqueté; (knife) dentelé.

jail /dʒeɪl/ n prison f. ● vt mettre en prison.

jam /dʒæm/ n confiture f; (traffic) ~ embouteillage m. ● vt/i (pt jammed) (wedge) (se) coincer; (cram) (s')entasser; (street) encombrer; (radio) brouiller.

Jamaica /dʒə'meɪkə/ n Jamaïque f.

jam-packed adj ▯ bondé; ~ with bourré de.

jangle /'dʒæŋgl/ n tintement m. ● vt/i (faire) tinter.

janitor /'dʒænɪtə(r)/ n (US) gardien m.

January /'dʒænjʊərɪ/ n janvier m.

Japan /dʒə'pæn/ n Japon m.

Japanese /dʒæpə'niːz/ n (person) Japonais/-e m/f; (Ling) japonais m. ● adj japonais.

jar /dʒɑː(r)/ n pot m, bocal m. ● vi (pt jarred) rendre un son discordant; (colours) détonner. ● vt ébranler.

jargon /'dʒɑːgən/ n jargon m.

jaundice /'dʒɔːndɪs/ n jaunisse f.

javelin /'dʒævlɪn/ n javelot m.

jaw /dʒɔː/ n mâchoire f.

jay /dʒeɪ/ n geai m.

jazz /dʒæz/ n jazz m. ● vt ~ up (dress) rajeunir; (event) animer.

jealous /'dʒeləs/ adj jaloux. **jealousy** n jalousie f.

jeans /dʒiːnz/ npl jean m.

jeer /dʒɪə(r)/ vt/i ~ (at) huer. ● n huée f.

jelly /'dʒelɪ/ n gelée f. ~fish n méduse f.

jeopardize /'dʒepədaɪz/ vt (career, chance) compromettre; (lives) mettre en péril.

jerk /dʒɜːk/ n secousse f; (fool ▣)

crétin m ▯. ● vt tirer brusquement. ● vi tressaillir. **jerky** adj saccadé.

jersey /'dʒɜːzɪ/ n (garment) pullover m; (fabric) jersey m.

jet /dʒet/ n (plane, stream) jet m; (mineral) jais m; ~ lag décalage m horaire.

jettison /'dʒetɪsn/ vt jeter pardessus bord; (Aviat) larguer; (fig) rejeter.

jetty /'dʒetɪ/ n jetée f.

Jew /dʒuː/ n juif/juive m/f.

jewel /'dʒuːəl/ n bijou m. **jeweller** n bijoutier/-ière m/f. **jeweller('s)** n (shop) bijouterie f. **jewellery** n bijoux mpl.

Jewish /'dʒuːɪʃ/ adj juif.

jibe /dʒaɪb/ n moquerie f.

jigsaw /'dʒɪgsɔː/ n puzzle m.

jingle /'dʒɪŋgl/ vt/i (faire) tinter. ● n tintement m; (advertising) refrain m publicitaire, sonal m.

jinx /dʒɪŋks/ n (person) portemalheur m inv; (curse) sort m.

jitters /'dʒɪtəz/ npl have the ~ ▯ être nerveux. **jittery** adj nerveux.

job /dʒɒb/ n emploi m; (post) poste m; out of a ~ sans emploi; it is a good ~ that heureusement que; just the ~ tout à fait ce qu'il faut. ~ centre n bureau m des services nationaux de l'emploi. **jobless** adj sans emploi.

jockey /'dʒɒkɪ/ n jockey m.

jog /dʒɒg/ n go for a ~ aller faire un jogging. ● vt (pt jogged) heurter; (memory) rafraîchir. ● vi faire du jogging. **jogging** n jogging m.

join /dʒɔɪn/ vt (attach) réunir, joindre; (club) devenir membre de; (company) entrer dans; (army) s'engager dans; (queue) se mettre dans; ~ sb (in activity) se joindre à qn; (meet) rejoindre qn. ● vi (become member) adhérer; (pieces) se joindre; (roads) se rejoindre. ● n raccord m. □ ~ **in** participer; ~ **up** (Mil) s'engager; ~ sth **up** relier qch. **joiner** n menuisier/-ière m/f.

joint /dʒɔɪnt/ adj (action) collectif; (measures, venture) commun; (winner) ex aequo inv; (account) joint; ~ author coauteur m. ● n (join) joint m; (Anat) articulation f; (Culin) rôti m; **out of** ~ déboîté.

joke /dʒəʊk/ n plaisanterie f; (trick) farce f; **it's no** ~ ce n'est pas drôle. ● vi plaisanter. **joker** n blagueur/-euse m/f; (cards) joker m.

jolly /'dʒɒlɪ/ adj (-ier, -iest) (person) enjoué; (tune) joyeux. ● adv [ǀ] drôlement.

jolt /dʒəʊlt/ vt secouer. ● vi cahoter. ● n secousse f; (shock) choc m.

jostle /'dʒɒsl/ vt/i (se) bousculer.

jot /dʒɒt/ vt (pt **jotted**) ~ (**down**) noter.

journal /'dʒɜːnl/ n journal m. **journalism** n journalisme m. **journalist** n journaliste mf.

journey /'dʒɜːnɪ/ n (trip) voyage m; (short or habitual) trajet m. ● vi voyager.

joy /dʒɔɪ/ n joie f. **joyful** adj joyeux. **joy**: ~**riding** n rodéo m à la voiture volée. ~**stick** n (Comput) manette f; (Aviat) manche m à balai.

jubilant /'dʒuːbɪlənt/ adj (person) exultant; (mood) réjoui.

Judaism /'dʒuːdeɪɪzəm/ n judaïsme m.

judge /dʒʌdʒ/ n juge m. ● vt juger; (distance) estimer; **judging by/from** à en juger par. **judg(e)ment** n jugement m.

judicial /dʒuːˈdɪʃl/ adj judiciaire. **judiciary** n magistrature f.

judo /'dʒuːdəʊ/ n judo m.

jug /dʒʌɡ/ n (glass) carafe f; (pottery) pichet m.

juggernaut /'dʒʌɡənɔːt/ n (lorry) poids m lourd.

juggle /'dʒʌɡl/ vt/i jongler (avec). **juggler** n jongleur/-euse m/f.

juice /dʒuːs/ n jus m. **juicy** adj juteux; (details [ǀ]) croustillant.

jukebox /'dʒuːkbɒks/ n juke-box m.

July /dʒuːˈlaɪ/ n juillet m.

jumble /'dʒʌmbl/ vt mélanger. ● n (of objects) tas m; (of ideas) fouillis m; ~ **sale** vente f de charité.

jumbo /'dʒʌmbəʊ/ n (also ~ **jet**) gros-porteur m.

jump /dʒʌmp/ vt sauter; ~ **the lights** passer au feu rouge; ~ **the queue** passer devant tout le monde. ● vi sauter; (in surprise) sursauter; (price) monter en flèche; ~ **at** (opportunity) sauter sur. ● n saut m, bond m; (increase) bond m.

jumper /'dʒʌmpə(r)/ n pull(-over) m; (dress: US) robe f chasuble.

jump-leads npl câbles mpl de démarrage.

jumpy /'dʒʌmpɪ/ adj nerveux.

junction /'dʒʌŋkʃn/ n (of roads) carrefour m; (on motorway) échangeur m.

June /dʒuːn/ n juin m.

jungle /'dʒʌŋɡl/ n jungle f.

junior /'dʒuːnɪə(r)/ adj (young) jeune; (in rank) subalterne; (school) primaire. ● n cadet/-te m/f; (School) élève mf du primaire.

junk /dʒʌŋk/ n bric-à-brac m inv; (poor quality) camelote f; ~ **food** nourriture f industrielle.

junkie /'dʒʌŋkɪ/ n ⊠ drogué/-e m/f.

junk: ~ **mail** n prospectus mpl. ~-**shop** n boutique f de bric-à-brac.

jurisdiction /dʒʊərɪsˈdɪkʃn/ n

compétence f; (Jur) juridiction f.

juror /'dʒʊərə(r)/ n juré m.

jury /'dʒʊərɪ/ n jury m.

just /dʒʌst/ adj (fair) juste. ● adv (immediately, slightly) juste; (simply) tout simplement; (exactly) exactement; he has/had ~ left il vient/venait de partir; have ~ missed avoir manqué de peu; I'm ~ leaving je suis sur le point de partir; it's ~ a cold ce n'est qu'un rhume; ~ as tall/well as tout aussi grand/bien que; ~ listen! écoutez donc!; it's ~ ridiculous c'est vraiment ridicule.

justice /'dʒʌstɪs/ n justice f; J~ of the Peace juge m de paix.

justification /dʒʌstɪfɪ'keɪʃn/ n justification f.

justify /'dʒʌstɪfaɪ/ vt justifier.

jut /dʒʌt/ vi (pt jutted) ~ (out) s'avancer en saillie.

juvenile /'dʒuːvənaɪl/ adj (childish) puéril; (offender) mineur; (delinquent) jeune. ● n jeune mf; (Jur) mineur/-e m/f.

juxtapose /dʒʌkstə'pəʊz/ vt juxtaposer.

Kk

kangaroo /kæŋɡə'ruː/ n kangourou m.

karate /kə'rɑːtɪ/ n karaté m.

kebab /kɪ'bæb/ n brochette f.

keel /kiːl/ n (of ship) quille f. ● vi ~ over (bateau) chavirer; (person) s'écrouler.

keen /kiːn/ adj (interest, wind, feeling) vif; (mind, analysis) pénétrant; (edge, appetite) aiguisé; (eager) enthousiaste; be ~ on être passionné de; be ~ to do or on doing tenir beaucoup à faire. **keenly** adv vivement. **keenness** n enthousiasme m.

keep /kiːp/ vt (pt kept) garder; (promise, shop, diary) tenir; (family) faire vivre; (animals) élever; (rule) respecter; (celebrate) célébrer; (delay) retenir; ~ sth clean/warm garder qch propre/au chaud; ~ sb in/out empêcher qn de sortir/d'entrer; ~ sb from doing empêcher qn de faire. ● vi (food) se conserver; ~ (on) continuer (doing à faire). ● n pension f; (of castle) donjon m. □ ~ **down** rester allongé; sth down limiter qch; ~ your voice down! baisse la voix!; ~ to (road) ne pas s'écarter de; (rules) respecter; ~ **up** (car, interest) suivre; (rain) continuer; ~ **up with sb** (in speed) aller aussi vite que; (class, inflation, fashion, news) suivre.

keeper /'kiːpə(r)/ n gardien/-ne m/f.

keepsake /'kiːpseɪk/ n souvenir m.

kennel /'kenl/ n niche f.

kept /kept/ →**KEEP**.

kerb /kɜːb/ n bord m du trottoir.

kernel /'kɜːnl/ n amande f; ~ of truth fond m de vérité.

kettle /'ketl/ n bouilloire f.

key /kiː/ n clé f; (of computer, piano) touche f. ● adj (industry, figure) clé (inv). ● vt ~ (in) saisir. ~**board** n clavier m. ~**hole** n trou m de serrure. ~-**pad** n (of telephone) clavier m numérique. ~-**ring** n porte-clés m inv. ~**stroke** n (Comput) frappe f.

khaki /'kɑːkɪ/ adj kaki inv.

kick /kɪk/ vt/i donner un coup de pied (à); (horse) botter. ● n coup m de pied; (of gun) recul m; get a ~ out of doing 🔢 prendre plaisir à faire. □ ~ **out** 🔢 virer 🔢.

kick-off n coup m d'envoi.

kid /kɪd/ n (goat, leather) chevreau m; (child 𝕀) gosse mf. ● vt/i (pt kidded) blaguer.

kidnap /'kɪdnæp/ vt (pt kidnapped) enlever. **kidnapping** n enlèvement m.

kidney /'kɪdnɪ/ n rein m; (Culin) rognon m.

kill /kɪl/ vt tuer; (rumour: fig) arrêter. ● n mise à mort. **killer** n tueur/-euse m/f. **killing** n meurtre m.

kiln /kɪln/ n four m.

kilo /'ki:ləʊ/ n kilo m.

kilobyte /'kɪləbaɪt/ n kilo-octet m.

kilogram /'kɪləgræm/ n kilogramme m.

kilometre, (US) **kilometer** /'kɪləmi:tə(r)/ n kilomètre m.

kilowatt /'kɪləwɒt/ n kilowatt m.

kin /kɪn/ n parents mpl.

kind /kaɪnd/ n genre m, sorte f; in ~ en nature; ~ of (somewhat 𝕀) assez. ● adj gentil, bon.

kindergarten /'kɪndəga:tn/ n jardin m d'enfants.

kindle /'kɪndl/ vt/i (s')allumer.

kindly /'kaɪndlɪ/ adj (-ier, -iest) (person) gentil; (interest) bienveillant. ● adv avec gentillesse; would you ~ do auriez-vous l'amabilité de faire.

kindness /'kaɪndnɪs/ n bonté f.

king /kɪŋ/ n roi m. **kingdom** n royaume m; (Bot) règne m. ~**fisher** n martin-pêcheur m. ~**size(d)** adj géant.

kiosk /'ki:ɒsk/ n kiosque m; telephone ~ cabine f téléphonique; (Internet) borne f interactive, kiosque m.

kiss /kɪs/ n baiser m. ● vt/i (s')embrasser.

kit /kɪt/ n (clothing) affaires fpl; (set of tools) trousse f; (for assembly) kit m. ● vt (pt kitted) ~ out équiper.

kitchen /'kɪtʃɪn/ n cuisine f.

kite /kaɪt/ n (toy) cerf-volant m; (bird) milan m.

kitten /'kɪtn/ n chaton m.

kitty /'kɪtɪ/ n (fund) cagnotte f.

knack /næk/ n tour m de main (of doing pour faire).

knead /ni:d/ vt pétrir.

knee /ni:/ n genou m. ~**cap** n rotule f.

kneel /ni:l/ vi (pt knelt) ~ (down) se mettre à genoux; (in prayer) s'agenouiller.

knew /nju:/ ⇒KNOW.

knickers /'nɪkəz/ npl petite culotte f, slip m.

knife /naɪf/ n (pl knives) couteau m. ● vt poignarder.

knight /naɪt/ n chevalier m; (chess) cavalier m. ● vt anoblir. ~**hood** n titre m de chevalier.

knit /nɪt/ vt/i (pt knitted or knit) tricoter; (bones) (se) souder. **knitting** n tricot m. **knitwear** n tricots mpl.

knob /nɒb/ n bouton m.

knock /nɒk/ vt/i cogner; (criticize 𝕀) critiquer; ~ sth off/out faire tomber qch. ● n coup m. ~ **down** (chair, pedestrian) renverser; (demolish) abattre; (reduce) baisser; ~ **off** (stop work 𝕀) arrêter de travailler; ~ £ 10 off faire une réduction de 10 livres; ~ **it off!** 𝕀 ça suffit!; ~ **out** assommer; ~ **over** renverser; ~ **up** (meal) préparer en vitesse.

knockout /'nɒkaʊt/ n (boxing) knock-out m.

knot /nɒt/ n nœud m. ● vt (pt knotted) nouer.

know /nəʊ/ vt/i (pt knew; pp

known (*answer, reason, language*) savoir (**that** que); (*person, place, name, rule, situation*) connaître; (*recognize*) reconnaître; ~ **how to** do savoir faire; ~ **about** (*event*) être au courant de; (*subject*) s'y connaître en; ~ **of** (*from experience*) connaître; (*from information*) avoir entendu parler de. ~**-how** n savoir-faire m inv.

knowingly /'nəʊɪŋlɪ/ adv (intentionally) délibérément; (meaningfully) d'un air entendu.

knowledge /'nɒlɪdʒ/ n connaissance f; (learning) connaissances fpl. **knowledgeable** adj savant.

knuckle /'nʌkl/ n jointure f, articulation f.

Koran /kəˈrɑːn/ n Coran m.

Korea /kəˈrɪə/ n Corée f.

kosher /'kəʊʃə(r)/ adj casher inv.

● ●

Ll

● ●

lab /læb/ n 🔲 labo m.

label /'leɪbl/ n étiquette f. ● vt (pt **labelled**) étiqueter.

laboratory /ləˈbɒrətrɪ/ n laboratoire m.

laborious /ləˈbɔːrɪəs/ adj laborieux.

labour, (US) **labor** /'leɪbə(r)/ n travail m; (workers) main-d'œuvre f; **in** ~ en train d'accoucher. ● vi peiner (to do à faire). ● vt trop insister sur.

Labour /'leɪbə(r)/ n le parti travailliste. ● adj travailliste.

laboured /'leɪbəd/ adj laborieux.

labourer /'leɪbərə(r)/ n ouvrier/-ière m/f; (on farm) ouvrier/-ière m/f

agricole.

lace /leɪs/ n dentelle f; (of shoe) lacet m. ● vt (shoe) lacer; (drink) arroser.

lacerate /'læsəreɪt/ vt lacérer.

lack /læk/ n manque m; **for** ~ **of** faute de. ● vt manquer de; **be** ~**ing** manquer (**in** de).

lad /læd/ n garçon m, gars m.

ladder /'lædə(r)/ n échelle f; (in stocking) maille f filée. ● vt/i (stocking) filer.

laden /'leɪdn/ adj chargé (with de).

ladle /'leɪdl/ n louche f.

lady /'leɪdɪ/ n (pl **ladies**) dame f; ladies and gentlemen mesdames et messieurs; young ~ jeune femme or fille f. ~**bird** n coccinelle f.

ladylike /'leɪdɪlaɪk/ adj distingué.

lag /læg/ vi (pt **lagged**) traîner. ● vt (pipes) calorifuger. ● n (interval) décalage m.

lager /'lɑːgə(r)/ n bière f blonde.

lagoon /ləˈguːn/ n lagune f.

laid /leɪd/ →LAY¹. ~ **back** adj décontracté.

lain /leɪn/ →LIE².

lake /leɪk/ n lac m.

lamb /læm/ n agneau m; leg of ~ gigot m d'agneau.

lame /leɪm/ adj boiteux.

lament /ləˈment/ n lamentation f. ● vt/i se lamenter (sur).

laminated /'læmɪneɪtɪd/ adj laminé.

lamp /læmp/ n lampe f. ~**post** n réverbère m. ~**shade** n abat-jour m inv.

lance /lɑːns/ vt (Med) inciser.

land /lænd/ n terre f; (plot) terrain m; (country) pays m. ● adj terrestre; (policy, reform) agraire. ● vt/i débarquer; (aircraft) (se) poser; (faire) atterrir; (fall) tomber; (obtain) décrocher; (*a blow*) porter; ~ up se retrouver.

landing /ˈlændɪŋ/ *n* débarquement *m*; (Aviat) atterrissage *m*; (top of stairs) palier *m*. ~**-stage** *n* débarcadère *m*.

land: ~**lady** *n* propriétaire *f*; (of pub) patronne *f*. ~**lord** *n* propriétaire *m*; (of pub) patron *m*. ~**mark** *n* (point de) repère *m*. ~**mine** *n* mine *f* terrestre.

landscape /ˈlænskeɪp/ *n* paysage *m*. ● *vt* aménager.

landslide /ˈlænslaɪd/ *n* glissement *m* de terrain; (Pol) raz-de-marée *m* *inv* (électoral).

lane /leɪn/ *n* (path, road) chemin *m*; (strip of road) voie *f*; (of traffic) file *f*; (Aviat) couloir *m*.

language /ˈlæŋgwɪdʒ/ *n* langue *f*; (speech, style) langage *m*. ~ **engineering** *n* ingénierie *f* des langues. ~ **laboratory** *n* laboratoire *m* de langue.

lank /læŋk/ *adj* (hair) plat.

lanky /ˈlæŋkɪ/ *adj* (-ier, -iest) grand et maigre.

lantern /ˈlæntən/ *n* lanterne *f*.

lap /læp/ *n* genoux *mpl*; (Sport) tour *m* (de piste). ● *vi* (*pt* lapped) (waves) clapoter. □ ~ **up** laper.

lapel /ləˈpel/ *n* revers *m*.

lapse /læps/ *vi* (decline) se dégrader; (expire) se périmer; ~ **into** retomber dans. ● *n* défaillance *f*, erreur *f*; (of time) intervalle *m*.

laptop /ˈlæptɒp/ *n* (Comput) portable *m*.

lard /lɑːd/ *n* saindoux *m*.

larder /ˈlɑːdə(r)/ *n* garde-manger *m* *inv*.

large /lɑːdʒ/ *adj* grand, gros; at ~ en liberté; by and ~ en général. **largely** *adv* en grande mesure.

lark /lɑːk/ *n* (bird) alouette *f*; (bit of

fun 🔢) rigolade *f*. ● *vi* 🔢 rigoler.

larva /ˈlɑːvə/ *n* (*pl* -vae) larve *f*.

laryngitis /lærɪnˈdʒaɪtɪs/ *n* laryngite *f*.

laser /ˈleɪzə(r)/ *n* laser *m*. ~ **printer** *n* imprimante *f* laser. ~ **treatment** *n* (Med) laserothérapie *f*.

lash /læʃ/ *vt* fouetter. ● *n* coup *m* de fouet; (eyelash) cil *m*. □ ~ **out** (spend) dépenser follement; ~ **out against** attaquer.

lass /læs/ *n* jeune fille *f*.

lasso /læˈsuː/ *n* lasso *m*.

last /lɑːst/ *adj* dernier; the ~ **straw** le comble; the ~ **word** le mot de la fin; on its ~ **legs** sur le point de rendre l'âme; ~ **night** hier soir. ● *adv* en dernier; (most recently) la dernière fois. ● *n* dernier/-ière *m/f*; (remainder) reste *m*; at (long) ~ enfin. ● *vi* durer. ~**-ditch** *adj* ultime. **lasting** *adj* durable. **lastly** *adv* en dernier lieu. ~**-minute** *adj* de dernière minute.

latch /lætʃ/ *n* loquet *m*.

late /leɪt/ *adj* (not on time) en retard; (former) ancien; (hour, meal) tardif; the ~ **Mrs X** feu Mme X. ● *adv* (not early) tard; (not on time) en retard; in ~ **July** fin juillet; of ~ dernièrement. **lately** *adv* dernièrement. **latest** *adj* ➡LATE; (last) dernier.

lathe /leɪð/ *n* tour *m*.

lather /ˈlɑːðə(r)/ *n* mousse *f*. ● *vt* savonner. ● *vi* mousser.

Latin /ˈlætɪn/ *n* (Ling) latin *m*. ● *adj* latin. ~ **America** *n* Amérique *f* latine.

latitude /ˈlætɪtjuːd/ *n* latitude *f*.

latter /ˈlætə(r)/ *adj* dernier. ● *the* ~ celui-ci, celle-ci.

Latvia /ˈlætvɪə/ *n* Lettonie *f*.

laudable /ˈlɔːdəbl/ *adj* louable.

laugh /lɑːf/ *vi* rire (at de). ● *n* rire

m. **laughable** *adj* ridicule.

laughing stock *n* risée *f.*

laughter /'lɑːftə(r)/ *n* (act) rire *m;* (sound of laughs) rires *mpl.*

launch /lɔːntʃ/ *vt* (rocket) lancer; (boat) mettre à l'eau; ~ (out) into se lancer dans. ● *n* lancement *m;* (boat) vedette *f.* **launching pad** *n* aire *f* de lancement.

launderette /lɔːndrəˈmæt/ *n* laverie *f* automatique.

laundry /'lɔːndrɪ/ *n* (place) blanchisserie *f;* (clothes) linge *m.*

laurel /'lɒrəl/ *n* laurier *m.*

lava /'lɑːvə/ *n* lave *f.*

lavatory /'lævətrɪ/ *n* toilettes *fpl.*

lavender /'lævəndə(r)/ *n* lavande *f.*

lavish /'lævɪʃ/ *adj* (person) généreux; (lush) somptueux. ● *vt* prodiguer (on à). **lavishly** *adv* luxueusement.

law /lɔː/ *n* loi *f;* (profession, subject of study) droit *m;* ~ and order l'ordre public. **~-abiding** *adj* respectueux des lois. **~court** *n* tribunal *m.*

lawful /'lɔːfl/ *adj* légal.

lawn /lɔːn/ *n* pelouse *f,* gazon *m.* **~-mower** *n* tondeuse *f* à gazon.

lawsuit /'lɔːsuːt/ *n* procès *m.*

lawyer /'lɔːjə(r)/ *n* avocat *m.*

lax /læks/ *adj* (government) laxiste; (security) relâché.

laxative /'læksətɪv/ *n* laxatif *m.*

lay[1] /leɪ/ *adj* (non-clerical) laïque; (worker) non-initié. ● *vt* (*pt* **laid**) poser, mettre; (trap) tendre; (table) mettre; (plan) former; (eggs) pondre. ● *vi* pondre; ~ **waste** ravager. □ ~ **aside** mettre de côté; ~ **down** (dé)poser; (condition) (im)poser; ~ **off** *vt* (worker) licencier; *vi* ⚁ arrêter; ~ **on** (provide) fournir; ~ **out** (design) dessiner; (display) disposer; (money) dépenser.

lay[2] /leɪ/ ⇒LIE[2].

lay-by /'leɪbaɪ/ *n* (*pl* **~s**) aire *f* de repos.

layer /'leɪə(r)/ *n* couche *f.*

layman /'leɪmən/ *n* (*pl* **-men**) profane *m.*

layout /'leɪaʊt/ *n* disposition *f.*

laze /leɪz/ *vi* paresser. **laziness** *n* paresse *f.* **lazy** *adj* (-ier, -iest) paresseux.

lead[1] /liːd/ *vt/i* (*pt* **led**) mener; (team) diriger; (life) mener; (induce) amener; ~ **to** conduire à, mener à. ● *n* avance *f;* (clue) indice *m;* (leash) laisse *f;* (Theat) premier rôle *m;* (wire) fil *m;* **in the** ~ en tête. □ ~ **away** emmener; ~ **up to** (come to) en venir à; (precede) précéder.

lead[2] /led/ *n* plomb *m;* (of pencil) mine *f.*

leader /'liːdə(r)/ *n* chef *m;* (of country, club) dirigeant/-e *m/f;* (leading article) éditorial *m.* **leadership** *n* direction *f.*

lead-free *adj* (petrol) sans plomb.

leading /'liːdɪŋ/ *adj* principal.

leaf /liːf/ *n* (*pl* **leaves**) feuille *f;* (of table) rallonge *f.* ● *vi* ~ **through** feuilleter.

leaflet /'liːflɪt/ *n* prospectus *m.*

leafy /'liːfɪ/ *adj* feuillu.

league /liːg/ *n* ligue *f;* (Sport) championnat *m;* **in** ~ **with** de mèche avec.

leak /liːk/ *n* fuite *f.* ● *vi* fuir; (news; fig) s'ébruiter. ● *vt* répandre; (fig) divulguer.

lean[1] /liːn/ *adj* maigre. ● *n* (of meat) maigre *m.*

lean[2] /liːn/ *vt/i* (*pt* **leaned** or **leant**) (rest) (s')appuyer; (slope) pencher. □ ~ **out** se pencher à l'extérieur; ~ **over** (of person) se pencher.

leaning /'liːnɪŋ/ *adj* penché. ● *n* tendance *f.*

leap /liːp/ *vi* (*pt* leaped *or* leapt) bondir. ● *n* bond *m*. ~ **year** *n* année *f* bissextile.

learn /lɜːn/ *vt/i* (*pt* learned *or* learnt) apprendre (to do à faire). **learned** *adj* érudit. **learner** *n* débutant/-e *m/f*. **learning curve** *n* courbe *f* d'apprentissage.

lease /liːs/ *n* bail *m*. ● *vt* louer à bail.

leash /liːʃ/ *n* laisse *f*.

least /liːst/ *adj* the ~ (smallest amount of) le moins de; (slightest) le *or* la moindre. ● le moins. ● *adv* le moins; (with adjective) le *or* la moins; at ~ au moins.

leather /ˈleðə(r)/ *n* cuir *m*.

leave /liːv/ *vt* (*pt* left) laisser; (depart from) quitter; (person) laisser tranquille; be left (over) rester. ● *n* (holiday) congé *m*; (consent) permission *f*; take one's ~ prendre congé (of de); on ~ (Mil) en permission. □ ~ alone (thing) ne pas toucher; (person) laisser tranquille; ~ **behind** laisser; ~ **out** omettre.

Lebanon /ˈlebanan/ *n* Liban *m*.

lecture /ˈlektʃə(r)/ *n* cours *m*, conférence *f*; (rebuke) réprimande *f*. ● *vt/i* faire un cours *or* une conférence (à); (rebuke) réprimander. **lecturer** *n* conférencier/-ière *m/f*; (Univ) enseignant/-e *m/f*.

led /led/ ⇒**LEAD**[1].

ledge /ledʒ/ *n* (window) rebord *m*; (rock) saillie *f*.

ledger /ˈledʒə(r)/ *n* grand livre *m*.

leech /liːtʃ/ *n* sangsue *f*.

leek /liːk/ *n* poireau *m*.

leer /lɪə(r)/ *vi* ~ (at) lorgner. ● *n* regard *m* sournois.

leeway /ˈliːweɪ/ *n* (fig) liberté *f* d'action; (Naut) dérive *f*.

left /left/ ⇒**LEAVE**. ● *adj* gauche. ● *adv* à gauche. ● *n* gauche *f*.

~-**hand** *adj* à *or* de gauche.

~-**handed** *adj* gaucher.

left luggage (office) *n* consigne *f*.

left-overs *npl* restes *mpl*.

left-wing *adj* de gauche.

leg /leg/ *n* jambe *f*; (of animal) patte *f*; (of table) pied *m*; (of chicken) cuisse *f*; (of lamb) gigot *m*; (of journey) étape *f*

legacy /ˈlegəsɪ/ *n* legs *m*.

legal /ˈliːgl/ *adj* légal; (affairs) juridique.

legend /ˈledʒənd/ *n* légende *f*.

leggings /ˈlegɪŋz/ *npl* (for woman) caleçon *m*.

legible /ˈledʒəbl/ *adj* lisible.

legionnaire /liːdʒəˈneə(r)/ *n* légionnaire *m*.

legislation /ledʒɪsˈleɪʃn/ *n* (body of laws) législation *f*; (law) loi *f*. **legislature** *n* corps *m* législatif.

legitimate /lɪˈdʒɪtɪmət/ *adj* légitime.

leisure /ˈleʒə(r)/ *n* loisirs *mpl*; at one's ~ à tête reposée. ● *adj* (centre) de loisirs.

leisurely /ˈleʒəlɪ/ *adj* lent. ● *adv* sans se presser.

lemon /ˈlemən/ *n* citron *m*.

lemonade /leməˈneɪd/ *n* (fizzy) limonade *f*; (still) citronnade *f*.

lend /lend/ *vt* (*pt* lent) prêter; (credibility) conférer; ~ **itself to** se prêter à.

length /leŋθ/ *n* longueur *f*; (in time) durée *f*; (section) morceau *m*; at ~ (at last) enfin; at (great) ~ longuement.

lengthen /ˈleŋθən/ *vt/i* (s')allonger.

lengthways /ˈleŋθweɪz/ *adv* dans le sens de la longueur.

lengthy /ˈleŋθɪ/ *adj* long.

lenient /ˈliːnɪənt/ *adj* indulgent.

lens /lenz/ n lentille f; (of spectacles) verre m; (Photo) objectif m.

lent /lent/ →LEND.

Lent /lent/ n Carême m.

lentil /ˈlentl/ n lentille f.

Leo /ˈliːəʊ/ n Lion m.

leopard /ˈlepəd/ n léopard m.

leotard /ˈliːətɑːd/ n body m.

leprosy /ˈleprəsɪ/ n lèpre f.

lesbian /ˈlezbɪən/ n lesbienne f.
● adj lesbien.

less /les/ adj (in quantity) moins de (than que). ● adv, n & prep moins de; ~ than (with numbers) moins de; ~ work ~ than travailler moins que; ten pounds ~ than dix livres de moins; ~ and ~ de moins en moins.

lessen vt/i diminuer. **lesser** adj moindre.

lesson /ˈlesn/ n leçon f.

let /let/ vt (pt **let**; pres p **letting**) laisser; (lease) louer. ● v aux ~ us do, ~'s do faisons; ~ him do qu'il fasse; ~ me know the results informe-moi des résultats. ● n location f. □ ~ **down** baisser; (deflate) dégonfler; (fig) décevoir; ~ **go** vt lâcher; vi lâcher prise; ~ **sb in/out** laisser ou faire entrer/sortir qn; ~ **a dress out** élargir une robe; ~ one-self in for (task) s'engager à; (trouble) s'attirer; ~ **off** (explode, fire) faire éclater ou partir; (excuse) dispenser; (not punish) ne pas punir; ~ **up** 🔢 s'arrêter.

let-down n déception f.

lethal /ˈliːθl/ adj mortel; (weapon) meurtrier.

letter /ˈletə(r)/ n lettre f ~**-bomb** n lettre f piégée. ~**-box** n boîte f à or aux lettres.

lettering /ˈletərɪŋ/ n (letters) caractères mpl.

lettuce /ˈletɪs/ n laitue f, salade f.

let-up /ˈletʌp/ n répit m.

leukaemia /luːˈkiːmɪə/ n leucémie f.

level /ˈlevl/ adj plat, uni; (on surface) horizontal; (in height) au même niveau (with que); (in score) à égalité. ● n niveau m; (spirit) ~ niveau m à bulle; be on the ~ 🔢 être franc. ● vt (pt **levelled**) niveler; (aim) diriger. ~ **crossing** n passage m à niveau. ~**-headed** adj équilibré.

lever /ˈliːvə(r)/ n levier m. ● vt soulever au moyen d'un levier.

leverage /ˈliːvərɪdʒ/ n influence f.

levy /ˈlevɪ/ vt (tax) prélever. ● n impôt m.

lexicon /ˈleksɪkən/ n lexique m.

liability /laɪəˈbɪlətɪ/ n responsabilité f; 🔢 handicap m; **liabilities** (debts) dettes fpl.

liable /ˈlaɪəbl/ adj be ~ to do avoir tendance à faire, pouvoir faire; ~ to (illness) sujet à; (fine) passible de; ~ for responsable de.

liaise /lɪˈeɪz/ vi 🔢 faire la liaison. **liaison** n liaison f.

liar /ˈlaɪə(r)/ n menteur/-euse m/f.

libel /ˈlaɪbl/ n diffamation f. ● vt (pt **libelled**) diffamer.

liberal /ˈlɪbərəl/ adj libéral; (generous) généreux, libéral.

Liberal /ˈlɪbərəl/ adj & n (Pol) libéral-e (m/f).

liberate /ˈlɪbəreɪt/ vt libérer.

liberty /ˈlɪbətɪ/ n liberté f; at ~ to libre de; take liberties prendre des libertés.

Libra /ˈliːbrə/ n Balance f.

librarian /laɪˈbreərɪən/ n bibliothécaire mf.

library /ˈlaɪbrərɪ/ n bibliothèque f.

libretto /lɪˈbretəʊ/ n livret m.

lice /laɪs/ n →LOUSE.

licence, (US) **license** /ˈlaɪsns/ n permis m; (for television) redevance f; (Comm) licence f; (liberty: fig) licence f. ~ **plate** n plaque f minéralogique.

license /'laɪsns/ vt accorder un permis à, autoriser.

lick /lɪk/ vt lécher; (defeat 🔲) rosser; (fig) a ~ of paint un petit coup de peinture. ● n coup de langue.

lid /lɪd/ n couvercle m.

lie[1] /laɪ/ n mensonge m. ● vi (pt lied; pres p lying) (tell lies) mentir.

lie[2] /laɪ/ vi (pt lay; pp lain; pres p lying) s'allonger; (remain) rester; (be) se trouver, être; (in grave) reposer; be lying être allongé. □ ~ **down** s'allonger; ~ **in** faire la grasse matinée; ~ **low** se cacher.

lieutenant /lefˈtenənt/ n lieutenant m.

life /laɪf/ n (pl lives) vie f. ~**belt** n bouée f de sauvetage. ~**boat** n canot m de sauvetage. ~**buoy** n bouée f de sauvetage. ~ **coach** n conseiller/ère m/f en développement personnel. ~**cycle** n cycle m de vie. ~**guard** n sauveteur m. ~ **insurance** n assurance-vie f. ~**jacket** n gilet m de sauvetage.

lifeless /'laɪflɪs/ adj inanimé.

lifelike /'laɪflaɪk/ adj très ressemblant.

life: ~**long** adj de toute la vie. ~ **sentence** n condamnation f à perpétuité. ~**size(d)** adj grandeur nature inv. ~ **story** n vie f. ~**style** n style m de vie. ~ **support machine** n appareil m de respiration artificielle.

lifetime /'laɪftaɪm/ n vie f; in one's ~ de son vivant.

lift /lɪft/ vt lever; (steal 🔲) voler. ● vi (of fog) se lever. ● n (in building) ascenseur m; give a ~ to emmener (en voiture). ~**off** n (Aviat)

décollage m.

light /laɪt/ n lumière f; (lamp) lampe f; (for fire, on vehicle) feu m; (headlight) phare m; **bring to** ~ révéler; **come to** ~ être révélé; have you got a ~? vous avez du feu? ● adj (not dark) clair; (not heavy) léger. ● vt (pt **lit** or **lighted**) allumer; (room) éclairer; (match) frotter. □ ~ **up** s'allumer; vt (room) éclairer. ~ **bulb** n ampoule f.

lighten[1] /'laɪtn/ vt (give light to) éclairer; (make brighter) éclaircir; (make less heavy) alléger.

lighter /'laɪtə(r)/ n briquet m; (for stove) allume-gaz m inv.

light: ~**headed** adj (dizzy) qui a un vertige; (frivolous) étourdi. ~**hearted** adj gai. ~**house** n phare m.

lighting /'laɪtɪŋ/ n éclairage m.

lightly /'laɪtlɪ/ adv légèrement.

lightning /'laɪtnɪŋ/ n éclair m, foudre f. ● adj (visit) éclair inv.

lightweight /'laɪtweɪt/ adj léger. ● n (boxing) poids m léger.

light year n année f lumière.

like[1] /laɪk/ adj semblable, pareil; be ~**minded** avoir les mêmes sentiments. ● prep comme. ● conj 🔲 comme. ● n pareil m; the ~s of you les gens comme vous.

like[2] /laɪk/ vt aimer (bien); I should ~ je voudrais, j'aimerais; would you ~? voudriez-vous?, voudrais-tu?; ~s goûts mpl. **likeable** adj sympathique.

likelihood /'laɪklɪhʊd/ n probabilité f.

likely /'laɪklɪ/ adj (**-ier, -iest**) probable. ● adv probablement; he is ~ to do il fera probablement; not ~! 🔲 pas question!

likeness /'laɪknɪs/ n ressemblance f.

likewise /'laɪkwaɪz/ adv également.

liking /'laɪkɪŋ/ n (for thing) penchant m; (for person) affection f.

lilac /'laɪlək/ n lilas m. ● adj lilas inv.

Lilo® /'laɪləʊ/ n matelas m pneumatique.

lily /'lɪlɪ/ n lis m, lys m.

limb /lɪm/ n membre m.

limber /'lɪmbə(r)/ vi ~ up faire des exercices d'assouplissement.

limbo /'lɪmbəʊ/ n be in ~ (forgotten) être tombé dans l'oubli.

lime /laɪm/ n (fruit) citron m vert; ~(-tree) tilleul m.

limelight /'laɪmlaɪt/ n in the ~ en vedette.

limestone /'laɪmstəʊn/ n calcaire m.

limit /'lɪmɪt/ n limite f. ● vt limiter.

limited company n société f anonyme.

limp /lɪmp/ vi boiter. ● n have a ~ boiter. ● adj mou.

line /laɪn/ n ligne f; (track) voie f; (wrinkle) ride f; (row) rangée f, file f; (of poem) vers m; (rope) corde f; (of goods) gamme f; (queue: US) queue f; be in ~ for avoir de bonnes chances de; hold the ~ ne quittez pas; in ~ with en accord avec; stand in ~ faire la queue. ● vt (paper) régler; (streets) border; (garment) doubler; (fill) remplir, garnir. □ ~ up (s')aligner; (in queue) faire la queue; ~ sth up prévoir qch. ~ dancing danse f en ligne.

linen /'lɪnɪn/ n (sheets) linge m; (material) lin m.

liner /'laɪnə(r)/ n paquebot m.

linesman /'laɪnzmən/ n (football) juge m de touche; (tennis) juge m de ligne.

linger /'lɪŋgə(r)/ vi s'attarder; (smells) persister.

linguist /'lɪŋgwɪst/ n linguiste mf.
linguistics n linguistique f.

lining /'laɪnɪŋ/ n doublure f.

link /lɪŋk/ n lien m; (of chain) maillon m. ● vt relier; (relate) (re)lier; ~ up (of roads) se rejoindre.
linkage n lien m. **links** n inv terrain m de golf. □~up n liaison f.

lino /'laɪnəʊ/ n lino m.

lion /'laɪən/ n lion m. **lioness** n lionne f.

lip /lɪp/ n lèvre f; (edge) rebord m; pay ~service to n'approuver que pour la forme. ~-read vt/i lire sur les lèvres. ~salve n baume m pour les lèvres. ~stick n rouge m (à lèvres).

liquid /'lɪkwɪd/ n & adj liquide (m).

liquidation /lɪkwɪ'deɪʃn/ n liquidation f; go into ~ déposer son bilan.

liquidize /'lɪkwɪdaɪz/ vt passer au mixeur. **liquidizer** n mixeur m.

liquor /'lɪkə(r)/ n alcool m.

liquorice /'lɪkərɪs/ n réglisse f.

lisp /lɪsp/ n zézaiement m; with a ~ en zézayant. ● vi zézayer.

list /lɪst/ n liste f. ● vt dresser la liste de. ● vi (ship) gîter.

listen /'lɪsn/ vi écouter; ~ to, ~ in (to) écouter. **listener** n auditeur/-trice m/f.

listless /'lɪstlɪs/ adj apathique.

lit /lɪt/ ➡LIGHT.

liter ➡LITRE.

literal /'lɪtərəl/ adj (meaning) littéral; (translation) mot à mot. **literally** adv littéralement; mot à mot.

literary /'lɪtərərɪ/ adj littéraire.

literate /'lɪtərət/ adj qui sait lire et écrire.

literature /'lɪtrətʃə(r)/ n littérature f; (brochures) documentation f.

Lithuania /lɪθju:'eɪnɪə/ n

Lituanie f.

litigation /lɪtɪ'geɪʃn/ n litiges mpl.

litre, (US) **liter** /'liːtə(r)/ n litre m.

litter /'lɪtə(r)/ n (rubbish) détritus mpl, papiers mpl; (animals) portée f. ● vt éparpiller; (make untidy) laisser des détritus dans; ~ed with jonché de. ~-bin n poubelle f.

little /'lɪtl/ adj petit; (not much) peu de. ● n peu m; a ~ un peu (de). ● adv peu.

live[1] /laɪv/ adj vivant; (wire) sous tension; (broadcast) en direct; be a ~ wire être très dynamique.

live[2] /lɪv/ vt/i vivre; (reside) habiter, vivre; ~ it up mener la belle vie. □ ~ **down** faire oublier; ~ **on** (feed oneself on) vivre de; (continue) survivre; ~ **up to** se montrer à la hauteur de.

livelihood /'laɪvlɪhʊd/ n moyens mpl d'existence.

lively /'laɪvlɪ/ adj (-ier, -iest) vif, vivant.

liven /'laɪvn/ vt/i ~ up (s')animer; (cheer up) (s')égayer.

liver /'lɪvə(r)/ n foie m.

livestock /'laɪvstɒk/ n bétail m.

livid /'lɪvɪd/ adj livide; (angry) furieux.

living /'lɪvɪŋ/ adj vivant. ● n vie f; make a ~ gagner sa vie; ~ conditions fpl de vie. ~-room n salle f de séjour.

lizard /'lɪzəd/ n lézard m.

load /ləʊd/ n charge f; (loaded goods) chargement m, charge f; (weight, strain) poids m; ~s of 🔲 des tas de 🔲. ● vt charger.

loaf /ləʊf/ n (pl **loaves**) pain m. ● vi ~ (about) fainéanter.

loan /ləʊn/ n prêt m; (money borrowed) emprunt m. ● vt prêter.

loathe /ləʊð/ vt détester (doing faire). **loathing** n dégoût m.

lobby /'lɒbɪ/ n entrée f, vestibule m; (Pol) lobby m, groupe m de pression. ● vt faire pression sur.

lobster /'lɒbstə(r)/ n homard m.

local /'ləʊkl/ adj local; (shops) du quartier; ~ **government** administration f locale. ● n personne f du coin; (pub 🔲) pub m du coin.

localization /ləʊkəlaɪ'zeɪʃn/ n localisation f.

locally /'ləʊklɪ/ adv localement; (nearby) dans les environs.

locate /ləʊ'keɪt/ vt (situate) situer; (find) repérer.

location /ləʊ'keɪʃn/ n emplacement m; on ~ (cinema) en extérieur.

lock /lɒk/ n (of door) serrure f; (on canal) écluse f; (of hair) mèche f. ● vt/i fermer à clef; (wheels: Auto) (se) bloquer. □ ~ **in** or **up** (person) enfermer; ~ **out** (by mistake) enfermer dehors.

locker /'lɒkə(r)/ n casier m.

locket /'lɒkɪt/ n médaillon m.

locksmith /'lɒksmɪθ/ n serrurier m.

locum /'ləʊkəm/ n (doctor) remplaçant/-e m/f.

lodge /lɒdʒ/ n (house) pavillon m (de gardien or de chasse); (of porter) loge f. ● vt (accommodate) loger; (money, complaint) déposer. ● vi être logé (with chez); (become fixed) se loger. **lodger** n locataire mf, pensionnaire mf. **lodgings** n logement m.

loft /lɒft/ n grenier m.

lofty /'lɒftɪ/ adj (-ier, -iest) (tall, noble) élevé; (haughty) hautain.

log /lɒg/ n (of wood) bûche f; ~ (~book) (Naut) journal m de bord; (Auto) ≈ carte f grise. ● vt (pt **logged**) noter; (distance) parcourir. □ ~ **on** (Comput) se connecter; ~

off (Comput) se déconnecter.

logic /'lɒdʒɪk/ *n* logique *f*. **logical** *adj* logique.

logistics /lə'dʒɪstɪks/ *n* logistique *f*.

loin /lɔɪn/ *n* (Culin) filet *m*; ∼s reins *mpl*.

loiter /'lɔɪtə(r)/ *vi* traîner.

loll /lɒl/ *vi* se prélasser.

lollipop /'lɒlɪpɒp/ *n* sucette *f*.

London /'lʌndən/ *n* Londres. **Londoner** *n* Londonien/-ne *m/f*.

lone /ləʊn/ *adj* solitaire.

lonely (-ier, -iest) solitaire; (person) seul, solitaire.

long /lɒŋ/ *adj* long; how ∼ is? quelle est la longueur de?; (in time) quelle est la durée de?; how ∼? combien de temps?; a ∼ **time** longtemps. ● *adv* longtemps; he will not be ∼ il n'en a pas pour longtemps; as or so ∼ as pourvu que; before ∼ avant peu; I no ∼er do je ne fais plus. ● *vi* avoir bien ou très envie (**for**, **to** de); ∼ **for** sb (pine) se languir de qn. ∼**-distance** *adj* (flight) sur long parcours; (phone call) interurbain; (runner) de fond. ∼**-face** grimace *f*. ∼**-hand** *n* écriture *f* courante.

longing /'lɒŋɪŋ/ *n* envie *f* (**for** de); (nostalgia) nostalgie *f* (**for** de).

longitude /'lɒndʒɪtjuːd/ *n* longitude *f*.

long: ∼ **jump** *m* en longueur. ∼**-range** *adj* (missile) à longue portée; (forecast) à long terme. ∼**-sighted** *adj* presbyte. ∼**-standing** *adj* de longue date. ∼**-term** *adj* à long terme. ∼ **wave** *n* grandes ondes *fpl*. ∼**-winded** *adj* verbeux.

loo /luː/ *n* 🔲 toilettes *fpl*.

look /lʊk/ *vi* regarder; (seem) avoir l'air; ∼ **like** ressembler à, avoir l'air de. ● *n* regard *m*; (appearance) air

m, aspect *m*; (good) ∼s beauté *f*. □ ∼ **after** s'occuper de, soigner; ∼ **at** regarder; ∼ **back on** repenser à; ∼ **down on** mépriser; ∼ **for** chercher; ∼ **forward to** attendre avec impatience; ∼ **in on** passer voir; ∼ **into** examiner; ∼ **out** faire attention; ∼ **out for** (person) guetter; (symptoms) guetter l'apparition de; ∼ **round** se retourner; ∼ **up** (word) chercher; (visit) passer voir; ∼ **up to** respecter.

lookout /'lʊkaʊt/ *n* (Mil) poste *m* de guet; (person) guetteur *m*; be on the ∼ **for** rechercher.

loom /luːm/ *vi* surgir; (war) menacer; (interview) être imminent. ● *n* métier *m* à tisser.

loony /'luːnɪ/ *n* & *adj* 🔲 fou, folle (*mf*).

loop /luːp/ *n* boucle *f*. ● *vt* boucler. ∼**hole** *n* lacune *f*.

loose /luːs/ *adj* (knot) desserré; (page) détaché; (clothes) ample, lâche; (tooth) qui bouge; (lax) relâché; (not packed) en vrac; (inexact) vague; (pej) immoral; at a ∼ **end** désœuvré; come ∼ bouger. **loosely** *adv* sans serrer; (roughly) vaguement. **loosen** *vt* (slacken) desserrer; (untie) défaire.

loot /luːt/ *n* butin *m*. ● *vt* piller.

lord /lɔːd/ *n* seigneur *m*; (British title) lord *m*; the L∼ le Seigneur; (good) L∼! mon Dieu!

lorry /'lɒrɪ/ *n* camion *m*.

lose /luːz/ *vt/i* (*pt* lost) perdre; get lost se perdre. **loser** *n* perdant/-e *m/f*

loss /lɒs/ *n* perte *f*; be at a ∼ être perplexe; be at a ∼ **to** être incapable de; **heat** ∼ déperdition *f* de chaleur.

lost /lɒst/ ⇒LOSE. ● *adj* perdu. ∼ **property** *n* objets *mpl* trouvés.

lot /lɒt/ n the ~ (le) tout m; (people) tous mpl, toutes fpl; a ~ (of), ~s (of) 𝕀 beaucoup (de); quite a ~ (of) 𝕀 pas mal (de); (fate) sort m; (at auction) lot m; (land) lotissement m.

lotion /ˈləʊʃn/ n lotion f.

lottery /ˈlɒtərɪ/ n loterie f.

loud /laʊd/ adj bruyant, fort. ● adv fort; out ~ tout haut. **loudly** adv fort. ~**speaker** n haut-parleur m.

lounge /laʊndʒ/ vi paresser. ● n salon m.

louse /laʊs/ n (pl lice) pou m.

lousy /ˈlaʊzɪ/ adj (-ier, -iest) 𝕀 infect.

lout /laʊt/ n rustre m.

lovable /ˈlʌvəbl/ adj adorable.

love /lʌv/ n amour m; (tennis) zéro m; in ~ amoureux (with de); make ~ faire l'amour. ● vt (person) aimer; (like greatly) aimer (beaucoup) (to do faire). ~ **affair** n liaison f amoureuse. ~ **life** n vie f amoureuse.

lovely /ˈlʌvlɪ/ adj (-ier, -iest) joli; (delightful 𝕀) très agréable.

lover /ˈlʌvə(r)/ n (male) amant m; (female) maîtresse f; (devotee) amateur m (of de).

loving /ˈlʌvɪŋ/ adj affectueux.

low /ləʊ/ adj & adv bas; ~ in sth à faible teneur en qch. ● n (low pressure) dépression f; reach a (new) ~ atteindre son niveau le plus bas. ● vi meugler. ~-**calorie** adj basses-calories. ~-**cut** adj décolleté.

lower /ˈləʊə(r)/ adj & adv LOW. ● vt baisser; ~ oneself s'abaisser.

low: ~-**fat** adj (diet) sans matières grasses; (cheese) allégé. ~-**key** adj modéré; (discreet) discret. ~**lands** npl plaine(s) f(pl). ~-**lying** adj à faible altitude.

loyal /ˈlɔɪəl/ adj loyal (to envers).

loyalty /ˈlɔɪəltɪ/ n fidélité f. ~**card** n carte f de fidélité.

lozenge /ˈlɒzəndʒ/ n (shape) losange m; (tablet) pastille f.

LP n (disque m) 33 tours m.

Ltd. abbr (Limited) SA.

lubricant /ˈluːbrɪkənt/ n lubrifiant m. **lubricate** vt lubrifier.

luck /lʌk/ n chance f; bad ~ malchance f; good ~! bonne chance!

luckily /ˈlʌkɪlɪ/ adv heureusement.

lucky /ˈlʌkɪ/ adj (-ier, -iest) qui a de la chance, heureux; (event) heureux; (number) qui porte bonheur; it's ~ that heureusement que.

ludicrous /ˈluːdɪkrəs/ adj ridicule.

lug /lʌg/ vt (pt lugged) traîner.

luggage /ˈlʌgɪdʒ/ n bagages mpl. ~-**rack** n porte-bagages m inv.

lukewarm /luːkˈwɔːm/ adj tiède.

lull /lʌl/ vt he ~ed them into thinking that il leur a fait croire que. ● n accalmie f.

lullaby /ˈlʌləbaɪ/ n berceuse f.

lumber /ˈlʌmbə(r)/ n bois m de charpente. ● vt 𝕀 ~ sb with (chore) coller à qn 𝕀. ~**jack** n bûcheron m.

luminous /ˈluːmɪnəs/ adj lumineux.

lump /lʌmp/ n morceau m; (swelling on body) grosseur f; (in liquid) grumeau m. ● vt ~ together réunir. ~ **sum** n somme f globale.

lunacy /ˈluːnəsɪ/ n folie f.

lunar /ˈluːnə(r)/ adj lunaire.

lunatic /ˈluːnətɪk/ n fou/folle m/f.

lunch /lʌntʃ/ n déjeuner m. ● vi déjeuner.

luncheon /ˈlʌntʃən/ n déjeuner m. ~ **voucher** n chèque-repas m.

lung /lʌŋ/ n poumon m.

lunge /lʌndʒ/ vi bondir (at sur; forward en avant).

lurch /lɜːtʃ/ *n* leave in the ~ planter là, laisser en plan. ● *vi* (*person*) tituber.

lure /lʊə(r)/ *vt* appâter, attirer. ● *n* (*attraction*) attrait *m*, appât *m*.

lurid /ˈlʊərɪd/ *adj* choquant, affreux; (*gaudy*) voyant.

lurk /lɜːk/ *vi* se cacher; (*in ambush*) s'embusquer; (*prowl*) rôder; (*suspicion, danger*) menacer.

luscious /ˈlʌʃəs/ *adj* appétissant.

lush /lʌʃ/ *adj* luxuriant.

lust /lʌst/ *n* luxure *f*.

Luxemburg /ˈlʌksəmbɜːg/ *n* Luxembourg *m*.

luxurious /lʌgˈzjʊərɪəs/ *adj* luxueux.

luxury /ˈlʌkʃərɪ/ *n* luxe *m*. ● *adj* de luxe.

lying /ˈlaɪɪŋ/ →LIE¹, →LIE². ● *n* mensonges *mpl*.

lyric /ˈlɪrɪk/ *adj* lyrique. **lyrical** *adj* lyrique. **lyrics** *npl* paroles *fpl*.

Mm

MA *abbr* →MASTER OF ARTS.

mac /mæk/ *n* 🔲 imper *m*.

machine /məˈʃiːn/ *n* machine *f*. ● *vt* (*sew*) coudre à la machine; (*Tech*) usiner. ~-**gun** *n* mitrailleuse *f*.

mackerel /ˈmækrəl/ *n inv* maquereau *m*.

mackintosh /ˈmækɪntɒʃ/ *n* imperméable *m*.

mad /mæd/ *adj* (**madder**, **maddest**) fou; (*foolish*) insensé; (*dog*) enragé; (*angry* 🔲) furieux; be ~ about se passionner pour; (*person*)

être fou de; drive sb ~ exaspérer qn; like ~ comme un fou. ~ **cow disease** *n* maladie *f* de la vache folle.

madam /ˈmædəm/ *n* madame *f*; (*unmarried*) mademoiselle *f*.

made /meɪd/ →MAKE.

madly /ˈmædlɪ/ *adv* (*interested, in love*) follement; (*frantically*) comme un fou.

madman /ˈmædmən/ *n* (*pl* -**men**) fou *m*.

madness /ˈmædnɪs/ *n* folie *f*.

magazine /mægəˈziːn/ *n* revue *f*, magazine *m*; (*of gun*) chargeur *m*.

maggot /ˈmægət/ *n* (*in fruit*) ver *m*, (*for fishing*) asticot *m*.

magic /ˈmædʒɪk/ *n* magie *f*. ● *adj* magique.

magician /məˈdʒɪʃn/ *n* magicien-ne *m/f*.

magistrate /ˈmædʒɪstreɪt/ *n* magistrat *m*.

magnet /ˈmægnɪt/ *n* aimant *m*. **magnetic** *adj* magnétique.

magnificent /mægˈnɪfɪsnt/ *adj* magnifique.

magnify /ˈmægnɪfaɪ/ *vt* grossir; (*sound*) amplifier; (*fig*) exagérer. **magnifying glass** *n* loupe *f*.

magpie /ˈmægpaɪ/ *n* pie *f*.

mahogany /məˈhɒgənɪ/ *n* acajou *m*.

maid /meɪd/ *n* (*servant*) bonne *f*; (*in hotel*) femme *f* de chambre.

maiden /ˈmeɪdn/ *n* (*old use*) jeune fille *f*. ● *adj* (*aunt*) célibataire; (*voyage*) premier. ~ **name** *n* nom *m* de jeune fille.

mail /meɪl/ *n* (*postal service*) poste *f*; (*letters*) courrier *m*; (*armour*) cotte *f* de mailles. ● *adj* (*bag, van*) postal. ● *vt* envoyer par la poste. ~ **box** *n* boîte *f* aux lettres; (*Comput*) boîte *f* aux lettres électronique. **mailing**

l
m

list n liste f d'adresses. ~man n (pl -men) (US) facteur m. ~ order n vente f par correspondance. ~ shot n publipostage m.

main /meɪn/ adj principal; a ~ road une grande route. ● n (water/gas) ~ conduite f d'eau/de gaz; the ~s (Electr) le secteur; in the ~ en général. ~frame n unité f centrale. ~land n continent m. ~stream n tendance f principale, ligne f.

maintain /meɪn'teɪn/ vt (continue, keep, assert) maintenir; (house, machine, family) entretenir; (rights) soutenir.

maintenance /'meɪntənəns/ n (care) entretien m; (continuation) maintien m; (allowance) pension f alimentaire.

maisonette /meɪzə'net/ n duplex m.

maize /meɪz/ n maïs m.

majestic /mə'dʒestɪk/ adj majestueux.

majesty /'mædʒəstɪ/ n majesté f.

major /'meɪdʒə(r)/ adj majeur. ● n commandant m. ● vi ~ in (Univ, US) se spécialiser en.

majority /mə'dʒɒrətɪ/ n majorité f; the ~ of people la plupart des gens. ● adj majoritaire.

make /meɪk/ vt/i (pt made) faire; (manufacture) fabriquer; (friends) se faire; (money) gagner; (decision) prendre; (place, position) arriver à; (cause to be) rendre; ~ sb do sth faire faire qch à qn; (force) obliger qn à faire qch; be made of être fait de; ~ oneself at home se mettre à l'aise; ~ sb happy rendre qn heureux; ~ it arriver; (succeed) réussir; I ~ it two o'clock j'ai deux heures; I ~ it 150 d'après moi, ça fait 150; I cannot ~ anything of it je n'y comprends rien; can you ~ Friday?

vendredi, c'est possible?; ~ as if to faire mine de. ● n (brand) marque f. □ ~ do (manage) se débrouiller (with avec); ~ for se diriger vers; (cause) tendre à créer; ~ good vi réussir; vt compenser; (repair) réparer; ~ off (flee) (with avec); ~ out distinguer; (understand) comprendre; (draw up) faire; (assert) prétendre; ~ up vt faire, former; (story) inventer; (deficit) combler; vi se réconcilier; ~ up for compenser; (time) rattraper; ~ up one's mind se décider.

make-believe adj feint, illusoire. ● n fantaisie f.

maker /'meɪkə(r)/ n fabricant m.

makeshift /'meɪkʃɪft/ adj improvisé.

make-up /'meɪkʌp/ n maquillage m; (of object) constitution f; (Psych) caractère m.

malaria /mə'leərɪə/ n paludisme m.

Malaysia /mə'leɪzɪə/ n Malaisie f.

male /meɪl/ adj (voice, sex) masculin; (Bot, Tech) mâle. ● n mâle m.

malfunction /mæl'fʌŋkʃn/ n mauvais fonctionnement m. ● vi mal fonctionner.

malice /'mælɪs/ n méchanceté f.
malicious /mə'lɪʃəs/ adj méchant.

malignant /mə'lɪɡnənt/ adj malveillant; (tumour) malin.

mall /mɔːl/ n (shopping) ~ (in suburbs) centre m commercial; (in town) galerie f marchande.

malnutrition /mælnjuː'trɪʃn/ n sousalimentation f.

Malta /'mɔːltə/ n Malte f.

mammal /'mæml/ n mammifère m.

mammoth /'mæməθ/ n mammouth m. ● adj (task) gigantesque; (organization) géant.

man /mæn/ n (pl **men**) homme m; (in sports team) joueur m; (chess) pièce f; **to man** d'homme à homme. ● vt (pt **manned**) (desk) tenir; (ship) armer; (guns) servir; (be on duty at) être de service à.

manage /ˈmænɪdʒ/ vt (project, organization) diriger; (shop, affairs) gérer; (handle) manier; **I could ~ another drink** 🔢 je prendrais bien encore un verre; **can you ~ Friday?** vendredi, c'est possible? ● vi se débrouiller; **~ to do** réussir à faire. **manageable** adj (tool, size, person) maniable; (job) faisable.

management /ˈmænɪdʒmənt/ n (managers) direction f; (of shop) gestion f.

manager /ˈmænɪdʒə(r)/ n directeur/-trice m/f; (of shop) gérant/-e m/f; (of actor) impresario m.

mandate /ˈmændeɪt/ n mandat m.

mandatory /ˈmændətərɪ/ adj obligatoire.

mane /meɪn/ n crinière f.

mango /ˈmæŋɡəʊ/ n (pl ~es) mangue f.

manhandle /ˈmænhændl/ vt maltraiter, malmener.

man: **~hole** n regard m. **~hood** n âge m d'homme; (quality) virilité f.

maniac /ˈmeɪnɪæk/ n maniaque m, fou m, folle f.

manicure /ˈmænɪkjʊə(r)/ n manicure f. ● vt soigner, manucurer.

manifest /ˈmænɪfest/ adj manifeste. ● vt manifester.

manipulate /məˈnɪpjʊleɪt/ vt (tool, person) manipuler.

mankind /mænˈkaɪnd/ n genre m humain.

manly /ˈmænlɪ/ adj viril.

man-made adj (fibre) synthétique; (pond) artificiel; (disaster)

d'origine humaine.

manned // adj (spacecraft) habité.

manner /ˈmænə(r)/ n manière f; (attitude) attitude f; (kind) sorte f; **~s** (social behaviour) manières fpl.

mannerism /ˈmænərɪzəm/ n particularité f; (quirk) manie f.

manoeuvre /məˈnuːvə(r)/ n manœuvre f. ● vt/i manœuvrer.

manor /ˈmænə(r)/ n manoir m.

manpower /ˈmænpaʊə(r)/ n main-d'œuvre f.

mansion /ˈmænʃn/ n (in countryside) demeure f; (in town) hôtel m particulier.

manslaughter /ˈmænslɔːtə(r)/ n homicide m involontaire.

mantelpiece /ˈmæntlˈself/ n (manteau m de) cheminée.

manual /ˈmænjʊəl/ adj (labour) manuel; (typewriter) mécanique. ● n (handbook) manuel m.

manufacture /mænjuˈfæktʃə(r)/ vt fabriquer. ● n fabrication f.

manure /məˈnjʊə(r)/ n fumier m.

many /ˈmenɪ/ adj & n beaucoup (de); **a great** or **good ~** un grand nombre (de); **~ a** bien des.

map /mæp/ n carte f; (of streets) plan m. ● vt (pt **mapped**) faire la carte de; **~ out** (route) tracer; (arrange) organiser.

mar /mɑː(r)/ vt (pt **marred**) gâcher.

marble /ˈmɑːbl/ n marbre m; (for game) bille f.

March /mɑːtʃ/ n mars m.

march /mɑːtʃ/ vi (Mil) marcher (au pas). ● vt **~ off** (lead away) emmener. ● n marche f.

margin /ˈmɑːdʒɪn/ n marge f.

marginal /ˈmɑːdʒɪnl/ adj marginal; (increase) léger, faible; (seat: Pol) disputé.

marinate /ˈmærɪneɪt/ vt faire

mariner (in dans).

marine /məˈriːn/ adj marin. ● n (shipping) marine f; (sailor) fusilier m marin.

marital /ˈmærɪtl/ adj conjugal. ~ **status** n situation f de famille.

mark /mɑːk/ n (currency) mark m; (stain) tache f; (trace) marque f; (School) note f; (target) but m. ● vt marquer; (exam) corriger; ~ out délimiter; (person) désigner; ~ time marquer le pas.

marker /ˈmɑːkə(r)/ n (pen) marqueur m; (tag) repère m; (School, Univ) examinateur/-trice m/f.

market /ˈmɑːkɪt/ n marché m; on the ~ en vente. ● vt (sell) vendre; (launch) commercialiser. ~ **research** n étude f de marché.

marmalade /ˈmɑːməleɪd/ n confiture f d'oranges.

maroon /məˈruːn/ n bordeaux m inv. ● adj bordeaux inv.

marooned /məˈruːnd/ adj abandonné; (snowbound) bloqué.

marquee /mɑːˈkiː/ n grande tente f; (of circus) chapiteau m; (awning; US) auvent m.

marriage /ˈmærɪdʒ/ n mariage m (to avec).

married /ˈmærɪd/ adj marié (to à); (life) conjugal; get ~ se marier (to avec).

marrow /ˈmærəʊ/ n (of bone) moelle f; (vegetable) courge f.

marry /ˈmærɪ/ vt épouser; (give or unite in marriage) marier. ● vi se marier.

marsh /mɑːʃ/ n marais m.

marshal /ˈmɑːʃl/ n maréchal m; (at event) membre m du service d'ordre. ● vt (pt marshalled) rassembler.

martyr /ˈmɑːtə(r)/ n martyr/-e m/f. ● vt martyriser.

marvel /ˈmɑːvl/ n merveille f. ● vi (pt marvelled) s'émerveiller (at de).

marvellous /ˈmɑːvələs/ adj merveilleux.

marzipan /ˈmɑːzɪpæn/ n pâte f d'amandes.

masculine /ˈmæskjʊlɪn/ adj & n masculin (m).

mash /mæʃ/ n (potatoes □) purée f. ● vt écraser. **mashed potatoes** npl purée f (de pommes de terre).

mask /mɑːsk/ n masque m. ● vt masquer.

Mason /ˈmeɪsn/ n franc-maçon m.

masonry /ˈmeɪsənrɪ/ n maçonnerie f.

mass /mæs/ n (Relig) messe f; masse f; the ~es les masses fpl. ● vt/i (se) masser.

massacre /ˈmæsəkə(r)/ n massacre m. ● vt massacrer.

massage /ˈmæsɑːʒ/ n massage m. ● vt masser.

massive /ˈmæsɪv/ adj (large) énorme; (heavy) massif.

mass media n médias mpl.

mass-produce vt fabriquer en série.

mast /mɑːst/ n (on ship) mât m; (for radio, TV) pylône m.

master /ˈmɑːstə(r)/ n maître m; (in secondary school) professeur m; M~ of Arts titulaire m/f d'une maîtrise ès lettres. ● vt maîtriser.

masterpiece /ˈmɑːstəpiːs/ n chef-d'œuvre m.

mastery /ˈmɑːstərɪ/ n maîtrise f.

mat /mæt/ n (petit) tapis m; (at door) paillasson m.

match /mætʃ/ n (for lighting fire) allumette f; (Sport) match m; (equal) égal/-e m/f; (marriage) mariage m; (sb to marry) parti m; be a

~ for pouvoir tenir tête à. ● vt opposer; (go with) aller avec; (cups) assortir; (equal) égaler. ● vi (be alike) être assorti. **matchbox** n boîte f à allumettes.

matching /'mætʃɪŋ/ adj assorti.

mate /meɪt/ n camarade mf; (of animal) compagnon m, compagne f; (assistant) aide mf; (chess) mat m. ● vt/i (s')accoupler (with avec).

material /mə'tɪərɪəl/ n matière f; (fabric) tissu m; (documents, for building) matériau(x) m(pl); ~s (equipment) matériel m. ● adj matériel; (fig) important. **materialistic** adj matérialiste.

materialize /mə'tɪərɪəlaɪz/ vi se matérialiser, se réaliser.

maternal /mə'tɜːnl/ adj maternel.

maternity /mə'tɜːnətɪ/ n maternité f. ● adj (clothes) de grossesse. ~ **hospital** n maternité f. ~ **leave** n congé m maternité.

mathematics /mæθə'mætɪks/ n & npl mathématiques fpl.

maths, (US) **math** /mæθs/ n maths fpl.

mating /'meɪtɪŋ/ n accouplement m.

matrimony /'mætrɪmənɪ/ n mariage m.

matron /'meɪtrən/ n (married, elderly) dame f âgée; (in hospital) infirmière f en chef.

matt /mæt/ adj mat.

matter /'mætə(r)/ n (substance) matière f; (affair) affaire f; as a ~ of fact en fait; what is the ~? qu'est-ce qu'il y a? ● vi importer; it does not ~ ça ne fait rien; no ~ what happens quoi qu'il arrive.

mattress /'mætrɪs/ n matelas m.

mature /mə'tjʊə(r)/ adj (psychologically) mûr; (plant) adulte. ● vt/i (se) mûrir. **maturity** n maturité f.

mauve /məʊv/ adj & n mauve (m).

maverick /'mævərɪk/ n non-conformiste mf.

maximize /'mæksɪmaɪz/ vt porter au maximum.

maximum /'mæksɪməm/ adj & n (pl -**ima**) maximum (m).

---

may /meɪ/

past **might**

● **auxiliary verb**

····▸ (possibility) they ~ be able to come ils pourront peut-être venir; she ~ not have seen him elle ne l'a peut-être pas vu; it ~rain il risque de pleuvoir; 'will you come?'—'I **might**' 'tu viendras?' —'peut-être'.

····▸ (permission) you ~ leave vous pouvez partir; ~ I smoke? puis-je fumer?

····▸ (wish) ~ he be happy qu'il soit heureux.

May /meɪ/ n mai m.

maybe /'meɪbiː/ adv peut-être.

mayhem /'meɪhem/ n (havoc) ravages mpl.

mayonnaise /meɪə'neɪz/ n mayonnaise f.

mayor /meə(r)/ n maire m.

maze /meɪz/ n labyrinthe m.

Mb abbr (**megabyte**) (Comput) Mo.

me /miː/ pron me, m'; (after prep.) moi; (indirect object) me, m'; he knows ~ il me connaît.

meadow /'medəʊ/ n pré m.

meagre /'miːɡə(r)/ adj maigre.

meal /miːl/ n repas m; (grain) farine f.

m

mean /miːn/ adj (poor) misérable; (miserly) avare; (unkind) méchant; (average) moyen. ● n milieu m; (average) moyenne f; in the ~-time en attendant. ● vt (pt meant) vouloir dire, signifier; (involve) entraîner; I ~ that! je suis sérieux; be meant for être destiné à; ~ to do avoir l'intention de faire.

meaning /ˈmiːnɪŋ/ n sens m, signification f. **meaningful** adj significatif. **meaningless** adj dénué de sens.

means /miːnz/ n moyen(s) m (pl); by ~ of sth au moyen de qch. ● npl (wealth) moyens mpl financiers; by all ~ certainement; by no ~ nullement.

meant /ment/ →MEAN.

meantime /ˈmiːntaɪm/, meanwhile adv en attendant.

measles /ˈmiːzlz/ n rougeole f.

measure /ˈmeʒə(r)/ n mesure f; (ruler) règle f. ● vt/i mesurer; ~up to être à la hauteur de. **measurement** n mesures fpl.

meat /miːt/ n viande f. **meaty** adj de viande; (fig) substantiel.

mechanic /mɪˈkænɪk/ n mécanicien/-ne m/f.

mechanical /mɪˈkænɪkl/ adj mécanique.

mechanism /ˈmekənɪzəm/ n mécanisme m.

medal /ˈmedl/ n médaille f.

meddle /ˈmedl/ vi (interfere) se mêler (in de); (tinker) toucher (with à).

media /ˈmiːdɪə/ n →MEDIUM. ● npl the~ les média mpl; talk to the ~ parler à la presse.

median /ˈmiːdɪən/ adj médian. ● n médiane f.

mediate /ˈmiːdɪeɪt/ vi servir d'intermédiaire.

medical /ˈmedɪkl/ adj médical; (student) en médecine. ● n visite f médicale.

medication /medɪˈkeɪʃn/ n médicaments mpl.

medicine /ˈmedsn/ n (science) médecine f; (substance) médicament m.

medieval /medɪˈiːvl/ adj médiéval.

mediocre /miːdɪˈəʊkə(r)/ adj médiocre.

meditate /ˈmedɪteɪt/ vt/i méditer.

Mediterranean /medɪtəˈreɪnɪən/ adj méditerranéen. ● n the ~ la Méditerranée f.

medium /ˈmiːdɪəm/ n (pl media) (mid-point) milieu m; (for transmitting data) support m; (pl mediums) (person) médium m. ● adj moyen.

medley /ˈmedlɪ/ n mélange m; (Mus) potpourri m.

meet /miːt/ vt (pt met) rencontrer; (see again) retrouver; (be introduced to) faire la connaissance de; (face) faire face à; (requirement) satisfaire. ● vi se rencontrer; (each other again) se retrouver; (in session) se réunir.

meeting /ˈmiːtɪŋ/ n réunion f; (between two people) rencontre f.

megabyte /ˈmegəbaɪt/ n (Comput) mégaoctet m.

melancholy /ˈmelənkəlɪ/ n mélancolie f. ● adj mélancolique.

mellow /ˈmeləʊ/ adj (fruit) mûr; (sound, colour) moelleux, doux; (person) mûri. ● vt/i (mature) mûrir; (soften) (s')adoucir.

melody /ˈmelədɪ/ n mélodie f.

melon /ˈmelən/ n melon m.

melt /melt/ vt/i (faire) fondre.

member /ˈmembə(r)/ n membre m. M~ of Parliament n député m. **membership** n adhésion f; (members) membres mpl; (fee) cotisation f.

memento /mɪˈmentəʊ/ n (pl ∼es) (object) souvenir m.

memo /ˈmeməʊ/ n note f.

memoir /ˈmemwɑː(r)/ n (record, essay) mémoire m.

memorandum /meməˈrændəm/ n note f.

memorial /məˈmɔːrɪəl/ n monument m. ● adj commémoratif.

memorize /ˈmeməraɪz/ vt apprendre par cœur.

memory /ˈmeməri/ n (mind, in computer) mémoire f; (thing remembered) souvenir m; from ∼ de mémoire; in ∼ of à la mémoire de.

men /men/ →MAN.

menace /ˈmenəs/ n menace f; (nuisance) peste f. ● vt menacer.

mend /mend/ vt réparer; (darn) raccommoder; ∼ one's ways s'amender. ● n raccommodage m; on the ∼ en voie de guérison.

meningitis /menɪnˈdʒaɪtɪs/ n méningite f.

menopause /ˈmenəpɔːz/ n ménopause f.

mental /ˈmentl/ adj mental; (hospital) psychiatrique.

mentality /menˈtæləti/ n mentalité f.

mention /ˈmenʃn/ vt mentionner; don't ∼it! il n'y a pas de quoi, je vous en prie! ● n mention f.

menu /ˈmenjuː/ n (food, on computer) menu m; (list) carte f.

MEP abbr (**Member of the European Parliament**) député m au Parlement européen.

mercenary /ˈmɜːsɪnəri/ adj & n mercenaire (m.)

merchandise /ˈmɜːtʃəndaɪz/ n marchandises fpl.

merchant /ˈmɜːtʃənt/ n marchand m. ● adj (ship, navy) marchand. ∼

bank n banque f de commerce.

merciful /ˈmɜːsɪfl/ adj miséricordieux.

mercury /ˈmɜːkjʊri/ n mercure m.

mercy /ˈmɜːsi/ n pitié f; at the ∼ of à la merci de.

mere /mɪə(r)/ adj simple. **merest** adj moindre.

merge /mɜːdʒ/ vt/i (se) mêler (with à); (companies: Comm) fusionner. **merger** n fusion f.

mermaid /ˈmɜːmeɪd/ n sirène f.

merrily /ˈmerɪli/ adv (happily) joyeusement; (unconcernedly) avec insouciance.

merry /ˈmeri/ adj (-ier, -iest) gai; make ∼ faire la fête. ∼-**go-round** n manège m.

mesh /meʃ/ n maille f; (fabric) tissu m à mailles; (network) réseau m.

mesmerize /ˈmezməraɪz/ vt hypnotiser.

mess /mes/ n désordre m, gâchis m; (dirt) saleté f; (Mil) mess m; make a ∼ of gâcher. ● vt ∼ up gâcher.; vi ∼ about s'amuser; (dawdle) traîner; ∼ with (tinker with) tripoter.

message /ˈmesɪdʒ/ n message m.

messenger /ˈmesɪndʒə(r)/ n messager/-ère m/f.

messy /ˈmesi/ adj (-ier, -iest) en désordre; (dirty) sale.

met /met/ →MEET.

metal /ˈmetl/ n métal m. ● adj de métal. **metallic** adj métallique; (paint, colour) métallisé.

metallurgy /mɪˈtælədʒi/ n métallurgie f.

metaphor /ˈmetəfɔː(r)/ n métaphore f.

meteor /ˈmiːtɪə(r)/ n météore m.

meteorite /ˈmiːtɪəraɪt/ n météorite m.

meteorology /miːtɪəˈrɒlədʒi/ n

m

météorologie f.

meter /'mi:tə(r)/ n compteur m; (US) →METRE.

method /'meθəd/ n méthode f.

methylated spirit(s) /'meθəleɪtɪd 'spɪrɪt(s)/ n alcool m à brûler.

meticulous /mɪ'tɪkjʊləs/ adj méticuleux.

metre, (US) **meter** /'mi:tə(r)/ n mètre m.

metric /'metrɪk/ adj métrique.

metropolis /mə'trɒpəlɪs/ n métropole f. **metropolitan** adj métropolitain.

mew /mju:/ n miaulement m. ● vi miauler.

mews /mju:z/ npl appartements mpl chic aménagés dans d'anciennes écuries.

Mexico /'meksɪkəʊ/ n Mexique m.

miaow /mi:'aʊ/ n & vi →MEW.

mice /maɪs/ →MOUSE.

mickey /'mɪkɪ/ n take the ~ out of 🅘 se moquer de.

microchip /'maɪkrəʊtʃɪp/ n puce f; circuit m intégré.

microlight /'maɪkrəʊlaɪt/ n ULM m.

microprocessor /'maɪkrəʊ prəʊsesə(r)/ n microprocesseur m.

microscope /'maɪkrəskəʊp/ n microscope m.

microwave /'maɪkrəweɪv/ n micro-onde f; ~ (oven) four m à micro-ondes. ● vt passer au four à micro-ondes.

mid /mɪd/ adj in ~ air en plein ciel; in ~ March à la mi-mars; in ~ afternoon milieu m de l'après-midi; he's in his ~ twenties il a environ vingt-cinq ans.

midday /mɪd'deɪ/ n midi m.

middle /'mɪdl/ adj (door, shelf) du

milieu; (size) moyen. ● n milieu m; in the ~ of au milieu de. **~-aged** adj d'âge mûr. **M~ Ages** n Moyen Âge m. ~ **class** n classe f moyenne. **M~ East** n Moyen-Orient m.

midge /mɪdʒ/ n moucheron m.

midget /'mɪdʒɪt/ n nain/-e m/f. ● adj minuscule.

midnight /'mɪdnaɪt/ n minuit f; it's ~ il est minuit.

midst /mɪdst/ n in the ~ of au beau milieu de; in our ~ parmi nous.

midsummer /mɪd'sʌmə(r)/ n milieu m de l'été; (solstice) solstice m d'été.

midway /mɪd'weɪ/ adv ~ between/along à mi-chemin entre/le long de.

midwife /'mɪdwaɪf/ n (pl -wives) sage-femme f.

might[1] /maɪt/ v aux I ~ have been killed j'aurais pu être tué; you ~ try doing sth vous pourriez faire qch; →MAY.

might[2] /maɪt/ n puissance f.

mighty /'maɪtɪ/ adj puissant; (huge 🅘) énorme. ● adv 🅘 vachement 🅘.

migrant /'maɪgrənt/ adj & n (bird) migrateur (m); (worker) migrant/-e (m/f).

migrate /maɪ'greɪt/ vi émigrer. **migration** n migration f.

mild /maɪld/ adj (surprise, taste, tobacco, attack) léger; (weather, cheese, soap, person) doux; (case, infection) bénin.

mile /maɪl/ n mile m (= 1,6 km); walk for ~s marcher pendant des kilomètres; ~s better 🅘 bien meilleur. **mileage** n nombre m de miles, kilométrage m.

milestone /'maɪlstəʊn/ n (lit) borne f; (fig) étape f importante.

military /ˈmɪlɪtrɪ/ adj militaire.

militia /mɪˈlɪʃə/ n milice f.

milk /mɪlk/ n lait m. ● vt (cow) traire; (fig) pomper.

milkman /ˈmɪlkmən/ n (pl -men) laitier m.

milky /ˈmɪlkɪ/ adj (skin, colour) laiteux; (tea) au lait; M~ Way Voie f lactée.

mill /mɪl/ n moulin m; (factory) usine f. ● vt moudre. ● vi ~ around grouiller.

millennium /mɪˈlenɪəm/ n (pl ~s) millénaire m.

millimetre, (US) **millimeter** /ˈmɪlɪmiːtə(r)/ n millimètre m.

million /ˈmɪljən/ n million m; a ~ pounds un million de livres. **millionaire** n millionnaire m.

millstone /ˈmɪlstəʊn/ n meule f; (fig) boulet m.

mime /maɪm/ n (actor) mime mf; (art) mime m. ● vt/i mimer.

mimic /ˈmɪmɪk/ vt (pt mimicked) imiter. ● n imitateur/-trice m/f.

mince /mɪns/ vt hacher; not to ~ matters ne pas mâcher ses mots. ● n viande f hachée.

mind /maɪnd/ n esprit m; (sanity) raison f; (opinion) avis m; be on sb's ~ préoccuper qn; bear that in ~ ne l'oubliez pas; change one's ~ changer d'avis; make up one's ~ se décider (to à). ● vt (have charge of) s'occuper de; (heed) faire attention à; I do not ~ the noise le bruit ne me dérange pas; I don't ~ ça m'est égal; would you ~ checking? je peux vous demander de vérifier?

minder /ˈmaɪndə(r)/ n (bodyguard) garde m de corps; (child) ~ nourrice f.

mindless /ˈmaɪndlɪs/ adj (programme) bête; (work) abrutissant;

(vandalism) gratuit.

mine /maɪn/ n mine f. ● vt extraire; (Mil) miner. ● pron le mien, la mienne, les mien(ne)s; the blue car is ~ la voiture bleue est la mienne or à moi.

minefield /ˈmaɪnfiːld/ n (lit) champ m de mines; (fig) terrain m miné.

miner /ˈmaɪnə(r)/ n mineur m.

mineral /ˈmɪnərəl/ n & adj minéral (m); ~ water eau f minérale.

minesweeper /ˈmaɪnswiːpə(r)/ n (ship) dragueur m de mines.

mingle /ˈmɪŋgl/ vt/i (se) mêler (with à).

minibus /ˈmɪnɪbʌs/ n minibus m.

minicab /ˈmɪnɪkæb/ n taxi m (non agréé).

minimal /ˈmɪnɪml/ adj minimal.

minimize /ˈmɪnɪmaɪz/ vt minimiser; (Comput) réduire.

minimum /ˈmɪnɪməm/ adj & n (pl -ima) minimum (m).

minister /ˈmɪnɪstə(r)/ n ministre m. **ministerial** adj ministériel. **ministry** n ministère m.

mink /mɪŋk/ n vison m.

minor /ˈmaɪnə(r)/ adj (change, surgery) mineur; (injury, burn) léger; (road) secondaire. ● n (Jur) mineur/-e m/f.

minority /maɪˈnɒrətɪ/ n minorité f; in the ~ en minorité. ● adj minoritaire.

mint /mɪnt/ n (Bot, Culin) menthe f; (sweet) bonbon m à la menthe; (fortune) fortune f. ● vt frapper; in ~ condition à l'état neuf.

minus /ˈmaɪnəs/ prep moins; (without 🔢) sans. ● n moins m; (drawback) inconvénient m.

minute[1] /ˈmɪnɪt/ n minute f; ~s (of meeting) compte-rendu m.

minute² /maɪˈnjuːt/ adj (object) minuscule; (risk, variation) minime.

miracle /ˈmɪrəkl/ n miracle m.

mirror /ˈmɪrə(r)/ n miroir m, glace f; (Auto) rétroviseur m. ● vt refléter.

misbehave /ˌmɪsbɪˈheɪv/ vi se conduire mal.

miscalculation /ˌmɪskælkjuˈleɪʃn/ n (lit) erreur f de calcul; (fig) mauvais calcul m.

miscarriage /ˈmɪskærɪdʒ/ n fausse couche f; ~ of justice erreur f judiciaire.

miscellaneous /ˌmɪsəˈleɪnɪəs/ adj divers.

mischief /ˈmɪstʃɪf/ n (playfulness) espièglerie f; (by children) bêtises fpl. **mischievous** adj espiègle; (malicious) méchant.

misconduct /ˌmɪsˈkɒndʌkt/ n mauvaise conduite f.

misconstrue /ˌmɪskənˈstruː/ vt mal interpréter.

misdemeanour, (US) **misdemeanor** /ˌmɪsdɪˈmiːnə(r)/ n (Jur) délit m.

miser /ˈmaɪzə(r)/ n avare mf.

miserable /ˈmɪzrəbl/ adj (sad) malheureux; (wretched) misérable; (performance, result) lamentable.

misery /ˈmɪzərɪ/ n (unhappiness) souffrance f; (misfortune) misère f; (person 🖪) rabat-joie mf inv.

misfit /ˈmɪsfɪt/ n inadapté/-e m/f.

misfortune /mɪsˈfɔːtʃuːn/ n malheur m.

misgiving /mɪsˈɡɪvɪŋ/ n (doubt) doute m; (apprehension) crainte f.

misguided /mɪsˈɡaɪdɪd/ adj (foolish) imprudent; (mistaken) erroné; be ~ (person) se tromper.

mishap /ˈmɪshæp/ n incident m.

misjudge /mɪsˈdʒʌdʒ/ vt (distance, speed) mal évaluer; (person)

mal juger.

mislay /mɪsˈleɪ/ vt (pt mislaid) égarer.

mislead /mɪsˈliːd/ vt (pt) misled tromper. **misleading** adj trompeur.

misplace /mɪsˈpleɪs/ vt mal ranger; (lose) égarer. **misplaced** adj (fear, criticism) déplacé.

misprint /ˈmɪsprɪnt/ n coquille f, faute f typographique.

misread /mɪsˈriːd/ vt (pt) misread mal lire; (intentions) mal interpréter.

miss /mɪs/ vt/i manquer; (bus) rater; he ~es her/Paris elle/Paris lui manque; you're ~ing the point tu n'as rien compris; ~ sth out omettre qch; ~ out on sth laisser passer qch. ● n coup m manqué; it was a near ~ on l'a échappé belle.

Miss /mɪs/ n Mademoiselle f; ~ Smith (written) Mlle Smith.

misshapen /mɪsˈʃeɪpən/ adj difforme.

missile /ˈmɪsaɪl/ n (Mil) missile m; (thrown) projectile m.

mission /ˈmɪʃn/ n mission f. **missionary** n missionnaire mf.

misspell /mɪsˈspel/ vt (pt misspelt or misspelled) mal écrire.

mist /mɪst/ n brume f; (on window) buée f. ● vt/i (s')embuer.

mistake /mɪˈsteɪk/ n erreur f; by ~ par erreur; make a ~ faire une erreur. ● vt (pt mistook; pp mistaken) (meaning) mal interpréter; ~ for prendre pour.

mistaken /mɪˈsteɪkən/ adj (enthusiasm) mal placé; be ~ avoir tort.

mistletoe /ˈmɪsltəʊ/ n gui m.

mistreat /mɪsˈtriːt/ vt maltraiter.

mistress /ˈmɪstrɪs/ n maîtresse f.

misty /ˈmɪstɪ/ adj (-ier, -iest) brumeux; (window) embué.

misunderstanding /mɪsʌndə-

'stændɪŋ/ n malentendu m.

misuse /mɪsˈjuːz/ vt (word) mal employer; (power) abuser de; (equipment) faire mauvais usage de.

mitten /ˈmɪtn/ n moufle f.

mix /mɪks/ n mélange m. ● vt mélanger; (drink) préparer; (cement) malaxer. ● vi se mélanger (with avec, à); (socially) être sociable; ~ with sb fréquenter qn. □ ~ **up** (confuse) confondre; (jumble up) mélanger; get ~ed up in se trouver mêlé à.

mixed /mɪkst/ adj (school) mixte; (collection, diet) mixte; (nuts, sweets) assorti.

mixer /ˈmɪksə(r)/ n (Culin) batteur m électrique; be a good ~ être sociable; ~ tap mélangeur m.

mixture /ˈmɪkstʃə(r)/ n mélange m.

mix-up /ˈmɪksʌp/ n confusion f (over sur).

moan /məʊn/ n gémissement m. ● vi gémir; (complain Ⓣ) râler Ⓣ.

mob /mɒb/ n (crowd) foule f; (gang) gang m; the M~ la Mafia. ● vt (pt mobbed) assaillir.

mobile /ˈməʊbaɪl/ adj mobile; ~ phone téléphone m portable. ● n mobile m.

mobilize /ˈməʊbɪlaɪz/ vt/i mobiliser.

mock /mɒk/ vt/i se moquer (de). ● adj faux.

mockery /ˈmɒkərɪ/ n moquerie f; a ~ of une parodie de.

mock-up n maquette f.

mode /məʊd/ n mode m.

model /ˈmɒdl/ n (Comput, Auto) modèle m; (scale representation) maquette f; (person showing clothes) mannequin m. ● adj modèle; (car) modèle réduit inv; (railway) miniature. ● vt (pt modelled)

modeler; (clothes) présenter. ● vi être mannequin; (pose) poser.

modelling n métier m de mannequin.

modem /ˈməʊdem/ n modem m.

moderate /ˈmɒdərət/ adj & n modéré/-e (m/f).

moderation /mɒdəˈreɪʃn/ n modération f; in ~ avec modération.

modern /ˈmɒdn/ adj moderne; ~ languages langues fpl vivantes. **modernize** vt moderniser.

modest /ˈmɒdɪst/ adj modeste. **modesty** n modestie f.

modification /mɒdɪfɪˈkeɪʃn/ n modification f. **modify** vt modifier.

module /ˈmɒdjuːl/ n module m.

moist /mɔɪst/ adj (soil) humide; (skin, palms) moite; (cake) moelleux. **moisten** vt humecter. **moisture** n humidité f. **moisturizer** n crème f hydratante.

molar /ˈməʊlə(r)/ n molaire f.

mold (US) →MOULD.

mole /məʊl/ n grain m de beauté; (animal) taupe f.

molecule /ˈmɒlɪkjuːl/ n molécule f.

molest /məˈlest/ vt (pester) importuner; (sexually) agresser sexuellement.

moment /ˈməʊmənt/ n (short time) instant m; (point in time) moment m. **momentarily** adv momentanément; (soon: US) très bientôt. **momentary** adj momentané.

momentum /məˈmentəm/ n élan m.

monarch /ˈmɒnək/ n monarque m. **monarchy** n monarchie f.

Monday /ˈmʌndeɪ/ n lundi m.

monetary /ˈmʌnɪtrɪ/ adj monétaire.

money /ˈmʌnɪ/ n argent m; make

m

~ (person) gagner de l'argent; (business) rapporter de l'argent. **~box** n tirelire f. **~ order** n mandat m postal.

monitor /ˈmɒnɪtə(r)/ n dispositif m de surveillance; (Comput) moniteur m. ● vt surveiller; (broadcast) être à l'écoute de.

monk /mʌŋk/ n moine m.

monkey /ˈmʌŋkɪ/ n singe m.

monopolize /məˈnɒpəlaɪz/ vt monopoliser. **monopoly** n monopole m.

monotonous /məˈnɒtənəs/ adj monotone. **monotony** n monotonie f.

monsoon /mɒnˈsuːn/ n mousson f.

monster /ˈmɒnstə(r)/ n monstre m. **monstrous** adj monstrueux.

month /mʌnθ/ n mois m.

monthly /ˈmʌnθlɪ/ adj mensuel. ● adv (pay) au mois; (publish) tous les mois. ● n (periodical) mensuel m.

monument /ˈmɒnjʊmənt/ n monument m.

moo /muː/ vi meugler.

mood /muːd/ n humeur f; in a good/bad ~ de bonne/mauvaise humeur. **moody** adj d'humeur changeante.

moon /muːn/ n lune f.

moonlight /ˈmuːnlaɪt/ n clair m de lune. **moonlighting** n ① travail m au noir.

moor /mɔː(r)/ n lande f. ● vt amarrer.

mop /mɒp/ n balai m à franges; ~ of hair crinière f ①. ● vt (pt mopped) ~ (up) éponger.

moped /ˈməʊped/ n vélomoteur m.

moral /ˈmɒrəl/ adj moral. ● n morale f; ~s moralité f.

morale /məˈrɑːl/ n moral m.

morbid /ˈmɔːbɪd/ adj morbide.

more /mɔː(r)/ adj plus; ~ serious plus sérieux; work ~ travailler plus; sleep ~ and ~ dormir de plus en plus; once ~ une fois de plus; I don't go there any ~ je n'y vais plus; ~ or less plus ou moins. ● det plus de; a little ~ wine un peu plus de vin; ~ bread encore un peu de pain; there's no ~ bread il n'y a plus de pain; nothing ~ rien de plus. ● pron plus; cost ~ than coûter plus cher que; I need ~ of it il m'en faut davantage.

moreover /mɔːˈrəʊvə(r)/ adv de plus.

morning /ˈmɔːnɪŋ/ n matin m; (whole morning) matinée f.

Morocco /məˈrɒkəʊ/ n Maroc m.

morsel /ˈmɔːsl/ n morceau m.

mortal /ˈmɔːtl/ adj & n mortel/-le (m/f).

mortgage /ˈmɔːɡɪdʒ/ n emprunt-logement m. ● vt hypothéquer.

mortuary /ˈmɔːtʃərɪ/ n morgue f.

mosaic /məʊˈzeɪɪk/ n mosaïque f.

mosque /mɒsk/ n mosquée f.

mosquito /məsˈkiːtəʊ/ n (pl ~es) moustique m.

moss /mɒs/ n mousse f.

most /məʊst/ det (nearly all) la plupart de; ~ people la plupart des gens; the ~ votes/money le plus de voix/d'argent. ● n le plus. ● pron la plupart; ~ of us la plupart d'entre nous; ~ of the money la plus grande partie de l'argent; the ~ I can do is ... tout ce que je peux faire c'est ... ● adv the ~ beautiful house/hotel in Oxford la maison la plus belle/l'hôtel le plus beau d'Oxford; ~ interesting très intéressant; what I like ~ (of all) is ce que j'aime le plus c'est. **mostly** adv surtout.

moth /mɒθ/ n papillon m de nuit; (in cloth) mite f.

mother /ˈmʌðə(r)/ n mère f. ● vt (lit) materner; (fig) dorloter. **motherhood** n maternité f. ~**-in-law** n (pl ~**s-in-law**) belle-mère f. ~**-of-pearl** n nacre f. **M**~**'s Day** n la fête des mères. ~**-to-be** n future maman f. ~ **tongue** n langue f maternelle.

motion /ˈməʊʃn/ n mouvement m; (proposal) motion f; ~ **picture** (US) film m. ● vt/i ~ (**to**) **sb** to faire signe à qn de. **motionless** adj immobile.

motivate /ˈməʊtɪveɪt/ vt motiver.

motive /ˈməʊtɪv/ n motif m; (Jur) mobile m.

motor /ˈməʊtə(r)/ n moteur m; (car) auto f. ● adj (industry, insurance, vehicle) automobile; (activity, disorder: Med) moteur. ~**bike** n moto f. ~ **car** n auto f. ~**-cyclist** n motocycliste mf. ~ **home** n autocaravane f.

motorist /ˈməʊtərɪst/ n automobiliste mf.

motorway /ˈməʊtəweɪ/ n autoroute f.

mottled /ˈmɒtld/ adj tacheté.

motto /ˈmɒtəʊ/ n (pl ~**es**) devise f.

mould /məʊld/ n (shape) moule m; (fungus) moisissure f. ● vt mouler; (influence) former. **moulding** n moulure f. **mouldy** adj moisi.

mount /maʊnt/ n (hill) mont m; (horse) monture f. ● vt (stairs) gravir; (platform, horse, bike) monter sur; (jewel, picture, campaign, exhibit) monter. ● vi monter; (number, toll) augmenter; (concern) grandir.

mountain /ˈmaʊntɪn/ n montagne f; ~ **bike** (vélo) tout terrain m, VTT m. **mountaineer** n alpiniste mf.

mourn /mɔːn/ vt/i ~ (**for**) pleurer.

mournful adj mélancolique.

mourning n deuil m.

mouse /maʊs/ n (pl **mice**) souris f. ~**trap** n souricière f.

mouth /maʊθ/ n bouche f; (of dog, cat) gueule f; (of cave, tunnel) entrée f. **mouthful** n bouchée f. ~**wash** n eau f dentifrice. ~**watering** adj appétissant.

move /muːv/ vt (object) déplacer; (limb, head) bouger; (emotionally) émouvoir; ~ **house** déménager. ● vi bouger; (vehicle) rouler; (change address) déménager; (act) agir. ● n mouvement m; (in game) coup m; (player's turn) tour m; (step, act) manœuvre f; (house change) déménagement m; **on the** ~ en mouvement. □ ~ **back** reculer; ~ **in** emménager. ~ **in with** s'installer avec; ~ **on** (person) se mettre en route; (vehicle) repartir; (time) passer; ~ **sth on** faire avancer qch; ~ **sb on** faire circuler qn; ~ **over** or **up** se pousser.

movement /ˈmuːvmənt/ n mouvement m.

movie /ˈmuːvɪ/ n (US) film m; **the** ~**s** le cinéma.

moving /ˈmuːvɪŋ/ adj (vehicle) en marche; (part, target) mobile; (staircase) roulant; (touching) émouvant.

mow /məʊ/ vt (pp **mowed** or **mown**) (lawn) tondre; (hay) couper; ~ **down** faucher. **mower** n tondeuse f.

MP abbr →**MEMBER OF PARLIAMENT**

Mr /ˈmɪstə(r)/ n (pl **Messrs**) ~ Smith Monsieur or M. Smith; ~ President Monsieur le Président.

Mrs /ˈmɪsɪz/ n (pl **Mrs**) ~ Smith Madame or Mme Smith.

Ms /məz/ n Mme.

much /mʌtʃ/ adv beaucoup; **too** ~ trop; **very** ~ beaucoup; **I like them**

m

as ~ as you (do) je les aime autant que toi. ● *pron* beaucoup; not ~ pas grand-chose; he didn't say ~ il n'a pas dit grand-chose; I ate so ~ that j'ai tellement mangé que. ● *det* beaucoup de; too ~ money trop d'argent; how ~ time is left? combien de temps reste-t-il?

muck /mʌk/ *n* saletés *fpl*; (*manure*) fumier *m*. □ ~ **about** T faire l'imbécile. **mucky** *adj* sale.

mud /mʌd/ *n* boue *f*.

muddle /'mʌdl/ *n* (mix-up) malentendu *m*; (mess) pagaille *f* T; get into a ~ s'embrouiller. □ ~ **through** se débrouiller; ~ **up** embrouiller.

muddy /'mʌdɪ/ *adj* couvert de boue.

muffle /'mʌfl/ *vt* emmitoufler; (*bell*) assourdir; (*noise*) étouffer.

mug /mʌɡ/ *n* grande tasse *f*; (for beer) chope *f*; (face T) gueule *f* ✗; (fool T) poire *f* T. ● *vt* (*pt* **mugged**) agresser. **mugger** *n* agresseur *m*.

muggy /'mʌɡɪ/ *adj* lourd.

mule /mjuːl/ *n* mulet *m*.

multicoloured /mʌltɪ'kʌləd/ *adj* multicolore.

multiple /'mʌltɪpl/ *adj* & *n* multiple (*m*); ~ **sclerosis** sclérose *f* en plaques.

multiplication /mʌltɪplɪ'keɪʃn/ *n* multiplication *f*. **multiply** *vt/i* (se) multiplier.

multistorey /mʌltɪ'stɔːrɪ/ *adj* (car park) à niveaux multiples.

mum /mʌm/ *n* T maman *f*.

mumble /'mʌmbl/ *vt/i* marmonner.

mummy /'mʌmɪ/ *n* (mother T) maman *f*; (embalmed body) momie *f*.

mumps /mʌmps/ *n* oreillons *mpl*.

munch /mʌntʃ/ *vt* mâcher.

mundane /mʌn'deɪn/ *adj* terre-à-terre.

municipal /mjuː'nɪsɪpl/ *adj* municipal.

mural /'mjʊərəl/ *adj* mural. ● *n* peinture *f* murale.

murder /'mɜːdə(r)/ *n* meurtre *m*. ● *vt* assassiner. **murderer** *n* meurtrier *m*, assassin *m*.

murky /'mɜːkɪ/ *adj* (**-ier, -iest**) (*water*) glauque; (*past*) trouble.

murmur /'mɜːmə(r)/ *n* murmure *m*. ● *vt/i* murmurer.

muscle /'mʌsl/ *n* muscle *m*. ● *vi* ~ **in** T s'imposer (on dans).

muscular /'mʌskjʊlə(r)/ *adj* (*tissue, disease*) musculaire; (*body, person*) musclé.

museum /mjuː'zɪəm/ *n* musée *m*.

mushroom /'mʌʃrʊm/ *n* champignon *m*. ● *vi* (*town*) proliférer; (*demand*) s'accroître rapidement.

music /'mjuːzɪk/ *n* musique *f*.

musical /'mjuːzɪkl/ *adj* (*person*) musicien; (*voice*) mélodieux; (*accompaniment*) musical; (*instrument*) de musique. ● *n* comédie *f* musicale.

musician /mjuː'zɪʃn/ *n* musicien/-ne *m/f*.

Muslim /'mʊzlɪm/ *n* Musulman/-e *m/f*. ● *adj* musulman.

mussel /'mʌsl/ *n* moule *f*.

must /mʌst/ *v aux* devoir; you ~ go vous devez partir, il faut que vous partiez; she ~ be consulted il faut la consulter; he ~ be old il doit être vieux; I ~ have done it j'ai dû le faire. ● *n* be a ~ T être indispensable.

mustard /'mʌstəd/ *n* moutarde *f*.

musty /'mʌstɪ/ *adj* (**-ier, -iest**) (*room*) qui sent le renfermé;

(*smell*) de moisi.

mute /mjuːt/ *adj & n* muet/-te (*m/f*). **muted** *adj* (*colour*) sourd; (*response*) tiède; (*celebration*) mitigé.

mutilate /'mjuːtɪleɪt/ *vt* mutiler.

mutter /'mʌtə(r)/ *vt/i* marmonner.

mutton /'mʌtn/ *n* mouton *m*.

mutual /'mjuːtʃʊəl/ *adj* (*reciprocal*) réciproque; (*common*) commun; (*consent*) mutuel. **mutually** *adv* mutuellement.

muzzle /'mʌzl/ *n* (*snout*) museau *m*; (*device*) muselière *f*; (*of gun*) canon *m*. ● *vt* museler.

my /maɪ/ *adj* mon, ma, *pl* mes.

myself /maɪ'self/ *pron* (*reflexive*) me, m'; I've hurt ~ je me suis fait mal; (*emphatic*) moi-même; I did it ~ je l'ai fait moi-même; (*after preposition*) moi, moi-même; I am proud of ~ je suis fier de moi.

mysterious /mɪ'stɪərɪəs/ *adj* mystérieux.

mystery /'mɪstərɪ/ *n* mystère *m*.

mystic /'mɪstɪk/ *adj & n* mystique (*mf*). **mystical** *adj* mystique.

myth /mɪθ/ *n* mythe *m*. **mythical** *adj* mythique. **mythology** *n* mythologie *f*.

Nn

nag /næg/ *vt/i* (*pt* **nagged**) critiquer; (*pester*) harceler. **nagging** *adj* persistant.

nail /neɪl/ *n* clou *m*; (*of finger, toe*) ongle *m*; on the ~ sans tarder, tout de suite. ● *vt* clouer. ~ **polish** *n* vernis *m* à ongles.

naïve /naɪ'iːv/ *adj* naïf.

naked /'neɪkɪd/ *adj* nu; to the ~

eye à l'œil nu.

name /neɪm/ *n* nom *m*; (*fig*) réputation *f*. ● *vt* nommer; (*terms*) fixer; be ~d after porter le nom de.

namely /'neɪmlɪ/ *adv* à savoir.

nanny /'nænɪ/ *n* nurse *f*.

nap /næp/ *n* somme *m*.

nape /neɪp/ *n* nuque *f*.

napkin /'næpkɪn/ *n* serviette *f*.

nappy /'næpɪ/ *n* couche *f*.

narcotic /nɑː'kɒtɪk/ *adj & n* narcotique (*m*).

narrative /'nærətɪv/ *n* récit *m*. **narrator** *n* narrateur-trice *m/f*.

narrow /'nærəʊ/ *adj* étroit. ● *vt/i* (se) rétrécir; (*limit*) (se) limiter; ~ down the choices limiter les choix. ~-**minded** *adj* à l'esprit étroit; (*ideas*) étroit.

nasal /'neɪzl/ *adj* nasal.

nasty /'nɑːstɪ/ *adj* (**-ier, -iest**) mauvais, désagréable; (*malicious*) méchant.

nation /'neɪʃn/ *n* nation *f*.

national /'næʃənl/ *adj* national. ● *n* ressortissant/-e *m/f*.

nationality /næʃə'nælətɪ/ *n* nationalité *f*.

nationalize /'næʃnəlaɪz/ *vt* nationaliser.

nationally /'næʃnəlɪ/ *adv* à l'échelle nationale.

National Trust Association caritative britannique fondée en 1895 pour assurer la protection de certains édifices ou parties de littoral menacés par l'industrialisation. Cette association est aujourd'hui le premier propriétaire foncier britannique car elle a acquis ou reçu en don beaucoup par sa création de nombreux sites et bâtiments; la plupart sont ouverts au public.

m
n

native /'neɪtɪv/ n (local inhabitant) autochtone mf; (non-European) indigène mf; be a ~ of être originaire de. ● adj indigène; (country) natal; (inborn) inné; ~ language langue f maternelle; ~ speaker of French personne f de langue maternelle française.

natural /'nætʃrəl/ adj naturel.

naturally /'nætʃrəlɪ/ adv (normally, of course) naturellement; (by nature) de nature.

nature /'neɪtʃə(r)/ n nature f.

naughty /'nɔ:tɪ/ adj (-ier, -iest) vilain, méchant; (indecent) grivois.

nausea /'nɔ:sɪə/ n nausée f. **nauseous** adj (smell) écœurant.

nautical /'nɔ:tɪkl/ adj nautique.

naval /'neɪvl/ adj (battle) naval; (officer) de marine.

navel /'neɪvl/ n nombril m.

navigate /'nævɪgeɪt/ vt (sea) naviguer sur; (ship) piloter. ● vi naviguer. **navigation** n navigation f.

navy /'neɪvɪ/ n marine f. ● adj ~ (blue) bleu inv marine.

near /nɪə(r)/ adv près; draw ~ (s')approcher (to de). ● prep près de. ● adj proche; ~ to près de. ● vt approcher de.

nearby /nɪə'baɪ/ adj proche. ● adv à proximité.

nearly /'nɪəlɪ/ adv presque; I ~ forgot j'ai failli oublier; not ~ as pretty as loin d'être aussi joli que.

nearness n proximité f.

nearside /'nɪəsaɪd/ adj (Auto) du côté du passager.

neat /ni:t/ adj soigné, net; (room) bien rangé; (clever) habile; (drink) sec. **neatly** adv avec soin; habilement.

necessarily /nesə'serəlɪ/ adv nécessairement.

necessary /'nesəsərɪ/ adj nécessaire.

necessitate /nɪ'sesɪteɪt/ vt nécessiter.

necessity /nɪ'sesətɪ/ n nécessité f; (thing) chose f indispensable.

neck /nek/ n cou m; (of dress) encolure f. ~ **and neck** adj à égalité. ~**lace** n collier m. ~**line** n encolure f. ~**tie** n cravate f.

nectarine /'nektərɪn/ n brugnon m, nectarine f.

need /ni:d/ n besoin m. ● vt avoir besoin de; (demand) demander; you ~ not come vous n'êtes pas obligé de venir.

needle /'ni:dl/ n aiguille f.

needless /'ni:dlɪs/ adj inutile.

needlework /'ni:dlwɜ:k/ n couture f; (object) ouvrage m (à l'aiguille).

needy /'ni:dɪ/ adj (-ier, -iest) nécessiteux. ● n the ~ les indigents.

negative /'negətɪv/ adj négatif. ● n (of photograph) négatif m; (word: Gram) négation f; in the ~ (answer) par la négative; (Gram) à la forme négative.

neglect /nɪ'glekt/ vt négliger, laisser à l'abandon; ~ to do négliger de faire. ● n manque m de soins; (state of) ~ abandon m.

negligent /'neglɪdʒənt/ adj négligent.

negotiate /nɪ'gəʊʃɪeɪt/ vt/i négocier. **negotiation** n négociation f.

neigh /neɪ/ n hennissement m. ● vi hennir.

neighbour, (US) **neighbor** /'neɪbə(r)/ n voisin/-e m/f. **neighbourhood** n voisinage m, quartier m; in the ~hood of aux alentours de. **neighbouring** adj voisin. **neighbourly** adj amical.

neither /'naɪðə(r)/ adj & pron

aucun/-e des deux, ni l'un/-e ni
l'autre. ● adv ni; ~ big nor small ni
grand ni petit. ● conj (ne) non plus;
~ am I coming je ne viendrai pas
non plus.
nephew /ˈnefjuː/ n neveu m.
nerve /nɜːv/ n nerf m; (courage)
courage m; (calm) sang-froid m; (impudence 🔢) culot m; ~s (before
exams) trac m. ~-**racking** adj
éprouvant.
nervous /ˈnɜːvəs/ adj nerveux; be
or feel ~ (afraid) avoir peur; ~
breakdown dépression f nerveuse.
nervousness n nervosité f; (fear)
crainte f.
nest /nest/ n nid m. ● vi nicher.
~-**egg** n pécule m.
nestle /ˈnesl/ vi se blottir.
net /net/ n filet m; (Comput) net m,
Internet m. ● vt (pt **netted**) prendre
au filet. ● adj (weight) net. ~**ball** n
netball m.
Netherlands /ˈneðələndz/ n the
~ les Pays-Bas mpl.
netiquette /ˈnetɪket/ n nétiquette f.
Netsurfer /ˈnetsɜːfər/ n Internaute mf.
nettle /ˈnetl/ n ortie f.
network /ˈnetwɜːk/ n réseau m.
neurotic /njʊəˈrɒtɪk/ adj & n
névrosé/-e (m/f).
neuter /ˈnjuːtə(r)/ adj & n neutre
(m). ● vt (castrate) castrer.
neutral /ˈnjuːtrəl/ adj neutre; ~
(gear) (Auto) point m mort.
never /ˈnevə(r)/ adv (ne) jamais; he
~ refuses il ne refuse jamais; I ~
saw him 🔢 je ne l'ai pas vu; ~
again plus jamais; ~ mind (don't
worry) ne vous en faites pas; (it
doesn't matter) peu importe.
nevertheless /nevəðəˈles/ adv
néanmoins, toutefois.

new /njuː/ adj nouveau; (brand-
new) neuf. ~-**born** adj nouveau-né.
~**comer** n nouveau venu m, nouvelle venue f.
newly /ˈnjuːlɪ/ adv nouvellement.
~-**weds** npl jeunes mariés mpl.
news /njuːz/ n nouvelle(s) f(pl);
(radio, press) informations fpl; (TV)
actualités fpl, informations fpl. ~
agency n agence f de presse.
~**agent** n marchand/-e m/f de journaux. ~**caster** n présentateur/-trice
m/f. ~**group** n (Internet) forum m
de discussion. ~**letter** n bulletin m.
~**paper** n journal m.
new year n nouvel an m. **New
Year's Day** n le jour de l'an. **New
Year's Eve** n la Saint-Sylvestre.
New Zealand /njuːˈziːlənd/ n
Nouvelle-Zélande f.
next /nekst/ adj prochain; (adjoining) voisin; (following) suivant; ~
to à côté de; ~ door à côté (to
de). ● adv la prochaine fois; (afterwards) ensuite. ● n suivant/-e m/f;
(e-mail) message m suivant.
~-**door** adj d'à côté. ~ **of kin** n
parent m le plus proche.
nib /nɪb/ n plume f.
nibble /ˈnɪbl/ vt/i grignoter.
nice /naɪs/ adj agréable, bon; (kind)
gentil; (pretty) joli; (respectable)
bien; inv; (subtle) délicat. **nicely** adv
agréablement; gentiment;
(well) bien.
nicety /ˈnaɪsətɪ/ n subtilité f.
niche /niːʃ/ n (recess) niche f; (fig)
place f, situation f.
nick /nɪk/ n petite entaille f; be in
good/bad ~ 🔢 être en bon/
mauvais état. ● vt (steal, arrest 🔢)
piquer.
nickel /ˈnɪkl/ n (metal) nickel m;
(US) pièce f de cinq cents.
nickname /ˈnɪkneɪm/ n surnom m.
● vt surnommer.

nicotine /ˈnɪkətiːn/ n nicotine f.

niece /niːs/ n nièce f.

niggling /ˈnɪɡlɪŋ/ adj (person) tatillon; (detail) insignifiant.

night /naɪt/ n nuit f; (evening) soir m. ● adj de nuit. ~-**cap** n boisson f (avant d'aller se coucher). ~-**club** n boîte f de nuit. ~-**dress** n chemise f de nuit. ~**fall** n tombée f de la nuit. **nightie** n chemise f de nuit.

nightingale /ˈnaɪtɪŋɡeɪl/ n rossignol m.

nightly /ˈnaɪtlɪ/ adj & adv (de) chaque nuit or soir.

night /naɪt/: ~**mare** n cauchemar m. ~-**time** n nuit f.

nil /nɪl/ n (Sport) zéro m. ● adj (chances, risk) nul.

nimble /ˈnɪmbl/ adj agile.

nine /naɪn/ adj & n neuf (m).

nineteen /naɪnˈtiːn/ adj & n dix-neuf (m).

ninety /ˈnaɪntɪ/ adj & n quatre-vingt-dix (m).

ninth /naɪnθ/ adj & n neuvième (mf).

nip /nɪp/ vt/i (pt **nipped**) (pinch) pincer; (rush 🔲) courir; ~ **out**/ **back** sortir/rentrer rapidement. ● n pincement m.

nipple /ˈnɪpl/ n mamelon m; (of baby's bottle) tétine f.

nippy /ˈnɪpɪ/ adj (-ier, -iest) (air) piquant; (car) rapide.

nitrogen /ˈnaɪtrədʒən/ n azote m.

no /nəʊ/ det aucun/-e; pas de; ~ **man** aucun homme; ~ **money**/ **time** pas d'argent/de temps; ~ **one** ➡NOBODY; ~ **smoking**/**entry** défense de fumer/d'entrer; ~ **way**! 🔲 pas question! ● adv non. ● n (pl **noes**) non m inv.

nobility /nəʊˈbɪlətɪ/ n noblesse f.

noble /ˈnəʊbl/ adj noble. ~**man** n

(pl -**men**) noble m.

nobody /ˈnəʊbədɪ/ pron (ne) personne; he knows ~ il ne connaît personne. ● n nullité f.

nocturnal /nɒkˈtɜːnl/ adj nocturne.

nod /nɒd/ vt/i (pt **nodded**); ~ (one's head) faire un signe de tête; ~ **off** s'endormir. ● n signe m de tête.

noise /nɔɪz/ n bruit m; make a ~ faire du bruit. **noisily** adv bruyamment. **noisy** adj (-ier, -iest) bruyant.

no man's land n no man's land m.

nominal /ˈnɒmɪnl/ adj symbolique, nominal; (value) nominal.

nominate /ˈnɒmɪneɪt/ vt nommer; (put forward) proposer.

none /nʌn/ pron aucun/-e; ~ **of us** aucun/-e de nous; I have ~ je n'en ai pas.

non-existent /nɒnɪɡˈzɪstənt/ adj inexistant.

nonplussed /nɒnˈplʌst/ adj perplexe.

nonsense /ˈnɒnsns/ n absurdités fpl.

non-smoker /nɒnˈsməʊkə(r)/ n non-fumeur m.

non-stick adj antiadhésif.

non-stop /nɒnˈstɒp/ adj (train, flight) direct. ● adv sans arrêt.

noodles /ˈnuːdlz/ npl nouilles fpl.

noon /nuːn/ n midi m.

nor /nɔː(r)/ adv ni. ● conj (ne) non plus; ~ **shall I come** je ne viendrai pas non plus.

norm /nɔːm/ n norme f.

normal /ˈnɔːml/ adj normal.

Norman /ˈnɔːmən/ n Normand/-e m/f. ● adj (village) normand; (arch) roman.

north /nɔːθ/ n nord m. ● adj nord inv, du nord. ● adv le nord.
North America n Amérique f du Nord.
north-east /nɔːθ'iːst/ n nord-est m.
northerly /'nɔːðəlɪ/ adj (wind, area) du nord; (point) au nord.
northern /'nɔːðən/ adj (accent) du nord; (coast) nord. **northerner** n habitant/-e m/f du nord.
northward /nɔːθwəd/ adj (side) nord inv; (journey) vers le nord.
north-west /nɔːθ'west/ n nord-ouest m.
Norway /'nɔːweɪ/ n Norvège f.
Norwegian /nɔː'wiːdʒən/ n (person) Norvégien/-ne m/f; (language) norvégien m. ● adj norvégien.
nose /nəʊz/ n nez m. ● vi ~ about fouiner.
nosedive /'nəʊzdaɪv/ n piqué m. ● vi descendre en piqué.
nostalgia /nɒ'stældʒə/ n nostalgie f.
nostril /'nɒstrɪl/ n narine f; (of horse) naseau m.
nosy /'nəʊzɪ/ adj (-ier, -iest) Ⅱ curieux, indiscret.
not /nɒt/ adv (ne) pas; I do not know je ne sais pas; ~ at all pas du tout; ~ yet pas encore; I suppose ~ je suppose que non.
notably /'nəʊtəblɪ/ adv notamment.
notch /nɒtʃ/ n entaille f. ● vt ~ up (score) marquer.
note /nəʊt/ n note f; (banknote) billet m; (short letter) mot m. ● vt noter; (notice) remarquer. ~book n carnet m.
nothing /'nʌθɪŋ/ pron (ne) rien; he eats ~ il ne mange rien; ~ else rien d'autre; ~ much pas grand-chose; for ~ pour rien, gratis. ● n

rien m; (person) nullité f. ● adv nullement.
notice /'nəʊtɪs/ n avis m, annonce f; (poster) affiche f; (advance) préavis m; at short ~ dans des délais très brefs; give in one's ~ donner sa démission; take ~ faire attention (of à). ● vt remarquer, observer. **noticeable** adj visible. ~board n tableau m d'affichage.
notify /'nəʊtɪfaɪ/ vt (inform) aviser; (make known) notifier.
notion /'nəʊʃn/ n idée f, notion f.
notorious /nəʊ'tɔːrɪəs/ adj (criminal) notoire; (district) mal famé; (case) tristement célèbre.
notwithstanding /nɒtwɪθ'stændɪŋ/ prep malgré. ● adv néanmoins.
nought /nɔːt/ n zéro m.
noun /naʊn/ n nom m.
nourish /'nʌrɪʃ/ vt nourrir. **nourishing** adj nourrissant. **nourishment** n nourriture f.
novel /'nɒvl/ n roman m. ● adj nouveau. **novelist** n romancier/-ière m/f. **novelty** n nouveauté f.
November /nə'vembə(r)/ n novembre m.
now /naʊ/ adv maintenant. ● conj maintenant que; just ~ maintenant; (a moment ago) tout à l'heure; ~ and again, ~ and then de temps à autre.
nowadays /'naʊədeɪz/ adv de nos jours.
nowhere /'nəʊweə(r)/ adv nulle part.
nozzle /'nɒzl/ n (tip) embout m; (of hose) jet m.
nuclear /'njuːklɪə(r)/ adj nucléaire.
nude /njuːd/ adj nu. ● n nu/-e m/f; in the ~ tout nu.
nudge /nʌdʒ/ vt pousser du coude. ● n coup m de coude.

n

nudism /'nju:dɪzəm/ n nudisme m.
nudity n nudité f.

nuisance /'nju:sns/ n (thing, event) ennui m; (person) peste f; be a ~ être embêtant.

null /nʌl/ adj nul.

numb /nʌm/ adj engourdi (with par). ● vt engourdir.

number /'nʌmbə(r)/ n nombre m; (of ticket, house, page) numéro m; (written figure) chiffre m; a ~ of people plusieurs personnes. ● vt numéroter; (count, include) compter. ~-**plate** n plaque f d'immatriculation.

numeral /'nju:mərəl/ n chiffre m.
numerate /'nju:mərət/ adj qui sait compter.
numerical /nju:'merɪkl/ adj numérique.
numerous /'nju:mərəs/ adj nombreux.

nun /nʌn/ n religieuse f.

nurse /nɜ:s/ n infirmier/-ière m/f; (nanny) nurse f. ● vt soigner; (hope) nourrir.

nursery /'nɜ:sərɪ/ n (room) chambre f d'enfants; (for plants) pépinière f; (day) ~ crèche f ~ **rhyme** n comptine f ~ **school** n (école) maternelle f.

nursing home n maison f de retraite.

nut /nʌt/ n (walnut, Brazil nut) noix f; (hazelnut) noisette f; (peanut) cacahuète f; (Tech) écrou m. ~**crackers** npl casse-noix m inv.

nutmeg /'nʌtmeg/ n muscade f.
nutrient /'nju:trɪənt/ n substance f nutritive.
nutritious /nju:'trɪʃəs/ adj nutritif.
nuts /nʌts/ adj (crazy [I]) cinglé.
nutshell /'nʌtʃel/ n coquille f de noix; in a ~ en un mot.

nylon /'naɪlɒn/ n nylon m.

Oo

oak /əʊk/ n chêne m.
OAP abbr old-age pensioner retraité/-e m/f.
oar /ɔ:(r)/ n rame f.
oath /əʊθ/ n (promise) serment m; (swearword) juron m.
oats /əʊts/ npl avoine f.
obedience /ə'bi:dɪəns/ n obéissance f obedient adj obéissant. **obediently** adv docilement.
obese /əʊ'bi:s/ adj obèse.
obey /ə'beɪ/ vt/i obéir (à).
object[1] /'ɒbdʒɪkt/ n (thing) objet m; (aim) but m; (Gram) complément m d'objet; money is no ~ l'argent n'est pas un problème.
object[2] /əb'dʒekt/ vi protester. ● vt ~ that objecter que; ~ to (behaviour) désapprouver; (plan) protester contre. **objection** n objection f; (drawback) inconvénient m.
objective /əb'dʒektɪv/ adj & n objectif (m)
obligation /ɒblɪ'geɪʃn/ n devoir m.
obligatory /ə'blɪɡətrɪ/ adj obligatoire.
oblige /ə'blaɪdʒ/ vt obliger (to do à faire).
oblivion /ə'blɪvɪən/ n oubli m. **oblivious** adj inconscient (to, of de).
oblong /'ɒblɒŋ/ adj oblong. ● n rectangle m.
obnoxious /əb'nɒkʃəs/ adj odieux.
oboe /'əʊbəʊ/ n hautbois m.
obscene /əb'si:n/ adj obscène.

obscure /əbˈskjʊə(r)/ adj obscur.
● vt obscurcir; (conceal) cacher.

observance /əbˈzɜːvəns/ n (of law) respect m; (of sabbath) observance f. **observant** adj observateur.

observation /ɒbzəˈveɪʃn/ n observation f.

observe /əbˈzɜːv/ vt observer; (remark) remarquer.

obsess /əbˈses/ vt obséder. **obsession** n obsession f. **obsessive** adj (person) maniaque; (thought) obsédant; (illness) obsessionnel.

obsolete /ˈɒbsəliːt/ adj dépassé.

obstacle /ˈɒbstəkl/ n obstacle m.

obstinate /ˈɒbstənət/ adj obstiné.

obstruct /əbˈstrʌkt/ vt (road) bloquer; (view) cacher; (progress) gêner. **obstruction** n (act) obstruction f; (thing) obstacle m; (in traffic) encombrement m.

obtain /əbˈteɪn/ vt obtenir. ● vi avoir cours. **obtainable** adj disponible.

obvious /ˈɒbvɪəs/ adj évident. **obviously** adv manifestement.

occasion /əˈkeɪʒn/ n occasion f; (big event) événement m; on ~ à l'occasion.

occasional /əˈkeɪʒənl/ adj (event) qui a lieu de temps en temps; the ~ letter une lettre de temps en temps. **occasionally** adv de temps à autre.

occupation /ɒkjʊˈpeɪʃn/ n (activity) occupation f; (job) métier m, profession f. **occupational therapy** n ergothérapie f.

occupier /ˈɒkjʊpaɪə(r)/ n occupant/-e m/f.

occupy /ˈɒkjʊpaɪ/ vt occuper.

occur /əˈkɜː(r)/ vi (pt occurred) se produire; (arise) se présenter; ~ to sb venir à l'esprit de qn.

occurrence /əˈkʌrəns/ n (event)

fait m; (instance) occurrence f.

ocean /ˈəʊʃn/ n océan m.

Oceania /əʊʃɪˈeɪnɪə/ n Océanie f.

o'clock /əˈklɒk/ adv it is six ~ il est six heures; at one ~ à une heure.

October /ɒkˈtəʊbə(r)/ n octobre m.

octopus /ˈɒktəpəs/ n (pl ~es) pieuvre f.

odd /ɒd/ adj bizarre; (number) impair; (left over) qui reste; (sock) dépareillé; write the ~ article écrire un article de temps en temps; ~ jobs menus travaux mpl; twenty ~ vingt et quelques. **oddity** n bizarrerie f.

odds /ɒdz/ npl chances fpl; (in betting) cote f (on de); at ~ en désaccord; it makes no ~ ça ne fait rien; ~ and ends des petites choses.

odour, (US) **odor** /ˈəʊdə(r)/ n odeur f. **odourless** adj inodore.

---

of /ɒv/

➡️ For expressions such as of course, consist of see ➡️course, consist.

● preposition
⋯▸ de; a photo ~ the dog une photo du chien; the king ~ the beasts le roi des animaux; (made) ~ gold en or; it's kind ~ you c'est très gentil de votre part; some ~ us quelques-uns d'entre nous; ~ it/them en; have you heard ~ it? est-ce que tu en as entendu parler?

---

off /ɒf/ adv be ~ partir, s'en aller; I'm ~ je m'en vais; 30 metres ~ à 30 mètres; a month ~ dans un mois. ● adj (gas, water) coupé; (tap) fermé; (light, TV) éteint; (party, match) annulé; (bad) (food) avarié; (milk) tourné; Friday is my day ~ je ne travaille pas le vendredi; 25% ~ 25% de remise. ● prep 3 metres ~ the ground 3 mètres (au-dessus) du sol; just ~ the kitchen juste à côté de la cuisine; that is ~ the point il n'est pas la question.

offal /'ɒfl/ n abats mpl.

offence /ə'fens/ n (Jur) infraction f; give ~ to offenser; take ~ s'offenser (at de).

offend /ə'fend/ vt offenser; be ~ed s'offenser (at de). ● vi (Jur) commettre une infraction. **offender** n délinquant/-e m/f.

offensive /ə'fensɪv/ adj (remark) injurieux; (language) grossier; (smell) repoussant; (weapon) offensif. ● n offensive f.

offer /'ɒfə(r)/ vt (pt offered) offrir. ● n offre f; on ~ en promotion.

offhand /ɒf'hænd/ adj désinvolte. ● adv à l'improviste.

office /'ɒfɪs/ n bureau m; (duty) fonction f; in ~ au pouvoir. ● adj de bureau.

officer /'ɒfɪsə(r)/ n (army) officier m; (police) policier m; (government ~) fonctionnaire mf.

official /ə'fɪʃl/ adj officiel. ● n (civil servant) fonctionnaire mf; (of party, union) officiel/-le m/f; (of police, customs) agent m.

off: ~-**licence** n magasin m de vins et spiritueux. ~-**line** adj autonome; (switched off) déconnecté; (Comput) hors connexion. ~-**load** vt (stock) écouler; (Comput) décharger. ~-**peak** adj (call) au tarif réduit; (travel) en période creuse. ~-**putting** adj rebutant. ~-**set** vt (pt -**set**, pres p -**setting**) compenser. ~-**shore** adj (out to sea) au large, en mer; (towards the shore) de terre; an

~ breeze une brise de terre. ● adv (funds) hors-lieu inv. ~-**side** adj (Sport) hors jeu inv; (Auto) du côté du conducteur. ~-**spring** n inv progéniture f.

often /'ɒfn/ adv souvent; how ~ do you meet? vous vous voyez tous les combien?; every so ~ de temps en temps.

oil /ɔɪl/ n (for lubrication, cooking) huile f; (for fuel) pétrole m; (for heating) mazout m. ● vt huiler. ~-**field** n gisement m pétrolifère. ~-**painting** n peinture f à l'huile. ~ **skins** npl ciré m. ~-**tanker** n pétrolier m.

oily /'ɔɪli/ adj graisseux.

ointment /'ɔɪntmənt/ n pommade f.

OK, okay /əʊ'keɪ/ adj d'accord; is it ~ if...? ça va si...?; feel ~ aller bien.

old /əʊld/ adj vieux; (person) vieux, âgé; (former) ancien; how ~ is he? quel âge a-t-il?; he is eight years ~ il a huit ans; ~er, ~est aîné. ~ **age** n vieillesse f. ~-**age pensioner** n retraité/-e m/f. ~-**fashioned** adj démodé; (person) vieux jeu inv. ~ **man** n vieillard m, vieux m. ~ **woman** n vieille f.

olive /'ɒlɪv/ n olive f. ~ **oil** huile f d'olive. ● adj olive inv.

Olympic /ə'lɪmpɪk/ adj olympique.

~ **Games** npl Jeux mpl olympiques.

omelette /'ɒmlɪt/ n omelette f.

omen /'əʊmən/ n augure m.

ominous /'ɒmɪnəs/ adj (presence, cloud) menaçant; (sign) de mauvais augure.

omission /ə'mɪʃn/ n omission f.

omit vt (pt **omitted**) omettre.

on /ɒn/ prep sur; ~ the table sur la table; put the key ~ the table mets la clé dessus; ~ 22 March le 22 mars; ~ Monday lundi; ~ TV à la télé; ~ video en vidéo; be ~ steroids prendre des stéroïdes; ~ arriving en arrivant. ● adj (TV, oven, light) allumé; (dishwasher, radio) en marche; (tap) ouvert; (lid) mis; the match is still ~ le match aura lieu quand même; the news is ~ in 10 minutes les informations sont dans 10 minutes. ● adv have sth ~ porter qch; 20 years ~ 20 ans plus tard; from that day ~ à partir de ce jour-là; **further** ~ plus loin; ~ **and off** (occasionally) de temps en temps; go ~ and ~ (person) parler pendant des heures.

once /wʌns/ adv une fois; (formerly) autrefois. ● conj une fois que; all at ~ tout d'un coup.

oncoming /'ɒnkʌmɪŋ/ adj (vehicle) qui approche.

one /wʌn/ det & n un (m) (f). ● pron un/e m/f; (impersonal) on; **(and only)** seul (et unique); a big ~ un grand/une grande; this/that ~ celui-ci/-là, celle-ci/-là; ~ **an-** other l'un/-e l'autre. ~**-off** adj ☐ unique, exceptionnel. ~**-self** pron soi-même; (reflexive) se. ~**-way** adj (street) à sens unique; (ticket) simple.

ongoing /'ɒngəʊɪŋ/ adj (process) continu; be ~ être en cours.

onion /'ʌnɪən/ n oignon m.

on-line /ɒn'laɪn/ adj & adv en ligne.

onlooker /'ɒnlʊkə(r)/ n spectateur/-trice m/f.

only /'əʊnlɪ/ adj seul; ~ son fils unique. ● adv seulement; he is ~ six il n'a que six ans.

onset /'ɒnset/ n début m.

onward(s) /'ɒnwəd(z)/ adv en avant.

open /'əʊpən/ adj ouvert; (view) dégagé; (free to all) public; (undisguised) manifeste; (question) en attente; in the ~ air en plein air. ● vt/i (door) (s')ouvrir; (shop, play) ouvrir; ~ **out** or **up** (s')ouvrir. ~**-ended** adj (stay) de durée indéterminée; (debate, question) ouvert. ~**-heart** adj (surgery) à cœur ouvert.

opening /'əʊpnɪŋ/ n (of book) début m; (of exhibition, shop) ouverture f; (of film) première f; (in market) débouché m; (job) poste m (disponible).

open: ~**-minded** adj ~**-minded** avoir l'esprit ouvert. ~**-plan** adj paysagé.

Open University Organisme britannique d'enseignement universitaire à distance. Les étudiants de tous âges travaillant chez eux et suivent les cours à la télévision ou sur Internet; ils envoient leurs travaux à leur directeur d'études (tutor) qu'ils peuvent rencontrer lors de stages en été. Les diplômes obtenus ont la même valeur que ceux délivrés par les universités traditionnelles.

opera /'ɒprə/ n opéra m.

operate /'ɒpəreɪt/ vt/i opérer; (Tech) (faire) fonctionner; ~ on (Med) opérer; **operating theatre** salle f d'opération.

operation /ɒpə'reɪʃn/ n opération f; have an ~ se faire opérer; in ~ (plan) en vigueur; (mine) en service.

operative /'ɒpərətɪv/ n employé/-e m/f. ● adj (law) en vigueur.

operator /'ɒpəreɪtə(r)/ n opérateur/-trice m/f; (telephonist) standardiste mf.

opinion /ə'pɪnɪən/ n opinion f, avis m. **opinionated** adj qui a des avis sur tout.

opponent /ə'pəʊnənt/ n adversaire mf.

opportunity /ɒpə'tjuːnətɪ/ n occasion f (to do de faire).

oppose /ə'pəʊz/ vt s'opposer à; as ~d to par opposition à. **opposing** adj opposé.

opposite /'ɒpəzɪt/ adj (direction, side) opposé; (building) d'en face. ● n contraire m. ● adv en face. ● prep ~ (to) en face de.

opposition /ɒpə'zɪʃn/ n opposition f.

oppress /ə'pres/ vt opprimer. **oppressive** adj (cruel) oppressif; (heat) oppressant.

opt /ɒpt/ vi ~ for opter pour; ~ out refuser de participer (of à); ~ to do choisir de faire.

optical /'ɒptɪkl/ adj optique. ~ illusion n illusion f d'optique. ~ scanner n lecteur m optique.

optician /ɒp'tɪʃn/ n opticien/-ne m/f.

optimism /'ɒptɪmɪzəm/ n optimisme m. **optimist** n optimiste mf. **optimistic** adj optimiste.

option /'ɒpʃn/ n option f; (choice) choix m.

optional /'ɒpʃənl/ adj facultatif; ~ extras accessoires mpl en option.

or /ɔː(r)/ conj ou; (with negative) ni.

oral /'ɔːrəl/ n & adj oral (m).

orange /'ɒrɪndʒ/ n (fruit) orange f; (colour) orange m. ● adj (colour) orange inv.

orbit /'ɔːbɪt/ n orbite f. ● vt décrire une orbite autour de.

orchard /'ɔːtʃəd/ n verger m.

orchestra /'ɔːkɪstrə/ n orchestre m.

orchid /'ɔːkɪd/ n orchidée f.

ordeal /ɔː'diːl/ n épreuve f.

order /'ɔːdə(r)/ n ordre m; (Comm) commande f; in ~ (tidy) en ordre; (document) en règle; in ~ that pour que; in ~ to pour. ● vt ordonner; (command) commander; ~ sb to ordonner à qn de.

orderly /'ɔːdəlɪ/ adj (tidy) ordonné; (not unruly) discipliné. ● n (Mil) planton m; (Med) aide-soignant/-e m/f.

ordinary /'ɔːdənrɪ/ adj (usual) ordinaire; (average) moyen.

ore /ɔː(r)/ n minerai m.

organ /'ɔːgən/ n organe m; (Mus) orgue m.

organic /ɔː'gænɪk/ adj organique; (produce) biologique.

organization /ɔːgənar'zeɪʃn/ n organisation f.

organize /'ɔːgənaɪz/ vt organiser.

organizer /'ɔːgənaɪzə(r)/ n organisateur/-trice m/f; electronic ~ agenda m électronique.

orgasm /'ɔːgæzəm/ n orgasme m.

Orient /'ɔːrɪənt/ n the ~ l'Orient m. **oriental** adj oriental.

origin /'ɒrɪdʒɪn/ n origine f.

original /ə'rɪdʒənl/ adj original; (inhabitant) premier; (member) d'origine; (naire. **originality** n originalité f. **originally** adv (at the outset) à l'origine.

originate /ə'rɪdʒɪneɪt/ vi (plan) prendre naissance; ~ from provenir de; (person) venir de. ● vt être l'auteur de. **originator** n (of idea) auteur m; (of invention) créateur -trice m/f.

ornament /ˈɔːnəmənt/ n (decoration) ornement m; (object) objet m décoratif.

orphan /ˈɔːfn/ n orphelin-e m/f. ● vt rendre orphelin. **orphanage** n orphelinat m.

orthopaedic /ɔːθəˈpiːdɪk/ adj orthopédique.

ostentatious /ɒstenˈteɪʃəs/ adj tape-à-l'œil inv.

osteopath /ˈɒstɪəpæθ/ n ostéopathe mf.

ostrich /ˈɒstrɪtʃ/ n autruche f.

other /ˈʌðə(r)/ adj autre; the ~ one l'autre mf. ● n & pron autre mf; (some) ~s d'autres. ● adv ~ than (apart from) à part; (otherwise than) autrement que. **otherwise** adv autrement.

otter /ˈɒtə(r)/ n loutre f.

ouch /aʊtʃ/ interj aïe!

ought /ɔːt/ v aux devoir; you ~ to stay vous devriez rester; he ~ to succeed il devrait réussir; I ~ to have done it j'aurais dû le faire.

ounce /aʊns/ n once f (= 28.35 g).

our /ˈaʊə(r)/ adj notre, pl nos.

ours /ˈaʊəz/ poss le or la nôtre, les nôtres.

ourselves /aʊəˈselvz/ pron (reflexive) nous; (emphatic) nous-mêmes; (after preposition) for ~ pour nous, pour nous-mêmes.

out /aʊt/ adv dehors; he's ~ il est sorti; further ~ plus loin; be ~ (book) être publié; (light) être éteint; (sun) briller; (flower) être épanoui; (tide) être bas; (player) être éliminé; ~ of hors de; go/walk/get ~ of sortir de; ~ of pity par pitié; made ~ of fait de; 5 ~ of 6 5 sur 6. **~break** n (of war) déclenchement m; (of violence, boils) éruption f. **~burst** n explosion f. **~cast** n paria m. **~class** vt surclasser. **~come** n résultat m. **~cry** n tollé m. **~dated** adj démodé. **~door** adj (activity) de plein air; (pool) en plein air. **~doors** adv dehors.

outer /ˈaʊtə(r)/ adj extérieur; ~ space espace m extra-atmosphérique.

outfit /ˈaʊtfɪt/ n (clothes) tenue f.

outgoing /ˈaʊtgəʊɪŋ/ adj (minister, tenant) sortant; (sociable) ouvert. **outgoings** npl dépenses fpl.

outgrow /aʊtˈgrəʊ/ vt (pt ~grew, pp ~grown) (clothes) devenir trop grand pour; (habit) dépasser.

outing /ˈaʊtɪŋ/ n sortie f.

outlaw /ˈaʊtlɔː/ n hors-la-loi m inv. ● vt déclarer illégal.

outlet /ˈaʊtlet/ n (for water, gas) tuyau m de sortie; (for goods) débouché m; (for feelings) exutoire m.

outline /ˈaʊtlaɪn/ n contour m; (of plan) grandes lignes fpl; (of essay) plan m. ● vt tracer le contour de; (summarize) exposer brièvement.

out: **~live** vt survivre à. **~look** n perspective f. **~number** vt surpasser en nombre. **~ of date** adj démodé; (expired) périmé. **~ of hand** adj incontrôlable. **~ of order** adj en panne. **~ of work** adj sans travail. **~patient** n malade mf externe.

output /ˈaʊtpʊt/ n rendement m; (Comput) sortie f. ● vt/i (Comput) sortir.

outrage /ˈaʊtreɪdʒ/ n (anger) indignation f; (atrocity) attentat m; (scandal) outrage m. ● vt (morals) outrager; (person) scandaliser. **outrageous** adj scandaleux.

outright /ˈaʊtraɪt/ adv (completely) catégoriquement; (killed) sur le coup. ● adj (majority) absolu; (ban) catégorique; (hostility) pur et simple.

outset /'aʊtset/ n début m.

outside /aʊt'saɪd/ n extérieur m. ● adv dehors. ● prep en dehors de; (in front of) devant. ● adj extérieur. **outsider** n étranger/-ère m/f; (Sport) outsider m.

out: ~ skirts npl périphérie f. ~spoken adj franc. ~standing adj exceptionnel; (not settled) en suspens.

outward /'aʊtwəd/ adj & adv vers l'extérieur; (sign) extérieur. (journey) d'aller. **outwards** adv vers l'extérieur.

oval /'əʊvl/ n & adj ovale (m).

> **Oval Office** Symbole
> même de la présidence
> américaine, le bureau ovale
> du président des États-Unis est
> situé dans l'aile ouest de la
> Maison-Blanche et a été inauguré
> en 1909. Le goût des pièces de
> forme ovale remonte à la prési-
> dence de George Washington
> (1789-1797) qui donnait des ré-
> ceptions à son domicile de Phila-
> delphie dans un salon ovale.

ovary /'əʊvərɪ/ n ovaire m.

oven /ˈʌvn/ n four m.

over /'əʊvə(r)/ prep (across) par-dessus; (above) au-dessus de; (covering) sur; (more than) plus de; it's ~ the road c'est de l'autre côté de la rue; ~ here/there par ici/là; children ~ six les enfants de plus de six ans; ~ the weekend pendant le weekend; all ~ the house partout dans la maison. ● adj, adv (term) terminé; (war) fini; get sth ~ with en finir avec qch;

ask sb ~ inviter qn; ~ and ~ (again) à plusieurs reprises; five times ~ cinq fois de suite.

overall /əʊvər'ɔːl/ adj global, d'en-semble; (length) total. ● adv globa-lement.

overalls /'əʊvərɔːls/npl combinai-son f.

over /'əʊvə(r)/ ~board adv par-dessus bord. ~cast adj couvert. ~charge vt faire payer trop cher à. ~coat n pardessus m.

overcome /əʊvə'kʌm/ vt (pt -came. pp -come) (enemy) vaincre; (difficulty, fear) surmonter; ~by ac-cablé de.

overcrowded /əʊvə'kraʊdɪd/ adj bondé; (country) surpeuplé.

overdo /əʊvə'duː/ vt (pt -did. pp -done) (Culin) trop cuire; ~ it (overwork) en faire trop.

over: ~ dose n surdose f. overdose f. ~draft n découvert m. ~draw vt (pt -drew. pp -drawn) faire un découvert sur. ~due adj en retard; (bill) impayé.

overflow[1] /əʊvə'fləʊ/ vi déborder.

overflow[2] /'əʊvəfləʊ/ n (outlet) trop-plein m. ~ car park n parking m de délestage.

overhaul /əʊvə'hɔːl/ vt réviser.

overhead[1] /əʊvə'hed/ adv au-dessus; (in sky) dans le ciel.

overhead[2] /'əʊvəhed/ adj aérien; ~ projector rétroprojecteur m. **overheads** npl frais mpl généraux.

over: ~hear vt (pt -heard) enten-dre par hasard. ~lap vt (pt -lapped) (se) chevaucher. ~leaf adv au verso. ~load vt surcharger. ~look vt (window) donner sur; (miss) ne pas voir.

overnight[1] /əʊvə'naɪt/ adv dans la nuit; (instantly: fig) du jour au len-demain.

overnight² /ˈəʊvənaɪt/ *adj* (*train*) de nuit; (*stay*) d'une nuit; (*fig*) soudain.

over: ∼**power** *vt* (*thief*) maîtriser; (*army*) vaincre; (*fig*) accabler. ∼**priced** *adj* trop cher. ∼**rate** *vt* surestimer. ∼**react** *vi* réagir de façon excessive. ∼**riding** *adj* (*consideration*) primordial. ∼**rule** *vt* (*decision*) annuler.

overrun /əʊvəˈrʌn/ *vt* (*pt* -**ran**. *pp* -**run**; *pres p* -**running**) (*country*) envahir; (*budget*) dépasser. ● *vi* (*meeting*) durer plus longtemps que prévu.

overseas /əʊvəˈsiːz/ *adj* étranger. ● *adv* outre-mer, à l'étranger.

over: ∼**see** *vt* (*pt* -**saw**. *pp* -**seen**) surveiller. ∼**sight** *n* omission *f*. ∼**sleep** *vi* (*pt* -**slept**) se réveiller trop tard. ∼**take** *vt/i* (*pt* -**took**. *pp* -**taken**) dépasser; (*fig*) frapper. ∼**time** *n* heures (*pl*) supplémentaires. ∼**turn** *vt/i* (se) renverser. ∼**weight** *adj* trop gros.

overwhelm /əʊvəˈwelm/ *vt* (*enemy*) écraser; (*shame*) accabler. **overwhelmed** *adj* (with offers, calls) submergé (*with*, *by* de); (with shame, work) accablé; (*by sight*) ébloui. **overwhelming** *adj* (*heat*, *grief*) accablant; (*defeat*, *victory*) écrasant; (*urge*) irrésistible.

overwork /əʊvəˈwɜːk/ *vt/i* (se) surmener. ● *n* surmenage *m*.

owe /əʊ/ *vt* devoir; **owing** *adj* dû; owing to en raison de.

owl /aʊl/ *n* hibou *m*.

own /əʊn/ *adj* propre. ● *pron* my ∼ le mien, la mienne; a house of one's ∼ sa propre maison; on one's ∼ tout seul. ● *vt* posséder; (*fig*) up to 🄸 avouer. **owner** *n* propriétaire *mf*. **ownership** *n* propriété *f*; (of land) possession *f*.

oxygen /ˈɒksɪdʒən/ *n* oxygène *m*.

oyster /ˈɔɪstə(r)/ *n* huître *f*.

ozone /ˈəʊzəʊn/ *n* ozone *m*; ∼ layer couche *f* d'ozone.

Pp

PA *abbr* ➡ **PERSONAL ASSISTANT**.

pace /peɪs/ *n* pas *m*; (speed) allure *f*; keep ∼ with suivre. ● *vt* (room) arpenter. ● *vi* ∼ (up and down) faire les cent pas.

Pacific /pəˈsɪfɪk/ *n* ∼ (Ocean) océan *m* Pacifique.

pack /pæk/ *n* paquet *m*; (Mil) sac *m*; (of hounds) meute *f*; (of thieves) bande *f*; (of lies) tissu *m*. ● *vt* (into case) mettre dans une valise; (into box, crate) emballer; (for sale) conditionner; (crowd) remplir complètement; ∼ one's suitcase faire sa valise. ● *vi* faire ses valises; ∼ into (cram) s'entasser dans; ∼ off expédier; send ∼ing envoyer promener.

package /ˈpækɪdʒ/ *n* paquet *m*; (Comput) progiciel *m*; ∼ **deal** offre *f* globale; ∼ **holiday** voyage *m* organisé. ● *vt* empaqueter.

packed /pækt/ *adj* (crowded) bondé; ∼ **lunch** repas *m* froid.

packet /ˈpækɪt/ *n* paquet *m*.

packing /'pækɪŋ/ n (action, material) emballage m.

pad /pæd/ n (of paper) bloc m; (to protect) protection f; (for ink) tampon m; (launch) ~ rampe f de lancement. ~ vt (pt **padded**) rembourrer; (text: fig) délayer. ● vi (pt **padded**) (walk) marcher à pas feutrés. **padding** n rembourrage m.

paddle /'pædl/ n pagaie f. ● vt ~ a canoe pagayer. ● vi patauger.

padlock /'pædlɒk/ n cadenas m. ● vt cadenasser.

paediatrician /ˌpiːdjə'trɪʃən/ n pédiatre mf.

pagan /'peɪgən/ adj & n païen/-ne (m/f).

page /peɪdʒ/ n (of book) page f. ● vt (on pager) rechercher; (over speaker) faire appeler. **pager** n radiomessageur m.

pain /peɪn/ n douleur f; ~s efforts mpl; be in ~ souffrir; take ~s to se donner du mal pour. ● vt (grieve) peiner. **painful** adj douloureux; (laborious) pénible. ~**killer** n analgésique m. **painless** adj (operation) indolore; (death) sans souffrance; (trouble-free) sans peine. **painstaking** adj minutieux.

paint /peɪnt/ n peinture f; ~s (in tube, box) couleurs fpl. ● vt/i peindre. ~ **brush** n pinceau m. **painter** n peintre m. **painting** n peinture f. ~**work** n peintures fpl.

pair /peə(r)/ n paire f; (of people) couple m; a ~ of trousers un pantalon. ● vi a ~ off former un couple.

pajamas /pə'dʒɑːməz/ npl (US) ►PYJAMAS.

Pakistan /pɑːkɪ'stɑːn/ n Pakistan m.

palace /'pælɪs/ n palais m.

palatable /'pælətəbl/ adj (food) savoureux; (solution) acceptable.

palate n palais m.

pale /peɪl/ adj pâle. ● vi pâlir.

Palestine /'pæləstaɪn/ n Palestine f.

pallid /'pælɪd/ adj pâle.

palm /pɑːm/ n (of hand) paume f; (tree) palmier m; (symbol) palme f. □ ~ **off** 🔁 ~ **sth off** sb faire passer qch pour; ~ **sth off on** sb refiler qch à sb 🔁.

palpitate /'pælpɪteɪt/ vi palpiter.

paltry /'pɔːltrɪ/ adj (-ier, -iest) dérisoire, piètre.

pamper /'pæmpə(r)/ vt choyer.

pamphlet /'pæmflɪt/ n brochure f.

pan /pæn/ n casserole f; (for frying) poêle f.

pancake /'pænkeɪk/ n crêpe f.

pandemonium /pændɪ'məʊnɪəm/ n tohu-bohu m.

pander /'pændə(r)/ vi ~ to (person, taste) flatter bassement.

pane /peɪn/ n carreau m, vitre f.

panel /'pænl/ n (of door) panneau m; (of experts, judges) commission f; (on discussion programme) invités mpl; (instrument) ~ tableau m de bord.

pang /pæŋ/ n serrement m au cœur; ~s of conscience remords mpl.

panic /'pænɪk/ n panique f. ● vt/i (pt **panicked**) (s')affoler. ~**stricken** adj pris de panique, affolé.

pansy /'pænzɪ/ n (Bot) pensée f.

pant /pænt/ vi haleter.

panther /'pænθə(r)/ n panthère f.

pantomime /'pæntəmaɪm/ n (show) spectacle m de Noël; (mime) mime m.

pantry /'pæntrɪ/ n garde-manger m inv.

pants /pænts/ npl (underwear) slip

m; (trousers: US) pantalon *m*.
paper /ˈpeɪpə(r)/ *n* papier *m*; (newspaper) journal *m*; (exam) épreuve *f*; (essay) exposé *m*; (wallpaper) papier *m* peint; (identity) ~s papiers *mpl* (d'identité); on ~ par écrit. ● *vt* (room) tapisser. ~**back** *n* livre *m* de poche. ~**clip** *n* trombone *m*. ~ **feed tray** *n* (Comput) bac *m* d'alimentation en papier. ~ **work** *n* (work) travail *m* administratif; (documentation) documents *mpl*.
par /pɑː(r)/ *n* be below ~ ne pas être en forme; on a ~ with (performance) comparable à; (person) l'égal de; (golf) par *m*.
parachute /ˈpærəʃuːt/ *n* parachute *m*. ● *vi* descendre en parachute.
parade /pəˈreɪd/ *n* (procession) parade *f*; (Mil) défilé *m*. ● *vi* défiler. ● *vt* faire étalage de.
paradise /ˈpærədaɪs/ *n* paradis *m*.
paradox /ˈpærədɒks/ *n* paradoxe *m*.
paraffin /ˈpærəfɪn/ *n* pétrole *m* (lampant); (wax) paraffine *f*.
paragliding /ˈpærəɡlaɪdɪŋ/ *n* parapente *m*.
paragon /ˈpærəɡən/ *n* modèle *m*.
paragraph /ˈpærəɡrɑːf/ *n* paragraphe *m*.
parallel /ˈpærəlel/ *adj* parallèle. ● *n* parallèle *m*; (maths) parallèle *f*.
Paralympics /pærəˈlɪmpɪks/ *npl* the ~ les jeux paralympiques.
paralyse /ˈpærəlaɪz/ *vt* paralyser. **paralysis** *n* paralysie *f*.
paramedic /pærəˈmedɪk/ *n* auxiliaire *mf* médical/-e.
parameter /pəˈræmɪtə(r)/ *n* paramètre *m*.
paramount /ˈpærəmaʊnt/ *adj* suprême.
paranoia /pærəˈnɔɪə/ *n* paranoïa *f*.

paranoid *adj* paranoïaque; (Psych) paranoïde.
paraphernalia /pærəfəˈneɪlɪə/ *n* attirail *m*.
parasol /ˈpærəsɒl/ *n* ombrelle *f*; (on table, at beach) parasol *m*.
paratrooper /ˈpærətruːpə(r)/ *n* (Mil) parachutiste *m*.
parcel /ˈpɑːsl/ *n* paquet *m*.
parchment /ˈpɑːtʃmənt/ *n* parchemin *m*.
pardon /ˈpɑːdn/ *n* pardon *m*; (Jur) grâce *f*; I beg your ~ je vous demande pardon. ● *vt* (*pt* **pardoned**) pardonner (sb for sth qch à qn); (Jur) gracier.
parent /ˈpeərənt/ *n* parent *m*.
parenthesis /pəˈrenθəsɪs/ *n* (*pl* -theses) parenthèse *f*.
parenthood /ˈpeərənthʊd/ *n* (fatherhood) paternité *f*; (motherhood) maternité *f*.
Paris /ˈpærɪs/ *n* Paris.
parish /ˈpærɪʃ/ *n* (Relig) paroisse *f*; (municipal) commune *f*.
park /pɑːk/ *n* parc *m*. ● *vt/i* (se) garer; (remain parked) stationner. ~ **and ride** *n* parc *m* relais.
parking /ˈpɑːkɪŋ/ *n* stationnement *m*; no ~ stationnement interdit. ~ **lot** *n* (US) parking *m*. ~ **meter** *n* parcmètre *m*. ~ **ticket** *n* (fine) contravention *f*, PV *m*🔢.
parliament /ˈpɑːləmənt/ *n* parlement *m*. **parliamentary** *adj* parlementaire.

Parliament Corps législatif britannique composé de la Chambre des communes (*House of Commons*) et de la Chambre des lords (*House of Lords*) qui siègent au Palais de Westminster. Le souverain convoque et dissout le Parlement, ouvre chaque

p

session parlementaire et signe les textes de lois. ▶SCOTTISH PARLIAMENT, ▶WELSH ASSEMBLY, ▶DÁIL

parlour, (US) **parlor** /'pɑːlə(r)/ n salon m.

parody /'pærədɪ/ n parodie f. ● vt parodier.

parole /pə'rəʊl/ n on ~ en liberté conditionnelle.

parrot /'pærət/ n perroquet m.

parry /'pærɪ/ vt (Sport) parer; (question) éluder. ● n parade f.

parsley /'pɑːslɪ/ n persil m.

parsnip /'pɑːsnɪp/ n panais m.

part /pɑːt/ n partie f; (of serial) épisode m; (of machine) pièce f; (Theat) rôle m; (side in dispute) parti m; in ~ en partie; on the ~ of de la part de; take ~ in participer à. ● adj partiel. ● adv en partie. ● vt/i (separate) (se) séparer; ~ with se séparer de.

part-exchange n reprise f; take sth in ~ reprendre qch.

partial /'pɑːʃl/ adj partiel; (biased) partial; be ~ to avoir un faible pour.

participant /pɑː'tɪsɪpənt/ n participant/-e m/f. **participate** vi participer (in à). **participation** n participation f.

participle /pɑː'tɪsɪpl/ n participe m.

particular /pə'tɪkjʊlə(r)/ n détail m; ~s détails mpl; in ~ en particulier. ● adj particulier; (fussy) difficile; (careful) méticuleux; that ~ man cet homme-là. **particularly** adv particulièrement.

parting /'pɑːtɪŋ/ n séparation f; (in hair) raie f. ● adj d'adieu.

partition /pɑː'tɪʃn/ n (of room) cloison f; (Pol) partition f. ● vt (room) cloisonner; (country)

partager.

partly /'pɑːtlɪ/ adv en partie.

partner /'pɑːtnə(r)/ n (professional) associé/-e m/f; (economic, sporting) partenaire m/f; (spouse) époux/-se m/f; (unmarried) partenaire m/f. **partnership** n association f.

partridge /'pɑːtrɪdʒ/ n perdrix f.

part-time adj & adv à temps partiel.

party /'pɑːtɪ/ n fête f; (formal) réception f; (group) groupe m; (Pol) parti m; (Jur) partie f.

pass /pɑːs/ vt/i (pt passed) passer; (overtake) dépasser; (in exam) réussir; (approve) (candidate) admettre; (invoice) approuver; (remark) faire; (judgement) prononcer; (law, bill) adopter; ~ (by) (building) passer devant; (person) croiser. ● n (permit) laisser-passer m inv; (ticket) carte f d'abonnement; (Geog) col m; (Sport) passe f; ~ (mark) (in exam) moyenne f. □ ~ away mourir; ~ out (faint) s'évanouir; ~ sth out distribuer qch; ~ over (overlook) délaisser; ~ up (forego) laisser passer.

passage /'pæsɪdʒ/ n (way through, text) passage m; (voyage) traversée f; (corridor) couloir m.

passenger /'pæsɪndʒə(r)/ n (in car, plane, ship) passager/-ère m/f; (in train, bus, tube) voyageur/-euse m/f.

passer-by /pɑːsə'baɪ/ n (pl passers-by) passant/-e m/f.

passing /'pɑːsɪŋ/ adj (motorist) qui passe; (whim) passager; (reference) en passant.

passion /'pæʃn/ n passion f. **passionate** adj passionné.

passive /'pæsɪv/ adj passif.

passport /'pɑːspɔːt/ n passeport m.

password /'pɑːswɜːd/ n mot m

de passe.

past /pɑːst/ adj (times, problems) passé; (president) ancien; the ∼ months ces derniers mois. ● n passé m. ● prep (beyond) après; walk/go ∼ sth passer devant qch; 10 ∼ 6 six heures dix; it's ∼ 11 il est 11 heures passées. ● adv go/walk ∼ passer.

pasta /'pæstə/ n pâtes fpl (alimentaires).

paste /peɪst/ n (glue) colle f; (dough) pâte f; (of fish, meat) pâté m; (jewellery) strass m. ● vt coller.

pasteurize /'pɑːstʃəraɪz/ vt pasteuriser.

pastime /'pɑːstaɪm/ n passe-temps m inv.

pastry /'peɪstrɪ/ n (dough) pâte f; (tart) pâtisserie f.

pat /pæt/ vt (pt patted) tapoter. ● n petite tape f.

patch /pætʃ/ n pièce f; (over eye) bandeau m; (spot) tache f; (of snow, ice) plaque f; (of vegetables) carré m; bad ∼ période f difficile. □ ∼ up (trousers) rapiécer; (quarrel) résoudre.

patent /'peɪtnt/ adj (obvious) manifeste; (patented) breveté; ∼ leather cuir m verni. ● n brevet m. ● vt faire breveter.

path /pɑːθ/ n (pl -s) sentier m, chemin m; (in park) allée f; (of rocket) trajectoire f.

pathetic /pə'θetɪk/ adj misérable; (bad 🄵) lamentable.

patience /'peɪʃns/ n patience f.

patient /'peɪʃnt/ adj patient. ● n patient/-e m/f. **patiently** adv patiemment.

patriotic /pætrɪ'ɒtɪk/ adj patriotique; (person) patriote.

patrol /pə'trəʊl/ n patrouille f; ∼ car voiture f de police. ● vt/i pa-

trouiller (dans).

patron /'peɪtrən/ n (of the arts) mécène m; (customer) client/-e m/f. **patronage** n clientèle f; (support) patronage m. **patronize** vt (person) traiter avec condescendance; (establishment) fréquenter.

patter /'pætə(r)/ n (of steps) bruit m; (of rain) crépitement m.

pattern /'pætn/ n motif m, dessin m; (for sewing) patron m; (for knitting) modèle m.

paunch /pɔːntʃ/ n ventre m.

pause /pɔːz/ n pause f. ● vi faire une pause; (hesitate) hésiter.

pave /peɪv/ vt paver; ∼ the way ouvrir la voie (for à).

pavement /'peɪvmənt/ n trottoir m; (US) chaussée f.

paving stone n pavé m.

paw /pɔː/ n patte f. ● vt (animal) donner des coups de patte à; (touch 🄵) peloter 🄵.

pawn /pɔːn/ n pion m. ● vt mettre en gage. ∼broker n prêteur/-euse m/f sur gages. ∼-shop n mont-de-piété m.

pay /peɪ/ vt (pt paid) payer; (interest) rapporter; (compliment, attention) faire; (visit, homage) rendre. ● vi payer; (business) rapporter; ∼ for sth payer qch. ● n salaire m; ∼ rise augmentation f (de salaire). ∼ back rembourser; ∼ in déposer; ∼ off (loan) rembourser; (worker) congédier; (succeed) être payant; ∼ out payer, débourser.

payable /'peɪəbl/ adj payable; ∼ to (cheque) à l'ordre de.

payment /'peɪmənt/ n paiement m; (regular) versement m; (reward) récompense f.

payroll /'peɪrəʊl/ n fichier m des salaires; be on the ∼ of être employé par.

P

PC abbr ➡ PERSONAL COMPUTER.

PDA abbr (personal digital assistant) assistant m personnel numérique.

PE abbr (physical education) éducation f physique, EPS f.

pea /piː/ n (petit) pois m.

peace /piːs/ n paix f; ~ of mind tranquillité f d'esprit. **peaceful** adj (tranquil) paisible; (peaceable) pacifique.

peach /piːtʃ/ n pêche f.

peacock /ˈpiːkɒk/ n paon m.

peak /piːk/ n (of mountain) pic m; (of cap) visière f; (maximum) maximum m; (on graph) sommet m; (of career) apogée m; (of fitness) meilleur m; ~ **hours** heures fpl de pointe.

peal /piːl/ n (of bells) carillon m; (of laughter) éclat m.

peanut /ˈpiːnʌt/ n cacahuète f; ~s (money) 🔢 clopinettes fpl 🔢.

pear /peə(r)/ n poire f.

pearl /pɜːl/ n perle f.

peasant /ˈpeznt/ n paysan/-ne m/f.

peat /piːt/ n tourbe f.

pebble /ˈpebl/ n caillou m; (on beach) galet m.

peck /pek/ vt/i (food) picorer; (attack) donner des coups de bec (à). ● n coup m de bec; a ~ on the cheek une bise.

peckish /ˈpekɪʃ/ adj be ~ 🔢 avoir faim.

peculiar /prˈkjuːlɪə(r)/ adj (odd) bizarre; (special) particulier (to à). **peculiarity** n bizarrerie f.

pedal /ˈpedl/ n pédale f. ● vi pédaler.

pedantic /prˈdæntɪk/ adj pédant.

peddle /ˈpedl/ vt colporter; (drugs) faire du trafic de.

pedestrian /prˈdestrɪən/ n piéton m. ● adj (precinct, street) piétonnier;

(fig) prosaïque; ~ **crossing** passage m pour piétons.

pedigree /ˈpedɪgriː/ n (of animal) pedigree m; (of person) ascendance f. ● adj (dog) de pure race.

pee /piː/ vi 🔢 faire pipi 🔢.

peek /piːk/ vi & n ➡ PEEP.

peel /piːl/ n (on fruit) peau m; (removed) épluchures fpl. ● vt (fruit, vegetables) éplucher; (prawn) décortiquer. ● vi (of skin) peler; (of paint) s'écailler.

peep /piːp/ vi jeter un coup d'œil (furtif) (at à). ● n coup m d'œil (furtif). ~**hole** n judas m.

peer /pɪə(r)/ vi ~ (at) regarder fixement. ● n (equal, noble) pair m. **peerage** n pairie f.

peg /peg/ n (for clothes) pince f à linge; (to hang coats) patère f; (for tent) piquet m. ● vt (pt pegged) (clothes) accrocher avec des pinces; (prices) indexer.

pejorative /prˈdʒɒrətɪv/ adj péjoratif.

pelican /ˈpelɪkən/ n pélican m; ~ **crossing** passage m pour piétons.

pellet /ˈpelɪt/ n (round mass) boulette f; (for gun) plomb m.

pelt /pelt/ vt bombarder (with de). ● n (skin) peau f.

pelvis /ˈpelvɪs/ n (Anat) bassin m.

pen /pen/ n stylo m; (for sheep) enclos m; (for baby, cattle) parc m.

penal /ˈpiːnl/ adj pénal. **penalize** vt pénaliser.

penalty /ˈpenltɪ/ n peine f; (fine) amende f; (in football) penalty m.

penance /ˈpenəns/ n pénitence f.

pence /pens/ ➡ PENNY.

pencil /ˈpensl/ n crayon m. ● vt (pt pencilled) crayonner; ~ **in** noter provisoirement. ~**sharpener** n taille-crayons m inv.

pending /'pendɪŋ/ adj (matter) en souffrance; (Jur) en instance. ● prep (until) en attendant.

penetrate /'penɪtreɪt/ vt pénétrer; (silence, defences) percer; (organization) infiltrer. ● vi pénétrer. **penetrating** adj pénétrant.

pen-friend n correspondant/ -e m/f.

penguin /'pengwɪn/ n manchot m, pingouin m.

pen: ~knife n (pl **~knives**) canif m. **~-name** n pseudonyme m.

penniless /'penɪlɪs/ adj sans le sou.

penny /'penɪ/ n (pl **pennies** or **pence**) (unit of currency) penny m; (small amount) centime m.

pension /'penʃn/ n (from state) pension f; (from employer) retraite f; ~ **scheme** plan m de retraite. ● vt ~ **off** mettre à la retraite. **pensioner** n retraité/-e m/f.

pensive /'pensɪv/ adj songeur.

penthouse /'penthaʊs/ n appartement m de luxe (au dernier étage).

penultimate /pen'ʌltɪmət/ adj avant-dernier.

people /'pi:pl/ npl gens mpl, personnes fpl; English ~ les Anglais mpl; ~ **say** on dit. ● n peuple m. ● vt peupler. ~ **carrier** n monospace m.

pepper /'pepə(r)/ n poivre m; (vegetable) poivron m. ● vt (Culin) poivrer.

peppermint /'pepəmɪnt/ n (plant) menthe f poivrée; (sweet) bonbon m à la menthe.

per /pɜː(r)/ prep par; ~ **annum** par an; ~ **cent** pour cent; ~ **kilo** le kilo; **ten km ~ hour** dix km à l'heure.

percentage /pə'sentɪdʒ/ n pourcentage m.

perception /pə'sepʃn/ n perception f; **perceptive** adj perspicace.

perch /pɜːtʃ/ n (of bird) perchoir m. ● vi (se) percher.

perennial /pə'renɪəl/ adj perpétuel; (plant) vivace.

perfect¹ /pə'fekt/ vt perfectionner.

perfect² /'pɜːfɪkt/ adj parfait. ● n (Ling) parfait m. **perfectly** adv parfaitement.

perfection /pə'fekʃn/ n perfection f; **to ~** à la perfection.

perforate /'pɜːfəreɪt/ vt perforer.

perform /pə'fɔːm/ vt (task) exécuter; (function) remplir; (operation) procéder à; (play) jouer; (song) chanter. ● vi (actor, musician, team) jouer; ~ **well/badly** (candidate, business) avoir de bons/de mauvais résultats. **performance** n interprétation f; (of car, team) performance f; (show) représentation f; (fuss) histoire f. **performer** n artiste mf.

perfume /'pɜːfjuːm/ n parfum m.

perhaps /pə'hæps/ adv peut-être.

peril /'perəl/ n péril m. **perilous** adj périlleux.

perimeter /pə'rɪmɪtə(r)/ n périmètre m.

period /'pɪərɪəd/ n période f; (era) époque f; (lesson) cours m; (Gram) point m; (Med) règles fpl. ● adj d'époque. **periodical** n périodique m.

peripheral /pə'rɪfərəl/ adj (vision, suburb) périphérique; (issue) annexe. ● n (Comput) périphérique m.

perish /'perɪʃ/ vi périr; (rubber) se détériorer.

perjury /'pɜːdʒərɪ/ n faux témoignage m.

perk /pɜːk/ n [T] avantage m. ● vt/i ~ **up** (se) remonter. **perky** adj [T] gai.

perm /pɜːm/ n permanente f. ● vt **have one's hair ~ed** se faire faire une permanente.

permanent /ˈpɜːmənənt/ adj permanent. **permanently** adv (happy) en permanence; (employed) de façon permanente.

permissible /pəˈmɪsɪbl/ adj permis.

permission /pəˈmɪʃn/ n permission f.

permissive /pəˈmɪsɪv/ adj libéral; (pej) permissif.

permit[1] /pəˈmɪt/ vt (pt permitted) permettre (sb to à qn de), autoriser (sb to qn à).

permit[2] /ˈpɜːmɪt/ n permis m.

perpendicular /ˌpɜːpən
ˈdɪkjʊlə(r)/ adj perpendiculaire.

perpetrator /ˈpɜːpɪtreɪtə(r)/ n auteur m.

perpetuate /pəˈpetjʊeɪt/ vt perpétuer.

perplexed /pəˈplekst/ adj perplexe.

persecute /ˈpɜːsɪkjuːt/ vt persécuter.

perseverance /ˌpɜːsɪˈvɪərəns/ n persévérance f. **persevere** vi persévérer.

persist /pəˈsɪst/ vi persister (in doing à faire). **persistence** n persistance f. **persistent** adj (cough, snow) persistant; (obstinate) obstiné; (noise, pressure) continuel.

person /ˈpɜːsn/ n personne f; in ~ en personne.

personal /ˈpɜːsənl/ adj (life, problem, opinion) personnel; (safety, freedom, insurance) individuel. ~ **ad** n petite annonce f. ~ **assistant** n secrétaire m/f de direction. ~ **computer** n ordinateur m (personnel), microordinateur m.

personality /ˌpɜːsəˈnælətɪ/ n sonnalité f; (star) vedette f.

personal: ~ **organizer** n agenda

m. ~ **stereo** n baladeur m.

personnel /ˌpɜːsəˈnel/ n personnel m.

perspiration /ˌpɜːspɪˈreɪʃn/ n (sweat) sueur f; (sweating) transpiration f. **perspire** vi transpirer.

persuade /pəˈsweɪd/ vt persuader (to de). **persuasion** n persuasion f. **persuasive** adj persuasif.

pertinent /ˈpɜːtɪnənt/ adj pertinent.

perturb /pəˈtɜːb/ vt troubler.

Peru /pəˈruː/ n Pérou m.

pervasive /pəˈveɪsɪv/ adj (smell) pénétrant; (feeling) envahissant.

perverse /pəˈvɜːs/ adj (desire) pervers; (refusal, attitude) illogique. **perversion** n perversion f.

pervert[1] /pəˈvɜːt/ vt (truth) travestir; (values) fausser; (justice) entraver.

pervert[2] /ˈpɜːvɜːt/ n pervers/-e m/f.

pessimist /ˈpesɪmɪst/ n pessimiste m/f. **pessimistic** adj pessimiste.

pest /pest/ n (insect) insecte m nuisible; (animal) animal m nuisible; (person Ⅰ) enquiquineur/-euse m/f Ⅰ.

pester /ˈpestə(r)/ vt harceler.

pet /pet/ n animal m de compagnie; (favourite) chouchou/-te m/f. ● adj (theory, charity) favori; ~ **hate** bête f noire; ~ **name** petit nom m. ● vt (pt petted) caresser; (spoil) chouchouter Ⅰ.

petal /ˈpetl/ n pétale m.

peter /ˈpiːtə(r)/ vi ~ **out** (conversation) tarir; (supplies) s'épuiser.

petite /pəˈtiːt/ adj (woman) menue.

petition /pəˈtɪʃn/ n pétition f. ● vt adresser une pétition à.

petrol /ˈpetrəl/ n essence f. ~ **bomb** n cocktail m molotov. ~ **station** n station-service f. ~ **tank** n réservoir *m* d'essence.

petticoat /ˈpetɪkəʊt/ *n* jupon *m*.

petty /ˈpetɪ/ *adj* (**-ier, -iest**) (minor) petit; (mean) mesquin; ~ **cash** petite caisse *f*.

pew /pjuː/ *n* banc *m* (d'église).

pharmacist /ˈfɑːməsɪst/ *n* pharmacien/-ne *m/f*. **pharmacy** *n* pharmacie *f*.

phase /feɪz/ *n* phase *f*. ● *vt* ~ **in/out** introduire/supprimer peu à peu.

PhD *abbr* (**Doctor of Philosophy**) doctorat *m*.

pheasant /ˈfeznt/ *n* faisan/-e *m/f*.

phenomenon /fəˈnɒmɪnən/ *n* (*pl* **-ena**) phénomène *m*.

phew /fjuː/ *interj* ouf.

philosopher /fɪˈlɒsəfə(r)/ *n* philosophe *mf*. **philosophical** *adj* philosophique; (resigned) philosophe. **philosophy** *n* philosophie *f*.

phlegm /flem/ *n* (Med) mucosité *f*.

phobia /ˈfəʊbɪə/ *n* phobie *f*.

phone /fəʊn/ *n* téléphone *m*; on the ~ au téléphone. ● *vt* (person) téléphoner à; ~ **England** téléphoner en Angleterre. ● *vi* téléphoner; ~ **back** rappeler. ~ **book** *n* annuaire *m*. ~ **booth**, ~ **box** *n* cabine *f* téléphonique. ~ **call** *n* coup *m* de fil 🔲. ~ **card** *n* télécarte *f*. ~**-in** *n* émission *f* à ligne ouverte. ~ **number** *n* numéro *m* de téléphone.

phonetic /fəˈnetɪk/ *adj* phonétique.

phoney /ˈfəʊnɪ/ *adj* (**-ier, -iest**) 🔲 faux. ● *n* (person) charlatan *m*; it's a ~ c'est un faux.

photocopier /ˈfəʊtəʊkɒpɪə(r)/ *n* photocopieuse *f*.

photocopy /ˈfəʊtəʊkɒpɪ/ *n* photocopie *f*. ● *vt* photocopier.

photograph /ˈfəʊtəɡrɑːf/ *n* photographie *f*. ● *vt* photographier. **photographer** *n* photographe *mf*.

phrase /freɪz/ *n* expression *f*; (idiom) locution *f*. ● *vt* exprimer, formuler. ~**-book** *n* guide *m* de conversation.

physical /ˈfɪzɪkl/ *adj* physique.

physicist /ˈfɪzɪsɪst/ *n* physicien/ -ne *m/f*.

physics /ˈfɪzɪks/ *n* physique *f*.

physiotherapist /fɪzɪəʊ ˈθerəpɪst/ *n* kinésithérapeute *mf*. **physiotherapy** *n* kinésithérapie *f*.

physique /fɪˈziːk/ *n* physique *m*.

piano /ˈpjænəʊ/ *n* piano *m*.

pick /pɪk/ *n* choix *m*; (best) meilleur/-e *m/f*; (tool) pioche *f*. ● *vt* choisir; (flower) cueillir; (lock) crocheter; ~ **a quarrel with** chercher querelle à; ~ **one's nose** se curer le nez. ◻ ~ **on** harceler; ~ **out** choisir; (identify) distinguer; ~ **up** *vt* ramasser; (sth fallen) relever; (weight) soulever; (habit, passenger, speed) prendre; (learn) apprendre; *vi* s'améliorer.

pickaxe /ˈpɪkæks/ *n* pioche *f*.

picket /ˈpɪkɪt/ *n* (striker) gréviste *mf*; (stake) piquet *m*; ~ **(line)** piquet *m* de grève. ● *vt* (*pt* **picketed**) installer un piquet de grève devant.

pickle /ˈpɪkl/ *n* conserves *fpl* au vinaigre; (gherkin) cornichon *m*. ● *vt* conserver dans du vinaigre.

pick-up /ˈpɪkʌp/ *n* (stylus-holder) lecteur *m*; (on guitar) capteur *m*; (collection) ramassage *m*; (improvement) reprise *f*.

picnic /ˈpɪknɪk/ *n* pique-nique *m*. ● *vi* (*pt* **picnicked**) pique-niquer.

pictorial /pɪkˈtɔːrɪəl/ *adj* (magazine) illustré; (record) graphique.

picture /ˈpɪktʃə(r)/ *n* image *f*; (painting) tableau *m*; (photograph) photo *f*; (drawing) dessin *m*; (film)

p

film *m*; (fig) description *f*: the ~s le cinéma. ● *vt* s'imaginer; be ~d (shown) être représenté.

picturesque /pɪktʃəˈresk/ *adj* pittoresque.

pie /paɪ/ *n* (sweet) tarte *f*; (savoury) tourte *f*.

piece /piːs/ *n* morceau *m*; (of string, ribbon) bout *m*; (of currency, machine) pièce *f*; a ~ of advice/furniture un conseil/meuble; go to ~s (fig) s'effondrer; take to ~s démonter.

pier /pɪə(r)/ *n* jetée *f*.

pierce /pɪəs/ *vt* percer.

pig /pɪg/ *n* porc *m*, cochon *m*.

pigeon /ˈpɪdʒɪn/ *n* pigeon *m*. ~-hole *n* casier *m*.

pig-headed *adj* entêté.

pigsty /ˈpɪgstaɪ/ *n* porcherie *f*.

pigtail /ˈpɪgteɪl/ *n* natte *f*.

pike /paɪk/ *n inv* (fish) brochet *m*.

pile /paɪl/ *n* (heap) tas *m*; (stack) pile *f*; (of carpet) poil *m*; ~s of 🗊 un tas de 🗊. ● *vt* ~ (up) entasser. ● *vi* ~ into s'engouffrer dans; ~ up (snow, leaves) s'entasser; (debts, work) s'accumuler. ~-up *n* (Auto) carambolage *m*.

pilgrim /ˈpɪlgrɪm/ *n* pèlerin *m*. **pilgrimage** *n* pèlerinage *m*.

pill /pɪl/ *n* pilule *f*.

pillar /ˈpɪlə(r)/ *n* pilier *m*. ~-box *n* boîte *f* aux lettres.

pillion /ˈpɪlɪən/ *n* siège *m* de passager; ride ~ monter en croupe.

pillow /ˈpɪləʊ/ *n* oreiller *m*. ~case *n* taie *f* d'oreiller.

pilot /ˈpaɪlət/ *n* pilote *m*. ● *adj* pilote. ● *vt* (*pt* piloted) piloter. ~-light *n* veilleuse *f*.

pimple /ˈpɪmpl/ *n* bouton *m*.

pin /pɪn/ *n* épingle *f*; (of plug) fiche *f*; (for wood, metal) goujon *m*; (in surgery) broche *f*; have ~s and needles avoir des fourmis. ● *vt* (*pt* pinned) épingler, attacher; (trap) coincer; ~ sb down (fig) forcer qn à se décider; ~ up accrocher.

pinafore /ˈpɪnəfɔː(r)/ *n* tablier *m*.

pincers /ˈpɪnsəz/ *npl* tenailles *fpl*.

pinch /pɪntʃ/ *vt* pincer; (steal 🗊) piquer. ● *vi* (be too tight) serrer. ● *n* (mark) pinçon *m*; (of salt) pincée *f*: at a ~ à la rigueur.

pine /paɪn/ *n* (tree) pin *m*. ● *vi* ~ (away) dépérir; ~ for languir après.

pineapple /ˈpaɪnæpl/ *n* ananas *m*.

pinecone /ˈpaɪnkəʊn/ *n* pomme *f* de pin.

pink /pɪŋk/ *adj* & *n* rose (*m*).

pinpoint /ˈpɪnpɔɪnt/ *vt* (problem, cause, location) indiquer; (time) déterminer.

pint /paɪnt/ *n* pinte *f* (GB = 0.57 litre; US = 0.47 litre).

pin-up /ˈpɪnʌp/ *n* 🗊 pin-up *f inv*. 🗊

pioneer /paɪəˈnɪə(r)/ *n* pionnier *m*. ● *vt* ~ the use of être le premier à utiliser.

pious /ˈpaɪəs/ *adj* pieux.

pip /pɪp/ *n* (seed) pépin *m*; (sound) top *m*.

pipe /paɪp/ *n* tuyau *m*; (to smoke) pipe *f*; (Mus) chalumeau *m*; ~s cornemuse *f*. ● *vt* transporter par tuyau. □ ~ down se taire.

pipeline /ˈpaɪplaɪn/ *n* oléoduc *m*; in the ~ en cours.

piping /ˈpaɪpɪŋ/ *n* tuyauterie *f*; ~ hot fumant.

pirate /ˈpaɪərət/ *n* pirate *m*. ● *vt* pirater.

Pisces /ˈpaɪsiːz/ *n* Poissons *mpl*.

pistol /ˈpɪstl/ *n* pistolet *m*.

pit /pɪt/ *n* fosse *f*; (mine) puits *m*; (quarry) carrière *f*; (for orchestra) fosse f; (of stomach) creux m; (of cherry: US) noyau m. ● vt (pt **pitted**) marquer; (fig) opposer; ~ oneself against se mesurer à.

pitch /pɪtʃ/ n (Sport) terrain m; (of voice, note) hauteur f; (degree) degré m; (Mus) ton m; (tar) brai m. ● vt jeter; (tent) planter. ● vi (ship) tanguer. □ ~ **in** 🔟 contribuer.

pitfall /ˈpɪtfɔːl/ n écueil m.

pitiful /ˈpɪtɪfl/ adj pitoyable. **pitiless** adj impitoyable.

pit stop n arrêt m mécanique.

pittance /ˈpɪtns/ n earn a ~ gagner trois fois rien.

pity /ˈpɪtɪ/ n pitié f; (regrettable fact) dommage m; take ~ on avoir pitié de; what a ~! quel dommage! ● vt avoir pitié de.

pivot /ˈpɪvət/ n pivot m. ● vi (pt **pivoted**) pivoter.

placard /ˈplækɑːd/ n affiche f.

place /pleɪs/ n endroit m, lieu m; (house) maison f; (seat, rank) place f; at or to my ~ chez moi; change ~s changer de place; in the first ~ d'abord; out of ~ déplacé; take ~ avoir lieu. ● vt placer; (order) passer; (remember) situer; be ~d (in race) se placer. □ ~**mat** n set m.

placid /ˈplæsɪd/ adj placide.

plagiarism /ˈpleɪdʒərɪzəm/ n plagiat m. **plagiarize** vt/i plagier.

plague /pleɪg/ n (bubonic) peste f; (epidemic) épidémie f; (of ants, locusts) invasion f. ● vt harceler.

plaice /pleɪs/ n inv carrelet m.

plain /pleɪn/ adj (obvious) clair; (candid) franc; (simple) simple; (not pretty) sans beauté; (not patterned) uni; ~ chocolate chocolat m noir; in ~ clothes en civil. ● adv franchement. ● n plaine f. **plainly** adv clairement; franchement; simplement.

plaintiff /ˈpleɪntɪf/ n (Jur)

plaignant/-e m/f.

plaintive /ˈpleɪntɪv/ adj plaintif.

plait /plæt/ vt tresser. ● n natte f.

plan /plæn/ n projet m, plan m; (diagram) plan m. ● vt (pt **planned**) projeter (to do de faire); (timetable, day) organiser; (economy, work) planifier. ● vi prévoir; ~ on s'attendre à.

plane /pleɪn/ n (level) plan m; (aeroplane) avion m; (tool) rabot m. ● adj plan. ● vt raboter.

planet /ˈplænɪt/ n planète f.

plank /plæŋk/ n planche f.

planning /ˈplænɪŋ/ n (of economy, work) planification f; (of holiday, party) organisation f; (of town) urbanisme m; family ~ planning m familial; ~ permission permis m de construire.

plant /plɑːnt/ n plante f; (Tech) matériel m; (factory) usine f. ● vt planter; (bomb) placer.

plaster /ˈplɑːstə(r)/ n plâtre m; (adhesive) sparadrap m. ● vt plâtrer; (cover) couvrir (with de).

plastic /ˈplæstɪk/ adj en plastique; (art, substance) plastique; ~ surgery chirurgie f esthétique. ● n plastique m.

plate /pleɪt/ n assiette f; (of metal) plaque f; (silverware) argenterie f; (in book) gravure f. ● vt (metal) plaquer.

plateau /ˈplætəʊ/ n (pl ~x) plateau m; (fig) palier m.

platform /ˈplætfɔːm/ n (stage) estrade f; (for speaking) tribune f; (Rail) quai m; (Pol) plate-forme f.

platoon /pləˈtuːn/ n (Mil) section f.

play /pleɪ/ vt/i jouer; (instrument) jouer de; (record) mettre; (game) jouer à; (opponent) jouer contre; (match) disputer; ~ safe ne pas prendre de risques. ● n jeu m;

p

(Theat) pièce f. □ ~ **down** minimiser; **~on** (fears) exploiter; **~ up** ⓘ commencer à faire des siennes ⓘ; ~ **up sth** mettre l'accent sur qch.

playful /'pleɪfl/ adj (remark) taquin; (child) joueur.

play: ~ground n cour f de récréation. **~group**, **~school** n garderie f.

playing /'pleɪɪŋ/ n (Sport) jeu m; (Theat) interprétation f. **~-card** n carte f à jouer. **~-field** n terrain m de sport.

play: ~pen n parc m (pour bébé). **~wright** n auteur m dramatique.

plc abbr (**public limited company**) SA.

plea /pliː/ n (for mercy, tolerance) appel m; (for food, money) demande f; (reason) excuse f; **make a ~ of guilty** plaider coupable.

plead /pliːd/ vt/i supplier; (Jur) plaider.

pleasant /'plezənt/ adj agréable.

please /pliːz/ vt/i plaire (à), faire plaisir (à); ~ **oneself, do as one ~s** faire ce qu'on veut. ● adv s'il vous ou te plaît. **pleased** adj content (with de). **pleasing** adj agréable.

pleasure /'pleʒə(r)/ n plaisir m; **with ~** avec plaisir; **my ~** je vous en prie.

pleat /pliːt/ n pli m. ● vt plisser.

pledge /pledʒ/ n (token) gage m; (promise) promesse f. ● vt promettre; (pawn) mettre en gage.

plentiful /'plentɪfl/ adj abondant.

plenty /'plentɪ/ n abondance f; **~ (of)** (a great deal) beaucoup (de); (enough) assez (de).

pliers /'plaɪəz/ npl pinces fpl.

plight /plaɪt/ n détresse f.

plinth /plɪnθ/ n socle m.

plod /plɒd/ vi (pt **plodded**) avancer péniblement.

plonk /plɒŋk/ n ⓘ pinard m ⓘ.

plot /plɒt/ n (conspiracy) complot m; (of novel) intrigue f; ~ **(of land)** terrain m. ● vt/i (pt **plotted**) (plan) comploter; (mark out) tracer.

plough /plaʊ/ n charrue f. ● vt/i labourer. □ ~ **back** réinvestir; ~ **through** avancer péniblement dans.

plow /plaʊ/ n & vt/i (US) ➜PLOUGH.

ploy /plɔɪ/ n stratagème m.

pluck /plʌk/ vt (flower, fruit) cueillir; (bird) plumer; (eyebrows) épiler; (strings: Mus) pincer; ~ **up courage** prendre son courage à deux mains. **plucky** adj courageux.

plug /plʌg/ n (for sink) bonde f; (Electr) fiche f, prise f. ● vt (pt **plugged**) (hole) boucher; (publicize) ⓘ faire du battage autour de. □ ~ **in** brancher. **~-hole** n bonde f.

plum /plʌm/ n prune f; ~ **pudding** (plum-)pudding m.

plumber /'plʌmə(r)/ n plombier m.

plume /pluːm/ n (of feathers) panache m.

plummet /'plʌmɪt/ vi tomber, plonger.

plump /plʌmp/ adj potelé, dodu.

plunge /plʌndʒ/ vt/i (dive, thrust) plonger; (fall) tomber. ● n plongeon m; (fall) chute f; **take the ~** se jeter à l'eau. **plunger** n (for sink) ventouse f.

plural /'plʊərəl/ adj pluriel; (noun) au pluriel; (ending) du pluriel. ● n pluriel m.

plus /plʌs/ prep plus; **ten ~** plus de dix. ● adj (Electr & fig) positif. ● n signe m plus; (fig) atout m.

ply /plaɪ/ vt (tool) manier; (trade) exercer. ● vi faire la navette; ~ **sb with drink** offrir continuellement à boire à qn.

plywood /ˈplaɪwʊd/ n contreplaqué m.

p.m. /piːˈem/ adv de l'après-midi ou du soir.

pneumatic drill /njuːˈmætɪk drɪl/ n marteaupiqueur m.

pneumonia /njuːˈməʊnɪə/ n pneumonie f.

PO abbr ►POST OFFICE.

poach /pəʊtʃ/ vt/i (game) braconner; (staff) débaucher; (Culin) pocher.

PO Box n boîte f postale.

pocket /ˈpɒkɪt/ n poche f; be out of ~ avoir perdu de l'argent. ● adj de poche. ● vt empocher. ~book n (notebook) carnet m; (wallet: US) portefeuille m; (handbag: US) sac m à main. ~money n argent m de poche.

pod /pɒd/ n (peas) cosse f; (vanilla) gousse f.

podgy /ˈpɒdʒɪ/ adj (-ier, -iest) dodu.

poem /ˈpəʊɪm/ n poème m. **poet** n poète m. **poetic** adj poétique. **poetry** n poésie f.

point /pɔɪnt/ n (position) point m; (tip) pointe f; (decimal point) virgule f; (remark) remarque f; good ~s qualités fpl; on the ~ of sur le point de; ~ in time moment m; ~ of view point m de vue; to the ~ pertinent; what is the ~? à quoi bon? ● vt (aim) braquer; (show) indiquer; ~ out signaler. ● vi indiquer du doigt; ~ out that, make the ~ that faire remarquer que. ~blank adj & adv à bout portant.

pointed /ˈpɔɪntɪd/ adj (sharp) pointu; (window) en pointe; (remark) lourd de sens.

pointless /ˈpɔɪntlɪs/ adj inutile.

poise /pɔɪz/ n (confidence) assurance f; (physical elegance)

poison /ˈpɔɪzn/ n poison m. ● vt empoisonner. **poisonous** adj (substance) toxique; (plant) vénéneux; (snake) venimeux.

poke /pəʊk/ vt/i (push) pousser; (fire) (thrust) fourrer; ~ fun at se moquer de. ● n (petit) coup m. □ ~out (head) sortir.

poker /ˈpəʊkə(r)/ n (for fire) tisonnier m; (cards) poker m.

Poland /ˈpəʊlənd/ n Pologne f.

polar /ˈpəʊlə(r)/ adj polaire.

pole /pəʊl/ n (stick) perche f; (for flag) mât m; (Geog) pôle m.

Pole /pəʊl/ n Polonais/-e m/f.

pole-vault n saut m à la perche.

police /pəˈliːs/ n (la) police f. ● vt faire la police dans. ~ **constable** n agent m de police. ~**man** n (pl -**men**) agent m de police. ~ **station** n commissariat m de police. ~**woman** n (pl -**women**) femme-agent f.

policy /ˈpɒləsɪ/ n politique f; (insurance) police f (d'assurance).

polish /ˈpɒlɪʃ/ vt polir; (shoes, floor) cirer. ● n (for shoes) cirage m; (for floor) encaustique f; (for nails) vernis m; (shine) poli m; (fig) raffinement m. □ ~ **off** finir en vitesse; ~ **up** (language) perfectionner.

Polish /ˈpəʊlɪʃ/ adj polonais. ● n (Ling) polonais m.

polished /ˈpɒlɪʃt/ adj raffiné.

polite /pəˈlaɪt/ adj poli.

political /pəˈlɪtɪkl/ adj politique.

politician /pɒlɪˈtɪʃn/ n homme m politique, femme f politique.

politics /ˈpɒlətɪks/ n politique f.

poll /pəʊl/ n (vote casting) scrutin m; (survey) sondage m; go to the ~s aller aux urnes. ● vt (votes) obtenir.

P

pollen /'pɒlən/ n pollen m.

polling booth n isoloir m.

polling station n bureau m de vote.

pollution /pə'luːʃn/ n pollution f.

polo /'pəʊləʊ/ n polo m. ~ **neck** n col m roulé.

pomegranate /'pɒmɪgrænɪt/ n grenade f.

pomp /pɒmp/ n pompe f.

pompous /'pɒmpəs/ adj pompeux.

pond /pɒnd/ n étang m; (artificial) bassin m; (stagnant) mare f.

ponder /'pɒndə(r)/ vt/i réfléchir (à), méditer (sur).

pong /pɒŋ/ n (stink 🔲) puanteur f. ● vi 🔲 puer.

pony /'pəʊnɪ/ n poney m. ~**tail** n queue f de cheval.

poodle /'puːdl/ n caniche f.

pool /puːl/ n (puddle) flaque f; (pond) étang m; (of blood) mare f; (for swimming) piscine f; (fund) fonds m commun; (of ideas) réservoir m; (snooker) billard m américain; ~s pari m mutuel sur le football. ● vt mettre en commun.

poor /pɔː(r)/ adj (not wealthy) pauvre; (not good) médiocre, mauvais.

poorly /'pɔːlɪ/ adj malade. ● adv mal.

pop /pɒp/ n (noise) pan m; (music) pop m. ● adj pop inv. ● vt/i (pp **popped**) (burst) crever; (put) mettre; ~ **in/out/off** entrer/sortir/partir. ☐ ~ **up** surgir. ~-**up** fenêtre f pop-up.

pope /pəʊp/ n pape m.

poppy /'pɒpɪ/ n pavot m; (wild) coquelicot m.

popular /'pɒpjʊlə(r)/ adj populaire; (in fashion) en vogue; be ~ **with** plaire à.

population /pɒpjʊ'leɪʃn/ n population f.

porcelain /'pɔːsəlɪn/ n porcelaine f.

porcupine /'pɔːkjʊpaɪn/ n porc-épic m.

pork /pɔːk/ n porc m.

pornography /pɔː'nɒgrəfɪ/ n pornographie f.

port /pɔːt/ n (harbour) port m; (left: Naut) bâbord m; ~ **of call** escale f; (wine) porto m.

portable /'pɔːtəbl/ adj portable.

porter /'pɔːtə(r)/ n (carrier) porteur m; (doorkeeper) portier m.

portfolio /pɔːt'fəʊlɪəʊ/ n (Pol, Comm) portefeuille m.

portion /'pɔːʃn/ n (at meal) portion f; (part) partie f.

portrait /'pɔːtreɪt/ n portrait m.

portray /pɔː'treɪ/ vt représenter.

Portugal /'pɔːtʃʊgl/ n Portugal m.

Portuguese /pɔːtʃʊ'giːz/ n (Ling) portugais m; (person) Portugais/-e m/f. ● adj portugais.

pose /pəʊz/ vt/i poser; ~ **as** (expert) se poser en. ● n pose f.

poser /'pəʊzə(r)/ n (person) frimeur/-euse m/f; (puzzle) colle f.

posh /pɒʃ/ adj 🔲 chic inv.

position /pə'zɪʃn/ n position f; (job, state) situation f. ● vt placer.

positive /'pɒzətɪv/ adj positif; (sure) sûr, certain; (real) réel, vrai.

possess /pə'zes/ vt posséder.

possession /pə'zeʃn/ n possession f; take ~ **of** prendre possession de.

possessive /pə'zesɪv/ adj possessif.

possible /'pɒsəbl/ adj possible.

possibly /'pɒsəblɪ/ adv peut-être; if I ~ **can** si cela m'est possible; I cannot ~ **leave** il m'est impossible de partir.

post /pəʊst/ n (pole) poteau m;

(station, job) poste m; (mail service) poste f; (letters) courrier m. ● adj postal. ● vt (letter) poster; keep ~ed tenir au courant; ~ (up) (a notice) afficher; (appoint) affecter.

postage /ˈpəʊstɪdʒ/ n affranchissement m; tarif m postal.

postal /ˈpəʊstl/ adj postal. ~ **order** n mandat m.

post: ~**box** n boîte f aux lettres. ~**card** n carte f postale. ~ **code** n code m postal.

poster /ˈpəʊstə(r)/ n (for information) affiche f; (for decoration) poster m.

postgraduate /pəʊstˈɡrædʒʊət/ n étudiant/-e m/f de troisième cycle.

posthumous /ˈpɒstjʊməs/ adj posthume.

post: ~**man** n (pl -**men**) facteur m. ~**mark** n cachet m de la poste.

post-mortem /pəʊstˈmɔːtəm/ n autopsie f.

post office n poste f.

postpone /pəˈspəʊn/ vt remettre.

postscript /ˈpəʊsskrɪpt/ n (to letter) postscriptum m inv.

posture /ˈpɒstʃə(r)/ n posture f. ● vi prendre des poses.

pot /pɒt/ n pot m; (drug 🆇) hasch m; go to ~ 🆇 aller à la ruine; take ~ luck tenter sa chance. ● vt (plants) mettre en pot.

potato /pəˈteɪtəʊ/ n (pl ~**es**) pomme f de terre.

pot-belly n bedaine f.

potential /pəˈtenʃl/ adj & n potentiel (m).

pothole /ˈpɒthəʊl/ n (in rock) caverne f; (in road) nid m de poule. **pot-holing** n spéléologie f.

potter /ˈpɒtə(r)/ n potier m. ● vi bricoler. **pottery** n (art) poterie f; (objects) poteries fpl.

potty /ˈpɒtɪ/ adj -**ier**, -**iest** (crazy 🆇) toqué. ● n pot m.

pouch /paʊtʃ/ n poche f; (for tobacco) blague f.

poultry /ˈpəʊltrɪ/ n volailles fpl.

pounce /paʊns/ vi bondir (on sur). ● n bond m.

pound /paʊnd/ n (weight) livre f (= 454 g); (money) livre f; (for dogs, cars) fourrière f. ● vt (crush) piler; (bombard) pilonner. ● vi frapper fort; (of heart) battre fort; (walk) marcher à pas lourds.

pour /pɔː(r)/ vt verser. ● vi couler, ruisseler (from de); (rain) pleuvoir à torrents. □ ~ **in/out** (people) arriver/sortir en masse; ~ **off** or **out** vider. **pouring rain** n pluie f torrentielle.

pout /paʊt/ vi faire la moue.

poverty /ˈpɒvətɪ/ n misère f, pauvreté f.

powder /ˈpaʊdə(r)/ n poudre f. ● vt poudrer.

power /ˈpaʊə(r)/ n (strength) puissance f; (control) pouvoir m; (energy) énergie f; (Electr) courant m. ● vt (engine) faire marcher; (plane) propulser; ~ed by (engine) propulsé par; (generator) alimenté par. ~ **cut** coupure f de courant.

powerful /ˈpaʊəfl/ adj puissant.

powerless /ˈpaʊəlɪs/ adj impuissant.

power: ~**point** n prise f de courant. ~-**station** n centrale f électrique.

practical /ˈpræktɪkl/ adj pratique. ~ **joke** n farce f.

practice /ˈpræktɪs/ n (procedure) pratique f; (of profession) exercice m; (Sport) entraînement m; **in** ~ (in fact) en pratique; (well-trained) en forme; **out of** ~ rouillé; **put into** ~ mettre en pratique.

practise /'præktɪs/ vt/i (musician, typist) s'exercer (à); (Sport) s'entraîner (à); (put into practice) pratiquer; (profession) exercer.

practitioner /præk'tɪʃənə(r)/ n praticien/-ienne m/f; dental ~ dentiste mf.

praise /preɪz/ vt faire l'éloge de; (God) louer. ● n éloges mpl, louanges fpl.

pram /præm/ n landau m.

prance /prɑːns/ vi caracoler.

prawn /prɔːn/ n crevette f rose.

pray /preɪ/ vi prier. **prayer** n prière f.

preach /priːtʃ/ vt/i prêcher; ~ at or to prêcher.

precarious /prɪ'keərɪəs/ adj précaire.

precaution /prɪ'kɔːʃn/ n précaution f.

precede /prɪ'siːd/ vt précéder.

precedence /'presɪdəns/ n (in importance) priorité f; (in rank) préséance f.

precedent /'presɪdənt/ n précédent m.

precinct /'priːsɪŋkt/ n quartier m commerçant; (pedestrian area) zone f piétonne; (district: US) circonscription f.

precious /'preʃəs/ adj précieux.

precipitate /prɪ'sɪpɪteɪt/ vt (person, event, chemical) précipiter.

précis /'preɪsiː/ n résumé m.

precise /prɪ'saɪs/ adj précis; (careful) méticuleux. **precision** n précision f.

precocious /prɪ'kəʊʃəs/ adj précoce.

preconceived /priːkən'siːvd/ adj préconçu.

predator /'predətə(r)/ n prédateur m.

predicament /prɪ'dɪkəmənt/ n situation f difficile.

predict /prɪ'dɪkt/ vt prédire. **predictable** adj prévisible. **prediction** n prédiction f.

predispose /priːdɪ'spəʊz/ vt prédisposer (to do à faire).

predominant /prɪ'dɒmɪnənt/ adj prédominant.

pre-empt /priː'empt/ vt (anticipate) anticiper; (person) devancer.

preface /'prefɪs/ n (to book) préface f; (to speech) préambule m.

prefect /'priːfekt/ n (pupil) élève m/f chargé/-e de la discipline; (official) préfet m.

prefer /prɪ'fɜː(r)/ vt (pt preferred) préférer (to do faire). **preferably** adv de préférence. **preference** n préférence f. **preferential** adj préférentiel.

prefix /'priːfɪks/ n préfixe m.

pregnancy /'pregnənsɪ/ n grossesse f. **pregnant** adj (woman) enceinte; (animal) pleine; (pause) éloquent.

prehistoric /priːhɪ'stɒrɪk/ adj préhistorique.

prejudge /priː'dʒʌdʒ/ vt (issue) préjuger de; (person) juger d'avance.

prejudice /'predʒʊdɪs/ n préjugé(s) m(pl); (harm) préjudice m. ● vt (claim) porter préjudice à; (person) léser. **prejudiced** adj partial; (person) qui a des préjugés.

premature /'premətjʊə(r)/ adj prématuré.

premeditated /priː'medɪteɪtɪd/ adj prémédité.

premises /'premɪsɪz/ npl locaux mpl; on the ~ sur les lieux.

premium /'priːmɪəm/ n (insurance) prime f; be at a ~ être précieux.

preoccupied /priːˈɒkjʊpaɪd/ adj préoccupé.

preparation /prepəˈreɪʃn/ n préparation f; ~s préparatifs mpl.

preparatory /prɪˈpærətrɪ/ adj préparatoire. ~ **school** n école f primaire privée; (US) école f secondaire privée.

prepare /prɪˈpeə(r)/ vt/i (se) préparer (for à); be ~d for (expect) s'attendre à; ~d to prêt à.

preposition /prepəˈzɪʃn/ n préposition f.

preposterous /prɪˈpɒstərəs/ adj absurde, ridicule.

prep school n →PREPARATORY SCHOOL.

prerequisite /priːˈrekwɪzɪt/ n condition f préalable.

prescribe /prɪˈskraɪb/ vt prescrire.

prescription /prɪˈskrɪpʃn/ n (Med) ordonnance f.

presence /ˈprezns/ n présence f; ~ of mind présence f d'esprit.

present¹ /ˈpreznt/ adj présent. ● n présent m; (gift) cadeau m; at ~ à présent; for the ~ pour le moment.

present² /prɪˈzent/ vt présenter; (film, concert) donner; ~ sb with offrir à qn. **presentation** n présentation f. **presenter** n présentateur/-trice m/f.

preservation /prezəˈveɪʃn/ n (of food) conservation f; (of wildlife) préservation f.

preservative /prɪˈzɜːvətɪv/ n (Culin) agent m de conservation.

preserve /prɪˈzɜːv/ vt préserver; (Culin) conserver. ● n réserve f; (fig) domaine m; (jam) confiture f.

presidency /ˈprezɪdənsɪ/ n présidence f.

president /ˈprezɪdənt/ n président/-e m/f.

press /pres/ vt/i (button) appuyer (sur); (squeeze) presser; (iron) repasser; (pursue) poursuivre; be ~ed for (time) manquer de; ~ for sth faire pression pour avoir qch; ~ sb to do sth pousser qn à faire qch; ~ on continuer (with sth qch). ● n (newspapers, machine) presse f; (for wine) pressoir m. ~ **cutting** n coupure f de presse.

pressing /ˈpresɪŋ/ adj pressant.

press: ~ **release** n communiqué m de presse. ~**stud** n bouton-pression m. ~**up** n pompe f.

pressure /ˈpreʃə(r)/ n pression f. ● vt faire pression sur. ~**cooker** n cocotte-minute f. ~ **group** n groupe m de pression.

pressurize /ˈpreʃəraɪz/ vt (cabin) pressuriser; (person) faire pression sur.

prestige /preˈstiːʒ/ n prestige m.

presumably /prɪˈzjuːməblɪ/ adv vraisemblablement.

presume /prɪˈzjuːm/ vt (suppose) présumer.

pretence, (US) **pretense** /prɪˈtens/ n feinte f, simulation f; (claim) prétention f; (pretext) prétexte m.

pretend /prɪˈtend/ vt/i faire semblant (to do de faire); ~ to (lay claim to) prétendre à.

pretentious /prɪˈtenʃəs/ adj prétentieux.

pretext /ˈpriːtekst/ n prétexte m.

pretty /ˈprɪtɪ/ adj (-ier, -iest) joli. ● adv assez; ~ much presque.

prevail /prɪˈveɪl/ vi (be usual) prédominer; (win) prévaloir; ~ on persuader (to do de faire). **prevailing** adj actuel; (wind) dominant.

prevalent /ˈprevələnt/ adj répandu.

prevent /prɪˈvent/ vt empêcher (from doing de faire). **prevention**

P

n prévention *f*. **preventive** *adj* préventif.

preview /'priːvjuː/ *n* avant-première *f*; (fig) aperçu *m*.

previous /'priːviəs/ *adj* précédent, antérieur; ~ to avant. **previously** *adv* auparavant.

prey /preɪ/ *n* proie *f*; bird of ~ rapace *m*. ● *vi* to ~ on faire sa proie de; (worry) préoccuper.

price /praɪs/ *n* prix *m*. ● *vt* fixer le prix de. **priceless** *adj* inestimable; (amusing) impayable 🄸.

prick /prɪk/ *vt* (with pin) piquer; ~ up one's ears dresser l'oreille. ● *n* piqûre *f*.

prickle /'prɪkl/ *n* piquant *m*.

pride /praɪd/ *n* orgueil *m*; (satisfaction) fierté *f*; ~ of place place *f* d'honneur. ● *vpr* ~ oneself on s'enorgueillir de.

priest /priːst/ *n* prêtre *m*.

prim /prɪm/ *adj* (**primmer**, **primmest**) guindé, méticuleux.

primarily /'praɪmərəli/ *adv* essentiellement.

primary /'praɪməri/ *adj* (school, elections) primaire; (chief, basic) premier, fondamental. ● *n* (Pol: US) primaire *f*.

prime /praɪm/ *adj* principal, premier; (first-rate) excellent. ● *vt* (pump, gun) amorcer; (surface) apprêter. **P~ Minister** *n* Premier Ministre *m*.

primitive /'prɪmɪtɪv/ *adj* primitif.

primrose /'prɪmrəʊz/ *n* primevère *f* (jaune).

prince /prɪns/ *n* prince *m*. **princess** *n* princesse *f*.

principal /'prɪnsəpl/ *adj* principal. ● *n* (of school) directeur/-trice *m/f*.

principle /'prɪnsəpl/ *n* principe *m*; in/on ~ en/par principe.

print /prɪnt/ *vt* imprimer; (write in

capitals) écrire en majuscules; ~ed matter imprimés *mpl*. ● *n* (of foot) empreinte *f*; (letters) caractères *mpl*; (photograph) épreuve *f*; (engraving) gravure *f*; in ~ disponible. out-of-~ épuisé. **printer** *n* (person) imprimeur *m*; (Comput) imprimante *f*.

prion /'priːɒn/ *n* prion *m*.

prior /'praɪə(r)/ *adj* précédent. ● *n* (Relig) prieur *m*. ~ **to** *prep* avant (de).

priority /praɪ'ɒrɪti/ *n* priorité *f*; take ~ avoir la priorité (over sur).

prise /praɪz/ *vt* forcer; ~ open ouvrir en forçant.

prison /'prɪzn/ *n* prison *f*. **prisoner** *n* prisonnier/-ière *m/f*. ~ **officer** *n* gardien/-ne *m/f* de prison.

pristine /'prɪstiːn/ *adj* be in ~ condition être comme neuf.

privacy /'prɪvəsi/ *n* intimité *f*, solitude *f*.

private /'praɪvɪt/ *adj* privé; (confidential) personnel; (lessons, house) particulier; (ceremony) intime; in ~ en privé; (of ceremony) dans l'intimité. ● *n* (soldier) simple soldat *m*. **privately** *adv* en privé; dans l'intimité; (inwardly) intérieurement.

privilege /'prɪvɪlɪdʒ/ *n* privilège *m*. **privileged** *adj* privilégié; be ~d to avoir le privilège de.

prize /praɪz/ *n* prix *m*. ● *vt* (value) priser.

pro /prəʊ/ *n* the ~s and cons le pour et le contre.

probable /'prɒbəbl/ *adj* probable. **probably** *adv* probablement.

probation /prə'beɪʃn/ *n* (testing) essai *m*; (Jur) liberté *f* surveillée.

probe /prəʊb/ *n* (device) sonde *f*; (fig) enquête *f*. ● *vt* sonder. ● *vi* ~ into sonder.

problem /'prɒbləm/ *n* problème *m*. ● *adj* difficile. **problematic** *adj* problématique.

procedure /prəˈsiːdʒə(r)/ n procédure f; (way of doing sth) démarche f à suivre.

proceed /prəˈsiːd/ vi (go) aller, avancer; (pass) passer (to à); (act) procéder; ~ (with) continuer; ~ to do se mettre à faire.

proceedings /prəˈsiːdɪŋz/ npl (discussions) débats mpl; (meeting) réunion f; (report) actes mpl; (Jur) poursuites fpl.

proceeds /ˈprəʊsiːdz/ npl (profits) produit m, bénéfices mpl.

process /ˈprəʊses/ n processus m; (method) procédé m; in ~ en cours; in the ~ of doing en train de faire. ~or n (Culin) robot m (ménager); (Comput) unité f centrale. ● vt (material, data) traiter.

procession /prəˈseʃn/ n défilé m.

procrastinate /prəʊˈkræstɪneɪt/ vi différer, tergiverser.

procure /prəˈkjʊə(r)/ vt obtenir.

prod /prɒd/ vt/i (pt prodded) pousser doucement. ● n petit coup m.

prodigy /ˈprɒdɪdʒɪ/ n prodige m.

produce[1] /ˈprɒdjuːs/ n produits mpl.

produce[2] /prəˈdjuːs/ vt/i produire; (bring out) sortir; (show) présenter; (cause) provoquer; (Theat, TV), mettre en scène; (radio) réaliser; (cinema) produire. **producer** n metteur m en scène; réalisateur m; producteur m.

product /ˈprɒdʌkt/ n produit m.

production /prəˈdʌkʃn/ n production f; (Theat, TV) mise f en scène; (radio) réalisation f.

productive /prəˈdʌktɪv/ adj productif. **productivity** n productivité f.

profession /prəˈfeʃn/ n profession f.

professional /prəˈfeʃənl/ adj fessionnel; (of high quality) de professionnel; (person) qui exerce une profession libérale. ● n professionnel/-le m/f.

professor /prəˈfesə(r)/ n professeur m (titulaire d'une chaire).

proficient /prəˈfɪʃnt/ adj compétent.

profile /ˈprəʊfaɪl/ n (of face) profil m; (of body, mountain) silhouette f; (by journalist) portrait m.

profit /ˈprɒfɪt/ n profit m, bénéfice m. ● vi ~ by tirer profit de. **profitable** adj rentable.

profound /prəˈfaʊnd/ adj profond.

profusely /prəˈfjuːslɪ/ adv (bleed) abondamment; (apologize) avec effusion. **profusion** n profusion f.

program /ˈprəʊɡræm/ n (US) ➡PROGRAMME; (computer) ~ programme m. ● vt (pt programmed) programmer.

programme /ˈprəʊɡræm/ n programme m; (broadcast) émission f.

programmer /ˈprəʊɡræmə(r)/ n programmeur/-euse m/f.

programming /ˈprəʊɡræmɪŋ/ n (Comput) programmation f.

progress[1] /ˈprəʊɡres/ n progrès m (pl) (in ~) en cours; make ~ faire des progrès; ~ report compterendu m.

progress[2] /prəˈɡres/ vi (advance, improve) progresser.

progressive /prəˈɡresɪv/ adj progressif; (reforming) progressiste.

prohibit /prəˈhɪbɪt/ vt interdire (sb from doing à qn de faire).

project[1] /prəˈdʒekt/ vt projeter. ● vi (jut out) être en saillie.

project[2] /ˈprɒdʒekt/ n (plan) projet m; (undertaking) entreprise f; (School) dossier m.

P

projection /prəˈdʒekʃn/ n projection f ; saillie f ; (estimate) prévision f.

projector /prəˈdʒektə(r)/ n projecteur m.

proliferate /prəˈlɪfəreɪt/ vi proliférer.

prolong /prəˈlɒŋ/ vt prolonger.

prominent /ˈprɒmɪnənt/ adj (projecting) proéminent; (conspicuous) bien en vue; (fig) important.

promiscuous /prəˈmɪskjʊəs/ adj de mœurs faciles.

promise /ˈprɒmɪs/ n promesse f. ● vt/i promettre. **promising** adj (person) qui promet.

promote /prəˈməʊt/ vt promouvoir; (advertise) faire la promotion de. **promotion** n promotion f.

prompt /prɒmpt/ adj rapide; (punctual) à l'heure, ponctuel. ● adv (on the dot) pile. ● vt inciter; (cause) provoquer; (Theat) souffler à. ● n (Comput) message m guide-opérateur. **prompter** n souffleur/-euse m/f. **promptly** adv rapidement; ponctuellement.

Proms Festival annuel de musique classique qui se déroule au Royal Albert Hall à Londres. Proms est l'abréviation de promenade concerts, car une partie des auditeurs reste debout. Aux États-Unis, prom (night) est un bal très habillé qui marque la fin des études secondaires.

prone /prəʊn/ adj ~ to sujet à.

pronoun /ˈprəʊnaʊn/ n pronom m.

pronounce /prəˈnaʊns/ vt prononcer. **pronunciation** n prononciation f.

proof /pruːf/ n (evidence) preuve f ; (test, trial copy) épreuve f ; (of alcohol) teneur f en alcool. ● adj ~ against en à l'épreuve de.

prop /prɒp/ n support m; (Theat) accessoire m. ● vt (pt **propped**) ~ (up) (support) étayer; (lean) appuyer.

propaganda /ˌprɒpəˈɡændə/ n propagande f.

propel /prəˈpel/ vt (pt **propelled**) (vehicle, ship) propulser; (person) pousser.

propeller /prəˈpelə(r)/ n hélice f.

proper /ˈprɒpə(r)/ adj correct, bon; (adequate) convenable; (real) vrai; (thorough 🔢) parfait. **properly** adv correctement, comme il faut; (adequately) convenablement.

proper noun n nom m propre.

property /ˈprɒpətɪ/ n (house) propriété f ; (things owned) biens mpl, propriété f. ● adj immobilier, foncier.

prophecy /ˈprɒfəsɪ/ n prophétie f.

prophet /ˈprɒfɪt/ n prophète m.

proportion /prəˈpɔːʃn/ n (ratio, dimension) proportion f ; (amount) partie f.

proposal /prəˈpəʊzl/ n proposition f ; (of marriage) demande f en mariage.

propose /prəˈpəʊz/ vt proposer. ● vi faire une demande en mariage; ~ to do se proposer de faire.

proposition /ˌprɒpəˈzɪʃn/ n proposition f ; (matter 🔢) affaire f. ● vt 🔢 faire des propositions malhonnêtes à.

proprietor /prəˈpraɪətə(r)/ n propriétaire mf.

propriety /prəˈpraɪətɪ/ n (correct behaviour) bienséance f.

prose /prəʊz/ n prose f ; (translation) thème m.

prosecute /ˈprɒsɪkjuːt/ vt poursuivre en justice.

prosecution n poursuites fpl. **prosecutor** n procureur m.

prospect¹ /ˈprɒspekt/ n (outlook) perspective f; (chance) espoir m.

prospect² /prəˈspekt/ vt/i prospecter.

prospective /prəˈspektɪv/ adj (future) futur; (possible) éventuel.

prospectus /prəˈspektəs/ n brochure f; (Univ) livret m de l'étudiant.

prosperity /prɒˈsperətɪ/ n prospérité f. **prosperous** adj prospère.

prostitute /ˈprɒstɪtjuːt/ n prostituée f.

prostrate /ˈprɒstreɪt/ adj (prone) à plat ventre; (exhausted) prostré.

protect /prəˈtekt/ vt protéger. **protection** n protection f. **protective** adj protecteur; (clothes) de protection.

protein /ˈprəʊtiːn/ n protéine f.

protest¹ /ˈprəʊtest/ n protestation f; under~ en protestant.

protest² /prəˈtest/ vt/i protester.

Protestant /ˈprɒtɪstənt/ adj & n protestant/-e (m/f).

protester /prəˈtestə(r)/ n manifestant/-e m/f.

protocol /ˈprəʊtəkɒl/ n protocole m.

protrude /prəˈtruːd/ vi dépasser.

proud /praʊd/ adj fier, orgueilleux.

prove /pruːv/ vt prouver. ● vi (~ to be) easy se révéler facile; ~ oneself faire ses preuves. **proven** adj éprouvé.

proverb /ˈprɒvɜːb/ n proverbe m.

provide /prəˈvaɪd/ vt fournir (sb with sth qch à qn). ● vi ~ for (allow for) prévoir; (guard against) parer à; (person) pourvoir aux besoins de.

provided /prəˈvaɪdɪd/ conj ~ that à condition que.

providing /prəˈvaɪdɪŋ/ conj →PROVIDED.

province /ˈprɒvɪns/ n province f; (fig) compétence f.

provision /prəˈvɪʒn/ n (stock) provision f; (supplying) fourniture f; (stipulation) dispositions fpl; ~s (food) provisions fpl.

provisional /prəˈvɪʒənl/ adj provisoire.

provocative /prəˈvɒkətɪv/ adj provocant.

provoke /prəˈvəʊk/ vt provoquer.

prow /praʊ/ n proue f.

prowess /ˈpraʊɪs/ n prouesses fpl.

prowl /praʊl/ vi rôder.

proxy /ˈprɒksɪ/ n by ~ par procuration.

prudish /ˈpruːdɪʃ/ adj pudibond, prude.

prune /pruːn/ n pruneau m. ● vt (cut) tailler.

pry /praɪ/ vi ~ into mettre son nez dans.

psalm /sɑːm/ n psaume m.

pseudonym /ˈsjuːdənɪm/ n pseudonyme m.

psychiatric /saɪkɪˈætrɪk/ adj psychiatrique. **psychiatrist** n psychiatre mf. **psychiatry** n psychiatrie f.

psychic /ˈsaɪkɪk/ adj (phenomenon) métapsychique; (person) doué de télépathie.

psychoanalyse /saɪkəʊˈænəlaɪz/ vt psychanalyser.

psychological /saɪkəˈlɒdʒɪkl/ adj psychologique. **psychologist** n psychologue mf. **psychology** n psychologie f.

PTO abbr (please turn over) TSVP.

pub /pʌb/ n pub m.

p

Pub Au Royaume-Uni, établissement où l'on sert des boissons (alcoolisées ou non) et parfois des repas légers. Certains appartiennent à une marque de bière alors que les *free houses* sont indépendants. C'est un lieu convivial où l'on vient passer un bon moment (fléchettes, billard, jeux de groupes). Aujourd'hui, la loi leur permet d'ouvrir de 11h à 23h.

puberty /'pjuːbətɪ/ *n* puberté *f*.

public /'pʌblɪk/ *adj* public; (library) municipal; **in ~** en public.

publican /'pʌblɪkən/ *n* patron/-ne *m/f* de pub.

publication /pʌblɪ'keɪʃn/ *n* publication *f*.

public house *n* pub *m*.

publicity /pʌb'lɪsɪtɪ/ *n* publicité *f*.

publicize /'pʌblɪsaɪz/ *vt* faire connaître au public.

public: **~ relations** *n* relations *fpl* publiques. **~ school** *n* école *f* privée; (US) école *f* publique. **~ transport** *n* transports *mpl* en commun.

Public schools Mis à part l'Écosse où ce terme désigne souvent une école publique, les *public schools* britanniques sont en réalité des écoles privées qui fonctionnent souvent sur le mode de l'internat et dont les frais de scolarité sont très élevés. Ces écoles accordent cependant des bourses aux élèves brillants mais peu fortunés. Les *public schools* américaines sont des écoles publiques et la scolarité y est gratuite. ▸ STATE SCHOOL.

publish /'pʌblɪʃ/ *vt* publier. **publisher** *n* éditeur *m*. **publishing** *n* édition *f*.

pudding /'pʊdɪŋ/ *n* dessert *m*; (steamed) pudding *m*.

puddle /'pʌdl/ *n* flaque *f* d'eau.

puff /pʌf/ *n* (of smoke) bouffée *f*; (of breath) souffle *m*. ● *vt/i* souffler. **~ at** (cigar) tirer sur. **~ out** (swell) (se) gonfler.

pull /pʊl/ *vt/i* tirer; (muscle) se froisser; **~ a face** faire une grimace; **~ one's weight** faire sa part du travail; **~ sb's leg** faire marcher qn. ● *n* traction *f*; (fig) attraction *f*; (influence) influence *f*; **give a ~** tirer. **~ away** (Auto) démarrer; **~ back** or **out** (withdraw) (se) retirer; **~ down** (building) démolir; **~ in** (enter) entrer; (stop) s'arrêter; **~ off** enlever; (fig) réussir; **~ out** (from bag) sortir; (extract) arracher; (Auto) déboîter; **~ over** (Auto) se ranger (sur le côté); **~ through** s'en tirer; **~ oneself together** se ressaisir.

pull-down menu *n* (Comput) menu *m* déroulant.

pulley /'pʊlɪ/ *n* poulie *f*.

pullover /'pʊləʊvə(r)/ *n* pull *m* (-over) *m*.

pulp /pʌlp/ *n* (of fruit) pulpe *f*; (for paper) pâte *f* à papier.

pulpit /'pʊlpɪt/ *n* chaire *f*.

pulsate /pʌl'seɪt/ *vi* battre.

pulse /pʌls/ *n* (Med) pouls *m*.

pump /pʌmp/ *n* pompe *f*; (plimsoll) chaussure *f* de sport. ● *vt* pomper; (person) soutirer des renseignements à; **~ up** gonfler.

pumpkin /'pʌmpkɪn/ *n* citrouille *f*.

pun /pʌn/ *n* jeu *m* de mots.

punch /pʌntʃ/ *vt* donner un coup de poing à; (ticket) poinçonner. ● *n* coup *m* de poing; (vigour 🗓) punch *m*; (device) poinçonneuse *f*; (drink) punch *m*. ~-line *n* chute *f*.

punctual /'pʌŋktʃʊəl/ *adj* à l'heure; (habitually) ponctuel.

punctuation /pʌŋktʃʊ'eɪʃn/ *n* ponctuation *f*.

puncture /'pʌŋktʃə(r)/ *n* crevaison *f*. ● *vt/i* crever.

pungent /'pʌndʒənt/ *adj* âcre.

punish /'pʌnɪʃ/ *vt* punir (for sth de qch). **punishment** *n* punition *f*.

punk /pʌŋk/ *n* (music, fan) punk *m*; (US: 🔟) voyou *m*.

punt /pʌnt/ *n* (boat) barque *f*; (Hist) (Irish pound) livre *f* irlandaise.

puny /'pjuːnɪ/ *adj* -ier, -iest chétif.

pupil /'pjuːpl/ *n* (person) élève *mf*; (of eye) pupille *f*.

puppet /'pʌpɪt/ *n* marionnette *f*.

puppy /'pʌpɪ/ *n* chiot *m*.

purchase /'pɜːtʃəs/ *vt* acheter (from sb à qn). ● *n* achat *m*.

pure /pjʊə(r)/ *adj* pur.

purgatory /'pɜːgətrɪ/ *n* purgatoire *m*.

purge /pɜːdʒ/ *vt* purger (of de). ● *n* purge *f*.

purification /pjʊərɪfɪ'keɪʃn/ *n* (of water, air) épuration *f*; (Relig) purification *f*. **purify** *vt* épurer; purifier.

puritan /'pjʊərɪtən/ *n* puritain/ -e *m/f*.

purity /'pjʊərətɪ/ *n* pureté *f*.

purple /'pɜːpl/ *adj* & *n* violet (*m*).

purpose /'pɜːpəs/ *n* but *m*; (determination) résolution *f*; on ~ exprès; to no ~ sans résultat.

purr /pɜː(r)/ *n* ronronnement *m*. ● *vi* ronronner.

purse /pɜːs/ *n* porte-monnaie *m inv*; (handbag: US) sac *m* à main. ● *vt* (lips) pincer.

pursue /pə'sjuː/ *vt* poursuivre.

pursuit /pə'sjuːt/ *n* poursuite *f*; (hobby) activité *f*, occupation *f*.

pus /pʌs/ *n* pus *m*.

push /pʊʃ/ *vt/i* pousser; (button) appuyer sur; (thrust) enfoncer; (recommend 🔟) proposer avec insistance; be ~ed for (time) manquer de; be ~ing thirty ~ friser la trentaine; ~ sb around bousculer qn. ● *n* poussée *f*; (effort) gros effort *m*; (drive) dynamisme *m*; give the ~ to 🔟 flanquer à la porte 🔟. ▫ ~ **in** resquiller; ~ **on** continuer; ~ **up** (lift) relever; (prices) faire monter.

pushchair /'pʊʃtʃeə(r)/ *n* poussette *f*.

pusher /'pʊʃə(r)/ *n* revendeur/ -euse *m/f* (de drogue).

push-up *n* pompe *f*.

put /pʊt/ *vt/i* (*pt* **put**; *pres p* **putting**) mettre, placer, poser; (question) poser; ~ **the damage at a million** estimer les dégâts à un million; ~ **sth tactfully** dire qch avec tact. ▫ ~ **across** communiquer; ~ **away** ranger; (in hospital, prison) enfermer; ~ **back** (postpone) remettre; (delay) retarder; ~ **down** (dé)poser; (write) inscrire; (pay) verser; (suppress) réprimer; ~ **forward** (plan) soumettre; ~ **in** (insert) introduire; (fix) installer; (submit) soumettre; ~ **in for** faire une demande de; ~ **off** (postpone) renvoyer à plus tard; (disconcert) déconcerter; (displease) rebuter; ~ **sb off sth** dégoûter qn de qch; ~ **on** (clothes, radio) mettre; (light) allumer; (accent, weight) prendre; ~ **out** sortir; (stretch) (é)tendre; (extinguish) éteindre; (disconcert) déconcerter; (inconvenience) déranger; ~ **up** lever, remonter; (building) construire; (notice) mettre; (price) augmenter; (guest) héberger; (offer) offrir; ~ **up with** supporter.

putt /pʌt/ *vi* putter. ● *n* putt *m*.

putty /'pʌtɪ/ *n* mastic *m*.

puzzle /'pʌzl/ n énigme f; (game) casse-tête m inv; (jigsaw) puzzle m. • vt rendre perplexe. • vi se creuser la tête.

pyjamas /pə'dʒɑːməz/ npl pyjama m.

pylon /'paɪlən/ n pylône m.

Qq

quack /kwæk/ n (of duck) coin-coin m inv; (doctor) charlatan m.

quadrangle /'kwɒdræŋgl/ (of college) n cour f.

quadruple /'kwɒdrʊpl/ adj & n quadruple (m). • vt/i quadrupler.

quail /kweɪl/ n (bird) caille f.

quaint /kweɪnt/ adj pittoresque; (old) vieillot; (odd) bizarre.

qualification /kwɒlɪfɪ'keɪʃn/ n diplôme m; (ability) compétence f; (fig) réserve f, restriction f.

qualified /'kwɒlɪfaɪd/ adj diplômé; (able) qualifié (to do pour faire); (fig) conditionnel.

qualify /'kwɒlɪfaɪ/ vt qualifier; (modify) mettre des réserves à; (statement) nuancer. • vi obtenir son diplôme (as de); (Sport) se qualifier; ~ for remplir les conditions requises pour.

quality /'kwɒlɪtɪ/ n qualité f.

qualm /kwɑːm/ n scrupule m.

quantity /'kwɒntɪtɪ/ n quantité f.

quarantine /'kwɒrəntiːn/ n quarantaine f.

quarrel /'kwɒrəl/ n dispute f, querelle f. • vi (pt quarrelled) se disputer.

quarry /'kwɒrɪ/ n (excavation) carrière f; (prey) proie f. • vt extraire.

quart /kwɔːt/ n ≈ litre m.

quarter /'kwɔːtə(r)/ n quart m; (of year) trimestre m; (25 cents: US) quart m de dollar; (district) quartier m; ~s logement m; from all ~s de toutes parts. • vt diviser en quatre; (troops) cantonner.

quarterly /'kwɔːtəlɪ/ adj trimestriel. • adv tous les trois mois.

quartet /kwɔː'tet/ n quatuor m.

quartz /kwɔːts/ n quartz m. • adj (watch) à quartz.

quash /kwɒʃ/ vt (suppress) étouffer; (Jur) annuler.

quaver /'kweɪvə(r)/ vi trembler, chevroter. • n (Mus) croche f.

quay /kiː/ n (Naut) quai m.

queasy /'kwiːzɪ/ adj feel ~ avoir mal au cœur.

queen /kwiːn/ n reine f; (cards) dame f.

queer /kwɪə(r)/ adj étrange; (dubious) louche; ⊠ homosexuel.

quench /kwentʃ/ vt éteindre; (thirst) étancher; (desire) étouffer.

query /'kwɪərɪ/ n question f. • vt mettre en question.

quest /kwest/ n recherche f.

question /'kwestʃən/ n question f; in ~ en question; out of the ~ hors de question. • vt interroger; (doubt) mettre en question; the question of. ~ mark n point m d'interrogation.

questionnaire /kwestʃə'neə(r)/ n questionnaire m.

queue /kjuː/ n queue f. • vi (pres p queuing) faire la queue.

quibble /'kwɪbl/ vi ergoter.

quick /kwɪk/ adj rapide; (clever) vif/vive; be ~ (hurry) se dépêcher. • adv vite. • n cut to the ~ piquer au vif. **quicken** vt/i (s')accélérer.

quickly adv rapidement, vite.

~sand n sables mpl mouvants.

quid /kwɪd/ n ① livre f sterling.

quiet /'kwaɪət/ adj (calm, still) tranquille; (silent) silencieux; (gentle) doux; (discreet) discret; **keep ~** se taire. ● n tranquillité f; **on the ~** en cachette. **quieten** vt/i (se) calmer.

quietly adv (speak) doucement; (sit) en silence.

quilt /kwɪlt/ n édredon m; (continental) ~ couette f.

quirk /kwɜːk/ n bizarrerie f.

quit /kwɪt/ vt (pt quitted) quitter; (smoking) arrêter de. ● vi abandonner; (resign) démissionner; ~ **doing** (US) cesser de faire.

quite /kwaɪt/ adv tout à fait, vraiment; (rather) assez; ~ **a few** un bon nombre (de).

quits /kwɪts/ adj quitte (with envers); **call it ~** en rester là.

quiver /'kwɪvə(r)/ vi trembler.

quiz /kwɪz/ n (pl **quizzes**) test m; (game) jeu-concours m. ● vt (pt **quizzed**) questionner.

quotation /kwəʊ'teɪʃn/ n citation f; (price) devis m; (stock exchange) cotation f; ~ **marks** guillemets mpl.

quote /kwəʊt/ vt citer; (reference, number) rappeler; (price) indiquer; (share price) coter. ● vi ~ **for** faire un devis pour; ~ **from** citer. ● n (quotation) citation f; (estimate) devis m; **in ~s** ① entre guillemets.

. . . .

Rr

. . . .

rabbi /'ræbaɪ/ n rabbin m.

rabbit /'ræbɪt/ n lapin m.

rabies /'reɪbiːz/ n (disease) rage f.

race /reɪs/ n (contest) course f; (group) race f. ● adj racial; rela-

tions relations fpl inter-raciales. ● vt (compete with) faire la course avec; (horse) faire courir. ● vi courir; (pulse) battre précipitamment; (engine) s'emballer. **~course** n champ m de courses. **~horse** n cheval m de course. **~track** n piste f; (for horses) champ m de courses.

racing /'reɪsɪŋ/ n courses fpl; ~ **car** voiture f de course.

racism /'reɪsɪzəm/ n racisme m. **racist** adj & n raciste (mf).

rack /ræk/ n (shelf) étagère f; (for clothes) portant m; (for luggage) compartiment m à bagages; (for dishes) égouttoir m. ● vt ~ **one's brains** se creuser la cervelle.

racket /'rækɪt/ n (Sport) raquette f; (noise) vacarme m; (swindle) escroquerie f; (crime) trafic m.

radar /'reɪdɑː(r)/ n & adj radar (m).

radial /'reɪdɪəl/ n ~ **(tyre)** pneu m radial.

radiate /'reɪdɪeɪt/ vt (happiness) rayonner de; (heat) émettre. ● vi rayonner (from de). **radiation** n (radioactivity) radiation f. **radiator** n radiateur m.

radical /'rædɪkl/ n & a radical/-e (m/f).

radio /'reɪdɪəʊ/ n radio f; **on the ~** à la radio. ● vt (message) envoyer par radio; (person) appeler par radio.

radioactive /ˌreɪdɪəʊ'æktɪv/ adj radioactif.

radiographer /ˌreɪdɪ'ɒɡrəfə(r)/ n manipulateur/-trice m/f radiographe.

radish /'rædɪʃ/ n radis m.

radius /'reɪdɪəs/ n (pl **-dii**) rayon m.

raffle /'ræfl/ n tombola f.

rag /ræɡ/ n chiffon m; **~s** loques fpl.

rage /reɪdʒ/ n rage f, colère f; **be all the ~** faire fureur. ● vi (person) tempêter; (*storm, battle*) faire rage.

ragged /'rægɪd/ *adj* (*clothes*) en loques; (*person*) dépenaillé.

raid /reɪd/ *n* (Mil, on stock market) raid *m*; (by police) rafle *f*; (by criminals) hold-up *m inv.* ● *vt* faire un raid ou une rafle ou un hold-up dans. **raider** *n* (*thief*) pillard *m*; (Mil) commando *m*; (corporate) raider *m*.

rail /reɪl/ *n* (on balcony) balustrade *f*; (stairs) rampe *f*; (for train) rail *m*; (for curtain) tringle *f*; **by** ~ par chemin de fer.

railing /'reɪlɪŋ/ *n* (also ~**s**) grille *f*.

railway /'reɪlweɪ/, (US) **railroad** *n* chemin *m* de fer. ~ **line** *n* voie *f* ferrée. ~ **station** *n* gare *f*.

rain /reɪn/ *n* pluie *f*. ● *vi* pleuvoir. ~**bow** *n* arc-en-ciel *m*. ~**coat** *n* imperméable *m*. ~**fall** *n* précipitation *f*. ~ **forest** *n* forêt *f* tropicale.

rainy /'reɪnɪ/ *adj* (**-ier, -iest**) pluvieux; (*season*) des pluies.

raise /reɪz/ *vt* (*barrier, curtain*) lever; (*child, cattle*) élever; (*question*) soulever; (*price, salary*) augmenter. ● *n* (US) augmentation *f*.

raisin /'reɪzn/ *n* raisin *m* sec.

rake /reɪk/ *n* râteau *m.* ● *vt* (*garden*) ratisser; (*search*) fouiller dans. □ ~ **in** (*money*) amasser; ~ **up** (*past*) remuer.

rally /'rælɪ/ *vt/i* (se) rallier; (*strength*) reprendre; (after illness) aller mieux; ~ **round** venir en aide. ● *n* rassemblement *m*; (Auto) rallye *m*; (tennis) échange *m*.

ram /ræm/ *n* bélier *m.* ● *vt* (*pt* **rammed**) (*thrust*) enfoncer; (*crash into*) rentrer dans.

RAM *abbr* (**random access memory**) RAM *f*.

ramble /'ræmbl/ *n* randonnée *f*. ● *vi* faire une randonnée. □ ~ **on** discourir.

ramp /ræmp/ *n* (*slope*) rampe *f*; (in garage) pont *m* de graissage.

rampage[1] /ræm'peɪdʒ/ *vi* se déchaîner (through dans).

rampage[2] /'ræmpeɪdʒ/ *n* **go on the** ~ tout saccager.

ran /ræn/ ⟹RUN.

rancid /'rænsɪd/ *adj* rance.

random /'rændəm/ *adj* (*fait*) au hasard. ● *n* **at** ~ au hasard.

rang /ræŋ/ ⟹RING².

range /reɪndʒ/ *n* (of prices, products) gamme *f*; (of people, beliefs) variété *f*; (of radar, weapon) portée *f*; (of aircraft) autonomie *f*; (of mountains) chaîne *f*. ● *vi* aller; (vary) varier.

rank /ræŋk/ *n* rang *m*; (Mil) grade *m*. ● *vt/i* ~ **among** (se) classer parmi.

ransack /'rænsæk/ *vt* (*search*) fouiller; (*pillage*) mettre à sac.

ransom /'rænsəm/ *n* rançon *f*.

rap /ræp/ *n* coup *m* sec; (Mus) rap *m.* ● *vt* (*pt* **rapped**) donner des coups secs (on sur).

rape /reɪp/ *vt* violer. ● *n* viol *m*.

rapid /'ræpɪd/ *adj* rapide.

rapist /'reɪpɪst/ *n* violeur *m*.

rapturous /'ræptʃərəs/ *adj* (*delight*) extasié; (*welcome*) enthousiaste.

rare /reə(r)/ *adj* rare; (Culin) saignant. **rarely** *adv* rarement.

rascal /'rɑːskl/ *n* coquin/-e *m/f*.

rash /ræʃ/ *n* (Med) rougeurs *fpl*. ● *adj* irréfléchi.

raspberry /'rɑːzbrɪ/ *n* framboise *f*.

rat /ræt/ *n* rat *m.* ● *vi* (*pt* **ratted**) on (desert) lâcher; (inform on) dénoncer.

rate /reɪt/ *n* (ratio, level) taux *m*; (speed) rythme *m*; (price) tarif *m*; (of exchange) taux *m*; **at any** ~ en tout cas. ● *vt* (value) estimer; (deserve) mériter; ~ **sth highly** admirer beaucoup qch. ● *vi* ~ **as** être considéré comme.

rather /ˈrɑːðə(r)/ *adv* (by preference) plutôt; (fairly) assez, plutôt; (a little) un peu; I would ~ go je préfère partir; I would ~ ... **than** go plutôt que de partir.

rating /ˈreɪtɪŋ/ *n* (score, value) cote *f*; **the** ~**s** (TV) l'indice *m* d'écoute, l'audimat® *m*.

ratio /ˈreɪʃɪəʊ/ *n* proportion *f*.

ration /ˈræʃn/ *n* ration *f*. ● *vt* rationner.

rational /ˈræʃənl/ *adj* rationnel; (person) sensé.

rationalize /ˈræʃnəlaɪz/ *vt* justifier; (organize) rationaliser.

rattle /ˈrætl/ *vi* (bottles, chains) s'entrechoquer; (window) vibrer. ● *vt* (bottles, chains) faire s'entrechoquer; (fig, ①) énerver. ● *n* cliquetis *m*; (toy) hochet *m*. ~**snake** *n* serpent *m* à sonnette, crotale *m*.

rave /reɪv/ *vi* (enthuse) s'emballer; (in fever) délirer; (in anger) tempêter.

raven /ˈreɪvn/ *n* corbeau *m*.

ravenous /ˈrævənəs/ *adj* **be** ~ avoir une faim de loup.

ravine /rəˈviːn/ *n* ravin *m*.

raving /ˈreɪvɪŋ/ *adj* ~ **lunatic** fou *m* furieux, folle *f* furieuse.

ravishing /ˈrævɪʃɪŋ/ *adj* ravissant.

raw /rɔː/ *adj* cru; (not processed) brut; (wound) à vif; (immature) inexpérimenté; **get a** ~ **deal** être mal traité; ~ **material** matière *f* première.

ray /reɪ/ *n* (of light) rayon *m*; ~ **of hope** lueur *f* d'espoir.

razor /ˈreɪzə(r)/ *n* rasoir *m*. ~**blade** *n* lame *f* de rasoir.

re /riː/ *prep* au sujet de; (at top of letter) objet.

reach /riːtʃ/ *vt* (place, level) atteindre; (decision) arriver à; (contact) joindre; (audience, market) toucher. ● *vi* ~ **up/down** lever/baisser le bras; ~ **across** étendre le bras. ● *n* **portée** *f*; **within** ~ **of** à portée de; (close to) à proximité de.

react /rɪˈækt/ *vi* réagir. **reaction** *n* réaction *f*. **reactor** *n* réacteur *m*.

read /riːd/ *vt/i* (pt **read**) lire; (study) étudier; (instrument) indiquer; ~ **about sb** lire quelque chose sur qn; ~ **out** lire à haute voix. **reader** *n* lecteur/-trice *m/f*. **reading** *n* lecture *f*; (measurement) indication *f*; (interpretation) interprétation *f*.

readjust /riːəˈdʒʌst/ *vt* rajuster. ● *vi* se réadapter (to à).

read-only memory, **ROM** *n* mémoire *f* morte.

ready /ˈredɪ/ *adj* (-**ier**, -**iest**) prêt; (quick) prompt. ~**made** *adj* tout fait. ~**to-wear** *adj* prêt-à-porter.

real /rɪəl/ *adj* (not imaginary) véritable, réel; (not artificial) vrai; **it's a** ~ **shame** c'est vraiment dommage. ~ **estate** *n* biens *mpl* immobiliers.

realism /ˈrɪəlɪzəm/ *n* réalisme *m*. **realistic** *adj* réaliste.

reality /rɪˈælətɪ/ *n* réalité *f*. ~ **TV** *n* télé-réalité *f*.

reasonable /ˈriːznəbl/ *adj* raisonnable.

realize /ˈrɪəlaɪz/ *vt* se rendre compte de, comprendre; (fulfil, turn into cash) réaliser; (price) atteindre.

really /ˈrɪəlɪ/ *adv* vraiment.

reap /riːp/ *vt* (crop) recueillir; (benefits) récolter.

reappear /riːəˈpɪə(r)/ *vi* reparaître.

rear /rɪə(r)/ *n* arrière *m*; (of person) derrière *m*. ① ● *adj* (seat) arrière *inv*;

(entrance) de derrière. ● vt élever.
● vi (horse) se cabrer. ~-view mirror n rétroviseur m.

reason /'ri:zn/ n raison f (to do,
for doing de faire); within (~ to dans
la limite du raisonnable.

reassurance /ri:ə'ʃɔːrəns/ n réconfort m. **reassure** vt rassurer.

rebate /'ri:beɪt/ n (refund) remboursement m; (discount) remise f.

rebel[1] /'rebl/ n & adj rebelle (mf).

rebel[2] /rɪ'bel/ vi (pt **rebelled**) se
rebeller. **rebellion** n rébellion f.

rebound[1] /rɪ'baʊnd/ vi rebondir;
~ on (backfire) se retourner contre.

rebound[2] /'ri:baʊnd/ n rebond m.

rebuke /rɪ'bju:k/ vt réprimander.
● n réprimande f.

recall /rɪ'kɔːl/ vt (remember) se
souvenir de; (call back) rappeler.
● n (memory) mémoire f; (Comput,
Mil) rappel m.

recap /ri:'kæp/ vt/i (pt **recapped**)
récapituler. ● n récapitulation f.

recede /rɪ'si:d/ vi s'éloigner; his
hair is receding son front se dégarnit.

receipt /rɪ'si:t/ n (written) reçu m;
(of letter) réception f; ~s (Comm)
recettes fpl.

receive /rɪ'si:v/ vt recevoir; (stolen
goods) receler. **receiver** n (telephone) combiné m; (TV) récepteur m.

recent /'ri:snt/ adj récent. **recently**
adv récemment.

receptacle /rɪ'septəkl/ n récipient m.

reception /rɪ'sepʃn/ n réception f;
give sb a warm ~ donner un accueil chaleureux à qn.

recess /rɪ'ses/ n (alcove) alcôve m;
(for door) embrasure f; (Jur, Pol) vacances fpl; (School, US) récréation f.

recession /rɪ'seʃn/ n récession f.

recharge /ri:'tʃɑːdʒ/ vt recharger.

recipe /'resəpɪ/ n recette f.

recipient /rɪ'sɪpɪənt/ n (of honour) récipiendaire mf; (of letter) destinataire mf.

reciprocate /rɪ'sɪprəkeɪt/ vt (compliment) retourner; (kindness) payer
de retour. ● vi en faire autant.

recite /rɪ'saɪt/ vt réciter.

reckless /'reklɪs/ adj imprudent.

reckon /'rekən/ vt/i calculer;
(judge) considérer; (think) penser;
~ on/with compter sur/avec. **reckoning** n (guess) estimation f; (calculation) calculs mpl.

reclaim /rɪ'kleɪm/ vt récupérer;
(flooded land) assécher.

recline /rɪ'klaɪn/ vi s'allonger;
(seat) s'incliner.

recluse /rɪ'klu:s/ n reclus/-e m/f.

recognition /rekəg'nɪʃn/ n reconnaissance f; beyond ~ méconnaissable; gain ~ être reconnu.

recognize /'rekəgnaɪz/ vt reconnaître.

recollect /rekə'lekt/ vt se souvenir
de, se rappeler. **recollection** n souvenir m.

recommend /rekə'mend/ vt recommander. **recommendation** n
recommandation f.

reconcile /'rekənsaɪl/ vt (people)
réconcilier; (facts) concilier; ~ oneself to se résigner à.

recondition /ri:kən'dɪʃn/ vt remettre à neuf.

reconsider /ri:kən'sɪdə(r)/ vt réexaminer. ● vi réfléchir.

reconstruct /ri:kən'strʌkt/ vt reconstruire; (crime) faire une reconstitution de.

record[1] /rɪ'kɔːd/ vt/i (in register,
on tape) enregistrer; (in diary)

noter; ~**that** rapporter que.

record² /ˈrekɔːd/ n (of events) compte-rendu m; (official) procès-verbal m; (personal, administrative) dossier m; (historical) archives fpl; (past history) réputation f; (Mus) disque m; (Sport) record m; (criminal) ~ casier m judiciaire; off the ~ officieusement. ● adj record inv.

recorder /rɪˈkɔːdə(r)/ n (Mus) flûte f à bec.

recording /rɪˈkɔːdɪŋ/ n enregistrement m.

record-player n tourne-disque m.

recover /rɪˈkʌvə(r)/ vt récupérer. ● vi se remettre; (economy) se redresser. **recovery** n (Med) rétablissement m; (of economy) relance f.

recreation /rekrɪˈeɪʃn/ n récréation f.

recruit /rɪˈkruːt/ n recrue f. ● vt recruter. **recruitment** n recrutement m.

rectangle /ˈrektæŋɡl/ n rectangle m.

rectify /ˈrektɪfaɪ/ vt rectifier.

recuperate /rɪˈkuːpəreɪt/ vt récupérer. ● vi se rétablir.

recur /rɪˈkɜː(r)/ vi (pt recurred) se reproduire.

recycle /riːˈsaɪkl/ vt recycler.

red /red/ adj (redder, reddest) rouge; (hair) roux. ● n rouge m; in the ~ en déficit. R~ **Cross** n Croix Rouge f. ~**currant** n groseille f.

redecorate /riːˈdekəreɪt/ vt repeindre, refaire.

redeploy /riːdɪˈplɔɪ/ vt réorganiser; (troops) répartir.

red: ~**-handed** adj en flagrant délit. ~**-hot** adj brûlant.

redirect /riːdɪˈrekt/ vt (traffic) dévier; (letter) faire suivre.

redness /ˈrednɪs/ n rougeur f.

redo /riːˈduː/ vt (pt -did; pp -done) refaire.

redress /rɪˈdres/ vt (wrong) redresser; (balance) rétablir. ● n réparation f.

reduce /rɪˈdjuːs/ vt réduire; (temperature) faire baisser. **reduction** n réduction f.

redundancy /rɪˈdʌndənsɪ/ n licenciement m.

redundant /rɪˈdʌndənt/ adj superflu; (worker) licencié; **make** ~ licencier.

reed /riːd/ n (plant) roseau m.

reef /riːf/ n récif m, écueil m.

reel /riːl/ n (of thread) bobine f; (of film) bande f; (winding device) dévidoir m. ● vi chanceler. ● vt ~ **off** réciter.

refectory /rɪˈfektrɪ/ n réfectoire m.

refer /rɪˈfɜː(r)/ vt/i (pt referred) ~ **to** (allude to) faire allusion à; (concern) s'appliquer à; (consult) consulter; (direct) renvoyer à.

referee /refəˈriː/ n (Sport) arbitre m. ● vt (pt refereed) arbitrer.

reference /ˈrefərəns/ n référence f; (mention) allusion f; (person) personne f pouvant fournir des références; in or with ~ **to** en ce qui concerne; (Comm) suite à.

referendum /refəˈrendəm/ n (pl ~s) référendum m.

refill¹ /riːˈfɪl/ vt (glass) remplir à nouveau; (pen) recharger.

refill² /ˈriːfɪl/ n recharge f.

refine /rɪˈfaɪn/ vt raffiner.

reflect /rɪˈflekt/ vt refléter; (heat, light) renvoyer. ● vi réfléchir (on à); ~ **well/badly** on sb faire honneur/du tort à qn.

reflection /rɪˈflekʃn/ n réflexion f; (image) reflet m; on ~ à la réflexion.

r

reflective /rɪˈflektɪv/ adj (surface) réfléchissant; (person) réfléchi.

reflector /rɪˈflektə(r)/ n (on car) catadioptre m.

reflex /ˈriːfleks/ adj & n réflexe (m).

reflexive /rɪˈfleksɪv/ adj (Gram) réfléchi.

reform /rɪˈfɔːm/ vt reformer. ● vi (person) s'amender. ● n réforme f.

refrain /rɪˈfreɪn/ n refrain m. ● vi s'abstenir (from de).

refresh /rɪˈfreʃ/ vt (drink) rafraîchir; (rest) reposer. **refreshments** npl rafraîchissements mpl.

refrigerate /rɪˈfrɪdʒəreɪt/ vt réfrigérer. **refrigerator** n réfrigérateur m.

refuel /ˈriːfjʊəl/ vt/i (pt refuelled) (se) ravitailler.

refuge /ˈrefjuːdʒ/ n refuge m; take ~ se réfugier. **refugee** n réfugié/-e m/f.

refund[1] /rɪˈfʌnd/ vt rembourser.

refund[2] /ˈriːfʌnd/ n remboursement m.

refurbish /riːˈfɜːbɪʃ/ vt remettre à neuf.

refuse[1] /rɪˈfjuːz/ vt/i refuser.

refuse[2] /ˈrefjuːs/ n ordures fpl.

regain /rɪˈɡeɪn/ vt retrouver; (lost ground) regagner.

regard /rɪˈɡɑːd/ vt considérer; as ~s en ce qui concerne. ● n égard m, estime f; in this ~ à cet égard; ~s amitiés fpl. **regarding** prep en ce qui concerne.

regardless /rɪˈɡɑːdlɪs/ adv malgré tout; ~ of sans tenir compte de.

regime /reɪˈʒiːm/ n régime m.

regiment /ˈredʒɪmənt/ n régiment m.

region /ˈriːdʒən/ n région f; in the ~ of environ.

register /ˈredʒɪstə(r)/ n registre m.

● vt (record) enregistrer; (vehicle) faire immatriculer; (birth) déclarer; (letter) recommander; (indicate) indiquer; (express) exprimer. ● vi (enrol) s'inscrire; (at hotel) se présenter; (fig) être compris.

registrar /ˌredʒɪˈstrɑː(r)/ n officier m de l'état civil; (Univ) responsable m du bureau de la scolarité.

registration /ˌredʒɪˈstreɪʃn/ n (of voter, student) inscription f; (of birth) déclaration f; ~ (number) (Auto) numéro m d'immatriculation.

registry office n bureau m de l'état civil.

regret /rɪˈɡret/ n regret m. ● vt (pt regretted) regretter (to do de faire). **regretfully** adv à regret.

regular /ˈreɡjʊlə(r)/ adj régulier; (usual) habituel. ● n habitué/-e m/f. **regularity** n régularité f. **regularly** adv régulièrement.

regulate /ˈreɡjʊleɪt/ vt régler. **regulation** n (rule) règlement m; (process) réglementation f.

rehabilitate /ˌriːəˈbɪlɪteɪt/ vt (in public esteem) réhabiliter; (prisoner) réinsérer.

rehearsal /rɪˈhɜːsl/ n répétition f. **rehearse** vt/i répéter.

reign /reɪn/ n règne m. ● vi régner (over sur).

reimburse /ˌriːɪmˈbɜːs/ vt rembourser.

reindeer /ˈreɪndɪə(r)/ n inv renne m.

reinforce /ˌriːɪnˈfɔːs/ vt renforcer. **reinforcement** n renforcement m; ~s renforts mpl.

reinstate /ˌriːɪnˈsteɪt/ vt (person) réintégrer; (law) rétablir.

reject[1] /ˈriːdʒekt/ n marchandise f de deuxième choix.

reject[2] /rɪˈdʒekt/ vt (offer, plea) rejeter; (goods) refuser. **rejection** n (personal) rejet m; (of candidate, work) refus m.

rejoice /rɪ'dʒɔɪs/ vi se réjouir.

relapse /'riːlæps/ n rechute f. ● vi rechuter; ~ into retomber dans.

relate /rɪ'leɪt/ vt raconter; (associate) associer. ● vi ~ to se rapporter à; (get on with) s'entendre avec. **related** adj (ideas) lié; we are ~d nous sommes parents.

relation /rɪ'leɪʃn/ n rapport m; (person) parent/-e m/f. **relationship** n relations fpl; (link) rapport m.

relative /'relətɪv/ n parent/-e m/f. ● adj relatif; (respective) respectif.

relax /rɪ'læks/ vt (grip) relâcher; (muscle) décontracter; (discipline) assouplir. ● vi (person) se détendre; (grip) se relâcher. **relaxation** n détente f. **relaxing** adj délassant.

relay¹ /'riːleɪ/ n (also ~ race) course f de relais.

relay² /rɪ'leɪ/ vt relayer.

release /rɪ'liːs/ vt (prisoner) libérer; (fastening) faire jouer; (object, hand) lâcher; (film) faire sortir; (news) publier. ● n libération f; (film) sortie f; (new record, film) nouveauté f.

relevance /'reləvəns/ n pertinence f, intérêt m.

relevant /'reləvənt/ adj pertinent; be ~ to avoir rapport à.

reliability /rɪlaɪə'bɪlɪtɪ/ n (of firm) sérieux m; (of car) fiabilité f; (of person) honnêteté f. **reliable** adj (firm) sérieux; (person, machine) fiable.

reliance /rɪ'laɪəns/ n dépendance f.

relic /'relɪk/ n vestige m; (object) relique f.

relief /rɪ'liːf/ n soulagement m (from à); (assistance) secours m; (outline) relief m; ~ road route f de délestage.

relieve /rɪ'liːv/ vt soulager; (help) secourir; (take over from) relayer.

religion /rɪ'lɪdʒən/ n religion f. **religious** adj religieux.

relish /'relɪʃ/ n plaisir m; (Culin) condiment m. ● vt (food) savourer; (idea) se réjouir de.

relocate /riːləʊ'keɪt/ vt muter. ● vi (company) déménager; (worker) être muté. **relocation** n délocalisation f.

reluctance /rɪ'lʌktəns/ n répugnance f.

reluctant /rɪ'lʌktənt/ adj (person) peu enthousiaste; (consent) accordé à contrecœur; ~ to peu disposé à. **reluctantly** adv à contrecœur.

rely /rɪ'laɪ/ vi ~ on (count) compter sur; (be dependent) dépendre de.

remain /rɪ'meɪn/ vi rester. **remainder** n reste m.

remand /rɪ'mɑːnd/ vt mettre en détention provisoire. ● n on ~ en détention provisoire.

remark /rɪ'mɑːk/ n remarque f. ● vt remarquer. ● vi ~ on faire des remarques sur. **remarkable** adj remarquable.

remedy /'remədɪ/ n remède m. ● vt remédier à.

remember /rɪ'membə(r)/ vt se souvenir de, se rappeler; ~ to do ne pas oublier de faire. **remembrance** n souvenir m.

remind /rɪ'maɪnd/ vt rappeler (sb of sth qch à qn); ~ sb to do rappeler à qn de faire. **reminder** n rappel m.

reminisce /remɪ'nɪs/ vi évoquer ses souvenirs.

remission /rɪ'mɪʃn/ n (Med) rémission f; (Jur) remise f.

remnant /'remnənt/ n reste m; (trace) vestige m; (of cloth) coupon *m*.

remodel /riːˈmɒdl/ *vt* (*pt* **remodelled**) remodeler.

remorse /rɪˈmɔːs/ *n* remords *m*.

remote /rɪˈməʊt/ *adj* (*place, time*) lointain; (*person*) distant; (*slight*) vague; ~ **control** télécommande *f*.

removable /rɪˈmuːvəbl/ *adj* amovible.

removal /rɪˈmuːvl/ *n* (of employee) renvoi *m*; (of threat) suppression *f*; (of troops) retrait *m*; (of stain) détachage *m*; (from house) déménagement *m*; ~ **men** déménageurs *mpl*.

remove /rɪˈmuːv/ *vt* enlever; (dismiss) renvoyer; (do away with) supprimer; (Comput) effacer.

remunerate /rɪˈmjuːnəreɪt/ *vt* rémunérer. **remuneration** *n* rémunération *f*.

render /ˈrendə(r)/ *vt* rendre.

renegade /ˈrenɪgeɪd/ *n* renégat/-e *m/f*.

renew /rɪˈnjuː/ *vt* renouveler; (resume) reprendre. **renewable** *adj* renouvelable.

renounce /rɪˈnaʊns/ *vt* renoncer à; (disown) renier.

renovate /ˈrenəveɪt/ *vt* rénover.

renown /rɪˈnaʊn/ *n* renommée *f*.

rent /rent/ *n* loyer *m*. ● *vt* louer; for ~ à louer. **rental** *n* prix *m* de location.

reopen /riːˈəʊpən/ *vt/i* rouvrir.

reorganize /riːˈɔːgənaɪz/ *vt* réorganiser.

rep /rep/ *n* (Comm) représentant/-e *m/f*.

repair /rɪˈpeə(r)/ *vt* réparer. ● *n* réparation *f*; in good/bad ~ en bon/mauvais état.

repatriate /riːˈpætrɪeɪt/ *vt* rapatrier. **repatriation** *n* rapatriement *m*.

repay /rɪˈpeɪ/ *vt* (*pt* **repaid**) rembourser; (reward) récompenser. **repayment** *n* remboursement *m*.

repeal /rɪˈpiːl/ *vt* abroger. ● *n* abrogation *f*.

repeat /rɪˈpiːt/ *vt/i* répéter; (renew) renouveler; ~ **itself**, ~ **oneself** se répéter. ● *n* répétition *f*; (broadcast) reprise *f*.

repel /rɪˈpel/ *vt* (*pt* **repelled**) repousser.

repent /rɪˈpent/ *vi* se repentir (of de).

repercussion /riːpəˈkʌʃn/ *n* répercussion *f*.

repetition /repɪˈtɪʃn/ *n* répétition *f*.

replace /rɪˈpleɪs/ *vt* (put back) remettre; (take the place of) remplacer. **replacement** *n* remplacement *m* (of de); (person) remplaçant/-e *m/f*; (new part) pièce *f* de rechange.

replay /ˈriːpleɪ/ *n* (Sport) match *m* rejoué; (recording) répétition *f* immédiate.

replenish /rɪˈplenɪʃ/ *vt* (refill) remplir; (renew) renouveler.

replica /ˈreplɪkə/ *n* copie *f* exacte.

reply /rɪˈplaɪ/ *vt/i* répondre. ● *n* réponse *f*.

report /rɪˈpɔːt/ *vt* rapporter, annoncer (that que); (notify) signaler; (denounce) dénoncer. ● *vi* faire un rapport; ~ **(on)** (news item) faire un reportage sur; ~ **to** (go) se présenter chez. ● *n* rapport *m*; (in press) reportage *m*; (School) bulletin *m*. **reporter** *n* reporter *m*.

repossess /riːpəˈzes/ *vt* reprendre.

represent /reprɪˈzent/ *vt* représenter.

representation /reprɪzenˈteɪʃn/ *n* représentation *f*; make ~s to protester auprès de.

representative /reprɪˈzentətɪv/ adj représentatif, typique (of de). ● n représentant/-e m/f.

repress /rɪˈpres/ vt réprimer.

reprieve /rɪˈpriːv/ n (delay) sursis m; (pardon) grâce f. ● vt accorder un sursis à; gracier.

reprimand /ˈreprɪmɑːnd/ vt réprimander. ● n réprimande f.

reprisals /rɪˈpraɪzlz/ npl représailles fpl.

reproach /rɪˈprəʊtʃ/ vt reprocher (sb for sth qch à qn). ● n reproche m.

reproduce /riːprəˈdjuːs/ vt/i (se) reproduire. **reproduction** n reproduction f. **reproductive** adj reproducteur.

reptile /ˈreptaɪl/ n reptile m.

republic /rɪˈpʌblɪk/ n république f. **republican** adj & n républicain/-e (m/f).

repudiate /rɪˈpjuːdɪeɪt/ vt répudier; (contract) refuser d'honorer.

reputable /ˈrepjʊtəbl/ adj honorable, de bonne réputation.

reputation /repjʊˈteɪʃn/ n réputation f.

repute /rɪˈpjuːt/ n réputation f.

request /rɪˈkwest/ n demande f. ● vt demander (of, from à).

require /rɪˈkwaɪə(r)/ vt (of thing) demander; (of person) avoir besoin de; (demand, order) exiger. **required** adj requis. **requirement** n exigence f; (condition) condition f (requise).

rescue /ˈreskjuː/ vt sauver. ● n sauvetage m (of de); (help) secours m.

research /rɪˈsɜːtʃ/ n recherche(s) f(pl). ● vt/i faire des recherches (sur). **researcher** n chercheur/ -euse m/f.

resemblance /rɪˈzembləns/ n ressemblance f. **resemble** vt

ressembler à.

resent /rɪˈzent/ vt être indigné de, s'offenser de. **resentment** n ressentiment m.

reservation /rezəˈveɪʃn/ n (doubt) réserve f; (booking) réservation f; (US) réserve f (indienne); make a ~ réserver.

reserve /rɪˈzɜːv/ vt réserver. ● n (stock, land) réserve f; (Sport) remplaçant/-e m/f; in ~ en réserve; the ~s (Mil) les réserves fpl. **reserved** adj (person, room) réservé.

reshuffle /riːˈʃʌfl/ vt (Pol) remanier. ● n (Pol) remaniement m (ministériel).

residence /ˈrezɪdəns/ n résidence f; (of students) foyer m; in ~ (doctor) résidant.

resident /ˈrezɪdənt/ adj résidant; be ~ résider. ● n habitant/-e m/f; (foreigner) résident/-e m/f; (in hotel) pensionnaire m/f. **residential** adj résidentiel.

resign /rɪˈzaɪn/ vt abandonner; (job) démissionner de. ● vi démissionner; ~ oneself to se résigner à. **resignation** n résignation f; (from job) démission f. **resigned** adj résigné.

resilience /rɪˈzɪlɪəns/ n élasticité f; ressort m.

resin /ˈrezɪn/ n résine f.

resist /rɪˈzɪst/ vt/i résister (à). **resistance** n résistance f. **resistant** adj (Med) rebelle; (metal) résistant.

resolution /rezəˈluːʃn/ n résolution f.

resolve /rɪˈzɒlv/ vt résoudre (to do de faire). ● n résolution f.

resort /rɪˈzɔːt/ vi ~ to avoir recours à. ● n (recourse) recours m; (place) station f; in the last ~ en dernier ressort.

resource /rɪˈsɔːs/ n ressource f;

~s (wealth) ressources *fpl*. **resourceful** *adj* ingénieux.

respect /rɪ'spekt/ *n* respect *m*; (aspect) égard *m*; with ~ to à l'égard de, relativement à. ● *vt* respecter.

respectability /rɪspektə'bɪlɪtɪ/ *n* respectabilité *f*. **respectable** *adj* respectable.

respectful /rɪ'spektfl/ *adj* respectueux.

respective /rɪ'spektɪv/ *adj* respectif.

respite /'respaɪt/ *n* répit *m*.

respond /rɪ'spɒnd/ *vi* répondre (to à); ~ to (react to) réagir à. **response** *n* réponse *f*.

responsibility /rɪspɒnsə'bɪlɪtɪ/ *n* responsabilité *f*. **responsible** *adj* responsable; (*job*) qui comporte des responsabilités.

responsive /rɪ'spɒnsɪv/ *adj* réceptif.

rest /rest/ *vt/i* (se) reposer; (lean) (s')appuyer (on sur); (be buried, lie) reposer; (remain) demeurer. ● *n* repos *m*; (support) support *m*; have a ~ se reposer; the ~ (remainder) le reste (of de); (other people) les autres.

restaurant /'restrɒnt/ *n* restaurant *m*.

restless /'restlɪs/ *adj* agité.

restoration /restə'reɪʃn/ *n* rétablissement *m*; restauration *f*.

restore /rɪ'stɔ:(r)/ *vt* rétablir; (building) restaurer; ~ sth to sb restituer qch à qn.

restrain /rɪ'streɪn/ *vt* contenir; ~ sb from retenir qn de. **restrained** *adj* (moderate) mesuré; (in control of self) maître de soi.

restrict /rɪ'strɪkt/ *vt* restreindre. **restriction** *n* restriction *f*.

rest room *n* (US) toilettes *fpl*.

result /rɪ'zʌlt/ *n* résultat *m*. ● *vi*

résulter; ~ in aboutir à.

resume /rɪ'zju:m/ *vt/i* reprendre.

résumé /'rezju:meɪ/ *n* résumé *m*; (of career: US) CV *m*, curriculum vitae *m*.

resurrect /rezə'rekt/ *vt* ressusciter.

resuscitate /rɪ'sʌsɪteɪt/ *vt* réanimer.

retail /'ri:teɪl/ *n* détail *m*. ● *adj* & *adv* au détail. ● *vt/i* (se) vendre (au détail). **retailer** *n* détaillant/-e *m/f*.

retain /rɪ'teɪn/ *vt* (hold back, remember) retenir; (keep) conserver.

retaliate /rɪ'tælɪeɪt/ *vi* riposter. **retaliation** *n* représailles *fpl*.

retch /retʃ/ *vi* avoir un haut-le-cœur.

retire /rɪ'taɪə(r)/ *vi* (from work) prendre sa retraite; (withdraw) se retirer; (go to bed) se coucher. **retired** *adj* retraité. **retirement** *n* retraite *f*.

retort /rɪ'tɔ:t/ *vt/i* répliquer. ● *n* réplique *f*.

retrace /ri:'treɪs/ *vt* ~ one's steps revenir sur ses pas.

retract /rɪ'trækt/ *vt/i* (se) rétracter.

retrain /ri:'treɪn/ *vt/i* (se) recycler.

retreat /rɪ'tri:t/ *vi* (Mil) battre en retraite. ● *n* retraite *f*.

retrieval /rɪ'tri:vl/ *n* (Comput) extraction *f*. **retrieve** *vt* (object) récupérer; (situation) redresser; (data) extraire.

retrospect /'retrəuspekt/ *n* in ~ rétrospectivement.

return /rɪ'tɜ:n/ *vi* (come back) revenir; (go back) retourner; (go home) rentrer. ● *vt* (give back) rendre; (bring back) rapporter; (send back) renvoyer; (put back) remettre. ● *n* retour *m*; (yield) rapport *m*; ~s (Comm) bénéfices *mpl*; in ~ for en échange de. ~ **ticket** n aller-retour m.

reunion /riːˈjuːnɪən/ n réunion f.

reunite /riːjuːˈnaɪt/ vt réunir.

rev /rev/ n (Auto 🔟) tour m. ● vt/i (pt **revved**) ~ (**up**) (engine 🔟) (s')emballer.

reveal /rɪˈviːl/ vt révéler; (allow to appear) laisser voir.

revelation /revəˈleɪʃn/ n révélation f.

revenge /rɪˈvendʒ/ n vengeance f. ● vt venger.

revenue /ˈrevənjuː/ n revenu m.

reverberate /rɪˈvɜːbəret/ vi (sound, light) se répercuter.

reverend /ˈrevərənd/ adj révérend.

reversal /rɪˈvɜːsl/ n renversement m; (of view) revirement m.

reverse /rɪˈvɜːs/ adj contraire, inverse. ● n contraire m; (back) revers m, envers m; (gear) marche f arrière. ● vt (situation, bracket) renverser; (order) inverser; (decision) annuler; ~ **the charges** appeler en PCV. ● vi (Auto) faire marche arrière.

review /rɪˈvjuː/ n (inspection, magazine) revue f; (of book) critique f. ● vt passer en revue; (situation, bracket) réexaminer; faire la critique de. **reviewer** n critique m.

revise /rɪˈvaɪz/ vt réviser; (text) revoir. **revision** n révision f.

revival /rɪˈvaɪvl/ n (of economy) reprise f; (of interest) regain m.

revive /rɪˈvaɪv/ vt (person, hopes) ranimer; (custom) rétablir. ● vi se ranimer.

revoke /rɪˈvəʊk/ vt révoquer.

revolt /rɪˈvəʊlt/ vt/i (se) révolter. ● n révolte f. **revolting** adj dégoûtant.

revolution /revəˈluːʃn/ n révolution f.

revolve /rɪˈvɒlv/ vi tourner.

revolver /rɪˈvɒlvə(r)/ n revolver m.

revolving door n porte f à tambour.

reward /rɪˈwɔːd/ n récompense f. ● vt récompenser (for de). **rewarding** adj rémunérateur; (worthwhile) qui (en) vaut la peine.

rewind /riːˈwaɪnd/ vt (pt **rewound**) rembobiner.

rewire /riːˈwaɪə(r)/ vt refaire l'installation électrique de.

rhetorical /rɪˈtɒrɪkl/ adj (de) rhétorique; (question) de pure forme.

rheumatism /ˈruːmətɪzəm/ n rhumatisme m.

rhinoceros /raɪˈnɒsərəs/ n (pl ~es) rhinocéros m.

rhubarb /ˈruːbɑːb/ n rhubarbe f.

rhyme /raɪm/ n rime f; (poem) vers mpl. ● vt/i (faire) rimer.

rhythm /ˈrɪðəm/ n rythme m. **rhythmic(-al)** adj rythmique.

rib /rɪb/ n côte f.

ribbon /ˈrɪbən/ n ruban m; in ~s en lambeaux.

rice /raɪs/ n riz m. ~ **pudding** n riz m au lait.

rich /rɪtʃ/ adj riche.

rid /rɪd/ vt (pt **rid**; pres p **ridding**) débarrasser (of de); get ~ of se débarrasser de.

ridden /ˈrɪdn/ ⇒RIDE.

riddle /ˈrɪdl/ n énigme f. ● vt ~ **with** (bullets) cribler de; (mistakes) bourrer de.

ride /raɪd/ vi (pt **rode**; pp **ridden**) aller (à bicyclette, à cheval); (in car) rouler; (on a horse as sport) monter à cheval. ● vt (a particular horse) monter; (distance) parcourir. ● n promenade f, tour m; (distance) trajet m; give sb a ~ (US) prendre qn en voiture; go for a ~ aller faire un tour (à bicyclette, à cheval). **rider** n cavalier/-ière m/f; (in horse race) jockey m; (cyclist) cycliste mf; (motorcyclist) motocycliste mf.

ridge /rɪdʒ/ n arête f, crête f.

ridiculous /rɪ'dɪkjʊləs/ adj ridicule.

riding /'raɪdɪŋ/ n équitation f.

rifle /'raɪfl/ n fusil m. ● vt (rob) dévaliser.

rift /rɪft/ n (crack) fissure f; (between people) désaccord m.

rig /rɪg/ vt (pt **rigged**) (equip) équiper; (election, match) truquer. ● n (for oil) derrick m. □ ~ **out** habiller; ~ **up** (arrange) arranger.

right /raɪt/ adj (morally) bon; (fair) juste; (best) bon, qu'il faut; (not left) droit; be ~ (person) avoir raison (to do); (calculation, watch) être exact; put ~ arranger, rectifier. ● n (entitlement) droit m; (not left) droite f; (not evil) le bien; be in the ~ avoir raison; on the ~ à droite. ● vt (a wrong, sth fallen) redresser. ● adv (not left) à droite; (directly) tout droit; (exactly) bien, juste; (completely) tout à fait); ~ away tout de suite; ~ **now** (at once) tout de suite; (at present) en ce moment.

righteous /'raɪtʃəs/ adj vertueux.

rightful /'raɪtfl/ adj légitime.

right-handed adj droitier.

rightly /'raɪtlɪ/ adv correctement; (with reason) à juste titre.

right of way n (Auto) priorité f.

right wing adj de droite.

rigid /'rɪdʒɪd/ adj rigide.

rigorous /'rɪgərəs/ adj rigoureux.

rim /rɪm/ n bord m.

rind /raɪnd/ n (on cheese) croûte f; (on bacon) couenne f; (on fruit) écorce f.

ring[1] /rɪŋ/ n (hoop) anneau m;

(jewellery) bague f; (circle) cercle m; (boxing) ring m; (wedding) ~ alliance f. ● vt entourer; (word in text) entourer d'un cercle.

ring[2] /rɪŋ/ vt/i (pt **rang**; pp **rung**) sonner; (of words) retentir; ~ **the bell** sonner. ● n sonnerie f; give sb a ~ donner un coup de fil à qn. □ ~ **back** rappeler; ~ **off** raccrocher; ~ **up** téléphoner (à). ~**tone** sonnerie f.

ring road n périphérique m.

rink /rɪŋk/ n patinoire f.

rinse /rɪns/ vt rincer; ~ **out** rincer. ● n rinçage m.

riot /'raɪət/ n émeute f; (of colours) profusion f; **run** ~ se déchaîner. ● vi faire une émeute.

rip /rɪp/ vt/i (pt **ripped**) (se) déchirer; **let** ~ (not check) laisser courir; ~ **off** ⊠ rouler. ● n déchirure f.

ripe /raɪp/ adj mûr. **ripen** /raɪp/ vt/i mûrir.

rip-off n ⊥ vol m; arnaque f ⊥.

ripple /'rɪpl/ n ride f, ondulation f. ● vt/i (water) (se) rider.

rise /raɪz/ vi (pt **rose**; pp **risen**) (increase) monter, s'élever; (stand up, get up) se lever; (rebel) se soulever; (sun) se lever; (water) monter; ~ **up** se soulever. ● n (slope) pente f; (increase) hausse f; (in pay) augmentation f; (progress, boom) essor m; **give** ~ **to** donner lieu à.

risk /rɪsk/ n risque m; **at** ~ menacé. ● vt risquer; ~ **doing** (venture) se risquer à faire. **risky** adj risqué.

rite /raɪt/ n rite m; **last** ~**s** derniers sacrements mpl.

rival /'raɪvl/ n rival/-e m/f. ● adj rival; (claim) opposé. ● vt (pt **rivalled**) rivaliser avec.

river /'rɪvə(r)/ n rivière f; (flowing into sea) fleuve m. ● adj (fishing, traffic) fluvial.

rivet /'rɪvɪt/ n (bolt) rivet m. ● vt (pt **riveted**), river, riveter.

Riviera /rɪvɪ'eərə/ n the (French) ~ la Côte d'Azur.

road /rəʊd/ n route f; (in town) rue f; (small) chemin m; the ~ to (glory: fig) le chemin de. ● adj (sign, safety) routier. ~**map** n carte f routière. ~ **rage** n violence f au volant. ~**worthy** adj en état de marche.

roam /rəʊm/ vi errer. ● vt (streets, seas) parcourir.

roar /rɔː(r)/ n hurlement m; (of lion, wind) rugissement m; (of lorry, thunder) grondement m. ● vt/i hurler; (lion, wind) rugir; (lorry, thunder) gronder; ~ **with laughter** rire aux éclats.

roast /rəʊst/ vt/i rôtir. ● n (meat) rôti m. ● adj rôti. ~ **beef** n rôti m de bœuf.

rob /rɒb/ vt (pt **robbed**) voler (sb of sth qch à qn); (bank, house) dévaliser; (deprive) priver of de). **robber** n voleur/-euse m/f. **robbery** n vol m.

robe /rəʊb/ n (of judge) robe f; (dressinggown) peignoir m.

robin /'rɒbɪn/ n rouge-gorge m.

robot /'rəʊbɒt/ n robot m.

robust /rəʊ'bʌst/ adj robuste.

rock /rɒk/ n roche f; (rock face, boulder) rocher m; (hurled stone) pierre f; (sweet) sucre m d'orge; (Mus) rock m; **on the** ~**s** (drink) avec des glaçons; (marriage) en crise. ● vt/i (se) balancer; (shake) (faire) trembler; (child) bercer. ~**climbing** n varappe f.

rocket /'rɒkɪt/ n fusée f.

rocking-chair n fauteuil m à bascule.

rocky /'rɒkɪ/ adj (**-ier, -iest**) (ground) rocailleux; (hill) rocheux; (shaky: fig) branlant.

rod /rɒd/ n (metal) tige f; (wooden) baguette f; (for fishing) canne f à pêche.

rode /rəʊd/ →RIDE.

roe /rəʊ/ n œufs mpl de poisson.

rogue /rəʊg/ n (dishonest) bandit m; (mischievous) coquin/-e m/f.

role /rəʊl/ n rôle m.

roll /rəʊl/ vt/i rouler; ~ (about) (child, dog) se rouler; **be** ~**ing (in money)** 🄸 rouler sur l'or. ● n rouleau m; (list) liste f; (bread) petit pain m; (of drum, thunder) roulement m; (of ship) roulis m. □ ~ **out** étendre; ~ **over** se retourner; ~ **up** (sleeves) retrousser.

roll-call n appel m.

roller /'rəʊlə(r)/ n rouleau m. ~ **blade** n patin m en ligne, roller m. ~**coaster** n montagnes fpl russes. ~**skate** n patin m à roulettes.

ROM abbr (**read-only memory**) mémoire f morte.

Roman /'rəʊmən/ adj & n romain/ -e (m/f). ~ **Catholic** adj & n catholique (mf).

romance /rəʊ'mæns/ n (novel) roman m d'amour; (love) amour m; (affair) idylle f; (fig) poésie f.

Romania /rəʊ'meɪnɪə/ n Roumanie f.

Romanian /rəʊ'meɪnɪən/ adj roumain. ● n (person) Roumain/-e m/f; (language) roumain m.

romantic /rəʊ'mæntɪk/ adj (love) romantique; (of the imagination) romanesque.

roof /ruːf/ n toit m; (of mouth) palais m. ● vt recouvrir. ~**rack** n galerie f. ~**top** n toit m.

room /ruːm/ n pièce f; (bedroom) chambre f; (large hall) salle f; (space) place f; ~ **for manoeuvre** marge f de manœuvre. ~**mate** n camarade *mf* de chambre.

roomy /'ruːmɪ/ *adj* spacieux; (*clothes*) ample.

root /ruːt/ *n* racine *f*; (*source*) origine *f*; take ~ prendre racine. ● *vt/i* (s')enraciner. □ ~ **about** fouiller; ~ **for** (US 🔲) encourager; ~ **out** extirper.

rope /rəup/ *n* corde *f*; know the ~s être au courant. ● *vt* attacher; ~ **in** (*person*) enrôler.

rose /rəuz/ *n* rose *f*.

rosé /'rəuzeɪ/ *n* rosé *m*.

rosy /'rəuzɪ/ *adj* (**-ier, -iest**) rose; (*hopeful*) plein d'espoir.

rot /rɒt/ *vt/i* (*pt* **rotted**) pourrir.

rota /'rəutə/ *n* liste *f* (de service).

rotary /'rəutərɪ/ *adj* rotatif.

rotate /rəu'teɪt/ *vt/i* (faire) tourner; (*change round*) alterner.

rotten /'rɒtn/ *adj* pourri; (*tooth*) gâté; (*bad* 🔲) mauvais, sale.

rough /rʌf/ *adj* (*manners*) rude; (*to touch*) rugueux; (*ground*) accidenté; (*violent*) brutal; (*bad*) mauvais; (*estimate*) approximatif. ● *adv* (*live*) à la dure.

roughage /'rʌfɪdʒ/ *n* fibres *fpl*.

roughly /'rʌflɪ/ *adv* rudement; (*approximately*) à peu près.

round /raund/ *adj* rond. ● *n* (*circle*) rond *m*; (*slice*) tranche *f*; (*of visits, drinks*) tournée *f*; (*competition*) partie *f*, manche *f*; (*boxing*) round *m*; (*of talks*) série *f*; ~ **of applause** applaudissements *mpl*; go the ~s circuler. ● *prep* autour de; she lives ~ here elle habite par ici; ~ **the clock** vingt-quatre heures sur vingt-quatre. ● *adv* autour; ~ **about** (*nearby*) par ici; (*fig*) à peu près; go or come ~ **to** (*a friend*) passer chez; enough to go ~ assez pour tout le monde. ● *vt* (*object*) arrondir; (*corner*) tourner. □ ~ **off** termi-

ner; ~ **up** rassembler

roundabout /'raundəbaut/ *n* (in fairground) manège *m*; (for traffic) rond-point *m* (à sens giratoire). ● *adj* indirect.

round trip *n* voyage *m* aller-retour.

round-up *n* rassemblement *m*; (of suspects) rafle *f*.

route /ruːt/ *n* itinéraire *m*, parcours *m*; (Naut, Aviat) route *f*.

routine /ruː'tiːn/ *n* routine *f*. ● *adj* de routine.

row[1] /rəu/ *n* rangée *f*, rang *m*; in a ~ (*consecutive*) consécutif. ● *vi* ramer; (Sport) faire de l'aviron. ● *vt* ~ **a boat up the river** remonter la rivière à la rame.

row[2] /rau/ *n* (noise 🔲) tapage *m*; (quarrel 🔲) dispute *f*. ● *vi* 🔲 se disputer.

rowdy /'raudɪ/ *adj* (**-ier, -iest**) tapageur.

rowing /'rəuɪŋ/ *n* aviron *m*. ~**-boat** *n* bateau *m* à rames.

royal /'rɔɪəl/ *adj* royal. **royalty** *n* famille *f* royale; **royalties** droits *mpl* d'auteur.

RSI *abbr* (repetitive strain injury) TMS *m*, trouble *m* musculo-squelettique.

rub /rʌb/ *vt/i* (*pt* **rubbed**) frotter; ~ **it in** insister, en rajouter. ● *n* friction *f*. □ ~ **out** (s')effacer.

rubber /'rʌbə(r)/ *n* caoutchouc *m*; (eraser) gomme *f*. ~ **band** *n* élastique *m*. ~ **stamp** *n* tampon *m*.

rubbish /'rʌbɪʃ/ *n* (refuse) ordures *fpl*; (junk) saletés *fpl*; (fig) bêtises *fpl*.

rubble /'rʌbl/ *n* décombres *mpl*.

ruby /'ruːbɪ/ *n* rubis *m*.

rucksack /'rʌksæk/ *n* sac *m* à dos.

rude /ruːd/ *adj* impoli, grossier; (improper) indécent; (blow) brutal.

ruffle /'rʌfl/ *vt* (hair) ébouriffer;

(*clothes*) froisser; (*person*) contrarier. ● n (frill) ruche f.

rug /rʌg/ n petit tapis m.

rugby /'rʌgbɪ/ n rugby m.

rugged /'rʌgɪd/ adj (*surface*) rude, rugueux; (*ground*) accidenté; (*character*, *features*) rude.

ruin /'ru:ɪn/ n ruine f. ● vt (destroy) ruiner; (damage) abîmer; (spoil) gâter.

rule /ru:l/ n règle f; (regulation) règlement m; (Pol) gouvernement m; as a ~ en règle générale. ● vt gouverner; (master) dominer; (decide) décider; ~ out exclure. ● vi régner. **ruler** n dirigeant-e m/f; gouvernant m; (measure) règle f.

ruling /'ru:lɪŋ/ adj (class) dirigeant; (*party*) au pouvoir. ● n décision f.

rum /rʌm/ n rhum m.

rumble /'rʌmbl/ vi gronder; (stomach) gargouiller. ● n grondement m; gargouillement m.

rumour, (US) **rumor** /'ru:mə(r)/ n bruit m, rumeur f; there's a ~ that le bruit court que.

rump /rʌmp/ n (of animal) croupe f; (of bird) croupion m; (steak) romsteck m.

run /rʌn/ vi (pt ran; pp run; pres p running) courir; (flow) couler; (pass) passer; (function) marcher; (melt) fondre; (extend) s'étendre; (of bus) circuler; (of play) se jouer; (last) durer; (of colour in washing) déteindre; (in election) être candidat. ● vt (manage) diriger; (event) organiser; (risk, race) courir; (house) tenir; (temperature, errand) faire; (Comput) exécuter. ● n course f; (journey) parcours m; (outing) promenade f; (rush) ruée f; (series) série f; (for chickens) enclos m; (in cricket) point m; in the long ~ avec le temps; on the ~ en fuite.

□ ~ **across** rencontrer par hasard; ~ **away** s'enfuir; ~ **down** descendre en courant; (of vehicle) renverser; (production) réduire progressivement; (belittle) dénigrer; ~ **into** (hit) heurter; ~ **off** (copies) tirer; ~ **out** (be used up) s'épuiser; (of lease) expirer; ~ **out of** manquer de; ~ **over** (of vehicle) écraser; (details) revoir; ~ **through** regarder qch rapidement; ~ **sth through** sth through sth à travers qch; ~ **up** (bill) accumuler.

runaway /'rʌnəweɪ/ n fugitif-ive m/f. ● adj fugitif; (horse, vehicle) fou; (inflation) galopant.

rung /rʌŋ/ ⇒**RING²**. ● n (of ladder) barreau m.

runner /'rʌnə(r)/ n coureur-euse m/f. ~ **bean** n haricot m d'Espagne. ~**up** n second-e m/f.

running /'rʌnɪŋ/ n course f à pied; (of business) gestion f; (of machine) marche f; be in the ~ for être sur les rangs pour. ● adj (commentary) suivi; (water) courant; four days ~ quatre jours de suite.

runway /'rʌnweɪ/ n piste f.

rural /'rʊərəl/ adj rural.

rush /rʌʃ/ vi (move) se précipiter; (be in a hurry) se dépêcher. ● vt (person) bousculer; (Mil) prendre d'assaut; ~ **to** envoyer d'urgence à. ● n ruée f; (haste) bousculade f; (plant) jonc m; in a ~ pressé. ~**hour** n heure f de pointe.

Russia /'rʌʃə/ n Russie f.

Russian /'rʌʃn/ adj russe. ● n (person) Russe mf; (language) russe.

rust /rʌst/ n rouille f. ● vt/i rouiller.

rustle /'rʌsl/ vt/i (papers) froisser.

rusty /'rʌstɪ/ adj rouillé.

ruthless /'ru:θlɪs/ adj impitoyable.

rye /raɪ/ n seigle m.

Ss

sabbath /'sæbəθ/ n (Jewish) sabbat m; (Christian) jour m du seigneur.

sabbatical /sə'bætɪkl/ adj (Univ) sabbatique.

sabotage /'sæbətɑːʒ/ n sabotage m. ● vt saboter.

saccharin /'sækərɪn/ n saccharine f.

sack /sæk/ n (bag) sac m; get the ~ 🇬🇧 être renvoyé. ● vt 🇬🇧 renvoyer; (plunder) saccager. **sacking** (cloth) toile f à sac; (dismissal 🇬🇧) renvoi m.

sacrament /'sækrəmənt/ n sacrement m.

sacred /'seɪkrɪd/ adj sacré.

sacrifice /'sækrɪfaɪs/ n sacrifice m. ● vt sacrifier.

sad /sæd/ adj (**sadder, saddest**) triste.

saddle /'sædl/ n selle f. ● vt (horse) seller.

sadist /'seɪdɪst/ n sadique mf. **sadistic** adj sadique.

sadly /'sædlɪ/ adv tristement; (unfortunately) malheureusement.

sadness /'sædnɪs/ n tristesse f.

safe /seɪf/ adj (not dangerous) sans danger; (reliable) sûr; (out of danger) en sécurité; (after accident) sain et sauf; ~ **from** à l'abri de. ● n coffre-fort m.

safeguard /'seɪfgɑːd/ n sauvegarde f. ● vt sauvegarder.

safely /'seɪflɪ/ adv sans danger; (in safe place) en sûreté.

safety /'seɪftɪ/ n sécurité f. ~**-belt** n ceinture f de sécurité. ~**-pin** n épingle f de sûreté. ~**-valve** n sou-

pape f de sûreté.

saffron /'sæfrən/ n safran m.

sag /sæg/ vi (pt **sagged**) (beam, mattress) s'affaisser; (flesh) être flasque.

sage /seɪdʒ/ n (herb) sauge f.

Sagittarius /sædʒɪ'teəriəs/ n Sagittaire m.

said /sed/ ⇒SAY.

sail /seɪl/ n voile f; (journey) tour m en bateau. ● vi (person) voyager en bateau; (as sport) faire de la voile; (set off) prendre la mer; ~ **across** traverser. ● vt (boat) piloter; (sea) traverser. **sailing-boat, sailing-ship** n voilier m.

sailor /'seɪlə(r)/ n marin m.

saint /seɪnt/ n saint/-e m/f.

sake /seɪk/ n **for the ~ of** pour.

salad /'sæləd/ n salade f.

salaried /'sælərɪd/ adj salarié.

salary /'sælərɪ/ n salaire m.

sale /seɪl/ n vente f; **for** ~ à vendre; **on** ~ en vente; (reduced) en solde; ~**s** (reductions) soldes mpl; ~**s assistant**, (US) ~**s clerk** vendeur/-euse m/f.

salesman /'seɪlzmən/ n (pl **-men**) (in shop) vendeur m; (traveller) représentant m.

saline /'seɪlaɪn/ adj salin. ● n sérum m physiologique.

saliva /sə'laɪvə/ n salive f.

salmon /'sæmən/ n inv saumon m.

salon /'sælɒn/ n salon m.

saloon /sə'luːn/ n (on ship) salon m; ~ (**car**) berline f.

salt /sɔːlt/ n sel m. ● vt saler. **salty** adj salé.

salutary /'sæljʊtrɪ/ adj salutaire.

salute /sə'luːt/ n salut m. ● vt saluer. ● vi faire un salut.

salvage /'sælvɪdʒ/ n sauvetage m; (of waste) récupération f. ● vt sauver; (for re-use) récupérer.

same /seɪm/ adj même (as que).
● pron the ~ le même, la même, les mêmes; at the ~ time en même temps; the ~ (thing) la même chose.

sample /'sɑːmpl/ n échantillon m; (of blood) prélèvement m. ● vt essayer; (food) goûter.

sanctimonious /sæŋktɪ'məʊnɪəs/ adj (pej) supérieur.

sanction /'sæŋkʃn/ n sanction f. ● vt sanctionner.

sanctity /'sæŋktɪtɪ/ n sainteté f.

sanctuary /'sæŋktʃʊərɪ/ n (safe place) refuge m; (Relig) sanctuaire m; (for animals) réserve f.

sand /sænd/ n sable m; ~s (beach) plage f.

sandal /'sændl/ n sandale f.

sandpaper /'sændpeɪpə(r)/ n papier m de verre. ● vt poncer.

sandpit /'sændpɪt/ n bac m à sable.

sandwich /'sænwɪdʒ/ n sandwich m; ~ course cours m avec stage pratique.

sandy /'sændɪ/ adj (beach) de sable; (soil) sablonneux; (hair) blond roux inv.

sane /seɪn/ adj (view) sensé; (person) sain d'esprit.

sang /sæŋ/ ⇒SING.

sanitary /'sænɪtrɪ/ adj (clean) hygiénique; (system) sanitaire; ~ towel serviette f hygiénique.

sanitation /sænɪ'teɪʃn/ n installations fpl sanitaires.

sanity /'sænətɪ/ n équilibre m mental; (sense) bon sens m.

sank /sæŋk/ ⇒SINK.

Santa (Claus) /'sæntə (klɔːz)/ n le père Noël.

sapphire /'sæfaɪə(r)/ n saphir m.

sarcasm /'sɑːkæzəm/ n sarcasme m. **sarcastic** adj sarcastique.

sash /sæʃ/ n (on uniform) écharpe f; (on dress) ceinture f.

sat /sæt/ ⇒SIT.

satchel /'sætʃəl/ n cartable m.

satellite /'sætəlaɪt/ n & adj satellite (m); ~ dish antenne f parabolique.

satire /'sætaɪə(r)/ n satire f. **satirical** adj satirique.

satisfaction /sætɪs'fækʃn/ n satisfaction f.

satisfactory /sætɪs'fæktərɪ/ adj satisfaisant.

satisfy /'sætɪsfaɪ/ vt satisfaire; (convince) convaincre.

satphone /'sætfəʊn/ n téléphone m satellite.

saturate /'sætʃəreɪt/ vt saturer. **saturated** adj (wet) trempé.

Saturday /'sætədeɪ/ n samedi m.

sauce /sɔːs/ n sauce f.

saucepan /'sɔːspən/ n casserole f.

saucer /'sɔːsə(r)/ n soucoupe f.

Saudi Arabia /saʊdɪ ə'reɪbɪə/ n Arabie f saoudite.

sausage /'sɒsɪdʒ/ n (for cooking) saucisse f; (ready to eat) saucisson m.

savage /'sævɪdʒ/ adj (blow, temper) violent; (attack) sauvage. ● n sauvage mf. ● vt attaquer sauvagement.

save /seɪv/ vt sauver; (money) économiser; (time) gagner; (keep) garder; ~ (sb) doing sth éviter (à qn) de faire qch. ● n (football) arrêt m. **saver** n épargnant/-e m/f. **saving** n économie f. **savings** npl économies fpl.

saviour, (US) **savior** /'seɪvɪə(r)/ n sauveur m.

savour, (US) **savor** /'seɪvə(r)/ n saveur f. ● vt savourer. **savoury** adj (tasty) savoureux; (Culin) salé.

s

saw /sɔː/ →SEE. ● n scie f. ● vt (pt sawed; pp sawn or sawed) scier.

sawdust /'sɔːdʌst/ n sciure f.

saxophone /'sæksəfəʊn/ n saxophone m.

say /seɪ/ vt/i (pt said) dire; (prayer) faire. ● n have a ~ dire son mot; (in decision) avoir voix au chapitre. **saying** n proverbe m.

scab /skæb/ n croûte f.

scaffolding /'skæfəldɪŋ/ n échafaudage m.

scald /skɔːld/ vt (injure, cleanse) ébouillanter. ● n brûlure f.

scale /skeɪl/ n (for measuring) échelle f; (extent) étendue f; (Mus) gamme f; (on fish) écaille f; on a small ~ sur une petite échelle; ~ model maquette f. ● vt (climb) escalader; ~ down réduire. **scales** npl (for weighing) balance f.

scallop /'skɒləp/ n coquille f Saint-Jacques.

scalp /skælp/ n cuir m chevelu.

scampi /'skæmpi/ npl (fresh) langoustines fpl; (breaded) scampi mpl.

scan /skæn/ vt (pt scanned) scruter; (quickly) parcourir. ● n (ultrasound) échographie f; (CAT) scanner m.

scandal /'skændl/ n scandale m; (gossip) potins mpl 🗓.

Scandinavia /skændɪ'neɪvɪə/ n Scandinavie f.

scanty /'skænti/ adj (-ier, -iest) maigre; (clothing) minuscule.

scapegoat /'skeɪpgəʊt/ n bouc m émissaire.

scar /skɑː(r)/ n cicatrice f. ● vt (pt scarred) marquer.

scarce /skeəs/ adj rare. **scarcely** adv à peine.

scare /skeə(r)/ vt faire peur à; be ~d avoir peur. ● n peur f; bomb ~ alerte f à la bombe. **scarecrow** n

épouvantail m.

scarf /skɑːf/ n (pl scarves) écharpe f; (over head) foulard m.

scarlet /'skɑːlət/ adj écarlate; ~ fever scarlatine f.

scary /'skeərɪ/ adj (-ier, -iest) 🗓 qui fait peur.

scathing /'skeɪðɪŋ/ adj cinglant.

scatter /'skætə(r)/ vt (throw) éparpiller, répandre; (disperse) disperser. ● vi se disperser.

scavenge /'skævɪndʒ/ vi fouiller (dans les ordures). **scavenger** n (animal) charognard m.

scene /siːn/ n scène f; (of accident, crime) lieu m; (sight) spectacle m; behind the ~s en coulisse. **scenery** n paysage m; (Theat) décors mpl.

scenic adj panoramique.

scent /sent/ n (perfume) parfum m; (trail) piste f. ● vt flairer; (make fragrant) parfumer.

sceptic /'skeptɪk/ n sceptique mf. **sceptical** adj sceptique. **scepticism** n scepticisme m.

schedule /'ʃedjuːl/, /'skedʒʊl/ n horaire m; (for job) planning m; behind ~ en retard; on ~ dans les temps. ● vt prévoir; ~d flight vol m régulier.

scheme /skiːm/ n projet m; (dishonest) combine f; pension ~ plan m de retraite. ● vi comploter.

schizophrenic /skɪtsəʊ'frenɪk/ adj & n schizophrène (mf).

scholar /'skɒlə(r)/ n érudit/-e m/f. **school** /skuːl/ n école f; go to ~ aller à l'école. ● adj (age, year, holidays) scolaire. ~**boy** n élève m. ~**girl** n élève f. **schooling** n scolarité f. ~**teacher** n (primary) instituteur/-trice m/f; (secondary) professeur m.

science /'saɪəns/ n science f; teach ~ enseigner les sciences. **scientific**

adj scientifique. **scientist** *n* scientifique *mf*.

scissors /'sɪzəz/ *npl* ciseaux *mpl*.

scold /skəʊld/ *vt* gronder.

scoop /sku:p/ *n* (shovel) pelle *f*; (measure) mesure *f*; (for ice cream) cuillère *f* à glace; (news) exclusivité *f*.

scooter /'sku:tə(r)/ *n* (child's) trottinette *f*; (motor cycle) scooter *m*.

scope /skəʊp/ *n* étendue *f*; (competence) compétence *f*; (opportunity) possibilité *f*.

scorch /skɔ:tʃ/ *vt* brûler; (iron) roussir.

score /skɔ:(r)/ *n* score *m*; (Mus) partition *f*; on that ~ à cet égard. ● *vt* marquer; (success) remporter. ● *vi* marquer un point; (football) marquer un but; (keep score) marquer les points. **scorer** *n* (Sport) marqueur *m*.

scorn /skɔ:n/ *n* mépris *m*. ● *vt* mépriser.

Scorpio /'skɔ:pɪəʊ/ *n* Scorpion *m*.

Scot /skɒt/ *n* écossais/-e *m/f*.

Scotland /'skɒtlənd/ *n* écosse *f*.

Scottish /'skɒtɪʃ/ *adj* écossais.

> **Scottish Parliament** En 1997, les Écossais se prononcèrent par référendum pour le rétablissement de leur parlement. Celui-ci siège depuis 1999 à Édimbourg et comprend 129 membres. Ses compétences s'étendent aux affaires internes à l'Écosse (santé, éducation, environnement, etc.), mais il dispose d'un pouvoir fiscal limité et la défense, les affaires étrangères et les finances restent contrôlées par Londres.

scoundrel /'skaʊndrəl/ *n* gredin *m*.

scour /'skaʊə(r)/ *vt* (pan) récurer; (search) parcourir. **scourer** *n* tampon *m* à récurer.

scourge /skɜ:dʒ/ *n* fléau *m*.

scout /skaʊt/ *n* éclaireur *m*. ● *vi* ~ around for rechercher.

scowl /skaʊl/ *n* air *m* renfrogné. ● *vi* prendre un air renfrogné.

scramble /'skræmbl/ *vi* (clamber) grimper. ● *vt* (eggs) brouiller. ● *n* (rush) course *f*.

scrap /skræp/ *n* petit morceau *m*; ~s (of metal, fabric) déchets *mpl*; (of food) restes *mpl*; (fight 🔲) bagarre *f*. ● *vt* (*pt* **scrapped**) abandonner; (car) détruire.

scrape /skreɪp/ *vt* gratter; (damage) érafler. ● *vi* ~ against érafler. □ ~ **through** réussir de justesse.

scrap: ~**-paper** *n* papier *m* brouillon. ~**yard** *n* casse *f*.

scratch /skrætʃ/ *vt/i* (se) gratter; (with claw, nail) griffer; (graze) érafler; (mark) rayer. ● *n* (on body) égratignure *f*; (on surface) éraflure *f*; start from ~ partir de zéro; up to ~ à la hauteur. ~ **card** *n* jeu *m* de grattage.

scrawl /skrɔ:l/ *n* gribouillage *m*. ● *vt/i* gribouiller.

scrawny /'skrɔ:nɪ/ *adj* (**-ier, -iest**) décharné.

scream /skri:m/ *vt/i* crier. ● *n* cri *m* (perçant).

screech /skri:tʃ/ *vi* (scream) hurler; (tyres) crisser. ● *n* cri *m* strident; (of tyres) crissement *m*.

screen /skri:n/ *n* écran *m*; (folding) paravent *m*. ● *vt* masquer; (protect) protéger; (film) projeter; (candidates) filtrer; (Med) faire subir un test de dépistage. **screening** *n* (cinema) projection *f*; (Med) dépistage *m*.

screen: ~**play** *n* scénario *m*. ~

saver n protecteur m d'écran.

screw /skru:/ n vis f. ● vt visser; ~ **up** (eyes) plisser; (ruin 🗊) cafouiller 🗊. **~driver** n tournevis m.

scribble /'skrɪbl/ vt/i griffonner. ● n griffonnage m.

script /skrɪpt/ n script m; (of play) texte m.

scroll /skrəʊl/ n rouleau m. ● vt/i (Comput) (faire) défiler. ~ **bar** n barre f de défilement.

scrounge /skraʊndʒ/ 🗊 vt (favour) quémander; (cigarette) piquer 🗊; ~ **money from sb** taper de l'argent à qn. ● vi ~ **off sb** vivre sur le dos de qn.

scrub /skrʌb/ n (land) broussailles fpl. ● vt/i (pt **scrubbed**) nettoyer (à la brosse), frotter.

scruffy /'skrʌfɪ/ adj (**-ier, -iest**) dépenaillé.

scrum /skrʌm/ n (rugby) mêlée f.

scruple /'skru:pl/ n scrupule m.

scrutinize /'skru:tɪnaɪz/ vt scruter. **scrutiny** n examen m minutieux.

scuba-diving /'sku:bədaɪvɪŋ/ n plongée f sousmarine.

scuffle /'skʌfl/ n bagarre f.

sculpt /skʌlpt/ vt/i sculpter. **sculptor** n sculpteur m.

sculpture /'skʌlptʃə(r)/ n sculpture f.

scum /skʌm/ n (on liquid) mousse f; (people: pej) racaille f.

scurry /'skʌrɪ/ vi se précipiter, courir (for pour chercher); ~ **off** se sauver.

sea /si:/ n mer f; **at** ~ en mer; **by** ~ par mer. ● adj (air) marin; (bird) de mer; (voyage) par mer. **~food** n fruits mpl de mer. **~gull** n mouette f.

seal /si:l/ n (animal) phoque m; (insignia) sceau m; (with wax) cachet m. ● vt sceller; cacheter; (stick

down) coller. □ ~ **off** (area) boucler.

seam /si:m/ n (in cloth) couture f; (of coal) veine f.

search /sɜ:tʃ/ vt/i (examine) fouiller; (seek) chercher; (study) examiner; (Comput) rechercher. ● n fouille f; (quest) recherches fpl; (Comput) recherche f; **in** ~ **of** à la recherche de. ~ **engine** n (Internet) moteur m de recherche. **~light** n projecteur m. **~-warrant** n mandat m de perquisition.

sea: **~shell** n coquillage m. **~shore** n (coast) littoral m; (beach) plage f.

seasick /'si:sɪk/ adj **be** ~ avoir le mal de mer.

seaside /'si:saɪd/ n bord m de la mer.

season /'si:zn/ n saison f; ~ **ticket** carte f d'abonnement. ● vt assaisonner. **seasonal** adj saisonnier. **seasoning** n assaisonnement m.

seat /si:t/ n siège m; (place) place f; (of trousers) fond m; **take a** ~ asseyez-vous. ● vt (put) placer; **the room** ~**s 30** la salle peut accueillir 30 personnes. **~-belt** n ceinture f (de sécurité).

seaweed /'si:wi:d/ n algue f marine.

secluded /sɪ'klu:dɪd/ adj retiré.

seclusion /sɪ'klu:ʒn/ n isolement m.

second[1] /'sekənd/ adj deuxième, second; **a** ~ **chance** une nouvelle chance; **have** ~ **thoughts** avoir des doutes. ● n deuxième mf, second/-e m/f; (unit of time) seconde f; ~ **s** (food) rab m. 🗊 ● adv (in race) deuxième; (secondly) deuxièmement. ● vt (proposal) appuyer.

second[2] /sɪ'kɒnd/ vt (transfer) détacher (to à).

secondary /ˈsekəndrɪ/ adj secondaire; ~school lycée m, école f secondaire.

second-best n pis-aller m.

second-class adj (Rail) de deuxième classe; (post) au tarif lent.

second hand n (on clock) trotteuse f.

second-hand adj & adv (article) d'occasion; (information) de seconde main.

secondly /ˈsekəndlɪ/ adv deuxièmement.

second-rate adj médiocre.

secrecy /ˈsiːkrəsɪ/ n secret m.

secret /ˈsiːkrɪt/ adj secret. ● n secret m; in ~ en secret.

secretarial /sekrəˈteərɪəl/ adj (work) de secrétaire.

secretary /ˈsekrətrɪ/ n secrétaire mf; S~ of State ministre m; (US) ministre m des Affaires étrangères.

secrete /sɪˈkriːt/ vt (Med) sécréter; (hide) cacher.

secretive /ˈsiːkrətɪv/ adj secret. **secretly** adv secrètement.

sect /sekt/ n secte f. **sectarian** adj sectaire.

section /ˈsekʃn/ n partie f; (in store) rayon m; (of newspaper) rubrique f; (of book) passage m.

sector /ˈsektə(r)/ n secteur m.

secular /ˈsekjʊlə(r)/ adj (school) laïque; (art, music) profane.

secure /sɪˈkjʊə(r)/ adj (job, marriage) stable; (knot, lock) solide; (window) bien fermé; (feeling) de sécurité; (person) sécurisé. ● vt attacher; (obtain) s'assurer; (ensure) assurer.

security /sɪˈkjʊərətɪ/ n (safety) sécurité f; (for loan) caution f; ~ guard vigile m.

sedate /sɪˈdeɪt/ adj calme. ● vt don-

ner un sédatif à. **sedative** n sédatif m.

seduce /sɪˈdjuːs/ vt séduire. **seducer** n séducteur/-trice m/f. **seduction** n séduction f. **seductive** adj séduisant.

see /siː/ vt/i (pt saw; pp seen) voir; see you (soon)! à bientôt!; ~ing that vu que. □ ~ **out** (person) raccompagner à la porte; ~ **through** (deception) déceler; (person) percer à jour; ~ **sth through** mener qch à bonne fin; ~ **to** s'occuper de; ~ **to it that** veiller à ce que.

seed /siːd/ n (Bot) graine f; (collectively) graines fpl; (origin: fig) germe m; (tennis) tête f de série. **seedling** n plant m.

seek /siːk/ vt (pt sought) chercher.

seem /siːm/ vi sembler; he ~s to think it a ~ il a l'air de croire.

seen /siːn/ ➔SEE.

seep /siːp/ vi suinter; ~ **into** s'infiltrer dans.

see-saw /ˈsiːsɔː/ n tapecul m. ● vi osciller.

seethe /siːð/ vi ~ **with** (anger) bouillir de; (people) grouiller de.

segment /ˈsegmənt/ n segment m; (of orange) quartier m.

segregate /ˈsegrɪgeɪt/ vt séparer.

seize /siːz/ vt saisir; (territory, prisoner) s'emparer de. ● vi ~ **on** (chance) saisir; ~ **up** (engine) se gripper.

seizure /ˈsiːʒə(r)/ n (Med) crise f.

seldom /ˈseldəm/ adv rarement.

select /sɪˈlekt/ vt sélectionner. ● adj privilégié. **selection** n sélection f. **selective** adj sélectif.

self /self/ n (pl selves) moi m; (on cheque) moi-même. ~-**assured** adj plein d'assurance. ~-**catering** adj (holiday) en location. ~-**centred**, (US) ~-**centered** adj égocentrique.

~-**confident** adj sûr de soi.
~-**conscious** adj timide.
~-**contained** adj (flat) indépendant. ~-**control** n sangfroid m.
~-**defence** n autodéfense f; (Jur) légitime défense f. ~-**employed** adj qui travaille à son compte.
~-**esteem** n amour-propre m.
~-**governing** adj autonome.
~-**indulgent** adj complaisant.
~-**interest** n intérêt m personnel.

selfish /ˈselfɪʃ/ adj égoïste.

selfless /ˈselflɪs/ adj désintéressé.

self: ~-**portrait** n autoportrait m.
~-**reliant** adj autosuffisant.
~-**respect** n respect m de soi.
~-**righteous** adj satisfait de soi.
~-**sacrifice** n abnégation f.
~-**satisfied** adj satisfait de soi.
~-**seeking** adj égoïste. ~-**service** n & adj libre-service (m).

sell /sel/ vt/i (pt sold) vendre; ~ well se vendre bien. □ ~ **off** liquider; ~ **out** (items) se vendre; have sold out avoir tout vendu.

Sellotape® /ˈseləʊteɪp/ n scotch® m.

sell-out n (betrayal) ⊤ revirement m; be a ~ (show) afficher complet.

semester /sɪˈmestə(r)/ n (Univ) semestre m.

semicircle /ˈsemɪsɜːkl/ n demi-cercle m.

semicolon /semɪˈkəʊlən/ n point-virgule m.

semi-detached /semɪdɪˈtætʃt/ adj ~ house maison f jumelée.

semifinal /semɪˈfaɪnl/ n demi-finale f.

seminar /ˈsemɪnɑː(r)/ n séminaire m.

semolina /seməˈliːnə/ n semoule f.

senate /ˈsenɪt/ n sénat m. **senator** n sénateur m.

send /send/ vt/i (pt sent) envoyer.

□ ~ **away** (dismiss) renvoyer; ~ **(away** or **off) for** commander (par la poste); ~ **back** renvoyer; ~ **for** (person, help) envoyer chercher; ~ **up** ⊤ parodier.

senile /ˈsiːnaɪl/ adj sénile.

senior /ˈsiːnɪə(r)/ adj plus âgé (to que); (in rank) haut placé; be ~ to sb être le supérieur de qn. ● n aîné/-e m/f. ~ **citizen** n personne f âgée. ~ **school** n lycée m.

sensation /senˈseɪʃn/ n sensation f. **sensational** adj sensationnel.

sense /sens/ n sens m; (mental impression) sentiment m; (common sense) bon sens m; ~s (mind) raison f; there's no ~ in doing cela ne sert à rien de faire; make ~ avoir un sens; make ~ of comprendre. ● vt (pres)entir. **senseless** adj insensé; (Med) sans connaissance.

sensible /ˈsensəbl/ adj raisonnable; (clothing) pratique.

sensitive /ˈsensətɪv/ adj sensible (to à); (issue) difficile.

sensory /ˈsensərɪ/ adj sensoriel.

sensual /ˈsenʃʊəl/ adj sensuel. **sensuality** n sensualité f.

sensuous /ˈsenʃʊəs/ adj sensuel.

sent /sent/ ⟶SEND.

sentence /ˈsentəns/ n phrase f; (punishment: Jur) peine f. ● vt ~ to condamner à.

sentiment /ˈsentɪmənt/ n sentiment m. **sentimental** adj sentimental.

sentry /ˈsentrɪ/ n sentinelle f.

separate[1] /ˈseprət/ adj (piece) à part; (issue) autre; (sections) différent; (organizations) distinct.

separate[2] /ˈsepəreɪt/ vt/i (se) séparer.

separately /ˈsepərətlɪ/ adv séparément.

separation /sepə'reɪʃn/ n séparation f.

September /sep'tembə(r)/ n septembre m.

septic /'septɪk/ adj (wound) infecté; ~ **tank** fosse f septique.

sequel /'si:kwəl/ n suite f.

sequence /'si:kwəns/ n (order) ordre m; (series) suite f; (in film) séquence f.

Serb /sɜːb/ adj serbe. ● n (person) Serbe mf; (Ling) serbe m.

Serbia /'sɜːbɪə/ n Serbie f.

sergeant /'sɑːdʒənt/ n (Mil) sergent m; (policeman) brigadier m.

serial /'sɪərɪəl/ n feuilleton m. ● adj (Comput) série inv.

series /'sɪəriːz/ n inv série f.

serious /'sɪərɪəs/ adj sérieux; (accident, crime) grave.

seriously /'sɪərɪəslɪ/ adv sérieusement; (ill) gravement; take ~ prendre au sérieux.

sermon /'sɜːmən/ n sermon m.

serpent /'sɜːpənt/ n serpent m.

serrated /sɪ'reɪtɪd/ adj dentelé.

serum /'sɪərəm/ n sérum m.

servant /'sɜːvənt/ n domestique mf.

serve /sɜːv/ vt/i servir; faire; (transport, hospital) desservir; ~ **as/to** servir de/à; ~ **a purpose** être utile; ~ **a sentence** (Jur) purger une peine. ● n (tennis) service m.

server /'sɜːvə(r)/ n serveur m; remote ~ téléserveur m.

service /'sɜːvɪs/ n service m; (maintenance) révision f; (Relig) office m; ~s (Mil) forces fpl armées. ● vt (car) réviser. ~**area** n (Auto) aire f de services. ~ **charge** n service m. ~ **station** n station-service f.

session /'seʃn/ n séance f; be in ~ (Jur) tenir séance.

set /set/ vt (pt) set; pres p setting placer; (table) mettre; (limit) fixer; (clock) mettre à l'heure; (example, task) donner; (TV), (cinema) situer; ~ **fire to** mettre le feu à; ~ **free** libérer; ~ **to music** mettre en musique. ● vi (sun) se coucher; (jelly) prendre; ~ **sail** partir. ● n (of chairs, stamps) série f; (of knives, keys) jeu m; (of people) groupe m; (TV), (radio) poste m; (Theat) décor m; (tennis) set m; (mathematics) ensemble m. ● adj (time, price) fixe; (book) au programme; (meal) à prix fixe; (procedure) bien déterminé; ~ **against sth** opposé à; be ~ **on doing** tenir absolument à faire. □ ~ **about** se mettre à; ~ **back** (delay) retarder; (cost Ⅰ) coûter; ~ **in** (take hold) s'installer, commencer; ~ **off** or **out** partir; ~ **off** (panic, riot) déclencher; (bomb) faire exploser; ~ **out** (state) présenter; (arrange) disposer; ~ **out** to do sth chercher à faire qch; ~ **up** (stall) monter; (equipment) assembler; (experiment) préparer; (company) créer; (meeting) organiser. ~**back** n revers m.

settee /se'tiː/ n canapé m.

setting /'setɪŋ/ n cadre m; (on dial) position f.

settle /'setl/ vt (arrange, pay) régler; (date) fixer; (nerves) calmer. ● vi (come to rest) (bird) se poser; (dust) se déposer; (live) s'installer. □ ~ **down** se calmer; (marry etc.) se ranger; ~ **for** accepter; ~ **in** s'installer; ~ **up** (with) régler.

settlement /'setlmənt/ n règlement m (of de); (agreement) accord m; (place) colonie f.

settler /'setlə(r)/ n colon m.

seven /'sevn/ adj & n sept (m).

seventeen /sevn'tiːn/ adj & n dix-sept (m).

s

seventh /'sevnθ/ adj & n septième (mf).

seventy /'sevntɪ/ adj & n soixante-dix (m).

sever /'sevə(r)/ vt (cut) couper; (relations) rompre.

several /'sevrəl/ adj & pron plusieurs; ~ of us plusieurs d'entre nous.

severe /sɪ'vɪə(r)/ adj (harsh) sévère; (serious) grave.

sew /səʊ/ vt/i (pt sewed; pp sewn or sewed) coudre.

sewage /'suːɪdʒ/ n eaux fpl usées.

sewer /'suːə(r)/ n égout m.

sewing /'səʊɪŋ/ n couture f. ~-machine n machine f à coudre.

sewn /səʊn/ ⇒SEW.

sex /seks/ n sexe m; have ~ avoir des rapports (sexuels). ● adj sexuel. **sexist** adj & n sexiste (mf). **sexual** adj sexuel.

shabby /'ʃæbɪ/ adj (-ier, -iest) (place, object) miteux; (person) habillé de façon miteuse; (treatment) mesquin.

shack /ʃæk/ n cabane f.

shade /ʃeɪd/ n ombre f; (of colour, opinion) nuance f; (of lamp) abat-jour m inv; a ~ bigger légèrement plus grand. ● vt (tree) ombrager; (hat) projeter un ombre sur.

shadow /'ʃædəʊ/ n ombre f. ● vt (follow) filer. S~ Cabinet n cabinet m fantôme.

shady /'ʃeɪdɪ/ adj (-ier, -iest) ombragé; (dubious) véreux.

shaft /ʃɑːft/ n (of tool) manche m; (of arrow) tige f; (in machine) axe m; (of mine) puits m; (of light) rayon m.

shake /ʃeɪk/ vt (pt shook; pp shaken) secouer; (bottle) agiter; (belief) ébranler; ~ hands with serrer la main à; ~ one's head dire non de la tête. ● vi trembler. ● n secousse f; give sth a ~ secouer qch. □ ~ off se débarrasser de. ~-up n (Pol) remaniement m.

shaky /'ʃeɪkɪ/ adj (-ier, -iest) (hand, voice) tremblant; (ladder) branlant; (weak: fig) instable.

shall /ʃæl/ v aux I ~ do je ferai; we ~ see nous verrons; we go. . . ? si on allait . . . ?

shallow /'ʃæləʊ/ adj peu profond; (fig) superficiel.

shame /ʃeɪm/ n honte f; it's a ~ c'est dommage. ● vt faire honte à.

shampoo /ʃæm'puː/ n shampooing m. ● vt faire un shampooing à.

shandy /'ʃændɪgæf/ n panaché m.

shan't ⇒SHALL NOT.

shanty /'ʃæntɪ/ n (shack) baraque f; ~ town bidonville m.

shape /ʃeɪp/ n forme f. ● vt (clay) modeler; (rock) façonner; (future: fig) déterminer; ~ sth into balls faire des boules avec qch. ● vi ~ up (plan) prendre tournure; (person) faire des progrès.

share /ʃeə(r)/ n part f; (Comm) action f. ● vt/i partager; (feature) avoir en commun. ~holder n actionnaire mf. ~ware n (Comput) logiciel m contributif.

shark /ʃɑːk/ n requin m.

sharp /ʃɑːp/ adj (knife) tranchant; (pin) pointu; (point, angle, cry) aigu; (person, mind) vif; (tone) acerbe. ● adv (stop) net; (sing, play) trop haut; six o'clock ~ six heures pile. ● n (Mus) dièse m.

sharpen /'ʃɑːpən/ vt aiguiser; (pencil) tailler.

shatter /'ʃætə(r)/ vt (glass) fracasser; (hope) briser. ● vi (glass) voler en éclats.

shave /ʃeɪv/ vt/i (se) raser. ● n have a ~ se raser. **shaver** n rasoir m électrique.

shaving /'ʃeɪvɪŋ/ n (of wood) copeau m. ● adj (cream, foam, gel) à
raser.

shawl /ʃɔːl/ n châle m.

she /ʃiː/ pron elle. ● n (animal) femelle f.

shear /ʃɪə(r)/ vt (pp **shorn** or
sheared) (sheep) tondre; ~ off se
détacher.

shears /ʃɪəz/ npl cisaille f.

shed /ʃed/ n remise f. ● vt (pt **shed**;
pres p **shedding**) perdre; (light,
tears) répandre.

sheen /ʃiːn/ n lustre m.

sheep /ʃiːp/ n inv mouton m.
~**-dog** n chien m de berger.

sheepish /'ʃiːpɪʃ/ adj penaud.

sheepskin /'ʃiːpskɪn/ n peau f de
mouton.

sheer /ʃɪə(r)/ adj pur; (steep) à pic;
(fabric) très fin. ● adv à pic.

sheet /ʃiːt/ n drap m; (of paper)
feuille f; (of glass, ice) plaque f.

shelf /ʃelf/ n (pl **shelves**) étagère f;
(in shop, fridge) rayon m; (in oven)
plaque f.

shell /ʃel/ n coquille f; (on beach)
coquillage m; (of building) carcasse
f; (explosive) obus m. ● vt (nut) décortiquer; (peas) écosser; (Mil) bombarder.

shellfish /'ʃelfɪʃ/ npl (lobster etc.)
crustacés mpl; (mollusc) coquilla-
ges mpl.

shelter /'ʃeltə(r)/ n abri m. ● vt/i
(s')abriter; (give lodging to) donner
asile à.

shelve /ʃelv/ vt (plan) mettre en
suspens.

shepherd /'ʃepəd/ n berger m;
~'s pie hachis m Parmentier. ● vt
(people) guider.

sherry /'ʃerɪ/ n xérès m.

shield /ʃiːld/ n bouclier m; (screen)
écran m. ● vt protéger.

shift /ʃɪft/ vt/i (se) déplacer, bouger; (exchange, alter) changer de.
● n changement m; (workers)
équipe f; (work) poste m; ~ work
travail m posté, travail m par roulement.

shifty /'ʃɪftɪ/ adj (-ier, -iest)
louche.

shimmer /'ʃɪmə(r)/ vi chatoyer.
● n chatoiement m.

shin /ʃɪn/ n tibia m.

shine /ʃaɪn/ vt (pt **shone**) (torch)
braquer (on sur). ● vi (light, sun,
hair) briller; (brass) reluire. ● n lustre m.

shingle /'ʃɪŋgl/ n (pebbles) galets
mpl; (on roof) bardeau m.

shingles /'ʃɪŋglz/ npl (Med)
zona m.

shiny /'ʃaɪnɪ/ adj (-ier, -iest)
brillant.

ship /ʃɪp/ n bateau m, navire m. ● vt
(pt **shipped**) transporter. **shipment**
n (by sea) cargaison f; (by air, land)
chargement m. **shipping** n (ships)
navigation f. ~**wreck** n épave f;
(event) naufrage m.

shirt /ʃɜːt/ n chemise f; (woman's)
chemisier m.

shiver /'ʃɪvə(r)/ vi frissonner. ● n
frisson m.

shock /ʃɒk/ n choc m; (Electr) décharge f; in ~ en état de choc; ~
absorber amortisseur m. ● adj (result) choc inv; (tactics) de choc. ● vt
choquer.

shoddy /'ʃɒdɪ/ adj (-ier, -iest) mal
fait; (behaviour) mesquin.

shoe /ʃuː/ n chaussure f; (of horse)
fer m; (brake) ~ sabot m (de frein).
● vt (pt **shod**; pres p **shoeing**)
(horse) ferrer. ~**lace** n lacet m. ~
size n pointure f

s

shone /ʃɒn/ →SHINE.

shook /ʃʊk/ →SHAKE.

shoot /ʃuːt/ vt (pt **shot**) (gun) tirer un coup de; (bullet) tirer; (missile, glance) lancer; (person) tirer sur; (kill) abattre; (execute) fusiller; (film) tourner. ● vi tirer (at sur). ● n (Bot) pousse f. □ ~ **down** abattre; ~ **out** (rush) sortir en vitesse; ~ **up** (spurt) jaillir; (grow) pousser vite.

shooting /ʃuːtɪŋ/ n (killing) meurtre m (par arme à feu) hear ~ entendre des coups de feu.

shop /ʃɒp/ n magasin m; (small) boutique f; (workshop) atelier m. ● vi (pt **shopped**) faire ses courses; ~ **around** comparer les prix. ~ **assistant** n vendeur/-euse m/f. ~-**floor** n (workers) ouvriers mpl. ~-**keeper** n commerçant/-e m/f. ~-**lifter** n voleur/-euse m/f à l'étalage.

shopper /ʃɒpə(r)/ n acheteur/-euse m/f.

shopping /ʃɒpɪŋ/ n (goods) achats mpl; go ~ (for food) faire les courses; (for clothes etc.) faire les magasins. ~ **bag** n sac à provisions. ~ **centre**, (US) ~ **center** n centre m commercial.

shop window n vitrine f.

shore /ʃɔː(r)/ n côte f, rivage m; ~ à terre.

short /ʃɔːt/ adj court; (person) petit; (brief) court, bref; (curt) brusque; be ~ (of) manquer (de); everything ~ of tout sauf; nothing ~ of rien de moins que; cut ~ écourter; cut sb ~ interrompre qn; fall ~ of ne pas arriver à; he is called Tom for ~ son diminutif est Tom; in ~ en bref. ● adv (stop) net. ● n (Electr) court-circuit m; (film) courtmétrage m; ~s (trousers) short m.

shortage /ʃɔːtɪdʒ/ n manque m.

short: ~**bread** n sablé m. ~-**change** vt (cheat) rouler ①. ~ **circuit** n court-circuit m. ~**coming** n défaut m. ~ **cut** n raccourci m.

shorten /ʃɔːtn/ vt raccourcir.

shortfall /ʃɔːtfɔːl/ n déficit m.

shorthand /ʃɔːthænd/ n sténographie f; ~ **typist** sténodactylo f

short: ~ **list** n liste f des candidats choisis. ~-**lived** adj de courte durée.

shortly /ʃɔːtlɪ/ adv bientôt.

short: ~-**sighted** adj myope. ~-**staffed** adj à court de personnel; ~ **story** nouvelle f. ~-**term** adj à court terme.

shot /ʃɒt/ →SHOOT. ● n (firing, attempt) coup m de feu; (person) tireur m; (bullet) balle f; (photograph) photo f; (injection) piqûre f; like a ~ sans hésiter. ~**gun** n fusil m de chasse.

should /ʃʊd/ v aux devoir; I ~ help me vous devriez m'aider; I ~ have stayed j'aurais dû rester; I ~ like to j'aimerais bien; if he ~ come s'il venait.

shoulder /ʃəʊldə(r)/ n épaule f. ● vt (responsibility) endosser; (burden) se charger de. ~ **bag** n sac m à bandoulière. ~ **blade** n omoplate f.

shout /ʃaʊt/ n cri m. ● vt/i crier (at après); ~ **sth out** lancer qch à haute voix.

shove /ʃʌv/ n give sth a ~ pousser qch. ● vt/i pousser; ~ **off!** ① tire-toi! ①.

shovel /ʃʌvl/ n pelle f. ● vt (pt **shovelled**) pelleter.

show /ʃəʊ/ vt (pt **showed**; pp **shown**) montrer; (dial, needle) indiquer; (put on display) exposer; (film) donner; (conduct) conduire;

~ sb in/out faire entrer/sortir qn.
● vi (be visible) se voir. ● n (exhibition) exposition f, salon m; (Theat) spectacle m; (cinema) séance f; (of strength) démonstration f; for ~ pour l'effet; on ~ exposé. □ ~ off faire le fier/la fière; ~ sth/sb off exhiber qch/qn; ~ up se voir; (appear) se montrer; ~ sb up 🛈 faire honte à qn.

shower /ˈʃaʊə(r)/ n douche f; (of rain) averse f. ● vt ~ with couvrir de. ● vi se doucher.

showing /ˈʃəʊɪŋ/ n performance f; (cinema) séance f.

show-jumping n concours m hippique.

shown /ʃəʊn/ ➡ SHOW.

show: ~-off n m'as-tu-vu mf inv. 🛈 ~room n salle f d'exposition.

shrank /ʃræŋk/ ➡ SHRINK.

shrapnel /ˈʃræpnl/ n éclats mpl d'obus.

shred /ʃred/ n lambeau m; (least amount: fig) parcelle f. ● vt (pt) **shredded** déchiqueter; (Culin) râper.

shrewd /ʃruːd/ adj (person) habile; (move) astucieux.

shriek /ʃriːk/ n hurlement m. ● vt/i hurler.

shrill /ʃrɪl/ adj (voice) perçant; (tone) strident.

shrimp /ʃrɪmp/ n crevette f.

shrine /ʃraɪn/ n (place) lieu m de pèlerinage.

shrink /ʃrɪŋk/ vt/i (pt **shrank**; pp **shrunk**) rétrécir; (lessen) diminuer; ~ from reculer devant.

shrivel /ˈʃrɪvl/ vt/i (pt **shrivelled**) (se) ratatiner.

shroud /ʃraʊd/ n linceul m. ● vt (veil) envelopper.

Shrove Tuesday n mardi m gras.

shrub /ʃrʌb/ n arbuste m.

shrug /ʃrʌg/ vt (pt **shrugged**) one's shoulders hausser les épaules; ~ sth off ignorer qch.

shrunk /ʃrʌŋk/ ➡ SHRINK.

shudder /ˈʃʌdə(r)/ vi frémir. ● n frémissement m.

shuffle /ˈʃʌfl/ vt (feet) traîner; (cards) battre. ● vi traîner les pieds.

shun /ʃʌn/ vt (pt **shunned**) fuir.

shut /ʃʌt/ vt (pt shut; pres p **shutting**) fermer. ● vi (door) se fermer; (shop) fermer. □ ~ in or up enfermer; ~ up 🛈 se taire; ~ sb up faire taire qn.

shutter /ˈʃʌtə(r)/ n volet m; (Photo) obturateur m.

shuttle /ˈʃʌtl/ n (bus) navette f; ~ service navette f. ● vi faire la navette. ● vt transporter.

shuttlecock /ˈʃʌtlkɒk/ n (badminton) volant m.

shy /ʃaɪ/ adj timide. ● vi ~ away from se tenir à l'écart de.

sibling /ˈsɪblɪŋ/ n frère/sœur m/f.

sick /sɪk/ adj malade; (humour) macabre; (mind) malsain; be ~ (vomit) vomir; be ~ of 🛈 en avoir assez or marre de 🛈 feel ~ avoir mal au cœur. ~-leave n congé m de maladie.

sickly /ˈsɪklɪ/ adj (-ier, -iest) (person) maladif; (taste, smell) écœurant.

sickness /ˈsɪknɪs/ n maladie f.

sick-pay n indemnité f de maladie.

side /saɪd/ n côté m; (of road, river) bord m; (of hill, body) flanc m; (Sport) équipe f; (TV 🛈) chaîne f; ~ by ~ côte à côte. ● adj latéral. ● vi ~ with se ranger du côté de. ~-board n buffet m. ~-effect n effet m secondaire. ~light n (Auto) feu m de position. ~-line n activité f secondaire. ~-show n attraction f. ~-step vt (pt) -**stepped** éviter.

s

~street n rue f latérale. **~track**
vt fourvoyer. **~ walk** n (US) trottoir m.

sideways /'saɪdweɪz/ adj (look) de travers. ● adv (move) latéralement; (look at) de travers.

siding /'saɪdɪŋ/ n voie f de garage.

sidle /'saɪdl/ vi s'avancer furtivement (up to vers).

siege /siːdʒ/ n siège m.

siesta /sɪ'estə/ n sieste f.

sieve /sɪv/ n tamis m; (for liquids) passoire f. ● vt tamiser.

sift /sɪft/ vt tamiser. ● vi ~ through examiner.

sigh /saɪ/ n soupir m. ● vt/i soupirer.

sight /saɪt/ n vue f; (scene) spectacle m; (on gun) mire f; at or on ~ à vue; catch ~ of apercevoir; in ~ visible; lose ~ of perdre de vue. ● vt apercevoir.

sightseeing /'saɪtsiːɪŋ/ n tourisme m.

sign /saɪn/ n signe m; (notice) panneau m. ● vt/i signer. □ ~ on (as unemployed) pointer au chômage; ~ up (s')engager.

signal /'sɪɡnl/ n signal m. ● vt (pt signalled) (gesture) faire signe (that que); (indicate) indiquer.

signatory /'sɪɡnətrɪ/ n signataire mf.

signature /'sɪɡnətʃə(r)/ n signature f; ~ tune indicatif m.

significance /sɪɡ'nɪfɪkəns/ n importance f; (meaning) signification f. **significant** adj important; (meaningful) significatif. **significantly** adv (much) sensiblement.

signify /'sɪɡnɪfaɪ/ vt signifier.

signpost /'saɪnpəʊst/ n panneau m indicateur.

silence /'saɪləns/ n silence m. ● vt faire taire.

silent /'saɪlənt/ adj silencieux; (film) muet. **silently** adv silencieusement.

silhouette /sɪluːet/ n silhouette f. ● vt be ~d against se profiler contre.

silicon /'sɪlɪkən/ n silicium m; ~ chip puce f électronique.

silk /sɪlk/ n soie f.

silly /'sɪlɪ/ adj (-ier, -iest) bête.

silver /'sɪlvə(r)/ n argent m; (silverware) argenterie f. ● adj en argent.

SIM card /'sɪmkɑːd/ n carte f SIM.

similar /'sɪmɪlə(r)/ adj semblable (to à). **similarity** n ressemblance f. **similarly** adv de même.

simile /'sɪmɪlɪ/ n comparaison f.

simmer /'sɪmə(r)/ vt/i (soup) mijoter; (water) (laisser) frémir.

simple /'sɪmpl/ adj simple.

simplicity /sɪm'plɪsətɪ/ n simplicité f.

simplify /'sɪmplɪfaɪ/ vt simplifier.

simplistic /sɪm'plɪstɪk/ adj simpliste.

simply /'sɪmplɪ/ adv simplement; (absolutely) absolument.

simulate /'sɪmjʊleɪt/ vt simuler.

simultaneous /sɪml'teɪnɪəs/ adj simultané.

sin /sɪn/ n péché m. ● vi (pt sinned) pécher.

---

since /sɪns/

● **preposition**

····▸ depuis; I haven't seen him ~ Monday je ne l'ai pas vu depuis lundi; I've been waiting ~ yesterday j'attends depuis hier; she had been living in Paris ~ 1985 elle habitait Paris depuis 1985.

● *conjunction*

····▸ (in time expressions) depuis que; ~ she's been working here depuis qu'elle travaille ici; ~ she left depuis qu'elle est partie or depuis son départ.

····▸ (because) comme; ~ he was ill, he couldn't go comme il était malade, il ne pouvait pas y aller.

● *adverb*

····▸ depuis; he hasn't been seen ~ on ne l'a pas vu depuis.

sincere /sɪn'sɪə(r)/ adj sincère. **sincerely** adv sincèrement. **sincerity** n sincérité f.

sinful /'sɪnfl/ adj immoral; ~ man pécheur m.

sing /sɪŋ/ vt/i (pt **sang**; pp **sung**) chanter.

singe /sɪndʒ/ vt (pres p **singeing**) brûler légèrement; (with iron) roussir.

singer /'sɪŋə(r)/ n chanteur/-euse m/f.

single /'sɪŋgl/ adj seul; (not double) simple; (unmarried) célibataire; (room, bed) pour une personne; (ticket) simple; in ~ file en file indienne. ● n (ticket) aller simple m; (record) 45 tours m inv; ~s (tennis) simple m. ● vt ~ out choisir. **~-handed** adj tout seul. **~-minded** adj tenace. ~ **parent** n parent m isolé.

singular /'sɪŋgjʊlə(r)/ n singulier m. ● adj (strange) singulier; (noun) au singulier.

sinister /'sɪnɪstə(r)/ adj sinistre.

sink /sɪŋk/ vt (pt **sank**; pp **sunk**) (boat) couler; (well) forer; (post) enfoncer. ● vi (boat) couler; (sun, level) baisser; (wall) s'effondrer. ● n (in kitchen) évier m; (wash-basin) lavabo m. □ ~ **in** (news) faire son chemin.

sinner /'sɪnə(r)/ n pécheur/-eresse m/f.

sip /sɪp/ n petite gorgée f. ● vt (pt **sipped**) boire à petites gorgées.

siphon /'saɪfn/ n siphon m. ● vt ~ **off** siphonner.

sir /sɜː(r)/ n Monsieur m; Sir (title) Sir M.

siren /'saɪərən/ n sirène f.

sirloin /'sɜːlɔɪn/ n aloyau m.

sister /'sɪstə(r)/ n sœur f; (nurse) infirmière f en chef. **~-in-law** n (pl **~s-in-law**) belle-sœur f.

sit /sɪt/ vt/i (pt **sat**; pres p **sitting**) (s')asseoir; (committee) siéger; ~ (for) (exam) se présenter à; ~ ting être assis. □ ~ **around** ne rien faire; ~ **down** s'asseoir.

site /saɪt/ n emplacement m; (building) ~ chantier m. ● vt construire.

sitting /'sɪtɪŋ/ n séance f. (in restaurant) service m. **~-room** n salon m.

situate /'sɪtjʊeɪt/ vt situer; be ~d être situé. **situation** n situation f.

six /sɪks/ adj & n six (m).

sixteen /sɪk'stiːn/ adj & n seize (m).

sixth /sɪksθ/ adj & n sixième (mf).

sixty /'sɪkstɪ/ adj & n soixante (m).

size /saɪz/ n dimension f; (of person, garment) taille f; (of shoes) pointure f; (of sum, salary) montant m; (extent) ampleur f. □ ~ **up** (person) se faire une opinion de; (situation) évaluer. **sizeable** adj assez grand.

skate /skeɪt/ n patin m; (fish) raie f. ● vi patiner.

skateboard /'skeɪtbɔːd/ n skateboard m, planche f à roulettes. ● vi faire du skateboard.

skating /'skeɪtɪɒːd/ n patinage m.

skeleton /'skelɪtn/ n squelette m; ~ **staff** effectifs mpl minimums.

sketch /sketʃ/ n esquisse f; (hasty) croquis m; (Theat) sketch m. ● vt faire une esquisse ou un croquis de. ● vi faire des esquisses.

sketchy /'sketʃɪ/ adj (-ier, -iest) (details) insuffisant; (memory) vague.

skewer /'skjuːə(r)/ n brochette f.

ski /skiː/ n ski m. ● adj de ski. ● vi (pt **ski'd** or **skied**; pres p **skiing**) skier; (go skiing) faire du ski.

skid /skɪd/ vi (pt **skidded**) déraper. ● n dérapage m.

skier /'skiːə(r)/ n skieur/-euse m/f.

skiing /'skiːɪŋ/ n ski m.

ski jump n saut m à ski.

skilful /'skɪlfl/ adj habile.

ski lift n remontée f mécanique.

skill /skɪl/ n habileté f; (craft) compétence f; ~s connaissances fpl.

skilled adj (worker) qualifié; (talented) consommé.

skim /skɪm/ vt (pt **skimmed**) écumer; (milk) écrémer; (pass over) effleurer. ● vi ~ **through** parcourir.

skimpy /'skɪmpɪ/ adj (clothes) étriqué.

skin /skɪn/ n peau f. ● vt (pt **skinned**) (animal) écorcher; (fruit) éplucher.

skinny /'skɪnɪ/ adj (-ier, -iest) 🔟 maigre.

skip /skɪp/ vi (pt **skipped**) sautiller; (with rope) sauter à la corde. ● vt (page, class) sauter. ● n petit saut m; (container) benne f.

skipper /'skɪpə(r)/ n capitaine m.

skirmish /'skɜːmɪʃ/ n escarmouche f.

skirt /skɜːt/ n jupe f. ● vt contourner. **skirting-board** n plinthe f.

skittle /'skɪtl/ n quille f.

skull /skʌl/ n crâne m.

sky /skaɪ/ n ciel m. ~-**blue** adj & n bleu ciel m inv. ~ **marshal** n garde m armé (à bord d'un avion.) ~**scraper** n gratte-ciel m inv.

slab /slæb/ n (of stone) dalle f.

slack /slæk/ adj (not tight) détendu; (person) négligent; (period) creux. ● n (in rope) mou m. ● vi se relâcher.

slacken /'slækən/ vt (rope) donner du mou à; (grip) relâcher; (pace) réduire. ● vi (grip, rope) se relâcher; (activity) ralentir; (rain) se calmer.

slam /slæm/ vt/i (pt **slammed**) (door) claquer; (throw) flanquer; (criticize 🔟) critiquer. ● n (noise) claquement m.

slander /'slɑːndə(r)/ n (offence) diffamation f; (statement) calomnie f. ● vt calomnier; (Jur) diffamer. **slanderous** adj diffamatoire.

slang /slæŋ/ n argot m.

slant /slɑːnt/ vt/i (faire) pencher; (news) présenter sous un certain jour. ● n inclinaison f; (bias) angle m. **slanted** adj (biased) orienté; (sloping) en pente.

slap /slæp/ vt (pt **slapped**) (strike) donner une tape à; (face) gifler; (put) flanquer 🔟. ● n (on face) gifle f. ● adv tout droit. **slapdash** /'slæpdæʃ/ adj (person) brouillon m; (work) bâclé 🔟.

slash /slæʃ/ vt (picture, tyre) taillader; (face) balafrer; (throat) couper; (fig) réduire (radicalement). ● n lacération f.

slat /slæt/ n (in blind) lamelle f; (on bed) latte f.

slate /sleɪt/ n ardoise f. ● vt 🔟 taper sur 🔟.

slaughter /'slɔːtə(r)/ vt massacrer; (animal) abattre. ● n massacre m; abattage m.

slave /sleɪv/ n esclave mf. ● vi trimer ①. **slavery** n esclavage m.

sleazy /'sli:zɪ/ adj (-ier, -iest) ① (story) scabreux; (club) louche.

sledge /sledʒ/ n luge f; (horse-drawn) traîneau m.

sleek /sli:k/ adj (hair) lisse, brillant; (shape) élégant.

sleep /sli:p/ n sommeil m; go to ~ s'endormir. ● vi (pt slept) dormir; (spend the night) coucher; ~ in faire la grasse matinée. ● vt loger.

sleeper /'sli:pə(r)/ n (Rail) (berth) couchette f; (on track) traverse f.

sleeping-bag n sac m de couchage.

sleeping-pill n somnifère m.

sleep-walker n somnambule mf.

sleepy /'sli:pɪ/ adj (-ier, -iest) somnolent; be ~ avoir sommeil.

sleet /sli:t/ n neige f fondue.

sleeve /sli:v/ n manche f; (of record) pochette f; up one's ~ en réserve.

sleigh /sleɪ/ n traîneau m.

slender /'slendə(r)/ adj (person) mince; (majority) faible.

slept /slept/ →SLEEP.

slice /slaɪs/ n tranche f. ● vt couper (en tranches).

slick /slɪk/ adj (adept) habile; (insincere) roublard ①. ● n (oil) ~ marée f noire.

slide /slaɪd/ vt/i (pt slid) glisser; ~ into (go silently) se glisser dans. ● n glissade f; (fall: fig) baisse f; (in playground) toboggan m; (for hair) barrette f; (Photo) diapositive f.

sliding /'slaɪdɪŋ/ adj (door) coulissant; ~ scale échelle f mobile.

slight /slaɪt/ adj petit, léger; (slender) mince; (frail) frêle. ● vt (insult) offenser. ● n affront m. **slightest** adj moindre. **slightly** adv légèrement,

un peu.

slim /slɪm/ adj (slimmer, slimmest) mince. ● vi (pt slimmed) maigrir.

slime /slaɪm/ n dépôt m gluant; (on riverbed) vase f. **slimy** adj visqueux; (fig) servile.

sling /slɪŋ/ n (weapon, toy) fronde f; (bandage) écharpe f. ● vt (pt slung) jeter, lancer.

slip /slɪp/ vt/i (pt slipped) glisser; ~ped disc hernie f discale; ~ sb's mind échapper à qn. ● n (mistake) erreur f; (petticoat) combinaison f; (paper) bout m de papier; ~ of the tongue lapsus m. □ away s'esquiver; □ into (go) se glisser dans; (clothes) mettre; □ up ① faire une gaffe ①.

slipper /'slɪpə(r)/ n pantoufle f.

slippery /'slɪpərɪ/ adj glissant.

slip road n bretelle f.

slit /slɪt/ n fente f. ● vt (pt slit; pres p slitting) déchirer; ~ sth open ouvrir qch; ~ sb's throat égorger qn.

slither /'slɪðə(r)/ vi glisser.

sliver /'slɪvə(r)/ n (of glass) éclat m; (of soap) reste m.

slobber /'slɒbə(r)/ vi baver.

slog /slɒg/ ① vt (pt slogged) (hit) frapper dur. ● vi (work) bosser ①. ● n (work) travail m dur.

slogan /'sləʊgən/ n slogan m.

slope /sləʊp/ vi être en pente; (handwriting) pencher. ● n pente f; (of mountain) flanc m.

sloppy /'slɒpɪ/ adj (-ier, -iest) (food) liquide; (work) négligé; (person) négligent.

slosh /slɒʃ/ vt ① répandre; (hit ①) frapper. ● vi clapoter.

slot /slɒt/ n fente f. ● vt/i (pt slotted) (s')insérer.

sloth /sləʊθ/ n paresse f.

slot-machine n distributeur m automatique; (for gambling) machine f à sous.

slouch /slaʊtʃ/ vi être avachi.

Slovakia /slə'vækɪə/ n Slovaquie f.

Slovenia /slə'viːnɪə/ n Slovénie f.

slovenly /'slʌvnlɪ/ adj débraillé.

slow /sləʊ/ adj lent; be ∼ (clock) retarder; in ∼ motion au ralenti. ● adv lentement. ● vt/i ralentir. **slowly** adv lentement. **slowness** n lenteur f.

sludge /slʌdʒ/ n vase f.

slug /slʌg/ n (mollusc) limace f; (bullet 🇺🇸) balle f; (blow 🇺🇸) coup m.

sluggish /'slʌgɪʃ/ adj (person) léthargique; (circulation) lent.

slum /slʌm/ n taudis m.

slump /slʌmp/ n (Econ) effondrement m; (in support) baisse f. ● vi (demand, trade) chuter; (economy) s'effondrer; (person) s'affaler.

slung slʌŋ// →SLING.

slur /slɜː(r)/ vt/i (pt slurred) (words) mal articuler. ● n calomnie f (on sur).

slush /slʌʃ/ n (snow) neige f fondue. ∼ **fund** n caisse f noire.

sly /slaɪ/ adj (crafty) rusé; (secretive) sournois. ● n on the ∼ en cachette.

smack /smæk/ n tape f; (on face) gifle f. ● vt donner une tape à; gifler. ● vi ∼ of sth sentir qch. ● adv 🇺🇸 tout droit.

small /smɔːl/ adj petit. ● n ∼ of the back creux m des reins. ● adv (cut) menu. ● ad n petite annonce f. ∼ **business** n petite entreprise f. ∼ **change** n petite monnaie f. ∼**-pox** n variole f. ∼ **print** n petits caractères mpl. ∼ **talk** n banalités fpl.

smart /smɑːt/ adj élégant; (clever 🇺🇸) malin, habile; (restaurant) chic

inv; (Comput) intelligent. ● vi (wound) brûler.

smarten /'smɑːtn/ vt/i ∼ (up) embellir; ∼ (oneself) up s'arranger.

smash /smæʃ/ vt/i (se) briser, (se) fracasser; (opponent, record) pulvériser. ● n (noise) fracas m; (blow) coup m; (car crash) collision f; (hit record 🇺🇸) tube m. 🇺🇸

smashing /'smæʃɪŋ/ adj 🇺🇸 épatant.

SME abbr (small and medium enterprises) PME.

smear /smɪə(r)/ vt (stain) tacher; (coat) enduire; (discredit: fig) diffamer. ● n tache f; (effort to discredit) propos m diffamatoire; ∼ (test) frottis m.

smell /smel/ n odeur f; (sense) odorat m. ● vt/i (pt smelt or smelled) sentir; ∼ of sentir mauvais. **smelly** adj qui sent mauvais.

smelt /smelt/ →SMELL.

smile /smaɪl/ n sourire m. ● vi sourire.

smiley /'smaɪlɪ/ n (Internet) binette f.

smirk /smɜːk/ n petit sourire m satisfait.

smitten /'smɪtn/ adj (in love) fou d'amour.

smog /smɒg/ n smog m.

smoke /sməʊk/ n fumée f; have a ∼ fumer. ● vt/i fumer. **smoked** adj fumé. **smokeless** adj (fuel) non polluant. **smoker** n fumeur/-euse m/f. **smoky** adj (air) enfumé.

smooth /smuːð/ adj lisse; (movement) aisé; (manners) onctueux; (flight) sans heurts. ● vt lisser; (process) faciliter.

smoothly /'smuːðlɪ/ adv (move, flow) doucement; (brake, start) en douceur; go ∼ marcher bien.

smother /'smʌðə(r)/ vt (stifle) étouffer; (cover) couvrir.

smoulder /'sməʊldə(r)/ *vi* (lit) se consumer; (fig) couver.

smudge /smʌdʒ/ *n* trace *f*. ● *vt/i* (ink) (s')étaler.

smug /smʌg/ *adj* (**smugger, smuggest**) suffisant.

smuggle /'smʌgl/ *vt* passer (en contrebande). **smuggler** *n* contrebandier/-ière *m/f*. **smuggling** *n* contrebande *f*.

smutty /'smʌti/ *adj* grivois.

snack /snæk/ *n* casse-croûte *m inv*.

snag /snæg/ *n* inconvénient *m*; (in cloth) accroc *m*.

snail /sneɪl/ *n* escargot *m*.

snake /sneɪk/ *n* serpent *m*.

snap /snæp/ *vt/i* (*pt* **snapped**) (whip, fingers) (faire) claquer; (break) (se) casser net; (say) dire sèchement. ● *n* claquement *m*; (Photo) photo *f*. ● *adj* soudain. □ ~ **up** (buy) sauter sur.

snapshot /'snæpʃɒt/ *n* photo *f*.

snare /sneə(r)/ *n* piège *m*.

snarl /snɑːl/ *vi* gronder (en montrant les dents). ● *n* grondement *m*. ~-**up** *n* embouteillage *m*.

snatch /snætʃ/ *vt* (grab) attraper; (steal) voler; (opportunity) saisir; ~ **sth from sb** arracher qch à qn. ● *n* (theft) vol *m*; (short part) fragment *m*.

sneak /sniːk/ *vi* aller furtivement. ● *n* 🔢 rapporteur/-euse *m/f*.

sneer /snɪə(r)/ *n* sourire *m* méprisant. ● *vi* sourire avec mépris.

sneeze /sniːz/ *n* éternuement *m*. ● *vi* éternuer.

snide /snaɪd/ *adj* narquois.

sniff /snɪf/ *vt/i* renifler. ● *n* reniflement *m*.

snigger /'snɪgə(r)/ *n* ricanement *m*. ● *vi* ricaner.

snip /snɪp/ *vt* (*pt* **snipped**) couper.

sniper /'snaɪpə(r)/ *n* tireur *m* embusqué.

snippet /'snɪpɪt/ *n* bribe *f*.

snivel /'snɪvl/ *vi* (*pt* **snivelled**) pleurnicher.

snob /snɒb/ *n* snob *mf*.

snooker /'snuːkə(r)/ *n* snooker *m*.

snoop /snuːp/ *vi* 🔢 fourrer son nez partout.

snooty /'snuːtɪ/ *adj* (**-ier, -iest**) 🔢 snob *inv*, hautain.

snooze /snuːz/ *n* petit somme *m*. ● *vi* sommeiller.

snore /snɔː(r)/ *n* ronflement *m*. ● *vi* ronfler.

snorkel /'snɔːkl/ *n* tuba *m*.

snort /snɔːt/ *n* grognement *m*. ● *vi* (person) grogner; (horse) s'ébrouer.

snout /snaʊt/ *n* museau *m*.

snow /snəʊ/ *n* neige *f*. ● *vi* neiger; **be** ~**ed under with** être submergé de.

snowball /'snəʊbɔːl/ *n* boule *f* de neige. ● *vi* faire boule de neige.

snow: ~**board** *n* snowboard *m*. ~**boarding** *n* surf *m* des neiges. ~-**bound** *adj* bloqué par la neige. ~**drift** *n* congère *f*. ~**drop** *n* perce-neige *m* or *f inv*. ~**flake** *n* flocon *m* de neige. ~**man** *n* (*pl* **-men**) bonhomme *m* de neige. ~-**plough** *n* chasse-neige *m inv*.

snub /snʌb/ *vt* (*pt* **snubbed**) rembarrer. ● *n* rebuffade *f*.

snuffle /'snʌfl/ *vi* renifler.

snug /snʌg/ *adj* (**snugger, snuggest**) (cosy) confortable; (tight) bien ajusté.

snuggle /'snʌgl/ *vi* se pelotonner.

so /səʊ/ *adv* si, tellement; (thus) ainsi; ~ **am I** moi aussi; ~ **good as** aussi bon que; **that is** ~ c'est ça; **I think** ~ je pense que oui; **five or** ~ environ cinq; ~ **as to** de ma-

s

nière à; ~ far jusqu'ici; ~ long! 🔲
à bientôt!; ~ that pour que. ● conj donc,
alors.

soak /səʊk/ vt/i (faire) tremper (in
dans). □~ **in** pénétrer; ~ **up** absorber. **soaking** adj trempé.

soap /səʊp/ n savon m. ● vt savonner. ~ **opera** n feuilleton m. ~
powder n lessive f.

soar /sɔː(r)/ vi monter (en flèche).

sob /sɒb/ n sanglot m. ● vi (pt
sobbed) sangloter.

sober /'səʊbə(r)/ adj qui n'a pas bu
d'alcool; (serious) sérieux. ● vi ~
up dessoûler.

soccer /'sɒkə(r)/ n football m.

sociable /'səʊʃəbl/ adj sociable.

social /'səʊʃl/ adj social. ● n réunion f (amicale), fête f.

socialism /'səʊʃəlɪzəm/ n socialisme m. **socialist** adj & n socialiste (mf).

socialize /'səʊʃəlaɪz/ vi se mêler
aux autres; ~ **with** fréquenter.

socially /'səʊʃəlɪ/ adv socialement;
(meet) en société.

social: ~ **security** n aide f sociale.
~ **worker** n travailleur/-euse m/f
social/-e.

society /sə'saɪətɪ/ n société f.

sociological /səʊsɪə'lɒdʒɪkl/ adj
sociologique. **sociologist** n sociolo-
gue mf. **sociology** n sociologie f.

sock /sɒk/ n chaussette f. ● vt (hit
🔲) flanquer un coup (de poing) à.

socket /'sɒkɪt/ n (for lamp) douille
f; (Electr) prise f (de courant); (of
eye) orbite f.

soda /'səʊdə/ n soude f; ~(-water)
eau f de Seltz.

sodden /'sɒdn/ adj détrempé.

sofa /'səʊfə/ n canapé m. ~ **bed** n
canapé-lit m.

soft /sɒft/ adj (gentle, lenient) doux;
(not hard) doux, mou; (heart, wood)
tendre; (silly) ramolli. ~ **drink** n
boisson f non alcoolisée.

soften /'sɒfn/ vt/i (se) ramollir;
(tone down, lessen) (s')adoucir.

soft spot n to have a ~ for sb
avoir un faible pour qn.

software /'sɒftweə(r)/ n logiciel m.

soggy /'sɒgɪ/ adj (-ier, -iest)
(ground) détrempé; (food) ramolli.

soil /sɔɪl/ n sol m, terre f. ● vt/i (se)
salir.

sold /səʊld/ ➡SELL. ● adj ~ out
épuisé.

solder /'səʊldə(r)/ n soudure f. ● vt
souder.

soldier /'səʊldʒə(r)/ n soldat m.
● vi ~ **on** 🔲 persévérer.

sole /səʊl/ n (of foot) plante f; (of
shoe) semelle f; (fish) sole f. ● adj
unique, seul. **solely** adv uniquement.

solemn /'sɒləm/ adj solennel.

solicitor /sə'lɪsɪtə(r)/ n notaire m;
(for court and police work) ≈
avocat/-e m/f.

solid /'sɒlɪd/ adj solide; (not hollow)
plein; (gold) massif; (mass) compact; (meal) substantiel. ● n solide
m; ~s (food) aliments mpl solides.

solidarity /sɒlɪ'dærətɪ/ n solidarité f.

solidify /sə'lɪdɪfaɪ/ vt/i (se) solidifier.

solitary /'sɒlɪtrɪ/ adj (alone) solitaire; (only) seul.

solo /'səʊləʊ/ n solo m. ● adj (Mus)
solo inv; (flight) en solitaire.

soluble /'sɒljʊbl/ adj soluble.

solution /sə'luːʃn/ n solution f.

solve /sɒlv/ vt résoudre.

solvent /'sɒlvənt/ adj (Comm)

solvable. ● *n* (dis)solvant *m*.

some /sʌm, səm/
● *determiner*
····▸ (unspecified amount) du/de l'/de la/des; I have to buy ~ bread je dois acheter du pain; have ~ water prenez de l'eau; ~ sweets des bonbons.
····▸ (certain) certains/certaines; ~ people say that certains disent que.
····▸ (unknown) un/une; ~ man came to the house un homme est venu à la maison.
····▸ (considerable amount) we stayed there for ~ time nous sommes restés là assez longtemps; it will take ~ doing ça ne va pas être facile à faire.

➡ In front of a plural adjective *des* changes to *de*: some pretty dresses *de jolies robes*.

● *pronoun*
····▸ en; he wants ~ il en veut; have ~ more reprenez-en.
····▸ (certain) certains/certaines; ~ are expensive certains sont chers.
● *adverb*
····▸ environ; ~ 20 people environ 20 personnes.

somebody /'sʌmbədɪ/ *pron* quelqu'un. ● *n* be a ~ être quelqu'un.
somehow /'sʌmhaʊ/ *adv* d'une manière ou d'une autre; (for some reason) je ne sais pas pourquoi.
someone /'sʌmwʌn/ *pron & n* →SOMEBODY.
someplace /'sʌmpleɪs/ *adv* (US)

→SOMEWHERE.
somersault /'sʌməsɒlt/ *n* roulade *f*. ● *vi* faire une roulade.
something /'sʌmθɪŋ/ *pron & n* quelque chose (*m*); ~ good quelque chose de bon; ~ like un peu comme.
sometime /'sʌmtaɪm/ *adv* un jour; ~ in June en juin. ● *adj* (former) ancien.
sometimes /'sʌmtaɪmz/ *adv* quelquefois, parfois.
somewhat /'sʌmwɒt/ *adv* quelque peu, un peu.
somewhere /'sʌmweə(r)/ *adv* quelque part.
son /sʌn/ *n* fils *m*.
song /sɒŋ/ *n* chanson *f*; (of bird) chant *m*.
son-in-law /'sʌnɪnlɔː/ *n* (pl sons-in-law) gendre *m*.
soon /suːn/ *adv* bientôt; (early) tôt; I would ~er stay j'aimerais mieux rester; ~ after peu après; ~er or later tôt ou tard.
soot /sʊt/ *n* suie *f*.
soothe /suːð/ *vt* calmer.
sophisticated /sə'fɪstɪkeɪtɪd/ *adj* raffiné; (machine) sophistiqué.
sopping /'sɒpɪŋ/ *adj* trempé.
soppy /'sɒpɪ/ *adj* (-ier, -iest) Ⓣ sentimental.
sorcerer /'sɔːsərə(r)/ *n* sorcier *m*.
sordid /'sɔːdɪd/ *adj* sordide.
sore /sɔː(r)/ *adj* douloureux; (vexed) en rogne (at, with contre). ● *n* plaie *f*.
sorely /'sɔːlɪ/ *adv* fortement.
sorrow /'sɒrəʊ/ *n* chagrin *m*.
sorry /'sɒrɪ/ *adj* (-ier, -iest) (regretful) désolé (to de; that que); (wretched) triste; feel ~ for plaindre; ~! pardon!
sort /sɔːt/ *n* genre *m*, sorte *f*, espèce

f; (person 🛈) type m; what ~ of? quel genre de?; be out of ~s ne pas être dans son assiette. ● vt ~ (out) (classify) trier; ~ out (tidy) ranger; (arrange) arranger; (problem) régler.

so-so /'sǝʊsǝʊ/ adj & adv comme ci comme ça.

sought /sɔːt/⟶SEEK.

soul /sǝʊl/ n âme f.

sound /saʊnd/ n son m, bruit m. ● adj solide; (healthy) sain; (sensible) sensé. ● vt/i sonner; (seem) sembler (as if que); (test) sonder; ~ out sonder; ~ a horn klaxonner; ~ like sembler être. ~ asleep adj profondément endormi. ~ barrier n mur m du son.

soundly /'saʊndlı/ adv (sleep) à poings fermés; (built) solidement.

sound-proof /'saʊndpruːf/ adj insonorisé. ● vt insonoriser.

sound-track /'saʊndtræk/ n bande f sonore.

soup /suːp/ n soupe f, potage m.

sour /'saʊǝ(r)/ adj aigre. ● vt/i (s')aigrir.

source /sɔːs/ n source f.

south /saʊθ/ n sud m. ● adj sud inv, du sud. ● adv vers le sud.

South Africa n Afrique f du Sud.

South America n Amérique f du Sud.

south-east n sud-est m.

southern /'sʌðǝn/ adj du sud. **southerner** n habitant/-e m/f du sud.

southward /'saʊθwǝd/ adj (side) sud inv; (journey) vers le sud.

south-west n sud-ouest m.

souvenir /suːvǝ'nıǝ(r)/ n souvenir m.

sovereign /'sɒvrın/ n & a souverain/-e (m/f).

sow[1] /sǝʊ/ vt (pt sowed or sown) (seed) semer; (land) ensemencer.

sow[2] /saʊ/ n (pig) truie f.

soya /'sɔıǝ/ n soja m. ~ **sauce** n sauce f soja.

spa /spaː/ n station f thermale.

space /speıs/ n espace m; (room) place f; (period) période f. ● vt ~ (out) espacer. ~**craft** n inv, ~**ship** n engin m spatial. ~**suit** n combinaison f spatiale.

spacious /'speıʃǝs/ adj spacieux.

spade /speıd/ n (for garden) bêche f; (child's) pelle f; (cards) pique m. ~**work** n (fig) travail m préparatoire.

spaghetti /spǝ'getı/ n spaghetti mpl.

spam /spæm/ n (Comput) multipostage m abusif.

Spain /speın/ n Espagne f.

span /spæn/ n (of arch) portée f; (of wings) envergure f; (of time) durée f. ● vt (pt spanned) enjamber; (in time) embrasser.

Spaniard /'spænjǝd/ n Espagnol/-e m/f.

spaniel /'spænjǝl/ n épagneul m.

Spanish /'spænıʃ/ adj espagnol. ● n (Ling) espagnol m.

spank /spæŋk/ vt donner une fessée à.

spanner /'spænǝ(r)/ n (tool) clé f (plate); (adjustable) clé f à molette.

spare /speǝ(r)/ vt (treat leniently) épargner; (do without) se passer de; (afford to give) donner, accorder. ● adj en réserve; (surplus) de trop; (tyre, shoes) de rechange; (room, bed) d'ami; are there any ~ tickets? y a-t-il encore des places? ● n ~ (part) pièce f de rechange. ~ **time** n loisirs mpl.

sparing /'speərɪŋ/ adj frugal. **sparingly** adv en petite quantité.

spark /spɑːk/ n étincelle f. ● vt ~ off (initiate) provoquer.

sparkle /'spɑːkl/ vi étinceler. ● n étincellement m. **sparkling** adj (wine) mousseux; (eyes) brillant.

spark-plug n bougie f.

sparrow /'spærəʊ/ n moineau m.

sparse /spɑːs/ adj clairsemé. **sparsely** adv (furnished) peu.

spasm /'spæzəm/ n (of muscle) spasme m; (of coughing, anger) accès m.

spat /spæt/ ⇒SPIT.

spate /speɪt/ n a ~ of (letters) une avalanche de.

spatter /'spætə(r)/ vt éclabousser (with de).

spawn /spɔːn/ n frai m, œufs mpl. ● vt pondre. ● vi frayer.

speak /spiːk/ vi (pt spoke; pp spoken) parler. ● vt (say) dire; (language) parler. ☐ ~ up parler plus fort.

speaker /'spiːkə(r)/ n (in public) orateur m; (Pol) président m; (loudspeaker) baffle m; be a French/a good ~ parler français/bien.

spear /spɪə(r)/ n lance f.

spearmint /'spɪəmɪnt/ n menthe f verte.

special /'speʃl/ adj spécial; (exceptional) exceptionnel.

specialist /'speʃəlɪst/ n spécialiste mf.

speciality, **specialty** /speʃɪ'ælətɪ/ n spécialité f.

specialize /'speʃəlaɪz/ vi se spécialiser (en en).

specially /'speʃəlɪ/ adv spécialement.

species /'spiːʃiːz/ n inv espèce f.

specific /spə'sɪfɪk/ adj précis,

explicite.

specification /spesɪfɪ'keɪʃn/ n (of design) spécification f; (of car equipment) caractéristiques fpl. **specify** vt spécifier.

specimen /'spesɪmən/ n spécimen m, échantillon m.

speck /spek/ n (stain) (petite) tache f; (particle) grain m.

specs /speks/ npl 🆃 lunettes fpl.

spectacle /'spektəkl/ n spectacle m. **spectacles** n lunettes fpl. **spectacular** adj spectaculaire.

spectator /spek'teɪtə(r)/ n spectateur/-trice m/f.

spectrum /'spektrəm/ n (pl -tra) spectre m; (of ideas) gamme f.

speculate /'spekjʊleɪt/ vi s'interroger (about sur); (Comm) spéculer. **speculation** n conjectures fpl; (Comm) spéculation f. **speculator** n spéculateur/-trice m/f.

speech /spiːtʃ/ n (faculty) parole f; (diction) élocution f; (dialect) langage m; (address) discours m. **speechless** adj muet (with de).

speed /spiːd/ n (of movement) vitesse f; (swiftness) rapidité f. ~ **camera** n radar m. ~ **dating**® n rencontres fpl rapides, speed dating m. ● vi (pt sped) aller vite; (pt speeded) (drive too fast) aller trop vite. ☐ ~ up accélérer; (of pace) s'accélérer.

speedboat /'spiːdbəʊt/ n vedette f.

speeding /'spiːdɪŋ/ n excès m de vitesse.

speed limit n limitation f de vitesse.

speedometer /spɪ'dɒmɪtə(r)/ n compteur m (de vitesse).

spell /spel/ n (magic) charme m, sortilège m; (curse) sort m; (of time) (courte) période f. ● vt/i (pt spelled

or spelt) écrire; (mean) signifier; ~ **out** épeler; (explain) expliquer. ~**checker** n correcteur m orthographique.

spelling /'spelɪŋ/ n orthographe f. ● adj (mistake) d'orthographe.

spend /spend/ vt (pt **spent**) (money) dépenser (on pour); (time, holiday) passer; (energy) consacrer (on à). ● vi dépenser.

spent /spent/ ➡SPEND. ● adj (used) utilisé; (person) épuisé.

sperm /spɜːm/ n (pl **sperms** or **sperm**) sperme m.

sphere /sfɪə(r)/ n sphère f.

spice /spaɪs/ n épice f; (fig) piquant m.

spick-and-span adj impeccable.

spicy /'spaɪsɪ/ adj épicé; piquant.

spider /'spaɪdə(r)/ n araignée f.

spike /spaɪk/ n pointe f.

spill /spɪl/ vt (pt **spilled** or **spilt**) renverser, répandre. ● vi se répandre; ~ **over** déborder.

spin /spɪn/ vt/i (pt **spun**; pres p **spinning**) (wool, web) filer; (turn) (faire) tourner; (story) sortir; ~ **out** faire durer. ● n (movement, excursion) tour m.

spinach /'spɪnɪdʒ/ n épinards mpl.

spinal /'spaɪnl/ adj vertébral. ~ **cord** n moelle f épinière.

spin-drier n essoreuse f.

spine /spaɪn/ n colonne f vertébrale; (prickle) piquant m.

spin-off n avantage m accessoire; (by-product) dérivé m.

spinster /'spɪnstə(r)/ n célibataire f; (pej) vieille fille f.

spiral /'spaɪərəl/ adj en spirale; (staircase) en colimaçon. ● n spirale f. ● vi (pt **spiralled**) (prices) monter (en flèche).

spire /'spaɪə(r)/ n flèche f.

spirit /'spɪrɪt/ n esprit m; (boldness) courage m; ~s (morale) moral m; (drink) spiritueux mpl. ● vt ~ **away** faire disparaître. **spirited** adj fougueux. ~-**level** n niveau m à bulle.

spiritual /'spɪrɪtʃʊəl/ adj spirituel.

spit /spɪt/ vt/i (pt **spat** or **spit**; pres p **spitting**) cracher; (of rain) crachiner; ~ **out** cracher; the ~**ting** image of le portrait craché or vivant de. ● n crachat(s) m(pl); (for meat) broche f.

spite /spaɪt/ n rancune f; in ~ **of** malgré. ● vt contrarier.

splash /splæʃ/ vt éclabousser. ● vi faire des éclaboussures; ~ (about) patauger. ● n (act, mark) éclaboussure f; (sound) plouf m; (of colour) tache f.

spleen /spliːn/ n (Anat) rate f.

splendid /'splendɪd/ adj magnifique, splendide.

splint /splɪnt/ n (Med) attelle f.

splinter /'splɪntə(r)/ n éclat m; (in finger) écharde f. ~ **group** n groupe m dissident.

split /splɪt/ vt/i (pt **split**; pres p **splitting**) (se) fendre; (tear) (se) déchirer; (divide) (se) diviser; (share) partager; ~ **one's sides** se tordre (de rire). ● n fente f; (tear) déchirure f; (share ▣) part f, partage f; (quarrel) rupture f; (Pol) scission f. □ ~ **up** (couple) rompre. ~ **second** n fraction f de seconde.

splutter /'splʌtə(r)/ vi crachoter; (stammer) bafouiller; (engine) tousser.

spoil /spɔɪl/ vt (pt **spoilt** or **spoiled**) (pamper) gâter; (ruin) abîmer; (mar) gâcher, gâter. ● n ~(s) butin m. ~-**sport** n trouble-fête mf inv.

spoke[1] /spəʊk/ n rayon m.

spoke[2], **spoken** ➡SPEAK.

spokesman /ˈspəʊksmən/ n (pl -men) porteparole m inv.

sponge /spʌndʒ/ n éponge f. ● vt éponger. ● vi ~ on vivre aux crochets de. ~bag n trousse f de toilette. ~cake n génoise f.

sponsor /ˈspɒnsə(r)/ n (of concert) parrain m, sponsor m; (surety) garant m; (for membership) parrain m, marraine f. ● vt parrainer, sponsoriser; (member) parrainer. **sponsorship** n patronage m; parrainage m.

spontaneous /spɒnˈteɪnɪəs/ adj spontané.

spoof /spuːf/ n ① parodie f.

spoon /spuːn/ n cuiller f, cuillère f.

spoonful /ˈspuːnfʊl/ n (pl ~s) cuillerée f.

sport /spɔːt/ n sport m; (good) ~ (person ①) chic type m; ~s car/coat voiture/veste f de sport; (display) exhiber, arborer. ● vt (display) exhiber, arborer.

sporting /ˈspɔːtɪŋ/ adj sportif; a ~ chance une assez bonne chance.

sportsman /ˈspɔːtsmən/ n (pl -men) sportif m.

sporty /ˈspɔːtɪ/ adj ① sportif.

spot /spɒt/ n (mark, stain) tache f; (dot) point m; (in pattern) pois m; (drop) goutte f; (place) endroit m; (pimple) bouton m; a ~ of ① un peu de; on the ~ sur place; (without delay) sur le coup. ● vt (pt **spotted**) ① apercevoir. ~ **check** n contrôle m ponctuel.

spotless /ˈspɒtlɪs/ adj impeccable.

spotlight /ˈspɒtlaɪt/ n (lamp) projecteur m, spot m.

spotty /ˈspɒtɪ/ adj (skin) boutonneux.

spouse /spaʊz/ n époux m, épouse f.

spout /spaʊt/ n (of teapot) bec m; (of liquid) jet m; up the ~ (ruined ①) fichu. ● vi jaillir.

sprain /spreɪn/ n entorse f, foulure f. ● vt ~ one's wrist se fouler le poignet.

sprang /spræŋ/ ➡SPRING.

sprawl /sprɔːl/ vi (town, person) s'étaler. ● n étalement m.

spray /spreɪ/ n (of flowers) gerbe f; (water) gerbe f d'eau; (from sea) embruns mpl; (device) bombe f, atomiseur m. ● vt (surface, insecticide, plant) vaporiser; (person) asperger; (crops) traiter.

spread /spred/ vt/i (pt **spread**) (stretch, extend) (s')étendre; (news, fear) (se) répandre; (illness) (se) propager; (butter) (s')étaler. ● n propagation f; (of population) distribution f; (paste) pâte f à tartiner; (food) belle table f. ~**eagled** adj bras et jambes écartés. ~**sheet** n tableur m.

spree /spriː/ n go on a ~ (have fun ①) faire la noce.

sprig /sprɪg/ n petite branche f.

sprightly /ˈspraɪtlɪ/ adj (-ier, -iest) alerte, vif.

spring /sprɪŋ/ vi (pt **sprang**; pp **sprung**) bondir. ● vt ~ sth on sb annoncer qch de but en blanc à qn. ● n bond m; (device) ressort m; (season) printemps m; (of water) source f. ~ **from** provenir de; ~ **up** surgir. ~**board** n tremplin m. ~**onion** n oignon m blanc.

springy /ˈsprɪŋɪ/ adj (-ier, -iest) élastique.

sprinkle /ˈsprɪŋkl/ vt (with liquid) arroser (with de); (with salt, flour) saupoudrer (with de); (sand) répandre. **sprinkler** n (in garden) arroseur m; (for fires) extincteur m (à déclenchement) automatique.

sprint /sprɪnt/ vi (Sport) sprinter. ● n sprint m.

sprout /spraʊt/ vt/i pousser. ● n

(on plant) pousse *f*; (Brussels) ∼s choux *mpl* de Bruxelles.

spruce /spruːs/ *adj* pimpant. ● *vt* ∼ oneself up se faire beau. ● *n* (tree) épicéa *m*.

sprung /sprʌŋ/ ➡SPRING.

spud /spʌd/ *n* 🔲 patate *f*.

spun /spʌn/ ➡SPIN.

spur /spɜː(r)/ *n* (of rider) éperon *m*; (stimulus) aiguillon *m*; on the ∼ of the moment sous l'impulsion du moment. ● *vt* (*pt* **spurred**) éperonner.

spurious /ˈspjʊəriəs/ *adj* faux.

spurn /spɜːn/ *vt* repousser.

spurt /spɜːt/ *vi* jaillir; (fig) accélérer. ● *n* jet *m*; (of energy) sursaut *m*.

spy /spaɪ/ *n* espion/-ne *m/f*. ● *vi* espionner. ● *vt* apercevoir.

squabble /ˈskwɒbl/ *vi* se chamailler. ● *n* chamaillerie *f*.

squad /skwɒd/ *n* (of soldiers) escouade *f*; (Sport) équipe *f*.

squadron /ˈskwɒdrən/ *n* (Mil) escadron *m*; (Aviat) escadrille *f*.

squalid /ˈskwɒlɪd/ *adj* sordide.

squander /ˈskwɒndə(r)/ *vt* (money, time) gaspiller.

square /skweə(r)/ *n* carré *m*; (open space in town) place *f*. ● *adj* carré; (honest) honnête; (meal) solide; (boring 🔲) ringard; (all) ∼ (quits) quitte; ∼ meal repas *m* copieux. ● *vt* (settle) régler; ∼ up to faire face à.

squash /skwɒʃ/ *vt* écraser; (crowd) serrer. ● *n* (game) squash *m*; (marrow: US) courge *f*; lemon ∼ citronnade *f*; orange ∼ orangeade *f*.

squat /skwɒt/ *vi* (*pt* **squatted**) s'accroupir; ∼ in a house squatteriser une maison. ● *adj* (dumpy) trapu. **squatter** *n* squatter *m*.

squawk /skwɔːk/ *n* cri *m* rauque. ● *vi* pousser un cri rauque.

squeak /skwiːk/ *n* petit cri *m*; (of door) grincement *m*. ● *vi* crier; grincer.

squeal /skwiːl/ *n* cri *m* aigu. ● *vi* pousser un cri aigu; ∼ on (inform on 🔲) dénoncer.

squeamish /ˈskwiːmɪʃ/ *adj* (trop) délicat.

squeeze /skwiːz/ *vt* presser; (hand, arm) serrer; (extract) exprimer (from de); (extort) soutirer (from à). ● *vi* (force one's way) se glisser. ● *n* pression *f*; (Comm) restrictions *fpl* de crédit.

squid /skwɪd/ *n* calmar *m*.

squint /skwɪnt/ *vi* loucher; (with half-shut eyes) plisser les yeux. ● *n* (Med) strabisme *m*.

squirm /skwɜːm/ *vi* se tortiller.

squirrel /ˈskwɪrəl/ *n* écureuil *m*.

squirt /skwɜːt/ *vt*/*i* (faire) jaillir. ● *n* jet *m*.

stab /stæb/ *vt* (*pt* **stabbed**) (with knife) poignarder. ● *n* coup *m* (de couteau); have a ∼ at sth essayer de faire qch.

stability /stəˈbɪlətɪ/ *n* stabilité *f*.

stabilize /ˈsteɪbɪlaɪz/ *vt* stabiliser.

stable /ˈsteɪbl/ *adj* stable. ● *n* écurie *f*. ∼**-boy** *n* lad *m*.

stack /stæk/ *n* tas *m*. ● *vt* (∼ up) entasser, empiler.

stadium /ˈsteɪdɪəm/ *n* stade *m*.

staff /stɑːf/ *n* personnel *m*; (in school) professeurs *mpl*; (Mil) état-major *m*; (stick) bâton *m*. ● *vt* pourvoir en personnel.

stag /stæg/ *n* cerf *m*.

stage /steɪdʒ/ *n* (Theat) scène *f*; (phase) stade *m*, étape *f*; (platform in hall) estrade *f*; go on the ∼ faire du théâtre. ● *vt* mettre en scène; (fig) organiser. ∼ **door** *n* entrée *f* des artistes. ∼ **fright** *n* trac *m*.

stagger /ˈstægə(r)/ *vi* chanceler.

● vt (shock) stupéfier; (payments) échelonner. **staggering** adj stupéfiant.

stagnate /stægˈneɪt/ vi stagner.

stag night n soirée f pour enterrer une vie de garçon.

staid /steɪd/ adj sérieux.

stain /steɪn/ vt tacher; (wood) colorer. ● n tache f; (colouring) colorant m. **stained glass window** n vitrail m.

stainless steel n acier m inoxydable.

stain remover n détachant m.

stair /steə(r)/ n marche f; the ~s l'escalier m. **~case**, **~way** n escalier m.

stake /steɪk/ n (post) pieu m; (wager) enjeu m; at ~ en jeu. ● vt (area) jalonner; (wager) jouer; ~ a claim to revendiquer.

stale /steɪl/ adj pas frais; (bread) rassis; (smell) de renfermé.

stalk /stɔːk/ n (of plant) tige f. ● vi marcher de façon guindée. ● vt (hunter) chasser; (murderer) suivre.

stall /stɔːl/ n (in stable) stalle f; (in market) éventaire m; ~s (Theat) orchestre m. ● vt/i (Auto) caler; ~ (for time) temporiser.

stallion /ˈstælɪən/ n étalon m.

stamina /ˈstæmɪnə/ n résistance f.

stammer /ˈstæmə(r)/ vt/i bégayer. ● n bégaiement m.

stamp /stæmp/ vt/i ~ (one's foot) taper du pied. ● vt (letter) timbrer. ● n (for postage, marking) timbre m; (mark: fig) sceau m. ~ **out** supprimer. **~-collecting** n philatélie f.

stampede /stæmˈpiːd/ n fuite f désordonnée; (rush: fig) ruée f. ● vi s'enfuir en désordre; se ruer.

stand /stænd/ vi (pt **stood**) être ou se tenir (debout); (rise) se lever; (be situated) se trouver; (Pol) être candidat (for à); ~ **in line** (US) faire la queue; ~ **to reason** être logique. ● vt mettre (debout); (tolerate) supporter; ~ **a chance** avoir une chance. ● n (stance) position f; (Mil) résistance f; (for lamp) support m; (at fair) stand m; (in street) kiosque m; (for spectators) tribune f; (Jur, US) barre f; **make a** ~ prendre position. ~ **back** reculer; ~ **by** or **around** ne rien faire; ~ **by** (be ready) se tenir prêt; (promise, person) rester fidèle à; ~ **down** se désister; ~ **for** représenter; Ⓣ supporter; ~ **in for** remplacer; ~ **out** ressortir; ~ **up** se lever; ~ **up for** défendre; ~ **up to** résister à.

standard /ˈstændəd/ n norme f; (level) niveau m (voulu); (flag) étendard m; ~ **of living** niveau m de vie; ~s (morals) principes mpl. ● adj ordinaire.

standard of living n niveau m de vie.

standby /ˈstændbaɪ/ adj de réserve. ● n be a ~ être de réserve.

stand-in /ˈstændɪn/ n remplaçant/-e m/f.

standing /ˈstændɪŋ/ adj debout inv. ● n réputation f; (duration) durée f; ~ **order** n prélèvement m bancaire.

standpoint /ˈstændpɔɪnt/ n point m de vue.

standstill /ˈstændstɪl/ n at a ~ immobile; **bring/come to a** ~ (s')immobiliser.

stank /stæŋk/ ⇒STINK.

staple /ˈsteɪpl/ n agrafe f. ● vt agrafer. ● adj principal, de base. **stapler** n agrafeuse f.

star /stɑː(r)/ n étoile f; (person) vedette f. ● vt (pt **starred**) (film) avoir pour vedette. ● vi ~ **in** être la vedette de.

starch /stɑːtʃ/ n amidon m; (in food) fécule f. ● vt amidonner.

s

stardom /'stɑːdəm/ n célébrité f.

stare /steə(r)/ vi ~ at regarder fixement. ● n regard m fixe.

starfish /'stɑːfɪʃ/ n étoile f de mer.

stark /stɑːk/ adj (desolate) désolé; (severe) austère; (utter) complet; (fact) brutal. ● adv complètement.

starling /'stɑːlɪŋ/ n étourneau m.

start /stɑːt/ vt/i commencer; (machine) (se) mettre en marche; (fashion) lancer; (cause) provoquer; (jump) sursauter; (of vehicle) démarrer; ~ to do commencer or se mettre à faire; ~ing tomorrow à partir de demain. ● n commencement m, début m; (of race) départ m; (lead) avance f; (jump) sursaut m. □ ~ off commencer (doing or faire); ~ out partir; ~ up (business) lancer. **starter** n (Auto) démarreur m; (runner) partant m; (Culin) entrée f.

starting point n point m de départ.

startle /'stɑːtl/ vt (make jump) faire tressaillir; (shock) alarmer.

starvation /stɑː'veɪʃn/ n faim f.

starve /stɑːv/ vi mourir de faim. ● vt affamer; (deprive) priver.

stash /stæʃ/ vt cacher.

state /steɪt/ n état m; (pomp) apparat m; S~ état m; the S~s les États-Unis; get into a ~ s'affoler. ● adj d'état, de l'état; (school) public. ● vt affirmer (that que); (views) exprimer; (fix) fixer.

intègrent normalement une comprehensive school, ou, à l'issue d'un examen d'entrée, une grammar school. ▷PUBLIC SCHOOLS.

stately /'steɪtlɪ/ adj (-ier, -iest) majestueux. ~ home n château m.

statement /'steɪtmənt/ n déclaration f; (of account) relevé m.

statesman /'steɪtsmən/ n (pl -men) homme m d'état.

static /'stætɪk/ adj statique. ● n (radio, TV) parasites mpl.

station /'steɪʃn/ n (Rail) gare f; (TV) chaîne f; (Mil) poste m; (rank) condition f. ● vt poster, placer; ~ed at or in (Mil) en garnison à.

stationary /'steɪʃənrɪ/ adj immobile, stationnaire; (vehicle) à l'arrêt.

stationery /'steɪʃənrɪ/ n papeterie f.

station wagon n (US) break m.

statistic /stə'tɪstɪk/ n statistique f; ~s statistique f.

statue /'stætʃuː/ n statue f.

status /'steɪtəs/ n (pl ~es) situation f, statut m; (prestige) standing m.

statute /'stætʃuːt/ n loi f; ~s (rules) statuts mpl. **statutory** adj statutaire; (holiday) légal.

staunch /stɔːntʃ/ adj (friend) loyal, fidèle.

stave /steɪv/ n (Mus) portée f. ● vt ~ off éviter, conjurer.

stay /steɪ/ vi rester; (spend time) séjourner; (reside) loger. ● vt (hunger) tromper. ● n séjour m. □ ~ away from (school) ne pas aller à; ~ behind or on rester; ~ in rester à la maison; ~ up veiller, se coucher tard.

stead /sted/ n stand sb in good ~ être utile à qn.

steadfast /'stedfɑːst/ adj ferme.

steady /ˈstedɪ/ adj (-ier, -iest) stable; (hand, voice) ferme; (regular) régulier; (staid) sérieux. ● vt maintenir, assurer; (calm) calmer.

steak /steɪk/ n steak m, bifteck m; (of fish) darne f.

steal /stiːl/ vt/i (pt stole; pp stolen) voler (from sb à qn).

steam /stiːm/ n vapeur f; (on glass) buée f. ● vt (cook) cuire à la vapeur. ● vi fumer. **~-engine** n locomotive f à vapeur.

steamer /ˈstiːmə(r)/ n (Culin) cuit-vapeur m; (boat) (bateau à) vapeur m.

steel /stiːl/ n acier m; ~ **industry** sidérurgie f. ● vpr ~ oneself s'endurcir, se cuirasser.

steep /stiːp/ adj raide, rapide; (price: 🔢) excessif. ● vt (soak) tremper; ~ed in (fig) imprégné de.

steeple /ˈstiːpl/ n clocher m.

steer /stɪə(r)/ vt diriger; (ship) gouverner; (fig) guider. ● vi (in ship) gouverner; ~ clear of éviter.

steering-wheel n volant m.

stem /stem/ n tige f; (of glass) pied m. ● vi (pt stemmed) ~ from provenir de. ● vt (pt stemmed) (check, stop) endiguer, contenir. ~ **cell** n cellule f souche.

stench /stentʃ/ n puanteur f.

stencil /ˈstensɪl/ n pochoir m. ● vt (pt stencilled) reproduire au pochoir.

step /step/ vi (pt stepped) marcher, aller. ● n pas m; (stair) marche f; (of train) marchepied m; (action) mesure f; ~s (ladder) escabeau m; in ~ au pas; (fig) conforme (with à). ~ **down** (resign) démissionner; (from ladder) descendre; ~ **forward** faire un pas en avant; ~ **in** (intervene) intervenir; ~ **up** (pressure) augmenter. **~brother** n demi-frère m. **~daughter** n belle-fille f.

~father n beau-père m. **~ladder** n escabeau m. **~mother** n belle-mère f. **~ stepping-stone** n (fig) tremplin m. **~sister** n demi-sœur f. **~son** n beau-fils m.

stereo /ˈsterɪəʊ/ n stéréo f; (record-player) chaîne f stéréo. ● adj stéréo inv.

stereotype /ˈsterɪətaɪp/ n stéréotype m.

sterile /ˈsteraɪl/ adj stérile. **sterility** n stérilité f.

sterilize /ˈsterəlaɪz/ vt stériliser.

sterling /ˈstɜːlɪŋ/ n livre(s) f (pl) sterling. ● adj sterling inv; (silver) fin; (fig) excellent.

stern /stɜːn/ adj sévère. ● n (of ship) arrière m.

steroid /ˈstɪərɔɪd/ n stéroïde m.

stew /stjuː/ vt/i cuire à la casserole; ~ed fruit compote f; ~ed tea thé m trop infusé. ● n ragoût m.

steward /ˈstjʊəd/ n (of club) intendant m; (on ship) steward m. **stewardess** n hôtesse f.

stick /stɪk/ vt (pt stuck) (glue) coller; (put 🔢) mettre; (endure 🔢) supporter. ● vi (adhere) coller, adhérer; (to pan) attacher; (remain 🔢) rester; (be jammed) être coincé; be stuck with sb 🔢 se farcir qn. ● n bâton m; (for walking) canne f; ~ **at** persévérer dans; ~ **out** vt (head) sortir; (tongue) tirer; vi (protrude) dépasser; ~ **to** (promise) rester fidèle à; ~ **up for** 🔢 défendre.

sticker /ˈstɪkə(r)/ n autocollant m.

sticky /ˈstɪkɪ/ adj -ier, -iest poisseux; (label, tape) adhésif.

stiff /stɪf/ adj raide; (limb, joint) ankylosé; (tough) dur; (drink) fort; (price) élevé; (manner) guindé; ~ **neck** torticolis m.

stifle /ˈstaɪfl/ vt/i étouffer.

stiletto /strˈletəʊ/ adj & n ~s, ~ heels talons mpl aiguille.

still /stɪl/ adj immobile; (quiet) calme, tranquille; keep ~ arrête de bouger! ● n silence m. ● adv encore, toujours; (even) encore; (nevertheless) tout de même.

stillborn /ˈstɪlbɔːn/ adj mort-né.

still life n nature f morte.

stimulate /ˈstɪmjʊleɪt/ vt stimuler. **stimulation** n stimulation f.

stimulus /ˈstɪmjʊləs/ n (pl -li) (spur) stimulant m.

sting /stɪŋ/ n piqûre f; (of insect) aiguillon m. ● vt/i (pt stung) piquer.

stingy /ˈstɪndʒɪ/ adj (-ier, -iest) avare (with de).

stink /stɪŋk/ n puanteur f. ● vi (pt stank or stunk; pp stunk) ~ (of) puer.

stipulate /ˈstɪpjʊleɪt/ vt stipuler.

stir /stɜː(r)/ vt/i (pt stirred) (move) remuer; (excite) exciter; ~ up (trouble) provoquer. ● n agitation f.

stirrup /ˈstɪrəp/ n étrier m.

stitch /stɪtʃ/ n point m; (in knitting) maille f; (Med) point m de suture; (muscle pain) point m de côté; be in ~es 🔒 avoir le fou rire. ● vt coudre.

stock /stɒk/ n réserve f; (Comm) stock m; (financial) valeurs fpl; (family) souche f; (soup) bouillon m; we're out of ~ il n'y en a plus; take ~ (fig) faire le point; in ~ en stock. ● adj (goods) courant. ● vt (shop) approvisionner; (sell) vendre. ● vi ~ up s'approvisionner (with de). ~**broker** n agent m de change. ~ **cube** n bouillon-cube m. **S~ Exchange** n Bourse f.

stocking /ˈstɒkɪŋ/ n bas m.

stock market n Bourse f.

stockpile /ˈstɒkpaɪl/ n stock m. ● vt stocker; (arms) amasser.

stock-taking n (Comm) inventaire m.

stocky /ˈstɒkɪ/ adj (-ier, -iest) trapu.

stodgy /ˈstɒdʒɪ/ adj lourd.

stole, stolen ➡STEAL.

stomach /ˈstʌmək/ n estomac m; (abdomen) ventre m. ● vt (put up with) supporter. ~**ache** n mal m à l'estomac or au ventre.

stone /stəʊn/ n pierre f; (pebble) caillou m; (in fruit) noyau m; (weight) 6,350 kg. ● adj de pierre; ~-cold/-deaf complètement froid/sourd. ● vt (throw stones) lapider; (fruit) dénoyauter.

stony /ˈstəʊnɪ/ adj pierreux.

stood /stʊd/ ➡STAND.

stool /stuːl/ n tabouret m.

stoop /stuːp/ vi (bend) se baisser; (condescend) s'abaisser. ● n have a ~ être voûté.

stop /stɒp/ vt/i (pt stopped) arrêter (doing de faire); (moving, talking) s'arrêter; (prevent) empêcher (from de); (hole, leak) boucher; (pain, noise) cesser; (stay 🔒) rester. ● n arrêt m; (full stop) point m; ~ (-over) halte f; (port of call) escale f ~ off s'arrêter; ~ up boucher,

stopgap /ˈstɒpgæp/ n bouche-trou m. ● adj intérimaire.

stoppage /ˈstɒpɪdʒ/ n arrêt m; (of work) arrêt m de travail; (of pay) retenue f.

stopper /ˈstɒpə(r)/ n bouchon m.

stop-watch n chronomètre m.

storage /ˈstɔːrɪdʒ/ n (of goods, food) emmagasinage m. ~ **heater** n radiateur m électrique à accumulation.

store /stɔː(r)/ n réserve f; (warehouse) entrepôt m; (shop) grand magasin m; (US) magasin m; have in ~ for réserver à; set ~ by attacher du prix à. ● vt (for future) mettre en réserve; (in warehouse, mind) emmagasiner. **~-room** n réserve f.

storey /'stɔːrɪ/ n étage m.

stork /stɔːk/ n cigogne f.

storm /stɔːm/ n tempête f, orage m. ● vt prendre d'assaut. ● vi (rage) tempêter.

story /'stɔːrɪ/ n histoire f; (in press) article m; (storey: US) étage m. **~-teller** n conteur/-euse m/f.

stout /staʊt/ adj corpulent; (strong) solide. ● n bière f brune.

stove /stəʊv/ n cuisinière f.

stow /stəʊ/ vt **~ away** (put away) ranger; (hide) cacher. ● vi voyager clandestinement.

straddle /'strædl/ vt être à cheval sur, enjamber.

straggler /'stræglə(r)/ n traînard/-e m/f.

straight /streɪt/ adj droit; (tidy) en ordre; (frank) franc; **~ face** visage m sérieux; **get sth ~** mettre qch au clair. ● adv (in straight line) droit; (direct) tout droit; **~ ahead** or on tout droit; **~ away** tout de suite; **~ off** ① sans hésiter. ● n (Sport) ligne f droite.

straighten /'streɪtn/ vt (nail, situation) redresser; (tidy) arranger.

straightforward /streɪt'fɔːwəd/ adj honnête; (easy) simple.

straight off ① sans hésiter.

strain /streɪn/ vt (rope, ears) tendre; (limb) fouler; (eyes) fatiguer; (muscle) froisser; (filter) passer; (vegetables) égoutter; (fig) mettre à l'épreuve. ● vi fournir des efforts. ● n tension f; (fig) effort m; (breed) race f; (of virus) variété f; **~s** (tune: Mus) accents mpl. **strained** adj forcé; (relations) tendu. **strainer** n passoire f.

strait /streɪt/ n détroit m; **~s** dé-

troit m; **be in dire ~s** être aux abois. **~-jacket** n camisole f de force.

strand /strænd/ n (thread) fil m, brin m; (of hair) mèche f.

stranded /'strændɪd/ adj (person) en rade; (ship) échoué.

strange /streɪndʒ/ adj étrange; (unknown) inconnu. **stranger** n inconnu/-e m/f.

strangle /'stræŋgl/ vt étrangler.

stranglehold /'stræŋglhəʊld/ n **have a ~ on** tenir à la gorge.

strap /stræp/ n (of leather) courroie f; (of dress) bretelle f; (of watch) bracelet m. ● vt (pt **strapped**) attacher.

strategic /strə'tiːdʒɪk/ adj stratégique. **strategy** n stratégie f.

straw /strɔː/ n paille f; **the last ~** le comble.

strawberry /'strɔːbrɪ/ n fraise f.

stray /streɪ/ vi s'égarer; (deviate) s'écarter. ● adj perdu; (isolated) isolé. ● n animal m perdu.

streak /striːk/ n raie f, bande f; (trace) trace f; (period) période f; (tendency) tendance f. ● vt (mark) strier. ● vi filer à toute allure.

stream /striːm/ n ruisseau m; (current) courant m; (in school) classe f (de niveau). ● vi ruisseler (with de); (eyes, nose) couler.

streamline /'striːmlaɪn/ vt rationaliser. **streamlined** adj (shape) aérodynamique.

street /striːt/ n rue f. **~-car** n (US) tramway m. **~ lamp** n réverbère m. **~ map** n indicateur m des rues.

strength /streŋθ/ n force f; (of wall, fabric) solidité f; **on the ~ of** en vertu de. **strengthen** vt renforcer, fortifier.

strenuous /'strenjʊəs/ adj (exercise) énergique; (work) ardu.

stress /stres/ n (emphasis) accent m; (pressure) pression f; (Med) stress m. ● vt souligner, insister sur.

stretch /stretʃ/ vt (pull taut) tendre; (arm, leg) étendre; (neck) tendre; (clothes) étirer; (truth) forcer; ∼ one's legs se dégourdir les jambes. ● vi s'étendre; (person) s'étirer; (clothes) se déformer. ● n étendue f; (period) période f; (of road) tronçon m; at a ∼ d'affilée. ● adj (fabric) extensible.

stretcher /ˈstretʃə(r)/ n brancard m.

strew /struː/ vt (pt strewed;pp strewed or strewn) (scatter) répandre; (cover) joncher.

strict /strɪkt/ adj strict.

stride /straɪd/ vi (pt strode; pp stridden) faire de grands pas. ● n grand pas m.

strife /straɪf/ n conflit(s) m(pl).

strike /straɪk/ vt (pt struck) frapper; (blow) donner; (match) frotter; (gold) trouver. ● vi faire grève; (attack) attaquer; (clock) sonner. ● n (of workers) grève f; (Mil) attaque f; (find) découverte f; on ∼ en grève. □ ∼ off or out rayer; ∼ up (a friendship) lier amitié (with avec).

striker n gréviste mf; (football) attaquant/-e m/f. **striking** adj frappant.

string /strɪŋ/ n ficelle f; (of violin, racket) corde f; (of pearls) collier m; (of lies) chapelet m; the ∼s (Mus) les cordes; pull ∼s faire jouer ses relations. ● vt (pt strung) (thread) enfiler. **stringed** adj (instrument) à cordes.

stringent /ˈstrɪndʒənt/ adj rigoureux, strict.

stringy /ˈstrɪŋɪ/ adj filandreux.

strip /strɪp/ vt/i (pt stripped) (undress) (se) déshabiller; (deprive) dépouiller. ● n bande f.

stripe /straɪp/ n rayure f; raie f. **striped** adj rayé.

strip light n néon m.

stripper /ˈstrɪpə(r)/ n strip-teaseur/-euse m/f; (solvent) décapant.

strip-tease n strip-tease m.

strive /straɪv/ vi (pt strove; pp striven) s'efforcer (to de).

strode /strəʊd/ ⇒STRIDE.

stroke /strəʊk/ vt (with hand) caresser. ● n coup m; (of pen) trait m; (swimming) nage f; (Med) attaque f, congestion f; at a∼ d'un seul coup.

stroll /strəʊl/ vi flâner; ∼ in entrer tranquillement. ● n petit tour m. **stroller** n (US) poussette f.

strong /strɒŋ/ adj fort; (shoes, fabric) solide; be fifty ∼ être fort de cinquante personnes. ∼hold n bastion m.

strongly /ˈstrɒŋlɪ/ adv (greatly) fortement; (with energy) avec force; (deeply) profondément.

strove /strəʊv/ ⇒STRIVE.

struck /strʌk/ ⇒STRIKE.

structure /ˈstrʌktʃə(r)/ n (of cell, poem) structure f; (building) construction f.

struggle /ˈstrʌgl/ vi lutter, se battre. ● n lutte f; (effort) effort m; have a ∼ to avoir du mal à.

strum /strʌm/ vt (pt strummed) gratter de.

strung /strʌŋ/ ⇒STRING. ● adj ∼ up (tense) nerveux.

strut /strʌt/ n (support) étai m. ● vi (pt) strutted se pavaner.

stub /stʌb/ n bout m; (counterfoil) talon m. ● vt (pt stubbed) ∼ one's toe se cogner le doigt de pied. □ ∼ out écraser.

stubble /'stʌbl/ n (on chin) barbe f de plusieurs jours; (remains of wheat) chaume m.

stubborn /'stʌbən/ adj obstiné.

stuck /stʌk/ →STICK.● adj (jammed) coincé; **I'm ~** (for answer) je sèche. **~-up** adj Ⅱ prétentieux.

stud /stʌd/ n (on jacket) clou m; (for collar) bouton m; (stallion) étalon m; (horse farm) haras m. ● vt (pt **studded**) clouter.

student /'stju:dnt/ n (Univ) étudiant/-e m/f; (School) élève m/f. ● adj (restaurant, life) universitaire.

studio /'stju:dɪəʊ/ n studio m.

studious /'stju:dɪəs/ adj (person) studieux; (deliberate) étudié.

study /'stʌdɪ/ n étude f; (office) bureau m. ● vt/i étudier.

stuff /stʌf/ n substance f; Ⅱ chose (s) f (pl). ● vt rembourrer; (animal) empailler; (cram) bourrer; (Culin) farcir; (block up) boucher; (put) fourrer. **stuffing** n bourre f; (Culin) farce f.

stuffy /'stʌfɪ/ adj (-ier, -iest) mal aéré; (dull Ⅱ) vieux jeu inv.

stumble /'stʌmbl/ vi trébucher; **~ across** or **on** tomber sur. **stumbling block** n obstacle m.

stump /stʌmp/ n (of tree) souche f; (of limb) moignon m; (of pencil) bout m.

stumped /stʌmpt/ adj embarrassé.

stun /stʌn/ vt (pt **stunned**) étourdir; (bewilder) stupéfier.

stung /stʌŋ/ →STING.

stunk /stʌŋk/ →STINK.

stunning /'stʌnɪŋ/ adj (delightful Ⅱ) sensationnel.

stunt /stʌnt/ vt (growth) retarder. ● n (feat Ⅱ) tour m de force; (trick Ⅱ) truc m; (dangerous) cascade f.

stupid /'stju:pɪd/ adj stupide, bête.

stupidity n stupidité f.

sturdy /'stɜ:dɪ/ adj (-ier, -iest) robuste.

stutter /'stʌtə(r)/ vi bégayer. ● n bégaiement m.

sty /staɪ/ n (pigsty) porcherie f; (on eye) orgelet m.

style /staɪl/ n style m; (fashion) mode f; (sort) genre m; (pattern) modèle m; **do sth in ~** faire qch avec classe. ● vt (design) créer; **~ sb's hair** coiffer qn.

stylish /'staɪlɪʃ/ adj élégant.

stylist /'staɪlɪst/ n (of hair) coiffeur/-euse m/f.

suave /swɑ:v/ adj (urbane) courtois; (smooth: pej) doucereux.

subconscious /ˌsʌb'kɒnʃəs/ adj & n subconscient (m), subconscient (m.)

subcontract /ˌsʌbkən'trækt/ vt sous-traiter.

subdue /səb'dju:/ vt (feeling) maîtriser; (country) subjuguer. **subdued** adj (person, mood) morose; (light) tamisé; (criticism) contenu.

subject[1] /'sʌbdʒɪkt/ adj (state) soumis; **~ to** soumis à; (liable to, dependent on) sujet à. ● n sujet m; (focus) objet m; (School,Univ) matière f; (citizen) ressortissant/-e m/f, sujet/-te m/f.

subject[2] /səb'dʒekt/ vt soumettre.

subjective /səb'dʒektɪv/ adj subjectif.

subject-matter n contenu m.

subjunctive /səb'dʒʌŋktɪv/ adj & n subjonctif (m.)

sublet /ˌsʌb'let/ vt sous-louer.

submarine /ˌsʌbmə'ri:n/ n sousmarin m.

submerge /səb'mɜ:dʒ/ vt submerger. ● vi plonger.

submissive /səb'mɪsɪv/ adj soumis.

s

submit /səb'mɪt/ vt/i (pt submitted) (se) soumettre (to à).

subordinate /sə'bɔːdɪnət/ adj subalterne; (Gram) subordonné. ● n subordonné-e m/f.

subpoena /sə'piːnə/ n (Jur) citation f, assignation f.

subscribe /səb'skraɪb/ vt/i verser (de l'argent) (to à); ~ to (loan, theory) souscrire à; (newspaper) s'abonner à, être abonné à. **subscriber** n abonné-e m/f. **subscription** n abonnement m; (membership dues) cotisation f.

subsequent /'sʌbsɪkwənt/ adj (later) ultérieur; (next) suivant. **subsequently** adv par la suite.

subside /səb'saɪd/ vi (land) s'affaisser; (flood, wind) baisser.

subsidiary /səb'sɪdɪərɪ/ adj accessoire. ● n (Comm) filiale f.

subsidize /'sʌbsɪdaɪz/ vt subventionner. **subsidy** n subvention f.

substance /'sʌbstəns/ n substance f.

substandard /sʌb'stændəd/ adj de qualité inférieure.

substantial /səb'stænʃl/ adj considérable; (meal) substantiel.

substitute /'sʌbstɪtjuːt/ n succédané m; (person) remplaçant-e m/f. ● vt substituer (for à).

subtitle /'sʌbtaɪtl/ n sous-titre m.

subtle /'sʌtl/ adj subtil.

subtract /səb'trækt/ vt soustraire.

suburb /'sʌbɜːb/ n faubourg m, banlieue f; ~s banlieue f. **suburban** adj de banlieue. **suburbia** n la banlieue.

subway /'sʌbweɪ/ n passage m souterrain; (US) métro m.

succeed /sək'siːd/ vi réussir (in doing à faire). ● vt (follow) succéder à.

success /sək'ses/ n succès m,

réussite f.

successful /sək'sesfl/ adj réussi, couronné de succès; (favourable) heureux; (in exam) reçu; be ~ in doing réussir à faire.

succession /sək'seʃn/ n succession f; in ~ de suite.

successive /sək'sesɪv/ adj successif; six ~ days six jours consécutifs.

successor /sək'sesə(r)/ n successeur m.

such /sʌtʃ/ det & pron tel(le), tel(le)s; (so much) tant(de). ● adv si; ~ a book un tel livre; ~ books de tels livres; ~ courage tant de courage; ~ a big house une si grande maison; ~ as comme, tel que; as ~ en tant que tel; there's no ~ thing ça n'existe pas. ~-and-~ adj tel ou tel.

suck /sʌk/ vt sucer. □ ~ in or up aspirer. **sucker** n (rubber pad) ventouse f; (person 🔲) dupe f.

suction /'sʌkʃn/ n succion f.

sudden /'sʌdn/ adj soudain, subit; all of a ~ tout à coup. **suddenly** adv subitement, brusquement.

sue /suː/ vt (pres p) suing poursuivre (en justice).

suede /sweɪd/ n daim m.

suffer /'sʌfə(r)/ vt/i souffrir; (loss, attack) subir. **sufferer** n victime f, malade m/f. **suffering** n souffrance(s) f(pl).

sufficient /sə'fɪʃnt/ adj (enough) suffisamment de; (big enough) suffisant.

suffix /'sʌfɪks/ n suffixe m.

suffocate /'sʌfəkeɪt/ vt/i suffoquer.

sugar /'ʃʊɡə(r)/ n sucre m. ● vt sucrer.

suggest /sə'dʒest/ vt suggérer. **suggestion** n suggestion f.

suicidal /suːɪ'saɪdl/ adj suicidaire.

suicide /'suːɪsaɪd/ n suicide m;

commit ~ se suicider.

suit /suːt/ n (man's) costume m; (woman's) tailleur m; (cards) couleur f. ● vt convenir à; (garment, style) aller à; (adapt) adapter.

suitable /'suːtəbl/ adj qui convient (for à), convenable. **suitably** adv convenablement.

suitcase /'suːtkeɪs/ n valise f.

suite /swiːt/ n (rooms) suite f; (furniture) mobilier m.

suited /'suːtɪd/ adj (well) ~ (matched) bien assorti; ~ to fait pour, apte à.

sulk /sʌlk/ vi bouder.

sullen /'sʌlən/ adj maussade.

sultana /sʌl'tɑːnə/ n raisin m de Smyrne, raisin m sec.

sultry /'sʌltrɪ/ adj (-ier, -iest) étouffant, lourd; (fig) sensuel.

sum /sʌm/ n somme f; (in arithmetic) calcul m. ● vt/i (pt summed) ~ up résumer, récapituler; (assess) évaluer.

summarize /'sʌməraɪz/ vt résumer.

summary /'sʌmərɪ/ n résumé m. ● adj sommaire.

summer /'sʌmə(r)/ n été m. ● adj d'été. **~time** n (season) été m.

Summer camps Les camps de vacances sont une composante importante des vacances d'été des jeunes Américains. Souvent situés dans des parc nationaux, ces camps proposent de multiples activités de plein air (canoë, escalade, équitation, natation, ski nautique, tennis, randonnée, etc.). Des milliers d'étudiants y sont recrutés chaque année en tant que moniteurs.

summery /'sʌmərɪ/ adj estival.

summit /'sʌmɪt/ n sommet m; ~ (conference) (Pol) (conférence f au) sommet m.

summon /'sʌmən/ vt appeler; ~ sb to a meeting convoquer qn à une réunion; ~ up (strength, courage) rassembler.

summons /'sʌmənz/ n (Jur) assignation f. ● vt assigner.

sun /sʌn/ n soleil m. ● vt (pt sunned) ~ oneself se chauffer au soleil. **~burn** n coup m de soleil.

Sunday /'sʌndeɪ/ n dimanche m. ~ **school** n catéchisme m.

sundry /'sʌndrɪ/ adj divers; sundries articles mpl divers; all and ~ tout le monde.

sunflower /'sʌnflaʊə(r)/ n tournesol m.

sung /sʌŋ/ ➡SING.

sun-glasses npl lunettes fpl de soleil.

sunk /sʌŋk/ ➡SINK.

sunken /'sʌŋkən/ adj (ship) submergé; (eyes) creux.

sunlight /'sʌnlaɪt/ n soleil m.

sunny /'sʌnɪ/ adj (-ier, -iest) ensoleillé.

sun: **~rise** n lever m du soleil. **~roof** n toit m ouvrant. ~ **screen** n filtre m solaire. **~set** n coucher m du soleil. **~shine** n soleil m. **~stroke** n insolation f.

sun-tan /'sʌntæn/ n bronzage m. ~ **lotion** n lotion f solaire. ~ **oil** n huile f solaire.

super /'suːpə(r)/ adj 🔢 formidable.

superb /suː'pɜːb/ adj superbe.

superficial /suːpə'fɪʃl/ adj superficiel.

superfluous /suː'pɜːfluəs/ adj superflu.

superimpose /suːpərɪm'pəʊz/ vt

s

superposer (on à).

superintendent /su:pərɪn
'tendənt/ n directeur/-trice m/f; (of police) commissaire m.

superior /su:'pɪərɪə(r)/ adj & n supérieur/-e (m/f).

superlative /su:'pɜ:lətɪv/ adj suprême. ● n (Gram) superlatif m.

supermarket /'su:pəmɑ:kɪt/ n supermarché m.

supersede /su:pə'si:d/ vt remplacer, supplanter.

superstition /su:pə'stɪʃn/ n superstition f. **superstitious** adj superstitieux.

superstore /'su:pəstɔ:(r)/ n hypermarché m.

supervise /'su:pəvaɪz/ vt surveiller, diriger. **supervision** n surveillance f. **supervisor** n surveillant/-e m/f; (shop) chef m de rayon; (firm) chef m de service.

supper /'sʌpə(r)/ n dîner m; (late at night) souper m.

supple /'sʌpl/ adj souple.

supplement[1] /'sʌplɪmənt/ n supplément m. **supplementary** adj supplémentaire.

supplement[2] /'sʌplɪmənt/ vt compléter.

supplier /sə'plaɪə(r)/ n fournisseur m.

supply /sə'plaɪ/ vt fournir; (equip) pourvoir; (feed) alimenter (with en). ● n provision f; (of gas) alimentation f; supplies (food) vivres mpl; (material) fournitures fpl.

support /sə'pɔ:t/ vt soutenir; (family) assurer la subsistance de. ● n soutien m, appui m; (Tech) support m. **supporter** n partisan/-e m/f; (Sport) supporter m. **supportive** adj qui soutient et encourage.

suppose /sə'pəʊz/ vt/i supposer; be ~d to do être censé faire, de-

voir faire; **supposing** he comes supposons qu'il vienne. **supposedly** adv soi-disant, prétendument.

suppress /sə'pres/ vt (put an end to) supprimer; (restrain) réprimer; (stifle) étouffer.

supreme /su:'pri:m/ adj suprême.

surcharge /'sɜ:tʃɑ:dʒ/ n supplément m; (tax) surtaxe f.

sure /ʃɔ:(r)/ adj sûr; make ~ of s'assurer de; make ~ that vérifier que. ● adv (US [!]) pour sûr. **surely** adv sûrement.

surf /sɜ:f/ n ressac m. ● vi faire du surf; (Internet) surfer.

surface /'sɜ:fɪs/ n surface f. ● adj superficiel. ● vt revêtir. ● vi faire surface; (fig) réapparaître.

surfer /'sɜ:fə(r)/ n surfeur/-euse m/f; (Internet) internaute mf.

surge /sɜ:dʒ/ vi (waves, crowd) déferler; (increase) monter. ● n (wave) vague f; (rise) montée f.

surgeon /'sɜ:dʒən/ n chirurgien m.

surgery /'sɜ:dʒərɪ/ n chirurgie f; (office) cabinet m; (session) consultation f; need ~ devoir être opéré.

surgical /'sɜ:dʒɪkl/ adj chirurgical. ~ **spirit** n alcool m à 90 degrés.

surly /'sɜ:lɪ/ adj (-ier, -iest) bourru.

surname /'sɜ:neɪm/ n nom m de famille.

surplus /'sɜ:pləs/ n surplus m. ● adj en surplus.

surprise /sə'praɪz/ n surprise f. ● vt surprendre. **surprised** adj surpris (at de). **surprising** adj surprenant.

surrender /sə'rendə(r)/ vi se rendre. ● vt (hand over) remettre; (Mil) rendre. ● n (Mil) reddition f; (of passport) remise f.

surround /sə'raʊnd/ vt entourer; (Mil) encercler. **surrounding** adj environnant. **surroundings** npl environs *mpl*; (setting) cadre *m*.

surveillance /sɜːˈveɪləns/ *n* surveillance *f*.

survey[1] /səˈveɪ/ *vt* (review) passer en revue; (inquire into) enquêter sur; (building) inspecter.

survey[2] /ˈsɜːveɪ/ *n* (inquiry) enquête *f*; inspection *f*; (general view) vue *f* d'ensemble.

surveyor /səˈveɪə(r)/ *n* expert *m* (géomètre).

survival /səˈvaɪvl/ *n* survie *f*.

survive /səˈvaɪv/ *vt/i* survivre (à). **survivor** *n* survivant/-e *m/f*.

susceptible /səˈseptəbl/ *adj* sensible (to à); ~ **to** (prone to) prédisposé à.

suspect[1] /səˈspekt/ *vt* soupçonner; (doubt) douter de.

suspect[2] /ˈsʌspekt/ *n & adj* suspect/-e *(m/f)*.

suspend /səˈspend/ *vt* (hang, stop) suspendre; (licence) retirer provisoirement. **suspended sentence** *n* condamnation *f* avec sursis.

suspender /səˈspendə(r)/ *n* jarretelle *f*; ~**s** (braces: US) bretelles *fpl*. ~ **belt** *n* porte-jarretelles *m*.

suspension /səˈspenʃn/ *n* suspension *f*; retrait *m* provisoire.

suspicion /səˈspɪʃn/ *n* soupçon *m*; (distrust) méfiance *f*.

suspicious /səˈspɪʃəs/ *adj* soupçonneux; (causing suspicion) suspect; **be** ~ **of** se méfier de. **suspiciously** *adv* de façon suspecte.

sustain /səˈsteɪn/ *vt* supporter; (effort) soutenir; (suffer) subir.

sustenance /ˈsʌstɪnəns/ *n* (food) nourriture *f*; (nourishment) valeur *f* nutritive.

swallow[1] /ˈswɒləʊ/ *vt/i* avaler; ~ **up** (absorb, engulf) engloutir. ● *n* hirondelle *f*.

swam /swæm/ ➡SWIM.

swamp /swɒmp/ *n* marais *m*. ● *vt* (flood, overwhelm) submerger.

swan /swɒn/ *n* cygne *m*.

swap /swɒp/ *vt/i* (*pt* **swapped**) 🔟 échanger. ● *n* 🔟 échange *m*.

swarm /swɔːm/ *n* essaim *m*. ● *vi* fourmiller; ~ **into** or **round** (crowd) envahir.

swat /swɒt/ *vt* (*pt* **swatted**) (fly) écraser.

sway /sweɪ/ *vt/i* (se) balancer; (influence) influencer. ● *n* balancement *m*; (rule) empire *m*.

swear /sweə(r)/ *vt/i* (*pt* **swore**; *pp* **sworn**) jurer (to sth de qch); ~ **at** injurier; ~ **by** 🔟 ne jurer que par qch. ~**-word** *n* juron *m*.

sweat /swet/ *n* sueur *f*. ● *vi* suer.

sweater /ˈswetə(r)/ *n* pull-over *m*.

sweat-shirt *n* sweat-shirt *m*.

swede /swiːd/ *n* rutabaga *m*.

Swede /swiːd/ *n* Suédois/-e *m/f*. **Sweden** *n* Suède *f*.

Swedish /ˈswiːdɪʃ/ *adj* suédois. ● *n* (Ling) suédois *m*.

sweep /swiːp/ *vt/i* (*pt* **swept**) (floor) balayer; (carry away) emporter, entraîner; (chimney) ramoner. ● *n* coup *m* de balai; (curve) courbe *f*; (movement) geste *m*, mouvement *m*; (for chimneys) ramoneur *m*. ~ **by** passer rapidement or majestueusement. **sweeper** *n* (for carpet) balai *m* mécanique; (football) libero *m*.

sweet /swiːt/ *adj* (not sour, pleasant) doux; (not savoury) sucré; (charming) 🔟 gentil; **have a** ~ **tooth** aimer les sucreries. ● *n* bonbon *m*; (dish) dessert *m*. ~**corn** *n* maïs *m*.

sweeten /ˈswiːtn/ *vt* sucrer; (fig) adoucir. **sweetener** *n* édulcorant *m*.

sweetheart /ˈswiːthɑːt/ *n* petit/-e ami/-e *m/f*; (term of endearment) chéri/-e m/f.

sweetly /'swiːtlɪ/ adv gentiment.

sweetness /'swiːtnɪs/ n douceur f; goût m sucré.

sweet pea n pois m de senteur.

swell /swel/ vt/i (pt swelled; pp swollen or swelled) (increase) grossir; (expand) (se) gonfler; (hand, face) enfler. ● n (of sea) houle f. **swelling** n (Med) enflure f.

sweltering /'sweltərɪŋ/ adj étouffant.

swept /swept/ →SWEEP.

swerve /swɜːv/ vi faire un écart.

swift /swɪft/ adj rapide. ● n (bird) martinet m.

swim /swɪm/ vi (pt swam; pp swum; pres p swimming) nager; (be dizzy) tourner. ● vt traverser à la nage; (distance) nager. ● n baignade f; go for a ~ aller se baigner. **swimmer** n nageur/-euse m/f. **swimming** n natation f.

swimming pool n piscine f.

swimsuit /'swɪmsuːt/ n maillot m (de bain).

swindle /'swɪndl/ vt escroquer. ● n escroquerie f.

swine /swaɪn/ npl (pigs) pourceaux mpl. ● n inv (person ⚠) salaud m.

swing /swɪŋ/ vt/i (pt swung) (se) balancer; (turn round) tourner; (pendulum) osciller. ● n balancement m; (seat) balançoire f; (of opinion) revirement m (towards en faveur de); (Mus) rythme m; be in full ~ battre son plein. □ ~ round (person) se retourner.

swipe /swaɪp/ vt (hit ⚠) frapper; (steal ⚠) piquer. ~ card n carte f magnétique, badge m.

swirl /swɜːl/ vi tourbillonner. ● n tourbillon m.

Swiss /swɪs/ adj suisse. ● n inv Suisse m/f.

switch /swɪtʃ/ n bouton m (électrique), interrupteur m; (shift) changement m, revirement m. ● vt (transfer) transférer; (exchange) échanger (for contre); (reverse positions of) changer de place; ~ trains (change) changer de train. ● vi changer. □ ~ off éteindre; ~ on mettre, allumer.

switchboard /'swɪtʃbɔːd/ n standard m.

Switzerland /'swɪtsələnd/ n Suisse f.

swivel /'swɪvl/ vt/i (pt swivelled) (faire) pivoter.

swollen /'swəʊlən/ →SWELL.

swoop /swuːp/ vi (bird) fondre; (police) faire une descente, foncer. ● n (police raid) descente f.

sword /sɔːd/ n épée f.

swore /swɔː(r)/ →SWEAR.

sworn /swɔːn/ →SWEAR. ● adj (enemy) juré; (ally) dévoué.

swot /swɒt/ vt/i (pt swotted) (study ⚠) bûcher ⚠. ● n ⚠ bûcheur/-euse m/f⚠.

swum /swʌm/ →SWIM.

swung /swʌŋ/ →SWING.

syllabus /'sɪləbəs/ n (pl ~es) (School, Univ) programme m.

symbol /'sɪmbl/ n symbole m. **symbolic (al)** adj symbolique. **symbolize** vt symboliser.

symmetrical /sɪ'metrɪkəl/ adj symétrique.

sympathetic /sɪmpə'θetɪk/ adj compatissant; (fig) compréhensif.

sympathize /'sɪmpəθaɪz/ vi ~ with (pity) plaindre; (fig) comprendre les sentiments de. **sympathizer** n sympathisant/-e m/f.

sympathy /'sɪmpəθɪ/ n (pity) compassion f; (understanding) compréhension f; (solidarity) solidarité f; (condolences) condoléances fpl; (affinity) affinité *f*; be in ~ with comprendre, être en accord avec.

symptom /'sɪmptəm/ *n* symptôme *m*.

synagogue /'sɪnəgɒg/ *n* synagogue *f*.

synonym /'sɪnənɪm/ *n* synonyme *m*.

synopsis /sɪ'nɒpsɪs/ *n* (*pl* **-opses**) résumé *m*.

syntax /'sɪntæks/ *n* syntaxe *f*.

synthesis /'sɪnθəsɪs/ *n* (*pl* **-theses**) synthèse *f*.

synthetic /sɪn'θetɪk/ *adj* synthétique.

syringe /sɪ'rɪndʒ/ *n* seringue *f*.

syrup /'sɪrəp/ *n* (liquid) sirop *m*; (treacle) mélasse *f* raffinée.

system /'sɪstəm/ *n* système *m*; (body) organisme *m*; (order) méthode *f*; **systematic** *adj* systématique.

systems analyst *n* analyste-programmeur/- euse *m/f*.

Tt

tab /tæb/ *n* (on can) languette *f*; (on garment) patte *f*; (label) étiquette *f*; (US ①) addition *f*; (Comput) tabulatrice *f*; (setting) tabulation *f*.

table /'teɪbl/ *n* table *f*; (at the) ~ à table; lay or set the ~ mettre la table. ● *vt* (motion) présenter. ~**cloth** *n* nappe *f*. ~**-mat** *n* set *m* de table. ~**spoon** *n* cuillère *f* de service.

tablet /'tæblɪt/ *n* (of stone) plaque *f*; (drug) comprimé *m*.

table tennis *n* tennis *m* de table;

ping-pong® *m*.

taboo /tə'buː/ *n* & *a* tabou (*m*).

tacit /'tæsɪt/ *adj* tacite.

tack /tæk/ *n* (nail) clou *m*; (stitch) point *m* de bâti; (course of action) voie *f*. ● *vt* (nail) clouer; (stitch) bâtir; (add) ajouter. ● *vi* (Naut) louvoyer.

tackle /'tækl/ *n* équipement *m*; (in soccer) tacle *m*; (in rugby) plaquage *m*. ● *vt* (problem) s'attaquer à; (player) tacler, plaquer.

tact /tækt/ *n* tact *m*. **tactful** *adj* plein de tact.

tactics /'tæktɪks/ *npl* tactique *f*.

tadpole /'tædpəʊl/ *n* têtard *m*.

tag /tæg/ *n* (label) étiquette *f*. ● *vt* (*pt* **tagged**) (label) étiqueter. ● *vi* ~ along *t* suivre.

tail /teɪl/ *n* queue *f*; ~s (coat) habit *m*; ~sl (on coin) pile! ● *vt* (follow) filer. ● *vi* ~ away or off diminuer. ~**-back** *n* bouchon *m*. ~**-gate** *n* hayon *m*.

tailor /'teɪlə(r)/ *n* tailleur *m*. ● *vt* (garment) façonner; (fig) adapter. ~**-made** *adj* fait sur mesure.

take /teɪk/ *vt/i* (*pt* **took**; *pp* **taken**) prendre (from sb à qn); (carry) porter, porter (to à); (escort) emmener; (contain) contenir; (tolerate) supporter; (accept) accepter; (prize) remporter; (exam) passer; (precedence) avoir; (view) adopter; ~ sb home ramener qn chez lui; be taken by or with être impressionné par; be taken ill tomber malade; it ~s time il faut du temps pour. □ ~ **after** tenir de; ~ **apart** démonter; (fig) descendre en flammes ①; ~ **away** (object) enlever; (person) emmener; (pain) supprimer; ~ **back** reprendre; (return) rendre; (accompany) raccompagner; (statement) retirer; ~ **down** (object) descendre; (notes) prendre; ~ **in** (object) rentrer; (include) inclure; (cheat) tromper; ~ **off** (Aviat) décoller; ~ sth **off** enlever qch; ~ sb **off** imiter qn; ~ **on** (task, staff, passenger) prendre; (challenger) relever le défi de; ~ **out** sortir; (stain) enlever; ~ **over** vt (country, firm) prendre le contrôle de; vi prendre le pouvoir; ~ **over from** remplacer; ~ **part** participer (in à); ~ **place** avoir lieu; ~ **to** se prendre d'amitié pour; (activity) prendre goût à; ~ **to** doing se mettre à faire; ~ up (object) monter; (hobby) se mettre à; (occupy) prendre; (resume) reprendre; ~ **up with** se lier avec. ~**away** n (meal) repas m à emporter. ~**off** n (Aviat) décollage m. ~**over** n (Pol) prise f de pouvoir; (Comm) rachat m.

tale /teɪl/ n conte m; (report) récit m; (lie) histoire f.

talent /'tælənt/ n talent m. **talented** adj doué.

talk /tɔ:k/ vt/i parler; (chat) bavarder; ~ sb **into** doing persuader qn de faire; ~ sth **over** discuter de qch. ● n (talking) propos mpl; (conversation) conversation f; (lecture) exposé m.

talkative /'tɔ:kətɪv/ adj bavard.

tall /tɔ:l/ adj (high) haut; (person) grand.

tame /teɪm/ adj apprivoisé; (dull) insipide. ● vt apprivoiser; (lion) dompter.

tamper /'tæmpə(r)/ vi ~ **with** (lock, machine) tripoter; (accounts, evidence) trafiquer.

tan /tæn/ vt/i (pt **tanned**) bronzer; (hide) tanner. ● n bronzage m.

tangerine /'tændʒəri:n/ n mandarine f.

tangle /'tæŋgl/ vt/i ~ (up) s'emmêler. ● n enchevêtrement m.

tank /tæŋk/ n réservoir m; (vat)

cuve f; (for fish) aquarium m; (Mil) char m (de combat).

tanker /'tæŋkə(r)/ n (lorry) camion-citerne m; (ship) navire-citerne m; oil/petrol ~ pétrolier m.

tantrum /'tæntrəm/ n crise f (de colère).

tap /tæp/ n (for water) robinet m; (knock) petit coup m; **on** ~ disponible. ● vt (pt **tapped**) (knock) taper (doucement); (resources) exploiter; (phone) mettre sur écoute.

tape /teɪp/ n bande f (magnétique); (cassette) cassette f; (video) cassette f vidéo; (fabric) ruban m; (sticky) scotch (r) m. ● vt (record) enregistrer; ~ sth **to** sth coller qch à qch. ~**measure** n mètre m ruban. ~ **recorder** n magnétophone m.

tapestry /'tæpəstri/ n tapisserie f.

tar /tɑ:(r)/ n goudron m. ● vt (pt **tarred**) goudronner.

target /'tɑ:gɪt/ n cible f; (objective) objectif m. ● vt (city) prendre pour cible; (weapon) diriger; (in marketing) viser.

tariff /'tærɪf/ n (price list) tarif m; (on imports) droit m de douane.

tarmac, Tarmac® /'tɑ:mæk/ n macadam m; (runway) piste f.

tarpaulin /tɑ:'pɔ:lɪn/ n bâche f.

tarragon /'tærəgən/ n estragon m.

tart /tɑ:t/ n tarte f. ● adj aigrelet.

task /tɑ:sk/ n tâche f.

taste /teɪst/ n goût m; (experience) aperçu m. ● vt (eat, enjoy) goûter à; (try) goûter; (perceive taste of) sentir (le goût de). ● vi ~ **of** or **like** avoir un goût de. **tasteful** adj de bon goût.

tattoo /tə'tu:/ vt tatouer. ● n tatouage m.

tatty /'tætɪ/ adj (**-ier, -iest**) ⚠ miteux.

taught /tɔːt/ ➡TEACH.

taunt /tɔːnt/ vt railler. ● n raillerie f.

Taurus /ˈtɔːrəs/ n Taureau m.

tax /tæks/ n (on goods, services) taxe f; (on income) impôt m. ● vt imposer; (put to test: fig) mettre à l'épreuve. **taxable** adj imposable.
taxation n imposition f; (taxes) impôts mpl.

tax: ~ **collector** n percepteur m. ~**-deductible** adj déductible des impôts. ~ **disc** n vignette f. ~**-free** adj exempt d'impôts. ~ **haven** n paradis m fiscal.

taxi /ˈtæksɪ/ n taxi m. ~ **rank** n station f de taxi.

tax: ~**payer** n contribuable mf. ~ **relief** n dégrèvement m fiscal. ~ **return** n déclaration f d'impôts.

tea /tiː/ n (drink, meal) thé m; (children's snack) goûter m; ~ **bag** sachet m de thé.

teach /tiːtʃ/ vt (pt taught) apprendre (sb sth qch à qn); (in school) enseigner (sb sth qch à qn). ● vi enseigner. **teacher** n enseignant/-e m/f; (secondary) professeur m; (primary) instituteur/-trice m/f.

team /tiːm/ n équipe f; (of animals) attelage m. ● vi ~ **up** faire équipe (with avec).

teapot /ˈtiːpɒt/ n théière f.

tear[1] /teə(r)/ vt/i (pt tore; pp torn) (se) déchirer; (snatch) arracher (from à); (rush) aller à toute vitesse. ● n déchirure f.

tear[2] /tɪə(r)/ n larme f. **in** ~**s** en larmes. ~**-gas** n gaz m lacrymogène.

tease /tiːz/ vt taquiner. ● n taquin/-e m/f.

tea: ~ **shop** n salon m de thé. ~**spoon** n petite cuillère f.

teat /tiːt/ n tétine f.

tea-towel n torchon m.

technical /ˈteknɪkl/ adj technique.

technician /tekˈnɪʃn/ n technicien/-ne m/f.

technique /tekˈniːk/ n technique f.

techno /ˈteknəʊ/ n (Mus) techno f.

technology /tekˈnɒlədʒɪ/ n technologie f.

technophobe /ˈteknəˈfəʊb/ n technophobe mf.

teddy /ˈtedɪ/ adj ~ **bear** ours m en peluche.

tedious /ˈtiːdɪəs/ adj ennuyeux.

tee /tiː/ n (golf) tee m.

teenage /ˈtiːneɪdʒ/ adj (girl, boy) adolescent; (fashion) des adolescents. **teenager** n jeune mf, adolescent/-e m/f.

teens /tiːnz/ npl in one's ~ adolescent.

teeth /tiːθ/ ➡TOOTH.

teethe /tiːð/ vi faire ses dents.

teetotaller /tiːˈtəʊtələ(r)/ n personne f qui ne boit pas d'alcool.

telecommunications /ˌtelɪkəmjuːnɪˈkeɪʃnz/ npl télécommunications fpl.

telecommuting /ˈtelɪkəˈmjuːtɪŋ/ n télétravail m.

teleconferencing /ˈtelɪˈkɒnfərənsɪŋ/ n téléconférence f.

telegram /ˈtelɪgræm/ n télégramme m.

telegraph /ˈtelɪgrɑːf/ n télégraphe m. ● adj télégraphique.

telephone /ˈtelɪfəʊn/ n téléphone m. ● vt (person) téléphoner à; (message) téléphoner. ● vi téléphoner. ~ **book** n annuaire m. ~ **booth**, ~ **box** n cabine f téléphonique. ~ **call** n coup m de téléphone. ~ **number** n numéro m de téléphone.

telephoto /ˈtelɪˈfəʊtəʊ/ adj ~ **lens** téléobjectif m.

telescope /ˈtelɪskəʊp/ n télescope

m. ● *vt/i* (se) télescoper.

teletext /'telɪtekst/ *n* télétexte *m.*

televise /'telɪvaɪz/ *vt* téléviser.

television /'telɪvɪʒn/ *n* télévision *f*; ~ **set** poste *m* de télévision, téléviseur *m.*

teleworking /'telɪwɜːkɪŋ/ *n* télétravail *m.*

telex /'teleks/ *n* télex *m.* ● *vt* envoyer par télex.

tell /tel/ *vt* (*pt* **told**) dire (sb qch à qn); (story) raconter; (distinguish) distinguer; ~ **sb to do sth** dire à qn de faire qch; ~ **sth from** sth voir la différence entre qch et qch. ● *vi* (show) avoir un effet; (know) savoir. □ ~ **off** 🔟 gronder.

temp /temp/ *n* intérimaire *mf.* ● *vi* faire de l'intérim.

temper /'tempə(r)/ *n* humeur *f*; (anger) colère *f*; **lose one's** ~ se mettre en colère.

temperament /'temprəmənt/ *n* tempérament *m.* **temperamental** *adj* capricieux.

temperature /'temprətʃə(r)/ *n* température *f*; **have a** ~ avoir de la fièvre *or* de la température.

temple /'templ/ *n* temple *m*; (of head) tempe *f.*

temporary /'temprərɪ/ *adj* temporaire, provisoire.

tempt /tempt/ *vt* tenter; ~ **sb to** **do** donner envie à qn de faire.

ten /ten/ *adj & n* dix (*m*).

tenacious /tɪ'neɪʃəs/ *adj* tenace.

tenancy /'tenənsɪ/ *n* location *f.* **tenant** *n* locataire *mf.*

tend /tend/ *vt* s'occuper de. ● *vi* ~ **to** (be apt to) avoir tendance à; (look after) s'occuper de. **tendency** *n* tendance *f.*

tender /'tendə(r)/ *adj* tendre; (sore, painful) sensible. ● *vt* offrir, donner. ● *vi* faire une soumission. ● *n*

(Comm) soumission *f*; **be legal** ~ (money) avoir cours.

tendon /'tendən/ *n* tendon *m.*

tennis /'tenɪs/ *n* tennis *m.* ● *adj* (court, match) de tennis.

tenor /'tenə(r)/ *n* (meaning) sens *m* général; (Mus) ténor *m.*

tense /tens/ *n* (Gram) temps *m.* ● *adj* tendu. ● *vt* (muscles) tendre, raidir. ● *vi* (face) se crisper.

tension /'tenʃn/ *n* tension *f.*

tent /tent/ *n* tente *f.*

tentative /'tentətɪv/ *adj* provisoire; (hesitant) timide.

tenth /tenθ/ *adj & n* dixième (*mf*).

tepid /'tepɪd/ *adj* tiède.

term /tɜːm/ *n* (word, limit) terme *m*; (of imprisonment) temps *m*; (School) trimestre *m*; ~**s** conditions *fpl*; **on good/bad** ~**s** en bons/ mauvais termes; **in the short/long** ~ à court/long terme; **come to** ~**s** **with sth** accepter qch; ~ **of office** (Pol) mandat *m.* ● *vt* appeler.

terminal /'tɜːmɪnl/ *adj* (point) terminal; (illness) incurable. ● *n* (oil, computer) terminal *m*; (Rail) terminus *m*; (Electr) borne *f*; **air** ~ aérogare *f.*

terminate /'tɜːmɪneɪt/ *vt* mettre fin à. ● *vi* prendre fin.

terminus /'tɜːmɪnəs/ *n* (*pl* **-ni**) (station) terminus *m.*

terrace /'terəs/ *n* terrasse *f*; (houses) rangée *f* de maisons contiguës; **the** ~**s** (Sport) les gradins *mpl.*

terracotta /terə'kɒtə/ *n* terre *f* cuite.

terrible /'terəbl/ *adj* affreux, atroce.

terrific /tə'rɪfɪk/ *adj* (huge) énorme; (great 🔟) formidable.

terrify /'terɪfaɪ/ *vt* terrifier; **be terrified of** avoir très peur de.

territory /'terətrɪ/ n territoire m.

terror /'terə(r)/ n terreur f.

terrorism /'terərɪzəm/ n terrorisme m. **terrorist** n terroriste mf.

test /test/ n épreuve f; (written exam) contrôle m; (of machine, product) essai m; (of sample) analyse f; driving ~ examen m du permis de conduire. ● vt évaluer; (School) contrôler; (machine, product) essayer; (sample) analyser; (patience, strength) mettre à l'épreuve. ● vi ~ for faire une recherche de.

testament /'testəmənt/ n testament m; Old/New T~ Ancien/Nouveau Testament m.

testicle /'testɪkl/ n testicule m.

testify /'testɪfaɪ/ vt/i témoigner (to de; that que).

testimony /'testɪmənɪ/ n témoignage m.

test tube n éprouvette f.

tetanus /'tetənəs/ n tétanos m.

text /tekst/ n texte m. ● vt ~ sb envoyer un texto à qn. ~book n manuel m. ~ **message** n texto m.

texture /'tekstʃə(r)/ n (of paper) grain m; (of fabric) texture f.

than /ðæn/, /ðən/ conj que, qu'; (with numbers) de; more/less ~ ten plus/moins de dix.

thank /θæŋk/ vt remercier; ~ you!, ~s! merci! ~ful adj reconnaissant (for de). thanks npl remerciements mpl; ~s to grâce à. **Thanksgiving (Day)** n (US) jour m d'Action de Grâces.

---

that /ðæt/ pl **those**

● **determiner**

···▸ ce, cet, cette, ces; ~ dog ce chien; ~ man cet homme; ~ woman cette femme; those books ces livres; at ~ moment à ce moment-là.

! To distinguish that/those from this/these, you add -là to the noun: I prefer that car je préfère cette voiture-là.

● **pronoun**

···▸ cela, ça, ce; what's ~?, what are those? qu'est-ce que c'est (que ça)?; who's ~? qui est-ce?; ~ is my brother c'est or voilà mon frère; those are my parents ce sont mes parents.

···▸ (emphatic) celui-là, celle-là, ceux-là, celles-là; all the dresses are nice but I like ~/those best toutes les robes sont jolies mais je préfère celle-là/celles-là.

● **relative pronoun**

···▸ (for subject) qui; the man ~ stole the car l'homme qui a volé la voiture.

···▸ (for object) que; the girl ~ I met la fille que j'ai rencontrée.

! With a preposition, use lequel/laquelle/lesquels/lesquelles: the chair ~ I was sitting on la chaise sur laquelle j'étais assis.
With a preposition that translates as à, use auquel/à laquelle/auxquels/auxquelles: the girls ~ I was talking to les filles auxquelles je parlais.
With a preposition that translates as de, use dont: the people ~ I've talked about les personnes dont j'ai parlé.

● **conjunction** que; she said ~ she would do it elle a dit qu'elle le ferait.

t

thatched /ˈθætʃd/ adj de chaume; ~ cottage chaumière f.

thaw /θɔː/ vt/i (faire) dégeler; (snow) (faire) fondre. ● n dégel m.

the /ðə, ðiː/ determiner
····▸ le, l', la, les; ~ dog le chien; ~ tree l'arbre; ~ chair la chaise; to ~ shops aux magasins.

! With a preposition that translates as à: à + le = au and à + les = aux.

theatre /ˈθɪətə(r)/ n théâtre m.

theft /θeft/ n vol m.

their /ðeə(r)/ adj leur, pl leurs.

theirs /ðeəz/ pron le or la leur, les leurs.

them /ðem/, /ðəm/ pron les; (after preposition) eux, elles; (to) ~ leur; phone ~! téléphone-leur!; I know ~ je les connais; both of ~ tous/toutes les deux.

theme /θiːm/ n thème m. ~ park n parc m de loisirs (à thème).

themselves /ðemˈselvz/ pron eux-mêmes, elles-mêmes; (reflexive) se; (after preposition) eux, elles.

then /ðen/ adv alors; (next) ensuite, puis; (therefore) alors, donc. ● adj d'alors; from ~ on dès lors.

theology /θɪˈɒlədʒɪ/ n théologie f.

theory /ˈθɪərɪ/ n théorie f.

therapy /ˈθerəpɪ/ n thérapie f.

there /ðeə(r)/ adv là; (with verb) y; (over there) là-bas; he goes ~ il y va; on ~ là-dessus; ~ is, ~ are il y a; (pointing) voilà. ● interj ~, ~! allons, allons!

therefore /ˈðeəfɔː(r)/ adv donc.

thermal /ˈθɜːml/ adj thermique f.

thermometer /θəˈmɒmɪtə(r)/ n thermomètre m.

Thermos® /ˈθɜːməs/ n thermos ® m or f inv.

thermostat /ˈθɜːməstæt/ n thermostat m.

thesaurus /θɪˈsɔːrəs/ n (pl -ri) dictionnaire m de synonymes.

these /ðiːz/ ▶THIS.

thesis /ˈθiːsɪs/ n (pl theses) thèse f.

they /ðeɪ/ pron ils, elles; (emphatic) eux, elles; (people in general) on.

thick /θɪk/ adj épais; (stupid) bête; be 6 cm ~ avoir 6 cm d'épaisseur.

thief /θiːf/ n (pl thieves) voleur/-euse m/f.

thigh /θaɪ/ n cuisse f.

thin /θɪn/ adj (thinner, thinnest) mince; (person) maigre, mince; (sparse) clairsemé; (fine) fin. ● vt/i (pt thinned) ~ (down) (paint) diluer; (soup) allonger.

thing /θɪŋ/ n chose f. ~s (belongings) affaires fpl; the best ~ is to le mieux est de; the (right) ~ ce qu'il faut (for sb à qn).

think /θɪŋk/ vt/i (pt thought) penser (about, of à); (carefully) réfléchir (about, of à); (believe) croire; I ~ so je crois que oui; ~ of doing envisager de faire; ~ over bien réfléchir à; □ ~ up inventer.

third /θɜːd/ adj troisième. ● n troisième m/f; (fraction) tiers m. T~ World n tiers-monde m.

thirst /θɜːst/ n soif f.

thirsty /ˈθɜːstɪ/ adj be ~ avoir soif; make ~ donner soif à.

thirteen /θɜːˈtiːn/ adj & n treize (m).

thirty /ˈθɜːtɪ/ adj & n trente (m).

this /ðɪs/ *pl* **these**

● *determiner*

···→ ce/cet/cette/ces; ∼ dog ce chien; ∼ man cet homme; ∼ woman cette femme; these books ces livres.

❗ To distinguish from that and those, you need to add *-ci* after the noun: I prefer this car je préfère cette voiture-ci.

● *pronoun*

···→ ce; what's ∼?, what are these? qu'est-ce que c'est? who is ∼? qui est-ce?; ∼ is the kitchen voici la cuisine; ∼ is Sophie je te or vous présente Sophie; these are your things ce sont tes affaires.

···→ (emphatic) celui-ci/celle-ci/ceux-ci/celles-ci; all the dresses are nice but I like ∼/these best toutes les robes sont jolies mais je préfère celle-ci/celles-ci.

thistle /ˈθɪsl/ *n* chardon *m*.

thorn /θɔːn/ *n* épine *f*.

thorough /ˈθʌrə/ *adj* (detailed) approfondi; (meticulous) minutieux. **thoroughly** *adv* (clean, study) à fond; (very) tout à fait.

those /ðəʊz/ ⇒**THAT**.

though /ðəʊ/ *conj* bien que. ● *adv* quand même.

thought /θɔːt/ ⇒**THINK**. ● *n* pensée *f*, idée *f*. **thoughtful** *adj* pensif; (kind) prévenant.

thousand /ˈθaʊznd/ *adj & n* mille (*m inv*); ∼s of des milliers de. **thousandth** *adj & n* millième (*mf*).

thread /θred/ *n* (yarn & fig) fil *m*; (of screw) pas *m*. ● *vt* enfiler; ∼ one's way se faufiler.

threat /θret/ *n* menace *f*. **threaten**

vt/i menacer (with de).

three /θriː/ *adj & n* trois (*m*).

threw /θruː/ ⇒**THROW**.

thrill /θrɪl/ *n* frisson *m*; (pleasure) plaisir *m*. ● *vt* transporter (de joie); be ∼ed être ravi. ● *vi* frissonner (de joie).

thrive /θraɪv/ *vi* (*pt* thrived or throve;*pp* thrived or thriven) prospérer; he ∼s on it cela lui réussit.

throat /θrəʊt/ *n* gorge *f*; have a sore ∼ avoir mal à la gorge.

throb /θrɒb/ *vi* (*pt* throbbed) (heart) battre; (engine) vibrer; (pain) élancement *m*; (of engine) vibration *f*. **throbbing** *adj* (pain) lancinant.

throne /θrəʊn/ *n* trône *m*.

through /θruː/ *prep* à travers; (during) pendant; (by means of or way of) par; (by reason of) grâce à, à cause de. ● *adv* à travers; (entirely) jusqu'au bout. ● *adj* (train) direct; be ∼ (finished) avoir fini; come or go ∼ (cross, pierce) traverser; I'm putting you ∼ je vous passe votre correspondant.

throughout /θruːˈaʊt/ *prep* ∼ the country dans tout le pays; ∼ the day pendant toute la journée. ● *adv* (place) partout; (time) tout le temps.

throw /θrəʊ/ *vt* (*pt* threw; *pp* thrown) jeter, lancer; (baffle) déconcerter; ∼ a party faire une fête. ● *n* jet *m*; (of dice) coup *m*. □ **away** jeter; **off** (get rid of) se débarrasser de; ∼ **out** (person) expulser; (reject) rejeter; ∼ **up** (arms) lever; (vomit 🔲) vomir.

thrust /θrʌst/ *vt* (*pt* thrust) pousser. ● *n* poussée *f*.

thud /θʌd/ *n* bruit *m* sourd.

thug /θʌg/ *n* voyou *m*.

thumb /θʌm/ *n* pouce *m*. ● *vt*

t

(book) feuilleter; ~ a lift faire de l'autostop. ~-**index** n répertoire m à onglets.

thump /θʌmp/ vt/i cogner (sur); (heart) battre fort. ● n coup m.

thunder /ˈθʌndə(r)/ n tonnerre m. ● vi (weather, person) tonner. ~-**storm** n orage m.

Thursday /ˈθɜːzdeɪ/ n jeudi m.

thus /ðʌs/ adv ainsi.

thwart /θwɔːt/ vt contrecarrer.

thyme /taɪm/ n thym m.

tick /tɪk/ n (sound) tic-tac m; (mark) coche f; (moment 🗉) instant m; (insect) tique f.● vi faire tic-tac. ● vt (~ off) cocher. □ ~ **over** tourner au ralenti.

ticket /ˈtɪkɪt/ n billet m; (for bus, cloakroom) ticket m; (label) étiquette f. ~-**collector** n contrôleur/-euse m/f.~-**office** n guichet m.

tickle /ˈtɪkl/ vt chatouiller; (amuse: fig) amuser.● n chatouillement m.

tidal /ˈtaɪdl/ adj (river) à marées; ~ **wave** raz-de-marée m inv.

tide /taɪd/ n marée f; (of events) cours m.

tidy /ˈtaɪdɪ/ adj (-ier, -iest) (room) bien rangé; (appearance, work) soigné; (methodical) ordonné; (amount 🗉) joli.● vt/i ~ (up) faire du rangement; ~ sth (up) ranger qch; ~ oneself up s'arranger.

tie /taɪ/ vt (pres p tying) attacher; (knot) faire; (scarf) nouer; (link) lier.● vi (in football) faire match nul; (in race) être ex aequo.● n cravate f; (fastener) attache f; (link) lien m; (draw) match m nul. ~-**down** attacher; ~ **in with** être lié à; ~ **up** attacher; (money) immobiliser; (occupy) occuper.

tier /tɪə(r)/ n étage m, niveau m; (in stadium) gradin m.

tiger /ˈtaɪɡə(r)/ n tigre m.

tight /taɪt/ adj (clothes, budget) serré; (grip) ferme; (rope) tendu; (security) strict; (angle) aigu. ● adv (hold, sleep) bien; (squeeze) fort.

tighten /ˈtaɪtn/ vt/i (se) tendre; (bolt) (se) resserrer; (control) renforcer.

tights /taɪts/ npl collant m.

tile /taɪl/ n (on wall, floor) carreau m; (on roof) tuile f.● vt carreler; couvrir de tuiles.

till /tɪl/ n caisse f (enregistreuse).● vt (land) cultiver. ● prep & conj →UNTIL.

timber /ˈtɪmbə(r)/ n bois m (de construction); (trees) arbres mpl.

time /taɪm/ n temps m; (moment) moment m; (epoch) époque f; (by clock) heure f; (occasion) fois f; (rhythm) mesure f; ~s (multiplying) fois fpl; any ~ n'importe quand; for the ~ being pour le moment; from ~ to ~ de temps en temps; have a good ~ s'amuser; in no ~ en un rien de temps; in ~ à temps; (eventually) avec le temps; a long ~ longtemps; on ~ à l'heure; what's the ~? quelle heure est-il?; ~ off du temps libre. ● vt choisir le moment de; (measure) minuter; (Sport) chronométrer. ~ **limit** n délai m.

timer /ˈtaɪmə(r)/ n minuterie f; (for cooker) minuteur m.

time: ~-**scale** n délais mpl. ~**table** n horaire m. ~ **zone** n fuseau m horaire.

timid /ˈtɪmɪd/ adj timide; (fearful) peureux.

tin /tɪn/ n étain m; (container) boîte f. ~**(plate)** fer-blanc m. ● vt (pt tinned) mettre en boîte. ~**foil** n papier m d'aluminium.

tingle /ˈtɪŋɡl/ vi picoter. ● n picotement m.

tin-opener n ouvre-boîtes m inv.

tint /tɪnt/ n teinte f; (for hair) shampooing m colorant. ● vt teinter.

tiny /'taɪnɪ/ adj (-ier, -iest) tout petit.

tip /tɪp/ n (of stick, pen, shoe, ski) pointe f; (of nose, finger, wing) bout m; (gratuity) pourboire m; (advice) tuyau m; (for rubbish) décharge f. ● vt/i (pt tipped) (tilt) pencher; (overturn) (faire) basculer; (pour) verser; (empty) déverser; (give money) donner un pourboire à. □ ~ off prévenir.

tiptoe /'tɪptəʊ/ n on ~ sur la pointe des pieds.

tire /'taɪə(r)/ vt/i (se) fatiguer; ~ of se lasser de. ● n (US) pneu m.

tired /'taɪəd/ adj fatigué; be ~ of en avoir assez de.

tiring /'taɪərɪŋ/ adj fatigant.

tissue /'tɪʃuː/ n tissu m; (handkerchief) mouchoir m en papier; ~ (paper) papier m de soie.

tit /tɪt/ n (bird) mésange f; give ~ for tat rendre coup pour coup.

title /'taɪtl/ n titre m. ~ **deed** n titre m de propriété.

to /tuː, tə/
● preposition

····▸ à; ~ Paris à Paris; give the book ~ Jane donne le livre à Jane; ~ the office au bureau; ~ the shops aux magasins.

····▸ (with various countries) en; ~ France en France.

····▸ (to + personal pronoun) me/te/lui/nous/vous/leur; she gave it ~ them elle le leur a donné; I'll say it ~ her je vais

le lui dire.

! à + le = au
à + les = aux.

● in an infinitive

to is not translated (to go aller; to sing chanter)

····▸ (in order to) pour; he's gone into town ~ buy a shirt il est parti en ville pour acheter une chemise.

····▸ (after adjectives) à; de; be easy/difficult ~ read être facile/difficile à lire; it's easy/difficult to read her writing c'est facile/difficile de lire son écriture.

➡ For verbal expressions using the infinitive 'to' such as to tell sb to do sth, to help sb to do sth ➡tell, help.

toad /təʊd/ n crapaud m.

toast /təʊst/ n pain m grillé, toast m; (drink) toast m. ● vt (bread) faire griller; (drink to) porter un toast à. **toaster** n grille-pain m inv.

tobacco /tə'bækəʊ/ n tabac m.

tobacconist /tə'bækənɪst/ n marchand-e m/f de tabac; ~'s (shop) tabac m.

toboggan /tə'bɒgən/ n toboggan m, luge f.

today /tə'deɪ/ n & adv aujourd'hui (m).

toddler /'tɒdlə(r)/ n bébé m (qui fait ses premiers pas).

toe /təʊ/ n orteil m; (of shoe) bout m; one's ~s vigilant. ● vt ~ the line se conformer.

together /tə'geðə(r)/ adv ensemble; (at same time) à la fois; ~ with avec.

t

toilet /ˈtɔɪlɪt/ n toilettes fpl.

toiletries /ˈtɔɪlɪtrɪz/ npl articles mpl de toilette.

token /ˈtəʊkən/ n (symbol) témoignage m; (voucher) bon m; (coin) jeton m. ● adj symbolique.

told /təʊld/ ⇒TELL.

tolerance /ˈtɒlərəns/ n tolérance f.

tolerate /ˈtɒləreɪt/ vt tolérer.

toll /təʊl/ n péage m; (count) nombre m de morts; take its ~ faire des ravages. ● vi (bell) sonner.

tomato /təˈmɑːtəʊ/ n (pl ~es) tomate f.

tomb /tuːm/ n tombeau m.

tomorrow /təˈmɒrəʊ/ n & adv demain (m); ~ morning/night demain matin/soir; the day after ~ après-demain.

ton /tʌn/ n tonne f (= 1016 kg); (metric) ~ tonne f (= 1000 kg); ~s of Ⅱ des masses de.

tone /təʊn/ n ton m; (of radio, telephone) tonalité f. ● vt ~ down atténuer. ● vi ~ (in) s'harmoniser (with avec).

tongs /tɒŋz/ npl (for coal) pincettes fpl; (for sugar) pince f; (for hair) fer m.

tongue /tʌŋ/ n langue f.

tonic /ˈtɒnɪk/ n (Med) tonique m. ● adj (effect, accent) tonique; ~ (water) tonic m, Schweppes® m.

tonight /təˈnaɪt/ n & adv (evening) ce soir; (night) cette nuit.

tonsil /ˈtɒnsl/ n amygdale f.

too /tuː/ adv trop; (also) aussi; ~ many people trop de gens; I've got ~much/many j'en ai trop; me ~ moi aussi.

took⇒TAKE.

tool /tuːl/ n outil m. ~bar n barre f d'outils. ~box n boîte f à outils.

toot /tuːt/ n coup m de klaxon®.

● vt/i ~ (the horn) klaxonner.

tooth /tuːθ/ n (pl teeth) dent f. ~ache n mal m de dents. ~brush n brosse f à dents. ~paste n dentifrice m. ~pick n cure-dents m inv.

top /tɒp/ n (highest point) sommet m; (upper part) haut m; (upper surface) dessus m; (lid) couvercle m; (of bottle, tube) bouchon m; (of beer bottle) capsule f; (of list) tête f; on ~ of sur; (fig) en plus de. ● adj (shelf) du haut; (step, floor) dernier; (in rank) premier; (best) meilleur; (distinguished) éminent; (maximum) maximum. ● vt (pt topped) (exceed) dépasser; (list) venir en tête de; ~ up remplir; ~ped with (dome) surmonté de; (cream) recouvert de.

topic /ˈtɒpɪk/ n sujet m.

topless /ˈtɒplɪs/ adj aux seins nus.

torch /tɔːtʃ/ n (electric) lampe f de poche; (flaming) torche f.

tore /tɔː(r)/ ⇒TEAR¹.

torment /tɔːˈment/ vt tourmenter.

torn /tɔːn/ ⇒TEAR¹.

torrent /ˈtɒrənt/ n torrent m.

tortoise /ˈtɔːtəs/ n tortue f. ~shell n écaille f.

torture /ˈtɔːtʃə(r)/ n torture f; (fig) supplice m. ● vt torturer.

Tory /ˈtɔːrɪ/ n & a tory (mf), conservateur/-trice (m/f).

toss /tɒs/ vt lancer; (salad) tourner; (pancake) faire sauter. ● vi se retourner; ~ a coin, ~ up tirer à pile ou face (for pour).

tot /tɒt/ n petit/-e enfant m/f; (drink) petit verre m.

total /ˈtəʊtl/ n & a total (m). ● vt (pt totalled) (add up) additionner; (amount to) se monter à.

touch /tʌtʃ/ vt toucher; (tamper with) toucher à. ● vi se toucher. ● n (sense) toucher m; (contact) contact m; (of artist, writer) touche f; a ~of (small amount) un petit peu de; get in ~ with se mettre en contact avec; out of ~ with déconnecté de. □ ~ **down** (Aviat) atterrir; ~ **up** retoucher. **~down** n atterrissage m; (Sport) essai m. ~ **line** n ligne f de touche. **~tone** adj (phone) à touches.

tough /tʌf/ adj (negotiator) coriace; (law) sévère; (time) difficile; (robust) robuste.

tour /tʊə(r)/ n voyage m; (visit) visite f; (by team) tournée f; on ~ en tournée. ● vt visiter.

tourist /'tʊərɪst/ n touriste mf. ● adj touristique. ~ **office** n syndicat m d'initiative.

tournament /'tɔːnəmənt/ n tournoi m.

tout /taʊt/ vi ~ (for) racoler 🇫. ● vt (sell) revendre. ● n racoleur/-euse m/f; revendeur/-euse m/f.

tow /təʊ/ vt remorquer. ● n remorque f; on ~ en remorque.

toward(s) /tə'wɔːd(z)/ prep vers; (of attitude) envers.

towel /'taʊəl/ n serviette f.

tower /'taʊə(r)/ n tour f. ● vi ~ **above** dominer.

town /taʊn/ n ville f; in ~ en ville. ~ **council** n conseil m municipal. ~ **hall** n mairie f.

tow: ~ **path** n chemin m de halage. ~ **truck** n dépanneuse f.

toxic /'tɒksɪk/ adj toxique.

toy /tɔɪ/ n jouet m. ● vi ~ **with** (object) jouer avec; (idea) caresser.

trace /treɪs/ n trace f. ● vt (person) retrouver; (cause) déterminer; (life) retracer; (draw) tracer; (with tracing paper) décalquer.

track /træk/ n (of person, car) traces fpl; (of missile) trajectoire f; (path) sentier m; (Sport) piste f;

(Rail) voie f; (on disc) morceau m; keep ~ of suivre. ● vt suivre la trace or la trajectoire de. □ ~ **down** retrouver. ~ **suit** n survêtement m.

tractor /'træktə(r)/ n tracteur m.

trade /treɪd/ n commerce m; (job) métier m; (swap) échange m. ● vi faire du commerce; ~**on** exploiter. ● vt échanger. ● adj (route, deficit) commercial. ~**in** n reprise f. ~ **mark** n marque f (de fabrique); (registered) marque f déposée.

trader /'treɪdə(r)/ n commerçant/ -e m/f; (on stockmarket) opérateur/ -trice m/f.

trade union n syndicat m.

trading /'treɪdɪŋ/ n commerce m; (on stockmarket) transactions fpl (boursières).

tradition /trə'dɪʃn/ n tradition f.

traffic /'træfɪk/ n trafic m; (on road) circulation f. ● vi (pt trafficked) faire du trafic (in de). ~ **jam** n embouteillage m. ~**lights** npl feux mpl (de circulation). ~ **warden** n contractuel/-le m/f.

trail /treɪl/ vt/i traîner; (plant) ramper; (track) suivre; ~ **behind** traîner. ● n (of powder) traînée f; (track) piste f; (path) sentier m.

trailer /'treɪlə(r)/ n remorque f; (caravan) caravane f; (film) bande-annonce f.

train /treɪn/ n (Rail) train m; (underground) rame f; (procession) file f; (of dress) traîne f. ● vt (instruct, develop) former; (sportsman) entraîner; (animal) dresser; (ear) exercer; (aim) braquer. ● vi être formé, étudier; (Sport) s'entraîner. **trained** adj (skilled) qualifié; (doctor) diplômé. **trainee** n stagiaire mf. **trainer** n (Sport) entraîneur/-euse m/f. **trainers** npl (shoes) chaussures fpl de sport. **training** n formation f;

t

(Sport) entraînement m.

tram /træm/ n tram(way) m.

tramp /træmp/ vi marcher (d'un pas lourd). ● vt parcourir. ● n (vagrant) clochard/-e m/f; (sound) bruit m.

trample /'træmpl/ vt/i ~ (on) piétiner; (fig) fouler aux pieds.

tranquil /'træŋkwɪl/ adj tranquille. **tranquillizer** n tranquillisant m.

transact /træn'zækt/ vt négocier. **transaction** n transaction f.

transcript /'trænskrɪpt/ n transcription f.

transfer[1] /træns'fɜ:(r)/ vt (pt **transferred**) transférer; (power) céder; (employee) muter. ● vi être transféré; (employee) être muté.

transfer[2] /'trænsfɜ:(r)/ n transfert m; (of employee) mutation f; (image) décalcomanie f.

transform /træns'fɔ:m/ vt transformer.

transitive /'trænzətɪv/ adj transitif.

translate /trænz'leɪt/ vt traduire. **translation** n traduction f; **translator** n traducteur/-trice m/f.

transmit /trænz'mɪt/ vt (pt **transmitted**) transmettre. **transmitter** n émetteur m.

transparency /træns'pærənsɪ/ n transparence f; (Photo) diapositive f.

transplant /træns'plɑːnt/ n transplantation f; (Med) greffe f.

transport[1] /træns'pɔ:t/ vt transporter.

transport[2] /'trænspɔ:t/ n transport m.

trap /træp/ n piège m. ● vt pt **trapped** (jam, pin down) coincer; (cut off) bloquer; (snare) prendre au piège.

trash /træʃ/ n (refuse) ordures fpl; (nonsense) idioties fpl. ~**-can** n (US)

poubelle f.

trauma /'trɔ:mə/ n traumatisme m. **traumatic** adj traumatisant.

travel /'trævl/ vi (pt **travelled**, US **traveled**) voyager; (vehicle, bullet) aller. ● vt parcourir. ● n voyages mpl. ~ **agency** n agence f de voyages.

traveller, (US) **traveler** /'trævlə(r)/ n voyageur/-euse m/f; ~'s **cheque** chèque m de voyage.

trawler /'trɔ:lə(r)/ n chalutier m.

tray /treɪ/ n plateau m; (on office desk) corbeille f.

treacle /'tri:kl/ n mélasse f.

tread /tred/ vi (pt **trod**; pp **trodden**) marcher (on sur). ● vt fouler. ● n (sound) pas m; (of tyre) chape f.

treasure /'treʒə(r)/ n trésor m. ● vt (gift, memory) chérir; (friendship, possession) tenir beaucoup à.

treasury /'treʒərɪ/ n trésorerie f; the T~ le ministère des Finances.

treat /tri:t/ vt traiter; ~ **sb to sth** offrir qch à qn. ● n (pleasure) plaisir m; (food) gâterie f. **treatment** n traitement m.

treaty /'tri:tɪ/ n traité m.

treble /'trebl/ adj triple; ~ **clef** clé f de sol. ● vt/i tripler. ● n (voice) soprano m.

tree /tri:/ n arbre m.

trek /trek/ n randonnée f. ● vi (pt **trekked**) ~ **across/through** traverser péniblement; **go** ~**king** faire de la randonnée.

tremble /'trembl/ vi trembler.

tremendous /trɪ'mendəs/ adj énorme; (excellent) formidable.

tremor /'tremə(r)/ n tremblement m; (earth) ~ secousse f.

trench /trentʃ/ n tranchée f.

trend /trend/ n tendance f; (fashion) mode f. **trendy** adj 🔲 branché 🔲.

trespass /'trespəs/ vi s'introduire illégalement (on dans). **trespasser** n intrus/-e m/f.

trial /'traɪəl/ n (Jur) procès m; (test) essai m; (ordeal) épreuve f; go on ~ passer en jugement; by ~ and error par expérience.

triangle /'traɪæŋgl/ n triangle m.

tribe /traɪb/ n tribu f.

tribunal /traɪ'bjuːnl/ n tribunal m.

tributary /'trɪbjʊtərɪ/ n affluent m.

tribute /'trɪbjuːt/ n tribut m; pay ~ to rendre hommage à.

trick /trɪk/ n tour m; (dishonest) combine f; (knack) astuce f; do the ⊡ faire l'affaire. ● vt tromper. **trickery** n ruse f.

trickle /'trɪkl/ vi dégouliner; ~ in/out arriver or partir en petit nombre. ● n filet m; (fig) petit nombre m.

tricky /'trɪkɪ/ adj (task) difficile; (question) épineux; (person) malin.

trifle /'traɪfl/ n bagatelle f; (cake) diplomate m; a ~ (small amount) un peu. ● vi ~ with jouer avec.

trigger /'trɪgə(r)/ n (of gun) gâchette f; (of machine) manette f. ● vt ~ (off) (initiate) déclencher.

trim /trɪm/ adj (trimmer, trimmest) soigné; (figure) svelte. ● vt (pt trimmed) (hair, grass) couper; (budget) réduire; (decorate) décorer. ● n (cut) coupe f d'entretien; (decoration) garniture f; in ~ en forme.

trinket /'trɪŋkɪt/ n babiole f.

trip /trɪp/ vt/i (pt tripped) (faire) trébucher. ● n (journey) voyage m; (outing) excursion f.

triple /'trɪpl/ adj triple. ● vt/i tripler. **triplets** npl triplés/-es m/fpl.

tripod /'traɪpɒd/ n trépied m.

trite /traɪt/ adj banal.

triumph /'traɪʌmf/ n triomphe m. ● vi triompher (over de).

trivial /'trɪvɪəl/ adj insignifiant.

trod, **trodden** /trɒd(ən)/ ➡TREAD.

trolley /'trɒlɪ/ n chariot m.

trombone /trɒm'bəʊn/ n (Mus) trombone m.

troop /truːp/ n bande f; ~s (Mil) troupes fpl. ● vi ~ in/out entrer/ sortir en bande.

trophy /'trəʊfɪ/ n trophée m.

tropic /'trɒpɪk/ n tropique m; ~s tropiques mpl.

trot /trɒt/ n trot m; on the ~ ⊡ coup sur coup. ● vi (pt trotted) trotter.

trouble /'trʌbl/ n problèmes mpl; ennuis mpl; (pains, effort) peine f; be in ~ avoir des ennuis; go to a lot of ~ se donner du mal; what's the ~? quel est le problème? ● vt (bother) déranger; (worry) tracasser. ● vi ~ (oneself) to do se donner la peine de faire. ~maker n provocateur/-trice m/f. ~shooter n conciliateur/-trice m/f; (Tech) expert m.

troublesome /'trʌblsəm/ adj ennuyeux.

trousers /'traʊzəz/ npl pantalon m; short ~ short m.

trout /traʊt/ n inv truite f.

trowel /'traʊəl/ n (garden) déplantoir m; (for mortar) truelle f.

truant /'truːənt/ n (School) élève mf qui fait l'école buissonnière; play ~ sécher les cours.

truce /truːs/ n trêve f.

truck /trʌk/ n (lorry) camion m; (cart) chariot m; (Rail) wagon m de marchandises. ~driver n routier m.

true /truː/ adj vrai; (accurate) exact; (faithful) fidèle.

truffle /'trʌfl/ n truffe f.

t

truly /'truːlɪ/ adv vraiment; (faithfully) fidèlement; (truthfully) sincèrement.

trumpet /'trʌmpɪt/ n trompette f.

trunk /trʌŋk/ n (of tree, body) tronc m; (of elephant) trompe f; (box) malle f; (Auto, US) coffre m; **~s** (for swimming) slip m de bain.

trust /trʌst/ n confiance f; (association) trust m; **in ~** en dépôt. ● vt avoir confiance en; **to ~ sb with** confier à qn. ● vi **~ in** or **to** s'en remettre à. **trustee** n administrateur/-trice m/f. **trustworthy** adj digne de confiance.

truth /truːθ/ n (pl **-s**) vérité f. **truthful** adj (account) véridique; (person) qui dit la vérité.

try /traɪ/ vt/i (pt **tried**) essayer; (be a strain on) éprouver; (Jur) juger; **~ on** or **out** essayer; **~ to do** essayer de faire. ● n (attempt) essai m; (rugby) essai m.

T-shirt /'tiːʃɜːt/ n tee-shirt m.

tub /tʌb/ n (for flowers) bac m; (of ice cream) pot m; (bath) baignoire f.

tube /tjuːb/ n tube m; the ~ Ⓣ le métro.

tuberculosis /tjuːbɜːkjʊ'ləʊsɪs/ n tuberculose f.

tuck /tʌk/ n pli m. ● vt (put away, place) ranger; (hide) cacher. ● vi **~ in** or **into** Ⓣ attaquer; **~ in** (shirt) rentrer; (blanket, person) border.

Tuesday /'tjuːzdeɪ/ n mardi m.

tug /tʌg/ vt (pt **tugged**) tirer. ● vi **~ at/on** tirer sur. ● n (boat) remorqueur m.

tuition /tjuː'ɪʃn/ n cours mpl; (fee) frais mpl pédagogiques.

tulip /'tjuːlɪp/ n tulipe f.

tumble /'tʌmbl/ vi (fall) dégringoler. ● n chute f. **~-drier** n sèche-linge m inv.

tumbler /'tʌmblə(r)/ n verre m droit.

tummy /'tʌmɪ/ n Ⓣ ventre m.

tumour /'tjuːmə(r)/ n tumeur f.

tuna /'tjuːnə/ n inv thon m.

tune /tjuːn/ n air m; **be in ~/out of ~** (instrument) être/ne pas être en accord; (singer) chanter juste/faux. ● vt (engine) régler; (Mus) accorder. ● vi **~ in (to)** (radio),TV écouter. □ **~ up** s'accorder.

Tunisia /tjuː'nɪzɪə/ n Tunisie f.

tunnel /'tʌnl/ n tunnel m; (in mine) galerie f. ● vi (pt **tunnelled**) creuser un tunnel (into dans).

turf /tɜːf/ n (pl **turf** or **turves**) gazon m; the ~ (racing) le turf. ● vt **~ out** Ⓣ jeter dehors.

Turk /tɜːk/ n Turc m, Turque f. **Turkey** n Turquie f.

turkey /'tɜːkɪ/ n dinde f.

Turkish /'tɜːkɪʃ/ adj turc. ● n (Ling) turc m.

turn /tɜːn/ vt/i tourner; (person) se tourner; (to other side) retourner; (change) (se) transformer (**into** en); (become) devenir; (deflect) détourner; (milk) tourner. ● n tour m; (in road) tournant m; (of mind, events) tournure f; **do a good ~** rendre service; **in ~** à tour de rôle; **take ~s** se relayer. □ **~ against** se retourner contre; **~ away** vi se détourner; vt (avert) détourner; (refuse) refuser; (send back) renvoyer; **~ back** (return) retourner; (vehicle) faire demi-tour; vt (fold) rabattre; **~ down** refuser; (fold) rabattre; (reduce) baisser; **~ off** (tap) éteindre; (engine) arrêter; (tap) fermer; (of driver) tourner; **~ on** (light) allumer; (engine) allumer; (tap) ouvrir; **~ out** vt (light) éteindre; (empty) vider; (produce) produire; vi it **~s out** that il se trouve que; **~ out well/badly** bien/mal se terminer; **~ over** se retourner; **~**

round (person) se retourner; ~ **up**
vi arriver; (be found) se retrouver; vt
(find) déterrer; (collar) remonter.

turning /ˈtɜːnɪŋ/ n rue f; (bend) virage m.

turnip /ˈtɜːnɪp/ n navet m.

turn: ~**out** n assistance f. ~**over** n
(pie) chausson m; (money) chiffre m
d'affaires. ~**table** n (for record)
platine f.

turquoise /ˈtɜːkwɔɪz/ adj turquoise inv.

turtle /ˈtɜːtl/ n tortue f (de mer).
~**neck** n col m montant.

tutor /ˈtjuːtə(r)/ n (private) professeur m particulier; (Univ) (GB)
chargé/-e m/f de travaux dirigés.

tutorial /tjuːˈtɔːrɪəl/ n (Univ) classe
f de travaux dirigés.

tuxedo /tʌkˈsiːdəʊ/ n (US) smoking m.

TV /tiːˈviː/ n télé f.

tweezers /ˈtwiːzəz/ npl pince f (à
épiler).

twelfth /twelfθ/ adj & n douzième (mf).

twelve /twelv/ adj & n douze (m);
~ (o'clock) midi m or minuit m.

twentieth /ˈtwentɪəθ/ adj & n
vingtième (mf).

twenty /ˈtwentɪ/ adj & n vingt (m).

twice /twaɪs/ adv deux fois.

twig /twɪg/ n brindille f.

twilight /ˈtwaɪlaɪt/ n crépuscule m.
● adj crépusculaire.

twin /twɪn/ n & a jumeau/-elle
(m/f).● vt (pt **twinned**) jumeler.

twinge /twɪndʒ/ n (of pain) élancement m; (of conscience, doubt)
accès m.

twinkle /ˈtwɪŋkl/ vi (star) scintiller;
(eye) pétiller. ● n scintillement m;
pétillement m.

twinning /ˈtwɪnɪŋ/ n jumelage m.

twist /twɪst/ vt tordre; (weave
together) entortiller; (roll) enrouler;
(distort) déformer. ● vi (rope) s'entortiller; (road) zigzaguer. ● n tor-
sion f; (in rope) tortillon m; (in road)
tournant m; (in play, story) coup m
de théâtre.

twitch /twɪtʃ/ vi (person) tremblo-
ter; (mouth) trembler; (string) vibrer.● n (tic) tic m; (jerk) secousse f.

two /tuː/ adj & n deux (m); **in** ~**s**
par deux; **break in** ~ casser
en deux.

tycoon /taɪˈkuːn/ n magnat m.

type /taɪp/ n type m, genre m;
(print) caractères mpl. ● vt/i (write)
taper (à la machine). ~**face** n police f (de caractères). ~**writer**
n machine f à écrire.

typical /ˈtɪpɪkl/ adj typique.

typist /ˈtaɪpɪst/ n dactylo mf.

tyrant /ˈtaɪərənt/ n tyran m.

tyre /ˈtaɪə(r)/ n pneu m.

Uu

udder /ˈʌdə(r)/ n pis m, mamelle f.

UFO /ˈjuːfəʊ/ n OVNI m inv.

UHT abbr ultra heat treated ~
milk lait m longue conservation.

ugly /ˈʌglɪ/ adj (**-ier, -iest**) laid.

UK abbr ➞UNITED KINGDOM.

Ukraine /juːˈkreɪn/ n Ukraine f.

ulcer /ˈʌlsə(r)/ n ulcère m.

ulterior /ʌlˈtɪərɪə(r)/ adj ultérieur;
~ **motive** arrière-pensée f.

ultimate /ˈʌltɪmət/ adj dernier, ultime; (definitive) définitif; (basic)
fondamental.

ultrasound /ˈʌltrəsaʊnd/ n

ultrason *m*.

umbilical cord /ʌmˈbɪlɪkl kɔːd/ *n* cordon *m* ombilical.

umbrella /ʌmˈbrelə/ *n* parapluie *m*.

umpire /ˈʌmpaɪə(r)/ *n* arbitre *m*. ● *vt* arbitrer.

umpteenth /ʌmpˈtiːnθ/ *adj* 🗓 énième.

UN *abbr* (**United Nations**) ONU *f*.

unable /ʌnˈeɪbl/ *adj* incapable; (through circumstances) dans l'impossibilité (to do de faire).

unacceptable /ʌnəkˈseptəbl/ *adj* (suggestion) inacceptable; (behaviour) inadmissible.

unanimous /juːˈnænɪməs/ *adj* unanime. **unanimously** *adv* à l'unanimité.

unattended /ʌnəˈtendɪd/ *adj* sans surveillance.

unattractive /ʌnəˈtræktɪv/ *adj* (idea) peu attrayant; (person) peu attirant.

unauthorized /ʌnˈɔːθəraɪzd/ *adj* non autorisé.

unavoidable /ʌnəˈvɔɪdəbl/ *adj* inévitable.

unbearable /ʌnˈbeərəbl/ *adj* insupportable.

unbelievable /ʌnbɪˈliːvəbl/ *adj* incroyable.

unbiased /ʌnˈbaɪəst/ *adj* impartial.

unblock /ʌnˈblɒk/ *vt* déboucher.

unborn /ʌnˈbɔːn/ *adj* (child) à naître; (generation) à venir.

uncalled-for /ʌnˈkɔːldfɔː(r)/ *adj* injustifié, déplacé.

uncanny /ʌnˈkænɪ/ *adj* (-ier, -iest) étrange, troublant.

uncivilized /ʌnˈsɪvɪlaɪzd/ *adj* barbare.

uncle /ˈʌŋkl/ *n* oncle *m*.

uncomfortable /ʌnˈkʌmftəbl/ *adj* (chair) inconfortable; (feeling) pénible; feel or be ~ (person) être mal à l'aise.

uncommon /ʌnˈkɒmən/ *adj* rare.

unconscious /ʌnˈkɒnʃəs/ *adj* sans connaissance, inanimé; (not aware) inconscient (of de). ● *n* inconscient *m*.

unconventional /ʌnkənˈvenʃənl/ *adj* peu conventionnel.

uncouth /ʌnˈkuːθ/ *adj* grossier.

uncover /ʌnˈkʌvə(r)/ *vt* découvrir.

undecided /ʌndɪˈsaɪdɪd/ *adj* indécis.

under /ˈʌndə(r)/ *prep* sous; (less than) moins de; (according to) selon. ● *adv* au-dessous; ~ it/there là-dessous. ~ **age** *adj* mineur. ~ **cover** *adj* secret. ~**cut** *vt* (*pt* -**cut**; *pres p* -**cutting**) (Comm) vendre moins cher que. ~**dog** *n* (Pol) opprimé/-e *m/f*; (socially) déshérité/-e *m/f*. ~**done** *adj* pas assez cuit. ~**estimate** *vt* sous-estimer. ~**fed** *adj* sous-alimenté. ~**go** *vt* (*pt* -**went**; *pp* -**gone**) subir. ~**graduate** *n* étudiant/-e *m/f* (qui prépare la licence).

underground /ˈʌndəɡraʊnd/ *adj* souterrain; (secret) clandestin. ● *adv* sous terre. ● *n* (rail) métro *m*.

under: ~line vt souligner. ~mine vt saper.

underneath /ʌndə'ni:θ/ prep sous. ● adv (en) dessous.

under: ~pants npl slip m. ~rate vt sous-estimer.

understand /ʌndə'stænd/ vt/i (pt -stood) comprendre.

understanding /ʌndə'stændɪŋ/ adj compréhensif. ● n compréhension f; (agreement) entente f.

undertake /ʌndə'teɪk/ vt (pt -took; pp -taken) entreprendre. ~taker n entrepreneur m de pompes funèbres. ~taking n (task) entreprise f; (promise) promesse f.

underwater /ʌndə'wɔ:tə(r)/ adj sous-marin. ● adv sous l'eau.

under: ~wear n sous-vêtements mpl. ~world n (of crime) milieu m, pègre f.

undo /ʌn'du:/ vt (pt -did; pp -done) défaire, détacher; (wrong) réparer; (Comput) annuler.

undress /ʌn'dres/ vt/i (se) déshabiller; get ~ed se déshabiller.

undue /ʌn'dju:/ adj excessif.

unearth /ʌn'ɜ:θ/ vt déterrer.

uneasy /ʌn'i:zi/ adj (ill at ease) mal à l'aise; (worried) inquiet; (situation) difficile.

uneducated /ʌn'edʒʊkeɪtɪd/ adj (person) inculte; (speech) populaire.

unemployed /ʌnɪm'plɔɪd/ adj en chômage. ● npl the ~ les chômeurs mpl.

unemployment /ʌnɪm 'plɔɪmənt/ n chômage m; ~ benefit allocations fpl de chômage.

uneven /ʌn'i:vn/ adj inégal.

unexpected /ʌnɪk'spektɪd/ adj inattendu, imprévu. **unexpectedly** adv (arrive) à l'improviste; (small, fast) étonnamment.

unfair /ʌn'feə(r)/ adj injuste.

unfaithful /ʌn'feɪθfl/ adj infidèle.

unfit /ʌn'fɪt/ adj (Med) pas en forme; (ill) malade; (unsuitable) impropre (for à); ~ to (unable) pas en état de.

unfold /ʌn'fəʊld/ vt déplier; (expose) exposer. ● vi se dérouler.

unforeseen /ʌnfɔ:'si:n/ adj imprévu.

unforgettable /ʌnfə'getəbl/ adj inoubliable.

unfortunate /ʌn'fɔ:tʃənət/ adj malheureux; (event) fâcheux.

ungrateful /ʌn'greɪtfl/ adj ingrat.

unhappy /ʌn'hæpɪ/ adj (-ier, -iest) (person) malheureux; (face) triste; (not pleased) mécontent (with de).

unharmed /ʌn'hɑ:md/ adj indemne, sain et sauf.

unhealthy /ʌn'helθɪ/ adj (-ier, -iest) (climate) malsain; (person) en mauvaise santé.

unheard-of /ʌn'hɜ:dɒv/ adj inouï.

unhurt /ʌn'hɜ:t/ adj indemne.

uniform /'ju:nɪfɔ:m/ n uniforme m.● adj uniforme.

unify /'ju:nɪfaɪ/ vt unifier.

unintentional /ʌnɪn'tenʃənl/ adj involontaire.

uninterested /ʌn'ɪntrəstɪd/ adj indifférent (in à).

union /'ju:nɪən/ n union f; (trade union) syndicat m; U~ Jack drapeau m du Royaume-Uni.

unique /ju:'ni:k/ adj unique.

unit /'ju:nɪt/ n unité f; (of furniture) élément m; ~ trust ≈ SICAV f.

unite /ju:'naɪt/ vt/i (s')unir.

United Kingdom n Royaume-Uni m.

United Nations npl Nations fpl Unies.

United States (of America)

npl états-Unis *mpl* (d'Amérique).

unity /ˈjuːnətɪ/ *n* unité *f.*

universal /juːnɪˈvɜːsl/ *adj* universel.

universe /ˈjuːnɪvɜːs/ *n* univers *m.*

university /juːnɪˈvɜːsətɪ/ *n* université *f.* ● *adj* universitaire; (*student, teacher*) d'université.

unkind /ʌnˈkaɪnd/ *adj* pas gentil, méchant.

unknown /ʌnˈnəʊn/ *adj* inconnu. ● *n* the ~ l'inconnu *m.*

unleaded /ʌnˈledɪd/ *adj* sans plomb.

unless /ənˈles/ *conj* à moins que.

unlike /ʌnˈlaɪk/ *adj* différent. ● *prep* contrairement à; (*different from*) différent de.

unlikely /ʌnˈlaɪklɪ/ *adj* improbable.

unload /ʌnˈləʊd/ *vt* décharger.

unlock /ʌnˈlɒk/ *vt* ouvrir.

unlucky /ʌnˈlʌkɪ/ *adj* **-ier, -iest** malheureux; (*number*) qui porte malheur.

unmarried /ʌnˈmærɪd/ *adj* célibataire.

unnatural /ʌnˈnætʃrəl/ *adj* pas naturel, anormal.

unnecessary /ʌnˈnesəsrɪ/ *adj* inutile.

unnoticed /ʌnˈnəʊtɪst/ *adj* inaperçu.

unofficial /ʌnəˈfɪʃl/ *adj* officieux.

unpack /ʌnˈpæk/ *vt* (*suitcase*) défaire; (*contents*) déballer. ● *vi* défaire sa valise.

unpleasant /ʌnˈpleznt/ *adj* désagréable (to avec).

unplug /ʌnˈplʌg/ *vt* débrancher.

unpopular /ʌnˈpɒpjʊlə(r)/ *adj* impopulaire; ~ with mal vu de.

unprofessional /ʌnprəˈfeʃənl/ *adj* peu professionnel.

unqualified /ʌnˈkwɒlɪfaɪd/ *adj*

non diplômé; (*success*) total; be ~ to ne pas être qualifié pour.

unravel /ʌnˈrævl/ *vt* (*pt* **unravelled**) démêler.

unreasonable /ʌnˈriːznəbl/ *adj* irréaliste.

unrelated /ʌnrɪˈleɪtɪd/ *adj* sans rapport (to avec).

unreliable /ʌnrɪˈlaɪəbl/ *adj* peu sérieux; (*machine*) peu fiable.

unrest /ʌnˈrest/ *n* troubles *mpl.*

unroll /ʌnˈrəʊl/ *vt* dérouler.

unruly /ʌnˈruːlɪ/ *adj* indiscipliné.

unsafe /ʌnˈseɪf/ *adj* (*dangerous*) dangereux; (*person*) en danger.

unscheduled /ʌnˈʃedjuːld/ *adj* pas prévu.

unscrupulous /ʌnˈskruːpjʊləs/ *adj* sans scrupules, malhonnête.

unsettled /ʌnˈsetld/ *adj* instable.

unsightly /ʌnˈsaɪtlɪ/ *adj* laid.

unskilled /ʌnˈskɪld/ *adj* (*worker*) non qualifié.

unsound /ʌnˈsaʊnd/ *adj* (*roof*) en mauvais état; (*investment*) douteux.

unsteady /ʌnˈstedɪ/ *adj* (*step*) chancelant; (*ladder*) instable; (*hand*) mal assuré.

unsuccessful /ʌnsəkˈsesfl/ *adj* (*result, candidate*) malheureux; (*attempt*) infructueux; be ~ ne pas réussir (in doing à faire).

unsuitable /ʌnˈsuːtəbl/ *adj* inapproprié; be ~ ne pas convenir.

unsure /ʌnˈʃɔː(r)/ *adj* incertain.

untidy /ʌnˈtaɪdɪ/ *adj* (**-ier, -iest**) (*person*) désordonné; (*room*) en désordre; (*work*) mal soigné.

untie /ʌnˈtaɪ/ *vt* (*knot, parcel*) défaire; (*person*) détacher.

until /ʌnˈtɪl/ *prep* jusqu'à; not ~ pas avant. ● *conj* jusqu'à ce que; not ~ pas avant que.

untrue /ʌnˈtruː/ *adj* faux.

unused /ʌnˈjuːst/ *adj* (new) neuf; (not in use) inutilisé.

unusual /ʌnˈjuːʒl/ *adj* exceptionnel; (strange) insolite, étrange.

unwanted /ʌnˈwɒntɪd/ *adj* (useless) superflu; (child) non désiré.

unwelcome /ʌnˈwelkəm/ *adj* fâcheux; (guest) importun.

unwell /ʌnˈwel/ *adj* souffrant.

unwilling /ʌnˈwɪlɪŋ/ *adj* peu disposé (to à); (accomplice) malgré soi.

unwind /ʌnˈwaɪnd/ *vt/i* (*pt* **unwound**) (se) dérouler; (relax 🄸) se détendre.

unwise /ʌnˈwaɪz/ *adj* imprudent.

unwrap /ʌnˈræp/ *vt* déballer.

up /ʌp/ *adv* en haut, en l'air; (sun, curtain) levé; (out of bed) levé, debout; (finished) fini; be ∼ (level, price) avoir monté. ● *prep* (a hill) en haut de; (a tree) dans; (a ladder) sur; come or go ∼ monter; ∼ in the bedroom là-haut dans la chambre; ∼ there là-haut; ∼ to jusqu'à; (task) à la hauteur de; it is ∼ to you ça dépend de vous (to de); be ∼ to sth (able) être capable de qch; (plot) préparer qch; be ∼ to (in book) en être à; be ∼ against faire face à; ∼ to date moderne; (news) récent. ● *n* ∼s and downs les hauts et les bas *mpl*.

up-and-coming *adj* prometteur.

upbringing /ˈʌpbrɪŋɪŋ/ *n* éducation *f*.

update /ʌpˈdeɪt/ *vt* mettre à jour.

upgrade /ʌpˈɡreɪd/ *vt* améliorer; (person) promouvoir.

upheaval /ʌpˈhiːvl/ *n* bouleversement *m*.

uphill /ʌpˈhɪl/ *adj* qui monte; (fig) difficile. ● *adv* go ∼ monter.

upholstery /ʌpˈhəʊlstərɪ/ *n* rembourrage *m*; (in vehicle) garniture *f*.

upkeep /ˈʌpkiːp/ *n* entretien *m*.

up-market *adj* haut-de-gamme.

upon /əˈpɒn/ *prep* sur.

upper /ˈʌpə(r)/ *adj* supérieur; have the ∼ hand avoir le dessus. ● *n* (of shoe) empeigne *f*. ∼ **class** *n* aristocratie *f*. ∼**most** *adj* (highest) le plus haut.

upright /ˈʌpraɪt/ *adj* droit. ● *n* (post) montant *m*.

uprising /ˈʌpraɪzɪŋ/ *n* soulèvement *m*.

uproar /ˈʌprɔː(r)/ *n* tumulte *m*.

uproot /ʌpˈruːt/ *vt* déraciner.

upset[1] /ʌpˈset/ *vt* (*pt* **upset**; *pres p* **upsetting**) (overturn) renverser; (plan, stomach) déranger; (person) contrarier, affliger. ● *adj* peiné.

upset[2] /ˈʌpset/ *n* dérangement *m*; (distress) chagrin *m*.

upside-down /ʌpsaɪd ˈdaʊn/ *adv* (lit) à l'envers; (fig) sens dessus dessous.

upstairs /ʌpˈsteəz/ *adv* en haut. ● *adj* (flat) du haut.

uptight /ʌpˈtaɪt/ *adj* 🄸 tendu, coincé 🄸.

up-to-date *adj* à la mode; (records) à jour.

upward /ˈʌpwəd/ *adj* & *adv*, **upwards** *adv* vers le haut.

urban /ˈɜːbən/ *adj* urbain.

urge /ɜːdʒ/ *vt* conseiller vivement (to do de). ∼ on encourager. ● *n* forte envie *f*.

urgency /ˈɜːdʒənsɪ/ *n* urgence *f*; (of request, tone) insistance *f*. **urgent** *adj* urgent; (request) pressant.

urinal /jʊəˈraɪnl/ *n* urinoir *m*.

urine /ˈjʊərɪn/ *n* urine *f*.

us /ʌs, əs/ *pron* nous; (to) ∼ nous; both of ∼ tous/toutes les deux.

US *abbr* ➡ **UNITED STATES**.

USA *abbr* ➡ **UNITED STATES OF AMERICA**.

u

use¹ /juːz/ vt se servir de, utiliser. (consume) consommer; ~ up épuiser.

use² /juːs/ n usage m, emploi m; in ~ en usage; it is no ~ doing ça ne sert à rien de faire; make ~ of se servir de; of ~ utile.

used¹ /juːzd/ adj (car) d'occasion.

used² /juːst/ v aux he ~ to smoke il fumait (autrefois). ● adj ~ to habitué à.

useful /ˈjuːsfl/ adj utile.

useless /ˈjuːslɪs/ adj inutile; (person) incompétent.

user /ˈjuːzə(r)/ n (of road, service) usager m; (of product) utilisateur/-trice m/f. ~-friendly adj facile d'emploi; (Comput) convivial. ~name nom m d'utilisateur.

usual /ˈjuːʒl/ adj habituel, normal; as ~ comme d'habitude. **usually** adv d'habitude.

utility /juːˈtɪlɪtɪ/ n utilité f; (public) ~ service m public.

utmost /ˈʌtməʊst/ adj (furthest, most intense) extrême; take ~ care le plus grand soin. ● n do one's ~ faire tout son possible.

utter /ˈʌtə(r)/ adj complet, absolu. ● vt prononcer.

U-turn /ˈjuːtɜːn/ n demi-tour m; (fig) volteface f inv.

·······························

·······························

vacancy /ˈveɪkənsɪ/ n (post) poste m vacant; (room) chambre f disponible.

vacant /ˈveɪkənt/ adj (post) vacant; (seat) libre; (look) vague.

vacate /vəˈkeɪt/ vt quitter.

vacation /vəˈkeɪʃn/ n vacances fpl.

vaccinate /ˈvæksɪneɪt/ vt vacciner.

vacuum /ˈvækjʊəm/ n vide m. ~ cleaner n aspirateur m. ~-packed adj emballé sous vide.

vagina /vəˈdʒaɪnə/ n vagin m.

vagrant /ˈveɪɡrənt/ n vagabond/-e m/f.

vague /veɪɡ/ adj vague; (outline) flou; be ~ about ne pas préciser.

vain /veɪn/ adj (conceited) vaniteux; (useless) vain; in ~ en vain.

valentine /ˈvæləntaɪn/ n ~ (card) carte f de la Saint-Valentin.

valid /ˈvælɪd/ adj (argument, ticket) valable; (passport) valide.

valley /ˈvælɪ/ n vallée f.

valuable /ˈvæljʊəbl/ adj (object) de valeur; (help) précieux. **valuables** npl objets mpl de valeur.

valuation /væljʊˈeɪʃn/ n (of painting) expertise f; (of house) évaluation f.

value /ˈvæljuː/ n valeur f; ~ added tax taxe f à la valeur ajoutée, TVA f. ● vt (appraise) évaluer; (cherish) attacher de la valeur à.

valve /vælv/ n (Tech) soupape f; (of tyre) valve f; (Med) valvule f.

van /væn/ n camionnette f.

vandal /ˈvændl/ n vandale mf.

vanguard /ˈvænɡɑːd/ n in the ~ of à l'avantgarde f de.

vanilla /vəˈnɪlə/ n vanille f.

vanish /ˈvænɪʃ/ vi disparaître.

vapour /ˈveɪpə(r)/ n vapeur f.

variable /ˈveərɪəbl/ adj variable.

varicose /ˈværɪkəʊs/ adj ~ veins varices fpl.

varied /ˈveərɪd/ adj varié.

variety /vəˈraɪətɪ/ n variété f; (entertainment) variétés fpl.

various /ˈveərɪəs/ adj divers.

varnish /ˈvɑːnɪʃ/ n vernis m. ● vt

vernir.

vary /'veərɪ/ vt/i varier.

vase /vɑːz/ n vase m.

vast /vɑːst/ adj (space) vaste; (in quantity) énorme.

vat /væt/ n cuve f.

VAT abbr (value added tax) TVA f.

vault /vɔːlt/ n (roof) voûte f; (in bank) chambre f forte; (tomb) caveau m; (jump) saut m. ● vt/i sauter.

VCR abbr →VIDEO CASSETTE RECORDER.

VDU abbr →VISUAL DISPLAY UNIT.

veal /viːl/ n veau m.

vegan /'viːɡən/ adj & n végétalien/-ne (m/f).

vegetable /'vedʒtəbl/ n légume m. ● adj végétal.

vegetarian /vedʒɪ'teərɪən/ adj & n végétarien/-ne (m/f).

vehicle /'vɪəkl/ n véhicule m.

veil /veɪl/ n voile m.

vein /veɪn/ n (in body, rock) veine f; (on leaf) nervure f.

velvet /'velvɪt/ n velours m.

vending-machine /'vendɪŋ mə'ʃiːn/ n distributeur m automatique.

veneer /vɪ'nɪə(r)/ n (on wood) placage m; (fig) vernis m.

venereal /və'nɪərɪəl/ adj vénérien.

venetian /vɪ'niːʃn/ adj ~ blind n jalousie f.

vengeance /'vendʒəns/ n vengeance f; with a ~ de plus belle.

venison /'venɪsn/ n venaison f.

venom /'venəm/ n venin m.

vent /vent/ n bouche f, conduit m; (in coat) fente f. ● vt (anger) décharger (on sur).

ventilate /'ventɪleɪt/ vt ventiler.

ventilator n ventilateur m.

venture /'ventʃə(r)/ n entreprise f.

● vt/i (se) risquer.

venue /'venjuː/ n lieu m.

verb /vɜːb/ n verbe m.

verbal /'vɜːbl/ adj verbal.

verdict /'vɜːdɪkt/ n verdict m.

verge /vɜːdʒ/ n bord m; on the ~ of doing sur le point de faire. ● vi ~ on friser, frôler.

verify /'verɪfaɪ/ vt vérifier.

vermin /'vɜːmɪn/ n vermine f.

versatile /'vɜːsətaɪl/ adj (person) aux talents variés; (mind) souple.

verse /vɜːs/ n strophe f; (of Bible) verset m; (poetry) vers mpl.

version /'vɜːʃn/ n version f.

versus /'vɜːsəs/ prep contre.

vertebra /'vɜːtɪbrə/ n (pl -brae) vertèbre f.

vertical /'vɜːtɪkl/ adj vertical.

vertigo /'vɜːtɪɡəʊ/ n vertige m.

very /'verɪ/ adv très. ● adj (actual) même; the ~ day le jour même; at the ~ end tout à la fin; the ~ first le tout premier; ~ much beaucoup.

vessel /'vesl/ n vaisseau m.

vest /vest/ n maillot m de corps; (waistcoat: US) gilet m.

vet /vet/ n vétérinaire mf. ● vt (pt vetted) (candidate) examiner (de près).

veteran /'vetərən/ n vétéran m; war ~ ancien combattant m.

veterinary /'vetrɪnrɪ/ adj vétérinaire; ~ surgeon vétérinaire mf.

veto /'viːtəʊ/ n (pl -es) veto m; (right) droit m de veto. ● vt mettre son veto à.

vibrate /vaɪ'breɪt/ vt/i (faire) vibrer.

vicar /'vɪkə(r)/ n pasteur m.

vice /vaɪs/ n (depravity) vice m; (Tech) étau m.

vicinity /vɪ'sɪnətɪ/ n environs mpl; in the ~ of à proximité de.

vicious /'vɪʃəs/ adj (spiteful) méchant; (violent) brutal; ~ circle cercle m vicieux.

victim /'vɪktɪm/ n victime f.

victor /'vɪktə(r)/ n vainqueur m. **victory** n victoire f.

video /'vɪdɪəʊ/ adj (game, camera) vidéo inv. ● n (recorder) magnétoscope m; (film) vidéo f; ~ (cassette) cassette f vidéo. ~ **game** n jeu m vidéo. **~phone** n vidéophone m. ● vt enregistrer.

videotape /'vɪdɪəʊteɪp/ n bande f vidéo. ● vt (programme) enregistrer; (wedding) filmer avec une caméra vidéo.

view /vju:/ n vue f; **in my** ~ à mon avis; **in** ~ **of** compte tenu de; **on** ~ exposé; **with a** ~ **to** dans le but de. ● vt (watch) regarder; (consider) considérer (as comme); (house) visiter. **viewer** n (TV) téléspectateur/-trice m/f.

view: **~finder** n viseur m. **~point** n point m de vue.

vigilant /'vɪdʒɪlənt/ adj vigilant.

vigour, (US) **vigor** /'vɪgə(r)/ n vigueur f.

vile /vaɪl/ adj (base) vil; (bad) abominable.

villa /'vɪlə/ n pavillon m; (for holiday) villa f.

village /'vɪlɪdʒ/ n village m.

villain /'vɪlən/ n scélérat m, bandit m; (in story) méchant m.

vindictive /vɪn'dɪktɪv/ adj vindicatif.

vine /vaɪn/ n vigne f.

vinegar /'vɪnɪgə(r)/ n vinaigre m.

vineyard /'vɪnjəd/ n vignoble m.

vintage /'vɪntɪdʒ/ n (year) année f, millésime m. ● adj (wine) de grand cru; (car) d'époque.

viola /vɪ'əʊlə/ n (Mus) alto m.

violate /'vaɪəleɪt/ vt violer.

violence /'vaɪələns/ n violence f. **violent** adj violent.

violet /'vaɪələt/ n (Bot) violette f; (colour) violet m.

violin /vaɪə'lɪn/ n violon m.

VIP abbr (**very important person**) personnalité f, VIP m.

virgin /'vɜ:dʒɪn/ n (woman) vierge f.

Virgo /'vɜ:gəʊ/ n Vierge f.

virtual /'vɜ:tʃʊəl/ adj quasi-total; (Comput) virtuel. **virtually** adv pratiquement.

virtue /'vɜ:tʃu:/ n vertu f; (advantage) mérite m; **by** ~ **of** en raison de.

virus /'vaɪərəs/ n virus m.

visa /'vi:zə/ n visa m.

visibility /vɪzə'bɪlətɪ/ n visibilité f. **visible** adj visible.

vision /'vɪʒn/ n vision f.

visit /'vɪzɪt/ vt (pt **visited**) (person) rendre visite à; (place) visiter. ● vi être en visite. ● n (tour, call) visite f; (stay) séjour m. **visitor** n visiteur/-euse m/f; (guest) invité/-e m/f.

visual /'vɪʒʊəl/ adj visuel. ~ **display unit** n visuel m, console f de visualisation.

visualize /'vɪʒʊəlaɪz/ vt se représenter; (foresee) envisager.

vital /'vaɪtl/ adj vital.

vitamin /'vɪtəmɪn/ n vitamine f.

vivacious /vɪ'veɪʃəs/ adj plein de vivacité.

vivid /'vɪvɪd/ adj (colour, imagination) vif; (description, dream) frappant.

vivisection /vɪvɪ'sekʃn/ n vivisection f.

vocabulary /vəˈkæbjʊlərɪ/ n vocabulaire m.

vocal /ˈvəʊkl/ adj vocal; (person) qui s'exprime franchement. ~ **cords** npl cordes fpl vocales.

vocation /vəʊˈkeɪʃn/ n vocation f. **vocational** adj professionnel.

voice /vɔɪs/ n voix f. ● vt (express) formuler. ~ **mail** n messagerie f vocale.

void /vɔɪd/ adj vide (of de); (not valid) nul. ● n vide m.

volatile /ˈvɒlətaɪl/ adj (person) versatile; (situation) explosif.

volcano /vɒlˈkeɪnəʊ/ n (pl ~es) volcan m.

volley /ˈvɒlɪ/ n (of blows, in tennis) volée f; (of gunfire) salve f.

volt /vəʊlt/ n (Electr) volt m. **voltage** n tension f.

volume /ˈvɒljuːm/ n volume m.

voluntary /ˈvɒləntrɪ/ adj volontaire; (unpaid) bénévole.

volunteer /vɒlənˈtɪə(r)/ n volontaire mf. ● vi s'offrir (to do pour faire); (Mil) s'engager comme volontaire. ● vt offrir.

vomit /ˈvɒmɪt/ vt/i (pt **vomited**) vomir. ● n vomi m.

vote /vəʊt/ n vote m; (right) droit de vote. ● vt/i voter; ~ **sb in** élire qn. **voter** n électeur-trice m/f. **voting** n vote m (of de); (poll) scrutin m.

vouch /vaʊtʃ/ vi ~ **for** se porter garant de.

voucher /ˈvaʊtʃə(r)/ n bon m.

vowel /ˈvaʊəl/ n voyelle f.

voyage /ˈvɔɪɪdʒ/ n voyage m (en mer).

vulgar /ˈvʌlɡə(r)/ adj vulgaire.

vulnerable /ˈvʌlnərəbl/ adj vulnérable.

Ww

wad /wɒd/ n (pad) tampon m; (bundle) liasse f.

wade /weɪd/ vi ~ **through** (mud) patauger dans. (book: fig) avancer péniblement dans.

wafer /ˈweɪfə(r)/ n (biscuit) gaufrette f.

waffle /ˈwɒfl/ n (talk 🔲) verbiage m; (cake) gaufre f. ● vi 🔲 divaguer.

wag /wæɡ/ vt/i (pt **wagged**) (tail) remuer.

wage /weɪdʒ/ n (campaign) mener; ~ **war** faire la guerre. ● n (weekly, daily) salaire m; ~**s** salaire m. ~**earner** n salarié-e m/f.

wagon /ˈwæɡən/ n (horse-drawn) chariot m; (Rail) wagon m (de marchandises).

wail /weɪl/ vi gémir. ● n gémissement m.

waist /weɪst/ n taille f. ~**coat** n gilet m.

wait /weɪt/ vt/i attendre; I can't ~ **to start** j'ai hâte de commencer; **let's** ~ **and see** attendons voir; ~ **for** attendre; ~ **on** servir. ● n attente f.

waiter /ˈweɪtə(r)/ n garçon m, serveur m.

waiting-list n liste f d'attente.

waiting-room n salle f d'attente.

waitress /ˈweɪtrɪs/ n serveuse f.

waive /weɪv/ vt renoncer à.

wake /weɪk/ vt/i (pt **woke**; pp **woken**) ~ **(up)** (se) réveiller. ● n (track) sillage m; **in the** ~ **of** (after) à la suite de. ~ **up call** n réveil m téléphonique.

Wales /weɪlz/ n pays m de Galles.

walk /wɔːk/ *vi* marcher; (*not ride*) aller à pied; (*stroll*) se promener. ● *vt* (*streets*) parcourir; (*distance*) faire à pied; (*dog*) promener. ● *n* promenade *f*, tour *m*; (*gait*) démarche *f*; (*pace*) marche *f*, pas *m*; (*path*) allée *f*; have a ∼ faire une promenade. □ ∼ out (*go away*) partir; (*worker*) faire grève; ∼ out on abandonner.

walkie-talkie /wɔːkɪˈtɔːkɪ/ *n* talkie-walkie *m*.

walking /ˈwɔːkɪŋ/ *n* marche *f* (à pied). ● *adj* (*corpse, dictionary*: *fig*) ambulant.

walkman® /ˈwɔːkmən/ *n* walkman® *m*, baladeur *m*.

walk: ∼-out *n* grève *f* surprise. ∼-over *n* victoire *f* facile.

wall /wɔːl/ *n* mur *m*; (*of tunnel, stomach*) paroi *f*. ● *adj* mural.
walled *adj* (*city*) fortifié.

> **Wall Street** Cette petite rue new yorkaise est le centre de la finance et des affaires aux États-Unis. *Wall Street* est souvent employé pour désigner la Bourse de New York, également située dans cette rue.

wallet /ˈwɒlɪt/ *n* portefeuille *m*.

wallpaper /ˈwɔːlpeɪpə(r)/ *n* papier *m* peint. ● *vt* tapisser.

walnut /ˈwɔːlnʌt/ *n* (*nut*) noix *f*; (*tree*) noyer *m*.

waltz /wɔːls/ *n* valse *f*. ● *vi* valser.

wander /ˈwɒndə(r)/ *vi* errer; (*stroll*) flâner; (*digress*) s'écarter du sujet; (*in mind*) divaguer.

wane /weɪn/ *vi* décroître.

want /wɒnt/ *vt* vouloir (to do faire); (*need*) avoir besoin de (doing d'être fait); (*ask for*) demander; I ∼ you to do it je veux que vous le fassiez. ● *vi* ∼ for manquer de. ● *n* (*need, poverty*) besoin *m*; (*desire*) désir *m*; (*lack*) manque *m*; for ∼ of faute de. **wanted** *adj* (*criminal*) recherché par la police.

war /wɔː(r)/ *n* guerre *f*; at ∼ en guerre; on the ∼path sur le sentier de la guerre.

ward /wɔːd/ *n* (*in hospital*) salle *f*; (*minor: Jur*) pupille *mf*; (*Pol*) division *f* électorale. ● *vt* ∼ off (*danger*) prévenir.

warden /ˈwɔːdn/ *n* directeur/-trice *m/f*; (*of park*) gardien/-ne *m/f*; (*traffic* ∼) contractuel/-le *m/f*.

wardrobe /ˈwɔːdrəʊb/ *n* (*furniture*) armoire *f*; (*clothes*) garde-robe *f*.

warehouse /ˈweəhaʊs/ *n* entrepôt *m*.

wares /weəz/ *npl* marchandises *fpl*.

warfare /ˈwɔːfeə(r)/ *n* guerre *f*.

warm /wɔːm/ *adj* chaud; (*hearty*) chaleureux; be or feel ∼ avoir chaud; it is ∼ il fait chaud. ● *vt/i* ∼ (up) (se) réchauffer; (*food*) chauffer; (*liven up*) (s')animer; (*exercise*) s'échauffer.

warmth /wɔːmθ/ *n* chaleur *f*.

warn /wɔːn/ *vt* avertir, prévenir; ∼ sb off sth (*advise against*) mettre qn en garde contre qch; (*forbid*) interdire qch à qn.

warning /ˈwɔːnɪŋ/ *n* avertissement *m*; (*notice*) avis *m*; without ∼ sans prévenir. ∼ light *n* voyant *m*. ∼ triangle *n* triangle *m* de sécurité.

warp /wɔːp/ *vt/i* (*wood*) (se) voiler; (*pervert*) pervertir; (*judgment*) fausser.

warrant /ˈwɒrənt/ *n* (*for arrest*) mandat *m* (d'arrêt); (*Comm*) autorisation *f*. ● *vt* justifier.

warranty /ˈwɒrəntɪ/ *n* garantie *f*.

wart /wɔːt/ *n* verrue *f*.

wartime /ˈwɔːtaɪm/ *n* in ∼ en

temps de guerre.

wary /ˈweərɪ/ *adj* (**-ier, -iest**) prudent.

was /wɒz, wəz/ ➡**BE**.

wash /wɒʃ/ *vt*/*i* (se) laver. (flow over) baigner; ~ one's hands of se laver les mains de. ● *n* lavage *m*; (clothes) lessive *f*; **have a** ~ se laver. ~ **up** faire la vaisselle; (US) se laver. ~-**basin** *n* lavabo *m*.

washer /ˈwɒʃə(r)/ *n* rondelle *f*.

washing /ˈwɒʃɪŋ/ *n* lessive *f*. ~-**machine** *n* machine *f* à laver. ~-**powder** *n* lessive *f*.

washing-up *n* vaisselle *f*. ~ **liquid** *n* liquide *m* vaisselle.

wash: ~-**out** *n* 🄴 fiasco *m*. ~-**room** *n* (US) toilettes *fpl*.

wasp /wɒsp/ *n* guêpe *f*.

wastage /ˈweɪstɪdʒ/ *n* gaspillage *m*.

waste /weɪst/ *vt* gaspiller; (time) perdre. ● *vi* ~ **away** dépérir. ● *adj* superflu; ~ **products** or **matter** déchets *mpl*. ● *n* gaspillage *m*; (of time) perte *f*; (rubbish) déchets *mpl*; **lay** ~ dévaster. **wasteful** *adj* peu économique; (person) gaspilleur.

waste: ~**land** *n* (desolate) terre *f* désolée; (unused) terre *f* inculte; (in town) terrain *m* vague. ~ **paper** *n* vieux papiers *mpl*. ~-**paper basket** *n* corbeille *f* (à papier).

watch /wɒtʃ/ *vt*/*i* (television) regarder; (observe) observer; (guard, spy on) surveiller; (be careful about) faire attention à. ● *n* (for telling time) montre *f*; (Naut) quart *m*; **be on the** ~ guetter; **keep** ~ on surveiller; ~ **out** (take care) faire attention (for à); ~ **out for** (keep watch) guetter.

water /ˈwɔːtə(r)/ *n* eau *f*; **by** ~ en bateau. ● *vt* arroser. ● *vi* (eyes) larmoyer; **my**/**his mouth** ~**s** l'eau

me/lui vient à la bouche. □ ~ **down** couper (d'eau); (tone down) édulcorer. ~-**colour** *n* (painting) aquarelle *f*. ~-**cress** *n* cresson *m* (de fontaine). ~-**fall** *n* chute *f* d'eau, cascade *f*. ~-**heater** *n* chauffe-eau *m*. **watering-can** *n* arrosoir *m*. ~-**lily** *n* nénuphar *m*. ~-**melon** *n* pastèque *f*. ~-**proof** *adj* (material) imperméable. ~ **shed** *n* (in affairs) tournant *m* décisif. ~-**skiing** *n* ski *m* nautique. ~-**tight** *adj* étanche. ~-**way** *n* voie *f* navigable.

watery /ˈwɔːtərɪ/ *adj* (colour) délavé; (eyes) humide; (soup) trop liquide.

wave /weɪv/ *n* vague *f*; (in hair) ondulation *f*; (radio) onde *f*; (sign) signe *m*. ● *vt* agiter. ● *vi* faire signe (de la main); (move in wind) flotter.

waver /ˈweɪvə(r)/ *vi* vaciller.

wavy /ˈweɪvɪ/ *adj* (line) onduleux; (hair) ondulé.

wax /wæks/ *n* cire *f*; (for skis) fart *m*. ● *vt* cirer; farter; (car) lustrer.

way /weɪ/ *n* (road, path) chemin *m* (to à); (distance) distance *f*; (direction) direction *f*; (manner) façon *f*; (means) moyen *m*; ~**s** (habits) habitudes *fpl*; **be in the** ~ bloquer le passage; (hindrance: fig) gêner (qn); **be on one's** ~ être sur son or le chemin; **by the** ~ à propos; **by** ~**side** au bord de la route; **by** ~ **of** comme; (via) par; **go out of one's** ~ se donner du mal; **in a** ~ dans un sens; **make one's** ~ somewhere se rendre quelque part; **push one's** ~ **through** se frayer un passage; **that** ~ par là; **this** ~ par ici; ~ **in** entrée *f*; ~ **out** sortie *f*. ● *adv* 🄴 loin.

we /wiː/ *pron* nous.

weak /wiːk/ *adj* faible; (delicate) fragile.

weakness /ˈwiːknɪs/ *n* faiblesse *f*;

(fault) point *m* faible; a ~ for (liking) un faible pour.

wealth /welθ/ *n* richesse *f*; (riches, resources) richesses *fpl*; (quantity) profusion *f*.

wealthy /'welθɪ/ *adj* (-ier, -iest) riche. ● *n* the ~ les riches *mpl*.

weapon /'wepən/ *n* arme *f*; ~s of mass destruction armes *fpl* de destruction massive.

wear /weə(r)/ *vt* (*pt* wore; *pp* worn) porter; (put on) mettre; (expression) avoir. ● *vi* (last) durer; ~ (out) (s')user. ● *n* (use) usage *m*; (damage) usure *f*. ~ down user; ~ off (colour, pain) passer; ~ out (exhaust) épuiser.

weary /'wɪərɪ/ *adj* (-ier, -iest) fatigué, las. ● *vi* ~ of se lasser de.

weather /'weðə(r)/ *n* temps *m*; under the ~ patraque. ● *adj* météorologique. ● *vt* (survive) réchapper de or à. ~ forecast *n* météo *f*.

weave /wi:v/ *vt/i* (*pt* wove; *pp* woven) tisser; (basket) tresser; (move) se faufiler. ● *n* (style) tissage *m*.

web /web/ *n* (of spider) toile *f*; (on foot) palmure *f*.

Web /web/ *n* (Comput) Web *m*. ~cam *n* webcam *f*. ~master *n* administrateur *m* de site Internet. ~ page *n* page *f* Web. ~ search *n* recherche *f* sur le Web. ~site *n* site *m* Internet.

wedding /'wedɪŋ/ *n* mariage *m*. ~ring *n* alliance *f*.

wedge /wedʒ/ *n* (of wood) coin *m*; (under wheel) cale *f*. ● *vt* caler; (push) enfoncer; (crowd) coincer.

Wednesday /'wenzdɪ/ *n* mercredi *m*.

weed /wi:d/ *n* mauvaise herbe *f*. ● *vt/i* désherber; ~ out extirper.

week /wi:k/ *n* semaine *f*; a ~ today/tomorrow aujourd'hui/demain en huit. ~day *n* jour *m* de semaine. ~end *n* week-end *m*, fin *f* de semaine.

weekly /'wi:klɪ/ *adv* toutes les semaines. ● *adj* & *n* (periodical) hebdomadaire (*m*).

weep /wi:p/ *vt/i* (*pt* wept) pleurer (for sb qn).

weigh /weɪ/ *vt/i* peser; ~ anchor lever l'ancre. ~ down lester (avec un poids); (bend) faire plier; (fig) accabler; ~ up calculer.

weight /weɪt/ *n* poids *m*; lose/put on ~ perdre/prendre du poids. ~-lifting *n* haltérophilie *f*. ~ training *n* musculation *f* en salle.

weird /wɪəd/ *adj* bizarre.

welcome /'welkəm/ *adj* agréable; (timely) opportun; be ~ être le or la bienvenu(e), être les bienvenu(e)s; you're ~ il n'y a pas de quoi; ~ to do libre de faire. ● *interj* soyez le or la bienvenu(e), soyez les bienvenu(e)s. ● *n* accueil *m*. ● *vt* accueillir; (as greeting) souhaiter la bienvenue à; (fig) se réjouir de.

weld /weld/ *vt* souder. ● *n* soudure *f*.

welfare /'welfeə(r)/ *n* bien-être *m*; (aid) aide *f* sociale. **W~ State** *n* état-providence *m*.

well[1] /wel/ *n* puits *m*.

well[2] /wel/ *adv* (better, best) bien; do ~ (succeed) réussir; ~ done! bravo! ● *adj* bien *inv*; as ~ aussi; be ~ (healthy) aller bien. ● *interj* eh bien; (surprise) tiens.

well-behaved *adj* sage. ~-being *n* bien-être *m* *inv*.

wellington /'welɪŋtən/ *n* (boot) botte *f* de caoutchouc.

well-known *adj* (bien) connu. ~-meaning *adj* bien intentionné. ~ off *adj* aisé, riche. ~-read *adj* ins-

truit. ~**-to-do** adj riche. ~**-wisher**
n admirateur/-trice m/f.
Welsh /welʃ/ adj gallois. ● n (Ling)
gallois m.

> ℹ️ **Welsh Assembly** L'Assem-
> blée du Pays de Galles a
> été établie à Cardiff en
> 1999, à l'issue d'un référendum
> auprès de la population galloise. À
> la différence du parlement écos-
> sais, elle n'a pas de réel pouvoir
> législatif, mais ses 60 membres
> peuvent aménager les lois nationa-
> les en fonction des besoins spécifi-
> ques des Gallois. ▷ **SCOTTISH PAR-**
> **LIAMENT**.

went /went/ ➡️ GO.
wept /wept/ ➡️ WEEP.
were /wɜː(r)/ ➡️ BE.
west /west/ n ouest m; the W~
(Pol) l'Occident m. ● adj d'ouest.
● adv vers l'ouest.
western /'westən/ adj de l'ouest;
(Pol) occidental. ● n (film) western
m. **westerner** n occidental/-e m/f.
West Indies /west 'ɪndiːz/ n Antilles fpl.
westward /'westwəd/ adj (side)
ouest inv; (journey) vers l'ouest.
wet /wet/ adj (wetter, wettest)
mouillé; (damp, rainy) humide;
(paint) frais; get ~ se mouiller. ● vt
(pt wetted) mouiller. ● n the ~
l'humidité f; (rain) la pluie f. ~**suit** n
combinaison f de plongée.
whale /weɪl/ n baleine f.
wharf /wɔːf/ n quai m.

what /wɒt/
● pronoun
····➤ (in questions as object pronoun) qu'est-ce que?; ~ are

we going to do? qu'est-ce que
nous allons faire?
····➤ (in questions as subject
pronoun) qu'est-ce qui?; ~
happened? qu'est-ce qui s'est
passé?
····➤ (introducing clause as object) ce que; I don't know ~
he wants je ne sais pas ce
qu'il veut.
····➤ (introducing clause as subject) ce qui; tell me ~ happened raconte moi ce qui s'est
passé.
····➤ (with prepositions) quoi; ~
are you thinking about? à
quoi penses-tu?

● determiner
····➤ quel/quelle/quels/quelles; ~
train did you catch? quel train
as-tu pris?; ~ time is it?
quelle heure est-il?

whatever /wɒt'evə(r)/ adj ~
book quel que soit le livre. ● pron
(no matter what) quoi que, quoi
qu'; (anything that) tout ce que;
(object) tout ce que or qu'; ~ happens quoi qu'il arrive; ~ happened? qu'est-ce qui est arrivé?;
the problems quels que soient les
problèmes; ~ you want tout ce
que vous voulez; nothing ~ rien
du tout.
whatsoever /wɒtsəʊ'evə(r)/ adj &
pron ➡️ WHATEVER.
wheat /wiːt/ n blé m, froment m.
wheel /wiːl/ n roue f; at the ~ (of
vehicle) au volant; (helm) au gouvernail. ● vt pousser. ● vi tourner;
~ and deal faire des combines.
~**barrow** n brouette f. ~**chair** n
fauteuil m roulant.
when /wen/ adv & pron quand.
● conj quand, lorsque; the day/mo-

W

ment ~ le jour/moment où.

whenever /wen'evə(r)/ *conj & adv* (at whatever time) quand; (every time that) chaque fois que.

where /weə(r)/ *adv, conj & pron* où; (whereas) alors que; (the place that) là où.

whereabouts /weərə'baʊts/ *adv* (à peu près) où. ● *n* sb's ~ l'endroit où se trouve qn.

whereas /weər'æz/ *conj* alors que.

wherever /weər'evə(r)/ *adv* où que; (everywhere) partout où; (anywhere) (là) où; (emphatic where) où donc.

whether /'weðə(r)/ *conj* si; not know ~ ne pas savoir si; ~ I go or not que j'aille ou non.

---

which /wɪtʃ/

● *pronoun*

····➤ (in questions) lequel/laquelle/lesquels/lesquelles; there are three peaches, ~ do you want? il y a trois pêches, laquelle veux-tu?

····➤ (in questions with superlative adjective) quel/quelle/quels/quelles; ~ (apple) is the biggest? quelle est la plus grosse?

····➤ (in relative clauses as subject) qui; the book ~ is on the table le livre qui est sur la table.

····➤ (in relative clauses as object) que; the book ~ Tina is reading le livre que lit Tina.

● *determiner*

····➤ quel/quelle/quels/quelles; ~ car did you choose? quelle voiture as-tu choisie?

---

whichever /wɪtʃ'evə(r)/ *adj* ~ book quel que soit le livre que ce qui; take ~ book you wish prenez le livre que vous voulez. ● *pron* celui/celle/ceux/celles qui or que.

while /waɪl/ *n* moment *m*. ● *conj* (when) pendant que; (although) bien que; (as long as) tant que. ● *vt* ~ away (time) passer.

whilst /waɪlst/ *conj* ➙WHILE.

whim /wɪm/ *n* caprice *m*.

whine /waɪn/ *vi* gémir, se plaindre. ● *n* gémissement *m*.

whip /wɪp/ *n* fouet *m*. ● *vt* (*pt* whipped) (Culin) fouetter, battre; (seize) enlever brusquement. ● *vi* (move) aller en vitesse. □ ~ up exciter; (cause) provoquer; (meal 🖪) préparer.

whirl /wɜːl/ *vt/i* (faire) tourbillonner. ● *n* tourbillon *m*. ~pool *n* tourbillon *m*. ~wind *n* tourbillon *m* (de vent).

whisk /wɪsk/ *vt* (snatch) enlever or emmener brusquement; (Culin) fouetter. ● *n* (Culin) fouet *m*.

whiskers /'wɪskə(r)s/ *npl* (of animal) moustaches *fpl*; (of man) favoris *mpl*.

whisper /'wɪspə(r)/ *vt/i* chuchoter. ● *n* chuchotement *m*; (rumour: fig) rumeur *f*, bruit *m*.

whistle /'wɪsl/ *n* sifflement *m*; (instrument) sifflet *m*. ● *vt/i* siffler; ~ at or for siffler.

white /waɪt/ *adj* blanc. ● *n* blanc *m*; (person) blanc/-che *m/f*. ~ coffee *n* café *m* au lait. ~-collar worker *n* employé/-e *m/f* de bureau. ~ elephant *n* projet *m* coûteux et peu rentable. ~ lie *n* pieux mensonge *m*. W~ Paper *n* livre *m* blanc.

whitewash /'waɪtwɒʃ/ *n* blanc *m* de chaux. ● *vt* blanchir à la chaux; (person: fig) blanchir.

Whitsun /ˈwɪtsn/ n la Pentecôte.

whiz /wɪz/ vi (pt **whizzed**) (through air) fendre l'air; (hiss) siffler; (rush) aller à toute vitesse. ∼-**kid** n jeune prodige m.

who /huː/ pron qui.

whoever /huːˈevə(r)/ pron (no matter who) qui que ce soit qui or que; (the one who) quiconque; ∼ you want dites-le à qui vous voulez.

whole /həʊl/ adj entier; (intact) intact; the ∼ house toute la maison. ● n totalité f; (unit) tout m; on the ∼ dans l'ensemble. ∼**foods** npl aliments mpl naturels et diététiques. ∼-**hearted** adj sans réserve. ∼**meal** adj complet.

wholesale /ˈhəʊlseɪl/ adj (firm) de gros; (fig) systématique. ● adv (in large quantities) en gros; (fig) en masse.

wholesome /ˈhəʊlsəm/ adj sain.

wholly /ˈhəʊllɪ/ adv entièrement.

whom /huːm/ pron (that) que, qu'; (after prepositions & in questions) qui; of ∼ dont; with ∼ avec qui.

whooping cough /ˈhuːpɪŋ kɒf/ n coqueluche f.

whose /huːz/ pron & a à qui, de qui; ∼ hat is this?, ∼ is this hat? à qui est ce chapeau?; ∼ son are you? de qui êtes-vous le fils?; the man ∼ hat I see l'homme dont je vois le chapeau.

why /waɪ/ adv pourquoi; the reason ∼ la raison pour laquelle.

wicked /ˈwɪkɪd/ adj méchant, mauvais, vilain.

wide /waɪd/ adj large; (ocean) vaste. ● adv (fall) loin du but; open ∼ ouvrir tout grand; ∼ open grand ouvert; ∼ awake éveillé. **widely** adv (spread, spaced) largement; (travel) beaucoup; (generally) géné-ralement; (extremely) extrêmement.

widespread /ˈwaɪdspred/ adj très répandu.

widow /ˈwɪdəʊ/ n veuve f. **widowed** adj (man) veuf; (woman) veuve. **widower** n veuf m.

width /wɪdθ/ n largeur f.

wield /wiːld/ vt (axe) manier; (power: fig) exercer.

wife /waɪf/ n (pl **wives**) femme f, épouse f.

wig /wɪg/ n perruque f.

wiggle /ˈwɪgl/ vt/i remuer; (hips) tortiller; (worm) se tortiller.

wild /waɪld/ adj sauvage; (sea, enthusiasm) déchaîné; (mad) fou; (angry) furieux. ● adv (grow) à l'état sauvage.

wildlife /ˈwaɪldlaɪf/ n faune f.

---

will¹ /wɪl/

present **will**; present negative **won't**, **will not**; past **would**

● auxiliary verb

····▸ (in future tense) he'll come il viendra; it ∼ be sunny tomorrow il va faire du soleil demain.

····▸ (inviting and requesting) ∼ you have some coffee? est-ce que vous voulez du café?

····▸ (making assumptions) they won't know what's happened ils ne doivent pas savoir ce qui s'est passé.

····▸ (in short questions and answers) you'll come again, won't you? tu reviendras, n'est-ce pas?; 'they won't forget'—'yes they ∼' ils n'oublieront pas'—'si'.

w

····→ (capacity) **the lift ~ hold 12** l'ascenseur peut transporter 12 personnes.

····→ (ability) **the car won't start** la voiture ne veut pas démarrer.

● *transitive verb* ~ **sb's death** souhaiter ardemment la mort de qn.

will² /wɪl/ n volonté f; (document) testament m; **at ~** quand or comme on veut.

willing /'wɪlɪŋ/ adj (help, offer) spontané; (helper) bien disposé; ~ **to** disposé à. **willingly** adv (with pleasure) volontiers; (not forced) volontairement. **willingness** n empressement m (to do à faire).

willow /'wɪləʊ/ n saule m.

will-power /'wɪlpaʊə(r)/ n volonté f.

win /wɪn/ vt/i (pt won; pres p **winning**) gagner; (prize) remporter; (fame) acquérir, trouver; ~ **round** convaincre. ● n victoire f.

winch /wɪntʃ/ n treuil m. ● vt hisser au treuil.

wind¹ /wɪnd/ n vent m; (breath) souffle m; **get ~ of** avoir vent de; **in the ~** dans l'air. ● vt essouffler. ~ **farm** n ferme f d'éoliennes. ~ **turbine** moteur m éolien.

wind² /waɪnd/ vt/i (pt wound) (s')enrouler; (of path, river) serpenter; ~ **(up)** (clock) remonter; ~ (end) (se) terminer; ~ **up in hospital** finir à l'hôpital.

windmill /'wɪndmɪl/ n moulin m à vent.

window /'wɪndəʊ/ n fenêtre f; (glass pane) vitre f; (in vehicle, train) vitre f; (in shop) vitrine f; (counter) guichet m; (Comput) fenêtre f. ~**-box** n jardinière f. ~**-cleaner** n laveur m de carreaux.

~**-dresser** n étalagiste mf. ~**-ledge** n rebord m de (la) fenêtre. ~**-shopping** n lèche-vitrines m. ~**-sill** n (inside) appui m de (la) fenêtre; (outside) rebord m de (la) fenêtre.

windscreen /'wɪndskriːn/ n pare-brise m inv. ~ **wiper** n essuie-glace m.

windshield /'wɪndʃiːld/ n (US) →WINDSCREEN.

windsurfing /'wɪndsɜːfɪŋ/ n planche f à voile.

windy /'wɪndɪ/ adj (-ier, -iest) venteux; **it is ~** il y a du vent.

wine /waɪn/ n vin m. ~**-cellar** n cave f (à vin). ~**glass** n verre m à vin. ~**-grower** n viticulteur m. ~ **list** n carte f des vins. ~**-tasting** n dégustation f de vins.

wing /wɪŋ/ n aile f; ~**s** (Theat) coulisses fpl; **under one's ~** sous son aile. ~ **mirror** n rétroviseur m extérieur.

wink /wɪŋk/ vi faire un clin d'œil; (light, star) clignoter. ● n clin m d'œil; clignotement m.

winner /'wɪnə(r)/ n (of game) gagnant/-e mf; (of fight) vainqueur m.

winning /'wɪnɪŋ/ ●adj →WIN. (number, horse) gagnant; (team) victorieux; (smile) engageant. **winnings** npl gains mpl.

winter /'wɪntə(r)/ n hiver m.

wipe /waɪp/ vt essuyer. ● vi ~ **up** essuyer la vaisselle. ● n coup m de torchon or d'éponge. □ ~ **out** (destroy) anéantir; (remove) effacer.

wire /'waɪə(r)/ n fil m; (US) télégramme m.

wiring /'waɪərɪŋ/ n (Electr) installation f électrique.

wisdom /'wɪzdəm/ n sagesse f.

wise /waɪz/ adj prudent, sage;

(look) averti.

wish /wɪʃ/ n (specific) souhait m, vœu m; (general) désir m; best ~es (in letter) amitiés fpl; (on greeting card) meilleurs vœux mpl. ● vt souhaiter, vouloir, désirer (to do faire); (bid) souhaiter. ● vi ~ for souhaiter; I ~ he'd leave je voudrais bien qu'il parte.

wishful /'wɪʃfl/ adj it's ~ thinking c'est prendre ses désirs pour des réalités.

wistful /'wɪstfl/ adj mélancolique.

wit /wɪt/ n intelligence f; (humour) esprit m; (person) homme m d'esprit, femme f d'esprit.

witch /wɪtʃ/ n sorcière f.

with /wɪð/ prep avec; (having) à; (because of) de; (at house of) chez; the man ~ the beard l'homme à la barbe; fill ~ remplir de; pleased/shaking ~ content/frémissant de.

withdraw /wɪð'drɔː/ vt/i (pt withdrew; pp withdrawn) (se) retirer. **withdrawal** n retrait m.

wither /'wɪðə(r)/ vt/i (se) flétrir.

withhold /wɪð'həʊld/ vt (pt withheld) refuser (de donner); (retain) retenir; (conceal) cacher (from à).

within /wɪ'ðɪn/ prep & adv à l'intérieur (de); (in distances) à moins de; ~ a month (before) avant un mois; ~ sight en vue.

without /wɪ'ðaʊt/ prep sans; ~ my knowing sans que je sache.

withstand /wɪð'stænd/ vt (pt withstood) résister à.

witness /'wɪtnɪs/ n témoin m; (evidence) témoignage m; bear ~ to témoigner de. ● vt être le témoin de, voir. ~ **box**, ~ **stand** n barre f des témoins.

witty /'wɪtɪ/ adj (-ier, -iest) spirituel.

wives /waɪvz/ ➞WIFE.

wizard /'wɪzəd/ n magicien m; (genius: fig) génie m.

WMD abbr (weapon of mass destruction) ADM f.

woke, woken ➞WAKE.

wolf /wʊlf/ n (pl wolves) loup m. ● vt (food) engloutir.

woman /'wʊmən/ n (pl women) femme f; ~ doctor femme f médecin; ~ driver femme f au volant.

women /'wɪmɪn/ ➞WOMAN.

won /wʌn/ ➞WIN.

wonder /'wʌndə(r)/ n émerveillement m; (thing) merveille f; it is no ~ ce or il n'est pas étonnant (that que). ● vi s'étonner (at de); (reflect) songer (about à).

wonderful /'wʌndəfl/ adj merveilleux.

won't /wəʊnt/ ➞WILL NOT.

wood /wʊd/ n bois m.

wooden /'wʊdn/ adj en or de bois. (stiff: fig) raide, contraint.

wood: ~**wind** n (Mus) bois mpl. ~**work** n (craft, objects) menuiserie f.

wool /wʊl/ n laine f. **woollen** adj de laine. **woollens** npl lainages mpl.

woolly /'wʊlɪ/ adj laineux; (vague) nébuleux. ● n (garment 🔲) lainage m.

word /wɜːd/ n mot m; (spoken) parole f, mot m; (promise) parole f; (news) nouvelles fpl; by ~ of mouth de vive voix; give/keep one's ~ donner/tenir sa parole; have a ~ with parler à; in other ~s autrement dit. ● vt rédiger. **wording** n termes mpl.

word processing n traitement m de texte. **word processor** n machine f à traitement de texte.

wore /wɔː(r)/ ➞WEAR.

work /wɜːk/ n travail m; (product,

book) œuvre *f*, ouvrage *m*; (building work) travaux *mpl*; ~s (Tech) mécanisme *m*; (factory) usine *f*. ● *vi* (person) travailler; (drug) agir; (Tech) fonctionner, marcher. ● *vt* (Tech) faire fonctionner, faire marcher; (land, mine) exploiter; (shape, hammer) travailler; ~ sb (make work) faire travailler qn. □ ~ **out** *vt* (solve) résoudre; (calculate) calculer; (elaborate) élaborer; *vi* (succeed) marcher; (Sport) s'entraîner; ~ **up** *vt* développer; *vi* (to climax) monter vers; ~**ed up** (person) énervé.

workaholic /wɜːkə'hɒlɪk/ *n* Ⓣ bourreau *m* de travail.

worker /'wɜːkə(r)/ *n* travailleur/-euse *m/f*; (manual) ouvrier/-ière *m/f*.

work-force *n* main-d'œuvre *f*.

working /'wɜːkɪŋ/ *adj* (day, lunch) de travail; ~s mécanisme *m*; in ~ order en état de marche.

working class *n* classe *f* ouvrière. ● *adj* ouvrier.

workman /'wɜːkmən/ *n* (*pl* -men) ouvrier *m*.

work: ~**out** *n* séance *f* de mise en forme. ~**shop** *n* atelier *m*. ~**station** *n* poste *m* de travail.

world /wɜːld/ *n* monde *m*; best in the ~ meilleur au monde. ● *adj* (power) mondial; (record) du monde.

world-wide *adj* universel.

World Wide Web, WWW *n* World Wide Web *m*, réseau *m* des réseaux.

worm /wɜːm/ *n* ver *m*. ● *vt* ~ one's way into s'insinuer dans.

worn /wɔːn/ ➡WEAR. ● *adj* usé. ~**out** *adj* (thing) complètement usé; (person) épuisé.

worried /'wʌrɪd/ *adj* inquiet.

worry /'wʌrɪ/ *vt/i* (s')inquiéter. ● *n*

souci *m*.

worse /wɜːs/ *adj* pire, plus mauvais; be ~ off perdre. ● *adv* plus mal. ● *n* pire *m*.

worsen /'wɜːsn/ *vt/i* empirer.

worship /'wɜːʃɪp/ *n* (adoration) culte *m*. ● *vt* (*pt* **worshipped**) adorer. ● *vi* faire ses dévotions.

worst /wɜːst/ *adj* pire, plus mauvais. ● *adv* (the) ~ (sing) le plus mal. ● *n* the ~ (one) (person, object) le or la pire; the ~ (thing) le pire.

worth /wɜːθ/ *adj* be ~ valoir; it is ~ waiting ça vaut la peine d'attendre; it is ~ (one's) while ça (en) vaut la peine. ● *n* valeur *f*; ten pence ~ of (pour) dix pence de.

worthless *adj* qui ne vaut rien.

worthwhile *adj* qui (en) vaut la peine.

worthy /'wɜːðɪ/ *adj* (-ier, -iest) digne (of de); (laudable) louable.

would /wʊd/ *v aux* he ~ do/you ~ sing (conditional tense) il ferait/ tu chanterais; he ~ have done il aurait fait; I ~ come every day (used to) je venais chaque jour; I ~ like some tea je voudrais du thé; ~ you come here? voulez-vous venir ici?; he wouldn't come il a refusé de venir. ~**be** *adj* soidisant.

wound[1] /wuːnd/ *n* blessure *f*. ● *vt* blesser; the ~ed les blessés *mpl*.

wound[2] /waʊnd/ ➡WIND[2].

wove, woven /wəʊv, 'wəʊvn/ ➡WEAVE.

wrap /ræp/ *vt* (*pt* **wrapped**) ~ (up) envelopper. ● *vi* ~ up (dress warmly) se couvrir; ~**ped up in** (engrossed) absorbé dans.

wrapping /'ræpɪŋ/ *n* emballage *m*.

wreak /riːk/ *vt* ~ havoc faire des ravages.

wreath /riːθ/ n (of flowers, leaves) couronne f.

wreck /rek/ n (sinking) naufrage m; (ship, remains, person) épave f; (vehicle) voiture f accidentée or délabrée. ● vt détruire; (ship) provoquer le naufrage de. **wreckage** n (pieces) débris mpl; (wrecked building) décombres mpl.

wrestle /ˈresl/ vi lutter, se débattre (with contre).

wrestling /ˈreslɪŋ/ n lutte f; (all-in) ~ catch m.

wriggle /ˈrɪgl/ vt/i (se) tortiller.

wring /rɪŋ/ vt (pt wrung) (twist) tordre; (clothes) essorer; ~ out of (obtain from) arracher à.

wrinkle /ˈrɪŋkl/ n (crease) pli m; (on skin) ride f. ● vt/i (se) rider.

wrist /rɪst/ n poignet m.

write /raɪt/ vt/i (pt wrote; pp written) écrire. □ ~ back répondre; ~ down noter; ~ off (debt) passer aux profits et pertes; (vehicle) considérer bon pour la casse; ~ up (from notes) rédiger.

write-off /ˈraɪtɒf/ n perte f totale.

writer /ˈraɪtə(r)/ n auteur m, écrivain m; ~ of auteur de.

write-up /ˈraɪtʌp/ n compte-rendu m.

writing /ˈraɪtɪŋ/ n écriture f; ~(s) (works) écrits mpl; in ~ par écrit. ~-paper n papier m à lettres.

written ⇒WRITE.

wrong /rɒŋ/ adj (incorrect, mistaken) faux, mauvais. (unfair) injuste; (amiss) qui ne va pas; (clock) pas à l'heure; be ~ (person) avoir tort (to de); (be mistaken) se tromper; go ~ (err) se tromper; (turn out badly) mal tourner; it is ~ to (morally) c'est mal de; what's ~? qu'est-ce qui ne va pas?; what is ~ with you? qu'est-ce que vous avez?

● adv mal. ● n injustice f; (evil) mal m; be in the ~ avoir tort. ● vt faire (du) tort à. **wrongful** adj injustifié, injuste. **wrongfully** adv à tort. **wrongly** adv mal; (blame) à tort.

wrote /rəʊt/ ⇒WRITE.

wrought iron /rɔːt ˈaɪən/ n fer m forgé.

wrung /rʌŋ/ ⇒WRING.

Xx

Xmas /ˈkrɪsməs/ n Noël m.

X-ray /ˈeksreɪ/ n rayon m X; (photograph) radio (graphie) f. ● vt radiographier.

Yy

yank /jæŋk/ vt tirer brusquement. ● n coup m brusque.

yard /jɑːd/ n (measure) yard m (= 0.9144 metre). (of house) cour f; (garden: US) jardin m; (for storage) chantier m, dépôt m. ~stick n mesure f.

yawn /jɔːn/ vi bâiller. ● n bâillement m.

yeah /jeə/ adv 🄸 ouais.

year /jɪə(r)/ n an m, année f; school/tax ~ année scolaire/fiscale; be ten ~s old avoir dix ans.

yearly /ˈjɪəlɪ/ adj annuel. ● adv annuellement.

yearn /jɜːn/ vi avoir bien or très envie (for, to de).

w
x
y

yeast /jiːst/ n levure f.

yell /jel/ vt/i hurler. ● n hurlement m.

yellow /ˈjeləʊ/ adj jaune; (cowardly 🗊) froussard. ● n jaune m.

yes /jes/ adv oui; (as answer to negative question) si. ● n oui m inv.

yesterday /ˈjestədeɪ/ n & adv hier (m).

yet /jet/ adv encore; (already) déjà. ● conj pourtant, néanmoins.

yew /juː/ n if m.

yield /jiːld/ vt (produce) produire, rendre; (profit) rapporter; (surrender) céder. ● n rendement m.

yoga /ˈjəʊgə/ n yoga m.

yoghurt /ˈjɒgət/ n yaourt m.

yolk /jəʊk/ n jaune m (d'œuf).

you /juː/ pron (familiar form) tu, pl vous; (polite form) vous; (object) te, t', pl vous; (polite) vous; (after prep.) toi, pl vous; (polite) vous; (indefinite) on; (object) vous; (to) ~ te, t', pl vous; (polite) vous; I gave ~ a pen je vous ai donné un stylo; I know ~ je te connais or je vous connais.

young /jʌŋ/ adj jeune. ● n (people) jeunes mpl; (of animals) petits mpl.

your /jɔː(r)/ adj (familiar form) ton, ta, pl tes; (polite form, & familiar form pl.) votre, pl vos.

yours /jɔːz/ pron (familiar form) le tien, la tienne, les tien(ne)s; (polite form, & familiar form pl.) le or la vôtre, les vôtres; ~ faithfully/sincerely je vous prie d'agréer mes salutations les meilleures.

yourself /jɔːˈself/ pron (familiar form) toimême; (polite form) vousmême; (reflexive & after pre-

positions) te, t'; vous; proud of ~ fier de toi. **yourselves** pron vousmêmes; (reflexive) vous.

youth /juːθ/ n jeunesse f; (young man) jeune m. ~ **hostel** n auberge f de jeunesse.

Yugoslav /ˈjuːgəʊslɑːv/ adj yougoslave. ● n Yougoslave mf.

Yugoslavia /juːgəʊˈslɑːvɪə/ n Yougoslavie f.

Zz

zap /zæp/ vt 🗊 (kill) descendre; (Comput) enlever.

zeal /ziːl/ n zèle m.

zebra /ˈzebrə/ n zèbre m. ~ **crossing** n passage m pour piétons.

zero /ˈzɪərəʊ/ n zéro m.

zest /zest/ n (gusto) entrain m; (spice: fig) piment m; (of orange or lemon peel) zeste m.

zip /zɪp/ n (vigour) allant m; ~(-fastener) fermeture f éclair(r). ● vt (pt **zipped**) fermer avec une fermeture éclair(r); (Comput) compresser. **Zip code** (US) n code m postal.

zodiac /ˈzəʊdɪæk/ n zodiaque m.

zone /zəʊn/ n zone f.

zoo /zuː/ n zoo m.

zoom /zuːm/ vi (rush) se précipiter. □ ~ **off** or **past** filer (comme une flèche). ~ **lens** n zoom m.

zucchini /zuːˈkiːnɪ/ n inv (US) courgette f.

French Verbs

1 chanter

Present indicative

je	chante
tu	chantes
il	chante
nous	chantons
vous	chantez
ils	chantent

Future indicative

je	chanterai
tu	chanteras
il	chantera
nous	chanterons
vous	chanterez
ils	chanteront

Imperfect indicative

je	chantais
tu	chantais
il	chantait
nous	chantions
vous	chantiez
ils	chantaient

Perfect indicative

j'	ai	chanté
tu	as	chanté
il	a	chanté
elle	a	chanté
nous	avons	chanté
vous	avez	chanté
ils	ont	chanté
elles	ont	chanté

Present subjunctive

(que)	je	chante
(que)	tu	chantes
(qu')	il	chante
(que)	nous	chantions
(que)	vous	chantiez
(qu')	ils	chantent

Present conditional

je	chanterais
tu	chanterais
il	chanterait
nous	chanterions
vous	chanteriez
ils	chanteraient

Past participle

chanté/chantée

Pluperfect indicative

j'	avais	chanté
tu	avais	chanté
il	avait	chanté
elle	avait	chanté
nous	avions	chanté
vous	aviez	chanté
ils	avaient	chanté
elles	avaient	chanté

2 finir

Present indicative

je	finis
tu	finis
il	finit
nous	finissons
vous	finissez
ils	finissent

Future indicative

je	finirai
tu	finiras
il	finira
nous	finirons
vous	finirez
ils	finiront

Imperfect indicative

je	finissais
tu	finissais
il	finissait
nous	finissions
vous	finissiez
ils	finissaient

Perfect indicative

j'	ai	fini
tu	as	fini
il	a	fini
elles	a	fini
nous	avons	fini
vous	avez	fini
ils	ont	fini
elles	ont	fini

Present subjunctive

(que)	je	finisse
(que)	tu	finisses
(qu')	il	finisse
(que)	nous	finissions
(que)	vous	finissiez
(qu')	ils	finissent

Present conditional

je	finirais
tu	finirais
il	finirait
nous	finirions
vous	finiriez
ils	finiraient

Past participle

fini/finie

Pluperfect indicative

j'	avais	fini
tu	avais	fini
il	avait	fini
elle	avait	fini
nous	avions	fini
vous	aviez	fini
ils	avaient	fini
elles	avaient	fini

3 attendre

Present indicative

j'	attends
tu	attends
il	attend
nous	attendons
vous	attendez
ils	attendent

Future indicative

j'	attendrai
tu	attendras
il	attendra
nous	attendrons
vous	attendrez
ils	attendront

Imperfect indicative

j'	attendais
tu	attendais
il	attendait
nous	attendions
vous	attendiez
ils	attendaient

Perfect indicative

j'	ai	attendu
tu	as	attendu
il	a	attendu
elle	a	attendu
nous	avons	attendu
vous	avez	attendu
ils	ont	attendu
elles	ont	attendu

Present subjunctive

(que)	j'	attende
(que)	tu	attendes
(qu')	il	attende
(que)	nous	attendions
(que)	vous	attendiez
(qu')	ils	attendent

Present conditional

j'	attendrais
tu	attendrais
il	attendrait
nous	attendrions
vous	attendriez
ils	attendraient

Past participle

attendu/attendue

Pluperfect indicative

j'	avais	attendu
tu	avais	attendu
il	avait	attendu
elle	avait	attendu
nous	avions	attendu
vous	aviez	attendu
ils	avaient	attendu
elles	avaient	attendu

4 être

Present indicative

je	suis
tu	es
il	est
nous	sommes
vous	êtes
ils	sont

Future indicative

je	serai
tu	seras
il	sera
nous	serons
vous	serez
ils	seront

Imperfect indicative

j'	étais
tu	étais
il	était
nous	étions
vous	étiez
ils	étaient

Perfect indicative

j'	ai	été
tu	as	été
il	a	été
elle	a	été
nous	avons	été
vous	avez	été
ils	ont	été
elles	ont	été

Present subjunctive

(que)	je	sois
(que)	tu	sois
(qu')	il	soit
(que)	nous	soyons
(que)	vous	soyez
(qu')	ils	soient

Present conditional

je	serais
tu	serais
il	serait
nous	serions
vous	seriez
ils	seraient

Past participle

été (*invariable*)

Pluperfect indicative

j'	avais	été
tu	avais	été
il	avait	été
elle	avait	été
nous	avions	été
vous	aviez	été
ils	avaient	été
elles	avaient	été

5 avoir

Present indicative

j'	ai
tu	as
il	a
nous	avons
vous	avez
ils	ont

Future indicative

j'	aurai
tu	auras
il	aura
nous	aurons
vous	aurez
ils	auront

Imperfect indicative

j'	avais
tu	avais
il	avait
nous	avions
vous	aviez
ils	avaient

Perfect indicative

j'	ai	eu
tu	as	eu
il	a	eu
elle	a	eu
nous	avons	eu
vous	avez	eu
ils	ont	eu
elles	ont	eu

Present subjunctive

(que)	j'	aie
(que)	tu	aies
(qu')	il	ait
(que)	nous	ayons
(que)	vous	ayez
(qu')	ils	aient

Present conditional

j'	aurais
tu	aurais
il	aurait
nous	aurions
vous	auriez
ils	auraient

Past participle

eu/eue

Pluperfect indicative

j'	avais	eu
tu	avais	eu
il	avait	eu
elle	avait	eu
nous	avions	eu
vous	aviez	eu
ils	avaient	eu
elles	avaient	eu

[6] acheter

1 j'achète 2 j'achèterai 3 j'achetais
4 que j'achète 5 acheté

[7] acquérir

1 j'acquiers, nous acquérons,
ils acquièrent 2 j'acquerrai
3 j'acquérais 4 que j'acquière
5 acquis

[8] aller

1 je vais, tu vas, il va, nous allons,
vous allez, ils vont 2 j'irai 3 j'allais
4 que j'aille, que nous allions, qu'ils
aillent 5 allé

[9] asseoir

1 j'assois, tu assois, il assoit, nous
assoyons, vous assoyez, ils assoient
2 j'assoirai 3 j'assoyais 4 que
j'assoie, que nous assoyions, qu'ils
assoient 5 assis

[10] avancer

1 nous avançons 3 j'avançais

[11] battre

1 je bats, il bat, nous battons
2 je battrai 3 je battais 4 que je
batte 5 battu

[12] boire

1 je bois, il boit, nous buvons,
ils boivent 2 je boirai 3 je buvais
4 que je boive 5 bu

[13] bouillir

1 je bous, il bout, nous bouillons,
ils bouillent 2 je bouillirai

3 je bouillais 4 que je bouille
5 bouilli

[14] céder

1 je cède, nous cédons, ils cèdent
2 je céderai 3 je cédais 4 que je
cède 5 cédé

[15] créer

1 je crée, nous créons 2 je créerai
3 je créais 4 que je crée 5 créé

[16] conclure

1 je conclus, il conclut, nous
concluons, ils concluent 2 je
conclurai 3 je concluais 4 que je
conclue 5 conclu (but inclus)

[17] conduire

1 je conduis, nous conduisons,
2 je conduirai 3 je conduisais
4 que je conduise 5 conduit (but
lui, nui)

[18] connaître

1 je connais, il connaît, nous
connaissons 2 je connaîtrai
3 je connaissais 4 que je connaisse
5 connu

[19] coudre

1 je couds, il coud, nous cousons,
ils cousent 2 je coudrai 3 je cousais
4 que je couse 5 cousu

[20] courir

1 je cours, il court, nous courons,
ils courent 2 je courrai 3 je courais
4 que je coure 5 couru

---

1 Present Indicative   2 Future Indicative   3 Imperfect Indicative
4 Present Subjunctive   5 Past Participle

[21] couvrir

1 je couvre 2 je couvrirai 3 je couvrais 4 que je couvre 5 couvert

[22] craindre

1 je crains, il craint, nous craignons, ils craignent 2 je craindrai 3 je craignais 4 que je craigne 5 craint

[23] croire

1 je crois, il croit, nous croyons, ils croient 2 je croirai 3 je croyais, nous croyions 4 que je croie, que nous croyions 5 cru

[24] croître1 1 je croîs, il croît, nous croissons

2 je croîtrai 3 je croissais 4 que je croisse 5 crû/crue (*but* accru, décru)

[25] cueillir

1 je cueille 2 je cueillerai 3 je cueillais 4 que je cueille 5 cueilli

[26] devoir

1 je dois, il doit, nous devons, ils doivent 2 je devrai 3 je devais 4 que je doive, que nous devions 5 dû/due

[27] dire

1 je dis, il dit, nous disons, vous dites, ils disent 2 je dirai 3 je disais 4 que je dise 5 dit

[28] dissoudre

1 je dissous, il dissout, nous dissolvons, ils dissolvent 2 je dissoudrai 3 je dissolvais 4 que je dissolve 5 dissous/dissoute

[29] distraire

1 je distrais, il distrait, nous distrayons 2 je distrairai 3 je distrayais 4 que je distraie 5 distrait

[30] écrire

1 j'écris, il écrit, nous écrivons 2 j'écrirai 3 j'écrivais 4 que j'écrive 5 écrit

[31] employer

1 j'emploie, nous employons, ils emploient 2 j'emploierai 3 j'employais, nous employions 4 que j'emploie, que nous employions 5 employé

[32] envoyer

1 j'envoie, nous envoyons, ils envoient 2 j'enverrai 3 j'envoyais, nous envoyions 4 que j'envoie, que nous envoyions 5 envoyé

[33] faire

1 je fais, nous faisons (*say* /fəzɔ̃/), vous faites, ils font 2 je ferai 3 je faisais (*say* /fəzɛ/) 4 que je fasse, que nous fassions 5 fait

[34] falloir *(impersonal)*

1 il faut 2 il faudra 3 il fallait 4 qu'il faille 5 fallu

[35] fuir

1 je fuis, nous fuyons 2 je fuirai 3 je fuyais, nous fuyions 4 que je fuie, que nous fuyions 5 fui

---

1 Present Indicative 2 Future Indicative 3 Imperfect Indicative
4 Present Subjunctive 5 Past Participle

[36] haïr
1 je hais, il hait, nous haïssons, ils haïssent 2 je haïrai 3 je haïssais 4 que je haïsse 5 haï

[37] interdire
1 j'interdis, vous interdisez 2 j'interdirai 3 j'interdisais 4 que j'interdise 5 interdit

[38] jeter
1 je jette, nous jetons, ils jettent 2 je jetterai 3 je jetais 4 que je jette 5 jeté

[39] lire
1 je lis, il lit, nous lisons 2 je lirai 3 je lisais 4 que je lise 5 lu

[40] manger
1 je mange, nous mangeons 2 je mangerai 3 je mangeais 4 que je mange, que nous mangions 5 mangé

[41] maudire
1 je maudis, il maudit, nous maudissons 2 je maudirai 3 je maudissais 4 que je maudisse 5 maudit

[42] mettre
1 je mets, tu mets, nous mettons 2 je mettrai 3 je mettais 4 que je mette 5 mis

[43] mourir
1 je meurs, il meurt, nous mourons 2 je mourrai 3 je mourais 4 que je meure 5 mort

[44] naître
1 je nais, il naît, nous naissons 2 je naîtrai 3 je naissais 4 que je naisse 5 né

[45] oublier
1 j'oublie, nous oublions, ils oublient 2 j'oublierai 3 j'oubliais, nous oubliions, vous oubliiez 4 que nous oubliions, que vous oubliiez 5 oublié

[46] partir
1 je pars, nous partons 2 je partirai 3 je partais 4 que je parte 5 parti

[47] plaire
1 je plais, il plaît (but il tait), nous plaisons 2 je plairai 3 je plaisais 4 que je plaise 5 plu

[48] pleuvoir *(impersonal)*
1 il pleut 2 il pleuvra 3 il pleuvait 4 qu'il pleuve 5 plu

[49] pouvoir
1 je peux, il peut, nous pouvons, ils peuvent 2 je pourrai 3 je pouvais 4 que je puisse, que nous puissions 5 pu

[50] prendre
1 je prends, il prend, nous prenons 2 je prendrai 3 je prenais 4 que je prenne 5 pris

---

1 Present Indicative   2 Future Indicative   3 Imperfect Indicative
4 Present Subjunctive   5 Past Participle

[51] prévoir

1 je prévois, il prévoit, nous prévoyons, ils prévoient 2 je prévoirai 3 je prévoyais, nous prévoyions 4 que je prévoie, que nous prévoyions 5 prévu

[52] recevoir

1 je reçois, il reçoit, nous recevons, ils reçoivent 2 je recevrai 3 je recevais 4 que je reçoive, que nous recevions 5 reçu

[53] résoudre

1 je résous, il résout, nous résolvons, ils résolvent 2 je résoudrai 3 je résolvais 4 que je résolve 5 résolu

[54] rire

1 je ris, nous rions, ils rient 2 je rirai 3 je riais, nous riions 4 que je rie, que nous riions 5 ri

[55] savoir

1 je sais, il sait, nous savons, ils savent 2 je saurai 3 je savais 4 que je sache, que nous sachions 5 su

[56] suffire

1 il suffit, ils suffisent 2 il suffira 3 il suffisait 4 qu'il suffise 5 suffi (but frit)

[57] suivre

1 je suis, il suit, nous suivons 2 je suivrai 3 je suivais 4 que je suive 5 suivi

[58] tenir

1 je tiens, il tient, nous tenons, ils tiennent 2 je tiendrai 3 je tenais 4 que je tienne, que nous tenions 5 tenu

[59] vaincre

1 je vaincs, il vainc, nous vainquons, ils vainquent 2 je vaincrai 3 je vainquais 4 que je vainque 5 vaincu

[60] valoir

1 je vaux, il vaut, nous valons 2 je vaudrai 3 je valais 4 que je vaille, que nous valions 5 valu

[61] vêtir

1 je vêts, il vêt, nous vêtons 2 je vêtirai 3 je vêtais 4 que je vête 5 vêtu

[62] vivre

1 je vis, il vit, nous vivons, ils vivent 2 je vivrai 3 je vivais 4 que je vive 5 vécu

[63] voir

1 je vois, nous voyons, ils voient 2 je verrai 3 je voyais, nous voyions 4 que je voie, que nous voyions 5 vu

[64] vouloir

1 je veux, il veut, nous voulons, ils veulent 2 je voudrai 3 je voulais 4 que je veuille, que nous voulions 5 voulu

1 Present Indicative   2 Future Indicative   3 Imperfect Indicative

4 Present Subjunctive   5 Past Participle

What are the equivalent tenses in English

Present indicative
je chante = I sing, I'm singing
Future indicative
je chanterai = I will sing
Imperfect indicative
je chantais = I was singing
Perfect indicative
j'ai chanté = I sang, I have sung
Pluperfect indicative
j'avais chanté = I had sung
Present subjunctive
bien que je chante = although I sing

Present conditional
si je pouvais, je chanterais
= if I could, I would sing
Past participle
chanté/chantée = sung

How to conjugate a reflexive verb

Present indicative and other simple tenses
je me lave
tu te laves
il se lave
elle se lave
nous nous lavons
vous vous lavez
ils se lavent
elles se lavent
in the negative form
je ne me lave pas
tu ne te laves pas
il ne se lave pas
elle ne se lave pas
nous ne nous lavons pas
vous ne vous lavez pas
ils ne se lavent pas
elles ne se lavent pas

Perfect indicative and other compound tenses
(always with auxiliary être)
je me suis lavé
tu t'es lavé
il s'est lavé
elle s'est lavée
nous nous sommes lavés
vous vous êtes lavés
ils se sont lavés
elles se sont lavées
in the negative form
je ne me suis pas lavé
tu ne t'es pas lavé
il ne s'est pas lavé
elle ne s'est pas lavée
nous ne nous sommes pas lavés
vous ne vous êtes pas lavés
ils ne se sont pas lavés
elles ne se sont pas lavées

Verbes irréguliers anglais

Infinitif	Prétérit	Participe passé	Infinitif	Prétérit	Participe passé
be	was	been	**drive**	drove	driven
bear	bore	borne	**eat**	ate	eaten
beat	beat	beaten	**fall**	fell	fallen
become	became	become	**feed**	fed	fed
begin	began	begun	**feel**	felt	felt
bend	bent	bent	**fight**	fought	fought
bet	bet,	bet,	**find**	found	found
	betted	betted	**flee**	fled	fled
bid	bade, bid	bidden, bid	**fly**	flew	flown
bind	bound	bound	**forecast**	forecast,	forecast,
bite	bit	bitten		forecasted	forecasted
bleed	bled	bled	**forget**	forgot	forgotten,
blow	blew	blown			forgot *US*
break	broke	broken	**freeze**	froze	frozen
breed	bred	bred	**get**	got	got, gotten *US*
bring	brought	brought	**give**	gave	given
build	built	built	**go**	went	gone
burn	burnt,	burnt,	**grow**	grew	grown
	burned	burned	**hang**	hung,	hung,
burst	burst	burst		hanged	hanged
buy	bought	bought	**have**	had	had
catch	caught	caught	**hear**	heard	heard
choose	chose	chosen	**hide**	hid	hidden
cling	clung	clung	**hit**	hit	hit
come	came	come	**hold**	held	held
cost	cost,	cost,	**hurt**	hurt	hurt
	costed (*vt*)	costed	**keep**	kept	kept
cut	cut	cut	**kneel**	knelt	knelt
deal	dealt	dealt	**know**	knew	known
dig	dug	dug	**lay**	laid	laid
do	did	done	**lead**	led	led
draw	drew	drawn	**lean**	leaned,	leaned,
dream	dreamt,	dreamt,		leant	leant
	dreamed	dreamed	**leap**	leaped,	leaped,
drink	drank	drunk		leapt	leapt

Infinitif	Prétérit	Participe passé	Infinitif	Prétérit	Participe passé
learn	learnt, learned	learnt, learned	**smell**	smelt, smelled	smelt, smelled
leave	left	left	**speak**	spoke	spoken
lend	lent	lent	**spell**	spelled, spelt	spelled, spelt
let	let	let	**spend**	spent	spent
lie	lay	lain	**spit**	spat	spat
lose	lost	lost	**spoil**	spoilt, spoiled	spoilt, spoiled
make	made	made			
mean	meant	meant	**spread**	spread	spread
meet	met	met	**spring**	sprang	sprung
pay	paid	paid	**stand**	stood	stood
put	put	put	**steal**	stole	stolen
quit	quitted, quit	quitted, quit	**stick**	stuck	stuck
			sting	stung	stung
read	read	read	**stride**	strode	stridden
ride	rode	ridden	**strike**	struck	struck
ring	rang	rung	**swear**	swore	sworn
rise	rose	risen	**sweep**	swept	swept
run	ran	run	**swell**	swelled	swollen, swelled
say	said	said			
see	saw	seen	**swim**	swam	swum
seek	sought	sought	**swing**	swung	swung
sell	sold	sold	**take**	took	taken
send	sent	sent	**teach**	taught	taught
set	set	set	**tear**	tore	torn
sew	sewed	sewn, sewed	**tell**	told	told
shake	shook	shaken	**think**	thought	thought
shine	shone	shone	**throw**	threw	thrown
shoe	shod	shod	**thrust**	thrust	thrust
shoot	shot	shot	**tread**	trod	trodden
show	showed	shown	**under-**	under-	understood
shut	shut	shut	**stand**	stood	
sing	sang	sung	**wake**	woke	woken
sink	sank	sunk	**wear**	wore	worn
sit	sat	sat	**win**	won	won
sleep	slept	slept	**write**	wrote	written
sling	slung	slung			

Numbers/Les nombres

Cardinal numbers/ Les nombres cardinaux

0	zero	**zéro**
1	one	**un**
2	two	**deux**
3	three	**trois**
4	four	**quatre**
5	five	**cinq**
6	six	**six**
7	seven	**sept**
8	eight	**huit**
9	nine	**neuf**
10	ten	**dix**
11	eleven	**onze**
12	twelve	**douze**
13	thirteen	**treize**
14	fourteen	**quatorze**
15	fifteen	**quinze**
16	sixteen	**seize**
17	seventeen	dix-**sept**
18	eighteen	dix-**huit**
19	nineteen	dix-**neuf**
20	twenty	**vingt**
21	twenty-one	**vingt et un**
22	twenty-two	**vingt-deux**
30	thirty	**trente**
40	forty	**quarante**
50	fifty	**cinquante**
60	sixty	**soixante**
70	seventy	**soixante-dix**
80	eighty	**quatre-vingt**
90	ninety	**quatre-vingt-dix**

100	a hundred	**cent**
101	a hundred and one	**cent un**
110	a hundred and ten	**cent dix**
200	two hundred	**deux cents**
250	two hundred and fifty	**deux cent cinquante**
1,000	one thousand	**mille**
1,001	one thousand and one	**mille un**
2,000	two thousand	**deux mille**
10,000	ten thousand	**dix mille**
100,000	a hundred thousand	**cent mille**
1,000,000	a million	**un million**

Ordinal numbers/ Les nombres ordinaux

1st	first	**premier**
2nd	second	**deuxième**
3rd	third	**troisième**
4th	fourth	**quatrième**
5th	fifth	**cinquième**
6th	sixth	**sixième**
7th	seventh	**septième**
8th	eighth	**huitième**
9th	ninth	**neuvième**
10th	tenth	**dixième**
11th	eleventh	**onzième**
12th	twelfth	**douzième**
13th	thirteenth	**treizième**
14th	fourteenth	**quatorzième**
15th	fifteenth	**quinzième**

Abbreviations/Abréviations

adjective	*adj*	adjectif
abbreviation	*abbr, abrév*	abréviation
adverb	*adv*	adverbe
anatomy	*Anat*	anatomie
archaeology	*Archaeol, Archéol*	archéologie
architecture	*Archit*	architecture
motoring	*Auto*	automobile
auxiliary	*aux*	auxiliaire
aviation	*Aviat*	aviation
botany	*Bot*	botanique
commerce	*Comm*	commerce
computing	*Comput*	informatique
conjunction	*conj*	conjonction
cookery	*Culin*	culinaire
determiner	*det, dét*	déterminant
electricity	*Electr, Électr*	électricité
figurative	*fig*	sens figuré
geography	*Geog, Géog*	géographie
geology	*Geol, Géol*	géologie
grammar	*Gram*	grammaire
humorous	*hum*	humoristique
interjection	*interj*	interjection
invariable	*inv*	invariable
law	*Jur*	droit
linguistics	*Ling*	linguistique
literal	*lit*	littéral
phrase	*loc*	locution
medicine	*Med, Méd*	médecine
military	*Mil*	armée
music	*Mus*	musique
noun	*n*	nom
nautical	*Naut*	nautisme
feminine noun	*nf*	nom féminin
masculine noun	*nm*	nom masculin
masculine and feminine noun	*nm,f or nmf or nm/f*	nom masculin et féminin